# Contemporary
# Literary Criticism

# Guide to Gale Literary Criticism Series

**When you need to review criticism of literary works, these are the Gale series to use:**

| If the author's death date is: | You should turn to: |
| --- | --- |

**If the author's death date is:**

After Dec. 31, 1959
(or author is still living)

1900 through 1959

1800 through 1899

1400 through 1799

Antiquity through 1399

**You should turn to:**

*CONTEMPORARY LITERARY CRITICISM*

for example: Jorge Luis Borges, Anthony Burgess,
William Faulkner, Mary Gordon,
Ernest Hemingway, Iris Murdoch

*TWENTIETH-CENTURY LITERARY CRITICISM*

for example: Willa Cather, F. Scott Fitzgerald,
Henry James, Mark Twain, Virginia Woolf

*NINETEENTH-CENTURY LITERATURE CRITICISM*

for example: Fedor Dostoevski, George Sand,
Gerard Manley Hopkins, Emily Dickinson

*LITERATURE CRITICISM FROM 1400 TO 1800*
*(excluding Shakespeare)*

for example: Anne Bradstreet, Pierre Corneille,
Daniel Defoe, Alexander Pope,
Jonathan Swift, Phillis Wheatley

*SHAKESPEAREAN CRITICISM*

Shakespeare's plays and poetry

*CLASSICAL AND MEDIEVAL LITERATURE CRITICISM*

for example: Dante, Homer, Plato, Sophocles, Vergil,
the Beowulf poet

---

**Gale also publishes related criticism series:**

*CHILDREN'S LITERATURE REVIEW*

This ongoing series covers authors of all eras.
Presents criticism on authors and author/illustrators
who write for the preschool to junior-high audience.

*CONTEMPORARY ISSUES CRITICISM*

This two-volume set presents criticism on
contemporary authors writing on current issues.
Topics covered include the social sciences,
philosophy, economics, natural science, law, and
related areas.

ISSN 0091-3421

Volume 33

# Contemporary Literary Criticism

Excerpts from Criticism of the
Works of Today's Novelists, Poets,
Playwrights, Short Story Writers, Scriptwriters,
and Other Creative Writers

**Daniel G. Marowski**
**Jean C. Stine**
EDITORS

Gale Research Company
Book Tower
Detroit, Michigan 48226

# STAFF

Daniel G. Marowski, Jean C. Stine, *Editors*

Roger Matuz, Jane E. Neidhardt, Marjorie Wachtel,
Robyn V. Young, *Senior Assistant Editors*

John G. Kuhnlein, Molly L. Norris, Sean R. Pollock,
Jane C. Thacker, Debra A. Wells, *Assistant Editors*

Phyllis Carmel Mendelson, *Contributing Editor*

Lizbeth A. Purdy, *Production Supervisor*
Denise Michlewicz Broderick, *Production Coordinator*
Eric Berger, *Assistant Production Coordinator*
Robin L. Du Blanc, Kelly King Howes, *Editorial Assistants*

Linda M. Pugliese, *Manuscript Coordinator*
Donna Craft, *Assistant Manuscript Coordinator*
Colleen M. Crane, Maureen A. Puhl, Rosetta Irene Simms, *Manuscript Assistants*

Victoria B. Cariappa, *Research Coordinator*
Jeannine Schiffman Davidson, *Assistant Research Coordinator*
Kevin John Campbell, Vincenza G. DiNoto, Daniel Kurt Gilbert, Kyle Schell,
Filomena Sgambati, Valerie Webster, *Research Assistants*

Jeanne A. Gough, *Permissions Supervisor*
Janice M. Mach, *Permissions Coordinator*
Susan D. Nobles, *Assistant Permissions Coordinator*
Patricia A. Seefelt, *Assistant Permissions Coordinator, Illustrations*
Margaret A. Chamberlain, Sandra C. Davis, Mary M. Matuz, *Senior Permissions Assistants*
Kathy Grell, Josephine M. Keene, *Permissions Assistants*
H. Diane Cooper, Dorothy J. Fowler, Yolanda Parker,
Mabel E. Schoening, *Permissions Clerks*

Frederick G. Ruffner, *Publisher*
James M. Ethridge, *Executive Vice-President/Editorial*
Dedria Bryfonski, *Editorial Director*
Christine Nasso, *Director, Literature Division*
Laurie Lanzen Harris, *Senior Editor, Literary Criticism Series*

Copyright © 1985 by Gale Research Company

Library of Congress Catalog Card Number 76-38938
ISBN 0-8103-4407-6
ISSN 0091-3421

Computerized photocomposition by
Typographics, Incorporated
Kansas City, Missouri

Printed in the United States

# Contents

5

# Preface

Literary criticism is, by definition, "the art of evaluating or analyzing with knowledge and propriety works of literature." The complexity and variety of the themes and forms of contemporary literature make the function of the critic especially important to today's reader. It is the critic who assists the reader in identifying significant new writers, recognizing trends in critical methods, mastering new terminology, and monitoring scholarly and popular sources of critical opinion.

Until the publication of the first volume of *Contemporary Literary Criticism (CLC)* in 1973, there existed no ongoing digest of current literary opinion. *CLC,* therefore, has fulfilled an essential need.

## Scope of the Work

*CLC* presents significant passages from published criticism of works by today's creative writers. Each volume of *CLC* includes excerpted criticism on about 60 authors who are now living or who died after December 31, 1959. Since the series began publication, more than 1,700 authors have been included. The majority of authors covered by *CLC* are living writers who continue to publish; therefore, an author frequently appears in more than one volume. There is, of course, no duplication of reprinted criticism.

Authors are selected for inclusion for a variety of reasons, among them the publication of a critically acclaimed new work, the reception of a major literary award, or the dramatization of a literary work as a movie or television screenplay. For example, the present volume includes Joyce Carol Oates, whose novels *Mysteries of Winterthurn* and *Solstice* were recently published; David Rabe, whose reputation grew with the Broadway production of his play *Hurlyburly;* and Thomas Pynchon, whose collection of short stories, *Slow Learner,* received much attention from the literary world. Perhaps most importantly, authors who appear frequently on the syllabuses of high school and college literature classes are heavily represented in *CLC;* Saul Bellow and Eudora Welty are examples of writers of this stature in the present volume. Attention is also given to several other groups of writers—authors of considerable public interest—about whose work criticism is often difficult to locate. These are the contributors to the well-loved but nonscholarly genres of mystery and science fiction, as well as writers who appeal specifically to young adults and writers for the nonprint media, including scriptwriters, lyricists, and cartoonists. Foreign writers and authors who represent particular ethnic groups in the United States are also featured in each volume.

## Format of the Book

Altogether there are about 750 individual excerpts in each volume—with an average of about 11 excerpts per author—taken from hundreds of literary reviews, general magazines, scholarly journals, and monographs. Contemporary criticism is loosely defined as that which is relevant to the evaluation of the author under discussion; this includes criticism written at the beginning of an author's career as well as current commentary. Emphasis has been placed on expanding the sources for criticism by including an increasing number of scholarly and specialized periodicals. Students, teachers, librarians, and researchers frequently find that the generous excerpts and supplementary material provided by the editors supply them with all the information needed to write a term paper, analyze a poem, or lead a book discussion group. However, complete bibliographical citations facilitate the location of the original source as well as provide all of the information necessary for a term paper footnote or bibliography.

A *CLC* author entry consists of the following elements:

- The **author heading** cites the author's full name, followed by birth date, and death date when applicable. The portion of the name outside the parentheses denotes the form under which the author has most commonly published. If an author has written consistently under a pseudonym, the pseudonym will be listed in the author heading and the real name given on the first line of the biographical and critical introduction. Also located at the beginning of the introduction to the author entry are any important name variations under which an author has written. Uncertainty as to a birth or death date is indicated by a question mark.

- A **portrait** of the author is included when available.

- A brief **biographical and critical introduction** to the author and his or her work precedes the excerpted criticism. However, *CLC* is not intended to be a definitive biographical source. Therefore, *cross-references* have been included to direct the reader to other useful sources published by the Gale Research Company: *Contemporary Authors* now includes detailed biographical and bibliographical sketches on almost 81,000 authors; *Children's Literature Review* presents excerpted criticism on the works of authors of children's books; *Something about the Author* contains heavily illustrated biographical sketches on writers and illustrators who create books for children and young adults; *Contemporary Issues Criticism* presents excerpted commentary on the nonfiction works of authors who influence contemporary thought; *Dictionary of Literary Biography* provides original evaluations of authors important to literary history; and the new *Contemporary Authors Autobiography Series* offers autobiographical essays by prominent writers. Previous volumes of *CLC* in which the author has been featured are also listed in the introduction.

- The **excerpted criticism** represents various kinds of critical writing—a particular essay may be normative, descriptive, interpretive, textual, appreciative, comparative, or generic. It may range in form from the brief review to the scholarly monograph. Essays are selected by the editors to reflect the spectrum of opinion about a specific work or about an author's literary career in general. The excerpts are presented chronologically, adding a useful perspective to the entry. All titles by the author featured in the entry are printed in boldface type, which enables the reader to easily identify the works being discussed.

- A complete **bibliographical citation** designed to help the user find the original essay or book follows each excerpt. An asterisk (*) at the end of a citation indicates the essay is on more than one author.

## Other Features

- A list of **Authors Forthcoming in *CLC*** previews the authors to be researched for future volumes.

- An **Appendix** lists the sources from which material in the volume has been reprinted. Many other sources have also been consulted during the preparation of the volume.

- A **Cumulative Index to Authors** lists all the authors who have appeared in *Contemporary Literary Criticism, Twentieth-Century Literary Criticism, Nineteenth-Century Literature Criticism,* and *Literature Criticism from 1400 to 1800,* along with cross-references to other Gale series: *Children's Literature Review, Authors in the News, Contemporary Authors, Contemporary Authors Autobiography Series, Dictionary of Literary Biography, Something about the Author,* and *Yesterday's Authors of Books for Children.* Users will welcome this cumulated author index as a useful tool for locating an author within the various series. The index, which lists birth and death dates when available, will be particularly valuable for those authors who are identified with a certain period but whose death date causes them to be placed in another, or for those authors whose careers span two periods. For example, F. Scott Fitzgerald is found in *Twentieth-Century Literary Criticism,* yet a writer often associated with him, Ernest Hemingway, is found in *Contemporary Literary Criticism.*

- A **Cumulative Index to Critics** lists the critics and the author entries in which their essays appear.

## Acknowledgments

The editors wish to thank the copyright holders of the excerpted articles included in this volume for permission to use the material and the photographers and other individuals who provided photographs for us. We are grateful to the staffs of the following libraries for making their resources available to us: Detroit Public Library and the libraries of Wayne State University, the University of Michigan, and the University of Detroit. We also wish to thank Jeri Yaryan for her assistance with copyright research.

## Suggestions Are Welcome

The editors welcome the comments and suggestions of readers to expand the coverage and enhance the usefulness of the series.

# Authors Forthcoming in *CLC*

*Contemporary Literary Criticism,* Volume 34 will be a yearbook devoted to an examination of the outstanding achievements and the trends in literature during 1984. Material in Volume 35 will be selected to be of special interest to young adult readers. Volume 36 will contain criticism on a number of authors not previously listed and will also feature criticism on recent works by authors included in earlier volumes.

### To Be Included in Volume 35

Maya Angelou (American novelist, poet, dramatist, and scriptwriter)—Best known for her series of autobiographical novels that began with *I Know Why the Caged Bird Sings,* Angelou has continued this acclaimed series with *The Heart of a Woman.*

Bruce Catton (American historian, essayist, journalist, and editor)—One of the foremost authorities on the Civil War, Catton is widely praised for the literary skills he brought to his historical works.

Peter Dickinson (Zambian-born English novelist, short story writer, scriptwriter, and editor)—Highly regarded for his ability to create intriguing storylines, Dickinson has recently written several works for both adults and young adults that will be covered in his entry, including *The Seventh Raven* and *Hindsight.*

Frank Herbert (American novelist, short story writer, nonfiction writer, and editor)—The best-selling author of the *Dune* series has added a fifth novel to this acclaimed science fiction saga with the publication of *Heretics of Dune.*

Langston Hughes (American novelist, poet, dramatist, short story writer, biographer, and essayist)—A leading member of the Harlem Renaissance, Hughes has earned a place of prominence among twentieth-century American authors for his endearing humor and his insightful examinations of racial injustice.

Aldous Huxley (English novelist, short story writer, dramatist, poet, essayist, and scriptwriter)—Criticism will focus on Huxley's utopian and dystopian fiction, with an emphasis on his classic novel *Brave New World.*

M.E. Kerr (American novelist)—A prolific author of fiction for young adults, Kerr has recently published the novels *What I Really Think of You* and **Him** *She Loves?* as well as her autobiography, *Me Me Me Me Me: Not a Novel.*

John Lennon (English songwriter and fiction writer)—One of contemporary music's most important figures, Lennon has influenced the lives of young people for over twenty years through his music and lyrics.

Paul McCartney (English songwriter)—McCartney has sustained much of the popular appeal he enjoyed as a member of the Beatles through solo projects and recordings with his band, Wings.

Margaret Mead (American anthropologist and nonfiction writer)—Mead is credited with having revolutionized the field of anthropology by broadening its scope to include such areas of scholarship as sociology, psychology, and economics.

Prince (American songwriter)—The enormous popular success of his first film, *Purple Rain,* has contributed to this sometimes controversial performer's rise to stardom.

Carl Sandburg (American poet, short story writer, novelist, editor, biographer, and essayist)—A recipient of two Pulitzer Prizes, Sandburg was one of America's most revered literary figures. He is often said to have captured the essence of the nation through the eloquence of his colloquial verse.

Thornton Wilder (American dramatist, novelist, and scriptwriter)—Criticism will focus on *Our Town,* a play about life in a small American town for which Wilder earned one of his three Pulitzer Prizes.

Vicente Aleixandre (Spanish poet and essayist)—The recent publication of *A Longing for Light: Selected Poems by Vicente Aleixandre* has increased appreciation of this Nobel laureate's work.

J.G. Ballard (English novelist and short story writer)—A distinguished science fiction writer, Ballard often explores the implications of new developments in science and technology for contemporary society. His recent novel, *Empire of the Sun,* evidences Ballard's concern with humanity's struggle for survival and its potential for self-destruction.

Marian Engel (Canadian novelist, short story writer, essayist, and nonfiction writer)—One of the most respected contemporary Canadian writers, Engel won the Governor General's award for her novel *Bear.* Her recent novel, *Lunatic Villas,* offers a satiric view of life in Toronto.

Nicolas Freeling (English novelist, short story writer, and nonfiction writer)—A prolific author of suspense and crime novels, Freeling created Inspector Peter Van der Valk, a sensitive and logical detective who appears in several works, including the award-winning *King of a Rainy Country.*

Allen Ginsberg (American poet and editor)—The publication of *Collected Poems: 1947-1980* has prompted reevaluation of the entire career of this controversial literary figure.

Joseph Heller (American novelist, dramatist, and scriptwriter)—*God Knows,* an irreverent account of the life of King David of Israel, displays the wit, inventiveness, and insight that distinguished earlier Heller novels, including *Catch-22* and *Something Happened.*

Ted Hughes (English poet, dramatist, and editor)—Among the most respected of contemporary poets, Hughes was named Poet Laureate of England in 1984. Recent publications that will be covered in his entry include *Selected Poems* and *River.*

Andrea Lee (American novelist, short story writer, and nonfiction writer)—Lee is best known as the author of the novel *Sarah Phillips,* a sensitive depiction of an intelligent and independent young black woman, and the nonfiction work *Russian Journal,* a highly praised view of life in the Soviet Union.

Edna O'Brien (Irish novelist, short story writer, dramatist, and scriptwriter)—Among the works that will be covered in this prolific author's entry are *Virginia,* a play about the life of Virginia Woolf, and *The Fanatic Heart: Selected Stories.*

George Plimpton (American nonfiction writer, journalist, and editor)—Often described as a "professional amateur," Plimpton is well regarded for his humorous accounts of his adventures in various sporting activities.

Josef Škvorecký (Czechoslovakian novelist, short story writer, editor, and translator)—The recent translation into English of Skvorecky's novel *The Engineer of Human Souls* has added to his international renown.

Michel Tournier (French novelist, short story writer, and essayist)—Considered one of France's most important contemporary writers, Tournier is widely praised for his philosophically speculative fiction. His entry will cover several works, including his recently translated short story collection, *The Fetishist.*

Lanford Wilson (American dramatist)—Wilson is best known for *The Hot l Baltimore* and for his series of plays about the Talley family, including *Talley's Folly,* for which he won the Pulitzer Prize.

# Nelson Algren

## 1909-1981

American novelist, journalist, short story writer, poet, and essayist.

Algren lived most of his life in Chicago and often explored in his fiction the gritty underworld of Chicago's impoverished neighborhoods. He depicted the tragedies of his born losers in a lyrical prose noted for concrete, earthy details and authentic street dialect. Saul Maloff called Algren's work "a species of literary populism and native romanticism," but many critics have placed his novels of social protest in the realistic or naturalistic traditions. Algren's reputation waned after the success of such early books as *The Man with the Golden Arm* (1948), winner of the National Book Award and the basis for a well-known film, but the posthumous publication of his novel *The Devil's Stocking* (1983) revived respect for Algren's compassionate portrayals of the "American Dream" gone awry.

Algren's fiction reflected his life experiences. He was born in Detroit and grew up in a poor Polish neighborhood in Chicago. He graduated with a degree in journalism from the University of Illinois and for many years worked as a journalist, often reporting on the victims of poverty and crime. During the depression Algren drifted in the Southwest and spent some time in New Orleans. He became involved with the Communist Party and, with Jack Conroy, edited a leftist magazine called the *New Anvil*. In the late 1930s he joined the Federal Writers Project, which gave him a chance to write full time. From 1942 to 1945 he served in the army. Algren knew many of the important writers of the period, including Ernest Hemingway, Richard Wright, James T. Farrell, Jean-Paul Sartre, and Simone de Beauvoir.

Algren's first two novels, *Somebody in Boots* (1935) and *Never Come Morning* (1942), center on young men whose unhappy fates are determined by their environments. Cass McKay of *Somebody in Boots* is a poor, illiterate Texan who drifts through America during the depression; Chicagoan Bruno Bicek of *Never Come Morning* dreams of being a champion boxer but is instead arrested for murder. Both novels dwell on violence and death and the effect of poverty on character. Algren touches on these themes again in *The Man with the Golden Arm,* the story of a morphine addict who works as a card dealer in a gambling house. In what some critics consider his finest book, *A Walk on the Wild Side* (1956), Algren reworked his first novel to portray a drifter similar to Cass McKay who is beaten and blinded after becoming involved with prostitutes and criminals in New Orleans. Completed immediately prior to Algren's death, *The Devil's Stocking* recounts the events surrounding the real-life conviction for murder of a well-known boxer.

In addition to his novels, Algren wrote short stories, criticism, poetry, and two travelogues: *Who Lost an American?* (1963) and *Notes from a Sea Diary: Hemingway All the Way* (1965). Algren's short stories, collected in *The Neon Wilderness* (1947), cover the familiar terrain of his novels, along with material from his army life. *The Last Carousel* (1973) contains memoirs, poetry, travel writing, and short stories. Although most of Algren's journalism and nonfiction received little attention,

*Chicago: A City on the Make* (1951), an essay in the form of a prose poem, attained substantial recognition.

(See also *CLC*, Vols. 4, 10; *Contemporary Authors*, Vols. 13-16, rev. ed., Vol. 103 [obituary]; *Dictionary of Literary Biography*, Vol. 9; and *Dictionary of Literary Biography Yearbook: 1981, 1982.*)

### BENJAMIN APPEL

Mr. Algren's new novel [*Never Come Morning*] is a knockout. Like a flare of light, it illumines one of our big industries—the crime racket. But the illumination is in human terms, the method of Richard Wright, and not of W. R. Burnett or James Cain. . . .

"Never Come Morning" deals with . . . [the petty criminals] who live in the Polish section of Chicago. Bruno Lefty Bicek, the chief character, is a sort of Polish-American Bigger Thomas. Bruno and Bigger are twins, but not identical twins. Unlike Bigger who ends up defying the whole white world like a human wolf, there is an out for Bruno. . . .

There is a great deal more here, enough to make "Never Come Morning" tower head and shoulders over most novels as "Native Son" towered over most novels in its publication year.

There is the hard bitter poetry of the street argot: "Don't gimme that hustle, Bicek. Don't gimme that executive hustle." There is the Céline-like horror of the split soul with Bruno thinking of himself as: "this Bicek wasn't the one to take advantage of man, woman or child. Just a big clean kid; he'd be a clean champ." There are the superbly done worlds of gang and street, of cop and jail, of whore and jukebox.

There are also, to my way of thinking, some loose ends. . . . I feel the author's own creative outlook has tripped him up. I think Algren is just a bit too fascinated by gang life as gang life, as Wright was to a far larger degree fascinated by murder for its own getting-rid-of-the-corpse sake. This fascination is reflected in the darkness of the title; in the dedication out of Walt Whitman, in dozens of lines and passages throughout the novel.

God knows there is darkness. But there is light, too. Not the light of the Klieg-like Pollyanna novelists, or the candlelight of the sentimentalist fictioneers. But the living light of ordinary human hopes. . . . However, these omissions are dwarfed by the powerful positive achievements on almost every page of character, of color, of poetry, of understanding.

*Benjamin Appel, "People of Crime," in* The Saturday Review of Literature, *Vol. XXV, No. 16, April 18, 1942, p. 7.*

## TIME

The kids around Chicago's tough, slummy Division Street had a game called Let Her Fly. It was easy to learn, and it was a dandy game because it made the winner feel good and the loser feel terrible. All the player had to do was wrap up some garbage, sneak up on his opponent and slam it in his face. (p. 104)

There was no use anyone's trying to understand Frankie Majcinek, a son of Division Street, unless he could understand a childhood geared to Let Her Fly. In *The Man with the Golden Arm,* Chicago Novelist Nelson Algren's compassionate understanding of Frankie and his world is the foundation of one of the finest novels so far this year. Readers with queasy stomachs may shrink from an environment in which the unbelievably sordid has become a way of life. They will also come away with some of Algren's own tender concern for his wretched, confused and hopelessly degenerate cast of characters. In that, Writer Algren scores a true novelist's triumph.

At 29, Frankie Majcinek had just one salable skill. In the dealer's slot at Schwiefka's gambling joint, he dealt cards with the impersonal fairness and nerveless accuracy of a machine. "Frankie Machine," the Division Street punks called him, or just Dealer. (pp. 104, 106)

Frankie Machine's world will be as new to most readers as if it were made up of whole fictional cloth. But it exists, and Algren has reproduced it with faithfulness to its speech, smells, gross humor and hopeless squalor. Some of the jailhouse scenes have a chilling rightness that goes far beyond inspired reporting, and aging, deeply troubled Police Captain Bednar is the most sympathetically understood cop in recent fiction.

*The Man with the Golden Arm* has its specks of dross, moments when it reads like the late Damon Runyon at his slapdash, sentimental worst. ("She had gone to that bookie in the brain where hustlers' hearts pay off to win, place or show. She had bet her health on a long one and waited each night to be paid off in her turn.") But Algren's ear and sense of pity betray

him very seldom. His book has humor as well as heart, and it shows up a rotted piece of U.S. life without indulging in a paragraph of preaching. (p. 107)

*"The Lower Depths," in* Time, *Vol. LIV, No. 11, September 12, 1949, pp. 104, 106-07.*

## WILLIAM BARRETT

In his novels Nelson Algren has always been a strict regionalist of Chicago's South Side, but in *Who Lost an American?* . . . he shows himself to be a surprisingly accomplished, if highly unorthodox, cosmopolitan. Taking us on a tour of the "seamier sides" of life in the great capitals—New York, Dublin, Paris, Barcelona, Istanbul—he is the tough-guy traveler never to be conned by any place or face, irreverently and raucously himself.

He is also, when he chooses, a very perceptive observer, though what he sees may not always be the whole truth. New York, for example, was for Mr. Algren mainly a city of rapacious publishers and authors' agents, where writers gather at cocktail parties to hurl their egos at each other. . . . He was more at home in Paris, where he was received in the circle of Sartre and Simone de Beauvoir, and in Spain; but Istanbul awakened the traveler's jitters once again as a place "where ancient and modern world meet and both are that much worse for meeting."

When Mr. Algren got home to Chicago, he found it changed and changing; and the last four pieces in this genially dyspeptic book go to work like a battery of air drills excavating the entrails of his native city. (pp. 132-33)

*William Barrett, "Citizens of the World," in* The Atlantic Monthly, *Vol. 211, No. 6, June, 1963, pp. 132-34.*

## SHELDON NORMAN GREBSTEIN

Nelson Algren evokes little attention these days. Although he has published nine books, his last work of fiction, *A Walk on the Wild Side,* appeared in 1956, and the journalistic writing he has done in recent years hardly warrants our concern. It seems understandable, then, that Algren should be ignored by serious critics. . . .

But upon reflection, such neglect is hardly justified. Far less able writers are winning far more attention. Indeed, a generation ago Nelson Algren was considered among our most promising writers. Although Algren's earliest writing originated in the '30's, no writer who matured during the war decade had a better claim to the recognition Algren received when his 1949 novel *The Man with the Golden Arm* was chosen for the National Book Award. The current critical neglect lends credence to Algren's own claim that he has of late refused to make the total commitment serious art requires because the economics of publishing and the vagaries of critical taste together prohibit his kind of work from earning any sort of just appreciation. (p. 299)

For Algren there are neither partial truths nor soft truths, but only the whole and hard truth. It is the compulsion to tell the whole, hard truth as a contradiction to our national lies that constitutes the basic impulse and moving spirit behind Algren's serious writing. . . . Algren's whole truth, to name it in the terms he used in *Conversations with Algren,* is that there is a world whose existence the middle-class American denies, "that there are people who have no alternative, that there are people who live in horror, that there are people whose lives are night-mares.''

Such is the nature of Algren's world. Whatever its universal human implications—and I intend to argue that Algren's world conveys such implications—Algren's fiction depicts but three milieus: life on the road or in the jails of the Southwest in the 1930's; life in the slums, bars, and whorehouses of New Orleans of the '30's; life in the poorer working-class neighbor-hoods, especially the Polish, in the Chicago of the 1930's and '40's. Similarly, the population of Algren's world consists of hobos, prostitutes, criminals, fighters, drug addicts, cops, drunks, losers, cripples, down-and-outers, and innocent boys from small towns soon mutilated by life. Nowhere in Algren are there people vibrantly healthy, free of guilt, clean, fulfilled, content. Their existence—*our* existence, we would prefer to say—is suggested only in the abstract: as the faceless and faintly hostile crowds through which Algren's underground men travel, or as the invisible but potent force behind the police who are the nemesis of Algren's characters. The whole truth for Algren could also be described in vivid dramatic metaphors, especially in the scenes of violence so graphically depicted as to be nearly unbearable, and once viewed, unforgettable: a man in a jail cell dying of gunshot wounds, too far gone in shock to give the assent (required by law) to perform the surgery that might save his life; a legless man smashing to a pulp what had been the face of a handsome youth, in a fight over a prostitute.

Algren's first novel *Somebody in Boots* (1935) was in part a picaresque and in part a proletarian novel; it contained in ep-isode, theme, and character the germ cells for some of Algren's later work, particularly a number of the stories in *The Neon Wilderness* (1949) and much of *A Walk on the Wild Side*. The theme of *Somebody in Boots* can be stated simplistically in Marxist terms: poverty corrupts. Men are driven to violence and crime by it; women are driven to prostitution by it; both men and women are degraded and dehumanized by it. Indeed, the novel's last two sections are prefaced with quotations from the Communist Manifesto. But there is much in the novel that derives from Algren's peculiar and consistent *weltanshauung*, rather than the social philosophy of Marxism which he was soon to abandon. The novel's protagonist has those qualities native to all of Algren's heroes; he is fundamentally innocent and well-intentioned, and he yearns most of all to love and be loved. His badness comes not from inherent viciousness but from the conditioning imposed by the jungle environment he inhabits. . . . Together with what are for Algren's work pro-totypical descriptions of filth, brutality, poverty, hunger, the novel also advances Algren's prototypical assertion of the pos-sibility of romantic love among even the criminal, the down-trodden, and the supposedly lost.

However, Algren's best work remains neither his first novel nor his last, but the two novels of the 1940's: *Never Come Morning*, 1942, and *The Man with the Golden Arm*, 1949. These books focus on the Chicago milieu which is the true center of Algren's world. They incorporate and integrate a number of the best stories published in *The Neon Wilderness*. They are largely free of the self-consciously florid writing that mars both Algren's earliest and most recent works. Their stron-gest effects come from keenly visualized dramatic scenes rather than from editorializing. They are of Algren's work the most fully realized in action, character, and structure. (pp. 300-02)

*Never Come Morning* and *The Man with the Golden Arm* are distinguished by great verisimilitude and authenticity of setting and language, given emotional force by the artist's profound involvement in the lives of his doomed characters, sharpened by irony, supported upon a carefully designed structure, and made resonant by symbolic undertones. The pattern of action of both novels is identical: the essentially innocent and poten-tially noble protagonists, though besmirched by crime and fallen into vice, seek and temporarily find fulfillment and expiation through love, and even momentarily attain a kind of success, only to be trapped by their earlier misdeeds at the very moment of their greatest triumph and happiness.

If these protagonists, Lefty Bicek and Frankie Machine, are already lost when we first meet them, or soon after, if, natu-ralistic heroes that they are, their fates have already been de-termined, they nevertheless remain within the range of our sympathies because they are brought to life as neither subhuman brutes nor noble savages. (p. 302)

The central theme of *Never Come Morning*, its whole truth, so to speak, is the refutation of what has been among the hallowed official truths of American society, a truth which Algren con-siders the blackest lie: the belief that the individual retains the power of choice, of deciding between two alternatives, in plot-ting his destiny. The novel's hero, Lefty Bicek, has no alter-natives. The police captain who arrests him, first for a mug-ging, and at the end of the novel for murder, keeps this legend on the wall of his office: I HAVE ONLY MYSELF TO BLAME FOR MY FALL. Yet, ironically, only after Lefty has already fallen, only after his doom is already sealed, does he assume the strength and wisdom to consider alternatives. The fall itself is totally the product of what his environment has made him. On the same night that Lefty has taken his girl, Steffi, to an amusement park and has promised to go to church with her, on the very night when he begins to realize that he loves her— although the code of his environment would never permit the utterance of the sentiment itself—on that night he surrenders her to the savage pleasures of his "friends." His motivation is basic and one conditioned by what he has lived, fear born of self-preservation, fear both of losing the respect of his com-rades, and the physical fear of the knife one of them carries. (p. 303)

[Working] against its harsh naturalism and brutality, which includes such horrendous scenes as the mass rape, there is a more complex interaction of themes. The themes of the novel are depicted as dualisms: love and betrayal, freedom and con-finement, guilt and expiation, victory and defeat. In Book I of the novel Steffi's love and trust of Lefty moves her to give herself to him; he then betrays her love and gives her to others. In the last Book Steffi enters into a plot to betray Lefty to his former friends. But just as Lefty redeems himself to Steffi by confessing his shame to her and pledging himself to fight for her and marry her, so she reveals the plot to Lefty and fights for him.

From the moment Steffi surrenders her virginity to Lefty, nei-ther is free. Ironically, the bond between them is permanently fixed when Lefty pretends to freedom by turning Steffi over to his gang. But the betrayal that is in part supposed to free Lefty from the sentiment of love and the obligations of sexual conquest produces slavery instead, slavery for both protago-nists. Lefty falls slave to his conscience; Steffi to the whore-house which is her only shelter after being used by the neigh-borhood toughs. Lefty must suffer the merciless inquisition of his thoughts; Steffi must suffer the entrance of any man who has her price. Each, too, has become a criminal in the same episode of betrayal, and thus permanently enslaved to the whims of the police and the machinations of the law. (pp. 303-04)

Although Algren's fiction is more notable for its mood, its rendition of milieu, and its individually powerful scenes than for completely integrated and symmetrical structure, the novel's architechture does support its themes, in corollary or analogous form. It is organized around three motifs: fight, prison, dream, each of which is also crucial to Algren's work at large. (p. 304)

As I have suggested, *Never Come Morning* demands a prominent place in an important literary mode, which, contrary to a current critical cliché, is far from dead. But good as it is, *The Man with the Golden Arm* excels it. Not only is Algren's novel the first serious treatment in our literature of the drug addict, it is also a profoundly felt and profoundly moving book. This novel marks the culmination of Algren's identification with characters the "normal" man might think beneath or beyond his sympathies, yet such is Algren's craft that he extends the norm. I know of no more powerful scene of its kind in any literature than that in which Frankie takes a shot of morphine from the peddler, Louie. This is a scene in which Algren makes us participate, regardless of our range of experience.

We participate because the novel is morally pertinent. As in Algren's other serious work the themes of love, freedom, and guilt are central to *The Man with the Golden Arm,* although expressed in different dramatic terms than in *Never Come Morning.* The particular conflict here is that between self-sacrifice and self-preservation, a conflict knotted into the relationship between Frankie Machine and his wife Sophie, his friend Sparrow, and his girl Molly. These are the dynamic relationships which fluctuate with the condition of the participants. Such is Algren's version of the whole truth that his people tend to prey on one another, whether in friendship or love. (pp. 305-06)

In this way the novel establishes a general pattern of self-preservation and self-sacrifice. But such is the harshness and fatalism of Algren's world view, that the pattern of give and take does not result in anything like justice or equality. Just as betrayal, slavery, and guilt dominated *Never Come Morning* and determined the fates of its characters, so the major characters in *The Man with the Golden Arm* suffer cruel destinies, regardless of what their self-preservation or self-sacrifice would seem to earn them in an equitable universe: Frankie dies a suicide, Sophie is committed to an asylum, Sparrow and Molly face long prison terms.

Although I have stressed the tragic aspects of Algren's work, I should also point out that his books are not comprised of total gloom and unrelieved misery. There is considerable gusto and comedy throughout his work, especially in *The Neon Wilderness* and *The Man with the Golden Arm.* Indeed, the alternation between comic and tragic episodes is perhaps the most distinctive structural principle of *The Man with the Golden Arm.* (pp. 306-07)

Algren's ambitions as a social novelist notwithstanding, his ambition to write "influential" books, books that ameliorate unfair conditions, he has perhaps already accomplished something more important for literature: the scenes he has created have become part of our imaginative life, and his people are now among those we know. Algren's version of the whole truth in such works as *Never Come Morning* and *The Man with the Golden Arm* convinces us no more that his is the *whole* truth than does Dostoyevsky's vision of truth in *Notes from Underground.* Algren's truth, like Dostoyevsky's, attains its greatest conviction as a particular and imagined truth. Whatever

validity it has to life, its larger validity is to art. I believe that Algren's truth attains this larger validity. (pp. 308-09)

> *Sheldon Norman Grebstein, "Nelson Algren and the Whole Truth," in* The Forties: Fiction, Poetry, Drama, *edited by Warren French, Everett/Edwards, Inc., 1969, pp. 299-309.*

**SAUL MALOFF**

No writer has been more relentlessly faithful to his scene and cast of characters than Nelson Algren. His scene is the "wild side," the "neon wilderness," the seamier sprawls of Chicago and its spiritual extensions across this broad land—America as Chicago. And his characters are . . . the born losers who constitute a half-world, an anti-society to the society that never appears, not even as a sensed or felt presence, in Algren's work. . . . The mythical time, whatever the calendar reads, is always the '30's, somewhere around the longest year of 1935.

Except when it's time for settling old scores. Since *The Last Carousel* is for the most part an ingathering of magazine pieces, many of them from the pages of *Playboy,* anything goes. So Algren allows himself yet another unpleasant portrait of Simone de Beauvoir and some small diversions in the form of vendettas—against Alfred Kazin in particular and critics in general; the University of Iowa Writers' Workshop in particular and, in general, workshops and other forms of corrupting the young and susceptible. As these and some other self-indulgent pieces do evident violence to the prevailing unity of tone and subject, the internal pressure to include them must have been tremendous. They succeed largely in getting off some cheap shots, though some of the objects so richly deserve savaging, one can't wholly begrudge the author these incidental pleasures, any more than one can deny him the pleasures of some fine childhood reminiscence, or of recording racetrack, baseball and boxing lore, in which Algren, in his best moments, is incomparably if lachrymosely good.

But the book takes its echoing tone from Algren's chronic weakness for "fine" writing, the kind of overblown elegiac lyricism—tremulous, quivering, cadenced, or wistful, celebratory, nostalgic, poignant—that used to be called prose-poetry. It was widely practiced by sensitive young writers in conscious quest of an American demotic voice, some suitable song for the open road—the endless, receding plains, prairies, rivers of the imagined West. Of that chorus, Algren's voice was the most prominent and is the longest lasting, the others have long since faded. Decidedly a literary manner, it came on aggressively anti-literary: tough-tender and bittersweet, sentimental and swaggering, robust, keen-eyed, sprung from the soil, epic, open to the full spectrum of American experience, defiantly outside the mainstream of literary modernism and contemptuous of it, a strong dose of salts for the university wits and nancies—in short a species of literary populism and native romanticism, a nervously American preoccupation of the '30's.

The trouble with "style," with any strongly marked literary manner, is that it can become its own object of contemplation. Algren has always been a gifted yarn-spinner, a teller of tall tales and manner as to be finally strangled by them. Helplessly our sorely strained attention shifts from story and character. Typically the story outgrows its limits, expands, without warrant, toward legend. Characters degenerate into "colorful characters"; and our attention, having been thus wrenched from its ostensible objects, centers on the evocative voice of the poet singing of summer with full-throated ease. Not a page is free from it.

Even in self-mockery it is enamored of itself. . . .

The collection includes actual quasi-balladic verse: **"Epitaph: The Man with the Golden Arm," "Ode to an Absconding Bookie," "Tricks Out of Times Long Gone"**; but always the prose aspires to that state, so that, disconcertingly, the movement from time to time comes to a full stop to allow space for the assertion of verses before movement toward status can be resumed. (p. 23)

Now tarts, with all due respect, may have hearts of gold, and no doubt they—together with drifters of *no* trade—have stories to tell; but their stories are few in number, drab in texture, small in scope—and, in the nature of things, somewhat similar in tone and substance. Aglren, our only poet of the lumpen proletariat, is the rambling minstrel of times that never were and are now long gone. He alone has remembered their voices and restored their lives. In order to make them memorable, the stuff of lore, figures in the American landscape, he provides the amplification, with reedy winds, often one lonesome oboe, off-key, and augmented strings, some of them snapped. (p. 24)

Saul Maloff, "Maverick in American Letters," in The New Republic, *Vol. 170, No. 3, January 19, 1974, pp. 23-4.*

### CHOICE

Advertised as a collection of stories, [*The last carousel*] is really an assortment of memoirs, travel writings, poems, and diatribes, with a few stories mixed in. It will do nothing for the reputation of the author of *The man with the golden arm* (1949). The style is self-indulgent and egocentric, the satire is trivial, and the pieces on Oriental massage parlors are simply embarrassing, though intended as social comment. One long piece on the fixing of the 1919 World Series has some interest, and there are meditations on Bonnie and Clyde worthy of Steinbeck, but this collection will only keep Algren's stove warm: the soup is very thin, because the pot never even came to a rolling boil.

A review of "The Last Carousel," *in* Choice, *Vol. 11, No. 1, March, 1974, p. 84.*

### MARTHA HEASLEY COX AND WAYNE CHATTERTON

Altogether, the published short stories of Algren are a considerable achievement. Though somewhat uneven, "a curious amalgam," the stories of *The Neon Wilderness* have elicited unexpected discipline from an author so often charged with looseness and with over-rhapsodizing in his novels. Catherine Meredith Brown justifiably says of the short stories what has rarely if ever been claimed for the novels: "the staccato precision of the writing must be read, remembered, and admired." (p. 57)

Nowhere outside the short stories has Algren been so free to exercise his ability to construct a tale from the single, self-revelatory catch-phrase; "Sometimes I stagger. But I don't fall down"; "The devil lives in a double-shot"; "I knew I'd never get to be twenty-one anyhow"; "We are all members of one another"; "Lies are a poor man's pennies"; "Tell 'em where you got it and how easy it was"; "I'm the girl that men forget." Nowhere else has he controlled so stringently his tendency to blend the sordid and poetic; as a result, the short stories have

largely escaped the adverse reaction which such a controversial mixture has brought against his novels.

Otherwise, however, the short stories are almost indistinguishable from the novels. In each genre are the same twilit shadow-world of alley, bar, brothel, jail, cave-like tenement, and flea-bag hotel room; the same maudlin and monotonous juke-box tunes punctuated by the rattling of the El above its thousand columns; the same hopheads, drunks, mackers, outworn prostitutes, sharpies, and general losers; the same grostequeries of tone and situation; the same concrete and specific insights; the same entrapments, vague unrest, and futile striving. Above all, these stories, despite their shortcomings, are a monument to the honesty, directness, and authority of a writer who has depicted a nightmare society which its parent world would rather disown but which Algren knows too well to let it endure unsung. (pp. 57-8)

Algren's compassion for society's lost and dispossessed had been clear from his earliest works; but, with the appearance of *A Walk on the Wild Side,* the already hostile critics, and some heretofore undecided ones, accused him of "Puerile sentimentality" and of wild excess. One complained that "in supposing that human virtue flourishes best among degenerates, Novelist Algren has dressed his sense of compassion in the rags of vulgarity.". . .

The general reaction to the novel was favorable, however. Most reviewers were willing to accept the premise that Algren had set himself "the extremely difficult literary task of showing how much basic human strength and worth can persist in lives which, outwardly, represent utter degradation." (p. 85)

As the critical reaction indicates, Algren's success is partly the result of his having developed convincing and entertaining characters, even though they are a "covey of queer quail." The queer quail include pimps and whores, sexual deviates, sadists, lushes, hoboes, "kleptoes," gamblers, con men, pickpockets, "cokies," and other assorted criminals and on-the-fringe people. But all are highly individualized, and none is ever dull. One of Algren's most remarkable achievements in *A Walk on the Wild Side* is his convincing, compassionate treatment of a group of characters who could, in less skillful hands, be little more than a gallery of freaks and sheer grotesques. Algren makes them believable and sometimes arouses sympathy in the reader by treating them as people with dreams and aspirations, however callous the world outside; with vitality, however debilitating the circumstances; with humor, however unfunny the situation; and with individuality, whatever the usual literary mold or stereotype.

The unforgettable legless man, Schmidt, who is Algren's own favorite character among his creations, is an example. Though a substantial literary tradition of partial or total amputees exists, Schmidt belongs to the family of neither Captain Ahab nor Porgy. Despite Schmidt's having displayed himself as a carnival freak, he as a man transcends his freakishness. Despite—or because of—his own virility, he is the only customer who turns away in disgust from Finnerty's peep show. Retaining all the original strength of his magnificent torso, yet doomed to move, however agilely, upon a wheeled platform, he bursts upon the reader as a complex and impressive human being rather than a cripple. To laugh *at* Schmidt is unthinkable, though it is sometimes possible to laugh *with* him. Even more formidable than the strength of his arms is the strength of his pride. That he should die of his wounded pride, and die in an almost Surrealistic scene of jungle-like barroom viciousness, is so fitting as to seem almost inevitable. (pp. 86-7)

In depicting "the girls," Algren, with a freshness and vividness unequaled in similar fiction, avoids the centuries-old stereotype of the "good-hearted whore." The house girls on old Perdido Street are no more the tragi-comic whores of the seventeenth- and eighteenth-century stage than they are the bland, generous girls of John Steinbeck's *Cannery Row*. To Algren, the "oldest profession" is a subject neither for righteous sermonizing nor for a romantic cliché; a business like any other, it is distinguished by its long history as a profession and by its location at the margin of the law. Otherwise, pimps and whores are bosses and workers; and the workers "are people, good, bad, and indifferent, like any other women. If they perform a good deed or an unselfish act their motives are as mixed as those of any wife or sweetheart—or any businessman on the make for a buck." In settling for the unvarnished view of a profession so long distorted by other considerations, Algren has studied his characters as people who have adopted a time- and self-consuming business, whatever the moral aspects of the business, and whatever the idiosyncrasies of the individuals. (pp. 88-9)

Algren's colorful, unorthodox prose style elicited even more critical comment after the appearance of *A Walk on the Wild Side* than it had in the past. Algren often speaks of his fiction as poetry, and his style is, in at least the broadest sense, poetic. Yet, like Whitman, he writes of matters which have not been historically acceptable as poetic; and, in his novels, he has been particularly vulnerable to the charge that his style is "blurred" because it alternates between the hard-cast realistic prose and passages of lyricism. In the ribald, Rabelaisian tone of *A Walk on the Wild Side*, however, this alternation creates precisely the effect which the subject matter demands.

Algren disclaims deliberate poetizing in this book, however, and the lyric tone is in general more closely integrated with the prose and less obtrusive than in the Chicago novels. For the most part, he relies upon snatches of popular jukebox tunes and upon an occasional short near-metrical passage that warrant the comment that he "frames his materials in back-country balladry and earthy lyricism." Otherwise, he concentrates upon capturing the true music of dialect and upon exercising his keen ear for prose rhythms in which the natural repetition and the metrical rise and fall of colloquial speech predominate. (p. 90)

But the true stylistic unorthodoxies appear in his syntax and imagery far more than in his propensity for borderline versifying. From the beginning of his career, he has experimented with unconventional techniques of punctuation to achieve special effects. By the time he was writing the Chicago novels, he had wrought the techniques into a distinctive stylistic manner that was unlike that of any other novelist. His basic technique is to bind together a succession of individual fragments through the syntax which normally controls a long single sentence. Sometimes he varies this effect by using a short, uncomplicated run-on sentence. By the time he wrote *A Walk on the Wild Side*, he had fine-tuned this technique, frequently omitting "spare parts," until it was capable of conveying subtle nuance and astonishing variety of effect.

The result is that, during moments of high emotional pitch, his sentences and paragraphs break into an almost limitless variety of specially designed sentence fragments—all controlled by their being part of an otherwise conventional set of antitheses, subordinates, or coordinates. The effect is that of

high rhythmic flexibility that has unusual prose control of pause and acceleration and that ranges from crackling staccato through crescendo. (pp. 90-1)

In *A Walk on the Wild Side*, Algren utilized his rhetoric to develop devices of imagery with which he had long practiced. Like Stephen Crane's, his color-imagery had always been startling. In the Chicago novels, for instance, he had developed almost to the point of mannerism the device of coupling figurative noun-modifiers with the participle *colored*. The effects of the practice were impressive but startling since the modifiers were generally not words with a true or specific color designation. In the Chicago novels a man's cap is almost habitually described as "pavement colored." Though to most readers the imagery is gray, the modifier compound offers a range or choice of hue with the added dimensions of texture and suggestive tone. Few such compounds in the Chicago novels, however, are such broad use of the device as is the description of evening as "slander-colored" in *A Walk on the Wild Side*. Further, by the time Algren was reworking *Somebody in Boots*, he had begun to use extensively such highly specialized figures as forms of inverted personification; "It was fantasy that had pursued them, every one, all their lives; they had not pursued it."

But in *A Walk on the Wild Side,* as in Algren's previous novels, the impressive verbal mortar which binds the other stylistic properties is still the concreteness and specificity of detail; the accurate terminology of road, gutter, bar, and brothel; the keen and comprehensive ear for dialect; the eye for significant idiosyncrasies of dress and behavior; the quick grasp of obsessive quirks of thought—the ring of authority. With the true novelist's ability to record and recall every detail which his senses register—especially all that he hears—Algren is able to recreate the little-known twilight world of the pander and the prostitute with a convincingness rarely matched in fiction. A 'curious blend of the poet and the reporter, a kind of prose Walt Whitman," he combines the sensitivity and emotion of the poet with the factual sense of the good journalist. One reads such writers as Algren not simply for the vigor and excitement, though *A Walk on the Wild Side* abounds in these, but also because of the unavoidable impression that one is learning something valuable from a writer who knows his material. (pp. 91-2)

All these elements—the ethic, the characterization, the style—are fused and raised to a higher caliber by the maturing of Algren's sense of comedy, the ribald, grotesque, near-Surrealistic humor which informs all of *A Walk on the Wild Side*. . . . Algren's whole career had tuned him, as it were, to write this book. It is his own favorite and, he believes, his best. (p. 92)

*The Man with the Golden Arm* is an estimable novel which occupies an important position in Algren's development as a novelist. Though not so neatly constructed as *Never Come Morning*, it is more densely packed, more intense, and in some ways more mature. The humorous scenes lead straight to Algren's last major work, the uniquely comic *A Walk on the Wild Side*, which Algren and many of his critics consider to be his best novel.

Like all important writers, Algren has been asked repeatedly to define the writer's role in modern society. He has struggled seriously to express the function he has sought to perform as a writer; and, though he has said it many different ways, the gist is much the same: "The role of the writer is always to stand against the culture he is in," or more specifically, "the writer's place today is with the accused, guilty or not guilty, with the accused.''

*The Man with the Golden Arm* is Algren's most comprehensive expression of his conviction that America's great middle class should be made to recognize the personal worth and dignity of the socially disinherited who do not live the spurious lives of the ''business cats'' and the country-club set, neither of whom has been willing to recognize ''the world underneath.'' In writing such novels as *The Man with the Golden Arm,* Algren has blended Naturalistic Determinism ''with a sympathy for his people that nevertheless cannot deter him from sending them to their miserable fates.'' In a style and language that are drawn from the world he depicts, he has ''managed to impart a dignity to material which would be merely sordid in the hands of a lesser writer.'' He regularly insists that the ''poetry'' which characterizes his Realism is a natural poetry, one taken from the people themselves: ''When I heard a convict who had just finished his stretch say, 'I made my time from bell to bell, now the rest of the way is by the stars,' if somebody was fusing poetry with realism it was the con, not me. My most successful poetry, the lines people threw back at me years after they were written, were lines I never wrote. They were lines I heard, and repeated, usually by someone who never read and couldn't write.''

For this reason, despite the concreteness and authoritative detail of his prose, Algren is ''more a singer than an explainer,'' one whose prose in *The Man with the Golden Arm* can become almost a ''kind of incantation, like the chanting of ritual itself.'' In such a form, the curb and tenement and half-shadow world of Frankie and Sophie and Molly with its unforgettable smoke-colored rain, its musk-colored murmuring, and its calamitous light have brought the world underneath a bit closer to the middle-class American consciousness and conscience. (pp. 132-33)

> *Martha Heasley Cox and Wayne Chatterton, in their* Nelson Algren, *Twayne Publishers, 1975, 163 p.*

## PHOEBE-LOU ADAMS

Algren began his last book [*The Devil's Stocking*] as a report on a murder case in Paterson, New Jersey—a case in which the guilt of the accused was doubted by sympathetic observers despite his conviction. Eventually, Algren decided to transform the material he had gathered into fiction. Although this process enabled him to enliven fact with the kind of gritty semi-underworld episodes that he handled with notable skill and assurance, it produced a loose-hung book in which the remains of reportage and the inventions of the novelist never quite fit together. But if the whole is a bit shaky, many of the parts are splendid, and worth reading for their own brilliant sake.

> *Phoebe-Lou Adams, in a review of ''The Devil's Stocking,'' in* The Atlantic Monthly, *Vol. 252, No. 4, October, 1983, p. 123.*

## JOHN W. ALDRIDGE

During their lifetimes Nelson Algren and James T. Farrell were often discussed together as two very similar and clearly important novelists of the Depression Thirties, although neither was considered quite worthy of promotion to first-rank eminence. But they did in fact have a good deal in common besides their modesty of status. Both were committed social realists who at various stages of their careers were in and out of sympathy with the Marxist movement. (p. 9)

[In *The Devil's Stocking* Algren] seems not to have aged but only matured and to be, as never before, in firm possession of his subject. His language throughout the novel is precise, controlled, almost entirely free of the lush lyrical excesses of the past, but nonetheless genuinely warm and alive. The story is recognizable as belonging to the classic Algren repertoire, yet is also freshly conceived and carried forward with an easy assurance that indicates Algren had it in him to write five or six more novels in the same vein.

''The Devil's Stocking'' is based on the true-life story of Rubin ''Hurricane'' Carter, a small-time middleweight boxer who was tried and imprisoned for murder in what Algren believed to have been a serious miscarriage of justice.... Algren has managed with remarkable success to transform the principal figures of the Carter case into fictive characters with lives that no longer conform to the mere facts but are freed to serve Algren's imaginative vision of their human and dramatic possibilities. Most of the familiar jungle types in his low-life menagerie are present once again—the call girls, petty crooks, gamblers and sadistic police officers. But the character of Carter himself has been transmogrified into Ruby Calhoun, a protagonist who grows in complexity as the action proceeds, until he becomes a fully realized, multidimensional tragic personage in a narrative that has all the vital signs of having been produced by a writer still fully confident of his inventive powers. (pp. 9, 32)

> *John W. Aldridge, ''Two Realists from Chicago,'' in* The New York Times Book Review, *October 9, 1983, pp. 9, 32-3.*\*

## ELAINE KENDALL

Rubin (Hurricane) Carter was a black middleweight boxer tried and jailed for a murder.... The stark outline of this story forms the basis for [''**The Devil's Stocking**'']..., demonstrating the same intense social consciousness characterizing the author's earlier work.... Artfully fictionalized, Carter acquires a depth and breadth of character exceeding expectation, forcing the most skeptical reader to see the central character as a man first and a metaphor second, insisting that we make the necessary connections between our systems and the people they both serve and victimize.

> *Elaine Kendall, in a review of ''The Devil's Stocking,'' in* Los Angeles Times Book Review, *October 30, 1983, p. 4.*

# Max (Isaac) Apple

## 1941-

American short story writer, novelist, scriptwriter, and critic.

In his fiction Apple affectionately satirizes various aspects of American culture. His stories are fast-paced, and his fictional characters often interact with well-known public figures. With his first book, *The Oranging of America and Other Stories* (1976), Apple established a reputation for comic inventiveness sparked by wit, slapstick humor, and farcical situations. Most reviews of this book were favorable, matching Eliot Fremont Smith's evaluation: "Apple proves once again that literary delight may engage the current mind in a rewarding way even though it does not confront great issues of immediate consequence."

In *Zip: A Novel of the Left and the Right* (1978), Apple maintains the same approach as in his short fiction. This novel centers on Ira Goldstein, a man lacking personal drive who latches onto other people displaying energy and ambition, or "zip." Apple uses the sport of boxing to satirize religion and politics, and he blends fictional characters named Jesús, Solomon, and Moses with such controversial figures as Fidel Castro, Jane Fonda, and J. Edgar Hoover. The stories collected in *Free Agents* (1983) are generally more autobiographical. In this book Apple finds humor in topics that include Disneyland, psychotherapy, jogging, and death. Critics found Apple's comic treatment of both trivial and serious themes to be honest and sympathetic.

(See also *CLC*, Vol. 9 and *Contemporary Authors*, Vols. 81-84.)

Marion Ettlinger/courtesy Esquire

## NICHOLAS DELBANCO

Max Apple has real comic talent. He has an eye for incongruity and an ear for intonation; his collection of short stories, *The Oranging of America*, proved him a social satirist with charm. *Zip: A Novel of the Left and the Right* is about politics and prize-fighting, and there's fancy footwork throughout. Though there's a slightly cloying coyness to the title's double entendre, Apple by and large avoids cheap shots. His books are better than their names.

The cast of characters teeters once again between the imagined and the actual. We have Ira Goldstein managing a middleweight called Jesus the Crab; the first-person narration, in both present and past tenses, is Ira's memoir. . . .

There are plots abounding. While Ira plans seduction and mounts an assault on the middleweight crown, his shadow-boxing secret sharer plots a coup. Though Jesus does road-work incessantly, he's no running dog; licking the spittle from his mouthpiece, later, he's no capitalist lickspittle lackey but the unchained proletarian champ. . . .

But as Ira and Jesus go public, so do the characters. Jane Fonda appears in Jesus's dressing room before his first big fight. She knees him in the groin; he's wearing a protective cup, however, and goes out to kidnap J. Edgar Hoover, and they fly him to Castro's Havana, where Hoover ends up in a chair suspended over the boxing ring—a fight-fan to the end—watching Tiger Williams demolish the crowd-pleasing ideologue while Grand-

mother Goldstein is dying back home, and LBJ invites the Solomons down to the ranch for ribs. Got that? This book winds up, folks, it doesn't run down, it's a regular slambang fantasia, replete with Howard Cosell and George Danton the trainer and Caluccio Salutatti, who should have been merely the Mafia but is, more dangerously, a Marxist, and Tom Hayden and baby and bathwater. (p. 35)

In a book so full of "low comedy," however, where should "high seriousness" reside? Character after character takes the world seriously, while their author takes it with a fistful of salt. And this produces [a] kind of vertigo . . . ; Grandmother Goldstein's vengeful integrity seems wrong-headed, mostly, and Jesus's deeply held convictions fail to convince. Apple is most effective when he goes for the sidelong effect. . . . But it's hard to know what this novel's about, or who's knocking whom for a loop. (pp. 35-6)

And the figures descend from prototype to stereotype; the women, in particular, have too few distinguishing marks. The courtship of Solomon and Frieda reads like warmed-over Bruce Jay Friedman, and the grandmother's complaints begin to bore. The book, though brief, feels windy by comparison with *The Oranging of America*'s shapely succinctness. Apple used the prizefight metaphor to as good advantage in his short story, **"Inside Norman Mailer,"** and the brilliant **"Understanding**

Alvarado'' did better by Castro and Cuba. The novel ends in a great burst of speed, but—to borrow the diction once more—it's as if he saved himself for the 15th round.

Still there's magic here. From the Goldstein's cellar in Detroit to the fight of the century in Havana—with J. Edgar Hoover as stakes—is a zany distance to travel, and Apple's a good-humored guide. His plot is absurd but admittedly so; his prose is sprightly throughout. There are no villains in this comic cosmos; even Tiger Williams, who batters Jesus senseless, is ''tired and in tears.'' The dialogue is excellent, and the closing sequence—an apotheosis of Jesus ascending—proves a *tour de force* as farce. Apple's imagination is fecund; if the book leaves the aftertaste of cotton candy, it's nonetheless been a well-spun sweet read. Take it with you to the beach and watch out for Jesus the Crab. (p. 36)

> *Nicholas Delbanco, in a review of ''Zip: A Novel of the Left and the Right,'' in* The New Republic, *Vol. 178, No. 25, June 24, 1978, pp. 35-6.*

### JOHN LEONARD

Max Apple is the author of a wonderful collection of short stories, **''The Oranging of America,''** in which Howard Johnson, Fidel Castro, the Arabs and other myth-afflicted riffraff wander around causing trouble and laughter. Whether Mr. Apple is also a novelist is problematic. **''Zip,''** for which Castro makes a return appearance as a promoter of a middleweight boxing match with J. Edgar Hoover as the prize, seems to me to be less a novel than a box of toys, epigrams, firecrackers, political pot shots, Talmudic maunderings, whistles and screams. What distinguishes it from other, similar exercises in Pop Modernism is its affection. Mr. Apple likes people, even crazy people. . . .

What are we to make of [all the goings-on in **''Zip''**], and do we have to? Well, there's more Jewish guilt—about history, about sex, about the darker races. This is the territory of Bernard Malamud, Philip Roth, Bruce Jay Friedman and Woody Allen. And there's more of the Jewish romance with America, the longing to belong. Such a longing, like his love of baseball and movies, leads Ira to inform on Jesus; he is another, comic version of Saul Bellow's Humboldt and Stanley Elkin's franchiser. And there's more of the politicizing of dreams, the sociologizing of the private life, the drama of the self distorted into headlines. See [Robert] Coover and E. L. Doctorow and Donald Barthelme and Thomas Pynchon.

I am not just making lists. Mr. Apple reminds me at one time or another of all these writers. He is, however, kind. He is not a nag. You have only to compare his portrait of Debby Silvers in **''Zip''** with Mr. Roth's portrait of Brenda Patimkin in ''Goodbye, Columbus'' to see what a difference two decades and a benign temperament can make. Inside Mr. Apple's cartoons of Bertha and Solomon are real people, with dimensions independent of politics and money and the mongering of a thesis. Mr. Apple uses a feather, not a blowtorch, on his characters. He would tickle politics out of business.

Still, Jesus just isn't interesting enough to seduce us out of our incredulity. Ira is too unfocused to care much about. A fine comic intelligence, a superb ear, and a brilliant way with slapstick do not automatically add up to a coherent, satisfying book. Once upon a time Ira's father told him, ''Impossible is not fair.'' This is true of novels, too, no matter how zippy.

> *John Leonard, in a review of ''Zip: A Novel of the Left and the Right,'' in* The New York Times, *July 17, 1978, p. C15.*

### TERENCE WINCH

Max Apple's *Zip* is an exposé of the spiritual bankruptcy of American life in which people trade virtue for ambition and love for success and no one is ever really satisfied. His novel is also a parody of the ongoing battle between The Flesh and The Spirit in contemporary American writing in which neither side is ever the clear-cut winner. . . .

[Right] off the bat, Apple mixes religion and boxing, with his new Jesús as the potential ''peoples' champion.'' . . .

Rather than be mocked by boxing or religion, Apple's approach is to do the mocking himself. *Zip* can be most successfully read as a parody of Christianity. The novel's comic method is reduction—Jesús is a middleweight, not a heavyweight; there is a Solomon who is smart, but not wise; the Crucifixion becomes a boxing match in Cuba; ''Zip'' (a blend of ambition and assertiveness) replaces grace as the ruling virtue. Jesús even takes on Ira's last name to become ''Jesús Goldstein''—a mixed metaphor in which the spirituality of one name is devalued by the material connotations of the other. . . .

Apple does not confine himself to boxing. *Zip,* the subtitle tells us cleverly, is ''A Novel of the Left and the Right.'' But when politics hits the fan, the plot starts to splatter.

In [the short stories] **''The Oranging of America''** and **''Disneyad,''** . . . Apple revealed a special talent for re-creating historical figures in his fiction. In *Zip,* J. Edgar Hoover, Jane Fonda and Tom Hayden all make appearances, and there are flashes of Apple's special talent at work. But because the narrative becomes too ridiculous to be convincing, Apple's ''real'' characters seem fake. In **''Disneyad,''** Apple made you feel you were right there with Will and Walt Disney as they built their cartoon empire. But there is no way a kidnapped Hoover, dangling from a basket suspended over a boxing ring in Cuba, can seem authentic. . . .

In the 1950s and '60s, the Jewish novel became an established tradition in American fiction and Apple's book belongs very much to this tradition. His prose has the humor and poise of Bellow's or Roth's. And his story of a Jew's relationship with a Puerto Rican owes a debt to several older writers. For Edward Lewis Wallant in *The Pawnbroker,* the characters were Sol Nazerman and Jesús Ortiz. In Bernard Malamud's *The Assistant,* they were Morris Bober and Frank Alpine. The spiritual exchange between Jew and Gentile was a parable of modern salvation that Wallant and Malamud took very seriously. In *Zip,* however, Apple parodies the salvation parable. But rather than transforming the myth through humor, he simply discredits it.

There is no question that Max Apple is a good writer. But in *Zip* he seems to be taking on too much in too brief a novel. Apple could learn a lesson from Henry James who, it has been said, ''chewed more than he bit off.''

> *Terence Winch, ''Down for the Count,'' in* Book World—The Washington Post, *August 6, 1978, p. F3.*

## PHILIP STEVICK

As the 1960s recede in the memory, [the era] seems less a drama of substantive tensions—ideological, political, and social—than a mélange of styles, most of them overdone and obsessive. Had we not all lived through the decade, it would be possible to call those styles surreal. In Max Apple's *Zip,* Ira Goldstein, his manic narrator, describes Debbie Silvers's living room. It contains pictures of Ho Chi Minh and napalmed children; she sits on her water bed, eats M&Ms, reads *The Structure of Music,* her brown nipples showing through her Indian shirt. The combination of napalmed children and M&Ms is what gives the passage both its power to amuse, for it is touching and grotesque, and its power to evoke, for the world, ten years ago, was full of Debbie Silverses. (p. 153)

"About" the '60s, the novel is also "about" zip. Zip is energy. Ira, energetic enough, God knows, is in quest of zip, that flush of adrenalin that gives passion and drive to life. Being parasitic, he finds zip from other people and that, perhaps, is Apple's most telling comment on the '60s, that depressing tendency to derive energy from other energetic people, irrespective of what those other people *do.*

Max Apple's first book was a bright, inventive collection of short fictions, *The Oranging of America.* Writers whose first success is in short forms always invite the criticism that their subsequent longer fictions lack the substance which the length demands, being only extended stories. Formulaic and predictable though the criticism is, in this case it is just. Apple sustains Ira's monologue with a kind of idiotic vigor that only Stanley Elkin can do better. And he renders the sense of the '60s as farce, giving that version as much justification as the heavier versions can carry. But the novel finally lacks the range that its premises lead one to expect. Apple is a virtuoso but Ira Goldstein can only do a limited number of things with words. Apple, no doubt, has a range of human responsiveness that is greater than most men's. But to Ira, everyone is something to be promoted, coped with, hectored, kvetched about. And so the impression is finally of a novel with wonderful moments, a splendid sense of verbal play, and a keen eye for the styles of the '60s but without the imaginative power of Apple's best shorter work. (pp. 153-54)

*Philip Stevick, "Napalm and M&Ms," in* The Nation, *Vol. 227, No. 5, August 19-26, 1978, pp. 153-54.*

## LYNN LURIA-SUKENICK

*Zip: A Novel of the Left and the Right* mates the schlemiel of the Jewish novel of the fifties with the whimsy and politics of the pop novels of the sixties and the result is a hybrid that should be palatable but is curiously uninteresting as an entire book.... Max Apple's astuteness about the complexities of political sentiments is visible in the book, but is not taken far. What he wants is a cartoon novel, a theme that's to be respected for its riffs and variations.... (p. 292)

Apple is a very good writer, a funny writer, and at times that seems to be enough: the fountain of genial chicken-flavored speech is delightful, his imagination is rich, he tells us interesting little stories. Yet the telling is finally too flavored for anything but talk to matter; the characters don't mean anything to one another but only to the author, whose pleasure in them derives from his opportunity to use language on them.... [The] localized felicities don't accumulate to move or involve us. Apple wants to do standup comedy, that's his secret. He

wants those one-liners ("To kiss her would be acupuncture."), those Yiddish cadences, those tics and nudges. And it would be a blessing to his readers if he would give them the *spritz* direct instead of asking his overworked plot and characters to carry his considerable wit around. (pp. 292-93)

*Lynn Luria-Sukenick, in a review of "Zip," in* Partisan Review, *Vol. XLVII, No. 2, 1980, pp. 292-93.*

## WILLIAM KOTZWINKLE

"My doctor said that because of my drinking I had developed little pockets of beer, not just the well-known belly but beer bulge at the wrists, behind the ears, between the vertebrae."

This is vintage Max Apple, the sort of line that takes you in at first, and you believe it, laugh, then laugh at yourself for believing it, and laugh again. I find myself laughing with Mr. Apple while driving my car, hours later, or much later in the night. He sneaks up on you that way, throughout the stories in **"Free Agents,"** his new collection. . . .

He is also willing to try most anything—ice fishing, for example, in which he catches the spirit of his deceased wife. He is honest about emotion, and it's infectious, for I think he's found a way of living that is like Lao-tze. All others are clear; he alone is clouded. And in that cloud, that constant puzzle that is Max Apple looking at himself, we see things as they are.

**"Blood Relatives"** is the story of his wealthy Uncle Jake, an elderly landlord for whom Max is afraid, because the old man lives in a poor black neighborhood. The old man is unperturbed and, in a wonderfully funny scene, Mr. Apple returns to find Uncle Jake and some of the neighborhood's shadier characters having a party, listening to 78-r.p.m. Hebrew melodies and "Mickey Katz singing 'Herring Boats Are Coming.'" . . .

Months later, when Uncle Jake gets sick, the only people to come to see him, other than Max, are the black hustlers, to give him a pint of their blood. Are they hustling him? Do they love him? Whichever way you look at it, it's a great story. . . .

At the other end of Mr. Apple's spectrum, the part more softly lighted, is [**"Bridging"**], the story of the Girl Scouts. His wife has died, young, tragically, and this isn't funny. But if humor is the only thing that makes us human, as some philosophers say, then Mr. Apple can't stop being funny even in his loss, for humor is his strength; he has many, many shades of it, exquisitely delicate, and perfectly appropriate.

*William Kotzwinkle, "The Father As Girl Scout, and Other Wonders," in* The New York Times Book Review, *June 17, 1984, p. 11.*

## WALTER CLEMONS

The narrator of the title story in Max Apple's new collection [*Free Agents*] declares himself "ready for everything." The phrase describes Apple's own stance. The author of **"The Oranging of America"** (1976) and **"Zip"** (1978) has a voice of unusual timbre. He is a satirist without scorn, an affectionate ironist. Apple masters the lingoes of postmodernism, incorporation and Washington lobbying and comes up grinning, as if he's found diamonds, not dreck. . . .

This book contains one story that I would, without embarrassment, call great. **"Bridging"** is about single parenting. A father becomes a Girl Scout assistant leader. His daughter prefers to stay home and watch baseball games on television. Both suffer grief at the loss of a wife and mother, and neither can talk about their loss. I never thought, on the basis of his earlier work, to compare Apple with Chekhov. But he here merits such praise. **"Bridging"** is one of the best stories anybody has ever written. It is at least as good as Chekhov's "Grief."

Walter Clemons, "Apple Blossoms," in Newsweek, Vol. CIII, No. 26, June 25, 1984, p. 68.

### SHIMON WINCELBERG

Over a year ago, knowing nothing about Max Apple, I began to read a book of his called, rather facetiously, *The Oranging of America*. In the gee-whiz style of a PR-inspired newspaper feature, its title story purported to tell how a man named Howard Johnson came to fulfill his American Dream from the back of a 1964 Cadillac limousine equipped with a battery-operated ice-cream freezer that held at least 18 flavors at all times, although Mr. Johnson ate only vanilla. Possibly not in the mood either for whimsy or for learning more than I wanted to know about the motel and ice-cream business, I gave up after a couple of pages.

My mistake. As I discovered upon being moved to pick it up again when I finished [*Free Agents*], *Oranging* is also a cheerful mixture of Apple's deceptively bland sense of fantasy and airy humor—a humor free of malice, aggression, or sly nudges to share a laugh at another's expense. The classic definitions will have to be rewritten.

**"Walt and Will,"** the first story in *Free Agents*, opens in the Johnson saga's upbeat, almost plodding expository manner. You could confuse it with the sort of authorized biography the Disney management might entrust to a tame, starry-eyed academic. Then, as imperceptibly as an airliner retracting its wheels, it drops its horizon and soars into a most un-Disneylike flight of fancy on how a diffident young genius-to-be hit on the original idea for his billion-dollar mouse. . . .

Further on, Apple records for us the conversation in which the true visionary, head-on-his-shoulders brother Will, has to virtually twist Walt's arm to get the go-ahead to build Disney World. . . .

I am willing to concede that the author's transcript of the brothers' exchange may not be historically accurate. But I have no difficulty believing—having myself often foolishly resisted arm-twistings by similarly inspired dreamers—that this is the kind of talk, the kind of icy-shrewd, childlike leap of faith that gave us the Empire of the Mouse. . . .

Much of Apple's writing encroaches on the private lives of the famous: Disney, Mailer, Velikovsky, Einstein. Yet with the possible exception of **"Inside Norman Mailer"** in *The Oranging of America*, his intent seems to me not so much satire as appropriation. He finds evident joy in his skill at making the bigwigs *his* fictional characters. Thus in *Free Agents* he doesn't even bother to include one of those smarmy disavowals of "any similarities to persons living or dead."

Other delightful rearrangements of our world occur in **"Small Island Republics,"** where a brilliant young Japanese-American lobbyist rides to the rescue of an abandoned, stagnating and forgotten Taiwan—by leasing it to Disneyland. The solution is arrived at with such perfect logic, one suspects it could not fail to earn Ronald Reagan's wholehearted approbation. (p. 15)

Apple's more overtly autobiographical stories, if equally sweet-natured, seem to me somewhat less magical. He is capable in these of putting you in mind of a Bellow protagonist recalling his impossible women. The Apple women, though, . . . are less formidable, less toxic, less mad. They may, on occasion, have "noticeable armpits," or "teeth like lightning rods," but they do not, à la Bellow's, "eat green salads and drink human blood."

Of the personal pieces, the one I have been pushing into friends' faces is **"Stranger at the Table."** Here Apple describes, with passion and good humor, what it is like to belong to "the minority of the minority" and go through life forever obliged to explain what it means to keep kosher.

The conventional wisdom is that short story collections do not sell. Readers—like johns prudently disinclined to fall in love with a hooker—are perceived as reluctant to invest a whole lot of emotion in an experience that is over so quickly. Nevertheless, the warm critical reception *Free Agents* has been receiving, and Max Apple's recent appearances in *Esquire*, lead me to hope it may still be enough for a writer to offer us an altogether new way of looking at our world while making us laugh out loud with pleasure. (pp. 15-16)

Shimon Wincelberg, "Delightfully Rearranging Our World," in The New Leader, Vol. LXVII, No. 13, July 9-23, 1984, pp. 15-16.

### TOM LeCLAIR

Much of Max Apple's new collection [*Free Agents*] could have been published in *Me Magazine*. There's Max growing up in the 1950s with a Yiddish-speaking grandmother in Grand Rapids, deserting his family and region, holding onto kosher food (**"The American Bakery,"** **"Blood Relatives,"** **"Stranger at the Table"**). From the "Me and Mine" section we have three stories: Max exploring fatherhood with children Jessica and Sam at Girl Scout meetings, in a "Pizza Time" restaurant, and on a Dallas movie set. In the "My Arts" department are **"The Four Apples,"** a piece about stories for kids, and **"An Offering,"** a fictional prospectus advertising shares in "Max Apple, Inc.," producer of "private fantasies." The title story, about Max Apple's organs' declaring independence from him, would be perfect for *Me*'s lead section: "My Body."

Four fictions told by single or separated men of Apple's age and two narrated by women (all about personal success in love or business) extend the narcissistic atmosphere. Only two stories—**"Walt and Will,"** about the Disney brothers, and **"Small Island Republics"**—and two sketches, **"Post-Modernism"** and **"The National Debt,"** are fully set in the public world. This wide vision is the appeal of his first collection, *The Oranging of America*, and *Zip: A Novel of the Left and the Right*. Rapid-fire effects or the "zip" of jammed fictional combinations have been Apple's trademark and reason for his admitted "shortcuts". . . . Self is the shortcut of *Free Agents*, the quick starter for a story, but Apple doesn't push far enough into that self or send it wide enough to matter in most of these twenty pieces. The free agent owns himself only to sell himself: that's the feeling here. (p. 46)

For all his Apple absorption, he's a likable fellow, a little nostalgic and guilty, well intentioned and concerned with continuity—his family's past and kids' future. Many of his stories, though, seem assigned or machined for magazine space—"Have Apple do 3,000 words on eating kosher." They are good first-person journalism but, with the exception of **"Blood Rela-tives,"** a story about Jews and blacks in Muskegon, mediocre art.

The non-Apple stories, though also sometimes perfunctory, are generally better: they imagine strangers and set them in a sharper popular culture. Entertainment is the prime subject that links the two sets of stories. . . .

While complaining about the cartooning of America, *Free Agents* too often shares complicity with it. "If you want long, go to art," says Apple's spleen. But with twice as many stories here as in *The Oranging of America,* it's speed Apple has chosen. Donald Barthelme, Robert Coover, and Leonard Michaels use some of the same shortcuts and have some of the same targets in Americaland, but entertaining as they are, they also have the power to disturb. Apple's Disney story, with its depressed Walt and ruthless Will, has this capacity, as does **"Eskimo Love,"** about a man who hooks (he thinks) his dead wife while ice-fishing. These disturbances come to be a welcome relief from self-irony, amusing fancy, and good-natured wit, the entertaining Apple. . . .

Because the Apple who narrates often tags along behind a journalistic situation, and because his surrogate tellers don't have his linguistic skills, the crafted verbal texture of *The Oranging of America* is lost in *Free Agents*. Yes, beltway dwellers on the Southern Rim do speak in the plain, unmetaphorical style Apple gives them; but the writer to whom Apple is most frequently compared, Stanley Elkin, manages to give his similarly undistinguished agents jobs or interests or passions that create individual voices and separate textures. While **"An Offering"** and **"Business Talk"** do mock commercial jargon, and **"Kitty Partners"** uses some card-playing argot, too many of these pieces run together stylistically, yet another unfortunate result of the same self's dominance.

I'd like to see another novel from Max Apple. Though largely autobiographical and rather brief, *Zip* gathered together the talents of *The Oranging of America. Free Agents*—and perhaps the title admits it—disperses those talents, lets each sign up as a specialist for a story or two. If Apple can lay off speed and miniaturization, he won't have to be, in his own joke, "Max Apple, Inc., P.C.," the Apple Personal Computer. He could be main-frame. (p. 48)

*Tom LeClair, in a review of "Free Agents," in* The New Republic, *Vol. 191, No. 17, October 22, 1984, pp. 46, 48.*

# Ayi Kwei Armah

## 1939-

Ghanaian novelist, short story writer, poet, and scriptwriter.

Considered one of Africa's leading prose stylists writing in English, Armah is noted for his insights into postcolonial Africa and his uncommon perception of human alienation. He writes vehemently of the direct and indirect psychological and moral effects of colonialism upon contemporary Ghana and Africa. Armah has been applauded for his attempts to stimulate public awareness toward the amelioration of existing conditions in his native country.

Armah's first three novels are heavily symbolic representations of life in contemporary Africa. *The Beautyful Ones Are Not Yet Born* (1968) tells the story of a simple railway clerk during the regime of Kwame Nkrumah, the African leader who took power when Ghana gained independence from Britain. The protagonist, known only as The Man, is caught between accepting the bribery that is a common method of Ghanaian upward mobility and retaining his personal values of communal allegiance with his neighbors. The central image of the novel, human excrement, serves as a metaphor for the corruption and moral decay of his country and, by extension, Africa. Although The Man overcomes his dilemma and the corrupt Nkrumah is overthrown, little actual change occurs. This conflict between the hope for change and the betrayal of that hope by his nation's leaders is central to Armah's fiction.

The protagonists of Armah's next two novels studied in the United States, as did Armah himself. In *Fragments* (1970) the returning student is expected to flaunt his education and status as a "been to" to gain prestige and wealth for his family and village. However, this passive young intellectual prefers a less pretentious life and rejects the corrupt values of the new Africa. The pressure of reconciling these contradictory values is too much for him, and he is eventually committed to a sanitarium. *Why Are We So Blest?* (1972) recounts the story of Modin, a would-be revolutionary who is ultimately destroyed by the conflict between his desire to reject Western values in pursuit of African independence and his involvement with a white American girl. The novel is complex in structure, abandoning the linear progression of Armah's previous works.

*Two Thousand Seasons* (1973) marks a striking change from Armah's earlier novels. In this work Armah's previous emphasis on individual characterization is replaced by cultural generalization. Another divergence is the change from a contemporary to a historical perspective. *Two Thousand Seasons* covers one thousand years of African history and approaches epic proportions in its compressed meanings, descriptions of battles, and use of folk mythology. Armah condemns the Arab "predators" and European "destroyers" and calls for the reclamation of Africa's traditional values. *The Healers* (1978) takes this hope a step further, developing the idea of spiritual inspiration as a reparative force. The young protagonist condemns violence and disunity among his people, embracing instead a communal philosophy. As with *Two Thousand Seasons*, *The Healers* emphasizes the need to return to traditional African culture as a model for the future.

(See also *CLC*, Vol. 5 and *Contemporary Authors*, Vols. 61-64.)

Photograph by Bhupendra Kavia; reproduced by permission of Heinemann Educational Books

## CHARLES MILLER

Ghana under Kwame Nkrumah is the scene of this oustanding novel [*The Beautyful Ones Are Not Yet Born*] by Ayi Kwei Armah, a Ghanaian television writer. But the story could take place in almost any new nation of Africa, since it deals with that handmaiden of fledgling African sovereignty: corruption in "people's" governments. . . .

*The Beautyful Ones Are Not Yet Born* turns on the purgatory of a railway clerk (we never learn his name) who will end his days as a railway clerk because he carries the terrible burden of principle in a climate of ethics that permits advancement only under the table. In and out of his job fast-buck offers abound but he spurns them all, to the bewilderment of the high-living mediocrities and incompetents who are eager to make him a man of means for a price. Although, being human, he's not entirely immune to temptation, the degrading payola atmosphere stiffens his resistance. . . .

Nor can he find inner reward in his virtue, tortured as he is by the memory of just a few years earlier, when a dynamic young leader brought the fruits of freedom within the Ghanaian people's reach—and then handed them over to a rookery of corner-cutting political hacks. The bitterness of hope betrayed has become poison in his mind; everyday life is a lockstep march through a prison yard. On February 24, 1966, the long-awaited day of reckoning, a shout of joy echoes across the nation as Nkrumah and his gang get the heave-ho—and the wheeling-dealing goes on under new management. Or at least so it seems to the clerk. He continues to walk his treadmill of hopelessness.

Armah's handling of the clerk's ordeal is, to put it mildly, unusual. In fact, quite a few readers are going to find it revolting. For his message almost seems to be that power corrupts while absolute power defecates. The extent to which Armah relies on human waste to symbolize the decay of personal integrity is all but breathtaking—and this can, if you wish, refer to holding the nose. In brief, it really hits the fan.

This is literary talent? You bet it is. And I say that as one who finds most scatological prose not only disgusting but badly written. It calls for no small gift to expound on excreta and neither offend nor bore, even greater ability if this unlovely topic is to be made valid within the context of a novel. Armah brings it off, his objective being, of course, to convey a moral lesson—by highlighting his protagonist's uncompromising ethical rectitude through personal fastidiousness. To the clerk, going to the toilet is a nightmare, not only because the public lavatories which he uses happen to violate every rule of hygiene but because they also represent, in a very physical sense, the moral contamination which surrounds him—sometimes even tempts him in its foul way—and against which he must always be on guard. Armah has treated a most indelicate function with remarkable skill—and force. (p. 24)

I register two small objections. Now and then, Armah's lampoonery may go below the belt. His portrayal of the old United Gold Coast Convention Party (although it's not identified by name) as an assemblage of Uncle Toms strikes me as unfair to a group that did much to spearhead Ghanaian independence. (It's also an injustice to the party's leader, Dr. J. B. Danquah, regarded by some, myself included, as Ghana's real founding father.) And I can't buy the impression he creates that despite Nkrumah's overthrow, nothing in Ghana has changed for the good. All right, the country has yet to become a model of freedom, but it would be very wrong to overlook certain impressive strides made by Ghana's National Liberation Council toward restoration of the constitutional democracy that Nkrumah so callously dismantled.

It would also be a mistake to let these two shortcomings prejudice the reader against a valid and uncommonly arresting view of the abuse of power in that part of the world which may be least able to afford so outrageous an indulgence. (pp. 24-5)

*Charles Miller, "The Arts of Venality," in* Saturday Review, *Vol. LI, No. 35, August 31, 1968, pp. 24-5.*

**GUY DAVENPORT**

Mr. Ayi Kwei Armah, a native of Ghana, has a degree in sociology from Harvard, a fact one would happily not guess from reading his first novel [*The Beautyful Ones Are Not Yet Born*]. Not since Joyce Cary's *Mister Johnson* has a novelist got onto paper quite so much of the taste and smell and moral weather of West Africa. With saprophiliac glee Mr. Armah creates a veritable hail of all possible mucoid effluences, of all African stinks and exhalations in which he moves his torpid, steaming characters. The story is simple: an account of a poor worker in Nkrumah's socialist model state, contrasted with a party official. The one has little but a popping, bone-dislocating bus painted with slogans (the title is one of these) to distinguish

his existence from that of primitive bush life. The other slides in vulgar elegance upon political corruption, until the coup unseats him.

Behind the plot is the humble fable of city mouse and country mouse, with a hint of the tortoise and the hare. Mr. Armah has no grindstone and no ax; his people are simply people, and the Redeemer's model state was a cruel fraud. The wonder of this colorful novel is in the hard-edged caricatures of officials, bribers, pretenders to Western luxury, socialist statesmen bediamonded and in Cadillacs. Mr. Armah is amused, but as only a bitter satirist is amused; he writes with compassion for the defrauded and with acid contempt for the defrauders. He achieves absolutes of the ridiculous: African petty officials with heavy British accents playing golf on links carved out of the edge of the jungle; a *nouveau riche* lady disdaining beer now that her palate has discovered Scotch; a German short-wave radio played at top volume in the conviction that a softer tone would be under-using a noble machine and would, besides, be hiding a light under a bushel.

This is a brash and powerfully colorful novel, and if it amounts to doing the laundry in public, we can only say *What a laundry!* and *What an heroic job at the scrub board!* (p. 1121)

*Guy Davenport, "Old Tunes and a Big New Beat," in* National Review, *Vol. XX, No. 44, November 5, 1968, pp. 1120-21.\**

**CHRISTINA AMA ATA AIDOO**

It must be said [of *The Beautyful Ones Are Not Yet Born*] . . . that any Ghanaian workers who are conscious of what their positions are, coupled with the kind of sensitivity "the man" [the hero of the novel] has, would, in a country like Ghana, end up in a lunatic asylum. And most likely that is exactly where they might be found. Because Ayi Kwei Armah is right. For all that Ghanaian society expects of the ordinary worker in the way of material proofs of his earning capacity, he might as well be the owner of the mines or the ships he works in. Whereas, in reality, the tale of his dealings, first with the colonial regime and then with their black representatives, has been full of promises followed by one betrayal after another. (p. xi)

That this story is no different from that of the proletariat in the greater part of the world does not make it any easier to swallow. What is fortunate or unfortunate, according to how you choose to look at it, is precisely that, in Ghana, international monopoly capital is very well represented by a local "petty bourgeoisie," the vulgarity of whose self-congratulation, complacency and rate of consumption of capital goods must be paralleled only in a few other places in the underdeveloped world, while, at the same time, their so-called intelligentsia daily trumpets the ultimate wholesomeness of Western values.

At this juncture, one could say that perhaps Mr. Armah has allowed his revulsion at all this to influence his use of visible symbols to describe the less visible but general decay of the people and the country. Even a "bad" Ghanaian (one who does not believe in the national uniqueness in all things) could find it difficult to accept in physical terms the necessity for hammering on every page the shit and stink from people and the environment. One has encountered similar and even worse physical decay in other parts of the world. Though again, like the fate of the workers, this does not make it any easier to put up with. But somehow one feels a slight unease that the ordinary people should be subjected to the rather hyperbolical exposure which this book makes. There are quite a few angles from which one can judge cleanliness, including the emotional and clinical. For instance, quite a few people might prefer to live any day in the city or town which forms the background to the book than in Santa Monica, near Los Angeles, with its cold, sterilized cleanliness. (pp. xi-xii)

What is clear, then, is that whatever is beautiful and genuinely pleasing in Ghana or about Ghanaians seems to have gone unmentioned in *The Beautyful Ones Are Not Yet Born*. Yet, what kind of beauty is that which is represented by a human being like that avaricious tinsel of an Estella? Or what could be pleasing in the heartless betrayal of a people's hopes? And can there be anything at all beautiful about the generation which does this betraying? Is it not true also that, when an atmosphere is polluted anyway, nothing escapes the general foulness? Besides, one has to grant Mr. Armah that there is a nightmarish possibility that a full awareness of all this can become so crippling, that its effect on even a potentially active individual might be to make him want to withdraw completely into himself—a tendency the Teacher already betrays and which this rather obscure and almost redundant figure in the book imparts to "the man."

These are some of the main propositions the author makes. Indeed his desire for writing the novel seems to have been to express with a view to destroying what he cannot take about Ghana. The contents of the book clearly delineate what his targets would be if words could kill. (p. xii)

> *Christina Ama Ata Aidoo, in an introduction to* The Beautyful Ones Are Not Yet Born: A Novel *by Ayi Kwei Armah, Collier Books, 1969, pp. vii-xii.*

## MARTIN TUCKER

*Fragments,* like Armah's first novel, is an expression of frustration and despairing hope. . . . [The old grandmother of the hero Baako] has lived a long time, seen the values of her society crumble in the rush of a new moneyed class of businessmen and government officials. She has been the only witness to the destruction of her grandson by the new order of values; the other members of the family all have been participants in the destruction. The grandmother hopes for the end to come—the final bestial crouch to devour everyone—for only from the end will come the beginning. The grandmother has faith that her faith is whispering to her the sustenance of truth.

The grandmother's hope is a muted one seeing despair as a precondition to a new harmony. It is a more passive view than the one in Armah's first novel. (p. 24)

In [*The Beautyful Ones Are Not Yet Born*] something strong and vital emanated from the journey of The Man. At the end of the novel, seeing a bus with this sign on it: "The Beautyful Ones Are Not Yet Born," The Man knew that the beautiful ones would come; having a conception of them meant they had to come. The grandmother's faith in *Fragments* is not so convincing. The book begins and ends with her; she is the preamble and the coda, and she is a completely passive character. Watching the downfall of the hero, her grandson Baako, she does not offer an alternative.

In a similar way the hero of *Fragments* is a passive man. He is a "been-to," an African who has been abroad. He is returning from America, where he has studied, and where he

decided to become a writer. He also has had a nervous breakdown in the States, and needs a special drug to counter any attack. Baako is a symbolic African figure, the educated young man torn between the values of the old and new. But the distinction that Armah brilliantly shows is that even the new values have turned. In early African novels of colonialist Africa when the educated here returned to his country he was adrift. He belonged neither to his tribesmen nor to the British who acknowledged his education but never accepted him socially and personally. Such heroes, in African novels, usually ended in despair and often self-inflicted violence. Now the "been-to" returns to his own country but finds the corrupt bureaucracy has changed from a white British to a black Ghanaian skin.

One of the most significant agents in Baako's destruction is his mother. Her dreams of Baako's providing a car and a showy home for her are turned into the drab realism of his moving into her small house and taking the bus every morning to work like any African commuter. Finally and tragically she fails to understand Baako's dream of writing; when she discovers his journal and concludes that he is writing to himself, she rationalizes that he is mad, for only a sick man writes and speaks to himself. She has her family forcibly take Baako to a mental asylum. (pp. 24, 26)

Baako's downfall from expected hero to mental waif on a cement floor takes a year, and during that time he is in such a poor state that he cannot participate in the affairs of his country. His retreat to private insularity is in effect his rejection of a Ghana gone mad on power and extortion and the fringe benefits of politics.

The novel, while a powerful moral indictment of the present state of his country makes its force felt through symbolism, not direct propagandistic means. This use of symbology is both Armah's weakness and virtue. The killing of a dog, the capture of gulls, the unfinished house in the hills—all these take on added layers of sense, as in a tone poem or painting—and sometimes the result is a wonderfully sensuous appreciation of the dissociation of life, the inward nature of each individual, the ultimate unknowingness of things. Yet the technique is so richly used that it becomes a drug. The pictorials, the moments are resonant phrases tossing suggestively in a dream.

I think the novel fails of its promise—for the first novel promised more than fragments. It still succeeds as a tone poem of powerful allegorical force. (p. 26)

> *Martin Tucker, "Tragedy of a Been-to," in* The New Republic, *Vol. 162, No. 5, January 31, 1970, pp. 24, 26.*

## GARETH GRIFFITHS

What Kwei Armah sets out to show [in *The Beautyful Ones Are Not Yet Born*] is the experience of living in a corrupt universe. The limitations and confusions of such distancing are overcome through the guide which metaphor and image offer the reader. (p. 1)

The world outside the individual reflects the world within. The novel operates through a series of remarkable metaphorical links which institute a set of correspondences between the body of man, his society and his landscape; between, too, the inner processes of feeding and reproduction and their social equivalents, inheritance and consumption; and, finally, between the personal rot of conscience and ideals and the physical decay and putresence of the world in which this rot occurs. Central to the exchange is the question: where does the rot begin? What is the relationship between the processes of corruption and decay in the individual and in the society around him? What, if any, are the causal relations between one and the other? . . .

The predominant metaphor is that of eating, or rather of eating, digestion and excretion. This metaphor is linked, as is common in African writing through oral usage, to the theme of corruption and bribery. Money is food. The metaphoric link is a graphic illustration of the primitive economic nature of even the wealthiest of the West African states. In this world the "consumer" society is a literal reality. (p. 2)

The novel dwells obsessively on the process by which the body converts food into excreta, reflecting the obsession with which society "consumes" goods, the "shining" things which it covets. But just as food must issue in excreta, so such consumption must issue in bribery and corruption, the excrement of an aggressive drive for the new life. Each man's bodily processes become a metaphor for the corruption in which he lives, his own body a paradigm for the landscape he inhabits. This metaphor helps to structure the book since it is instrumental in relating the hero's discovery of the relationship between the bloom of life and the dung and filth which feeds it. (pp. 2-3)

[We] are given little direct help towards understanding the significance of the action of the novel, except in the sixth chapter which is pivotal to the structure and which I shall examine. But a careful reading of this difficult novel reveals that Armah has brought into play a pattern of images which defines the issues, and complements the limited viewpoints of characters and narrators.

The novel falls into three distinct sections. The first . . . introduces us to the daily round of the man's life, and to the pressure of family and friends which he feels to join in the struggle for the "good things" of life. We are introduced towards the end of this section (Chapter 4) to the figure of Koomson, the black-whiteman who is pre-eminently one of the "heroes of the gleam", the possessors of the Mercedes and the new suits. . . . Armah dwells on Koomson's suit, which replaces the man entirely. He is the white man because he is a white shirt, gleaming through a darkness into which his body merges. He is literally the gleaming clothes he stands up in. . . . The black-whiteman is invisible because he is merely a caricature. He has no social or economic reality, no personal identity. His reality is defined solely by the objects with which he surrounds himself, and from which he builds a "personality". (p. 3)

In the following chapter we meet the complex figure of Teacher, for the first time, a juxtaposition which is significant since he represents the opposite extreme from Koomson as I shall show. It is necessary to be very precise here. The figure we meet originally is NOT Teacher, but an extension of the role he plays in the symbolic patterning the book operates. . . . The confusion of persona, the multiple characterisation, shifting time-sequences and rapidly alternating narrative viewpoint which this episode establishes is continued throughout the crucial chapter six. The effect of introducing this Doppelganger for Teacher is to prepare us for the realisation that Teacher's stance, although directly opposed to that of Koomson's, is equally dangerous. . . . His ultimate solution, "the one way" to salvation that he discovers "Near the end" is a rejection of life. He rejects women, and through yoga attempts to convert the life-giving seminal fluid to the purpose of rejuvenation. But

he is rotting inside, and when he dies his heart is seen to be "only a living lot of worms gathered together tightly in the shape of a heart". . . . [When the real] Teacher is finally introduced he is naked, for if Koomson's life has reduced him to a mere suit of clothes, then Teacher's life has had a reductive effect too. Without the guidance of the imagery we might assume Teacher's nakedness a pure symbol of innocence. But in the context Armah so carefully establishes we are able to see the extremism of his stance, to see how it too depends on a selected notion of life, a refusal to accept the inevitable relationship . . . between the dung and the blossom. Teacher, the naked man, is as far removed from reality as Koomson, the suit. They both represent extremes which fail to meet the requirements of reality, that the ideal and the sordid should be seen to coexist in the same universe, and in the same compass of experience. (pp. 3-4)

[Teacher] is both a figure from the past and the character existing in the novel's "present". He is Rama Krishna, the lost friend, and Teacher, the present comforter. To try and fit him into a realistic category is to fail to see the novel's intention. Teacher is a symbol of a kind of African experience, a symbol of the timeless, non-technological, romantic and anthropological African experience. He is juxtaposed to Koomson, the black-whiteman, the modern elitist, the hatchet man of the consumer revolution. But Teacher's stance is as dangerous as Koomson's, for his withdrawal is ultimately no answer to the challenge posed to the hero by the "blinding gleam of beautiful new houses and the shine of powerful new Mercedes cars." Because of this, he has become a figure without hope. . . . Teacher is clearly identified with the old sources of African culture, the non-European, the non-technological sources, the world of the dead gods where spirit and matter are interfused. But in him they are separate. He is dead. His only answer now is withdrawal and death. (p. 4)

[In chapter six we] are presented with a symbolic history of the childhood and youth of a man which embodies the history of the liberation movement itself. . . . The narrative viewpoint moves between Teacher and the hero. The confusion of the two is deliberate since later, in the final chapter, we note that the hero inherits memories (the figure of Maanan) which belong to the portions of chapter six narrated by Teacher. This confusion merely stresses once again that we have to frame demands other than those satisfied by conventional novel structure. The figures and events are not merely aspects of an autobiography, but aspects of an historical process and a general cultural experience. . . . The chapter begins with an image of birth, but a strangely ambiguous one. . . . It is a birth which is described in terms of an ending. We come into the world like dung. Our birth is like the end of the chain of life, the excretion that follows the eating of food. The end of sexual love is this squalid and undignified entrance into the world, an entrance which reminds us forcibly that in our end is our beginning, and that in dung and blood we must go out again. To be born is to commit oneself to a process over which one has no control. Our adult pretensions to direction and choice are illusions. Our dreams of withdrawal and security, of the ability to remain still above the flux are illusions. . . . This inevitable aging and decay is the fate of movements and ideals as well as individuals. The birth and the youth of the liberation movement seemed to offer a new beginning, but that too was subject to decay. The story of a life and the story of a nation are fused in the imagery. The man struggling in the squalor of compromise and disillusion is a vision of Ghana itself, and its whole people. The reminiscences and memories of chapter six are not merely flashbacks in the story of a life, they are also images of the pilgrimage of the colonised through oppression to liberation and independence and on into disillusion and decay. (p. 5)

The novel pictures vividly the process by which in the colonial period the envy and aggression of the colonised people finds expression in a self-destructive process in which each turns upon his fellow. The war acted as a catalyst, revealing to the African that the white men were not always and everywhere the tin gods of the colonial landscape, and that he too was a potential source of power and force, that he too could move mountains and change the conditions of his life. Upon their return the soldiers find no outlet in the colonial situation for their new confidence and aggressiveness, and find it impossible to live happily under the old dispensations. The aggression released by war is in a heightened form the continual aggression bred by colonialism in the subject people, an aggression founded in envy, and in the desire to appropriate for themselves the status of the white settler, to win back the enchanted garden guarded by force and cruelty which they now see as their lost inheritance. (p. 6)

[The] increasing sense of the universality and the inevitability of the corrupting process culminates in the third section of the book in the visit of Koomson, now deposed and fleeing arrest. Koomson, terrified and broken, is a literal body of corruption. . . . [The escape into the latrine by Koomson and "the man"] provides a return to the initial birth image of chapter six. The two men must force their way through the latrine hole, "trailing dung and exhausted blood" to reenter the world. This second birth ironically mocks the first, when it was still possible to believe that 'growth' from youth to age, from purity to decay, might be arrested by choice. This second birth is a deliberate acknowledgement that all life is caught in the tension between vigour and decay, between the symbolic blossom which has appeared time and again in the narrative and the hidden dung which sustains it and to which it must ultimately return. . . . The birth struggle and the excretory struggle are only foci for a universal action, a mastering peristalsis by which the world digests the human aspirations which each birth renews and each old age destroys. Questions of individual motive are again irrelevant in such a context. The issue of why the man saves Koomson is not answerable, except perhaps in terms of a recognized kinship of all those who experience. The latrine episode draws together the metaphorical skeins of the book, and insists vividly on the structural identity of birth, excretion, copulation and death. Metaphorical theme has become the immediate tool of insight and compassion. (pp. 7-8)

*Gareth Griffiths, "Structure and Image in Kwei Armah's 'The Beautyful Ones Are Not Yet Born'," in* Studies in Black Literature, *Vol. 2, No. 2, Summer, 1971, pp. 1-9.*

**CHARLES R. LARSON**

When Ayi Kwei Armah published his first two novels, *The Beautyful Ones Are Not Yet Born* and *Fragments,* many of his countrymen were offended at the picture he presented of life in post-Independence Day Ghana. Armah depicted an African wasteland, where corruption in the government was rampant and where the African intellectual, educated abroad, felt totally out of place, frustrated to the point of rage or despair by his inability to make any change in the system. Although Armah's criticism was specifically aimed at the sterility of contemporary

Ghanaian life, indirectly it was pointed away from Africa—especially at Western commercialism and neo-colonialism. (p. 73)

In *Why Are We So Blest?* Armah has presented the quintessential learning experience for the African student—education in the United States. Although the main action takes place in North Africa, lengthy sections of the narrative flash back to record the main character's higher education in Cambridge, Massachusetts. When the novel opens, Modin Dofu, who has been a student at Harvard, has come to North Africa in hopes of joining a revolutionary group plotting the liberation of Portugal's African colonies. With him is Aimée Reitsch, a white American student whose sexual fantasies, rooted in her stereotyped dreams of deepest, darkest Africa, underlie the master-slave relationship she has established over Modin.

Solo Nkonam is another Ghanaian who has been educated overseas—in Lisbon. His function within *Why Are We So Blest?* is much like Marlow's in Conrad's *The Heart of Darkness*: to act as the recording consciousness for the protagonist's moral disintegration. Solo realizes that previously he himself has played a variant of the slave role Modin is now enacting with Aimée, but Solo has temporarily found release by working as a translator in North Africa—far from his own people. . . . Solo sees himself as a ghostly wanderer, a man diminished by his Western education. (pp. 73-4)

The heart of the novel, however, is Modin's plight in America. His education, he realizes, has been designed to make him a cog in the neo-colonial machine. Frigid white women throw themselves at him, expecting that he will liberate them from their sexual fetters. As Modin reflects, "These women I have known have had deep needs to wound their men. I have been an instrument in their hands." . . .

Armah's new novel may offend some readers. The ending, for example, is the most graphic and sickening portrayal of physical torture I can recall having encountered. At the same time, this violent denouement is by no means arbitrary: the author has carefully prepared his reader for it. Masterfully constructed, *Why Are We So Blest?* is disturbing in many ways: in the sharpness of its focus on the psychological by-products of racial prejudice—among others, emasculation and self-contempt—and in the implications it makes about race relations. Yet it is these very elements which, I predict, will make people talk about this book for a long time to come. (p. 74)

*Charles R. Larson, in a review of "Why Are We So Blest?" in* Saturday Review, *Vol. LV, No. 10, March 18, 1972, pp. 73-4.*

**JAMES GAFFNEY**

Implicit [in *Why Are We So Blest?*] is the author's conviction that African independence is not primarily a political or economic ideal, but a spiritual and cultural one. It is freedom to develop in a uniquely African way, alien and indeed antipathetic to "Europe"—a kind of radical *négritude*. But it remains one of the book's major disappointments that it fails even to try to convey any clear impression of what this ideal is conceived positively to mean.

The meaning of "Europe," on the other hand, is painfully clear: a familiar caricature whose details are debatable but whose foundation is all too real. It is the America of *Zabriskie Point,* dissatisfied in its opulence, destructive in its power, sterile in its lust: a rapacious parasite, materially strong enough to supply its spiritual void by draining the vitality of its victims.

For Africa, the prototype of "Europe" is forever the slaver, the exchanger of material unnecessities for human lives. But the slaver of the old days had also his "factor," an African accomplice, rewarded for his quickness to assimilate the foreigner's ways by being employed to manage, from a position of safe concealment, the wholesaling of his brothers.

Modin's ultimate despairing conclusion is that the new African leadership are merely the old "factors" in new guises, and that the only real alternatives for Africans are to be "factors" or to be slaves. Modin's own destiny is slavery. His destruction is wrought by the one token of "Europe" he proved unable to relinquish: the predatory libido of a frustrated American girl who leaves him at the end mutilated in the very sex to which she had sacrificed everything else that was in him.

When the day comes, I suppose it must, for somebody to write *Love and Death in the African Novel,* that volume ought to contain abundant references to Ayi Kwei Armah and *Why Are We So Blest?* (pp. 434-35)

James Gaffney, "An African in Exile, Camelot Revisited and Espionage Uncloaked," in America, *Vol. 126, No. 16, April 22, 1972, pp. 434-35.**

## CHINUA ACHEBE

[*The essay from which this excerpt is taken was written in 1973.*]

There is a brilliant Ghanaian novelist, Ayi Kwei Armah, who seems to me to be in grave danger of squandering his enormous talents and energy in pursuit of the *human condition.* In an impressive first novel, **The Beautyful Ones Are Not Yet Born,** he gives us a striking parable of corruption in Ghana society and of one man who refuses to be contaminated by this filth.

It is a well-written book. Armah's command of language and imagery is of a very high order indeed. But it is a sick book. Sick, not with the sickness of Ghana, but with the sickness of the *human condition.* The hero, pale and passive and nameless—a creation in the best manner of existentialist writing—wanders through the story in an anguished half-sleep, neck-deep in despair and human excrement of which we see rather a lot in the book. Did I say he *refused* to be corrupted? He did not do anything as positive as refusing. He reminded me very strongly of that man and woman in a Jean-Paul Sartre novel who sit in anguished gloom in a restaurant and then in a sudden access of nihilistic energy seize table knives and stab their hands right through to the wood—to prove some very obscure point to each other. Except that Armah's hero would be quite incapable of suffering any seizure.

Ultimately the novel failed to convince me. And this was because Armah insists that this story is happening in Ghana and not in some modern, existentialist no man's land. He throws in quite a few realistic ingredients like Kwame Nkrumah to prove it. And that is a mistake. Just as the hero is nameless, so should everything else be; and Armah might have gotten away with a modern, "universal" story. Why did he not opt simply for that easy choice? I don't know. But I am going to be superstitious and say that Africa probably seized hold of his subconscious and insinuated there this deadly obligation—deadly, that is, to universalistic pretentions—to use his considerable talents in the service of a particular people and a particular place. Could it be that under this pressure Armah

attempts to tell what Europe would call a modern story and Africa a moral fable, at the same time; to relate the fashions of European literature to the men and women of Ghana? He tried very hard. But his Ghana is unrecognizable. This aura of cosmic sorrow and despair is as foreign and unusable as those monstrous machines Nkrumah was said to have imported from Eastern European countries. Said, that is, by critics like Armah.

True, Ghana was sick. And what country is not? But everybody has his own brand of ailment. Ayi Kwei Armah imposes so much foreign metaphor on the sickness of Ghana that it ceases to be true. And finally, the suggestion (albeit existentially tentative) of the hero's personal justification without faith nor works is grossly inadequate in a society where even a lunatic walking stark naked through the highways of Accra has an extended family somewhere suffering vicarious shame.

Armah is clearly an alienated writer, a modern writer complete with all the symptoms. Unfortunately Ghana is not a modern existentialist country. It is just a Western African state struggling to become a nation. So there is enormous distance between Armah and Ghana. There is something scornful, cold and remote about Armah's obsession with the filth of Ghana. . . . (pp. 38-40)

Armah is quoted somewhere as saying that he is not an African writer but just a writer. Some other writers (and friends of mine, all) have said the same thing. It is a sentiment guaranteed to win applause in Western circles. But it is a statement of defeat. A man is never more defeated than when he is running away from himself. (pp. 41-2)

Chinua Achebe, "Africa and Her Writers," in his Morning Yet on Creation Day: Essays, *Anchor Press/ Doubleday, 1975, pp. 29-45.**

## "TWO THOUSAND SEASONS" STUDY GROUP

Like all of Armah's previous works, **Two Thousand Seasons** is forcefully written and compelling. The sheer beauty of Armah's prose is almost enough to make this novel outstanding, but the power of his ideas is what brings this book into the realm of the extraordinary. Armah has succeeded in taking the historical facts of the Empire of Ghana and recreating these facts into a story that moves with passion, purpose, conviction and truth. This book is much more than a novel; it is also an invocation to the "hearers," "seers," "rememberers," "imaginers," "thinkers," and "prophets" in the Afrikan community to come to the aid of the Afrikan people who have through years of destruction and oppression lost the Afrikan way (the giving and receiving way that is in the best interests of the masses of Afrikan people). . . .

Armah's use of penetrating concise symbols—the desert, predators, destroyers, the way, ostentatious cripples, parasites—helps to bring a deeper meaning to this story. The entire novel revolves around the concept of time, two thousand seasons. These two thousand seasons represent the one thousand years (Ghana only has two seasons) of destruction suffered by the Afrikan people at the hands of the Arabs (predators) and the Europeans (destroyers). Armah seems to believe that time is on the side of the Afrikan people and that eventually the two thousand seasons (time) will turn in favor of Afrika. . . .

Vitriolically, Armah attacks the enemies from within, those "Zombies" among his own people—ostentatious cripples, parasites, askaris, and others who have completely lost their souls—who have chosen the white way as opposed to the Afrikan

Way. These "zombies" are each unique in their manner of embracing the white way, but they share the common bond of "fidelity to those who spat on them." The most lamentable aspect of these traitors from within is that their minds belong to the conqueror. Armah states that these "victims had one aim: to help to destroy their people, forcing the yet undestroyed surrounding into unison with their lost selves." . . .

The conclusion of *Two Thousand Seasons* offers hope and inspiration for the Afrikan people in the struggle for Afrikan minds. (p. 56)

In *Two Thousand Seasons,* Armah has succeeded in revealing the nature of oppression while addressing the profound ideas of revolution and liberation within the novel format. We commend him for this monumental task. (p. 57)

*"Two Thousand Seasons" Study Group, "'Two Thousand Seasons': Ayi Kwei Armah," in* Black Books Bulletin, *Vol. 4, No. 4, Winter, 1976, pp. 55-7.*

## S. NYAMFUKUDZA

*Two Thousand Seasons* presents a considerable departure from what [Armah] has done before. Indeed, one of the questions likely to preoccupy the reader is whether it is a novel at all. The collective racial memory of the black people is given voice through their pilgrimage of self-assertion in received versions of the long years of collision, destruction and enslavement by the white man, 'the destroyers', both Arab and Caucasian, who have colonised and plundered Africa. The distinction between We, Us, the Black people—the plural narrative voice of the novel—and Them, the white destroyers, is absolute and uncompromising. The quest is largely a spiritual one, to recapture as well as create a saving vision of a time when black people were one and their relationship was one of 'reciprocity' between individuals, variously termed 'the way', 'our way'.

The story itself is of a group migrating south to the coast, presumably the West African coast, from Arab invaders, only to collide with white slave-dealers raiding inland. A period of capture and enslavement follows, but the prisoners escape from the ship due to take them across the Atlantic and from then on wage a guerrilla struggle against the white men and a collaborating local chief. Strong meat indeed, but what the reader is likely to find even less comfortable is the abandonment of naturalistic delineation of individual character, setting and time itself, as the story ranges back and forth, speaking insistently to the present. The message is relentlessly at the fore-front and we are much closer to the traditional tribal story teller, whose purpose is to educate and preserve the group's identity, history and traditions, than to any familiar novelistic form. The sombre, sometimes outraged biblical cadence of the prose bears the epic on. The theory and attempt are bold and admirable, but the resulting simplification and polarisation are an impoverishment of Armah's art. The message too is none too clear in its implications for the much more complex present.

*The Healers,* Armah's latest novel, is by contrast, a straight-forward historical narrative and deals with the fall of the Ashanti empire under the onslaught of the British. Why was the empire such a pushover for the colonists? Disunity, greed for power and internal contradictions inherent in a slave-holding and war-like society undermined its capacity and spirit for resistance.

The prose is pared down into a beautifully taut and evocative instrument, with the novel at its best in the first half where it revolves round one of the main characters, Densu, disenchanted

and ill-at-ease with the manipulative local politics. Ababio, the Machiavel of the novel, comes over as a truly sinister and frightening figure, plotting away against the royal household and ready to ally himself to the invading white men in his quest for power. Densu resists his enticements, choosing instead to dedicate himself to the calling of the healers under the tutelage of one of the sages. They receive such scant recognition that at this stage they have removed to their own healer's village deep in the forest. It is a lonely and ascetic way of life, study and self-communing, knowing oneself and trusting to inspiration rather than leaping into the thick of short-term political battles. Towards the end, when the battles take place, the novel tends to read like a Cowboys-and-Indians tale. It ends on an optimistic note, however, with the villain Ababio exposed and tried, ironically, by his former white allies. Although under the shadow of defeat and alien domination, West Indian slaves and Black Africans dance on the beach in symbolic reconciliation. It seemed hardly possible that Armah's commitment could be pushed further, but so it has, towards a more general and specifically African reading public. (p. 363)

*S. Nyamfukudza, "Drought & Rain," in* New Statesman, *Vol. 99, No. 2555, March 7, 1980, pp. 362-63.*

## CHARLES R. LARSON

With the publication of *The Beautyful Ones Are Not Yet Born* in 1968, Ayi Kwei Armah, the young exiled Ghanaian writer, became the leading light of a new movement in contemporary African fiction: realistic, hard-hitting and critical of post-independence African societies. That first novel—a scathing account of Nkrumah's Ghana caught in a death grip with Western capitalism—won for Armah instant recognition from his African contemporaries, though his elders were not always so enthusiastic about his writing. The neorealism continued in two subsequent novels, *Fragments* (1970) and *Why Are We So Blest?* (1972), as Armah continued to flail away at the problem of African leadership. Each work was uniquely different from the previous one, and each one won for the author further accolades—especially for his poetic style.

A subtle change in focus began with *Two Thousand Seasons,* published in 1973. In that volume Armah shifted his concern to the African past: the historical sweep of violence and repression in its precolonial, colonial and neocolonial stages. That novel was also a further delving into the heroic past supplanted by the inglorious present. Armah's new novel *The Healers* . . . returns to the past as a further exploration of the source of contemporary African political disharmony.

In this lengthy but relatively loosely-structured novel Armah's theme is once again cultural disintegration. The root source is perceived as tribal disunity—a "disease" that plagued African societies before the coming of the Europeans. Though the focus is upon the Ashanti Empire (and its decline after the historic battle with the British at Kumase), Armah means for us to regard this tribe emblematically. Its confrontation with the West reduplicates the age-old question of power and leadership. (pp. 246-47)

Though I admire the epic qualities of *The Healers* and the richness of its use of traditional folk materials, there is an unsatisfying verbosity to much of the central narrative. The main revenge story (involving a young acolyte healer named Densu who is accused of killing the heir apparent to one of the Ashanti villages) often borders on the pedestrian. I believe

I preferred the early Armah, in his more realistic stages, to the vague mysticism of *The Healers*. (p. 247)

Charles R. Larson, "Books in English from the Third World," in World Literature Today, Vol. 54, No. 2, Spring, 1980, pp. 246-48.*

## JAMES BOOTH

*Why Are We So Blest?* is not only an analysis of the psychological effects of racism, it is itself a racist book. This needs to be said since the fact that it is also the most powerful work of a novelist of genius may make the humane critic reluctant to admit the fact—even to him or herself. But racism is a subtle and infinitely varied phenomenon, the understanding of which is not helped by reticences and taboos which oversimplify it in the minds of those who wish to feel themselves above such things. . . . [In much African literature the] black is a projection (or to use Armah's word, a 'shadow') in the white imagination and conducts him- or herself in accordance with the complex demands of a white myth, in this case a liberal white myth. The common humanity which blacks share with the white author is subsumed in archetype or lost in fantasy, fantasy the more powerful for its explicit *opposition* to racism.

At this point it is necessary to clarify a fundamental confusion in the way the term 'racism' is used. The word has in fact two related but different meanings which are frequently confounded together. On the personal, subjective level 'racism' presents itself to the individual as a matter of personal choice. A person is either racist or not depending on the level of his or her moral development or sense of common humanity. The true liberal will see little beyond than this meaning. It may however tend to obscure the social and economic determinants of racism. As has frequently been remarked racism follows and justifies social and economic oppression in those parts of the world where the exploiting class happens to be different in colour from the exploited. On this wider level the individual seems to have no real choice whether to be racist or not. Racism is an unavoidable *communal* reality and all his or her relations will be affected by it. . . . On the crudest level the laws of a society may compel racism by force as is the case in South Africa with its notorious pass regulations and Immorality Act. But on every other level too, even in matters apparently in the realm of individual morality or taste alone, racism, in some form or other, will be inevitable. Hence the contradictions of an Alan Paton. The disturbing power of Armah's novel is that it confronts this individual/communal dichotomy in racism and ruthlessly insists that there is *no* personal or individual escape. The liberal white illusion of a personal escape from racism attainable through 'love' or 'humanity' for Armah reveals a misunderstanding of the nature of racism. Indeed such liberalism is itself merely an inverted form of racism—one which attempts to obscure the objective situation under subjective good will. This is the lesson we are meant to draw from Armah's Aimée, whose apparent lack of personal racism in her love affair with Modin and her enthusiasm for the liberation struggle reveal themselves in the end to be a mere veneer covering the fundamental viciousness inherited from her colonial background. It is also the lesson of Modin who, deluded into thinking that a personal relation with a white can transcend the cultural norm, is drawn by this relation to humiliation and death. (pp. 51-2)

The characterisation [of Aimée] is a subtle and compelling blend of naturalism and symbol. On the level of realism Aimée is clearly portrayed as a psychopathic sado-masochist. More symbolically she derives from the *femme fatale* of Romanticism, but brilliantly reinterpreted in the modern American context. The love scenes are masterly in the indefinable uneasiness and distrust which they evoke in the reader through an ostensibly frank and naturalistic portrayal of a difficult human relationship. Throughout, her symbolic dimension as the agent of white rapacity and destructiveness is firmly rooted in realistic psychology and description. Even the apparent implausibility of her entrusting Modin's and her own journals to Solo after Modin's murder could be interpreted as a realistic psychological subtlety, the result of her subconscious wish to boast about her destructive handiwork.

Modin is treated in more detail, and at first his experiences resemble those in a novel of a much more conventional kind of social satire on race-relations. . . . But Modin is much more than a Clarkian *ingénu* against whom Western hypocrisy is measured. Armah goes beyond the easy attitudinising of other writers. It is not in this social-satiric aspect but in Modin's own prolonged self-analysis that his full symbolic significance emerges. He begins to realise that his life is totally a creation of the whites, and that his independent identity is an illusion. Economically, socially, culturally, he is dominated. He sees himself as like the 'factors' of the colonial period, black employees of the whites who handled black slaves for them. As an educated modern black, spirited away by an arbitrary scholarship from his own culture, he is being trained to plunder his own people on behalf of his masters, as did his factor predecessors. His soul, he slowly realizes, has become the property of the whites, he has been subsumed in their rapacious search for material wealth and spiritual domination. Even his spontaneous emotions are all white dictated, and his wish to assimilate himself into whiteness, like some morbid disease, begins to involve the destruction of his black self—in reality his only self. (pp. 55-6)

The treatment of Modin's relations with women reverses the usual white stereotype which opposes a purely physical black virility to the greater spirituality of whites. Here it is the whites who, having crushed their own spirit under a crude physicality, are turning their sexual rapacity on the souls of blacks. . . . Similarly Europe is seen in terms of a bright fiery sun, consuming Africa in its 'hell', reversing the Western stereotype of cool dispassionate Europe as against hot demonic Africa. (p. 57)

All this adds up to a brilliant counter-myth to that of Europe. And again its symbolic force grows out of the novel's realism. The conclusions of this inward self-exploration are corroborated by Modin's experiences with particular whites. His own reinterpreted myth of the relations between the races seems grounded in the reality he encounters. As a study in neo-colonial psychology he is only too believable.

On the realistic level of the novel, then, we find two characters compulsively acting out racially predetermined roles which deform their humanity. So far the novel is masterly. And so far it might be construed as an attack on the racial myth-making process itself and its destructiveness of human values. However it early becomes clear that this is not Armah's intention, and it is here that one begins to feel uneasy with Armah's deductions. It is one thing to portray the tragedy of two particular individuals dominated and spiritually destroyed by the cultural stereotypes which history has imposed on them. It is one thing also to go a stage further and imply, as Armah does, that such tragedies are inevitable, given the brutal socio-economic realities—that theirs is a typical, symbolic case. But it is quite another to imply that this symbolic relationship is the key to *all* personal relations between black and white. And this is what the novel attempts to do. This is to push the metaphorical dimension too far. The organisation of the narrative insistently suggests that this is not simply one typical, significant, even symbolic case history. It is intended as a paradigm, as an alternative myth to that of the white culture. For all its insight and psychological truth it is ultimately as much racial propaganda as Conton's novel [*The African*] or those of Alan Paton.

One of the most formidably persuasive elements in Armah's attempt to elevate this case-history into a universal metaphor of relations between white and black is the novel's narrative strategy. The entire story comes to us through Solo Nkonam, either in his own words or through passages from Aimée's and Modin's journals edited by him. He is a brilliant narrative device. As a would-be revolutionary who has travelled the same road as Modin, he is ideally placed to reinforce and generalise the lessons of the African's fate. He persistently parallels Modin's experiences with his own. . . . He parallels Modin's self-analysis in his journals with his own and draws universal lessons. He, too, cannot find any identity apart from that of a 'factor' for, or a 'lover' of, the whites. . . . So not only are the two main black characters in the novel illustrations of the paralysis of their race, but the outermost narrative voice with all its impressive authority belongs to one of these characters and controls our response to the entire story. The reader is allowed no avenue of escape.

Nor can the reader easily find refuge in simply doubting Solo's authority, as he doubts that of the narrator in Conton's *The African*. Many readers might like to feel that for all the massive rhetorical certitude of his tone Solo is not wholly trustworthy. He is, like Modin, simply an illustration of a particular perversion of mind due to colonialism. But the whole posture of the novel attacks such relativism. The characters in it seem somehow permanent: realistic but also larger than life. They have symbolic names to imply their universality: 'the African', Solo, Aimée ('beloved'). The man who first meets Modin in the United States is named Blanchard ('whitener'). And more disturbingly, Armah has already anticipated his reader's rebellion and attempted to counter it within the book. Solo himself is continually doubting his own objectivity within the novel itself thus adding authority to his final conclusions. (pp. 57-8)

Most subtly and persuasively of all, Solo's personal reluctance to draw the 'rational' racist conclusion is seen as only another aspect of his own enslavement to sub-white status. He has been corrupted to the point where he cannot hate whites, however much cause they give him to do so. (p. 59)

Armah's narrative strategy is thus designed to allow the reader no alternative but to accept the universality of his conclusion. It must surely be admitted, however, that these conclusions are not in the final analysis supported by adequate evidence. What the novel *shows* is a plausible single relationship between members of different races: but then, as it were, it tries to sell this to the reader by masterly technical manipulation as a universal law of such relationships. (p. 60)

But perhaps even more powerful than its narrative voice in compelling the reader's imaginative assent to Armah's racism is the novel's metaphoric power. The harrowing end of the book must serve as our focus here. The symbolism is shockingly explicit and resonant, and brilliantly consummates the psychological realism we have already examined. Several European men use the American girl to arouse the helpless Af-

rican, who has been tied to a car. The wider racial implications about the relations between the three continents are almost diagrammatic, even the car might be thought to have its significance as representative of dominant Western technology. The woman, in accordance with her culture's myth, is desperately eager to reach Modin and sate her lust for sexual domination on his captive and defenceless body. At the same time she is the more profoundly roused by the white men's restraint upon her and their contempt of her for her sexual desire for the black man. Modin's own erection shows that, however involuntarily, he too cannot help but continue to play his part as 'lover' and servant of the whites. On the realistic level the action fulfils Aimée's Mwangi fantasy (which explains her strange eagerness and exhilaration); and it also echoes Modin's previous experience with the Jeffersons, when he was similarly sexually used by a white woman and assaulted by a white man. The final twist to the symbolism comes when the men finally mutilate the African. It is significant that they cut off only the tip of his penis, since this makes possible the most appallingly symbolic act of the novel, when Aimée kneels before him, drinking the blood pulsing from his penis in a parody of orgasm and asking him "Do you love me?" No more horrifying concrete and appropriate embodiment than this could be imagined of Solo's verdict on the relations between Africa and the West.

> Of what other use have Africa's tremendous
> energies been these many centuries but to serve
> the lusts of the whites.

Here, quite literally, 'Africa's' creative life blood flows to satisfy the destructive and sterile lust of 'Europe' and 'America' combined.

But surely the exquisite appropriateness of all the details at this point, though it makes the scene nightmarishly unforgettable, is in itself suspect artistically. Is there not a cynicism (or is it sentimentalism?) in the aesthetic completeness and appropriateness of it all? Real life would surely be messier and more ambiguous. Aimée's parody of fellatio would not be possible for instance if the men castrated Modin more crudely (which would surely be more likely on a realistic level). More radically one might ask whether Armah seriously wishes to imply that all white women are sado-masochists like Aimée, as Solo's comments and her resonant symbolic qualities seem to suggest. In my view Armah is attempting here by careful simplification and dazzling symbolism to shock his readers into accepting a crude and subjective deduction from the dubiousness and relativity of real individual experience. Armah's work gains much of its distinctive power from such emotive symbolism. He sees life instinctively in terms of brilliant, resonant images, which usually express a moral or spiritual attitude in shocking physical terms. In this he resembles Dickens. . . . At their most artistically successful his symbols embody complex and subtle ideas inexpressible perhaps in any other form: Koomson farting in fear in a darkened back room at the end of *The Beautyful Ones Are Not Yet Born,* for instance, or the axing of the mad dog at the beginning of *Fragments.* Such images are compulsive and unforgettable, especially when, as is the case with the final scene of *Why Are We So Blest?* the concrete action is in terms of something so emotion-laden and set about with cultural myths as race, rape and murder. But they can also mislead. Hitler may have imagined that his disgusting imagery of maggots in *Mein Kampf* was a means of informing his readers as to the objective nature of Jews. In fact the metaphorical tenor has escaped its vehicle and all it tells us about is Hitler's own subjective emotions.

Armah's work represents a peculiarly sophisticated version of the familiar dangers of theoretical commitment to 'black consciousness' or 'négritude': dangers which, ironically, he himself has clearly analysed, in their political manifestation, in his article "African Socialism: Utopian or Scientific?" . . . Armah asserts against the European "I think therefore I am", an "African" "I feel therefore I am". The protagonists of his first three novels are all desperately, wincingly sensitive beings. His original variation is to substitute for "Hoorah for those who never invented anything!", "Alas for those who are being prevented from inventing anything!". His characters possess a crushing negativity and passivity. . . . The authorial or quasi-authorial voices in these works are voices of despair. There is no sense of positive or active identity, except that gained through suffering and attempting to understand and live with inevitable suffering. . . . The problem becomes even more acute in Armah's next novel, *Two Thousand Seasons,* where he attempts to throw off his previous passivity by imaginatively realising this non-European 'paradise' in the form of 'the way'. But the only inherent qualities of 'the way' which convey themselves are a kind of puritanical lack of sexism and a grim and humourless communalism. Otherwise 'the way' seems rather anti-European than non-European, defining itself mainly in terms of its opposition to, and grimly brutal killing of, 'the destroyers'.

Armah then becomes in his later work a figure of negativity in African literature. . . . But in *The Beautyful Ones Are Not Yet Born* and *Fragments* a certain dignity and human warmth *does* occasionally invest the protagonists, making the pessimism of Armah's vision doubly poignant. In *Why Are We So Blest?* this human warmth is quite overwhelmed by pathos and bitter despair. At the bottom of *Why Are We So Blest?* lies the ultimately sentimental desire to blame all the problems of the contemporary African on the whites. And the fact that, instead of the usual gentle and innocent African victim beloved of the soft liberal imagination one finds in Armah a powerfully evoked self-disgust, should not blind us to this. *Why Are We So Blest?* is in the end just such a 'justificatory hallucination' as Solo sees in all self-images created by blacks, if a subtle one, one even half-aware of its own hallucinatory quality. As a cry of resentment and suffering the book is unparalleled. As a universal myth of race relations it is deceptive. (pp. 60-3)

James Booth, "'Why Are We So Blest?' and the Limits of Metaphor," in Journal of Commonwealth Literature, Vol. XV, No. 1, August, 1980, pp. 50-64.

## BERNTH LINDFORS

[Both *Two Thousand Seasons* and *The Healers*] present Africa as a victim of outside forces that it resists but cannot contain. These depradations of the past are responsible for the chaos one sees in Africa at present, and only by properly understanding that past and present will Africans collectively be able to tackle the problems of the future: how to get the victim back on its feet, how to raise the materially oppressed and downtrodden, how to heal the spiritually sick. Instead of merely cursing various symptoms of the colonial disease, as he had done in his first three books, Armah now wants to work towards effecting a cure. (p. 87)

[*Two Thousand Seasons*] is an interesting scenario and a fascinating contrast to Armah's earlier fiction. Instead of watching one man struggle fruitlessly to maintain his purity or sanity in an atmosphere of rank corruption, we see a communal group,

activated by the highest ideals, actually *succeed* in their military manoeuvres against extraordinarily powerful antagonists. Instead of witnessing the anguish of a doomed, fragmented individual, we are shown the joy of a mini-tribe united in the struggle against evil. Instead of existential despair, there is revolutionary hope. Instead of defeat, victory.

But the optimism in Armah's new view of man and society in Africa is predicated on certain assumptions which it is difficult to credit as reasonable. Foremost among these is the belief that Africa, before being polluted by contact with the outside world, was a Garden of Eden, at least in terms of social organization. People lived in harmonious communities, sharing the fruits of their labour and never striving to compete against their neighbours for the acquisition of superior status or material goods. Rulers did not exist; the communities were acephalous, completely democratic and devoted to the principle of reciprocity. This principle was the very essence of what Armah calls 'our way, the way'. . . . Africans were a creative, productive, hospitable, non-oppressive, healthy and sharing people—until the invaders came. Africans should now strive to return to 'our way, the way' by destroying the destroyers of their former paradise.

The villains in this stark melodrama are portrayed as the obverse of the heroes. This may be a dramatic necessity, in as much as one needs very potent Manichean forces to overwhelm such a superabundance of virtue as is said to have existed in prehistoric Africa. But it also assumes that entire races of people can be reduced to the level of primal forces, that one be characterized as inherently predisposed towards good, another addicted to evil. This kind of xenophobic oversimplification used to be found in B-grade films manufactured in Hollywood during the Second World War, in which fanatical kamikaze pilots and fat, stupid, goose-stepping German generals represented all that was reprehensible in the world. (pp. 89-90)

The trouble with Armah's cartoon history of Africa is that it ultimately is not a positive vision, even though it promises future happiness. All it really offers is negation of negation. The most creative act imaginable is destruction of the destroyers. . . . This is a philosophy of paranoia, an anti-racist racism—in short, negritude reborn. In place of a usable historical myth, *Two Thousand Seasons* overschematizes the past, creating the dangerous kind of lie that Frantz Fanon used to call a 'mystification'. (p. 90)

In his latest novel *The Healers* Armah moves a step closer to fleshing out his nightmare vision of the past by substituting concrete substance for abstract symbol. If *Two Thousand Seasons* was his theory of history, *The Healers* is an adumbration of the theory using actual recorded events as proof of the hypotheses advanced. Armah takes the fall of the Ashanti Empire as emblematic of Africa's destruction, and he attributes the calamity not only to the rapacity of the West but also to the disunity within Africa itself. It is towards the reunification of Africa tomorrow that Africans must work today if they wish to repair the damage done yesterday. History is again seen as a guide to a better future.

The novel itself is unified by the imagery of disease. Africa has been prostrated by a foreign plague against which it had no natural immunity, and some of its members, infected beyond all possibility of recovery, have turned against the parent body itself, spreading the disabling disorder still further. Any manifestation of division in society is regarded as a symptom of the malady, a crippling indisposition requiring a cure. (p. 91)

It is clear that Armah himself wants to assist in the healing process. The role of the writer, he seems to be saying, is to inspire Africa to be true to its own spirit so it can be reunited as the harmonious community it once was before the predators and destroyers came. This is a noble goal, even if the 'paradise lost' theme is rather naïve as an interpretation of human history. Armah evidently is trying to do something constructive in his fiction, something far more positive than he had done in his first three novels. Giving Africa a new, clean image of itself is a much more wholesome occupation than rubbing its nose in dung.

And, indeed, *The Healers* is a better-balanced book, a saner piece of fiction, than *Two Thousand Seasons*. Gone, but not totally forgotten, are the Arab and European demons who were objects of such intense hatred in Armah's earlier venture into history. Gone, too, are the scenes of sexual perversion and the almost Homeric descriptions of bloodshed, gore and corporeal mutilation, descriptions which told in gleeful, gloating detail exactly where a bullet or blade entered an enemy's body and where it exited. Gone as well is the over-idealized band of forest guerrillas, those glamorous outlaws descended from a romantic blend of Mao, Mau Mau and Robin Hood, who, instead of offering the reader some semblance of fidelity to African life, gave imaginary life to African fidelity. Gone, in short, are the delirious fantasies that pushed *Two Thousand Seasons* beyond the dimensions of viable myth into the wilder liberties of nightmare.

*The Healers*, it must be admitted, also has its good guys and bad guys, its heavy-handed moralizing and its propensity to force history to fit a predetermined ideological paradigm, but it is not a harmful book to put into the hands of young people. For one thing, it does not encourage xenophobia. For another, it emphasizes creativity ('inspiration') rather than destruction. And by concentrating on real events and weaving fiction into the fabric of fact, it could help young Africans to reshape their perspective on the past and come to a better understanding of the world in which they currently live. In other words, it offers an interpretation of human experience that seems valid because it is rooted in an imaginable reality.

Yet it is still a cartoon, still comic-strip history. It will not persuade many adults because it falsifies far more than it authenticates and in the process fails to avoid the pitfalls of oversimplification. Nevertheless, some grown-ups will be able to enjoy it at the level of popular fiction, for it is good cops-and-robbers, cowboys-and-indians stuff. It even includes a murder mystery to bait the reader's interest. But basically it is juvenile adventure fiction of the *Treasure Island* or *King Solomon's Mines* sort, the only major difference being that it is thoroughly *African* juvenile adventure fiction. (pp. 94-5)

I am not saying this to belittle the novel's importance. Obviously, *The Healers* is a major attempt by a major African writer to reinterpret a major event in African history. But I think it will have its major impact on young people, and this is as it should be in any remythologizing of Africa. One must aim at winning the hearts and minds of the young, imbuing them with the highest ideals and making them proud and happy to be Africans. This *The Healers* does better than any other novel Armah has written. And this is why it is potentially his most important book and certainly his healthiest. One can no longer complain that his vision is warped or his art sick. (p. 95)

Bernth Lindfors, "Armah's Histories," in African Literature Today, *No. 11, 1980, pp. 85-96.*

### ROBERT FRASER

[In *The Healers*] historicity is here to be viewed, not as an eternally flowing stream, or an endlessly repetitive cycle, but rather as a multi-layered texture whose subtler depths may best be plumbed by inserting the narrative instrument at one precise point; the more precise the more accurate the findings. To put it another way, the historical method in *Two Thousand Seasons* was deductive. Starting from certain clearly defined tenets or premises, it set out to establish their relevance, taking the entire span of the racial memory as its example. *The Healers,* on the other hand, may be viewed as an inductive work. Taking as its field of inquiry a particular moment when the stresses to which one society was habitually subject arose to overwhelm it, it sets out to demonstrate the reasons for this failure and hence to illustrate something about the nature, not only of this culture, but perhaps also of all comparable societies which succumb to external pressure in this way. It thus tells us something very important about the whole colonial experience. At the heart of the novel there lies an overriding question: why were the immensely proud and resourceful Ashanti people subjected in this ignoble manner? In answering it, the novel helps us to understand some basic truths about the social interaction of different and hostile cultures. (pp. 84-5)

The historical episode on which Armah chooses to concentrate is one which has been subject to a peculiar amount of misrepresentation by European historians. Seen from the Western point of view, the history of the late nineteenth century has often been seen as a process of rapid expansion of colonial frontiers, the bringing of the light to 'darkest Africa' being but a benign offshoot of this development. In this scenario the final humiliation of a remote African people during the Second Asante War features as a minor, though piquant peccadillo, an obscure and often ignored sub-paragraph in school textbooks. . . . [In] the popular mind the overwhelming impression persists of an incident that was both fitting and inevitable, the irresistible impact of a technically superior force on a bewildered but headstrong people stuck in a cultural backwater. The sad fact is that this notion not only retains its hold over the minds of most people in the West, but, thanks to the importation of metropolitan ideas through the colonial educational system, has come to determine the way that some Africans regard their own history.

It is this state of affairs which Armah takes it upon himself to challenge. The book is thus not merely a reinstatement of a neglected and misunderstood phase of the colonial past, but part of the total reclamation of history on behalf of those whose contribution received opinion has traditionally slighted or abused. In attempting to achieve this Armah has availed himself of all the latest advances in the field: the novel shows abundant evidence of extensive research, and a subtle appreciation of the various factors involved in a complex historical issue. Yet his attitude to established fact is far from slavish. Armah is a novelist, not an academic historian, and, in time honoured fashion, he has used and shaped the available material so as to tailor history to a particular vision. . . . Armah, in pursuit of his ideal of spiritual health, has used history as a medicine for rankling sores, and hence acted as a healer of his own people. It is important to realize that his purpose, however, has not been simply to dull the pain; as well as the soothing salve he has also applied in several places the rack, since to cure one has often to cause pain.

What are the crucial weaknesses of Asante society as portrayed in the book? Despite a superficial solidarity it is gradually revealed as a culture barely at ease with itself. . . . Despite the system of aristocratic inheritance, great stress is placed on the element of competition and personal excellence. The system of ascribed hereditary status is hence subject to certain meritocratic qualifications. Yet the meritocratic system itself is uneven, since apparently only certain qualities count. The deeper, more searching qualities are left almost totally out of consideration. For instance, Damfo, the master healer, in introducing the protagonist Densu to his art. . . , informs him that one of the penalties of being a healer is that you must live without respect. . . . (pp. 85-6)

In order to adopt the healing vocation, Densu has to embrace what in many ways is a despised office. The fact that he is eventually willing to make this sacrifice marks him out as someone deeply at odds with the mainstream of Asante life. (p. 86)

Densu is not, however, like the visionary heroes of some of Armah's earlier books, completely and irrevocably alone. There are others among both his elders and his contemporaries who share his sympathies. First and foremost among these, as we soon learn, are the eponymous healers themselves. But there are others who, though not healers themselves, share something of their hardy serenity, notably the nimble and resourceful Anan who, before he dies in his attempted escape from the trial scene, is able to lend Densu much moral support in his altercation with the society's more typical elements. Densu senses in Anan a deep, inventive confidence, and beyond that a core of abiding peace greater than any elation to be gained from a cheap victory over others. (p. 87)

The deep divide in Asante society between those, like Anan, who prize peace and those, in the vast majority, who favour aggression, is not confined to the individual level. It is even reproduced at the pinnacle of Asante among the very Council of State. Any simplistic notions of the Asante as a proud, warlike people are countered by Armah's shrewd portrayal of a people sorely divided on the crucial issue as to whether or not to fight the British. (p. 88)

[The] main advocate of the peace party is Asamoa Nkwanta, a general of vast experience and prestige and by his title of 'ruler of the battles' hailed as the brightest star in the military firmament. (p. 89)

From the moment when we meet him, when he comes to the healer's village at Praso seeking advice, the great general acts as a living paradox: a military craftsman, a man of war who has increasingly become committed to the cause of peace. There is little doubt that the healers' influence serves to deepen his convictions in this respect, since abstention from violence is one of the foundations of their order. The anomalous position in which the general thus finds himself has the effect for us of raising the essential philosophical question of the validity of war as an instrument in the service of patriotic ideals. Throughout the novel Asante is portrayed as a nation at war, one which moreover is obliged to sustain a fighting posture in order to safeguard its territorial integrity. For instance, Amankwa Tia's expedition, which starts at the beginning of the novel as an enterprise of acquisition and conquest, has by the end transformed itself into a desperate rearguard action, a vital life-saving operation. To what extent can the healers, and Asamoa

Nkwanka too with his newly acquired pacificism, condone the actions of an army which is defending itself against overwhelming odds? In the context of Armah's work this question has far-reaching implications, for it corresponds almost exactly to the query with which *Two Thousand Seasons* ended. There the seer Isanusi, regarded as a repository of spiritual wisdom with convictions not dissimilar to those of the healers, concluded with a slightly ambiguous pronouncement about the simplistic 'praise of arms'. In *The Healers* the same issue is raised perhaps more directly, in a manner which, however, refrains from eliciting an easy, complacent answer.

This clash of opinion and interest within Ashanti society forms a framework within which the plot, a skilful compound of fiction and recorded fact, weaves its way, illuminating in its course various facets of the central philosophical debate. . . . (pp. 89-90)

In opting for a life of relative seclusion among those dedicated to medical skill Densu is not merely responding to sentimentality, nostalgia, or immature idealism. The healers' way of life and outlook represent a feasible though demanding alternative to the practices of the tribe, one only embraced after a considerable period of training and a system of spiritual exercises almost as gruelling as Ignatius Loyola's. In his interviews with Damfo, Densu is introduced to the ground rules of the community. If he wishes to join he must refrain from alcoholic drink, violence and political involvement. These, however, are only the superficial mannerisms of commitment. At its heart lies an attitude to the quality of life which cuts at the root of Asante political organization. The novel's word for this is 'inspiration' by which is meant a creative alignment at odds with those who would force instinctual self-expression into alien channels, those whom the novel distinguishes as 'manipulators'. (p. 91)

The original ideal of Akan 'wholeness' has been ditched in a surfeit of social competitiveness and a notion of purely individual advancement. The inevitable concomitants of this process—slavery, the rise of an oligarchic ruling class, fragmentation into jostling ethnic sub-groups—act as a blight on the whole texture of the community's life. It is part of the healers' ultimate purpose to wean society away from enslavement to these false idols, to which it is seemingly as addicted as were the emergent bourgeoisie of Armah's earlier books to the bright gleam emanating from the cocktail cabinet and the chrome panelling. That this analogy occurs is hardly surprising since both sets of phenomena are seen as imports, a prestigious mimicry of alien superfluities. But the healers, as Damfo later informs Densu, have to move carefully, surrounded as they are by social ignominy, and the resistance of those . . . whose whole activity is directed towards encouraging a whole society to be untrue to itself. (p. 92)

Asamoa Nkwanta, despite his celebrity, is in many ways taken to be a very typical figure, one who epitomizes the virtues and vices of a proud, imperialistic but morally complacent society. In him the process of self-questioning to which the Asante are currently prone is also enacted to an unusual degree. . . . [The general has] been guilty of self-betrayal, but as his nature is so congruent with the public personality of the nation he serves, his betrayal also possesses a social dimension. It is not merely he, but also the whole of Asante, that has been untrue to itself. Thus Asamoa Nkwanta cannot begin to examine his own motivations without by the same token casting doubt on the very foundations of the empire, and especially the cherished institutions of kingship and slavery. It is at this juncture that the links between the healers' medical and their social mission make themselves manifest. The kinds of disease to which Damfo and his colleagues apply themselves are the products of that long process of social disintegration which has brought Asante to the crisis in which it currently finds itself. (pp. 93-4)

If violence, as the healers clearly believe, is a symptom of a deep social disease, are passivity and surrender to be taken as signs of health? The problem is a convoluted one, since there are moments in the text which would seem to lend support to either view. For instance, some time before the final holocaust, the return of Amankwa Tia's dejected army to Kumasi after their coastal exploits is described in terms which suggest eloquently the terrible pathos of defeat.... The paradox of values is very deep here. The army's retreat is clearly seen as an instance of lack of nerve, yet there are hints ... which would appear to be distinctly disparaging of the consequences which would have accrued from a possible victory. Moreover, retrenchment is in direct compliance with Asamoa Nkwanta's already formulated policy of passive resistance and would even seem to be pertinent to his design of drawing the British armies into the trap of invading Ashanti territory.

The contradiction in tone is acute, yet capable of a kind of resolution. It is Damfo the healer who, on withdrawing from the war front on completion of his work, sets the context inside which the dilemmas facing Ashanti territory must be solved. Indeed the paradox we have already noted in the authorial attitude is also observable to a certain extent in the healer's own behaviour. In returning one of the army's prize leaders to fighting shape and then releasing him to unleash violence, however reluctantly, on the advancing British line, is he not renouncing his sacred trust as a man of peace? When this discrepancy is put to him, Damfo feels obliged to counsel realism. After all Asamoa Nkwanta is by trade a general, a servant of the State who, as such, is called upon to fulfill certain requirements. To ask him to refrain from acting in his country's defence would be to demand that he should violate an important aspect both of his calling and of the social network which sustains it. Like everybody else the healers are forced to achieve whatever they can within the conditions which currently obtain, hoping in the long run to work towards the ultimate ideals of brotherhood and peace.... (pp. 98-9)

The distant perspective—complete social cohesion, peace both within the community and the individual mind—is deftly suggested by the culmination of the plot. In sorrow of heart, Densu retires from Kumasi, but not before he has witnessed the execution of the bully Buntui in a manner befitting his crimes. Passing through Praso he observes the burning of the healers' village by disgruntled elements within its midst. Eventually, after rejoining Damfo and Ajoa, he makes his way to the palace at Esuano, only to find that his arch-enemy Ababio has now been enstooled as chief. No sooner has Densu confronted him than Ababio has the young man arrested for the alleged murder of Appia. Hauled off to Cape Coast for a trial in the British manner, he is rescued at the eleventh hour by Araba Jesiwa who, now well both in body and soul, is able to testify to Buntui's guilt and Ababio's complicity. After the latter's arrest, the British expeditionary force embarks from the Protectorate, sent off by a carnival of rejoicing from the varied ethnic groups gathered in this place for a campaign intended originally as divisive, but giving rise in the event to a paradoxical cohesion.... (p. 99)

In their determination to set the black race against itself and hence exacerbate the already severe process of fragmentation,

the British have only succeeded in bringing it, however fleetingly, together. A mercurial conclusion, perhaps, but one which serves to project poetically the longed for ideal of wholeness, from which the rest of the novel marks a retreat. Thus, figuratively, the end of history rejoins its beginning, and, in terms of a circular vision of time here latent, though simultaneously localized, the cycle at length becomes complete. (p. 100)

> *Robert Fraser, in his* The Novels of Ayi Kwei Armah: A Study in Polemical Fiction, *Heinemann, 1980, 113 p.*

## EUSTACE PALMER

In one majestic sweep of Africa's history, Armah seeks to demonstrate in *Two Thousand Seasons* how those pure African values and traditions which used to exist in an almost prehistoric past were largely annihilated through the exploits of Arab predators and European destroyers.... Armah adopts an essentially Negritudist posture, the net effect of his presentation being the total condemnation of the Arabs and Europeans as the destroyers of the pristine values of a once pure Africa. He sees imperialism as a destructive force obscuring the essential truths of "the way," interrupting its reign and inducing people to forget their origins. Armah sees a number of features of modern society as deviations from "the way" introduced by the forces of imperialism. Monarchial systems of government and the tyranny in which they resulted, the individual ownership of land, and the subordinate role accorded to women in many African societies, were all imported by the Moslem predators and European destroyers. So, for that matter, were trade and materialism....

The most significant fact about *Two Thousand Seasons* is Armah's positing of a far distant past when all black peoples belonged to one vast African nation with its own genuine, pure system of values or way of life that the author consistently refers to as "the way"—"our way." ... According to Armah, the distinguishing characteristic of this African "way" is the principle of reciprocity—mutual giving and receiving. These two components of reciprocity are intertwined and together constitute an essential principle of life; death, both spiritual and physical, ensues when the two are separated. "The way" is, therefore, a creative life-affirming principle as opposed to the destroyers' way of death; "the way" had its own clearly defined political and religious systems. In political organization it emerges as Communistic and egalitarian with "each participant an equal working together with all others for the welfare of the whole." ... The people of "the way" could not be regarded as materialistic, since materialism implied the individual hoarding of possessions. Though they loved possessions, they used them for the enrichment of the whole.... (p. 4)

Armah also posits a religion of "the way" quite distinct from Islam or Christianity which he sees as alien religions associated with the death-dealing Arab predators and European destroyers. In this, Armah goes much further than avowedly Negritudist writers such as Laye and Kane who present Islam as a traditional African religion accepted by the people. He groups Islam with Christianity as "shrieking theologies" with which the Arab predators and white destroyers assail the black people, and he refers to the myths of both religions as "fables." The religion of "the way" is indeed closely linked with Armah's principle of communalism. For if there is a supreme force in the world at all, it is not a supernatural being, but the collective will and determination of the people. It "is an energy in us, strongest in our working, breathing, thinking together as one people; weakest when we are scattered, confused, broken into individual, unconnected fragments." . . . (p. 5)

It is unfortunate that Armah does not give a really extended presentation of this ancient African traditional society which he is recommending as a model for the restructuring of our modern societies. . . . There is much talk in *Two Thousand Seasons* about the ideals and values of "the way"; a lot of our information about it comes through the mouths of prophetesses and seers, but there is little actual demonstration of "the way" in action, most of the book being taken up, in fact, by the attempts of the virtuous to rediscover "the way" after the disasters of colonialism and postcolonialism. Furthermore, one is not quite certain that Armah has succeeded in his intention of convincing us that the destruction of the values associated with "the way" was entirely the responsibility of the white destroyers. The disintegration had started before the advent of the imperialists due to the people's deviation from the path of reciprocity to that of unbridled generosity. But even before this period of prosperity when generosity became a vice, there had been the savage period of the rule of the fathers—a harsh time characterized by warring gangs and clans and leaders determined to cling to power. This harshness and tyranny, this deviation from "the way" was surely not caused by the destroyers; the uncharitable might suggest that "the way" must itself have possessed the seeds of its own destruction.

Armah's strong racial consciousness appears almost negative when he equates whiteness with death and destruction, not just because in the African imagination it is the color of death and disease, but because it is also the color of the destructive imperialists. Significantly, he regards both Arab predators and European destroyers as being white. On the other hand, black is the color associated with racial triumph and eventual fulfillment. It is also possible to argue that the relish with which Armah describes the assassination of the Arab predators and white destroyers smacks of racialism. . . . [And yet] one can argue, with Wole Soyinka, that the work is rescued from a negative racism by the positive nature of its message. It seeks to recreate a genuine traditional African past and calls rousingly to all Africans to liberate themselves from all those alien forces—economic, political, and spiritual—which, in his view, initially led to the destruction of African traditional values and which are the real cause of the present decadence on the continent. (pp. 5-6)

[For Armah] this exercise in racial retrieval, this return to origins, is part of the strategy for the transformation of modern society. It is much more therefore than a complacent, self-regarding idealization of blackness and black culture. The values thus retrieved must be actively used as the leaven for humanizing contemporary society. The ultimate target, therefore, is not so much the white man, as was the case with Negritude, as black men and contemporary black society. The retrieval of these pristine African values is not the end, merely the means. . . . The new Negritude, therefore, while sharing many of the characteristics of the old, is more positive, more confident, less introspective, more aggressive. It derives its inspiration not so much from a contemplation of what Africa was, as from a determination to bring about what it ought to be. (pp. 10-11)

*Eustace Palmer, "Negritude Rediscovered: A Reading of the Recent Novels of Armah, Ngugi, and Soyinka," in* The International Fiction Review, *Vol. 8, No. 1, Winter, 1981, pp. 1-11.**

## JOYCE JOHNSON

In ex-colonial Africa, Prometheus is important first as the prototype of the revolutionary intellectual. In the classical myth, Prometheus, a Titan, allied with Zeus to overthrow the unimaginative rule of brother Titans, but was later forced by Zeus's uncompromising exercise of power against mankind to rebel against him. . . . For those African intellectuals who welcomed the new order of political independence in various African societies and who became increasingly alienated from their political regimes, the myth of Prometheus supplies an appropriate symbolic structure for depicting the opposition of forces in contemporary African societies. This is one of the ways in which Ayi Kwei Armah has used the myth in *Fragments* and in *Why Are We So Blest*. In both novels, Armah depicts the attempt of a conscientious intellectual to dissociate himself from the new political élite that emerged during the struggle for independence in African societies and to serve the interests of the ordinary people whose lot remained unchanged in the post-independence era.

An important point in the myth of Prometheus is his gift to mankind of fire stolen from the Olympians. In modern interpretations of the myth the fire symbolizes the power to reflect upon experience, to acquire knowledge and to use it to improve human existence. The relevance of this aspect of the myth to the situation of the African intellectual is clear. Just as control of the tools of Western culture has placed Western-educated Africans in privileged positions within their societies, so control of technology by developed Western societies has placed them ahead of African societies in economic matters. The result is a chasm between rich and poor nations. An important question for the African intellectual, Armah suggests in *Fragments* and in *Why Are We So Blest,* is the nature of the transfer of knowledge and "technique" that should be made from the West to Africa. In these novels Armah compares the relationship that existed between the Olympians and humanity in the myth of Prometheus and that existing between rich and poor nations and between the political élite and the masses in contemporary African societies. The heroes of both novels are concerned about the situation of ordinary individuals in the ex-colonial society and the lack of self-direction in the society as a whole.

Second, Prometheus has specific reference to ex-colonial Africa because he is a hero who attempted to bridge two worlds. This aspect of the myth, which relates to Prometheus' attempt to cross over from a position of privilege to the side of oppressed humanity, is especially relevant to the situation of the Western-educated African who is attempting to re-establish links with his traditional cultural background or to identify with the ordinary people. In *Fragments* and in *Why Are We So Blest* the heroes are shown attempting to give up social privilege available to them because of their Western education. They offend the privileged class, whose principles they reject, but are isolated from the masses because of their special abilities. In the world of the privileged they are regarded as betrayers of their own kind; in the world of the oppressed they are regarded as strangers. As a result they are isolated figures between two worlds.

Armah's interpretation of the myth of Prometheus differs from the traditional Western one. Where in the European context the myth has served to confirm the idea of mankind's progress towards a new and better world, in the African context, Armah suggests, it has quite a different application. Armah interprets the myth to show the futility of endeavor for the African intellectual who is attempting to discover a model of progress for his society and emphasizes the extent to which "the arrangements for fighting privilege were themselves structures of privilege." In both *Fragments* and *Why Are We So Blest* the Promethean hero's attempt to intervene on behalf of the oppressed reveals the ineradicable patterns of dominance and dependence in the society. (pp. 497-99)

The theme of the divided worlds and of an élite above the masses, which is further developed in *Why Are We So Blest,* is clearly one which underlies the structure of *Fragments.* So too are the ideas of the crossover and the picture of an élite formed by individuals who "rise from the plains" to enjoy extraordinary privilege. Baako, with his desire to see the oppressed break out of the circle of oppression, his rejection of privilege and his "foolhardy" attempt to defy an entrenched power structure, is clearly a hero in the Promethean mould. *Why Are We So Blest* may therefore be seen as a further attempt to deal with a theme previously introduced in *Fragments.* (p. 501)

The first chapter of *Fragments* is narrated by Naana, Baako's grandmother. . . . Naana's imaginative projections about Baako's departure and return are important to the overall structure of the novel. Armah uses them as a means of relating the elements of Western myth and African folklore that have been incorporated into the novel. In Naana's imagination Baako is associated with beings who live in the sky. . . . Several images converge in [Naana's imagination]. . . . There is the image of "the departed one" entering the world of the spirits, the initiate in the rites of passage "entombed at a place where the sky meets the earth," and Prometheus on his rock exposed to the elements. All three images are of individuals placed between two worlds. Through this convergence of images, Armah associates Prometheus, who rescued mankind from the persecution of the Olympians, with the departed ancestor who, in African religious belief, acts as an intermediary between the worlds of the living and of the ancestors and ensures the well-being of the former.

The imaginative projection of Baako as the departed one elevates him to the status of an ancestor and places him, like a god, above the people he has left behind and who look to him for help. It also leads to a further perception of Baako as one who is transformed by his separation from his society and who, like Prometheus, may be regarded as stranger among those on whose behalf he feels compelled to intervene. The reference to the initiate in the rites of passage emphasizes the notion of transition by relating the situation of Baako, who is separated from his society in order to acquire new knowledge, to that of the member of the traditional society who is moving between the "structure of positions" in the society. (pp. 501-02)

In *Fragments,* the airplane which takes the traveller to and from the West is a visible symbol of the knowledge and technique the Olympians possess. Metallic, luminous and white, it is associated with the realm of the gods, the world of technology and the realm of death. Flying in an airplane to the West expresses in a concrete way the idea of moving between two worlds. Those who have flown to the West in an airplane acquire a god-like status in the society. (p. 503)

[Armah] shows the extent to which the masses are responsible for perpetuating their own servile condition. . . . The Ghanaian masses, Armah suggests . . . , need to be rescued not only from the abuses of those with power but also from the destructive tendencies within themselves. Throughout the novel he contrasts the people's idea of their needs, material goods brought back by travellers returning from the technologically developed

societies, with their real need, which is to develop their own potential for progress. This contrast between what the people desire and what they need is brought out, for example, in the description of Juana's drive through the outskirts of Accra. Armah's description of the incidents Juana witnesses not only illustrates the plight of the society but also reinforces the classical associations of the novel. The people express themselves mainly through violent action directed at the weakest among them. . . .

In *Fragments,* there is . . . a clear analogy made between the situation described in the myth of Prometheus in which the Olympians dominated an "impotent" and "blind" humanity and a contemporary situation in which privileged individuals dominate an unenlightened community. These privileged individuals are further associated with Western societies which have developed a knowledge and a control of technology which make them rich and powerful and enable them to dominate poor and technologically underdeveloped societies. Armah's allusions to the myth of Prometheus give the seemingly commonplace events of modern Ghanaian family life strong impact and give point to the resolution of events in the novel, for reference to the myth explains Baako's inability to act effectively. Although Baako decries the social fragmentation which has resulted from his society's interaction with the West, the power which he has to adjust the balance comes, like that of Prometheus, from the knowledge and technique he shares with "Olympians." Baako's understanding of the irony of his situation weakens his capacity for confident action. (p. 505)

In *Why Are We So Blest,* as in *Fragments,* Armah depicts two opposed worlds. The separation of the élite and the masses obtains even within the revolutionary movement, which had developed its own hierarchical structure. Seen in a wider context, the opposed worlds of the "Olympians" and the "plain-dwellers" correspond with those of colonizers and colonized, European and African societies and rich and poor nations. The events of the novel show that the Promethean hero who attempts to intervene between the two worlds is doomed to futility and despair. (pp. 506-07)

Modin's situation in *Why Are We So Blest* recalls Prometheus' later punishment by the eagle daily devouring his liver. This association arises especially from Armah's description of Modin's relationship with Aimée. Modin's spiritual and physical resources are drained by his continued intercourse with her. The dominant image of such a relationship, Solo reflects, is that of "carrion—fastened onto by a beast of prey." . . . The image of Aimée as a predator remorselessly consuming experience at the cost of Modin's suffering is sustained throughout the novel. (p. 507)

In *Why Are We So Blest,* Aimée clearly embodies the decadent aspects of Western civilization. Modin's situation thus reflects the predicament of the African intellectual who is involved with Western civilization but is, at the same time, attempting to develop a commitment to his own people. Aimée is presented both as an exploiter and as someone needing to be rescued. As the entries in her diary show, she is seeking a source from which to enliven an existence which is daily becoming more futile and boring. As in the original myth, Armah uses fire to symbolize the creative energy which can give meaning to existence. . . . Fire is, of course, an agent for purifying and transforming things, but it is also, Monica Wilson has observed [in *Religion and the Transformation of Society: A Study of Social Change in Africa*], a symbol for sex in Africa. As Armah shows throughout the novel, the stimulation which Aimée seeks is largely sexual. Her involvement in revolutionary activity satisfies a craving for excitement. Using Aimée as representative of Western culture, Armah suggests that there is no longer any relationship between the Western idea of progress and the sense of moral achievement which is emphasized in the interpretations of the myth of Prometheus. (pp. 507-08)

Like Baako in *Fragments,* Modin achieves nothing by his act of rebellion. His awareness of the equivocal nature of the role of the revolutionary intellectual in Africa renders him ineffectual. In Modin's case, as in Baako's, the inability to develop a clear purpose or to influence events is due to his recognition of the strange inconsistency in the Promethean role when it is viewed in relation to the situation of the ex-colonial. In this situation, one cannot ignore the point that although Prometheus' intervention started mankind on the path to progress, it introduced progress on a model developed by the Olympians, since it was their fire which he stole and gave to mankind. By comparing the relationship which existed between Olympians and humans before Prometheus' intervention with that which

exists between dominant and oppressed groups in contemporary society, Armah highlights the problems of ex-colonial societies which seek to become self-directing. In *Fragments* and *Why Are We So Blest,* he shows no hope for adjusting the balance of power between the two worlds and between the two levels of society which he has depicted.

Armah's interest in exposing the inadequacies of the Western myth of progress accounts for the pessimistic outlook of his heroes and their general ineffectiveness. The Promethean hero in the African context, Armah suggests, is inevitably the vector of a "foreign" culture. Although he makes the "descent from Olympus," he cannot become part of the lives of the people whom he attempts to serve. Having voluntarily left the "realm of the gods," the hero becomes trapped within the gulf which lies between two worlds. (p. 508)

*Joyce Johnson, "The Promethean 'Factor' in Ayi Kwei Armah's 'Fragments' and 'Why Are We So Blest?'" in* World Literature Written in English, *Vol. 21, No. 3, Autumn, 1982, pp. 497-510.*

# Alan Ayckbourn
## 1939-

(Has also written under pseudonym of Roland Allen) English dramatist and lyricist.

One of England's most popular and prolific playwrights, Ayckbourn uses the forms of bourgeois comedy and farce to explore the monotony and emotional torment underlying daily middle-class life and marriage. The inability of Ayckbourn's characters to communicate forms the locus of conflict; further complications reveal their loneliness, unintentional cruelty, self-interest, and obliviousness to others. An Ayckbourn play may be recognized not only by these features, but also by the intricate and unconventional staging techniques that he has invented.

Ayckbourn's staging techniques often allow his characters to transcend space and time. In *How the Other Half Loves* (1969), for example, two separate settings are superimposed onstage so that actions which occur in different places, at different times, are seen simultaneously. Similarly, in *Bedroom Farce* (1975), three bedrooms in three different homes are the setting for continuous, cross-cutting action. In *Taking Steps* (1979), multiple levels of a house are thrust from a single-level stage, and *Way Upstream* (1981) is performed on a boat suspended in a fiberglass tank of water.

*Standing Room Only* (1961), one of Ayckbourn's most popular plays under the pseudonym Roland Allen, concerns a London bus driver and his family caught in a bus during a twenty-year traffic jam. Despite the farcical overtones in his later plays, *Standing Room Only* is Ayckbourn's only truly absurdist work. His first production under his own name was *Meet My Father* (1965; subsequently retitled *Relatively Speaking*). *Relatively Speaking* is a "well-made play," modeled after Oscar Wilde's *The Importance of Being Earnest*. The humor in this play about infidelity derives from audience awareness of a misunderstanding among the characters. *How the Other Half Loves* also explores infidelity and misunderstanding in a humorous way. When a man's affair is about to be discovered by his wife, he invents a marital dispute between another couple as an excuse for coming home in the middle of the night. By the play's end, the undertones are serious, as three marriages are nearly destroyed through the gradual multiplication of the husband's lies. The same themes are again manifest in *Bedroom Farce,* a lighter work about a married couple who attempt to reconcile their differences by individually disrupting the sleep of three other couples, causing each of them to reevaluate their own sagging marriages.

*Time and Time Again* (1971) and *Absurd Person Singular* (1972) mark the beginning of Ayckbourn's search for a form combining his interests in farce and Chekhovian melodrama, or what he called "the truly hilarious dark play." *Absurd Person Singular* (1972), widely considered an early Ayckbourn masterpiece of dark comedy, is about three unhappily married couples who take turns entertaining one another on three successive Christmas Eves. Ayckbourn's traditional themes of class and sex antagonisms, cruelty, and self-interest are evident in such famous scenes as when the hostess of a party drinks herself into a stupor while buried offstage beneath a pile of

*Photograph by Mark Gerson*

coats thrown over her by her uncomprehending guests. In another scene, the woman repeatedly attempts suicide in front of her guests, who remain cruelly incognizant of her pain. In *Absent Friends* (1974), a young man whose fiancée has died visits some married friends who wish to comfort him. However, his astonishing openness and the happiness of his memories force the couples to contemplate the lesser happiness of their own marriages. This trend toward darker, sadder comedy continues in such plays as *Just Between Ourselves* (1976), *Joking Apart* (1978), and *Way Upstream.*

Related to Ayckbourn's interest in unconventional staging is his tendency to alter chronology and plot in what some critics have called a "jigsaw" fashion. *The Norman Conquests* (1973), one of Ayckbourn's best-known works, is a trilogy of interlocking plays that are comprehensible when viewed either individually or in any order. In the three plays, *Table Manners, Living Together,* and *Round and Round the Garden,* action that occurs offstage in one play becomes onstage action in another. The plays center around Norman, an amoral, womanizing assistant librarian whose fundamentally innocent wish to please all the women he knows sets him at odds with his in-laws. Ayckbourn wrote two versions of the second and third scenes of another play, *Sisterly Feelings* (1979). The version performed on a given night is determined by an actress's choice or the flip of a coin. Though the emphasis of the play becomes very different when focused on either of the possible protagonists, the fourth and final scene is invariable, illustrating that decisions only appear to change people's lives. In *Intimate Exchanges* (1982), thirty-one different scenes may be performed in sixteen different combinations.

Ayckbourn is probably the most commercially successful dramatist in England today. London's West End regularly produces at least one of his plays, and frequently more. Early in his career, Ayckbourn received a warm critical reception. In 1971, John Russell Taylor wrote that while Ayckbourn "has . . . consistently and uncompromisingly avoided any suggestion of deeper meaning in his plays," he is so adept at keeping his audience laughing that he does not need a "safety net of deeper significance." Later in his career, when Ayckbourn's plays became increasingly laden with meaning, critics praised him for his ability to write hilarious comedy while portraying the dark side of human nature and the constant frustration of daily life. However, in recent years, Ayckbourn has been less consistently praised by critics, some of whom find his plays overly crafted and repetitive of his earlier successes.

(See also *CLC*, Vols. 5, 8, 18; *Contemporary Authors*, Vols. 21-24, rev. ed.; and *Dictionary of Literary Biography*, Vol. 13.)

## OLEG KERENSKY

*Mr. Whatnot,* Ayckbourn's first work to reach London, was largely a mime play with a complex taped sound track. His first big success was *Relatively Speaking,* which established him as a writer of ingenious farcical comedy, with an ear for dialogue and with a penchant for complex situations and misunderstandings, and ingenious plots. His delight in playing games with the English language is evident from the play's punning title, which aptly describes the plot. There are just four characters; Greg and Ginny who are having an affair, Philip, an older man who was Ginny's previous lover, and Sheila, Philip's wife. After an introductory scene in Ginny's London apartment, with Greg getting suspicious that she still has other men and not understanding why he can't go with her to her parents' for the week-end, the scene shifts to Philip and Sheila's country cottage. Greg, having found the address lying around Ginny's apartment, arrives to surprise her, assuming that he is visiting her parents. Ginny arrives to try to persuade Philip to stop pestering her with his attentions. The main humour of the play derives from Greg's continuing misconception that he is visiting Ginny's parents and the various misunderstandings that result. In addition to the amusement generated by these, there is also some mild social satire. The play ends with a typical Ayckbourn twist. Greg has earlier shown Sheila a pair of men's slippers which he found under Ginny's bed; Sheila recognized them as Philip's and thus learnt of his affair with Ginny. But at the final curtain Philip discovers that they are not his slippers: Ginny had yet another man.

The opening scene of *Relatively Speaking* is a slightly contrived way of preparing for the main action of the play; with greater experience Ayckbourn would probably have started the play differently. In the rest of the play, however, he is astonishingly skilful in maintaining various permutations of his basic situation and holding the audience's attention, an achievement which is all the more remarkable when one considers that in real life either Sheila or Philip would surely have asked Greg what he was doing in their house and who he was, or he would have discovered that they were not actually Ginny's parents. (pp. 116-17)

*Time and Time Again* . . . shows Ayckbourn getting more interested in pillorying the manners and social conventions of the middle classes. This time the cast consists of two couples and an odd man out, Leonard, who is the central character. He is a 'pale, alert, darting' young man who is bored by the idle chit-chat of those around him, and who has a disturbing effect on them with his mixture of selfishness and naïveté. His sister Anna is down-trodden by her husband Graham and has retreated into a routine of domestic chores. Leonard talks to the garden gnome, hides in cupboards and lusts after Joan, the fiancée of Graham's employee Peter. Graham a cold, practical bully, impatient of Leonard's fantasies and keen to get him out of the house, has invited Joan and Peter to tea. The action takes place in a garden with the back of the house at one end and a sports ground at the other. The plot is not quite so elaborate as in the earlier plays, while the characterization is deeper. But a great deal of fun is extracted from the misunderstandings when Leonard contrives to make Peter think it is Graham who is flirting with Joan. In the end Leonard pretends to have no idea what has been going on, Joan leaves in disgust with both Leonard and Peter, who make it up and go off to play football together. Ayckbourn regards this as a happy ending, as Leonard would have been 'trampled to death' in a few years if he had married Joan. Peter, a typical Englishman of a certain sort, is happier 'playing the game' than in emotional relationships. (p. 118)

*Confusions,* five one-act plays loosely strung together to make a two-hour evening, . . . [is] spiced with a strong element of social satire and with a vague linking theme of man's loneliness and selfishness. The last of the five plays epitomizes this theme and the central 'confusion' of the evening:—five strangers sit close to each other on park benches and each in turn unburdens his worries to his uninterested but mildly irritated neighbour. The final line is spoken in frustration, when the wheel has come full circle and the first speaker realizes that his neighbour is not listening: 'You might as well talk to yourself.' That, in effect, is what the characters of *Confusions* all do.

Ayckbourn shows his customary ingenuity in using just three actors and two actresses to play twenty-one characters, arranging their costume and make-up changes so that one play follows another with scarcely any break. The first two are linked in the sense that the husband of the central character in the first actually appears in the second. Similarly, a woman whom we see quarrelling with her husband in the third play appears without her husband in the fourth. . . . The plays can in any case be performed separately, and Ayckbourn hopes they will be, when they are done by amateur groups.

*Mother Figure,* the opening sketch, is about Lucy, a woman so obsessed with her children that she also addresses her neighbours in baby talk and treats their marital squabbles with an old-fashioned nanny's mixture of bullying and cajolery. She succeeds in making the husband apologize to his wife, while forcing them to drink milk and orange juice, and she stops the wife crying by holding up a toy and asking if she wants it to see her cry! The result is amusing, and strangely moving. *Drinking Companion,* the least successful of the five plays, shows Lucy's husband trying to pick up two girls in the bar of a provincial hotel; he persists in thinking they are going to come to his bedroom, and gets drunker and drunker while forcing them to accept drinks. The play takes rather too long to reach its inevitable denouement, when they walk out on him.

*Between Mouthfuls,* which ends the first act of *Confusions,* has a typical Ayckbourn gimmick. Two couples are dining in a restaurant, but the audience can only hear as much of their conversation as is overheard by the waiter. As soon as he leaves one of the tables, the conversation there reverts to dumb show. One couple is quarrelling, with the wife demanding to know what her husband was doing while allegedly on business in Rome. The man at the other table is an employee of the man at the first, while the second man's wife was the boss's mistress in Rome. A great deal of laughter is extracted from this situation, from the sudden interruptions of conversation as the waiter moves from table to table and to the kitchen, and from the waiter's 'tactful' hoverings and occasional deft intrusions with the food and wine.

*Gosforth's Fête,* which opens the second act, is the funniest of the five sections. Everything goes wrong at a village fête:— one couple discuss their affair and the girl's pregnancy over the public address system by mistake, the lady councillor who opens the fête gets her dress ruined in the mud, the tea urn cannot be switched off, so that a manic procession of tea cups is carried to it while the councillor is trying to make her speech. The sound system short circuits and nearly electrocutes the councillor, while the pregnant girl's fiancée gets drunk and bawls obscene songs over a megaphone. The climax, when most of these things are happening simultaneously, is hilarious.

Finally *A Talk in The Park* has five solitaries in turn complaining to their neighbours that they have just been bored by their other neighbours, though of course they would never do such a thing themselves. It sums up the self-centeredness and confusion of the entire evening, and of most of the characters in Ayckbourn's plays. As with the other plays, it is possible to enjoy *Confusions* without noticing its social satire or its implicit criticism of our behaviour, but nevertheless it is much more than the mere commercial farce which it superficially resembles.

So, despite its deceptive title, is *Bedroom Farce.* Traditionally a bedroom farce is a romp in which various characters jump in and out of bed together, or are caught in embarrassing circumstances in the same bedroom. Ayckbourn's play is set in three bedrooms, shown side by side on the stage, and involves four couples, but the married couples stay together and never get sexually intermingled, while their characters and problems are probed much more deeply than is usual in farce. Trevor and Susannah are infuriatingly self-absorbed; they think nothing of having a row in their hosts' bedroom at a party or of visiting their friends in the middle of the night to pour out their troubles. This couple provides the link between the others and the three bedrooms; their own bedroom is never shown.... There is a lot of humour, ... but it is wry humour. *Bedroom Farce* is mainly notable for the sympathetic irony of its characterizations and for the ingenuity with which Ayckbourn links his couples and keeps the action—consecutively and sometimes simultaneously—in their bedrooms. (pp. 126-28)

[Ayckbourn's] plays have to be easily understood by a seaside audience, drawn from many walks of life and not consisting mainly of regular theatregoers. Apart from that, being a professional man of the theatre, Ayckbourn believes that plays should be skilfully put together. (p. 130)

Ayckbourn's progress from traditional farce 'into the Chekhovian field' remarkably parallels the development of the American playwright Neil Simon. Both seem increasingly interested in the comic side of the more bitter and tragic aspects of modern society. Perhaps because they are so closely concerned with their own societies, both of them have had difficulty in crossing the Atlantic. (p. 131)

*Oleg Kerensky, "Alan Ayckbourn," in his* The New British Drama: Fourteen Playwrights Since Osborne and Pinter, *1977. Reprint by Taplinger Publishing Company, 1979, pp. 115-31.*

## ANTHONY CURTIS

[In *Ten Times Table,* the] ballroom of the Swan Hotel somewhere in the shires of England is being used as the venue for the Committee which is planning the pageant that is to be the climax of the town's anniversary celebrations. Need I go on? Only perhaps to observe how strictly Ayckbourn sticks to his own rules. He has decided here that we shall not move from this place with its ... long table composed of several small ones around which for most of the action our committee sits.

Yet action there is and plenty of it, arising out of the sedentary state. Factions form; personal lives intrude; the local issues mirror national politics.... [A] Tory lady is pitted against ... [a] Marxist lecturer; ... [a] drunk confronts ... [an] impeccably smooth Chairman who has his own problem in the shape of his wife; ... [a] councillor is still dominated by his deaf mother (a wonderful study of an old woman with all her wits if not her faculties about her ...). And so on and so on.... [Ayckbourn] has managed to find in the divisiveness that afflicts every committee a perfect comic metaphor for contemporary England. (pp. 56-7)

*Anthony Curtis, in a review of "Ten Times Table," in* Drama, *No. 129, Summer, 1978, pp. 55-7.*

## BENEDICT NIGHTINGALE

[*Family Circles*] ... is an extremely interesting addition to the Ayckbourn archives; but one can see why the West End impresarios might shy away even from what is, it seems, its third and final version. Two daughters bring their husbands, and the third her latest lay, to celebrate the wedding anniversary of their parents, who may and may not be trying to murder one another. It is a party whose spirit-level may be gauged, not only by this grisly suspicion, but by the father's first-act remark that 'whoever you choose to share the rest of your life, it invariably turns out to be the worst choice you ever made'. And this, in fact, is the proposition that Ayckbourn then proceeds to test. The visitors arrive, take an awkward tea together, go out to a spectacularly unsuccessful dinner, then return home; and each girl spends the time attached to one after the other of the three men. Technically, the piece is as taxing as anything yet attempted by an author well known for his jigsaw mind and acrostic artefacts. Emotionally, it is bleaker than any of his plays except *Just Between Ourselves,* and no less cynical about the domestic dove-cote, the mock-Tudor love-nest. Once again, Ayckbourn is taking risks not easily reconciled with popular comedy.

To a large extent, the canny observation and funny encounters justify those risks. As Ayckbourn sees it, the ugly sisters change awesomely little, whoever their partners may be. But one husband, resilient enough when he's married to the most bloody-minded, sinks into apathetic hypochondria when he moves on to the earnest, flustered one. Another, who flaunts a seedy grandeur when this fusspot is his wife, visibly coarsens when he's with the family flibbertygibbet and actually becomes violent when he's taken over by the commuter-belt Regan. This is revealing and instructive as far as it goes. The trouble is that we've hardly got a bearing on any relationship before it has flashed past, and in the fourth and last act the compass is snatched from our collective hands and sent spinning from north to south and back again. The characters bustle on and off, more often than not married to a different person, and the effect is frantic, giddy, and disorientating, not a mental state in which laughter can be easily generated. *Family Circles* is a good idea that ends with its wits turned by its own bravura. (p. 763)

Benedict Nightingale, "Stay Single," in New States-man, Vol. 96, No. 2489, December 1, 1978, pp. 762-63.*

## RONALD HAYMAN

Alan Ayckbourn cannot be ranked as an innovative playwright, though he has made some interesting experiments in some of his comedies. In *Mr. Whatnot* . . . most of the action is word-less. Like Harpo Marx, the eponymous piano-tuner never speaks, but mimes his farcically anarchic way into marrying the daugh-ter of a lord. *How the Other Half Loves* . . . uses the two halves of the set to represent two living rooms in different houses with contrasting furniture. The two households are linked by an adulterous liaison, and the plot develops a series of con-fusions involving a third couple used by both lovers for an alibi. In *Absurd Person Singular* . . . Ayckbourn succeeded in making a girl's suicide attempts into a subject for farcical comedy. *The Norman Conquests* . . . is an ambitious trilogy, each play involving the same characters, the same time-span, and the same events, but each set in a different part of the house or garden. Allusions in the dialogue are criss-crossed ingeniously so that each play is comprehensible by itself, but each illuminates the incidents of the others by going into detail about what was happening at the same time in a different place.

Having written his early farces under the influence of Feydeau, Ayckbourn began to feel at the beginning of the Seventies that he wanted to put Chekhovian characters into an absurd frame-work. But Chekhov contrived a brilliantly judged mixture of absurdity and pathos as the framework for the existence of his characters, while Ayckbourn's, well observed and entertaining though they are, get put into situations too patently contrived. (pp. 68-9)

Ronald Hayman, "Innovation and Conservatism," in his British Theatre Since 1955: A Reassessment, Oxford University Press, Oxford, 1979, pp. 30-79.*

## ROBIN THORNBER

As a demonstration of technical virtuosity [*Taking Steps*] sim-ply leaves you gasping. The stagecraft which characterises [Ayckbourn's] earlier work—the meticulous construction of farcical hysteria, the toying with split-stage techniques—is de-veloped to new lengths.

This time we have three floors of a decrepit old mansion su-perimposed on the one small arena set, with razor-edge lighting shifting the action from sitting-room to bedroom to attic and the characters breathlessly running up and down imaginary but completely convincing staircases. It's a three-storeyed symbol of disintegration; not only is the house falling apart, but the family building firm which owns it is on the verge of collapse and the relationships—between the boozy tycoon who's buying it and his ex-dancer wife, and between her boring brother and his fiancee—are also breaking down. (pp. 61-2)

Robin Thornber, in a review of "Taking Steps," in Drama, No. 135, January, 1980, pp. 61-2.

## IRVING WARDLE

*Suburban Strains* tells the story of Caroline, a trusting young English teacher who first turns her flat over to an open marriage with an unemployed actor, and recoils from that disaster into a deadly affair with a priggish doctor who specializes in un-ravelling women like pieces of knitting. Caroline finally throws him out, too, and achieves a happy ending with her first man. The piece explores territory as bleak as any Ayckbourn has touched, but this time he relents and allows his heroine fairy tale privileges.

Paul Todd's music, intrusive in too prolonged overtures, but wholly self-effacing as a support to the action, is not there for decorative purposes. Like other technical devices Ayckbourn has used, its purpose is functional; in this case, to present material that will be so familiar to the average middle-class spectator that it bursts out of the lives of this particular group of characters. A ghastly dinner party, for instance, becomes a sextet involving three simultaneous lines of conversation. . . .

Ayckbourn has mounted his production on two concentric re-volves (a device I have not seen before), which not only secure speedy changes of scene and present the same scene from different angles, but also enable him to shuffle past and present in the bewildered Caroline's mind; allowing her absent husband to walk through the set in the midst of a tender encounter with the new man; and showing her twice returning home from dinner parties to hold double conversations with the two men she brings back on the two different occasions.

The piece shows Ayckbourn as alert as ever to the absurdities of marital experiment; surrounding Caroline with domineering friends, all telling her what to do with her life, while they themselves are as lost as she is.

Irving Wardle, in a review of "Suburban Strains," in The Times, London, January 19, 1980, p. 8.

## JOHN PETER

["**Sisterly Feelings**"] might have been written by someone who felt caged in by the limitations of the stage. That may sound like an odd thing to say about a consummate craftsman like Ayckbourn. But consider. If "**Norman Conquests**" was written as three plays because Ayckbourn wanted to show us what happened off stage in each of them, then "**Sisterly Feelings**" may have been written because he wanted to show us what might have happened if some of his characters had made dif-ferent choices.

The solution has a brazen simplicity about it. How would things have turned out if rangy, athletic Simon had walked home with Dorcas instead of her sister Abigail? The answer is, write two different sequels and see. Now then. Suppose he walks home with Abigail, starts an affair with her, and later (in Scene Two, to be precise) her husband surprises them at a family picnic? The picnic ends in confusion and pouring rain. Abigail might cycle home again with Simon; or she might opt for her hus-band's plushy car. What will she do? The answer is, write another two alternative sequels (Scene Three) and see. The family will then foregather for the inevitable wedding in Scene Four. These scenes will combine into four alternative plays: people who see one might want to see more.

The thing requires the temerity of a circus manager and the skill of a high-precision instrument maker, and Ayckbourn has both in ample supply. But if I make it sound like a box of tricks—which it is—there is more to it than that.

The play opens on the village common, after the funeral of the sisters' mother. Pa . . . an ageing eccentric, and like all eccentrics utterly self-centred, rambles on desultorily about the past like a cross between Winston Churchill and Cyril Cusack. His brother-in-law Len, a policeman, a barrel-chested old hardliner with the eyes of a puritanical basilisk . . . growls grimly about vandalism. The middle-aged relations look on with indifference, the young with undisguised hostility.

Ayckbourn is at his best in such scenes. All his plays are about families or small communities engaged in the great tribal rituals of Christmas party, cricket, tennis, selling the car, funeral, picnic—scenes in which he observes the English Middle Class in the bizarre activity it calls Life. The dialogue is seamlessly commonplace; it has the ghastly inevitability of everyday life, full of dim impulses and pathetic self-revelations. Its banal eloquence is the work of a master. For more than a decade, Ayckbourn has been drawing up a great comic map of middle-class malevolence, dottiness and insecurity. **"Sisterly Feelings"** confidently extends the view.

Is it a view to a life or a view to a death? A bit of both, actually. Dorcas and Abigail have their affairs but in the end everyone ends up paired off as before. It is almost as if Ayckbourn were quizzically saying that neither chance nor choice can change a thing: the family remains each time as we first saw it, in full possession of its victims, its obsessions and its insecurities. . . .

[The] story unfolds like a slow, strange tribal dance. This is one of the most consummately organised pieces of comedy you can hope to see. . . . Observe . . . Abigail, in full command of the marital snarl and displaying a gauche but ravenous sexuality. Or her sister . . . , one of nature's put-upon organisers, full of bouncy, fretful competence.

I am not sure that I am entirely convinced by her dreadful lover Stafford; his reconciliation with Dorcas made me think that Ayckbourn was in a hurry to make his ends meet. . . . As for Abigail's husband, Patrick, he is really two men loosely stitched together. Did Ayckbourn want to show how different the same person could be in different circumstances? If so, he has not quite made his point. . . .

For the sake of objectivity I have to say that **"Sisterly Feelings"** is not as good as **"Norman Conquests"**: it is not as tightly knit and does not have quite the same sense of comic opulence. But it is tough, sharp, full of vitriolic observation and cretinous, fumbling humanity. This is the real people show and nobody should miss it. (I mean miss them.)

*John Peter, "Ayckbourn's Double Deal," in The Sunday Times, London, June 8, 1980, p. 38.*

## JOHN RUSSELL TAYLOR

Everyone seems to have found Alan Ayckbourn's new play-and-a-half disappointing. We know of old that Ayckbourn is turned on by technical challenges, but *Sisterly Feelings* . . . seemed like an instance of too far or not far enough. Whichever way you see it, it consists of four scenes, and the first and last are identical. But in the second scene it is decided by the toss of a coin (sometimes literally) which of the sisters shall go off with the attractive spare man at their mother's funeral. If it is

Abigail, the respectably married one, then this leads to a disastrous family picnic in which her husband and her new lover look daggers over the insufficiently mixed sandwiches. If it is Dorcas, the free-living local broadcaster, then the picnic instead (and more feebly) requires her discarded poet lover to lurk obtrusively behind bushes. Either way, this leads to another decision, by which the new lover can either change ladies at midpoint or continue as he is. If he has Abigail in the third scene they are involved in a farcical attempt to camp out on the heath, constantly interrupted by a policeman uncle's conviction that they are a coven of witches; if Dorcas, then they fall foul of a very disorganized cross-country race over the same terrain. Either way they end up as they began in the fourth scene.

It all sounds very ingenious, but unfortunately it is not this time ingenious enough. The two sisters are supposed to be widely contrasted, but in the first and last scenes they have to be written so ambiguously (to take account of the various things that may befall or have befallen) that they could be interchangeable. Also, it is very easy, even without having seen all four possible combinations (I saw two, one all with Abigail, the other all with Dorcas), to work out what would be the happiest. The picnic with Abigail coupled with the available Simon is much funnier and more pointed, and the cross-country run scene is a decided improvement on the pseudo-coven routine. And of course if it were done that way both sisters would have a fair innings, and both their alternative men, Abigail's husband . . . and Dorcas's scruffy boyfriend Stafford . . . , would have decent roles too. If Ayckbourn had made up his mind to this at the outset, he could have lavished more detailed care and attention on the play as a comic exploration of real human beings (however incidentally caricatured) rather than as a dehumanised conjuring trick. Even so, I doubt if it would have been vintage Ayckbourn, since it would remain thin and not very inventive in its humour. . . . (pp. 19-20)

*John Russell Taylor, in a review of "Sisterly Feelings," in Drama, No. 138, October, 1980, pp. 19-20.*

## JOHN RUSSELL TAYLOR

I think *Season's Greetings* . . . is not exactly vintage Ayckbourn. . . . It takes the relationship between the two sisters almost straight from *Sisterly Feelings*, along with the character of the obsessed policeman uncle and his idiotic wife (as we may divine, though we never see her here). It is remarkably straightforward for Ayckbourn—even more so than *Taking Steps*—and simply chronicles the innumerable mishaps of an uncomfortable family Christmas, leading up to an irresistible *scène à faire* in which the wife's attempts to drag her sister's boy-friend into bed (or finally on to the rug in the hall) are constantly, cumulatively thwarted. The character of the incompetent doctor is one of Ayckbourn's happier inventions . . . , and the whole thing is amusing enough. But the play is much too long (three sprawling acts), and seems absolutely right as an occasional piece for family consumption rather than an important London contender.

*John Russell Taylor, in a review of "Season's Greetings," in Drama, No. 139, 1st Quarter, 1981, p. 37.*

## LINDA BROWN

[*Suburban Strains*] revolves, literally as well as figuratively, around a young teacher: her marriage and its break-up; her subsequent *affaire* (with a doctor who has an alarming penchant for personality destruction and feels that people owe it to the world to clean their shoes) and its break-up; her well-meaning, dinner-party-giving friends and their attempts to help; her job and what its long-term effects might be on her and her chances of happiness; her need for individuality.

Universal strains, every one, but as presented by Ayckbourn they have a distinct suburban edge. So devastating fun is made not only of dinner parties in general but in particular those where the hosting couple's relationship results in his doing the cooking—all the time—because he likes to.

There he is in a navy-blue striped apron with matching oven gloves, flapping when the lateness of the guests threatens to turn his poulet l'estragon into chicken broth. One of the guests is another male cordon bleu aficionado who accordingly is more worried about the food than the emotional traumas fast overtaking his fellow guests. He reports soothingly from the kitchen while hysteria rages that no one need worry since the host/chef is "keeping the sauce at bay".

The message bubbling in this musical stew is that no one wants to go it alone and that all of us are prepared to make compromises to that end.

> Linda Brown, "Traumas in the Suburbs," in Tribune, Vol. 45, No. 7, February 13, 1981, p. 7.*

## JOHN RUSSELL TAYLOR

One wonders from play to play just when [Ayckbourn] is going to run out of material altogether, especially since in recent plays (with the exception of the all-out farce *Taking Steps*) he seems to be playing variations on the same characters and going less and less, instead of, as one would hope, more and more, deeply into what makes his suburban stereotypes tick. *Suburban Strains* . . . is unfortunately a prime example. . . . It contains a number of familiar Ayckbourn devices, such as the simultaneous presence on stage of past and present, two different actions cunningly intercut, and since it is a musical it . . . [enables] us through song to know what the characters are thinking while they are saying something quite different or doing nothing at all.

One of the troubles, which must inevitably weigh heavy in a musical with fourteen numbers, is that on the whole the musical side of it, provided by Paul Todd, goes for very little. Some of the blame for this seems to attach itself to Ayckbourn's lyrics, which are sometimes ingenious but tend to have rather too intricate rhyme-schemes and varying line-lengths to lend themselves readily to setting and singing. But this trouble is overcome quite satisfactorily in a couple of instances: **"Nice Feeling Tonight"**, buried in the midst of the long **"Table Talk"** number, is catchy, and **"Dorothy and Me"**, an elaborate piece of Forties nostalgia, is very funny. And it would not matter too much if the surrounding text told you enough about any of the characters to believe in them or to care. As it is, though, we are not told even some very basic things, like, how old are Caroline and Kevin? They would seem to be in their early twenties, to judge by a lot of their behaviour and by Caroline's assumption that a fellow teacher of 47 is immensely old. And yet other indicators—the belief at school that she is a confirmed "old bachelor", the age of her parents—suggest they may be well into their thirties; and our attitudes towards them would be very different if they are. But this is perhaps splitting hairs, since neither character comes over as more than a collection of conventional attitudes, and one knows right from the start

how this thin and eminently prunable show is going to end— with Caroline making the right vaguely feminist gesture of independence and self-realization ("I'm an individual") then going straight back to where she was before.

> John Russell Taylor, in a review of "Suburban Strains," in Drama, No. 140, 2nd Quarter, 1981, p. 22.

## JOHN RUSSELL TAYLOR

The main distinguishing feature of the New Drama [of the 1960s] was that in various ways its writers challenged our view of reality, or even denied that it existed at all ('What have I seen', inquired one of Pinter's characters, 'the scum or the essence?'). Traditional dramatists, on the other hand, however much they might challenge our received ideas about intellectual, social, political or moral issues, usually left reality as such alone: maybe they recognized that it was 'a joint pretence' on which we all depended to continue (Pinter again), but if so they were certainly not going to hint as much to their audiences. In the 1970s two important dramatists at least diverged from the New Drama norm by seeming to assume, and allowing us comfortably to assume, that while the whole truth might not be known, it was not of its nature unknowable.

They were, of course, Alan Ayckbourn and Simon Gray. Apart from their success with a vast, non-specialized public they have virtually nothing else in common. (pp. 182-83)

Ayckbourn, happily, has never been troubled with delusions of deeper significance. Of his whole very theatrically orientated generation (he was born in 1939) he has probably been the most complete, all-round man of the theatre. . . . Since [the 1967 London production of *Meet My Father*] he has established himself as far and away our most prolific dramatist as well as our most staggering commercial success, with, at one point, no fewer than five plays running simultaneously in London. (It might be added, parenthetically, that he seems to be very specifically a British taste; his plays have never done so well elsewhere, and certainly not in New York.) (p. 183)

At least Ayckbourn's plays are all of a piece, middle-class plays for middle-class audiences, set wherever in the scampi-belt the garden gnomes grow thickest. Certainly he began with out-and-out farce, and has moved little by little into character comedy, but not, apparently, with any of the comedian's traditional desire to play Hamlet. Rather, he has created his own comic world, and if from time to time he feels inclined to probe it a little deeper, he never shows any signs of ceasing to see it as comic at all. One or two of his plays manage a hint or two of melancholy just beneath the surface: *Time and Time Again* (1971-72), perhaps, and *Joking Apart* (1979) begin, particularly the latter, to mirror a certain menopausal dissatisfaction with life on the part of Ayckbourn's characters if not, we presume, of Ayckbourn himself. But in general he is content to recolonize for the English theatre those territories of society which have been lying fallow since *French Without Tears* began to seem intolerably elitist and out of touch with life (which is to say, some time before it came to look like a charming period piece and long before it began to seem again to be a play which had something of lasting validity to say about youth and growing up and life).

Ayckbourn is in fact an interesting and exceptional dramatist because what turns him on in his plays is so evenly divided between the creation of character and milieu, and the element of purely technical challenge. In *Relatively Speaking* the technical challenge seems to be uppermost: one would guess that Ayckbourn has set out quite deliberately to make the most out of the least, to see just how far one farcical joke (a misunderstanding involving a girl's fiancé in the belief that her older lover is actually her father) can be taken without cracking under the strain. Admittedly, this is your basic stuff of farce, and that is the way it is developed. But to make so much capital out of the one simple situation—especially for an author who, as we have subsequently had ample evidence, is hardly short of ideas—does appear to invite comment on the prestidigitatory side of the proceedings: we must, surely, be meant to be aware of (to vary the metaphor) just how dangerous a tightrope our dramatist is treading. Hope/fear that he will fall is all part of the fun.

But since *Relatively Speaking* Ayckbourn has managed to keep his elements in better balance. If the human element is more prominent and important in *How the Other Half Loves* (1970), so is the purely technical. The trick of the play, in fact, resides . . . in one technical device which, once the audience grasps it, becomes an enjoyable talking-point in itself, being not only used, but displayed for all it is worth. In this case it is the notion of combining two households in one set, super-imposed and intertwined. The set is half pseudo-grand, with damask wallpaper and Harrods' traditional furniture, half struggling *Guardian*-reader, with distemper and nappies drying; the two households are equally contrasted, linked only by the fact that the two husbands work in the same firm and that, secretly, Mrs. Foster (grand) is having an affair with Mr. Phillips (ambitious). The actions that go on in the two rooms alternate and often get inextricably involved with each other as a character in one will narrowly miss collision with a character in the other or apparently (from the audience's point of view) deliver a resounding insult fairly and squarely in the face of his victim, without either party on stage being aware of it. The climax of farcical ingenuity comes with the dinner scene, when an innocent third family, which has been used as an alibi by both philanderers, finds itself embarrassingly involved in two simultaneous dinner parties, full of ambiguity and devastating cross-reference, at a table which is half linen and crystal, half paper napkins and tumblers from the local supermarket.

It is possible to suspect that without the mechanical complication Ayckbourn's plays might turn out to be pretty thin. But one might as well wonder what Feydeau would be like without his clockwork precision of intrigue: that, after all, is the prime source of his creativity. Ayckbourn is a little bit more interested in his people than Feydeau, but finally he is interested in them only within the context of the complex structures he devises to set them in motion, and it would be unrealistic to complain that these structures are only an elaborate cover he adopts to disguise from us the limitations of his human vision. Certainly when he does not have the structural complexity, as in, say, *Ten Times Table* (1978), his plays can seem pretty frail and long drawn out. (pp. 183-85)

But on the other hand, in one of his really complicated works, like *The Norman Conquests* (1974), the characters do take on intricacy too. The three plays which make up *The Norman Conquests* . . . are in some ways an extension of the idea of *How the Other Half Loves,* turning it, in a sense, inside out. This time all the romantic and other intrigues are going on in the same house at the same time, during another ghastly weekend. So while we are watching people popping in and out of the garden at just the right wrong moments, we are probably wondering what on earth can be going on in the dining room or the drawing room. The classical answer is that nothing is: the characters are existent only when and where we see them, and there is no point asking how many children Lady Macbeth had or other such questions which presuppose that there is a larger reality of which what we see in the theatre is but a small segment. But, says Ayckbourn, what if I, the dramatist, know perfectly well what is going on elsewhere, and choose to tell you? Hence, we have these three plays, the action of which is for the most part simultaneous: put them together in your mind, and you know exactly where everyone is and what he or she is doing for just about every moment of the time covered. (p. 185)

By the time of Ayckbourn's real emergence as a dramatist the New Drama itself was already old and settled enough to make questions of whether he really belonged to it, or was, rather, an entrenched conservative dressed up in a certain amount of technical gimmickry but none the less catering essentially for the complacencies of Aunt Edna, seem completely beside the point. New drama, old drama, what's the difference? The world is divided into plays that work and plays that don't. Most of Ayckbourn's do, and if he is finally Ben Travers for the 1970s, at least it is for the 1970s, not the 1930s. The New Drama has changed the expectations even of audiences who would never dream of enjoying one of those modern plays—very much as Shaw remarked in the 1890s 'A modern manager need not produce *The Wild Duck,* but he must be very careful not to produce a play which will seem insipid and old-fashioned to playgoers who have seen *The Wild Duck,* even though they may have hissed it.' Even a conservative audience is quite a bit different in its expectations today from how it was ten years ago, and it is ridiculous to berate a commercially successful dramatist for taking advantage of this difference without, as it were, having put in his stint of experimental unpopularity in order to deserve it. (pp. 185-86)

*John Russell Taylor, "Art and Commerce: The New Drama in the West End Marketplace," in* Contemporary English Drama, *Stratford-Upon-Avon Studies, No. 19, edited by C.W.E. Bigsby, Holmes & Meier Publishers, Inc., 1981, pp. 177-88.\**

## PAUL ALLEN

Ayckbourn has given us all a good shaking with *Way Upstream*. The master of comic and slightly cynical observation allied to dazzling gifts for technical problem-solving, and therefore theatrical coups, seems to be starting much as usual. The set is devastating; a cabin cruiser moored to a towpath and settled in real and murky water. The couples climb aboard, the directors of a small firm (manufacturing some sort of ornamental trash) and their wives. The boat moves out into the stream, complete with a little bow-wave, and the first mooring is as funny as any set-piece Ayckbourn has given us, with husbands cursing their own wives, and vice versa, while being icily polite to opposite numbers as bow and stern swing alternately into the current and the boat assumes brief, mad control of floundering humanity.

But from there on everything grows darker and, at the last, positively apocalyptic. One couple is characterised as aggressive, acquisitive, insensitive, domineering and bitchy (it is almost a saving grace that they hate each other). When a sort of embittered buccaneer and his female accomplice more or less hijack the boat from the self-styled skipper, we are glad, along with the nice but dangerously inactive "middle" couple

But as the pirates turn their thirst for vengeance on the pleasant couple too all sorts of ugly birds come home to roost. Finally Mr. and Mrs. Worm turn, forced into violence, against their tormentors, and the couple free themselves and cruise the boat up to and beyond the point at which the River Orb (on which they are holidaying) is said to be navigable. There they enact a dream of paradise by taking off their clothes to jump in the water. The point they've reached? It's the far side of Armageddon Bridge.

The names would make you look for messages if nothing else did. The journey of the nice people up the river named after the world through to the far side of Armageddon has been described in my hearing as a party political broadcast for the Social Democrats. It is possible to take it as that; it may even be intended as that. But I prefer to believe it is something related to that but at once both more simple and more deeply significant, the statement of a profound myth which the English cherish above all that the nice guys eventually win through. . . .

I don't myself think the play finally supports this myth, not in the sense of giving it the force of realism, whether intended or not. The final "frozen frame" of the nice couple poised naked over the water while already bathed in a warm light told me that the whole story was a hymn to wishful thinking. I hope Ayckbourn thinks that too, but he may not. . . . I enjoyed myself enormously.

*Paul Allen, in a review of "Way Upstream," in* Drama, *No. 143, Spring, 1982, p. 46.*

### PAUL ALLEN

Ayckbourn doesn't need to believe in the need to have music if you want to entertain the "ordinary" audience, but he does like writing musicals. Perhaps he still wants to prove himself in the medium. After the Jeeves fiasco he seems to like easing himself gently back with gentle shows for home consumption: *Making Tracks* . . . was a lively and sometimes sharp entertainment well worth crossing the street for but not, perhaps, in the usual Ayckbourn straight drama class.

In a recording studio a failing record producer desperately needs a hit in order to pay off the loan shark who wants his money back. The girl he's picked up virtually off the street is clearly inadequate, and the one who could work the magic just happens to be his own ex-wife and the shark's current floozy. The plot is tense enough and there's a good running gag in the fact that people in a recording studio are, to all intents and purposes, silent when they aren't at the microphone. . . . [The] record producer [is] seedy, hectoring, simpering and sly, but a lover for all that and eventually a man asking for and getting love too. . . .

It was another highly polished, highly enjoyable, good-time evening.

*Paul Allen, in a review of "Making Tracks," in* Drama, *No. 144, Summer, 1982, p. 37.*

### BRYAN APPLEYARD

Alan Ayckbourn is generally known to resemble one of his own characters—middle-class, amiable but at the mercy of forces he cannot control. So perhaps the National Theatre should have expected the odd plumbing problem when he asked them to flood the stage for his new play, *Way Upstream.* Sure enough the vast fibre-glass tank sprang a leak, a typical Ayckbourn

accident which in one of his plays might be taken to symbolize a deeper British malaise. . . .

A boat is an image of a grotesque national miscalculation, an image of escape and adventure unfortunately curtailed in its resonance by the technical incompetence of those who would partake of its liberating mysteries. For, in a boat, you have to make decisions and Ayckbourn's middle class are incapable of making decisions. They put off the evil hour of definitive choice until it is too late, until some megalomaniac has taken the whole thing out of their pathetic hands.

It is a theme the simplicity of which appears to embarrass Ayckbourn somewhat: "If you boil down your themes they sound terribly banal. Mainly I want to say things about the fear and distrust people have for each other, the fact that men and women still don't seem to understand each other very well. There are too many people in the world who are likely to leave important decisions they should make until far too late. . . ."

[Ayckbourn's] words have a habit of pursuing themselves back and forth between jokes and semi-visionary worries about a collapsing society. The dark side of Ayckbourn for which the critics have been calling has always been there. It is just that his effortless dramatic technique and inescapable comic talent—the theatrical equivalent of his amiably fluent conversation—have prompted them to demand more. Is it not time we had Ayckbourn's *Hamlet*? But he has persisted in ploughing a narrow furrow, inspired by an actor's sense of what the public wants and a pragmatic desire first to fill the theatre and second to convince his audience.

"The first thing is to get people in. Once you've got them in and once you've kept their minds wedged open—it's the easiest thing in the world to say something punishing and serious. . . ."

*Way Upstream,* he happily admits, is his darkest play so far. One actor in Scarborough commented on the terrible sense of evil that seemed to lurk within it. Indeed at the age of 42 Ayckbourn senses the serious side closing in and he feels able, if not obliged, to speak more plainly about the horrors that may lie ahead.

"I feel threatened by the fact that the fabric of society is under tremendous tension at the moment. Occasionally you get the odd Toxteth or bomb in the Park—we all forget it very quickly, thank God—but it keeps occurring." So Ayckbourn, the fluid farceur, has begun to realize why the laughter in his plays makes people sad.

"I used to think there was no such thing as evil—one used to think it was just bad upbringing or something—but some people are just plain horrible and they take delight and pleasure from it. . . . I suppose it's not a particularly startling revelation for a man of 42—some kids of eight could tell you as much—but before I just sort of liberalled along saying these people haven't had enough bread and butter. Really some sort of opposition is necessary."

He appears to be entering a visionary middle age and the long-term effect on his plays is liable to be stronger polarization. Villains will really be villains—like Vince in *Way Upstream,* "a very dangerous smiling villain"—and heroes may well at last begin to be heroes, like Alistair. "He is a man who is forced eventually to make a decision and wins . . . just."

Alistair, probably Ayckbourn's first hero, thus threatens to become the material for the as-yet-unwritten tragedy, a man who breaks free from the suffocating social and psychological conventions to which Ayckbourn's every creation has been subject. The signs are all there. Encroaching middle age and visionary pessimism are beginning to mark Ayckbourn's work. *Intimate Exchanges* . . . includes his first stage death.

He still claims it is laughter that brings in the crowds. . . . *Absent Friends* would appear to be a fairly clear exception.

"What the extreme left and the extreme right have in common is absolutely no sense of humour. Perhaps I can spread a sense of balance through comedy. I don't think it will do very much. It's like throwing a bucket of sand on a forest fire, but it might serve to save a small proportion."

It is all a triumph of technique, a realization that the joke in his early plays—that human beings were hopelessly incompetent at managing their lives—was in fact more deeply true than he realized when he exploited it as a structural device. Indeed the depth of the gag has revealed a steady strain of pessimism in his insight, better put by Yeats, that "the best lack all conviction, while the worst are full of passionate intensity".

Ayckbourn giggles or chuckles in the course of almost every sentence he speaks, yet the fact is that he is clearly not entirely convinced by Alistair's liberation. He is dubious about the validity of heroes in any form. If Alistair is his first hero, he might also prove to be his last; after all, when it comes to heroes, he is obviously making it all up.

"Well, I'd like to think they existed."

"Do you know any?"

"No."

> Bryan Appleyard, *"Still Hoping for Heroes," in* The Times, *London, August 18, 1982, p. 7.*

## HAROLD HOBSON

I believe the public like Ayckbourn because he is both a highly comic writer and, dramatically speaking, a first-class conjuror. The tricks he plays in some of his work are stupendous. They are miracles of human ingenuity. *Relatively Speaking,* the first of his plays to make a serious impact on London, turned entirely on Ayckbourn's skill in seeing to it that a simple piece of information which the audience knew should not be passed on to various characters in the piece. Time and again they skirted the edge of discovery, and time and time again, they missed the vital clue. (p. 4)

There is in at least two of [Ayckbourn's plays] (the two most popular) an element of sadism in its ingenuity. In *How the Other Half Loves* there was a rather foolish wife. Every time she made a stupid remark her husband slapped her on the wrists. This humiliation of a quite harmless woman before her friends delighted the audience and disgusted me. I do not enjoy seeing such women being made publicly ridiculous. In this I appear to differ from most audiences (consisting, strangely enough, mainly of women). Again, in *Absurd Person Singular,* [a woman] . . . spent the entire central act vainly attempting to commit suicide. Every means she attempted ludicrously failed to succeed. No matter how hard she tried, she failed every time to kill herself. This seemed very funny to the audience, but it did not seem funny to me. It is quite possible that I have no sense of humour. Yet I think that there is in British audiences a taste for cruelty which the most popular plays of Ayckbourn satisfy.

But I have to reckon with the awful possibility that I misunderstand Ayckbourn. This, I think, was undoubtedly the case with the play of his which moved me most and gave me most dramatic satisfaction. Let us turn for a moment to Henry James. Nowadays everyone knows that James's most famous short story, *The Turn of the Screw,* can be read in two diametrically opposite senses. . . . The same is true of James's greatest novel, *The Golden Bowl.* Adam Verver and his daughter can be either the most morally valid characters in the book, or the worst. It depends on which way you look at it. (p. 5)

[It] is in the least popular of Ayckbourn's work that I find his greatest achievement. Nothing of his has moved me so much as *Absent Friends.* And yet according to many readers and, as I finally discovered, to Ayckbourn himself I interpreted it wrongly. . . .

Now I took this play to be a triumphant manifestation of the splendour of true love. Colin's happiness, or so it seemed to me, was rooted in the joyous memory of his fiancèe when she lived. To have known such an affection and to have experienced such happiness was enough to make a whole life rich. I found this deeply moving. But many people who saw the play interpreted it quite differently. They took it that Colin's present happiness was a sign, not of supreme love, but of callousness. They pointed out that his effect on everyone was to increase, not lessen, their misery. This last argument, however, does not mean much. For in nearly all his plays Ayckbourn is a dramatist convinced that in marriage there is no joy. And yet I think that on the whole Ayckbourn would agree with them rather than with me. For on [a] television programme . . . he said that *Absent Friends* was about the death of love.

This brings up an interesting question. Is one's enjoyment of a work of art any less valid if one interprets it differently from the author? I do not think necessarily so. Presumably one of the possible explanations of *The Turn of the Screw* and *The Golden Bowl* is the one that Henry James intended, and no one knows which that is. But these stories are valid aesthetic experiences even if the explanation one chooses is not the one that James meant. *So* I continue to feel that the emotions I had at *Absent Friends* were justifiable—even if Mr. Ayckbourn had never intended that I should have them.

Anyway, it all comes to this. The things that the public most appreciates in Ayckbourn—the jokes, the leger-de-main, the farce, the high spirits—are all worth appreciating. They are first-class theatre. But they are not, in my opinion, the things which are most valuable in him, and by which it is possible that his work may live. Behind all his foolery he has this sad conviction that marriage is a thing that will not endure. Men and women may get instant satisfaction from life, but it is not a satisfaction that will last long. I think of the forlorn and weary commercial traveller, in one of the plays in *Confusions* trying to hit it off with a couple of girls in the bar, and miserably failing; or of the tycoon in *Joking Apart* whose confidence is vanishing, and of the desperate game of tennis, with which a well-meaning but blundering friend tried to restore it, and of this game's disastrous results. It is when Ayckbourn sees the tears of life, its underlying, ineradicable sadness, that he is at his superb best. (p. 6)

> Harold Hobson, *"Alan Ayckbourn: Playwright of Ineradicable Sadness," in* Drama, *No. 146, Winter, 1982, pp. 4-6.*

## FELIX BARKER

Before we get out of our depth in rough waters during this naval review [of *Way Upstream*] I should perhaps advise a lifebelt if you wish to avoid being drowned in watery metaphors. They are as inescapable as my conclusion that the author has taken us up a creek and abandoned us there without a paddle. . . .

How she goes probably doesn't need much logging by now. Your compass is likely to be boxed already, so you will know the basic situation is about a pair of mismatched married couples on a hired cruiser whom the author sends up a winding and mysterious river. (p. 24)

Oh, it's a splendid trip to start with. All aboard the lugger and the mirth is fine. No one excells Ayckbourn in pointing up the follies and social pretensions of people without the humour to see their own absurdities. . . .

All four bicker amusingly up as far as Gessing Lock (Warning to All Shipping: here you are meant to start guessing) where they encounter a seemingly helpful young man full of virile charm called Vince. . . . After ingratiating himself on board, this devious Iago slowly imposes his will, and by Stumble Lock has made himself the tyrannical skipper. (p. 24)

The ship's capture and the degradation of the actual hirers is as rapid and ruthless as the occupation of a country by a victorious army. Stripped of his captaincy, Keith abandons ship; his flighty wife June is willingly seduced by Vince who subjects her to a bout of cabin bondage with fancy knots; the other husband is cast off on an island; and his wife is forced to walk the plank.

When the boarders run up the Jolly Roger it becomes clear that we cannot cling to realism. Giggles are no longer in order. Storm cones are flying and Ayckbourn is ordering us to climb into a lifeboat of considerable allegorical dimensions.

The Ship of State, divided against itself, is the victim of menacing forces and has succumbed with abysmal ease to evil. Preoccupied by their own internal disputes, the conquered people have ignored the maxim that the price of peace is eternal vigilance. Armageddon (Bridge) ahead threatens their ultimate destruction. If you happen to spot any more Ayckbourn symbolism, just run it up the mast. I don't promise to salute.

In fact, Ayckbourn relents. Fascism does not prevail. Vince gets a bloody nose. The fearful bridge is successfully negotiated, and the older couple find themselves in calm water, 'at the limits of navigation'. In search of naked innocence, they strip off and, happily reconciled, plunge into the now tranquil river. Decode the morse, and the message would seem to read: 'The meek shall inherit the earth'. Always good news, but hardly a denouement worthy of the Book of Revelation.

I can imagine a grinning Ayckbourn pretending that all these interpretations are in the mind of the beholder, and well, oh yes, he supposes you could read that into the play but why not just accept it as a comedy? The answer I am afraid is that the screw is too hopelessly entangled in symbolic weeds: a jolly cruise has run aground. (pp. 24-5)

> *Felix Barker, in a review of "Way Upstream," in* Plays and Players, *No. 352, January, 1983, pp. 24-5.*

## MALCOLM PAGE

Ayckbourn claims our attention for his insights about people: he prompts us to laugh, then to care about the character and to make a connection with ourselves, our own behaviour, and possibly beyond to the world in which we live. Through *Absurd Person Singular*, Ayckbourn first explores a dual response: that these are his creations to amuse us, and that they are also suffering human beings. Here he turns from displaying the fatuity and absurdity of his people to examining their unhappiness and what might be done about it. . . . [But not] till *Just Between Ourselves* does Ayckbourn manage to write the scene that is both amusing and disturbing. *Just Between Ourselves*, the earlier *Absent Friends*, and the later *Joking Apart* are the three Plays Serious—which are nevertheless also comedies.

*Absent Friends* (1974), the first piece that is a "play" rather than a "comedy," remains Ayckbourn's most restrained, sombre, and subdued work. Five friends gather for a Saturday afternoon tea-party to cheer Colin, whom they have not seen for three years and whose fiancée, Carol, drowned two months before. They expect that Colin will not want to talk about Carol, but in fact he speaks of her both readily and cheerfully. The end of the first act reveals the basic notion of *Absent Friends*. . . . There is, of course, a paradox . . . : the people with ample reason to be happy are not. Further, the contented Colin lacks the tact and sensitivity to understand his impact.

The three women emerge as very unhappy people. Marge, for example, is married to a sick, bedridden man who wanted to be a cricketer but became a fire-prevention officer instead; she puts her energy into choosing shoes and cleaning stains off chairs. Evelyn's husband, John, seems to have placed Evelyn accurately: "she has absolutely no sense of humour. Which is very useful since it means you never have to waste your time trying to cheer her up. Because she's permanently unhappy. Misery is her natural state." . . . Unlike most Ayckbourn males, John sees something of the situation, but not his own responsibility or what might be done. Diana is Ayckbourn's fullest study of a woman in decline after marrying and entering her thirties. . . . (pp. 38-9)

*Absent Friends* is sad because youth is behind all of the characters and only Colin, lucky in his temperament, can take a rose-tinted-spectacles view. . . . Colin's return has a disastrous impact on Diana and [her husband] Paul. Perhaps, however, if we seek affirmation, his impact on Marge and John may be judged beneficial. Although Ayckbourn's plays are not located with geographical precision . . . it is nevertheless clear that *Absent friends* sketches in the limitations, the boredom, the humdrum of a small town rather than suburbia.

*Just Between Ourselves* (1976) shows how a well-meaning husband drives his wife to insanity through relentless cheerfulness and optimism. . . . This is typical of Ayckbourn in his vein of lightly concealed seriousness: [in the first scene] we laugh twice at Dennis's amusing lines [about his wife's nervous clumsiness] then wince and recognize the implications of being always on the receiving end of put-down humour. (pp. 39-40)

Taking place on Dennis's birthday, the second scene ends in a melancholy way with a disastrous tea-party at which everyone tries not to focus on the forgotten birthday cake and the likelihood of accidents by the tense Vera. The third scene concludes with the greatest moment in Ayckbourn's work, an episode wildly funny and deeply tragic, when Vera goes insane. While Dennis has become entangled inside the car with the steering-wheel, seat-belts, and a neighbouring woman Pam, to whom he is demonstrating the car, Vera quarrels with her mother-in-law and pursues her with a roaring electric drill. Then Pam slumps onto the car horn, which *"blasts loudly and continu-*

*ously''*; and Neil comes in with a birthday cake, switching on lights, thus *"bathing the scene in a glorious technicolour,"* and singing "Happy birthday to you." . . . Ayckbourn dreams of writing *"a truly hilarious dark play"*: this he has achieved, at least for these five minutes.

Four months later we see Vera again, sitting silently in her garden in January. The people responsible hover round her, assuring each other that she is getting better. Throughout this chilling scene, Vera stares out blankly, speechless, motionless, as grim an image as any in Beckett, grimmer than almost any scene anywhere in comedy. Here the laughter of the first three scenes dies on the lips, as the audience see what poor Vera has come to and how the man responsible is as far as ever from realizing his responsibility. (pp. 40-1)

*Just Between Ourselves* is really Vera and Dennis's play. [Michael] Billington is . . . accurate in describing the theme as "what Terence Rattigan once called the real *vice Anglais:* fear of expressing emotion . . . The total gesture is one of fierce attack on what E. M. Forster called 'the under-developed heart'." Yet Dennis is no villain: he can be faulted only for insensitivity, ignorance, thoughtlessness. (pp. 41-2)

The third "serious" play, *Joking Apart* (1978), sets its four scenes on special occasions: Guy Fawkes's Night, Boxing Day, a girl's eighteenth birthday. The stage includes the corner of a tennis-court, offering glimpses of the action in two games, and a croquet-lawn just off, with balls rolling on from time to time. The structural innovation is that the scenes are four years apart, so that we see seven characters over a period of twelve years, from their twenties to their thirties.

*Joking Apart* is a study of winners and losers. Richard and Anthea, for example, are likeable, generous, hospitable people. They are also enormously successful: happy, energetic, their two children a credit to them, Richard's furniture-import business flourishing. No one can put a finger on the secret of their success—some mixture of luck, instinct, talent. In contrast, their neighbours Hugh and Louise are losers. (p. 42)

There are three other characters in the picture. Another couple are Richard's business partners: Sven, a Finn, and his wife, Olive. Richard's business acumen gradually makes Sven think himself a failure, so that he becomes resigned to being second-rate—and Olive takes her mood from him. . . . In the sad decline of this couple, Richard and Anthea's immediate role is slight. Finally, there is Brian. Like Hugh, he is silently devoted to Anthea; and Anthea seems insensitive in not grasping this devotion, ready though she is to be a week-end hostess to Brian and his girl-friends.

In general, the degree of blame attached to Richard and Anthea is small. Perhaps a critic should more accurately emphasize Sven's envy and resentment, and to a degree the same flaws in the other four hangers-on. Ayckbourn illuminates the sadness intrinsic to the condition that the world has its born winners, and the less obvious fact that other people shrink through contrasting themselves with these winners. The final mood is wistful, downbeat, even elegiac—though the occasion is a girl's eighteenth birthday party, and she may be able to shrug off the middle-aged losers, and winners.

These three "serious" plays at first look to be very different from the rest of the *oeuvre*. Ayckbourn himself encouraged the distinction by describing *Just Between Ourselves* and *Joking Apart* (but not *Absent Friends*) as his "winter plays, written

for the winter months when his theatre performs for the local Scarborough audience rather than for the summer visitors who seek only laughter from the theatre. Consequently, when *Bedroom Farce* was advertised throughout its long London run with the quotation from the *Daily Express,* "If you don't laugh, sue me," it clearly identified the kind of play it was. Yet some of the lighter plays of the seventies also challenge an accepted rule of contemporary comedy: that the audience does not take home the sorrows of the characters after the show. This convention—a matter of both the dramatist's style and the audience's expectations—verges on breakdown when Ayckbourn shifts from farce to real people in real trouble.

These realistic plays leave much to the director and actors: whether or not suffering humanity is to be drawn out, perhaps at the expense of our laughing so readily at the action. *The Norman Conquests* extensively studies two troubled marriages, and shows pity for unfortunate Annie as well, trapped into looking after her bedridden mother and unable in the end to take off for even one stolen week-end in East Grinstead. In watching *Bedroom Farce,* the audience can laugh only as long as they remember that the man contorted with the pain of a bad back is an actor exercising his craft (as with suicidal Eva in *Absurd Person Singular,* this is one of the moments when Ayckbourn is either heartless or audacious). The neurotic Susannah in *Bedroom Farce* is not so far from victims like Vera of *Just Between Ourselves* and Louise of *Joking Apart:* whereas Susannah is distanced by the familiar framework of comedy, the other two women are not.

While Ayckbourn was writing shrewdly and on the whole sadly of human behavior, *Absurd Person Singular* suggested that he aspired to be a social critic, too. In this play, the property-speculating shopkeeper rises during the dramatic action to pass the architect and bank manager, reversing the normal pecking order. . . . Such precise attention to occupations and social change is not found again in Ayckbourn's work. The playwright is not faulting society for the madness of Vera and the decline of Louise; he indicts the insensitive people around them. (pp. 42-4)

Looking at individuals, Ayckbourn shows and condemns thoughtlessness and insensitivity. He studies people who are cheerful, well-meaning, and amiable, yet stir up every kind of trouble and unhappiness in their circles. Dennis of *Just Between Ourselves* is most savagely treated, confident that he understands his wife while he drives her insane. . . . Ayckbourn looks steadily at people in pain and shows that being human, having any involvement with others, is difficult and fraught with problems. Which aspect of human nature will he next examine? Ayckbourn is forty-three in 1983, his writing career probably less than half over. I look forward especially to more winter plays—more efforts to write "the truly hilarious dark play." (p. 44)

*Malcolm Page, "The Serious Side of Alan Ayckbourn," in* Modern Drama, *Vol. XXVI, No. 1, March, 1983, pp. 36-46.*

## CHRISTOPHER EDWARDS

Alan Ayckbourn's reputation is secure enough to bear the occasional flop. The British Musical is not so rich in talent that it can afford to decline the attentions of a writer of his prolific invention; unfortunately [*Making Tracks*] is cringe-making, and with the memory of his recent dull collaboration with Paul Todd in *Me, Myself and I* in the wake years ago of *Jeeves* I'm not convinced that Ayckbourn's abilities will ever find a true home in this genre.

He has set the action in a tacky recording studio run by Stan and Rog. Rog is a gauche Sound Engineer whose conversation, like his seduction routine, sound like extracts from *Computer Weekly*. Stan is a divorced, paunchy failure of a song writer turned would-be recording tycoon. All he and Rog need is a Chart Buster, and Stan thinks he has found the job when, through the bottom of an oft-drained glass, he spots a singer called Sandie Beige at a local talent contest. (pp. 37-8)

I thought the plot lacked any elementary suspense, and relied too much upon unexciting running gags. Nor did I really believe in the minor characters—Gus the guitarist suffering from marital angst, or Chris the drummer who had to get home to celebrate his (dead) father's birthday. . . . [The character of] Sandie was the most successful effort to move the production into Ayckbourn Country, where ordinary folk's flighty aspirations are seen poignantly to bump against their inescapable ordinariness; she discovers a genuine comic pathos in the huge incongruity represented by her shrinking manner, monotonal voice and gawky arms trying to establish themselves amid the 'heavy' world of session musicians. But in the end Ayckbourn's lyrics set Paul Todd too painfully difficult a task. It must be hard to make anything appealing out of lines like . . . 'I don't remember you—were you the man who fixed my fridge?' (p. 38)

*Christopher Edwards, in a review of "Making Tracks," in* Plays and Players, *No. 356, May, 1983, pp. 37-8.*

## JOHN SIMON

[*Taking Steps*] is not top Ayckbourn, but there is enough wit and resourcefulness afoot to keep the occasionally sagging interest from lagging. There is the usual master gimmick, in this case three floors of a house, along with connecting staircases and corridors, represented by a continuous flat stage surface but with the different elements clearly marked by large lettering and architectural drawings on the floorboards. The topographical disorientation enhances the general discombobulation, indeed becomes its objective correlative. . . .

[Once] again, Ayckbourn demonstrates how much a farce can benefit from a fanciful choreography. Ascents and descents along a spiral staircase as flat as a pancake ought not to be unceasingly amusing, but the play neatly turns that trick. With an assortment of other sight and sound gags all around, *Taking Steps* manages to be a superior piece of *esprit d'escalier*. (p. 67)

*John Simon, "East, West, and in Between," in* New York *Magazine, Vol. 17, No. 14, April 2, 1984, pp. 66-7.\**

## RICHARD CORLISS

The exhaustively inventive Ayckbourn . . . has now devised a pyramid of farcical possibilities. *Intimate Exchanges* begins with one of two different scenes; each of those scenes offers two more variants; and so on, and so on, and so on. It makes for 31 scenes in 16 possible permutations—all on the author's familiar theme of suburban swinishness. This is a prodigious stunt of dramatic construction and performers' memory, but hardly worth 16 nights of anyone's time. Or one night. (p. 95)

*Richard Corliss, "With a Little Help from Our Friends," in* Time, *Vol. 124, No. 7, August 13, 1984, pp. 94-5.\**

# Amiri Baraka

## 1934-

(Born Everett LeRoi Jones; has also written as LeRoi Jones and Imamu Amiri Baraka) American poet, dramatist, short story writer, novelist, essayist, critic, and editor.

A controversial literary figure, Baraka uses his writing to reveal his radical philosophies and convey his personal ideology. Baraka's work reflects the political and social tensions of race relations in contemporary America. He employs a variety of literary genres, most notably drama, poetry, and the essay, through which he develops strong social messages and attempts to educate the American public. An interest in Afro-American music is evident in Baraka's work, influencing his diction and signifying his affinity with black culture. Recognized primarily as a radical voice of the 1960s, Baraka's literary career has encompassed the Beat movement, black nationalism, and Marxist-Leninist philosophy.

A sense of rebellion is the one consistent theme throughout Baraka's canon. This rebellion first surfaced when he integrated himself with the Beat movement of Greenwich Village in the late 1950s. The literary avant-garde were flourishing in their revolt against the traditional values of American society. Associating with such prominent members of the movement as Allen Ginsberg, Gregory Corso, and Jack Kerouac, Baraka began his career by publishing *Yugen*, a magazine that provided a forum for the new poetry of the Beats. Following the Beats' abandonment of traditional poetic structure and adopting their free use of slang, Baraka earned praise and respect as a poet with his first volume of poetry, *Preface to a Twenty Volume Suicide Note. . . .* (1961). That same year he published *Cuba Libre*, an essay describing his trip to Cuba to join in the anniversary celebration of Fidel Castro's first revolutionary attempt. The trip proved essential to Baraka's evolution as a writer by introducing him to committed political activists, thereby starting the process of his eventual metamorphosis from literary bohemian to black nationalist. During this transitional period Baraka produced some of his best-known works, including an analysis of contemporary black music, *Blues People. . . . Negro Music in White America* (1963), and a second volume of poetry, *The Dead Lecturer* (1964).

Although Baraka wrote a number of plays during this period, *Dutchman* (1964) is widely considered his masterpiece. The play received the Obie Award for best Off-Broadway play and brought him to the attention of the American public. Involving a conflict between a black middle-class college student and a flirtatious white woman, *Dutchman* is said to mark the emergence of Baraka's heightened racial awareness. It was hailed for its powerful evocation of the black man's oppression and homogenization in the Euro-American culture of the United States. *The Slave* (1964) also demonstrates the philosophical change Baraka was undergoing. This play revolves around a black revolutionary leader who confronts his ex-wife and her husband, both of whom are white. Critics suggest that the ambiguous emotions of the protagonist represent Baraka's own uncertainties as he moved away from his role as a mediator between blacks and whites toward an antiwhite, problack stance.

© *Kelly Wise*

In 1965 Baraka divorced his white wife, deserted the white literary colony of Greenwich Village, and moved to Harlem. Completely dissociating himself from the white race, Baraka dedicated himself to creating works that were inspired by and spoke to the black community. With increasingly violent overtones, Baraka's writing called for blacks to unite and establish their own nation. Experimenting with ritual forms in his drama, he penned *Slave Ship* (1967), a recreation of the desperate circumstances experienced by slaves during their passage to America. Other works written during Baraka's black nationalist period are *The System of Dante's Hell* (1965), his only novel, and *Tales* (1967), a collection of short stories. Hoping to withdraw further from the conventionality of his middle-class past, Baraka became a Muslim and in 1968 changed his name from LeRoi Jones to Imamu Amiri Baraka. As his ideologies became of primary concern, Baraka began to move away from fiction and drama in order to concentrate on expository prose.

By 1974, Baraka had dropped the spiritual title of Imamu and declared himself an adherent of Marxist-Leninist thought. Again shifting the focus of his rebellion, Baraka now called for a working-class revolt against the bourgeoisie. During his socialist period Baraka has produced such works as *Hard Facts* (1975), a volume of poetry, and the plays *S-1* (1978), *The Motion of History* (1978), and *The Sidney Poet Heroical* (1979).

More recently Baraka has written *The Autobiography of LeRoi Jones/Amiri Baraka* (1984). Since becoming a vocal proponent of socialism, Baraka has been faulted for polemicism. His work does, however, reflect the changes in racial attitudes over the past thirty years. As Lloyd W. Brown asserts, Baraka's "significance as a mirror of his society has been one of his most enduring characteristics."

(See also *CLC*, Vols. 1, 2, 3, 5, 10, 14; *Contemporary Authors*, Vols. 21-24, rev. ed.; and *Dictionary of Literary Biography*, Vols. 5, 7, 16.)

## EMILE CAPOUYA

We have grown fairly accustomed to the idea that hell is a city much like Seville, but we may need to be reminded that Seville in turn is South Newark or Shreveport. LeRoi Jones, already well known as a most original poet and playwright, has written a novel ["The System of Dante's Hell"] that induces us to make that necessary connection in our imagination. Borrowing features of the moral geography of Dante's "Inferno," Mr. Jones is nevertheless scarcely concerned with allegory. As befits the poet of a secular age, he abandons the idea that hell is a fixed department of the cosmos. He is rather inclined to follow Jean-Paul Sartre's suggestion that hell is other people—and, ultimately, one's self.

Accordingly, the episodes of "The System of Dante's Hell" tend to be representations of states of mind and states of soul rather than sections of conventional narrative. . . .

The prose is poetic or simply telegraphic, but not out of a desire to represent the Joycean stream of consciousness. That innocent naturalism has been left far behind. Mr. Jones rejects the formal logic of exposition; he invites verbal and emotional accidents, willingly or wilfully connecting ideas and impressions that have no common focus outside his own mind. Thus, he puts into practice the essential program of contemporary art—to find esthetic value in chaos, accidental juxtapositions, happenings. The difference between Dante and Jones, in this respect alone, is an absolute measure of the distance between two epochs in the development of a single civilization.

To Dante's fierce certainties the 20th century opposes its despair of any certainty. It is remarkable, in this connection, how reverting to older patterns of thought has an immediate tonic effect—at least when a powerful imagination is doing the reverting. (p. 4)

The static and fragmentary lyricism of much of the novel . . . is an expression of the intellectual and moral lost motion of the age. Here, Mr. Jones chooses rather to embrace than to defy it. This is not true of his plays, which are concerned with social, almost topical, themes, and are explicit and shocking. It is not true of the brief epilogue to "The System of Dante's Hell," which appears to be of later composition than the text, refers to the special agony of the American Negro, and offers another clue to the meaning of the author's own notorious public rejection of the white world. (pp. 4, 42)

> Emile Capouya, "States of Mind, of Soul," in The New York Times Book Review, *November 28, 1965, pp. 4, 42.*

## GRANVILLE HICKS

*The System of Dante's Hell* is described by the publisher as a novel, and if that seems to me a rather strange name for it, I can't think of a more suitable one. As the title indicates, the book is organized in a general way on the plan of Dante's *Inferno,* with various circles and subdivisions; heretics, panderers, and seducers, thieves, fraudulent counsellors, and so on. In actuality it is made up of sketches from the author's early years, which fit only approximately into the categories in which they have been placed.

Jones writes mostly in a violent staccato. . . .

This kind of writing can grow tiresome, but there is a strong cumulative effect. It is a tough, dirty world that Jones is writing about, with a good deal of raw sex, both heterosexual and homosexual, some violence, and many unpleasant details. The author-narrator remembers his acquaintances at various stages of their development, and we have a gallery of warped persons. As we get the sense of it from these fragments, his was a grim young manhood.

The best of the book is the last part. . . . It is a fairly long piece of continuous narrative, describing the author during his Air Force training in Louisiana. He and a companion go into the Negro section of Shreveport, where they take up with a couple of whores. (p. 31)

After a night of drunkenness and fornication, he is tempted to accept the prostitute's invitation to stay with her. . . . But he runs away, to go back to his camp and take his punishment. Before he has gone far, he is beaten by three Negroes. The whole nightmare experience comes through powerfully. (pp. 31-2)

Jones's boyhood in a Negro section of Newark is for the most part stark and terrible. But it is interesting to note that in the course of the book he refers to Eliot, Pound, Cummings, Apollinaire, Joyce, Keats, Hardy, Kafka, Dylan Thomas, and Baudelaire. Somehow, then, in the midst of all this squalor and desperation, the young man managed to get a literary education. . . .

[Jones] was and is an heir of Western civilization, but he gives only slight indication of that fact in his book and doesn't tell us how he became acquainted with the modern masters, even though that process must have been as important a part of his experience as anything he describes. The plan upon which the book is organized compares and contrasts his view of life with that of one of the greatest poets of our culture. I am not sure that the parallels with the *Inferno* do much to enrich the book, but at least the scheme is a claim to kinship with the makers of Western culture. (p. 32)

> Granville Hicks, "The Poets in Prose," in Saturday Review, *Vol. XLVIII, No. 50, December 11, 1965, pp. 31-2.**

## BERNARD BERGONZI

LeRoi Jones uses the descending circles of the *Inferno* as the structure of [*The System of Dante's Hell*], an autobiographical novel about a Negro childhood and adolescence in Newark, N. J. This scaffolding gives the book an ambitious appearance, but it doesn't seem to me to serve much organic function, except, possibly, providing guide-lines to the author's memory and imagination. Certainly, the reader can do without it: the Hell that Mr. Jones writes about is terrible enough without bringing in factitious echoes of Dante. Early on Mr. Jones gives a brutally uncompromising warning: "This thing, if you read it, will jam your face in my shit. Now say something intelligent!'' Faced with a challenge like that, the reviewer needs all the help he can get; fortunately, Mr. Jones makes his intentions clear in a short epilogue to the novel called ''Sound and Image'':

> What is hell? Your definitions.
>
> I am and was and will be a social animal. Hell is definable only in those terms. I can get no place else; it wdn't exist. Hell in this book which moves from sound and image (''association complexes'') into fast narrative is what vision I had of it around 1960-61 and that fix on my life, and my interpretation of my earlier life. . . .

''Hell,'' he concludes, ''was the inferno of my frustration. But the world is clearer to me now, and many of its features more easily definable.''

Mr. Jones's conclusion is almost serene, but the preceding narrative is anything but that. The first part of his book is a rapid, disjunctive series of impressions of the vitality, squalor, violence, and promiscuity of urban slum life, in which any kind of coherence or organization is sacrificed to the demands of immediacy and intensity. . . .

[This prose style] is probably satisfying to write but soon gets monotonous to read. In spite of the endeavors of some recent writers, language remains a frail instrument that can rarely perform all that is asked of it. And nothing is harder than to convey the sensation of direct, unmediated physical experience; verbalism soon starts intruding. Perhaps Mr. Jones wants to break down what he may regard as ''white man's syntax'': but the larger problem involved in using white man's language at all is still with him.

The ''fast narrative'' in the second part of the book is much better; here Mr. Jones's authentic literary powers are brought into play, notably in the final section about the experiences of a young northern Negro drafted into the Air Force and sent to a base in the South. This is a brutal but superbly written piece of narrative, which reaches its climax when the airman is beaten up by three local Negroes. . . .

This novel sticks in the mind, vividly if not very pleasantly. But it doesn't seem to me a success, not, at least, by any of the standards I am used to employing. At the risk of sounding square, one can only reaffirm the weary truism that it is not the businenss of art to use chaos to express chaos (whether physical or moral), and this, in spite of the achievement of the later sections, is what Mr. Jones's book, taken as a whole, seems to do. If, as he says, he wants to jam the reader's face in his shit, then this is ultimately a political act rather than an imaginative or creative one. And not, I think, all that effective. Despite everything, Mr. Jones is a powerful writer; but many works of popular sociology or journalism would contain more immediate directives in the cause of Negro emancipation. (p. 22)

> *Bernard Bergonzi, ''Out Our Way,'' in* The New York Review of Books, *Vol. V, No. 12, January 20, 1966, pp. 22-3.**

**ROBERT BONE**

LeRoi Jones writes in the mood of a Prodigal Son who has returned at last to his blackness. He celebrates his homecoming in some 20 essays [collected in *Home: Social Essays*], written between 1960 and 1965. In the title piece, Mr. Jones asks us to take note of the movement of these essays, and to view it as a linear progression toward his Negritude. Actually it represents the swing of a pendulum from assimilationism to Negro nationalism, from an extreme hatred of self to an extreme hatred of whites. . . .

As the pendulum moves through the middle ranges . . . Jones has some important things to say. The early pieces, written between 1960 and 1963, are often arresting and sometimes persuasive. Thereafter Jones enters the fantasyland of black nationalism.

At the heart of these early essays is a dispute over the nature of reality. The view from the top of the hill and the view from the bottom, Jones insists, are not the same. It follows that the Negro writer, in assuming the burden of self-definition, must liberate himself from the white man's definitions of reality. For the truth about the Negro has never been admitted to the consciousness of his oppressor. Preventing it has been a screen of twisted images and grotesque stereotypes. Hence the Negro writer's determination to ''tell it like it is,'' and not the way the white man says it is.

An official version of reality, for example, permeates the thinking of the white South: ''Governor Wallace, on television, admonishes his black housekeeper warmly, 'Y'all take care of everything, heah?' The old woman smiles, and goes off to take care of his baby. That is the Negro that really exists for him.'' . . .

The white Southerner, we may perhaps agree, is the victim of his own hallucinations. But when Jones extends his discussion to the realm of foreign policy, we begin to feel uneasy. Is it possible that America is responding to the colonial revolution in the jaundiced spirit of a James Eastland? ''The Negro who wants the foot off his neck must be inspired by Communists.'' So the whites believe in Mississippi. But time and again, says Jones, confronted with national liberation movements in Asia, Africa, and Latin America, we have opposed the legitimate aspirations of the people in the name of anti-Communism. Here too are twisted images, falsified reality, and often enough a course of action based on dangerous hallucinations. . . .

About a third of the collection is devoted to literary subjects, and here Jones is distinctly at his best. Three essays in particular contain the most considered writing of the present volume. ''The Myth of a Negro Literature'' states the case for disaffiliation from the value system and the world view of the white middle class. ''Expressive Language'' explores the relationship between Negro speech, emotional nuance and cultural expression. ''Hunting Is Not Those Heads on the Wall'' attempts to define an esthetic. In his emphatic rejection of formal art, of tradition and of classical restraint, Jones betrays his affinity for that neo-Romantic permissiveness, that unbridled self-indulgence, which links him to the poets of the Beat generation.

We have finally to deal with five or six pieces which are not so much essays as fulminations. Ostensibly they announce the author's conversion to black nationalism; in reality they signal an esthetic breakdown, a fatal loss of artistic control. The prose disintegrates, the tone becomes hysterical, and all pretense of logical argument is abandoned. The style, shall we say, is severely disturbed.

The consequences are apparent in the following passage, from an essay called ''The Legacy of Malcolm X and the Coming of the Black Nation'': ''The Concepts of National Consciousness and the Black Nation, after the death of Malik, have moved to the point where now some Black People are demanding national sovereignty as well as National (and Cultural) Consciousness. In Harlem, for instance, *as director of the Black Arts Repertory Theater School,* I have issued a call for a Black Nation. In Harlem where 600,000 Black People reside. *The first act* must be the nationalization of all properties and resources belonging to white people, within the boundaries of the Black Nation.'' (My italics).

LeRoi Jones, it is now apparent, is hoping to assume the mantle of the late Malcolm X. But pass over the self-aggrandizement; pass over the element of fantasy; concentrate on the unintended ambiguity of *first act.* Here is a playwright who has lost the fundamental distinction between image and event, between a scenario and a political program. This blurring of boundaries, this loss of discriminative power, is the price that Jones has paid for the unrestrained indulgence of his hate.

> *Robert Bone, "Action and Reaction," in* The New York Times Book Review, *May 8, 1966, p. 3.*

## FAITH BERRY

Into our now-the-story-of-the-Negro-can-be-told period come some new and added versions from LeRoi Jones; twenty-four pieces of social criticism about America the *un*beautiful: *Home.* (p. 23)

Little of his personal life is mentioned in the book, but the little that is, added to the blurbs that have appeared elsewhere in the past, tell part of the story of what he was trying to do during the five years the book covers: to break away from the image he thought he was a part of, "the middle-class chump," the Ivy Leaguer, "the new Negro," "the Negro writer"; to abandon the poetry workshop and Greenwich Village and make it Harlem; to gather what allies he could for the beginning of Blackhope, Black Writing, and The Black Arts Repertory Theatre.

And the reasons are repeated in one way or another, from beginning to end in the chronology of these essays, a few of them stressing ideas he's already mentioned in *Blues People*: the belief that "Negro culture" in America except for blues and jazz has been assassinated; that Negro literature has never moved to create its own myths and symbols, but to imitate, to protest, or to commercialize; the anxiety over having to lose dissent in order to enter mainstream America; that non-violence is encouraged to protect certain economic interests; that American Negroes have been converted to help kill non-white peoples in Africa, Asia, and Latin America; that the whole of western civilization is dying, and when it dies, American Negroes will die with it—at the same time for the same reasons.

The reflection that most Negroes might be on the way to becoming "white" is one Ralph Ellison's *Invisible Man* had twenty years ago; he comforted himself by staying in his hole in the ground. Jones has another idea: the founding of a Black Nation, one he's "calling for" in Harlem as Director of The Black Arts Repertory Theatre. (pp. 23-4)

The book will likely give Mr. Jones the titles of racist, demagogue, and exhibitionist that he gained from *The Toilet, Dutchman,* and *The Slave. Home* is not racism; it's race pride that has gone too far in one direction. And what might be termed culture resistance with a capital "C"—the kind of resistance that doesn't allow him to eat his dinner, listen to his records, or read his books without wondering where in each one the "Black experience" lies; and where each bite he takes,

each tone he hears, and each word he reads fits into his historical time and place. (p. 24)

The book, if it's to be thought anti-white, can't be called altogether so pro-Negro either. In the end, he stops using this word ("Negro") partly because it's an adjective (somebody should have put a stop to it a long time ago), and because he considers "Negroes" as "strait-jacketed lazy clowns whose only joy is carrying out the white man's will." Race doesn't count if you see part of the world as Jones does. Joyce, Sartre, Burroughs and Allen Ginsberg come out higher on the scoreboard than Phillis Wheatley, Arna Bontemps, Langston Hughes and James Baldwin. But Feiffer, Harrington and *The Village Voice* get pounced. And since he makes a distinction between "Negroes" and Black People, Martin Luther King is a loser, but the late W.E.B. DuBois is a champion; an educator like Booker T. Washington gets the image of an Uncle Tom, but another one like E. Franklin Frazier is heroic. The Jones heroes are usually dissenters, some of whom have been called extremists, Communists, Black Nationalists and revolutionists.

The book is a refusal of American foreign and domestic policy on most issues. It rejects the civil rights movement and the right to register and to vote, on the judgment there's not much worth voting for and both political parties are the same; likewise the fight for education and employment, on the premise the struggle is not worth what comes with it. Otherwise, on hopes for home, he has none. He disregards the idea of the New World or "the free world," as such, and takes on allegiance to the part of the globe the French call *Tiers Monde:* Africa, Asia, and Latin America.

What may be said about this book is that it is more a part of home than it may seem. It belongs, in its way, on American bookshelves next to some essays like William Harper's, Thomas R. Dew's, James Hammond's and George Fitzhugh's—a few men as convinced about the way affairs should have gone in their era as LeRoi Jones is in his. Its visions also of a Black Nation take on some visions Jefferson, Monroe, Madison, Marshall, and Clay had with The American Colonization Society—though theirs, alas, were to try and get all Black Nations off American shores.

*Home* sets out in its own way to tell part of this story, but finally, in the end, what it does is to parody itself, and it fails.

But it succeeds in part, in doing what it most wanted to do; to have "Black Writing" tell some of what LeRoi Jones believes has been left untold—and in the terms he thinks it should tell it.

He notes midway through the book in a piece called *LeRoi Jones Talking,* that "something else I aspire to is the craziness of all honest men." In certain passages, before his own beliefs overtake him, he fulfills it, not only with the craziness of his own honesty, but with moments of truth. (pp. 24-5)

> *Faith Berry, "Black Artist, Black Prophet," in* The New Republic, *Vol. 154, No. 22, May 28, 1966, pp. 23-5.*

## HENRY S. RESNIK

The sense of Jones's capabilities does not come easy . . . either to himself or to the reader, for his writing is a continual experiment. Indirectly acknowledging the influence of Joyce, Eliot, Pound, and Yeats, among others, he explores their idioms almost at random. The earlier tales [in the collection

*Tales*] are done in a frequently bewildering telegraphic style that is more notation than expression. Moreover, the writing fluctuates between the precision and elegance (not necessarily virtues) of "white" language and the crude strength of "black" slang. *Tales* is a potpourri reflecting a wide spectrum of linguistic styles as they relate to Jones's life and as they exist in contemporary America. That Jones transcends this chaos is one of the chief merits of his book, for it emerges as a unified whole, ultimately providing a rationale for what seems at first to be self-defeating obliqueness.

Although many of the sixteen tales appeared originally in various magazines and can be read independently, the book is more a novel than a collection of stories. Characters, names, places, and symbols, most of them rooted in Jones's earlier work, recur throughout. There are . . . several personifications of Jones himself. . . . Jones's life is merely the basis for *Tales,* however; his sense of poetry carries him far beyond the mere telling of his own story.

Most of the pieces are isolated moments conceived as lyric poem-stories. The first, **"A Chase (Alighieri's Dream)"** (almost a continuation of *The System of Dante's Hell*), shows the protagonist running, from "lies," from the past, from threats of which even he is scarcely aware, through his nightmare-city. . . .

He passes the people he knows . . . , and as he reaches the top of the hill he changes on the street "to a black suit. Black wool." ("Black wool," in Jones's unfortunately private iconology, is gray flannel.) Thus cryptically, the stage is set for the conflict within himself between Negro and white that will plague him throughout the book. (p. 28)

Fortunately, most of the stories are immediately understandable without keys to Jones's private world. **"The Alternative"** vividly represents him as the leader (presumably at Howard University) who nervously controls his group by dint of superior verbal powers; these give him the "whiteness" to which the others aspire. But his leadership is shattered when the others, probing his weaknesses, discover that he cannot cope with his emotional shock when they tease one of his homosexual friends. Finally they rebel, torment the homosexual in an ecstasy of malice, turn on the leader, and literally push him to the floor. He lies there, defeated—"My face pushed hard against the floor. And the wood, old, and protestant. And their voices, all these other selves screaming for blood. For blood, or whatever it is fills their noble livies." The self-pity is obvious, but Jones has a remarkable capacity for getting past such faults— again the paradox: the sensitivity to words and events that, in his eyes, weakens him as a man saves him as a writer.

Even though Jones rejects *Hamlet* as a purely white manifestation of Western culture, his stories show a preoccupation with one of Shakespeare's classic problems, the conflict between words and action (with overtones of "black" and "white"). On the one hand, words are the supreme power of both the black world and the white; on the other, they disgust him. "How can you read *Pierre*," he asks in a mediocre story about his marital problems, "when your wife's doing something weird?" And, in a far better story about his failure to respond when two policemen torment a pathetic bum in a hospital ward, "It is the measure of my dwindling life that I returned to the book to rub out their images, and studied very closely another doomed man's life." At one point he even implies that because he is a writer he is less manly; he is thus

a victim of American stereotypes about writers as well as about Negroes, but he seems often to delight in them.

There is a progression in *Tales,* however, away from the word-centered world to a world of intense emotion and violent action. In one of the best stories, **"The Screamers,"** Jones describes a nightclub in Newark, surging to the sound of jazz which takes on a raging life of its own and pushes the Negro dancers into the street, where they astonish white onlookers. But this rather joyful prophecy only begins to anticipate the grimness of what actually happened in Newark.

Finally the conflict between words and action reaches a resolution: the words become weapons, white weapons wielded by Jones's new-found black consciousness. "Many years ago I wanted to be myself," he writes. "And still I walk that same line . . . But in a stark black and white tube. With my brothers and sisters on benches for sale. And the beasts themselves darting in and out inside, in their capes and revenge . . . I couldn't walk stupid or unfeeling or in hip germany, forever . . . This is an exact crevice. This is sunrise like seeing the logic of the white castle."

The final story, **"Answers in Progress,"** is a fantasy in which the blacks completely destroy the white world, burning the white cities; they are joined by a group of whimsical, jazz-loving, blue-colored spacemen who have just arrived from another planet in search of Art Blakey records. The tone is hilariously bitter.

It is understatement to say that the quality of these stories is uneven. The strain of anti-intellectualism and the cultivation of spontaneous self-expression are so strong that the writing frequently gets out of control. Despite redeeming paragraphs or episodes, a few of the stories are downright amateurish.

But, while it spoils some of the pieces, this method is the source of the book's strength. Lesser writers should beware of it; Jones triumphs because he is consistently able to inspire language with new life and rhythm. Sensitive to himself and the world around him, he is at the center of the drama of contemporary America. The white world might be more comfortable if LeRoi Jones stayed in his jails, both real and imagined; but it needs his voice. (pp. 28-9)

> *Henry S. Resnik, "Brave New Words," in* Saturday Review, *Vol. L, No. 49, December 9, 1967, pp. 28-9.*

**S. K. OBERBECK**

[In Jones'] fiction he tries to chart his break with rotten white society. Jones' imaginary gutters are torrential with our blood, and in his efforts to glorify total immersion in a new life of utter negritude, he obsessively compounds all the supposed sickness of white society that afflicted him when he moved among it.

And yet he writes much better now than he did. There is still a familiar, childish narcissism in his prose, and an unsurprising revving-up of vindictive violence often more funny than fearsome. But several stories [in *Tales*] are rare cameos in onyx. In **"Heroes Are Gang Leaders,"** the obviously autobiographical narrator occupies a hospital bed next to that of a Pole who has drunk paint remover and can only "gurgle" pathetically. Two detectives, out of ignorance or spite, relentlessly question the babbling Pole. Finally, the narrator, who has been reading Ford Madox Ford's sad chronicle of Christopher Tietjens in

*No More Parades,* says to them: "That man can't speak. His voice is gone." "And who the ——— asked you?" snaps one gumshoe. "It is the measure of my dwindling life," the next sentence concludes with crystalline irony, "that I returned to the book to rub out their image, and studied very closely another doomed man's life."

But the telling moments are always overcast with darkness; Jones' daydreams are a white man's nightmares. The frequency of his pathological fantasies, some of which have come true in Newark and Detroit, are key to an understanding of his angry soul. "Blood Everywhere," ends one story. "And the heroes march thru smiling." Another tale, like Black Power science fiction, has creatures from outer space helping black people annihilate whites. In **"The Screamers,"** a sweating saxophone player becomes a Black Power Pied Piper leading a happenstance-protest string of snake-dancers. "It would be the sweetest form of revolution," writes Jones, "to hucklebuck into the fallen capital, and let the oppressors lindy hop out."

The majority of the stories, however, contemplate no sweet revolutions. The blood-letting refrain rings loudest, and saddest, in **"New-Sense,"** a paean to militant negritude: "O world I want to change you, and these fantasies are sundays in the wet silence, gathering my strength about me, clear and free, for a hard thing. Which must be done, and gotten, in order that peace come, and be free, and unconditional." Which reminds me of what Andrei Sinyavsky wrote about the Russian revolution: "So that not one more drop of blood should be shed, we killed and killed and killed."

> S. K. Oberbeck, "Black Daydreams, White Man's Nightmares," in Book World—The Washington Post, December 24, 1967, p. 7.*

### ALFRED KAZIN

To some Black writers, there is nothing so exciting just now as Race. Or as Imamu Amiri Baraka . . . puts it in the title, theme, and thrust of his "essays since 1965," *Raise Race Rays Raze.* Of course, Baraka has an insurrectionary pun there that those (more or less white) liberals who would rather buy and read books than move in on City Hall will not necessarily identify with. But to some black writers, Race and Black are the exciting, creative, uplifting terms just now. (p. 33)

Both Richard Wright and James Baldwin seem old hat now to many black militants. Ralph Ellison's faith in the Western literary tradition is scorned by them with the kind of bitterness that is never found in their contemptuous, condescending references to Nixon and George Wallace. Still, given the charged-up, wholly "political," militant Black nationalism and Black esthetic of so many young black writers, the hatred of "crazy individualism," and the mystical faith in "blackness" expressed by the most quirky and talented of black writers since Baldwin, LeRoi Jones himself, isn't it interesting that Jones is the most idiosyncratic stylist of the lot, the writer with the most original and individual rhythms? Even in the two explicitly propagandistic books under review [*Raise Race Rays Raze* and *In Our Terribleness*], books supposedly written to stir up his own people, Jones dreamily fuses poetry with prose, politics with religion, symbolism with invective. This is Western bourgeois elitist writing at its most luxurious and fanciful. No one since Whitman has so spread himself and indulged himself, loafing and inviting his own soul! . . .

[Jones'] incantations resemble the lonely dithyrambs of Nietzsche's Zarathustra more than they reflect the everyday life of the black people in Newark. Jones, as a political leader, has so skillfully organized Newark blacks that *The New York Times* credits him with greater political clout in Newark than Mayor Gibson! Yet, despite the dreamy, mystic, self-communing quality of Baraka's prose, it is obvious that he addresses "his" people from on high, in the classic stance of the prophet and deliverer; he seeks to move them, to awaken them to a prouder awareness of themselves. It is all pep talk—in the scriptural sense a lifting of the spirit for those who are black, black, black. If you are outside, you may find it just a bit precious. Jones is particularly gifted as a dramatist, writes fiction cleverly but without much interest in the form, and seems less interested in books than in being a Voice, a Personality, a Leader. He is probably not so much the Lenin of Black Nationalism as its Ralph Waldo Emerson. He has to be read, but he writes in patches, like a genius in a trance. (p. 34)

> Alfred Kazin, "Brothers Crying Out for More Access to Life," in Saturday Review, Vol. LIV, No. 40, October 2, 1971, pp. 33-5.*

### LLOYD W. BROWN

[Amiri Baraka] has been a controversial figure in American politics and literature for the last sixteen years. . . . [While] his poetry, drama, and political activism continue to make him a significant figure in black America, his work as art critic represents an important contribution to the debates of the 1960s and early 1970s. Consequently he has become one of the leading representatives of what is now known as the black aesthetic, or black arts movement, which still seeks to define the alleged peculiarities of the black American's art and art criticism.

But, curiously, for some time serious study of Baraka's work lagged far behind his undoubted achievements and his undeniable reputation. This neglect can be traced, in part, to the fact that Baraka's work has frequently attracted political reaction, or more precisely, political invective, rather than informed and informative analysis. In one sense this kind of reaction is understandable, even inevitable, though not really excusable for all that. Baraka's visibility as black political activist and his frank insistence on the political significance of his literary art have usually aroused unease about his racial militancy, and have encouraged the assumption that his work is political propaganda rather than "serious" art.

However, this kind of assumption has not been very helpful. Although Baraka has been adamant about his political role and vision he has never ceased to produce works that are recognizably distinct from the pamphlets, essays, and speeches that comprise direct political statement. Although he attacks the usual academic insistence on art for its own sake, Baraka clearly makes a distinction between art, even politically committed art, and the tracts, speeches, and other tools of his political activism. Otherwise it would be difficult to account for the fact that during his most politically committed periods he has continued to write as poet and dramatist. In the process he has obviously continued to invite study as a writer whose political activism is integrated with his art (at least on his own terms). And his continuing interest in the creation of literary art forms—albeit fervently committed art forms—implies more than political commitment as such. It also represents a continuing and deep-rooted interest in all of those definable constructs and indeterminate traits which are peculiar to art, whether art is viewed as a self-contained, self-justifying mode or seen as an integral part of a political process. (pp. 7-8)

Each of Baraka's genres—essay, novel, short story, poetry, and drama—reflects certain aspects of his development as politically committed writer, and it simultaneously helps to define the very nature of the experience which it contains. Thus the essays are the direct statements of the political activist and critic. That directness clarifies the relationship between Baraka's personal development and his political ideas. Moreover the special role of the expository essays underlines Baraka's clear distinction between his interest in the written word as committed art and his use of unadorned political statement.

The prose fiction is distinct in Baraka's work, not only as a genre, but also as a form which he abandons relatively early in his career. This abandonment is significant, particularly in view of Baraka's personal view of prose fiction as an inherently white, Western mode. Precisely because of its "alien" cultural sources, Baraka's prose fiction is peculiarly suited to the central themes of his novel (*The System of Dante's Hell*) and his short stories (*Tales*)—the conflict between an "alien" white value system and black identity. This cultural conflict is perversely appropriate for a fictive form since Baraka is always able to dramatize the struggle by continuously striking out at the form itself. Narrative patterns in these works arise, paradoxically, from a violent assault on preconceived notions of fictive form and on the (white, Western) culture that is the source of those notions.

Baraka's dual perception of form and language—both as form of communication and target of attack—runs throughout the poetry. Here, in a genre which spans most of Baraka's career as writer, form and structure have evolved to cohere with his themes in a direct way, rather than by virtue of the paradoxical ironies of the prose fiction. Poetry allows Baraka an unparalleled latitude, accommodating his need to destroy forms, create new structures, and to exploit language itself while demonstrating its limitations. And part of this accomplishment rests in the fact that Baraka's use of black folk forms (music and language, for example) invests his poetry with an "ethnic" legitimacy that the "alien" forms of prose fiction seem to lack in his view.

But in spite of the relatively consistent successes of the poetry it is the drama that most seems to attract Baraka. This fascination lies in his perception of art as commitment and in the peculiar identity of drama itself. As both word and action the form has a special appeal to the political activist who requires, even demands, an artistic mode that is distinct from but complementary to straightforward political activism. This probably explains why, as Baraka's personal activism has intensified and broadened, he has turned more and more to the stage. For example, his most significant work as a convert to socialism has been drama—*The Motion of History* (1976) and *S-1* (1976).

As a result the drama reflects much of Baraka's recent growth as a writer. But for a similar reason his plays comprise his most uneven achievements, ranging from the penetrating insights of *Dutchman* and *The Slave* to the unimaginative baldness of later pieces where committed art seems to have degenerated into a mere preachiness. (pp. 9-10)

[The] unevenness of Baraka's drama is fairly representative of his general achievements as a writer. For even at its least distinguished his writing reflects a continuing tension between the decidedly unsubtle ideologue and the committed artist, between a passion for literal political statement and an interest in art as an imaginatively conceived, expressive, and committed design. And this tension remains in the background even when the interest in imaginative art is merely theoretical. Moreover, as the genre that spans his writing career his drama appropriately reflects a major constant in his writings. That is, despite his ideological shifts, his themes and their underlying social attitudes have remained fairly consistent.

Consequently, his perception of American society is invariably bleak. He always envisions a society of moral corruption and human decay whenever he contemplates America. This moral revulsion at America as a wasteland has a twofold effect. On the one hand it inspires those images of violence and death which characterize much of Baraka's work, ranging from the early radicalism and the black protests and moving to the later revolutionism of the black nationalist and socialist periods. And, on the other hand, this revulsion also triggers a passionate commitment to life, that is, to the moral and social rebirth which he envisages in his successive alternatives (ethnic, socialist, and so forth) to the American wasteland.

Moreover, the moral overview of America is always integrated with his racial themes. The black American's plight as racial victim is both a primary concern in its own right and an important symptom of America's pervasive ills. And this remains true even in the deliberate emphasis on nonracial criteria in the socialist drama where the issue of racial violence and divisiveness is emphasized as the sign of an exploitive and oppressive ruling elite. Racial anger and moral outrage have always been inextricably interwoven in Baraka's work. Consequently, the thematic complexity of his more substantial work has easily eluded critics, both hostile and sympathetic, who respond only to his ethnic militancy. Finally, it is necessary to recognize the degree to which the shock tactics of moral outrage really arise from the fact that Baraka is a familiar kind of moral idealist, one whose idealism motivates the wasteland images of the "Beat" poetry, the black revolutionism of the middle years, and the more recent themes of socialist revolution.

The underlying thematic continuities of Baraka's work are complemented by certain consistencies in his approach to certain forms or techniques. The images of sight and sound which he emphasizes as a narrative technique in his only novel and in his short stories go back to his earliest poetry. And at the same time these images are adapted to the requirements of the black nationalist poems where the sounds of political statement are indistinguishable from the forms of politically committed art. In the drama the morality play tradition and the interest in ritual forms continue from the earliest plays to the later revolutionary works.

The continuity of certain forms attests to a strong degree of artistic self-awareness in Baraka the writer. This is the kind of self-awareness that springs from his lifelong commitment to the integration of theme with artistic form, and even when that integration is more a matter of promise than practice it makes for a complex context in which to examine Baraka, one in which the reader must be constantly alert to the actual or possible relationship between form and content, rather than neglecting one in favor of the other. This is the major reason for the enormous demands that Baraka's work, even at its worst, places on the reader. At its worst the work suffers from a narrowness of vision and a shrillness of tone that frequently distort the effects of whatever structural achievements might exist. But his best writing is challenging in the other sense: the closely knit relationship between theme and form requires a painstaking attention to the manner as well as the substance of statement—a requirement that has often proven too difficult for those who are overly hostile toward or enthusiastic about the substance.

Finally, Baraka's achievement as a writer should also be weighed on the representative nature of his political activism and art. In fact his career as a whole can be seen as a political weather vane of sorts. The early period reflects that combination of concerns which influences much of American literature and politics in the late 1950s and early 1960s: there is a growing uneasiness about America's world role and the country's relationship with the Third World; and there is increasing recognition that the black civil rights movement raised questions about American society in general as well as about racial relationships. The middle period, the years of Baraka's black nationalism, coincides with the militancy of black America's black power movement and the racial riots in the cities. Finally even the more recent conversion to socialism is symptomatic, notwithstanding the fact that scientific socialism is not a popular movement in America at this time. His current ideology and writings are representative in that they reflect a general turning away from cultural nationalism and racial confrontation in black American politics since the early 1970s. Although Baraka denounces the "black petite bourgeoisie" who simply exploited black nationalism in order to feather their nests in the mainstream culture, Baraka's own switch to scientific socialism is as much an admission of the failure of black nationalism as is the opportunism that he condemns in the black middle class.

The decline of ethnic politics in black America reflects a marked decrease in political energies, a decrease that can be attributed to the opening of some doors to the mainstream and to the death, imprisonment, or discrediting of the political leaders of the 1960s. Baraka himself is a good example of this decline of political energies. As a scientific socialist he is in the least imaginative phase of his life as a political writer. This relative lack of creativity is not really the fault of the ideology itself. It seems, more likely, to be the reflection of a certain intellectual flabbiness on Baraka's part. Not only in the forgettable poems of *Hard Facts* but also in the plays and essays of the later years, Baraka seems to find it increasingly difficult to go beyond the accepted clichés of political dogma. It has appeared progressively easier for him to offer hackneyed and literal statements in lieu of artistic forms that are both imaginative and sociopolitically significant. Of course the current flabbiness is not necessarily terminal. In light of his career as a whole Baraka is unlikely to remain pedestrian as a political activist or mediocre as an artist. And whatever further developments occur in that career they will, in all likelihood, be closely linked with the literary and political atmosphere of his time. His significance as a mirror of his society has been one of his most enduring characteristics. (pp. 166-68)

> *Lloyd W. Brown, in his* Amiri Baraka, *Twayne Publishers, 1980, 180 p.*

## C.W.E. BIGSBY

In terms of the 1960s, black theatre became less a question of establishing specific repertory groups ... than of creating a drama responsive to the needs and interests of black people and performed in the black communities which it serves. And at the heart of this enterprise, creating the institutions which could facilitate it and elaborating the images, the myths, and the forms of this new theatre, was, most crucially, a single man—LeRoi Jones. It was as a modernist poet, drawing on European and American models, that LeRoi Jones first came to prominence; it was as the colleague of white writers that he first established a reputation, founding *Yugen* Magazine and Totem Press in 1958 and coediting *The Floating Bear* magazine with Diane DiPrima in 1961.

But a changing social world, nationally and internationally, exerted the same moral pressure on Jones that it did on James Baldwin who had been living in Paris while the first events of the civil rights movement were being enacted in America. The change which eventually came over LeRoi Jones was a profound one, one which affected his private, public, and artistic life and made him the most important black writer of the 1960s— a shift, moreover, symbolized by a change of name. He abandoned his "slave name" for an appellation which indicated his new stance—Imamu (leader) Amiri (warrior) Baraka (blessing). In fact, from the beginning, his work had grown out of his own sense of cultural identity but where that had been simply the circumstance of his art, in the late 1960s it became the basis of an artistic and political philosophy. In many ways Baraka has contained within himself the conflict within the black community: avant-garde artist and committed spokesman, putative Black Muslim and secular politician, black nationalist and Marxist ideologue. And the gap between these opposing compulsions—like the space between American promise and fulfillment, revolutionary rhetoric and reality—is always liable to be filled with violence sublimated in artistic form. And it was partly as a writer whose powerful plays were luminous with violent images and articulate anger that he became the leading black playwright of the last decade and a half.

Baraka's arguments with himself have, in essence, been the arguments which split the black community. The irony is that now, as a Marxist-Leninist, he has spent the last few years struggling to escape from a myth of his own construction, that of black political and cultural separation, as in the late 1960s he had had to exorcise his earlier career as experimental writer and proponent of a modernist aesthetic. The alliance which he now seeks between black and white members of the "advanced" working class constitutes a synthesis of the terms of the dialectic which he had identified in the 1960s as constituting mutually exclusive symbolic systems and socially unassimilable propositions. If he was never the true poet of violence which he was taken to be, he was a writer for whom social action and imaginative fiat were symbiotically related. And though he retains that conviction, the components which form his imaginative universe today differ fundamentally from the Manichean elements which constituted his moral battleground a few years ago.

Although his early poetry lays claim to the modernist tradition, there was from the beginning a social compulsion in his work, a drive through the word to the fact. And his admiration for the Beats was, in part at least, an admiration for people who located a specific environment which became not merely the reason for the literal and stylistic quest, but also, in some ways, its subject. (pp. 235-36)

But the public situation was changing. Africa now stood as a model of revolution rather than as a romantic image of primal innocence as it had in the 1920s. ... [Jones's] work, too, was changing. In 1963, he published *Blue People: Negro Music in White America,* and, in 1964, his powerful one-act play, *Dutchman,* was produced at the Cherry Lane Theatre with the assistance of Edward Albee's Playwrights Unit. It was not his first play. *A Good Girl Is Hard to Find* had been produced in Montclair, New Jersey, in 1958, and early in 1964 *The 8th Ditch* (an excerpt from his forthcoming novel, *The System of Dante's Hell*) and *The Baptism* made brief appearances. But it was *Dutchman,* a powerful fable of American race relations, which established his reputation as a dramatist and which turned his career in a new direction. (pp. 236-37)

*Dutchman* remains one of the best plays ever written by a black author and one of the most impressive works of recent American theatre. Like [Edward Albee's] *The Zoo Story,* it is a potent parable of alienation. If Jones's control of language is reminiscent of Albee's, as is his sense of musical structure, in the person of Clay he has created a far more complex character than Albee's Peter, whose stereotypical role is the one serious flaw in what is otherwise the most impressive first play ever written by an American dramatist. *Dutchman* is a reflexive work. At its heart is a consideration of the artistic process, a debate over the legitimacy of sublimating social anguish into aesthetic form. It addresses itself to a central problem of the black artist who is alive to the evasion which may be implied in the act of writing. It is a debate which Jones has continued throughout his career without ever finding a wholly satisfactory answer.

In part, of course, the play can be read as Jones's confession or critique of his own safe refuge in words, of his own attempts to sublimate racial tensions in art. If this is so it was even more true of a subsequent play, *The Slave,* which is intensely autobiographical and in which he accuses himself and others of remaining slaves to a liberalism which can no longer be validated by reality. (p. 239)

Later the same year, two of his plays were performed at St. Marks Playhouse, *The Toilet* and *The Slave.* The former is a one-act play in which racial violence breaks out in a school lavatory. Yet, beneath the apocalyptic clash is a curiously contradictory belief in the efficacy of love—a Baldwin-like sentimentality expressed in a sexual grace which transcends social realities. The ending, which he explains to have been "tacked on," is strangely out of key with the main thrust of the play. But it does appear to validate his own continuing commitment to the interracial ethos of his Greenwich Village existence. So, black and white come together in the concluding moment of the play in an epiphany, suggesting thereby that dispossession and exclusion are not exclusively racial experiences.

*The Slave,* however, pursues racial tensions to their logical conclusion. It takes place at the moment of a black revolt in America. The revolutionary leader, Walker Vessels, formerly married to a middle-class white woman, now visits her and her husband, a white liberal professor, as his troops move in on the city. Himself a writer, he had abandoned the word for the act. But his own presence in his ex-wife's apartment shows that he has not escaped his past, he is still a slave to old ideas and associations. His denunciation of the white liberal is thus largely an exorcism of his own former self. But it is also an assertion that it is precisely liberal equivocation that has transformed the slave into the rebel. Despite his own reservations, however, the logic of his position and of the history in which they are all trapped leads to his shooting the white professor. The play ends as shells hit the building, his former wife is crushed underneath a fallen beam, and the screams of his two children are heard.

For all the violence of the action, the most striking aspect of the play lies in the reservations which it expresses about the

act of revolt. He is aware of, and in part still feels, liberal ambiguities about violence and about a social transformation which depends on simple inversion. Lacking any ideological structure for his work, he is left with presenting revolt as generating its own values. In some ways, therefore, it is a work, like Lowell's *The Old Glory,* dedicated to presenting the paradox of revolution. Change is necessary, but the violence of revolt closes the moral gap between oppressed and oppressor. (pp. 239-40)

On the verge of a profound change in his personal life and in the racial situation in America, Jones is all too aware that ideas need judging, that revolutionary symbols fail to deal adequately with the complexity of private or public action. But the play deploys a level of subtlety and ambiguity which he rapidly dispensed with as his own analysis of American society and the racial situation led him to a more stringent and unambiguous stance.

The ironies of the play are magnified when one realizes that shortly afterwards Jones left his white Jewish wife and his two daughters and moved his activities to Harlem where he became the focus for the Black Arts movement of the late 1960s. *The Slave,* therefore, stands as a personal act of exorcism, and the works which followed advocated a clear cultural and political nationalism of a kind which left no space for self-doubt. (p. 242)

Asked, in 1977, what his view of the whole Black Arts movement of the 1960s was, he replied, "There are still progressive black artists who relate what they are doing to the Black Liberation Movement, and to revolution, which is the positive aspect of that. I think the negative aspect has actually been co-opted by the bourgeoisie—I mean the part of black art that just rested with skin identification, so that the very people who first opposed us are given the grants and the money to open the Black Arts Theatres, all around the country, the Negro Ensemble Company, the New Lafayette Company. And now you have exploitation flicks talking about black arts, and there are several people on television who were in plays of mine in the 1960s, who considered themselves revolutionary black artists but who became involved simply with the skin aspect of it. What is black art? It's about black people, they thought. But the point is, it's supposed to be about revolution." It is a view, of course, which necessarily makes him blind to the accomplishments of a work like Ntozake Shange's "Choreopoem" *For Coloured Girls Who Have Considered Suicide When the Rainbow Is Enuf.* . . . But, then, he has replaced the rigors of one ideological stance by those of another which leaves little space for lyricism.

In his own eyes, of course, the development from *Dutchman* [which espouses Black Nationalism] to *S-1* [which emphasizes the need for blacks and whites to come together and form a Marxist-Leninist Communist Party] represents "a leap from partial truth to a more wholesided reality," from "the feeling and rage against oppression to the beginnings of actual scientific analysis of this oppression and its true sources." To others, it might appear that he had simply moved from one ideology to another, pressing experience to its extreme edges, to the point at which meaning seems to render itself up only in moral absolutes of chilling determinism. There is indeed a clear line of development visible in his work. Whether or not it is a move in the direction of truth, however, is more debatable. Dramatically, he has abandoned rituals as "bourgeois nationalism" and forsworn the subtleties of his own early work as simply inadequate to confront what he takes to be the unsubtle conflicts of capital and labor. His plays are, he admits, "vehicles for a simple message," and their weakness is perhaps apparent in that description.

His work is now, I suspect, overarticulate. It operates wholly on the surface. All hidden powers are exposed, and the result is both an oversimplified view of political process and a dissipation of dramatic power. No longer interested in the energy generated by the collision of conscious and subconscious or in the potent rhythms of submerged passions, he resolves all tensions into the battle for economic hegemony; all violence becomes literal and political. Character is crushed as effectively by the playwright as it is by the reactionary forces against which he pitches his work. And the risk, clearly, is that in identifying those historical forces which account for the drive towards Marxist-Leninism, he fails to dramatize those human forces which must finally validate it. (pp. 245-46)

But Baraka is not unaware of the problems involved in creating ideological drama. His artistic credo is taken from Mao Tsetung's *Yenan Forum on Art and Literature:* "What we demand is the unity of politics and art, the unity of content and form, the unity of revolutionary political content and the highest possible perfection of artistic form; . . . we oppose both works of art with a wrong political viewpoint and the tendency towards the 'poster and slogan style' which is correct in political viewpoint but lacking in artistic power." As he has indicated in a recent interview, this still eludes him. But he obviously believes that what he has lost—the imaginative brilliance of *Dutchman,* the subtle analysis of *The Slave,* the controlled rhythms and potent rituals of *Slaveship*—is adequately compensated for by the historical significance of his new career. At the moment it is difficult to endorse that view. The question is whether he can yet find a form and a language adequate to his self-imposed task or whether the logic of his present position may not drive him beyond theatre altogether.

Clearly, the pressure for ideological commitment in Baraka is strong, whether it be the shaping myths of black nationalism or those of Marxist-Leninism. But he is a writer of genuine integrity for whom art must always be seen as a public act. His struggle to find a structure capable of expressing the needs of the individual and those of society, his search for a form of transcendence which lies neither in aestheticism nor in a convenient surrender of historical truth, has in essence been that of all black writers in the last two decades. (pp. 246-47)

*C.W.E. Bigsby, "Black Drama: The Public Voice," in his* The Second Black Renaissance: Essays in Black Literature, *Greenwood Press, 1980, pp. 207-56.**

### HENRY C. LACEY

Perhaps more so than any other writer, Baraka captures the idiom and style of modern urban black life. The uniqueness and authenticity of his work is largely attributable to his thorough knowledge of the speech and music of urban blacks. In his best work, he exploits these two powerful and rich possessions of an otherwise weak and impoverished people. He shows, especially in his later works, an understanding of the full range of black speech patterns, an element which invigorates and renders dramatic even his short stories and poems. Baraka's flawless ear retained also the sounds of modern jazz, the most important artistic creation of black America. Along with the frequent evidence of the traditional jazz framework, we see also in the poems the following characteristics of modern jazz: spontaneity of line, moving by sheer suggestiveness of impetus; elliptical phrasing; polyrhythmic thrust. Although

similar musical qualities have been attributed to the work of other modern American poets, the conscious and effective employment of these qualities cannot be questioned in Baraka's case, for his musical insights are not only integrated into the artistic methods of his plays, poems, and stories. They have been articulated in a number of perceptive essays, as well as the extremely important study *Blues People.* Throughout his literary career, Baraka has been concerned greatly with the sounds of black life. During the latter 1960's and early 1970's, this concern took on even more importance in his attempts to reach a largely non-reading audience.

Baraka is among the most influential of black American writers because his example has been followed by younger black artists of every conceivable medium. In forsaking the closed circle of Village literati, Baraka turned to the creation of a more "functional" or socially committed art, an art concerned with shaping the minds of black Americans. His example inflamed the imaginations of many aspiring writers, musicians, and visual artists during the late '60's. We can trace Baraka's influence in the mature work of such black writers as Ed Bullins (drama), David Henderson (poetry), and Ishmael Reed (poetry and fiction), to name only a few. Although these and other Baraka-influenced writers have since eschewed the leader's extreme didacticism, Baraka was vital to their development in that he taught them to value their own experiences and to understand that they, too, had "access to a real world," one as open to artistic recreation as any other.

Not the least of Baraka's contributions to the younger writers is his demonstration, rather paradoxically, of the limitations of "protest" writing. Faced with Baraka's bitter but finely crafted studies of black-white conflict, conflict surpassing that of Wright or Baldwin, and presented in the most immediate genre, drama, the more talented disciples were forced to seek new directions. They began to deal, as does Baraka himself, more intensely with the intragroup experiences of blacks. Thus, in a very real sense, Baraka frees the younger writers to create instead of react. (pp. viii-ix)

*Henry C. Lacey, in a preface to his* To Raise, Destroy, and Create: The Poetry, Drama, and Fiction of Imamu Amiri Baraka (Le Roi Jones), *The Whitston Publishing Company, 1981, pp. vii-xii.*

### CHRISTOPHER LEHMANN-HAUPT

One reason I was drawn to this autobiography ["**The Autobiography of LeRoi Jones**"] was to learn what eventually happened to LeRoi Jones. What became of him after he changed his name to Amiri Baraka . . . and disappeared into the black cultural nationalist movement? . . .

[He's] not a black nationalist anymore; he's a Marxist who believes in "scientific socialism" now. And he's just a little apologetic about what he's put us through—and himself too— in the previous, densely packed 300 pages. . . .

One just wishes he'd expressed this note of self-doubt a little sooner, because you can't really tell from reading his book that he ever thought he, himself, was responsible for anything. True, he concedes along the way that certain errors were made. He was dumb enough at times nearly to be taken in by the white man's devilish game. By attending Howard University, he aspired to being "yellow"—a Negro in the white man's system—and thereby turned his back on the true "black" souls of his people. In the Air Force and in his Village days, he fell in love with art for art's sake.

It bothered his conscience a little when his growing hatred of "whitey" forced him to leave his first wife and their two children, though he was never loyal to her, or any of his subsequent women for that matter. (Chauvinism had him in its clutches.) He and the people who backed Kenneth Gibson should have taken him "for a long ride and" threatened "to blow his head off if he pulled any funny Negro" tricks. "But we didn't, and I have to take the weight for this." And finally, he concedes, cultural nationalism turned out to be "some kind of complex and funny Rube Goldberg machine of the mind."

And yet in describing all these stages he passed through, he writes as if he still believes in their validity. His narrative is clogged with cant phrases and revolutionary political slogans, yet in a book denouncing art used for anything less than political ends, he expresses admiration of Joyce's "Portrait of the Artist as a Young Man" and pays homage to it by describing his early childhood in the language of that childhood.

Despite all his charges of racism, his glorification of the mystical supremacy of blackness resembles nothing quite so much as Hitler's celebrations of Aryanism. He tries to justify his attempts to practice polygamy by suggesting that he was only moving a little closer to his Islamic roots. When a woman he's been seeing casually tells him she's pregnant, he writes: "Hey, goddamnit, I felt, we only made it a couple of times. But apparently, according to some scientists, one shot can do it." (He had taken chemistry as a pre-med student at Howard, but he had flunked it.)

Now it may be that there's a plan behind the author's stunning ability to have it both ways. Maybe his irony is so arch that I passed under it without ever having noticed it. Or maybe his homage to "Portrait of the Artist" is deeper than I realized; perhaps despite his expressed disdain for European art, he has attempted, like Joyce, to recreate his life in his prose style.

Or maybe he wants to provoke reviewers like me into denouncing his book so that it will confirm for him the hostility of the establishment's media. That would certainly be consistent with a pattern established in his book, and he most assuredly succeeds in provoking when he concludes after returning from a visit to Africa: "I realized, also, that the US was my home. As painful and complicated as that was. I realized that the 30 million African Americans would play a major role in the transformation of black people's lives all over this planet. It was no mere truism, we lived where the head of world oppression lived and when the people of the world united to bring this giant oppressor to its knees we would be part of that contingent (of not only blacks, but of other oppressed nationalities and workers of all nationalities) chosen by the accident of history to cut this thing's head off and send it rolling through the streets of North America."

I'm afraid that this last motive may have been uppermost in Amiri Baraka's mind when he wrote his book, because for several moments it made me sympathize with those many people in Newark he contends were out to destroy him. But whatever his hidden plan was in writing **"The Autobiography of LeRoi Jones,"** one doesn't feel altogether confident in his concluding promise that now at last "I do understand the world better."

Why, when he consistently endorses a past that has failed him, should we suddenly believe in his future?

*Christopher Lehmann-Haupt, in a review of "The Autobiography of LeRoi Jones," in* The New York Times, *January 23, 1984, p. C22.*

## MARK R. YERBURGH

Those who enjoyed Baraka's *Autobiography of Leroi Jones* . . . will be disappointed with this polemical brew of essays, speeches, and lecture notes [*Daggers and Javelins: Essays, 1974-1979*]. The 31 items, some previously published, fall into three categories: revolutionary politics and change, black literature, and the Afro-American experience. Despite the merits of such pieces as "Malcolm X and Paul Robeson" and "Langston Hughes and the Harlem Renaissance," the collection is sloppily written (by any definition), digressive, and repetitive.

*Mark R. Yerburgh, in a review of "Daggers and Javelins: Essays, 1974-1979," in* Library Journal, *Vol. 109, No. 8, May 1, 1984, p. 900.*

## JOYCE ANN JOYCE

*The Autobiography of LeRoi Jones/Amiri Baraka* is a most recent example of how the genre of autobiography continues to be an effusive, contemporary expression of black art and life. Baraka—the author of at least 11 volumes of poetry, three works of fiction, six collections of essays, 15 plays and four anthologies—persistently forges a synthesis between his role as black literary artist and political activist. . . .

Admirably honest, open and revelatory of a personality much softer than the persona of his poetry and personal appearances, this autobiography maps out the steps in Baraka's realization of his cultural, personal, artistic and political sensibility. His life in the Village and his early readings demonstrate an Americanness that connected him to the white mainstream, but his affairs with numerous black women, his second marriage, his profound experiences with the Black Arts Theater, the political struggles in Newark and the black nationalists illuminate the evolution and synthesis of his role as black man, literary artist and political activist.

He provides us with the image of the public figure who stumbles through life like the rest of us. The reader perceives how the artist-activist was created from experiences and ideologies derived from hard struggle, haphazard occurrences and improvisational ideas set into motion. However, while he gives a carefully orchestrated, detailed analysis of his involvement in political activities, he neglects to look at his active role as father of seven children. Thus we leave *The Autobiography* with the idea that his role as artist-political activist is the umbrella under which all other elements of his life must fit.

In this account of approximately 40 years of Baraka's life, the reader profits enormously from a succinct look at history in which the most innovative blues and jazz musicians, New York restaurants, politicians and political figures, black show business personalities, the civil rights movement and the black power movement became integral elements of the chronicler's story. Written predominantly in the rebellious, polyrhythmic style that characterizes Baraka's poetry, essays and dramas, *The Autobiography* measures time through experiences rather than by numbers. The syntax—like the author—is sometimes difficult and tricky. The tone is personal and conversational, reflecting a subjectivity and rebelliousness that is antiacademic and politically motivated.

The many humorous asides within parentheses, the salient black speech and the choppy abbreviated sentences attest to Amiri Baraka's ongoing use of language as a political weapon both to free the spirits of oppressed people and to force them to question the established order of things. The humor that pervades the book and often forces the reader to laugh aloud reflects a seasoned, serious artist-activist capable of the self-criticism necessary if the autobiographer is to be successful at the dual role of moving into the self and stepping out at the same time.

> *Joyce Ann Joyce, in a review of "The Autobiography of LeRoi Jones/Amiri Baraka," in* America, *Vol. 150, No. 20, May 26, 1984, p. 406.*

## C. WERNER

[*Daggers and Javelins: Essays, 1974-1979,* a] collection of speeches and writings on political and literary topics, complements *The Autobiography of LeRoi Jones/Amiri Baraka* (1984) in charting Baraka's movement from black nationalism to a perspective based on "Marxist-Leninist-Mao Tse Tung thought." Whatever the topic of a given selection . . . Baraka focuses on its relationship to a basic set of themes: the threat of war emanating from the contradictions facing the imperialist powers, the US and the USSR; the need for a US communist party with a clear ideological line; the need for the self-determination of the Afro-American nation in the Black Belt South; the relationship between cultural expression and economic base. Frequently effective as an oratorical approach in a specific situation, this tactic when fixed in written form paradoxically emphasizes the technique rather than the content of Baraka's rhetoric, effectively undercutting both its political and aesthetic impact.

> *C. Werner, in a review of "Daggers and Javelins: Essays, 1974-1979," in* Choice, *Vol. 22, No. 2, October, 1984, p. 265.*

## GREG TATE

In [Baraka's] sharpest and his shoddiest work, the subjective wars for space with the sociological, the political with the personal, the existentialist with the engagé. In [*The Autobiography of LeRoi Jones*] Baraka jokingly (perhaps) points up how his sense of good and evil came from radio mystery plays—like to say the evils of his imagining and the evils of the world were but one and the same, both disposable at will. Beneath his desire to have his morality plays go gate-crashing reality, to have art change society, lies Baraka's need to do his growing up in public—to have the world take heed of what changes it's been putting him through.

Portrait of the artist plotting revenge on society: Take *Dutchman*—which we all thought was an allegory on the seduction of the black man by white America. No, says its author; he only wanted to get back at his first white girlfriend for running mindgames on him when he were just a naive young colored boy flush from the Air Force. Which again, however, points up the beauty of the cat: his ability to turn his navel observations into a mirror of society. Baraka's gift for converting introspection into racial commentary probably derives from his moments of alienation and communion with both the black and white worlds. . . .

I owe Baraka one for turning me on to the music (jazz, that is) and writing through his tomes *Blues People* and *Black Music,* which not only made me run out and cop my first Trane, Dolphy, and Miles sides but taught me music could be made with words and ideas as well as notes and tones. Then I discovered his poetry. Lord, how can I begin to tell how in love I am with this man's poetry! Not only for its scope, sweep, and invention, but for the voodoo it runs on modernism's icons (Pound, Williams, Joyce, Eliot, Genet, et al.), and its empathy for life—the sort you'd expect from some versifying naturalist rather than a product of . . . [a] concrete jungle. . . . The black poetry circuit Baraka sparked in the '60s practically made John Coltrane a national hero in the black community. And if Baraka has been dubbed the Father of the Black Arts Movement it's because, as poet Mae Jackson recently related, he gave young black artists a place to go outside of white bohemia and black academia, a place more open to communion with black working-class culture. . . . (p. 41)

The most valuable lesson I've learned from the breadth, depth, and volume of Baraka's work is not unlike the one I learned from Langston Hughes. Which is: yes, my sister/brother, you can actually make a career out of vexing the King's English until it speaks in tongues. Even more instructive has been Baraka's recombinant splicing of black life and Western literary modernism, which sez yo, homegirl/homeboy, you can talk that arty talk and walk that walk, slide in your stride, zip in your hip; so go on 'head with your baad self, mix that intellectual shit in with a few healthy doses of yang and you'll still be cool. Reminding us always, as he admonishes his bohemian incarnation in the autobiography, "Be careful in giving up the provincial that you don't give up the fundamental and the profound."

In Baraka's case, this warning also begs the inverse: Be careful in celebrating the provincial that you don't cast out the cosmopolitan and the complex. Because the tragedy of Baraka's writing, for a lifetime reader of the mug like me, is that in what critic Werner Sollors has termed his quest for a populist modernism Baraka hasn't been able, like García Márquez, Cortázar, and Cabrera Infante (not to mention Sembene, Césaire, and Ngugi wa Thiong'o, if we really want to up the ante), to radically fuse his comprehensive knowledge of Western literature with his need to address the condition and complexity of his people. Least not lately, though if you go back to **"The Screamers"** you got my man laying the groundwork for a modernist black novel which evokes the provincial and the cosmopolitan, the political and the personal without ever leaving the scene of a screamin' and honkin' Newark cabaret.

The Cabrera Infante of *Three Trapped Tigers* got nothing on this Baraka when it comes to making orchestra music out of adolescent memory; nor the Cortázar of *Hopscotch* if we're talking about mapping the interior city; nor the García Márquez of *Chronicle of a Death Foretold* if we want to study up on how journalism can be surrendered to magic realism without missing a beat. . . . Only like I said, that was a whole 'nutha Baraka ago y'all. And much as I love my main mutha, I got to say his output over the past decade ain't been nothing but a muthafunkin' disappointment, give or take a few gems he stole out along the way, like the poems **"Das Kapital"** and **"In the Tradition,"** the liner notes for Woody Shaw, a few other scraps of verse here and there. Because otherwise we talking about some diatribe disguised as literature. Stuff so lame I sometimes had to do the serious doubletake and ask myself, is this the same cat made me want to throw down on a typewriter in the first place? Sheee, you lying to me. Which isn't to say hearing Baraka recite some of this mess couldn't make your ass snap to, 'cause he's still one of the meanest rap acts around. (pp. 41-2)

Popular opinion likes to tell you how Baraka's politics, first those of black nationalism and later those of Marxism, fucked up his writing; that as he got more race and class conscious he got progressively less craft conscious. And there's truth to that. Reading and listening to some of the more polemical work, you do feel yourself in the presence of a revolutionary shaman, out to chase his devils away with rhetorical spells and incantations rather than artful literary strategies. (p. 42)

The strangest thing about the memoirs is that they formally and structurally recreate the process of Baraka's literary degeneration, the book tracking his personal, political, and literary changes in a way that's very schizzy, to say the least. The various sections read like lost pages from former works, almost as if in writing them he was reliving not just their historical occurrence but their point of literary origin as well. The chapter on his Newark upbringing reads like parts of *The System of Dante's Hell*, sometimes fractured and associative, other times given over to straight narrative about his childhood. My favorite of his remembrances is of going to black baseball games and the sense of ethnic communion and celebration he took from them. . . . The sections on Howard University, the Air Force, and Greenwich Village remind me of *Tales* and *Home*, full as they are of angst and intellectual awakening. . . . The Howard section of the memoirs won me out because of how fluidly it reads and because like my mentor I dropped out first chance I got. It also proves the Tombstone of Negro Education ain't changed in 30 years and points up Baraka's genius at crystallizing the Northern urban black male experience—his gifts for making prose poetry out of the body of cultural attitudes toward music, speech, style, and women which bind and shape big city brothers. . . . Narratively, the memoirs begin to take a turn for the worse (and let me add that this is one of the worst edited and proofed books in years) in recounting the nationalist period, reading as it does exactly like the hipty dip rhetoric he was printing back when he was under the gun, trying to juggle double lives in art and politics and beginning to let art take the fatal plunge. And as much as the book reworks Baraka's literary descent, there's also something to be said for how unreconstructed it reveals his ideas to be about the revolution that never came, black supremacy, homosexuals, women (ever the ideologue, he comes off good on "the woman question"; it's the spiteful way he deals with old flames that rankles), and high yella nigras. While, remarkably, there's not a trace of anti-Semitism, the caste aspersions are really vile.

After giving one whole chapter over to divvying the world up into his version of the good, the bad, and the ugly (read: the black and brown, the yellow, and the white) Baraka does a pretty fair job throughout the rest of the tome convincing us how little love is lost between him and fair-skinned black folk. (pp. 42-3)

Baraka is obviously full of contradictions, emotional and intellectual, that no party line is ever gonna resolve for him. Not to say he hasn't spent a lifetime trying to make good on the attempt. I once asked a friend of his why Baraka had gone through so many changes. He replied it was because, more than anyone he'd ever met, Baraka was tortured by always wanting to do the right thing. More cynical folk would tell you the negro just likes being contrary, more hard-nosed analysts would tell you

while his literary gifts border on genius his powers of reason tend to fail him miserably when it comes to choosing ideologies and ideological partners. . . .

T'ain't his changes per se which have made Baraka so hard to take seriously as a political person, but the vociferousness with which he proclaims himself a true believer in one dogma only to just as vociferously vilify it when he's ready to move on to the next. So that we find the ultimate bohemian literati only publishing his white fellow travelers, the ultimate nationalist becoming a devout believer in black separatism, the ultimate Marxist gleefully declaring the death of black nationalism upon deliverance of his first pro-Marxist speech. Somehow the ultimate revisionist fails to mention the devout who got left in the lurch when he changed his line from get-whitey to workers of the world unite, the lefty version of "We Shall Overcome." Growing up in public again, only this time leaving a mess of young minds trapped and confused, and wiser colleagues doubtful about his commitment to the cause of black liberation. (Though if you talk to some of these citizens, they'll tell you how of late he's come back to black. And certainly the excellent essays he's been writing in *Black Nation* bear this out.)

Reentering the black nationalist period through the memoirs is like stepping into the twilight zone for real. When you consider what black folks' mass energy level was then and what it is now you feel like that era maybe never happened at all, like bebop and the Harlem Renaissance even were more recent and likely occurrences in African-American history. The fire that time, where'd it go, up in smoke? The din having died down from all those readings, riots, and rebellions, you could almost think black folk just packed up the circus one day and went home. . . . [When] you reconsider the procession of demagogues Baraka drags out from under the rug of history, Carmichael, Cleaver, Karenga, himself, and the trips they put us through, you relive the tension and intensity of a people caught in a crossfire between shamanism and hard struggle, outraged emotion and wasted energy, and wonder why in the hell did we go through all of that. Did it get us where we are today, Jesse dreaming on at the Democratic national convention, or Farrakhan running mindgames on Ted Koppel, or did it accomplish something more?

I know the answer is affirmative. These characters really did raise the consciousness of people a lot more naive, sincere, and committed than themselves. . . . Certainly they have something to do with the way my head turns when I see the fine sisters in the braids or dreads, check their ebony elegance (yeah, nationalism really turns me on), what I feel when I listen to Trane or wade through the crowd at Harlem day. . . .

Something to do with black art and style on one level and deeper still with a sense of community, culture, and love for self. And since Baraka helped precipitate a big part of that transformation in my consciousness, I can overlook some of his failings and end up respecting him. . . . See, you can take comrade Baraka to task, chump him for cuttin' the fool growing up in public; but can't nobody say he grew up to chump out on black people. Not unless, of course, you're a bookworm like me who thinks highbrow culture matters in the struggle too and wishes he'd finished what he started with **"The Screamers."** (p. 43)

*Greg Tate, "Growing Up in Public: Amiri Baraka Changes His Mind," in* The Village Voice, *Vol. XXIX, No. 40, October 2, 1984, pp. 41-3.*

# Saul Bellow

## 1915-

Canadian-born American novelist, short story writer, essayist, dramatist, editor, nonfiction writer, and translator.

One of the most celebrated and respected of contemporary writers, Bellow pursues the question of what it is to be fully human in an increasingly impersonal and mechanistic world. In humorous, philosophical fiction, Bellow depicts sensitive, introspective individuals who strive to understand their personal anxieties and aspirations. In a period when it has become common for writers to champion antiheroes, Bellow has been commended for creating deeply human characters with whom readers can identify. He has also been praised for his recreation of such urban environments as Chicago and New York and for showing how they can overwhelm the individual. Malcolm Bradbury lauds Bellow's work as "a moral, intellectual and metaphysical undertaking of great and classic power." Bellow has won three National Book Awards and a Pulitzer Prize in fiction. He was also awarded the 1976 Nobel Prize in literature.

Critics often concentrate on two aspects of Bellow's fiction: his skillfully crafted protagonists, who collectively exemplify the "Bellow hero," and his expansive prose style, through which Bellow literally talks his characters into existence. The typical Bellow hero, male and often Jewish, tries to find a personal balance while rebelling against the chaos of the modern world. The Bellow hero was described by the Nobel Committee as a man "who keeps trying to find a foothold during his wanderings in our tottering world, one who can never relinquish his faith that the value of life depends on its dignity, not its success." In developing his characters Bellow emphasizes dialogue and interior monologue; his prose style features a rich mixture of street slang and philosophical musings, sudden flashes of wit, and thought-provoking epigrams. As his protagonists speak to themselves and to others, the reader is drawn into their struggle with self and society. Irving Howe has claimed that Bellow evolved "the first major new style in American prose fiction since those of Hemingway and Faulkner."

Bellow developed two distinctive styles in his early works. Disciplined technique and realistic detail characterize his first two novels, *Dangling Man* (1944) and *The Victim* (1947). In *Dangling Man*, a young man named Joseph anticipates being drafted into the United States army. When his induction is delayed by bureaucratic snafus, Joseph tries to decide how to lead his life; when he is inducted, he is released from having to make the crucial choice that could define his future. *The Victim* focuses on Asa Leventhal, an established editor who is challenged by a series of encounters to face his repressed feelings. Critics praised Bellow's sensitive, naturalistic depiction of these tormented characters. Bellow's most successful work in his early formal style is the novella *Seize the Day* (1956). This work centers on Tommy Wilhelm, a middle-aged man who aspired to become rich and famous but has become a failure in business and in human relationships. Wilhelm gains a better understanding of himself and an appreciation for others during the course of this work by overcoming his fear

of mortality. This is a major theme throughout Bellow's fiction.

During the 1950s, Bellow developed a looser prose style that could accommodate comic misadventures and profound metaphysical musings. He began writing sweeping, picaresque novels that feature larger-than-life protagonists, and he employed various rhetorical elements to effect a livelier prose style. In *The Adventures of Augie March* (1953), for example, Augie, an extroverted, happy-go-lucky character, believes that "A man's character is his fate." Disregarding his brother's materialistic values, Augie undergoes a series of adventures through which he learns to channel his energy toward positive ends. After *Seize the Day,* in which he returned to his austere early style, Bellow wrote *Henderson the Rain King* (1959). Henderson, a huge man who is at once sensitive and brutal, suffers from a deep-rooted sense of anomie. He undertakes a journey through Africa, which some critics view as a journey into his subconscious, and learns to surrender his excessive egoism in order to experience love.

With *Herzog* (1964), Bellow successfully fused the formal realism of his early works with the exuberance of his large novels of the 1950s. Like the typical Bellow hero, Herzog is a suffering "joker" who has trouble maintaining human relationships, especially with woman. In response to his wife's infidelity,

Herzog retreats from what he views as the corrupting influence of the urban environment. Nevertheless, he continues to examine himself and to remain responsive to the world. Bellow explores various Western intellectual traditions in this work; he also introduces a series of poignant events and a host of colorful minor characters. *Herzog* gained for Bellow a large readership to match the respect he had previously garnered from critics.

Critical reception to Bellow's later works has varied. *Mr. Sammler's Planet* (1970) has been called his most pessimistic work due to the title character's melancholy presentiments on the passing of Western culture. Mr. Sammler, an old man who has experienced the promises and horrors of twentieth-century life, undertakes an extensive critique of modern values and speculates on the future. Critics expressed surprise over the somber tone of this novel and were divided as to whether Mr. Sammler succeeds as a wry commentator on contemporary life. *Humboldt's Gift* (1975) was more roundly praised. This novel centers on the conflict between materialistic values and the claims of art and high culture. The protagonist, Charles Citrine, is a writer who examines the role of the artist in contemporary American society. Citrine endures an exhaustive series of encounters with divorce lawyers, hoodlums, artists, and other representative figures of modern urban life. He also recalls his relationship with the flamboyant artist Von Humboldt Fleisher, a composite of several actual American writers who despaired in their attempts to reconcile their artistic ideals with the indifference and the materialistic values of American society. Citrine concludes that he can maintain artistic order by dealing with the enormous complexities of life through ironic, comic detachment. Many critics contend that Citrine's beliefs reflect those of Bellow himself and that Von Humboldt is modeled on the poet Delmore Schwartz, Bellow's close personal friend and a strong influence early in Bellow's career.

In *The Dean's December* (1982), Bellow undertakes a more direct attack against the negative social forces that challenge human dignity. Set in depressed areas of Chicago and Bucharest, Romania, this novel focuses on Albert Corde, a respected journalist who has recently returned to academic life in order to revive his love for high culture. In the course of the novel, Corde admonishes those who have failed to maintain humanistic values, including politicians, liberal intellectuals, journalists, and bureaucrats, in both democratic and communist nations. Critics often note the novel's many autobiographical elements and debate whether or not they are as skillfully employed as in Bellow's previous fiction. In the five stories collected in *Him with His Foot in His Mouth* (1984) Bellow depicts sensitive ordinary people and intellectuals who struggle to maintain personal dignity and to reaffirm humanistic qualities. These stories have helped reinforce Bellow's reputation as a thoughtful purveyor of the value of life.

(See also *CLC*, Vols. 1, 2, 3, 6, 8, 10, 13, 15, 25; *Contemporary Authors*, Vols. 5-8, rev. ed.; *Dictionary of Literary Biography*, Vols. 2, 28; *Dictionary of Literary Biography Yearbook: 1982*; and *Dictionary of Literary Biography Documentary Series*, Vol. 3.)

## MALCOLM BRADBURY

[Bellow's works] are intensely contemporary and are certainly firmly placed amid the directions, tendencies and epistemologies that have shaped and then been amended in the novel of today. Bellow is an intellectual writer, and his sense of

literary debts and derivations is serious and explicit: they are debts of great variousness. There is a clear debt to Emerson, Melville and the American Transcendentalists (Bellow refers to them often, either directly or by allusion, conspicuously, for example, in the ending of *Herzog*) and to the massed heritage of European Romanticism. There is another clear debt to Dreiser and the tradition of naturalism, deeply powerful in both its bleak and its optimistic forms in American fiction. Bellow often refers to this tradition, in both its ironizing and its vitalistic aspects (especially in *The Adventures of Augie March*), and has praised Dreiser, another Chicago novelist, for opening the American novel to the power of the unmediated, the open fact of American life, the commanding chaotic force of the American city. The debt also goes further, shaping Bellow's lasting struggle with the deterministic inheritance. His books show a deep sense of environmental intrusion, of the power of the conditioned, of life as competitive struggle chaotically releasing and suppressing energy. As a novelist he encounters an urban, mechanical, massed world—in which the self may be ironized, displaced or sapped by dominant processes and the laws of social placing, where victimization is real, and the assertion of self and the distillation of an act of will or a humanistic value is a lasting problem. Much of this naturalistic lore Bellow inherited from the 1930s, at the end of which he began to write. But what intersects with all this, and makes his work so convincing, is the deep penetration of his work by the classic stock of European modernism, especially that modernism in its more historically alert, post-romantic and humanistically defeated forms.

Bellow is thus a novelist of a very different generation from that of Lewis, Faulkner, Hemingway, Steinbeck or James T. Farrell, all of whom might in different ways be associated with the centralizing of the American novel as a major twentieth-century form of expression. He is a novelist writing beyond the end of American pastoral; his works belong to a new order of American and world history. (pp. 24-5)

Politically active in the Depression, he none the less started to write in the mood of abeyance to dialectical politics that came with the Second World War.... His earliest fictional publication thus immediately precedes the Japanese attack on Pearl Harbor which plunged America into the Second World War, collapsed the thirties political spectrum and allied Americans with the bleakness and bloodiness of modern world history. It was a history that disoriented the liberal progressive expectations of the American left, challenged naturalism as a language of political attention, and raised the question of art's response to a totalitarian and genocidal world. Bellow's response was to write about an America newly exposed to history, affected by the desperations of existentialism and absurdism, war-pained, urban, materialist, *Angst*-ridden, troubled with global responsibility, struggling to distil meaning and morality from the chaos of utopian and progressive thought.

All this was very apparent in *Dangling Man*, Bellow's first full-length novel, which appeared in 1944, as the war moved to an end—an extraordinary book which displays clear debts to a modern European writing of romantic disorientation and historical enclosure that comes from Dostoevsky, Conrad, Sartre and Camus. It is not hard to draw links between his and Dostoevsky's spiritually agonized heroes—caught in the fragmentations of a culture collapsing into urban strangeness, political disorder and waning faith which struggles with existential desire; nor between his world and Conrad's, where civilization is a thin veneer overlying anarchy, calling forth 'absurd' existential affirmations; nor between his imaginings and Kafka's, where the self moves solipsistically through an onerously powerful yet incomprehensible historical world. Yet it is as if this was a tradition which Bellow felt he had the power to qualify and amend, to recall toward humanism; and here his Jewish sources are deeply relevant, constituting another force that 'Europeanizes' his fiction.

Perhaps Isaac Bashevis Singer rather than Kafka—Bellow translated Singer's story 'Gimpel the Fool'—better suggests this origin, with his classic images of suffering and victimization irradiated with transcendental and mystical hopes; the recovering victim and the 'suffering joker' are part of the essential stuff of Bellow's writing, but so is that sense of human bonding which allows him to struggle toward a latter-day humanism and a new civility. Indeed it was that new civility, accommodating the experience of persecution and the path of survival, that made Bellow seem so central a figure in the postwar world, a world post-holocaust and post-atomic, urban and material, where progressive naturalism and innocent liberalism no longer spoke recognizably to experience.

Bellow thus went on to become a primary voice of a time when the Jewish-American writer, urban, historically alert, concerned to distil a morality and a possible humanism from a bland, material, encroaching reality in which all substantial meanings seemed hidden, moved to the centre of American writing. (pp. 25-7)

Bellow thus developed as a writer in a period when a distinct stylistic and aesthetic climate, which was also a political climate, was forming. It was a period of revived liberalism, invigorated by the reaction against totalitarianism that arose with the battle against and then the defeat of Nazism, and then with the new cold war struggle of the superpowers. The politics and aesthetics of liberalism were an important version of recovered pluralism and democracy; yet at the same time the post-war social order, with its materialism, its pressure toward conformity, its move toward mass society, threatened the liberal self. (p. 28)

It was the Jewish writers, with their sense of traditional alienation and exile, their profoundly relevant witness to the recent holocaust, their awareness of the inadequacies of an older liberalism that could not cope with what Reinhold Niebuhr called 'the ultimately religious problem of the evil in man', who concentrated the spirit of the necessary imagination. Lionel Trilling would call this 'the liberal imagination', whose natural centre lies in the novel, the testing place where the ideal is perpetually forced to mediate with the contingent and the real, where ideology meets 'the hum and buzz of culture', where history and individual are compelled into encounter.

Bellow's fiction, as it developed from the tight form of *Dangling Man* (1944) and *The Victim* (1947) into the looser and more picaresque structures of *The Adventures of Augie March* (1953) and *Henderson the Rain King* (1959), thus seemed to gesture toward a revival of the liberal novel—a form that has had a strained history in our modern and modernist century. . . . Bellow's novels have certainly moved toward the salvaging of a liberal form. They are hero-centred to a degree unusual in modern fiction; the hero often gives his name to the novel. He is always a man and often a Jew, and often a writer or intellectual; he is anxious about 'self', concerned with exploring its inward claim, and about 'mind', which may be our salvation or the real source of our suffering. At the same time he is driven by an irritable desire to recognize his relation with oth-

ers, with society as such, with the felt texture of common existence, with nature and the universe. Around such battles certain prime reminders occur: man is mortal, and death must be weighed; man is biologically in process, part of nature, and must find his measure in it; man is consciousness, and consciousness is indeed in history; man is real, but so is the world in its historical evolution, and the two substantialities evade understandable relation. So we are drawn toward thoughts of extreme alienation, urgent romantic selfhood, apocalyptic awareness, while at the same time we know ourselves to be in a post-romantic universe, Lenin's age of wars and revolutions, where our conditioning is inescapable. Social and historical existence may thus contend with mythical or metaphysical existence, but neither can finally outweigh the other, and the effort must be toward reconciliation—an end displayed in Bellow's own fictional endings, which frequently take the form of some complex contractual renewal between the self and the world, though, despite critical suspicion of them, these endings are less some rhetorical resolution than a suspended anxiety, often returned to in the next novel. (pp. 28-30)

As for the balance and nature of Bellow's work, that too changed. In the 1950s he had explored the expansive epic, testing out whether man can set himself free in history. By the 1960s that enquiry had tightened again, into the complex structural form of *Herzog* (1964), where historical presence becomes a form of madness, and the bleak irony of *Mr Sammler's Planet* (1970), which now looks less a bitter assault on the new radicalism than the beginning of a new kind of enquiry into the elements of evil secreted in our modern history, and in modern America, in an age marked by postcultural energy, a new rootless barbarism in which possibility and monstrosity contend for the soul. Bellow's books have grown not easier but harder to read. They have become in some ways more meditative, philosophical, transcendental. (pp. 31-2)

Bellow is not, in the fashionable sense of the term, a 'postmodern' or even an 'experimental' novelist. He does not question reflexively his own fictionality, or adopt the nihilist stoicism of black humour. His books still grant the dominant materiality of the outer world, which is process, system and power; and they continue to explore consciousness and mind in struggle with that power, as they hunt to find a significant human meaning, an inward presence and a sense of personal immediacy, and an outward awareness of the nature of the cosmic world. Consciousness and history still struggle at odds, but in an ever-compelled and ever-changing intimacy. His books have, indeed, largely changed by circling their own known subjects, intensifying the elements, deepening the enquiry. Bellow's perception of the nature, the substance and the pressure of the historical world has moved increasingly toward a definition of a new, post-cultural America, most clearly manifest in his own home city of Chicago, that 'cultureless city pervaded nonetheless by Mind', as its life has changed, accumulated and massed; as its old localities and ways of life fall under the hands of the new developers, as crime and terror haunt its inner city and the *inner* inner city of its inhabitants, as the doors are triple-locked and bourgeois life goes on under siege in some strange modern compact with a new barbarism, it becomes a central image of what the mind and the novel alike must come to terms with. His perception of the world of consciousness has also grown more intense and avid for right feeling, as it finds itself bereft yet busy, having nowhere else but history from which to draw versions of reality in its endless quest for awareness and fulfilment.

A novelist who registers the enormous pressure of modern life, and also the peculiar sense of existence, on a scale rare in fiction, Bellow has thus reacted with a considerable formal flexibility and variousness. Coming into being over four transforming decades of American life, his books have registered them with a vital historical *and* aesthetic attention, taking the novel form as *the* necessary mode of mediation between the world of process and the world of consciousness. A critic of apocalyptics, Bellow has grown more apocalyptic; a doubter of concepts, he has grown more conceptual and abstract, though searching always for those moments of immediacy and humanity when the soul feels its presence and its need to value existence. A voice of moral liberalism, he has grown more conservative, in a large sense, become a writer who explores the contrast between a culturally coherent past and a post-cultural present. A novelist who defends the novel's humanism, he has shown us, more than most novelists, the powers that point toward a post-humanist world, and hence challenge the novel's capacities to explore it. His books, especially his most recent, portraits of writers making the crucial attempt, show both the challenge and the indeterminacy of the solutions; in a sense, it is their indeterminacy that makes every new Bellow novel possible. Bellow not only has been, but remains, one of the most essential American writers of his age. . . . (pp. 32-4)

Bellow remains one of our most serious novelists, and our most commanding, because he is a great modern novelist of the attempt to reconcile mind, in all its resource and confusion, its fantastic fertility and unending anguish, with a life that is itself absurd, extravagant, pressing us not only with material forces but with ideas and forms of consciousness, information and concepts, boredoms and rewards. It is a world where the measure of man can hardly be taken, the right form of expression or idea never be found; but where our mind as a sense of felt existence insists that we take it. The resulting perception is indeed comedy in its seriousness: which is an observation of disparity, an awareness that we are, indeed, 'suffering jokers', vital but absurd, and of a secret freedom, lying in our gift to know. History, environment, concept and the reality-instructors tell us much, and much of it makes us despair; but against that there is a self-presence, vivid and curious, and of it Bellow is surely one of the great modern metaphysical comedians. (pp. 103-04)

> *Malcolm Bradbury, in his* Saul Bellow, Methuen, *1982, 110 p.*

ANATOLE BROYARD

In "Cousins," the last of the five stories in ["**Him With His Foot in His Mouth and Other Stories**"], a man's former wife says: "You have an exuberance that you keep to yourself. You have a crazy high energy absolutely peculiar to you. Because of this high charge you can defy the plain dirty facts that other people have to suffer through, whether they like it or not. What you are is an exuberance-hoarder."

This passage comes nine pages from the end of **Him With His Foot in His Mouth and Other Stories,** and it was not until I read it that I understood what had been troubling me. It seems to me that Saul Bellow himself is an exuberance-hoarder and that, in this book at least, his crazy high energy is so very peculiar to him that it is only imperfectly communicated to the reader.

Another character, also in "Cousins," says, "I'd have more confidence in Scholem if he weren't so statuesque." Too many

of the characters in this book strike me as statuesque—especially Victor Wulpy, the famous art critic and ideologue of "**What Kind of Day Did You Have?**" Still another character in "Cousins" is described as "crowded with masses of feeling for which there was no language." With all the elaborateness of Mr. Bellow's language, I still found most of his characters inchoate, unarticulated, trapped in their mysterious and frustrating exuberance. . . .

Mr. Bellow is in a perorating mood, full of summations, retrospectives, revisitings. The dizzying family connections in "**Cousins**" is not much more appealing than an anthropologist's study of kinship systems. The protagonist in this story seems driven back on his family by nothing better than his own alienation. The reader feels like a stranger at an immense family reunion, where everyone is talking at once in almost indecipherable accents.

In his earlier collection of stories, "**Mosby's Memoirs,**" Mr. Bellow was at his best and his most lyrical. His ideas were full of barely repressed affection and amusement. But the mood in these mortality haunted later stories reminds me of a man who is angry at the thought of dying in an unsatisfactory landscape.

To my mind, these characters suffer from a lack of palpable wanting. They seem so much after the fact, past the moment of climax, like so many bitter footnotes or appendixes. Mr. Bellow is obsessed with power here: the power, or lack of it, of intellectuals and the power of those who live on the fringe of the law. For Mr. Bellow, this fringe resembles the old idea of the American frontier, as if we have moved from geographical to legal boundaries. Mr. Bellow's intelligence appears to have grown exasperated with everything about people but their fates. Epistemology and eschatology seem to have shouldered out love, hate and the ordinary business of living. . . .

Mr. Bellow seems to resent [the] need to paddle in the ordinary. Disdaining plot or character development, he appears to be out of patience with fiction, with its necessary foolishness. His protagonists keep examining the people around them, but without real concern or curiosity. They are mere flaneurs of the human condition.

> *Anatole Broyard, in a review of "Him with His Foot in His Mouth and Other Stories," in* The New York Times, *May 11, 1984, p. C27.*

CYNTHIA OZICK

A concordance, a reprise, a summary, all the old themes and obsessions hauled up by a single tough rope—does there come a time when, out of the blue, a writer offers to decode himself? . . .

[For Saul Bellow] the moment for decoding is now, and the decoding itself turns up unexpectedly in the shape of a volume of five stories ["**Him with His Foot in His Mouth**"], awesome yet imperfect, at least one of them overtly a fragment, and none malleable enough to achieve a real "ending." Not that these high-pressure stories are inconclusive. With all their brilliant wiliness of predicament and brainy language shocked into originality, they are magisterially the opposite. They tell us, in the clarified tight compass Bellow has not been so at home in since "**Seize the Day,**" what drives Bellow. (p. 1)

When "**The Dean's December**" was published in 1982, it was not so much reviewed as scrutinized like sacred entrails: Had this idiosyncratically independent writer turned "conservative"? Had he soured on Augiesque America? . . . In short, it seemed impossible to rid Bellow's novel of Bellow's presence, to free it as fiction.

In consequence of which, one is obliged to put a riddle: If you found **"Him with His Foot in His Mouth and Other Stories"** at the foot of your bed one morning, with the title page torn away and the author's name concealed, would you know it, after all, to be Bellow? . . .

Yes, absolutely; a thousand times yes. It is Bellow's Chicago, Bellow's portraiture—these faces, these heads!—above all, Bellow's motor. That he himself may acknowledge a handful of biographical sources—"germs," textured shells—does not excite. The life on the page resists the dust of flesh, and is indifferent to external origins. Victor Wulpy is who he is as Bellow's invention; and certainly Zetland is. These inventions take us not to Bellow as man, eminence, and friend of eminences (why should I care whom Bellow knows?), but to the private clamor in the writing. And it is this clamor, this sound of a thrashing soul—comic because metaphysical, metaphysical because aware of itself as a farcical combatant on a busy planet—that is unequivocally distinguishable as the pure Bellovian note. . . .

**"What Kind of Day Did You Have?,"** the novella that is the centerpiece of this volume, also its masterpiece, gives us a day in the life of "one of the intellectual captains of the modern world"—Victor Wulpy, who, if love is sublime and lovers foolish, qualifies as a reacher both high and absurd. . . .

What emerges . . . is a mind at the pitch of majesty. The agitated, untamable, yet flagging figure of the dying Victor Wulpy, a giant in the last days of his greatness, seizes us not so much for the skein of shrewd sympathy and small pathos in which he is bound and exposed, as for the claims of these furious moments of insatiable connection: "Katrina had tried to keep track of the subjects covered between Seventy-Sixth Street and Washington Square: the politics of modern Germany from the Holy Roman Empire through the Molotov-Ribbentrop Pact; what surrealist communism had *really* been about; Kiesler's architecture; Hans Hofmann's influence; what limits were set by liberal democracy for the development of the arts. . . . Various views on the crises in economics, cold war, metaphysics, sexaphysics."

Not that particular "subjects" appear fundamentally to matter to Bellow, though they thrillingly engage him. . . .

It is the hound of heaven living in the bony box of intelligence that dogs Bellow, and has always dogged him. If the soul is the mind at its purest, best, clearest, busiest, profoundest, then Bellow's charge has been to restore the soul to American literature.

The five stories in **"Him with His Foot in His Mouth"** are the distillation of that charge. Their method is to leave nothing unobserved and unremarked, to give way to the unprogrammed pressure of language and intellect, never to retreat while imagination goes off like kites. (p. 44)

A light flavoring of Jewish social history dusts through it all: Victor Wulpy reading the Pentateuch in Hebrew in a cheder on the Lower East Side in 1912; or Zetland's immigrant father, who, in a Chicago neighborhood "largely Polish and Ukrainian, Swedish, Catholic, Orthodox, and Evangelical Lutheran," "preferred the company of musical people and artists, bohemian garment workers, Tolstoyans, followers of Emma

Goldman and of Isadora Duncan, revolutionaries who wore pince-nez, Russian blouses, Lenin or Trotsky beards."

What this profane and holy comedy of dazzling, beating, multiform profusion hints at, paradoxically, is that Bellow is as notable for what isn't in his pages as for what is. No preciousness, of the ventriloquist kind or any other; no carelessness either (formidably the opposite); no romantic aping of archaisms or nostalgias; no restraints born out of theories of form or faddish tenets of experimentalism or ideological crypticness; no Neanderthal flatness in the name of cleanliness of prose; no gods of nihilism; no gods of subjectivity; no philosophy of parody. As a consequence of these and other salubrious omissions and insouciant dismissals, Bellow's detractors have accused him of being "old-fashioned," "conventional," of continuing to write a last-gasp American version of the 19-century European novel; his omnivorous "Russianness" is held against him, and at the same time he is suspected of expressing the deadly middle class.

The grain of truth in these disparagements takes note, I think, not of regression or lagging behind, but of the condition of local fiction, which has more and more closeted itself monkishly away in worship of its own liturgies—of its own literariness. Whereas Bellow, seeing American writing in isolation from America itself, remembered Whitman and Whitman's cornucopia, in homage to which he fabricated a new American sentence. All this, of course, has been copiously remarked ever since Augie March; but these five stories say something else. What Bellow is up to here is nothing short of a reprise of Western intellectual civilization. (pp. 44-5)

But even this is not the decoding or revelation I spoke of earlier. It has not been enough for Bellow simply to have restored attention to society—the density and entanglements of its urban textures, as in **"A Silver Dish."** . . .

[To] thickness of community and . . . passions of mind Bellow has added a distinctive ingredient, not new on any landscape, but shamelessly daring just now in American imaginative prose. . . . Bellow, it seems, has risked mentioning—who can admit to this without literary embarrassment?—the Eye of God.

And that is perhaps what his intellectual fevers have always pointed to. **"Cousins"** speaks of it explicitly: "As a man is, so he sees. As the Eye is formed, such are its powers." Yet **"Cousins"** is overtly about "the observation of cousins," and moves from cousin Tanky of the rackets to cousin Seckel whose "talent was for picking up strange languages" to cousin Motty, who, "approaching ninety, still latched on to people to tell them funny things." All this reflects a powerfully recognizable Jewish family feeling—call it, in fact, family love, though it is love typically mixed with amazement and disorder.

The professor-narrator of **"Him with His Foot in His Mouth"**— the title story—like cousin Motty is also a funny fellow, the author of a long letter conscientiously recording his compulsion to make jokes that humiliate and destroy, put-downs recollected in tranquillity. But the inescapable drive to insult through wit is equated with "seizure, rapture, demonic possession, frenzy, *Fatum*, divine madness, or even solar storm," so this lambent set of comic needlings is somehow more than a joke, and may touch on the Eye of Dionysus. . . .

The commanding image of this volume—the concordance, so to speak, to Bellow's work—turns up in the reflections of one of the cousins, Ijah Brodsky: " 'To long for the best that ever was': this was not an abstract project. I did not learn it over a seminar table. It was a constitutional necessity, physiological, temperamental, based on sympathies which could not be acquired. Human absorption in faces, deeds, bodies, drew me toward metaphysical grounds. I had these peculiar metaphysics as flying creatures have their radar.''

This metaphysical radar (suspiciously akin to the Eye of God) ''decodes'' Saul Bellow; and these five ravishing stories honor and augment his genius. (p. 45)

> *Cynthia Ozick, ''Farcical Combat in a Busy World,''*
> *in* The New York Times Book Review, *May 20,*
> *1984, pp. 1, 44-5.*

## OLIVER CONANT

No other writer has dramatized what used to be called the life of the mind with Saul Bellow's confidence and wit. Some of his creations—Asa Leventhal, Augie March, Moses Herzog, the redoubtable Mr. Sammler—have an exemplary stature that we associate with characters in the great 19th-century novels. In one work after another, Bellow has demonstrated a high degree of imaginative generosity, of sympathy. And he can move, has moved, from high anthroposophical realms of speculation to realistic action and suffering.

With important exceptions, there also is much to be grateful for in [*Him With His Foot in His Mouth*]. It is not as powerful as *Mosby's Memoirs*. But the yeasty brew of Bellow's language; the ease, boldness, *sprezzatura* of his imagination; his pageant, or rather carnival of ideas; his fine, satiric insight into the deficiencies as well as his cherishing of the valuable in American life—all are here. A gangster's face resembles ''an edema of deadly secrets.'' An evangelical home is ''full of Bibles and pictures of Jesus and the Holy Land and that faint Gentile odor, as if things had been rinsed in a weak vinegar solution.'' . . .

Our foremost chronicler of 1930s immigrant Chicago further remains as acute as ever on the incongruities of period and place: The black coal-heaver wears a woman's fur coat against the cold, the ''fur collar spikey with the wet and sprinkled with soot.'' At the little Division Street Savings Bank that became a fish store after the '29 crash, ''a tank for live carp was made of the bank marble.'' The dialogue similarly reproduces the variety and exactitude of colloquial speech amid Bellow's own inimitable idiolect. Thus the stories are linguistically and in other ways meaty, even where one disagrees with their arguments—a far cry from the desiccated avant-gardism or the deliberate ordinariness and minimalism of too much of today's fiction.

The collection is uneven, however. In the title piece and in a story called **''What Kind of Day Did You Have?''** the author's long-standing ambivalence toward intellectuals often turns nasty. Such phrases as ''neurotic, gutless, conniving intellectual types'' are a little too frequent for my taste.

To be sure, Bellow's feelings about intellectuals are complicated (he *is* one, after all), have many sources and are honorably come by. . . .

Bellow's quarrel with intellectuals has in the past inspired some of his best work, including his second and perhaps finest novel, *The Victim. Herzog* and *Mr. Sammler's Planet* extend the argument, taking on fashionable irrationalism and theorists of ''alienation.'' In the present volume, though, his annoyance expends itself in bumptiousness.

As the prevalence of neoconservative politics and deconstructionist criticism suggests, the times hardly lack high-flown tendencies inimical to the creative enterprise. But these are not the author's targets; he flails about, observing the operation of *ressentiment*, greed and arrogance among academics and intellectuals with a cruel unsparingness and (to my mind) a distressing lack of purpose. Most disappointing of all, his admirable figures, born of past noble battles, have been replaced by Shawmutt and Wulpy, characters out of some kind of burlesque. (p. 16)

Invariably protean, Bellow sounds a new note . . . of persistent nostalgia, of regret for vanished folkways. In **''Zetland: By A Character Witness,''** the protagonist, a young prodigy, exhibits cultural ambitions and a range of adolescent reading which, we are given to understand, have vanished. ''Books in Chicago were obtainable,'' remarks the narrator, and the pensiveness of the statement makes one almost believe that they no longer are.

Nearly all of the stories in *Him With His Foot in His Mouth* are set in the past, or return to the past. When this feeds the author's intelligent cultural pessimism it is extremely valuable; it is much less so when the result is merely gloom and intensified ambivalence about intellectual success. (p. 17)

> *Oliver Conant, ''Burlesquing Intellectuals,'' in* The
> New Leader, *Vol. LXVII, No. 11, June 11, 1984,*
> *pp. 16-17.*

## ROBERT ALTER

Admirers of Saul Bellow will find this new collection of stories an assortment of delights. For readers less acquainted with Bellow, as well as for those who have been wondering what all the fuss is about, *Him with His Foot in His Mouth* offers a vivid introduction to the distinctive allure of his fictional world.

Bellow is essentially a novelist rather than a short-story writer because he is drawn to large panoramic views of contemporary life. . . . But where most contemporary American novels (examples from Updike, Malamud, and Roth come readily to mind) collapse disastrously along their obvious fault-lines, Bellow's books have shown a remarkable ability to survive, splendidly, their own flaws. Conversely, the new stories read more like brilliant fragments than like well-made wholes with discernible form and neat closure; nonetheless, the series of vignettes repeatedly illustrates within small compass what it is about Bellow's writing in general that provides deep imaginative pleasure from sentence to sentence and perception to perception.

There is a special quality of zest in virtually everything Bellow has written from *Augie March* onward—even, I would say, in his darker, more mordant books—and this derives above all from his untiring interest in and affection for the varieties of human character. Perhaps this curiosity about character is what has seemed most ''old-fashioned'' in Bellow's novels to the proponents of more avant-garde fiction. At a time when character in the novel so often becomes the facelessness of figures in an apocalyptic landscape, or the transparent manipulation of an ideological argument, or an epiphenomenon of sexual organs, it is unusual to find an American novelist still absorbed in the quirkiness, the stubborn and often wacky self-assertions of individual character. (pp. 33-4)

To bring to the light, through an act of inventive empathy, the secret ideas and dreams of variegated humanity is precisely a major task of the traditional novelist. The special Bellow emphasis is the attraction to mantic vision, crazy intensities. He loves human excess, extravagance, flamboyance, the looniness of adherence to self-consistency at all costs. . . . The gamut of extravagant types in the new volume runs from (Jewish) mafiosi, con men, ne'er-do-well spongers, and cab-driving metaphysicians, to fugitive musicologists (the narrator of the title story), septuagenarian art critics (the main figure of **"What Kind of Day Did You Have?"** obviously based on Harold Rosenberg), and philosophers-turned-bohemians (the hero of **"Zetland,"** an homage to Bellow's friend Isaac Rosenfeld). (pp. 34-5)

It may begin to sound as though Bellow's fiction were a neo-Dickensian gallery of comic grotesques. What makes the modern difference is the sense his protagonists have, alternatively brooding, bemused, perplexed, of the unfathomable nature of an individual life amidst this bewildering variety of characters, which is to say, this bewildering variety of modes of being, existential routes traversed. Toward the end of *The Dean's December,* we are told that the Dean "was only now discovering how many important things he had neglected to think about." It is a discovery that is made by one Bellow protagonist after another; and, at least for this reader, it remains an abidingly salutary discovery because Bellow is able, through the different destinies of his various heroes, to imagine this difficult business of moral growth freshly, as a revelation that dawns on them from the particular circumstances of their lives. Bellow, as has often been observed, is a writer who delights in the sounds and smells and colors of urban reality and in the colloquial language and anecdotal styles associated with that reality. He is also, however, a writer who repeatedly raises questions about what we are and why we are here, and his ability to combine racy realism with philosophic reflection is one of his greatest strengths. (p. 35)

Bellow is a philosophic writer in two, complementary senses. The more obvious one is the intense intellectuality of so many of his characters, who in dialogue and monologue wrestle with Schopenhauer and Nietzsche and Freud and Whitehead on everything from the constitution of the psyche and the nature of historical process to cognition and being. What gives much of this talk resonance is something I would describe as a trapdoor effect in Bellow's depiction of reality. The eye adheres patiently, lovingly, to the grainy, vivid surfaces of the material world, but things have an uncanny way of opening up to surprising vistas below or behind them. Thus, a familiar everyday experience like the ascent of a passenger plane to the brightness above the clouds becomes a leap into "the lucid sunlight coming through infinite space"—at once a lyric moment and an intimation for the character of another realm of being. The trapdoor may open up, as we have seen, into the reaches of zoology or geography or space, or, perhaps most poignantly, into the visionary depths of personal memory. (p. 36)

The sense of energies and the image of things whirling—that "palpitating universe"—are at the heart of Bellow's fiction. The tense balance of opposing perspectives here should be noted. Despite the colloidal eyes and the bony box of the brain, Bellow is not the sort of literary metaphysician T. S. Eliot detected in John Webster, who "saw the skull beneath the skin," for he also sees a gorgeous world streaming with radiant colors. The seeing, moreover, is rarely an isolated act of observation in his books. It is undertaken within an entangling web of relations and feelings, in the midst of all those human messages given and received. One takes in the bright world through the translucence of the eye but also, necessarily, with the cloudy heart. Throughout his career as a novelist, Bellow has been enchanted by the play of movement in the circumambient world and at the same time a patient student of the shifting inner cloud patterns that obfuscate vision, distort it, and perhaps sometimes simply shape it. His success in holding both views together, embracing the whirl of the world and the uncertainties of the heart, makes him one of the few living novelists whose work often evinces the imaginative authority to address our lives. (pp. 36-7)

*Robert Alter, "Mr. Bellow's Planet," in* The New Republic, *Vol. 190, No. 23, June 11, 1984, pp. 33-7.*

## MARTIN AMIS

Saul Bellow's last novel, **'The Dean's December,'** promised the arrival of a fresh inspiration in his work, and this stirring collection of stories [**'Him with His Foot in His Mouth'**] confirms that it is here to stay. Without tempting providence too much, I think we can call the new phase Late Bellow. It has to do with last things, leavetaking, and final lucidities.

Late Bellow expresses itself through the familiar opposition: a rich, generously comic and fanatically detailed record of the human experience and habitat, set against a wayward dreaminess or mooniness, an intoxicated receptivity to ideas—Bellow's own poetry of meditation. None of these delights is withheld, but there are now two changes of emphasis. First, a more formal artistry, with sharper focus, a keener sense of shape and balance. And secondly a countervailing ferocity in his apprehension of the peculiar disorders and distortions of the modern era. 'I don't know what the world's coming to' may not sound like much of a topic-sentence when you hear it at the bus-stop—yet this is Bellow's subject. Actually it is the central subject, and always has been. . . .

These are stories about Chicago (new and old), and about families. They shore up one's impression that Bellow's greatness has always been endorsed by two lucky accidents—and this is to belittle neither the strenuousness of his discipline nor the luck of literary talent itself. First, Chicago. When Chicagoans call their hometown 'the city that works' they have more in mind than efficiency and high employment, bustle and brawn. They mean that they have accepted money as the only 'vital substance'; and they regard the ubiquitous corruption that results from this as the definition of realistic maturity: 'If you're so smart, how come you ain't rich?' Such distortions, which include an aggressive, even a disgusted philistinism, provide the writer with a wonderfully graphic reversal of human values. . . .

Bellow's second slice of congenital good fortune lies in his Jewishness, which, along with much else, provides him with an unusual tenderness for the human ties of race and blood. . . . In [one] story Bellow's narrator asks why the Jews have always been such energetic anthropologists, virtually the founders of the science (Durkheim, Lévy-Bruhl, Mauss, Boas, *et al*). Was it that they were 'demystifiers,' their ultimate aim to 'increase universalism'? The narrator demurs. 'A truer explanation is the nearness of the ghettos to the sphere of Revelation, an easy move for the mind from rotting streets and rancid dishes, a direct ascent into transcendence.'

This describes Bellow's origins as a writer, and perhaps accounts also for the strong vein of (heterodox) transcendentalism in his work. In the middle-period novels the transcendental 'alternative' takes on structural status, affording a radiant backdrop against which the protagonists shuffle and blunder. The primitive princeliness of Africa in **'Henderson the Rain King,'** the Wellsian dreams of lunar escape in **'Mr Sammler's Planet,'** the 'invisible sciences' of **'Humboldt's Gift'**: these are respectively ranged against the nullity of New England, the hysteria of New York, and the gangsterism—both emotional and actual—of bleak Chicago.

The emphasis on these illusory otherworlds was probably too heavy, laying Bellow open to charges of crankery and self-indulgence. In Late Bellow, however, the transcendentalism has found its true function, which is Yeatsian—a source of metaphor, a system of imagery that gives the reader an enduring mortal pang, a sense of his situation in larger orders of time and space. . . . Bellow has made the real world realer (sharper, harsher), and has confronted its perversities; but human destiny still 'depends on what you think, feel and will about such manifestations or apparitions, on the kabbalistic skill you develop in the interpretation of these contemporary formations.' He keeps a soul's watch upon the world, as passionate as ever and yet disinterested now, with no stake in the outcome.

There aren't any weaklings in the new book: each story has the same consistency of brilliance and vigour. . . . In the title story an old man languishes in British Columbia, facing extradition to Chicago, a fall-guy for various financial crimes committed by his family. *His* only sin has been his spontaneity, whereas the sins of his adversaries were always shrewdly premeditated. . . . Up in Canada, the only company is the landlady, a mad widow who babbles of the Divine Spirit. No one wants to hear all this, but the old boy finds that he is more than ready to listen:

> The Divine Spirit, she tells me, has withdrawn in our time from the outer, visible world. You can see what it once wrought, you are surrounded by its created forms. But although natural processes continue, Divinity has absented itself. The wrought work is brightly divine but Divinity is not now active within it. The world's grandeur is fading. And this is our human setting. . . .

Of course, the myth of decline—the elegiac vision, which insists that all the good has gone and only the worst remains—has never looked less like a myth and more like a reality. But perhaps the world always looks that way, especially when you start your preparations for leaving it. At the height of his earthly powers, Bellow makes generous reparations to the credit side of the ledger, helping 'to bring back the light that has gone from these molded likenesses.'

> *Martin Amis, "Saul's December," in* The Observer, *June 24, 1984, p. 20.*

### GEORGE SIM JOHNSTON

Since his last collection of stories appeared in 1968, Saul Bellow, like his most famous creation, Moses Herzog, has felt the need to explain, to have it out, to put into perspective. *Mr. Sammler's Planet* and *The Dean's December* gave the impression that their author had written a hundred or so jeremiads for the *New York Times* op-ed page and decided instead to slice them up and serve with fictional filler. Not since H. G. Wells

wrote *Mr. Brittling Sees It Through* has such a plague of unsolicited opinion ravaged the work of a first-rate novelist. *Humboldt's Gift* was several cuts above its two neighbors; the characters at least seemed to exist for reasons other than sounding off; and although the narrator, Charles Citrine, does manage to get in his two bits at every opportunity, he is not, like Sammler and Dean Corde, looking down from a crow's nest halfway to heaven. Not that I mind Bellow's ideas or the way he puts them. If you lifted all of the digressions since *Herzog* and pasted them in a book, you would have a chrestomathy of superb journalism. Bellow is one of the best intellectual break dancers around. (p. 37)

So far as the fiction goes, the long short story **"The Old System,"** which appeared in *Mosby's Memoirs and Other Stories,* is, for my money, his best work since *Herzog.* A perceptive study of the assimilation of Old World immigrants into America, it covers more ground in forty pages than most novels. It is also the only fiction Bellow has written since *Seize the Day* in which not a single world-class intellectual or school of philosophy is mentioned. Not one! Bellow has a weakness for the virtuosic manipulation of brand-name intellectuals. You can't go for more than a dozen pages in his later work without running into Hegel or Freud or Sartre or Merleau-Ponty or André Breton. Sometimes they appear in job lots on a single page. I don't think his fiction would suffer much if he had excised every one. . . . Bellow has a slangy way with high-brow thought which is charming (". . . nihilism, too, has its no-no's"). But all this intellection seldom fuses with the fiction proper. There have been novelists obsessed with intellectual categories—Stendhal and Mann, for example—who nonetheless have managed to keep the name-dropping to a minimum and get on with the story.

When Bellow does get on with the story, he shows a canny sense of his strengths and weaknesses. He is not a dramatic writer, which he made abundantly clear in his full-length play *The Last Analysis,* and steers clear of the sort of immediate scene setting one finds, say, in James and Waugh. His method is the flashback, the monologue, the character sketch; his narrators are often alone in a room (or lying in a hammock in an overgrown garden) recalling the past. This filter of sensibility allows him to avoid the problem, as Mailer once put it, of getting his characters out of a room; the narrative intelligence can jump wherever it pleases. Bellow once said that Gide's work is full of excellent monologuists who want to advance to dialogue, which is exactly his own case.

All these characteristics make the short story or novella, and not the novel, Bellow's natural form. With the exception of *The Victim,* which he later referred to as "small and correct," an exercise in restraint before he let it rip in *The Adventures of Augie March,* Bellow's full-length novels could all be chopped up into smaller pieces without losing anything essential. . . . Reading the wonderful collection of new stories in *Him with His Foot in His Mouth,* one is thankful that Bellow chose not to bury the odd assortment of intellectuals, Chicago mobsters, and night school existentialist tile contractors who appear in them in another long, amorphous novel. Each is more entertaining and instructive for being on his own fictional patch. (pp. 37-8)

Back in 1949, Bellow wrote a story for the *Partisan Review* called **"A Sermon by Doctor Pep,"** which could serve as a subtitle to much of his work. Bellow has been an eloquent dissenter from the Wasteland mentality which he once called "the Established Church in modern literature." A somber note runs through this new collection of stories, however. "The humanistic music has ceased, and now there is a different barbarous music welling up,'' says one of the characters. It is not an observation Augie March or Moses Herzog would have made. Whether this late pessimism is justified or not, it does not have the designer label affixed to the *angst* of most of our "serious" novelists. Among the pleasures of reading Bellow is the impression that one is dealing with a mature and powerful mind which makes its own markets on the intellectual exchange. (p. 38)

> *George Sim Johnston, in a review of "Him with His Foot in His Mouth and Other Stories," in* The American Spectator, *Vol. 17, No. 11, November, 1984, pp. 37-8.*

# Frank Bidart

## 19??-

**American poet.**

**Bidart is a leading figure in the generation of American poets that emerged during the 1970s and 1980s. He writes confessional poetry noted for its distinctive prosody; his unusual verse approximates, both visually and orally, American speech patterns. Bidart explains that his style evolved from his efforts to figure out "how to write down, how to 'fasten to the page' the voice—and the movements of the voice—in my head." To accomplish this purpose, Bidart uses unevenly spaced indentations and lines, italics, unconventional capitalization, and other stylistic devices.**

**Bidart's poetry is essentially autobiographical, and several critics suggest that it demonstrates his obsession with guilt. In *Golden State* (1973), Bidart relives his past and strives to overcome the guilt engendered by his parents. Erotic desires are the focus of *The Book of the Body* (1977); guilt in this volume stems from the conflict between the physical and the mental. Bidart's protagonists in the several parts of *The Sacrifice* (1983) struggle with guilt and feel the need to sacrifice in order to expiate their sins.**

**Bidart's poetry takes many forms. Perhaps his most disquieting poems are the dramatic monologues in which Bidart speaks through various personae: a young girl suffering from anorexia exposes her inner feelings in "Ellen West," a child-murderer and necrophiliac confesses in the shocking "Herbert White," and the factually based protagonist of "The War of Vaslav Nijinsky" equates personal guilt with responsibility for the tragedy of World War I.**

© *Kelly Wise*

## JONATHAN GALASSI

Frank Bidart's *Golden State* is "naked poetry", revolutionary in comparison with the work of [such writers as Peter Porter, Charles Tomlinson, Seamus Heaney, and Robert Graves]. Like most of them, Bidart is concerned with the past, but he approaches it through an examination of the making of the individual personality. In a bare-boned diction which mimics the cadence and intonation of talk with the help of precisely maneuvered punctuation and spacing, he dissects his family history, attempting "to see myself / as a piece of history, having a past / which shapes, and informs, and thus inevitably / limits". *Golden State* acts out, in a certain sense, the process of analysis. Bidart's attitudes develop organically through the poems from a rigid, desperate faith in psychotherapy and the power of "experience" to "inform . . . life" to an acknowledgement of the "surprising; unknowable; unpossessable" nature of the past. (pp. 118-19)

I can't call Bidart's method experimental; it's too accomplished and too successful for that. But these obsessive meditations on the uses of the past, articulated in the simple speech in which we talk to ourselves, go beyond "the lies / of mere, neat poetry". The allusive thematic unity of *Golden State* and its exciting, dangerous independence from the distancing conventions of most poetry make it one of the most rewarding first books to appear in a long time. (p. 119)

Jonathan Galassi, "Dealing with Tradition," in Poetry, Vol. CXXIII, No. 2, November, 1973, pp. 113-19.*

## RICHARD HOWARD

A young man, a young poet, cannot discover the true goals of his endeavor without discarding the false ones. The wrong turns, the missing links and mistaken signals are no more than evidence of what may be right, given, understood. Over this book [*Golden State*] is suspended, like a ceiling of swords, the threat and indeed the doom of the negative. In his prosody, as in his convulsive pursuit of a voice which will, accountably, speak in the first person singular—and of course the achieved value here is that the prosody is not apart from but is a part of the pursuit, it *is* the pursuit at its incandescent brimstone pitch—Frank Bidart is as evasive as he is venturesome. "Don't turn into the lies / of mere, neat poetry . . ." he implores his father *in his own poetry,* and he will be at pains to keep the utterance from being *mere,* from becoming neat. Everywhere is the effort to vary the cadence, to elude that kind of recuperation of energy, that avowal of a constant in verbal behavior which (precisely because it can be repeated, violated, returned to) we call *verse.* This is a poetry which is, as Heidegger calls it in his 1950 essay "Language," *purely spoken;* its roots are not in assent, which is silent, but in declaration, in contestation, which is the lesson of all speech. "The opposite of what is purely spoken, the opposite of the poem," Heidegger says, "is not prose. Pure prose is never 'prosaic'. It is as poetic and hence as rare as poetry." Prose, then, is the basis of Frank Bidart's prosody, his organization of language to suit and serve his need, which is his quest: a poetry in search of itself. Such a petition will necessarily invoke a warp of the formal enterprises—the novel and the play, ever since Proust and Pirandello made the Search explicit thematically, which is to say formally, afford the clue here, the way into the labyrinth. The way out, however, is one that Bidart has had to find by himself: if poetry is prose, then the poem must have that form of its own which is *not* a novel, *not* a play. And he has found that form (cunningly enjambed, weighted with the varying shifts of the raised voice, the wounded utterance) in the *terrain vague* between the dream and the letter, the only two forms of human expression which are not subject to revision, but merely to creation. Bidart's *dream letters,* then, are that form, as astounding in their mythologizing remove as in their intimacy, their avowals.

Undressing, Oscar Wilde once told someone, is romance, dressing philanthropy; and the poet who is neither romantic nor philanthropic, merely questing his own creation as a poet, is indeed endangered, likely to be severed from himself by the one sword or the other. It is interesting to see how Bidart avoids the cutting edges: he begins and ends his book with "other lives," mirror-images of what, in his center section, he explores indeed as the *given.* Shocking as **"Herbert White"** is intended to be—and shocking it is—there is every reason for it to precede the rest, for this poem's real horror is its parallel with the discovery made in the closing poem **"Another Life,"** the *identical* discovery that the self must become one with its unacknowledged obsession, that there is only the one life, not other lives. Dressing, then, is how the book begins, for it is Bidart's tactical decision to open with an "autobiographical" narrative which is not his own, thereby preparing us to accept his ulterior revelations, his undressing as fictions, as mythologized identities, not confessions. . . . (pp. vii-viii)

Richard Howard, "A Note on Frank Bidart," in Golden State *by Frank Bidart, George Braziller, 1973, pp. vii-ix.*

## ALAN WILLIAMSON

Frank Bidart's **Golden State** is a very original first book, though its originality may be expected to repel as well as to attract. Bidart is a stylistic ascetic, who avoids metaphor and even descriptive language; he writes a plainer prose, but also a more explanatory, a more *intelligentsia* kind of prose ("I've been reading Jung, and he says" . . . ) than we are used to in poetry, even in 1974. Yet Bidart is, in his own way, a consummate craftsman. His fluid and inventive visual form, with its shifting margins and stanza shapes, its odd and profuse punctuation, is at the service of an ear exquisitely attuned to the rushes and hesitations of speech, the subliminally characteristic rhythms. Only the real masters of the conversational mode—Frost, Jarrell—give us more of the unforgettable immediacy of the speaking voice. But Bidart's poems, unlike theirs, must often carry on voice alone, and on the naked importance of what is said.

The book begins with a harrowing *tour de force*—the confession of **"Herbert White,"** a child-murderer and necrophiliac. But what is most harrowing about Herbert White, as Richard

Howard suggests in his introductory Note [see excerpt above] is his similarity to the Frank Bidart we come to know in the book. Beyond the common anger at parental neglect and sexual cheapness, there is the desire "to *feel* things make sense," to complete a pattern, to make the world "somehow, come alive," that White experiences, horribly but convincingly, in his crimes. "When I hit her over the head, it was good," White's voice opens the book; five pages later, Bidart asks in a **"Self-Portrait,"** "What *reaches* him except disaster?" Another of White's traits that will haunt Bidart is his technique of fragmenting himself, to protect his essence from his actions: "somebody else did it . . . " The terrible effects of the inability to confront oneself whole dominate the central autobiographical sequence, incarnate in a culture and a man. The culture is Southern California, no Golden State for Bidart, but an endless, over-stylized Hollywood set, an imaginary frontier with real corpses in it. The man is Bidart's father. . . . The story of the father and son's struggle and ultimate failure to accept each other is—despite a jejune scornfulness in the earliest of the poems—one of the most painfully moving of its kind in contemporary literature. Bidart succeeds in his intention of becoming "not merely . . . the 'eye,' but a character," as he charts his rebellious shaping of the Eastern intellectual identity which, for him, must always mean both weakness and sanity. (pp. 89-90)

Bidart's stylistic bareness works, I think, because it is a part of the drama, the outward sign of the spiritual poverty in which the self must remain fragmented or else—as in the dream-poem **"Another Life"**—prey on itself. To approach the matter differently, one might recall Hemingway's dictum that the artist can always afford to leave out what he knows. The magnetic power of emotional indulgence, of decadence and the apocalyptic, is so completely known in the story itself, that it would be a kind of insult to work such feelings up in the reader through a more sensuous, alluring style. And yet, strong as the destructive powers are, Richard Howard is wrong, I think, to romanticize a "Satanic" element in the book. Much of Mr. Howard's recent criticism has been obsessed with a vision of the contemporary poem as a self-destruct mechanism, an *unsaying* of itself, and of the poet as (ergo) a self-destructive personality. But in Mr. Bidart's case, the unsayings are preparatory to a degree of commitment, of final and memorable utterance, too rare among younger poets. And, tragic as his book is, Mr. Bidart insists, "I want to change." He seeks a second birth, not a "colonization of inferno" (Mr. Howard); and he seeks it through the difficult Marriage of William Blake's Heaven and Hell, "Insight" and "mere life." (pp. 90-1)

Alan Williamson, "History Has to Live with What Was Here," in Shenandoah, *Vol. XXV, No. 2, Winter, 1974, pp. 85-91.**

## SHARON MAYER LIBERA

Frank Bidart's **Golden State** [is] the autobiographical inquest of a reluctant Californian, conducted with spareness and precision. **Golden State** begins, paradoxically, not with the self, but with a quintessential ugliness, a monstrosity:

"when I hit her on the head, it was good,
and then I did it to her a couple of times,—
but it was funny,—afterwards,
it was as if somebody else did it . . .

This is the dramatic monologue of **"Herbert White,"** psychopath and necrophiliac. If not Bidart's alter ego, he is certainly well understood by him; as if Bidart were playing Dante to

White's Francesca. White (pure white?) is known to most of us through the lurid silhouettes of newsprint; Bidart's achievement, even a *tour de force,* is to have made him human. The narrator's gruesome adventures become the least important aspect of the monologue—what is significant is his reaching out, in a language both awkward and alive, for the reasons he seeks power over his experience in peculiar and violent ways.... ''Come alive'' is the key phrase [in this poem], for White to himself feels dead. He is separated from himself—and when he awakes to his actions it is always ''as if somebody else did it.'' The only reintegration possible for him is to accept responsibility, to know finally that ''there was just me there, / and her,'' even though this realization constitutes ''Hell.'' This agonizing necessity of accepting that part of one's personality which is a ''monster'' is the essence of Bidart's hard-won wisdom.

In the three central poems of the book, which deal with his strident California background, the poet, like White, is trying to find a whole self, and, like White, is blocked from doing so by a flawed relationship to flawed parents, especially the father.... The subject could be maudlin or idiosyncratic, except that Bidart's theme is highly traditional—the search for articulation, which is the essence of culture both personal and social.... His task, like that of so many American writers, is to articulate the meaning of a past which lacks traditions or any obvious nobility. (pp. 259-61)

[Initially] it will seem that Bidart's use of the personal material, the confessing, probing ''I'' which is the voice of these poems, derives from [Robert] Lowell. But Bidart is more properly the inheritor of Dr. Williams of *Paterson.* If we can imagine Lowell writing in the language of Williams, *Golden State* might be the result. Paterson, New Jersey, and Bishop, California, are two places seemingly unredeemable, comparable in their resistance to ''taste.'' (p. 261)

In deciding to use the pacing of spoken language . . . , Bidart must have known he was taking a considerable risk. He hasn't completely succeeded, for the poetry often comes across as flat. It *is* poetry, there's no doubt about that, but the extreme scrupulosity which is the sign of Bidart's control also inhibits the unpredictable from happening. (p. 262)

Bidart's poems explore his California experience with an almost painful intelligence; even his two translations from Vergil and Catullus comment upon his fate, so that what emerges from this first book, in spite of its limitations, is a remarkable formal integrity and the power keenly to move us. (p. 263)

*Sharon Mayer Libera, ''Bartholomew Fair,'' in* Parnassus: Poetry in Review, *Vol. 3, No. 2, Spring/Summer, 1975, pp. 259-69.\**

## ROBERT PINSKY

Bidart's diction is often ''abstract,'' but in the way that the colloquial speech of the poet's class, place, and time can be abstract. The rhythms, too, are based on the serious, intense speech of the poet and his contemporaries, as [J. V.] Cunningham's rhythms are based on the iambic tradition of Jonson. Bidart's prosody relies on the way line-endings and white space can indicate or heighten the pauses and emphases of conversation. And in structure, too, Bidart often relies on a slowly expanding, inclusive form analogous to speech. If it is necessary to test how a Cunningham epigram makes known the mind, it is necessary to ask what, in Bidart's work, gives the

statement the firmness of poetry. The answer, I think, lies in a determination like Cunningham's to pursue a statement beyond or outside such matters as the nominalist tradition, the inclination to wit, or the appeal of the exquisite image.

The title poem of Bidart's book *Golden State* is an address, in ten numbered parts, to the poet's father.... There is an initial shock at reading a poem which bases itself so genuinely upon the writer's way of speaking.... We are not used to poems which actually base their diction upon a heightened version of the earnest speech used by the poet's social class. This is not merely the familiar literary version of speech which poets, in order to be colloquial, create from sources like Williams, Hemingway, country music, and the phrases used by advertising or by teen-aged informants. That constructed idiom is ''literary'' partly because it is bound to avoid too many phrases which evoke the speech of people who read or try to make literature; that is, a poet who undertakes diction like ''insight'' and ''disaffection,'' contriving to use it along with ''bag of money'' and ''movie star,'' as naturally as he would in speech, sets out to claim an almost revolutionary freedom. (pp. 139-41)

[Such] freedom involves limitations and risks. Most obvious is the risk of flatness, which **''Golden State''** meets by limiting itself to a gravely linear development, a careful adherence to the moral issues. Such a style sacrifices unpredictability; the poem offers revelations, but no surprises of a radical kind. This discipline gives the texture of the writing a firm, vigorous quality; the abstract terms and speaking voice turn out, repeatedly, to have their own, rather investigative, kind of precision. But such poetry depends in a special way upon what it will say about its subject, in the way that we expect of prose. To put it another way, where and what, specifically, is the emotion here?

The desires of the opening lines of the section are for ease of different kinds: ''relief,'' ''more money,'' easiness of life clothed in avoidance or in progress toward health, the nudity of conflict and of yearning almost hidden away. None of this is ironic—very little in **''Golden State''** is ironic—for the poet does not hold ease, or peace, cheap; and for what it is worth, therapy can be ''good.'' These desires are true not ironically but, characteristically, ''in many ways.''

In relation to the father, however, that scheme of desired ends becomes wishful thinking. The compromises of progress toward the good and avoidance of evil appear to be wishful thinking, or evasions, before the father's massive unhappiness. The question is, does a craving for some absolute glory or pleasure, beyond the apparent possibilities and compromises of actual life, constitute something infantile and trivial, or something irresistibly heroic, demanding loyalty? For the reasonable, decent-sounding poet, characterized by his careful honesty in the opening lines, the answer seems to lean away from such careful compromise and toward the unreasonable, indecently hungry shapes of desire. In the language of compromise and caution, the poem expresses its own radical impatience with the limits of life. The father's needs were too simple or too complex for any easy survival in the world, and also too simple or too complex to be dismissed in the name of an ideal based upon the limits of the world.

Thus, the element of abstract diction in the writing, like the reliance on definition and statement, has two different effects. On the surface, the effect is an air of dogged sincerity, an almost clinical honesty patterned by the rhythms of a naturalistic voice. In a deeper way, the abstractions do what abstractions always tend to do: they assert the presence or pursuit of an absolute, some value transcending the particulars of experience. (pp. 141-42)

Because of the snapshot-image of the well-turned-out father, some readers of **"Golden State"** will think of the possible influence of Robert Lowell's *Life Studies.* Stylistically, however, Lowell's poems often rely upon a series of bitter or ironic incongruities, surprises of contrasted or unexpectedly extended images. . . . This grim, unpredictable wandering into invention has the effect of relieving the potential banality or pointlessness of the material; we feel the poet needing the inventive language as a kind of polished shield in which he can regard the father's reflection without being overcome by pity or some other emotion. The rich catalogue of details and figures supplies a varied, many-colored background; against that background of nearly random colors, the plainness of closing lines like "I feel awful" can stand out.

The method of Bidart's **"Golden State"** is quite different. Most biography is potentially banal or pointless, a circumstance which **"Golden State"** meets with the stylistic opposite of Lowell's nervously varied surface texture. Instead, we have the speaking voice described above, and the implied promise to penetrate the subject, however "unpoetic" it may seem at times. If that commitment and its voice are—like Cunningham's pentameter abstractions—confining, they are also liberating. (pp. 143-44)

> *Robert Pinsky, "The Discursive Aspect of Poetry, 'Earnestness': Cunningham, Bidart," in his* The Situation of Poetry: Contemporary Poetry and Its Traditions, *Princeton University Press, 1976, pp. 134-44.**

## JAMES ATLAS

[In *The Book of the Body,* Frank Bidart has moved] toward a poetry that depends on sheer force of utterance to distinguish it from prose.

"Don't turn into the lies / of mere, neat poetry," Bidart implored his father in *Golden State,* a series of autobiographical poems published four years ago. Perhaps his greatest accomplishment has been to violate those "lies"—of decorum, grace, reticence—without sacrificing his art. The sprawl and apparent randomness of Bidart's prosody belie an exacting sense of composition that has nothing to do with "free verse"; every word, line and stanza is justified by Bidart's will to reproduce the character of speech, its cadences and hesitations. (p. 763)

The California poems in Bidart's first book provide a striking image of that fascinating, desolate landscape, better even than Joan Didion's essays because less self-consciously apocalyptic. But they depend on the same deliberate accretion of detail one expects from prose; there are few striking lines in Bidart's poetry. It owes its effect to the cumulative intensity of the story he relates, and its "poetry" derives from the stark *montage* of words clustered on the page. . . . Bidart's is a poetry of emphasis, of pauses and insistent repetitions. It could not be written as prose because it demands the concentrated economies of the line and stanza to give it urgency. The portrait of his father acquires its vividness from compression and brusque reportage. . . . And Bidart's ear for his parents' speech is perfect. (pp. 763-64)

Every poetic renovation since Wordsworth has made a claim for the importance of the demotic, but few American poets have really tried to write American speech, and when they

have, the result has been more or less disastrous. . . . The virtue of Bidart's poetry is that it records what is interesting, characteristic, self-revelatory about the way his parents talk, and uses that expressiveness to dramatize their lives. His gift for illustrating failure and emptiness, inarticulate feelings and unspoken regret by means of quotation is infallible.

Bidart's dramatic monologues are disconcerting, to put it mildly. **"Herbert White,"** the first poem in *Golden State,* is spoken by a murderer of young girls who likes to "jack off" over their bodies, and *The Book of the Body* opens with the meditations of an amputee; instructions about how to bandage his stump introduce the poem. **"Ellen West"** is based on a case history by Ludwig Binswanger of an anorexic woman who loathes her body and ends a suicide. But there is far more to these lurid histories than a desire to shock; the myth of Philoctetes, which Edmund Wilson made a parable of the artist's estrangement from society in *The Wound and the Bow,* is a tacit parable for Bidart as well. Philoctetes's offensive, suppurating wound prevents him from using his great bow, just as Bidart's characters—not gifted precisely, but with sufficient human attributes to warrant their being salvaged—are crippled by their psychic wounds. (p. 764)

What enables Bidart to fathom and interpret others' warped lives with such apparent ease is the recognition that his own damaged experience requires

> An adult's forgiveness of his parents
> born out of increasing age and empathy
>
> which really forgives nothing,—
> but is loathing, rage, revenge,
>
> yet forgiveness as well—;

Perhaps this is why his most impressive poems are autobiographical. The dramatic monologues, convincing as they are often sound like the poet himself; their traumas, rehearsals of betrayal, even the inflections of their voices recall the more intimate confessions that resonate through the poems about Bidart's own life. In *The Book of the Body,* he returns to the familiar themes of mother and father—the "family romance" in its most destructive form—and his precarious journey toward a tolerant self-estimate. **"Elegy"** begins with the death of his mother's dog (a scene of pure bathos, but incredibly moving all the same), then takes up her own death from cancer, concluding with a brilliant villanelle about the grotesque menace of a past that resists resolution and yet insists on its primacy. . . . (pp. 764-65)

**"Happy Birthday"** and the title poem offer minor variations on poems in *Golden State*: **"Self-Portrait, 1969,"** where, staring at himself in a mirror, he wonders, "What *reaches* him except disaster?" and **"To my Father,"** "whose name was not in my language." But of course it is, and the danger is that Bidart will find himself pronouncing that name, in the form of poems that bind him ever closer to their source, until he has exhausted the subject. As for the dramatic monologues, they too threaten to become repetitive, and one can only hope that ideas other than "disaster" will eventually reach his imagination. If they do, Bidart promises to become one of the significant poets of our time. (p. 765)

> *James Atlas, "The Poetry of Mere Prose," in* The Nation, *Vol. 224, No. 24, June 18, 1977, pp. 763-66.**

## HELEN VENDLER

Frank Bidart's best poems in his second volume, *The Book of the Body*, are case-studies, but case-studies motivated not by the projection of the usual dramatic monologue, nor by a covert social history, nor by a sympathy for the grotesque—though they might seem to spring from all of these. Rather, the grotesque becomes in Bidart the figure for the ordinary, the human, the "normal," and casts an eerie oblique cloud over "normalcy" itself. The personages in Bidart's two central poems of this story are, respectively, an amputee and an anorexic who have—the one by accident, the other by compulsion—been placed outside "Nature." *"I loathed 'Nature',"* says the anorexic Ellen West (her story borrowed from Binswanger's account): "I shall *defeat* 'Nature'." "Nature," Bidart reminds us through Ellen West's tortured perceptions, is loathed even by those of us who won't admit it: a short student carries his body "as if forcing / it to be taller," and a woman who shows her gums when she smiled "often held her / hand up to hide them." (p. 78)

Bidart's method is not narrative; unlike the seamless dramatic monologues we are used to, his are spliced together, as harrowing bits of speech, an anecdote, a reminiscence, a doctor's journal notes, a letter, an analogy, follow each other in a cinematic progression. These fragments are further fragmented by interpolation, captions, parentheses, blank spaces on the page, idiosyncratic punctuation, quotations, italics, capitals, asterisks, printed matter, lists, and flashes of interior speech. All this violence to the printed page seems to be comparable to cinematic forms of italicizing—the freeze-frame, the speed-up, the zoom, the panning, the slow-motion, the shift from color to black-and-white and back, the angle-shot. All of these are devices to forbid the audience's sinking into conventional expectation of mimetic art: not for more than a few lines at once can we read Bidart without being jolted out of any mimetic illusion. Someone—an author—is "placing" the voices in these poems, accompanying them with his typographical devices as with a weird orchestration, making the voices just slightly inhuman, hitting our ears at a pitch strangely above the level of hearing, jangling one line against another into quarter-tones that abrade the ear. . . . (pp. 78-9)

Bidart's poetry in propria persona is less severely controlled. The title poem and the long central elegy (partly spoken by his mother) exhibit some unsteadiness, explicable in terms of Bidart's chosen voice—exhibitionistic, disdainful of metaphor, questioning, pleading, qualifying, naked. In these poems he still puts the extreme case with an absoluteness which denies that it is anything other than the universal one. As we stand in Bidart's universe, convention calls up, as responses natural to the event of life, postures as contorted, deformed, and racked as the figures in the greenish light of an El Greco. (p. 79)

*Helen Vendler, in a review of "The Book of the Body," in* The Yale Review, *Vol. LXVII, No. 1, Autumn, 1977, pp. 78-9.*

## HAROLD BLOOM

Frank Bidart is a poet of extraordinary talent who is both sustained and damaged by the narrow, obsessive range of his imagery and thematic concerns. *The Book of the Body* . . . follows the earlier *Golden State* in its almost compulsive association of the family romance with tropes of mutilation. Bidart writes narrative so harrowing in design and detail that all of his acute intelligence, moral force and devoted skill at language may continue to be neglected, since very few readers can sustain poems so uncompromising in facing reductive and very unpleasant truths. (p. 26)

*Harold Bloom, in a review of "The Book of the Body," in* The New Republic, *Vol. 177, No. 22, November 26, 1977, p. 26.*

## PETER STITT

Each of the five long poems in [Frank Bidart's *The Sacrifice*] presents a central character who is so obsessed with the notion of human guilt that he or she ends up believing in the necessity of sacrifice in order that sin may be expiated.

The Platonic system is central to human thought, which recognizes the mind/body problem as a real issue touching upon the very nature of existence as we know it. The same cannot be said of the moral notion Bidart plays with in his book. In fact, it is a chilling, arbitrary, and thoroughly questionable concept that has survived into our age from much more primitive times. With respect to the book, one has to wonder why Bidart is giving such an idea so much attention. Does he himself find it believable, operative within reality? The fact that each of his major characters, the ones who believe in the necessity of sacrifice, is insane would seem to indicate Bidart's own reservations about the concept. On this issue, however, we must reserve judgment until after we have looked more closely at the poems.

The insanity of these characters is clear from what they do, from what they say, and from how they say it. The longest poem in the volume, **"The War of Vaslav Nijinsky,"** is a subtle portrait of the dancer which centers on his reaction to the First World War. Nijinsky came to feel that he, like everyone else, was responsible for the moral ravages of that war. Unlike everyone else, he believes he can do something about his feeling—he presents a dance which enacts his own personal sacrifice as expiation for it. The beliefs that underlie his action are presented in a passage near the end of the poem:

But then,—
        he LEARNED SOMETHING.

He learned that

        *All life exists*

*at the expense of other life* . . .
. . . . . . . . . . . . . . . . . . . . . . . . . . . . . . . . . . . . . . . . . . . .
THE ROCK
        THAT GIVES SHADE TO ONE CREATURE,—

*FOR ANOTHER CREATURE*

                *JUST BLOCKS THE SUN.*

Nijinsky's craziness is easy to see. Does all life exist at the expense of other life? Of course. Should that fact create in the thriving individual a feeling of guilt? Of course not. And when the rock shades one person but discomfits another, is that the first person's fault? Should he commit suicide to expiate his guilt? Well, Nijinsky thinks so—and so do the other characters in the book.

Nijinsky is upset about the First World War; another character was mean to her sister once when they were little; still another . . . is distraught because she couldn't stop her mother from dying of cancer. Some of this is serious business indeed, but the underlying idea is still questionable. The most interesting of all these poems is **"Confessional,"** in which yet another of these tormented souls talks with the only character in the book who might actually be sane, the "confessor." As we read this poem, in fact, we begin to wonder if its context is not perhaps more psychological than religious.

The supplicant's primary concern is that his mother died before the two of them could exchange forgiveness for their various mutual sins. The poem consists of this man's anguished recital of his thinking on their entire relationship, a monologue which is occasionally and briefly interrupted by the confessor/psychiatrist. The supplicant is clearly disturbed and feels, like the other central characters in these poems, that he must perform some act of self-sacrifice in order to expiate both his and his mother's guilt. The confessor generally carries the burden of wisdom, rationality, and truth in the poem, and corrects the more egregious errors of the supplicant. At the end of the poem's first section, the confessor says: *"Forgiveness doesn't exist."* Because of its inherent realism, this is a refreshing statement within the context of the book. At the end of the second section, the confessor concludes the poem by saying (less refreshingly): *"Man needs a metaphysics; / he cannot have one."*

This statement seems, finally, to be the idea which is really central to this book, the idea which . . . Bidart is imposing upon reality in order to understand experience more accurately. Unfortunately, rather than undermining the thinking which causes trouble for the major characters in this book, the confessor's idea turns out subtly to support the basis of that thinking. The statement has two parts; with respect to the first, we cannot help but feel that, could these characters free themselves from the burden of needing a metaphysics, they would certainly be less unhappy than they are; they might also be less insane. The second half of the statement seems to present a solution to this problem—but only seems. In fact, it actually asserts the existence of a metaphysical structure while (paranoically) denying its efficacy to mankind. By saying man cannot have a metaphysics, the confessor establishes a Prime Giver who chooses, in this instance, not to give. Thus the escape from insanity offered at the end of this poem turns out to be just the same old trap in disguise, and we end up feeling that the confessor may not be so much more rational than his patient after all.

Stylistically, the book seems to end up at a similarly indecisive point. The problem is that there is virtually no stylistic modulation anywhere in the volume, nothing to distinguish the author's voice from those of his characters. The stylistic devices used here seem calculated to emphasize the insanity of the characters who speak. Bidart relies on a very simple level of diction, which—in the absence of assonance, consonance, meter, rhyme—is enlivened primarily through the use of capitalized words at some times, italicized words at other times, capitalized words *and* italicized words at still other times. All three varieties are illustrated in the lines from **"The War of Vaslav Nijinsky"** quoted above; the effect is of a kind of irrational shouting. The only voice that is at all different is that of the confessor, and his is (as I have shown) not different enough. One wishes that Bidart had seen fit somehow to differentiate himself, his own voice, from the relentless perspective expressed by his central characters. The only way such a thing could have been accomplished is through style, and finally it is style which is the greatest failure in this book. *The Sacrifice* is an eerie volume, presenting as it does a short tour through one wing of an asylum. The poems are powerful and have a way of sticking in the mind, but the reader ends up

wishing he had a more clearly defined guide to show him through the intricacies of this maze. (pp. 900-03)

*Peter Stitt, "A Variegation of Styles: Inductive, Deductive, and Linguistic," in* The Georgia Review, *Vol. XXXVII, No. 4, Winter, 1983, pp. 894-905.**

### BRAD CRENSHAW

[In *The Book of the Body*] Frank Bidart has taken the dualism inherited from his modernist fathers, has accepted the separation between what he can say and what he can know, and has sexualized it, so that the felt mode of his alienation is at once anxious and erotic. This association is what is so distinctive about his poetry, and accounts for the often skewed characters that have peopled his imagination. For the human condition, according to Bidart, is doubly bound by epistemological traumas—at the root of which is language and its inadequacies—and by the ethical dilemmas put in force by his bodily incarnation. The two modes—the linguistic and the physical, the epistemological and the ethical—frequently abrade each other. Discourse isolates him, as Pound, Valéry and their brethren explain, within the cultural locutions of his particular historical circumstances, buffered by language from other social realities as well as from the physical world. His body, on the other hand, as it materially individuates him, locates him existentially in that very world, that very time and physical place from which the self's linguistic closures divide him. The body is a social ground, a prime requisite for public life, because it permits proximity by mooring the diffuse self within its concrete and alien condition.

It also introduces him into the ethical morass of its carnal appetites. If language is primarily concerned with cognition, then the body is, in Bidart's cosmology, the matrix of desire. As such it ushers him into a moral world, a public place that requires, because of the body's potential sensual excesses—its capacity to sin—some principles of proper social behavior. If you are inclined to doubt this, read **"Herbert White,"** the title character of which is an avowed child molester and murderer, *and* a necrophiliac until natural processes put a halt to it: "When the body got too decomposed, / I'd just jack off, letting it fall on her. . . ." Though he is the sole character to date whose disaffection is actually criminal, yet Herbert White is only the first of the poet's several personas to be inspired by an extraordinary disgust for the human body—a disgust not only for its lusts and gluttonies and sloths, but as well for its *life*, the principles of which transcend what we know about it. (pp. 58-9)

It is no accident that Bidart typically chooses to imagine not only profoundly troubled characters—characters whose bodily repugnance is in many cases pathological—but *inarticulate* ones as well. . . . Linguistic facility is seldom a virtue since its tropes are more likely than not to mislead or confound the thinking subject—who nevertheless has little other recourse than to struggle through his or her conceptual fogs. The poet is not inclined to praise ignorance or to celebrate primitivism. Rather, he cares to account for the values engendered in people by desire in a world from which their language severs them, though into which their bodies have set them nevertheless and there spurred them to actions neither the significance nor the consequences of which can they comprehend. Bidart is, in short, first a student of moral philosophy, not linguistics. His desire is to articulate the right relation of human beings to their universe, the principles of which involves the value, or the lack of value, inherent in material embodiment. (pp. 59-60)

Brad Crenshaw, "The Sin of the Body: Frank Bidart's Human Bondage," in Chicago Review, Vol. 33, No. 4, Summer, 1983, pp. 57-70.

## HELEN VENDLER

In the harrowing poems of Frank Bidart's new book [*The Sacrifice*] it is difficult to distinguish the cries of the saint from the shrieks of the damned. The forms that Bidart used earlier in *Golden State* (1973) and *The Book of the Body* (1977)—the dramatic monologue, the case history, and an eccentric punctuation—recur here, but they are put to new uses in the six poems that make up the book. In Bidart's strange combination of excruciating confession and clinical detachment, the book considers the war to the death between mental (or spiritual or aesthetic) life and the life of the body (sexual, appetitive, seductive). The desires of the Christian saints to mortify the flesh, to refuse food and sexual experience, and to abjure society, become here only special instances of the universal asceticism demanded, at least to some extent, of everyone who finds himself living the life of the mind. The grim words of St. Paul, that the spirit lusts against the flesh, and the flesh against the spirit, concern the same struggle that appears here centrally placed in a poem by Catullus, *Odi et amo*. Bidart treats the poem as a rebuttal; an opponent says, "Why do you hate the world so much?" and the poet answers,

> I hate *and* love. Ignorant fish, who even
> wants the fly while writhing.

The writhing of this book between desire and disgust reappears in the elegy on a friend who died of cancer. The friend has vacillated in life between a grasping at experience and a repudiation of it.... At death, offered the cup of "Forgetfulness," does the divided soul reach for it gratefully? The poem decides not: to become pure spirit, solitary, is not within human capacity. On the contrary, souls at the general Resurrection, given another chance at life, would choose a life of the body more social and more human than before: *"The phone is plugged in, please call, / I will answer it."* This fantasy is guaranteed by the final act of the dying friend, who staves off death in order to see her sister once more and mend the relationship, asking.

DO YOU FORGIVE ME?
Then: WILL YOU MISS ME?

—the voice reduced to the barest of exchanges.

The soul's need to acknowledge and enter into the social and domestic world, and the absolute irreconcilability of that world with the mental world—solitary, estranged, fierce, concentrated—brings Bidart's chief protagonists toward either suicide or madness. In the long poem that begins this book . . . , **"The War of Vaslav Nijinsky,"** Nijinsky's madness moves within a double guilt, the personal guilt felt by the dancer toward his family, whom he attempts to kill, and the common or collective guilt for which the artist is the expressive channel—in the case of Nijinsky, the collective sin of World War I. (p. 24)

The contorted drama of Bidart's **"Nijinsky"** is pieced together from factual sources, but it arises from these pages as a play of voices (in this sense, too, it descends from *The Waste Land*), Nijinsky's voice is by turns hysterical, grief stricken, horrified, elegiac, manic, and sane—but always intense, uninterruptible, compelling, as he holds us with his glittering eye. Nijinsky possesses three type fonts: CAPS for important words and axiomatic truths (chiefly ghastly ones); *italics* for a rise in pitch,

an insistence; and roman for a base line. Nijinsky's wife and friends talk and write in prose printed in roman. They use normal punctuation; Nijinsky uses Bidart's full repertoire of notation, including ellipses, dashes . . . , exclamation points, quotation marks, and so on. Nijinsky also speaks in verse, in short bursts of one or two lines, some beginning at the left margin, some along different tabstops (so to speak) across the page. We may conclude from this that "ordinary people," who feel (either by nature or by will) none of the divisions which disturb artists, keep an even and uninterrupted "prose" tenor; divided souls have italic intensities, irregularities of emotional pulse, elliptic reveries, exclamatory excitements, and upper case insights. The irreconcilability of the two styles—Nijinsky's feverish broken utterance and the world's "sane," reasonable, and offended prose—enacts Bidart's aesthetic dilemma. He avoids the sentimentality attending the stereotype of the *poète maudit* by making Nijinsky both dangerous and unjust toward his wife and children. In his wish to throw pure lyric up against the most ordinary prose, as if to say that lyric had to take stock of its relation to the everyday management of life, Bidart is a descendant of Pound and Williams. The mutually critical relation of solitary lyric and the social world (to put the quarrel in only one set of many possible terms) can no longer, after the modernists, be avoided.

Bidart's sympathies with the lyric side of the quarrel are evident; but in making his poem one about guilt, he also reflects the predicament of the innocent bystanders who suffer from their contact with genius, and asserts the falsity of any claim that the artist, however pure his aesthetic intent, can escape human error, evil, or destructiveness. (p. 25)

The rhythm of life that lies behind this book is phrased most baldly in the title poem, **"The Sacrifice,"** which takes the life of Jesus as the paradigm of earthly life, but not in the usual religious fashion. Here, the essential factors are Christ and Judas, the betrayed and the betrayer. Jesus loved the world, underwent betrayal by someone who purported to love him, and sacrificed his life, shouldering the guilt of the world; Judas, shouldering the guilt of his action, killed himself. The modern instance offered by the poem is that of a daughter unable to bear her mother's death agony, yet unable to kill her; feeling she has betrayed her mother, she kills herself. By taking such a banal instance—filial helplessness at the parental deathbed—Bidart forces the issue with each reader, refusing to euphemize one of the commonest causes for "irrational" guilt:

> Christ knew the Secret. Betrayal
> is necessary; as is woe for the betrayer.

One could almost be reading graffiti; the melodrama of the style derives from the modern ripping away of veils.

A far more successful poem, I think, is **"The Confessional,"** a long imitation of a psychiatric session, or series of sessions, in which the analyst speaks in italics and the client in the fantastic "lyric" mode of Nijinsky. The client exposes the relation between himself and his mother—their *folie à deux* caused by her obsessive love for him, her "nervous breakdown," her demands, his obsessive love for her, his success in supplanting both his father and stepfather.... The result, when the client grew to adulthood, was a stranglehold he felt he had to break.... This relation is compared to the relation of Augustine and his mother Monica: they, according to the *Confessions*, succeeded in attaining an idyllic relation, both aspiring, in a joint project, to sainthood. The wretched veiled hostility between the client and his mother, mutually critical in adulthood (*"Forgiveness doesn't exist"*), lasted until death.

In the poem, the idyll between Augustine and his mother takes place in a long lyric flight, with musically sustained sentences generating clause after clause of aspiration and rapture. The poem sees this as a fantasy no longer available to us, and it ends crucified on its twin analytic truths:

> *Man needs a metaphysics;*
> *he cannot have one.*

Against this voice of reason, Bidart's volume places its last idyll, a "translation" of Genesis 1-2:4, the *ur*-poem. In the modern manner, this is a re-creation, depending on various previous English translations, with help from commentators about the meaning of the Hebrew. Here there are no frenzied or analytical italics: God speaks in caps and the narrator speaks in roman with caps for the large items in the universe (HEAVEN, EARTH, OCEAN, SEASONS, and so on). The punctuation, too, is seemly—commas and periods. But we see (tutored by Bidart's previous practice) that the narrator and God are both composing poetry. . . . Can there be a poetry of this sort, the "translation" asks—a poetry of creation without madness, destruction, "intensity," hysteria, betrayal? Can a measured and rhythmic lyricism be attained in this century?

In reaching back to the moment before guilt and betrayal entered the world, Bidart asks whether there is an imagination as benevolent as it is grim, one that in the midst of conflict can stop to imagine harmony. The Genesis poet lived in a fallen world; he knew the story of Adam and Eve, and Cain and Abel. And yet he was able to write of something idyllic. . . . In ending his volume with the prelapsarian ideal invented by the Genesis poet or by his culture, Bidart allies himself with those artists who say, like Yeats's father, that poetry concerns itself with the creation of paradises—but, Bidart would add, only in the exceptional instance.

The purposes of lyric, as they emerge from Bidart's book, are several. In the first place, lyric serves as a repository for the visionary and the harmonious, as in Augustine's and Monica's joint heavenly flight, or as in God's supreme invention of the cosmos. In the second place, lyric serves as a vehicle for emotions and actions too "intense" for "prose"; lyric is needed for the reproach to the conditions of existence underlying **"The Confessional,"** for the violent incorporative act of the artist in taking the whole activity of his culture into consciousness and re-enacting it in expressive form, for deathbed betrayals and erotic paradox. Thirdly, lyric serves as the genre for literary aria; surrounded by the *recitative* of every day, the voice in lyric elaborates itself into the *bel canto* of words (for which Bidart's inventive notation is of course a symbol). Lastly, lyric is the genre of pressure; it compresses into a few pages, in a montage of cinematic flashes, the strains of a whole life, and it compresses as well, by means of a few symbols, the metaphysical dilemmas of mind and flesh. (pp. 26-8)

> Helen Vendler, *"Body and Soul,"* in The New Republic, *Vol. 189, No. 15, October 10, 1983, pp. 24-8.*

## DON BOGEN

[Frank Bidart] writes about guilt. His first book, *Golden State* (1973), centered on parents as the source of guilt. In *The Book of the Body* (1977) he looked at guilt stemming from physical desires. His new volume, *The Sacrifice,* examines guilt as a fundamental condition of human existence. While Bidart's work contains a great deal of intense, often tortured emotion, his general approach is analytical rather than merely expressive. He is a poet of rationality and dramatic argument. . . . There is little "poetic" atmosphere in *The Sacrifice,* and the volume is hardly a smooth presentation of individual sensitivity. To open a book and find Vaslav Nijinsky discussing *Ecce Homo* and concluding, "I am not Nietzsche. I am the bride of Christ" is to enter a more complex and disturbing world than the poetry of sensibility allows.

With its portentous and rather bleak subject, *The Sacrifice* could easily be weighed down by the seriousness of its concerns. Indeed, Bidart's closing poem, **"Genesis 1-2:4,"** is at times slow going despite its intriguing variations on the King James text. But the writing is generally so diverse and energetic that the book never feels like a sermon or a treatise. The volume contains a broad range of poems: the Genesis passage, a long historical poem spoken primarily by Nijinsky, two elegies for friends, an extended self-analysis and a two-line translation from Catullus. And the poems abound in different voices. **"The War of Vaslav Nijinsky,"** the thirty-page poem that opens the book, for example, includes passages of dramatic monologue spoken by the dancer, prose observations by his wife and different biographers and a framing device in which Bidart summarizes Nijinsky's life in relation to his time. Though the frame may be too obvious, the poem as a whole combines dramatic tension with the sustained power of a meditation on a theme.

Bidart's ability to retain variety and energy in the long poem without losing focus is particularly impressive in **"Confessional."** This exploration of the poet's symbiotic relationship with his mother convinces in the sheer exasperation it evokes. But Bidart is not content merely to pour out his guilt and suffering in the standard confessional manner. He includes in the poem a terrifying "confessor," part priest, part shrink, whose repeated questions—*"Did you forgive her?" "Why are you angry?" "How do you explain it?"*—force the poet to analyze and interpret his experience. In its exhaustive clarification of an insoluble problem, **"Confessional"** is one of the most intelligent and moving poems on family relations to appear in recent years.

Bidart's work quite literally looks like no one else's. Long, often complex sentences wind across lines varying from one word to extensive lists. Capital letters, italics, italicized capitals and other forms of emphasis stand out like neon signs all over the page. Tone shifts rapidly: a speaker may be hushed and reverent in one line, hysterical in the next. Bidart's voices speed up and slow down, make sudden interjections, contradict themselves and go off on tangents. They use authorities, events in their lives and deductive reasoning interchangeably to make their points. . . . The overall effect of this protean texture is not one of chaos but rather one of intense introspection—the halting, often involuted progress of minds turned in on themselves.

With its introspective focus, *The Sacrifice* is a highly self-conscious work. Yet it contains none of the coyness that can afflict books that include references to their own creation. When Bidart follows his initial analysis of a friend's life and death in **"For Mary Ann Youngren"** with "No, that's *not* enough,— / *not* true, wrong," we are led not so much to admire his cleverness in turning the poem back on itself as to consider the final inability of language to resolve experience. In this sense *The Sacrifice* is a fundamentally tragic book. Nijinsky, Catullus and Bidart himself devise myriad strategies for coming to terms with guilt, all of which, at least on one level, fail.

The aura of failure haunts Bidart's language. It is not that words cannot clarify experience—many of the speakers understand their predicaments quite well—but that they cannot provide relief from the past and the guilt it has set in motion. Obsessive, paradoxical, Bidart's vocabulary struggles against its own powerlessness. There is a strange music to this struggle, grounded in careful use of abstract, seemingly "unpoetic" terms. . . . Bidart uses repetition and the tonal variation created by different emphases and placement to develop an unusual lyric effect. When his work sings it is not with the traditional illusion of effortless ease but with a baroque intricacy that comes out of his distinctly uneasy struggle for clarity. The poems are marked with the effort of their creation.

Bidart's odd music will not appeal to all readers. Drenched in obsession, his poems have the obsessive's resistance to easy conclusions. These examinations of guilt are jagged, disquieting and finally illuminating. *The Sacrifice* seems unresolved—not because it is vague but because it is clear. It makes much of contemporary poetry look like mere posing. (pp. 610-11)

*Don Bogen, "Guilt-Edged Poems," in* The Nation, *Vol. 237, No. 19, December 10, 1983, pp. 610-11.*

## DAVID LEHMAN

With his first two collections, **"Golden State"** (1973) and **"The Book of the Body"** (1977), Frank Bidart established himself as a poet of uncommon intelligence and uncompromising originality. **"The Sacrifice"** should add to that reputation. . . . (p. 71)

"Verse, whatever else it may or may not be, is itself a system of *punctuation*," T. S. Eliot once wrote, and Bidart demonstrates the truth of this axiom. Making liberal use of italics and capital letters, Bidart plays the keyboard with dash and brio.

Through his distinctive "system of punctuation," he achieves the rhythm of emphasis that makes the speakers in his poems sound so powerfully, urgently present: if you thought that nothing new could be done with the dramatic monologue, think again.

**"The War of Vaslav Nijinsky"** begins and ends with the premise that "the Nineteenth Century's / guilt, *World War One*, / was danced / by Nijinsky on January 19, 1919." Like virtually all of Bidart's protagonists in **"The Sacrifice,"** Nijinsky is obsessed with guilt—his own and the world's. . . . The dancer's "essential innocence" transforms his madness into something holy without for a moment diminishing his anguish. Like Kafka's Joseph K. in the cathedral episode of "The Trial," Nijinsky begins to acknowledge distinctions that are paradoxes in disguise. Expiation is "necessary" but "NOT possible." Therefore, *"my life is the expiation for my life."* Bidart employs a collage technique to get us inside his character's skin; Nijinsky's ravings alternate with prose passages lifted from biographical accounts. The result combines a documentary effect with an intensity rare in contemporary poetry.

**"Confessional,"** the other long poem in **"The Sacrifice,"** doesn't work nearly as well. An analysand's attempt to come to terms with his mother ("TO SURVIVE, I HAD TO KILL HER INSIDE ME"), the poem is overwhelmed by its emotional burden. Nor do the several shorter poems fare any better; Bidart's imagination requires a broad canvas. But none of this lessens the book's ultimate impact. **"The Sacrifice"** does for the treatment of guilt what **"The Book of the Body"** did for the mind-body schism: it transmutes an obsession into poetry that is innovative in its means and rich in moral and psychological implication. (pp. 71-2)

*David Lehman, "Demons of the Mind," in* Newsweek, *Vol. CIII, No. 5, January 30, 1984, pp. 71-2.*

# Robert (Albert) Bloch

## 1917-

(Also writes under pseudonyms of Tarleton Fiske, Will Folke, Nathan Hindin, E. K. Jarvis, Wilson Kane, John Sheldon, and Collier Young) American novelist, short story writer, and scriptwriter.

Bloch has written many novels and hundreds of short stories in the horror, fantasy, and mystery genres. Stephen King commented that "Bloch has been scaring the bejammers out of people for more than forty-five years, and he is still going strong." Bloch is also the author of many film, radio, and television scripts, including episodes for such programs as "Stay Tuned for Terror," "Alfred Hitchcock Presents," "Thriller," "I Spy," "Night Gallery," and "Star Trek." Recently, Bloch novelized the four segments of *Twilight Zone—The Movie* and wrote *Psycho II* (1982), a sequel to his 1959 novel *Psycho*, made famous by Alfred Hitchcock's classic horror film of the same title.

Bloch began his writing career at the suggestion of H. P. Lovecraft and made his first major sale in 1935 to the horror-fantasy pulp magazine *Weird Tales*. He became one of the "Weird Tales Group," which included Ray Bradbury, August Derleth, Clark Ashton Smith, and Donald Wandrei. In his first decade as a writer, Bloch sold over a hundred stories, primarily horror tales, to a variety of publications. Toward the end of that period he began his popular "Lefty Feep" series of fantasy stories. Probably the best-known story from this early period is "Yours Truly, Jack the Ripper" (1943). Initially emulating Lovecraft in such works as *The Opener of the Way* (1945), Bloch later established an individual style characterized by conversational, seemingly innocent beginnings that quickly develop ominous undercurrents and build to terrifying conclusions.

Many of Bloch's stories center on psychopaths. His first novel, *The Scarf* (1947), is the first-person narrative of a strangler; *The Dead Beat* (1960) follows the exploits of a dangerous con artist; *Firebug* (1961) details the crimes of a pyromaniac; and *Night-World* (1972) outlines the search for an escaped killer. Two of his books are based on real people and actual events. *Psycho* is taken from accounts of mild-mannered Ed Gein's grisly activities in a small Wisconsin town during the 1950s, and *American Gothic* (1974) resurrects Herman W. Mudgett, a notorious murderer in turn-of-the-century Chicago.

(See also *Contemporary Authors*, Vols. 5-8, rev. ed.; *Contemporary Authors New Revision Series*, Vol. 5; and *Something about the Author*, Vol. 12.)

## H. R. HAYS

The genre of the weird tale which Mr. Bloch practices [in **"The Opener of the Way"**] is concerned with fantastic or unpleasant events. It embraces both the supernatural and inexplicable, and pure grand guignol. In the past such writers as Kipling, H. G. Wells, W. W. Jacobs and even James have written stories of this type, and have pretty well standardized the form. Currently the trend is in the direction of psychological terror with a

*Photograph by Jay Kay Klein*

realistic setting, while the old-fashioned weird tale continues to be published in one or two specialized pulp magazines.

In consequence, Mr. Bloch's stories are aimed at a certain group which reads these magazines. The idol and master craftsman of this group was the late H. P. Lovecraft. . . . Bloch is one of his disciples. In some of his stories he takes over the master's mythology and even reworks the latter's themes.

The philosophy of Lovecraft (and Bloch) is simple. A set of Elder Gods (imperfectly banished by later and more respectable deities) is always trying to break through from outer space and bring about Evil. . . .

It is rather difficult to review a collection of stories about which both author and publisher are so apologetic. Both are anxious to point out that the tales "are not written for posterity—only for immediate reader reaction." However, a formula is a formula whether it appears in The Saturday Evening Post or in Weird Tales. Over and over again Bloch makes use of such worn-out devices as the Egyptian curse, vampirism, demonic possession, etc. Moreover, he is constantly trying for surprise endings which don't come off. Even if Bloch's stories did not, in the words of the author's introduction, "cause the reader to shudder over the style rather than the content," the type of horror which he employs arouses no reaction other than mild discomfort. . . .

It is the waxwork macabre of Mrs. Radcliff and Walpole and, yes, Poe, which still lives on in the tales of Mr. Bloch. The fear of the unknown, of those things in human life which defy science, the strange and terrible irrationality of the human heart have inspired some of the most profound achievements in literature, from the Greeks to Franz Kafka. By comparison, those who deal in terror without moral significance seem pretty much in a class with the vendors of dirty postcards.

All this will mean nothing to Mr. Bloch's fans, who will doubtless welcome the appearance of his stories in book form. From the point of view of a fan, Bloch is more successful in working up a thrill the nearer he comes to Lovecraft. He has already achieved a reputation as one of the better practitioners of a highly specialized genre.

> *H. R. Hays, in a review of "The Opener of the Way," in* The New York Times Book Review, *December 9, 1945, p. 24.*

## DONALD BARR

For his first novel Robert Bloch has chosen a tested melodramatic theme, used a tricky but reliable form to project it, sauced it copiously with psychiatry. **"The Scarf"** is the case-history of a pathological murderer, told in the strangler's own words. It is true that these words, which by rights ought to be full of anguish and passion and bewilderment, are actually full of teasing professional artifice, but Mr. Bloch accounts for this nicely by making Daniel Morley a popular novelist as well as an extremely efficient butcher of young ladies.

Dan is started on both his careers by a Miss Frazer, his high school English teacher. She is a spinster, and in the hot flush of her autumnal infatuation . . . she makes him a maroon scarf for a graduation present. As she gives it to him at her apartment, she plies him with muscatel, and then kisses him. He is only 18; he passes out. Then he revives. She has tied his hands with the maroon scarf and turned on the gas, that they may die together, having betrayed Beauty. But he pushes her off, staggers to a window and breaks the glass with his head.

Mr. Bloch tries hard to keep this episode from being richly comic, but it gets the better of him. That is bad for the book, because everything young Morley does afterward is supposed to be explained by this traumatic experience. . . .

Later, Dan finds time to become a novelist. It takes him only three months to change completely—from a drunken bum to a writer about sex. This, too, becomes symbolic: he murders everyone he puts into his books. Hollywood, the graveyard of so much talent, is fatal to Dan. As a novelist, it is clear that he has no talent to ruin, but when he tries to strangle Verna at Laguna and Pat at San Diego, he bungles both times. The ending is conventionally neat, but clears up nothing.

> *Donald Barr, "Silken Death," in* The New York Times Book Review, *September 28, 1947, p. 31.*

## ANTHONY BOUCHER

[In **"Psycho,"** Bloch] is more chillingly effective than any writer might reasonably be expected to be. . . .

Here Mr. Bloch demonstrates, almost like a male Margaret Millar, that a believable history of mental illness can be more icily terrifying than all the arcane horrors summoned up by a collaboration of Poe and Lovecraft. The narrative surprises and shocks are so cunningly arrayed that it's unwise even to hint at plot and theme beyond mentioning that they seem suggested by a recent real-life monstrosity in the Middle West. It's a short book, powerfully and speedily told. . . .

> *Anthony Boucher, in a review of "Psycho," in* The New York Times, *Section VII, April 19, 1959, p. 25.*

## JAMES SANDOE

Grand Guignol is Robert Bloch's mode in **"Psycho"** . . . , and he manages as splendid a set of creeps as we've enjoyed in some time. His materials look commonplace enough (a motel bypassed by the new highway, its pudgy proprietor, his dominating mama and a girl wondering whether she'd better be on the lam), but Mr. Bloch's employment of them is adroit and blood-curdling. He doesn't (perhaps by intention) keep his ultimate surprise for the close and, as a pretty crawly sort of fact, this is probably kindness. Of the plot nothing more should be said here, but a hint in a press release seems worth reprinting: "Once a Robert Bloch fan asked what he, Bloch, was like, to which Bloch replied: 'I have the heart of a small boy. I keep it on my desk in a bottle.'"

> *James Sandoe, in a review of "Psycho," in* New York Herald Tribune Book Review, *April 26, 1959, p. 11.*

## THE NEW YORKER

[**"Psycho"** is a] thoroughly creepy tale about a middle-aged mother's boy, a pretty girl with forty thousand stolen dollars in her handbag, and a rundown motel on a back road in the wastes of western Kansas. The writing is a little smudgy, but the story moves at an admirably measured tread, and it contains (as all such entertainments should but only a handful do) a series of absolutely jaw-dropping curtains. (pp. 159-60)

> *A review of "Psycho," in* The New Yorker, *Vol. XXXV, No. 16, June 6, 1959, pp. 159-60.*

## JAMES SANDOE

[In **"The Dead Beat"**] Robert Bloch sketches the later history of a young heel who plays pretty good piano but is trying to parlay himself into means by blackmail. . . . Mr. Bloch manipulates his narrative with speed, economy, bite and with appropriately less ruthlessness than he needed last year for the compulsive **"Psycho."** But then this is a different book, not by any means a lesser one.

> *James Sandoe, in a review of "The Dead Beat," in* New York Herald Tribune Book Review, *May 29, 1960, p. 12.*

## NEWGATE CALLENDAR

[**"Night-World,"**] alas, is a very conventional account of a psychotic mass murderer who, along with several other inmates, escapes from an asylum. Bloch is a professional enough writer to keep things moving, but everything in **"Night-World"** is so predictable that the book is something of a bore.

> *Newgate Callendar, in a review of "Night-World," in* The New York Times Book Review, *August 6, 1972, p. 24.*

## O. L. BAILEY

[*Night World*] is an arresting little thriller. There is a psychopathic killer on the loose, a populace alarmed, a police force methodically pursuing its schizoid role of detection and protection, and the wife of a mental patient snared in a web of love, fear, and uncertainty. These are the elements that unsettlingly juxtapose the sane and the psychopathic.

The writing is taut, never deviating from the classic concept that the shortest distance between two points is a straight plot line. *Night World* is a fast read. Bloch . . . demonstrates a commanding display of sensitivity to the variety of language and life-styles and the social heterogeneity that typify the Los Angeles scene. (p. 62)

> O. L. Bailey, "On the Docket," in Saturday Review, Vol. LV, No. 35, August 26, 1972, pp. 61-2.*

## NEWGATE CALLENDAR

Robert Bloch has based his "American Gothic" . . . on an actual criminal who operated during the Chicago exposition of 1893. Bloch in this book really has created an American gothic, complete with castle, hidden passageways and terrified females. (p. 32)

Unfortunately, Bloch's book is not as good as some of his previous ones. His ingredients are all too familiar: the evil doctor, the bright girl reporter, the scalpels and dismemberment chamber, and so on. The ending contains no surprises, and the writing is not much above a juvenile level. (pp. 32-3)

> Newgate Callendar, in a review of "American Gothic," in The New York Times Book Review, June 30, 1974, pp. 32-3.

## DAN MILLER

[*Cold Chills* is a collection of fourteen] recently published stories by the author of *Psycho,* each with an afterword challenging the reader to decide whether the inspiration came from God or the devil. The owner of a novelty shop who gets caught up in the incarnation of his cynical bumper stickers, an aging movie extra who sees a familiar but impossible face in old movies, the manager of a chicken fight who ends up in the ring, and the vengeance of a father whose daughter was killed by a crazed drug freak are among the psychological suspenses. Bloch's cinematic background injects the thrillers with highly visual imagery, quick dialogue, fast action, and chilling punches to the psyche. (pp. 1484-85)

> Dan Miller, in a review of "Cold Chills," in Booklist, Vol. 73, No. 19, June 1, 1977, pp. 1484-85.

## ALGIS BUDRYS

[The twenty-one stories in *Such Stuff as Screams Are Made Of*] all bear the Bloch cachet of easy entertainment. In addition, some of them bear direct evidence of Bloch's very sharp intelligence and of a wit that now and then penetrates beyond the first ready chuckle and stops amusement hard in the vicinity of the Adam's apple. Those who read fantasy for relaxation

from weightier concerns may find that there is more here than facile escapism.

> Algis Budrys, in a review of "Such Stuff As Screams Are Made Of," in Booklist, Vol. 75, No. 13, March 1, 1979, p. 1042.

## PETER D. PAUTZ

[*Strange Eons*], Robert Bloch's first novel since *American Gothic* (1974), is at once a homage to H. P. Lovecraft and the conclusive Cthulhu Mythos work. Bloch's 44-year-old, self-imposed debt to the Providence fantasist is herein repaid as the World Fantasy Award winner for Life Achievement weaves his characters through horror and nightmare until your heart bleeds for them. And at your own peril.

As violent earthquakes riddle the entire Pacific Ocean and sunken R'lyeh rises to release the Great Old One, Albert and Kay Keith learn of HPL and his horrid fantasies. Or are they fantasies? And, worse yet, are the people around them as totally ignorant as they seem? You never know until it's too late to save yourself; you never know whose side you are really on.

The only drawback here is the constant reference to HPL's seminal works as protagonist after protagonist is informed, remembers, or discovers that what is happening to him was written about, in startling repetitious detail, over fifty years ago. For the Lovecraft fan this provides the blessed opportunity to relive some of the more gruesome and shuddering chills of the original tales. But for those unfamiliar with Lovecraft's pantheon of sinister beings, their impact, threat, and continuing terror might be dispelled forever.

> Peter D. Pautz, in a review of "Strange Eons," in Science Fiction & Fantasy Book Review, Vol. 1, No. 8, September, 1979, p. 104.

## CONNIE FLETCHER

[*Psycho II,* the] sequel to the popular *Psycho,* will probably be in big demand. But the story that picks up where *Psycho* left off—with murderer Norman Bates now in a state hospital for the criminally insane—is a predictable "gore-fest" that falls far short of the original *Psycho*'s finely plotted maze of terror. Bates escapes from the hospital by murdering a nun and dressing in her habit. He then hitchhikes and kills his way to Hollywood, where a movie is being made about him. There he proceeds to slash his way through the set. Instead of the brooding, introverted madman of the original *Psycho,* we are now given a murder machine, a Cuisinart of killing. Bloch tries so hard to equal the suspense of *Psycho* that he subverts its sequel in the process; this reads more like a teenage monster movie than a sophisticated psychological shocker.

> Connie Fletcher, in a review of "Psycho II," in Booklist, Vol. 78, No. 21, July, 1982, p. 1393.

## WALTER KENDRICK

[Robert Bloch was inspired to write a novel by the horrific circumstances surrounding a Wisconsin murder in 1957. There were questions in the case for which he wanted to provide answers, albeit speculative ones.] Bloch's hero would rob only one grave (his mother's); his isolated motel would bring him a steady supply of victims. He would be an amateur taxidermist and an occasional transvestite, like [Ed Gein, the actual murderer], and his pathological mother-fixation would explain everything. Bloch called his novel *Psycho* and its hero Norman Bates—under which name Ed has been a celebrity ever since.

Not, of course, on account of Bloch's novel, which is a pretty trashy piece of work, about on a par with his 50 other paperback potboilers. Ed/Norman's fame is almost wholly due to the Hitchcock film, released in 1960 (a year after the novel) and an instant classic. The novel has been out of print for some time, but now Warner is bringing it back as a companion volume to its sequel. A film called *Psycho II* is also in production, but it has nothing to do with the book *Psycho II*. . . .

The most striking thing about *Psycho,* the novel, is how pat and reassuring it is by comparison to both the real-life horror that inspired it and the wickedly funny film it gave rise to. Headshrinkers (as they were called in 1957) had a field day while Ed Gein was famous. . . . But this was tap-dancing at the brink of Ed's abyss: no one could chart his mind then, and no one has done so since.

Norman Bates à la Bloch, however, is simple. Much of the novel is told from Norman's point of view, so although we're kept in the dark till nearly the end about the fact that he *is* his mother, we're let in on his obsessions: sex, death, embalming, Mom. And when, at the end, the psychiatric accounting comes, it clears away all shadows. The novel displays a strong, very '50s trust in Freudian phrases: Norman himself reads psychiatry books and at one point even considers discussing "the Oedipus situation" with his mother. . . .

Hitchcock confines the Freudianism to the end, where it rings ghoulishly hollow. . . .

[As a film], *Psycho* unties many of the loose ends that still dangle from the Gein case but that Bloch bound up in his novel. This was, I presume, not done deliberately, but only with the aim of making the film as horrible, and as horribly funny, as possible. Because the film *is* funny (especially when you know what's coming), while the novel is driven by an unrelenting earnestness that palls very fast. (p. 46)

The film's two most audacious strokes—killing off the heroine a third of the way through, and doing it in the spectacular shower scene—are both derived from the novel, but in Bloch they're rudimentary and undeveloped. Bloch's Mary Crane (for some reason she's Marion in the film) is an only partly sympathetic character, and we know a lot about Norman and his mother before she ever meets him. So her sudden death, though shocking enough, is nothing like the total derailment of feeling that Hitchcock's version made it. And in the novel her death is very briefly told: "Mary started to scream, and then the curtains parted further and a hand appeared, holding a butcher knife. It was the knife that, a moment later, cut off her scream. And her head." That's all there is to it.

This brilliant scene is the feature of *Psycho,* the film, that has enshrined itself most firmly in popular myth. The exploitative psychology of it is clear and simple: blinded, deafened, naked, and cornered, we're never more vulnerable than when we're in the shower. A whole generation has grown up with an irrational fear of cleanliness—and Robert Bloch started it all. Yet it's apparent from comparing the novel and the film that though the root ideas were Bloch's, he had no inkling of their potential impact. It took a much greater genius than Bloch's to recognize a power that Bloch threw blithely away.

Reading *Psycho* today is an antiquarian experience, like digging through old newspaper files for facts about Ed Gein. There's

pleasure in it, though of a rather outré sort—not the kind of thing that's likely to take America by storm. No doubt Bloch knows that nobody would read his old novel now if it weren't for Hitchcock; Bloch's creation isn't his own anymore. Maybe that's why it took him 23 years to get around to a sequel, and why the sequel reads more like *Psycho III* than *II*. Even Norman Bates's creator now must see him mostly through Hitchcock's eyes.

In *Psycho,* the novel, for example, Norman is short, fat, and 40. In *Psycho,* the film, he's tall, slender, boyish Anthony Perkins. In *Psycho II,* Norman ought to be 63, but he's much too agile for that; he's also grown at least a foot and lost a great deal of weight. The first Norman was pathetic, unattractive, and impotent. Hitchcock gussied him up and gave him sex appeal, and now Bloch himself has accepted the Master's revisions.

The same is true of the shower scene. . . . The preeminence of the shower scene was entirely Hitchcock's invention, but in *Psycho II* Bloch has to contend with an audience weaned on Hitchcock, not Bloch. So he keeps us waiting till nearly the end before he springs a new shower scene on us, and this one—well, it's a joke.

I feel obliged not to give away the details of *Psycho II:* like its predecessor (though unlike Hitchcock), it depends for its effect entirely on two or three little tricks, and if you know them in advance there's no point in reading it. As a novel, *Psycho II* is no better or worse than the run of Bloch's other pulp: efficient, fast moving, and clever enough to sustain the slight interest it solicits. But it's a haunted book. Hitchcock made *Psycho* immortal in spite of itself and allowed *Psycho II* to come into being, but the fate of the sequel is in its own hands. Read it quickly, before the paper-shredders arrive. (pp. 46, 48)

> Walter Kendrick, "The Real Norman Bates," in The
> Village Voice, *Vol. XXVII, No. 39, September 28,*
> *1982, pp. 1, 46, 48.*

### MICHAEL E. STAMM

Twenty-three years ago *Psycho* was published. The next year, the Hitchcock movie came out. The rest, as they say, is history. (p. 17)

Now we have Bloch's . . . [sequel, *Psycho II*,] and it's the *definitive* version. Is it as good as the original? No . . . and yes.

*Psycho* was a nightmare of intensity, a compact story with few characters, centering on the grim Bates Motel. *Psycho II* has more scope: it moves from a sanitarium, where Norman Bates has been since 1959, to Fairvale and beyond to Hollywood. And therein lies the tale: in 1959 Norman Bates was merely a psychopath. In 1982 he's become a legend about to be immortalized on the silver screen. So *Psycho II* can't have the impact of the original. It isn't as much an exercise in sustained terror as it is a *tour de force,* for it takes place in a world wherein Norman Bates finds himself to be an institution, something beyond himself. And if he wasn't sane before . . .

Technically the book is a mixture. It's not as carefully written as the original; on this scale Bloch is working in territory others are more familiar with, and his style does not always mesh with the need for detailing a larger world. (And the master has learned from the student—in some ways, stylistically at least, ***Psycho II*** owes something, I think, to the work of Stephen King.) But the novel says significant things about modern society, the nature of man, and the nature of evil. What is more surprising—and a pleasure—is that Bloch's often none-too-subtle wit is more controlled, more neatly applied, than I've ever seen it.

The plot has a number of twists, among which the end is not the least. (I don't think that end indicates a *Psycho III*—or beyond—to come, as some have feared; but what it says is more frightening, in its way.) The book is not perfectly satisfying, and I might have done several things differently—but this is pure-quill Bloch. (pp. 17-18)

> *Michael E. Stamm, in a review of "Psycho II," in*
> Science Fiction & Fantasy Book Review, *No. 10,*
> *December, 1982, pp. 17-18.*

# Art(hur) Buchwald

## 1925-

American journalist, novelist, and dramatist.

Buchwald's widely-syndicated newspaper columns of political and social satire have established him as one of America's foremost humorists. He has been variously dubbed "Will Rogers with chutzpah," "the Voltaire of the Breakfast Table," "the Poor man's Swift," and even "the Grandma Moses of the humorous columnists." Buchwald's topical political commentary is couched in hyperbole but balanced by a lack of malice. He has been both the recipient of praise and the target of censure; some critics and readers find his light humor engaging, but others feel that his satire lacks sting. Dean Acheson has suggested that Buchwald "is probably the greatest satirist in English since Pope and Swift" yet goes on to say, "perhaps he must share the honors for this with the times he satirizes." Buchwald himself notes: "The world itself is a satire. All you're doing is recording it."

Buchwald began working in the newspaper business in 1948, first as a correspondent for *Variety* in France, and shortly afterwards as a columnist for the Paris edition of the *New York Herald Tribune* under the heading "Paris After Dark." Buchwald's readership grew with his column's syndication, and in 1962 he moved to Washington, D.C., where he still lives.

The essays Buchwald composed in France capture an American view of Europe. They satirize cultural differences, French politics, the urban and domestic world, and Buchwald himself. Collections from these years include *Art Buchwald's Paris* (1953), *The Brave Coward* (1957), *More Caviar* (1959), *Don't Forget to Write* (1961), *How Much Is That in Dollars?* (1962), and *Is It Safe to Drink the Water?* (1962).

Buchwald's first novel, *A Gift from the Boys* (1958), is a farcical comedy about a deported mobster's mishaps with government officials, criminals, and revolutionaries. *The Bollo Caper,* (1974), his next work of fiction, is an ecological fairy tale about a leopard who is hunted for his fur by zealous rich people. Billed as a children's story, this novel is of interest to adults as well.

Buchwald's collections of his American newspaper columns satirize politics and social concerns of the last twenty-five years. Their titles indicate the tone of Buchwald's humor; they include *And Then I Told the President* (1965), *Son of the Great Society* (1966), *The Establishment Is Alive and Well in Washington* (1969), *Getting High in Government Circles* (1971), *I Am Not a Crook* (1974), *Washington Is Leaking* (1976), *The Buchwald Stops Here* (1978), and his recent *While Reagan Slept* (1984). *Down the Seine and Up the Potomac* (1979) is a collection of Buchwald's best columns.

(See also *Contemporary Authors,* Vols. 5-8, rev. ed. and *Something about the Author,* Vol. 10.)

## ILKA CHASE

"Art Buchwald's Paris," from the city of the same name, may not mirror the Paris of the Faubourg Saint Germain or Notre Dame, but it details in sprightly fashion the town of the tourist's dream. . . .

*Photograph by Donal F. Holway*

Many of the pieces in his current glossary of learning and mellow experience have appeared in [the Paris edition of the *New York Herald Tribune*] . . . and Buchwald fans will recognize with pleasure such old favorites as the letters to friends about to visit the City of Light (if they want to enjoy themselves after receiving an account of what awaits them in the French capital—a single bed for two and a threat of polio—they will turn in ecstasy to Paris, Arkansas) and the learned treatise on "Le Bazbal Made Easy" with the central position so aptly described as *l'aisiette maison.*

There are a few solid and highly readable essays—the one on art speculation as big business and the engaging account of Europe's first omnibus—but probably the most popular chapters for any reader anticipating a trip abroad will prove to be the authoritative and straightforward pieces on tipping and night life.

Ilka Chase, "Happyville-on-the-Seine," in New York Herald Tribune Book Review, *November 21, 1954, p. 4.*

## ALAN LEVY

Buchwald's latest book, *The Brave Coward,* is a collection of 43 dispatches from Africa, Europe, and America. He contemplates every place with the eye of a foreign correspondent and gives even a journey through the Empire State Building the flavor of a trip up Everest by elevator. But, while the emphasis is on places, Buchwald does not overlook people. In his name-dropping moments, he can hold his own with Bennett Cerf. (p. 18)

The most recurrent person in Buchwald's book is Buchwald. You are there as Buchwald is manhandled by Leena, a woman who administers the best *sauna* (the native Finnish bath) in all Helsinki. You are there as he becomes entangled in East Berlin's May Day parade; spends a Sunday beagling in Ireland; bobsleds at St. Moritz, and hunts an honest jeweler named Davud in the Istanbul bazaar. (pp. 18-19)

The cumulative effect of these short pieces—in which the scenery changes, but Buchwald remains the same—tends to make the author seem a trifle pale and quite repetitious. There is really just one joke—Buchwald's joyous cowardice when confronted by any situation. This can be as tiresome as its opposite number, the heroics in a comic strip or adventure story.

Perhaps that is why the most fantastic and amusing episode in *The Brave Coward* is one called *The Six-Minute Louvre,* in which Buchwald has only a bit part. It tells how Peter Stone, an American tourist, got through the museum in 5:56, making the required pauses at the Big Three—the "Winged Victory," the "Venus de Milo" and the "Mona Lisa"—and the innocuous tourist remark that must be made at the "Mona Lisa." ("I don't see what's so great about it.") . . .

The voyage from *The Herald Tribune* to . . . [book form] has made a few of the pieces look seasick. But disappointing as it may be, it is likely to bring Buchwald new readers and admirers. You can sense that almost all this stuff must have looked good in a newspaper column. And every now and then you realize that Buchwald is—on a part-time basis—one of the few satirists practicing in the columns of newspapers. His alleged visit to the Dallas Petroleum Club indicates that even Texas still has fertile soil for a humorist. . . .

[In the aforementioned article] and in a section on the origin of the Parker pens sold on Rome's sidewalks (they're made by an unauthorized Parker Pen Company in Torino), Buchwald is a wonderful combination of satirist and reporter. In these moments, he outgrows his chosen world where the common brand names are TWA Constellation, Neiman-Marcus, The Istanbul Hilton, the Simca Aronde auto, and Balenciaga costumes. The International Set's life could be more than a beat for a man of Buchwald's energy. It could be the take-off point for a talented satirist who should be able to make fun of more promising targets than himself. (p. 19)

> *Alan Levy, "Shaking Knees with Buchwald," in* The New Republic, *Vol. 136, No. 16, April 22, 1957, pp. 18-19.*

### AL MORGAN

"A Gift From the Boys" has all the Buchwald virtues. It is the easiest reading since Henny Penny felt a piece of the sky fall on her tail. It is a book that always seems on the verge of being realistic but happily goes barreling off into the realm of fantasy and the never-never land of Mr. B's cockeyed appraisal of life. It is more an entertainment than a novel but since the world is full of novels and reasonably short on entertainment, it is a welcome addition to our reading.

The hero of "A Gift From the Boys" is an American gangster named Frank Bartlett (born Bartelini) who finds himself suffering from an occupational disease known as "Deportation." While his appeal on an income tax evasion charge is still pending before a higher court, he is hustled aboard a luxury liner bound for the land of his birth, La Coma, Sicily. In his party are his faithful body guard, an American crime reporter, who has conned his newspaper into sending him along to do a series on the deported gangster, and the "Gift From the Boys" . . . a luscious hunk of blonde womanhood named Karen who is along to keep the long ocean voyage from becoming too dull. . . .

If Mr. Buchwald seems to run out of invention and interest two-thirds of the way through, it is not completely fatal to his first excursion into novel-writing. Most of the way, "A Gift From the Boys" is entertaining, amusing and fun. These days that's well under par for this particular course.

> *Al Morgan, "A Mobster's Comic Woes," in* New York Herald Tribune Book Review, *September 7, 1958, p. 7.*

### MARTIN LEVIN

Art Buchwald, whose novel "A Gift From the Boys" . . . is the merry travel log of a deported mobster, remarks philosophically: "Even if they should get me, at least there'll be money for the wife and kids." However, Mr. Buchwald has more to fear from Italian officialdom than the underworld. Frank Bartlett, the too rugged individualist exiled to his native La Coma, is treated with the deference Edward Everett Hale accorded Philip Norton. . . .

It would be unsporting to cavil at an unpretentiously funny charade, written by one of the deftest humorists around. But if there is something lacking in "A Gift from the Boys," it is a mite of solid construction, which should keep a novel rolling unpredictably along. Actually, all that happens to poor Bartlett is one damn thing after another, and eventually the reader begins to feel as overwhelmed as the deportee.

> *Martin Levin, "Italian Spree," in* Saturday Review, *Vol. XLI, No. 47, November 22, 1958, p. 20.*

### BEN CRISLER

At book length Art Buchwald seems an original and altogether diverting anomaly, like a banquet of sumptuous splendor and endless variety composed exclusively of hors d'oeuvres. But, if Art is fleeting, Time is long. Hence this fortunate accumulation ["More Caviar"], from the Paris edition, more or less of The New York Herald Tribune, a dossier of satirical whimsies which Buchwald's adoptive France, fittingly enough, alone has a word for.

The word is not merely *feuilletons* but *mitrailles,* designating small but deadly and strictly nonpartisan missiles, something like paper airplanes armed with hypodermic warheads. Many are aimed at the French who, luckily, as a rule, are insensitive to anything written in English. A fusillade entitled "Russian Caviar" clangs drolly against the Iron Curtain, while others patter like unseasonal hail along the Côte d'Azur or ricochet from ancient impervious monuments (as in "The Mona Lisa Crouch") to wound visiting Americans.

On the whole, however, Buchwald respects Americans abroad as a true sportsman honors sitting ducks. His sweetest havoc is wreaked among a certain supra-national noblesse who prey on tourists as piranhas prey on outboard Brazilians. In a blistering étude entitled "A Heart-Warming Christmas Story," Buchwald enshrines one of these ghastly cannibals in formaldehyde.

**"More Caviar"** deals with live-coal issues—such as the great dry-martini reaction of the mid-Fifties which promises to restore Count Rossi, the vermouth king, to his ancient estates. . . .

The Bourbonic-plague of French civil servants; the acute shortage of guests on the Riviera (resulting in several ugly incidents between competing villa and yacht people, including rumors of cruise-guests shanghaied from hotels) are among dozens of unlikely topics, too numerous and too wonderfully intricate to catalogue.

Incidentally, Buchwald's prose—composed largely of inverse hyperbole—remains the surest antidote for travel-page fatigue which American journalism affords. What's more, **"More Caviar"** is probably the most amusing . . . substitute for an All-Inclusive European Tour at present obtainable between book covers.

> Ben Crisler, *"Notes for, and of, Innocents Abroad,"* in The New York Times Book Review, *April 19, 1959, p. 10.*

**BEN CRISLER**

Art Buchwald's column from Paris in The New York Herald Tribune has consistently endeared itself to students of undignified foreign affairs. **"Don't Forget to Write"** is a welcome addition to the collected works of Buchwald, frankly frivolous, in some cases, outrageously rigged, but, nevertheless, highly recommendable.

Although a typical Buchwald column is usually a prankish intercontinental missile, as harmless as a paper airplane, it tends to be accurately aimed and is frequently fitted with a dummy warhead of potential or implied satire calculated to keep his celebrity-patrons on pins and needles. . . .

Like Boswell, Buchwald has a happy knack for midwifing great thoughts, as when he draws out Al Capp, the cartoonist, on the subject: "Don't Be a Pal to Your Son," with fruitful results. And his reportage, though technically trivial, sometimes develops an illuminating, fourth-dimensional quality, as when he reveals why Paul Getty, the oil billionaire, bought the Duke of Sutherland's ancestral estate. It seems he did it to save hotel expenses.

Some of Buchwald's best columns are inspired by non-celebrity friends such as Jean Tinguely, sculptor-inventor of an antimechanical machine which embodies "the functional use of hazard." On this monstrous juke device, it seems, anyone may turn out an impressive abstract painting for one dollar. This sort of thing is fun: still, Buchwald doesn't let fame or riches prejudice him against a subject. When celebrityism gets too thick, as with the twin luminaries, Dinah Shore and husband, George Montgomery, he simply interviews their children on "Problems of Traveling With Parents."

Perhaps, on the whole, Buchwald's happiest effects consist in transposing the obvious into pure hoax and fantasy, as in "A Talk With the Nubam of Lemon" or "Little-Known Festivals in Europe." In the latter he glowingly describes Gazpacho's colorful fiesta which is climaxed by the stoning of tourists; also a friendly interchange of crop burnings between Upper

and Lower Gesundheit, a famine-producing but traditional and hence, unavoidable custom. . . .

In short, Mr. Buchwald's topics, numerous and diverse as they are, form a practically flawless necklace of non sequiturs, reducing the chaos of our world and time to small, pleasantly assimilable doses.

> Ben Crisler, *"Frankly Frivolous,"* in The New York Times Book Review, *September 25, 1960, p. 38.*

**SUSAN M. BLACK**

***Don't Forget to Write*** consists of 85 pieces divided into 8 sections beginning with "What's Nous" ("Nous" is a happy family of five: Buchwald, wife and three small, expensive children—supplemented by friends and an occasional nanny or mother-in-law). The scene is usually Paris but Buchwald will go almost anywhere, by train, plane, letter, telephone or imagination. . . .

The virtues of Buchwald's writing are many: good reporting, good satire, good taste. As for his vices, I wish he didn't push the funny business so hard. Still, I find him the funniest newspaper columnist today. If you are stunned by the sameness of his columns (and you will be, upon reading them *en masse*), remember how good they looked when they appeared one at a time, three times a week, alongside gloomy headlines and gloomier interpretations by the more serious pundits.

> Susan M. Black, *"The Unquiet American in Paris,"* in The New Republic, *Vol. 143, No. 21, November 14, 1960, p. 18.*

**AL MORGAN**

Art Buchwald, the Breakfast Table Voltaire, has committed a book again. A whopping collection of eighty of his most recent columns has been packaged under the all-inclusive title: **"How Much Is That in Dollars?"** There is nothing particularly newsworthy in the fact alone. What is newsworthy is this yearly reminder that the roly-poly young man with the horn-rimmed glasses is perhaps the last living practitioner of the funny essay. What is more surprising and important is that he is able to hit his target a good three-quarters of the time.

The basic difference between Buchwald and his fellow syndicated pundits is that over the years he has managed to create a character as rounded, as three-dimensional and as real as, for instance, Jack Benny's skinflint or Bob Hope's coward. Buchwald has built up a public personality for himself as the lovable schnook in Paris. . . .

In the current volume of columns, only slightly less than half of the material concerns the Buchwald family and you may be surprised to discover that beneath the obvious style, the puns and the pure entertainment content there is a solid, valid portrait of what it is like to be part of an American family with one foot in the Hudson and the other in the Seine. His Paris eye view of French politics owes its point of view to the district club in the Bronx, he is always the innocent abroad who has the jaundiced eye of a New York cab driver. He is skillful and superbly readable.

To say that Buchwald is a funny writer is to belabor the obvious. What may not be obvious is the fact that he is a satirist of no mean ability. Get Jim Hagerty to show you his scars, sometime. Or read the column in this current volume on a plane conversation with a German industrialist.

To the regular reader of the Buchwald columns the appearance of a new collection is reason enough for rejoicing. To the retarded few who have not read him in three-a-week dosage . . . here is an opportunity to be exposed to one of the unique entertainers of our time . . . everybody's man in Paris.

> Al Morgan, "Our Man by the Seine," in Books, November 19, 1961, p. 11.

## ROSALIE PACKARD

This scissors-and-paste job of Art Buchwald's columns [*How Much is That in Dollars?*] . . . creates an unfortunate first impression. . . . [The] first few pieces are abysmally dull: but stick with it, if you have the time, and the whole deal gathers speed. One reads on with a gentle smile playing about the lips. The cumulative effect is of charm and kindness.

The humour of Art Buchwald, to get this seminar off its unpleasant cavilling note, is very American, very poker-faced. He is no Thurber or S. J. Perelman (it is one of the world's great sadnesses that there are only the two of them), but he has a lot in common with Abe Burroughs, well-known Broadway play-doctor. . . .

Perhaps Buchwald's finest effort in this book is the story of Lovlost-by-the-Sea, 'that tiny European country that has been a bulwark against Communism and friend of the United States since the early days of 1946.' Lovlost's currency is the bardot, and it has the only carrier-pigeon station in NATO. There are two stalwart members of the American armed forces on duty in Lovlost who are catered for by a PX with 500 civilian employees. How Dean Rusk stays so calm in the face of all this is more than I can understand.

> Rosalie Packard, "Art for Art's Sake," in The Spectator, Vol. 208, No. 6982, April 20, 1962, p. 518.

## M. J. ARLEN

"Is It Safe to Drink the Water?" is Buchwald's third collection of columns to be published in hardcover, and it contains what must be nearly all the columns he's written in the past two years. Buchwald is especially good when burlesquing a topical theme or event and there are funny pieces here on "new-wave" Westerns, on imaginary interviews with de Gaulle and Khrushchev, on the Japanese sailor who missed sinking PT-109, and on a Ban the Peace Movement. In fact, when you consider that these interviews and sketches were turned out for a newspaper deadline, at a rate of three per week, it's amazing how high a level of quality, of being amusing, he maintains over what must have been a long and tiring course indeed.

Unfortunately this isn't a collection of columns in a newspaper; it is a collection of newspaper columns in a book. The words are the same, but the setting is different and our expectations are somehow different too. Mr. Buchwald's collection is certainly not skimpy in the variety of its material. He has 94 different columns reprinted here. Nor is it hindered by topicality, or lack of it. What the collection suffers from is that the individual pieces don't seem to travel very far, or far enough; which is not to say they are too short, but that they are too sketchy and incomplete.

Of course Mr. Buchwald, in this instance, hasn't really written a book, but he has published one. It is a genial book, a merry book, here and there a downright funny book. It shouldn't be any particular discredit to this master columnist to say that although his are the best humorous columns in the business, they still read to greatest effect in the pages of the newspapers for which they were originally written.

> M. J. Arlen, "Footnotes for Fun," in The New York Times Book Review, November 4, 1962, p. 24.

## LEONARD C. LEWIN

For those who have yet to be exposed to Art Buchwald, this current collection of his recent columns ["**And Then I Told the President**"] is a fine place to start. . . .

Describing Buchwald as a *political* columnist says as much about our times as it does about him. The quantity, and especially the quality, of political criticism currently expressed in the form of satire or simple humor would have been unimaginable 10 years ago. . . . The dead-pan ironies of Buchwald, the mordant apperceptions of Russell Baker and the ebullient imagination of Arthur Hoppe (to name only the first of a dozen who come to mind) are already reaching millions of readers through syndication, and the prospects for reaching more are bullish.

Wide distribution, I am happy to note, has not led to dilution of the product; on the contrary, the satirists are increasingly inclined to take on big issues rather than to stick to safe ones. It is now possible to appreciate their work for its wit, its grace and its effectiveness, without necessarily feeling obliged to make allowances for its daring or the lack of it. I am not suggesting that the flag of Free Expression already flies unchallenged over its allotted sector of the Great Society. But we have at least recaptured territory that had been lost between Hiroshima and the fall of McCarthy.

Buchwald at his best has a deceptive simplicity which can be devastating; he is concise, unelaborate and, incidentally, very funny. At his worst he is heavy-handed. But his ratio of hits to misses rises steadily; every now and then he scores a bull's-eye that demolishes his target. (p. 3)

A few short quotes will indicate the typical directness of his attack, though not the relentless logic of his exposition. . . . On overkill: "We must build bigger targets to fit our bombs." On economics: "I have discovered that America is a nation of middlemen and subcontractors and that there is only one man in the entire nation that actually does the work. His name is Harold." . . .

Although the work of today's new wave of American popular satirists can stand comparison with that of earlier periods in our history, there seems to be no evidence that it has—as yet—had any but the most indirect influence on public affairs. If and when the time should come that Buchwald and his peers receive the kind of serious political attention enjoyed by Artemus Ward a hundred years ago, or by Finley Peter Dunne at the turn of the century, it will be, I think, a good day for all of us. (p. 20)

> Leonard C. Lewin, "Politics and Pins," in The New York Times Book Review, May 2, 1965, pp. 3, 20.

## JAMES F. FIXX

Why hasn't President Johnson asked J. Edgar Hoover to resign? Simple. Hoover doesn't exist. He's a mythical person invented in 1925 by *Reader's Digest*. The myth has been so successful that over the years no fewer than twenty-six people have had to be recruited to play the role, and now it's too late to back out. Only once was there a real slip-up—when one of the J. Edgar Hoovers was photographed arresting John Dillinger in Chicago while another was simultaneously accepting a DAR Americanism Award in Philadelphia. As a result of that boner, the man in charge of keeping the various Hoovers on schedule was banished from his job.

So, at any rate, goes a slice of contemporary Americana as refracted by the fertile, fanciful mind of Art Buchwald, a syndicated newspaper columnist who delights in turning a wisp of fact into an astonishing tangle of improbabilities. Part parodist and part national demon-in-residence, Buchwald clearly delights in his self-appointed assignment of exposing Washington, D.C., as the sort of city one might expect to find at the bottom of Alice's rabbit hole. . . .

Buchwald's wild and wily wit . . . is pleasantly revisited in his new book, . . . *And Then I Told the President* . . . , a sprightly accumulation of columns rather casually edited to arrest, if not quite cure, that congenital malady of such collections, paste-and-scissors disease. The book is clearly dated in more than one spot, roaming as far back in time as that faintly recalled yesterday when, in one Buchwald political allegory, the Arizona Kid stalked the land, terrorizing such rivals as Pennsylvania Bill and Deputy Dick. But Buchwald, in his daily stint at the typewriter, is writing for now, not for some book to be published months from now, and the wonder of it is that his writing keeps as well as it does.

Take, for example, one of his columns on the John Birch Society, written after the Birchers unwittingly helped the UNICEF Christmas card campaign by trying to stop it in Monterey, California. Buchwald first reports the facts, as plainly as any other Washington newspaperman might do. But then that strange gleam comes into his prose, and before his readers know it he's off to Wonderland, gleefully speculating on the fund-raising possibilities inherent in widespread John Birch Society opposition. . . .

Then, too, there are columns on . . . praying in school ("They're going to do it anyway, and it's better to have them pray openly in class than sneak into the locker room or into the washroom for a quick prayer where no one will see them"), and on a whole circus of other subjects that would occur only to the quixotic wit of American journalism's Mad Hatter. . . . *And Then I Told the President* is, in short, just the antidote for those days when you have the uneasy suspicion that everything is going right.

> James F. Fixx, "Arthur in Wonderland," in Saturday Review, Vol. XLVIII, No. 19, May 8, 1965, p. 67.*

## JOHN WESLEY FULLER

The latest collection of Art Buchwald's short satiric essays [*Son of the Great Society*] will surely add to the numerous Buchwald fans who enjoy his rollicking, but incisive comments. His earliest collection focused mainly on life abroad, but this book focuses mainly on American politics, mores, and foibles.

The President and his close associates have to bear the brunt of Buchwald's ribbing. Isn't it fortunate, Buchwald asks, that Goldwater was not elected? If he had been, we would probably right now be landing marines in South Vietnam, bombing North Vietnam, and generally escalating the conflict at an alarming rate! . . .

In addition to party politics and Vietnam, the essays touch on inflation, segregation, taxes, husbands and wives, parents and children, the new math, fashions, the Dominican Republic, South American dictatorships, Africa, the CIA, Batman, Dr. Spock, Elizabeth Taylor, toothpaste ads, the great power blackout—the list is as varied as life itself.

But Buchwald's underlying topic is neither the Great Society nor its son (himself), but human foibles. His satire devastates phony political poses and suspect public pronouncements. In addition to such satiric devices as irony and understatement, he has mastered the method of exaggerating a point of view until it is reduced to absurdity.

Such fare might be expected to cloy in a collection of more than one hundred essays, but the constant flow of unexpected turns and clever insights piques the reader's interest from beginning to end. Anyone may find here and there an essay that, for his taste falls rather flat—as perhaps the proposal for automation in the circus. But then he is likely to find that the piece next to it—a sketch satirizing the way TV announcers have to pad out the time while waiting for a delayed blast-off—more than compensates.

Court jesters of old played a role in relieving tensions and maintaining sanity and perspective. We need skillful jesters like Art Buchwald today. However tragic, tense—or even humdrum—the daily news, his mercurial wit extracts from it not only laughter, but a balance of common sense and common humanity. This book reassures one that, for all its weaknesses and mistakes, a society that is free enough to laugh at itself and its leaders in print is also resilient enough to endure.

> John Wesley Fuller, "A Skillful Jester," in The Christian Science Monitor, October 18, 1966, p. 9.

## ROBERT J. MANNING

The quality that distinguishes [Art Buchwald] from other Washington columnists, save for his somewhat subtler colleague at *The New York Times*, Russell Baker, is that he is intentionally funny. Hardly a week passes that some Congressman or Cabinet officer or Chief Executive or international pundit doesn't top him, but these unwitting forays into ridiculousness or comedy are usually by-products of some solemn enterprise, such as . . . the defense of free enterprise as a reason for denying Social Security coverage to elderly charladies.

But Buchwald is a pro, and for the day-to-day haul, his humor [in *Son of the Great Society*] is consistently amusing, even more so than the society pages of *The Washington Post* and *The Washington Star*. And at its best, his satirical commentary on the somber and even fearful cares of state is sometimes more illuminating—and sometimes even tells us more—than do the ponderings of his more serious brethren. . . .

Buchwald deliberately does not try to moralize nor to probe deeply. He is no Thurber, gliding tellingly through human fancy and foible, nor a Perelman sending spirals of nonsense into happy orbit; nor does he have the sardonic tone that brought a touch of gloom if not despair even to the funniest of Mark

Twain's work. His forte is the cartoon brought to life, the campus skit or vaudeville blackout raised to a certain This-Is-The-Week-That-Was maturity and social relevance. . . .

Many of his most effective pieces are built around a certain "in" humor (though the spread of his column and the rise of his affluence suggest that the "in-group" is growing rapidly). Some of his most consistent fans are the Washingtonians whose manners, or sacred cows, or personalities he most likes to mimic or satirize. This is because he writes without malice. One day he can pin wry plaudits on Sen. Robert Kennedy for his valiant non-effort to help Mayor John Lindsay solve the New York transit strike; a week or two later he may be . . . crewing for Bobby and Teddy in a sailboat race off Hyannisport (and explain that he can't give it the old Kennedy try because it might hurt his tennis game, an unlikelihood comparable to Galli-Curci's worrying about losing her knuckle-ball). He's a funny man and who doesn't want to have a funny man around?

> Robert J. Manning, "Capitol Jester," in Book Week—World Journal Tribune, October 23, 1966, p. 14.

## PAMELA MARSH

[Art Buchwald's] column is one big trick that is not meant to deceive for a second. He likes to pretend that his highly individual style and opinions do not belong to him at all. His specialty is to seize on some topic in the news, hand it over to two imaginary characters (one of them is usually a self-deprecatory interviewer operating under the name Buchwald), and allow us to eavesdrop. Then his points are made, his punch-lines fired off inside quotation marks, with never a nudge administered or a verdict pronounced by the columnist.

[In *Have I Ever Lied to You?*] Mr. Buchwald talks to a mythical father who has run through his savings before his son has graduated (from nursery school that is) or to another who has managed college fees but not bail. Draft card destroying came expensive; burning the gym along with the card, exorbitant. . . .

Mr. Buchwald is not always funny. He is sometimes irritating (perhaps when it is my prejudices he is pricking), and he can be ponderous. But at his deftest and lightest, he can knock you down with his feathers.

> Pamela Marsh, "Buchwald Interviewing Buch-wald," in The Christian Science Monitor, April 16, 1968, p. 9.

## DEAN ACHESON

One of the few propositions one can put forward today without high risk of being proved wrong tomorrow is that Art Buchwald is probably the greatest satirist in English since Pope and Swift. Perhaps he must share the honors for this with the times he satirizes. . . .

Out of Buchwald's gift for laughter comes his genial humor, without which satire edges toward bitterness and invective. He has none of that. [In *Have I Ever Lied to You?*, his] humor, though keen, is tolerant. It springs from his sense that the world is mad, which saves him from ethical or moral purpose. "'Tis a mad world, my Masters!" he says with his Elizabethan kindred spirit, John Taylor, and hence nothing can be done about it. Since his literary form is the newspaper column, rather than the grander forms of the 18th-century satirists, one can say of him without derogation that he is the poor man's Swift. But

one refers only to form and not to his art and observation. They are worthy of his illustrious predecessors from Horace down. Today periodical publication and particularly the newspaper has rejected the essay and verse. Form must be adapted to the times. Yet Lincoln would have reveled in Buchwald; even the column form is akin to Lincoln's vehicle for satire, the epigram and fable.

That Buchwald not only sees the world as mad, but that it is mad gives him—as the British say—a leg up. When he holds the mirror to life, he finds with both Molière and Shaw the mockery of sense and reason so well blocked in to begin with that he has only to add a gay touch of exaggeration and the grotesque to produce satire. One wonders, for instance, when Buchwald writes of one of his favorite characters, Mr. Allstop, how the newspaper compositors know whose photograph to attach to which column.

Another debt which Buchwald owes to his times was owed also by the 18th-century satirists to theirs—the decline of current political writing. One has only to glance at the columns among which Buchwald appears to be struck by their triviality, repetitiveness and utter boredom. Their content has been reduced almost entirely to discussion of personalities—in other words, gossip—about people whose only claim to attention is public position and ambition. The outpourings of such columnists become those of village Horace Walpoles. Collections of them are not apt to rank with *The Federalist Papers*.

Satire alone makes the current scene bearable. Buchwald brings to his satire the genius of hitting upon the most absurd of the absurdities around him and a rare gift for dialogue that runs the gamut of humor from the subtle to the Rabelaisian to the hilarious. Dialogue has always played a large part in satire, whether in the form of drama or fable. (p. 1)

Art Buchwald's book is a bedside book, but in quite the opposite sense from what is usually meant by that phrase. It should be there not to put one to sleep but to comfort one on waking up in the ghastly dawn of another day, wondering whether one can churn another batch of the same sour cream. Then is the time to turn on the light and reach for Buchwald. "'Tis a mad world, my Masters!" he will greet you cheerfully, and after a half hour's transfusion you will be up eager to test how mad it is. (p. 3)

> Dean Acheson, "Gift of Laughter in a Mad, Mad, Mad, Mad World," in Book World—The Washington Post, May 26, 1968, pp. 1, 3.

## NATHANIEL BENCHLEY

Trying to write a rational review of a collection of Art Buchwald pieces is like trying to report on a riot in a madhouse; it looks as though most of the characters are crazy, but there's a streak of cold sanity lurking in the background, and you occasionally get the feeling you should be screaming instead of laughing. Sometimes you do both, and sometimes neither. It's all very confusing.

The present volume [*The Establishment Is Alive and Well in Washington*] consists of 119 pieces, written over two years, and it is Buchwald's tenth such collection. Quick addition will show that this represents a prodigious amount of work, and to be funny—or even to try to be funny—in print, three or four times a week, year in and year out, is a job that would flatten most aspiring humorists. That Buchwald's eyes bulge every now and then, and a glisten of sweat appears on his forehead, should not be held against him; his batting average is remarkably high. He is an American institution, the Grandma Moses of the humorous columnists, and to snipe at him would be like hurling tomatoes at the Iwo Jima monument. . . .

To me, one of the neatest pieces in the present book, possibly because of its simplicity, is the one in which he explains the entire international situation in terms of the comic strip "Peanuts": Lucy as France, Linus as Great Britain (with his blanket marked "Made in U.S.A."), Charlie Brown the United States, Schroeder West Germany, and Snoopy Italy. With this established, everything falls into place with quiet perfection; Lucy wants to be leader of the gang and keeps berating Charlie Brown, who can say nothing but "good grief," and so on. It is a masterpiece of explanation, and once understood it simplifies everything except Russia and China, who have no place in a "Peanuts" strip anyway. Of course, without de Gaulle, France has assumed a somewhat different mien, but this doesn't change the point of the piece. . . .

In his domestic pieces, Buchwald concentrates most heavily on Washington and the political scene, which by its very nature is made to order for satire, but he is by no means unaware of the domestic—in the sense of household—scene as well. Preferences here must naturally be a matter of taste, and I prefer the home-front pieces to the political-front ones simply because they're harder to do, and therefore more rewarding when they work. There's something deceptive about domestic comedy: it looks so easy to write that a lot of people think they can do it, and most of them fail. When Buchwald succeeds, as with "God Bless You, Mrs. Robinson," he is splendid. Here he has a suburban matron turning her coincidental name with the leading lady in *The Graduate* into an asset instead of an embarrassment, and it is neat and deft and a small triumph.

When he doesn't succeed, it is either because the punch telegraphs itself in the beginning, or the idea becomes too tricky to be handled without straining. In either case, the result is nothing worse than a mild letdown. Furthermore, the reader's eyes tend to become glazed with too much humor; it is fairer to the book to read the pieces a few at a time and at varying intervals, so that the inevitable pattern doesn't become too obvious. And also to skip around among the subjects; they are lumped together in various categories, and too much of one category at one time can bring on a nibbling ennui.

These are, however, minor quibbles, and will probably outrage his fans. . . . He is, as he has always been, a sort of Will Rogers with chutzpah, and if that doesn't make Grandma Moses turn over in her grave than nothing ever will.

> *Nathaniel Benchley, "Would You Believe a Will Rogers with Chutzpah?" in* Book World—The Washington Post, *October 5, 1969, p. 3.*

**PAUL SHOWERS**

For absent-minded Buchwald fanciers who are forever clipping his columns and mislaying them, this book is an unmixed blessing. . . .

[The 117 sketches in **"The Establishment Is Alive and Well in Washington"**] review most of the major points of public interest in the last couple of years: the Pueblo, Jackie Kennedy's remarriage, student unrest, deGaulle and NATO, the ABM hearings, black power, crime and violence, Russia's invasion of Czechoslovakia and the new four-letter vogue.

The beauty of Buchwald is that he is not only a devastatingly brilliant satirist; he is also terribly funny, which is not always true of serious satirists. He can, for instance, toss off a low-comedy lead with the greatest of the masters: "My friend Mulligan was in a stew." It's why Buchwald addicts are never cured.

> *Paul Showers, in a review of "The Establishment Is Alive and Well in Washington," in* The New York Times Book Review, *November 30, 1969, p. 38.*

**E. S. TURNER**

Art Buchwald's style [in *Oh, To Be a Swinger*] is unladen with ornament. The idea is all. Sometimes it looks too easy: all he's doing is the humorist's stand-by, the Simple Inversion Trick. Men arrive on Earth from space and find it a desert of concrete covered with deadly gases in which nothing can live. But even if Buchwald relies on some familiar devices you never hear the groan of the crankhandle. His pieces are shorter than those of his fellow practitioners: the idea must spin instantly and then compression increases its velocity. No one has a sharper ear for the humbug of official spokesmen. . . . Buchwald suggests all too plausibly how the media build up terrorists and how society embraces them; only slightly less plausibly he shows us a CIA man subsidising student action.

> *E. S. Turner, "Cod and Blod," in* The Listener, *Vol. 84, No. 2174, November 26, 1970, p. 747.\**

**A. J. ANDERSON**

[*Getting High in Government Circles*] is a collection of short vignettes. . . . In this set of fables Buchwald conveys a sense of the often incongruous and absurd things that humans do, particularly those in high office, when they think they are acting in an intelligent and prudent way. He achieves his effects by juxtaposing exaggeration and understatement, and the point of his fantasies is always unmistakably clear. The book should have wide appeal, and is recommended heartily. (pp. 2772-73)

> *A. J. Anderson, in a review of "Getting High in Government Circles," in* Library Journal, *Vol. 96, No. 16, September 15, 1971, pp. 2772-73.*

**DAVID K. WILLIS**

[*I Never Danced At The White House*] is not to be read straight through: 84,000 words of Buchwald is for dipping into, not submerging beneath. Some columns, inevitably, are weaker than others.

Besides sustained inventiveness, Buchwald's virtue is his relentless topicality; the collection reawakens many past headlines more effectively than re-reading the headlines themselves. . . .

Often the columns have an uncanny ring to them: they are so almost-true that the laughter they evoke—usually through dialogue—is, suddenly, not so funny after all.

This latest collection is Buchwald unadorned: no author's note, no foreword, postscript, analysis, footnotes, annotation. Just columns, roughly divided into Watergate, Vietnam, campaigning, etc. This, perhaps is the best way: to let the columns speak for themselves.

David K. Willis, "Washington through Fogged-Up Glasses," in The Christian Science Monitor, October 24, 1973, p. 9.

## CLEVELAND AMORY

"High on the list of [Buchwald's] pet hates," says the jacket of this book [*The Bollo Caper*], "are Big Game Hunters who like to shoot rare animals for the sport of it. Next on his list are people who kill animals for their fur."

This book, in a word, is about that. A shorty—56 pages—and ostensibly a children's book it is far too good to waste on their unappreciative little minds. It is in fact subtitled "A Fable for Children of All Ages."

Bollo, our hero here and the one from whose point of view the story is told, is a leopard—one with the most beautiful skin in the world. And the $30,000 question is will he retain this skin or will he go to the Hollywood Academy Awards on the back of the already frontally satisfactory Miss Lulu La Looche. Miss La Looche greets everyone as "Dahling" and is pictured in the illustrations by Julie Brinckloe as, if not the person you think she is, at least as close as the law allows.

The style here is Buchwald at his best—a rippling, bubbly surface of chuckles which can be checked only so long and then breaks out into a spouting guffaw....

We will not spoil it for you except to say that from the moment the boom boom of the native drums begins to the incredible end, an awful lot happens. The scenes shift in rapid succession from Africa to Kennedy Airport to the top of a Manhattan Yellow Taxi to the Central Park Zoo to the top of a Metroliner to the White House lawn. At one point a tiger in a Washington, D.C. circus—not the one at the White House—tells Bollo, "Wow, I've heard some wild animal stories in my time, but this one takes the cake."

A tiger like that is wasted in a circus. He should be writing reviews.

*Cleveland Amory, "Hide and Seek," in* Book World—The Washington Post, *May 19, 1974, p. 3.*

## SUSAN WOOD

One of the things that makes Buchwald so endearing ... is that he can turn a wry eye on himself, as well as the rest of us. In the fantasy that begins [*Washington Is Leaking*], he imagines himself as a "tall, handsome man" so powerful that he can afford to snub Teddy Kennedy. In another he becomes the czar of the family Monopoly board, while in a third he is "the world's greatest lobber." Buchwald also offers advice to those of us wondering how to cope. If you want to know what you can do to help avert another gas shortage, take a sheikh to lunch.

What becomes clear in reading *Washington is Leaking* is that as long as we can laugh along with Art Buchwald we may be leaking but we're not sinking.

*Susan Wood, in a review of "Washington Is Leaking," in* Book World—The Washington Post, *November 7, 1976, p. G4.*

## JEFF GREENFIELD

["**Down the Seine and Up the Potomac**"] brings together a sampler from 25 years of newspaper and magazine columns by one of America's best-known contemporary humorists. From his days covering and spoofing the European jet set to his days as a Washington columnist, Buchwald has managed to touch a responsive nerve in an American readership that sometimes regards humor as a suspect, if not black, art.

The remarkable longevity of Buchwald is due to the simplicity of his satirical approach. He has been smart enough to develop a form that is, above all, predictable. Once the comic pretense is set up—stores suspect cash customers in an age of credit, lack of driving is un-American, bureaucrats work hard to avoid working—the column works that premise again and again....

Two caveats: first, the lack of dates sometimes makes the point of many columns obscure. Did Buchwald mock hysterical anti-Communism in the 1950's, when such satire was risky, or in the 1960's, when it was relatively safe (answer: the latter). Second, Buchwald is often lacking in the sheer malice that turns humor into a deadly art. Except for his brilliant, and early, mocking of the premises of the Vietnam War—set in South Nonamura—most of these satires are written by someone who will meet his targets at a party that evening.

*Jeff Greenfield, in a review of "Down the Seine and Up the Potomac with Art Buchwald," in* The New York Times Book Review, *September 25, 1977, p. 16.*

## ARNOLD BEICHMAN

Two of America's most popular syndicated columnists have just published ... two volumes of their most recent writings [*The Buchwald Stops Here* by Art Buchwald and *A Hymnal: The Controversial Arts* by William F. Buckley, Jr.].... Why are they so popular that they are about to be declared national institutions? I think I know the secret. While they deal harshly with our betters, usually politicians, bureaucrats and other semi-skilled intellectuals, they love us, Everyman. They are on our side; who else?

When B & B complete their dissection of the Other Side ... we revel in a sense of victory over our betters who, in the B & B lexicon, usually betray the very virtues in which we are presumably badly instructed.

The difference between the two columnists is more a matter of style and technique than content since, for them, The Enemy is everywhere. Their agenda is Political Man and his corruptions, the inevitable fall from grace of the high-minded who seek to rule our lives by all sorts of chicanery. Occasionally, B & B miss because they allow their respective "ideologies" to divert them from their targets—Buchwald, the liberal who sometimes wittingly spears a liberal but not often and Buckley who dislikes Democrats although he is sometimes dismayed by his fellow Republicans.

Buckley's penchant for dealing in facts is his greatest weakness, whereas Buchwald's strength is that he deals with only one fact per column and then reduces it to the absurdity it usually is. While Buckley, the master logician, can always find a periphrasis or an excluded middle concealed in the Enemy's prose, Buchwald cunningly acts the part of Figaro, victimized at the beginning but, with a broad wink at us, triumphant at the end.

*Arnold Beichman, "Buckley and Buchwald: Absurdity in High Places," in* The Christian Science Monitor, *December 20, 1978, p. 19.\**

## MICHAEL G. HYDAK

A compendium of Buchwald's best articles during the past 25 years, ***Down the Seine and up the Potomac with Art Buchwald*** can be used very effectively by the French teacher in quest of a fresh and humorous look at contemporary France. . . .

The book is divided into 15 parts, with most of the French material in the beginning sections. The titles of some of the more memorable ones include "The Six-Minute Louvre," an account of the famous international contest to "do" the Louvre in under six minutes; "Dear Mary—Please Come Home," the naive plea by an American coed's parents to come home from the dangers of Paris to the safety of small-town U.S.A.; and "Salesmanship in Europe," a telling description of how national character is manifested when the hapless author attempts to buy a shirt in Great Britain, Italy, and France. (p. 82)

The non-French pieces of Buchwald's work make for very good reading. His wit ranges over the problems and the fads that have beset the United States in the past 20 years, from civil rights to Vietnam, from Earth Day to no-frill airplane tickets. Buchwald's trenchant comments about the Vietnamese war, for example, have lost none of their bite. There is even a piece entitled "The Truth About Book Reviews."

***Down the Seine and up the Potomac with Art Buchwald*** is an excellent source for cultural insight into modern France and modern America. Many sections can be extrapolated wholesale for use in the language classroom, but rare is the teacher who will be able to limit his reading to the strictly utilitarian aspects of this marvelous book. (pp. 82-3)

*Michael G. Hydak, in a review of "Down the Seine and Up the Potomac with Art Buchwald," in* The Modern Language Journal, *Vol. LXIII, Nos. 1 & 2, January & February, 1979, pp. 82-3.*

## CLIFFORD D. MAY

In the introduction to this collection of Art Buchwald columns ["**Laid Back in Washington**"], the author reluctantly confesses to a cigarette-smoking blonde with whom he has just spent an amorous night at a motel that he steals his ideas from newspapers, television, his kids and "even from Barbara Walters." "But why?" asks the shocked blonde (later revealed to be his wife). "Because that's where the money is," Mr. Buchwald confesses, "stealing ideas."

Evidently, the money is also in recycling those stolen ideas into books. Still, it's hard to hold a grudge against someone as consistently funny as Art Buchwald. . . . Not every [column] has been a gem, but all have had at least a touch of sparkle. . . .

Perhaps the most surprising thing about looking at Mr. Buchwald's columns the second time around is to find that they hold up well. Sure, jokes about Teddy Kennedy and Jimmy Carter are beginning to go a little moldy around the edges. But Mr. Buchwald's digs at such perennial bugbears as oil executives, bureaucrats and the I.R.S. remain fresh and pungent.

So if Mr. Buchwald wants his columns bound between hard covers and sitting on bookshelves rather than lining the bottoms of bird cages, I suppose he's got a right.

*Clifford D. May, in a review of "Laid Back in Washington," in* The New York Times Book Review, *January 3, 1982, p. 10.*

## ROBERT SHERRILL

The title [***While Reagan Slept***] is, of course, a takeoff on *While England Slept,* the book allegedly written by John Kennedy but which many people believe was written, or at least doctored in large part, by Arthur Krock of *The New York Times.* I suspect there is something phony about ***While Reagan Slept,*** too. It's supposed to be a collection of Art Buchwald's columns, but some of it is so wacky it couldn't possibly be the work of a mere humorist. I expect we'll learn someday that many of these pieces were written, or at least contributed to, by Reagan himself, working in dead seriousness. . . .

And if not from Ronnie, much of this material obviously came from very high up. For example, the stuff about Bonzo getting loose in the White House, while the Reagans were away, and making Reaganomics and foreign policy that passed for real. And the eerily accurate account of the top-level meeting of advisers who proposed that Reagan throw a black tie cheddar-cheese dinner for poor people.

Aside from top sources inside the White House, Buchwald has an incredible network of spies in the bureaucracy. How else could he obtain a transcript of the phone conversation between the State Department and the ambassador in a certain Latin American country, who reported that it deserves our military aid because it has improved so greatly in the human rights area? . . .

Buchwald can pretend he made that up if he wants to, but it's obviously *real.*

*Robert Sherrill, in a review of "While Reagan Slept," in* Book World—The Washington Post, *October 9, 1983, p. 4.*

# Italo Calvino

## 1923-

Cuban-born Italian novelist, short story writer, translator, essayist, and journalist.

A leading figure in contemporary literature, Calvino investigates what it means to be an individual in the twentieth century. Renowned as a master storyteller, he employs elaborately inventive techniques while examining humanistic and ideological concerns of the modern world, particularly those of postwar Italian society. Calvino has acknowledged that his work is strongly influenced by the playful fantasy and moral content of the fable. Accordingly, he often creates fantastic settings, characters, and situations to comment on the modern world through such devices as allegory, irony, and satire. In all of his works Calvino displays his great knowledge of literature and the natural sciences, which he uses to extend the implications of his themes.

During World War II, Calvino joined the Italian Resistance movement in its attempt to undermine Fascist control of Italy. Following the war he wrote his first novel, *Il sentiero dei nidi di ragno* (1947; *The Path to the Nest of Spiders*), which depicts the activities of Resistance members as observed by a small boy. Calvino's first collection of short stories, *Ultimo viene il corvo* (1949; *Adam, One Afternoon and Other Stories*), also centers on the Resistance and on life in postwar Italy. These socially oriented works are written in the colloquial language of rural Italy and present moral and political responses to such issues as war, fascist policies, and the rebuilding of Italian society after World War II. On the basis of these two books, Calvino was linked with Cesare Pavese and Elio Vittorini as a member of the Italian neorealist literary movement. However, unlike the neorealist writers, who documented the problems of society in a straightforward, factual manner, Calvino employed artistic embellishments in his work, including subtle twists of plot and rhetorical elements of the fable.

During the 1950s, Calvino's fiction moved away from neorealism as he began to address contemporary social issues through works of fantasy. He wrote a trilogy of novels, published collectively as *Il nostri antenati* (1960; *Our Ancestors*), in which he created an allegory for the social situation in postwar Italy. *Il visconte dimezzato* (1952; *The Cloven Viscount*), the first novel of the trilogy, is set in the seventeenth century and depicts a knight who is severed in half by a cannonball. The halves, one good, the other evil, return separately to a village, where they expound upon their differing moral viewpoints. This work has been read as an examination of the problem of identity. In *Il barone rampante* (1957; *The Baron in the Trees*), a twelve-year-old boy leaves his family home to live in a tree and remains there for the rest of his life. Critics have interpreted this work as an analysis of an individual's attempt to live a self-determined existence and also as a critique of society. *Il cavaliere inesistente* (1959; *The Nonexistent Knight*), which completes the trilogy, depicts a suit of armor inhabited by an intangible being. Calvino won wide acclaim for these works, particularly for treating his fabulous inventions as though they were part of everyday life. Critics found stimulating the plurality of meanings suggested in the trilogy and praised Cal-

vino for his poignant, ironic commentary on life in Italy after World War II.

Calvino developed further as a fantasist during the 1960s, composing two of his most popular works, *Le cosmicomiche* (1965; *Cosmicomics*) and *Ti con zero* (1967; *t zero*). In these collections of interrelated short stories, Calvino introduces a character named Qfwfq who passes through all the crucial transitional stages of evolution. Calvino draws extensively on modern theories in physics, chemistry, and astronomy to dramatize the unfolding history of the universe, and he relates ordinary human problems to complicated scientific concepts. Critics praised Calvino's imaginative application of scientific postulations and his self-conscious investigation of the narrative aspect of storytelling.

Calvino wrote three highly acclaimed novels during the 1970s, and many critics began to regard him as the foremost writer of postwar Italy. *Le città invisibili* (1972; *Invisible Cities*), based on the journals of Marco Polo, centers on a fictionalized Marco Polo describing imaginary cities to an aged Kublai Khan. While the experiences of Marco Polo impart moral lessons on how to appreciate life, this work also focuses on the relationship between writer and reader. Kublai Khan serves as a spokesman for the reader as he interprets, questions, argues, and attempts to find patterns that will yield meaning to the tales.

Calvino's next major work, *Il castello dei destini incrociati* (1973; *The Castle of Crossed Destinies*), follows a group of travelers who lose their power of speech while passing through an enchanted forest. The travelers learn to communicate by using tarot cards that they find in a castle. Calvino relies on the random sequence of turning over cards to inform and influence the shape of his story; the fate of his characters hinges upon what the cards reveal. In addition, this novel intricately develops a network of allusions to such literary legends as Faust, Parsifal, and Oedipus. *Se una notte d'inverno un viaggiatore* (1979; *If on a winter's night a traveler*) contains Calvino's most extensive investigation of the relationship between writer, reader, and text. This novel is composed of a series of beginnings of novels, none of which are concluded, and a frame story in which a man and a woman meet and enter into a relationship based on their love of reading. While focusing on how the fictive imagination interacts with reality and how reality is perceived through art, this work provides samples of writing styles employed by various contemporary authors. For example, the sequence of novels begun in *If on a winter's night a traveler* are written in such modes as modernism, magic realism, detective fiction, and the politically committed style of East European authors. While some critics have argued that the novel's structure and Calvino's long digressions inhibit the enjoyment of his frame story, many regard this work as a virtuoso performance.

(See also *CLC*, Vols. 5, 8, 11, 22 and *Contemporary Authors*, Vols. 85-88.)

## SALMAN RUSHDIE

*If on a winter's night a traveller* distils into a single volume what is perhaps the dominant characteristic of Calvino's entire output: his protean, metamorphic genius for never doing the same thing twice. In the space of 260 pages, we are given the beginnings of no fewer than ten novels, each of which is a transmogrified avatar of the previous one; we also have a more or less fully-developed love story between [You, the Reader] and Ludmilla, the Other Reader; plus, for good measure, a conspiracy-theory fiction about a secret society known as the Organisation of Apocryphal Power, run by a fiendish translator named Ermes Marana, whose purpose may or may not be the subversion of fiction itself. The OAP is vaguely reminiscent of Thomas Pynchon's underground postal service, the Tristero System, and almost certainly has covert links with Bunuel's Revolutionary Army of the Infant Jesus, the only comic terrorist organisation in the history of the cinema. . . .

It is entirely possible that Calvino is not a human being at all, but a planet, something like the planet Solaris of Stanislaw Lem's great novel. Solaris, like Calvino, possesses the power of seeing into the deepest recesses of human minds and then bringing their dreams to life. Reading Calvino, you're constantly assailed by the notion that he is writing down what you have always known, except that you've never thought of it before. This is highly unnerving: fortunately, you're usually too busy laughing to go mad.

The first message from the planet Calvino was received on Earth as long ago as 1947. This was *The Path to the Nest of Spiders,* a war story sired by Ernest Hemingway out of Italian neo-realist cinema about a cobbler's apprentice who joins the Partisans and finds the friend he has always longed to have. Although this book has one of the great titles of 20th-century literature, it's really no better than worthy, and the last sentence

appears to have dipped its feet in slush. It reads: 'And they walk on, the big man and the child, into the night, amid the fireflies, holding each other by the hand.'

I have quoted this line in full because it is the last example on record of a bad sentence by Italo Calvino. After *Spiders,* he tells us, 'instead of making myself write the book I *ought* to write, the (''neo-realistic'') novel that was expected of me, I conjured up the book I myself would have liked to read, the sort by an unknown writer, from another age and another country, discovered in an attic.'

Shazam! Instant metamorphosis, caterpillar into butterfly, Samsa into giant bug, Clark Kent into Superman, politically-committed Calvino into Captain Italo Marvel. In 1952, he published *The Cloven Viscount,* which, along with its successors *The Baron in the Trees* and *The Non-Existent Knight,* he has . . . collected in the volume entitled *Our Ancestors.*

These three novels possess a clarity, a simplicity which I'm going to have to compare with *One Hundred Years of Solitude,* because Calvino shares with Marquez the effortless ability of seeing the miraculous in the quotidian. *The Cloven Viscount* is about a cloven viscount, vertically bisected by a cannon-ball in medieval Bohemia. The two halves continue to live, the one fiendishly evil, the other impossibly good. Both halves are unbearable. In the end they fight a duel. The Bad 'Un and the Good 'Un reopen the terrible wounds of their bisection, and are sewn back together by the story's most appealing character, a refugee from the works of Calvino's favourite writer, Robert Louis Stevenson: Dr Trelawney it is who performs the operation. This is a happy ending, but for the story's youthful narrator it is also the moment of childhood's end. . . .

*The Baron in the Trees* is the story of Cosimo Piovasco di Rondo, who, at the age of 12, refuses to eat the repellent snail soup prepared by his sister Battista (who also cooks 'some pâté toast, really exquisite, of rats' livers . . . and some grasshoppers' claws . . . laid on an open tart in a mosaic; and pigs' tails roasted as if they were little cakes'), is ordered from the table by his crusty father, climbs a tree and never sets foot on solid ground for the rest of his life. His affair with the capricious Viola, his adventures with the local bandits, his encounter with a group of exiled Spanish grandees and his meticulous strategies for making a successful life in the trees twine and intertwine to form thick forests of marvellous ideas, and make *The Baron in the Trees* one of the most haunting images of rebellion, of determined nay-saying, that exists in the literature of this rebellious century.

In *The Baron,* and in the third novel in the trilogy, *The Non-Existent Knight,* Calvino is also getting interested in narration as a process. . . .

*The Non-Existent Knight,* which is the story of an empty suit of armour that thinks it's a knight of the Emperor Charlemagne and keeps itself/himself going by sheer willpower, discipline and devotion to duty, is also a very 'narrated' tale, told by Sister Theodora, a nun locked up in a convent, who can have no possible experience, as she is very well aware, of the scenes of chivalry she is required to describe. . . . And yet, heroically, she writes on and on, inventing the unknown and making it seem truer than the truth, and providing Calvino with a marvellous metaphor for himself. This growing preoccupation with the Book as opposed to the World will come to its true fruition in *If on a winter's night* . . . . . .

Six years later, Calvino published a collection of stories about an even more fluid time. The 12 *Cosmicomics* take, for their modest theme, nothing more nor less than the creation of the universe, as narrated by a polymorphous immortal being masquerading under the muffled, spluttering title of Qfwfq, whom we instantly perceive to be Calvino himself.... We see the galaxies form, we see life crawl out of the waters of the Earth: the miracle of these stories is that somehow Calvino gives it all a richly comic and wholly human scale. In '**The Aquatic Uncle**', for instance, Qfwfq and his family have just 'abandoned aquatic life for terrestrial', and Qfwfq is in love with a fellow land-creature. But: 'Yes, we had a great-uncle who was a fish, on my paternal grandmother's side, to be precise, of the Coelacanthus family of the Devonian period'; and this Uncle N'ba N'ga obstinately refuses to give up his watery life. What's more, when an embarrassed Qfwfq is forced by his loved one to introduce her to his stubbornly primitive relative, the aquatic uncle seduces her back into the water . . . I could go on, but what's the point? . . .

What do you do when you've just reinvented the world? What Calvino did was to turn himself into Marco Polo and go travelling in it. *Invisible Cities* is not really a novel at all, but a sort of fugue on the nature of the City. Polo and Kublai Khan are the only attempts at 'characters' in this book: its true star is Calvino's descriptive prose. Others (well, Gore Vidal, anyway) have called this Calvino's 'most beautiful work' [see *CLC*, Vol. 5], and perhaps it is. But it's an oppressive and finally cloying beauty, all those jewelled sentences and glittering notions and no story-telling worth a damn. You will notice I'm in two minds about this book: but it's worth keeping it by your bedside and reading it a paragraph at a time, because even though I wasn't convinced by the whole, I'm bound to admit that the separate parts are pretty dazzling....

Next, Calvino turned himself into two packs of Tarot cards and used them as the basis of the stories in *The Castle of Crossed Destinies*, the only one of his books which I actually find too clever to like. Travellers meet by chance, in the first part in a castle and in the second in a tavern, and fall miraculously dumb, so that they are obliged to tell their travellers' tales by laying out the Tarot cards. Calvino uses these card-sequences as texts which he then interprets for us, telling us the stories which the cards may or may not be intending to tell: a form, I suppose, of mystical structuralism. Ho hum.

*If* . . . is a book to praise without buts. This is Calvino rampant in the world of books, Calvino joyously playing with the possibilities of fiction, of story-telling, which is, after all, also a nursery euphemism for lying. You, the Reader, is (or are) a sort of dogged Lemmy Caution-figure trying to find Your way through the literary labyrinths of Calvino's city of words, his Alphabetaville.

You buy the new Calvino. You begin reading a story called *If on a winter's night a traveler*. I note that an 'l' has fallen out of this last word in its journey from the dust-jacket. The story is a thriller set at a train station. But suddenly You have to stop reading: there is a binding error in Your copy. You take it back to the bookshop and find that the story You began wasn't the new Calvino at all. The wrong pages, the bookseller tells You, were bound between the wrong covers. What You started (and now want to finish) was *Outside the town of Malbork* by one Tazio Bazakbal. You, and Your new friend Ludmilla, who has had the same problem with her copy of the Calvino, go off to read this second book. But it turns out to be an entirely different story, some kind of rural novel, and

then another binding mistake is discovered just when You're getting interested: blank pages have been bound in by mistake. You ring Ludmilla, speak first to her sister Lotaria, eventually to this girl in whom You have become very interested indeed. (p. 16)

*If on a winter's night a traveller* is quite possibly the most complicated book you (and You, too) will ever read. But Calvino's conjuring trick works because he makes the complications so funny, and makes you (though not You) share the joke. The ten transformations of the eternally-beginning story are carried off with an inventiveness so dazzling that it never becomes tiresome; the gradual weaving together of the texts and their readers is nothing less than—to use an archaically appropriate piece of slang—wizard. Calvino has left Stevenson far behind; he has avoided sounding like imitation Borges, which is what happens to him when he isn't on peak form; and his great gift, the ability to give human scale to the most extravagant of his inventions, has never been more in evidence. In *Cosmicomics*, the explosion of the universe outwards from a single point is precipitated by the first generous impulse, the first-ever 'true outburst of general love', when a proto-being called, astonishingly, Mrs Ph(i)Nk$_0$, cries out: 'Oh, if I only had some room, how I'd like to make some noodles for you boys!' And in *If* . . . , the most outrageous fiction about fiction ever conceived, we stumble in every paragraph over nuggets of hard, irreducible truth: "'Nobody these days holds the written word in such high esteem as police states do,'' Arkadian Porphyrich says. ''What statistic allows one to identify the nations where literature enjoys true consideration better than the sums appropriated for controlling it and suppressing it?'''

Why, finally, should we bother with Calvino, a word-juggler, a fantasist, in an age in which our cities burn and our leaders blame our parents? What does it mean to write about nonexistent knights, or the formation of the Moon, or how a reader reads, while the neutron bomb gets the go-ahead in Washington, and plans are made to station germ-warfare weaponry in Europe? Not escapism, because although the reader of Italo Calvino will be taken further out of himself than most readers, he will also discover that the experience is not a flight from, but an enrichment of himself. No, the reason Calvino is such an indispensable writer is precisely that he tells us, joyfully, wickedly, that there are things in the world worth loving as well as hating; and that such things exist in people, too. I can think of no finer writer to have beside me while Italy explodes, while Britain burns, while the world ends. (p. 17)

*Salman Rushdie, ''Calvino,'' in* London Review of Books, *September 17 to September 30, 1981, pp. 16-17.*

## HARRIETT GILBERT

The Second World War in Italy is Italo Calvino's war—one of starving civilians, partisans, traitors. It permeates the stories of *Adam, One Afternoon*.... Unlike Calvino's more recent work, these stories are quite traditional, maintaining a respectable distance between the reader and the author. Already, however, Calvino is playing with fairy tales—his writing refined, impersonal, formal; his frame of reference extending beyond the 'human' to the 'natural' and 'animal' worlds. Even in the urban comedies there is a sensuality, a comedy less of 'manners' than of 'life', that gives both weight and depth to his slightest anecdote. By accepting that beauty co-exists with cruelty, absurdity with dignity, tragedy with farce, Calvino does more than refuse to judge—he indicates one possible way we might learn to live with ourselves. (p. 28)

*Harriett Gilbert, "Stomaching It," in* New States-man, *Vol. 105, No. 2711, March 4, 1983, pp. 27-8.\**

## JUDY ASTOR

[Italy is] the setting for the most chilling stories in Italo Calvino's collection, *Adam, One Afternoon.* . . . It is the Italy of the Partisans rather than the Red Brigade, and the two best stories, **'Going to Headquarters'** and **'One of the Three is Still Alive'**, both chart the anguished alternation between hope and fear of men faced with death: in one case, a suspected spy who is being taken into the woods to be shot by a partisan; in the other, three Germans about to be executed as a reprisal.

Calvino's strength is his economy and subtlety, shown at its best when, for instance, he describes through the eyes of a 15-year-old boy the reactions of his middle-class family to the newly-arrived goatherd, a huge shy peasant of his own age, whom his father in an expansive moment invites to join them at lunch. The mother's chilly condescension, the father's hollow heartiness, the son's unhappy awareness of their lack of intelligent sympathy for the peasant boy's dumb, homesick misery, are suggested in a masterly way.

The best of his allegorical fantasies have the power of the Brothers Grimm, rollicking stories on the surface, with an underlying savagery. Those that seem the weakest now, the ones with a political message, like **'The Enchanted Garden'**, come across as both pat and patronising, the moral too obvious, the pill all too visible through the gilt.

*Judy Astor, "On the Run," in* The Listener, *Vol. 109, No. 2803, March 17, 1983, p. 24.\**

## MIRANDA SEYMOUR

Calvino, always the most skittishly elusive of writers, has become increasingly absorbed in making impenetrable filigree pagodas of his books and the hidden implications are difficult to extricate. But in reserving their highest admiration for the elaborate craftsmanship of the artifice Calvino's devotees risk turning him into a writer's writer, directing himself to an elite audience of enthusiasts. There are not many people who would contemplate buying one of his novels for the sheer fun of it. And that is a pity, for Calvino is a jester and an entertainer as much as he is a scholarly magician. The general reader should not be frightened off him.

It is to be hoped that the publication . . . of Calvino's earliest and most accessible works will do something to redress the balance. . . . We have already been given the enchanting collection of Italian folk-tales selected and re-told by Calvino. *Adam, One Afternoon* . . . introduced us to the author as a masterly teller of fables which are both cynical and gay, set mostly in the poor villages of wartime Italy. Mood and time link them closely to *Marcovaldo,* notably in the title story of Liberoso, the country boy who tries to court an urban Miss with offerings of grasshoppers and beetles and—the final horror—live frogs which he sends hopping through her kitchen.

Liberoso is a sketch for the portrait of Marcovaldo, a countryman struggling to accommodate himself to city life. Genial, well-intentioned and not very bright, Marcovaldo's attempts to reconcile peasant lore with urban existence lead him into comic disasters and Chagall-like fantasies. He can fall asleep

on a rubbish heap with a bunch of buttercups pressed to his nose, but a visit to the supermarket conveys only the hurried impartial greed of the housewives and a roar of trolley wheels before fantasy takes over with a vast crane descending to scoop all their purchases back on to the shelves.

All artefacts are enemies to Marcovaldo. He can make sense of them only by translating them into familiar objects. A row of hoardings is transformed into a forest where he goes to chop down wood until the police discover and reprimand the culprit. A rabbit being used for toxic experiments is seen as a fellow stranger from the country and carried home for reassurance until the civic authorities burst in to retrieve it. A rubber plant rescued from its tub in a foyer is magically changed into a tropical monster of prodigious size before the evening wind snatches it from Marcovaldo's hands and blows it away in a gust of yellow leaves.

Undeterred by the catastrophes he is causing, Marcovaldo stumbles on, attaching himself to anything that looks familiar in an alien world. Imagination and invention are his weapons. (pp. 23-4)

Merry and entertaining, the history of Marcovaldo reflects the young Calvino's sense of the stultifying effect of everyday urban life among the workers. If Marcovaldo is in part a clown, he is also an individualist who refuses to fit into the expected pattern. A displaced Hesiod, he remains staunchly and endearingly himself. (p. 24)

*Miranda Seymour, "Shimmering," in* The Spectator, *Vol. 251, No. 8098, September 24, 1983, pp. 23-4.\**

## ANATOLE BROYARD

Italo Calvino is the Italian writer who seems to cause the most excitement among American readers. With three books especially—**"Cosmicomics,"** **"Invisible Cities"** and **"If on a winter's night a traveler"**—Mr. Calvino has earned comparisons with Jorge Luis Borges and Gabriel Garcia Marquez. After decades of Italian neo-realism in the works of authors like Alberto Moravia, Elio Vittorini and Cesare Pavese, Mr. Calvino's fictions appear to be closer to the fantastic Italy of a Fellini film or a painting by Giorgio de Chirico.

He is seen by some critics as an emancipation, as a writer who has brought back humor, lightness and freedom of invention to contemporary Italian fiction. Others find him too light, or all light and no shadow, no substance. He is clever and witty, they concede, but all surface. Italy, it seems, has grown used to taking itself very seriously and is resisting, in fiction at least, the anarchic pleasures of the international modern style.

**"Marcovaldo"** reads like an attempt to satisfy both schools of thought. The hero for whom the book is named is a Chaplinesque figure posed against the background of a drab and nameless industrial city in the north of Italy. Marcovaldo is Mr. Calvino's Candide, his image of an innocent who survives the 1950's and 60's in a modern metropolis by willfully misreading reality, as Chaplin did, by opposing his optimism to its negative influences.

Since all 20 of these very short stories feature the same character, **"Marcovaldo"** might just as easily be read as a novel. In fact, some of the stories are so slight that without the support of the others, they seem negligible. Taken together, they have a mild charm. . . .

An unskilled laborer with a wife and several children to feed, Marcovaldo is always searching his city for some sign of a relenting. In one story, he finds this relenting in the form of mushrooms springing up under the city's trees. As it turns out, the mushrooms are poisonous. Yet, because there are not enough of them, the poison is not fatal. Marcovaldo and his family enjoy the poisoned, metropolitan pleasure of eating the mushrooms and surviving them. In Mr. Calvino's work, irony too springs up underneath the city's trees. . . .

In another story or chapter, Marcovaldo comes out of a Technicolor movie to find the city shrouded in fog, blurred and disguised, as it were, by his uncritical and romantic imagination. As the only remaining inhabitant of the city during August, the traditional month for European vacations, Marcovaldo is interviewed by a television crew. But after another interesting beginning, the story slips away into a series of familiar ironies.

This may be the trouble with Marcovaldo and with Mr. Calvino's work in general: It leans almost entirely on irony, but of a rather bland or schematic kind. One feels, in reading the book, a sort of fatigue in regard to irony, like the fatigue some of us felt with novels about sex in the 60's. Like sex, irony needs flesh on its bones or it becomes just one more of Ezra Pound's "accelerated grimaces."

Mr. Calvino invents, but he does not persevere. His most popular book in America, **"If on a winter's night a traveler,"** consists of 10 beginnings of novels, and one is reminded of the writer in the Donald Barthelme story who could not do middles. For all his supposed "freedom" of imagination, Mr. Calvino is like a blocked writer who is forever starting brilliant books and not quite finishing them. It may be a sign of our restless times. One can imagine a literature composed exclusively of beginnings, incomplete stories and novels for people too impatient, or too clever, to follow anything to a conclusion.

> *Anatole Broyard, in a review of "Marcovaldo, or The Seasons in the City," in* The New York Times, *November 9, 1983, p. C20.*

## FRANCO FERRUCCI

A sentence from Italo Calvino's introduction to his **"Italian Folktales"** reveals the secret behind the magic of the earlier stories in **"Marcovaldo":** "I believe that fables are true." Conversely, Mr. Calvino believes that reality is fabulous. When he began the stories of **"Marcovaldo"** in the 1950's and 60's he did not know he was creating a masterwork in the narrative trend labeled the *nouveau roman* by French critics. He simply followed his instincts as a storyteller and achieved a durable balance between the heritage of 20th-century Italian neorealism and a fabulous vision of reality. . . .

[**"Marcovaldo"**] is a series of ecological allegories in the form of urban tales. Psychological insights are held back in favor of cartoons in which facts and people succeed one another with the geometrical smoothness of movie animation. . . . Even early in his career, his rhetorical virtuosity disguised the subtlety and depth of his vision—especially in some of the stories in **"Marcovaldo,"** like **"The City Lost in the Snow," "A Saturday of Sun, Sand and Sleep"** and **"The Wrong Stop."** He writes lightly and jauntily; any trace of effort is concealed. But what catches the reader goes beyond the unspotted perfection of the style; it is his uninhibited poetic sense of life.

Each story belongs to a season, and all of them together take their shape from the cycle of the seasons. Marcovaldo lives through the stories as the double of the writer, observing, reflecting and comparing in a perfectly detached way. He is a humble and romantic blue-collar worker lost in the big city, which perverts rhythms and obfuscates cycles. He is trapped in the unreality of this modern city (the setting is vividly evoked in **"Marcovaldo at the Supermarket"**), a place that even suffocates the life of the animals in the stories **"The Garden of Stubborn Cats"** and **"The Poisonous Rabbit."** He longs for nature, and nature rewards him in surprising ways. Mushrooms sprout out of the cement in **"Mushrooms in the City";** the sky suddenly opens wide in **"Park-Bench Vacation";** the moon shines brighter than the neon signs in **"The Moon and GNAC."**

What is so much admired by the readers of Mr. Calvino's later **"Invisible Cities"** was already at work in **"Marcovaldo"** and with a more cogent narrative drive. **"Invisible Cities"** seems like a memory, while **"Marcovaldo"** conveys the sensuous, tangible qualities of life.

> *Franco Ferrucci, "Calvino's Urban Allegories," in* The New York Times Book Review, *January 22, 1984, p. 8.*

## HARRIETT GILBERT

The stories collected in *Difficult Loves* have been dug from the 1950s, and it has to be said that the two longer tales, **'Smog'** and **'A Plunge into Real Estate',** give the impression of having been printed as ballast. Bad, they certainly are not; neither, however, is as startling, as magically strange and inventive, as Calvino's more recent work. Their greatest value lies, perhaps, in the picture they sketch of an Italy dazedly trying to pull itself together in the wake of the Second World War.

The shorter tales—to which, in fact, the title *Difficult Loves* refers—are a better reason for the book's publication. A *Decameron*-type package of stories . . . , they are, superficially, all concerned with more-or-less tortuous sexual, romantic or simply affectionate encounters. A man of obsessively meticulous habits confronts the hazards of an overnight train to visit his lover in Rome; a woman, swimming, discovers that she has somehow lost her bathing-suit and is forced to tread water in growing despair until rescued by a passing fisherman. But what the stories are really about (of course, this being Calvino) is the difficulty not of love itself, but of verbalising, of making *sense* of the chaos of emotional experience. Delicate, funny, compassionate and wise, these tales are the obvious seedlings of later Calvino flowers.

> *Harriett Gilbert, "Truth Games," in* New Statesman, *Vol. 107, No. 2768, April 6, 1984, p. 35.\**

## DEAN FLOWER

The awareness of social class typically taken for granted by American writers is never forgotten in Italo Calvino's most recently translated book [*Marcovaldo, or The Seasons in the City*]. . . . Readers familiar with the fabulous ingenuities of *Invisible Cities* and *The Castle of Crossed Destinies,* which are less novels than meditations on the mysteries of fictive structures, may be surprised at the charming simplicity of these tales. . . . For the hero, Marcovaldo, illusions flourish in every story. Hard pressed by poverty, demanding wife and children, peremptory employers, a dreary industrial city, his own aging body, Marcovaldo schemes endlessly to outwit his fate. . . . If you've seen "Big Deal on Madonna Street" or any Vittorio Gassmann comedy, you will know Marcovaldo at once: touchingly earnest, full of romantic notions, a big talker yet a gentle man, certain to fail.

Calvino deepens the comedy by constant reminders of social reality. If Marcovaldo trades lunches with a boy of wealthy family, someone instantly steps in to call him a thief. Lured into a supermarket but without any money, playing Santa Claus for the spoiled children of the rich, or trying to dispose of too many free samples of detergent, Marcovaldo is only driven back where he came from. Affluence is a soap bubble in the sky, glimpsed for a moment, then leaving "only smoke, smoke, smoke." Emphasizing this naturalistic trap, as the book's subtitle indicates, are the seasons: the twenty stories carry us through the yearly cycle five times, without the slightest suggestion that anything will change. (pp. 308-09)

[There are] flights in almost all of these stories, fantastic swerves up, up and away from reality, as readers of Calvino's better known works will have guessed. Marcovaldo is literally aloft at the end of one story when in a thick fog the bus he boards turns out to be an airplane bound for Singapore. This is not just another joke at Marcovaldo's expense. Calvino ends the tale with a mysteriously resonant uplift: "The night beyond the windows was full of stars, now that the plane had passed through the thick blanket of fog, and was flying in the limpid sky of the great altitudes." For all his Chaplinesque foolishness, Marcovaldo seems to know about such things: *the* great altitudes. In another story he finds himself the only inhabitant left in the city during a mid-August holiday, and he begins to explore it as a wholly new world: a building he sees every day becomes "in its reality" a quarry of gray sandstone; an old wooden fence has fresh pine boards. He discovers a whole realm of "bark and scales and clots and nerve-systems." Even after being violently pulled back through the looking-glass, interviewed by a TV crew, and put to work on the floodlights while a famous film star dives into the city fountain for the cameras, Marcovaldo is "blinded and dazed" by overlapping versions of reality. He concludes that his dream city probably wasn't real, but Calvino and the reader know better. For anyone curious about the foundations of Calvino's many fictions of invisible cities, these stories should be required reading. They *are* a guide to the night. (p. 309)

*Dean Flower, in a review of "Marcovaldo, or The Seasons in the City," in* The Hudson Review, *Vol. XXXVII, No. 2, Summer, 1984, pp. 308-09.*

## URSULA K. LE GUIN

Calvino's early stories, exact, delicate, kind, dry, crazy, often follow [the] theme of invasion or interpenetration of animal life and artificial life—a subversion of order by the strange. I can't come at the distinction more precisely, for it is a complex one, not to be pulled out of the stories as a mere idea. It is a political, a social, and a psychological theme, and a fascinating one. Indeed Calvino is such an interesting writer intellectually that one tends to forget the powerful gift of narrative that has let him pull off such "anti-narrative" stunts as *Invisible Cities* or *If on a winter's night a traveler*. In [*Difficult Loves*] you can see the storyteller pure and simple in "Mine Field," a paradigm of suspense. Will he get blown up or won't he? I didn't know I could hold my breath for seven pages. (p. 3)

Calvino's stories from the '40s have the mood of the great postwar films of Rossellini and De Sica, with their strange

clarity of feeling, a vernal power springing in release from the long, dead grip of fascist lying and bullying. These tales are loving and terrible, very tender, never truly hopeful.

The stories from the '50s might make you think of Fellini— the farce, the fantasy, the wit, delight, and vitality, and the marvelous gift of image. Where Fellini errs toward incoherence, Calvino overcontrols, erring towards the cerebral—but seldom, and never fatally. He is far too intelligent to become really cerebral.

"**The Adventure of a Bather**" won't become a myth or byword like Andersen's "The Emperor's New Clothes," because it isn't quite simplistic enough. The plot is certainly simple: Swimming alone at a big beach resort, a bather loses the bottom half of her swimsuit. Now how can you make anything out of that but a wink, a snicker? Calvino makes it a story worthy of Chekhov, a tiny comedy that touches the greatest chords. The smart-aleck kid who says the Emperor has no clothes speaks for the child in us, but Calvino's swimmer is an adult, and her peculiar problem is an adult problem, in fact you could say that her problem is that she is adult—that she is fully human.

Repeatedly in the later stories the metaphor of happiness is a man's sexual enjoyment of a woman. I found this a bit tiresome. A male writer may expect a female reader to accept description of sex from the man's point of view as a satisfactory representation of human sexual experience, but he can't ask her to agree that male pleasure defines human bliss. Not these days. Under the patriarchy "the nude" could stand for "beauty," but these days she's likely to be seen as a naked woman painted by a clothed man. There is nothing pornographic in Calvino, of course. His sensuality is free and real, as exact, mysterious, and enjoyable as everything in his writing. But the metaphor, repeated, trivializes. (p. 14)

*Ursula K. Le Guin, "The Marvels of Italo Calvino,"
in* Book World—The Washington Post, *November 18, 1984, pp. 3, 14.*

## ROBERT TOWERS

When the early work of a famous writer rides in on the coattails, so to speak, of the later work that has made him famous, one is inclined either to dismiss it with a knowing wink at the cupidity of publishers or else, if a devotee of the writer in question, to examine it for signs pointing to subsequent maturations and triumphs. Neither response is appropriate in the case of *Difficult Loves*. Calvino's stories stand on their own as finished performances, as distinctive and seductive in their own way as the more spectacular "metafictions" that followed them. . . .

The first section of *Difficult Loves* consists of the "Riviera Stories," which date back to the beginning of Calvino's career in the 1940s. For the most part they are nearly plotless sketches, many of them dealing with children, that shift delicately between realism and fantasy; a major pleasure in reading them is to watch the way Calvino maintains a light but perfect control as he allows the material to veer slightly to one side of the line and then to the other. . . .

In ["**Adam, One Afternoon**"], as in "**The Enchanted Garden**" and in "**Lazy Sons**" (the droll account of two narcoleptic young men who shamelessly resist all appeals for help from their hard-working, hard-pressed parents), one keeps expecting a metamorphosis into fairy tale that never quite takes place. The slightly teasing effect is nicely calculated.

In "Wartime Stories" and "Postwar Stories" the cruelties of partisan warfare and the exigencies of poverty invite a more grimly realistic treatment of the peasants, migrant workers, prostitutes, and black marketeers who populate them. . . . But metaphysical, fabulist, or farcical elements keep breaking in. In the most impressive of the war stories, a trigger-happy soldier-boy, "a mountaineer with an apple face," keeps shooting, with miraculous accuracy, at everything that catches his eye—birds, pine cones, trout, toadstools, and the gilt buttons on the uniforms of German soldiers—in an effort to transcend his separateness from the rest of creation. . . .

The humor of some of the "Postwar Stories" is of a kind that Boccacio might have relished. Crowded sleeping arrangements figure in two of them, **"Sleeping like Dogs"** and **"Transit Bed,"** while in another, **"Desire in November,"** a poor old man, Barbagallo, who wears a military overcoat and nothing else (his clothes having been stolen from the riverbank the preceding summer), forces his way into an elegant furrier's shop where, in the company of one of the saleswomen, he spends the night lapped in the softest and richest pelts that luxury can provide.

The final section, "Stories of Love and Loneliness," consists of eight "adventures," which, far more than the earlier pieces, resemble the Calvino we have come to know. . . . [Each] adventure proposes a problem which is then explored with a kind of philosophical thoroughness, mitigated by wit. While the explicitly Italian setting is retained, character and action are strictly subordinated to the working out of the chosen perplexity. In **"The Adventure of a Bather"** we meet a respectable woman who loses her bikini bottom while enjoying a swim at a populous beach. The sea is crowded with men eager for a look. Exhausted after swimming for hours, Signora Isotta cannot even allow herself the "indefensible, excessive remedy" of drowning. . . . (p. 33)

The wittiest of all is **"The Adventure of a Reader,"** in which Amedeo, whose interest in an active life has given way to a passion for reading thick novels—especially those of the nineteenth century—settles himself on a rocky shelf overlooking a secluded patch of beach with just such a volume. The identity of the work changes as he reads: sometimes it is *War and Peace,* sometimes *Crime and Punishment, The Charterhouse of Parma, Lost Illusions,* or *Remembrance of Things Past.* His absorption in the narration of events, the tangle of human

situations, is nearly total. Nearly total—for occasionally, at the end of a chapter, he dives into the tepid, translucent water. Even as he swims, he can't wait to get back to the story of Albertine—"would Marcel find her again, or not?"

He has also become aware of a deeply tanned lady sunning herself on a rubber mattress not far from his perch. One thing leads to another, they take a dip together, and a desultory conversation ensues, interrupted by long intervals during which Amedeo returns to his book with a devouring curiosity to find out what happens next. The day is waning. The lady, whose intentions are clearly amorous, undoes the halter of her bathing suit under the pretext of getting dressed. Having reached a climax in the book, "Amedeo didn't know whether to look at her, pretending to read, or to read, pretending to look at her." Finally aroused, he embraces the lady, falling onto the mattress with her, but as he does so he slightly turns his head toward the book to make sure it has not fallen into the sea. Even in the ecstasy of his lovemaking, Amedeo tries "to free one hand to put the bookmark at the right page.". . . As Calvino develops the situation, his ambivalence toward the entire world of traditional fiction . . . becomes incandescent, shedding gleams of comic irony in every direction.

The collection possesses great charm. It can only enhance Calvino's already towering reputation. The stories are "lightweight" in the most favorable sense of that term: never, in his exploration of the possibilities latent in each "adventure," does Calvino allow himself to become tedious. More obviously than his later books, with their cosmopolitan or cosmological settings, *Difficult Loves* reveals Calvino as a classically Italian writer—a writer, that is, for whom clarity of outline and brilliantly lighted surfaces seem preferable to thickness of atmosphere and the weight of social and psychological documentation. Gesture and act count more than introspection; shame, as in the case of the poor bather, is a more palpable emotion than guilt. While Calvino plays with abstractions, is engaged by conundrums, and is drawn toward symmetry, his inventions, however fanciful, are always embedded in sharply observed or vividly imagined sensory detail. Boccaccio, Pirandello, and the early De Chirico—these are among the Italian artists with whom his genius is aligned. (pp. 33-4)

*Robert Towers, "Light and Lively," in* The New York Review of Books, *Vol. XXXI, No. 19, December 6, 1984, pp. 33-4.**

# Henry (Coffin) Carlisle

## 1926-

American novelist, editor, and translator.

Carlisle writes popular novels within a number of genres, including satire, mystery, and historical fiction. His first novel, *Ilyitch Slept Here* (1965), satirizes American-Soviet diplomatic relations in a tale of an American vice-consul who buys a Swiss villa formerly owned by Lenin. *The Contract* (1968) is a spoof of murder mysteries in which three cousins plot to do away with one another's wealthy aunts. *Voyage to the First of December* (1972) marks Carlisle's switch to historical fiction. The novel dramatizes the discovery of a plot to mutiny aboard the United States navy brig *Somers* in 1842, the executions of three men, and the subsequent inquiry. Although Paul Theroux praised the accuracy of the historical narrative, Christopher Lehmann-Haupt faulted the book because "the author is more occupied with history and its ironies than with freely exploring the story's characters." *The Jonah Man* (1984) fictionalizes another sea story—that of Nantucket whaler Captain George Pollard and his crew, who resorted to cannibalism after their ship was sunk by a whale in 1820.

(See also *Contemporary Authors*, Vols. 13-16, rev. ed. and *Contemporary Authors New Revision Series*, Vol. 15.)

## MARTIN LEVIN

In the delightful vein of "Ninotchka," Henry Carlisle's [*Ilyitch Slept Here*] . . . makes light of American-Soviet relations. This is a tricky assignment, if a certain respect for the facts is to be observed—and if the whole business is not to degenerate into elephantine allegory. Happily, Mr. Carlisle avoids the obvious pitfalls and derives his humor from Russian and American prototypes whom he launches on a collision course in the diplomatic channels of Switzerland. . . . [The characters interested in Lenin's villa] rattle around in Lenin's former home, where, with the aid of a connecting double agent, they make explosively funny contact.

> Martin Levin, in a review of "Ilyitch Slept Here,"
> in The New York Times Book Review, *January 3,
> 1965, p. 20.*

## DAVID F. SHARPE

Some novels are worthwhile if only for the pleasant diversion they bring. "**The Contract,**" a second effort by the author, Henry Carlisle, is just such a number. The work is certainly not the rollicking comedy and spoof of the "generation gap" that the dust jacket seems to promise, but it is an interesting and enjoyable story for anyone desiring an evening's light reading. (p. 313)

"**The Contract**" is expertly written as Carlisle has obvious style and wit. After finishing the book, one is reminded of the Saturday morning TV cartoons, where the good guys are good and the bad guys are bad. When the latter meet their total, but somehow harmless demise, it is with embarrassment that one mildly anticipates going through the same thing next week. (pp. 313-14)

Photograph by Barbara Hall

> David F. Sharpe, in a review of "The Contract," in
> Best Sellers, *Vol. 28, No. 15, November 1, 1968,
> pp. 313-14.*

## PAUL THEROUX

Fiction must persuade us, and when a novel supplies credible details in imaginative form it is the best because it is indistinguishable from truth. Henry Carlisle's book [*Voyage to the First of December*] is an excellent example of this. It describes the consequences of a disruptive plot discovered on board the U.S. Navy brig *Somers* in 1842. The captain, Alexander Mackenzie, dealt swiftly with those he took to be the rebels—there were floggings, and three of the accused were hanged.

A single bureaucratic report might have ended the business, except that the principal accused, the hanged ringleader, was Philip Spencer, the son of the United States Secretary of War. So a Court of Inquiry was convened; this novel is a record of that inquiry, an examination of the characters of the captain, officers, and the dead men. It is a complex anatomizing of justice in which ideas of authority are explained and tested.

Seen through the eyes of the ship's doctor, Robert Leacock, this sometimes makes for cumbersome revelation, for although

Leacock seemed to agree with the captain's original decision, he later changes his mind. . . .

Leacock is the perfect narrator; he has seen it all from the beginning, and he is articulate, describing and questioning "the age, the whole God-crazed westward-hopping country." Mackenzie is vindicated by the tribunal, but not by Leacock: the book ends with the facts of his suicide. It is a novel that is sometimes unnecessarily dense, but always compelling, and as important as if the events it relates happened yesterday— Carlisle's point is that they might well have done, and he's right.

*Paul Theroux, in a review of "Voyage to the First of December," in* Book World—The Washington Post, *January 23, 1972, p. 2.*

### CHRISTOPHER LEHMANN-HAUPT

[In **"Voyage to the First of December"**] the characters are not so much answering the call of Manifest Destiny as paving the way for America's expansion westward. For at the end of Mr. Carlisle's novel, when his narrator walks out on a lonely beach in Nantucket and puts a bullet through his head, a debate is symbolically ended, and henceforth those who would justify immoral behavior by invoking "our country's destiny" will presumably have their way.

**"Voyage to the First of December"** comes within a halyard's thickness of being a crackling good sea yarn, with its authentic 19th-century narrative voice and its double bonus of shipboard intrigue and courtroom drama. So why bother with historical implications?

Because Mr. Carlisle's story misses by just that halyard's width, and it misses, I think, because the author is more preoccupied with history and its ironies than with freely exploring the story's characters. By portraying his chief mutineer as a rebel with so many causes that none of them seems plausible or convincing, and by focusing the subsequent Naval Court inquiry on the question of whether a second (and less interesting) man was actually part of the conspiracy, Mr. Carlisle may have stuck to the record . . . , but he has fuzzied the drama.

For we never really learn what is supposed to be at stake, other than the vague theoretical right to possess a nonconformist nature. We only understand that the outcome—which leaves four men dead (including the narrator, who is the star witness against the ship's commander) but which upholds old American Glory, law and order and the wrong side (presumably) of several other contemporary issues—is *meant* to be hugely ironic. We can't be sure.

*Christopher Lehmann-Haupt, "A Pair of Revisionist Novels," in* The New York Times, *February 2, 1972, p. 37.\**

### ALDEN WHITMAN

Historical fiction is difficult to pull off. Either the author so distorts the basic incident that its reliability as recreation strains the credulity of even the hardiest reader, or he gallops off into Freudland on a psychological hobbyhorse. [In *Voyage to the First of December*] Henry Carlisle has wisely done neither in recounting the purported conspiracy to mutiny aboard the United States Navy brig *Somers* in 1842. . . .

Mr. Carlisle retells the episode through the eyes of Dr. Robert Leacock, the brig's surgeon, who was skeptical of young Spencer's guilt and that of his two friends. He draws also on the records of the Naval Court and contemporary newspaper articles. One result, and a gratifying one, is character keenly etched in authentic background.

Although the mutiny story might easily have been presented as a period piece, Mr. Carlisle has skillfully managed to make it a thoroughly 1970s tale. He does so by posing the gist of the dispute between the antagonists as both generational and ideological—authority being represented by Mackenzie; the subtle subversion of it, by the nineteen-year-old Spencer.

By focusing on these differences as the central tragedy of the *Somers*, Mr. Carlisle has produced a taut, suspenseful, and provocative novel. And one, moreover, that because of its fidelity to the historical record is completely credible.

*Alden Whitman, in a review of "Voyage to the First of December," in* Saturday Review, *Vol. LV, No. 7, February 12, 1972, p. 74.*

### PUBLISHERS WEEKLY

This impressive novel [*The Jonah Man*] goes far beyond an adventure story in chronicling the life of Captain George Pollard, a Nantucket whaler who takes command of the ill-fated ship the *Essex* in 1819, when he is not yet 30. Reading as the aging captain's memoirs, the book describes his youthful ambition, his sense of separateness due to this farm upbringing and his loss of virginity to his doomsaying mother's beautiful and much younger sister, Nancy Coffin. At the time he sets sail with the *Essex,* he feels that he is living out a wonderful destiny. The ship, however, is destroyed by a whale, and before rescue, Pollard is forced to implement an ancient custom of the sea: to draw lots for the sacrifice of one man for the nourishment of the rest. The loser in the lottery is Owen Coffin, Nancy's son. Pollard's obedience to a different set of moral laws—and the consequences of returning to a society that cannot accept them—mold his ensuing struggles and what seems to be a final existential embrace of his act. Although Carlisle . . . doesn't completely address the religious questions raised at the start of Pollard's saga, he has crafted a vivid, believable and deftly written account of one man's journey through hell.

*A review of "The Jonah Man," in* Publishers Weekly, *Vol. 225, No. 17, April 27, 1984, p. 72.*

### TIMOTHY FOOTE

For over a century, ["Moby Dick"] has pretty well pre-empted whaling as a subject for serious fiction. Now comes **"The Jonah Man"** by Henry Carlisle, . . . recording and recreating as fiction the life and fate of the Essex' crew and especially its ill-starred captain, George Pollard. . . .

[The] dramatic real-life givens, richly specific and encouraging reflection on destiny and design in life (or their absence), do not make Mr. Carlisle's attempt at an imaginative biography of George Pollard either easy or successful. Reading **"The Jonah Man,"** one's attention is steadily sabotaged by the distracting question of exactly what Mr. Carlisle has or has not created, with incidents that fail as fiction highly suspect of invention.

Especially at the beginning, "The Jonah Man" fairly clanks with stagy portents of Things to Come. But the book is always interesting, in part because the reader can so clearly watch the writer work. Mr. Carlisle finally achieves a mildly philosophical novel about a man's aging, about coming to terms with wordly failure and personal blame, in Pollard's case while playing hide-and-seek with most of the moral absolutes his century adhered to. Aboard the Essex, Pollard is not much more than a boy's book protagonist. But ruined and ashore for life, despite some attempts by Mr. Carlisle to melodramatize the story, he becomes a satisfactory character.

The conclusion reached by so many Graham Greene characters, that with God for a friend you don't need an enemy, does not explicitly occur to Pollard. He seems to lean toward the notion that perfect peace resides in the sure knowledge of God's utter absence. Yet he finally passes a kind of existential judgment on the events in the whaleboat (this is difficult in part because nobody ashore understands or wants to talk about it), deciding there are things worse than death, especially inner personal dishonor. . . .

"The Jonah Man" does not succeed in making George Pollard impressive. But it amply demonstrates that this quondam cannibal died old and full of memories.

> *Timothy Foote, "In the Whale's Wake," in* The New York Times Book Review, *July 22, 1984, p. 7.*

## CAMPBELL GEESLIN

Two minor defects mar this fascinating book [*The Jonah Man*] (caused perhaps by the author's desire to please a contemporary audience): The novel is presented as a first-person journal, as if written by Pollard himself, though no 19th-century person ever wrote sentences as short and abrupt as these; and no self-respecting 19th-century male would ever—in public memoirs—include a scene describing his seduction by his mother's sister.

> *Campbell Geeslin, in a review of "The Jonah Man," in* People Weekly, *Vol. 22, No. 4, July 23, 1984, p. 12.*

# J(ohn) M. Coetzee

## 1940-

South African novelist and translator.

Coetzee's novels focus on underprivileged and abused characters. Although his interest in injustice stems from social and political oppression in South Africa, Coetzee's fiction extends beyond the geographic and social boundaries of his native country to encompass universal themes and characters. He combines elements of allegory and fable with an understated prose style and an apolitical narrative viewpoint, projecting a world where an offense against an individual becomes an offense against humanity. Coetzee earned increasing international respect for each of his first three novels, *Dusklands* (1974), *In the Heart of the Country* (1977), and *Waiting for the Barbarians* (1980). *Life & Times of Michael K* (1983), for which Coetzee received the Booker McConnell Prize, has further reinforced his reputation as an important contemporary author.

*In the Heart of the Country* is written in diary form and relates the experiences of Magda, a white woman who murders her father, ostensibly due to his affair with a young black woman. Magda's mental state gradually deteriorates within the grim environment of the isolated sheep farm where she lives. Employing such modernist techniques as nonlinear progression and emphasis on interior monologue, Coetzee creates a surreal atmosphere in which both the woman and the reader are uncertain whether her participation in patricide, rape, and incest was real or imagined. *Waiting for the Barbarians* is set in a nameless land where a totalitarian regime rules over a group of people known as "the Barbarians." The story traces a magistrate's struggle between his official role in helping dominate the Barbarians and his desire to ally himself with them. Critics lauded Coetzee's ability to universalize his themes through allegory, symbolism, and abstraction. He was also praised for his insight into the mentality of people who promote brutality and injustice.

*Life & Times of Michael K* corresponds thematically to Coetzee's earlier work but also includes a new dimension in its focus on the oppression of a single character. The novel follows the journey of Michael K., a disfigured, slow-witted young man taking his dying mother to a place she fondly remembers from her youth. Along the way his mother dies and he suffers a series of misfortunes. Critics have cited similarities between Michael K and the character K in Franz Kafka's novel *The Trial*. Like Kafka's K, Michael K is victimized by social forces he can neither control nor understand. Although some critics objected to Coetzee's use of Kafkaesque elements, most applauded the novel's powerful social and political implications. As Cynthia Ozick stated, "Mr. Coetzee's subdued yet urgent lament is for the sadness of a South Africa that has made dependents and parasites and prisoners of its own children, black and white."

(See also *CLC*, Vol. 23 and *Contemporary Authors*, Vols. 77-80.)

## CHRISTOPHER LEHMANN-HAUPT

J. M. Coetzee's "Waiting for the Barbarians" was an astonishment. By relaxing the prose style he had used in an earlier

novel, "In the Heart of the Country," and by generalizing his vision, the author succeeded in creating a tragic fable of colonialism that surpassed the boundaries of his native South Africa and made universal the agony of its conscience-stricken European protagonist.

In his new novel, "Life & Times of Michael K," Mr. Coetzee goes even further in the same direction. True, the geography of the book is more specifically South African—during his wanderings the story's protagonist makes his way east from Cape Town to the Great Karoo and back again—yet the setting might be any third-world country in the throes of war.

The tone of "Michael K" is more stark and impersonal than that created by the self-conscious "I" of "Barbarians." . . .

One reads "Life & Times of Michael K" with an absorption bordering on compulsion. The deadpan tone of the narrative creates a vacuum that sucks you along, and as you get more involved you grow to identify with the stoic hero as the ultimate "escape artist" in a world of violent and brutal contention.

There are stabbing touches of irony in the scenes where police put down Cape Town rioters from apartment buildings called the Côte d'Azur, the Côte d'Or and the Copacabana, or when someone wearing a San Jose State sweatshirt shows up as a volunteer-helper in what for all intents is a concentration camp.

Not merely stabbing is the irony that Michael K—trying to survive by raising pumpkins and living in a hole in the ground on an abandoned farm—is assumed to be part of a mountain guerilla force and is tortured for information. But that's the sort of irony we have grown accustomed to in Mr. Coetzee's writing.

Still, for all its effectiveness, **"Michael K"** does not generate the force that **"Waiting for the Barbarians"** does. Several things combine to weaken its impact. There is, to begin with, the novel's heavy debt to Franz Kafka—not only the references to "K" and even once to a telephone call placed to "the Castle," but also the insistent comparisons of Michael K to various insects, and his gradual mastery of the role of hunger artist. These are doubtless meant to be tributes to a master as much as borrowings from him, but they are overdone and call an unnecessary amount of attention to themselves.

Then there is the shift in the second of the three sections to the narrative point of view of a doctor in a hospital where Michael K shows up. The doctor sees meaning in this strange little hare-lipped figure who, like Melville's Bartleby, refuses all offers to help him survive. The doctor makes imaginary speeches to the man he insists on referring to as "Michaels": "Slowly, as your persistent *No*, day after day, gathered weight, I began to feel that you were more than just another patient." ...

"This sense of gathering meaningfulness," the doctor continues, "is not something like a ray that I project to bathe this or that bed, or a robe in which I wrap this or that patient according to whim. Michaels means something, and the meaning he has is not private to me."

The problem here is that this meaning the doctor detects is evident without his pointing it out. Sufficient unto **"Waiting for the Barbarians"** was the presence of the conscience-stricken colonialist. Here it is excessive and only serves to sentimentalize Michael K.

Finally, there is a problem raised by Michael's supposed slow-wittedness. In fact he is not in the least slow-witted. He is clever with his hands; he often perceives other people's motives even before they do, and he is, as the doctor-narrator of Part Two keeps pointing out, a genius of an escape-artist. Of course, it is certain Cape Town authorities who once perceived Michael K as feeble-minded. The narrator knows better, and this becomes still another source of the novel's irony.

Still, often when I read yet another passage that implicitly celebrates Michael's cleverness, I found myself wishing I could see him as those anonymous Cape Town authorities had done. One trouble with the novel is that the omniscient narrator tells us too much about what is going on inside Michael's head. Not only does this work against the Kafkaesque mysteriousness Mr. Coetzee is trying to achieve, it frequently dissipates the novel's most basic drama.

> *Christopher Lehmann-Haupt, in a review of "Life & Times of Michael K," in* The New York Times, *December 6, 1983, p. C22.*

## CYNTHIA OZICK

The literature of conscience is ultimately about the bewilderment of the naïve. Why do men carry guns and build prison camps, when the nurturing earth is made for freedom? To the outcast, the stray, the simpleton, the unsuspecting—to the in-nocent—the ideologies that order society are inane, incomprehensible. To the innocent, comprehension comes unaccoutered, stripped, uninstructed—Huck Finn on the loose, who merely knows what he knows. And what the pariah Huck knows, against the weight and law and common logic of his slave-holding "sivilization," is that the black man is whole, the rightful owner of his life and times.

In **"Life & Times of Michael K,"** J. M. Coetzee ... has rewritten the travail of Huck's insight, but from Nigger Jim's point of view, and set in a country more terrible—because it is a living bitter hard-hearted contemporary place, the parable-world of an unregenerate soon-after-now, with little pity and no comedy. Conscience, insight, innocence: Michael K cannot aspire to such high recognitions—he is "dull," his mind is "not quick." He was born fatherless and with a disfigurement: a harelip that prevented him from being nourished at his mother's breast. When he needs some tools to make a cart to transport his dying mother, he breaks into a locked shed and takes them. The smallest transgression, undetected and unpunished, the single offense of life; yet nearly every moment of his life is judged as if he were guilty of some huge and undisclosed crime—not for nothing is his surname resonant with the Kafkan "K." His crime is his birth. When as a schoolchild he is perplexed by long division, he is "committed to the protection" of a state-run orphanage for the "variously afflicted." From then on he is consistently protected—subject to curfews, police permits, patrols, convoys, sentries, guns, a work camp with wire fences, a semi-benevolent prison hospital: tyranny, like his school, "at the expense of the state." (p. 1)

The country is at war.

The purpose of the war, from one standpoint—that of a reasonable-minded prison-master—is "so that minorities will have a say in their destinies." This is indisputably the language of democratic idealism. In a South African context such a creed unexpectedly turns Orwellian: It means repression of the black majority by the white minority. Yet in Mr. Coetzee's tale we are not told who is black and who is white, who is in power and who is not. Except for the reference to Cape Town and to place-names that are recognizably Afrikaans, we are not even told that this is the physical and moral landscape of South Africa. We remain largely uninstructed because we are privy solely to Michael K's heart, an organ that does not deal in color or power, a territory foreign to abstractions and doctrines; it knows only what is obvious and elemental. Though there is little mention anywhere of piety or faith, and though it is the prison-masters alone who speak sympathetically and conscientiously of rights and of freedom, Michael K responds only to what appears to be divinely ordered—despite every implacable decree and man-made restraint. He names no tyranny and no ideal. He cares for his mother; he cares for the earth; he will learn how they come to the same in the end.

Mr. Coetzee is a writer of clarifying inventiveness and translucent conviction. Both are given voice gradually, seepingly, as if time itself were a character in the narrative. "There is time enough for everything." As in his previous novel, **"Waiting for the Barbarians,"** Mr. Coetzee's landscapes of suffering are defined by the little-by-little art of moral disclosure—his stories might be about anyone and anyplace. At the same time they defy the vice of abstraction; they are engrossed in the minute and the concrete. It would be possible, following Mr. Coetzee's dazzlingly precise illuminations, to learn how to sow, or use a pump, or make a house of earth. The grain of his sentences is flat and austere, but also so purifying to the senses that one comes away feeling that one's eye has been sharpened, one's hearing vivified, not only for the bright proliferations of nature, but for human unexpectedness. (pp. 1, 26)

[After the scene where Michael K buries his mother's ashes] begins the parable of Michael K's freedom and resourcefulness; here begins Michael K's brief bliss. He is Robinson Crusoe, he is the lord of his life. It is his mother's own earth; it is his motherland; he lives in a womblike burrow; he tills the fruitful soil. Miracles sprout from a handful of discovered seeds.... When he has grown almost unafraid, civilization intrudes.

A whining boy who is a runaway soldier takes over the farmhouse and declares himself in need of a servant. A group of guerrillas and their donkeys pass through by night and trample the seedlings. Michael K flees; he is picked up as a "parasite" and confined to a work camp. But because he has lived in the field as a free man—in the field "he was not a prisoner or a castaway . . . he was himself"—he has learned how to think and judge....

From the seed of freedom Michael K has raised up a metaphysics. It is not the coarse dogma of a killer-rebel or a terrorist; he does not join the guerrillas. He sees vulnerable children on all sides—the runaway who wants to be taken care of, the careless insurgents who are like "young men come off the field after a hard game," even the young camp guard with diabetes, callous and threatening, yet willing to share his food, who will end up as a prisoner himself. "How many people are there left who are neither locked up nor standing guard at the gate?"

But behind the gate Michael K cannot eat, cannot swallow, cannot get nourishment, and now Mr. Coetzee turns his parable to one of starvation. Repression wastes. Tyranny makes skeletons. Injustice will be vomited up. (p. 26)

If "Life & Times of Michael K" has a flaw, it is in the last-minute imposition of an interior choral interpretation. In the final quarter we are removed, temporarily, from the plain seeing of Michael K to the self-indulgent diary of the prison doctor who struggles with the entanglements of an increasingly abusive regime. But the doctor's commentary is superfluous; he thickens the clear tongue of the novel by naming its "message" and thumping out ironies. For one thing, he spells out what we have long ago taken in with the immediacy of intuition and possession. He construes, he translates.... All this is redundant. The sister-melons and the brother-pumpkins have already had their eloquent say. And the lip of the child kept from its mother's milk has had its say. And the man who grows strong and intelligent when he is at peace in his motherland has had his say.

Mr. Coetzee's subdued yet urgent lament is for the sadness of a South Africa that has made dependents and parasites and prisoners of its own children, black and white.... Moreover, Mr. Coetzee makes plain that the noble endurances and passionate revelations of Michael K are not to be taken for a covert defense of terrorism; although he evades no horrors, existing or to come, Mr. Coetzee has not written a symbolic novel about the inevitability of guerilla war and revolution in a country where oppression and dependency are breathed with the air. Instead, he discloses, in the language of imagination, the lumbering hoaxes and self-deceptions of stupidity. His theme is the wild and merciless power of inanity. Michael K suffers from the obdurate callowness of both sides, rulers and rebels— one tramples the vines, the other blows up the pump. At the end of the story, he dreams of drinking the living water drawn

out of his mother's earth, if only drop by drop, if only from a teaspoon.

For the sake of the innocent, time is Mr. Coetzee's hope. (pp. 26, 28)

Cynthia Ozick, "A Tale of Heroic Anonymity," in The New York Times Book Review, December 11, 1983, pp. 1, 26, 28.

BRUCE ALLEN

Of all the writers of recent eminence, South African novelist J. M. Coetzee embodies, as do few of his contemporaries, the idea that fiction should serve social and political uses. His divided, dangerous country is his subject, its injustice and its repressive impact on human personality his obsessive theme....

["Life and Times of Michael K" offers] pungent and challenging allegory: On one level, it's an impassioned (though understated) criticism of apartheid and its effects; on another it's a tale of ordeal and survival that reminds me of works as different (and, I suppose, similar) as "The Adventures of Robinson Crusoe" and Jerzy Kosinski's "The Painted Bird." It's a strong, involving book, though deeply flawed by occasional redundancy and overwriting....

[Perhaps the redundancy is unavoidable] given Coetzee's emphasis on his character's quiet, stubborn resilience.

More serious problems arise from the frequently elevated thoughts and language attributed to this simple soul. For example, we're told Michael thinks of himself, "not as something heavy that left tracks behind it, but if anything as a speck upon the surface of an earth too deeply asleep to notice the scratch of ant-feet, the rasp of butterfly teeth, the tumbling of dust." Though the prose is lovely and haunting, I don't believe *this* character thinks *those* thoughts.

The book succeeds best when Coetzee presents Michael K as a kind of enigmatic, stubborn force. We see frequent evidence of his strange, delicately precise visionary ability: Ransacking somebody's vegetable garden, and hearing a sharp sound, "he imagined a shot cracking out from the back window of the farm house, he imagined a huge Alsatian streaking out to attack him." This is powerful and convincing.

I don't discount this novel's excesses and awkwardnesses, but I do suggest that, with it, Coetzee has moved a step beyond the criticism of inhumanity, which . . . made memorable his "Waiting for the Barbarians." In Michael K. he has given us a character who is nothing less than an embodiment of the survival instinct—and, in doing so, has taken his particular brand of allegorical fiction perhaps as far as it can possibly go.

Bruce Allen, "A Pungent Tale of Ordeal and Survival Set in South Africa," in The Christian Science Monitor, December 12, 1983, p. 29.

JAMES LASDUN

J. M. Coetzee's new novel is even better than its remarkable predecessor. *Waiting for the Barbarians,* a study of the paranoia that at once fosters and undermines the ambitions of imperialism, was essentially a fable, with all the strengths and limitations that word implies. *Life and Times of Michael K* is something of a fable too, but it works also as a piece of vivid, palpable realism. Its themes are suffering and oppression—a passive man, isolated by a hare lip and a simple mind, trying to make sense of life in a state that subjects him to a series of atrocious physical and psychological assaults. One thinks immediately of Kafka, and of course the hero's—or rather the victim's—name is an explicit reference to Kafka. But the point of that reference is as much to invoke contrast as comparison. It is no longer necessary to hold a distorting mirror to reality, Coetzee implies, in order to expose the psychosis in the relation of state to individual—or not when the state in question happens to be South Africa. The things that happen to Michael K make harrowing reading, the more so because one never doubts they could happen one day to any of South Africa's dispossessed. (p. 69)

Coetzee describes [K's journey] with a calm, dispassionate precision. There is no revelling in horror. Understatement is employed, sometimes quite brilliantly, to show how barbarity can become institutionalised, and enter the minds of its agents so thoroughly that they perpetrate it without any particular sense of malice: "'You climb the fence and I'll shoot you dead, mister. No hard feelings'", says a guard at a camp for the homeless. And the word *explained* takes on a grotesque resonance when a dog handler in the same camp confiscates a radio from a woman: "He dropped it to the earth and stamped on it. 'No radios', he explained."

Simple-minded as he is, K is a complex character, sometimes problematically so. As a paradigm of passive suffering he is an awesome creation. A frightening vacancy of spirit brings him close to complete immobility. . . . And even his one major act of resistance, refusing prison food (in itself a decidedly passive form of revolt), is presented as something forced on him by an ineluctable natural law, rather than his own intention.

Coetzee is marginally less convincing when he tries to interpret K for us, instead of letting us do the work for ourselves. In the short section dealing with K's hunger strike, he switches from an authorial point of view to that of the prison doctor—an archetypal white liberal, plagued with uncertainty about the role assigned him (not unlike the magistrate in *Waiting for the Barbarians*). In contrast to Coetzee's own impassive coolness, the doctor's appraisal of K is highly emotional, a series of pat formulae grabbed at in an effort to turn this wretched man who refuses his help into a symbol he can accommodate:

> "I see you as . . . a soul blessedly untouched by doctrine, untouched by history . . . a creature left over from an earlier age, like the coelacanth or the last man to speak Yanqui. . . ."

There is perhaps a mild satire intended, on the kind of megalomaniac guilt to which white liberals are prone, but it is hard to be sure, and one is glad to leave the doctor behind.

In the course of the book, K's past as a municipal gardener is revived. He does find the farm—now derelict—at Prince Albert, and becomes obsessed with a continually thwarted project to raise pumpkins and supply his own minuscule needs. Here Coetzee shows a hint of greed over his character, trying to impose on K's role as indomitable victim that of Crusoe; the two do not always sit comfortably together.

But these are minor blemishes on what remains a work of tremendous depth and force—one that fully deserves its 1983 Booker Prize. The final pages (in which K, barely alive, is casually befriended and pickpocketed by a pimp, and as casually fellated by a silver-wigged prostitute, before returning at last to his dismal cupboard room) provide a conclusion of powerful and appropriate chilliness to a study of life at one of its furthest extremities. (pp. 69-70)

*James Lasdun, "Life's Victims," in* Encounter, *Vol. LXII, No. 1, January, 1984, pp. 69-73.**

**MARK ABLEY**

When times become difficult, literature begins to reassume its ancient function of prophecy. In South Africa, where political stability seems less and less likely to endure, such writers as Nadine Gordimer and André Brink have visualized the crumbling future in detail. *Life & Times of Michael K* . . . provides an acute insight into a society about to undergo a gradual collective breakdown. . . .

Coetzee concentrates not on the sweeping manifestations of power, race and class, but on a humble individual who becomes trapped in political turmoil. The novel's hero is not alluring. He is an inarticulate, friendless gardener with a hare lip. . . .

Although it is rooted in the scarred and lovely landscape of South Africa, Coetzee's vision is not limited to his own country. The arbitrary violence and oppression that he evokes are known to many other nations. To underscore the book's universality, Coetzee deliberately invites comparison with one of the greatest of modern novelists, the German-Jewish author Franz Kafka. Michael's name points to Kafka's *The Trial* and *The Castle,* in which the hero is called "K"; it is as audacious a move as a contemporary playwright calling a character "Hamlet." Both writers create an atmosphere of brooding menace and actions that seem both utterly necessary and bizarre. But, unlike Kafka, Coetzee infuses a surprising amount of optimism into his fiction. *The Trial* ends bleakly: "It was as if he meant the shame of it to outlive him." *Life & Times of Michael K* finishes with the hopeful words, "One can live."

Michael can never rid himself of politics, because it is impossible to escape from history. The forces around him shape his destiny even more than his own actions do. Throughout the novel he does make political decisions—at one point, he refuses to become the servant of a white deserter who is trying to hide from the police in the wilderness. Yet Michael's imagination has not been harmed by the worst effects of the wars, leaving him free from rhetoric and abstract ideology. As a result, Coetzee may be no more popular with Marxists than with apologists for apartheid. His book serves as a reminder that dignity has nothing to do with comfort, security or even good health, but with the resilience to endure the hardships of fate without cynicism or surrender. An attention to small things—the feel of a dried seed, the smell of bitter water—distinguishes both Michael's life and Coetzee's prose. *Life & Times of Michael K* begins as a study of an apparently ordinary man; it develops into a portrait of an exceptional human being, written with unusual power and beauty.

*Mark Abley, "An Outcast in a Tormented Country," in* Maclean's Magazine, *Vol. 97, No. 5, January 30, 1984, p. 49.*

**NADINE GORDIMER**

J. M. Coetzee, a writer with an imagination that soars like a lark and sees from up there like an eagle, chose allegory for his first few novels. It seemed he did so out of a kind of opposing desire to hold himself clear of events and their daily, grubby, tragic consequences in which, like everybody else living in South Africa, he is up to the neck, and about which he had an inner compulsion to write. So here was allegory as a stately fastidiousness; or a state of shock. He seemed able to deal with the horror . . . only—if brilliantly—if this were to be projected into another time and plane. His *Waiting for the Barbarians* was the North Pole to which the agitprop of agonized black writers (and some white ones hitching a lift to the bookmart on the armored car) was the South Pole; a world to be dealt with lies in between. . . . Coetzee has taken it up now [in *The Life and Times of Michael K*].

Michael K (the initial probably stands for Kotze or Koekemoer and has no reference, nor need it have, to Kafka) is not Everyman. In fact he is marked out, from birth, by a harelip indelibly described as curled like a snail's foot. . . . His deformity distorts his speech and his actual and self-images. He shrinks from the difficulty of communication through words and the repugnance he sees holding him off, in people's eyes; thus he appears to be, and perhaps is, retarded—one of those unclassifiable beings that fascinated Dostoevsky, a "simple." . . .

This, then, is the simple story of a "simple" man. And it begins unexceptionally, anybody's refugee plodding predictably away from hunger and homelessness without much hope that these will not be waiting again at the end of the journey. You can shake your head decently over yet another evocation of commonplace misery; the only particular reaction, this time, a slight sense of impatience—did it all have to be laid on so thick? Does the man have to be harelipped, etc., on top of everything else?

But Coetzee's mode, from the beginning, is soon seen to have arisen solely out of the needs of content, and is purely and perfectly achieved. As the reader is drawn into the novel there comes the extraordinarily rare occurrence of one's response to its events opening up along with that of the central character himself. This is the reverse of facile identification: a prehensile comprehension stirs to take hold where the grasp of familiarity doesn't reach. A fellow inmate of the labor camp says to Michael K, "You've been asleep all your life. It's time to wake up." For the reader, too.

It is here that allegorical symbols occur. The work speaks: a voice inside the reader. Michael K is a real human being experiencing an individual body, but for some of us he will be the whole black people of South Africa, whatever gradations of color the South African Population Registration Act sorts them into; for some he will be the inmate of Auschwitz or Stalin's camps. Others will see the split lip and strangled speech as the distortion of personality that South African race laws have effected, one way or another, in all of us who live there, black and white. (p. 3)

The abstraction of allegory and symbol will not give access to what is most important in this magnificent novel, however. Neither will seeing it as a vision of the future. If it is set ahead in time at all, then this is done as a way of looking, as if it had come to the surface, at what lies under the surface of the present. The harried homelessness of Michael K and his mother is the experience, in 1984, of hundreds of thousands of black people in South African squatter towns and "resettlement" camps. A civil war is going on in 1984 on South Africa's borders, between black and white, and bombings by underground liberation movements within the country. . . . Coetzee

has won (or lost?) his inner struggle and now writes, from among the smell of weary flesh, a work of the closest and deepest engagement with the victimized people of Michael K's life and times.

Political statements are made implicitly through the situations and reactions of Michael K that have no obvious political meaning. The deserter who comes to the farm is the grandson of the white farmer from Michael's mother's girlhood: Visagie's descendant and that of his laborer are living a parallel life now that the old structure is destroyed, one a fugitive from duty within the army that hunts and kills, the other fugitive from its pursuit. In the presence of the two on the farm is contained the core of tenure—this is the land that was taken by conquest, and then by deeds of sale that denied blacks the right even to buy back what had been taken from them. Can't the fugitives accommodate each other? Neither knows how to do this outside the ghostly pattern of master-servant. So Michael instinctively runs; and when he returns to find the boy has gone, he does not even then move into the Visagie house.

When he articulates the reason, it comes not as from an author's mouthpiece, but as what lies developing inside Michael, unsaid, unable to be shaped by his misformed lip. "Whatever I have returned for, it is not to live as the Visagies lived, sleep where they slept, sit on their stoep looking out over their land. . . . The worst mistake, he told himself, would be to try to found a new house, a rival line, on his small beginnings." (His hidden pumpkins.) Here is the concrete expression, through the creative imagination, of political debate about the future of South Africa under black majority rule: whether or not it should take over what has been the white South African version of the capitalist system.

Yet the unique and controversial aspect of this work is that while it is implicitly and highly political, Coetzee's heroes are those who ignore history, not make it. That is clear not only in the person of Michael K, but in other characters, for example the white doctor and nurse in the "rehabilitation" camp, who are "living in suspension," although for the woman, washing sheets, time is as full with such tasks as it has ever been, and for the doctor it is a state of being "alive but not alive," while for both "history hesitated over what course it should take." No one in this novel has any sense of taking part in determining that course; no one is shown to believe he knows what that course should be. The sense is of the ultimate malaise: of destruction. Not even the oppressor really believes in what he is doing, anymore, let alone the revolutionary.

This is a challengingly questionable position for a writer to take up in South Africa, make no mistake about it. The presentation of the truth and meaning of what white has done to black stands out on every page, celebrating its writer's superb, unafraid creative energy as it does; yet it denies the energy of the will to resist evil. That *this* superb energy exists with indefatigable and undefeatable persistence among the black people of South Africa—Michael K's people—is made evident, yes, heroically, every grinding day. It is not present in the novel.

Except in the person of Michael K?

If so, then this can be only because Coetzee, while fiercely moved far beyond commonplace understanding of their plight, does not believe in the possibility of blacks establishing a new regime that will do much better. . . . While "we have all tumbled over the lip into the cauldron," the doctor, who takes over the narrative in the first person toward the close of the novel, finds Michael K "a soul blessedly untouched by doctrine, untouched by history," a creature no "organ of state" would recruit as one of its agents. This white liberal feels *chosen* by the victim of his own society; wasted Michael K becomes the doctor's burden and his only hope of salvation. He believes Michael K can lead him out of history to those "areas that lie between camps and belong to no camp." A revulsion against all political and revolutionary solutions rises with the insistence of the song of cicadas to the climax of this novel.

I don't think the author would deny that it is his own revulsion.

And so J. M. Coetzee has written a marvelous work that leaves nothing unsaid—and could not be better said—about what human beings do to fellow human beings in South Africa; but he does not recognize what the victims, seeing themselves as victims no longer, have done, are doing, and believe they must do for themselves. Does this prevent his from being a great novel? My instinct is to say a vehement "No." But the organicism that George Lukács defines as the integral relation between private and social destiny is distorted here more than is allowed for by the subjectivity that is in every writer. The exclusion is a central one that may eat out the heart of the work's unity of art and life.

For is there an idea of survival that can be realized entirely outside a political doctrine? Is there a space that lies between camps? Again, this book is unusual in positing its answer while writers customarily say it is their business only to explore questions. The place is the earth, not in the cosmic but the plain dirt sense. The idea is the idea of gardening. And with it floods into the book, yet again, much more than it seemed to be about: the presence of the threat not only of mutual destruction of whites and blacks in South Africa, but of killing, everywhere, by scorching, polluting, neglecting, charging with radioactivity, the dirt beneath our feet. From this perspective the long history of terrible wars whose reason has been advanced as "to augment human happiness" could, I suppose, be turned away from; only the death of the soil is the end of life. The single sure joy Michael K can experience is the taste of a pumpkin he has grown, hidden from the just and unjust of marauding history. Under the noise of the cicadas, with delicacy and sureness, Coetzee has been drawing upon the strength of the earth to keep his deceptively passive protagonist and the passionate vitality of this book alive. (pp. 3, 6)

> Nadine Gordimer, "The Idea of Gardening," in The New York Review of Books, Vol. XXXI, No. 1, February 2, 1984, pp. 3, 6.

**VIVIAN GORNICK**

The literature of most of the world—Latin America, Eastern Europe, South Africa—is a literature of allegory and fable infused with modernist sensibility. Here, the grotesque and the fantastical are elemental, the language of hallucination is common, and the controlling metaphor is the image of a human being steadily broken by a gathering force that calls itself The State, composed of people who not only look and speak as we do but are in fact our friends, relatives, and neighbors. The urgency and sense of mission in these books is unmistakable: let the record show that at this time in this place human beings did unspeakable things to one another and suffered at each other's hands as none could have suffered through famine, flood, disease, or economic devastation.

J. M. Coetzee . . . inherits both fable and hallucination as literary givens. He writes short, dense, visionary novels sustained by allegorical intent and driven by an anxiety common to writers from his part of the world. His prose is suffused with the preoccupations of a man who lives in a country where, in the course of daily life, black people are hunted like animals: picked up off city streets and country roads, forced to live under a curfew, herded into camps, townships, and centers. Which of us, Coetzee's novels ask, can look daily into the eyes of black men and women and not be made crazy by the flat stare, the silent compliance? Who can avoid knowing the fear that begins to take on mythic proportions and seems to portend awesome and terrible things? There *is* no living with oneself in such a world. Coetzee, among other South Africans, seems to write in order to say precisely that.

Yet fable and allegory are problematic (only rarely is an allegorical vision of life strong enough to prevail over the absence of human particularity), and so is the self-conscious application of sensibility. In Coetzee's novels, the power of fable, in conjunction with a contemporary usage of derangement and disconnect, works with varying degrees of success. . . . *In the Heart of the Country* captures and reflects an essence of South African writing. Even when the story fails to hold the reader's interest, these mad doings on an empty plain where nothing stirs and the most ordinary human sympathies are long dead, their skeletons swarming with flesh-eating insects—all this accumulates into a penetrating atmosphere, oppressive and peculiarly South African. The sense of remove is extraordinary. Remoteness induces fear and dread, becomes a compelling metaphor for human degeneration. What are these people *doing* here? And why are they doing it? In the name of what does all this go forward?

*Waiting for the Barbarians,* a far more ambitious novel, is overwhelmed by allegory: the atmosphere is abstract, the people are symbolic representations. . . . Much in this book is wise and moving. . . . [But] *Barbarians* is nevertheless severely limited by the absence of real people or felt atmosphere. Indeed, the intelligence makes painfully clear how much of another century apartheid is, and how hard it is to make of its existence a contemporary fable that will resonate for those of us who, in every way, are living on the other side of the world.

In *Life & Times of Michael K,* the most complex and memorable of the three novels, allegory and modernist technique struggle admirably with felt life. . . .

The power of *Michael K* lies in Coetzee's ability to describe in hour-by-hour, day-by-day, week-by-week detail Michael's involvement with survival and how he comes to realize that the only way he can be free is to need nothing, absolutely nothing, from the world that begins at the end of his own body. This realization comes to him gradually, as the cumulative experience of his days and nights penetrates his feeling body, and it penetrates us as well. As Michael moves dumbly about, wanting only to be safe and at rest, it slowly dawns on him that every human encounter is a source of threat and humiliation. He feels this truth eating into his emaciated body—and we feel it, too. The profound isolation at the heart of Coetzee's metaphor—the sheer speechlessness of it—is evoked with strength and skill; *this* book is pain. *Michael K* succeeds as a work of the imagination to the degree that Coetzee's allegorical and modernist intentions are foiled rather than sustained. The use of K is mannered and pretentious—K belongs to Kafka for the millennium, and to the overformed world of the modern

West, where the crime is anonymity. Michael belongs to the underformed world of South Africa, where the crime is infantilization. Indeed, Michael himself is complicated proof of the kind of reduced life one associates with South Africa. What Michael feels any sentient creature in his position would feel—the full pain of not being allowed to live free. Beyond this, we know very little of who or what Michael is. Coetzee tries to make him a holy idiot, but what emerges is a human being who fails to arrive at articulation because he has been kept in a childlike state all his life: exactly what a man like Coetzee might observe of a man like Michael, the two of them passing each other daily on the streets of Cape Town.

The war, as well, is an abstraction, a background that is declared but not experienced. I found myself thinking of the work of Israelis—who also write from a part of the world, remote and under a burning sun, where life is such that people have a hard time remembering why it is they must remain human—and how naturally "the war" weaves in and out of their stories, gaining metaphoric authority precisely because it is a felt reality. In *Michael K,* "the war" does not ring true. What *is* a felt reality in Coetzee's writing (as it is in much South African writing) is the remoteness and the peculiar silence: as of an unholy quiet at the center. The sense of human beings struggling in this muffled airless dream—sex and spirit coming up hot, quick, unbidden—lends great power to much of the literature coming out of this desperately unhappy country. J. M. Coetzee's novels, at their best, remind one of the South African silence. They enrich a body of work that is, finally, a testament to the irreducible in human life.

*Vivian Gornick, "When Silence Speaks Louder than Words," in* The Village Voice, *Vol. XXIX, No. 12, March 20, 1984, p. 40.*

# Alfred (DeWitt) Corn (III)

## 1943-

**American poet and critic.**

Corn has been widely praised as an important contemporary poet. His informal, controlled style synthesizes elements from such traditional poets as Hart Crane and Walt Whitman and such modern poets as James Merrill and John Ashbery. Among Corn's prominent themes are love, nature, and loss of innocence. His poetry has been commended for making the familiar seem refreshingly new. Accordingly, Corn has stated that "when I write, I try to bring all the resources of experience and language to bear on what I say, in the belief that the result will strike the reader as rare and valuable, beautiful and useful."

As Robert B. Shaw has noted, Corn is "especially good at the topographical lyric, the poem which mingles place with an observing mind's meditation." Many of the poems in his first collection, *All Roads at Once* (1976), begin with descriptions of particular objects or locales and lead into penetrating examinations of experience. In subsequent volumes, including *A Call in the Midst of the Crowd* (1978), Corn concentrates on the long poem. The title poem in this volume is about New York City. Like William Carlos Williams in *Paterson,* Corn intersperses throughout the poem quotations about the city from various documentary sources and from other authors, including Herman Melville, Edgar Allan Poe, Walt Whitman, and Wallace Stevens. The long title piece gained considerably more critical notice than the shorter poems in the volume; Corn has remarked that more attention should have been given "to how the lyrics in the first part shape response to the New York poem."

Corn grew up in Georgia. He later lived in New York City for eleven years and moved to New Haven, Connecticut, in 1976. The poems in his third collection, *The Various Light* (1980), reflect this change in milieu. Some of them examine New England towns and their seasonal changes. The most notable piece in this volume is another long poem, "The Outdoor Amphitheater." Set in Valdosta, Georgia, this poem contrasts Corn's idealistic boyhood with the insight of mature acceptance. In a similar vein, *Notes from a Child of Paradise* (1984) is a book-length poem chronicling Corn's coming-of-age and his marriage during the 1960s. The structure and style of this poem owe much to works of other writers, particularly Dante's *Inferno* and Wallace Stevens's *Notes Toward a Supreme Fiction.* Corn's unsentimental evocation of a turbulent era has been widely praised.

(See also *Contemporary Authors,* Vol. 104 and *Dictionary of Literary Biography Yearbook: 1980.*)

## J. D. McCLATCHY

[Alfred Corn's] work is what Keats called . . . "ethereal." That is . . . almost the keynote in James Merrill's jacket-blurb for *All Roads At Once:* "Airy, all-seeing, a new window onto the world—this is an extremely beautiful first book. Among Mr. Corn's contemporaries I know of no poet more accomplished." That high praise is entirely deserved, and its source

© *Rollie McKenna*

is apposite if one were to cite the influences on this book: clearly Merrill's urbane angle of vision is one, along with John Ashbery's intelligent insouciance, and Elizabeth Bishop's eye for the charged detail. None of these very different poets is Corn's model, though aspects of his art might remind a reader of any one of them. His manner and matter are entirely his own, and in more than the question of technique he has refused to narrow his poetic choices, so that his book has a variety and weight that are not only promising but already assured.

Corn's maturity is immediately apparent in his ability to attend to the things of this world, and he conjugates them with a verbal felicity and subtlety rare among his contemporaries, who often lack the patience to see a subject through or an object thoroughly. His poems closely scan the shades and surfaces of their environments—whether white everlastings on the Oregon coast or oil slicks on a Soho street, a case of Chinese porcelains or a Fairfield Porter print. Yet neither the transient natural detail nor art's ambivalent permanence is his real concern. Instead, they function as the composition of place for his meditations, since "nothing really appears unless we try / to see it as something else"—"The world is made in our own images." To compare is more than to conjure; it is to restore the world to our ideas of it, which, for Corn, are the true *matière première.* He is, at times, suspicious of thought. . . . And his meditations are occasionally skittish, as if to respect the essential obscurity of purpose and consequence in this life. . . .

Still, his poems are contingency plans to counter the hazards of overdetermined or undermining circumstance, and he sets out—on all roads at once, but in the footsteps of Wallace Stevens and Hart Crane—to discover or devise "eternity / on a human scale," in the instant or the instance. . . .

A typical Corn poem is a measured *aria parlante*, domestic or solitary, working its way word-over-word toward what is implicit in experience—his, ours, the poem's. Here is a new poet—one is tempted to add "at last!"—with faith in the expressive and imaginative resources of his craft, and to read such poems as **"Interim in a Waiting Room," "Images for Piano,"** or **"Pages from a Voyage"** allows us his convictions. It is apparent, too, that Corn has read other books than the one he has written, and he risks invoking the visionary company to which he clearly belongs; his moving poem on Hart Crane, **"The Bridge, Palm Sunday, 1973,"** asks help for his ambition and project from that voyager. It is a touching gesture, and bids to bridge our strongest American line of poetry into the new generation. But Alfred Corn is also on his own, and the pleasure his characteristic work gives is itself a moving experience—no less moving than the realization that many of these poems have a stature that encourages comparison with artists already acknowledged as our best. (p. 506)

> J. D. McClatchy, "The World Rendered, the World Restored," in The Nation, Vol. 223, No. 16, November 13, 1976, pp. 505-06.*

### HAROLD BLOOM

[Alfred Corn's *All Roads At Once*] comes with accurate endorsements from Merrill and Ashbery, both of whom are indubitable influences upon this superb book, which ultimately however goes back to Hart Crane. Corn . . . is very nearly Crane's reincarnation. Many of his lyrics would fit into Crane's *White Buildings,* and his *The Bridge, Palm Sunday, 1973* and the beautiful sequence, *Pages from a Voyage,* precisely evoke Crane's spirit. Yet the effect is one of loving struggle, of the highest agony of identity-and-opposition, and not of mere imitation. Corn, already a fully formed poet, may become for his generation what Merrill and Ashbery have become for theirs—indispensable.

> Harold Bloom, in a review of "All Roads at Once," in The New Republic, Vol. 175, No. 21, November 20, 1976, p. 26.

### RICHARD HOWARD

To his extravagant purpose—which is a kind of saturation in the welter, even in the dither of experience until the world makes sense only when his senses make it—Alfred Corn brings a first-rate talent [in *All Roads at Once*]: the poet sees, and he sees that what he sees changes, and that in fact

> Nothing really appears unless we try
> to see it as something else.

But the seeing comes first, before the transformations into meaning ("really appears" is Corn's characteristic oxymoron for this process), and it is capital that Corn sees—and senses—so well; he had better, for there is an extremity in his enterprise which the aesthete's gentleness, so readily mistaken for languor, would seem to belie. . . . There is an extremity, even a

kind of heroism, in Corn's insistence that the poem be realized on its own terms, without much conceptual meddling on the poet's part. . . . So we get a number of observant lyrics "at the dark fold of the revealed world", the best of which is **Interim in a Waiting Room** (life itself?), and a group of extended pieces not so much narrative as ruminative, cud-chewing of an excruciatingly conscious man invariably at that "limit / where light is less and mood more," the best of which is **Pages from a Voyage** (that part of life itself which can be subtracted from death?). Corn breathes a good deal about the bush, trusting it will burst into flame, and it does so often enough, though the touch is sometimes very feathery indeed. . . . [There are] limitations of a mode which relies so much upon what Conrad called doing justice to the visible world. We long, now and then, for governance, for shape, even that imposed shape which we call meter and rhyme, that derived identity which comes from Authority rather than from Temperament. (pp. 226-27)

[A] note of complacency is sounded [in some of the poems] . . . , and sorts a little too comfortably with a sense of helpless *tristesse* ("We see our flaws but not how to mend"). But Corn is victorious for the most part in his submission, his submersion: "to be read and dreamed / until the secret order appears." He examines his movements through a bout of illness, a spell of city life—a visit to a Corot in the museum, a reading of Darwin's *Voyage,* time with friends, time alone—and the secret order does appear. Travel and disease are the great solvents, of course, for all the chromatics, the "pastel quarters, plumed dens"; what appears is wisdom, along with that wonderful willingness to give the self away, to let go, to "fall forward into words". Like Ashbery's, Alfred Corn's poems are about what it is like for him to be alive and conscious; like Merrill's, they are about how much must be gainsaid, renounced and foregone in order to have, at least, themselves; but they are like no one else's in their zealous disposition to let the world speak through them, to praise being. . . . (p. 227)

> Richard Howard, "Art or Knack?" in Poetry, Vol. CXXIX, No. 4, January, 1977, pp. 226-32.*

### DAVID KALSTONE

For a poet the second book is often the hardest to write, especially if he has been praised, as Alfred Corn was, for the first. His readers are no longer looking for single gifted poems so much as for staying power, a plotted version of the self—even more, for robustness, for signs of the poet's own particular heresies and power. Those signs are present in the confident and mysterious privacy of the shorter poems in *A Call in the Midst of the Crowd* and in some of the virtuoso moments of the long ambitious "poem in four parts on New York City" which gives the book its title.

*A Call in the Midst of the Crowd* is less resolved and more agitated than its hale title from Whitman suggests. The book falls into two parts which seem to tap two different levels of psychological pressure and assurance. In the long New York poem the protagonist measures himself against Whitman's extroverts and optimists and comes out saddened, irritated, still full of puzzled pride about the relation of city to solitude, of experience to writing. The apparent plot is a "portrait of the artist as a young man." But the emotional subtext—not realized fully enough on the surface of the poem—is a lovers' separation and tentative reunion. The shorter poems in the book are more focused: they find their strength precisely in those moments of absence, isolation and bereavement which are memorable in the longer poem. In **"Darkening Hotel Room,"** for example, a son trying and failing to remember his mother lost in early childhood recalls what it is like

> To reach in confidence for efficient,
> Bony arms and only find—
> A bereavement, immaterially goes on,
> An asceticism, for a lifetime.

The wisdom here has a lot to do with finding the right rhythm and syntax; illumination comes in a plain and pained phrase ("an asceticism"), stern truth, almost masked as an afterthought. I find these accents more authentic and self-possessed than those of the protagonist of **"A Call in the Midst of the Crowd,"** who spends perhaps too much time wandering the city, on foot or bicycle, eating alone in restaurants, "trying to feel actual in the absence of a human echo." The triumphs of this book come in moments when Corn stops thinking in terms of an echo, a self repeated by the world, and begins to feel "actual" *because* the self is imperfectly received and transmitted by others. His best passages and poems suggest human relationships like those in Chekhov plays: characters reach out for one another, and, as if under water, fail to touch because they misjudge the space between them. . . .

[In **"A Call in the Midst of the Crowd,"** Corn] alternates his lyrics with collages from famous and anonymous writing about New York: Whitman, Poe, Henry James, Edith Wharton, guidebooks, encyclopedias, *The New York Times*. At their best the quotations stand in provocative relation to the private preoccupations of the poet. A documentary account of Henry Hudson's disappearance at sea, set adrift by his own crew, is followed by a poem which transforms history, turns it inward. . . .

At . . . times Corn's "documents" threaten to overwhelm his poems. Is it that he doesn't trust the latter or is this willed juxtaposition meant to show us how little the public life has to do with the private? In either case the scheme of the poem— a year, the four seasons, city landmarks visited, the Bicentennial—obligates the poet to respond to and include far more of the stimuli of the outside world than he really cares to. Yet, at one point (JULY: Fire: The People) the public challenge launches him into apocalyptic language of wonderful power. His oceanic phrases subject the city to a transfiguring wish which makes it, momentarily, entirely his own. . . . (p. 120)

[The] most valuable apprenticeship in the book is to the poetry of James Merrill and John Ashbery. Not only has studying their work enriched Corn's way of seeing and writing . . . , but it has also given him the courage to explore his instinct for remote states of mind. Some of the most telling details in this book are not external observations but sharp outer detail transferred to Corn's own inner "land of unlikeness." The language is rich, but its purpose is paradoxically ascetic: it allows him to pursue what seems at this stage his subject, the psyche's quarrel with the world. (pp. 120-21)

>           *David Kalstone, "The Psyche's Quarrel with the World," in* The Nation, *Vol. 227, No. 4, August 5-12, 1978, pp. 120-21.*

## GEORGE KEARNS

The long [title poem of Alfred Corn's *A Call in the Midst of the Crowd*], subtitled "A Poem in Four Parts on New York City," has a plot of sorts. The poet is a youngish man whom we discover characteristically staring from his apartment window, or walking, cruising, biking around the streets of New York, trying to make sense of himself and what he sees. A Byronic melancholy, reported with good humor and high spirits, is upon him, the causes several and properly confused. . . . (p. 157)

[The poem] gives us more (*less*, some will say) than the symbolist residue of experience; yet with its overt romantic-visionary themes, its brilliant urban spots of time, it avoids the merely chatty-anecdotal. The experience *and* the fruit of experience . . . are each given their due, are allowed to play across each other in a variety of intensities and relationships. The twenty-six lyrical sections are rooted in recognizable occasions and move across the four seasons of a year, from winter to autumn, as the plot moves autobiographically and thematically to a precariously happy ending. The poet is reunited with his lover; but on the chilly deck of a ferry back to Manhattan . . . he bears a chastened sense of the fragility of romantic love and of its potential as a structure for experience. . . . He's gathered the confidence to assert—why, one isn't sure, though it lies beyond argument—that "The world has become manageable again." Power over experience appears identical with power over language, the ability to have brought a modestly dazzling poem into being.

The lyrical pages that form the journal of a year are interleaved with a miscellany of short prose passages, all about New York, gathered from guidebooks, encyclopedias, letters, memoirs, the daily papers. The mixture of lyric with prose "found objects," combined with the theme of a walker through the streets of an American city, suggests an obligatory comparison with *Paterson;* but Williams is enormously more complex and abandoned, and can risk, more than Corn dares, getting out of control. In *Paterson*, the city, its people, its language, have an irreducible life of their own, while Corn's New York and its people are trapped within his egotistical sublime—he's frankly looking into "the mirror of this self-imposed city." The poem would not be at all as amiable as it is without the space cleared by the prose *intermezzi*, where other voices, other experiences may be heard. The relations between prose and poetry, various and witty, now clear, now elusive, suggest a game whose only rule is the poet's implicit meditation that *somehow* these other New Yorks converge upon his. Many of the prose fragments are by and about other writers in New York—Whitman, Crane, Melville, Stevens, Lorca, James, O'Hara, Poe—though—a marvelous inspiration of restraint—we don't see them *as poets*, but as men, like the central character in this poem, walking about, observing . . . , coping with life in the city. (pp. 158-59)

If Corn remains a bit cautious with form and language, he's willing to take risks of another kind. Along the way, he'll report anything that comes into his head, revealing the sophomoric musings we all have (I suppose) but . . . have learned to keep to ourselves. Whitman, of course—Corn's master in this—never learned to keep them to himself, and if he makes us wince at times, we have to come round to seeing his unedited openness as the source of his charm and strength. (p. 159)

Of artifice [Corn] has plenty. He likes to set up formal games for himself, then ignore them as he chooses. In the first seven lyric passages in **"A Call in the Midst of the Crowd,"** apparent spontaneity of experience and diction is meticulously shaped into sixteen-line stanzas; the stanzas are abandoned in the central section of the poem for flexible verse-paragraphs; then they reappear . . . for the final seven lyrics. In an earlier poem, **"To the End of the Pier,"** he establishes Marianne Moore eccentric-syllabics, which he then doesn't quite bother to stick with. The demonstration of mastery, combined with a studied carelessness with form, seems to mimic the kind of self he's fashioning in the poems, whose control won't screen out possibilities, who fuses random events in moments of vision, while continuing to accept things as they appear. He is lavish with poetic self-awareness. (p. 160)

Neither sentiment nor skill, however, even in the combination that he's made his own, marks the limits of Corn's sensibility. He can convince us, as well, that flashes of vision inform his verse. . . . His inspired passages can be rapturous and dazzling, and at times display something like the sophisticated afflatus that drives Browning's "A Toccata of Galuppi's." For Corn unashamedly wants to write within a high tradition: if Pegasus has thrown him he's determined to remount. . . . (pp. 160-61)

Corn is more convincing the more I read him, the more I become familiar with his elegies for the ever-vanishing moment. Yet the shorter poems are not always as accessible as **"A Call in the Midst of the Crowd,"** in part because they sometimes sound as if they retain private messages, polished for our eyes, but not wholly made public. Among them I particularly like the bright assurance of **"To a Muse"** and the shades of melancholy in **"Synecdoche"** and **"Deception."** . . .

Corn has learned the manners of lordlier, more fastidious and aristocratic poets. One of the pleasures of reading him has been to discover behind the New York sophisticate a visionary whom one imagines as friendly and vulnerable. (p. 162)

*George Kearns, "Alfred Corn's Speaking Gift," in Canto: Review of the Arts, Vol. 2, No. 3, Fall, 1978, pp. 157-62.*

## ALAN WILLIAMSON

Whether the long title poem [of *A Call in the Midst of the Crowd*] . . . is, as has been said, a "major" American personal epic, is a difficult question. The plot-line is thin: a love affair broken and repaired—in both cases, for mysterious reasons—with the time of estrangement ironically coinciding with the traditional seasons of hope and desire. Perhaps it is this irony that directs the speaker's attention to what I take to be the poem's real subject: the excess or tumidity of feeling which the city, with its intimations of possibility and insignificance, superimposes on the individual emotions lived out within it. Corn strains, to my mind, gallantly but self-consciously when he tries to render this tumidity, in **"Fire: The People,"** as a mystical experience. . . . Corn is more surely moving when the painful elusiveness, goallessness, of the feeling is the point, as in **"Summer Vertigo,"** or **"Spring and Summer,"** or **"Awakened before I meant."** . . . Perhaps this is why my heart sinks a little at seeing the poem compared, without qualification, to *The Bridge*. . . . Whatever else it is, **"A Call in the Midst of the Crowd"** is not a great poem of history. The political statements in it (**"Some New Ruins," "Declaration, July 4"**) are all too characteristic of the 1970s: good-natured, folksy, irresolute on any large issue. The prose quotations from earlier American writings, which constitute about half of the poem, seem too available a way of including the past, after *Paterson*; they are, moreover, rarely a challenge to received ideas of the past, as Williams's quotations so often, and brilliantly, are. What they do contribute is a sense of how many minds New York has impinged on in the same way; thus they extend, and aerate, the lyric themes. And I think it is as an assemblage of poignant, accomplished lyrical writing, on Romantic subjects, possibility and evanescence—rather than as

epic or vision—that this, when all is said, quite remarkable poem is most likely to be remembered. (pp. 106-07)

*Alan Williamson, "'Fool,' Said My Muse to Me . . . ," in Poetry, Vol. 133, No. 2, November, 1978, pp. 100-07.***

## JOYCE CAROL OATES

[*A Call in the Midst of the Crowd*] is sharply disappointing. Its center is a very long poem about New York City that is not only unfortunately reminiscent of Williams's *Paterson*, but seems to possess no distinctive poetic voice of its own. So much of it is excerpts from other writers . . . that it is hardly more than a sort of commonplace book; and not all of the excerpts are really very interesting. There are paragraphs about New York from the *Encyclopedia Americana*, a pedestrian guide to the "Empire State," an advertising brochure, threaded in with Corn's own extremely minimal thoughts on the subject. . . . There are awkward figures of speech . . . , and lapses of taste that are dreadful even if deliberate. . . . Corn's talent seems to be for the purely lyric, the emotional. Indeed, he confesses that he has "moods—often mistaken for morals or philosophy."

From time to time personalities emerge in *A Call in the Midst of the Crowd*, but they are disappointingly anemic. The poet, evidently accompanied by another man, takes a ferry ride on a day that "prosiness feels right"; what might have been a poignant and dramatic poem if written by Adrienne Rich sinks into banalities as the issue of the men's relationship is raised, and feebly dropped. . . . (pp. 29-30)

When lyric poetry is not imaginatively written its most fundamental (perhaps its basest) motive becomes painfully clear: it is a record of thinking and doing, a way of making the temporary appear to be permanent. But the desultory jottings of a diary cannot be transposed into poetry, especially when the poet's ostensible subject is so large as New York City, and his viewpoint fragmented and superficial. Other work of Corn's, though reminiscent of the brooding, meditative poetry of Stevens, Wilbur, and Nemerov, is at least more rigorously shaped and more deserving of the accolade art—if we mean by "art" that which can interest people beyond the artist and his intimate circle. (p. 30)

*Joyce Carol Oates, in a review of "A Call in the Midst of the Crowd," in The New Republic, Vol. 179, No. 24, December 9, 1978, pp. 29-30.*

## STANLEY PLUMLY

[Alfred Corn's *The Various Light*] promotes the same polish and wit and high verbal energy and exhilaration as his earlier books. No doubt he writes in a hurry—not that his work is careless or unfinished, not even that it feels particularly spontaneous. It simply reads *fast*, moves easily at the surface, partly because experience is received and returned at a rapid rate and partly because the pitch of the poems is invariably in the direction of the language—often as if to announce that the artifice itself is at issue. Sometimes it is, sometimes the poet's language overloads the poem. . . . [A] number of whole poems seem to be extra added attractions. **"Debates," "Songs for Five Companionable Singers,"** and **"Lacrimae Rerum,"** for example, begin and end in idea, in thinking that takes place mostly in shadow, in a chiaroscuro and subtlety almost too abstract to recognize, too rich with meaning to differentiate. These are poems that are lonely with sensibility. They make the Symbolists sound like literalists of the imagination.

At his best, however, Corn has a wonderful facility with form and phrasing, and the intellectual's gift for absorbing and making information immediately available. His good poems fix on the object, locate the place, focus an actual, articulate emotional source. . . . [In] poems such as **"Grass"** and **"A Bid,"** he avoids any trace of rhetorical chat that might exhaust the subject before letting go of the language. These two poems in particular raise the ante on what talk, as direct address, can be in a poem, how even in the middle of the action the mind is sorting and selecting and converting. . . . Corn is a committed formalist, which means that he perceives the world not only in language but as language. He sees it in the very speech of symbolization. That is why the risk in his work is always toward verbal excess or cleverness. Words live in the world as well; they depend, like birds and beachstones, on the resources of gravity. In his book's longest poem, **"The Outdoor Amphitheater,"** Corn frees himself in order to extend himself. For more than 350 lines the poet explores and entertains "those first scenes, lapidary, paint-box bright" that help qualify his past—whether he is on stage, as an 8-year-old alto, or watching his sister crowned beauty queen, "odd but touching, there, out of doors." In this piece more than any other he becomes "the spectator, / Taking it all in." The poem moves at the speed of the mind in recitation, over primary emotional material, making the hard choices about what the words should be and where they come from.

> *Stanley Plumly, "Of Lyricism, Verbal Energy, the Sonnet, and Gallows Humor," in* Book World—The Washington Post, *November 2, 1980, p. 10.**

## PHOEBE PETTINGELL

[*The Various Light*] finds Corn coming to terms with what he takes to be his limitations, the boundaries of his poetic gift. He still feels the need to reconcile the vagaries of human feeling, and tries to unify and arrange fragments into a mosaic pattern: yet where his earlier works often forced this vision of wholeness, straining for an unjustified triumph, *The Various Light* makes no more of a situation than what the poet can see. His manner is subdued and honest. . . .

As expectations diminish, there is a compensating perception of what is imperfect and unfinished. In **"Reading *Pericles* in New London"** . . . , Corn asks whether minor Shakespeare contains less of the bard's essence than *The Tempest* or *King Lear*. Compared with the timelessness of the great plays, *Pericles* strikes the modern reader as a period piece, but Corn has an abiding faith that no matter how different the circumstances, people remain essentially themselves. . . . Through Shakespeare Corn considers his own styles and purposes, his latest change of heart.

Juxtapositions and shifts of perspective haunt Corn's latest poems as he studies a chiaroscuro of shadows and bright patches, savoring slants of light, of feeling, of season. Subtle changes become subjects for dramatic insight. An erotic play staged in a desanctified church prompts a wry inquiry into the true nature of God. . . . Observing a New England landscape, he ruminates on how points of view change as relationships and directions alter, how continuities are broken as high points fade into the background and obscurities become prominent: Our confidence is shaken and our neat ideas must be revised. Nevertheless, the reassessment is benign. . . . (p. 11)

Corn treats his swerve from the cosmopolitan to the provincial symbolically in **"Moving: New York—New Haven Line,"** assuaging his sense of loss when circumstances forced him to move to Connecticut. "How is it possible to be moved in so many ways at once?" he wonders, watching scenery from the train window and contemplating alterations in his life. He asserts at the end of his journey, "Though I've kept to one spot, the place has changed." Has he changed too?

Corn's reasons for setting aside his earlier expansiveness can be found in **"The Outdoor Amphitheater."** On this fixture of his Southern childhood he hangs memories of his first appearance as a poet-performer, and then as a spectator at plays, vaudeville productions, concerts, revival meetings, a beauty pageant—all those rituals of small town life that suggest a broader world beyond. The older Corn, imagining himself as a boy walking through the empty amphitheater out of season, takes stock of their respective dreams. . . . But if Corn gently mocks himself for daring to wish that his art could transcend natural limitations, he nonetheless feels he did learn from the amphitheater the hope that "this stage not be the last; / And that the performance move from strength to strength." Alfred Corn is obviously in a time of transition. I believe from the evidence of this book that he will become more of a regional poet in the future. Certainly, in *The Various Light* Corn has discovered a deeper, more authoritative voice. Sometimes less is more. (pp. 11-12)

> *Phoebe Pettingell, "Sharpened Visions," in* The New Leader, *Vol. LXII, No. 20, November 3, 1980, pp. 11-12.**

## ROBERT B. SHAW

Corn's prodigious gifts, evident from the beginning, have reached such a peak of articulation in [*The Various Light*] that it no longer suffices to describe him as a promising poet. Potentiality has been swallowed up in the splendor of achievement. The title of the book comes from Andrew Marvell, and Corn may be said to have earned a comparison with that seventeenth-century master, with whom he shares urbanity, wit, authoritative phrasing and an exciting tension between skeptical intelligence and mystical intuition. For all that, Corn's style is not that of a latter-day metaphysical poet. He has assimilated tendencies of his own century. The most discernible influence on his style is that of Stevens, and by being fully aware of his debt Corn turns what could have been an inhibiting factor into a creative opportunity. **"Gloze"** is an allusion to Stevens's "The Death of the Soldier," not a parody but in its own words a "ghostly echo" of the earlier text. The two poems relate to each other as a composer's variations may adapt an earlier composer's theme. **"At the Grave of Wallace Stevens"** succeeds as homage by observing scale; it eschews inflated rhetoric and mounts one of the more effective tributes directed by one poet to another, strongly felt and felicitous. . . .

In most of the other poems one is less aware of influences than of Corn's formal and descriptive strengths. He is especially good at what might be called the topographical lyric, the poem which mingles place with an observing mind's meditations. **"Cornwall," "Remembering Mykinai"** and the beautiful poem about Stonington, **"The Village,"** are examples. Best of all, and grander in scope than any of these successes, is **"The Outdoor Amphitheater,"** a various and luminous account of the poet's Georgia childhood, running to twelve awesomely sustained pages.

When Pound said of *The Waste Land* that it was the longest poem in the English language, he meant that nothing in it was superfluous. The same can be said of **"The Outdoor Amphitheater."** Its texture is so closely woven that paraphrase is bound to do it injustice. The drama of the growth of the poet's mind is deftly re-enacted by invoking memories of the summer plays and pageants he witnessed or took part in as a boy. His humorous and affectionate recalling of the limitless array of life's possibilities symbolized by the theater is balanced against a delicate and austere sense of regret for the losses time has brought upon him. Neither feeling predominates; but expressed through Corn's rendering of "those first scenes, lapidary, paintbox bright" they merge to yield a complex vision of life. Few poets of our time have drawn upon the wisdom of experience with such unaffected honesty and tactful skill. If Corn continues to write verse of such resonance he will be a very important American poet indeed; as it is, at the age of 37, he stands in the forefront of his generation. (p. 478)

> Robert B. Shaw, "'Utensils Down the Dream'," in The Nation, *Vol. 231, No. 15, November 8, 1980, pp. 476-78.*

### DANA GIOIA

*The Various Light* is Alfred Corn's third and finest book of poetry. Each of his earlier volumes contained much interesting work . . . but this new collection shows a consistency of concentration and inspiration unmatched in the earlier books. Corn has always cultivated a relaxed, informal voice. "Prosiness feels right," he once commented in a poem, and while this informality has made his work engaging and witty, it sometimes allowed his verse to become too diffuse. In *The Various Light* Corn has overcome this one weakness without losing any of his many strengths. The result is a fully realized volume by an important new poet.

Corn's poems are moments of intense attention. When this attention is turned to the outer world, his visual sense dominates, and the reader often has the excitement of seeing something familiar as if for the first time. . . . When this attention is turned inward, Corn's auditory sense predominates. Here the poems move forward obliquely through association, wordplay, and allusion. It is no surprise then that the sequence, **"Songs for Five Companionable Singers,"** which is one of the most private poems in the volume, is an auditory *tour de force* composed of three villanelles, a sestina, and a pantoum. Corn's imagination tends to be quiet and reflective, and occasionally these meditative poems become almost inaccessible, like brilliant but private messages read out of context. . . . (pp. 624-25)

There is much to praise in Corn's work—its scope, its verbal inventiveness, its rare balance of sophistication and honesty— but what I most admire is its intelligence. One does not often praise an American poet for intelligence. Quite the opposite. Listening to most critics applaud strength, speed, passion, and intensity, one might easily conclude that a poet was good only insofar as he resembled a prizefighter. But Corn's work packs an intellectual punch as much as a visceral one. One cannot read poems like **"Town Center in December"** or **"Reading Pericles in New London"** without learning something about contemporary life. In this way Corn's work recalls Auden's underrated and often misunderstood later poetry. The comparison with Auden is not gratuitous. Corn obviously sees himself as a successor in the tradition Auden created in American poetry. Maybe Corn and Sugar Ray Leonard do have something

in common after all—they both are serious contenders for a heavy-weight title. (pp. 625-26)

> Dana Gioia, in a review of "The Various Light," in The Hudson Review, *Vol. XXXIII, No. 4, Winter, 1980-81, pp. 624-26.*

### G. E. MURRAY

Alfred Corn is a poet able to manage and merge two distinct and often contradictory instincts, namely, to articulate a sharp verbal discipline within the broader framework of a narrative posture. As such, the consequence of Corn's poetry is immediate, attentive to both past and present, to emotional setting and physical event. This is apparent early in Corn's second collection *A Call in the Midst of the Crowd.* . . . [What] finally impresses is his ability to alter mood with the slightest shift in description. It is as if one is sitting in a room alone when the glass in a window cracks, giving an entirely different sense to the room's unexplained forces. A change in atmospheric pressure, you guess. Or, put differently, indulging a need to reanimate the landscape of childhood, Corn investigates the deep sources of that need. So what begins with matter moves slowly into mind, and psychology replaces event.

This discursive mode in which Corn most successfully operates leads through indirection, creates nuance amid fact, pays verbal respect to a repertoire of emblems. . . . For as much statement as Corn packs into his lines, his strength resides in the implications of a few well-conceived details. . . . [The] sensuous surface of Corn's language is so smoothly polished that one rarely notices how much is going on. Each phrase and contour of thought contributes to a lasting effect, but the effect never seems contrived or labored, only steadily delivered. (pp. 277-78)

The bulk of *A Call in the Midst of the Crowd* . . . is devoted to the title work—a homage to the vagaries, both past and present, of the *magnum opus* that is New York City. This is a poem in four parts, not uniquely divided among the seasons. Further, it stands as a piecemeal report on a critical year in the poet's life set against New York's varied seasonal background, the underlying design of which indirectly relates a love connection lost and regained. (pp. 278-79)

Corn intersperses his own poetic tracts with three centuries of documentary notations, excerpts from histories, newspapers, diaries and letters. In effect, it is a long poem of moving parts, echoes of place and time and person, a smokescreen of original poetry and socio-historical fragments intended to unify and relate a new experience. In this sense, the idea of New York City at large becomes as much a harbor as predicament, where the fearful can presume that "death may be served as the consommé." The subject geography, of course, is a huge prismatic reality, a common ground for every taste and tongue: the arts, business, communications, society as it breathes and heaves. . . . There is an astonishing sense of sensual excitement . . . , however routine the city landscape. Even when Corn simply observes the dawning of still another street scene, . . . his sight proves both subtle and complex, his sense intricate and sometimes elusive. He does not lay out every step the reader must take but rather requires active collaboration in making connections . . . , especially in thinking through the full associations of his compiled images. (pp. 279-80)

Corn renders his poem with patience and authority. Indeed, eventually the mammoth, dispassionate portrait of New York softens, rationalizes, and makes possible the poet's own emotional tours. Frequently, the sadness and fear and folly are eviscerated, the irony heightened, with this record of personal spirit. (p. 281)

[In] *The Various Light,* Corn shifts his intense attention from crowded urban settings to open-ended landscapes, connecting his world of words to the world's visceral appeal. In the first two sections of this book, Corn discovers in the raw backdrops of New England and Europe a certain regenerative force ideal for his imaginings and observations.... More than ever, Corn is attuned to the natural world and its dissociated participants.... The quality of Corn's descriptive powers, and the precision of his vocabulary which he often displays like an arsenal, help fuse what's evolving in the mind's eye to the "Uninsurable things" discovered in a richly apprehended world. But these abundant skills mainly enable the poet to sustain in quiet, unassuming ways a continuous tension between intelligence and intuition.... (pp. 282-83)

Corn's real virtue is his pursuit of vision's high ground, some pinnacle from which to assess

> The middle distances, a touch farther
> Off from fact; if only to discover
>
> Perspectives where such a limited thing
> Multiplies into so much of everything....

From these theoretical musings, Corn comes to reason the purpose of his place in time. Corn's finest achievement in this regard is **"The Outdoor Amphitheater,"** a beautifully sustained 12-page reflection on the rites of childhood and its impending passages. The title location—a setting from summers past—serves as a focal point for the initiation of "Memory's hide-and-seek." And Corn, quickly handed over to the swell and drama of recollecting "Those first scenes, lapidary, paint-box-bright," fully understands his essential task: "The idea hard to get in focus is not how things / Looked but how the look felt, then—and then, now." Again we have the poet transgressing time so as to arrive at a psychological place in which to fix assessment and perspective. It is a far more demanding process than just rummaging in the family photo album or leisurely indexing life's gains and losses. Instead, Corn yields to a complex vision of the nurturing and care of his Being as first fostered by "Those demented and inspiring acts" at the rural open-air playhouse. Then, as the seasons turn, the poet's expectation heightens, and requires symbol....

Corn's purpose [in this section of the poem] is to repossess "the slow length of a homeward mile" and learn again both the delights and trepidation of each facet of journey. Thus he shares with readers the very core of his newly realized appreciations. The poem concludes with the poet's sister "Crowned Queen of the Beauty Pageant," a ritual Corn employs as platform for the hope of both communal and individualized spirit.... (p. 284)

Throughout Corn's poetry, the happenings he seizes upon are made significant by the intimacy he reveals, the affections he shares, and the mysteries he plumbs. For all of this, he celebrates and suffers. Doing so, he comes to instruct how, variously, all things are gospel, all things unknown, as he continues to make adjustments to "The pondered weight of what we are." (pp. 284-85)

> *G. E. Murray, "In the Place of Time," in* Parnassus:
> Poetry in Review, *Vol. 11, No. 1, Spring-Summer,
> 1983, pp. 277-85.*

## ALAN WILLIAMSON

[In *Notes from a Child of Paradise*] Corn has again undertaken a book-length poem, this time in an effort to come to terms with the experience of growing up in the 1960s—a subject which, considering its importance, has had singularly little direct attention in our poetry.... *Notes from a Child of Paradise* is, I hasten to add, a book about but not of the '60s. It is not militant, not—in the catchphrase Corn quotes a little scornfully—"the latest / Naked Poem." Rather, it is urbane, well-crafted, rueful, tragicomic, mixing "The serious and the broad" in the tradition of Ariosto, of Byron's *Don Juan,* of James Merrill's "The Book of Ephraim."

Corn's title comes from the great French film *Les Enfants du Paradis,* which was something of a cult object in the '60s. I believe the phrase is roughly equivalent to our "peanut gallery"—a meaning which is not inappropriate to Corn's sense of being a helpless, if sometimes an exhilarated, spectator of cataclysmic public events. But in a deeper sense, I think, Corn means to imply that any child of the '60s was a "child of paradise." What the decade imposed on all of us was an extraordinary hope: that by breaking boundaries, whether of class, custom, or psyche, one would somehow arrive at a place where every moment was vivid and charged with significance, every impulse uninhibited yet somehow harmonious, good. That hope was political, but it was both more and less than politics in any normal sense. If it generated a more humane and psychological concept of revolution than the Old Left had known, it also led off into a dozen artificial paradises. The summers in Europe were part of it—those summers which postwar prosperity had made available to thousands of middle-class American students.... No writer before Corn has captured so perfectly the poignant comedy of that little world: those American kids, some brilliant, some not, all sophomoric and a little scared, managing and mismanaging their love affairs in a blinding radiance of mythic parallel. (pp. 39-40)

[In one section, Corn recounts his courtship of and marriage to Ann Jones.] It is a tale whose appeal is simple and irresistible, for all the worldly elegance of the telling. How can one not love two lovers who are brave enough to overleap such obstacles—not only of physical distance, but his homosexual side, and her proto-feminist ideas of freedom? And yet, once together, Ann and Alfred cannot be simple constant lovers, or even intellectual companions, though they are that. They must believe that their love is, as Rimbaud demanded, "reinvented," free of all bourgeois precedent and prescriptiveness. Marriage, for them, is not a confirmation, but a chilling brush with an alien way of being serious about life.... A certain dimness enters into their feeling for each other thereafter; and finally, in "the long, dogged recessional" of the Vietnam War years, they part, Ann however remaining a central presence in Alfred's life, as friend, as lost paradise, and as Muse.

In the meantime, however, much else happens. From the beginning, the poem is punctuated with initially puzzling interpolations retelling a favorite children's book about the Lewis and Clark expedition. In these American sections, the rhetoric is soberer, less tongue-in-cheek (even imitating, at times, the rapt tone of Hart Crane's *The Bridge*). The subplot and the main plot converge toward the end, when Ann and Alfred, back, slightly disillusioned, from the French *événements* of 1968, decide to drive across the country. The Midwestern and Western landscapes that follow bring out the best of Corn's gifts as a descriptive poet.... Though Corn doesn't say so explicitly, this love of American places seems to bring him to his true vocation as a poet, away from the higher but colder-hearted ambitions, "black and new as Burroughs," of his radical years. In a different way, the journey West becomes a final emblem of the marriage. Like the relationship between Lewis and Clark and the Indian woman Sacajawea, this too is a love "outside history," only possible in a wilderness—the 1960s' wilderness of hope.

American long poems are almost by definition imperfect; so I hope it won't seem churlish to point out the flaws in this one. The strictly political scenes are a bit wooden, lacking the electric tension they have in Lowell and Mailer. Metaphysical passages, on the other hand, are often disastrously overwritten. . . . The poem also repeatedly compares itself to *The Divine Comedy*, in a way I found presumptuous. It simply isn't that large; moreover, Corn should know that such comparisons only succeed when they are tacit, like Dante's own self-comparison to Virgil. Finally, and perhaps most damagingly, Corn finds it difficult to write as frankly about the end of the marriage as about its beginning; so the dimness of feeling that afflicts the couple themselves also afflicts us as readers in the last third of the book.

What one remembers, however, is the touching, headlong bravery of Ann and Alfred's early commitment to each other; and how that quality comes back, in a strange way, at the very end. There *is* something unaffectedly Dantean about the vision of love as an educative experience, and therefore eternally part of the soul, that shines through Ann's final words to Alfred. . . . (pp. 40-1)

I have to say that I read this extraordinary book haunted . . . by how many events in our private lives somehow rhymed. Truly, as Corn writes, "We were all like that": naïvely solemn, as the '20s were not; introspective, unlike the radical '30s; utterly unlike the '50s in our demand for New Heaven and New Earth. This book gives a definitive account of the private impact, at least, of the decade's sense of the "mythic." It made me feel, for the first time, the truth of Robert Lowell's lines to John Berryman: "really we had the same life, / the generic one / our generation offered. . . ." (p. 41)

*Alan Williamson, "Taking Account of the '60s," in The New Republic, Vol. 190, No. 23, June 11, 1984, pp. 39-41.*

### GWYNETH LEWIS

*Notes from a Child of Paradise* takes love as its subject and recounts Corn's relationship with Ann, his former wife. . . .

This book-length poem has a hectic itinerary: the boy-meets-girl narrative takes us to France . . . , Italy, New York, and the Pacific Northwest. The couple falls in love and gets married. As graduate students in the late '60s, they are in the thick of intellectual and sexual ferment. Alfred protests against the war in Vietnam: "A dove, / Those days, seldom kept to the olive branch," either because it was stoned out of its tiny feathered head, or because it was away on a march somewhere. Woven into these discoveries is the narrative of Lewis and Clark's Northwest Expedition—Corn's version of the American Spirit. We zip out West on I-80, back again on U.S. 2, a journey that marks the growing distance between husband and wife. The causes of the rift are left unclear, and the reticence feels absolutely appropriate—this is poetic autobiography, not soap opera.

Corn is a graceful writer, witty in the James Merrill vein: the "Instamatic has earned its vacation"; Ann, walking by his side, is "Peripatetic but on shapely legs"; in a peevish moment "a former self grabs the mike to sigh, 'How bored and lonely we are!'" Some passages are downright lush. . . . Occasionally the grandiose language becomes too cumbersome for him to wield, even in jest, and it slips into high corn, though these lapses are rarer than you might expect in such an ambitious poem. Corn aims high, but seldom overreaches himself.

*Gwyneth Lewis, "Leaves of Corn," in The Village Voice, Vol. XXIX, No. 30, July 24, 1984, p. 50.*

### JAY PARINI

[*Notes from a Child of Paradise*] is a brilliant *tour de force* and shows off Corn's various skills in just the right way. As he wrote in **"Grass,"** from *The Various Light* (1980): "There's always more going on / than anyone has the wit to notice." The new book-length poem, a *comédie humaine* loosely modeled on Dante's *Divine Comedy*, offers the reader a glittering (but fragmentary) autobiography wherein there is always more going on than anyone will have the wit to comprehend in less than several readings. This is Alfred Corn's *Prelude*, chronicling "the growth of a poet's mind," and the poem's hero is the naive idealist, the apprentice-poet, who wades out over his head in the deep waters of the late '60s to find himself caught up and nearly swept away. The Paradise of the title is an earthly and, hence, fragile Eden, and this late epic of loss and recovery is tinged with a melancholic (and elegiac) irony that has come to mark a whole generation of American writers.

Corn's personal history *is* the history of his generation, and his adventures—projected in the illumined falsework of this exemplary *mythos*—describe the standard arc of a generation's progress from innocence to experience. (pp. 27-8)

Corn is the inheritor of a long tradition, that of the personal epic, with Dante, Milton, and Wordsworth as the leading figures to whom Corn alludes. Quite obviously, Dante provides the paradigm for *Notes*. . . . Corn's modestly entitled *Notes* traces the poet-hero's journey through an academic *Inferno* in Paris and New York made all the more intense by sexual confusions and longings. . . .

[The] reader will marvel at Corn's vivid writing throughout— a near embarrassment of riches. In fact, it's almost overdone. The profusion (and occasional confusion) of metaphors gluts the eye and ear. . . . One might also quarrel with Corn's excessively easy use of allusion—a near mania for bringing all of his (prodigious) learning to bear on the poem. Less might well have been, in this case, more.

But there is no doubting the veracity, the fierce brilliance, of this poem. It is an important work, a worthy heir to Stevens's *Notes Toward a Supreme Fiction*, to which Corn owes a good deal. His style is deeply reminiscent of Stevens, with its endless qualifications, its apposites and shrewd proleptic echoes. One puts down *Notes from a Child of Paradise* convinced, as Stevens says, that "Life's nonsense pierces us with strange relation." And Corn brings this sense of a strange relation to the surface cannily as he portrays a young man's self-exploration and self-creation. The poem's final turn is westward, beginning at the end of Part Two, where [Corn and his wife Ann] board the *United States*. They travel toward the Pacific Northwest, crossing America, in the third and final section. . . . Corn's poem reminds us repeatedly of Emerson's remark that America is a poem in our eyes. In Part Three, the physical journey is transformed into a spiritual one as the poet discovers the mysteries of his craft and the complex destiny of human love. (p. 28)

*Jay Parini, in a review of "Notes from a Child of Paradise," in* Boston Review, *Vol. IX, No. 4, July-August, 1984, pp. 27-8.*

## JOEL CONARROE

[Alfred Corn] has given us a detailed recollection of youth called *Notes From a Child of Paradise,* a long narrative in which he alludes to some major influences, including Dante, Wordsworth, Melville, and the three B's—Byron, Baudelaire, and Berryman.

And, of course, there is another relevant influence, the 1944 film *Les Enfants du Paradis.* Like Barrault's Jean-Louis-Pierrot, Corn's narrator, Albert, is a pacific young man of unusual sensitivity. In elegant, articulate stanzas, he describes his travels in Europe with a fellow student ("friends, lovers, then married") and their life together before they separate. Their youthful courtship and private marital drama are played out against a backdrop of public events, including Haight-Ashbury, the moon landing, and the Vietnam protests. In the third and final section, musings on the travels of Lewis and Clark provide counterpoint to diary-like passages describing the couple's trip to Oregon, where the young man discovers his vocation as poet.

And what a poet he is! Whether working variations on Wordsworth's five-stress line, sometimes rhyming, sometimes not, or on Dante's terza rima, Corn is always in control, obviously unintimidated by the challenge of sustaining momentum through hundreds of carefully wrought stanzas. That the lines often sound like natural speech—the words of a lucid man talking to a friend—belies the fact that they are fitted within a highly artificial framework, every syllable patted into place, and are polished to a fine gloss.

The book's considerable charm derives largely from the narrator's combination of intelligence and verbal dexterity. The poem is, by turns, learned, impassioned, touching, lyrical, and droll. . . . It also shifts from quest romance to travelogue, documentary, erotic autobiography, and artful confession. This is not, to be sure, confession in the heart-on-sleeve mode. Corn is too crafty for that; even passages dealing with sexual ambiguity are handled with restraint. The book, far from a purgative outpouring, is a finely etched portrait of an artist coming of age during a turbulent time. . . .

The poet's intention is "to find words that would fall in love" with what he saw. He succeeds splendidly. His poetry can be savored line by line; it is poetry to read aloud. With this book, his fourth, Alfred Corn establishes his standing as one of our finest poets. (p. 3)

*Joel Conarroe, "Poets of Innocence and Experience," in* Book World—The Washington Post, *August 5, 1984, pp. 3, 11.**

# Julio Cortázar

## 1914-1984

(Also wrote under pseudonym of Julio Denis) Argentine novelist, short story writer, poet, essayist, critic, and translator.

Cortázar is one of the seminal figures of the "Boom," a surge of excellence and innovation in Latin American letters during the 1950s and 1960s. His novel *Rayuela* (1963; *Hopscotch*) has been called Latin America's first great novel, and Carlos Fuentes hailed it as "one of the great manifestos of Latin American modernity." Like Gabriel García Márquez and other contemporary Latin American writers, Cortázar combined fantastic and often bizarre plots with commonplace events and characters. Much of Cortázar's fiction is a reaction to the Western tradition of rationalism and is an attempt to create new ways in which literature can represent life. To this end he experimented with language, form, and narrative identity. He often narrated his stories from unusual perspectives; "Axolotl" (1956), one of his most famous stories, is told by a man who has been transformed into a salamander after spending many days watching salamanders in an aquarium. In his many metafictional works Cortázar also addressed the complex relationship between art and life. The creation of art or literature plays a central role in most of these works. Perhaps the best known of these is "Las babas del diablo" (1956; "Devil's Drool"), upon which Michelangelo Antonioni's film "Blow Up" is loosely based. In this story, a photographer discovers a new and troubling reality after developing a photograph of a scene he has witnessed. Cortazar is regarded as a liberator for having enlarged and revitalized literary tradition with a consistent inventiveness of style, language, and theme.

Among Cortázar's early works are three short story collections: *Final del juego* (1956; *End of the Game and Other Stories*), *Historias de cronopios y de famas* (1962; *Cronopios and Famas*), and *Todos los fuegos el fuego* (1966; *All Fires the Fire*). In many of these stories Cortázar expresses the conflict between imagination and reality by letting the fantastic take gradual control of the mundane lives of his characters. Cortázar's interest in the way in which the unknown or the unusual can suddenly terrorize everyday lives is evident in his first novel, *Los premios* (1960; *The Winners*). Passengers on a luxury cruise begin to feel threatened when they are restricted to certain areas of the ship and forbidden to communicate with the crew. Cortázar examines the diverse ways in which the passengers react to this enigmatic and concealed threat. *Hopscotch*, Cortázar's best-known work, concerns an expatriate's attempt to break free of the rationalist slant of contemporary culture in order to find his "kibbutz of desire." The novel is considered a stylistic masterpiece: its one hundred and fifty-five chapters can be read in at least two logical sequences. Cortázar uses this technique to encourage the active participation of the reader and to emphasize his disdain for linear narrative.

Cortázar also wrote fiction that reflected his strong concern for political and human rights causes. For example, the novel *Libro de Manuel* (1973; *A Manual for Manuel*) is in part an exposé of the torture of political prisoners in Latin America. Cortázar believed that art should serve politics, although aesthetic ideals should never be sacrificed to political ones. He

was an advocate of socialism, both in his fiction and his essays, and a vocal supporter of the Cuban and Nicaraguan revolutions. Because of his opposition to the authoritarian regimes in Argentina, including those of Juan and Evita Peron and the military dictatorship established in 1974, Cortázar exiled himself to Paris in 1951 and lived there until his death.

Cortázar's last books include two short story collections, *A Change of Light and Other Stories* (1980; contains stories originally published in *Octaedro* [1974] and *Alguien que anda por ahí* [1978]) and *Queremos tanto a Glenda* (1983; *We Love Glenda So Much*), and a novel, *Un tal Lucas* (1979; *A Certain Lucas*). *A Change of Light* reflects the range of Cortázar's earlier fiction, from stories of political oppression and tales of hidden terror to works of fantasy. The stories in *We Love Glenda So Much* explore similar themes and also examine the nature of reality and those patterns and forms that people impose upon the world to maintain a sense of order and definition. In the title story, members of a fan club steal and edit copies of the films of their favorite actress in order to perfect them, but the actress is murdered by her admirers when she plans to make films that will not meet their standards. *A Certain Lucas* is divided into three sections composed of short musings and observations. The first and third sections describe episodes and dreams from the life of Lucas, an aging Argentine writer. The middle section contains some of Lucas's own writings.

Through Lucas, Cortázar ruminates on many of the ideas that were important to him throughout all of his writings; the nature of reality, the exploration of form, and the search for new ways to reveal the world.

(See also *CLC*, Vols. 2, 3, 5, 10, 13, 15; *Contemporary Authors, Vols. 21-24*, rev. ed.; and *Contemporary Authors New Revision Series*, Vol. 12.)

## JOYCE CAROL OATES

"A Change of Light" is Cortázar's eighth book of fiction to appear in English, and it is in many ways a change: of tone, of manner, of style, of emphasis, of "light" itself.

Here one does not find the lush and motile openness of "Hopscotch" [1966], or the risky, funny, ceaselessly inventive predicaments of "End of the Game" (1967). The penchant for exploring obsessions—the more futile, the more fertile for the ravenous imagination—that was a thematic undercurrent in "All Fires the Fire" (1973) is given in these 20 stories an unexpected delicacy, a surprising Jamesian dignity, by the elegiac tone of Cortázar's language and a less hurried (and more dramatic) pace. . . .

Throughout "A Change of Light" one is always aware that a story, an artifact, is being created. The political context is sometimes in the foreground, sometimes an ominous assumption, but at all times we are aware of the words that constitute the story as words, for the most part judiciously chosen. "He" frequently shifts to "I" and back again to "he" and then again to "I." The narrator may suddenly announce his own befuddlement. One of the more self-consciously literary of the stories, "Footsteps in the Footprints," is prefaced, not altogether unfairly, by the author's terse summary, as a "rather tedious chronicle, more in the style of an exercise than in the exercise of a style, say that of a Henry James who might have sipped maté in some Buenos Aires or Mar del Plata courtyard in the twenties"; the least satisfactory story, "The Ferry, or Another Trip to Venice," written in 1954, is "revised" here in a high-spirited gesture of defiance—the author, acknowledging the story's inferiority, is nevertheless intrigued by it and cannot let it go: "I like it, and it's so bad." . . . But even the most willfully self-conscious stories, even the "bad" story, are so finely written, sentence by sentence, and the author's melancholy intelligence so evident in every line, that the actual reading of "A Change of Light" is an invariable pleasure. And the incursions of fantasy, of improbability and nightmare, do not deflect from the stories' "realist" emotional authority: Several stories in this collection have the power to move us as Kafka's stories do. . . .

[In "Summer"] the pleasurable monotonous marriage of a quite ordinary couple is interrupted, perhaps fatally, by the overnight visit of a young daughter of a friend. The girl is innocent enough, a mere child, yet she appears to be accompanied by an enormous white horse who gallops snorting around the house, a ferocious white blur, a "rabid" creature, or anyway one maddened enough to want to enter a house. The white horse has stepped magnificently out of a dream recorded in Kafka's diary. . . . In fact the horse does not enter the house, though the little girl—accidentally or deliberately—leaves the front door open for him. But the marriage has been altered, the "new day that had nothing new about it" has been irrevocably lost. Cortázar's most sympathetic poeple are those who believe in compulsions (which they call rituals or games) as a response to death and nothingness. . . . But no ritual can ac-

commodate the snorting white horse, or even the overnight visit of a friend's child. (p. 9)

This collection's most compelling stories are unambiguous elegies. The narrator of "Liliana Weeping" imagines not only his own poignant death but a future for his wife that guarantees her survival; the narrator of "The Faces of the Medal" addresses a woman he has loved but to whom he cannot, inexplicably, make love. . . . And in the volume's title story two "lovers" are victims of their own self-absorbed fantasies about love: They are real enough people, but not so real as their obsessive dreams.

There are one or two stories here that seem out of place in the volume—fairly conventional "suspense" stories that dissolve to sheer plot, despite the fastidious writing. And no story is so irresistible, so immediately engaging as the classic "Axolotl" of "End of the Game"—my favorite Cortázar. . . . (p. 34)

> *Joyce Carol Oates, "Triumphant Tales of Obsession," in* The New York Times Book Review, *November 9, 1980, pp. 9, 34-5.*

## JOSEPH CHADWICK

[A] fundamental feature of Julio Cortázar's fiction [is] the attempt to collapse conventionalized distinctions between the "real" and the "imaginary," between the world of the spectator/reader and the world of the work. This effort is nothing new for Cortázar, nor does it show itself in a single guise. His juxtaposing of fictional with "found" or factual texts in *Hopscotch* and *A Manual for Manuel;* his metaphysical instruction-sheets and ethnographies of imaginary "races" in *Cronopios and Famas;* his combining of a comic book, a political fantasy involving numerous well-known writers, and an account of the Bertrand Russell Tribunal's investigation of human rights in Latin America in *Fantomas contra los vampiros multinacionales (Fantomas Against the Multinational Vampires)*—all attest to the centrality of this effort and to the variety of forms it takes. And in all of these texts, Cortázar at least partially fulfills the ultimate aim toward which this effort is directed: that of liberating the imagination and its works from the gilded cage (or rather, the quiet library or even print gallery) we call the "aesthetic"—that realm of very comfortable chairs where not only the books themselves, but also our responses to them, get put back a little too neatly on nicely dusted shelves.

All of which goes to say that, like a good many other contemporary Latin American authors, and for similar, brutally obvious reasons, Cortázar is a writer *engagé*. His political commitments, however, do not appear only in depictions of emphatically political situations. They also, and even more frequently, appear as challenges to a wide variety of conventions: the habitualized codes and languages by which we order our daily lives (or which order us in those lives), the narrative conventions which define our relations to what we read, the neat, categorical distinctions by which we separate fiction from history, art from life. The reason his political commitments often find expression through such apparently oblique strategies is that those commitments are accompanied by, and seem to have been preceded by, a sense of metaphysical rebelliousness that Cortázar has always expressed in very personal terms. Such rebelliousness leads quite naturally to challenges against the conventions that organize literature and everyday life, and Cortázar's political conscience seems, guerilla-like, to have infiltrated those challenges, transforming them in accordance with its own concerns.

For a writer engaged, as Cortázar is, in both metaphysical and political kinds of challenges, the short story as a form offers peculiar advantages and disadvantages. On the one hand, one can formulate a particularly radical challenge—a challenge which might be almost intolerable if extended to a novel's length—without so much fear of losing one's readers. On the other hand, the short story, like the lyric poem, has a long association with aspirations toward perfect, crystalline unity. And this association makes it particularly susceptible to being assigned that position of privileged irrelevance which lyric poetry has come to occupy in contemporary Western culture. In *A Change of Light* . . . Cortázar manages for the most part to sidestep deftly the disadvantages of the short story form, and to exploit—through some astonishing devices—the possibilities it offers.

One of the most intriguing challenges Cortázar poses in this volume appears in **"The Ferry, Or Another Trip to Venice."** The story centers on three characters: Valentina and Dora, two women who strike up a friendship at an American Express counter and decide to travel through Italy together, and Adriano, another traveler whom Valentina meets in a bar in Rome and with whom she rather reluctantly falls in love. . . . But this account only covers the original draft of the story, which Cortázar never published for reasons he explains in the story's preface: "On the last page of the rough draft I find this notation: 'How awful! I wrote this in Venice in 1954; I reread it ten years later and I like it, and it's so bad.'" In order to resolve this discord between his fondness for the story and his awareness that a good deal of the writing and many of the situations in it are rather hackneyed, he rejects the ordinary recourse of rewriting it. Instead he interrupts the original draft from time to time with comments from Dora, comments in which she accuses the story's original narrator not only of bad writing ("a perfect dialogue for a best seller," she remarks of one of Valentina and Adriano's impassioned exchanges, "meant to fill up two pages with nothing in particular"), but also of distorting her role in the story's action and denying the depth—and erotic nature—of her affection for Valentina.

Dora's accusations against the original narrator are really, of course, Cortázar's way of criticizing his own earlier unwillingness to depict love between two women and—as "perhaps . . . the reciprocal effect of a cause that is one and the same"—the conventionality of the rough draft's style and action. They are a way of measuring the degree to which his thinking has changed in the twenty-odd years that separate the two versions. But just as important as *what* Dora says is *how* she gets to say it—the device Cortázar uses to let her speak. By having Dora comment not only on what Valentina and Adriano say and do (which he could have managed by giving an account of her reactions *within* the narrative), but also on what the third-person narrator says, Cortázar challenges the conventional relations between reader and narrative which are embodied in the voice of such a narrator. For instead of placing our faith in a single omniscient voice, we must rather suspiciously . . . listen to two equally unreliable voices, one of which belongs to a character in the other's story. (pp. 10-11)

**"The Ferry"** is by no means the sole example of such a double-barreled challenge in *A Change of Light*, though it is certainly one of the most striking. Other stories, like **"Liliana Weeping," "A Place Named Kindberg," "Trade Winds," "Manuscript Found in a Pocket,"** and **"The Faces of the Medal,"** make use of similarly innovative strategies to complement challenges to the more personal, but equally conventionalized, codes by which their characters live. . . .

Using an informal, colloquial tone and an occasionally zig-zagging syntax, Cortázar allows us to approach his characters at a level made intimate by close attention to how they respond to the most trivial events. This skill serves him especially well in stories like **"Severo's Phases"** or **"Encounter within a Red Circle,"** where the fantastic plays an important role. For by creating such a casual intimacy between characters and reader, he shows us how easy it is to accept whatever code—however fantastic by contrast to our own—the character is acting out. And by demonstrating how such codes operate even in the everyday movement of his characters' thoughts, he shows us how hard they are to escape—and how easy they are to misinterpret.

Cortázar combines the fantastic most effectively with the colloquial interior monologue in **"Apocalypse at Solentiname."** This story also shows how his colloquial style helps to open the sealed doors of the library or gallery of the "aesthetic" to the noise of the street, even to the sound of gunfire. It begins as a chatty, autobiographical account of Cortazar's visit to Solentiname, a peasant community organized by the poet/priest Ernesto Cardenal. Only when the fantastic, with shocking force, erupts into the action of this "memoir" does it become a "story"—a work of "fiction"—at all. But since the political importance of what happens in the fantastic episode makes the autobiographical events seem almost trivial by comparison, fantasy turns out to show us a more compelling vision of political reality than does fact. The conflation of autobiographical and fantastic elements—of fantasy, fact, and political reality—in **"Apocalypse"** seems to be Cortázar's way of asserting the continuity between what happens in his writing and what happens in the social world. And his style implicitly makes the same assertion. By shaping it on the patterns of informal speech and the quirky twists of the inner, mental voice, he gives us a sense of immediate participation in events and ideas which are not restricted to the pages of a book. . . . I don't mean to imply that Cortázar creates, in a passage like this, an utterly convincing realistic image of a situation (though that is entirely within his powers), but rather to show that he gives us a sense of taking part in a conversation between close friends. The same impulse which led to the transformation of **"The Ferry"** from a univocal narrative into a kind of colloquy between narrator, character, and reader makes itself felt in **"Apocalypse"** through this conversational style. . . .

To insist that a contemporary writer's strength lies in creating such provocations, in isolating and challenging conventionalized codes that operate in both life and art, may itself seem a rather conventional reaction to that writer's work. By citing writers like Cervantes or Sterne, one can easily argue that many of Cortázar's innovations are as old as the genre of prose fiction itself; and certainly a concern with challenging conventional techniques is nothing unusual in contemporary fiction. Nor is the effort to make the hearts of the bourgeoisie go pitter-pat particularly novel for a writer of fiction. What makes Cortázar's work stand out is the intimate link he forges between the codes of art and the codes of life, a link which insures that a challenge to one will always be felt as a challenge to the other. (p. 11)

*Joseph Chadwick, "Cracking the Codes," in* The Threepenny Review, *Vol. II, No. 1, Spring, 1981, pp. 10-11.*

**LOIS PARKINSON ZAMORA**

[*A Change of Light and Other Stories*] contains eighteen stories which were originally published in two collections, *Octaedro*

(1974) and *Alguien que anda por ahí* (1978). Much in terms of both theme and narrative technique will be familiar to readers of Cortázar's previous work, but this should not be taken to mean that the author's creative powers have waned or that he is floundering in sterile repetition. On the contrary, Cortázar in these stories sharpens his focus on certain characteristic aesthetic and social preoccupations. The perils of finding love and the difficulties of maintaining it have perhaps increased for these characters; death is more threatening than it has been in earlier works; and the phenomenal world seems ever more resistant to the artist's attempts at aesthetic transcendence. There is less humor, less fantasy, less sheer playfulness than one might expect, judging from Cortázar's past fiction. Nevertheless, these stories explore and extend in a variety of ways Cortázar's previous forms and concerns.

A constant in Cortázar is the questioning of the relationship between reality and its verbal representation, and once again, in several of these stories, we find the author at work undermining the discursive, serial nature of prose fiction and of language itself by means of shifting points of view, disordered syntax, unexpected juxtaposition, dislocated sequence. "**The Faces of the Medal**," like the opening paragraphs of "**Blow-up**," shifts person and tense in what seems a desperate search for a sufficiently inclusive narrative perspective to convey the complexity of experience. The story of the union and dissolution of a lovers' world is revealed as the narration shifts from external omniscient third person to internal first person singular and plural points of view even within the space of a single sentence. The lovers are as united and yet as irrevocably separated as the two sides of a single coin, and the narrative technique expresses that paradox in the oscillation of its perspectives. (pp. 78-9)

Cortázar has often explored the problems of the artistic representation of experience, whether in words, pictures, or music, and his artist characters are in some sense alter egos, whether Roberto Michel, in "**Blow-up**," Johnny Carter in "**The Pursuer**," Horacio Oliveira in *Hopscotch,* or the frankly autobiographical character in "**There But Where, How**," in this collection. In this story, the narrator struggles to tell his recurrent, wrenching dream of a "dead friend," the same friend to whom Cortázar dedicated his collection, *Bestiario,* in 1951. One of the epigraphs of the story repeats that dedication ("To Paco, who liked my tales"), and the other pays homage to René Magritte: "*A painting by René Magritte shows a pipe that occupies the center of the canvas. At the bottom of the picture its title:* THIS IS NOT A PIPE." Magritte's painting, like Cortázar's story, points to the problematic nature of representation itself, the contradiction between the three-dimensional space which objects occupy and where lives are lived on the one hand, and the two-dimensional space of the canvas or the printed page on the other.... Magritte was interested in exploring not only the disjunction between the object and its *visual* image but also the disjunction between the object and its *verbal* symbol.... Magritte, with the words on his painting, and Cortázar, with his epigraph, remove their art from the sphere of representational illusionism, proposing a world and then inscribing it in a framework which denounces (or at least modifies) its reality.

The narrator of "**There But Where, How**," who is in fact a verbal image of Cortázar himself—he is an Argentine translator working in Geneva—constantly considers the irreconcilability of space and spatial illusion, the unbreachable gulf between being and representing. While trying desperately to explain to himself and to a reader whom he addresses directly the death of a promising young man and his own life in terms of that death, the narrator rails against the impossibility of expressing his experience in "neat rows—the knife blade of words I keep writing and which are no longer what follow there, but when, how." Once again, although language may betray the complexity of experience with its inherent linearity, it is nonetheless the artistic medium with which the narrator must work.... [The] dialectic between the soundless past, the silent dead, and the narrator's attempt at articulation in the living present creates a tension which permeates the story. (p. 79)

With the publication of his novel, *A Manual for Manuel,* in 1973, Cortázar's fiction assumed a stronger political stance than had been the case earlier, and there are several stories in this collection that continue that stance. These stories may also be said to conform to Magritte's "art of resemblance," for here as elsewhere, Cortázar portrays perception, "images of thought." Nevertheless, one senses an important difference in aesthetic intention, an intention to use art for social commentary and correction and to turn the problematic connection between the word and the world into an instrument for the accomplishment of that end. In "**Second Time Around**," a story which suggests the politics of torture but never calls it by its name, a young man simply disappears, thus evoking the horrible reality of thousands of *desaparecidos* in Argentina today. The story is presented from the viewpoints of both victimizers and victims: the victimizers sanitize their language into vague euphemisms in order to deny the moral responsibility—indeed, the reality—of what they are doing, and the language of the victims is equally vague through ignorance and/or fear. Arrest and torture become "procedures," the sites of such activities "offices," and the people summoned to these offices are likened to patients sitting in doctors' waiting rooms. The ominously ambiguous language, perfectly captured in English, communicates the unspeakable with dreadful clarity; such activity is sanctioned under the rubric of yet other deformations of language such as "governmental efficiency" and "the good of the country." (pp. 79-80)

One story, "**The Ferry, or another Trip to Venice**," should never have been included. Cortázar claims that it is an early story, interpolated with italicized comments on the prose and plot ostensibly added later by an older and wiser writer. This seems to me to be self-indulgent on Cortázar's part (or perhaps, to be generous, it is a story about a self-indulgent writer,) and forty-four unsuccessful pages long. But with so many good stories, to mention this one seems almost ungrateful. Several of these stories confirm Cortázar's status as a contemporary master of the genre. (p. 80)

> *Lois Parkinson Zamora, in a review of "A Change of Light and Other Stories," in* Review, *No. 29, May-August, 1981, pp. 78-80.*

## PAUL ZWEIG

With this intriguing collection of stories ["**We Love Glenda So Much**"], we are once again in the familiar territory of the Argentine writer Julio Cortázar: the compulsive eruptions of thought and memory; the slightly ominous characters who never seem to be located anywhere, or to look like anything, so absorbed are they in their own inner speech. They are named Alana, Diana, Sandro or Robert. But often they have no names at all, for names are gifts of self, and Cortázar's world exists below the threshold of the social, in a kind of no man's land that is, only incidentally, Paris, Buenos Aires or some anonymous bit of countryside. In Cortázar's stories, places, too, are merely traces of color among the clauses and parenthetical remarks, which, for him, form the mind's substance and language. There is something marvelous, almost mystically intense, about all this, as if thinking and talking were all a man could be expected to do in this world.

The stories themselves are curiously deliberate and mannered, resembling the patterns of a dance. (p. 1)

Some of the stories verge on the supernatural, but here too the reader is kept off balance by Cortázar's irony: Since a mind is capable of thinking all thoughts, the distinction between natural and supernatural may mean nothing to it. For example, in **"Stories I Tell Myself,"** a man can daydream that he is a truck driver who stops to pick up a woman at the side of the road, the wife of one of his friends, and that he makes love to her in his truck. Some time later, when he and the woman actually meet socially, she tells him of a peculiar incident. One night, her car broke down, a truck driver picked her up, and they made love in the back of his truck. Curiously enough, the story's emphasis is not on the ominous convergence of the daydream and the reality but on the breathless, unrushing substance of the man's mind. It is as if Proust and Edgar Allan Poe had collaborated to write an episode for "Twilight Zone." . . .

Cortázar enjoys . . . games. As an author, he refuses to be bound by any rules; his stories are puzzles which he is free to construct according to his whim. The mind itself is a form of play which, in his view, gives the stories a sort of verisimilitude.

It is the old argument between art and life, and Cortázar pursues it with a kind of savagery, as if he were updating Oscar Wilde's witty remark about nature imitating art. We get the flavor of Cortázar's view in his remarkable title story, **"We Love Glenda So Much."** A group of idle Argentines are mad about the American movie star Glenda Garson. (p. 37)

The group decides to buy up every extant copy of every one of Glenda Garson's films, editing out the flawed segments and inserting remakes which give the true inflection of her art. . . . Finally, they receive the consecration they most long for. Glenda announces her retirement. Intuitively she has understood. Perfection is a closed space which the living cannot enter. But life has pressures of its own, and a year or two later rumors circulate that the star is thinking of making another film. The group comes to a decision: Art must be defended against life, even by the sternest measures. Through the glimmerings of Cortázar's elusive style, we guess what the decision must be: Glenda Garson will be killed; she will die into her art.

Like his countryman Jorge Luis Borges, Cortázar is a juggler of skepticisms and intellectual games. His stories really are anti-stories, as if in the intense, inward realm his characters inhabit, stories were remote chains of events that hardly mattered. And all the time, we hear, as an undertone, Cortázar's ironic assault on his own creations; his mockery of these esthetic solitudes that hover like alternative spaces. (He calls a character in his novel **"Hopscotch"** a "materialized nebula.") In **"Press Clippings,"** a writer and a sculptor read a clipping from a newspaper in which a mother tells how her daughter was murdered by the Argentine Army and her amputated hands sent back in a jar. The clumsy dignity of the mother's newspaper testimony shatters their artistic games, and they are momentarily hushed.

Cortázar has lived in Paris for 30 years, and the self-exile of his characters, caught up in their ballooning interiors, may replicate the writer's actual exile, expressing a fundamental homelessness that Cortázar has made into his subject matter. His opposite is probably Gabriel García Márquez, whose fables tell of a mysterious home woven out of folklore, market smells and the common folk sleepwalking in myth. Yet Cortázar, no less than García Márquez, writes out of a cornucopia of imagery, an outpouring and a richness of language that has become the signature of Latin American fiction. It is as if the Latin Americans had taken as their motto William Blake's proverb of hell: "Enough! or Too Much." (pp. 37-8)

*Paul Zweig, "Ominous People Doing Odd Things,"* in The New York Times Book Review, *March 27, 1983, pp. 1, 37-8.*

## LANIN A. GYURKO

Throughout his work, both in novels like *62: Modelo para armar* and in numerous short stories, Cortázar links the artistic experience not with creative self-transcendence or liberation but with entrapment and destruction. Three of his short stories, two from his most recent collection to date, *Queremos tanto a Glenda,* including the title story itself and **"Clone,"** as well as **"Las ménades,"** from the collection *Final del juego,* strikingly demonstrate the perversion of art—its use as a force that summons up a nightmarish, demonic world for the audience/spectators of the artistic experience and for the artists themselves.

In narratives such as **"El otro cielo"** and **"El perseguidor,"** Cortázar has manifested a marked ambivalence toward the creative experience, one which he carries to a negative extreme in the three stories to be analyzed here. (p. 17)

In **"Queremos tanto a Glenda,"** **"Clone,"** and **"Las ménades,"** the creative impulse becomes twisted into the urge to manipulate and dominate. It is ironic that the function of art, instead of being to achieve a spiritual expression, to seek or to express a universal truth, to provide aesthetic pleasure, or to extend the boundaries of perception and feeling, instead becomes perverted into a display of power, violence, and even murder. At times the fusion of art with the supernatural is achieved by the artists themselves, and against one another, as in **"Clone."** At times the demonic is unleashed as a result of a bizarre "co-operation" between artists and audience, as in **"Las ménades."** And in **"Queremos tanto a Glenda,"** the demonic is incarnated in a group of fans turned initially into fierce critics of the cinematic superstar Glenda Garson, and finally into self-styled gods, re-creators of her image while they destroy her in reality. In **"Clone,"** the malevolent spirit of the fifteenth-century artist/murderer Gesualdo seems to invade the soul of the twentieth-century artist Mario, infusing him with the will and strength necessary to kill his faithless lover. In this regard, **"Clone"** parallels Cortázar's story **"Las armas secretas,"** where the demonic spirit of the dead Nazi that invades and rapidly erodes the sanity and the identity of the French protagonist Pierre, provides him with the monstrous extreme of the *machismo* that he has desired in order to seduce Michele.

Like many of Cortázar's short stories, **"Clone,"** **"Glenda"** and **"Las ménades"** are characterized by an intense air of fatalism. (pp. 17-18)

In all three of these stories, among the most powerful and the most compelling of Cortázar's narratives, the demonic is linked with a monstrous *amour propre* for which the archetype is the egomania of Lucifer, who dared to challenge and to rival God. The title "Queremos tanto a Glenda," is deliberately misleading. The adoration of the select group of fans is not for the living actress Glenda Garson, despite their oft-professed devotion to her. Indeed, the cinematic star is more and more vilified by them. Instead, the adoration of the group is for the mere image of Glenda—the image they themselves have fabricated by painstakingly modifying her movies to suit their own aesthetic criteria. Thus their love is only for their own creation, and, ultimately, for themselves. In "Clone," the self-centeredness of the members of the madrigal group is carried to such a bizarre extreme that one of their own members must be killed in order to preserve the "artistic perfection" toward which they, like the re-creators of Glenda, are fanatically striving. Finally, in "Las ménades," the arrogance of the Maestro is equalled and then surpassed by the megalomania of the audience, who insist not only on being recognized by the conductor but on his abject submission to their will, as they physically overwhelm and almost destroy the man who has dared to place himself, literally and culturally, above them. In "Queremos tanto a Glenda," the inveterate narcissism of the members of the "fan club" even reaches the extreme of self-deification—another perversion of the creator's role.

All three stories display a masterful style, which exercises a hypnotic effect over the reader. This is a complex style that in its rhythms, its repetitions, its manic intensity, both captures the surface reality of the characters, and, far more importantly, conveys their hidden, submerged or suppressed essence. All three stories function on multiple levels. Often the central narrator establishes, through an eloquent, even breezy style, an atmosphere of nonchalance. Yet the subterranean, psychological reality—a negative state of pent-up emotion, of frustration, hatred, jealousy, vindictiveness, that is masked by the narrator—is conveyed through the style, which places the reader directly in contact with the mind of the characters. (p. 19)

Ironically, although the concept of cloning for many is a dehumanizing one, since it signifies that the individual in effect ceases to exist and is but one more "carbon copy," the members of the choral group [in "Clone"] actually lose their status as clones—because this apparently voluntary suppression of the self creates a group that functions perfectly. Cloning therefore becomes an essential element in the artistic process—each one of the eight relinquishes his or her individual identity to create a totality that does not merely function as a unity but lives and breathes as one. (p. 20)

The members of the choral group strive for a state of transcendental unity not only with one another but, beyond that, through space and time, to attempt to unite with the spirit of the artist—the composer of the madrigals they are performing, Gesualdo. They seek not merely to offer one more rendition of his music but to become Gesualdo—to convey him as a living entity. Perhaps without their realizing it consciously, their desire is to relive Gesualdo's life in order to perform his madrigals with full authenticity—in all of their shades and nuances. The irony is, of course, that the spirit from the fifteenth century that they strive to summon up and to fuse with, in effect using the music of Gesualdo as a type of incantation, conjures up instead a creative monster—one who in a fit of jealous rage has murdered both his wife and her lover. For its perfect realization, Gesualdo's art requires duplication of the same ghastly circumstances that led to its initial creation, as Gesualdo escaped into artistic endeavor as a salvation from the torment of guilt, remorse, and lost love. The group's fascination with Gesualdo and their obsessive desire to portray a living Gesualdo lead them to create among themselves a situation in which the same forces—infidelity, passion, desire for brutal vengeance—will be acted out again. (p. 21)

Ironically, and perhaps fatalistically, instead of choosing another, less controversial composer, the group add madrigal after madrigal to their repertoire. Testimony to the manner in which their obsession has perverted their art is that the madrigals now function not as artistic creations but as weapons—symbolic of the infusion into the group of the murderous spirit necessary for them to purge themselves of the unwanted leader, Sandro, whom they hold responsible for what they perceive as a decline in their previously perfect performances. . . . (p. 21)

Art functions in a complex manner within this bizarre narrative. For Gesualdo, it is a release from personal affliction—the creative urge that, ironically, is born from the destructive one, the masterful sublimation of all the tragedy of his personal life. But in the twentieth century, the group of madrigal singers completes the cycle—turning the creative impulse back into the destructive. Even though their behavior is motivated by a desire to protect their own creative center, Gesualdo's art, in which they seek salvation, proves to be the condemnation of the group, finally resulting in its permanent dissolution. (p. 22)

Another important aspect of all three of these narratives of Cortázar is the role of the group—the body that achieves a weird life of its own. . . . Like the characters of *62: Modelo para armar,* whose existence is linked with fatalistic patterns of vampirism . . . , the group in "Clone" finds its ultimate significance not in the present or in the future but within the mold of a fated past. . . . In "Queremos tanto a Glenda," the group is transmogrified from a casual, spontaneous, open gathering of fans into a closed, sinister, highly organized cabal, imbued with demonic energy. And in "Las ménades," the audience becomes infused, as an effect of the catalyst that is the supernatural music of the Maestro, with a superhuman power. In all three stories the emphasis is on anonymity—none of the narrators is ever identified, a circumstance that further underscores the importance of the collectivity. (pp. 22-3)

The same continual ambivalence, the same story-within-a-story, and the same surface action concealing deep and obsessive passion and ultimately, a desire for murder, characterize Cortázar's "Queremos tanto a Glenda." Beneath the apparent adulation of Glenda lies a secret jealousy of her, one that finally hardens into hatred of the world famous star, just as the prolonged and ecstatic applause for the Maestro in "Las ménades" conceals a desire by his "loyal" fans not only to humiliate but, finally, to destroy him. Just as in "Clone," the striving for artistic perfection dominates the group in "Glenda." Here, however, the irony is more pronounced, because, first of all, all-consuming desire exists not in the artist but in a group of dilettantes who merely pose as enthusiastic fans and, secondly, these fans are fanatically dedicated to the cinema—the most open and democratic of the arts. The group, on the other hand, is extraordinarily élitist. It is thus ironic that they should fasten on this popular art form, so often dominated by commercial, box-office concerns. (pp. 25-6)

Perhaps, since more than any other art form, the cinema provides a means through which the actor or actress, who achieves the status of a demigod, can immortalize the personal self, it is to share in this semidivine status and immortality that the fans are attracted to Glenda. Indeed, the reality of the aging and for them increasingly imperfect Glenda is an abomination, a blot or stain on the cinematic Glenda whose image and whose performance they have labored so incessantly to perfect. Thus the real-life Glenda must be destroyed in order that the immortal Glenda—her film image—may continue unsullied. . . . [The] ending of "Clone" traces the sudden and permanent collapse of the artistic group. Similarly, in both "Queremos tanto a Glenda" and "Las ménades," the artist is defeated, as the audience turned co-creators score a diabolic triumph over the artists. (p. 26)

"Glenda" is one of the most chilling of Cortázar's stories. In this narrative as in "Las ménades," the cult of the artist is carried to a gruesome extreme. Like "Clone," "Queremos tanto a Glenda" functions on several levels. As in so many of Cortázar's narratives, short stories like "Lejana" and "Las puertas del cielo," and novels like *Rayuela,* we witness, from the outset of "Glenda," emphasis on both separation and superiority. (p. 27)

What motivates this group to go to the absurd extreme of obtaining all existing copies of the films of Glenda in order to "correct" the scenes they condemn as imperfect? . . . Perhaps their extreme act—the murder of Glenda—can be seen as the ultimate retribution by the fans, for being forced to surrender their identity in order to sustain the legend of a cinematic goddess.

In a sense, what Cortázar does in both "Queremos tanto a Glenda" and "Las ménades" is to burlesque his own concept, articulated in *Rayuela,* of the *lector macho*—the active reader, the fan or critic who collaborates with the artist, in contrast with the passive, receptive *lector hembra* who welcomes the omniscient author, who explains or interprets everything for him. It is this *lector macho* whom Cortázar—at least in *Rayuela*—desires as a co-creator of the novel, the inventive reader who must take the myriad fragments of the work, its atemporal structure, its uncompleted characters, scenes, and plot, to enter the zone of contingency and ambiguity that Cortázar as author has deliberately left open for him. In "Queremos tanto a Glenda" are a group of highly intelligent individuals who, not content with the many obvious defects in the films of Glenda, seek to become *espectadores machos,* actively and diligently recreating these films. And, in "Las ménades," the ardent fans also conceive of themselves not as mere appreciators of the music but as co-creators. Both welcoming and yet resenting the powerful impact made on them by the stupendous music of the Maestro, the audience uses a force of their own—their applause—as a means not only of celebrating, but of rivalling, even of opposing the force of that music. Perhaps Cortázar is showing us the logical—and disastrous—consequences of the process of this co-creation of a work of art.

Cortázar seems to be satirizing the fan—or the critic—of a work of art, who, never having created an art object himself, dares to set himself up as evaluator and, at times, even condemns the production of the artist. (pp. 28-9)

"Glenda" burlesques not only the "crítico macho" but also the apparently inexhaustible controversy, the polemic that has been waged in Latin America for generations, between those advocating "art for art's sake" and those dedicated to "arte comprometido." This often bitter polemic has engulfed Cortázar himself, and has prompted him to answer in writing charges by the critic Oscar Collazos that he is not an *engagé* artist. . . .

But in "Glenda" he seems to be caricaturing the heated polemic, as he places it within the midst of a group of fanatics devoting their lives to the absurd. . . . They view their "work" not as a mere pastime of the idle rich but as an ennobling crusade, a mission that, in their delusions of grandeur, they even see as saving mankind. . . . Here again, style expertly conveys their grandiose intent. Instead of a mere dissolution of the group, should it be wracked by infighting, there would be a "diáspora." Use of the *esdrujúla* in words such as "diáspora," "espléndida," "filósofos" and "escrúpulos" further contributes to the creation of a lofty self-image. Schisms in the group prove to be only temporary. (pp. 31-2)

The final attitude of the clan toward the living Glenda is one of scarcely disguised contempt, now that they no longer need the real-life artist. (p. 32)

Cortázar's short story parallels the poem by Yeats entitled "The Dolls," which also treats the antagonism between art and life, and shows the callous suppression of life, deemed inferior to art, in favor of the closed, perfect realm of artistic creation. Yet, through his poem, itself an artistic masterpiece, Yeats, paradoxically, provides an indictment of art and a defense of life. Cortázar does the same, through his evocation of the fans/critics/re-creators as lunatics and monsters. In Yeats's poem as in Cortázar's narrative, art triumphs over life—life is considered as an intrusion into the perfect, immortal, even divine sphere of art. (pp. 33-4)

How can we interpret "Queremos tanto a Glenda"? Like so many of Cortázar's narratives, works like "Las babas del diablo" or "Casa tomada" or "Bestiario," it is a bizarre story that lends itself to multiple interpretations—psychological, as an example of collective dementia; supernatural, as the infusion of the demonic into a group of religious fanatics; political, as a veiled critique of fascism, and, finally, as an allegory of élitist versus popular art. Perhaps in "Glenda" Cortázar is tracing the elaborate vengeance of the intellectual, cultural, and financial élite against the popular taste, in the form of the person, Glenda Garson, whom that taste has falsely enshrined. If so, then the reverse of this situation is presented in "Las ménades," which forcefully depicts the revolt and the triumph of the popular, the bourgeois audience who hate the élitist conductor and his musicians, by whom they feel tyrannized and degraded. Here the masses are depicted as cultural *poseurs,* as a crass, boorish audience that has but little understanding of or appreciation for classical music. (p. 35)

The full, violent, overwhelming eruption of the demonic linked directly to art, in ["Queremos tanto a Glenda"] as in "Clone" with the spellbinding, supernatural power of music, occurs in one of Cortázar's most vivid and dramatic stories, "Las ménades." Once more, as in both of the preceding narratives, as in "El perseguidor" as well, it is the artist, in this case the venerable Maestro, who is victimized by the very art at which he so excels. The undercurrents of sadism that permeate both "Clone" and "Glenda" become a raging torrent in "Las ménades." Here Cortázar demonstrates how quickly the façade of reason and cultural sophistication can fall away to reveal the bestial. It is ironic that the concert master, who has been engaged in a life-long attempt to bring culture to the masses, to "civilize" his unruly provincial audience, is finally conquered by the barbaric.

In "Las ménades" Cortázar astutely mixes the humorous and the grotesque, the savage and the sublime, the celestial and the bestial. Epitomizing the fusion of opposites is the figure of the narrator, who constantly vacillates in his interpretations of both personalities and events. At first he chides, then he identifies fully with the Maestro, yet he finally desires to join the audience against him. (pp. 35-6)

As in the two preceding stories, the surface behavior of the characters masks deep frustration and an intense desire for vengeance. Perhaps the members of the vast audience resent the attitude of marked disdain toward them manifested by the Maestro. Perhaps they also resent that the arrogant conductor, although dependent upon them for his reputation and livelihood, nevertheless deceives and exploits them. As in **"Queremos tanto a Glenda,"** the fans have come to the theatre ostensibly to pay homage to the Maestro but in reality to celebrate their own triumph, to manifest their own terrible power.

Similar to the fans of Glenda, who are acutely conscious of the passivity and even nullity of their role vis-a-vis that of the artist . . . , the audience in **"Las ménades"** chafes at having been reduced to an inferior position—and at having to be pandered to. (p. 37)

The charged atmosphere predominates from the very beginning of the concert. The members of the audience cannot tolerate even the slightest criticism of their idol; they are ready to come to blows in their rabid devotion to the Maestro. The musicians are reluctant to perform for such a group as, unlike the totally self-absorbed Maestro, they sense the malevolence behind the façade of approbation. They come on stage more like prisoners being thrown to the lions than proud performers. . . . The brazen leader of the group of attackers, a woman dressed in brilliant red, underscores the desire of the fans to free themselves once and for all from the gray, passive, nonentity role of mere spectators. The irony is that, as the applause increases in mountainous waves, the Maestro for the first time in his career is being manipulated by his audience. . . . (p. 40)

As in **"Clone"** and **"Glenda,"** and stories from other collections of Cortázar such as **"El otro cielo,"** we notice a fervid desire on the part of the audience not merely to experience art as an aesthetic phenomenon—one that will grant them pleasure or delight or even catharsis—but to live that art. Thus Beethoven's *Fifth Symphony,* expressive of the *Götterdämmerung,* turns out to be a very poor choice for the Maestro to have made, instead of something more soothing like Brahms' *Lullaby.* Ironically, the conductor, a master showman, has planned his program all too well. In his quest for universal fame and glory, he further excites his already mercurial audience. Music in **"Las ménades"** not only symbolizes the tragic, it produces it; here as in **"Clone"** the music rears up as a living and demonic force. . . . **"Las ménades"** traces the submission of even the narrator himself to the spell of the concert hall—his absorption into the demonic. (pp. 40-1)

As in the two previous stories, many of the incidents of **"Las ménades"** have a double meaning. On the surface, it seems as if the lady in red is approaching the Maestro to render him homage, like a penitent before an altar. . . . But her rapturous enthusiasm is in fact exhibitionist, like her flaming red dress, and her positioning herself close to the Maestro is in order to obtain the most advantageous point from which to strike. (p. 41)

Similar to the infernal atmosphere—the hell without flames—that permeates other Cortázar stories about art and the demonic, like **"Siestas,"** in which the haunting paintings of Delvaux become the hellworld into which the young protagonist of the story becomes permanently absorbed, the atmosphere in the immense concert hall becomes hellish. . . . The dimming of the theatre lights produces a reddish glow which, combined with the epileptic shadows cast by the hysteric fans, gives the hall the air of a world populated by souls writhing in torment, a monstrous world of chaotic shapes. . . . (pp. 41-2)

**"Las ménades"** is important not only for its fusion of contemporary reality and classical myth but also as a peculiarly Latin American work, for one of its central themes—the conflict between civilization and barbarism—continues the portrayal that this important theme has received in other major literary works, such as Sarmiento's *Civilización y barbarie,* Güiraldes' *Doña Bárbara,* and Asturias' *El Señor Presidente.* All these works portray the ambivalent attitude, of both repulsion and fascination, their authors adopt toward the barbaric, whether incarnated in a caudillo, as in *Civilización y barbarie,* or in a dictator, as in *El Señor Presidente,* or a witch, as in *Doña Bárbara.* (pp. 42-3)

**"Las ménades"** demonstrates the . . . triumph of barbarism, always lurking beneath the thin veneer of civilized appearance, that, like the jungle in [*Los pasos perdidos,* by Alejandro Carpentier] . . . , seems to be checked by the force of civilization, yet quickly asserts its primacy and its dominance over technological man whenever his grip is relaxed. Just as in Carpentier's novel, the barbaric in **"Las ménades,"** when it explodes, carries away everything in its awesome wake. . . . (p. 43)

The ending of **"Las ménades,"** like that of **"Glenda,"** is chilling. As in both of the preceding stories by Cortázar, it manifests the final triumph of the demonic. Although the fury has subsided, the triumphant leader of the attack, the woman in red, has still not recovered from her transport, and the indication is that she will return to lead the audience again. Although most have recovered their sense of shame, indicating that perhaps the norms of civilized life have once again been restored, the continued power of the barbaric is frighteningly symbolized by the demented countenance of the woman in red, who is still savoring her triumph, and who still has her retinue. . . . (p. 44)

Art is linked with the demonic in many of the other stories of Cortázar, such as **"Siestas,"** **"El ídolo de las Cícladas,"** **"Las babas del diablo,"** and **"Carta a una señorita en Paris."** As in **"Las ménades,"** art becomes a sinister powerful force, one that leaps out to overwhelm the spectators, possessing and even destroying them. (p. 45)

**"Clone,"** **"Glenda,"** and **"Las ménades"** are very unsettling narratives, stories in which the boundaries between reality and fantasy, present and mythic or historical past, sanity and madness, art and life, are constantly being crossed. In these stories of the uncanny and the absurd, the characters—the choral group in **"Clone,"** the clan in **"Glenda,"** and the audience in **"Las ménades"**—gain a weird type of self-expression and even self-fulfillment through their pact with the demonic. (p. 46)

*Lanin A. Gyurko, "Art and the Demonic in Three Stories by Cortázar," in Symposium, Vol. XXXVII, No. 1, Spring, 1983, pp. 17-47.*

**STEPHEN DOBYNS**

Webs, nets, mosaics, tapestries—the 10 stories in Julio Cortázar's new collection *We Love Glenda So Much and Other Tales* deal with the human need to impose order and sense on imperfectly connected phenomena: what the narrator of **"Return Trip Tango"** calls "that baroque necessity of the intelligence that leads it to fill every hollow until its perfect web has been spun and it can go on to something new."

Cortázar often presents these webs by means of the fantastic which he calls "the dominant feature of my work." . . .

Cortázar wants to jolt people out of their self-complacency, to make them doubt their own definitions of the world. In an early essay, he described his writing as "seeking an alternative to that false realism which assumed that everything could be neatly described as was upheld by the philosophic and scientific optimism of the eighteenth century."

Cortázar is one of the world's great writers. His range of styles, his ability to paint a scene, his humor, his endlessly peculiar mind make many of his stories wonderful. His novel *Hopscotch* is considered one of the best novels written by a South American, while his first collection of short stories in English *End of the Game* constantly startles and moves the reader by its brilliance. Unfortunately, that earlier collection is still superior to this new book *We Love Glenda So Much*.

What partly made the stories in *End of the Game* so good was that they dealt with people in states of extreme loneliness, isolation, separation from the world. One cared about these characters and was moved by their difficulties. The problem with too many of these new stories is that while they may be striking, one doesn't care about them.

This is best seen in the story **"Clone"** which concerns eight men and women who tour South America singing madrigals and whose perfect singing relationship is destroyed by a complicated love triangle within the group. In a note at the end of the story, Cortázar explains the structure was based on Johann Sebastian Bach's *A Musical Offering,* that the eight characters match the eight instruments and that "the development of each passage tries to resemble the musical form." The result is brilliant but not very satisfying. There is nothing to prop up the story's intricate surface with the result that it seems to tumble in on itself.

A more successful story, **"Text in a Notebook,"** deals with a man trying to impose sense on a passenger survey of the Buenos Aires subway after he learns that on one day 113,987 entered the subway and only 113,983 came out. Actually, the story is about the narrator's need to make sense of this unexplained phenomenon which leads to madness when he decides the subway system is being taken over by thousands of people who go into the subways but never return. . . .

The narrator's inability to accept the idea that the difference was accidental damages all his definitions of reality. This certainly becomes more interesting than the situation itself. When Cortázar transcends the fantastic to the human, the stories stop being surface and one comes to care about them. This happens in the best stories like **"Graffiti," "Return Trip Tango"** and **"Stories I Tell Myself."** In others, however, he seems so concerned with challenging the reader's definitions of reality, the story doesn't go past that original challenge. One is aware of brilliant writing and brilliant structure but most of the stories aren't emotionally engaging.

One of the reasons that people read is to find evidence of human life which jars them out of their own sense of isolation. With the fantastic it is all too easy for the situation to overwhelm that evidence of human life. The need to impose order on disorder, to see patterns where none exist is a common enough human need but too often the stories don't go past the situation which exemplifies this need. The fans of Glenda Garson end up creating for her a perfect body of work. Like the man dealing with the subways of Buenos Aires, they are driven to increas-

ingly extreme behavior in order to protect their definitions as to how the world should be. This also becomes Cortázar's weakness: to challenge our accustomed ways of seeing the world, he is forced to use ever greater degrees of the fantastic. The problem is that after having got the reader's attention, many of the stories don't take him anywhere. The reader responds as he might to a shout in a library reading room. He glances up, then after a moment returns to his book, his business and the usual definitions of the world.

Stephen Dobyns, "The Cortázar Treatment," in Book World—The Washington Post, *May 1, 1983, p. 9.*

## GEORGE KEARNS

Cortázar's tales [in *We Love Glenda So Much*] are filled with the familiar game-playing signs that signify "postmodern": if we are to have something that looks like a story we must pay the cost of being self-consciously reminded that fiction is about fiction, writing about writing, and all that. (p. 558)

Cortázar's stories are generally short and light, even when they deal with serious subjects such as political oppression in his native Argentina. He likes to play tricks with time, space, reality, illusion. . . . Behind their modish trappings and tricky narrative styles, Cortázar's stories are really nice old-fashioned "surprise ending" magazine tales in the tradition of Maupassant, O. Henry, Somerset Maugham, and "The Lady or the Tiger?" Seen that way, they have a certain antique charm and inconsequence. Back in the old days, when short story writers made real money, Cortázar could have done very nicely in *Colliers* or *The Saturday Evening Post*. The title story, about an international conspiracy of narrowly-specialized film fans, is based on some tricky work with film, and could make an amusing movie, just as an earlier story by Cortázar was blown up into *Blow Up*. (pp. 558-59)

George Kearns, "World Well Lost," in The Hudson Review, *Vol. XXXVI, No. 3, Autumn, 1983, pp. 549-62.**

## HARRY L. ROSSER

In the narratives of Julio Cortázar there is an intense preoccupation with the unexplainable phenomena which invade individual and collective experience. This restless, self-exiled Argentine rejects the rational, convenient, and limiting interpretations of the every-day world. He defies man-made formulae and simplistic explanations of reality. Cortázar believes that human beings can change and act upon their limitless potential for self-realization, for spiritual fulfillment, for a totality of life.

Cortázar uses the word "fantastic" in defining his fiction and his own special way of understanding reality. By "fantastic" he means the alternative to what he calls "false realism" or the view that "everything can be described and explained in line with the philosophical and scientific optimism of the eighteenth century, that is, within a world governed by a system of laws, of principles, of causal relations, of well-defined psychologies, of well-mapped geographies." He has emphasized that for him there exists "the suspicion of another order, more secret and less communicable" in which the true study of reality is found in the exceptions to the laws rather than in those laws themselves. For Cortázar, the approach to this order requires a loosening of the mind in order to make it a more receptive instrument of knowledge and to stimulate authentic transformations in man. This approach is evident in many of the short stories of this imaginative non-conformist.

Of the several stories that reflect Cortázar's fascination with fantastic incursions into the rational world of the self, "Axolotl" most memorably portrays a transformation experience and raises questions about the nature of that experience. While the story can be read as a direct narration of novelistic events, it lends itself to elucidation on another level as well. The purpose here is to offer an interpretation of Cortázar's narrative within the context of his unusual view of reality. (p. 419)

Cortázar uses a variety of literary techniques in "Axolotl." The events of the story take place over a period of a few days during which the narrator-protagonist focuses on critical phases of the transformation process. There is no linear sequence or spatial constancy. There appears to be no plot development, an impression conveyed by a circular kind of narrative procedure. The central idea established in the first few lines of the story is regularly reiterated: "There was a time when I thought a great deal about the axolotls. I went to see them in the aquarium at the Jardin des Plantes and stayed for hours watching them, observing their immobility, their faint movements. Now I am an axolotl." (p. 420)

As in a number of Cortázar's stories, suspense in "Axolotl" is not dependent upon the element of surprise but upon the particular experience described and upon the atmosphere of tension in which that experience takes place. Cortázar has stated that it is of utmost importance to him to hold the attention of his reader-accomplices, as he likes to call them, and to widen their horizons. . . . "Axolotl" is typical of Cortázar in other ways: it introduces a protagonist in a situation characterized by a routine existence; it recounts the way in which an alien presence interrupts that routine; and it reveals—at least partially—the consequences of that intervention.

"Axolotl" is a story in which the line between reality and fantasy gradually blurs in the reader's mind. It is narrated from several different perspectives that shift unpredictably and whose sources are somewhat ambiguous. Intentional confusion is caused by the skillful use of personal pronouns, verbal suffixes, and several verb tenses that are associated with the varying points of view. (p. 421)

The multiple pespectives established through the use of various pronouns and verbal suffixes is developed even further by a constant change in the temporal context. Several verb tenses appear in the same short paragraph or even in the same sentence: "The axolotls huddled on the wretched, narrow (only I can know how narrow and wretched) floor of stone and moss." . . . The story begins in the past ("There was a time when I thought a great deal about the axolotls." . . .), skips back and forth in time and then draws to a close in the present. The use of the present tense imbues the account with a sense of open-endedness. The last words of the salamander are: "And in this final solitude, to which he no longer comes, I console myself by thinking that perhaps he is going to write a story about us, that, believing he's making up a story, he's going to write all this about axolotls." (pp. 421-22)

Taken together, these literary techniques underscore the multiplicity of reality which Cortázar is so intent upon conveying through his fiction. The constant interchange of perspectives and temporal planes that the techniques create undermines the reliability of rational thought. Cortázar's innovative methods are meant to revitalize language as well as people. "I've always found it absurd," he says, "to talk about transforming man if

man doesn't simultaneously, or previously, transform his instruments of knowledge. How to transform oneself if oneself continues to use the same language Plato used?"

In "Axolotl" Cortázar has sought to express something for which there is no verbal concept within the realist mode of writing. He rejects writing on the basis of logical conceptualizations, for the mode he refers to as "fantastic" is not practiced from an intellectual standpoint. In fact, he has explained that, for the most part, writing just happens to him. It is a kind of literary exorcism. . . . On occasion it is as though he were a medium receiving a force over which he has no conscious control. The story under analysis, therefore, can be seen as a metaphor because it clearly has that mysterious quality of suggesting meaning beyond the mere anecdote of the narrative.

The meanings implied in the transformation may be numerous. The interpretation offered here is that the significance of the event described in "Axolotl" closely coincides with Carl Gustav Jung's views on the dynamics and development of the self. . . . What happens in "Axolotl" strongly suggests that Cortázar means to represent an ego-conscious personality striving for wholeness, or what Jung describes as "the ultimate integration of conscious and unconscious, or better, the assimilation of the ego to a wider personality."

Throughout the narrative it is suggested that Cortázar is actually portraying aspects of a process of self-realization. The solitary, routine existence in which the protagonist is mired is interrupted by an unexpected obsession for the salamanders. He is unable to think of anything else. Through the function of intuition he senses the attractive power of a collective image: "I knew that we were linked, that something infinitely lost and distant kept pulling us together." . . . In Jungian terms the unconscious component of the self—that is, those personal psychic activities and contents which are "forgotten, repressed or subliminally perceived, thought, and felt"—erupts into consciousness. It does this on its own accord, requiring the ego somehow to assimilate the new content. Cortázar's protagonist describes psychic associations which suggest that the activity originates in the unconscious, not only on a personal but on a collective level as well. In the unconscious, as Jung explains, there is interaction between "the acquisitions of the personal existence" and "the inherited possibility of psychic functioning in general, namely, in the inherited brain structure." Being the base of the psyche of every individual, the collective unconscious is a kind of heritage passed on to all human beings, and maybe even to all animals as well.

With these concepts in mind, the salamander in Cortázar's story may be seen as an archetypal representation of basic drives and appetites which include the urge for self-fulfillment. (pp. 422-23)

The narrator-protagonist gives even more weight to the primordial image that amphibians convey by his persistent attention to the eyes of the salamanders. . . . Apart from the hypnotic effect that is suggested through the man's reaction to the eyes, they may be understood to have psychological meaning as well. The eye is traditionally considered to be a window to the soul. Like sparks and stars, it is an artistic motif associated with the illumination of consciousness. Indeed, consciousness has commonly been described in terms related to light. (p. 423)

It is understood that what the man in "Axolotl" has undergone is not only fantastic but primitive and symbolic as well. The more primordial the experience seems, the more it represents the potentiality of being. The contents of the unconscious can provide a more complete way of living and perceiving. The salamanders' eyes speak to the man "of the presence of a different life, of another way of seeing." . . . Such subjective perception and introverted sensation have been discussed at length by Jung. He believes that primordial images, in their totality, constitute a "psychic mirror world" that represents the present contents of consciousness, not in their familiar form but in the way a million-year old consciousness might see them.

More primordial imagery can be found in **"Axolotl."** The narrator protagonist reiterates that to his way of thinking the salamanders are not human beings, but that they are not animals either. In comparing the two, he insists on the positive value of the animal. This is a recurring theme in Cortázar's fiction. (p. 424)

Cortázar's protagonist, then, has been caught up in an unsettling development process which leads to a kind of synthesis of conscious and unconscious elements. As it is explained in the story "what was his obsession is now an axolotl." . . . In other words, the narrator's momentous transformation signifies that he has become consciously aware of the effects of an instinctual side that he had neglected or suppressed. He has now integrated its valuable elements into his being. He no longer yields entirely to his rational conception of himself. He has discovered that he has a larger capacity for self-awareness. The details of what the hidden mind and spirit reveal to the narrator-protagonist are not disclosed specifically to the reader, but it is suggested that he has gained a deeper understanding of life. In relating to the amphibious creatures of the aquarium he acquires the insights, the means of comparison, that he needed for self-knowledge and for a sense of continuity as a living being. "Only the person who can consciously assent to the power of the inner voice becomes a personality," Jung has written. The man in **"Axolotl"** has heard that voice in the salamander and has gained the psychological advantage of a larger sense of life and of a reaffirmation of the spirit. He is now a changed, more complete being.

There may be disagreement over whether or not the transformation experience depicted in **"Axolotl"** has positive connotations. Some readers are of the opinion that Cortázar has told a story about a personal failure, about a defeat. The argument is that the salamander abandons the man, that a lack of communication ensues, and that at the end the man is left impoverished by the experience. "The 'I' is denied the possibility of living on two planes," concludes one critic. The interpretation that has been presented here views the transformation as positive. The conflicts over the matter arise from the enigmatic qualities of Cortázar's fiction, which reflects the inherent ambiguities of reality itself. Most likely, debate over the issue will go on. In any event, what is clear is that the readers of Cortázar's **"Axolotl"** are left with a heightened sense of awe regarding the potentialities of biological, spiritual and, most of all, literary realities. (p. 425)

> Harry L. Rosser, "The Voice of the Salamander: Cortázar's 'Axolotl' and the Transformation of the Self," in Kentucky Romance Quarterly, Vol. 30, No. 4, 1983, pp. 419-27.

## HARRIETT GILBERT

Julio Cortázar is, like all good modernists, intrigued by the symbiosis of life and art—of experience and its expression—and the stories in *We Love Glenda So Much* play with such explaining-and-containing devices as music, painting, the cinema; or, less predictably, graffiti.

Not only are the stories *about* form, they are themselves strictly formal. In tone precise to the point of pendantry (sometimes even obscurity), their structure is defined solely by an intellectual concept—with the minimum of plot, physical description, social location or characterisation to clutter up the lines. In the title story, . . . it is not only difficult, but pointless to remember which fan exactly 'Diana' is; just as it is irrelevant to try to locate, with precision, the story in time or place.

Where a concept has its own dynamic, this chucking away of the personal frills works quite astonishingly well. In **'Glenda'** itself, it is not altogether successful. The theme is exhausted too early for the climax to have any impact—it just looks contrived (as it is). In **'Graffiti'**, however (a terrible solo of outrage at political repression), or in **'Text in a Notebook'** (where 'official reports' are peeled from their covering of sanity) Cortázar's correctness is so ruthless that his formal designs expose, in themselves, the violence, cruelty and fear from which they were abstracted.

> Harriett Gilbert, "Emblematic," in New Statesman, Vol. 107, No. 2756, January 13, 1984, p. 28.*

## KEITH COHEN

A text that proposes to recount its own generation: nothing particularly new about that, except, perhaps, the recognition of its prevalence. . . . Writing about writing has indeed become a cornerstone of that still dimly lit edifice called modernism. (p. 15)

What constitutes the machinery of writing? It is at this point that technology becomes important, along with models of artistic continuity other than literary. It is also here that Julio Cortázar's **"Blow-Up"** can serve as a useful case in redefining the dynamics of the modernist text.

I place emphasis not so much on the purely literary divergences between nineteenth- and twentieth-century narrative as on the technological awareness of craft that is thrust upon the twentieth-century writer. The prime mover in this modern coming-to-awareness is, as I have argued elsewhere, the cinema. (p. 16)

It is now generally agreed that a principal aim of the dominant form of cinematic representationality—Hollywood cinema of the 1930s and '40s—was to minimize in whatever way possible the telltale signs of the interloping apparatus. Counter to this trend were the self-conscious Russians, Eisenstein and Vertov, and the surrealist and "impressionist" filmmakers in France during the 1920s, whose metalinguistic cinema reappears in the New Wave of the 1960s and in the American "underground" movement of the same period. In the meantime, there develops a peculiarly self-aware prose, which proceeds to lay bare the means of its own engendering in ways remarkably similar to those of the avant-garde cinema.

**"Blow-Up"** complicates its fictional content primarily within the two areas in which cinema has always offered a unique practice: perspective and voice. From the outset we are told that this story can have no consistent voice or person: "It'll never be known how this has to be told, in the first person or in the second, using the third person plural or continually inventing modes that will serve for nothing." . . . If the question, "Who speaks?" (dear to Genette) yields only a vexed answer, the question, "Who sees?" offers equivalent problems. In this case, however, the kink lies more in the "seeing" than in the "who." Aside from the constant vacillation within the subject Roberto Michel between "yo" and "él," it is the always uncertain perspective with which he views first the scene, then the photo, that concerns us most of all. (pp. 17-18)

"**Blow-Up**" deals with an action whose understanding depends on a complex and subtle perspective and whose very existence is, in the end, undecidable. The voice of narration reflects this perspectival instability by constantly switching from first to third person and by constantly wavering between the "now" of the writing and the actual time of the events. It is ironic in this respect that, given Cortázar's natural affinities with the narrative practices of filmmakers like Godard and Resnais, Antonioni should have chosen this text to adapt into a movie that transforms nearly all the problems of the apparatus into problems of the story, into the relatively banal problem of appearance vs. reality for the protagonist.

In Cortázar's text, we are never allowed to forget the apparatus of writing. The text opens and closes with a hypostatized moment of writing. The opening includes references to the apparatus most traditionally associated with writing: the typewriter. But the fantasy of the narrator suggests an impossible function for the typewriter: the power to take over the writing all by itself while he goes off to have a beer. Nor is this, he adds, "a manner of speaking," since poetically speaking, the writing machine might know better than he how to tell the story of another machine: the camera. . . . At the outset, then, is a humorous reference to two fundamental aspects of the text—the highly desired though impossible situation of a story without a human narrator, and the assignment of such a condition to another area of technology, photography, or rather to sequentialized photography: cinema. (pp. 18-19)

Up to this point, the text can be seen to call attention to its own production in a more or less traditional manner—compare the parenthetical digressions by Proust on the moment of writing. But as forewarned, we discover that the body of this text has for its principal protagonist a different machine, a machine that writes merely with light: the camera. Here the cinematic aspects of Cortázar's text take a new turn, for the peculiar issues of vision and perspective raised in this context would never be possible without the convenience of the camera itself. One third-person character—more spectator than actor—is therefore introduced to us as an amateur photographer and, in a few lines, goes out with his Contax. (p. 19)

Photography is introduced both as a primary narrative element and as a metaphoric means of alluding to verbal and visual perspective. We have been told that Michel wants to avoid becoming distracted as he writes . . . , and here the diaphragm of the camera serves as a useful emblem for the framework his verbal discourse seeks. Since we are not to find out until the last pages of the text why this discourse is such that its verbal boundaries are difficult to determine, we pursue this visual analogy by itself, witnessing the gradual "framing" of Michel's subject in terms of the camera. (p. 20)

Vision holds surprises. Such might be the innocent motto for a good deal of this story, as when Michel is unable to decide if it's a couple he's watching or a mother and a son. . . . But photographic vision has an entirely different dynamic and forgoes innocence altogether. Photography appropriates: one *takes* a picture. Hence the world offers itself not so much for purposeless observation as for consumption. In photographic terms, then, "every looking oozes with mendacity." Michel's whole

enterprise consists in choosing between this innocent observation and the interested voyeurism afforded by the camera: "to choose between looking and the reality looked at." . . .

The scene of the couple, with all its unheard yet undoubtedly erotic overtones, has for the voyeur a "disquieting aura." . . . The anxiety associated with the scene must be returned to later. For the moment, it is important to note how Michel convinces himself that the photo—far from revealing something hidden to his naked eye—will objectify the situation, neutralize the aura, "reconstitute things in their true stupidity." . . . The entire question of what he is really seeing—mother and child, lovers, sex by proxy—is displaced onto the camera. . . . (pp. 20-1)

The transformation of the lived into the photographed—"the seeing" into "the seen"—cannot for Michel dispel the disquieting aspects of the scene. The photo has an uncanny ability to repeat "exactly the position and the vision of the lens." . . . Far from producing a tranquil fixation of that morning onto photographic paper, the camera has turned out to be the machine that recapitulates, Michel realizes as he stares beyond his typewriter, all the undecidability of the scene. What is foregrounded for Michel in the photographic process, what distinguishes it, for example, most notably from verbal transcription, is the doubleness of its objects. First the scene, then the scene seen again, as in the recounting of a dream. While at the first stage taking the photo gave Michel the impression of calming the anxiety produced by the scene, at the second stage he is a victim of "the seen." . . . (p. 21)

Through the figure of photography, the text goes beyond simple metalanguage. It traces succinctly its own generation, as though we were watching the colors define themselves in a chemical bath. The figure of photography, in other words, doubles for literary description. Just as the first stage of the experience is demolished by the photo, so the initial pretextual experience is by definition demolished—and hence redefined, clarified—through the process of writing. (pp. 21-2)

Jean-Louis Baudry points out that the dominant Western idealist metaphor for reality, Plato's cave, is arranged in exactly the manner of a cinema projection and that, furthermore, this same manner of projection resembles one of Freud's dominant metaphors for explaining the activity of the unconscious during a dream. Baudry finds that "Dream is 'an hallucinatory psychosis of desire'—i.e. a state in which mental perceptions are taken for perception of reality." We need merely change the term "mental perceptions" to "the perception of cinematic projections" and the definition of dream becomes the definition of watching a film.

The connection between film viewing and dreaming depends on the notion of the apparatus. The apparatus of cinema includes the various recording and projecting devices along with the celluloid and screen. In the case of dreaming, it includes the complex network of conscious and unconscious perceptions, memories, and fantasies: the mind. . . . If we return at this point to Cortázar's text, I think it becomes evident that Roberto Michel begs to be interpreted in terms of the psychoanalytic model of the subject. Michel's initial experience, in these terms, takes on all the qualities of a dream, or of some trauma that is later dreamed about. His position as voyeur, both during the scene and afterwards as he stares at the photo, has been established above. But it may well be asked what pertinence this line of reasoning has, or how it can possibly explain Michel's final bursting into tears, followed by a mysterious, unsettling serenity.

Let us return, then, to the initial scene, that scene which returns to Michel with the force, of course, of something repressed. Mother and child, or lover and mistress? This is the fundamental undecidable as Michel first catches sight of the two people. He resolves that question to his satisfaction for the moment, dissolving its "disquieting" quality, by deciding in favor of an older woman propositioning a boy.... It is only when the "real" presents itself in photographic form that the motivation for this fantasy comes into question. What Michel fantasized seeing was what unconsciously he saw from the start: mother and child. But now mother and child coupled sexually. In other words, Michel projected himself onto the boy and saw in a moment of pure distraction what every young child wishes to see: himself about to make love to his mother. (pp. 22-3)

Now those subsidiary effects of photography mentioned above should be clear. The camera becomes, in short, an extension of the human apparatus. Michel transfers the disquieting sensations he is experiencing onto the physical apparatus of the camera and derives an infantile pleasure at eluding the parent figures, who are left to perform "the classical and absurd gesture of someone pursued looking for a way out."... But what has been boxed up has only been temporarily eluded— for just as long as the negative withholds its positive print potential. The photographic process has merely *displaced* the sacredness—and taboo—of the original, in the same manner that the true human apparatus, that of the subject, Michel, displaces his eye-witness of a fantasized primal scene.

The weakly understood significance of the scission of the writing subject now also becomes clearer. The text has three distinct parts, as suggested above: the moment of writing, the morning that Michel sees the couple and takes the photo ("the seeing"), and the moment of Michel's hallucination and collapse upon staring at the photo ("the seen"). To each of these parts corresponds one aspect of the living subject—somewhat in the manner of Fuentes's Artemio Cruz. Roberto Michel is the third-person observer who takes the photo: the subject in action. There is then one "I," the speculative subject, who, like the questioning Oedipus, persists in interrogating the photo, and the other "I," the reflective subject, recovered, who sits down to write about it. This scission would in itself be of little interest, were it not for the fact that these three parts also mirror the tripartite division of the subject in the dream state. (p. 24)

It may seem as though I have used the photographic and cinematic resonances of **"Blow-Up"** as pretexts to suggest a psychoanalytic reading of this text. The two, I would argue, are today scarcely separable. From the moment we admit the fundamental similarity between the filmic apparatus and the human apparatus of the mind, the unconscious forces itself to the forefront and introduces us to what Freud declared as the "other scene."

But one further scene has so far eluded my interpretation: that of the text's closing, where Michel sits in beatitude before a photo of almost nothing—just clouds and birds. The photograph, it would seem, has been emptied of its contents. Though still a rectangle tacked up on Michel's wall, the photo is now devoid of human figuration. It has become a double, or metaphoric depository, for all those clouds and birds that went irrelevantly by as interruptions to the main story.

Here we have the total identification between the cinematic apparatus and the apparatus of writing. Cortázar's short text is replete with references to blankness and nothingness. The entire drama is, in one sense, a play on presence and absence. The scene itself is at an early point parenthetically equated with "almost nothing" ..., and once the photo is developed "this nothing" takes on a paradoxical role as "the true solidifier of the scene" ..., i.e., as some predetermined emptiness—which will only be realized at the end—or as the chemical bath, the fixer, that makes possible the final appearance of the image. This appearing/disappearing power of "nothingness" is important, since it seems to mark a no-man's-land in between perception and representation, between fantasy and corporeality. As he describes the images of boy and woman initially, Michel says "I remember the image before his actual body." ... And again, their bodies seem somehow safely tucked away into nothingness once they are "ignominiously recorded on a small chemical image." ...

Cortázar thus plays with the ambiguous capacity of photography to hide, to take prisoner, the very thing it seeks to record, then to delude the spectator into believing he or she can experience reality by means of the photographed image. The hallucinated emptying of Michel's photo at the end of the story could be taken as a metaphor for the "writerly" text as a text that can take away or proffer with equal facility. (pp. 25-6)

Cortázar's closing, then, accomplishes what the narrator merely fantasized at the opening: a textual space devoid of human manipulation. The human subject is left as a raw apparatus of perception ("That was what I saw when I opened my eyes and dried them with my fingers"). Gone is the typewriter. We are here within the realm of something for now only momentarily possible, that of the apparently auto-generating text, seated with the mesmerized narrator before the cinema-like screen of the unconscious. (p. 27)

*Keith Cohen, "Cortázar and the Apparatus of Writing," in* Contemporary Literature, *Vol. 25, No. 1, Spring, 1984, pp. 15-27.*

### LOIS PARKINSON ZAMORA

[In *Deshoras*] the narrator of the title story begins by questioning his own motives for writing down his childhood memories.... This is a question which Cortázar's readers have come to expect, for Cortázar's best fiction has often pondered, as does this narrator, the relationship between reality and its verbal representation, between experience and words....

The stories of *Deshoras* continue Cortázar's exploration of the problematic nature of representation itself, the contradiction between the three-dimensional, changing space which objects occupy and where lives are lived on the one hand, and the two-dimensional, linear space of the printed page on the other. In these stories, as in his earlier fiction, Cortázar challenges the discursive, serial nature of prose fiction and of language itself by means of shifting points of view, disordered syntax, unexpected juxtapositions, dislocated sequence. So the multiple, shifting facets of experience, its rational *and* irrational aspects, are suggested in the narrative style and structure of these stories as well as in their content.

How to capture the images of the remembered past and fix them in words becomes the obsession of the narrator of the title story, **"Deshoras."** Sara, the object of his adolescent fantasy, is less remembered than invented by the narrator, and then framed with words like a faded daguerreotype. (p. 172)

This is not the only character in these stories who struggles with his memories. The narrator of **"Diario de un cuento"** also hopes to place his past beyond forgetting by writing a story about his former mistress, Anabel. However, his effort to create a verbal realm beyond the chronological succession of clocks and calendars is rendered ironically: he writes not a story but a diary, each entry labelled precisely with date and time. Cortázar creates this structural irony to suggest the inevitable tension between literary structure and human experience. I repeat: between words and the world.

And yet another story poses the problem of memory. In **"Escuela de noche,"** however, the narrator does *not* want to remember a past incident, but he cannot manage to forget it. Unspeakable cruelty, perversion, and intolerance are not so easily left unspoken: words, it is implied, may denounce inhumanity and may even ameliorate it.

Indeed, this story and others in this collection may be described by Cortázar's term, "la literatura de denuncia." The author's fervent commitment to social reform and his equally fervent opposition to political repression in Latin America have led him to write fiction which is increasingly polemical (in the best sense of that word). (pp. 172-73)

It is perhaps evident from the little that I have said here that the title of this collection has a broader application than to just the title story. The word *deshoras* conveys the feeling, implicit throughout, that "the time is out of joint," to use Hamlet's desperate phrase. (Hamlet, we remember, uses the phrase after confronting the ghost of his dead father on the ramparts of Elsinor: the confrontation symbolizes the irrational intrusion of the past into the present as well as the senseless violence of political intrigue . . . the two essential themes of this collection.) The title suggests as well the *process*, so evident in these stories, of creating alternative temporal orders of words— "deshoras"—which both reflect and revise historical reality, whether personal or political.

Such fictions have never been more necessary. (p. 173)

*Lois Parkinson Zamora, in a review of "Deshoras," in* Hispanic Journal, *Vol. 5, No. 2, Spring, 1984, pp. 172-73.*

## CHARLES CHAMPLIN

The Surrealist strain enriches and enlivens **"A Certain Lucas,"** a sort of literary Roman candle, as Cortazar builds a portrait, montage-like, through a succession of short sketches (humorous set-pieces, really) full of outrageous inventions, leaping and dream-like associations and funny turns of phrase. (The translator is too often an anonymous and undernoted figure, but Gregory Rabassa's rendering of Cortazar's kaleidoscopic language is so easy and expert it becomes hard to believe Cortazar was not, in fact, working directly in English.)

It is not astonishing to find that the emergent Lucas is the fantasy life, memory life, wishful life and, in certain moments of bizarre circumstance, the actual life of someone hardly distinguishable from Cortázar himself.

In the nearest thing to the memoir as short story, Lucas' wife sends him into the night to buy some matches, a matter so simple to accomplish that Lucas goes out in pajamas and robe. Through a series of confrontations and mischances, each more logical than the other, Lucas is at last stranded in a distant part of the city, still in pajamas and robe, penniless and still without

the matches. He is, in that scene, a Thurberesque figure widely transported, but still good-hearted and forever fumbling.

More often, the spirit is closer to the Bunuel and Dali of "The Andalusian Dog," full of zest for the bawdy, the anti-social, the ingeniously *outre*. . . .

If **"A Certain Lucas"** were no more than a series of extravagant jokes, it would be an exceptional passing entertainment but no more than that. Yet under the cover of raillery, self-indicting foolishness and extremely tall tales, Cortazar is discovered to be a thoughtful, deep-feeling man, impassioned, sentimental, angry, complicated, a philosopher exploring appearances vs. realities in the way of philosophers ever.

**"A Certain Lucas"** is, when the uproars have passed and the essays on soft-boiled eggs and on snail-years (as opposed to light-years) have been absorbed, an unexpectedly affecting book.

*Charles Champlin, "In the Robe of Ridicule, an Ironist Presses True," in* Los Angeles Times Book Review, *May 27, 1984, p. 3.*

## STEPHEN DOBYNS

In one of the 44 short pieces that make up Julio Cortázar's *A Certain Lucas,* he defines a polygraph as "a writer who deals with diverse material," those people "who cast their fishing poles in all directions, pretending at the same time to be half-asleep." Ostensibly, he is writing about Samuel Johnson, but then he adds, "When all is said and done, that's what I'm doing with this book."

*A Certain Lucas* is an odd and delightful book. This is Cortázar's eighth work to appear in English and it slightly resembles his popular *Cronopios and Famas,* published in 1962. In length, the pieces range from a paragraph to about six pages and they deal with life's absurdities and the sort of absurd bravery that is required if one is to endure and triumph. But despite the humor, this new book is also darker with intimations of age and illness. Cortázar himself never lived to see it published. (p. 4)

In *A Certain Lucas* the ideas and language . . . dance as the reader is drawn through one bit of extravagance after another. One piece argues that cats are really telephones. . . . In another, the people living under General Orangu in an unnamed country are kept happy by having tiny gold fish put into their blood. Another discusses "the reasons why many international athletes show an ever-growing proclivity for swimming in grits."

One of the world's great writers, Cortázar was sometimes criticized for his almost militant sense of play. Yet he also could write eloquently about life's various awfulnesses and the barbarity that human beings are capable of. What we see in Lucas and in much of Cortázar's work is a fierce love of this earth, despite the awfulness, and a fierce respect for life's ridiculousness. And in the midst of this ridiculousness, Cortázar dances—part Stravinsky and part Chaplin—and that dance comforts and eases our own course through the world. (p. 14)

*Stephen Dobyns, "Hopscotch with Julio," in* Book World—The Washington Post, *June 24, 1984, pp. 4, 14.*

## CARL SENNA

**"The Winners"** . . . was the first novel by Julio Cortázar to be published in the United States.

Readers of the author's daring fictional experiments such as the novel **"Hopscotch"** and the filmscript **"Blow-Up"** will find **"The Winners"** surprisingly conventional in structure.

But the form will prove deceptive; upon closer reading, **"The Winners"** is a masterly novel of ideas, sparkling with vivid satire on chance and the mortal games of human imposture.

A group of lottery-prize winners is on a celebratory cruise that has been planned by the state. . . .

No sooner has the ship put out to sea than something seems wrong. No one will reveal the ship's destination; the stern is declared off limits. A sense of dark menace and gloom pervades the winners.

Suspicion that the ship is contaminated with a plague induces divisions among the passengers. . . .

Finally a confrontation ensues between the passengers and crew. Characterizations deepen into extravagant portraits of humanity; isolated and fearful, each character seems to be acting haphazardly to achieve singular goals.

Plans are made to break through to the stern of the Malcolm in defiance of the crew. Who will discover the secret? The stern becomes a forbidden challenge, a symbol of repressive authority; one by one the characters find in it a vision of their past and a clue to their destination. In relationships born of desperation, the travelers achieve a special kind of communion.

**"The Winners"** is a powerful allegory, both comic and lyrical in the tradition of Latin American social realism. Characterizations are so numerous they are sometimes bewildering, but then character is less important here than fate.

As Cortázar once explained in an interview, **"The Winners"** is not (despite what it achieves) meant to be an allegory, but "an exercise in style." It is also a remarkable novel.

*Carl Senna, "Julio Cortázar's Vivid Satire on Chance," in* The Christian Science Monitor, *July 17, 1984, p. 24.*

**JIM MILLER**

[*A Certain Lucas*] consists of fragments grouped into three parts. Parts I and III concern Lucas, an aging Argentine writer exiled in Paris, living on memories and fantasies. Dreaming of himself as Heracles and Hydra rolled into one, Lucas imagines defeating his own monstrous habits, cutting off "the head that collects records" or "the one that invariably lays his pipe down on the left-hand side of the desk." . . .

In part II, Cortázar—or is it Lucas?—illustrates this "dialectical encounter" with a miscellany of parodies, whimsies and paradoxes. . . .

Coy and hermetic, Cortázar's prose is laced with labyrinthine run-on sentences and clotted with bizarre polysyllabic terms. Yet "even in his most delirious inventions," as Lucas puts it, "there's something so simple, so little bird, and so gin rummy. It's not a matter of writing for others but for oneself." The book sometimes seems tricked-up, yet the final effect is curiously touching, particularly when Lucas, in one of two scenes set in a hospital, comes face to face with "the other, the unknown, the disguised reality." It "leaps like a toad into the middle of his face."

*Jim Miller, "Delirium Tremens," in* Newsweek, *Vol. CVI, No. 12, September 17, 1984, p. 82.*

# William Empson

## 1906-1984

**English critic, poet, and editor.**

Best known for *Seven Types of Ambiguity* (1930), his seminal contribution to the formalist school of New Criticism, Empson is also highly regarded for his other critical works and his poetry. Empson wrote *Seven Types of Ambiguity* as well as the majority of his poems while he was a student at Cambridge University in the late 1920s, where he began as a mathematics student and later studied English under the distinguished critic I. A. Richards. Much of Empson's work reflects the influence of Richards and the atmosphere at Cambridge during this time: scientific thought and theory strongly influenced the arts; literature emphasized complex, rational techniques and themes; and critical approaches were likewise based on the belief that literature could be analyzed using formal, objective criteria derived from the scientific method. Empson's criticism is thus characterized by close textual analysis which focuses on the ambiguities of poetic diction, and his poetry is noted for its precision of style and form.

Empson's poetic output was small, totaling sixty-three poems collected in three main volumes: *Poems* (1935), *The Gathering Storm* (1940), and *Collected Poems* (1949; revised, 1955). While Empson's highly logical, intellectual manner was faulted by some critics and discouraged a large readership, his poetry has elicited significant praise. Richard Eberhart has declared, "for perfection of form, precision of statement, and delight of language, some of Empson's early poems will last as long as any of those of his contemporaries." Empson's poems often present an argument and follow it through its various complexities. This tendency to "argufy" has led many critics to link Empson with the seventeenth-century "metaphysical" poets. In his essay "Ambiguous Gifts," which helped renew interest in Empson's poetry in the 1950s, John Wain maintains that Empson's lines "seem to me a miraculous blend of the colloquial immediacy of Donne and the immense weight of Hopkins; and in the middle of a quiet, meditative poem he will suddenly introduce lines of an enormous Marlovian grandeur."

Empson's critical theory is based on the assumption that all great poetic works are ambiguous and that this ambiguity can often be traced to the multiple meanings of words. Empson analyzes a text by enumerating and discussing these various meanings and examining how they fit together to communicate the poem's ideas and emotions. His method of "puzzling" a poem has been widely attacked as well as praised. While Empson is almost unanimously respected for his intelligence, ingenuity, and exhaustive readings of a text, he has been faulted for the limitations of his approach. Elder Olson charges that Empson "confuses the diction with the poem." Citing the importance of a reader's emotional response, Olson states: "Where no such impression of humanity is engaged, we remain largely indifferent in the face of the finest diction." He thus faults Empson's criticism on the grounds that "what he misses entirely is the governance of metaphor by thought, of thought by character, or character by action" and concludes that "what is missing is the nature of poetry." Likewise, John Crowe Ransom, while claiming that "every critic would be

*Photograph by Mark Gerson*

well advised to own and read his Empson, in order to humble, and then to quicken, his own wit," also maintains that Empson can "overread" a poem. Citing as an example Empson's analysis of Andrew Marvell's "The Garden," Ransom points out that this "is a merry and witty poem," yet Empson's approach is highly serious, and to "direct the formidable apparatus upon a 'metaphysical' poem is to miss it." However, despite such charges, few have contested the significance of Empson's contribution to formalist criticism. His critical works, in addition to *Seven Types of Ambiguity*, are *Some Versions of Pastoral* (1935), *The Structure of Complex Words* (1951), *Milton's God* (1961), and *Using Biography* (1984).

(See also *CLC*, Vols. 3, 8, 19; *Contemporary Authors*, Vols. 17-20, rev. ed., Vol. 112 [obituary]; and *Dictionary of Literary Biography*, Vol. 20.)

## M. C. BRADBROOK

To estimate the importance of Mr. Empson's criticism is difficult for several reasons: because *Seven Types of Ambiguity* provides a demonstration of method and a test of critical intelligence which it is not simple to view with detachment; and because there is an uneasy suspicion lest the dissecting knife should have been supplied or at least sharpened, by the reading of Mr. Empson's own work. It is not comfortable to be a self-conscious Scythian.

Mr. Empson's criticism may be conveniently if arbitrarily considered with regard first to its results and then to its technique. The obvious brilliance of *Seven Types of Ambiguity* lies in the closeness of the work, the 'niggling' for which Mr. Empson apologised. Any pure literary criticism, unadulterated with the anecdotal, the historic or the pseudo-philosophic dilutions which temper the Pierean spring to the consistency of the river Fleet will appear 'difficult' and 'pedantic.' Mr. Empson's demands for specialized knowledge and interest are no more than every literary critic has the right to assume in his readers. The result is that *Seven Types of Ambiguity* provides three hundred pages of literary criticism and hardly a page of anything else: an achievement to justify some applause in these pursy times. Where it is simply a question of intellectual closeness and keenness Mr. Empson can hardly ever be caught out.

Secondly, his work has, as has been said, unusual fertilizing power. His methods can be adapted to deal with quite different problems from those he has chosen to tackle, and can be 'crossed' with those of other literary critics: in short the book's educating function is invaluable, and is perhaps an even rarer quality.

These are methods rather than results, and in fact if one were to adopt Mr. Empson's division between analytic and appreciative criticism, 'showing the modes of action of poetic effect' and 'producing a literary effect similar to the one you wish to isolate from the passage, both to show which particular one you mean and to convince the reader you know what you are talking about' it would be noticed how much more adequate and fully stressed is the former function. To a question of analysis and elucidation Mr. Empson will be all alive, but there is little attempt in his book to evaluate the experience analysed and presented.

Sympathy is apparently enough. (pp. 253-54)

[But] there is obviously a third factor. It is not enough to analyse dispassionately and enjoy sympathetically, there must be a simultaneous act of judgment. 'No poet, no artist of any art has his complete meaning alone. His significance, his appreciation is the appreciation of his relation to the dead poets and artists and also the relationship of the experience of the poetry to all the past experience, the total personality of the reader. This testing is the binding force between the cognitive-affective aspects: indeed, if Mr. Empson is using appreciative in the exact and not the popular meaning it is included in that term: yet his definition gives not a hint of any but the affective element, and in point of fact there are very few judgments of comparative values in *Seven Types of Ambiguity,* and scarcely one where response and judgment are fused.

Without this erective factor, the work of the critic will split into the exercise of intellectual ingenuity and the gusto of emotional stimulation. Though Mr. Empson declares that both elements are necessary, his very suggestion that they can be given separately (first the analysis, then the feeling) is a little suspect. It indicates why his best work is more apt to produce a feeling of assent, 'That's good; I agree to that' rather than a feeling of identification 'That's right; that is it' such as the best work of Mr. Eliot produces.

Because Mr. Empson is pre-occupied with analysis, the scope of his work is considerably curtailed. *Seven Types of Ambiguity* is not a survey of the whole of English poetry but of the rise and decline of Wit. It has high lights; the treatment of Donne,

Shakespeare, the Metaphysicals, Pope: but the width of reference is really illusory: there is no mention of Blake or Hardy, hardly any of the later eighteenth century, Wordsworth or Coleridge. (pp. 254-55)

Mr. Empson might reply that he had no intention of considering the whole of English literature; but those curious little trimmings of Egyptian semantics and Chaucerian red herrings indicate that he did not deliberately limit the field, nor was he exactly conscious of the architectonics of his work. . . .

His intellectual ingenuity can be seen working in dissociation from his sensibility in those passages where he forces an ambiguity regardless of the odds. For example, his interpretation of 'the untented woundings of a father's curse' . . . is unbalanced by the fact that *untented* was a common word medically and almost unheard of as *roofless* so that instead of a pair of alternatives he is presenting a very close shot and a very long one. (p. 255)

Mr. Empson drives a very frisky pen. Sometimes his facetiousness is embarrassing. . . . It can be felt most strongly in his analysis of . . . [a] passage from *Tintern Abbey*. . . . The sense of when to sneer is difficult to cultivate; but to sneer at Wordsworth at least should be classed with literary Hitlerisms. . . .

At the end of his analysis Mr. Empson adds 'I must protest that I enjoy these lines very much.' But since he has completely condemned them intellectually, one must assume that by a detached act of sympathy or gusto he blots out all his objections. The quality of Mr. Empson's gusto may be sampled from his comment on Sidney's sestines . . . 'This form has no direction or momentum: it beats, however rich its orchestration, with a wailing and immovable monotony for ever upon the same doors in vain.' . . . (p. 256)

In short, Mr. Empson's intellectual analysis and his emotional stimulation are each apt to get dissociated and out of focus. This can be seen very plainly in his article on Marvell which appeared in a recent number of *Scrutiny*. To state one's objections would be a lengthy business, but it may be suggested that *The Garden* is more than the sum of its parts, that simple addition and analysis will not work, that Mr. Empson has overstressed the sexual themes and neglected the others (*e.g.* the equally important one of the double metamorphosis of time and the individual, which he only touched) and above all that he has mistaken Marvell's tone for something a little too jaunty and smug, too like the early Donne. Mr. Empson's acute intelligence and natural exuberance can be seen operating here, but not that third factor which has been desiderated, and which his criticism seems to lack: judgment, a sense of relative values without which criticism is no more than a game for the intelligent and an emotional showerbath. Mr. Empson's criticism is of the very first importance in 'showing how a properly qualified mind works when it reads poetry, showing how those properly qualified minds have worked which have not at all understood their own working,' but something more than the working of a properly qualified mind and the expression of a lively sensibility goes to the making of a great critic. (p. 257)

*M. C. Bradbrook, "The Criticism of William Empson," in* Scrutiny, *Vol. II, No. 3, December, 1933, pp. 253-57.*

## JOHN CROWE RANSOM

Mr. William Empson is one of the closest living readers of poetry. He is willing to work harder than other readers to elicit the whole poetic experience from the text. But the impression one takes away from one of his exciting expositions may be that the poet and his expositor have collaborated in order to offer the biggest poetic experience possible; the impression supporting a suspicion that Mr. Empson has wanted to help out the poet, putting his own resources at the poet's service and making the poem bigger than the poet really dared to intend. (p. 322)

But we had better not dismiss the Empson commentaries as easily as that. The ordinary critic cannot read them and be the same critic again, and that in itself is not an inconsiderable advantage. Every critic would be well advised to own and read his Empson, in order to humble, and then to quicken, his own wit, and to avoid the dismal contingency that he may sometimes read with a dull wit that which is subtle, and stultify it. Besides, it is significant that Mr. Empson's writings win more agreement on the second reading than on the first; and win still more on the third.

I suspect there will generally remain in Mr. Empson's commentaries a residue from which we will withhold our consent. So far as I have tried them, the fourth and fifth readings do not help much.

For my part I approach Mr. Empson's critical work with admiration, and also with caution, because I do not wish to compete with so much learning, taste, and ingenuity. I hesitate only over his sense of proportion, and I mean by that, his sense of poetic occasion. But perhaps it should be said in justice that he seems to recognize two separate situations with respect to the poet-expositor relation.

The first occurs when Mr. Empson tells us what the poem means to him, and judges that it meant all that to the poet. In most cases, it is certain that other critics will find the poet's meaning not so complex as he represents it. Mr. Empson may urge in modesty that poets, or at least many of them, have had just as ingenious meanings in their heads as he has, and just as many at the same moment. The other critics will probably answer by denying it, which is a soft impeachment of Mr. Empson; or they may argue that poets give out what meanings they please, but do not ordinarily take pains to hide them, and do not conceive of poems as charades, or marvels of ratiocination.

The second situation occurs when the poet has not been conscious of all the meanings discovered by the critic for the excellent reason that some of them came out of his unconscious mind; they would not necessarily be for that less willed than the others, nor less important. (This much of their thesis the Freudians have seen carried overwhelmingly.) But here too Mr. Empson will have an argument on his hands, for we know from experience how the Freudians and the less imaginative persons can quarrel as to when a subterranean significance attaches to words and acts that think they are innocent. I must remark in passing that Mr. Empson's kinds of unconscious meaning are generally more comprehensive and therefore more sober than the lurid Freudian ones.

It is in this second situation, as I understand Mr. Empson, that he regards his critical elucidation as following a "psychological" method; though I believe he has not made the distinction systematically. The word turns up in his essay on Milton. He fears that it may be offensive, since it seems to imply that "Milton wrote in a muddle without knowing his own mind." He offers his feeling that Milton generally understood what he

was doing, though there really are places "where there is a muddle whose effect is unsatisfying."

Perhaps the critical method that applies in the other sort of situation, where the poetic effects were fully intended, might rate as "logical." The poem is satisfying if all its effects are logical; which would mean that they are objective, and public or universal, since all men are rational.

And surely there must be effects apparent to certain qualified readers which were concealed from the poet by the disorder in his own mind, the feud between its conscious and unconscious levels. These are effects which would seem to invite the attentions of the subtlest critic, who in Mr. Empson's view would be the psychologist. For some years we have been hearing about what psychology is going to do for the study of poetry. Mr. Empson's performance is far the finest fruit this tree has yet borne us. Yet I would remark that it is not psychology in its technical or formal aspect that gives us Mr. Empson's kind of criticism. What we have is the reading of the poet's muddled mind by some later, freer, and more self-conscious mind. Perhaps this is the definition of the mind of a Doctor of Psychology who has built up a "general practice," but it equally looks like a good version of the well-schooled literary mind.

Logical or psychological, indifferently, Mr. Empson's interpretations increase immensely the range of the experience, and therefore the density of the lines, beyond what the ordinary reader finds of these elements in the poem. Another way of putting it: he wants the language of poetry to bear a heavier burden than other readers think it can bear. He almost makes of poetry a cryptogram. But on the whole it may be a healthier policy to overestimate and strain the art's capacity for revelation than not to tax it at all. If I reproach his extravagances, I do not like the risk I run of giving comfort to the commonplace critic who likes to reduce the meaning of poetry to fit into his own cozy little apartment.

The essay on the Alices (of the Wonderland and the Looking-glass) is as admirable as it is subtle. For the first time we have this job completely done, so that it will not need to be done again. We may appropriate as much as we like of the detail of this comprehensive interpretation, and leave the rest; enough is there to furnish the most ambitious expositor. Here was a literary puzzle requiring a man of exactly Mr. Empson's attainments. The Alice books are deliberate nonsense, but with emphasis on the deliberate; we could not read them if they did not cover up a sense, and they exercise their fascination upon us—if they really do—in that we actually obtain from them a confused secret sense which is fascinating because it feels important, and hideous. It is evidently Mr. Empson's understanding that some of the sense was conscious in Carroll's mind, and some was unconscious, so that he can employ both logic and psychology. The psychology runs far beyond the Freudian analysis.

Not much behind this one in effectiveness, and likely to be of telling importance, I would rate the essay on the *Paradise Lost,* though I would have some qualification. His tone is as respectful to Milton as the pious reader ought to require. His occasion is the reading of Bentley's Eighteenth Century notes on the work, and Bentley is on the whole commended for his sharp eyes. Bentley was properly open-minded, perfectionist, and intensive, therefore distinguished among all Milton's critics. There have really been few intensive critics of Milton, and it is no wonder this has been true since Bentley, because an odium came to rest upon his honest and blunt performance which frightened the critics. Mr. Empson is of course more intensive than Bentley, and much more imaginative. Too imaginative sometimes. . . . (pp. 322-25)

The essay on Marvell's poem *The Garden* is the most extreme example of what I regard as Mr. Empson's almost inveterate habit of over-reading poetry. It is a charming piece, of the school called "metaphysical," and a little more elaborate than Marvell's other poems. The sixth of its nine stanzas has been picked up by many readers of our generation as a passage with a strangely modern note. . . . The last couplet [of this stanza] contains the apparent modernism, which is located principally in the phrase "green Thought." . . . I find it hard to tell whether a phrase so startling is usual, or generic, in the metaphysical poetry; I think not, though it might be a frequent kind of thing in our own poetry since the Symbolists appeared in French, and Mr. Eliot and others in English. But I think at any rate we do well just to observe it and let it pass, rather than build it into some big system of knowledge to load upon the consciousness of Marvell, who was merely a poet. It is as if Marvell had [meant]. . . that the mind finds every possible type of existence in the miniature complexity of the garden, which becomes a microcosm. . . . (pp. 331-32)

But for Mr. Empson such a paraphrase is not sufficient. It is as if he had prescribed to himself an exercise: Write several thousand words expanding the terms of the sixth stanza. (They are certainly very handsome and taking terms.) The expansion would take place within the locus of Mr. Empson's own ideas, which is a large and fertile area; not within the set of ideas fairly attributable to the poet. Mr. Empson is a solipsistic critic, because he has much to say about anything, and not the strictest conscience about making what he says "correspond" with what the poet says. The idea of the garden as an epitome of everything in the world is translated, as it were, into the idea of a poem as an epitome of everything in Mr. Empson's mind, so that when he once begins to tell what the poem makes him think of he cannot go wrong.

I do not mean to abuse the privileges of an essay, and that is why I will not try to indicate the philosophical meanings which Mr. Empson reads out of this poem. So intricate, not to say laborious, would be the argument, and so difficult to support it, at least for plain readers like myself, upon the phrases here and there in the poem which have to serve as scaffolding. But my reader may recall it, or he may look it up.

Yet for almost any experienced and grateful reader it is a merry and witty poem, not to be read with the last degree of seriousness. A common historical sort of consideration should have solicited Mr. Empson not to read it in a manner which violated the law of its kind. For what was the idea of those "metaphysical" poems which Donne and Marvell and others gave out so excitingly? It was the genius of this poetry to take an arresting metaphor and work it out in detail, with a great show of logic. (Such a metaphor might be, for instance, "The world is contained in my garden.") The result was fairly startling, but, if you demurred to it, the poet with a tantalizing smile could ask you, on the one hand, if you did not find the original metaphor "natural" enough, if you did not sometimes use it yourself; and, on the other hand, if you did not believe in being systematic. The metaphysical procedure was singularly like the theological, with a rather important difference: the poet was playful, while the theologians were in dead earnest. (pp. 332-33)

Mr. Empson's critical equipment, his deep-sea diving suit, would seem principally to enable his entry into some tortured

and dead-serious kind of poem which intended to be a theology and not a work of art. It would be very good for mining the hidden references in *The Waste Land,* which need, and with ingenuous confidence await, their explications; in Blake, and perhaps in Yeats; in Auden, Spender, and Lewis, if you will; or in any poetry that deals loosely but esoterically in religious symbols. To direct the formidable apparatus upon a "metaphysical" poem is to miss it. (p. 334)

In the matter of literary origins I derive Mr. Empson of course from Mr. I. A. Richards; so I think does the general public, so does Mr. Empson himself. (He wrote the monumental *Seven Types of Ambiguity* for Mr. Richards at Cambridge.) It works something like this. Mr. Richards has advocated a psychological view of poetry in preference to a logical. As an articulate doctrine I suppose he originated it, though it has governed careless critics for a long time (a century at least), and is the doctrine which had to be declared in an age of psychology. It argues that the end of poetry is the "satisfaction" of a subject (the poet, and his beneficiary the reader), and not the affirmation of an object. Under this view a poem might be complete enough, and "satisfactory," though it contained no predication at all; and the poem should be content to exhibit precious objects and blissful situations without making any effort to realize them logically. And under it, as a corollary, would be the view which encouraged in poetry not the single unified meaning but the largest possible multiplicity of meanings; because we enjoy them. Mr. Empson has slipped easily into this corollary view. The "ambiguity" which he has hallmarked as the object of his criticism is generally multiplicity. And the multiple meanings have no special unity except the loose psychological one of being tied up in the same moment of thought; they may be irrelevant to each other, and again they may be inconsistent, and at the worst they may be positively contradictory. (p. 336)

I have the notion that Mr. Richards and Mr. Empson confuse the kinds of psychological effect when they admire all possible complications, all muddles, indiscriminately. The really impressive effect comes, I should think, when the complications support and enforce a central meaning and do not diffuse it or dissolve it. A logical whole may have as much complication really as a muddle; that is, as many and as unique items discoverable in it. In fact it permits complication up to any particular limit, if that is what these psychologists want. The thing that makes a lyrical poem supreme over the other literary forms, and indeed the epitome and standard of literary forms, is its range of content; or, what is the same thing, its density. But the logic of the poem is supposed to control this range, and if it does not the exhibit falls short of a poem. It is the same principle which works in the meter . . . ; if there is no governing pattern to assimilate the sounds, they are but sounds, and wasted; their independence dooms them from engaging in a society, which would be a poetic melody, and they remain in their state of nature, as a prose.

Mr. Empson in the epilogue to his essay on Ambiguity, and everywhere for that matter, displays a perfect willingness to be "reasonable" in the matter of whether we must read the poems as he advises. He thinks of every objection, but it does not seem to affect his practice. And he actually displays an innocence, it seems to me, in several places where he moralizes on the contradictory meanings he finds in a poem. . . . His argument if reduced to simple terms is, I think, that the poem presents the one alternative, and then presents the other; till there they both are, spread out before our eyes in the poem;

so that evidently it is a lie to say that contradictories may not coexist, for they do it in poetry, though nowhere else; which makes poetry superior, and indeed supreme, among all human experiences. In these terms the idea does not deserve refutation. And under the name of "resolution" its case is hardly any better, for what is resolution? Mr. Empson likes to show a poet clinging to both his alternatives, as if from some eminence which exempts him from having to choose between them. But if the poet does not choose, his poem simply does not advance to the stage of logic and truth. I should like to see Mr. Empson's comment on the *Ode on a Grecian Urn*. It appears to me to be an exercise trying to see if a work of art can really evade the logic of alternatives. It does not so much ask, Whether the pleasure of anticipation is greater than the pleasure of realization, as it declares, Here is a way not to have to decide between them. It catches the act at a point half-way between, fixes it in the immortal verse, and gloats over its superiority this way to the mortal and consummated act. But there can be no "truth" to such "beauty." (The identification of these entities is just about what Mr. Richards has come to as an aesthetician.) Our liking for the poem, or our disliking, depends on whether we decide that its tone is playful, in a charming, melancholy way, or is serious. If the latter, the poem is not more lovely than an ineptitude can be, and that is not entirely the construction I prefer to give it. (pp. 337-38)

John Crowe Ransom, "Mr. Empson's Muddles," in *The Southern Review*, Vol. IV, No. 2, Autumn, 1938, pp. 322-39.

## JOHN WAIN

[*The essay from which this excerpt is taken was originally written in 1949 as "Ambiguous Gifts: Notes on a Twentieth-Century Poet" for publication in* Penguin New Writing.]

In an age when nine out of ten people who bother about literature do so because they are drawing a salary for it, it may well be that criticism will be read and remembered while poetry is forgotten, for criticism breeds fresh criticism more easily than poetry breeds fresh poetry; but in Empson's case it would be a pity if he were known simply as the 'ambiguity' man, and not as a poet. Of course it is the penalty of silence—he has published nothing in verse since *The Gathering Storm* in 1940—and in these scribbling days, out of print is out of mind. The position is made all the more difficult by the fact that Empson, as poet no less than as critic, has very firm local associations, and that these associations have themselves ceased to count for much. He was always placed, rightly or wrongly, as a product of the Cambridge English school: certainly the influence of Richards is very evident in *Seven Types*. . . . [When] a writer begins his career by closely identifying himself with one particular movement, he is likely to be left high and dry when that movement has spent itself. This is true to some extent of all the poets who were breaking new ground in the 'thirties; the conditions (social, political, and literary) which did so much to form their characteristics, have vanished, leaving them without any source of nourishment, and a little beyond the age at which it is possible to make a major adjustment. It is true that Messrs. Spender, Auden, Day Lewis, and MacNeice are still more or less firmly in possession of the public ear, but that is really due to the mediocrity of the younger poetic generation; they are likely to stay in fashion, however little they have to say, simply because their juniors have even less. Still, it is depressing to see poets carrying on from sheer force of habit, and one of the reassuring things about Empson is that, having

produced two very remarkable volumes of verse before the rot set in, he has since had the wisdom to hold his peace, even though this means being described in American reviews as 'British critic'. (pp. 169-70)

The trouble with the 'thirties, as a literary epoch, is that they happened a long time ago. . . . It is thus an act of the historical imagination to discuss such matters as the storm that blew up over the use, in verse, of the names of machinery and other 'anti-poetic' material. . . . All one can say at this distance of time is the obvious thing, that it is useful, like any other material, when it is properly assimilated, and not lugged along in the form of compulsory equipment. Many ludicrous failures could be listed, but they are usually cases where such imagery was slapped on with a trowel. . . . Empson [when he uses such imagery] never jars. . . . He places concrete for abstract in a way that, even in its least exciting passages, is recognizable as English poetry. . . . What is more, when he introduces scientific or mechanical imagery, he does so because it has a genuine function in the poem; whereas Auden, for instance, is clever at placing such imagery at the fringe of the poem, where it can do small harm and little good. (pp. 170-71)

But this question is really part of a bigger one, into which we must go more fully. How far ought scientific ideas to be incorporated into poetry? Poets, from Wordsworth on, have been better at talking about the relevance of science than actually doing anything about it, and this seems to be one of the ways in which Empson has made a real advance. It is worth noticing that in both prose and verse his mind flies to the scientific for analogy and metaphor. In his prose it is merely irritating. *Seven Types* is not really impregnated with the scientific spirit, despite its title; it is a collection of *aperçus* based on a method of analysis inaugurated by Riding and Graves in *Survey of Modernist Poetry*. But the reek of the laboratory was so strong in the author's nostrils as he wrote that we have to endure a barrage of not very illuminating asides like 'Here as in recent atomic physics there is a shift in progress' or 'having fixed the reaction, properly stained, on a slide, they must be able to turn the microscope on it with a certain indifference and without smudging it with their fingers'. . . . At all events this is probably not a mere affectation, since Empson started as a mathematician and probably knows a certain amount of science as well; but in the attempt to bring scientific ideas into poetry, it is not enough to know what you are talking about. . . . [It] is useless merely to *describe* in verse the things of which science tells us, while to introduce them in the form of simile and metaphor when the poem is really about something quite non-scientific is not much better. The only way to treat such material is to form it into a series of conceits on which the general meaning of the poem can be made to turn. This was Donne's way, and it is Empson's. In *The World's End* he uses the perfectly straightforward idea that, since space is 'curved', there is no such thing as the end of the world; you are always beginning your journey afresh, and so the world is a more oppressive prison than you ever suspected. (pp.172-73)

In the same way *Arachne* is not really about either soap-tension, or molecular structure, or the habits of water-spiders. These things are pivots on which a tragically sardonic love-poem is made to turn; the whole thing is a triumphant *tour de force*. . . . (p. 173)

Another distant echo from the past is the question of 'obscurity'. . . . As regards prose, where obscurity really is intolerable, Cyril Connolly's remark seems all that is required: 'A writer who thinks himself cleverer than his readers will write simply, one who is afraid they are cleverer than he, will make use of mystification; good style is arrived at when the language chosen represents what the author requires of it without shyness.' As regards verse, the issue is not so simple. . . . It is harder to produce an accurate statement than a careless rapture, harder still to combine the two, yet poetry *is* this combination. Tired of it though we all are, the question of 'obscurity' forces itself on our attention in discussing a poet whose blurb describes him as 'the most brilliantly obscure of modern poets': unfortunately Empson's own statement on the subject is itself of uncertain significance. In his Note on the Notes to *The Gathering Storm* he says, 'partly they are meant to be like answers to a crossword puzzle; a sort of puzzle interest is part of the pleasure you are meant to get from the verse, and that I get myself when I go back to it.' Obviously this is not wholly serious . . . , but neither is a good enough joke to be that and nothing more. One has to take Empson's remark about puzzles at least partly in good faith, because it really represents a feature of his mind; a 'puzzle interest' is evidently part of the pleasure he gets from all poetry. . . . Indeed, his two books of criticism are valuable chiefly as a very telling attack on the idea that we understand what we read. (pp. 173-75)

Empson has often been called 'metaphysical'. . . . (p. 177)

During the last twenty-five years the seventeenth century has been much in the air, and apologists for 'modern' poetry have found the appeal to Donne and the late Shakespeare a very useful weapon (we are not forced, like the French, to choose finally between the present and the past in our poetic theory). Yet, while it is legitimate to defend intellectualized and elliptical poetry by calling on the 'metaphysicals', the theory is, after all, propaganda, and must be modified when the shouting has died down. This, evidently, is not yet: in 1948 English reviewers could still hail Cleanth Brooks's ten-year-old *Modern Poetry and the Tradition,* which argues along these lines, as if it were the last word on its subject. How much twentieth-century poetry, examined in cold blood, really resembles Donne or Marvell? I should say that only John Crowe Ransom, Robert Graves since 1926, and possibly the early dandified Eliot, ever consistently recalled the metaphysical way of setting about poetry. Whether the theory about 'dissociation of sensibility' is true or not, that particular blend of thinking and feeling has been very rare since 1700, and the claim that it has been revived in our own time does not bear much examination: Auden, for instance, has not been blending them at all, but slipping from one to the other—hence the utter lack of repose and certainty even in his best work. For the rest, there are a few traces of Donne, but generally through one of the conventional intermediaries—Hopkins, Browning, Eliot himself—and there the matter rests. So that, historically speaking, the renascence of (in any precise sense of the word) 'metaphysical' poetry boils down to a few poems by a few poets.

Empson, however, is one of these poets. It is not easy to define metaphysical poetry, but obviously there are two features which distinguish it at once—a kind of general modernity which leads poets to bring in current ideas and current language, and a strong, at times almost perverse, desire to follow the argument wherever it leads the poem. Donne's poetry has no more 'conceits' in it than anyone else's, but the conceits are taken seriously and allowed to lead the poem from one point to another. It is this trait which links Empson most firmly to the seventeenth century. (pp. 177-78)

[It] would be impossible to assess Empson's achievement without some reference to the slow, heavy fulness of his lines; they

seem to me a miraculous blend of the colloquial immediacy of Donne and the immense weight of Hopkins; and in the middle of a quiet, meditative poem he will suddenly introduce lines of an enormous Marlovian grandeur. . . . (p. 179)

Of course no landscape is made up entirely of peaks; Empson has published, even in his small output, a number of pieces that are too slight to be worth sustained attention—*Just a Smack at Auden* and *Your Teeth are Ivory Towers* would be good if made up extempore at a party. . . . At the other end of the scale is the over-elaboration of a poem like *Bacchus,* which requires six pages of notes ('A mythological chemical operation to distil drink is going on in the first four verses') and seems hardly worth the fuss. But he has, after all, written at least a dozen poems which pass every known test of greatness: and who has done more?

Whether Empson will ever write any more poetry is not my business. If he does, it will be interesting to see whether the landslide in English literary taste has left us with a public capable of appreciating him. For the plain fact is that many of the reputations which today occupy the poetic limelight are such as would crumble immediately if poetry such as Empson's, with its passion, logic, and formal beauty, were to become widely known. If the day ever comes when poems like *This Last Pain, To an Old Lady, Manchouli, Note on Local Flora,* are read and pondered, and their lessons heeded, it will be a sad day for many of our punch-drunk random 'romantic' scribblers. But I suppose it never will. (pp. 179-80)

> *John Wain, "Three Contemporary Poets: Ambiguous Gifts, Notes on the Poetry of William Empson," in his* Preliminary Essays, *St. Martin's Press, 1957, pp. 169-80.*

### ELDER OLSON

[*The essay from which this excerpt is taken was originally published in* Modern Philology, *May 1950.*]

The last quarter of a century has seen the rise, in England and America, of a new critical movement. Its mere longevity would perhaps entitle it to some importance in the eyes of future literary historians; but that importance is guaranteed and augmented by the esteem which it has won and by the distinction and persistent fame of the persons who are regarded as its chief practitioners. The "new criticism," as this movement is called by both its friends and its foes, seems to be almost universally regarded as having at last brought literary study to a condition rivaling that of the sciences. . . .

Mr. William Empson is among the principal exponents of this movement, and it might almost be said that where he is mentioned, it is mentioned, and where it is, he is. Nor is this extraordinary; in certain respects it can be said that he has produced it, and it, him. His prestige, briefly, is enormous; his theories, never too vigorously assailed, have gained wider acceptance with the years, and his particular interpretations of texts are regarded as pretty nearly exhaustive and definitive. (p. 24)

For Empson, as for his master I. A. Richards, poetry is simply an aspect or condition of language; it is therefore definable in terms of its medium; it is language differentiated from other language by a certain attribute. Richards first proposed that this distinguishing feature was ambiguity, and occupied himself with exhibiting the complexities of response which ambiguity engenders; Empson has followed by enumerating seven kinds of ambiguity.

The term "ambiguity" here does not carry its usual meaning. Ambiguity as Empson conceives it is not the mere possession of double meaning. . . . Nor is ambiguity simply concision, nor the quality of language which produces mixed emotions; it is, rather, "any verbal nuance, however slight, which gives room for alternative reactions to the same piece of language." The important point here is that of alternative reactions; Empson illustrates his meaning by remarking that a child might view the sentence "The brown cat sat on the red mat" as part of a fairy story or as an excerpt from *Reading without Tears*.

The ambiguities are types of "logical disorder," arranged as stages of advancing disorder, or, what is apparently the same thing, "in order of increasing distance from simple statement and logical exposition." The seven types, then, are kinds in which (1) "a detail is effective in several ways at once"; (2) "two or more alternative meanings are fully resolved into one"; (3) "two apparently unconnected meanings are given simultaneously"; (4) "alternative meanings combine to make a complicated state of mind in the author"; (5) "a fortunate confusion" is present, "as when the author is discovering his idea in the act of writing or not holding it all in his mind at once"; (6) "what is said is contradictory or irrelevant and the reader is forced to invent interpretations"; and (7) "full contradiction" is present, "marking a division in the author's mind." (p. 25)

The broad theory underlying Empson's method seems to be as follows: Poetry uses language, and language is meaningful and communicative; hence poetry is communicative. In analyzing communication, there are three possibilities: one may speak about what happened in the author's mind, about what is likely to happen in the reader's mind, or "about both parties at once," as involved in the communication itself. The first two kinds of discussion, according to Empson, make the claim of knowing too much; "the rules as to what is conveyable are so much more mysterious even than the rules governing the effects of ambiguity" that the third possibility is best. Hence in the main he talks about the third, although he is by no means, he says, "puristic" about this. Apparently the poet communicates ideas, like everyone else, and the reader is affected by these ideas according to their kind; the poet, however, would seem to be a poet, not in virtue of the emotional quality of his ideas, but in virtue of the devices of ambiguity which he consciously or unconsciously employs. Moreover, the effects *proper* to poetry are not the emotions evoked by the ideas; rather, since ambiguity is the essence of poetry, the process of reading is a process of "inventing reasons" why certain elements should have been selected for a poem . . . and the peculiar pleasure derived from poetry is produced by the mental activity in response to these ambiguities. It is, to use Empson's own word, a pleasure of "puzzling," apparently different from the pleasure afforded by riddles, charades, and anagrams in that these latter involve matters emotionally indifferent.

The method of interpretation which rests upon this theory is, as we might expect, one reducing all poetic considerations to considerations of poetic diction, and one reducing all discussion of diction, even, to problems of ambiguities. The method might be described as the permutation and combination of all the various "meanings" of the parts of a given discourse, whether these parts be simple or complex; out of the mass of "meanings" so found, Empson selects those which "give room for alternative reactions," i.e., which satisfy the fundamental con-

dition of ambiguity. The instrument by which he detects the possible meanings of words is the *Oxford English Dictionary;* although it is seldom mentioned by name, its presence everywhere is neither invisible nor subtle. Its lengthy lists of meanings seem to have impressed no one so much as Empson. Apparently he reasons that, since poetry is language highly charged with meaning, the poetic word must invariably stagger under the full weight of its dictionary significances. Since the mass of significances achieved by permutation and combination is often very great, and since ambiguity is so extensive a principle of selection, the discovery of the main meaning or meanings of a passage often becomes for Empson an embarrassing matter. At such points he invokes the aid of rather general and often highly dubious historical, ethical, and psychological propositions about the poet and the audience. I suspect that such propositions are mainly conveniences for him; he does not, at any rate, worry too greatly when he finds them false.

The resulting interpretation is not always . . . prettily fanciful . . . ; fanciful it is always, indeed, but the method of "permutation and combination," as I have called it, is a mechanical method, and it is capable of all the mindless brutality of a machine. (pp. 26-7)

[Empson's treatment of a famous speech by Macbeth] is a wrenching of a text if I ever saw one; what is worse, it is a wrenching to no rational purpose. The remark about "double syntax" is typical; there is no double syntax in

> If it were done, when 'tis done, 'twere well
> It were done quickly . . . ;

for if you pause at the end of the line, as Empson suggests, you leave an unaccounted-for and absolutely unintelligible residue in the next line; and as a matter of fact you make nonsense, anyway, of the first. In short, the "double syntax" here owes its existence only to the supposition that poetry is necessarily ambiguous.

There are many other marvels of interpretation: at one point Empson not only confuses Macbeth with the witches, but the play itself with *King Lear;* [and] in *Hamlet*, the line "In the dead vast and middle of the night" is made to suggest a personification of Night as one of the terrible women of destiny, on the grounds of possible puns (*vast: waste: waist, middle* of night: *middle* of body). . . . But one of the most common results of Empson's procedure is that poets appear to him unintelligible, or to use his own word, "muddled." For example, Shakespeare's Sonnet XVI, with which I imagine few readers have found difficulty, is "muddled."

These things of course result, as I have said, from the theory of ambiguity; and one would suppose that a principle so ruthlessly applied would be of absolute force, especially since it is the "essence" of poetry. As a matter of fact, Empson is not quite willing to credit it with as much authority as he demands from it. An ambiguity, while it can be "beautiful," is "not satisfying in itself, nor is it, considered on its own, a thing to be attempted; it must in each case arise from, and be justified by, the peculiar requirements of the situation." "On the other hand, it is a thing which the more interesting and valuable situations are more likely to justify." This is an admission, I take it, that ambiguity is not even in Empson's view the *principle* of poetry, since its propriety or impropriety is determined by something else—an unanalyzed thing vaguely called "the situation." Rather, it is a sign, and by no means an infallible sign even for Empson, that an interesting and valuable situation is involved. (The statement even of that much is, by the way, left undefended and unsupported by Empson, although his whole position depends upon it.) And he seems to discuss the sign—ambiguity—rather than the "interesting and valuable situation" of which it is a sign only because the sign is "less mysterious." In short, he appears to be in the position of many of the ancient theorists who sought to discuss the elevated style; the style itself evaded their formulations, but since it predominantly involved certain tropes, the tropes might be analyzed, although, it was recognized, the mere production of tropes would not constitute elevation of style.

Indeed, Empson is really a tropist *manqué,* and the seven types are really tropes, as can be seen from the fact that the regular tropes fall under his divisions; the first type, for instance, includes metaphor and antithesis, and the subclasses are clearly subclasses of tropes. But there are certain important differences between the types of ambiguity and the ancient tropes; the types are not nearly so comprehensive; they do not offer nearly such clear distinctions between figures of language; they are not organized upon nearly so clear a principle; and, what is more crucial, they are not nearly so useful. The main difficulty with the tropes, as they were generally treated, was that, in Samuel Butler's phrase, "All a rhetorician's rules / Teach nothing but to name his tools"; that is, their treatment was not sufficiently functional; but they did offer a precise and exhaustive distinction, at their best, between kinds of grammatical devices. Hence, once a trope has been identified, one is in a position to inquire how it has been used, and thereby arrive ultimately at judgments of value. Empson's types, however, do not even permit the distinction of the device; I fear that only Empson can find instances of them, and even he is sometimes unsure. (pp. 28-30)

[However, he] is pointing to a problem; whatever we may think about his statement and treatment of it, the problem itself undoubtedly exists: what kind of minute and precise discussion of poetic language is requisite in order to make manifest the subtleties of genius and art? His principal difficulty is that contemporary criticism . . . affords no devices by which such a problem can be handled. . . . Possessing no clear or adequate poetic principles, he nevertheless has his intuitions. . . . Recognizing that poetic language can be enormously effective, he supposes that this is due to denseness of meaning; and since denseness of meaning implies ambiguity, one must discuss ambiguity.

It is, indeed, on this topic of meaning, so crucial to his system as well as to that of Richards, that his confusions are least manifest and most serious. Perhaps most serious of all is that between meaning and implication or inference. (pp. 31-2)

The confusion becomes particularly important when Empson is talking of the "meaning" of poetry. For, strictly speaking, a *mimetic* poem, an imitation—and he is mainly concerned with poems of this kind—has no meaning at all. It is a certain kind of product, like a picture, a symphony, or a statue; like an ax, a bed, a chair; it has no more meaning *as a poem* than these have. It is a fact; from that fact we may make inferences, to which we respond emotionally and about which we make judgments; but it means nothing; it is. In short, to speak of the "meaning" of a poem is to confuse meaning with the implication of fact.

Presumably, however, Empson means the diction of the poem when he speaks of poetry. In that case he confuses the diction with the poem, but his question may be very readily answered.

In the broadest sense, what the diction means, precisely, is the poem itself.

The importance of these distinctions, which at first sight may seem pedantic and useless, is that they lead, so far as poetics is concerned, to a distinction—a very important one for the problems in which Empson is interested—between *lexis* and *praxis;* between speech as meaningful and speech as action. What the poetic character says in the mimetic poem is speech and has meaning; his *saying it* is action, an act of persuading, confessing, commanding, informing, torturing, or what not. His diction may be accounted for in grammatical and lexicographical terms; not so his action. And the profundity and complexity in poetry which so much interests Empson is due primarily to action and character, which cannot be handled in grammatical terms, rather than to diction, which can. That profundity is only in a small degree verbal, in the sense that verbal analysis will yield the whole of it; and even then it is very seldom a matter of verbal ambiguity. Shakespeare's profoundest touches are a case in point. "Pray you, undo this button" and "The table's full" are profound, not as meaningful verbal expressions but as actions permitting an extraordinary number of implications, in that they are revelatory of many aspects of character and situation. We shall not explain them by jumbling the dictionary meanings of "button" and "table," but by asking, among other things, why Lear requested the unfastening of a button and why Macbeth thought the table was full. (pp. 33-4)

The theories of Richards and Empson illustrate a tendency, very prevalent among critics who rate diction as important, to rate it as entirely too important. In the order of our coming to know the poem, it is true, the words are all-important; without them we could not know the poem. But when we grasp the structure we see that in the poetic order they are the least important element; they are governed by everything else in the poem. We are in fact far less moved by the words as mere words than we think; we think ourselves moved mainly by them because they are the only visible or audible part of the poem. As soon as we grasp the grammatical meaning of an expression in a mimetic poem, we begin drawing inferences which we scarcely recognize as inferences, because they are just such as we habitually make in life; inferences from the speech as to the character, his situation, his thought, his passion, suddenly set the speaker vividly before us and arouse our emotions in sympathy or antipathy; our humanity is engaged, and it is engaged by humanity. But where we can draw no such inferences, where no such impression of humanity is conveyed, we remain largely indifferent in the face of the finest diction. These inferences, moreover, largely determine our interpretation of the language itself; we recognize a pun or an ambiguity when we see a human reason why the character should deal in puns and ambiguities, and not when the dictionary lists a variety of meanings. (p. 34)

If the words, then, are not what is primarily responsible for the effect, purely verbal interpretation, however essential, will not explain poetry, any more than stringing fine diction together will constitute it. Indeed, even Empson in a manner admits this; for he tells us that ambiguity must be justified by the "situation"; but he makes the fatal error of supposing that, because the situation is not something verbal, it is therefore outside the bounds of poetic consideration. As a consequence of this, he defines the poetic pleasure itself much too loosely; that pleasure is not, as he thinks, a logical pleasure produced by puzzling over the relation between statements; it is a pleasure produced by a play of emotions aroused in us by an exhibition of the actions and fortunes of men. (p. 34-5)

This looseness of treatment might seem to broaden the scope of Empson's inquiry; but it tends rather to restrict. He can conceive of metaphors, for instance, only as comparisons based upon real similarity; the more real likenesses present, the better the metaphor; the better the metaphor, the better the poem. His treatment of "Bare ruined choirs" is an instance. What he misses entirely is the governance of metaphor by thought, of thought by character, or character by action. For a metaphor is not simply a figure of diction in poetry; it is also someone's thinking, significantly, that something resembles something; it is the thought, that is, of a certain character in a certain situation, and it is significant of these things. The best similitudes are not always good metaphors in a given poem, and the best metaphors are not always good similitudes.

In short, something is missing in all this; and what is missing is the nature of poetry. (p. 35)

> Elder Olson, "William Empson, Contemporary Criticism, and Poetic Diction," in Critics and Criticism: Essays in Method, *edited by R. S. Crane, revised edition, The University of Chicago Press, 1957, pp. 24-61.*

## HUGH KENNER

[The Structure of Complex Words is] in intention a systematic treatise, a work meant to issue in a theory of language abstractly defensible, a landmark of speculative linguistics, applicable in numerous critical and pedagogical situations beyond those tackled in exemplification by the ingenious author. Parts of it will interest many sorts of specialists. Critics may pick up one or two terms, lexicographers some excellent stimulus, annotators various insights, semanticists some controversial bones to gnaw. It is difficult to say who will want the whole of it. The book is disappointing, and its disappointingness illuminates . . . the principles behind Mr. Empson's influential career. The lamp by which he hunted for a generalized theory of ambiguity illuminated everything to which he held it; the theory, now found, proves to be rather phosphorescent than enlightening.

Despite the symbolic notation or the tone of the opening pages, the organization of the book isn't particularly rigorous. The uniform and conscientiously arid terminology merely gives the appearance of holding together what are in effect disjunct critical essays written over the past fifteen years. . . . [The] essays, unlike those in *Some Versions of Pastoral* [published in the United States as *English Pastoral Poetry*], aren't particularly engaging apart from the theory whose usefulness they are meant to illustrate. It is not that they are spoiled by the theory; the theory remains the most interesting part of the book. There is no sign that the chapters in question—on the *Essay on Criticism, The Prelude, Paradise Lost,* and four Shakespeare plays—might have been interesting if they had been written differently. What has happened is that Mr. Empson's old exploratory zest in the face of poems and plays has evaporated because he has discovered a shortcut to the answers he sought. He no longer, necktie flying, paces off triangles; he has worked out a table of sines.

What he has actually done is tidy up the concept of Ambiguity, the very vagueness of which lent picaresque zest to the early book. It is characteristic of a new evasiveness about the scope he claims that only in a footnote on p. 103 do we learn that he knows it is old ground that is being ordered, rather than

new ground that is being broken. The old ground was canvassed early in the first chapter of *Ambiguity*:

> Thus a word may have several distinct meanings; several meanings connected with one another; several meanings which need one another to complete their meaning; or several meanings which unite together so that the word means one relation or one process.

A poem calls these components of its complex words into explicit play; what Mr. Empson was doing in *Ambiguity* and *Pastoral* was tracing out the lines of interaction in a passage one at a time:

> . . . the words of the poet will, as a rule, be more justly words, what they represent will be more effectively a unit in the mind, than the more numerous words with which I shall imitate their meaning so as to show how it is conveyed.

For old-style paraphrase, that *bête noir,* the "prose sense", which assumes that words are atoms, he substituted multiple paraphrase, a sort of hedonistic calculus, the assumption behind which is that the word-atom can be split into smaller particles, or that the effect of a piece of verse is like the synthetic colours in a magazine reproduction, resolvable into dots of varying sizes but standard hues. The analyst takes the "effect" for granted; he is interested in showing us how it arises. The technique is not one for arriving at evaluations, nor for enforcing evaluations once arrived at. It simply locks poet, poem, language, and reader inside a "communicative situation" and explores the intricacies of that. Suggestively, Mr. Empson's analogy for the fact that the good reader can get the effect without doing the analysis is "the way some people can do anagrams at a shot, and feel sure the letters all fit." (pp. 137-39)

[In the chapters on specific works of art, the] spectrum of a key word—"honest" in *Othello,* "fool" in *Lear,* "dog" in *Timon,* "sense" in *The Prelude*—is displayed, in part by logical analysis, in part by combing the N.E.D. (which receives repeated sententious homage as "the great work"), in part by etymology, and the results are put into symbolic notation. This lexicographic feat once performed—and no one is going to underrate its impressiveness, in a case like "honest" or "sense"—the various uses of the word are extracted from the text in hand and each is shown to correspond to something in the schema. This will seem like a parody to anyone who has worked through one of these chapters, but it is what the chapters amount to, with the parenthetic insights trimmed off. Mr. Empson tells us all he can in his first deployment of the word; the rest reads like a laborious attempt to convince himself—and us—that the machinery of notation is indeed adequate.

If the chapters are dull, it is because the method is wrong for discussing poetry. Long poems deploy a far more complex weight than Mr. Empson appears to suppose. They can't really be reduced to the intricacies of their key-words—it is a little like discussing a motor car solely in terms of the weight borne by its ball-bearings. As a way of showing off the analytic machinery, however, the method succeeds quite well; the machinery is usually adequate, for the words he picks. These are rather blank words, frequently, like Pope's "wit", great puzzles, which derive most of their body from context and tone. Mr. Empson's symbols depend on his supposition that a complex meaning can be resolved into linked senses plus a blend of attitudes and intentions. . . . Mr. Empson conceives "sense" mathematically. A sense is like a number, atomic and drastically invariable. A word doesn't pull an image into the matrix of discourse. It posits a sense, to be lit obliquely by attitudes. Naturally, the poetic image gives him trouble, as it always has; but he is cannier than he was in *Ambiguity,* and plays down the trouble by careful choice of cases. Of all the words Mr. Empson discusses, the only ones which carry an image are "fool" in *Lear,* which was troublesome enough to yield a rather flat chapter, and "dog" in *Timon,* where the perspective is forced by a preliminary chapter transforming "dog" from an animal into an epithet packed with complex and shifting attitudes. When Timon says to Alcibiades, "I do wish thou wert a dog", Mr. Empson doesn't talk about dogs but about the "logical puzzle" of railing against mankind. He can live with an image if it is really a gesture. If it is not that, it must be a Ricardian "vehicle" for saying something else, and is so discussed under "Metaphor". . . . (p. 140)

Behind this suppressed assumption that words are more the property of speakers than of things, one hears the voice of Humpty Dumpty saying, "When I use a word it means what I want it to—neither more nor less." Mr. Empson's charm has always depended on a sort of Alice-persona: the cool-headed quizzer of semantic monsters, seeking to adequate his understanding to the verdicts of his taste. He comes to poetry with an air of being surrounded by plangent irrationalities which can be shown to be quite orderly at bottom; a characteristic key-word in his earlier books was "absurd". In fact, as he explains in the present book, "What Humpty Dumpty gives is not the 'connotations' but the 'central meaning' and then the reason for the 'connotation'; 'That'll do very well', says Alice, who had the feeling already, as a person of taste, and only wanted the plain sense to fit in." They have to fit in, they have to be shown to be orderly, because the inexplicable has terrors. The motive behind such criticism as is contained in *Seven Types of Ambiguity* is not the enlightenment of the reader but the satisfaction of the author: "The object of life, after all", he tells us late in *Ambiguity,* "is not to understand things, but to maintain one's defences and equilibrium and live as well as one can; it is not only maiden aunts who are placed like this." Hence his usefulness to the sort of academic who does not want poetry to disturb him or change him. Hence the absence of intellectual gymnastics in his second volume of poetry. . . . An equilibrium has been discovered; it consists in contemplating the way your peripheral emotions get entangled with the absurd.

Hence, too, his very curious tastes, and tone, and blindnesses. His real focus of interest has always been Alice's nineteenth century. It is surely no accident that his finest piece of sustained writing is his exegesis of *Alice.* Like Lewis Carroll, he maintains a mathematical self (he started in mathematics at Cambridge) which is always trying to tidy up the decayed fish carried into the kitchen by the "sensitive" self. The analytic machinery is a Carrollean invention, too complex for the uses to which it is suited, like the "Nyctograph" Carroll invented for taking notes in the dark, and tried, naively, to put on sale. We are told in the preface to the revised *Ambiguity* that one of the motives of composition was a desire to get Swinburnean plangencies into stereoscopic focus with rediscovered Wit. Nothing, for Mr. Empson, has happened in poetry since the nineteenth century, except rounder and defter examples of the same thing. Eliot is the only contemporary poet he has tackled, and then only Eliot reverberating amid Victorian submarine darkness: the dressing-table scene in *The Waste Land,* the leaning creatures in *Whispers of Immortality.* He finds *Finnegans*

*Wake* "a gigantic corpse", essentially because you can't tell, in a Joycean compound, which of the meanings is primary: this is the howl of the machine striking granite. (pp. 141-42)

That he pushes discussion of a complex poetic work back into a discussion of writer-audience relations is, though it has a specious validity for drama, fundamentally indicative of Mr. Empson's attitude to poetry in general. His own early poems are full of images derived from exploration of interstellar space, "That network without fish, that mere / Extended idleness, those pointless places". Language is a kind of heliographic signalling, a faint and desperate attempt to stretch filaments from monad to monad. Style is narcissistic, like Alice's poise; a kind of pathetic elegance in manipulating the inconsequential; it is as if a cockroach should wave his feelers with an air. . . . Hence "All styles can come down to noise", and language is a collection of devices whereby we are perpetually well-deceived. (pp. 142-43)

When you are making up your world as you go along there is no safeguard against ingenious exegesis of the null (such as a whole page on a bad distich from a 1913 Cambridge anthology), or against subtleties about pronunciation (*God* "begins at the back of your throat, a profound sound, with which you are intimately connected—'ich'—, and then stretches right across to a point above the teeth, from back to front, from low to high, with a maximum of extension and exaltation"). And the Ricardian tenor-vehicle treatment of metaphor comes in patly because words are a way of saying something else, not of placing an intelligible structure of analogies on the page; at bottom nothing is really intelligible anyway, although almost anything turns out to be explicable.

It is no dispraise to Mr. Empson's ingenuity, energy, and industry to find something in their quality consonant with the poems and passages on which he employs them best; low-pressure entertainments like *The Beggar's Opera,* whose strength consists in a jaunty flexibility of tone; or flyweight acrobats of pathos like Hood; or the more colloquial parts of Pope and Chaucer, continuous with the spectrum of urbane chat; or (in works less conducive to composure) the moments when a character is sententiously weighing his wit against the will of a mistress or his littleness against a universe of murk or tragic machinery or fate; and the point of the analysis is to show how the tumult of language reflects the way the speaker is placed.

The infectious zest of *Ambiguity* was like that of a boy taking watches apart, but it was at least related to a sense of the wonders of watches. Mr. Empson has always taken poetry seriously, though like Alice confronted by vanishing cats he has always maintained in its presence a disconcerting composure; since poetry like everything else was to his supple Carrollean intelligence a trick we conspire to believe in. It is melancholy that in a book from which much of the enthusiasm has retired he is Alice no longer; he has accommodated himself at length to his own image of the Victorian scientist, who was "believed to have discovered a new kind of Roman virtue", and whom the public could always surprise, as Alice did the White Knight, obliviously head down in his suit of armour, hung with bellows and beehives, "patiently labouring at his absurd but fruitful conceptions." (pp. 143-44)

*Hugh Kenner, "Alice in Empsonland," in* The Hudson Review, *Vol. V, No. 1, Spring, 1952, pp. 137-44.*

**KENNETH BURKE**

The underlying structure of Empson's latest book [*Milton's God*], which has the virtues and vices of a protracted pamphlet, might be reduced to the following strands, though the actual exposition is more complex: (1) He builds up a repugnant picture of Milton's God, especially as depicted in *Paradise Lost*; (2) these notions involve him in more sympathetic treatments of Christ, Satan, Adam, Eve and the angels, whether loyal or fallen (sentiments that Empson also extends to Delilah, as portrayed in *Samson Agonistes*); (3) he holds that Milton's God, "wicked" as he is, is much better than the traditional God of the Christians; (4) these considerations involve the author in attacks upon current "neo-Christianizing literary critics"; (5) to round things out, there are some perfervid curses uttered against Christianity in general (a somewhat bloodthirsty diatribe against bloodthirstiness). Here Christianity gets blamed for a lot, and any virtues that persons trained as Christians may possess are likely to be thought of rather as surviving in spite of Christianity.

All told, William Empson, who is best known for his book, *Seven Types of Ambiguity* (later followed by a similarly mercurial book, *The Structure of Complex Words*) and whose book, *Some Versions of Pastoral*, is equally ingenious (it is the book of his that I prefer, along with its imaginatively Marxist twist, though I doubt whether any orthodox Marxist would agree with my description), has chosen this time to exercise in a more "controversial" fashion. And he rises to a pitch of righteous indignation that will either reinforce your own righteous indignation, if you agree with it, or will call forth a contrary kind of righteous indignation, if you as righteously disagree with it. Or, in case you simply enjoy watching a good scrap, these pages should entertain you. They should entertain you particularly if, like this reviewer, you are sick of the dismal gossip-novels that are regularly heralded by spokesmen for the trade as great works of literature. In this case, you will be relieved to see how, whatever the problems of Christian doctrine and of a great blind Christian poet who had wrestled so sturdily with them, the orbit of the damned dingy gossip that currently passes for the ideal of fiction or biography or autobiography is necessarily transcended. You can't talk about a brainy and temperamental poet like Milton without finding that you are automatically involved in livelier matters.

True, I'd flatly assert that Empson does not live up to the requirements of his subject. But, at least, he's free of the gossip racket. Milton inevitably did that for him. And in reading his book, you're in a realm where genuine literary exercising really counts. So, regardless of your righteous indignations, be they pro or con, I'd suggest that when confronting this book you relax and enjoy it. (p. 540)

Empson builds his interpretations, first of all, by relevant quotations from the text. He also employs paraphrases, often deliberately crude, designed to bring out the nature of the tactics. Thus, "God answers the petition of Adam by saying, in effect: 'What d'you want a woman for, hey? *I* don't want a woman.'" He makes effective polemic use of Milton's references to God's "derision." He plays up the fact that one-third of the angels revolted (a rebellion that would suggest the presence of tyrannical conditions in Heaven), and plays down Milton's explanation, according to which they got into a state of disobedience to God through hierarchically *obeying* their immediate superior, Satan. . . . He acts more as a debater than as an analyst in failing to bring out the fact that, in *Paradise Regained*, Milton stresses not Christ's "torture" but Christ's resistance to Satan's temptations. And by his stress upon "torture" rather than upon the sacrificial principle in general, he picturesquely deflects attention from the central relationship between religion and the social order. In sum, Empson is being Impson.

But above all, Empson commits what is surely the unpardonable sin as regards his concern with language: for he almost willfully fails to develop a mature, terministic or "logological" analysis of Milton's theological and poetic problems. This is no place to argue the matter in detail. But one point is obvious from the start: If only by reason of its borrowings from Judaism, the Greeks, the pagan Mediterranean cultures in general, the successive stages of secular Western thought and many other sources besides the "Neolithic," Christianity could not be so efficiently horrendous as Empson would want us to believe. Thus, though my own approach to the terminology of any and all theologies is secular, I have the uneasy feeling that something of the old Puritan fury shows through Empson's rabid brand of secularism. (p. 541)

*Kenneth Burke, "Invective against the Father," in* The Nation, *Vol. 194, No. 24, June 16, 1962, pp. 540-41.*

## GEORGE FRASER

The imagination of a poet seems to me to suffuse Empson's criticism. Nothing surprised me more in T. S. Eliot's posthumously published essay, 'To Criticise the Critic', than his description of Empson as primarily a theoretical critic, whose criticism had no obvious connection with his poetry. There is after all a very striking contrast between the tone, the voice, of Eliot's own criticism, and the tone, the voice of his poetry. Eliot, the publisher, and the public personage, seemed again, on the few occasions when one was privileged to meet him, something different from Eliot the poet or the critic. (p. 53)

Empson, on the other hand, is all of a piece throughout. There is the same directness, bluntness, and lack of assumption or disguise in his writing and in his personal manners. He is what one expects him, from his writings, to be. And I think, in fact, that it is this plain directness of manner that has helped to give him his wide influence. Dr Johnson noted of Donne, Empson's favourite English poet, that though he expresses very difficult thoughts he expresses them in very plain language. . . . [Empson is] an example of something rather rare in modern writing, that wholeness which Yeats called 'unity of being'. I think most, though not all, of the literature of our own time that we think of as typically 'modern' is literature of the divided self.

This may be one reason why Empson, in spite of his very great influence, particularly in the early 1950s, on many younger poets does not genuinely like very much modern poetry very much. . . . Empson has on the whole avoided writing about his contemporaries. . . . He knows, of course, what century he is writing in; he loves, and has written appreciatively about, the Joyce of *Ulysses*. But his great achievement as a critic has lain, I think, in making us read a number of writers, dating from the late sixteenth to the late nineteenth century, *as if* they were our contemporaries.

Eliot's odd observation, cited above, may have been based on the fact that Empson's first fame was won as a critic. (pp. 53-4)

He began, I think, not exactly as a theoretical critic, as Eliot calls him, but, to use an uglier but more precise word, as a methodological one. He was not interested, that is, in theories about what literature is but in new methods of analysing literature: in a sense, the approach was practical or technical, the very opposite of theoretical. (p. 54)

I read *Seven Types of Ambiguity* almost as soon as it came out, when I was about sixteen years old, and the sheer cleverness bowled me over, as I suppose it still bowls over most young readers. I. A. Richards's *Practical Criticism,* published two years earlier, in 1928, had a similar revolutionary effect on receptive young readers, but it has not quite to the same degree *le diable au corps.* (p. 55)

It was impossible, of course, and Empson did not expect one, to keep clear in one's mind when one had closed the book, or even in the course of reading it, which type of ambiguity was which. But *Seven Types* was, and remains, an indispensable primer of close reading.

Richards's *Practical Criticism,* still an indispensable text-book for undergraduates, was primarily concerned with teaching us not to be stupid through laziness or self-complacency, not to project irrelevant obsessions or *idées fixes* of our own into poems, not to rush our fences, not to make up our minds till we have really grasped sense, tone, feeling, and (that much more slippery concept) intention. It was essentially a great text-book about the morality of reading, and perhaps about morality in general. . . . But in so far as he was merely giving technical advice about how to read, Richards, I think, was concerned with making us read poems as wholes, suspending our judgment till we have grasped the whole; if you have grasped a whole, the parts must be the parts that fit into it.

Empson, not always but often in *Seven Types,* was a brilliant reader of *parts* of poems. Temperamentally the opposite of Richards (it is often useful for students to have teachers, as for teachers to have students, temperamentally the opposite of themselves), frank, haughty, rash, the Rupert of debate, but a Rupert who never came but to conquer or to fall. In brilliant wrong-headedness, some of the interpretations in *Seven Types* equal Dr Johnson on Gray's poem about the cat drowned in a bowl of goldfish or on Milton's *Lycidas*: but the wrong-headedness, in Empson's case as in Johnson's, expresses a wonderful quality of mind and spirit, an exultation in the exercise of careless power. Some of the passages, like that on Keats's 'Ode on Melancholy', are still among the most brilliantly exciting short specimens of English criticism and moreover, as in this instance, *right.* (pp. 55-6)

*Some Versions of Pastoral* is, at first sight, an oddly titled book (even more oddly titled in the American edition, *English Pastoral Poetry*). *The Shepherd's Kalendar, Lycidas,* Pope's pastorals, Thomson's *The Seasons,* Goldsmith's *Deserted Village,* Wordsworth's *Michael,* Shelley's *Adonais,* Arnold's *Thyrsis* are among the masterpieces of English pastoral poetry with which it does not deal. The only work it does deal with which its author ironically *called* a pastoral is Gay's 'Newgate Pastoral', *The Beggar's Opera.* But Empson is not merely being whimsical or perverse. Pastoral poetry from the days of Theocritus onwards has not been written by shepherds but about them. Courtiers or men leading a complicated and difficult city life have either romantically idealized the simplicity of rustic existence or, more interestingly, used a simplified picture to express criticisms of their own complex existence, which it might be dangerous to express directly. Both Spenser and Milton, for instance, use pastoral as a vehicle for satirical invective, from a Puritan point of view, against what they regard as the corruptions of church government under the Anglican settlement.

But one of the elements of the pastoral mode in this much wider sense, Empson points out, is that, like the narrower kind of merely verbal ambiguity, this structural mode of translating the complex into the simple, or setting it alongside the simple

for contrast, can express mixed feelings, notably a secret hankering after pagan and primitive ways of feeling that are consciously disapproved. . . . These two books of criticism coincide roughly with Empson's most productive poetic period. *Some Versions of Pastoral* is to me his most satisfying critical book, and in some ways also his most poetic. (pp. 59-60)

Neither of Empson's two post-Second World War critical books, *The Structure of Complex Words* and *Milton's God* (though I think the latter is a very fine book), have meant as much to my middle age as the two earlier critical books meant to my youth. I. A. Richards once said to me that *The Structure of Complex Words* was too much of a palimpsest, embodied too many layers of interest in Empson's thinking at separate times, to be wholly satisfactory. It is, of course, partly an attack on Richards's early theory of a fairly simple division between the referential and the emotive use of language. Roughly, one thing that Empson is saying is that words move us very largely *because* of what they refer to: the words 'child', 'rose', 'summer', 'kitten' will arouse pro-feelings in a large number of people and the words 'bully', 'pig', 'hyena', 'leprosy', 'cancer' will rather similarly arouse contra-feelings. The emotive charge of words is to a very large degree the charge of our habitual feelings about the things the words refer to. Yvor Winters made the same kind of point, quite independently, and it is a good point. More interesting and original was the point about how words like 'honest' or 'native', which ought to arouse pro-feelings, arouse condescending feelings, since we use them of those we think of as inferiors. Honesty is a virtue of tradesmen or servants and in Elizabethan times, in the very narrow sense of chastity, of women, thought of also as natural inferiors. Dark-skinned people, whom we rule, are natives, but we do not usually refer to ourselves as British natives. It was a good insight, but applied in rather too rough and ready a fashion. We were not getting quite pure historical textual analysis, but not getting quite pure theoretical semantics either. (p. 71)

*Milton's God* is a work of splendid vigour, inspired by Empson's growing animus over the years against what he calls neo-Christians (many of whom may be simply cradle Christians, who have come back to their childhood faith late in life). I do not know whether he believes the God of orthodox Christianity to exist, but he seems to hate Him almost as if he did exist: he blames him for being very cruel, and Christianity for being a very cruel religion, but if you were a whole-hearted atheist you would have to say that it is because men are cruel that they invent a cruel and frightening religion (and because they are not wholly cruel that they bring in love and charity too, and that Christianity can inspire self-sacrifice and service to the poor and the sick as well as sectarian hatred, bigotry, and persecution). Men are both cruel and kind, whatever religion they have, I think, and I believe that Christian morality at its best, in Dr Johnson or Jane Austen say, is the best morality. It is about this, I suppose, that Empson and I have had our worst quarrels: the Christian hell is certainly a very horrible concept and I could not believe anybody deserves to go there, except, in black moods, myself sometimes.

But Milton's Hell in *Paradise Lost* is not particularly horrible. His devils with their long parliamentary debates and their interminable philosophical arguments are, as Empson once said . . . , 'noble creatures'. There is a hell of a lot to admire in Satan, and C. S. Lewis is very mean to treat him as ridiculous, as a comic figure, simply because his cause is lost from the start. . . . One is all with Empson about Satan and about the beautiful human centrality to the story of Paradise (how right he is to say, against Eliot's theory of 'the great blind musician', that Milton paints like Claude) and of the great human love of Adam and Eve. Where I cannot go with him is in being either frightened or impressed by Milton's God. . . . *Paradise Lost* remains, in a sense, a great Christian poem, as St Paul's cathedral remains a great Christian church: but a Shintoist Japanese walking around St Paul's might be forgiven for thinking that it is a magnificent shrine devoted to the worship of great English admirals. One of Empson's points, of course, is that Milton deserves all credit for remaining so magnificently a humanist in spite of having such a horrible religion. My point is that, in the sense of which one speaks of having a disease, Milton hardly had the religion at all. So, though *Milton's God* is a fine book, Milton is a bad stick to beat Christianity with. (pp. 72-3)

> *George Fraser, "The Man within the Name: William Empson As Poet, Critic, and Friend," in* William Empson: The Man and His Work, *edited by Roma Gill, Routledge & Kegan Paul, 1974, pp. 52-75.*

## I. A. RICHARDS

When the editor of [*William Empson: The Man and his Work*], as reasonably as eloquently, asked me to try to make my first draft of this piece be more about *Complex Words*, 'Why, of course,' I thought, 'she is quite right. It is a real work and it's absurd to have such anxieties about it!' That settled, I went to bed, and began turning its well-known pages over in what I sometimes call 'my mind'. What was this? Aches and ague-shakes: the real thing! Ten days of the London flu. Recovered, if tottery, and back home from travel, there were the remembered hopeful green covers and the scribbled margins back in my hands. What now? Down again! A full battery, weeks more of Aix les Pains and with what additions!

Maybe this alibi will be enough to get me out of dealing at once with what has been the real source all through of those anxieties. They spring from my own inability to deal fairly and properly with the definitions and notations introduced in the first two chapters. If I could understand this inability more clearly, the anxieties might fade out. But I don't; and the best thing I can do for the moment will be to jump over these first two chapters and try instead to say why Empson's minute examinations have been, are and always will be of so much value to literary semantics. To put it solidly, they raised the standards of ambition and achievement in a difficult and very hazardous art. This sort of thing often happens in sports and the sciences—great examples might be: in sport, the entire transformation of the possible that has occurred since the thirties, with the developments of aids in rock- and ice-climbing; and, in science, the consequences, shall we say, of the transistor. But in the arts of reading, arts tedious and devious as they must be, such sudden revelations of new powers are perhaps even more surprising. What I ought to point out, if I can, is some of the ways by which Empson seems to have done this.

There are of course scientific sides to all this. The very title, *The Structure of Complex Words*, shrunken down though it be from 'Theory of the functions of the complex variable', suggests a quasi-mathematic treatment that Empson disowns. (I admit I find his fondness for the word 'equation' distracting.) But lexicographically, he very properly discusses, in his last chapter, the use his work may be to future dictionaries. With the new compacted *NED* so handy I do not myself see 'a still

bigger dictionary than the *NED*' as either 'obviously impracticable' or 'ludicrous.' . . . And this is a main part of why I think his work so important. His general proposal is that the *interactions* of the senses of a word should be included and his extremely acute, detailed (and diverting) account of what the *NED* actually does offers a very powerful case to show how this could be done without making it either much bigger or any harder to use. On the contrary, rather. Indeed, it is so convincing that I am astonished his services have not, long since, been retained as advisor and consultant upon how the major dictionaries of the future should be planned. (pp. 98-9)

So much for the lexicographic discernment, the expositional technique, brilliantly—even dazzlingly—displayed in this final and germinal chapter. *Where* to put *what,* so that it may be most conveniently, most safely, most economically apprehended: command of that is what I would signal here as Empson's chief contribution towards a possible scientific semantics. As a semanticist (queer though the label still seems) myself, I believe that what he has done should be taken very seriously. It is not merely a joke that we should hail The Dictionary as the true successor to Holy Writ. There, in the Dictionary, is the record, as well arranged as we can contrive, of the best (*and the worst*) that has been thought and said by prior users of the language—inspired, prophet-wise, or not, and by heavenly and infernal voices; or drearily uninspired. It is all there. . . .

Having argued this claim—as consequential as it is incontestable—I will turn now to my earlier remark, I believe fully as secure, that *Seven Types* and *Complex Words* did 'raise the standards' of the elucidative commentary on literature. This is far from being a lesser service than that I have been reporting. After all, we are by now accustomed to science advancing; but are we exactly expecting literature (and criticism, the perception of the literary endeavour—its triumphs and lapses) to tower up, endlessly, to new heights? In sad truth, we have been watching, almost all through our active days, little but dismal decline in people's power to do or say anything of significance *and* in people's ability to make out, and even less to appraise, the sorts of things being said. (p. 100)

In saying that Empson's best work in elucidative comment 'raised the standards' I have obviously to guard against misapprehensions. I am *not* saying that people in general, after studying him, did such work better—became more enterprising and effective. Far from it, as I have just been lamenting. And I am *not* saying that *all* of Empson's elucidative (or would-be elucidative) writing is on this new high level. I am saying only that *at his best* he is able to point out, describe, and make evident cooperations and interactions among meanings on a scale and with a subtlety and resource not to be found in previous critics. I am not claiming, either, that the new sorts of perceptions he conveys have in general the reconstitutive or seminal powers of those of Johnson or Coleridge. I *am* reporting, though, that his admiring reader often finds himself remarking: 'I never knew before that it was possible to see so much. I realize anew how much we ordinary readers may be missing.' The effect is in many ways like using a microscope. This again is a remark that can be taken amiss. As C. A. Mace wisely observed, 'A microscope is a poor instrument through which to find your way about a town.' None the less, in good hands, and on the right occasion, it can be extremely useful. (pp. 100-01)

[Not] all Empson's readers have been admiring. . . . Not every reader enjoys the feeling that something is being done that he could not possibly try to rival. That there should have been an ungenerous note in some of the reception of Empson's displays is not surprising. It is only fair, however, to add that he has not been (and indeed could not be) free from some responsibility for this.

Let me revert now to those two opening chapters of *Complex Words* which I alluded to above as occasioning for me bewilderments and anxieties. As I have said, I miss too many points and the issues grow cloudy. The 'little machine' of equations and notations causes me troubles which I am unable to diagnose helpfully. And I will not be the only one who has found these pages excessively difficult. I read on. Now and then, for a few tense sentences all seems beautifully clear, far-reaching vistas open, the taxed mind breathes deep, but alack, before long, the clouds crowd in, and one is again only *groping* through a paragraph hardly able even to see one's feet. Usually what illumines is an example. One ought, I suppose, to be able to carry it with one; but my candles—however skilfully Empson lights them—blow out. And I see moreover from the layers of marginalia that have been accumulating since the first weeks after *Complex Words* appeared and from my repeated efforts to set out Empson's symbols as a *ready vade-mecum* in table or diagram, that my uncertainties are not to be so simply set right. And yet, somehow I have to try to say what, I think, makes these two chapters such hard going—in comparison with the free felicities of so many of the specific studies that follow.

To begin with I am as certain as the case allows that Empson is right all through, well aware enough of what he is pointing out. My difficulties do not stem from faulty percipience there, but from his sentences being, as I struggle to grasp and use them, insufficient to make and maintain the relations and distinctions he employs them for. I am reminded of H. G. Wells' dread remark about trying to cut up an atom with a penknife. For me his percipiences, as I conjecture towards them, are incommensurably more refined than the clumsy terms through which he is, in these two chapters, trying to control and expound them. These terms serve him because he does not need them: he has his examples and his ways of taking them to keep his thinking in order. But his readers (at least, this one of them) has to try to follow the account without that guidance. And its terms get in his way. He is lost too often. (pp. 101-02)

Some time ago I ventured to observe, in *Speculative Instruments*, that 'It is not easy to let up on the pressure we are under to get (as we hope) something *said* in favour of awareness of the process of *saying*.' Which led Empson in a review to comment: 'This endeavour might seem wrong headed.' It is in fact the endeavour most of *Complex Words* is devoted to. But let me try again to say, with Niels Bohr's help, what, in part at least, is the trouble.

In the course of speculating about how widely his Complementarity Principle may apply, Bohr recorded two potentially dismaying observations. Both are germane to these bold explorations in *Seven Types* and *Complex Words*; they might indeed be pointedly discerning comments upon them:

> Words like 'thoughts' and 'sentiments', equally indispensable to illustrate the diversity of psychical experience, pertain to mutually exclusive situations characterized by a different drawing of the line of separation between subject and object.

To read this lingeringly is a good way of preparing ourselves for the other:

Our task can only be to aim at communicating experiences and views to others by means of language in which the practical use of every word stands in a complementary relation to attempts at its strict definition.

It is not clear (can't be, I conjecture) how far we are to take these. They could be pretty subversive. After all, the Complementarity Principle itself was once thought that: it has its saving limitary side. But how rich in outcomes it has been: enabling inquirers to combine results obtained by using formally incompatible assumptions. Get on with the inquiry and let *Ir*reconcilabilities cool their heels in the waiting room! May it continue to be so too with these semantic enterprises!

Certainly these two books have got on with the inquiry. And those who have bothered themselves for more than a brief spell about their methodological grounding have been missing an essential point as well as much wonderful fun. Conscientious scruples are out of place. However irremediably circular and reflexive our definitions and accounts are, to know that this is so is more than a little. The semantic situation that semantics itself is in, is really very entertaining. Empson has an infinity of means of making us enjoy it. (pp. 103-04)

I may fitly conclude with mention of another aspect of Empson's literary gifts: his very remarkable virtuosity as a writer of Basic English. His discussions of Swinburne and Wordsworth in Basic are truly notable achievements in a medium which can for some writers prove over-exacting. That he should have been thus interested in language control is certainly a notable aspect of his manifold venturesomeness as a writer. I see a certain appropriateness, therefore . . . , in ending this paper with a reminder that he has been as fully concerned with the problems of a truly elementary English as with its highest and most complex poetry. (p. 108)

*I. A. Richards, "Semantic Frontiersman," in* William Empson: The Man and His Work, *edited by Roma Gill, Routledge & Kegal Paul, 1974, pp. 98-108.*

**CHRISTOPHER NORRIS**

William Empson is perhaps the best known and least understood of modern critics. *Seven Types of Ambiguity* (1930) was a brilliant first book but tended to strike attitudes and pile up examples which Empson has too often been called to defend, in later years, from humourless scholarly attack. *Some Versions of Pastoral* (1935) avoided this provokingly obvious subtlety by absorbing it, translating its ingenuities and complications, into a basic metaphor and, by extension, an entire genre of literary history. *Some Versions* invited misunderstanding, not because its subtleties seemed too insistent, but because, on the contrary, they were so far left implicit and unspoken.

In *The Structure of Complex Words* (1951) Empson gave his readers further reasons for disquiet. Here he returned, through the structure of attitudes learned from Pastoral, to a linguistics of criticism which was more accountable, more historically secure and philosophically generalised, than anything in *Seven Types*. *Complex Words* is beyond doubt Empson's critical *summa*. Yet it, like the other books, has attracted little more than superficial or downright hostile attention. In this case it is perhaps the rather abstract theoretical machinery, prominent in his first two chapters, which has cost Empson his readers' sustained application. These theoretical sections of the book are inevitable by way of philosophic completeness—and ***Complex Words*** is . . . a real contribution to the philosophy of criticism. But they do come to seem inessential, at times, to the chapters of practical criticism. They provide both the assumed background and the ultimate formalisation of the insights gained in Empson's 'practical' chapters, the major part and central section of the book. ***Complex Words*** is, among other things, a rationalist theory of language and interpretation. (p. 1)

Like much of Empson's recent writing, [***Milton's God*** (1961)] incorporates an outspoken hatred of Christianity which largely governs and sometimes appears to distort his reading of the poetry. . . . Empson's humanistic rationalism is present in his earliest writings, and forms a coherent and developing background to each of his books. But in ***Milton's God*** and the later essays it becomes such a palpable design that one must, in fair assessment, try to sort out the biassed from the merely unorthodox in his criticism. Whatever the balance, it is I think possible . . . that Empson's 'eccentricity', as remarked upon by many of his critics, is less disabling—more a positive, consistent set of alternatives—than is commonly recognised. (p. 2)

> *Christopher Norris, in his* William Empson and the Philosophy of Literary Criticism, *The Athlone Press, 1978, 222 p.*

# Harvey Fierstein

## 1954-

American dramatist and actor.

Fierstein won Tony Awards for Best Play and Best Actor for *Torch Song Trilogy* (1981). This largely autobiographical work depicts three periods in the life of Arnold Beckoff, a young Jewish homosexual in search of a secure love relationship. Fierstein began his acting career as a founding member of the Brooklyn-based Gallery Players and as a "drag queen" in East Village clubs in New York City. He made his professional debut in 1971 in a similar role with the gay troupe La Mama ETC in Andy Warhol's *Pork* before turning to playwriting in 1973.

Originally conceived as three separate one-act plays (*The International Stud, Fugue in a Nursery*, and *Widows and Children First!*), *Torch Song Trilogy* attempts to reveal love as a universal theme independent of heterosexually defined conceptions of moral propriety. This concern is also evident in Fierstein's second major play, *La Cage aux folles* (1983), a musical version of the comic French play of the same name by Jean Poiret. The story is about two homosexuals, Albin and Georges, whose love affair is nearly ruined when Georges's son, conceived during a brief heterosexual encounter, falls in love with the daughter of a moral crusader. The play won a Tony Award for Best Musical. *Spookhouse* (1984), written before *Torch Song Trilogy* and *La Cage aux folles*, also deals with nontraditional family relationships but incorporates elements of horror and violence.

Photograph by Kenn Duncan

## MEL GUSSOW

Arnold Beckoff, the lonely but far-from-forlorn hero of Harvey Fierstein's "**Torch Song Trilogy**," is a die-hard romantic who takes his heart, soul and fatalism from the 1920's ballads that give the work its title and its tone. At the end of a long, infinitely rewarding evening in the company of . . . his family and friends, [Arnold] confesses with a sigh that he has always wanted exactly the life that his mother has had—"with certain minor alterations."

Those alterations—Arnold is a homosexual and a professional "drag queen"—are the substance but not the sum of Mr. Fierstein's work, three plays that give us a progressively dramatic and illuminating portrait of a man who laughs, and makes us laugh, to keep from collapsing. The evening is a double tour de force for Mr. Fierstein, who, with his throaty Tallulah voice and manner, stars in his own touching triptych.

We first met Arnold in "**The International Stud**," produced Off Broadway in 1978. At the time, I felt it was a sincere but sentimentalized view of a transvestite in extremis. Seeing the play again, in a carefully abridged version in a vastly superior staging by Peter Pope, I found myself enjoying Arnold's wit—he has the pithy humor of a Fran Lebowitz—at the same time that I was moved by his dilemma. He is a man of principle who compulsively plays the fool.

[In "**Torch Song Trilogy**"], "**The International Stud**" becomes the first chapter in a cycle of tales about Arnold. . . .

The current evening is designed as a trilogy of related plays, but it turns out to be one cohesive three-act play.

Each succeeding "act" adds to our understanding and fully justifies what has gone before. Instead of reiterating positions, Arnold's story becomes richer as it unfolds. There are still flashes of sentimentality in Mr. Fierstein's performance as well as in the text. The author is so accomplished at playing Arnold that he cannot resist an extra flourish or an easy wisecrack, and the ending is too neatly symbolic. But the cumulative event is one to be experienced and savored.

Among other things, it deals fairly—without any attempt at exploiting the situation or manipulating our emotions—with varieties of sexual orientation. For example, Arnold's lover is a bisexual who is caught between two magnets: what he thinks he needs and what he feels. The evening studies self-love and self-hate, headstrong passion and heartfelt compassion.

In the first part, the two men meet—to a counterpoint of torch songs, sung pensively—and after a sequence of on-again, off-again encounters, many of them humorous, they separate. In the second part, "**Fugue in a Nursery**," Arnold and his new lover, a male model, visit Arnold's "ex" and his new girlfriend at their farmhouse. The tinseled cynicism of the first play sweetens as the quartet conducts a roundelay that is both fanciful and immensely civilized. The four switch partners, conversationally as well as romantically, with the irrepressibly sympathetic Arnold trying, but not succeeding, in turning a deaf ear to the problems of others.

In the third and best play, **"Widows and Children First!"** we meet Arnold's past and present family. First there is his Jewish mother, fresh from Miami with an archetypal self-salute, "I'm the mother," and an unextinguishable hope that her son may yet blossom into heterosexuality. The final addition is a troubled teenager whom Arnold has rescued from the streets and wants to adopt. The sociological implications are complex and the author treats them with equanimity, demonstrating that the flamboyant Arnold is truly a reflection of his assertive mother, which is why they are destined to spend their lives at loggerheads. . . .

All of the characters are of course subsidiary to Arnold's dominant personality. He is his own torch song, and the role is inseparable from the actor-author. Mr. Fierstein's self-incarnation is an act of compelling virtuosity.

> *Mel Gussow, "Fierstein's 'Torch Song'," in* The
> New York Times, *November 1, 1981, p. 81.*

## JOHN SIMON

Kenneth Tynan created a stir some years ago by asserting that the two principal types of humor in the American theater were the Jewish and the homosexual. If this is so, and it well may be, the good news is that the two strains have been successfully crossbred in Harvey Fierstein's **Torch Song Trilogy**, which is a very amusing as well as moving affair for whose enjoyment, be it said right off, neither Jewishness nor homosexuality is a prerequisite.

This trilogy of shortish plays that lasts, all told (and is all ever told!), a little over four hours . . . [has] much to tell us about the way we live now. And when I say *we*, I mean people, any people, except perhaps those living in an offshore lighthouse or in the very buckle of the Bible Belt. Fierstein wrote, and performed the lead in, these three plays one at a time, but it is much better to see them as they are now: the long acts of one extended but not excessive work that gathers meaning as it progresses until, at last, all parts of it resonate in the mind in a bittersweet harmony made of dissonances, pain, resignation, and a little daredevil hope.

Arnold Beckoff, the protagonist, has all the earmarks of a stylized projection of the actor-author himself; yet even though one feels this potentially stifling closeness, one is not, or not for long, an embarrassed voyeur. Buttonholing immediacy is transmuted—by wit, irony, fair play to one and all—first into a bearable distance, then into a sense of wonder. For Beckoff-Fierstein emerges at the far end of identification in a state of liberated semi-detachment that is not quite so good as serenity but that will—will have to—do.

In the first play [*The International Stud*] Arnold, a drag queen, is either backstage at the nightclub where he performs (a performance we do not see—an unfortunate evasion), or at a gay bar called the International Stud, which gives the play its name, or in his apartment, when not in that of his new lover, Ed, a bisexual who is also involved with a young woman called Laurel. The themes here are Arnold's drifting into the orgiastic back rooms of gay hotspots versus his yearning for a solid relationship, Ed's shuttling between two kinds of sexuality and styles of life, and the difficulties with commitment to anything, even noncommitment. In dialogues, monologues, phone conversations with a homosexual friend, Arnold reveals himself and his world with a sweet campiness, an outrageousness whose bark is worse than its bite, an arrested development that does not preclude perceptions of devastating lucidity. . . .

In the second play, **Fugue in a Nursery,** it is a year later in the upstate farmhouse shared by Ed and Laurel, now living together and playing weekend hosts to Arnold and his new lover, Alan, a very young male model. Fierstein situates the entire action in an enormous symbolic bed in which the two couples talk, argue, copulate, and crisscross both emotionally and sexually. The writing is in the form of a fugue, which is clever, but also means something: The overlapping, intermingling dialogue, in which we are often not sure about who is talking to whom, conveys thought-provoking parallels between homo- and heterosexual relationships—though the captious might argue that Ed's bisexuality muddies the analogies. In any case, **Fugue** is an extremely droll and ingenious scrutiny of sexual politics whose humor, honorably, never hides the underlying cruelty or, still deeper down, the underlying pathos. (p. 110)

It is the last play, **Widows and Children First!,** that rises to true heights and ties all the foregoing together. Ed is unhappily married to Laurel, has had a fight with her and is temporarily bunking *chez* Arnold, after whom he still hankers; Alan, who had been living with Arnold, has met a horrible, homosexual death; Arnold is trying to adopt legally a problem teenager, David, a tough, street-wise, homosexual kid, chock-full of precocious knowledge and sarcasm, but not without a touching residue of childishness. Into this *ménage,* on a visit from Florida, comes Mrs. Beckoff, Arnold's widowed mother. She knows about her son's homosexuality, but cannot really accept it, and keeps needling him. Mother and son try to love each other, but cannot quite make it; their defense, which is also an offense, is wit: her Jewish wit against his homosexual one. While they fumble for each other's affection out of one side of their mouths, they cleverly lacerate each other out of the other side. The combat, fought with bare tongues and occasional desperate gestures, is verbal Grand Guignol of matchless humor and horror.

It turns out that the two widowed creatures, mother and son, are, except for their different sexualities, deeply alike down to their very jokes. The Jewish ones, to be sure, suggest a sad, lonely stand-up comedian resorting to an almost metaphysical sardonicism; the homosexual ones suggest a sarcastic masquerader, flamboyantly theatricalizing everything. But they climax in a very similar, murderous and suicidal, bitchiness: envenomed chicken soup against poisoned paillettes. (pp. 110-11)

All values are inverted and subverted. . . . There are ironies within ironies in this, a whole topsy-turvy world. And alongside the mother conflict are, cunningly and touchingly orchestrated, the David problem, the Ed problem, and even the Laurel problem. The author's ultimate achievement is the perfect blend of hard justice and warm empathy with which he embraces all characters, his own alter ego included. . . .

There are flaws. Arnold's source of income grows unclear: Could a drag-queen single parent adopt even as unwanted a kid as David? Alan was presented as a fling in the second play; the third makes him out to have been a beloved spouse. No matter: Peter Pope's staging and the production values are good; the play is better. What are you waiting for? (p. 111)

> *John Simon, "The Gay Desperado," in* New York
> Magazine, *Vol. 14, No. 49, December 14, 1981, pp.
> 110-11.*

## WALTER KERR

[In "**Torch Song Trilogy**," the] rambling and, because it can only move in circles, repetitive plot might do well enough. . . . But that self-mockery Mr. Fierstein delights in begins to pose problems as the performance now stands. It tends to become a permanent shield, concealing the man beneath it. Sometimes it is simply playful: two men on a telephone cooking up names for female singers, Kitty Litter, Bertha Vanation. Sometimes it is waspishly knowing: "I'm aging about as well as a Beach Party movie." Sometimes it makes "in" use of its homosexual background: "What's the matter—you catch your tongue on the closet door?" And sometimes it collapses of its own effort: speaking boastfully of all the "Hims" he knows well, Mr. Fierstein includes "The Battle Him of the Republic."

The quality of the jokes varies, but that's not the point. The point is that there's no knowing the joker. His defenses are, and remain, impenetrable. The author-actor is adding to this . . . by making certain of his gestures and reactions Road-Runner-broad: trying to arrange a date by telephone, he squirms in the armchair as though it had been invaded by red ants. Since none of the evening's other characters behave in this fashion (including two homosexuals and one bisexual), the excesses cannot be ascribed to his sexual patterns; neither can they be fitted into an over-all style that legitimately embraces the balance of the company. . . .

"I feel like freeze-dried death" isn't an unimaginative phrase; yet it is too self-conscious to make us think about, or feel for, the man uttering it. The phrase seems to be listening to itself, which makes it quite impersonal. Does this matter? I think it does. I found the constant tattoo of attempted left-field laughs ultimately wearing; and the barrage did get between the actor and any feelings I might have had for him. How much of this, I wondered, has come about during the weeks since the play opened downtown? Has that hard, ready-made laughter from out front hurt the complexity of the leading performances, helped turn it into a grab for the next guffaw?

The laughter—at least at the performance I saw—is peculiar because it is so unvaried and so unselective. Normally, audiences like to choose what they will laugh at. Perhaps a little laugh, a kind of chuckle of recognition. Or a medium size one, to indicate that the friendship is growing but the commitment is not yet permanent. Then, when surrender does come, the boffs. Here it's all boffs, which means that some of them simply cannot be genuine. For instance, I doubt that Mr. Fierstein makes a single campy gesture—or what a straight parodist would consider a homosexual gesture—that isn't greeted with instant hilarity. But this surely cannot be what Mr. Fierstein, as playwright, must once have had in mind. "**Torch Song Trilogy**" is certainly not a play meant to poke fun at homosexuals minute by minute. Laughter is legitimate, but other responses are called for. (p. H3)

It's strictly gag-time as things now stand. Has playing the show for some weeks or more, and finding new ways to nudge the audience's funny-bone nightly, finally hollowed out the play, erased variety and nuance, robbed it of its possible range of moods? The play's director, Peter Pope, might be well advised to take another, sterner look at it. (p. H16)

*Walter Kerr, " 'Torch Song Trilogy'—Self-Mockery As a Shield," in* The New York Times, *Section II, June 27, 1982, pp. H3, H16.*

## EDWIN WILSON

Aside from Mr. Fierstein's talents as a performer, how does "**Torch Song Trilogy**" hold up as drama? One would have to answer intermittently. The first play, the most blatantly homosexual, sacrifices dramatic action for the funny or the outre.

The second play, the foursome at the farmhouse, is often downright dull. But the third has real drama. Though Mr. Fierstein cannot resist making both his mother and the young David inexhaustible sources of comic one-liners, he also gives us true poignance in the experiences of Arnold as he attempts to deal with the loss of Alan—who has been brutally murdered—and to come to terms with his mother. In this play Mr. Fierstein transcends the homosexual emphasis of the evening and makes Arnold a person with whom everyone can empathize.

*Edwin Wilson, "A Drama of Homosexuality," in* The Wall Street Journal, *June 30, 1982, p. 22.*

## CLIVE BARNES

[In *Torch Song Trilogy*] Fierstein has written a devastatingly comic play with just the right resonances. It is a play about love and the merciless mayhem love wreaks. But by looking singlemindedly at the underbelly of that tragedy, the play is gorgeously funny. . . .

Like New York cockroaches, Arnold survives. Indeed like that archetypal cockroach, Archy, once celebrated in the pages of The New Yorker by Don Marquis, Arnold remains *toujours gai*. But at what cost.

All three plays of *Torch Song Trilogy* started as separate entities, and the present evening—their final form—are tightened, grimmed-down versions. It nevertheless makes a long evening, somewhat better than four hours with two brief intermissions, but it is a marathon very much worth running. It is—through Fierstein's fluent invention and buoyant humor—strangely untiring. (p. 245)

The play is both idealized and at times a little unlikely. The kid [Arnold adopts], for example, is provided with street smarts that show astonishing understanding of the human soul. Alan dies in sensationally heroic circumstances.

Also Fierstein can never resist a joke. If he were writing *Macbeth*, depend upon it, the murders would be incidental to the comic relief provided by the Porter.

Yet there is an appealing self-mockery and even bitterness to the relentless, bitchy camp-fiery humor. *Toujours gai*, as Archy would have said. . . .

For gays *Torch Song Trilogy* could, with its positiveness, be a sort of manifesto. For straights it could be a tourist trip to an alternative country. For playgoers it is a fun evening in the theater, with sad undercurrents of what makes the fun funny. (p. 246)

*Clive Barnes, " 'Song' of Love and Laughter," in* New York Post, *July 15, 1982. Reprinted in* New York Theatre Critics' Reviews, *Vol. XLIV, No. 9, May 30-June 6, 1983, pp. 245-46.*

## KIM POWERS

There are two types of scream in Harvey Fierstein's *Torch Song Trilogy*. The first, and less painful, is the scream of the Camp comedian. . . . [Fierstein's] humor is that of the hysterical 'queen'—a sort of Martha Raye on speed. The second, more lasting, and profound scream in the play is the shriek of horror that comes from a victim or prophet. Fierstein has been both; this second ''voice'' is his response to the ignorance about and bigotry against homosexuality in our society. Appropriately, he uses a language of extremity: loneliness becomes death, and death, ultimate extinction. Through Arnold's stories, Fierstein creates a personal, necessary history of obsession. Both screams, comic and death-defying, are of equal importance and volume in his storytelling, because they are equal parts of Fierstein's personality and dramatic strategy. (pp. 63-4)

The unifying spine of the three separate acts of *Torch Song Trilogy* is the persona and acting style of Fierstein himself, who plays Arnold.... Regardless of the line-by-line parallels in Fierstein's life and that of the character Arnold, we accept that we are watching something that approaches a loose autobiography. This gives an added dimension to the event: we experience an even more intense feeling of community because of the truthfulness of the revelations, the recreations performed by the same person who had the original experience.

The acting of Fierstein takes on a vaudevillian or even Brechtian quality. He seems continually to illustrate his life, the play. When Ed tells him over the phone that he is seeing a woman, Arnold/Fierstein torturously asks, ''Do you like her?'' He goes through an odd contortion of the word ''her'', stretching it out to control and disguise his emotion. He registers disgust, but at the same time seems to silently comment that this is a conversation he once had.... This 'commenting' continues in non-autobiographical scenes. In the third act, when Mrs. Beckoff finds out that Arnold is adopting a boy, she says, ''He sees you, living like this . . . don't you think it's going to affect him?'' Arnold: ''Ma, David is gay.'' Mrs. Beckoff: ''But he's only been here six months!'' Fierstein turns an incredulous face to the audience: a comment on both characters. Perhaps Fierstein's comic turns are the modern-day embodiment of Brecht's epic acting technique. (p. 64)

[*Torch Song Trilogy*] remains more important for its political achievement than for its aesthetic value. In its lengthy Broadway run, *Torch Song Trilogy* has been championed by major establishment critics, straight and gay audiences alike. Some gay presses have accused favorable straight critics of liberal patronization, or, conversely, of usurping something that was once their private domain. Regardless of orientation, most reviewers have been hesitant to criticize the pioneering *Trilogy*. The play does have its faults (the first act is an extended stand-up comedy routine; the second act a clever but diffuse exercise in expositional orchestration), yet it has an overriding significance as a sociological phenomenon, both in the present and implicative for the future....

Ben Cameron, in his article *''Bent'' on Broadway'' (Theater,* Summer 1980), calls for a new dramaturgy that will fuse a radical gay social message with an appropriate aesthetic. He mentions Fierstein as an artist working toward that new aesthetic, citing his ''implosion'' of form from within. Although Fierstein does incorporate a non-traditional dramatic structure into the first two acts of *Trilogy,* it is ironic and telling that the most significant and mature third, *Widows and Children First!,* is the most conventionally structured. It observes the classical unities of time and place and offers the reenactment of a sort of Prodigal Son story. Fierstein arranges with the audience a trade-off that provides the forward movement and tension of the act: a powerful though uneasy statement of gay

politics against the security of a conventional dramatic structure. Fierstein strategically uses this structure as an escape valve for the audience. It is almost as if he needed the perimeter of a known quantity (structure) to contain his explosiveness, something that would have been overwhelming in a new form. Content and form are symbiotic: the act's story of Mother and Son both tempers and expands Fierstein's quiet anarchy, his unbending petition for acceptance. The act of confrontation between Fierstein and his stage mother parallels the confrontation that takes place between Fierstein and the audience. There is a perfect continuum from the small-scale emotion of a parent/child encounter to the dynamics of mass education. The explicitness of his ultimatum for gay acceptance is new enough for Broadway; it is this location (both geographically and attitudinally) that must be at least part of the new dramaturgy. (p. 65)

[In the third act, it] is easy and convenient to build a case against the mother: she is part of an old regime, a delegate from straight society and a scapegoat for gay society, and she seems to have committed the ultimate maternal blasphemy—cursing the birth of her child. Much of the anger from both combatants can be excused by the heat of battle, but a new and difficult truthfulness has been uncovered. The eternal bond (Mother/Son) has become less important than the sexual, societal conflict (homosexual/heterosexual). (p. 66)

Because of the exact storytelling in this act, the 'work' the audience must do in understanding the physical events is minimal. One of the most direct passages in the play comes in this act from Arnold: (One last try) ''Ma, look, I'm gay. I don't know why. I don't think anyone else does. But that's what I am. For as far back as I can remember.'' The direction ''One last try'' is as important as the actual text. It informs Arnold's sincerity and desire for reconciliation. The context is no longer a one-upmanship of grief; the fact of the play has become ''Ma, look: I'm gay'' and its assumed counterpart, ''And there's nothing I can do about it.'' Arnold's simple statement eradicates any remorseful past for the present.

A different type of work then comes into play for the audience. They must make a decision. That process is inherent in the performance. The extremity of Fierstein's personality forces some sort of judgement. He is abrasive, shocking, flamboyant; the audience must resolve, or at least come to understand, any discomfort it may feel in dealing with an effeminate man. It must see beyond the bitchy gestures to the basic issues. This is Fierstein's responsibility: has he provoked any new considerations, or has he only confirmed old convictions? Which 'widowing' is more allowable—mother's or son's? I made the wrong decision before I discovered the craft and humanity of the playwright. One of the mother's final speeches is: ''You want me to leave? I'm leaving. You want me to fight? I'm too tired. You want me to change? I'm too old and I can't. I can't, I can't, I can't. So you do what you have to do, and I'll do what I have to do, and I hope you're satisfied.'' I interpreted this as the mother's final statement, a representative social attitude, and was infuriated at Fierstein's failure—his inclusion of this slice of life was inappropriate to his political vision; his allowing a potential convert to escape cowardly. I misinterpreted his strategies, and missed the rest of the play. A second reading showed me that Arnold (if not Fierstein) is beyond narrow, exclusive politics: his life, and his final understanding and acceptance of Alan's death, lead him to a transcendent world view. Fierstein has as many lessons for angry homosexuals as he does for ill-at-ease heterosexuals. (pp. 66-7)

Fierstein has translated his specific masculine/feminine concerns into a universal statement about acceptance. The narrowly political route would have been for him to disavow the mother, to settle only with the images of male love. This is a time for radical scenarios for problem solving. But perhaps Fierstein's final, all-inclusive choice is the radical one: to exorcise anger, vengeance, and martyrdom that make minority drama didactic and exclusive. Fierstein has accomplished by his move to Broadway an expansion of the narrow gay community for which the plays were first performed. He has enhanced the quality of thought in this new community with a model for acceptance that is built on the respect that comes from understanding. Not only has he invited outsiders into this society, he has armed them with the codes of social conduct with which to create a utopian future. (p. 67)

> Kim Powers, "Fragments of a Trilogy: Harvey Fierstein's 'Torch Song'," in Theater, Vol. 14, No. 2, Spring, 1983, pp. 63-7.

## FRANK RICH

"La Cage aux Folles" is the first Broadway musical ever to give center stage to a homosexual love affair—but don't go expecting an earthquake. The show . . . is the schmaltziest, most old-fashioned major musical Broadway has seen since "Annie," and it's likely to be just as popular with children of all ages. Were you hoping for a little more? I must confess that I was. The glitz, showmanship, good cheer and almost unflagging tunefulness of **"La Cage aux Folles"** are all highly enjoyable and welcome, but, in its eagerness to please all comers, this musical is sometimes as shamelessly calculating as a candidate for public office.

Sometimes, but, happily, not always. There are more than a few startling occasions in this rapaciously busy extravaganza when the vast machinery comes to a halt—when David Mitchell's glorious pastel-hued scenic visions of St.-Tropez stop flying, when the transvestite dancing girls vanish, when the running gags about whips and wigs limp away. . . .

[Albin], as Zaza, is the headline attraction at the nightclub that gives the musical its title. For 20 years, Albin has had a tranquil domestic life with Georges . . . , the club's impresario. Albin is the more flamboyant of the pair. It is he who must dress up in drag every night to entertain the customers and who has the most to fear from growing old. . . .

Whether in his female impersonations or in civilian guise, [Albin] is neither campy nor macho here: he could be any run-of-the-mill nightclub entertainer in midlife crisis. But it is precisely his ordinariness that makes him so moving. When [Albin] sits in front of his dressing-room mirror to sing plaintively of how he applies "a little more mascara" to make himself feel beautiful, we care much more about what the illusion of feminine glamour means to the otherwise humdrum Albin than we do about the rather routine illusion itself.

That's how it should be. By making us see so clearly how precariously his self-esteem is maintained, [Albin] makes it all the more upsetting to watch what happens when that identity is attacked. And, as in the French film of "La Cage aux Folles" . . . , that shock quickly arrives. Albin and Georges's "son" — fathered by Georges in a long-ago, one-night heterosexual fling — announces his intention to marry the daughter of a bigoted politician. To help the young man perpetuate the fiction

that he had a standard upbringing, Georges cruelly asks Albin to disappear when the prospective in-laws come to call.

What follows, at the end of Act I, is the evening's moment of triumph. [Albin] rushes on the stage of La Cage to perform as Zaza—only to stop in midstride and let loose with his real feelings of rejection and betrayal. In drag though he may be, the actor sings in a full-throttle baritone—with a pulsating force that induces shivers. The song, titled "I Am What I Am," is full of rage but, better still, of pride: even as Albin defends his right to live as he wishes, he pointedly asks not for either "praise" or "pity." . . .

When the stars aren't delivering . . . [their] songs, **"La Cage aux Folles"** can be as synthetic and padded as the transvestites' cleavage. . . . Harvey Fierstein, writer of the book, has misplaced his craftsmanship and bite on this outing; he's exercised few of his options to bolster a property that was thin and coarse to begin with. The tiny plot of **"La Cage"** is dribbled out with painful lethargy in Act I, then resolved chaotically (and confusingly) for the final curtain. Worse, there is a homogenized, sit-com tone to the script, which suggests that Mr. Fierstein is pandering to what he apparently regards as a squeamish Broadway-musical audience.

The ostensibly tart backstage wisecracks of Zaza's fellow transvestites are so tame and tired that they make the equivalent jokes of, say, "Victor/Victoria" or Mr. Fierstein's own **"Torch Song Trilogy"** sound like hardcore porn. . . . In the book scenes, unlike the songs, Georges and Albin are so relentlessly square that they become homogenized homosexuals in the manner of the scrupulously genteel black people of Hollywood's "Guess Who's Coming to Dinner" era. The lovers' turncoat son . . . is too wanly characterized for us to understand his casual callousness; the parents of the bride are such caricatured villains that even the more zealous homophobes in the audience can feel morally superior to them—and thereby escape the reach of the show's plea for tolerance. . . .

[Even when Fierstein and lyricist Jerry Herman] are cautiously watering down their material, their splashy entertainment usually hums along in its unabashedly conventional way. Wait for those privileged occasions when [the actors and] Mr. Herman summon up the full courage of the show's convictions, and you'll hear **"La Cage aux Folles"** stop humming and sing.

> Frank Rich, "The Musical 'Cage aux folles'," in The New York Times, August 22, 1983, p. C13.

## HOWARD KISSEL

In our period, the major figures in musicals are predominantly homosexual, and the openness about this fact that first emerged in "A Chorus Line" has reached its apogee in ["La Cage aux Folles"]. What is remarkable about "Cage" is its lack of preachiness. It submerges any tendency to lecture or browbeat in its consummate theatricality.

Its avoidance of politics is apparent even in the casting. The chorus has not been culled from the ranks of full-time drag queens. At one point, the same young men who play Cagelles do a funny number illustrating modes of masculinity. At the end, they take their curtain calls as clean-cut kids, like those in any Broadway show. Thus "Cage" presents itself not as special pleading but as entertainment.

Moreover, "Cage" is not a parochial show about a special kind of love. It has a warmth and tenderness we have not experienced in the musical theater since ''Ballroom,'' which was also about a middle-aged love defying social conventions. . . .

''Cage'' is not without its blemishes—Harvey Fierstein's funny book has awkward moments in the second act, and the treatment of women is sometimes crude (aren't they people too?).

But director Arthur Laurents has drawn superb and polished performances from the large cast. . . .

The most exciting performance, of course, is that of [George] Hearn, who, with enormous style and understatement, makes us see Albin not as a freak but as the outsider who uses his imagination to make the world a more enchanting place. So does ''Cage'' itself. (p. 191)

> *Howard Kissel, in a review of ''La Cage aux folles,'' in* Women's Wear Daily, *August 22, 1983. Reprinted in* New York Theatre Critics' Reviews, *Vol. XLIV, No. 11, July 11-July 17, 1983, pp. 190-91.*

## EDWIN WILSON

The public side of [''La Cage aux Folles''] is all splash and spectacle, but the behind-the-scenes action is in a different key. In a departure from the film, Harvey Fierstein, author of the show's book, has tried to make the story more human. In part he has succeeded: The love between Albin and Georges is entirely believable.

But Mr. Fierstein also wants to make ''La Cage'' teach a lesson, and here he runs into trouble. His Georges and Albin are a happily married couple—a monogamous couple, if you will—while the son who wants to deny their life style and the prospective father-in-law who maligns them are villains. In setting the contest, however, Mr. Fierstein has only gone halfway, humanizing the good guys while the bad guys remain cardboard cutouts.

In any case, realism and farce don't mix. And ''La Cage'' is essentially a farce. One of the hallmarks of farce is that the premise is always absurd. In asking us, however, to condemn the cruel way that Jean-Michel treats his ''parents,'' Mr. Fierstein raises awkwardly serious, nonfarcical questions.

Fortunately, Mr. Fierstein insists on being serious only part of the time. The rest is pure fun. . . .

> *Edwin Wilson, ''A Gay Evening on the Great White Way,'' in* The Wall Street Journal, *August 26, 1983, p. 15.*

## JACK KROLL

Broadway history is being made this week. ''La Cage aux Folles'' is not only going to be a gigantic hit, but the spectacular new musical, with its theme of homosexual love, its lavish transvestite costumes, its clever blending of blue material and true-blue domesticity, drags (so to speak) the Broadway audience laughing and cheering into the wide-open '80s. . . .

The show's creators, producer Allan Carr, book-writer Harvey Fierstein, composer-lyricist Jerry Herman and director Arthur Laurents, go right for the bottom line—energy and sentiment. The show attacks like a commando raid in its very first number, the drag-queen chorus line defiantly singing, ''We are what we are and what we are is an illusion, / We love how it feels putting on heels, causing confusion'' and dancing, not just in

a potent parody of a chorus line, but with a special manic energy. Any uneasiness floating around the theater is blown away by sheer showbiz power. . . .

What saves ''La Cage'' from being a glitzy tear-jerker is what saves most successful popular art—it has the courage of its sentimentality. When Georges sings ''Song on the Sand'' to Albin, a remembrance of things past in their romance, you do think of Maurice Chevalier singing ''I Remember It Well'' to Hermione Gingold in ''Gigi,'' and, give or take a chromosome or two, it's the same sweet situation here. And when Albin, wounded by Jean-Michel's rebuff, belts out a defiant ''I Am What I Am,'' only Jerry Falwell would refuse to admit the emotional validity of this prideful anthem—not to mention that it's that rarity these days, a classic first-act close that slugs the customers in their solar plexuses and leaves them gasping for more.

The more doesn't quite eventuate in the second act, with its overly broad farce of the meeting with the uptight Dindons and a few details in dubious taste, such as Jean-Michel accidentally groping his girlfriend's *maman* and turning her on. This put-on of heterosexual sensuality might have worked if ''La Cage'' had not chosen to bypass the theme of homosexual sensuality, concentrating instead on the family values which, Fierstein's book insists, are not the exclusive preserve of heterosexuals. This is exactly what Fierstein wrote about in his play ''Torch Song Trilogy.'' . . . ''Torch Song'' is wiser and wittier about love, sex, parents and children than ''La Cage.'' But ''La Cage'' is a musical—and an old-fashioned musical at that despite its *outré* trappings. That's why it packs such a jolt, because it brings to bear the straight audience's own ideals on a supposedly deviant universe. (p. 70)

Fierstein's campy brashness, Herman's apple-pie lyricism, Laurents's clear-eyed realism all meshed to make a success out of a project that many showbiz savants thought would never work. (p. 71)

> *Jack Kroll, ''Broadway Glitters and Is Oh So Gay,'' in* Newsweek, *Vol. CII, No. 9, August 29, 1983, pp. 70-1.*

## EDITH OLIVER

[''Spookhouse''] was a horror comic about a meddlesome social worker who tried to force a woman to accept and take care of her elder son, an adolescent drug addict, after the boy had raped and set afire an eight-year-old girl and then either fallen or been pushed off a roof. The rest of his family—mother, father, kid sister, and mentally defective younger brother— were shattered, but the zealous Ph.D. was adamant. The action took place in an apartment above the Spookhouse in Coney Island, which the parents owned and operated, and the effects— *son et lumière*—were appropriately shocking and obtrusive. As for the script, ''Spookhouse'' was less a play than a cluster of monologues. Those in the first act—the mother's desperate, sarcastic routines . . .—were often entertaining in a campy kind of way. They were the comic part. The second act was the horror: tears (on part of father), blood, and murder—though not murder of social worker, which I was rooting for. It would be tempting to dismiss the show as rubbish and leave it at that were it not for some skill in the writing and delineation of the characters.

> *Edith Oliver, ''Boo!'' in* The New Yorker, *Vol. LX, No. 13, May 14, 1984, p. 131.*

# John (Robert) Fowles

## 1926-

English novelist, short story writer, poet, and nonfiction writer.

Fowles's reputation as an important contemporary author rests on novels that combine myth and mystery with realism and existentialist thought. He experiments with such traditional prose forms as the mystery novel, the Victorian novel, the medieval tale, and the autobiography. Through these forms he comments on twentieth-century art and society. Fowles is an allusive, descriptive writer who creates complicated situations and lavish backgrounds permeated with legend, history, and art. Among the recurrent elements in his novels are strong narration and vital, resourceful characters. Many of these characters live outside the impositions of society; dramatic tension is provided when they reach crucial turning points requiring reevaluation of self. The women are intelligent and independent, while the men are usually uncertain and isolated, in search of answers to the enigmas in their lives. In most cases, however, simple solutions are not provided, and their quests result in further mystery. Fowles rejects the role of omniscient narrator, and readers have been annoyed at his refusal to offer satisfactory conclusions. Fowles believes that part of his responsibility includes allowing his characters freedom to choose and to act within their limitations. This practice parallels his conception of "authentic" human beings, or people who resist conformity by exercising free will and independent thought, thereby limiting the influence of chance.

Fowles's first novel, *The Collector* (1963), was a commercial success and was initially reviewed as a thriller or a product of the new class-conscious writing which evolved in the 1950s. Subsequent evaluations have suggested that the story concerns the struggle between the Few, or the elite, and the Many, or the masses. This concept was adapted from the pre-Socratic philosopher Heraclitus. One common interpretation of *The Collector* is that the authentic individual, who represents a code of behavioral excellence, is endangered by the pressures exerted by conventional society. These ideas are also discussed in *The Aristos* (1964), a nonfiction work that contains Fowles's thoughts on art, religion, politics, and society. The concept Fowles propounds in its summary, "to accept limited freedom, ... one's isolation ..., to learn one's particular powers, and then with them to humanize the whole," is integral to *The Magus* (1965) and *The French Lieutenant's Woman* (1969). Fowles revised *The Aristos* in 1968 in an attempt to clarify his ideas and organize them within an expanded context.

*The Magus* demonstrates Fowles's skill in narration and his unique approach to the novel form. While many critics found its labyrinthine structure disconcerting, the book was widely read by young adults. Fowles began the first draft in 1952, but he was not satisfied with it even after its publication in 1965. He revised it in 1977, incorporating many stylistic and structural changes designed to streamline the story and clarify some of its confusing aspects.

*The French Lieutenant's Woman* has been called Fowles's most ambitious and innovative work. In this novel he examines Victorian manners and morals from a present-day perspective. While Fowles's time-and-space manipulations in this book al-

*Photograph by Mark Gerson*

low truths to be discovered by the characters, they also lead to further ambiguities. Fowles has expressed the opinion that the world needs mysteries more than solutions because curiosity about the unknown prompts active participation in the quest for answers. Fowles offers a number of possible resolutions to the novel, any of which would be consistent with what has taken place. In this way, he emphasizes that reality is illusory and can be altered.

The short fictions contained in *The Ebony Tower* (1974) are variations on Fowles's previous themes and narrative methods. They also imitate and expand upon elements contained in Marie de France's medieval tale *Eliduc*, a translation of which is included in the book. Each story is connected to a form of art and concerns some aspect of the creative process.

*Daniel Martin* (1977) is a long, discursive work about a man's search for himself. Fowles calls the book "emotionally autobiographical," and some critics regard it as an attempt at a more realistic style. In this book he turns from a preoccupation with literary skill toward a greater involvement with substance. Events from different time periods intertwine and are told from different points of view by Daniel in an attempt to see himself objectively. Some critics consider the characters to be symbols of the relationship between individuals and generations. The ending is uncharacteristically happy, with promise for social and moral reintegration.

Fowles's next novel, *Mantissa* (1982), combines such diverse topics as sex and literary theory and centers on the role of the writer in modern literature. The sexual scenario between patient and psychiatrist becomes a literary debate between a writer and Erato, the Greek muse of poetry. Erato changes both shape and attitude throughout the novel, with each change intended to represent a condition of contemporary fiction.

Fowles's related but varied approaches to literature attest to his ability to combine traditional literary techniques with his personal beliefs and methods to produce fresh and unusual perspectives. He has delineated the restrictions of attempting to represent reality in art, but within those restrictions he still tries to achieve freedom and authenticity for himself, his characters, and his readers.

(See also *CLC*, Vols. 1, 2, 3, 4, 6, 9, 10, 15; *Contemporary Authors*, Vols. 5-8, rev. ed.; *Something about the Author*, Vol. 22; and *Dictionary of Literary Biography*, Vol. 14.)

## PETER WOLFE

[*The Collector*] tells the story of a clerk who wins £73,000 in a football pool and then kidnaps a young art student, whom he holds prisoner in his cellar till her death. The clerk has no friends, feels strongly about nothing, lacks a sense of humor, and displays no sexual force. His language is stiff and stale; badly educated and void of ideas, he cannot conceive of anything existing beyond his whims. He has never voted, had sex, nor lived away from home except for his military service. He holds too low an opinion of himself to attempt growth—moral, intellectual, or spiritual. (p. 51)

Out of this shriveled subject matter, Fowles paints one of modern literature's best portraits of a weak man. He describes Frederick Clegg's weakness, shows its effects on others, and explores both the psychological and historical realities that brought it about. Clegg's memoir gives Clegg pure and unadorned; he has nothing to give and he learns nothing. Fowles's feat of making him both predictable and chilling gains force from the novel's continuity. As soon as Miranda is captured, the reader fears for her, and his worst fears are realized. . . . Fowles gets his main ideas and dramatic tensions out early and sees them through rigorously. But in the process he destroys plot, story, and suspense. In their place he poses the questions of how and when Miranda will discover what is happening. The challenge he gives himself in *The Collector* is enormous. So long as Miranda remains a captive, her life brings no change or hope. No action depends on an earlier action. The book goes nowhere. It is contained, actionless, and without motion. Because Clegg has blocked sequence, each event exists for itself. He has no plan. He keeps Miranda prisoner in order to keep her prisoner. He backs the status quo; though she gives him nothing, he wants to prolong her imprisonment as long as he can. No issue builds between them. The only action he takes—besides restraining her—is to disavow action.

How, then, does Fowles hold our attention? How can he bypass so many of the resources of prose narrative and still keep us turning pages? Even though he handicaps himself, he has no symptoms of artistic cramp. He does not grope, cheat, or force conclusions. Incidents convey meaning, and these he develops with power and craft. Miranda says at one point, "This isn't just a fantastic situation; it's a fantastic variation of a fantastic situation." Fowles's inventiveness thrums so sharply—even in a first novel—that only composite terms like realist-fantasist or empiricist-illusionist can compass it. *The Collector* is a fantasy told in precise, realistic details. . . . Wildly original novels like *Robinson Crusoe* . . . and Golding's *Lord of the Flies* do not break loose from realism. Like them, *The Collector* succeeds because of its vision, its truth to human motives, and its workmanly narrative technique.

*The Collector* explores human possibilities. To grant it plausibility is to raise questions that probe a universal level of consequence. Does Clegg's willingness to give Miranda anything but freedom bring her situation close to ours? And while Clegg shows that lethal people exist *around* us, does he not also touch something lethal *within* us? . . . The plausibility of *The Collector* goes beyond technique. It gives a long, many-sided look at human reality. (pp. 51-3)

*The Collector* turns on the statistical and biological fact that independent, creative people have always been outnumbered by their apathetic counterparts. These, the Many, have distrusted and resented the Few because of their resistance to easy, prefabricated moralities. Unashamedly didactic, Fowles calls *The Collector* a parable whose point is that we must build a society where the Few can live freely and teach the Many. Clegg's capture of Miranda is an act of revenge, spurred by class difference. But Clegg does not need to play the avenger. Fowles dislikes the contemporary ideal of the inarticulate hero, based on Salinger's Holden Caulfield (*Catcher in the Rye*) and Sillitoe's Arthur Seaton (*Saturday Night and Sunday Morning*). Overgrown maladjusted adolescents like these need schooling, not power or vengeance. Fowles's remarks . . . show that he geared *The Collector* to the double requirements of topicality and timelessness: "What I tried to say in the book was this . . . In societies dominated by the Many, the Few are in grave danger of being suffocated. This is why the Many often seems like a terrible tyranny."

Fowles's view of the "biologically irrefutable" split between Few and Many goes past Heraclitus. Forces like chance, heredity, and environment condition the split. Often, a person cannot choose to belong to the Few or the Many. Nor is the Few-Many division always clearly marked. Everybody has in him elements from both strains. . . . Clegg and Miranda, too, though they never switch roles, sometimes display traits more characteristic of their opposite than of themselves. The inconsistency is deliberate, for it both humanizes the clash between Clegg and Miranda and gives the action a realistic moral reference.

Before looking into moral complexities, though, we have to review Clegg's suitability as an archetype of the common man and also the particular threat posed by his commonness in our day. . . . Though Clegg is no factory hand, he does come from the working class and shares some of their faults. He resents people with more education or money than he has, and he does not use his freedom well. Relieved of the burden of supporting himself, he is independent but also rudderless. . . . Money and the responsibilities it brings create challenges beyond Clegg's powers. Not only does his luck deny the equation of wealth and happiness. Though it frees him from a boring job, it brings out the worst traits in him. . . . His class consciousness spoils his outing to a London restaurant, where he goes to celebrate his winnings. To raise his spirits, he goes to a prostitute; but, unable to have sex, he feels still more depressed and left out. The separating and corrupting effects of money go through him as through water. He leaves his job and gives up all his personal ties. He collects his winnings and buys a camera, "the best, telephoto lens," which he uses to take pornographic photos. He is cruelly reminded of his social and sexual inadequacies.

He becomes a snob, saying of his aunt and cousin, with whom he has lived since age two, "You could see what they were at once, even more than me . . . small people who'd never left home." Then he kidnaps Miranda.

None of these acts is free. What he wants keeps clashing with what he does. He finds himself continually going against his wishes, interests, and comforts, and he never understands his conduct well enough to change it. He had wanted a new house but buys an old one. He says of Miranda, "I would do anything to know her, to please her, to be her friend." Yet capturing her defeats these hopes. From the outset he is trapped; whatever he does turns out wrong. . . . This failure shows clearly in his first conversation with Miranda. "My mind was really quick that morning," he recalls. But he is easily ruffled and routed. On the next page he says, "I knew what I said was confused." That Miranda, recently chloroformed and kidnapped, is both sick and shocked degrades Clegg still more. He shrinks quickly. Like the self-division hinted at by his chosen name, Ferdinand Clegg, and the omission of quotation marks around his speeches in his memoir, Miranda's easy rout nearly whips him out of reality altogether.

Other people invigorate Miranda, but they inhibit him. He has been hemmed in so long that when a beautiful girl comes his way he gets confused and then kills her. He lacks the self-acceptance, intelligence, and information to have a human relationship. A product of capitalism, he shrills at Miranda, "Tell me what you want, I'll buy you anything." Money, his words imply, solves all problems. His money *has* created a perfect society; all his needs are filled and nobody else's opinion counts. But he and Miranda are bored stiff. Because it is unnatural, his society of one is doomed; hazard, mystery, and the responsibility of nourishing human ties must infuse all social arrangements. . . . Though Clegg's facile identification of money, power, and happiness comes to grief, *The Collector* sustains no quarrel with capitalism. The variety and leisure that money brings are worthwhile. But they need to be shared, not hoarded.

Clegg's background proves him not fully accountable for his crimes. None of the forces that led him to kidnap Miranda has prepared him to deal with her. Many of them, in fact, were outside his control—his genes, his social class, his maleducation. Clegg suffers from what Fowles calls a *pawn complex*. He has no sense of importance; his *individuality* menaced. *The Aristos* calls this anxiety the *Nemo*, "The state of being nobody—'nobodiness.'" It comes from comparing oneself unfavorably to others. Though vexing, the practice is useful. It brings to mind the inequality of existence, and, along with its counterpole, the ego, aids independence of judgment and freedom of action. It helps evolution. Unfortunately, the threat of nonentity also disconcerts. Whereas we preen and prettify the ego, the Nemo brings panic. We are terrified by our ephemerality. We must cheat the Nemo.

This compulsion has had ruinous effects. The need for identity and security has exalted action; action is the best way to hold the Nemo at bay. Man substitutes action for security. Anybody threatened by ephemerality will prefer action over plain good conduct, because action attracts more notice. But the creed of action for action's sake blunts moral values and spurs a desperate search for uniqueness. . . . The social pressures exerted by the Nemo have robbed him of his role as a discoverer or adventurer. Content or substance always takes precedence in Fowles over form. As soon as style, surface, and visual appeal encroach on content, mechanical values drive out organic ones. This trend has gained force since 1945, and Clegg is the product

of it. His photography and butterfly collection negate mystery. They deny change and chance. They have made Clegg both a commodity-fetishist and, as Miranda says, a "visual." To delve beneath surfaces would be to go against the spirit of his society. A weak person, Clegg does not learn to cope with profundity or uniqueness. Nearly all his values are collective. His inarticulateness . . . signals a dreary conformity and a failure in both imagination and depth. It also makes him very dull company.

One force that shriveled him was the home he grew up in . . . [From an early age] he grows up in a home without a man to emulate or identify with. Lacking this healthful influence, he becomes twisted, especially in his attitude toward women. His Aunt Annie and her invalid daughter Mabel he resents for their shabby-genteel narrowness, just as he resents his mother for her moral vagrancy. Privileged people he learns to resent because of his family's low-church ties. So after he sends his aunt and cousin to Australia, he is free to vent his social and sexual wrath on Miranda.

He tells Miranda that he was never punished as a schoolboy, and he usually wears a hangdog look the reverse of wrathful energy. Yet the only thing that kept him decent as a boy and young man was his obscurity. . . . [Miranda's] attempts to help him cannot lift him above his slum mentality. What he cannot solve or cope with is her individuality—as a person, a mind, and a channel of communication. Her beauty and surprise first confuse and then anger him. He only goes to touch her—except for restraining her—when she is either unconscious or dead. So beauty-starved and self-distrustful is he that he degrades all attempts at communication. He keeps crawling beneath her. Flattery will not lower his guard because he lacks both the imagination and self-respect to accept flattery. His low opinion of himself blocks interchange. Lacking humanity, he cannot perceive it in others; his habit is to degrade all motives. Perhaps his pathological fear of sex stems from sex's democratic nature. Miranda's sexual overture drives a wedge between them so great that it divides them completely. . . . Their relationship tailspins quickly after this episode: motives clash more openly, hostility mounts, and she dies in less than a month.

The only way she can stay alive is to act like one of the butterflies in his collection. (pp. 54-60)

His reducing her to an object has political import. As Fowles says in *The Aristos,* any freedom must respect other freedoms: "All denigration of the rights to choose what shall make one happy . . . is fundamentally totalitarian." Clegg does not let Miranda choose her life, let alone her pleasures. . . . [His] severing her from the outside world constitutes the absolute censorship of the fascist state. . . . The only time she looks at his butterfly collection, she reproves him, "You don't even share it. Who sees these? You're like a miser, you hoard up all the beauty in these drawers." *The Aristos* insists several times that existence is countersupporting and that human values come from countertension. By denying Miranda force, Clegg denies the polarity needed for normal life. . . . His will has created a closed circle that nothing human can pierce. He has declared himself the only sentient being in his perfect state. Because he has everything, need does not exist; because he is asocial, his realm has no society and no politics. His will is absolute; his end is his beginning. Miranda's first moments as his prisoner resemble her last; she is lying on a cot, her breathing congested. Inevitably, Clegg looks for another girl to take her place after she dies. "Another M!" he notes when he learns that Miranda's replacement has the name of Marian. Yet the differences between the two girls are as sharp as those between the white magic of *The Tempest* and the sullenness of *Measure for Measure,* where Marian of the moated grange appears. A shop assistant at Woolworth's, Marian is less resourceful than Miranda, less able to teach Clegg, and less suited to a prisoner's life. (pp. 61-2)

Their differences notwithstanding, the two girls die cruel, wasteful deaths; totalitarianism does not respect human difference or individuality. Its success, in fact, depends on the eradication of differences. It cannot tolerate individuality. No one-party state can survive if it permits its aims and methods to be questioned. Miranda falls victim to the same controls exercised by the police state. (p. 62)

Arrogating to himself the roles of jailer, judge, and executioner seals all possible outlets of negotiation for Clegg. He epitomizes noncommunication. Soon after he moves into his house, he disconnects the phone, locks all gates and doors, and rudely dismisses the local vicar. Before he captured Miranda, he had wanted to send her two £5 notes anonymously but did not. After the capture, besides denying her access to radio, television, and the newspapers, he refuses to let her parents know she is still alive; he lies to her about sending a check for £100 to the Council for Nuclear Disarmament; he fails at sex. Where he never falters, though, is in the routine of locking and unlocking the doors of Miranda's cell during his visits. He even bolts her in after her death. Anything that puts barriers between people comes easily to him. . . . Clegg's power over Miranda is so total that it inhibits nature. Besides removing the bracing countertension of social relations, it reorders space and time. It deprives Miranda of fresh air and sunshine, essential to all growing things. Ironically, this power defeats Clegg's pleasure; as has been said, his freedom and general well-being decline inversely with his growing power. Power loosens his control of the realities of his life. (p. 63)

Contrary to his aims, the police-state Clegg sets up by taking away Miranda's rights hampers him, the tyrant, more than her. Because she resists him she must be put down. As a result he denies himself a living source of human values. Rather than dealing openly with her he lies, and he either changes the subject or walks away when she raises the question of her freedom. All emergencies involving her health bring the same response—inaction; if the emergency is not faked, he reasons, then it will either right itself or, past help, kill Miranda in spite of his efforts to keep her alive. He cannot admit any contingencies besides those imposed by holding her prisoner. This is the gangster outlook of modern fascism. In that he destroys her rather than revising his credo, he is much more of a prisoner than she. . . . Once again, this denial of process between Miranda and Clegg makes their life together a closed circle. Nothing new can come from their association; no stale value can be refreshed. Clegg's sexual failure is a logical corollary of his death drift. A natural act shared by people, sex is beyond him. He can communicate neither intellectually nor physically. Inaction and violence are the only two responses open to him. As has been said, *The Collector* has a severe logic. Miranda's humanity keeps flaring out in search of warm contacts. Since these outbursts oppose Clegg's wishes, he can only kill her.

A sure sign of his failure is his disregard of chance or hazard. Hazard, Fowles keeps insisting, defines freedom. If intelligence can be called the ability to handle the unforeseen, then hazard hones the intelligence. In his thick, dull way, Clegg never adapts to the needs created by hazard. He is immobilized by the unexpected and accidental. . . . He has never been self-

acting. He says that capturing her is "the first wicked thing I've ever done." But it is also the first thing of *any* kind he has done. As soon as he and Miranda meet and reverse their roles of agent and acted-upon, they are done for. Although the irony escapes him, the hazard situation that made him rich also brought Miranda to him. But by converting his luck to destruction, he misuses luck. Miranda is only the first in a series. The chance appearance of a policeman outside the doctor's home where Clegg goes to get help for Miranda clinches the hazard theme. Besides deepening Clegg's failure, the scene, coming at the end, balances his winning the lottery at the outset. Both ends of the book feature hazard. His fantasy cannot pad the impact that hazard makes on his life.

Another impact the novel delivers comes from the idea that every life is redeemable. Clegg is weak, but not stupid; unimaginative, but not slipshod. He prepares for Miranda's arrival with amazing cunning. . . . Nor is he tasteless or aesthetically blind. His attraction to Miranda bears out his sense of beauty. And while she despises him, her view of him relative to herself does vary. She admits, "He really had a sort of dignity," and on the next page she adds, "He had more dignity than I did then and I felt small, mean." The pure primitive contact of sex with him excites her. . . . There is much more to him than mechanical efficiency. His occasional oversights, like carelessly leaving his odd-jobs axe where she can lay hands on it, show that he is human. Were he completely mechanized, he would overlook nothing.

Yet he throws away his gift for organization and compassion. A self-declared existentialist, Fowles claims that what man does with his natural endowments counts more than the endowments themselves. Any potential must be translated into performance before it has value. Clegg squanders his potential because he cannot rise above his mania for collecting. The book's title encompasses him; to blot out the collector in him would leave nothing. His possessions possess him. A 1970 statement by Fowles points out the totalitarian dangers of collecting: "Any one who still collects (*i.e.,* kills) some field of living life just for pleasure and vanity has all the makings of a concentration-camp commandant." Then Fowles calls collecting "a narcissistic and parasitical" hobby. Killing, collecting, and exercising power are continuous and interchangeable. (pp. 64-6)

Clegg and his butterfly collection pollute British culture. He spoils his "lovely old house" with hideous furnishings and decorations. "A house as old as this has a soul," Miranda tells him, revolted by the house's tacky appointments. . . . By shutting a scheduled house and turning its chapel into a prison, Clegg defiles tradition. (pp. 67-8)

But why should he worry about wrecking tradition? What has tradition done for him to make him want to protect it? He has never owned property nor learned a skill. . . . His ignorance of due process leads him to take what he wants. Everything tallies. Clegg has not learned respect for the law because the law did not respect *him* enough to educate him properly. His problem is universal; social equality and justice cannot come from material possessions. What is needed above all is educational reform. (p. 68)

The encounter of Miranda and Clegg spells out this need. Being one of the Few does not confer superiority so much as the responsibility to teach and help the Many. Her physical death and his moral death express the difficulty of making good the responsibility. Miranda voices Fowles's humanistic objections as well as his passion for educational reform. She probably carries her narrative burden less well than Clegg, though. Readers have complained that Fowles's liberal-humanist conception of her makes her merely a literary man's model of an ideal girl. The following extract from her diary, though, describes her as more of a sociology major on the rampage than a humanities student:

> I hate the uneducated and the ignorant. I hate the pompous and the phoney. I hate the jealous and resentful. I hate the crabbed and the mean and the petty. I hate all ordinary dull little people who aren't ashamed of being dull and little. I hate . . . the New People, the new-class people with their cars and their money and their tellies and their stupid vulgarities and their stupid crawling imitation of the bourgeoisie.

The declaration has the shrillness of a platform manifesto. Silly and overcharged Miranda is. But her melodrama comes from a surplus of youthful moral passion. Her gropings are honest and forceful. Had she lived, she would have outgrown her romantic posturing and become somebody exceptional, perhaps even an evolutionary force. (pp. 68-9)

Though this potential good is snuffed out by the actuality of Clegg's evil, she does win a major battle. Clegg stoops to lies, evasiveness, and violence, but she maintains dignity by refusing to respond in kind. . . . The only advantages he enjoys over her are his superior physical strength and his money; and money, as it is in D. H. Lawrence, is a form of violence.

A major theme in the book is the battle between spirit and dull, sluggish matter. The winner here is Miranda, and though its moral lesson escapes Clegg, her victory constitutes a major triumph. Only a clear, strong spirit could wrest gains from her situation. Her captivity makes incredible demands on her. Clegg will give her anything but freedom; at the same time, his submissiveness puts her in charge of everything except her being. He gives her nothing human to work with. He and she are remote without enjoying any of the dignity and reserve of remoteness; they are extremely close but not intimate. By demanding nothing but her extended captivity, he makes her ordeal one of terror and boredom, claustrophobia and endless blankness. . . . That her body breaks before her mind celebrates her steely creativity. This tragic victory shows most clearly in the scene where she hits Clegg with an axe. Her humanity outweighs her instinct for survival. She never wanted to kill him. But by not following her temporary advantage, she does not knock him out either. Violence is simply not her way. Though Clegg deserves to be axed, she repents her outburst the next morning by apologizing and then dressing his wound.

Fowles neither resolves nor dissolves moral complexities. Miranda's death does not smoothe the spirit-matter dualism. In fact, it makes us ask whether we *should* fight to preserve what we love and live by. Miranda's failure to knock Clegg unconscious leads to her own death as well as to a number of other deaths. Life makes strange demands. Clegg has created an airless, bloodless realm whose laws deny good conduct. He has created this unnatural order without consulting Miranda. By adopting his measures to defend herself, she outrages her principles. But moral principle only prolongs the terror she lives under. Her life is at stake. And to gainsay life is to gainsay all. If she defends herself immorally, her range of choice has shrunk so far that the only alternative is death. Miranda sticks by her principles and dies.

But are principles worth dying for? Fowles's dislike of the pat answer and his fascination for the region of "what might have been" lead him to sidestep the question in favor of portraying Miranda as an existential heroine-in-the-making. (pp. 69-71)

The religious theme of *The Collector* is hinted at by the supposition that Miranda is being held prisoner in an old priest's chapel. The date of the house, 1621, puts the theme in a severe context: the Pilgrims landed at Plymouth Rock in 1620, and the Puritans set up their American commonwealth in 1629. Clegg's family is also nonconformist. The harshness of their low-church outlook, which includes the loveless notion of original sin, explains much of Clegg's conduct. Clegg plays God with Miranda. The only freedom she has is the freedom he gives her. Instead of treating her as a child of God, he makes her an idea in his mind. She only exists when he thinks of her. In a hideous parallel to Berkeleian idealism, he has her at his mercy. Her being is enclosed by his. Her survival depends wholly on him. . . . (pp. 72-3)

It has been seen how collecting inhibits process. As a harsh God who gives and takes away life, Clegg violates natural and supernatural law. He denies Miranda many of the necessities of animal, let alone, human survival. . . . [Hope] does not even exist marginally in *The Collector*. Nothing like the Holy Ghost joins Miranda to the graceless Clegg. He is without heart. He buys her a heart-shaped necklace in sapphires and diamonds, and, while she has it on, hears her say, "We don't have the same sort of heart." Elsewhere she says, referring to the fiction he uses to kidnap her, "That story about the dog. He uses my heart. Then turns and tramples on it." This heartlessness sharpens the Christian parallel. God, foreseeing the crucifixion, sent Christ to earth because the divine attribute of perfection rules out suffering. Clegg has no more ability to suffer than the God of Christianity; a pitiless iron law grips him with all the strength of a metaphysical necessity. But he lacks God's compassion and wisdom. He also lacks the heart to inspire the devotion Christ demanded from his followers. His violation of Miranda's nature and his denial of renewability make him a poor God-surrogate. The divine power he arrogates to himself, having no natural or supernatural sanction, can only lead to death.

This down-dragging inertia, his underground dungeon, and his sense of injured merit all suggest Satan. Clegg sins against the Holy Ghost, and his moral darkness tallies with an affinity for the dark. Darkness is his natural milieu. He prowls around London's parks in the dark, he develops his fetishist pictures in his dark room, and he admits that he could not have captured Miranda in clear weather. But there is nothing flashy about his evil. A mousy, fawning Satan, he has no imagination or verbal wit. His unworldliness is the demonic principle, not sophistication. The innocence-experience dualism does not apply in *The Collector*. The experience of sin need not taint or maim; more often, innocence is what destroys. Maleducation and "the horrid timid genteel in-between class" whose values he has inherited lead him to lie, degrade, and finally kill. His frequent blushes recall Satan's redness. And his cringing, run-down evil is Satanic in a way continuous with his social class, where the New People have more money and power than they can use responsibly.

But what of Miranda's blushes? And why does Fowles have her say that her heart differs from Clegg's while she has on the heart-shaped necklace he gives her? Although he does trample her heart, he only puts on the necklace because she asks him to. . . . Fowles's moral preference for Miranda is not as thoroughgoing as it appears. (pp. 73-5)

The moral ambiguities lengthen. Fowles even obscures pronoun references in her diary to keep the reader from knowing whether she is talking about Clegg or George Paston. The tremendous human distance between the two men matches the distance in outlook dividing Miranda from Clegg. Fowles's ironical dovetailings do more than just point out the characters' common humanity. They also turn his drama beyond causality and bend his indirect questions about guilt and responsibility to the unchartered depths of primitive experience.

The device of the alternating diaries captures the major irony of the book—the difference between Clegg's view of the abduction and Miranda's. The diaries convey the minds of the characters, so that the reader knows more about their common situation than either of them does. Motives, private histories, and strategies of each character come into view. Clegg's sexual impotence and Miranda's carefully planned attempt to dig her way out of the dungeon, coming as diary or memoir entries, give the reader more information about the abduction than either character alone has. Specifically, Miranda's chance for freedom shrinks progressively with our growing knowledge of Clegg. He will resort to any oversight, distortion, or lie to justify holding Miranda prisoner. So dogged is he in his rectitude that when the first part ends, nearly halfway into the book, his confession hurls the reader into Part Two, which is Miranda's diary; his confession reads:

> What I am trying to say is that it all came unexpected. I know what I did next day was a mistake, but up to that day I thought I was acting for the best and within my rights.

While Clegg's memoir describes his moral darkness, it also humanizes him. The effortless drive and fluency of the memoir, by giving a sustained private view, commits us to him imaginatively. This intimate self-disclosure is necessary, for a third-person narrative about someone as repellent as Clegg would set so much distance between him and us that he would come to us as a caricature or a monster. The memoir's mad, twisted logic, flat, colorless voice, and autobiographical data cohere as a self-portrait. Certain recurring attitudes deepen his madness. There is the withering disclosure voiced as a vague afterthought: Sexual magnetism is "some crude animal thing I was born without. (And I'm glad I was, if more people were like me, in my opinion, the world would be better.)": "I think people like Mabel [his invalid cousin] should be put out painlessly, but that's beside the point." There is also the protest of innocence, like his disclaiming responsibility for Miranda's death. . . . (pp. 76-8)

Fowles interposes Miranda's diary (Part Two) after she catches cold but before her last illness. Part Two goes up to the time of her delirium; there is no time lag between the end of Part One, the end of Part Two, and the start of Part Three, where Clegg's voice takes over again. The stylistic differences between the two accounts are jolting. Clegg's style is blunt, flat, and conservative. His shrunken, timorous mind prefers facts to speculation and interpretation. Miranda's style bespeaks her artistic, outgoing nature. It sparkles with color and sound. She uses language like daubs of paint on a sketchpad. Her lyrical, loose-jointed sentences hold together by free association; she sometimes uses one-word paragraphs; whereas Clegg abides slavishly by grammatical rules, her rippling, imagistic prose abounds in sentence fragments. (p. 78)

Though her diary repeats some of the events Clegg related, it cannot be faulted for repetitiousness. The diary is not infor-mational in thrust; its main job is to describe the staleness of prison life and also her creative responses to her enslavement. Clegg has not imprisoned her mind along with her body. He says, "It was like we were the only two people in the world." But her diary proves him wrong. She spends much time discussing George Paston, or G.P., whereas Clegg discusses only her. The entries devoted to G.P. explain that she has a life Clegg cannot touch; her world is not limited to him as his is to her. Instead of endearing her to him, her enslavement has the reverse effect of heightening her awareness of Paston. The entries dealing with Clegg are mostly short, choppy, and factual; those on Paston are more speculative, expansive, and expressive of her personality. Sometimes an entry . . . will start out discussing Clegg but will end by talking about Paston.

As with Clegg, whose terror sharpens by being couched in a blunt, matter-of-fact idiom, Miranda's literary style gauges her personality, her values, and her ability to adapt to chance. The stylistic inventiveness and control of *The Collector* fuel the novel's theme. *The Collector* is not a perfect novel. The symbolism at the end thickens and obtrudes: Clegg denies three pleas from Miranda for a doctor; her last words are, "I forgive you"; he buries her under an apple tree. Offsetting these blemishes is a marvelous narrative gift. No simplistic diversion, *The Collector* is a brilliant first novel. It features two people who have nothing in common and nothing to say to each other. The end of the book finds them more apart than ever. Yet the book overcomes these plot handicaps to strike roots in postwar British society and to flower in all time. Only an artist could have written it. (pp. 78-9)

> *Peter Wolfe, in his* John Fowles, Magus and Moralist, *Bucknell University Press, 1976, 178 p.*

## BARRY N. OLSHEN

Fowles's imagination, as glimpsed through his fiction and occasional remarks, is densely associative and highly erotic. He tends to view himself in terms of his imaginative life, and his prose fiction he sees as the embodiment of it. (p. 8)

Invention of character, situation, even dialogue seem to come very easily to Fowles. . . . He generally enjoys the rich profusion and eroticism of his fantasy life. In fact, some of the initial creative process seems to occur in the state between his sleeping and waking, when images float uncontrollably through his mind. (pp. 8-9)

While writing the rough draft of a novel, Fowles is principally attentive to the flow of the story-line and the overall narrative technique. After its completion, he will often shelve a manuscript for many months, sometimes indefinitely. The first draft of *The Magus*, for instance, was written more than a decade before the novel was published. *The Collector,* albeit the first work he sent to his publisher, was actually his eighth or ninth manuscript. He is, then, usually at work on more than one book at a time.

This fact may help to account for the remarkable consistency of thought and the regular occurrence of certain fundamental concepts from one book to the next. Also, of course, Fowles was thirty-seven years of age and a mature thinker by the time his first book was published. He was a man with breadth and depth of experience. He was (and still is) a habitual and omnivorous reader of considerable erudition, with certain central thoughts and moral convictions around which might crystallize a personal philosophy of life and art.

Still, considering the stylistic variety of his corpus, it is surprising that the work should be so consistent in terms of the thought. Regardless of the time, place, or action of his plots, the essential human situations and problems described remain quite similar, as do the philosophical questions raised and the moral judgments stated or implied. The recurrence of the same or similar ideas in his essays and even in the most recently published *Daniel Martin*, however, unfortunately give the impression of redundancy as well as consistency. He seems preoccupied—obsessed is an equally apt description—with certain ideas and situations to which he returns again and again.

Fowles is a moralist. He has very strong likes and especially dislikes, and tends to express these plainly and forcefully. His works possess obvious moral or didactic elements. . . . [A] key statement characterizing his work: "I think the serious writer has to have his view of the purpose of literature absolutely clear. I don't see that you can write seriously without having a philosophy of both life and literature to back you." (pp. 10-11)

When asked if there were a particular picture of the world that he wanted to develop in his work, Fowles responded:

> Freedom, yes. How you achieve freedom. That obsesses me. All my books are about that. The question is, is there really free-will? Can we choose freely? Can we act freely? Can we *choose*? How do we do it?

*The Aristos* makes it clear that Fowles dismisses simplistic answers to these questions. (p. 11)

While *The Aristos* presents the issues, the novels are predicated on the supposition of individual free will and the ideal of self-realization. Their conceptual focus remains on the nature and limits of human freedom, the power and responsibility that freedom entails, and the cruelty and necessity of conscious choice. The conditions of freedom and self-knowledge are everywhere conjoined in Fowles's work. Self-knowledge is the goal of life experience and formal education. It is the end toward which all of his protagonists grope.

Human freedom and the existence of a god who intervenes in the affairs of men are, for Fowles, mutually exclusive conditions. (pp. 11-12).

Fowles's fiction tends to focus upon those crucial moments when important choices are made and when they are set in motion by ensuing actions. The fiction stresses the existential shock so often necessary to jolt us into a full awareness of the moment of choice and the need to act upon this awareness. Freedom is generally explored along two paths simultaneously: the ethical or moral path, by involving us in the quest of the fictional characters; and the aesthetic, by illuminating the liberating possibilities, for reader and writer alike, of fiction itself.

Creating a work of art, for Fowles, is the supreme expression of the freedom to be who you are: "Being an artist is first discovering the self and then stating the self in self-chosen terms." In addition to its basic functions of teaching and amusing, Fowles believes that art also has the unorthodox function of stimulating insecurity, of making us aware of the rule of hazard in our lives. (p. 12)

Although Fowles equivocates in his use of the term, the central meaning of "mystery" in his work . . . is the antithesis of that which is known or knowable. It is conceived as man's source of energy, the dynamic spur to human achievement, because the very fact of mystery allows for the continued existential

quest. To live with it and to harness, not eliminate, the dynamic power of such a life is the ultimate goal. Fowles's fiction assumes a function almost religious in nature when it is able to evoke the unknown and to involve the reader relationally with it. These moments provide us with experiences akin to what is traditionally associated with the realm of the holy or sacred. The concept, however, need not be confined to the sphere of religion. (p. 13)

The fundamental fact of existence, for Fowles, is the tension or conflict of opposites. . . . These unresolved tensions, however, are a blessing to humanity for they promote and foster the basic activities of living.

Love and sexuality play a crucial role in causing and relieving the tensions of human existence. Perhaps for this reason, Fowles, in his writing, is engaged in the exploration and exposition of the nature of love and the criteria for harmonious relations between the sexes. (pp. 13-14)

Heterosexual love and the nature of freedom are at the thematic center of all of Fowles's work. In fact, in the novels, the two are inextricably bound: the realization of love brings with it a sense of freedom, and the responsible assumption of one's freedom allows for the full realization of the possibilities of love. (p. 14)

While *The Collector* is less elaborate than [his] other novels in terms of its structure and more modest in terms of its plot and themes, it is perhaps Fowles's most finely wrought and carefully organized long piece of fiction.

The plot is highly compressed, uncomplicated by the subplots and digressions that characterize his other novels. It is the very carefully controlled, often horrifying account of a lepidopterist who turns his attention from rare butterflies to young and beautiful women. (p. 15)

The "collector" is one Frederick (though he prefers to call himself Ferdinand) Clegg. . . . Clegg suffers from an acute sense of class inferiority and personal inadequacy, coupled with a fear of failure and criticism. This self-conscious and small-minded, friendless and graceless young man has little prospect for personal development or fulfillment of any kind until the day he strikes it rich. . . . It is his sudden wealth that incites Clegg to turn his secret, psychopathic fantasy into a concrete reality, and it is his plans and their eventualities that form the basis for the plot of the novel.

The object of his fantasy is the beautiful art student, Miranda Grey. She is everything he is not: imaginative, open-minded, gifted, liberal, humane. She possesses a vitality and a capacity for love and sympathy that are quite incomprehensible to the petty clerk. While she, in her own way, is also smug and priggish, it is clear that Miranda is to be seen as the flawed but certainly more positive product of the upper-middle class, with the sadly unrealized potential to become, as Fowles himself says, "the kind of being humanity so desperately needs." These two characters, then, embody individual and social polarities, and it is largely through the clash of their personalities and perspectives that the meaning of the novel emerges. (pp. 16-17)

Clegg purchases in Sussex an old, secluded cottage with a secret cellar, renovates and decorates the place, and outfits it with clothes, books, and other things he imagines will please Miranda. With diabolical precision he secures the place against her escape. One night, while she is returning from the cinema, he entices her to his van, chloroforms her, and abducts her to his new home, where she is to remain indefinitely as his "guest." (p. 18)

The remainder of the story deals with the intimate but perverse relationship that develops between the collector and his specimen, with Frederick's demented efforts to satisfy her needs and Miranda's repeated attempts to secure her release. The reader is at once repelled and fascinated by [the] apparently fantastic series of events. It seems perfectly plausible, however, because it is presented realistically and in minute detail. Though titillating throughout, the material is always handled with decorum and control. It is greatly to his credit that Fowles never allows the novel to descend to the level of sadism or sensationalism on the one hand, nor to sentimentality on the other. . . .

Despite their physical proximity, there is no bridge to span the separation between them. After wooing and seducing; after bargaining, begging, pleading, and play acting; after desperately trying every possible means of escape, including an attempt to burrow out and even an attack on his person with an axe, Miranda contracts pneumonia in the dank basement. Her incarceration ends implacably with a lonely, frightening, miserable death. (p. 19)

[The open-ended conclusion] suggests that the collector is bound to the cyclical enactment of his psychopathic fantasies. In Fowles's later novels the open-ended conclusions will suggest fresh beginnings and hitherto unthought-of potentialities in the lives of the protagonists.

The story, then, is quite simple. . . . Its subtlety and its extraordinary portraiture, however, arise almost entirely from the complexity of the narrative technique. Fowles allows his antagonists to tell their own stories, thus achieving a double perspective on the otherwise straightforward sequence of events. . . . From the conflation of these partial, subjective accounts, the reader gains a more objective and inclusive perspective on the events and their meaning, and a much fuller, more sophisticated understanding of the motives of the title character.

Clegg, of course, is allowed to condemn himself even before Miranda fills in the details from her point of view. His banal confession reveals much more clearly than Clegg himself ever realizes just how repressive his upbringing has been and how warped are his values. Indeed, much of the irony of his story arises from the fact that he unwittingly reveals more than he understands. Much of its horror arises from the apparently clinical, matter-of-fact manner in which he recounts his fiendish plot. A considerable part of his narrative is devoted to rationalizing or justifying his actions, and especially to denying his culpability, until we come to realize that Clegg does not fully understand what he is doing and therefore is not fully accountable for his actions. He frequently suggests that the plot was unpremeditated, that the events occurred by chance not by choice. (pp. 20-1)

When we turn from Clegg's narrative to Miranda's diary, comprising Part Two of *The Collector,* we are immediately aware of a radical departure in perspective and style. The events beginning with her capture and ending with her loss of consciousness are retold from her point of view, with, of course, changes of emphasis, deletions and additions, as well as long passages about her past life, her goals, and her social and aesthetic values. . . . She rightly identifies power as the major force governing their relationship. And yet, typical of Miran-

da's complex and ambivalent viewpoint, she still must admit: "A strange thing. He fascinates me."

One of the most interesting aspects of the diary is the way it records Miranda's coming to terms with her situation, trying to make sense of its evident absurdity and trying to understand the motives of her captor. It is the testimony of her repeated efforts to sympathize with Clegg and to educate him, of her refusal to relinquish hope, to admit that humaneness, sympathy, and intelligence count for nothing in the crypt room. The insight she provides into their growing intimacy is especially noteworthy. . . . (pp. 22-3)

Part Two is far from the clinical, uncritical, unimaginative matter-of-factness characteristic of so much of Part One. Instead of the unwitting irony in Clegg's account, we are treated to Miranda's conscious irony and even an occasional display of humor. . . . (p. 23)

The basis for the perception of humor . . . lies in the disparity between the energy exerted and the importance of the task, a perception that entirely escapes the monomaniacal Clegg. We are used to laughing at overly fastidious, obsessive, or purely mechanical behavior in comedy, but *The Collector* is in no way a comedy and its humor (the little that there is) is far from pure. Rather than providing "comic relief" from the situation, the humorous moments of the novel, more often than not, augment the feelings of anxiety and menace. (pp. 23-4)

Because of the conventional assumption in the diary form that the writer is the only reader (or, as Miranda says, that she is "talking to herself"), we must assume that we are getting a very private glimpse into the innermost thoughts and feelings of the diarist. We are thus ironically required to imagine ourselves in an analogous role to Clegg's, the role of the voyeur, reading what was never intended for us to read, and gaining vicarious enjoyment from this experience.

Miranda keeps her diary as a means of maintaining her sanity, as an imaginative and intellectual retreat—"to escape," as she says, "in spirit if not in fact." Naturally enough, she devotes much of her time to nostalgic reminiscence of the joy and excitement of life outside her prison, and especially of the influence of one particular artist friend, "G.P." (George Paston). He was Miranda's first and only mentor, and the pages of her diary reveal his influence on her intellectual, emotional, and aesthetic development, a development cut pathetically short. The sections recalling G.P.'s thought and life style contain embryonic expressions of Fowles's own philosophy. . . . Too often . . . , however, the reader senses that Miranda has stepped out of character and is serving mainly and too obviously as her author's mouthpiece. Despite this stylistic flaw, these overtly didactic passages do make a primary contribution to the development of the themes of the novel.

Miranda depicts herself (perhaps a little too melodramatically) as a martyred representative of "the few" and Clegg as the embodiment of what she calls "the Calibans" and what G.P. calls "the New People." Each of these two terms is associated with a separate pattern of imagery in *The Collector,* one exclusively literary in its reference, the other social. The first, "the Calibans," involves an elaborate analogy between *The Collector* and Shakespeare's *The Tempest.* (pp. 24-5)

The other image pattern, with its social implications, is associated with G.P.'s coinage "the New People." According to this line of interpretation, the struggle between Frederick and Miranda is an allegory (Fowles himself uses the term "parable''). The characters' situation represents the omnipresent struggle between two much greater opponents: the faithless and visionless, the materialist and philistine masses on the one hand, and the few imaginative individuals who create and maintain the best of our civilization on the other. Furthermore, the story of Frederick and Miranda stresses the mindless oppression and ultimate destruction of the physically weak but gifted few by, in Miranda's words, those possessed of the "great deadweight of pettiness and selfishness and meanness."

This conflict between the Few and the Many (as it is called in *The Aristos*) is at least as much an admonition for the future as it is a depiction of the present. Both Frederick and Miranda are products of their very different environments, their vastly unequal educations and opportunities. In the preface to the second edition of *The Aristos,* Fowles states quite explicitly that it was his intention in *The Collector* to illuminate the invidious consequences of these gross social inequalities so characteristic of Western society. Clegg's tyranny and Miranda's abortive attempts to understand and to educate her oppressor point to the need to create a society in which the Many will be tolerant of the Few and the Few will feel responsible for the education and betterment of the Many. If there is a positive morality that emerges from *The Collector,* it is surely this, an idea which also forms a central thesis of *The Aristos.* (pp. 26-7)

The fundamental significance of *The Collector* is in its depiction of the drive for possession as the ubiquitous substitute in the impotent for their inability to love and in the unimaginative for their inability to create. This theme holds a central position in the Fowles corpus. (p. 29)

> *Barry N. Olshen, in his* John Fowles, *Frederick Ungar Publishing Co., 1978, 140 p.*

## SYHAMAL BAGCHEE

Speaking about *The Collector* a few months after its publication, John Fowles commented that he was "shocked" to find British "intellectual" periodicals treating the novel as mere crime fiction. He explained that it was really a serious novel dealing with important philosophical questions about authentic and inauthentic existence. However, eleven years later Fowles described the same novel as "a sort of cold-blooded book . . . a small or narrow book . . . really a casebook for me." As far as the author was now concerned, the book had merely demonstrated that he could "write well-enough to get published." I think today most critics would agree with Fowles's later view and consider *The Collector* a work less distinguished than *The Magus, The French Lieutenant's Woman,* and *Daniel Martin.*

*The Collector* is popular mainly with critics who like novels with pronounced thematic and moralistic content. Such critics classify the book variously as a class novel, or a novel about the struggle between good and evil, light and darkness, life and death, or creative impulse and destructive mentality. Because of its sharply delineated contrasting characters and distinct two-part narrative with two unmistakably separate narrative voices, *The Collector* encourages such thematic white-versus-black readings where Miranda can be taken to represent goodness, beauty, and high morality; her captor, Clegg, evil, ugliness, and immorality.

This clear-cut thematic view of the novel is difficult to reconcile with the overall impression created by Fowles's fiction. His later works have demonstrated that his moral view is emo-

tionally finer and intellectually much more complex than what we apparently find in *The Collector.* Especially in *Daniel Martin,* his most compassionate book, Fowles's mature moral position is tentative and largely nonjudgmental. . . . [Yet] even *The Collector* contains intimations of Fowles's later moral and aesthetic complexity.

I have said "even *The Collector*" because it is clear that Fowles intended the book to be successful mainly by immediately contemporary standards. Whatever he might have said about its philosophical content, the book was primarily an exercise in a kind of fiction that later proved uncharacteristic of its author. Because the book lacks at least three important elements invariably found in his later fiction—a heightened sense of style, a subjective or metaphysical interest, and a sense of mystery—it seems likely that Fowles deliberately restrained himself from writing in his natural vein. (pp. 219-20)

*The Collector* was designed to succeed . . . [by making the artist seem to be a limited man]. It was seemingly both technically competent and intellectually limited. And its success gave Fowles the much-needed courage and clout to publish books more compatible with his imagination.

Notwithstanding the authorial design, *The Collector* deserves to be read with care and discrimination, for even if it is less dazzling and spiritually less engaging than Fowles's later works, it still contains evidence of intricate workmanship and unexpectedly complex storytelling. Read carefully, *The Collector* reveals a profoundly ironic view of the absurd that escapes the notice of readers interested only in broad thematic generalities. Both artistically and thematically—but not merely in terms of large themes—*The Collector* is a rewarding introduction to a study of Fowles's works, though at times it proves Fowles's novelistic strength only in an oblique fashion.

To use modern jargon, *The Collector* is an "instant" book, yet it displays Fowles's great command over plot structuring, creation of dramatic scenes, and the building up of a nerve-racking climax. Working within a severely limited setting—mostly in a cellar—and with an inarticulate main character and inexperienced heroine, physically restricting them to one place, with almost no other characters, and writing in a prose style that is very rarely modulated, Fowles gave himself the nearly impossible task of creating an effective story out of little tangible material. But he succeeded. The result is that one can only talk in paradoxes when describing this novel.

Compared with Fowles's other novels, *The Collector* is a timid book, but it is also remarkably daring in seeking to be perfect within such small compass. Stylistically drab, the novel yet has a style that suits the subject very well, particularly in the sections narrated by Clegg. . . . The meticulous way in which Fowles arranged the story's unfolding, matched and contrasted the double narrations, and executed the detailed descriptions of the encounters between Miranda and Clegg shows that he never slackened his artistic control over *The Collector.*

In this novel Fowles found the best compromise between his exacting sense of art and the age's demand for reality-oriented fiction. In treating an ostensibly topical theme Fowles was able to avoid being labeled an "experimental" writer. The book's characters are stably realized, and on the most obvious level the novel addresses itself to useful social and moral problems. The prophetic mode is entirely avoided. The book is not essentially symbolic; it uses symbols only of the most predictable kind: dead butterflies, paintings, photographs, sunlight, a cellar, and the old historical house in which most of the action takes place. The literary and linguistic allusions and hints are no less obvious: the references to Miranda, Caliban, and Ferdinand—ironical in the last case—and the derivation of Clegg's name from *clef*, a key. *The Collector* tells a suspenseful story with considerable cleverness and control. But within the framework of this narrow popular work Fowles has incorporated some interesting and vital features. At the surface level the novel prompts thematic readings, but because its hidden narrative thrust is ironic, its real meaning is often ambiguous and tentative. (pp. 220-22)

The inherent uniqueness of the particular drama contained in *The Collector* has been frequently overlooked. When examined closely and objectively, the novel reveals many unexpected elements that, while being real within the story, seem to contradict well-established thematic patterns. (p. 222)

The curious thing about the novel is that in spite of the immeasurable spiritual gulf between Miranda and Clegg their narrations rhetorically illuminate each other. *Together* they present a complex drama of conflict, tension, clash of personalities, as well as intimate insights and unexpected emotional reactions. It is not enough to read Clegg's narration as raw data for the psychological case study of a madman.

The two narrations frequently agree not only about physical descriptions of incidents that take place, but often also in the way two very different characters react similarly to given situations or display similar attitudes. The most obvious instance of this is in their opinion of God. A close examination of the text shows how surprisingly close their views are, and the seemingly inappropriate agreement between Miranda and Clegg in this matter points to an extremely involved ironic vision.

Neither Miranda nor Clegg is a believer. . . . Since Fowles himself is an atheist, he appears to be using Clegg as a highly improbable spokesman of his own views. Similarly, when Miranda writes . . . in her diary, she echoes sentiments often found in Hardy, an author whose view of chance or hazard has significant influence on Fowles's imagination. . . . (pp. 222-23)

The underlying dual narrative technique is, therefore, richly ironic and reveals a sombre and frightening view of life's hazards. The novel's reliance on the element of chance, the gloomy ending, the utter bungling by Clegg of all possibilities for a happier ending makes it Fowles's darkest book. Although Miranda expresses some existential robustness, a determination to take the plunge, it is all in vain because the overriding view of life in the book is unrelentingly gloomy. In fact, only a year later, in *The Aristos*, Fowles expresses a more cheerful existentialist attitude . . . almost as if caricaturing the pessimism of *The Collector*. . . . Hazard still dominates Fowles's view of life, but it is "hazard within bounds." Unless hazard is finite, the robust existentialist stance to perform a soul-redeeming *acte gratuit* becomes merely an ineffectual attitude of the mind, as Miranda is forced to realize in *The Collector*. (pp. 223-24)

In *The Collector* things happen by chance, by absurd combinations of events, and usually in a manner quite different from the way participants intend them to be. This is the basic ironic-absurdist view of the book. The world of *The Collector*, especially towards the end, is *not our world;* however, it is similar to the view of the world we have in our darkest hours. It is an absurd world that moves inexorably in its own willful manner. It is difficult to accept most humanistic and existentialist readings of *The Collector* because the final outcome of events here does not appear to spring so much from character or the nature of the individual as from the general condition of the novel's

world. This view, of course, is not unique to Fowles. Rather it is part of a persistent minor tradition of modern literature.

The irony of this story can be seen also in the fact that Miranda seals her own fate by *being herself*. With each successive escape attempt she alienates and embitters Clegg the more. Clegg is *not* predisposed to hating Miranda. In fact it is amazing how much trouble from Miranda he is willing to put up with. He is quickly able to get over his annoyance after each escape bid by Miranda.

In an early entry in her diary Miranda speaks of the "other side" of Clegg's character, the violent, cruel side of his personality. . . . Curiously enough, Clegg seldom displays this side; and Miranda herself admits soon after making the above comment that Clegg has "tremendous self-control." . . . She chips away at this self-control and near the end of the book makes him feel openly antagonistic towards her. She does not merely do this by attempting to escape, but also by continually taunting Clegg about his poor taste, cultural ignorance, and lack of education. The two incidents that finally effect the change in him are her desperate and unfeeling assault on his sexual timidity and the physical assault with the ax.

At this point in the novel Clegg's character undergoes a drastic change, and much of his attitude towards Miranda after this is rooted in her two-fold assault on him. Although most critics ignore this climactic point in the novel, both Miranda and Clegg indicate an awareness of the change.

Miranda says, "There is a great rift between us now. It can never be bridged." . . . Clegg's own view of the time when Miranda tried to seduce him is no less definite. . . . One of the implications of this "great rift" is that the deductions we make about Clegg's character up to this point in the story do not remain altogether valid in the remaining part of the book. For instance, the Clegg who decides to undertake an "experiment" with an "ordinary common shopgirl" (and perhaps many others after her) at the end of the novel is essentially *not* the same person as the Clegg at its beginning. (pp. 224-25)

Despite the shocking result of Clegg's love or "romance" the novel is, indeed, a love story. Once we recognize the basic ironic-absurdist thrust of the rhetoric of the book, we will see that love is an entirely appropriate theme of the story—because it is so paradoxical. Especially ironic is the fact that Clegg causes terrible and irreversible destruction even though his love is in many ways timid, self-effacing, dreamy, and idealistic. . . .

But *The Collector* is a love story in less horrifying but no less ironic ways as well. In the first place, there is the unfolding of an unusual relationship between Miranda and Clegg. Clegg is not an ordinary evil character. Fowles has taken great care to show that Clegg is like no other person we know. It takes Miranda a long time to get rid of her successive stereotyped views of Clegg as a rapist, an extortionist, or a psychotic. She admits to an uneasy sense of admiration for him, and this baffles her. Clegg defies stereotypical description.

We know that Miranda is a very special kind of young person. She is a radiant, albeit incomplete, character. In his painfully inarticulate fashion Clegg knows this too. There is much in his early description of her that suggests that, in spite of his obtuseness, he is aware of her preciousness and uniqueness. He cannot define it, he cannot fathom it, and his way of showing his admiration for her is unimaginably cruel. But even Miranda is overwhelmed by the steadfastness of his devotion and the selflessness of his attachment. He wishes to keep her with him—in his initial plan the captivity was only a temporary measure—but his need for her is not in the main self-assertive or solipsistic. He values her almost more than his own life.

Clegg stands apart from the depressingly small-minded class of people among whom he has had to live most of his life. In spite of winning an enormous amount of money in the pool, he does not lose his head easily. (p. 226)

Clegg has a moral restraint that is recognized by Miranda when she calculates her risks in trying to seduce him. . . . Ironically, however, Miranda fails to calculate the . . . risk she takes in threatening *his* sense of dignity and privacy. She precipitates her tragic end by her planned assault on Clegg's sense of masculinity.

Although Clegg becomes increasingly cruel towards Miranda after the rift, his unkindness contrasts vividly against an early scene like the following:

> "Put them on," she said. "If you give a girl jewellery, you must put it on yourself."
>
> She stood there and watched me, right up close to me, then she turned as I picked up the stones and put them round her neck. I had a job fastening them, my hands were trembling, it was the first time I had touched her skin except her hand. She smelt so nice I could have stood like that all the evening.

This is one of the few nearly epiphanous moments in this stylistically bare novel. Another is when Clegg takes Miranda out of the cellar and into the garden for a walk. There, too, he is stirred by a vague surge of passion but is content not to let himself get carried away. Even Miranda recognizes the power of this moment over Clegg. . . . In each case Clegg is not only greatly moved, but is also painfully conscious of an affection that can only be the sign of a deeper but inarticulated sensibility, however ill-grounded in reason.

Finally, this outrageous love story contains some unusual scenes of harmony. There are times when such uncharacteristic tranquility exists between Miranda and Clegg—at least on the surface—that the reader has to remind himself with a shock that it is a story about a kidnapper and his victim. Even Miranda feels touched by this tranquility. . . .

Clegg's description of these unusual moments of calm are remarkably similar to hers. . . . Again we see how the double-narrative technique is sometimes used by Fowles to unfold a remarkable similarity in perspective. Also, it is important to notice . . . that Clegg is aware of the intellectual and emotional differences that exist between him and Miranda. He does not fool himself into believing that Miranda's reaction to every experience is similar to his, although he senses correctly that on rare occasions their feelings match.

As one may expect, this complex, ironic technique also requires us to readjust our view of Miranda's character. She is a remarkable person, and often she is a dependable interpreter of Clegg's character. But she, too, is not merely an allegorical figure. Her sensibility is not determined by what we think she should properly be, but by what she is and by what happens to her.

Miranda is placed between two men who are in every possible way different from each other. George Paston is the object of Miranda's love, devotion, and admiration. Clegg, whom she names Caliban with only partial justice, is mostly the object of her scorn.

Miranda's admiration of Paston is due, at least partly, to her easy predisposition towards aestheticism. If Clegg is stubbornly opposed to aesthetic sensibilities, Miranda is much too willing to venerate them. Even though our knowledge of Paston is based entirely on Miranda's admiring account of him, Paston often appears to be a "fantastical" character in the Renaissance sense of the word. He cultivates a rude insularity and can be unnecessarily cruel towards people he does not like.

Although he has some valid opinions on art and morality, there is a degree of calculated shrewdness about the way he expresses them in order to impress Miranda. He is clever enough to size up Miranda, and to know what effect he can have on a person of her sensibilities and exactly how he can go about producing such an effect. He may not be a sham, but nor is he an ideal romantic hero. Of course, a typical romantic character is not likely to impress Miranda very much.

Miranda derives much of her ideas about life, art, and morality from Paston; frequently she judges people and experience in terms of his ideas. Nevertheless, in spite of Paston's views of the Few and the Many, and the New People, she is often conscious that her confinement by Clegg is something more than the symptom of a predictable class conflict or aesthetic conflict. She realizes, as we too must, that Clegg is not really a "type" character. Even his ordinariness, she admits, is extraordinary. . . . (pp. 227-29)

Miranda is only twenty years old, and one of the most frequently noted ironies in this story is that she really begins to grow up while in captivity; this she herself realizes. . . . Her growing up is finally futile; she learns the true meaning of existentialist choice when, in fact, she has very limited actual choice. And she learns to understand herself and her life when, in effect, that life has come to a standstill.

But even granting her immaturity and youth, I suspect that she is so extraordinarily under Paston's intellectual influence mainly because she is predisposed towards such domination. Notwithstanding the mild annoyance she occasionally feels in being so attracted by Paston, she is both in need of a person like him and is inclined to like his fantasticality. (pp. 229-30)

[It] is clear from Miranda's account of their early relationship that he had been manipulating the relationship throughout to his advantage.

Admittedly the advantage towards which Paston works is neither sexual nor financial. He makes no attempt to seduce Miranda. What he seems to desire most is to control her mind, to dominate her intellectually, morally, and aesthetically. He is, therefore, the first of Fowles's many teacher-inspirer-enchanter figures. (p. 230)

What corrupts Paston is his enjoyment of power. In spite of his avowedly ascetic lifestyle, he exercises considerable power in his role as a mentor. He overwhelms Miranda, and his process of instructing her—for which he makes himself responsible after making sure she deserves to be taught—includes playing fairly merciless games with her heart. (p. 231)

However, Fowles's view of power is unequivocally existentialist, for he does not approve of any force that seeks to dominate an individual. This creates a peculiar moral ambiguity in most of his novels.

From Miranda to Daniel, all of Fowles's protagonists are marked by an aestheticizing-intellectualizing sensibility. If it were not for this element of personality they would have been ordinary characters. But Fowles consistently creates protagonists who display spiritual and emotional liveliness even when they are morally imperfect. His characters are chosen for special attention by the instructor-enchanter figures because they are potential "elects." They have the special mental stuff that fascinates Fowles. It is characteristic of their mentality, in turn, to be fascinated by mystery.

However, this very predilection for the mysterious makes the characters the more subject to the instructor-enchanter's exercise of power. Necessarily, therefore, the protagonists invite the enchanters to trick, bully, and outwit them. This inflictor-afflicted relationship between the instructor and the protagonist is, unfortunately, not very satisfactory to anyone who, like Fowles, believes in the paramount importance of freedom and choice. (pp. 231-32)

It is well-known that power and freedom are among the central concerns of *The Collector.* The blatant and immoral exercise of power and control by Clegg has been clearly and helpfully discussed by most commentators of the novel. Miranda's struggle to escape, and her even more admirable struggle to keep her mind and soul free ought not to escape the reader's notice. But it is important to note that Paston and Miranda, too, indulge in power play—although not of a vicious kind—in this ironic novel.

In spite of Miranda's complaint that Clegg is constantly trying to force her to change her nature . . . , it is Miranda herself who tries to alter Clegg's personality. . . . One of the altruistic tasks Miranda sets before herself during her captivity is to educate Clegg. . . . She seems determined to help him out because he is so inferior to her: "I'm so superior to him," she tells herself. . . . Although her intentions are well-meaning, and even generous, they are not untouched by a desire to play a mild version of the godgame.

Some critics have justifiably complained about the sententiousness of Miranda's moral and aesthetic statements. Both the sententiousness and the air of righteous self-satisfaction with which she often speaks indicate that she is much too immaturely caught up in aesthetic idealism. (pp. 232-33)

At one point in the novel she pities Clegg for his inability to speak about his feelings clearly: "terrible not being able to speak" she remarks. . . . It seems equally true that Paston speaks much too well. If Clegg cannot articulate his feelings well, Paston can manipulate his words with extreme agility. Again, when Miranda diagnoses that Clegg needs a mother figure, we may conclude with equal justification that she looks upon Paston as a much-needed father figure. Miranda, in turn, tries to play a Paston to Clegg.

Increasingly towards the end of her narration she elevates Paston to the level of a symbol, as standing for life, light, art, individuality, and a host of other values. Yet there has to be an element of fantasy in these descriptions, because her earlier accounts of the encounter with the man reveal him to be, at least partly, cold-blooded, arrogant, cynical, and offensive. He is caustic, autocratic, and overbearing; what is worse he uses his intelligence to hurt people. He appears to get pleasure out of outwitting others and in being rude and unpredictable in his behavior. . . . (p. 233)

None of the foregoing criticism of Paston's character is meant to present him as a villain. At one level, at least, he is the spokesman for many of Fowles's own ideas. Paston's principles of art, morality, and life are accepted by Miranda, and they give her an inner strength all through the crisis and prevent her from giving in to the wishes of Clegg. Moreover, these secondhand notions become the basis of much that Miranda comes truly to realize about life during her incredibly fast spiritual growth in captivity. My point is simply that Fowles's imagination, even in *The Collector,* is more paradoxical than antithetical.

In the final analysis, *The Collector* must be considered a minor work; but it is not as slight as some critics have assumed. Nor is it a *roman á thèse.* The book contains a relatively complex philosophy of life, and its ironical technique is quite thorough. This is so in spite of the fact that Fowles has created it as a deliberately limited book, as a clever concession to the literary taste of the time. (p. 234)

> *Syhamal Bagchee, "'The Collector': The Paradoxical Imagination of John Fowles," in* Journal of Modern Literature, *Vol. 8, No. 2, 1980-81, pp. 219-34.*

## PATRICIA V. BEATTY

The one undisputed triumph of John Fowles' first published novel, *The Collector,* was the chilling portrait of Frederick Clegg, the drab and colourless clerk grown suddenly powerful with the winning of a large fortune in a football pool. The relevance of Clegg's presentation as an ill-educated, resentful social misfit has not faded with the passing years, and critics have rightly focused on Fowles' analysis through this character of the social and political forces which have shaped the Cleggs of this world. But what of the individual Clegg rather than the type? Paradoxically, an archetypal approach to Clegg allows us to locate the core of his personality; more specifically, an investigation of the archetypal associations of Eden as Fowles employs them in *The Collector* to establish the psychological dimensions of Clegg's personality reveals one of Fowles' central themes: the destructiveness of a failure to develop psychological strength and insight through a dialectical tension, as well as the pathos of an inability to acquire an attitude of imaginative consciousness toward life, which might be termed existentially aesthetic.

Fowles himself has said that being a writer means "being able to put your finger on the archetypal things in people's minds," and taking this cue, critics have explicated his later novels, especially *The Magus* and *The French Lieutenant's Woman,* in terms of Jungian archetypes as active personality fragments, such as the shadow or the anima or animus. . . . But I am concerned here with the *place* aspect of this class, as these structures may also be examined in their metaphoric form in literature as a means of communicating the "kind of transformation" being presented, or, as in Clegg's case, the "kind of transformation" which does not take place.

For Jung, places of "magic transformation and rebirth, together with the underworld and its inhabitants, are presided over by the Mother [archetype]." Such places as Paradise, churches, the sea, and gardens may symbolically represent "the goal of our longing for redemption," reverence, or creativity because they are representations of the complex of unconscious instincts associated with the mother-child relationship and its experience. But also associated with this complex is fear of personal obliteration, the dark, hidden power of the unconscious, and thus other representative associations with the mother are terrifying caves, the underworld of Classical mythology, or the Hell of Christian theology.

Or, in *The Collector,* the cellar of the isolated Sussex cottage which Clegg sees as an opportunity to create his own Eden. . . . (pp. 73-4)

The kind of Eden that Clegg creates is pictured in this remote cottage. Walled in on two sides, hedged on another, and with only one side open to the woods and fields surrounding it, it serves as an objectification of Clegg's own alienated, shuttered personality. Inside the house, the tasteless, mass-produced items provided by decorators are analogous to the conventional moral and social ideas which furnish Clegg's conscious mind. He has "bought" them without thought or involvement. It is the cellar, however, for which Clegg buys the cottage. . . . Although Clegg lacks any real insight into himself or his motivations, he feels intuitively drawn by a dream-like atmosphere; with its separation from the upstairs, "it was like down there didn't exist. It was two worlds." (pp. 74-5)

The cellar is a place where Clegg can realize his fantasies and thereby create his own paradise. But because his mind is unable to conceive of paradise except in possessive, infantile, claustrophobic terms, what he creates is a demonic parody of Eden, the lowest end of the scale on which representations of the Edenic archetype might be arranged. The conventional elements of paradise are all present—the walled-in enclosure, the exclusiveness, the unchanging climate, the provision of all things without toil or pain, the expectation of supreme happiness, and, especially, Adam and Eve. Clegg says at one point, "It was like we were the only two people in the world" (p. 65). Yet because this Eden is a projection of an unconscious trapped in arrested development, it is a travesty. The magical qualities of transformation, so prominent in Edenic sites, do not operate here for Clegg, although, ironically, for Miranda the cellar does become the "special place" where the creativity and rebirth associated with the archetype are evidenced in her reaction to imprisonment. (p. 75)

That Clegg is drawn to Miranda as his anima has been mentioned by a number of commentators. . . . Their observations are apt but perhaps not precise enough. Clegg is attracted to Miranda as his *potential* anima, but because his ego is underdeveloped, he is unable to move beyond the uroboric mother stage. His personality lacks the strong self-consciousness that would enable him to encorporate in his psychic structure the fragmented archetypes, thus unifying his self. He conceives of his relationship with Miranda in mother-son terms, and when Miranda mistakenly attempts to humanize him by offering herself to him sexually, he feels threatened. From this point on, he sees her as not the Good Mother but the Terrible Mother, and he must destroy her in order to preserve his illusion of autonomy and control. However, as his plan to receive another "guest" unfolds, it is quite clear that he is trapped in a pattern of action signifying his growing submission to the destructive unconscious.

While it may be coincidental that the cottage Clegg buys is named "Fosters," a word associated with maternal solicitude, and equally coincidental that most of the women in *The Collector* have names beginning with *M,* Clegg's mother fixation is established explicity in the narrative. Abandoned by his mother and raised by a cold, rigid, conventionally pious and hypocritical aunt, Clegg reaches adulthood with two conflicting concepts of women. Because his aunt has encouraged him to

think of his mother as a prostitute, Clegg has a low opinion of most women, yet he retains an ideal concept, which he believes he sees in Miranda. . . . The dreams he admits to consciously place her in a sexually neutral role as hostess and companion, and he repeats often that Miranda would "understand" him or that she would know how to love him, the implication being, as only a mother could. After he kidnaps her, she sees very early on that he is looking for a mother. . . . (pp. 76-7)

Although acute embarrassment in a man of Clegg's weak ego is enough to explain the extreme reaction Clegg has when he fails to respond to Miranda's sexual advances, his identification of her with the maternal archetype makes his sudden revulsion even more understandable. She becomes for him like the real mother, "no better than a common street-woman," . . . rather than the ideal mother he hoped to regain. . . . Thus he must assert his power by degrading her through forcing her to pose for pornographic pictures and eventually allow her to die. Potential anima, Miranda is not strong enough to lure Clegg from his inertness; he destroys the burgeoning soul within him and with it his chances for transformation. Instead, he plans for another *M,* Marian, a clerk, appropriately enough, in a dime store, a typical sign of the cheap, consumer society which has provided Clegg with his values. Clegg may hope to assert his superiority over his next victim, but his quest for recovery of maternal love, for the key to Eden's gate, is, of course, doomed to defeat.

Fowles himself has explicitly linked the quest for the irrecoverable "eternal other woman, the mother" to *The Collector.* In his "Hardy and the Hag," Fowles discusses the mother as providing for the infant Edenic security, pleasure, and a sense of magical power. . . . [Thus], the writer in his fiction repeatedly attempts to recapture Eden in the form of a feminine ideal, but, to ensure the continuation of his creative life, he must fail, for success would mean the end of the writer's motivation. (p. 78)

We may then see Clegg as an early, ironic presentation of the artist that Fowles believes each person must strive to become in shaping his life. Clegg is, of course, a failed artist doomed to write himself as a monster, as Caliban rather than the Ferdinand he would like to be. (p. 79)

In addition, Clegg fails as creator of fiction: in his first conversation with Miranda, he tries to make up a story to explain the kidnapping to her, a wild tale about being in the power of the bank president, and Miranda sees through it immediately. . . . His own narrative lacks the artistic objectivity even to allow for quotation marks around his own statements, although he does quote Miranda. His trite, cliché-ridden, dead language is put to the service of confused self-rationalization, and the lack of aesthetic shaping in his narrative is thrown into sharp relief when it is contrasted with Miranda's section, which is an exercise in self-examination and written in a variety of forms, including drama and fairy tales.

*The Collector's* ending is bleak; Clegg's burial of Miranda under an apple tree seems a savagely ironic commentary on the travesty of Eden that Clegg has created, Adam's ultimate revenge for Eve's betrayal. By arresting in flight and trapping the animating force of life, by attempting to hold in stasis what must by its very nature exist in a state of flux, of change and growth, Clegg ensures his own enslavement to forces which he can never understand and which will eventually effect his psychic death. (pp. 79-80)

For Fowles, the mind is truly its own place, and it carries within it an Eden universally experienced and universally lost. In *The Collector,* he shows us through Clegg negative and destructive responses to this loss. (p. 80)

Patricia V. Beatty, "John Fowles' Clegg: Captive Landlord of Eden," in Ariel, Vol. 13, No. 3, July, 1982, pp. 73-81.

## BENJAMIN DeMOTT

["**Mantissa**"] is a somewhat sluggishly played jeu d'esprit about sex, creativity and theories of literature. The hero is an amnesiac novelist named Miles Green who is hospitalized under the care of the heroine, a self-metamorphosing physician named Dr. Delfie. (From page to page the Delphic Delfie variously reconstitutes herself as oracle, muse, slut, siren and rock star.) The treatment prescribed for the amnesiac is a course of sex therapy which, in Mr. Fowles's description, edges intermittently (as Miles Green himself notes) toward soft-core porn. The overall effect achieved is that of conscious yet lumbering self-parody. Miles Green's references to his own work indicate that he shares his creator's tendency to run at the philosophical mouth when invention flags, as well as his addiction to multiple endings. . . .

The book opens with an account of an attempt by Dr. Delfie to rape her patient for his own good. The justifications offered for the deed range from the suggestion that "this procedure bears some resemblance to mouth-to-mouth resuscitation" to the claim that Green's memory lapse is attributable to a hyperactive superego.

In subsequent chapters of the book the initial patient-doctor conflict is redefined as a debate, sort of, between new-style and old-style literary theory. Dr. Delfie figures as Erato, sexually hungry muse of lyric; Miles Green steps forth as spokesman for "serious modern authors." Laying it down that modern fiction has only one subject ("the difficulty of writing serious modern fiction"), Green explains that fiction "has no business at all tampering with real life" and argues that "writing *about* fiction has become a far more important matter than writing fiction itself." He slips briefly into deconstructionist babble about the absence of connection between authors and texts but adheres mainly to fatuous self-celebration. . . .

There is a minority view of John Fowles (one that I confess I share) according to which, despite the quantity of intellectual rumination in his pages, the man is essentially a yarnsmith who is at his best when producing page-turners such as "**The Collector.**" . . . Admirable and immensely successful as a suspense engineer . . . , Mr. Fowles has gifts that are essentially for romance and glamour, not for the penetration of heart and not really for subtle intellection either.

It is a fact, though, that this author stands high at the moment in those quarters where one might expect jeux d'esprit about literary art to be best received; university literature departments. Early in his career, in "**The Aristos**" (a "self-portrait in ideas"), Mr. Fowles put himself forward as one capable of thinking interestingly about free will, determination, "the Few and the Many" and other philosophical themes. His narrative designs—in "**The French Lieutenant's Woman,**" in two of the stories collected in "**The Ebony Tower,**" even in "**The Collector**"—clearly invited explication and analysis. Equally alluring, to not quite first-class academic minds, was the chatter in "**The French Lieutenant's Woman**" about the Victorian

suppression of sexuality and the knowledge of the underclass, and the discourses in "**Daniel Martin**" about film writing versus novel writing. Signs abound in his work of exceptional responsiveness to intellectual fashion. . . . And the combination of knowingness, commitment to large topics (humanism, nature) and prolixity . . . has worked in support of the academic conception of John Fowles as Major Figure.

I think there's a chance that "**Mantissa**" will contribute in time to a sensible downward revision of Mr. Fowles's reputation. Its pages are bare of the pleasures that, in his other books, mask the comparative ordinariness of this novelist's performance as thinker. . . . What comes into sight is an author tentatively, self-protectively exploring, through the creation of an absurdly pretentious novelist, the possibility that the easygoing yarnsmith may in truth be his own best self. Literary theorists may find themselves troubled by this exploration; they may realize that Mr. Fowles is not merely unsympathetic with their cause but really rather dim about what that cause was in the first place. And this uneasiness could result in a situation in which Mr. Fowles loses a measure of his power to inspire critical monographs, but is thereby encouraged to resume writing tales that people read with hands running.

With luck, in short, "**Mantissa**" could emerge as a wonderful breakthrough for us all.

Benjamin DeMott, "The Yarnsmith in Search of Himself," in The New York Times Book Review, August 29, 1982, p. 3.

## ROBERTSON DAVIES

Here is a splendid *jeu d'esprit* by John Fowles, which will give delight to anyone who is truly fond of literature, though it may cause annoyance to readers who have little sense of humor.

[*Mantissa*] cannot be called a novel, for it has no story to tell. . . . [Yet what] Fowles has given us is no trifle, though it is not physically bulky, and not theological in any ordinary sense of the word.

It reaches toward the world of the gods, however, for it is about the relationship of an author with his Muse, in this case Erato, traditionally associated with erotic poetry (and geometry, for these Muses were versatile), whom Fowles thinks most likely to be interested in the modern novel.

Erato appears in several guises, and in all of them her concern for erotic poetry, or anything simply erotic, is amply apparent. Her occasional associate, in the mind of her author, is Persephone, or Kore, who turns up in the book as Nurse Cory, a beautiful Barbadian who is simpler and more generously erotic than Erato, who occasionally appears as the minatory Dr. Delfie. As you can see it is a book of some verbal complexity, and you have to be wide awake as you read it. (p. 1)

[The] author has every reason to be in the book, for Erato, or Dr. Delfie, is as distracting, capricious, tender, critical, admiring, captious, bossy, yielding, cold, hot and in every way such a mingling of opposites that one might say there was no knowing where to have her if it were not that the author (whose name is Miles Green) seems to manage pretty capably in that respect. The relation between author and Muse is a powerfully erotic one, although that is not all there is to it, and here again Erato is tease, prude, tough expert and untouched virgin in a series of bewildering changes. What is the book about, you are asking. It is about what I have been describing; it is about how an author—or better say how Miles Green—encounters and is inspired by his Muse, and it is quite the liveliest description of this fairly common encounter that I have ever read.

Muses are usually dealt with respectfully, not to say gingerly, by poets and prose writers who speak of them at all. . . .

Not so in *Mantissa;* Erato is touched, and indeed sometimes thumped, and in her turn she lands several shrewd blows on the author whose inspiration she is. Not only do they fight and make love; they talk, splendidly and entertainingly, and Miles Green's attempts to bring Erato up to date on the latest developments in the novel are hilarious, particularly those in which he explains the necessity for the thickest and most impenetrable existentialist gloom.

There is little here to give comfort to academic devotees of the latest fashions in the novel, or to the earnest proponents of Women's Lib. Erato is a partner, and sometimes senior partner, in what Miles Green writes, but she is not herself a writer. She is the Eternal Feminine, who does not need to be freed because she has never been bound, though now and then she is sat on, and for good reasons.

The book is a splendid lark, but no trifle. It is the best possible evidence of the relationship between John Fowles and his own Muse that he can spin a web like this which is so light, and yet so strong. (p. 8)

*Robertson Davies, "How to Make Love to a Muse," in* Book World—The Washington Post, *September 19, 1982, pp. 1, 8.*

MICHAEL POOLE

If the recent history of modernist fiction in England has largely been a case of having one's cake and eating it—of taking on board the baggage of experimentation while continuing to work within the traditional framework of the realist novel—then few practitioners can be said to have gorged themselves more fully on the confection than John Fowles. His first novel, a somewhat sensationalist thriller called *The Collector,* revealed a talent for psychological manipulation that was transferred to the narrative process itself in *The Magus* and *The French Lieutenant's Woman*: two wilfully deceptive fictions which begin in straightforwardly realist manner—as existential *Bildungsroman* and historical novel, respectively—only to end up playing a spectacular game of hide-and-seek with the reader.

This hybrid style, a combination of the slickly readable and the fashionably 'difficult', rocketed both books into the bestselling lists, much to the delight of Fowles's many critics who had dismissed them as the work of a vulgarising pasticheur, a literary magpie with an eye for writing modish Parisian theories about fiction into fiction itself. And when, after a gap of some eight years, Fowles could only come up with the disappointingly conventional *Daniel Martin,* a turgid meditation on Englishness of three-decker length and feel, it seemed as if they might have been right. . . . (pp. 26-7)

Well, after another longish interval . . . , the news is that Fowles has rediscovered some of his old élan in [*Mantissa*] which unequivocally turns its back on realism and, at the considerable risk of self-parody, both personal and artistic, attempts a sort of summation of all his previous concerns as a novelist to date. Which is to say that it is about sex and literature. First, though, a word about the title, which I immediately took to be a reference to the praying mantis and thus a further register of the

profound sense of unease generated by female sexuality in all Fowles's work. He himself is at pains to point to the word's strictly literary provenance, quoting the *OED*'s definition of it as 'an addition of comparatively small importance, especially to a literary effort or discourse'. In fact, both meanings are operative—and in a sense form the key to a novel centred on the apparition of a mythic Woman seeking a terrible revenge on a representative Novelist for his complicity in the literary conspiracy that has reduced her gender to a fantasy trope in the hands of male authors.

The novelist, though called Miles Green, is of course Fowles himself; while his antagonist is none other than Erato, the Greek Muse of erotic poetry. . . . They confront each other in the grey, quilt-lined walls of a psychiatric hospital where the novelist is undergoing sex-therapy, but which, as many an allusion to literature-as-neurosis makes clear, also approximates to the inside of his own head. The narrative unfolds as a series of increasingly violent exchanges, with the Erato figure assuming a bewildering variety of guises—now a character in one of Green's own novels, now in one of Fowles's own and now an historical personage—the better to berate the hapless scribbler for his sexist mythologising.

Anyone who knows Fowles's work will recognise that this scenario apparently represents a quite extraordinary about-face on his part. Normally in his novels it is women who are on the receiving end, albeit from flawed, limited men—in *The Collector,* a girl is imprisoned by a psychopath; in *The Magus,* the central female character is shabbily deserted; and in *The French Lieutenant's Woman* she is hypocritically betrayed. Are we to conclude, then, that the intervening growth of feminism has prompted a change of consciousness in Fowles? Probably not. The sexual dialectics of *Mantissa* are such that the Erato figure can still be made to conform to male desire when it suits the author: 'Take brutal possession of me against my will.' There is, in short, no happy medium—female sexuality remains either threatening or masochistic. Nor is Fowles beyond exploiting his theme for the kind of frisson associated with 'upper thigh' bestsellerdom. . . .

To be sure, there is serious intent here. Fowles, as ever, is toying with us, couching his narrative as one long tease in order to make a point about the erotic imperative at work in all literary endeavour. Sex *and* literature, then, and perhaps not in that order either, because *Mantissa* is packed solid with speculation about the nature of fiction and Fowles's own previous attempts to expose its mechanisms in his work. Constantly gesturing towards the reader and alluding throughout to its status within the institution of literature—in terms of the market, the reviewing establishment and the latest theoretical finery of the academy—it would seem, in fact, to be principally about Fowles's own rather fraught relationship to his audience. The novel's sexual revisionism turns out to have been something of a blind, a means of taking account of his feminist critics, while at the same time allowing him to squeeze yet another book out of his career-long obsession: the enigmatic woman.

Genuinely challenging, and thoroughly un-English in the energy it gives ideas *Mantissa* may be; but it is also an extremely arid book and one, it has to be said, that reeks too much of narcissism to offer any lasting sustenance. (p. 27)

*Michael Poole, "A Battle with Erato," in* The Listener, *Vol. 108, No. 2781, October 7, 1982, pp. 26-7.*

## GEOFFREY WOLFF

Not since William Faulkner abetted the publication of *Pylon* has a sillier novel [than *Mantissa*] appeared above the signature of a better novelist. No need to review John Fowles's manifest and manifold virtues, his happy way with a yarn (*The Collector* and *The French Lieutenant's Woman*), his narrative flexibility (*The Collector* and *The French Lieutenant's Woman*), his ambition (*The Magus*), his stamina (the recently revised version of *The Magus*), his learning (*The Aristos*), his humanism (*Daniel Martin*). He has before now written short fictions (*The Ebony Tower*) but never anything so meager, so pinchfist of invention and scruple, so ungenerous. To read *Mantissa* is like watching a train wreck, but a world less interesting and consequential. . . .

A contemporary novelist, Miles Green, awakes in the gray, puff-padded room (cell?) of a kind of hospital. He has amnesia, does not recognize (nor wish to recollect) his wife. He is slightly more interested in his doctor, called Delphie (for Delphic). She is his muse, . . . and the room of course is Green's brain, but in case you don't apprehend this Fowles will tell you as much. . . .

[Fowles's] work has always had a powerful erotic component, but never before so sleazy and mechanical. . . . [Listen] to Dr. Delphie talk to Miles Green as she works him over:

> The memory nerve-center in the brain is closely associated with the one controlling gonadic activity. We have to check that the latter is functioning normally. This is standard procedure. No reason to feel shy. Now please—close your eyes again. . . .

Certainly the preoccupation here with t & a . . . is conventionally juvenile. No offense, except against prose, to muse about breasts that "were in themselves warm and firm, pleasant handfuls.". . .

No, the shame of *Mantissa* is its nastiness, the gloom of weariness that fogs a listless light touch. No sooner does Miles begin to resemble Benny Hill . . . than sourness breaks out again. Sappho is "that poor old bent teaspoon on Lesbos," temperature rising to see Erato in her swimsuit. . . . (p. 34)

No real heart to press forward, show the whole hand. Miles Green's complaining, less a threnody than a whine, is like late-night bellyaching at Elaine's. Modern writing is arid, no one appreciates quality, reviewers don't read the books they review, "how sick one gets of writing—and even sicker of being read." This otherwise unlocalized ennui has earlier had a special reference, to the investigations into *seems* and *is* that have been Fowles's particular strength, what Green here repudiates as "all this crap about reality and unreality.". . .

The whole of *Mantissa* couldn't possibly be as bad as the parts I have displayed, and it isn't. The final chapter is crisp and smart (or crisper and smarter) than the first three, a languid bedroom battle-farce. . . .

The most troubling aspect of *Mantissa* is the considerable evidence to suggest that Fowles disbelieves utterly in its givens. Surely he has made previous references in his work, lightly, to the Muses. But he has also written, from what seems to have been the heart, that writing, unlike screenplaying, and unlike a collaboration between a Muse and her mouthpiece, is *not* a community work project. . . .

Or does the heart not recognize what the mind asserts? If *Mantissa* is about anything, and it isn't about much, its subject is manipulation and dominion. Fowles has often been charged with being a "manipulative" novelist, which is no charge at all, merely a tautology. By this his critics resent something duplicitous in his plots and narrative shifts, something I have always admired, an opening rather than foreclosing of possibilities. Even when the magician has seemed the most admiring fan of his own trick, there has been energy in the illusion, wonder in it. The manipulations here, however, are dutifully despotic, arbitrary, shows of force, habitual, unreflecting.

In the same 1968 essay in which he celebrated the singularity of the novel's creation, Fowles remarked that "my female characters tend to dominate the male." This was a curious, interestingly rich aside from the author of *The Collector* told by a man who kidnaps a young woman to *have* as he has the butterflies he likewise collects. But she tells her side, too, and in this world narrative rules. In the sexual combat of *Mantissa's* bloodless porn, man's contempt for woman is as plain and simple as woman's for man, a question of which rider spurs which horse. Human creatures are not so diminished as *Mantissa* pretends to believe. (p. 35)

*Geoffrey Wolff, "Bloodless Porn," in* The New Republic, *Vol, 187, No. 16, October 18, 1982, pp. 34-5.*

## ROBERT TAUBMAN

In 1964 John Fowles published 'a self-portrait in ideas' called *The Aristos,* of which he has said: 'I hate to think of the awful pages of bad philosophy that would be in my novels if I hadn't written that.' Perhaps time will find a similar use for *Mantissa:* at the moment, there's little else to say for it. Before fantasy was liberated by some modern writers, it often tended to the facetious: arch encounters between a fanciful nymph or two, muses and such. *Mantissa* is that sort of thing. It is an encounter between a writer and his muse, in a series of quick-change acts they have been developing ever since Erato came down from Olympus. There's no evidence this time that the writer is a self-portrait of John Fowles, but the ideas look like his all right. His ideas about literary theory, mythic recurrence or sexual politics may have done some service in the best of his novels, where they're not altogether out of contact with narrative and the reality principle—though even there they look a bit sententious. Here they have everything else wrong with them as well. . . .

[Erato] talks in all the ways women have ever been supposed to talk. The [writer] pompous Miles Green, on the other hand, talks like a book; what's worse, like this book—which advances its narrative by such means as: 'This somewhat abrupt ending (or aposiopesis) is caused by a previous movement from the figure on the bed.' Couched in every cant phrase ever used between man and woman, their exchanges are immensely boring. Serious points are intended—on the connection between sexuality and language, for instance. And there's the let-out that Erato isn't really responsible for her fantasies or her awful script: it's *his* fantasies about women that she's acting out. . . . But nothing serious stands a chance against the facetiousness of it all. Better to be facetious about silly ideas rather than serious ones. It's no consolation that Fowles is serious. (p. 16)

*Robert Taubman, "Beckett's Buttonhook," in* London Review of Books, *October 21 to November 3, 1982, pp. 16-17.\**

## PETER CONRADI

John Fowles's achievement has proved a hard one to assess, and not merely in the way that all contemporary writing is properly resistant to a just critical focus. . . . His fictions display anxieties about being serious as well as about being entertaining, and his flamboyantly showy fluency is itself a value he clearly suspects; the novels worry at it in the attempt to solicit a series of impossible liberations. In *The Collector* a beautiful kidnapped girl struggles to free herself from her deranged captor. In *The Magus* the struggle is against the authorial surrogate Conchis, whose totalitarian yet benign fantasy is paradoxically to educate the protagonist into a properly difficult sense of his own freedom. In *The French Lieutenant's Woman*, his most important work so far, it is the emancipation of the reader as well as the major characters from the coercions of the text which is part of the programme. Imprisonment and liberation, seduction and betrayal, are both thematic and formal obsessions for Fowles. He makes adroit use of the collaborative privileges of verbal form, soliciting the reader in fiction's felt need to authenticate itself (capturing/seducing the reader) and in its equal, contrary need to expose its own tricksterism, the artifice upon which any such authentication must ultimately rest (betraying/liberating the reader).

Fowles writes romances, gothic stories that exploit the ancient erotic sources and opportunities of narrative and whose designs on the reader are palpable; and through which a series of Persecuted Maidens and *princesses lointaines* are pursued and prompted, like the mystical and psychological truths they embody, to deny the text that closure they seek. In the magical enclosure in which his fictions abound, love is feudalized. He is a paradoxical figure: a didactic and coercive libertarian; an evolutionary socialist profoundly committed to the values of a Romantic individualism, which his existentialism is called upon to validate; an apologist for the female-principle much given to imagining the sexual exploitation and salvation of women; a writer of fables of erotic quest who does not present adult sexual relations, and who has been read as a bourgeois pornographer expert in the aesthetics of frustration—but which expertise is itself put at the service of a censorious sexual moralism.

Fowles has an evident willingness to risk himself in each of his fictions in something new, so that each novel can also be read as an innovatory attack on his own fluency. What each fiction also shares is a curiosity about the technical and ethical potentialities of what have traditionally been regarded as 'low' sub-genres of fiction, all of them broadly categories of romance. . . . Both *The Magus* and '**The Ebony Tower**' differently approach romance in its pure state; '**Poor Koko**' and *The Collector* utilize the thriller, *The French Lieutenant's Woman* the historical romance and sensation novel, and '**The Enigma**' the detective tale. In each, the interest of the fiction lies in the consequences of disconfirming the expectations raised by the genre. (pp. 15-17)

The romance, it is worth recalling, has traditionally been regarded with more suspicion in England than in America, and has been liable to derogation as a mode of lowbrow entertainment, of sentimental and fantastic escape. . . . British criticism at its least generous has tended to blame Fowles's novels simultaneously for stooping and aspiring, treating them—like the Hollywood fantasies excoriated in *Daniel Martin*—as both ruthlessly sensationalist in their manipulation of expectation and relentlessly high-minded in their moral tenor. . . . The American critic Robert Scholes suggests that it is a 'fair and

important question' whether Fowles's passion in *The Magus* is 'equal to his virtuosity, whether the book is merely sensational or truly meaningful'. Through moralizing his romances so insistently, however . . . , Fowles has made himself vulnerable to attack both from those critics whose aesthetic puritanism finds his ethically controlled fantasies didactic, and from those whose humanist puritanism finds them escapist. From some of those critics characterized by Paul de Man as content to be communal moralists in the morning and formalists in the afternoon, and from a vast non-academic audience, he has had a responsive reading. (p. 17)

All his novels differently marry literary modes and embattle styles. What distinguishes *The Magus* (1965) and *The French Lieutenant's Woman* (1969) is the way the conventions of realism and romance are made in the first to cohabit uneasily, in the second to collide openly. In *The Magus* Urfe's extraordinary adventures on a remote Greek island are subject by him to a constant, impossible series of attempts to authenticate them, to verify their basis; in *The French Lieutenant's Woman* the reader is wryly invited from the first page to test out the 'truths' of the narration, an invitation the novel extends in a variety of ways. . . .

But Fowles is, as I shall argue, himself a romantic artist as well as a writer utilizing the romance tradition, and for romantic artists, as W. H. Auden wittily put it, 'the Boojum [is] waiting at the next cross-roads where they will be asked whether or not they have become their actual selves.' The Fowlesian novel is always a new quest for personal authenticity, a place in which the self of the protagonist is to be tested, tried, stripped and subjected to ordeal. In his best books this testing is formal as well as thematic. In *The Magus* and *The French Lieutenant's Woman* Urfe and Smithson search for authenticity and are consequently denounced, in books that equally denounce themselves and try to purge their own inauthenticities by publicizing them. (p. 18)

The search for an absolute existential wholeness can never be fully achieved by either work or hero. Even the work that gleefully announces itself as a garden of forking paths, as *The French Lieutenant's Woman* tries to, is still a reticent accomplice of the world's bad conscience: that novel awards us and its characters three possible endings and proclaims our liberation and that of the protagonists to be a settled matter. (Life, as Christopher Ricks pointed out, would give us not three possibilities but an infinity of them.) If to be oneself is the aim of everything romantic, it is not an aim that can ever be wholly achieved. And indeed Fowles has acknowledged this: 'But *The French Lieutenant's Woman* was a cheat, you see. I thought it was an obvious cheat.' . . . Total self-coincidence always lies in the future—for the work and its agents as for the reader—or in the past where, in one necessary map of misreading, the Victorian novel can be pastoralized as a place Edenically unaware of its own conventionalization, awaiting like Milton's Adam that *felix culpa* of a Fall into Modernity which will enable it to start to know itself. The cloud of formal unknowing in which the nineteenth-century realist novel innocently and sinfully moves is itself a part of the subject-matter of *The French Lieutenant's Woman*. That mutual criticism of realism and romance which in *The Magus* made for an uncomfortable liaison reappears in *The French Lieutenant's Woman* as a more controlled formal irony. This novel, like certain mannerist art, puts its own conventions on a kind of show trial, convicting itself in public of deception, but oddly intensifying its own illusionism in so doing. The show trial turns out to be (like that of Urfe in *The Magus,* and like those of the 1930s) itself a kind of *trompe-l'œil.*

Closure, illusionism and a hierarchy of discourse figure in a recent critical work as the defining characteristics of classic realism, that quintessentially inauthentic mode. Fowles's novels show disturbances in all three areas. The hierarchy of discourse—which asserts the subordination of most levels in favour of one privileged level of discourse whose hegemony is finally asserted (closure)—is challenged in *The French Lieutenant's Woman,* where two endings are granted near equality: the expectation of a simple closure is frustrated. In *The Magus* the denial of closure is accompanied by an equivocation about whether the illusionism of the opening section, or the very different style of illusionism asserted at Bourani, will win the implied competition between them; neither level wholly agrees to accept subordinate status. Even *The Collector,* which apart from *Daniel Martin* shows the greatest debt to realism, has a penultimate chapter in which Clegg offers his ideal ending, an ending invalidated by the real last chapter. And this real ending in its turn is undercut by Clegg's plan to kidnap a new victim and re-establish the cycle of imprisonment. The open ending of *The Magus* and of some of the short stories, and the trick endings of *The French Lieutenant's Woman,* are also all part of 'a sort of theory that the energy is in the ill-defined' . . . , an attempt to imprison contingency or institutionalize provisionality. The same dedication to the provisional led Fowles to recall the text of *The Magus* and issue a revised version in 1977. (pp. 19-20)

The tension between . . . satisfying our credulity and appeasing our scepticism, as David Lodge has it—differently energizes each of Fowles's first three novels. When as in *Daniel Martin* such tensions are relaxed, the result is an unhappily indulgent and incontinent solipsism, the more singular in that it is apparently unwitting. (p. 21)

In a period in which the debate about the degree of integrity available to either the 'self' or the 'text' is an urgent cultural issue as well as a literary-critical battleground, it is not surprising that Fowles's work, impenitently hybrid as it is, should have received such diverse readings. Each of his novels can best be read as in pursuit of the peculiar integrity of its own incompleteness, which is to say as braving a new kind of fictional logic by which to foreground, however inconclusively, its necessary inauthenticities. (p. 22)

*Peter Conradi, in his* John Fowles, *Methuen, 1982, 109 p.*

## EUGENE GOODHEART

*Mantissa* fits the Oxford English Dictionary definition of the title: "an addition of comparatively small importance, especially to a literary effort or discourse." The action of the novel is a dialogue between a novelist—Miles Green—and his muse. Their relationship is polymorphously perverse, since the muse constantly changes shape and attitude throughout the novel. Each alteration in the relationship between muse and novelist illustrates a condition of contemporary fiction.

The first section, for example, shows the muse as both doctor and nurse administering, in or through their own persons, sexual therapy to Miles, who is suffering from amnesia. Sex is supposed to be the great stimulant of memory. What, in fact, it does stimulate is a sense of outrage in the novelist. . . . It would seem that from the point of view of the doctor-muse, the novelist Green/Fowles is neurotically repressed, unlike perhaps some of his erotically avant-garde contemporaries. "The reason I can already detect [remarks Dr. Delfie] is that you are overattached to the verbalization of feeling instead of to the direct act of feeling itself, which in turn means that—." Miles aptly responds "For God's sake—who's doing all the talking?" Fowles, through Miles, means to register his traditionalist suspicion that the erotics of contemporary art is so much cold-blooded talk.

In the hands of a novelist of ideas, a dialogue between novelist and muse might turn into literature as well as criticism. Neither achievement occurs in *Mantissa.* A vein of resentment runs through the attitudes (they never achieve the integrity of ideas) expressed by novelist and muse, who show each other off to disadvantage. Fowles has it in for post-structuralism and post-modernism against which he can mount only the easiest kind of parody. . . .

Strange that Fowles, who gives us a large sense of life in his other work, should in *Mantissa* write an example of the impoverished reflexive mode of contemporary fiction against which he protests.

*Eugene Goodheart, in a review of "Mantissa," in* Boston Review, *Vol. VIII, No. 1, February, 1983, p. 34.*

# Nadine Gordimer

## 1923-

South African novelist, short story writer, critic, and editor.

Gordimer has gained international stature as a writer who explores the effects of the South African apartheid system on both ruling whites and oppressed blacks. Although the political conditions in South Africa are an essential part of her work, Gordimer focuses primarily on the complex tensions they generate within and between individuals. Her novels and short stories are widely praised as unsentimental yet sensitive and insightful. Her prose style is noted for precise detail capable of evoking both the physical landscape of South Africa and the predicament of being trapped in an unjust multiracial society. She is also lauded for her nonstereotypical portrayal of black culture. Of her characters, Mervyn Jones says, "she writes not so much with sympathy, as with a cool, meditative understanding." Although some critics fault her detached narrative voice, claiming it results in a lack of emotional immediacy, many contend that the excellence of Gordimer's fiction is largely due to what Richard Hayes describes as the "elegance and sobriety" of her prose.

Gordimer often writes about the intrusion of external reality upon the sheltered existence of South Africa's middle-class whites. Her first novel, *The Lying Days* (1953), chronicles the coming-of-age of a young white woman who gradually gains a widened social perspective. Likewise, in *The Conservationist* (1974), which was awarded the Booker McConnell Prize, the protagonist must come to terms with his sense of guilt and displacement as he feels increasingly threatened by the pervasive presence of the black man. For many of Gordimer's characters, their efforts to rationalize their situation and repress their fears result in restricted emotional and personal growth. *A World of Strangers* (1958), which depicts an alienated and stratified society, and *The Late Bourgeois World* (1966), which centers on the arid isolation of the white middle class, further express Gordimer's belief that whites as well as blacks are victims of the apartheid system. Many of Gordimer's white characters are progressive and work against the existing social order. For example, *A Guest of Honor* (1970) tells of Colonel James Bray's return to an African country from which he had been exiled for supporting black revolutionaries. Considered by some Gordimer's best novel, *A Guest of Honor* won the James Tait Black Memorial Prize in 1972.

Critics have noted a connection between the development of Gordimer's themes and the deterioration of race relations in South Africa during her literary career. Although *The Lying Days* offered hope for the future, a recent novel, *July's People* (1984), confirms Gordimer's progressively pessimistic attitude. This novel, set in the future, takes place in the aftermath of a revolution and centers on a white family forced to depend on a former manservant to provide refuge for them. Through this reversal of roles the novel reveals deep-rooted feelings of prejudice and racial supremacy in even the most liberal-minded people.

The themes of Gordimer's short stories are similar to those of her novels. From her first major collection, *The Soft Voice of the Serpent* (1952), through *Something Out There* (1981), she

© Jerry Bauer

portrays individuals who struggle to avoid, confront, or change the conditions under which they live.

(See also *CLC*, Vols. 3, 5, 7, 10, 18; *Contemporary Authors*, Vols. 5-8, rev. ed.; and *Contemporary Authors New Revision Series*, Vol. 3.)

## JOHN BARKHAM

To the chorus of eloquent voices emerging from South Africa, add a new one, that of Nadine Gordimer. It is a fast growing chorus. Paton, Lessing, Rooke, Van der Post, and now Gordimer—until a few years ago none of these names was known here; but they have begun to speak and their voice is heard in the land. They will be heard from again, especially Nadine Gordimer. . . .

Miss Gordimer is a subtle writer who makes her points delicately and obliquely [in *The Soft Voice of the Serpent*]. A beach interlude with an Indian fisherman, as in "The Catch," will indirectly tell you as much about the color bar in South Africa as any editorial. A young couple (white, of course) grow to admire an Indian fisherman who has landed a big fish. Driving into the city later, they offer him a lift. The presence of other white passengers suddenly makes them conscious of his color— and therefore of his "inferiority."

But most of these stories are not even remotely concerned with headline types or affairs; rather with the happiness and disappointments of daily living. Anyone who has lived in South Africa, as this reviewer has done, will recognize the accuracy of Miss Gordimer's types, the validity of her situations, and the acuteness of her perception. This is South Africa as it really is, not as it is painted for this purpose or that.

Easily the best story in the book is **"A Watcher of the Dead,"** an account of a family death and its attendant ceremony that is a marvel of selective detail and artistic sensibility. But each of these tales will strike its own chord of significance. . . .

Not all of Miss Gordimer's stories come off, but her batting average is high. **"The Defeated"** might have been a poignant study of the unbridgeable gap between the first two generations of immigrant Jews, but the point is blunted by the over-coolness of the narrative style. Nor is the author sufficiently emotional in handling the incipient love affair that climaxes **"The Hour and the Years."**

But these are minor blemishes in what amounts to an unusually impressive debut.

> John Barkham, "African Smiles," in The Saturday Review, *New York, Vol. XXXV, No. 21, May 24, 1952, p. 22.*

### ISAAC ROSENFELD

[Miss O'Connor's *The Wise Blood*] gains something from being set alongside *The Soft Voice of the Serpent,* a collection of short stories by a South African writer. Miss Gordimer is much more articulate than Miss O'Connor, has a larger vocabulary (which she makes too much use of, especially in descriptions) and an interest in the surface and qualities of things, which produces in her writing, in its best passages, a considerable amount of objectivity, and in its poorest moments a case of adjectivitis, the "feminine" style. She is also a much more correct writer than Miss O'Connor, her pacing seems to have been timed with a stop-watch and the various characters in this collection, when it suits her purpose, are observed sharply enough to remain distinct from one another, even when there is nothing particularly memorable in the stories in which they happen to occur. (p. 19)

But while her collection is certainly not a waste of talent, one might well wish to see her talent at work on themes which have at least the same potential as Miss O'Connor's. Even a little of *The Wise Blood*'s agony might do her good. She keeps everything at arm's length, and the emotion in her stories is seldom more than suspiration in middle register. (One big exception is **"A Watcher of the Dead,"** which is apparently written from direct experience on a Jewish theme and attains a degree of emotional involvement not to be found in the rest.) For the most part I could not help feeling that nothing matters enough. (pp. 19-20)

> Isaac Rosenfeld, "To Win by Default," in The New Republic, *Vol. 127, No. 1, July 7, 1952, pp. 19-20.\**

### NATHAN ROTHMAN

Thomas Wolfe's wonderful subtitle for "Of Time and the River": "A Legend of Man's Hunger in his Youth," comes often to mind as a reviewer turns to a romantic, talented first novel of a writer's youth, such as Nadine Gordimer's **"The Lying Days."** It is what so many good first novels have always been about,

this seeking backward towards past experience. It is the first meat upon which writers feed, and only the thoughtless will complain of its recurrent materials: first friend, first love, first bitterness, school, sex, the discovery of the world. . . .

Given all the marvelous processes of sensitiveness and perception at the command of a writer like Miss Gordimer, it is still to be demanded of her that she spend her powers upon what is perceived, and leave the perceiver to us. In her novel of South Africa, where Miss Gordimer has spent much of her life, we have far too little of South Africa and far too much of the coming-of-age of an adolescent, which might have happened anywhere. This is my chief quarrel with her book, which is, as I have indicated, unquestionably well written, emotional and sensitive in feeling.

Her Helen Shaw is a girl who has lived the sheltered life of a young white girl in South Africa for the first seventeen years of her life. Her father is superintendent of a gold mine at Atherton, and Helen lives within the accepted pattern of social relationships, carefully walled away from the blacks. It is when she goes off to study at the University of Johannesburg that she first discovers there are other lives, other dimensions of thinking. (p. 27)

Such are the beginnings of education, and the rest is a furthering of the process, mainly a deepening of sex experience. An affair with a fascinating and worldly man wears off and breaks at last, ending the book upon a note of further search as Helen puts Africa behind her and escapes to Europe. She is leaving Africa, as it happens, just as the tension is rising, as the Malan Government is establishing its policy of *apartheid* and pushing the black people further and further behind walls.

Yet this, which might have appeared as an apocalyptic surge in the book and in her own history, is noted as a melancholy footnote to Helen's disappointment in love, her world-weariness. Her eye is still turned inward; not all of her discoveries about sex and love and social distinctions have served to draw her out into the world and to make her feel *it* as the primary source of her life, rather than her reactions, her moods, her urges, her disappointments. Helen retains the immature personality of the bright child, not profound and not impressive. We lack the growth to maturity, and we lack also the mature vision of her African home. . . . (p. 28)

> Nathan Rothman, "When Africa Sighs," in The Saturday Review, *New York, Vol. XXXVI, No. 40, October 3, 1953, pp. 27-8.*

### JAMES STERN

Some years ago I was sent for review a novel called "Cry the Beloved Country" and was so moved that for a long time I did not know how to express properly my conviction that here was a book that millions must read. Now the same predicament assails me again.

Strangely enough, Miss Gordimer comes from the same part of Africa and writes of much the same society (if the fuming melting pot of Johannesburg can be given that name) as does Alan Paton. Of the two books, if comparisons must be made, **"The Lying Days"** is the longer, the richer, intellectually the more exciting. It is exciting above all because its author is still in her twenties, and her book is in many respects as mature, as packed with insight into human nature, as void of conceit and banality, as original and as beautifully written as a novel by Virginia Woolf. This name springs to one's mind because

Miss Gordimer is a writer who can not only capture but express in the lives of human beings those moments which are so fleeting, so impalpable, as well as so common that they are overlooked by all but a very rare artist. I can think of no modern first "novel" superior to Miss Gordimer's.

The word has been placed in quotes because this book does not read like, and can hardly be described as, a novel. Written in that most difficult of all forms, the first person, it has no plot, no dénouement. It is a biography—the first twenty-four years in the life of Helen Shaw, a white girl brought up by conventional middle-class Protestant parents in a mining suburb of Johannesburg. (pp. 4-5)

By the time we have seen, through the eyes of Helen and her lover, the rags and hovels in which [the poor] . . . exist, have witnessed scenes of mob violence and sudden death such as possibly only Johannesburg knows, we have looked down upon the whole panorama of this explosive continent's most explosive corner, Dr. Malan's South Africa. Through a work of literature of a very high order we have been made to feel the sense of doom that pervades it, been inoculated once again with the guilt of the white man, the fear and the fury of the black, and we are left with no reason to wonder why the latter feel and behave as they do in this terrifying, terrified land. (p. 5)

*James Stern, "Out of Rags and Hovels," in* The New York Times Book Review, *October 4, 1953, pp. 4-5.*

### RICHARD HAYES

Miss Nadine Gordimer draws title and theme of her first novel [*The Lying Days*] from a melancholy quatrain of Yeats, "The Coming of Wisdom With Time":

> Though leaves are many, the root is one;
> Through all the lying days of my youth
> I swayed my leaves and flowers in the sun;
> Now I may wither into the truth.

Something of that lyric's wry and perfect surface, its elegance and sobriety, has invaded Miss Gordimer's prose. A young South African girl, she published last year a volume of short fiction distinguished and impressive, but tentative. What these stories disclosed was a sensibility tremulous and exacerbated, slowly feeling its way out of numbness and pain into sentience. But in the interval, Miss Gordimer's writing has taken on particularity and shape, an impeccable clarity of focus and a poetic texture of range and intensity. She excels in (even abuses) the power of generalized statement, and her control of scene is considerable. A fastidious taste governs her mind, and as a dramatist of the subtle impingement of place on a reflective consciousness, she seems to me unequalled.

The theme of *The Lying Days* is the turbulent adolescent passage into wisdom and reconciliation: the hardest subject of all, exhausted, a plundered vein. . . . Miss Gordimer solicits the attention with a portrait sure and eloquent: no one will dispute the authenticity of this grave and humorless young heroine, immensely touching in her over-riding egotism, blindly groping into the adult world of love and responsibility and human commitment. Indeed, in Miss Gordimer's drawing of her shy response to the charm and pleasure of the sensuous, physical world, the novel achieves a kind of hazy bloom of perfection which cannot but be called masterful.

When the center of her narrative moves, however, from the idyllic pastoral landscape—a tissue of life beautifully rendered—to the complex implications of an urban scene, Miss Gordimer's writing declines in chastity and poise. I would ascribe this softening to an improper discrimination the novelist has made between the two imaginative modes of recollection and re-creation. She has indulged herself with remembrance, and in consequence her subject, which importunes the shaping of art, is bound only by the tenuous unity of personality. She cannot dominate her experience—the venomous family ruptures, the slow attritions of a compulsive love affair—because she does not exist at a sufficient distance from it; the page is still freshly dusted with the heat and squalor of battle.

Nor has Miss Gordimer, with absolute success, imposed her private drama on the larger context of South African actuality. This is, of course, a generous, possibly a noble, failure. In the humiliating presence of *apartheid,* under the sullen eye of Dr. Malan, how is one even to sustain the illusion of personal worth? With guilt suppurating at every pore of a society, to counsel the refinements of moral taste is tantamount to an act of frivolity. Numbness or hysteria would seem to be the logical alternatives, and for all the tact of her conscience and the restraint of her art, Miss Gordimer has completely eschewed neither. . . .

I would suggest then, in full awareness of the impertinence here involved, that a more relentless attention to the formal exactions of the fictional convention would give Miss Gordimer's next work the precision and structural power in which *The Lying Days* is deficient. She is, wonderful to say, a novelist in whom sensibility is not debilitating, but a strong, enriching and affirmative force; and the special conditions of her life—her ambiguous position as a humane spirit in a society courting disaster—may at the last be her salvation as a writer, by presenting her with a raw imaginative substance of richness and implication. It is only because she herself is a talent of so austere and primary an order, and has set so intransigent a mark of excellence, that she is able to invoke in us the impulse of enthusiasm and concern.

*Richard Hayes, "A Coming of Age in South Africa," in* Commonweal, *Vol. LIX, No. 3, October 23, 1953, p. 66.*

### THE TIMES LITERARY SUPPLEMENT

Miss Gordimer's second collection of short stories [*Six Feet of the Country*] shows a broadening and deepening of the talent already evident in *The Soft Voice of the Serpent.* The best stories are again about South Africa, small incidents enlarged into pieces with a social or moral point, investigations of the abysms of feeling that make a natural bar between white and coloured people. Stories like **"Which New Era Would That Be?"** (the knowing young liberal white woman determined to show that she understands how a native feels, even to the point of calling him a liar), **"The Smell of Death and Flowers"** (another liberal white girl hesitates to make a final gesture of identification with the native cause), and the macabre title story could hardly be bettered. In some other stories her touch is less certain, but she never offers less than the kind of intelligent irony that gains its strength, and at the same time acknowledges a limitation, through some kind of self-involvement. Almost all these stories are told from a woman's point of view, and the women in them are much more keenly observed than the men.

*"Faces in Africa," in* The Times Literary Supplement, *No. 2837, July 13, 1956, p. 421.\**

## WALTER ALLEN

But life, in spite of everything, goes on. . . . It is, surely, the sense we have of this in a writer's work as much as anything else that marks the difference between art and propaganda. It is a quality, this awareness that suffering "takes place while someone else is eating or opening a window or just walking dully along," that Miss Gordimer, it seems to me, has beyond almost all of the other young novelists and short-story writers who have recently emerged from the Union of South Africa. For a young South African writer not to be aware, almost to the point of obsession, of the racial tensions of his country would be an impossibility, and if it were possible a monstrosity. It is the context in which he lives; but within that context life still goes on, for Black and White alike: normality continues to assert itself, exactly as in wartime. The interesting thing is the clash between this striving for the normal and the abnormal situation which constantly perverts it. This is the dominant theme running through this excellent collection of stories [*Six Feet of the Country*], even in those in which the race struggle is not implicit. Miss Gordimer is a writer of great gifts. She can illuminate life, and not merely South African life; yet it is when her material is specifically South African that she has most to offer, since, for English readers at any rate, it is the specifically South African scene that calls especially for illumination. She seems to understand her coloured characters as readily as her White and to penetrate into them as deeply. . . . Stories such as [*Which New Era Would That Be?* and *The Smell of Death and Flowers*] seem to enclose and express a whole world; and when she wants to, as in *Horn of Plenty*, Miss Gordimer can also, in the space of a single story, present a sharp and valid contrast between two different worlds, between those of New York and Johannesburg. (pp. 191-92)

*Walter Allen, in a review of "Six Feet of the Country," in* The New Statesman & Nation, *Vol. LII, No. 1327, August 18, 1956, pp. 191-92.*

## JAMES STERN

[In "**Six Feet of the Country**"] Nadine Gordimer's range is far wider, the observation even keener, than that shown in her volume "**The Soft Voice of the Serpent**." The quality of the prose, the authority and intelligence behind it, are surely unsurpassed by any other writer in South Africa today. What Miss Gordimer's admirers may miss here, however, is the abiding compassion of her novel, "**The Lying Days**."

In "**Six Feet of the Country**" the author's primary concerns seem to be twofold: the behavior—usually malicious, occasionally shocking—of highly sophisticated white South African women toward members of their own sex; and the dilemma of serious, liberal-minded white South African women whose lives have been warped by the gulf separating them from the colored people. (p. 5)

Brilliant as the stories dealing with South Africa's colored problem are, there is in this collection one story which concerns only white people and which could have taken place in any civilized country at any time. Appearing originally in different form in The New Yorker under the title "**The Pretender**," the story is now called "**My First Two Women**." In this reviewer's opinion it surpasses all Miss Gordimer's other stories in its

simplicity and insight into human nature. The theme is the universal one of the child whose father has divorced his wife and married again. The pretender is the stepmother over whom the child, who tells the story in retrospect, realizes at the age of 5 that he possesses a power—"something of which I am convinced there is no innocence this side of the womb." What the boy does with this power and what the stepmother is unable to do for all her awareness, decency and love, is a story that can act as a lesson to "progressive" parents as well as to budding authors who may be under the illusion that the working of a child's mind is simple, and as simple to describe. (p. 34)

*James Stern, "Troubled Souls," in* The New York Times Book Review, *October 7, 1956, pp. 5, 34.*

## EDWARD WEEKS

In an age of dearth, it is a rare pleasure to read Nadine Gordimer; she is one of the most gifted practitioners of the short story anywhere in English, and her new collection of twelve stories and a novella, *Friday's Footprint* . . ., holds a beauty not to be missed. It is impossible for a sensitive writer in South Africa to avoid taking sides. Miss Gordimer, who is a Johannesburger now in her mid-thirties, takes her stand with Alan Paton as a liberal opposed to apartheid and to the coarsening, tough-fibered materialism which she perceives to be the result of the Afrikaner's racial privilege. She has a keen sense of injustice, and there are times, as in "**The Last Kiss**" and "**Little Willie**," when her disgust betrays her and she writes too obviously against the insensibility she loathes. But at her best, as in "**The Bridegroom**," she achieves the perfect balance, and then her portraiture of the young white overseer of the road gang, fourteen miles from nowhere in the Kalahari dust, as he prepares the camp for the arrival of his bride, speaks volumes for the delicate tissue of relations between white and black. (p. 95)

*Edward Weeks, "Accept with Pleasure," in* The Atlantic Monthly, *Vol. 205, No. 1, January, 1960, pp. 95-6.\**

## MARY ELLEN CHASE

Whenever a careful reader makes the rare discovery that what is purposely *not* said on the pages before him is clearly far more important and filled with meaning than what *is* said, he reads yet again and with sharpened perception. . . . [Nadine Gordimer in her collection *Friday's Footprint*] often obscures or upon occasion omits occurrences, surroundings, dialogue, but only because by so doing she can more acutely and fully capture, or make, or at times restore a complete experience. The actual happenings which she deals with in these remarkably real and moving stories take place in various parts of her native Africa from Cairo to Johannesburg. They have to do with crocodile hunting at night, with the ironic and painful degradation of men and women, with a generous invitation which brings ruin and desolation in its wake, with a tropical river and its awful toll exacted both of the living and the dead, and with a wide variety of persons, Afrikaners and blacks, construction engineers and naturalists, small children, adolescents, and the old.

Yet the fact that all her characters and situations are engrossing as pure story material really means comparatively little in the face of their superb—shall we even say perfect?—presentation. They may and do "spread knowledge of things new," in Sainte-

Beuve's words; but their real accomplishment through Miss Gordimer's gifted mind is, as the French critic adds, "to lend freshness to things known." Each story or incident probes mercilessly into human motives and human weaknesses, into guilt, fear, disillusionment, ambition, despair. Each reveals the universal human condition, whether in a Boer community or in Chicago, Paris, Hollywood, or the most isolated village anywhere at all. . . .

Anthologists who compile volumes of "the best stories" must not miss this book. College instructors whose task it is "to teach the short story" will find enough here to teach themselves as well as their students. And most of us who try to write fiction will find reason for despair, or, if we are generous enough, for hope in its larger sense as well as for unqualified admiration.

> Mary Ellen Chase, "Miss Gordimer's Fine, True Art in Another Brilliant Collection," in New York Herald Tribune Book Review, January 10, 1960, p. 1.

### MARY DOYLE CURRAN

Nadine Gordimer's new collection of short stories (and a novella) is not the work of a novice. She has two other short story collections as well as two novels to her credit. Unfortunately, "Friday's Footprint," the latest addition to her South African saga, betrays the enervation of the contemporary short story. The major flaw can be summed up in a quotation from one of the stories, "The Last Kiss": "When people become characters, they cease to be regarded as human . . ." There is a lack of warmth and compassion here that is typical of the "objective" short story. Casting a cold eye is the dominant attitude of the book. And when another approach is taken, as in the novella, "An Image of Success," and in the story "The Last Kiss," it degenerates into the falsity of undeserved pathos.

Miss Gordimer is trapped by the contemporary fad for the unresolved ending, leaving it to the reader to trek back through the veld to resolve the meaning. But the trek does not result in resolution. Stories such as "Friday's Footprint," "A Thing of the Past," and "Our Bovary" do not have the linear complexity that in Joyce led so inevitably and justifiably to the final revelation. The stories play on gratuitous shock. They suggest a psychological complexity that is, in fact, simply not there. . . .

There is no question that Miss Gordimer has technical skill—as demonstrated by "The Bridegroom." But most of her stories echo with compromise and acceptance. . . .

The great test, finally, of fiction, is how interesting it is, how long it stays in the memory, how often it recurs to the reader. Few of Miss Gordimer's stories will haunt one. "The Path of the Moon's Dark Fortnight," "Little Willie," "The Bridegroom" are the only selections in "Friday's Footprint" that speak with a memorable voice of their own.

> Mary Doyle Curran, "Many Views from the Veld," in Saturday Review, Vol. XLIII, No. 3, January 16, 1960, p. 64.

### HONOR TRACY

There is no living writer of short stories more interesting, varied and fertile than Miss Gordimer at her best. In this new collection [Not for Publication and Other Stories], however, she does not always come up to her standard. The lyrical freshness

is dulled, as so often in the works of maturity: now and again, humanity degenerates into motherliness; and several pieces are too long for their weight. This may be due to their being written in the first place for American magazines, for American editors love stories to be "extended," either from a simple respect for quantity as such or from the need to lure their readers through the jungle of advertisement. . . .

The opening story, "Not for Publication," is not merely too long but reads as if the writer were tired. There are too frequent lapses into what is death to any story, a bold, lazy summarizing where all should be illumined and made manifest. . . .

With "The African Magician," she is back to her own superb form. . . .

The story is memorable for the unity of feeling, the brilliant use of background in the heightening of mood and the honesty. . . .

She succeeds again, beautifully, with "A Company of Laughing Faces," where a young girl is taken by her jolly commonplace mother to a seaside resort full of similar people. (p. 25)

I should mention "Message In a Bottle," a tour de force concerned with the haphazard cruelty of life, told with apparent inconsequence and deeply moving; and "Tenants of the Last Tree-House," dealing once more with the world of adolescence and the failure of communication between children and parents. "There was a math test on Thursday and I got 61 percent. . . ." In this vein Cavada writes her weekly letter home: but in a nursery cupboard among the outgrown clothes her mother finds a diary with an entry: "I love Peter—and adore him—and need him—for ever and ever," stands a little while thinking, then carefully hides the book away again. It is often in her simplest moments that Miss Gordimer is most poignant. (p. 26)

> Honor Tracy, "A Bouquet from Nadine Gordimer," in The New Republic, Vol. 152, No. 19, May 8, 1965, pp. 25-6.

### EDWARD HICKMAN BROWN

This superb collection of stories [Not for Publication and Other Stories] most decidedly is for publication. And I believe it represents a giant step forward for Nadine Gordimer.

What has always puzzled me profoundly about her writing in the past was why so small a proportion of her deftly executed, perspicacious stories made a really deep impression upon me. Hers was clearly more than an exceedingly skillful technique allied to a perceptive eye and an acute ear. One was constantly aware that a sensitive and intelligent mind was at work behind the stories that generally depicted—with rare accuracy—people caught in varied postures of human frailty. I found them infinitely superior to her two earliest novels (I missed the last one); but, although I enjoyed and respected most of the stories at the time of reading, relatively few of them remained impaled upon my consciousness through the ultimate test of the passage of time.

My far from certain conclusion, when last I considered this matter several years ago, was that it might perhaps be a case of too much dispassion and detachment on Miss Gordimer's part, for one should surely not be so everlastingly conscious of the author's own cool intelligence hovering above her stories. But the entire issue now appears to be academic. For this collection confirms, quite dramatically, a new authority that I believed I had noticed in the odd story read in various periodicals over the past couple of years. Some indefinable additional ingredient has been added. For lack of a better term, we can only (and inaccurately) label it experience. . . .

It is a measure of Miss Gordimer's mastery over her subject that she moves one so easily and swiftly into the grip of each story, giving her art the illusion of effortlessness. Whatever the subtle extra element might be, the amalgam has magically jelled. This writer who has never been sufficiently honored in her native land can now surely rank with the finest exponents of the short-story medium. . . .

Miss Gordimer is a master at capturing a single electric moment of illumination. In **"A Company of Laughing Faces"** a sensitive girl of seventeen finds beauty and meaning in an initial confrontation with death that abruptly clarifies the confusion she had experienced during a seaside holiday while working so hard at the business of "having the time of her life" predicted by her mother. **"The Worst Thing of All"** ends in a different kind of moment, but with an equal dramatic force: here a husband stands revealed in all his shabby superficiality before the wife who had previously clothed him in qualities of her own imagining. . . .

These excellent stories have the unmistakable ring of truth, and will not easily fade. Most should prove well worth rereading; half their number will in all likelihood become well-thumbed favorites of mine.

> *Edward Hickman Brown, "A Sudden Shaft of Light," in Saturday Review, Vol. XLVIII, No. 19, May 8, 1965, p. 33.*

## ANNE TYLER

Bam and Maureen Smales [of **"July's People"**], middle-class white liberals from Johannesburg, South Africa, begin their day with a tea tray carried in by their black manservant, July. However, there's something wrong here. The tea is served in two cheap glass cups, along with a jaggedly opened tin of milk. The door at which July knocks is only an aperture in the thick mud wall of an African hut.

The Smales are people who have overstayed. Extensions of Nadine Gordimer's earlier characters—those uneasy, conscience-stricken whites attempting to come to terms with the ambiguities of South African life—they find themselves face to face with the ultimate: total revolution. The time is the very near future, when rioting blacks have taken over the country. Airports are being bombed, and whites cannot leave. Bam and Maureen, with their three young children, have no choice but to flee to July's isolated village.

On a superficial level, this is a wonderful adventure story. It has the ingenuity and suspense of "Robinson Crusoe," the wry twists of "The Admirable Crichton." The Smales, whose hastily packed baggage includes a gadget for removing dry cleaners' tags without damaging the fingernails, are forced to adapt to a life of weed gathering and mealie cooking, of shivering in a rainstorm while the hut walls grow sodden and flying cockroaches zip through the dark. The clay vessels of the sort that Maureen used to collect as ornaments are now her kitchen utensils. . . .

On a deeper level, of course, **"July's People"** is much more than another survival story; and this level succeeds so extraordinarily because of the Smaleses' liberalism. It would have been too easy to make them racists, who finally see the light

while roughing it with the natives. Instead, they are from the outset sensitive, politically aware, genuinely concerned with the welfare of black South Africans. How ironic, then, is their discovery that even in the underbrush, reactionaries exist! And how much subtler and more complicated is the hostility that develops between Maureen and July! (p. 1)

Certain moments in this book seem to leap right off the page. They are so vivid that I expect to see them clearly, in full color, ten or twenty years from now just by glimpsing the title on a shelf. . . .

The details are so concrete that you're tempted to slap at the mosquitoes as you read, but they never slow the story. They are active details, humming with motion. It's hard for the reader to believe, when the last page is turned, that he's still sitting in the same easy chair after living through so much.

Nadine Gordimer has always been an admirable writer, combining skill with social conscience; but here she has outdone herself. **"July's People"** demonstrates with breathtaking clarity the tensions and complex interdependencies between whites and blacks in South Africa. It is so flawlessly written that every one of its events seems chillingly, ominously possible. (p. 26)

> *Anne Tyler, "South Africa After Revolution," in The New York Times Book Review, June 7, 1981, pp. 1, 26.*

## JUDITH CHETTLE

The possibility of bloody revolution has long been a staple of political debate about South Africa. Such a revolution is regarded as inevitable, desirable, or unthinkable, depending on individual beliefs. Nadine Gordimer has been increasingly preoccupied in her writings with its inevitability, and in her latest novel, *July's People,* she writes of the revolution accomplished and its immediate aftermath. Revolutions are messy things to write about, so perhaps Miss Gordimer can be forgiven for being brief and somewhat vague about the revolution itself. She prefers to tell about a white family. . . . [But] because her people think more than they feel, Miss Gordimer never seems to grapple seriously with the questions she has raised. The situation may be revolutionary, but the insights are not.

> *Judith Chettle, in a review of "July's People," in National Review, Vol. XXXIII, No. 25, December 25, 1981, p. 1561.*

## BETTY THOMPSON

For more than 30 years Nadine Gordimer, a white South African, has been recording the delicate nuances of change in the externally unchanged situation of South Africa—unchanged in that the black majority remains without basic human rights. But [in *July's People*] the delicate seismograph of Gordimer's sensibility takes us to the tomorrow that is looming for her native land. (p. 642)

For her epigraph, Gordimer chooses an extract from Antonio Gramsci's *Prison Notebooks:* "The old is dying and the new cannot be born; in this interregnum there arises a great diversity of morbid symptoms." In seven previous novels and an equal number of collections of short stories, Gordimer has chronicled this morbidity. She has shown us every shading of feeling, of truth and deception, between black and white, men and women, old and young. (pp. 642-43)

If white South Africans did not care for her earlier work, there will be naught for their comfort here. Gordimer brings to the apocalyptic vision of white flight and fright in a country under siege the same delicate attention to irony and detail as ever. Here the white man and woman, stripped of everything but a desire to survive, are in the state of total dependence. . . .

*July's People* is a slim book, but it conveys all that is necessary to understand the situation of whites and blacks in Africa, of masters and servants everywhere, and of how quickly it all can be reversed. (p. 643)

> Betty Thompson, in a review of "July's People," in The Christian Century, Vol. 99, No. 19, May 26, 1982, pp. 642-43.

### CHRISTOPHER HEYWOOD

Six collections of short stories, the first of which appeared in 1949 through the vigorous indigenous publishing channels of South Africa, provide a brilliant extension of the themes and techniques used in [Gordimer's] novels. The penetration of social situations, the delineation of character and the use of metaphor and narrative method are in general, as in the hands of many other South African and American writers, more assured in the short stories than in the novels. Each collection of stories has an accent of its own, and each represents a turning point in the development of Nadine Gordimer's art and thought. This discussion will follow the selection made by Nadine Gordimer from the six collections, published as *Some Monday For Sure* (1975). (p. 38)

The stories are generally in advance of the novels, which frequently develop aspects of thought and of social processes which had made a first appearance in stories of several years earlier. The story **'Some Monday for Sure'** develops the black involvement in an incident of the type which lies in the background of *The Late Bourgeois World* [1966] and which reflects the inevitable development towards armed conflict of the long standing tradition of black protest within South Africa. Thus, the anthology which takes its title from this story represents a more studied adoption of a politically committed and dangerous position, than anything that can be found in the more inclusive selection made in the *Selected Stories* (1975). The adoption of a point of view approximating to that of the submerged majority in southern Africa calls for no superhuman effort, since there is abundant evidence and experience, and a tradition of writing stemming from the American writer W. E. DuBois, and from the English writers such as E. D. Morel and D. H. Lawrence, upon which it can be based. . . . The failure to adopt this view is exposed, however, in unexpected quarters, notably those of well-wishing expatriates of British origin, and in the entrenched view of the old but by then moribund South African Liberal party. In contrast, modes of life and thought compatible with the expressed ideals of these defeated groups are suggested, in the stories as in the novels, to subsist within the overlooked minorities such as the 'detribalised' Afrikaners, members of the Indian community, and blacks of ambivalent orientation towards the culture of industrialized societies. Nadine Gordimer's view that the colour-bar . . . can be best repudiated and destroyed from within . . . entails the further recognition that among South African black writers, this is an ambition leading to suicide, exile and imprisonment. . . . The stories [in *Some Monday for Sure*] are made possible by the relatively privileged position of the white writer in South African society. The need

to lay bare the nerves of the process which lead to this situation is thereby intensified rather than removed. (pp. 38-40)

The story **'Some Monday for Sure'** tells of the holdup of a lorry carrying explosives for the mines, and the use of the captured materials for sedition, by a group whose members scatter after the incident. . . . As in many of the stories, a symbol drawn from the other arts provides a focus which helps to clarify the action. Against the male world of violence in which the processes of industry are scarcely distinguishable from those of war, the traditional world of women asserts an alternative rendering, through art, of the ambiguity of existence. The walls of a hut near the scene of the hold-up have on them patterns drawn by women, fascinating even to violent men who despise the opposite sex: 'the shape of things like big leaves and moons', and 'as you looked at the walls in the sun, some shapes were dark and some were light, and if you moved, the light ones went dark and the dark ones got light instead'. . . . Recalling the week of the action proves difficult owing to the cyclic nature of time, but it was 'some Monday for sure'. In the story, the phrase conveys the difficulty of pinning down historical events; but by an ambiguous application to the future, it changes meaning in Nadine Gordimer's own hands, and imparts prophetic certainty to future time: 'some perfectly ordinary day, for sure, black South Africans will free themselves and rule themselves' (Introduction). In the Introduction, Nadine Gordimer insists on the irony which dominates all aspects of her art, especially the short stories. The point of the story is not to phrophesy the date of the event, but to emphasise both the certainty and the danger of revolution, its severance of fragile links with the past, and its essentially male origins.

Thus, irony and ambiguity are persistent in Nadine Gordimer's writing; yet the stories point to clearly marked choices, and embody a consistently developed set of views. Few characters carry the author's full approval or endorsement, but the degree of sympathy with the character is a pointer to her interpretation of the dilemma. (pp. 40-1)

The direction of Nadine Gordimer's social and moral criticism may seem surprising when it includes the internationally recognized sources of benevolent philanthropy which stem from the anti-slavery movement in England and America. The position embodied in the story **'Not for Publication'**, a story which provided the title for a collection of stories published in 1965, foreshadows the criticism of pre- and post-independence attitudes which emerged in full scale in the novel *An Honoured Guest*. The attitude of these works remains consistent, however, with the alternative tradition of radical reform stemming from revolutionary processes within colonial society. . . . In the story **'Not for Publication'**, a black schoolboy absconds from the best school for black children in South Africa, when triumph in the examinations seems to lie in his grasp and he will become, in the burgeoning ambition of his form master, the first black Rhodes Scholar to come up from South Africa, or at the very least the holder of a scholarship from the overseas mission for study overseas. But a combination of the boy's failure of nerve, his inability to sustain the hothouse atmosphere of the school, and his rejection of the Western tradition which is moulding his personality, lead to a breakdown. He disappears; we are not told where, and also, we are not told how he achieves the ending which is stated at the start of the story. He rejects the life of schooling which could at best perpetuate itself by leading to his becoming a headmaster. The subtle flaw in the approach of his well-wishers is suggested in the hollow expectation of black schoolboys which vitiates the praise he earns at school '. . . : everyone was overanxious about the boy. Right from the start he'd shown that there was nothing mechanistic about his thought process; he had a brain, not just a set of conditioned reflexes'. . . . At his disappearance it is suggested by the women that he might have joined the *tsotsis* in the street; but the reader knows that Praise Baretse went on to become Prime Minister of a former Protectorate which emerges into independence.

The rejection of the tradition of overseas benevolence is matched in the later collection by the rejection of paternalistic liberalism, both indigenous and international. The story **'Africa Emergent'** (from the collection *Livingstone's Companions,* 1972), which marks the onset of this phase in Nadine Gordimer's thought, directs its irony both against the opportunism of blacks who exploit white patronage, and against the fumbling complacency of the whites who offer it. (pp. 42-3)

'From the start, then, modern African literature has been essentially a committed literature', Nadine Gordimer wrote in her most substantial essay in criticism, *The Black Interpreters* (1973 . . .). The literary tradition which provides the basis for her art is an amalgam of the urbane European and the American literary heritage. Nevertheless, her view of the African writer's mode of work is true to the central preoccupation in her own work. Her view of the African writer's inescapable commitment to the problems posed by the past, 'Black writers choose their plots, characters and literary styles; their themes choose *them*' . . . , is largely true of her own novels and stories. Her themes spring from the dilemmas of the South African colonial and industrial past. Whites as well as blacks feel themselves trapped and crushed, in [Matthew] Arnold's phrase 'between two worlds', torn apart by the tension between the demands of the metropolitan culture and the pressure to survive in a harsh environment. The artistic response to that tension was explored most potently in the nineteenth century by Melville, Hawthorne and Mark Twain. The later work of Dickens and the novels of George Eliot and Hardy return echoes to notes first struck on the American continent. Leaning at first towards late Victorians of the latter type, that is, towards George Eliot and D. H. Lawrence, and finding an early African model in Olive Schreiner's *The Story of an African Farm,* Nadine Gordimer in her later work leaned more towards the literature of the American continent. Together with the novels and stories of the 1970s, the essays in *The Black Interpreters* reflect her completion of this development by turning towards the literature of Africa. Her work includes the assimilation of lessons from American writers such as Carson McCullers, J. D. Salinger and Saul Bellow, who dramatise the society as it impinges on the tortured minds of individuals within it. In *A Guest of Honour* and *The Conservationist,* however, she re-explores themes first traced by Peter Abrahams and Wole Soyinka. These two African writers first traced the forces lined up against the Pan-Africanist ideals of the 1940s, and the search within a modern African society for a redemptive vision based on a fusion of western and African traditions. As in the best of these writers, the ambiguity of commitment emerges through the symbolism. The explosives truck in the story **'Some Monday for Sure'**, the graveyard landscape of the baobab trees in *Occasion for Loving,* and the recurrent image of the egg in *The Conservationist,* convey meaning by their simultaneous suggestions to the reader of the processes of liberation and extinction.

In this analysis, Nadine Gordimer emerges as a figure of international status, rooted in her experience of an important aspect of the African past. Models for the criticism of African writers stem from a diversity of intellectual traditions. It is suggested here that the vocabulary of anarchy and despair, and the awareness of literature as a body of redemptive expression coming from the mind of man in all societies, a pattern of critical discussion emerging first in English in the writings of Matthew Arnold, provides a fruitful avenue of approach to the understanding of this great modern writer. Arnold saw in the internationalised voice of Greece before and after its submergence in the Roman empire, that is, in 'Hellenism', the cure for the ills of a society which was destroying itself. Mark Twain and Melville pressed the analogy further. Like them, Nadine Gordimer proposes that the best that has been thought and said in the world includes the languages and literatures of Africa, and the moral attitudes which have survived from its invasion, its despoiling and re-ordering by the whites. Her heroes and martyrs are the renegades and castaways, the multifariously insulted and injured, but always sentient and perceiving, mysteriously enduring and delighting, emerging blacks of southern Africa. The apparently urbane surface of her prose carries a message of prophetic dimensions. (pp. 45-7)

> *Christopher Heywood, in his* Nadine Gordimer, *Profile Books Ltd., 1983, 50 p.*

### LEON WIESELTIER

''Each torpid turn of the world has such disinherited children, / to whom no longer what's been, and not yet what's coming, belongs,'' Rilke wrote in 1922, in a castle. In 1930, in a prison, a similar inspiration about the inconclusiveness of the modern age came to Gramsci. ''The crisis consists precisely in the fact that the old is dying and the new cannot be born,'' he wrote; and went on to add, in the manner of an intellectual, ''in this interregnum a great variety of morbid symptoms appear.'' In 1981 Nadine Gordimer, whose work has married lyricism to criticism in a way that tempts you to talk of greatness, chose Gramsci's sentence for the epigraph of *July's People,* perhaps her most representative fiction; and in a lecture a year later, referring again to Gramsci (and casually to Rilke), she rigorously described the present period in South Africa, a country of a few castles constructed over many prisons, as an interregnum. It is a time, she said, in which white superiority has begun to crumble before ''the black state that is coming.'' Into this gap this writer steps. Gordimer's work is classic in its debt to crisis and to change. . . .

I have read some of Gordimer's novels and stories, but not nearly all. Like any situation in which evil is easy to spot, the South African situation is one I think I know; but I suspect that I don't. Enormity is not simple; it is merely large. It is hard for me to separate Gordimer, therefore, from the news that she brings. (p. 193)

[In the novella *Something Out There*], as in some of her other writings, Gordimer continues to describe the forms of corrupted consciousness that characterize the morally demented domain of apartheid. Her people may be divided into those that are aware of their corruption and those that are not; but all are corrupted. There are some things you cannot see and stay whole. Obviously this plays itself out differently in blacks and whites. About blacks, Gordimer is utterly unsentimental. There is nothing votive in her portraits of the victims, no sanctity about their suffering of the kind that would put an end to the activity of the analyzing mind. That hatred distorts the hater is commonly known; it must not be forgotten, however, that it distorts the hated, too. In the pathological relationship of power between blacks and whites, nobody is not crippled. . . . Black terrorism in South Africa is growing more frequent, as it is in Gordimer's work, but even in South Africa, where terrorism would seem to make the most human sense, it makes no human sense. The fatuities of Fanon, for example, who made romance out of an earlier generation of African violence, and thought to settle the moral problem by calling healthy the innocently sick, are missing from Gordimer. She chronicles, instead, the steady inflammation of the blacks' inner lives, the full foul seething in their suffering souls. There emerges the impression of a class of victims that is obviously in the right, and turning to the wrong. . . . The guilt of the innocent; that is the most profound plot of many liberation stories, slavery's last scar. Where there is logic, there are no heroes. (pp. 194-95)

[A large part of Gordimer's] achievement is to have refused the choice between the work of the mind and the work of the heart; to have banished sentimentality but not sentiment; to have detached herself from the scene for the purposes of understanding, but not removed herself from it completely. It is increasingly clear from Gordimer's recent work that this gifted writer is also a gifted intellectual. Ideas appear as the stuff of fiction—ideas are the most natural product of an interregnum and they are handled with rigor. Despite its sometimes showy surfaces, then, the fiction reveals a mind calmly at work, and aimed everywhere equally. . . . You can learn from her about the compatibility of the commitment to truth with the commitment to justice. You can learn that the activity of the mind does not always require you to live nowhere. . . . She sees that the fights for freedom have unanticipated consequences, but she does not become ironic. She sees that the story of masters and slaves is a great spectacle, but she does not become aesthetic. She plays it straight. And playing it straight is an old form of high seriousness, a method of work which honors the magnitude of the subject more than it honors even the most exquisite sensibilities.

It is not the blacks that Gordimer writes with most authority about, however, but the whites. She is the supreme chronicler of their awakening, or of the failure of their awakening. The process itself consists in a competition between fear and knowledge. Their society, it turns out, is not so obvious. Life in South Africa is a vast system of common ceremonies and unarticulated arrangements by means of which its gross social division endures. As this system comes cracked, its privileged few learn for the first time about their real position, about the position of moral, historical, and social weakness in which minority tyrants always find themselves. They discover that in the depths of their dictatorship they were dependent; moreover, that they knew almost not at all the population whose docility they needed for their delusions. (pp. 195-96)

A word about Gordimer's style. It is the perfect instrument of her intention. The style sticks to you, like unwanted information. It is precise, indeed it is too precise, as it must be if it is to deliver an environment that is estranged. It is poetic, but it is awkwardly poetic, as it must be to communicate the spiritual state of living in the aftermath of ancient assumptions. Sometimes it reminds you of Virginia Woolf—there is a passage in this novella about a woman in a bath that recalls Clarissa Dalloway's sober spell of self-knowledge in her attic bedroom—but tougher, more persuaded of things that last, of the full measure of moral and historical gravity that an ordinary perception may hold. Gordimer's people have outer agonies to go with their inner agonies. She is a master of impressions,

and of interiority; but she is (to paraphrase Gautier) a woman for whom the outside world exists. (p. 196)

*Leon Wieseltier, in an afterword to "Something Out There," in* Salmagundi, *No. 62, Winter, 1984, pp. 193-96.*

### MERVYN JONES

Two of the stories in [*Something Out There*] present women—in one case black, in the other case white—who find themselves giving shelter to a man on the run from the police. . . . Life, hitherto, for each woman has been based on an assumption, accepted rather than thought out: she is against the power system (Nanike because she's black, Pat because she moves in liberal circles) but she isn't among those who prepare themselves by deliberate resistance for danger and suffering. Now she is confronted, not merely with a dilemma, but with a sudden withdrawal of inner as well as external protection. She comes up against an invisible line; on the far side of this line she would be a different person, someone she never meant to be. This is the kind of predicament that Nadine Gordimer explores, never giving the uplifting answers that the reader would like. She writes not so much with sympathy, as with a cool, meditative understanding.

As an admirer, I've sometimes wondered what sort of writer Nadine Gordimer would be if she were not South African. Doubtless a very good writer, given her formidable equipment: an unerring insight into human fallibilities, a superlative skill in portraiture, an easy (I don't mean facile) sureness in social observation, a clean and sinewy style. The novels might rank with the earlier novels of Virginia Woolf, the stories with Katherine Mansfield's. In other words, perhaps a bit thin? . . .

Yet, if Nadine Gordimer is a writer of predicaments, she has a predicament of her own. There is Nadine Gordimer the artist, who does indeed share some of the aims of a Katherine Mansfield, and whose literary values derive from the dominant European-American cultural tradition—a tradition in which a personal treachery or a disappointment in love can be a disaster of supreme gravity. And there is Nadine Gordimer the prophet, the defiant and minatory voice of a tormented country, bearing a responsibility which (like some of her characters) she must sometimes feel to have been forced upon her. Several times, and most notably in *July's People,* she has triumphantly resolved the contradiction. I don't feel that she has managed it again in '**Something Out There**', the novella which gives its title to the collection. (p. 29)

[In this novella] the symbolism feels rather forced, the point rather laboured, and the whole story rather too long. The characters, especially the conventional Afrikaners, are—for once—sketched without individuality. Where the best Gordimer stories end on a questioning note, this one is too neatly wrapped up. It leaves an impression of honourable but dutiful writing.

I prefer, as a depiction of the inhumanity and destructiveness of life in South Africa, a very much shorter story called '**Crimes of Conscience**'. . . . It tells us, not indeed all that we ought to know, but all that is essential about South Africa. (p. 30)

*Mervyn Jones, "Breaking-Point," in* The Listener, *Vol. 111, No. 2851, March 29, 1984, pp. 29-30.*

## PAUL MARX

Nadine Gordimer by now has established an unquestionable claim on a Nobel Prize, whether for her nine volumes of short fiction—including this latest collection [*Something Out There*]— or for her eight novels. As a novelist, her courage and lack of hypocrisy in probing moral and political questions puts her in the class of George Eliot, Dostoevsky, Conrad, and Mann. Of the title novella and nine stories in *Something Out There*, three— **"A City of the Dead, A City of the Living," "Sins of the Third Age,"** and **"Blinder"**—could easily be ranked among the best of the century. (p. 18)

Her 1981 novel *July's People* took us ahead in time to the full-scale racial war that seems inevitable in South Africa. **"Something Out There"** returns to the present, with its quickening pace of black violence. The "something out there" scaring white Johannesburg is a baboon that treads occasionally on its tidy lawns. Gordimer suggests that the community's response to the intruder parallels its reaction to the first, sporadic guerrilla actions. . . .

Gordimer is no sentimentalist; indeed, her honesty is one of her greatest literary resources. If her blacks are invariably less than perfect, her Afrikaners are far from inhuman caricatures. . . .

Nadine Gordimer's empathy, demonstrated again and again in over 30 years of writing, is remarkable. One marvels at how much this well-off white woman knows of black townships. . . . (p. 19)

Like other internationally recognized figures living in oppressive lands, Nadine Gordimer faces the temptation of giving up on the country where she was born. But the accident of birth imposes obligations she accepts. She frequently goes abroad yet always returns to South Africa, where morality extends only to one's kin and the very air smells of corruption. She understands that it is where a writer of her power is most badly needed—to bespeak the inevitable, expose the rot, and demonstrate the possibility of clear vision, courage and compassion. (p. 320)

*Paul Marx, "A South African Literary Conscience," in* The New Leader, *Vol. LXVII, No. 12, June 25, 1984, pp. 18-20.**

# Nicholas M. Guild
## 1944-

**American novelist and critic.**

**Guild is an author of suspense novels and has gained a reputation as a competent and entertaining storyteller. His protagonists are unlikely heroes who become involved in matters of espionage. William Lukas in *The Lost and Found Man* (1975) and Ray Guinness in *The Summer Soldier* (1978) were spies during World War II, after which they both became English professors. After years of civilian life, Lukas and Guinness are drawn into undercover operations by people from their pasts. *The Summer Soldier* is generally considered Guild's most successful work. Guinness is also the main character in the novels *Old Acquaintance* (1978) and *The Favor* (1981).**

**Both *Chain Reaction* (1983) and *Berlin Warning* (1984) take place during World War II. *Chain Reaction* revolves around Hitler's plan to have the atomic bomb stolen from the Americans. In *Berlin Warning*, the complicated story line pits Guild's hero against the British as well as the Nazis.**

**A professor of English literature, Guild has published essays and reviews in several literary journals, including *Modern Fiction Studies* and *Studies in English Literature*.**

**(See also *Contemporary Authors*, Vols. 93-96.)**

## KELLY FITZPATRICK

With the CIA hitting the front pages for its drug-induced suicides, disregard of federal orders to destroy dangerous drugs and weapons, and general dirty tricks, Nicholas Guild has . . . a timely suspense story [in *The Lost and Found Man*].

The hero is shambling William Lukas, a border-line failure, divorced, middle-aged, and a less-than-inspiring college instructor. (p. 237)

Lukas is a strange combination of Lew Archer and James Bond, with a touch of some of LeCarre's despondent men. . . . There is the usual introduction of a love interest, madly passionate and consuming in three days' time. There is some violence, a charming and cultured Mafia type, and some violence and shooting in the isolation of a country estate.

This is a yarn for an easy evening and will be devoured by the patron of the international suspense rack. It will not demand re-reading, however. (pp. 237-38)

> *Kelly Fitzpatrick, in a review of "The Lost and Found Man," in* Best Sellers, *Vol. 35, No. 8, November, 1975, pp. 237-38.*

## NEWGATE CALLENDAR

On the face of it, "The Lost and Found Man" by Nicholas Guild . . . is no different from any number of espionage novels. The hero is a sort of superman; the plot complications rival Kant's "Critique of Pure Reason" in their involved reasonings; not until the very last pages do we know the good guys from the bad. Sound familiar? It is.

But "The Lost and Found Man" has a couple of extra-special things working for it. Guild writes better than most. And, even more than that, he has the ability to dream up a fantasy figure with which we can all identify. Every veteran of World War II most likely has imagined himself, at one time or another, to be something like William Lukas, Guild's hero. . . .

Just about all of the recent espionage agents of fiction are rolled into this protagonist. Yet Lukas is anything but an epigone of Bond, Quiller or you-name-him; Guild has made him his own man. One can only hope that he will turn up again—Lukas is a valuable and believable addition to the field.

> *Newgate Callendar, in a review of "The Lost and Found Man," in* The New York Times Book Review, *December 21, 1975, p. 16.*

## KIRKUS REVIEWS

[In *The Summer Soldier,* when] Ray Guinness' wife Louise is found ice-picked and half burned to death in their San Francisco Bay Area kitchen, English prof. Ray . . . knows that his past has caught up with him: 15 years before, a totally down-and-out grad student at the U. of London, he somehow became British Security's smoothest, smartest, most prized hit-man—code name "Summer Soldier." That line of work cost Ray his first marriage, so he quit and tried to forget, but Misha Vlasov hasn't forgotten that Ray blew up Mrs. Vlasov during a bungled assassination attempt in Italy. Now Vlasov, who defected to the West for one reason only, has evened the score, but he wants more: a showdown, in Los Angeles, at Griffith Park. . . . The Griffith Park showdown is just about the least satisfying moment in this extremely well-crafted chunk of amoral, stiff-upper-lipped suspense: Guild's pacing between Ray's recollected past and nightmare present is razor-perfectly timed, readers with the proper bloodthirsty leanings will savor each choreographed execution, and only those with a prejudice against hired killers will fail to be thoroughly absorbed in Ray's tensely shifting, darkly shaded moods.

> *A review of "The Summer Soldier," in* Kirkus Reviews, *Vol. XLVI, No. 5, March 1, 1978, p. 258.*

## ALLAN A. RYAN, JR.

One of the sublime pleasures of summer is the sense of anticipation when one realizes that there is nothing half so much worth doing in the afternoon or evening ahead than settling down with a good book in the nearest hammock or beach blanket or easy chair. . . . One needn't be challenged or provoked or educated. . . . In the summer, it is enough sometimes simply to be entertained.

*The Summer Soldier* is a summer book, at least if your tastes run anywhere close to spy novels. Nicholas Guild is quite a capable writer—more's the pleasure of those hours—and the story itself is engrossing enough to pull you in without demanding utter concentration.

The protagonist here is Raymond Guinness, an instructor of English at a sleepy California college, who, we gradually see, has a past rather atypical of English teachers. While an American student of literature in London, he was recruited by the MI-6 to eliminate a particularly bothersome agent of the Other Side. Guinness stayed on to become the very best killer the British had. . . .

He executed every job perfectly, except his last—a particularly crafty KGB agent whose wife got in the way of two sticks of dynamite which Guinness had placed under the driver's seat of the family car. Seven years later, well out of the spy business and back in California, Guinness comes home from the campus for lunch and finds that someone has dispatched his wife with an ice pick—the widowed KGB agent's way of letting Guinness know that the agent is in town and settling old scores in preparation for a one-on-one showdown. Like any good spy novel, of course, murder and mayhem quickly take on their proper perspective—the tools of the trade, steps toward the inexorable confrontation of two supremely professional hunters. . . .

Much of *The Summer Soldier* is laid out in flashbacks, and many of the flashbacks themselves contain further ones and even flash-forwards to some intermediate point short of the present. This is treacherous terrain for even the slightly clumsy writer, but Guild is as surefooted as a mountain goat, never leaving the reader confused as to where he is, though the reminiscences often run into many pages. Guild's sense of pace seldom falters, and the reader is aware of where everyone in the drama is at any given moment.

Guild's prose, to be sure, sometimes lapses into a side-of-the-mouth tempo, a la Mickey Spillane. And what, alas, is one to make of this observation of two lovers seen in an ice-cream parlor: "And tonight they would lie in each other's arms, after

making wonderful, prelapsarian love, and dream no dreams. So it had been destined from the first star swirls." Guild has not only graded freshman English papers but perhaps has read too many of them in the process.

Such lapses are fortunately rare, and anyone who allows them to detract unduly from the enjoyment simply hasn't gotten the hang of summer reading.

> Allan A. Ryan, Jr., "A Wife for a Wife," in Book World—The Washington Post, *June 11, 1978, p. E5.*

## KIRKUS REVIEWS

[In *Old Acquaintance* Ray Guinness, the protagonist of *The Summer Soldier,*] has gone to work for the CIA, giving up on his attempts to be a mild-mannered English professor, and his first assignment takes him to a South Carolina college town where an atomic research project is being undermined by a foreign spy's threats on the families of the scientists involved. And the wife and daughter currently threatened turn out to be . . . *Ray's* wife #1 (now remarried) and daughter (now adopted), whom he hasn't seen in ten years, ever since wife Katey found out about his assassin job and deserted him. This is no coincidence—the CIA is testing Ray's resilience—and it's a promising premise. But whereas in *The Summer Soldier* Guild found just the right see-saw tension between unadorned action and Ray's interior monologue, here the ratio is a disaster: for each page of activity, there are three or four pages of reminiscing or musing—repetitive, self-pitying, mawkish thoughts about winning back the love of wife and daughter, The Way We Were, etc. As a result, the rather thin and implausible plot seems to be going on in cinematic slow motion—or, worse yet, as a jerky series of still photographs. In dozens of lines and in one strong sequence . . . , Guild reminds us how sharp a suspense writer he can be. But the windy self-consciousness and soap-operatic tendencies make Guinness and Guild old acquaintances whom we'll prefer to remember from *The Summer Soldier.* (pp. 1083-84)

> *A review of "Old Acquaintance," in* Kirkus Reviews, *Vol. XLVI, No. 19, October 1, 1978, pp. 1083-84.*

## NEWGATE CALLENDAR

"*Old Acquaintance*" is heavy, labored and padded. It seems to take [Nicholas Guild] forever to get to a point. Despite the hyped-up situation, hardly anything *happens:* there are too many flashbacks, too much philosophizing and moralizing; and the book moves with all the speed of a tank mired in quicksand.

> Newgate Callendar, in a review of "Old Acquaintance," in The New York Times Book Review, *March 4, 1979, p. 31.*

## KIRKUS REVIEWS

Though heavy with flashbacks and introspection, [*The Favor*, Guild's third novel featuring Ray Guinness,] . . . is actually just a thin violence orgy, disappointing work from the author of *The Summer Soldier* (though not quite so turgid as *Old Acquaintance*). This time Guinness, on assignment in Munich, is contacted by enemy agent Katzner, who once spared Guinness' life and now wants a favor: Guinness must save the life of Katzner's daughter Amalia, who has become the idealistic socialist pawn in some Communist spy-scheme in Holland involving a treasonous NATO officer from Belgium. Guinness has to agree, of course—and it just so happens that the spymaster behind the Holland scheme turns out to be Guinness' nemesis, "Flycatcher," whom Guinness has vowed to kill.... The final twist (which will surprise few readers): the whole thing with Katzner and Amalia was probably a setup, part of a "disinformation" scam.... Okay, intermittent action—but the espionage plotting seems little more than an excuse for some more of Guinness' revenge-killing; and, most crucially, Guinness has lost any of the recognizable motivations and sympathy he once had. All in all, it seems time for Guild to retire his thoroughly unlikable and dreary hero ... before the super-hitman does in what's left of this author's once-promising talent. (pp. 93-4)

> *A review of "The Favor," in* Kirkus Reviews, *Vol. XLIX, No. 2, January 15, 1981, pp. 93-4.*

### GEORGE COHEN

Ray Guinness is back for the third time [in *The Favor*] and again Guild has written a far-better-than-average suspense novel.... Guinness stalks his personal nemesis, the evil Flycatcher, convinced that the world would be a better place without him. There are several subplots to heighten the action. Guild makes the reader care about Guinness despite the fact that his character kills for a living.

> *George Cohen, in a review of "The Favor," in* Booklist, *Vol. 77, No. 14, March 15, 1981, p. 1012.*

### GREGG EASTERBROOK

Power. Bold, sweeping power. Awesome, radiant power. Power as dazzling as only one city in the entire history of the known universe, Washington, could express. He wanted that kind of power. No, he needed it, burned for it. And he would get it the only way he knew how: by writing a Washington thriller....

For a moment he savored it. Then he slammed his dynamic, masculine fist down on the priceless teak credenza. It was too late. Nicholas Guild, veteran writer of thrillers, had just beaten him to it with *The President's Man.*

Powerful book, he thought. Awesome, sweeping book. *The President's Man* was a book where people had names like Simon Faircliff, Pete Freestone, and Frank Austen. A book with lines like, "Simon Faircliff was a man of considerable physical presence—six three and built on a large scale; he reminded you of a wall.... The guy radiated power.... It was like having a light directed into your eyes." And, "Hell, Freestone had been followed before; it was the sort of thing that happened to political reporters." Staggering, stunning lines, yet Guild wrote them down without flinching, the way a man does.

Too bad, he thought, *The President's Man* had logical holes the Sixth Fleet could sail through. During its course Simon Faircliff's entire family, boyhood companions, congressional opponent, presidential nomination opponent, presidential election opponent, wife and official biographer all get knocked off under highly suspicious circumstances, yet no one raises an eyebrow. (No one ... except Frank Austen.) And though Faircliff has been president a complete term, not a single reporter has even visited his home town. Where, it seems, the damning evidence of Faircliff's true identity is practically on display at city hall.

Still, he knew, *The President's Man* was a book Washington-thriller fans would love, even if its characters did remind you of walls. It had a sort of goofy charm. It had ... power! ...

[Yet the book was sending him a message.] Suddenly he realized what it was! To write novels about how Washington works, you have to ignore how Washington works!

There was the central element of *The President's Man,* for instance. Awesome notion. A 50-year-long, globe-spanning conspiracy involving thousands of people which was executed like clockwork, no one ever suspecting a thing. (No one ... except Frank Austen.) In the real Washington, any program still running as planned by the end of its first week is the stuff of legends. In the real Washington power is diffuse and confused, not concentrated in the hands of a few wall-like men. Even presidents, in recent decades, have found that maddeningly true.

> *Gregg Easterbrook, "The Plot to Write a Washington Novel," in* Book World—The Washington Post, *April 11, 1982, p. 5.*

### FRANCIS T. DeANDREA

It is Nicholas Guild's ability at turning a phrase that saves *The President's Man.* Guild ... has concocted a story that is too unbelievable.

The main character is Frank Austen, a young, sharp, ruthless individual who lands a job as an assistant to Simon Faircliff, a liberal California congressman seeking a seat in the U.S. Senate. Faircliff wins the election, thanks in no small part to Austen's undercover work. The senator-elect appoints Austen his top aide....

Eventually, Faircliff wins the presidency and Austen is named director of the Central Intelligence Agency. He also ends up marrying Faircliff's only daughter, Dottie.

Up to this point, Guild manages to keep the reader's interest at a high level. The book's believability then takes a sharp nosedive. Prior to getting Faircliff elected president, Austen had considerable loyalty and affection for his father-in-law. But, when relations with the U.S.S.R. changed dramatically, Austen begins to question the president's leadership. At this juncture, Guild uses a terribly contrived device....

Guild's failure to make *The President's Man* believable comes from placing young Russian spies in positions in American society from which they—any one of them—can reach a point of control.

> *Francis T. DeAndrea, in a review of "The President's Man," in* Best Sellers, *Vol. 42, No. 2, May, 1982, p. 47.*

### PUBLISHERS WEEKLY

[Joachim von Niehauser] is landed on the coast of Maine in 1944 with one desperate mission: get the Manhattan Project secrets from a Nazi mole in Los Alamos and get them back to Germany via Mexico. After von Niehauser's first murder in Maine his trail is picked up by FBI agent George Havens. ["**Chain Reaction**"] is the taut, fast-paced story of a chase from New England to New Mexico to the Mexican border. Von Niehauser, Havens and Jenny Springer, a young army wife caught in a loveless affair, are the main characters, all of them disillusioned by the war and life. They are superbly drawn, as are even the minor characters. Despite some real humor, the atmosphere is bleak with each person trapped in a feeling of despair. The ending isn't happy, but the chief characters leave echoes. This is more than just another World War II thriller. It's good solid fiction.

*A review of "Chain Reaction," in* Publishers Weekly, *Vol. 223, No. 6, February 11, 1983, p. 58.*

## MARTIN J. HUDACS

*Chain Reaction* is appropriately titled because each event leads to the next, with swift and continuous action. This spy thriller grabs attention immediately and holds it hostage until the inevitable confrontation at the end.

Guild . . . ironically chooses two men who are loyal to their country but suspects in the organizations for which they work. When some of the great scientific minds of Germany began to defect to the West, the SS planted their own man in the scientific community. Now their man is part of the Manhattan Project. With the war going badly for Hitler, it is time to get their man out. His information and expertise offer the key to turning the war around.

Guild deftly develops his characters. It is a strength here, as in many of his novels, that the characters are well drawn and always true to form. Von Niehauser, for example, is an aristocrat by birth and by nature. . . . His manner and carriage always reflect his cultured, aristocratic background. He wants to succeed for his country although he harbors no loyalty to the Nazi regime. His antagonist is George Havens, an FBI agent on loan to the U.S. Army for the specific purpose of stopping von Niehauser. Havens feels no particular loyalty to the Agency since they prevented his enlistment into the Army.

Each man realizes the importance of his mission. Guild weaves into his tale the twists, double crosses, and brief encounters typical of the suspense thriller. In a style comparable to Jack Higgins and Ken Follett, Guild is establishing himself as a master of the genre.

*Martin J. Hudacs, in a review of "Chain Reaction," in* Best Sellers, *Vol. 43, No. 2, May, 1983, p. 49.*

## *KIRKUS REVIEWS*

[In *The Berlin Warning,* rich] young David Steadman, who fought the Fascists in Spain, is in love with lovely English war-widow Karen, now working for British Intelligence. So Steadman agrees to undertake a mission for Britain: he must prevent a German courier from reaching America with a mysterious attaché case. The proposed plan? Steadman's supposed to follow the courier aboard a US-bound ship in Sweden, then kill the courier and deliver the attaché case to London *un-*opened*. But David decides to do it *his* way: he steals the case from the German Embassy in Stockholm (booby-trapped floor, tricky safe-cracking), opens it, and discovers that it contains a Hitler letter warning FDR about Pearl Harbor—a bid to prevent the US from entering the war! What to do? Well, "as much as he disliked the idea of being Hitler's mailman, the letter to Roosevelt had to get there." Thus, Steadman is on the run—heading for Lisbon via Denmark, Germany, and France. The British are after him, of course (they *want* the US in the war), especially since the Intelligence chief is Steadman's lethal rival for dear Karen. But the Nazis are after Steadman too: the Himmler forces oppose the overture to FDR (inspired by von Ribbentrop); furthermore, SS-man Weinschenck has hated Steadman ever since they scuffled in Spain. And the upshot is a lively, violent series of confrontations. . . . [Finally], Steadman brings the warning-letter to Washington . . . with predictably ironic results. Guild . . . doesn't supply the character-texture or the gripping twists to rival *Eye of the Needle:* Karen is cardboard, the love-interest is drippy. But, with killings, break-ins, disguises, captures, escapes, and showdowns, the action here is constant and varied: a sturdy bet for WW II adventure fans. (pp. 99-100)

*A review of "The Berlin Warning," in* Kirkus Reviews, *Vol. LII, No. 3, February 1, 1984, pp. 99-100.*

## ALAN CHEUSE

Read a novel as cleanly composed and well-paced as Nicholas Guild's **"The Berlin Warning"** and you'll never again be satisfied with ordinary thrillers. Although the characters in his seventh book don't stand out as masterly handiworks of psychological insight, they function perfectly in a complicated plot that would take its toll of lesser writers. . . .

In the autumn of 1941 [David] Steadman finds himself in London, paying a call on the beautiful wife of his shell-shocked best friend. She, at the urging of yet another failed suitor, a biggie in British intelligence, recruits Steadman for a nearly suicidal mission in Nazi-occupied Europe. He is instructed to secure for the British a secret document that the Nazi high command had dispatched by courier for delivery to President Roosevelt. . . .

Steadman's life, of course, depends on his efforts to secure the document, though his honor, as it turns out, depends on his efforts to use it for his own purposes. Before long he's got both the Nazis and the British on his tail, and a trail of corpses behind him. If his ability to survive torture by both the Axis and the Allies seems less than credible, the fact that he is captured first by one side and then the other makes the novel quite engrossing.

*Alan Cheuse, "Don't Stop the War," in* The New York Times Book Review, *June 3, 1984, p. 41.*

# (Eugène) Guillevic

## 1907-

(Has also written under pseudonym of Serpières) French poet and translator.

Guillevic's poems typically are brief and free of rhetorical elements. He uses precise language and simple verse structure to probe the mysteries of nature. Many of Guillevic's poems were inspired by the landscape of Brittany, the region of his birth. Rocks, water, trees, sky, and animals are subjects of contemplation in much of his poetry. Guillevic seeks the essence of objects apart from their human intellectual and emotional associations, and he emphasizes the inherent organic unity in the natural world. According to Teo Savory, Guillevic "has extracted from the things of this world not their meaning to man, or their lesson for man, but rather their philosophy of themselves in an alien world peopled by those strange beings, men."

Guillevic gained recognition in France with his first book-length collection, *Terraqué* (1942). These poems feature his concise phrasing and understated style and subtly reveal cosmic significance in common objects. Following World War II, Guillevic departed from his early style and subject matter to comment on humanistic themes. The poems in *Exécutoire* (1947) concern the effects of war; *Gagner* (1949) and *Trente et un sonnets* (1954) address social and political issues of postwar France. With *Carnac* (1961) Guillevic returned to his distinctive early style. Several of his later volumes vary from his usual perspective and offer sequences of poems on such topics as Paris in *Ville* (1969) and the poet's relationship to other people in *Autres* (1980).

While only a portion of Guillevic's poetic output has been translated into English, he has won consistent praise in the English-speaking world for his original style and his sensitivity. According to one critic, "Guillevic is noted above all for having discovered a way of writing genuinely cosmic poetry without the least hint of strained portentousness."

(See also *Contemporary Authors*, Vols. 93-96.)

© Lütfi Özkök

### DENISE LEVERTOV

Guillevic is a Breton, born at Carnac of peasant stock. His poetry has deep roots in that inheritance. The great ritual places of the Celts, whether in Wales or Cornwall, Ireland or Brittany, the places where the great and small stones or *menhirs* are gathered in powerful and enigmatic testimony to forgotten certainties, are landscapes of a profound austerity. In such landscapes the senses are undistracted from the elemental: rock, sky, sea are there not backgrounds but presences. Beginning in such a place, Guillevic learned to recognize all else in life likewise as *presence,* not as incidental properties. Man, bird, cloud, lake, night, death, the sunlight—he knows them as Powers and Principalities, meets them face to face, and disdains the folly of attempting to use them as mere autobiographical adornments. This atheist is a radically religious poet.

His indignation at the use and misuse of some human beings by others, at the depersonalization of men by industrial and military interests, takes its force from the same source, that recognition of irreducible *presence* in all creation, animate and inanimate; but he is also a Marxist and a professional economist, and his moral indignation is accompanied by a cold and clear understanding of historical process.

The scrupulous simplicity of his diction often reminds me of that of Antonio Machado. (Guillevic does not read Spanish and does not know Machado's work.) Like Machado's, the shortest and seemingly plainest poems of Guillevic are often the most difficult to translate. In such short poems of Machado, the play of sound is essential, and the translator, without room to maneuver, is left with a flat literal. (p. vii)

Again like Machado, Guillevic avoids the easily opulent image, the blurred emotive impression. He trusts the hard, the plain, the stripped, to speak for itself. He refuses to say more than he feels.... But his feeling, his passion for life..., his passionate awareness of death, everywhere inseparable from life, his sharp and sensuous eye and ear are complex. And so the simplicity of diction, the plain and hard naming of things without descriptive qualification, reverberates, in the highly charged condensation of Guillevic's poems, with the ambiguity, the unfathomable mystery, of natural objects. To enter his work is to enter a kind of verbal Carnac, a gathering of sacred stones. (pp. viii-ix)

Like Francis Ponge—and like, in a very different manner, Rilke—Guillevic has many poems devoted to *things;* in [*Selected Poems*], "**A Hammer**" and "**A Nail**" are obvious examples, or, in a deeper vein, "**The Rocks**," and "**Gulls**." His relation to *the thing* is, however, less objective than Ponge's . . . and less self-identifying, or empathic, than Rilke's. Guillevic regards the primordial object with a kind of terror; it seems sometimes that he names it . . . to exorcize it—rather than either to reveal it or to extend his own life by identifying with it. Yet that passion for the world (and "there is no other world / in which to rest" he says) of which I have spoken, subsumes that terror, that recurring sense of the malignity of nature, makes it an element of passion, an awe-full means of adoration. And the sense of nature's malignity alternates, or coexists, with his humane grief and anger at man's inhumanity to man. . . . (pp. x-xi)

His Communism, and perhaps the poverty of his own youth, sometimes seem to make him divide mankind rather too sharply into the oppressors (see "**Big Business**") and the oppressed (see "**Portrait**"). However, anyone who supposes an avowed Communist will write only social-realist or propagandistic poetry will find themselves confuted by the ambiguity and even mysticism of Guillevic's writing. When I said to him that he was a religious poet he replied, "Of course. But mine is a religion of earth, not of heaven."

There seems to have been a crisis in his development in the middle 1950's, when *31 Sonnets* appeared, with a preface by Aragon. These are by no means his only "political" or overtly "engaged" poems (*Exécutoire*, 1947, and *Gagner*, 1949, in particular, contain many), but in these he seems—in the adoption of the sonnet form itself, as if to give to the common reader an absolutely familiar point of entry—to have been making a deliberate effort to write a kind of poem he felt (or had by external pressures, from the intellectual milieu in which he at that time found himself, been made to feel) he *ought* to be writing: which he owed to the social struggle. A number of the sonnets . . . seem to me admirable works in their way. But Guillevic himself seems to have felt it was not *his* way, for after a lapse of five years the next work he published was *Carnac*, a major sequence in which he reverted to, and further refined, the distinctive voice, the condensed and usually unrhymed forms, that characterized his earlier volumes and which he had continued to develop in his books of the last seven years.

I have spoken of the affinity I feel exists, unknown to Guillevic, between his work and some, at least, of Antonio Machado's. Even more notable, I believe, are the parallels between Guillevic and William Carlos Williams. No doubt, loving Williams as I do, and important for me as he has been, it was some sense of this likeness that first drew me to Guillevic. (pp. xi-xii)

Guillevic's poems have tended, on the whole, to get shorter (though often these short poems form long sequences) while Williams, not only in the epic *Paterson* but in *The Desert Music*, in "Asphodel, That Greeny Flower" and in the grandeur of other late poems, expanded his forms. In *Carnac* Guillevic has created a sustained and profound booklength poem, but formally his method in it remains the sequence of short poems, each paradoxically autonomous yet closely related to one another. (p. xiii)

*Denise Levertov, in an introduction to* Selected Poems *by Eugène Guillevic, translated by Denise Levertov, New Directions, 1969, pp. vii-xv.*

**DAVID KLEINBARD**

Guillevic's work [in *Guillevic*] reflects a struggle to maintain the greatest possible concision and lucidity. Often his poems concentrate his extraordinary perceptions of ordinary objects into a few starkly simple lines. A chair made of old wood, resting, forgetting its tree and its rancor, powerless. It wants nothing more, owes nothing more. "It contains its own whirlwind." Implicitly the poem evokes an old person's existence; and it comments upon people who live in a world of objects without noticing them or who make such objects without feeling for them and for the trees from which they come. The extreme simplicity and repetitiousness of the original give it an incantatory tone, as if it were a religious litany. For Guillevic, as for Rilke, who influenced him, the penetration "into the confidence of things" is a sacred act, a religious experience, as well as an act of completely devoted love. But no fuzzy mysticism or elusively subjective fantasy bars the reader who wishes to follow Guillevic into this region of awareness. Like the singing carpenter to whom he compares himself he has planed and sanded away all the superfluous words and images from these gnomic revelations. (pp. 291, 293)

*David Kleinbard, "Unicorn French Poets," in* The Nation, *Vol. 209, No. 9, September 22, 1969, pp. 290-91, 293.**

**STEPHEN BERG**

I have a picture of my two daughters standing naked in a large field overlooking a river blurred by the first morning haze of an August day. The energy of expectation and joy makes them come toward me out of the picture: the branches of two big shaggy pines lean down toward them from both sides like the arms of a very patient animal. A heavy tenderness. This snapshot reminds me of a kind of faith I may still have, for there is something about the attitude of those kids in that field which frightens me and yet makes me feel good about life. So with the poems of Guillevic [in *Selected Poems*]—raw telegraphic stanzas sent into things until they withdraw from their deep entering of the world, then offer very careful statements that reconcile what is between you and it. These poems have grown slowly, matured inside the objects they discuss until they have returned to us as language that matches the souls of the things they grew in. Seeds of language planted inside a hammer, big business, the poet's own death, inside language itself. . . . Guillevic's poems reflect the mind that has found itself in what is other. When Guillevic explains, and it is often, his logic maps the inexplicable presence of what he has lived in, and shows how it survives. This is given to the man who will not dream, who instead makes his task the penetration of the real until it speaks. It is as if the object or the scene or the event grows irritated by the poet that inhabits it, and can only send the poet back to us by giving him speech which corresponds to itself. This may be an extreme form of empathy, open to a man who has transcended his insecurities and can forget nothing but himself. It is at least one of the few satisfactory, fully convincing expressions of intellect. And though Guillevic's poems are simple, part by part, they contain the odor of roots, the granular jagged damp feel of thought that has gone down to the bottom and returned stripped of everything but truth. The poems are thorns, hard stations of a vision. (p. 260)

In Guillevic's poems there is no gap between the spirit and the flesh, nothing so silly and cruel. You have the process of the mind turning outward, being realized by its involvement with the world. The direction of the poems is reverence and thankfulness, a religion of grateful giving back, through the gift of understanding, as much as the twig, bird, death, or loved mouth gave the poet in the first place. A freedom to worship without giving in to the injustices of idolatry. The poems do not understand; they continue a process of birth, which means they reconcile by means of an attitude that praises the questions all things raise by being here. (p. 261)

Stephen Berg, "Transparencies," in Poetry, Vol. CXVI, No. 4, July, 1970, pp. 260-64.*

## TEO SAVORY

It is tempting to believe that Guillevic's concern is really us, mankind, and not nature with which he has imbued much that we have hitherto applied only to ourselves. That when he says "Nightingale, your song / Is what we need," the nightingale is only a symbol, the traditional symbol of peace of mind for *man*. We would like to believe that all Guillevic's poems are *lessons*. "I've lived in the flower," the poet tells us in **"Dwellings,"** and we wish to interpret this as a challenge to move out of the suburbs. Guillevic, unfortunately for the sentimental among us, means none of these things.

The flower, the ant, the blackbird, the rocks—especially the rocks—are exactly what their names imply. And he has extracted from the things of this world not their meaning to man, or their lessons for man, but, rather, their philosophy of themselves in an alien world peopled by those strange beings, men.

To grasp an object's philosophy of itself rather than the philosophy of nature, the poet contemplates his subjects intensely and silently and lets them communicate with him. This communication is different from speech, closer to intuition. Things are poems themselves, living by inspiration. His book, *Carnac*, makes Guillevic's approach to his writing clear. When he fills a page with two lines, "A whole system of arithmetic / Died in your waves," we sense that hours and days of contemplative communication with the Brittany shore have gone into them. And they have baffled our world of symbolic discourse, of assigning disintegrating arithmetical systems to the parts of this world. Nouns, our only means of naming things, are, to the nouns themselves, not simple statements but complete galaxies of meaning . . .

In his **"Euclidians"** Guillevic has gone far from poetry as it had been known. By including geometric designs on his pages, he has continued and advanced an earlier, surrealist idea into a new system of graphic poetry which even reflects some of the goals of concrete poetry. But unlike the latter, Guillevic's poetics are not new ways of looking at things, using eye as well as ear: his things are looking *at themselves*—and we are privileged to observe. The "you" and "me" of his geometry are not the poet and the circle but circle and circle. "Boredom vanquished," the circle says. "Repose," says the sinusoid. "Only connect," says the tangent.

Guillevic makes no distinction between natural objects—a rock, a tree—and the man-made objects that we have fashioned from those rocks and trees. . . .

Plastics and inorganic substances are completely missing from this world he has brought to our attention. (p. 43)

In Guillevic's world, events bring objects together, to their purpose, to themselves; what happens in nature is exactly right, right in the sense of surpassing what was meant to happen: "A

bridge, then, was the thing / For this spot." The bridge is also all the planning that went into its location, its shape, and especially the laborer who fashioned it, and it, him.

One expects such a poet, with this precise, almost mechanical viewpoint, to be lacking in compassion, in feeling, in empathy with *man's* world. Our perplexity is caused by our traditional view of nature; there is no contradiction between Guillevic's observation of nature—sympathetic rather than detached—and his compassion for the suffering of mankind. But one feels that his poems, and there are many, inspired by World War II, by revolution or any tragedies stemming from man's inhumanity to man are equalled by those in which his mission is to describe nature to itself, in which he uses his poetic tools to redescribe to us man's longing. The result is a curious understatement of our situation, with analytical descriptions of corpses, blood, rotting flesh, death, torture. (p. 44)

And yet, in this kind of protective detachment, there is so much tenderness, so exact a sense of time and place and rhythm, that one's heart is stirred by commonplaces whereas, under emotional bombardment, it would remain unmoved. . . .

The appeal of Guillevic must, as far as analysis of his work goes, remain mysterious. Only through the poems themselves can we attempt to understand his many facets, his unique philosophy. He is enjoyable and shocking, obtuse and aggravating, humane and unhuman. But it takes no time at all for us to begin to inhabit his world. And, as he begins to be translated into more and more languages, admiration for his skill as an artist, his poetic ability, becomes international.

Our difficulty, after reading his work, is to return to our former viewpoints, our previous focus on the world of cause and effect, of apathy and self-interest. Guillevic's ultimate artistry transcends that of either content or aesthetics: in that integrated fourth dimension within which he lives and writes, he has reconciled political and social concerns with an almost mathematical dissection of nature. And through reading his poetry, we are led toward a reconciliation, inward and outward, ourselves. (p. 45)

Teo Savory, "An Introduction to Guillevic," in Books Abroad, Vol. 45, No. 1, Winter, 1971, pp. 43-5.

## MICHAEL BISHOP

[*Du domaine*] is the latest in a long succession of books revealing Guillevic's unflagging exploration of matter and man's relationship to it through language. As so often with Guillevic's work, from *Terraqué* or *Gagner* to *Carnac* or *Inclus*, there is a crisp, terse quality about his writing, a use of words and typographical space that, while not rhetorically eccentric, nevertheless allows language's potentialities, like those of the phenomena with which he is concerned, to assume a certain conspicuousness. Yet this conspicuousness, of language, of sense, of things, remains veiled. Mishandled—either by poet or reader—it could become banal, irritatingly ineffectual. This kind of *rapport exact, exigu* that Guillevic's long poem offers of things may retain its full capacity for delicate, oblique revelation only if the reader establishes the right equilibrium between the text's continuity (and, therefore, demand that we neglect the detail in favor of the whole) and discontinuity (and, therefore, contrary demand that we immerse ourselves in the widening semantic circles that invisibly go out from each detail), between its air of fragility and minimality and the potential infinite expansiveness of its every component. Too rapid a reading of *Du domaine,* as of much of Guillevic's other work, would, oddly, heighten the effect of discontinuity, not reduce it. Fermentation must be allowed to occur, the gnomic must be allowed to tease itself out, the slight to inflate fully, in the space, allotted for this purpose, lying expectantly around each "stanza."

The significance of the act of writing for Guillevic is, of course, of a profoundly ontological order. Poetry implies, as for that most lucidly penetrating of all modern theoreticians of art, the poet Pierre Reverdy, a level of having and being that, while strictly never transcendent, cannot be thought of as flatly immanent. The point at which Guillevic's poetry generates its maximum power, the domain in which it attains to its highest degree of liberation and illumination, is neither exclusively of matter nor of man: it is always between, a fusion of the imaginary and the real, . . . the locus of a new dimensionality wherein the here and the beyond-here, the now and the forever, may be conjoined in fragile, even vulnerable equilibrium. Certainly, Guillevic's fundamental concern is to respond to the willingness and appeal of the world, that need things betray for attention and "care" to which Ponge and Heidegger have in different ways rendered us increasingly sensitive. Soot, water, ivy, walls, slugs—the most improbable as well as the most archetypally inviting of phenomena, therefore—are capable of opening up the way to a mode of co-being, of mutually advantageous conviviality, almost. The question that constantly confronts Guillevic, however, is *how* to reach the place of mediation, how to "étreindre la distance," how to respond to the injunction of matter . . . in order to realize the desired and ever-potential process of ontological intermingling of self and world. . . . And it is at this point that we appreciate to what extent the poet, in effect highly dependent upon and humbly solicitous of such a contact or "marriage"—despite any misgivings or, even, very real revulsions—must fall back upon his own resources, his personal capacity for "conjugation" of what only appears to be given, but which would remain inert but for this injection of vitality, of "poetic" being. (pp. 512-13)

> *Michael Bishop, in a review of "Du domaine," in* The French Review, *Vol. LII, No. 3, February, 1979, pp. 512-13.*

### SARAH N. LAWALL

Guillevic's latest book of poems [*Étier, poèmes 1965-1975*] is a collection of separate pieces . . . : many new, some reprinted from brief separate volumes . . . , some reprinted with minor changes from [*Guillevic*]. . . . Yet there is a definite coherence and growth in the course of the book's eight sections. . . .

The form is similar to Guillevic's earlier poetry; short, gnomic poems in stanzas for the most part of two or three brief lines, "free" in that there is no predictable pattern but also falling easily into the traditional even rhythms of 4-, 6-, 10-, and 12-syllable lines. The thought is discursive, the tone meditative and inquiring, avoiding the rhetorical tricks of imagery and verbal play unless to poke fun at them ("**Rose,**" "**Image**"), and emphasizing instead the development and variation of a single thought over a series of connected short poems. . . . The vocabulary is characteristically spare, conversational, yet analytic; the landscape, Guillevic's familiar Breton countryside, is depopulated by human beings, but truly inhabited by the lively interplay of light, water, stones, plants, and the occasional cry of a bird (or slaughtered pig). The only truly human

figure is that of the narrator: observing, questioning, "accepting in himself" what he can see or touch. . . . (p. 193)

If Guillevic writes "materialist" poetry, which he claims to and certainly does, it is also a poetry that asks all the old "transcendental" questions about the possibilities of knowledge, about fate, and about the yearning for balance and perfection in a tortured universe. . . . The answer, insofar as there is one, comes in a lively sense of our common material existence, symbolized perhaps in the final "**Herbier de Bretagne,**" where the daily revelation of leaf and flower reverses transcendental explanations to show "ce que la terre / Fait de l'univers". . . , and where the poet himself exists, simply to register the whole. . . . The poet's "place," here, is a channel of movement and relation, an *étier* between complementary states of being, and is presented in a collection of sober and subtly formed verse that increasingly rewards rereading. (p. 194)

> *Sarah N. Lawall, in a review of "Étier, poèmes 1965-1975," in* The French Review, *Vol. LIV, No. 1, October, 1980, pp. 193-94.*

### MICHAEL BISHOP

Despite his advancing years Guillevic continues to publish work at once varied and consistent. The long poem *Du domaine* appeared in 1977 . . . , *Étier* in 1978-79 . . . , "**Magnificat**" in 1978, and today *Autres,* a collection of "poetic" *contes et nouvelles,* dialogues, "suppositions" and one long text entitled "**Dit du pérégrin,**" all of which have been written during the past decade.

As always, Guillevic is concerned with those relationships between self and world that constitute his act of writing. The questioning that is his book takes place out of ignorance and is preferable not in itself so much as in contrast with the silence it defies. Guillevic seeks to explore the enigmas of relationship, the secrecy of our being there, with things and others. He is thus endlessly fascinated by our "presence," our ways of going forth into the world, through the body, through the senses, but also through the mind, through our mental/poetic creation of ourselves via relationships.

In all this Guillevic remains painfully conscious of his/our limitations, of the difficulty of being and what I have recently called the "imperfection of apotheosis." Not only is there still a floundering in spite of (the) language (of things), but there is, even worse, a floundering *in* this language. There is, in consequence, both an inaccessibility of ends and an inadequacy of means, though writing moves forward, in Guillevic's poetics, as a gesture that, while lucid, dismisses this imperfection. Speaking does not reduce the void or remove the necessity for speech. It merely moves the speaker on to a further void, a further necessity. Guillevic's final long poem, "**Dit du pérégrin,**" is especially revealing in this regard and shows, in its existential character, a good deal in common with his contemporary André Frénaud.

The discourse of the world/poetry is "cracked," fragmented, mysterious, open. Guillevic's writing, struggling constantly with such imperfections, continues also to know how to relax with them. (pp. 272-73)

> *Michael Bishop, in a review of "Autres," in* World Literature Today, *Vol. 55, No. 2, Spring, 1981, pp. 272-73.*

## WORLD LITERATURE TODAY

Though Guillevic began writing verse at twenty-two and published his first small collection, *Requiem,* in 1938, it was not until the appearance of *Terraqué* (Terraqueous—i.e., a verbal fusion of "land" and "water") in 1942 that his poetry started to receive recognition. The avowed purpose of his brief, dense, intensely imagistic poems is to isolate the essences of creatures and things—birds, animals, flowers, rocks—and to purge them of the intellectual and emotional associations man has imposed on them.... *Exécutoire* (Writ of Execution; 1947) collected the poetry of the war years written under the pseudonymn of "Serpières" and the verses of three small postwar volumes, all of them powerful in their brevity and concreteness in depicting the bloody nature of war. In *Gagner* (To Earn; 1949) and *Trente et un sonnets* (Thirty-One Sonnets; 1954) Guillevic turned to traditional, regular poetic forms and to discursive verse of events and social conditions; many critics find the poems of this period more formulaic statements of political creed than concise expressions of personal feeling, but Aragon, for one, sees the verses as "carved out of the flesh of the poet's heart." *Carnac* (1961) revives the concise, monolithic verse of the earlier volumes and regains force and vitality in like measure. *Sphère* (1963) concentrates its attention on this one simple figure, while the epigrams and geometric shapes of *Euclidiennes* (1968; transl. *Euclidians*) carry the poet's striving for concision and simplicity to its ultimate fulfillment, at the same time evincing some affinity with concrete poetry.

*Ville* (City; 1969) isolates the objects and aspects of Paris life and "moves swiftly to an appraisal of the infringement of things upon people"; *Paroi* (Wall; 1970) unfolds the whole dialectic of the poet's relationship to the "wall" which prevents us from entering a half-glimpsed, magnetic, other world beyond; and *Inclus* (Enclosed; 1974) is a long, fragmentary meditation on the art of poetry, viewing the poet alternately as Narcissus and Priest, Clown and Craftsman. *Du domaine* (Domain; 1977) again evokes stark images of boulders, pebbles, oaks, deer and, above all, water as "the very stuff of consciousness," in the words of ... Eric Sellin. *Étier* (Channel; 1979), collecting the poetry of the years 1965-75, proceeds from "elegies" on seascape and sky, through a series of meditative "pauses" and "exercises" that reestablish contact through the sensory organs, to an "analysis" of the surrounding world that leads toward a modest "Herbal of Brittany"—all clearly indicating a "continuing interest in the simplest things as cornerstone of his ars poetica." His newest publication, *Autres* (Other Things; 1980), is an amalgam of "poetic" *contes et nouvelles*, dialogues, "suppositions" and one long text entitled **"Dit de pérégrin,"** all written in the 1970s. "The innovative force of Guillevic's poetry," writes Sicilian-born poet and editor Mimmo Morina in nominating Guillevic for the 1982 Neustadt Prize, "is like a bazooka which opens the first breach in the armored door of academic conservatism. French literary language underwent, thanks to him, a process of lexical grafting which it had awaited for several decades in order to liberate itself from formal calcification. His poetry is spare, concise, free from any superfluous objectification, and this simplicity suffices to evoke a state of mind for witnessing a drama and penetrating the world of today with its violence and cruelty." (p. 631)

*"Candidate: (Eugène) Guillevic," in* World Literature Today, *Vol. 55, No. 4, Autumn, 1981, pp. 630-31.*

## SARAH LAWALL

Guillevic's latest book of poems [*Autres, poèmes 1969-79*] has a more personal, autobiographic tone than usual, and the poet "pérégrin" at the end seems to be weighing the challenges and choices of a lifetime.... Not that Guillevic's poetry is ever separate from personal experience, whether sensing other life forms in rocks, ocean, or plants, reacting against alienation and oppression in human society, or simply meditating on shapes of being. Yet here there is the hint of an overview of the poet's own life and relations with "others": with other people, with the partner of numerous dialogues, with a society of activists or squatters, *pestiférés* or *non-pestiférés*, or with the material world itself. Despite the apparent "make-believe" of the section titles—"Contes et nouvelles" (1972-76), "Bergeries" (1969-75), "Dialogues" (1971-76), and "Dit du Pérégrin" (1977-79)—there is recurrent emphasis on truth and value judgments: truth tested in question and response, in definitions, in poetic situations anticipated and weighed.... Fear, loneliness, hope, human needs and aspirations are all conveyed as truths throughout the imaginary visions of *Autres,* in images of interrelationships and experience that may or may not be practically unrealistic, but are all emotionally true.

Guillevic's characteristic themes and scenes appear throughout. The everyday ... space of his poetry is the isolated, humble space of an attic ... or an unassuming spot of land inhabited by dogs, flies, and the glory of a dandelion.... He speaks of fear, hostility, and violence, and of a poet's escape through the imagination—whether on the back of this fairytale giraffe ... or in the absorbing study of a small slate vase.... Writing as if he himself is *un autre,* he foreshadows a time when he will no longer be looking into the future and saying "plus tard, plus tard—"; the world will have lost one of its dimensions.... The subtlety and force of this poem, where the lost dimension includes both the sense of the future and the poet's voice, is typical of the best in this collection, which remains, however, somewhat uneven. Guillevic is consummately able to evoke complicated states of being in simple words describing interwoven perceptions; yet sometimes ... one feels a strained effort at significance inside this very simplicity.... This occasional awkwardness is only one part of Guillevic's great ability to evoke physical sensation as if he himself participated in all its forms, absorbing and redefining its implications for human existence. His is a participatory poetry that aims beyond words and is always worth reading. (pp. 159-60)

*Sarah Lawall, in a review of "Autres, poèmes 1969-79," in* The French Review, *Vol. LV, No. 1, October, 1981, pp. 159-60.*

## MICHAEL BISHOP

The past four years have seen the publication by Eugène Guillevic ... of no less than five volumes: four major collections of poetry—*Du domaine* (1977), *Étier* (1979), *Autres* (1980) and now *Trouées*—and one quasi-biography, *Vivre en poésie* (1980), which offers many insights into one of the most distinctive poetic imaginations of our day.... *Trouées* gives us the same cryptic yet open, available mode of articulation, the same rhythmic continuity of thought ..., the same dramatic yet soft, smiling intensity that his other recent work has so often revealed. Never heavy-handed or "trumpeted" in its expression, Guillevic's perspective is at once personal and objective, his gesture one of a delicate prying apart rather than of deep, insistent incision and blatant tracing. Maintaining a vital flux, a continuing, never-congealing dynamic exchange, is what matters most to Guillevic. The page may fascinate as much as the plain; the signs the poet conjures and distills may be ardently and doggedly sought, but Guillevic never aims to develop and impose a permanency of structure, an ideology and artifact that overawe, dazzle as ultimate law, becoming coagulated end instead of raw, throbbing way and means.

From the point of view of the thought or meaning to which it insistently directs, *Trouées* is in fact wonderfully rich, seething and frothing like the world itself, never still, never self-satisfied. (p. 481)

In all of this it is important to note the stress that is laid upon the here and now, yet in such a way as to evoke the endlessly peeling masks of all reality, its consequently inaccessible absoluteness or infiniteness, which nevertheless haunts and allures in a finiteness that is at once more and no more than itself. . . . In this way, as Guillevic had sensed as a young boy—he tells us in the opening pages of *Vivre en poésie*—that rich minimality, that apparent absurdity and insignificance all around us, in the sea, a blade of grass, a leaf, offers, amazingly, in its fleeting presence an intuitable sense of the eternity within it and a feeling of strange joy. Of his recent collections, *Trouées* is perhaps the finest, and of the texts it contains, **"Vitrail"** is perhaps the most compelling. (p. 482)

*Michael Bishop, in a review of "Trouées," in* World Literature Today, *Vol. 56, No. 3, Summer, 1982, pp. 481-82.*

# Jim Harrison
## 1937-

(Born James Thomas Harrison; also writes as James Harrison) American poet, novelist, scriptwriter, and critic.

Harrison writes in a variety of styles and forms: in his prose, he has created adventure stories, historically-based fiction, and accounts of spiritual quests; his poetry is written in both free verse and more formal structures. Central to most of his work is a strong sense of the outdoors. Harrison frequently combines nature imagery, ecological awareness, a keen attention to sensual details, and an outdoorsman's toughness. His roots in rural northern Michigan, his tendency toward understatement, and the theme of violence in much of his work have inevitably led to comparisons with Ernest Hemingway. Unlike Hemingway, however, Harrison has received almost as much acclaim for his poetry as for his prose.

Harrison's *Selected & New Poems 1961-1981* (1982) contains both new work and poems from his five major volumes: *Plain Song* (1965), *Locations* (1968), *Outlyer and Ghazals* (1971), *Letters to Yesinin* (1973), and *Returning to Earth* (1977). His poetry is generally unrhetorical and colloquial, gaining its power through the intensity and immediacy of its imagery. Although he writes mostly open, unstructured verse, Harrison has also written suites and ghazals, which depend on images to develop their central themes. A ghazal, as Harrison explains, is a "lyrical explosion"; indeed, Harrison's lyrics are sometimes considered explosive.

Harrison's fiction includes *Wolf: A False Memoir* (1971), *A Good Day to Die* (1973), *Farmer* (1976), *Legends of the Fall* (1979), *Warlock* (1981), and the recent *Sundog* (1984). *Wolf* and *Farmer* are novels which examine the quest for personal identity. *A Good Day to Die* and *Warlock* are thrillers, revealing Harrison's admiration for detective fiction in the tradition of John D. MacDonald. *Sundog* studies the ideals and values of contemporary America through an individual's search for self-knowledge, and *Legends of the Fall* consists of three interrelated novellas which explore the themes of violence and revenge.

(See also *CLC*, Vols. 6, 14; *Contemporary Authors*, Vols. 13-16, rev. ed.; *Contemporary Authors New Revision Series*, Vol. 8; and *Dictionary of Literary Biography Yearbook: 1982*.)

## JOHN BUCKLEY

In Jim Harrison's new novel [*Warlock*], Johnny Lundgren, an unemployed, housebound, middle-aged, neophyte gourmet, takes to calling himself "Warlock," his old Cub Scout name. And from the outset this assures that his actions will be puerile. . . .

*Warlock* is Harrison's fourth full-length novel and follows his fine collection of novellas, *Legends of the Fall* (1979). The problem here is that *Warlock* could have made an excellent novella, but Harrison has extended it to novel length by accumulating temporal data. *Warlock* has some exciting scenes, some well-drawn characters and, eventually, a good story. But it's flawed in its timing, taking forever to start then no time to end. There is rich irony in that ending, but it is less conclusion than punch line.

John Buckley, in a review of "Warlock," in Saturday Review, *Vol. 8, No. 10, October, 1981, p. 76.*

## J. D. REED

If Henry Miller, S. J. Perelman and Walt Whitman had holed up in a Michigan roadhouse to concoct a mystery yarn, the resulting mélange of cosmic erotica, snappish humor and hirsute lyricism might resemble this send-up of the "tecs" [*Warlock*] by Poet and Novelist Jim Harrison. . . . His mock hero, Johnny Lundgren, nicknamed Warlock, is a reluctant Swedish-American gumshoe who has been fired from his job as a foundation executive. He flees to the comforting semi-poverty of rural northern Michigan where irrelevance turns to comic Scandinavian angst. Trysts in his overheated Subaru prove difficult; his forays at gourmet cooking are disasters; insolvency threatens. Then, in the nick of time, Lundgren's wife Diana gets him a job with Dr. Rabun, a prosthetic Edison who designs sexual aids that imitate the motion of swimming porpoises. The doctor's problems: his extensive investments in timber and real estate are being skimmed, and his gay son and free-spending wife are bleeding him dry. Warlock's assignment: remove the bad apples from the barrel. (p. K12)

Harrison's humor in *Warlock* puts the wrong man in the trench coat. Lundgren is a poet, not a flatfoot, a satyr trying his hoof at logic and deduction. Like most literary fools since Don Quixote saddled up Rosinante, Lundgren is redeemed by his own goodness. Harrison's taste for the batty sometimes cloys: "He really wasn't so much a fool as he was giddy about still being alive." Lengthy erotic descriptions tend to become post-coital arias. But Harrison scores well on the firing range: his humor usually strikes in the killing zone. Dashiell Hammett's low-rent realism made the mystery novel fun to read. *Warlock* demonstrates that it is equally enjoyable to spoof. (pp. K12, K16)

> J. D. Reed, "Hick Gumshoe," in Time, Vol. 118, No. 19, November 9, 1981, pp. K12, K16.

## JOHN D. CASEY

"*Warlock*" is a sort of detective story by a poet and serious novelist who obviously loves reading American thrillers. In fact, with this book Jim Harrison may well be trying to repay a debt of pleasure to the best of the pulp caper writers of the past and their most recent descendants; he even mentions Travis McGee, John D. MacDonald's sleuth, in the novel.

The story takes some time getting cranked up. The first 90 pages don't have a lot of action, but they're enjoyable. This opening section is reminiscent of Thomas Berger's fictional series about Carlo Reinhart, particularly "Reinhart in Love." Mr. Harrison's hero, Johnny Lundgren (a.k.a. Warlock), has a lot of Carlo Reinhart's style abut him, including his amiable, energetic innocence and his penchant for rich inner monologues about his own desires and the vagaries of American life.

The novel picks up with the entrance of Dr. Rabun, a cracked genius doctor who employs our hero as a trouble-shooter. . . . I won't reveal the plot, which is full of fast turns. But things aren't what they seem. Mr. Harrison's narrative moves from the glee of charade, adventure and discovery—as Warlock philosophizes, wisecracks, alters his senses and falls into bed with the various women he encounters on the job—to some sorrow and anger.

The only flaw in this book is its pacing. Mr. Harrison takes the first lap too slowly and the last lap too fast. But that's better than starting out too fast and winding up too slow. More-over, the flaw is noticeable mainly because of the affection one develops for the novel's characters. Warlock is an engaging fellow, and his wife is a pretty nifty woman. I even liked his old dad and his mutt of a dog. So I didn't want to see these good creatures get so roughly tumbled about for the sake of the novel's big finish. Warlock, for instance, seems to get more comeuppance than he deserves. When the dust settles, however, Warlock and his wife are reconciled, and we are assured that they are going to get back to their normal lives.

For all its unevenness of pacing, there are pleasures of all sorts to be had—farcical, reflective, luscious, gritty—in this stylish entertainment. (p. 14)

> John D. Casey, "American Settings," in The New York Times Book Review, November 22, 1981, pp. 14, 45.*

## PAUL STUEWE

*Legends of the Fall* demonstrated that macho ideas and literary refinement needn't be incompatible bedfellows, but *Warlock* rejects this symbiosis for a frenetic hyper-masculinity that produces merely a substandard novel. The book attempts to bring comedy, tragedy and irony into a simple moral tale of good versus evil but succeeds only in making a pretentious mess out of some not terribly promising material.

> Paul Stuewe, "Sex in Venice, Essays from Blooms-bury and Uris's 'Jerusalem'," in Quill and Quire, Vol. 48, No. 1, January, 1982, p. 39.*

## PUBLISHERS WEEKLY

Harrison is classified as a novelist—which is not surprising, considering the unclassifiable nature of his poetry. He doesn't write like anyone else, relying entirely on the toughness of his vision and intensity of feeling to form the poem. Or, we should say, relying on the untrammeled renegade genius that has made him one of the most unappreciated writers in America. Anyone who missed "**Plain Song**," "**Outlyer & Ghazals**," "**Letters to Yesinin**" and "**Returning to Earth**" first time around has a treat in store [in "**Selected and New Poems 1961-1981**"]. Harrison will shock and delight readers who think they already know what a poem is supposed to be. The experience is something like coming across a Whitman or Dickinson, a Keats or Rimbaud after a long diet of formal and classical verse: here's a poet talking to you instead of around himself, while doing absolutely brilliant and outrageous things with language.

> A review of "Selected and New Poems: 1961-1981," in Publishers Weekly, Vol. 221, No. 26, June 25, 1982, p. 114.

## RICHARD TILLLINGHAST

Reading Jim Harrison's poetry I find I agree with Denise Levertov that Mr. Harrison is "one of the most authentic voices of his time." That is high praise, deservedly high. But to me it suggests something less than total enthusiasm about Mr. Harrison as a poet: In poetry "voice" is not everything. The colloquial, uncontrived style does allow him the effect of spontaneity and the freedom to speak about the most personal emotions and details of his life. Behind the words one always feels the presence of a passionate, exuberant man who is at the same time possessed of a quick, subtle intelligence and a deeply questioning attitude toward life.

A native of northern Michigan, a part of the country Ernest Hemingway also loved—and there are, both [in "**Selected and New Poems**"] and in Mr. Harrison's novels, resemblances to Hemingway's work, both the good and the bad—Mr. Harrison has few equals as a writer on outdoor life, the traditional heritage and proving ground of the American male. . . .

Mr. Harrison has been condemned, fashionably, for being aggressively "macho," but like many hunters he has a precise and empathetic knowledge of the natural world. . . .

Jim Harrison unfortunately has little feeling for form, rhythm, pacing and development in a poem. While the language is often vivid and colorful, a typical poem of his will not conclude; it will simply stop. One sometimes feels, particularly in the long poems, that one is reading diary entries chopped into lines. At his best, however, he writes so winningly that one ignores the formlessness and is simply content to be in the presence of a writer this vital, this large-spirited, who is "hanging on to nothing today and / with confidence." (p. 14)

Richard Tillinghast, "From Michigan and Tennessee," in The New York Times Book Review, December 12, 1982, pp. 14, 31.*

## GEORGE HELD

Jim Harrison can be grouped with his better-known WASP contemporaries Richard Brautigan, Ken Kesey, and Tom Robbins, and Tom McGuane. . . . All now well into their forties, these style-conscious novelists often use a Western or Midwestern rural setting and share a respect for nonconformity, a delight in sex, and a reverence for nature. All have an eye for the incongruous and speak to the conflict between our "natural" selves and the various synthetic effects of creeping urbanization and advanced technology. More like Kesey than like the others, Harrison is a ballsy writer true to his roots, in the Upper Peninsula of Michigan, where he was born and where he locates at least part of the action in a majority of his fictions. . . . [In] *Warlock* Harrison returns to the Upper Peninsula, to his current home in Leelanau County, and creates an alter ego in Johnny Lundgren. . . .

[Parody is] often the mode of *Warlock*. Thus after the fashion of Ben Franklin and Jay Gatsby, Johnny Lundgren sets down rules of conduct ("EAT SPARINGLY," "AVOID ADULTERY," "GET IN FIRST RATE SHAPE," etc.), none of which he follows. This comical good-natured book tries to work both the high-brow and the low-life sides of the street, alternating a description of Joycean significance—"He had grasped the future like a chalice, pursued it as a knight setting off for Jerusalem through the dank forests of Europe, and down through Turkey to the burning sands of the Middle East, where he no doubt swapped his cumbersome horse for a camel"—with an obscene aside—"What the fuck." Since the passage to which the first quotation alludes in Joyce's "Araby" is already parodic, Harrison's parody sinks into facetiousness. Elsewhere, Harrison undercuts a literary image with a touch of colloquial vulgarity: "A dark temptress had almost got his ass in a sling." Again, this sort of shifting tone sometimes makes the whole project seem less parodic than facetious.

Harrison's style is in any case mixed, and includes a playful use of cliché and allusion; like Warlock, he owns "an imponderable urge to both create and consume low-rent information." The novel thus contains quotations from Baudelaire and Blake, as well as allusions to *Gone With the Wind*, NFL football, and *Saturday Night Live*. And Harrison is no more likely to parody Joyce than he is Coppola. . . . In other words, Jim Harrison in *Warlock* is a lot like those of us who read *ABR*: he tries to fuse literary culture and pop culture without becoming totally confused.

In this, his fifth volume of fiction, James Harrison, a.k.a. Jim, faces a mid-career crisis. Having published five critically acclaimed books of poetry and numerous magazine articles, mainly in *Sports Illustrated* in the early seventies, Harrison has lately aimed at making a living from his fiction. . . . [Three] hard-edged adventure stories made plausible *Esquire*'s claim for him as "a superb storyteller," if not as "a writer of serious consequence." But now *Warlock* casts doubt on Harrison's art. Though the novel is tricked out with epigraphs from, among other sources, *A Midsummer-Night's Dream*, *Warlock* has a spirit derived less from Shakespeare than from contemporary popular literature. Still, Harrison's ribald and playful imagination makes *Warlock* a good read, if not a work of "serious consequence."

George Held, "Outside Men," in The American Book Review, Vol. 5, No. 4, May-June, 1983, p. 20.

## WILLIAM HARMON

> Then it becomes so dark
> and still
> that I shatter the moon with an oar.
>     **("Dusk")**

> Yesterday I fired a rifle into the lake.
>     **("A Year's Changes")**

> The child is fully clothed but sits in the puddle madly
> slapping the warm water on which the sun ripples
>     and churns.
>
>     **("Ghazals")**

These and similar passages [in *Selected and New Poems*] distill the essence of Harrison's idiom, which works most faithfully in a momentary image of peace disturbed, almost always figured as a body of water aimlessly but needfully hit by hand, slug, or oar. The perfection of Harrison's focus and attention here recalls a number of similar episodes: near to hand, Salinger's young Seymour throwing a rock at Charlotte Mayhew because she looks so beautiful in her yellow dress; farther away and three hundred years ago, Bashō's supremely froggy frog jumping impromptu into the old pond, *mizu no oto*, sound of water, period.

Harrison's visions are there, spaced throughout these poems of two decades, and one cannot avoid appreciating their clarity and rightness. And it may be that the rest is *remplissage*, idle random padding and stuffing that are neither here nor there. Harrison seems to devote an extravagant amount of language to disavowals and dismissals, strenuously working out what the blurb claims to be "a new approach to his poetry" by means of which he hopes "to avoid both academic formalism and the vogue of hygienic confessions." I do not find much in Harrison's poetry that could be called formalist or hygienic, but there is a good deal that is academic (mannered, burdened by learning, predictable, repetitious) and a great deal that certainly looks like autobiography, if not outright solipsistic confession. Reading the poems in chronological order, one can see a number of habits that Harrison has had to work through and cast off; although not exactly in the collegiate genre (e.g., freshmen, preregistration, dorms), these habits *are* academic in the sense of demonstrating attitudes that are not vital or original. The early Harrison had a problem with diction, for example, and he solved it in two antithetical ways, both of them academic. He will say "lay" for "lie" and "like" for "as," and the effect is not easy colloquial familiarity but a rather pained sloppiness. . . . (pp. 138-39)

Harrison repeats himself. "Pink" must appear three dozen times in these 212 pages, and several clichés, such as "still point" and images of clouds that look like brains, appear and then come back for unnecessary encores. Another heavily repeated item, also academic and also unnecessary, is the rhetorical hectoring about what the poem is *not* going to do. After a time, I got the feeling that a talented tightrope walker was interrupting himself every few steps to proclaim, "This is not scuba-diving." I wanted to paraphrase Eliot's family motto, *Tace et Fac*, and say to the poem, "Shut up and do it! I know you *can*." . . . Harrison frequently sounds as though he is unwilling to let his percussive lucidity speak for itself. Instead, he editorializes, and in Harrison's kind of personal lyric editorializing, forever rhetorical, is forever self-defeating. . . . (pp. 139-41)

William Harmon, "Nimsism and Kindred Delights," in Parnassus: Poetry in Review, *Vol. 11, No. 1, Spring-Summer, 1983, pp. 129-46.**

## MICHIKO KAKUTANI

Like **"Warlock,"** Jim Harrison's last novel, **"Sundog"** is a kind of detective story concerned with the "mystery of personality"—specifically that of an eccentric and larger-than-life adventurer named Robert Corvus Strang.

Strang, it appears, embodies all the optimism, vitality and raw, frontier values of an older and now almost defunct America; and by turning a journalist's pursuit of him into a "Heart of Darkness"-like quest for knowledge, Mr. Harrison would seem to have found a narrative strategy perfectly designed for showing off the gift for epic storytelling that he used to such effect in his fine novella, **"Legends of the Fall."**

Unfortunately, something has gone seriously awry in Mr. Harrison's execution of this book. His characters are neither mythic personages resonant with meaning, nor the kind of well-rounded figures one meets in the best naturalistic fiction; rather, they remain an assortment of clichés—unlikable line-drawings, rendered with a shaky hand.

As for the story of their overlapping lives, it never becomes more than a string of reminiscences held together by portentiously withheld secrets later revealed with a heavy clunk. Not only does this device make for crude storytelling, but in this book, it doesn't even have the desired effect of sustaining the reader's interest. By the end, we care so little about Strang that we really have no interest in his sister or whether that sister may actually have been his mother. It is even more difficult for us to understand why he exerts such an obsessive hold on the narrator's imagination.

To readers of Mr. Harrison's earlier books, the narrator of **"Sundog"** will be a familiar figure. Like the heroes in **"Farmer"** and **"Wolf,"** he is a randy, hard-drinking fellow, suffering from the anxieties of middle-age. What makes him different from so many previous Harrison males is that he is supposed to be a jaded city slicker—a symbol of what happens when we exchange the hard, manly ways of Strang for the self-indulgent ones of our overcivilized society. The trouble is, his life as a member of a fashionable literary set fails to come alive. Though we are told he once owned a Manhattan co-op and a house in Sag Harbor, and has dined at expensive restaurants around the world, such details hardly suffice to evoke his fictional world. . . .

Whatever curiosity Mr. Harrison succeeds in eliciting in the reader . . . is never fully satisfied. . . . Strang's life history dribbles out through his own words and through the narrator's tape-recorded impressions of him. . . .

[The narrator] admires Strang's code of self-reliance, his unbounded sexuality, his exuberant enjoyment of such male pleasures as hunting, fishing, drinking and wenching—his enormous will to live. Strang, in fact, makes the narrator feel that his own writerly life is attenuated and passive, and apparently inspires him to change his lethargic ways.

In his previous books, Mr. Harrison has celebrated a similar macho esthetic, and he presumably shares the narrator's attitude toward Strang. Readers of **"Sundog,"** however, may very well find Strang anything but heroic. If at times he is courageous,

guilt-free and willfully independent, he is also reckless, selfish and highly irresponsible. Given Mr. Harrison's two-dimensional depiction of Strang, he is not a character capable of supporting an entire novel.

Michiko Kakutani, in a review of "Sundog," in The New York Times, *May 21, 1984, p. C14.*

## JAMES B. HEMESATH

The narrator [of *Sundog*]—an unnamed writer of some renown—spends five months on Michigan's Upper Peninsula tape-recording the dying Strang's life story. From this framework of a tale within a tale, poet/fiction writer Harrison has fashioned a novel of considerable stature. Place setting, characterization, and a strong sense of humor are some of the key elements to the novel's success. Humor especially provides a needed antidote to the "macho" aspects of Strang's adventuresome life and the narrator's Hemingway-like world view.

James B. Hemesath, in a review of "Sundog," in Library Journal, *Vol. 109, No. 10, June 1, 1984, p. 1144.*

## PICO IYER

Jim Harrison is one of that renegade band of drifters and dreamers—including Sam Shepard, Tom McGuane, Jack Kerouac and sometimes Norman Mailer—who regard their homeland with the tenderness and solicitude of lovelorn swains. . . . Harrison's lyric flights are, at heart, songs of innocence and experience, chanting his country's praises, mourning its losses. These vagabond visionaries are not flag-waving patriots so much as votaries of America as symbol, promise and ideal; they suffer not from parochialism so much as from a romantic's expanded sense of boundary. And all these freethinking hobos constantly yearn to rescue and recover their country's lost youth—its vanished pastures, its Indian relics, the clear-cut rituals of the Wild West. All, in the end, lust after innocence and are hungry for a state of grace, a home.

In Harrison this longing becomes a search for the natural sanctuaries he knew as a boy. Thus, in the midst of confused wanderings and strung-out aspirations, his characters invariably return, in reverie or reminiscence, to the sylvan places that were their childhood haunts. ("In the woods," writes Emerson, "we return to reason and faith.") Harrison's fiction is drenched in nostalgia, in wistful memories of fathers, first loves and discoveries in the woods (to some extent, of course, all these things are America; it seemed most grand when he was small).

In *Sundog* two such voyages dovetail: the physical pilgrimage of a brittle New York City journalist to a homestead in the wilds of Michigan inhabited by an old wanderer named Strang; and the weathered ancient mariner's account of his own hegira. Dwelling in a cabin in the woods near a running stream, the old codger has fashioned what amounts in Harrison's world to a lease on the Garden of Eden: he is attended by a loyal dog and a lovely Costa Rican nymph, and is treated to hearty home cooking (Harrison is the most exacting gourmand west of his urban counterpart, Robert Parker) and Stravinsky all around. Settled within this Henry Millerish shrine, Strang spends most of the novel rambling along the byways of his memory and imagination, collecting en route flashes of beauty and a handful of stories, short and tall. And, as elsewhere in Harrison, the return to boyhood becomes a kind of religious revival—a reawakening of possibility, a rehearsal of a leap of faith. Strang is the lay preacher of this natural religion. "Of all beautiful things, I take to rivers the strongest," he admits in a typical moment. "They give me that incredible sweet feeling I once got from religion."

Naturally enough, the patron saint of such a faith is the household god of woody cabins, the guru of all craftsmen, isolatos and pioneers, the yogi who turned common values on their heads, Thoreau. It was he, after all, who first forged a way of living at an angle to American society—and there is no more ardent angler than Jim Harrison. . . .

Like Thoreau, too, Harrison observes nature not only with a believer's eye but with a painter's care and a scientist's precision; he carpenters his prose, building its constructions as a beaver might his dam (to invoke a favorite Harrison prop). His sentences, like Thoreau's, are sturdy and sound and sometimes sly. (p. 767)

Most important, perhaps, in dedicating his novel to hero worship and turning Strang's life into art, Harrison is following firmly in the footsteps of the Sage of Walden, whose grand mission was to rehabilitate the very notion of heroism by making himself its central example. Strang consistently embodies both the theory and the practice of Thoreau: in his craggy self-definition and gruff self-sufficiency, in his catholic collection of natural scriptures and his refusal to keep purity and scatology apart, in his habits and his premises. . . .

Sure, the Harrison hero is prepared to brawl if innocence is compromised, but he's just as ready to sing lullabies to keep it intact. No, he does not stand on ceremony, but he maintains a touching respect for civility. Yes, he may sometimes seem a tough-talking roughneck whose love of women and indifference to etiquette betray an excess of animal high spirits, but he is also a purist of elevated habits and erudite tastes. In *Sundog,* he admires boys who quote Lorca and civil engineers who compose poems. . . .

Harrison is driven . . . by a quintessentially American openness of heart and innocence of spirit that enable him to glimpse and then to chase ideals. Yet that same simplicity often disqualifies him from assessing realities. For those who write in the American grain seem always to issue blessings more naturally, and more effectively, than curses. . . . The finest American writing specializes in the erection of ideals, not the execution of satire. Whitman, Miller, Shepard and the rest may hymn their country's greatness, but the dirty work of adroit and cutting social observation is best left to sophisticated aliens—Nabokov, perhaps, or Waugh.

Harrison fits this model all too well: the part of his writing that explores possibilities, scouting new ground and scanning the horizon, is irradiated with a remarkable glow; the part that would expose social shortcomings is callow, jejune. He has a boy's unguarded gentleness with his idols, but that same boy's unrefined coarseness around his enemies. Here, then, is a craftsman who takes fastidious pains to sketch exquisite pictures of harmony and idyll, yet resorts to condemning all oil men because of "their utter greed and the direct venality of their business," writing off all Congressmen as "a bilious clot of lawyers" and twice in eleven pages calling politicians "swine."

Worst of all, perhaps, Harrison's caricature of the cynical New York writer is broader than the Grand Canyon and cheaper than a bargain-basement trinket. This so-called sophisticate blithely condemns himself out of his own mouth, announcing,

"I crave the topical, the ephemeral" and advertising his yearning for "an embittered career woman with whom to exchange caresses." (p. 768)

Keeping his senses more about him than his wits, Harrison has little taste for argument, and no talent for it. But his miscalculations seem only typical of his breed. Unable to embrace the private world without reviling the public, Thoreau squandered much of his fathomless dignity when he took to railing crankily against the society he had so nobly transcended. Mailer, so electric and fresh when pursuing unorthodox theories, never seems more foolish than when flogging the dead horses of plastics or totalitarian architecture. . . . Though the desperadoes' points are well taken, their polemics are often ill chosen.

Harrison also brings to mind those writers like Henry Miller and his spiritual descendant Charles Bukowski, who boast voices so strong and compelling that they can speak in no voice except their own. In *Sundog* he tries to disguise this by switching back and forth between the writer's narration, Strang's *apologia sua vita* and the narrator's taped diary. But all three blur into one indistinguishable sound, and characters develop no more than trees.

By the same token, Harrison's portrayal of women is terrible, even as his portrayal of a man's lustful, lyrical longing for a woman, driven by an avidity that is at once reproved and refined by tenderness, is wonderful. "We 'love' before we know how to protect ourselves, pure and simple," he writes. Beyond the pure and simple, Harrison himself often seems unprotected and lost.

More fundamentally, he has yet to find a way to fuse the two impulses he describes. All his books swing between gypsy narrative and tranquil meditation, adventure and reminiscence, Kerouac, in a sense, and Thoreau. In his first novel, *Wolf,* Harrison placed himself in the woods and there recalled his wanderings; in his next novel, *A Good Day to Die,* he drove cross-country while dreaming of the calmness of the woods. Now, in his sixth novel, he divides the two forces into two characters, seeker and sage, jaded skeptic and settled pundit. . . . But still he can find no unity. Harrison's novels are often hailed as "poet's novels," and that may well be their problem: they amount in effect to nothing more than generous anthologies of sweet visions, tingling epiphanies and lyrical tableaux. Since their highlights are still lifes, their climaxes are often stillborn. Sometimes they seem as serene, and as motionless, as the beautiful Zen-like paintings that grace their covers.

And yet, for all their lack of momentum, Harrison's novels are rarely unmoving, and there is no denying his strong, luminous—even numinous—talent. (pp. 768, 770)

Pico Iyer, "Romancing the Home," in The Nation, Vol. 238, No. 24, June 23, 1984, pp. 767-68, 770-71.

## A. C. GREENE

Jim Harrison has proved himself an author of many talents and a stylist of many styles. Some readers think **"Legends of the Fall"** displays the ultimate beauty of recent American storytelling; others hold **"Warlock"** to be the most hilarious bumbling-tough-guy detective story since Jonathan Latimer's "Headed for a Hearse"; still others believe the powerful poignancy of **"Farmer"** is scarcely touched in modern literature. But **"Farmer"** lovers can't abide the farce of **"Warlock,"** dedicated **"Warlock"** cultists reject "the pretty stuff," and followers of Mr. Harrison's poetry are dismayed he should even consider prose.

Picking up a new work by Mr. Harrison, a reader doesn't know what to expect, and such is the case with **"Sundog."** One thinks the amusing machismo of **"Warlock"** is coming through, then another passage seems to reflect the poet, or a sentence takes you back to the tormented realism of **"Farmer."** But, unfortunately, the reader of **"Sundog"** never arrives at any of these destinations, and as an editor once said of my own efforts, it doesn't come to enough.

**"Sundog"** is supposed to be an "as told to" story about a man named Robert Corvus Strang, a self-taught, middle-aged construction foreman whose career has taken him over the globe on such vast projects as hydroelectric dams and irrigation systems. Strang is presented as something of a giant work himself—a crippled, doomed guru with understanding, wisdom, tenderness and strength. . . .

**"Sundog"** is an unsatisfying book, as fragmentary as though it were the middle part of a series. The story's paramount weakness is its inability to make Strang the wise, attractive master of the inappropriate we are promised he is or to make the narrator into a believable literary figure. Strang, as man or god, is never effectively delivered, his supposedly heightened sensibilities and solutions to life are unpersuasive, and his insistent idolizing of an older brother is baffling. It is hard to convince us that a mean, sneering jerk like Strang is charming.

As for the narrator, he can be amusing when facing barmaids and hotelkeepers and candid in admitting the power sex has over him, but he is annoying when he reports things like "There is nothing so fatiguing as real emotion" or "At Harvard in the nineteenth century there was a scientist named Agassiz." The quality of Strang's aphorisms varies from wise to witty to cliché. The narrative often resembles an old agitprop movie, carefully explaining the well known. And the novel is unformed—three stories struggling to get out of one slim book. One reads on, hoping one tale or another will take over the narrative and drive us to some end. One of the strengths of Mr. Harrison's writing has been his ability to turn a resisting reader into a cheering supporter of unlikely, even unlikable, characters. Sometimes, however, even the strong stumble.

*A. C. Greene, "The Man-God of the Michigan Jungles," in* The New York Times Book Review, *July 15, 1984, p. 14.*

# Stratis Haviaras

## 1935-

**Greek-born American novelist, poet, and editor.**

**Haviaras is best known to the English-speaking world as the author of two semiautobiographical novels, *When the Tree Sings* (1979) and *The Heroic Age* (1984), that are narrated by young boys and examine turbulent events in recent Greek history. Before emigrating to the United States in 1967, Haviaras was respected in Greece as a poet; both *When the Tree Sings* and *The Heroic Age* reflect his background in their attention to detail and conciseness of language. *When the Tree Sings* is composed of short episodes which recount in graphic detail the horrors of life during the Nazi occupation of Greece in World War II. *The Heroic Age* centers on a group of children attempting to flee Greece during the Greek civil war. Both works blend realism with fantasy and myth in their depiction of violent struggles for survival.**

**(See also *Contemporary Authors*, Vol. 105.)**

*Photograph by Shvla Irving*

### KOSTAS MYRSIADES

In the four books of verse Haviarás has published so far, the growth of a personal lyrical voice has been steady and sequential. After "**The Lady with the Compass**" (1963), "**Berlin**" (1965) and "**The Night of the Man on Stilts**" (1967), his recent *Nekrofánia* (Apparent Death) is another painful step toward recovering the fragments of a self suddenly deprived of childhood and youth by the merciless reality of the war, the Occupation and what has followed them. His fragmentary personal "myth" of recollection and reality, of event and dream, of affection and irony, is very much the testimony of a generation that grew in the midst of deprivation, inhumanity, terror, deracination, alienation, further enriched in his poetry by his experience as a sensitive boy, destitute, homeless, parentless, driven by a heartless circumstance into hard labor for a living.

His poetry, however, is far from being a lengthy self-lament, a Jeremiad, a waste of words. A gentle and dignified equanimity and a highly suggestive simplicity, a mixing of the graceful with the grotesque, the poetic with the colloquial, the dreamy with the factual, the tragic with the humorous, transcends with unfailing sincerity and emotion what life has given him. He is, unquestionably, among the few of his and the subsequent generations of Greek poets that have not fallen into the impersonal cultism of the absurd and the shock technique of endless invention of stringless images in a formless vacuum. The absurd and the shock are certainly not absent in Haviarás, but they are controlled by a warmth and a fine sensibility and a sense of form. His creative longing constantly wonders, 'When will the eye of fire / open in my bosom?,' where fire is life itself, but it may also be a fatal wound, and it is also the Promethean fire of creativity, of poetry in particular. Life and poetic creativity are homonymous. The poet longs for both as one, both being a recovery of the self. In this "Apparent Death" of his he temporarily has the illusion of such a recovery, an illusion, however, cruelly dispersed by reality. (pp. 195-96)

*Kostas Myrsiades, in a review of "Nekrofánia," in* Books Abroad, *Vol. 48, No. 1, Winter, 1974, pp. 195-96.*

### CHOICE

Stratis Haviaras, a native of Greece and author of four collections of poetry in Greek, has now published his first collection written originally in English [*Crossing the River Twice*]. Although he has been living in the U.S. only since 1967, Haviaras demonstrates an enviable mastery of English and achieves effective results from the grafting of Greek sensibility to the English language. A love of story-telling comes through; fragments of folk tales heard as a child and now repeated for a new generation underscore the prose poem form which Haviaras prefers. The fable is at home here and attaches easily to the surreal elements, which in themselves seem to come from a breakdown in the usual distinction between man and nature. Haviaras returns in the poet's mind and in mankind's experience to where diffusion has not yet been replaced by differentiation.

*A review of "Crossing the River Twice," in* Choice, *Vol. 14, No. 8, October, 1977, p. 1048.*

## FRANCINE DU PLESSIX GRAY

"**When the Tree Sings**," the first work of prose Mr. Haviaras has published in English, is a novel of formidable lyric power, narrative gift and emotional resonance.

"**When the Tree Sings**" is an epic narrative about a young boy who comes of age in a Greek mountain village during the German occupation. No work I've read in recent years has dealt more eloquently with the subject of heroism and resistance or with a community's attempt to survive the holocaustal forces of the 1940's. Mr. Haviaras has structured his novel into brief episodic vignettes seldom more than four pages in length. His lyric gift is such that each sequence holds its own as a prose poem. But the episodes are also highly psychological in intent, documenting the characters' growing militancy and the mounting hallucination induced by the extreme famine that Greece experienced during World War II.

The almost brutal forthrightness of the narrator's voice, the fact that the events described take place between his 9th and 13th year, and the frequent horror of the facts narrated bring to mind the atmosphere of Jerzy Kosinski's "The Painted Bird." But Mr. Haviaras's style is both more lyric and more surreal than Mr. Kosinski's. And, unlike Mr. Kosinski, who deals with the impact of World War II on just one child, Mr. Haviaras gathers his episodes into a single large mosaic that encompasses the psychic experience of an entire community.

Save for the infamous village informer, Mr. Haviaras's protagonists are all *Maquisards* who survive oppression and starvation through intractable tribal loyalty and the solace of native tradition and myth. . . . Haviaras's women are even more memorable and more heroic than his men. Along with the reflective, acerbic young narrator, the novel's central character is the aging grandmother who holds together whatever is left of the family and answers all queries with cryptic, koan-like wit: "How come we don't kill fifty enemy soldiers when they kill one of us?" the child asks. "Our kill has quality," she answers.

Like the most gifted European documentors of Nazi atrocities—Tadeusz Borowski, Bruno Schulz—Mr. Haviaras manages to bring to the primal horror of his theme (constant executions, partisan reprisals, growing starvation) a vastly acerbic irony. (pp. 14-15)

"When the tree sings," Grandmother explains, "it's because somebody dies or somebody comes back from the dead." There's a hallucinatory and shamanistic quality to Mr. Haviaras's narrative, both in style and in content. However sophisticated their guerrilla tactics, the Mountain Fighters are a people still steeped in supernatural beliefs and ancient myths who live in pagan communion with the forces of nature. Tales of reincarnation and transfiguration abound; rocks sigh and whisper as readily as trees sing; the narrator remembers his previous lives as a sparrow, a mouse and a dog; virgins are rumored to give birth to monsters, children levitate to escape the attacks of hungry dogs. The Greek partisans take their *noms de combat* from Greek mythology. . . . And children control pain and starvation like veteran fakirs.

In one of the book's most haunting moments, the narrator tells how a German soldier promises him a roasted chestnut (his first morsel of food in days) if he can pick it out of the fire with his bare fingers and hold it until it cools. "It burned. I concentrated by staring into the soldier's eyes. They were light gray. I thought of two moist, cool marbles I wouldn't mind playing with."

The same lyric sparseness informs Mr. Haviaras's superb novel throughout. The magic precision of his prose, the relentless emotional tension he sustains throughout his narrative is typified by the following passage about a particularly acute moment of hunger the narrator suffers:

"I tapped the sparrow's hard little head, asked him, 'What do you know about hunger?' He cracked open his beak, letting out a small cry. 'I don't know either,' I said. He pecked at my hand. His tongue and the inside of his mouth were like a tiny silver and gold spoon, the spoon the priest used to give us communion with. Warmer in my hands, he started to close his eyes. . . . Quickly I twisted his neck full circle until I felt his tiny spine snap. . . . A spasm in my own neck, but it passed. I plucked the sparrow, touched the last warmth of his blood. I gutted him, broke his ribcage open, flattened him. Quickly onto the fire, a minute or so on each side. The end of his ribs crisped, the blood, his little blood, turning to juice, and dripping. And then it was my mouth embracing the sparrow. I was warmer, my throat was warmer, as if I had taken in his voice, singing with it for hours." (p. 15)

*Francine du Plessix Gray, "Germans in Greece," in* The New York Times Book Review, *June 24, 1979, pp. 14-15.*

## ANNE BERNAYS

Like the ideally instructed poet, some novelists try to make the ordinary appear extraordinary; others try to make the extraordinary appear ordinary. It seems to me that Stratis Haviaras has, in [**When the Tree Sings**], done both at once, an achievement so dazzling it defies the reader to analyze just what is going on.

The main element of the ordinary in this book is a boy's emotional, intellectual and physical growth. Even if we recognize by a clue here and there that this boy Teo—named only once in the entire novel—is special, gifted with a magical imagination, we are also aware that all children possess this gift in some measure. The extraordinary is the presence of an enemy force in Teo's small village and the terror it produces. These two elements fuse in an exchange so complete that readers must draw their own inferences as to which, the ordinary or the other, has been the more powerful force in the creation of this semi-autobiographical work or if, in fact, the blend is as balanced as that of an archetypal myth. (p. 183)

Episodic in form, the narrative of **When the Tree Sings** parallels the sort of attention-span a small boy would have, whose worlds—both imaginative and real—are constantly interrupted by the unspeakable: his father killed in front of his eyes, his mother mysteriously gone, his house burned to the ground, a close-up view of torture and murder. The plot does not proceed in the conventional sense but rather builds outwards from a central vision, more or less like the mosaic Teo constructs, a portrait of Angelica, the girl he loves and sees as a mermaid. "I used sparkling white pebbles for the upper part of her body and marbled silvery ones for her tail, black pebbles for her eyebrows and lashes, and for hair waving in the wind." The pieces of this novel fit together in a complete human picture that contains death, beauty and the entire range of "pebbles" in between.

That Haviaras can convince us Teo can sustain "ordinary" emotions like love in the face of the grotesque events taking place around him is tribute to his artistry, part of which, I'm convinced, has to do with his handling of horror. (pp. 183-84)

Horror weaves through this book like a beautiful but poisonous snake in the house. (If there is one danger in this novel, it is that Haviaras transforms horror into images so "poetic" that it can be read as a form of beauty and thus, seductive.) Horror is always there, in the torture of prisoners whose screams are baffled by the motorcycle the enemy keeps and accelerates while they go about their business; and in the hunger, "the sweet and burning sensation . . . between my throat and stomach. . . ."

The words "Greece" and "German" are never set down in this novel; but we know them for what they are. By skipping these particulars, Haviaras makes the experience universal. And by concentrating on the particular in almost every other instance, he grounds his story in a reality, which, if it does not exactly match our own, we can recognize psychically. (p. 185)

While horror plays a grand role in *When the Tree Sings* so do the urgency of love and growth. Teo is wildly curious; it is his questions which in large part keep the narrative moving. He is always asking. "Grandma, why do your knees bleed when you kneel?" "How do you recognize a spy?" "Were there real trees and water then, Grandfather?" Neither the presence of the enemy in the town nor the awareness that for . . . the townspeople life, and so time, has in effect stopped, can stunt Teo's spiritual and imaginative growth. Never was it clearer in fiction that the child is father to the man. (p. 186)

*Anne Bernays, in a review of "When the Tree Sings,"*
*in* Ploughshares, *Vol. 5, No. 3, 1979, pp. 183-86.*

### ROSS WETZSTEON

[Stratis Haviaras] has some *Painted Bird*-style stories to tell about a young boy growing up in Nazi-occupied Greece [in *When the Tree Sings*]. Unfortunately, Haviaras's pretentiously simple, self-consciously fabulistic prose (accompanied by tiny wash decorations) makes this widely reviewed and much adored first novel more emotionally fraudulent than historically engrossing.

Take the last paragraph . . . : "Mother had gone to bed and fallen asleep with a black scarf over her face. I got up and clipped my hair and dressed, and when I looked at her again I saw two wet darker patches where the scarf covered her eyes. I opened the window and climbed down quietly, being careful not to wake the neighborhood dogs, and walked out of town toward the fields, shuddering at the sound of bats on the wing and the luminous stare of the owl." What's supposed to be noticed here . . . is that it's a gem of Beautiful Writing. Every word has been so carefully chosen, so lovingly polished, so delicately placed in the paragraph—how Haviaras must have shivered with delight at the suspirating sound of that series of s's—that he can't see he's been laboring over a rhinestone.

Haviaras relentlessly keeps all emotion out of the telling of his tale—then they shot him, then he died, etc.—on the too obvious assumption that this will flood the *reader* with emotion. The trouble is that rather than leaving the reader free to respond to horrific events, the overly calculated simplicity, the purple silences, seem intended to coerce admiration for the author's Unbearable Sensitivity. The only difference between Haviaras's exquisiteness and that of vanity-press poets is that he

leaves out the gush—what's infuriating is that he so obviously expects the reader to provide it for him.

*Ross Wetzsteon, in a review of "When the Tree Sings,"*
*in* The Village Voice, *Vol. XXIV, No. 28, July 9, 1979, p. 70.*

### EDMUND KEELEY

[*When the Tree Sings*] is a poet's work of fiction in many ways. Most of the sections (often no more than a page long) that build its 30 short chapters are essentially prose poems, each meant to convey an immediate poetic statement as well as contribute to the novel's progress. That progress can be described as a developing portrait of the artist as child exile in his home country, specifically Greece during World War II.

The landscape that surrounds the first-person voice in the novel belongs to the same region delineated by the late poems of Yannis Ritsos, which in turn reflect the waste land of George Seferis' poetry. . . . And the figures who inhabit this often symbolic landscape are, again as in Ritsos, the dispossessed: a blind man, an itinerant puppeteer, a one-eyed playmate, a castoff whore, a gold-toothed grandmother wise as her years, and a troupe of cruel, changing enemies. . . .

The perspective of a child-poet whose vision develops dramatically under the pressures of terror and deprivation allows the author to project the poetic, sometimes mythic, aspects of the harsh reality that almost overwhelm his young hero. It also allows him to move back and forth with grace from horror to comedy, from violence to lyricism. . . .

Some episodes in the novel seem rigged too arbitrarily by the author's manipulating hand rather than emanating from a plausible vision in the narrator. One example is the predictable victory of our hero over the forces of evil in the battle of kites, and another, the most blatant perhaps, is the sudden entrance by the local priest "out of the bushes, his black cassock flying behind him," to scream "Paganists! Satanists!" at the villagers taking part in an unlikely orgy during a festival honoring "the Goat-legged One and the Nymphs." . . .

The implicit political commentary, which hides for the best part of the novel behind vague terms such as "the enemy," "The Mountain Fighters," "the Allies," comes in more overtly and obtrusively at the end, oversimplified, almost as black and white as the drawings of Fred Marcellino that decorate the book's margins, though without that artist's redeeming verisimilitude.

But the lapses in control are not so many as to diminish the cumulative impact of Stratis Haviaras' novel. We emerge from it with the sense of having heard a distinctive new voice, of having shared a special sensibility, one that usually succeeds in guiding us safely along the dangerous border between the real and the unreal, inspired as it is by a poet's courage, cunning and insight.

*Edmund Keeley, "Myths of a Modern Greek," in*
Book World—The Washington Post, *July 15, 1979, p. H3.*

### DORIS GRUMBACH

*When the Tree Sings* is a lovely book. A joyous, tragic, funny book. A book composed of anecdotes and parables about war and famine, treachery and fidelity, traitors and loyalists, children and grandparents. In every way—the quality of the prose, the power of the boy's mind who tells the stories, the contents of the short, graphic chapters, the impression the whole makes upon the reader—it is a triumph of poetic narration.

It may be that author Stratis Haviaras is almost the right age to have experienced all these things at first-hand. . . . He writes of a boy who seems older than 10 in the last years of the war, whose parents are "missing," and who lives with his grandmother, a memorable fictional creation. His chapters are full of such characters, and of the superstitions, story-telling, folklore, and life histories of the people of a village that is occupied by the Nazi army. . . .

Self-contained vignettes are the heart of the book: the story of the cage, filled with Greek prisoners, that is attached to the front of trains so that the Mountain Fighters will not dynamite them; the story of poor Dando, who is shot at and missed by the Germans and who dies the next day from believing he had been killed; the boy's tale of eating a starving sparrow and of being compelled to eat a burning chestnut and of defying God by throwing mud into His sky-face; of Uncle Spanos and of the beautiful Ermina, who is tortured by the informer Lekas; of the town doctor so sickened by what he has seen the Nazis do that he treats his patients from his own sickbed.

As I said, it is a lovely and moving novel. (p. R8)

> Doris Grumbach, "August Fiction: Serious Reading for a Searing Month," in The Chronicle of Higher Education: Books & Arts, August 6, 1979, pp. R7-R8.*

### PUBLISHERS WEEKLY

Haviaras's marvelous second novel [*The Heroic Age*] . . . is as full of clarity, human understanding and sharp poetic imagery as one would expect from the author of five volumes of verse in Greek. Set during the bitter civil war in Greece that followed World War II (and keyed to historical events by scraps of wire copy and memoirs), it tells how thousands of hungry, orphaned children became the ill-equipped army of the socialist Andartes faction in a hopeless fight against the American-backed royalists. . . . With the writer's powerful images, we feel as much despair at the weakness that comes from hunger as delight at the love epidemic that sweeps the youthful cave dwellers (and is swiftly "seared off" as a "bourgeois affliction"). This beautifully written book deserves wide readership.

> A review of "The Heroic Age," in Publishers Weekly, Vol. 225, No. 9, March 2, 1984, p. 84.

### CORINNE DEMAS BLISS

*The Heroic Age* put me in a quandary I too rarely encounter when I read contemporary fiction: I was caught up in the drama of the book's plot and wanted to race to its conclusion, but I felt compelled to linger in each paragraph and savor the beauty of the language. *The Heroic Age*, like Stratis Haviaras's highly acclaimed first novel, *When the Tree Sings*, is brilliantly descriptive. But in this second novel Haviaras has also managed to sustain a fast-paced, suspenseful narrative without ever sacrificing the radiance of his prose.

*The Heroic Age* is the first-person story of an extraordinarily sensitive and perspicacious boy named Panagis who grows up in the period after World War II, when Greece was torn apart by civil war. . . .

The first part of *The Heroic Age,* called "The Children's War," is the chilling adventure tale of a small band of orphans who try to escape out of Greece through the north and get conscripted by the Andartes. They endure a harrowing existence in the Grammos Mountains and are among the few survivors of the partisans' final battle. In the second part of the novel, ironically titled "Peace and Reconstruction," Panagis and his surviving friends are rescued from their mountain hide-out, shipped south with other children, and incarcerated on Antikalamos, an island so bare that the boys can't find "even a blade of grass." . . .

This is a brutal novel—a novel that describes great suffering and savagery—yet there is no gratuitous violence. Stratis Haviaras came to fiction after a successful career as a poet. . . . A poet's skill is evident throughout *The Heroic Age*. We are taken on a journey that is hair-raising and troubling, but, because we're in the hands of a poet, the experiences settle in the mind rather than the gut. . . .

*The Heroic Age* is a novel rich with metaphors, mysteries, and echoes. The pelting of pine-cones becomes the pelting of bombs, becomes the pelting of a storm. Marianna, Panagis's lover at the end of the novel, is a kind of reincarnation of his youthful love, Marina. A cave at the forbidden end of Antikalamos is a storehouse of marble statues that recall the children who froze to death in the Andartes' hide-out. . . .

*The Heroic Age* is also a novel of many textures. Characters relate their dreams, hallucinate, entertain each other with tales and jokes. The children live with myths while their own adventure turns into myth. Although the hero and his friends have been robbed of their childhood, they're children still. There's humor throughout. . . .

One technique Haviaras has employed to reinforce the verisimilitude of his novel is to separate his chapters with quotations from news sources. These articles—selections from sources like UPI and Reuters—place the story in its historical context and give the reader essential background material (material that would have bogged down the narrative and been inappropriate for the point of view). The contrast between the cold summaries of events and Panagis's moving personal story underscores a basic irony. We soon realize that it is the news accounts, with their omissions and distortions, that are the fiction, and it is the fictionalized narrative that has the power of truth. (p. 31)

The central characters in *The Heroic Age* are boys, but this novel has a supporting cast of some of the strongest female characters I've encountered in literature—from the narrator's aunt, whose definition of heroism frames the whole story, to his first love, Marina, who stays by the wounded rather than try to escape the last bombardment.

Panagis's tragedy is disquietingly timely. The parallels between the civil war in *The Heroic Age* and more familiar battle grounds—in Vietnam, in El Salvador—are unmistakable. Most disturbingly, perhaps, it is American bombers that drop napalm on children hiding in the mountains. It is the American-based Nationalist regime that rounds up the survivors and exiles them to concentration camps in the name of "repatriation." . . .

Haviaras does a remarkable job with the limitations of his first-person narrator. He manages to convey to his reader critical information about time and place and at the same time remains true to Panagis's subjective rendering of his surroundings and his experiences.

Panagis is a narrator who is both innocent and wise, and through him Haviaras is able to say a great deal about both politics and religion. Panagis's integrity and capacity for love survive the injustices and cruelties he is subjected to. Although he describes his suffering, he never complains. Because he doesn't pity himself his tale is ultimately exhilarating, rather than depressing. We rejoice with Panagis in all the small blessings of survival when the storm abates or rations are increased, and feel the poignancy of his pleasures. . . .

I can easily imagine *The Heroic Age* in the hands of an eager screenwriter. It is the stuff of films—an adventure story, an epic tale of humanity and heroism. But like all fine works of literature, its true power could not be realized in any film. What makes *The Heroic Age* so compelling is the way the author brings his reader so close to the soul of his character. This is a story that covers dramatic external events, but the more memorable story is the interior journey that Panagis makes in order to discover himself. (p. 32)

> Corinne Demas Bliss, in a review of "The Heroic Age," in Boston Review, Vol. IX, No. 3, June, 1984, pp. 31-2.

## EDWARD M. WHITE

The young protagonist of this stunning new novel ["**The Heroic Age**"], set in battle-torn Greece after World War II, asks his aunt what exactly is meant by "the heroic age" in that country. She tells him, early in the book, that for men, it is between 6 and 14 years old: "At 6," she said, "one is too old to be a child, and at 14 he is too young to be a soldier."

At the end of the novel, as the boy is about to turn 15, after passing through almost incredible suffering and disorder, he remembers his aunt, now dead, and her sarcastic wisdom. His heroic age, he knows is over, but he has learned much about life and is in the arms of a lover. The heroic age for women in Greece, according to his aunt, "was from the moment they were born to the moment they died." But for the reader, the heroic age for Greece remains alive in the pages of the novel, a saga of human endurance enriched by wit and warmth. . . .

This is a novel about lost childhood, lost identity, lost humanity. All the important characters are children and all choose new names to meet the barbarity they must face. Nonetheless— and this is the great triumph of the book—we never lose sight of the childishness of these characters, who adapt in order to make it through. . . .

Some readers will find the upbeat ending a bit implausible after the appalling experiences the characters suffer. Other readers will agree with me that even the grimmest epic vision allows a triumph through suffering, and that these characters have earned their way to a new life. Surely, the interspersed news releases and diplomatic notes (beginning with Churchill's casual agreement with Stalin about the fate of the Balkan states), and the ignoble role played by America in the novel, keep us from lightly dismissing this fictional world with its modern vision of a deracinated reality. "**The Heroic Age**" requires strong readers: They will be well-rewarded with a powerful and memorable experience.

> Edward M. White, "Too Old to Be a Child, Too Young for War," in Los Angeles Times Book Review, June 3, 1984, p. 1.

## MARCELLE THIÉBAUX

Children entrusted with grenades and guns can play at games of war with solemn gravity and an immense sense of style. Learning to die before you have learned to live is just part of the child guerrilla's code, according to [Stratis Haviaras], the author of this intriguing novel ["**The Heroic Age**"]. . . . In a kind of sequel to his first novel, "**When the Tree Sings**" (1979), "**The Heroic Age**" once more combines political actuality and myth in dealing with the extraordinary stresses experienced by children at war. But where the earlier novel reflected Greek village life as Mr. Haviaras knew it, during World War II and the Resistance to the Nazis, "**The Heroic Age**" turns to a later time when the country confronts bloody civil conflict. . . .

Despite the grimness of the war he describes, Mr. Haviaras's sensibility does not permit him to stick to unrelenting realism. Rather, the story keeps billowing away into the realms of fantasy. . . . What is unique about "**The Heroic Age**" is that the fantasy grows out of a mythic memory, with an ease and whimsy that appear as natural as breathing. Both Homeric and Christian, this mythic memory gives resonance to the fate of nearly 30,000 Greek children of our times.

There is an underlying imagery of metamorphosis involving the transformation of children from "birds" into "stone." Panagis himself crosses various thresholds of experience before outgrowing the heroic age, and these passages are immersed in the vocabulary of myth and legend—a picaresque journey with guides and ordeals, an epic battle and finally a purgatory. (p. 14)

A dissipation of energy, a lessening of concentration, besets the closing chapters, as if the story had lost its way. There is an unraveling at the seams rather than a denouement. True, the children are glad to be out alive, and the adult world into which the heroic-agers are allowed to graduate seems trivial and complacent, caring little for the recent agonies of the young on the road, the mountain, and the rock. But too many minor events are introduced and left unresolved, too many new characters (caricatures, really) are brought forth too late.

These are small imperfections in what is essentially a poignant and irresistible work of fiction. Mr. Haviaras tells a good story and his writing has a rugged grace. There is a band of children on Antikalamos who while celebrating spring cut a crocus and a bird out of the rock. The novel itself achieves something like this—hewing a vital fantasy out of the war's harsh materials. (p. 15)

> Marcelle Thiébaux, "Children Changed to Stone," in The New York Times Book Review, June 10, 1984, pp. 14-15.

## JOHN DOMINI

About two-thirds of the way through this sweet nightmare of a novel [*The Heroic Age*], the narrator meditates on stone. Although barely into his teens, he has been assigned to cut blocks of stone in a prison camp on a tiny and desolate Greek island. The rock, naturally enough, has him thinking of history: "Year by year our glorious history, the whole history, and throughout the years the starving and the dispossessed, the disabled and the thoroughly dead—unnamed and unclaimed forever." Harsh thinking. Yet *The Heroic Age*, for all its napalm and hard labor, ends up proving the boy wrong. Stratis Haviaras, who lived in Greece during the devastation his book portrays, has brought off a masterful act of reclamation. Tender about its smallest losses but ferocious in assigning their blame, full of sly laughs at a child's way of seeing but always respectful of the dream lives that only the young can know, *The Heroic Age* combines more of history's wallop and poetry's song than any novel this year. Indeed, despite its relative brevity, Haviaras's book has the epic authority and imaginative freedom of the great figures in the current Latin American literary boom. The accomplishment of this work might best be measured against theirs.

Moreover, his story, like theirs, takes much of its clout from the desperate circumstances it describes. His Greece is the gutted and self-destructive country that emerged at the end of World War II. His narrator is one of the many children who fought for the left-leaning Resistance, the Andartes, who carried on a hopeless guerrilla war for nearly five years against a regime backed by the full power of the American Sixth Fleet. The most horrific sequence comes when the government forces finish off the last Andartes by using an experimental weapon called napalm. Adding still more historical weight, Haviaras often heads his chapters with excerpts from news reports and other source works of those years—thus he builds upon the final ironies of his first novel, *When the Tree Sings* (1979), most of which concerns the earlier resistance against the Nazis. At that book's end the "Mountain Fighters" are betrayed by their Allied liberators and condemned to struggle on against new oppressors.

The earlier novel's narrator could have been a younger version of this one's, a boy less aware of his sexual self and more dependent on his family. Indeed, *When the Tree Sings* is about a child's escape from family, whereas *The Heroic Age* begins with a child's independence. The title refers to the time in a boy's life between six and 15—it's a definition that's provided early on by the narrator's aunt, his sole surviving relative. Shortly after that she dies, in a spectacular example of rightist neglect: she's allowed to make bread only from flour that's been tainted by fungus. In the peyote-like trance that follows, the boy is set free even as he hallucinates about reunion with his lost family. . . .

The episode provides the unnamed boy's first gropings toward a deeper communion, a family beyond his home's battered walls; at the same time it demonstrates, before 20 pages have passed, the kind of stylistic flights Haviaras is capable of. The tone throughout remains feverish and awestruck. This child, after all, is making up his world as he scrabbles through it. Yet most details and the shape of most incidents have a quasi-magical familiarity. . . . Like Gabriel García Márquez or Carlos Fuentes, this author relates intriguingly bent revisions of stories we've heard before. And his child's-eye view aids him, making things seem extraordinary whenever the sentences lengthen and the wording becomes a bit complicated. (p. 3)

[The] first encounter with the civil war plays like a child's game; the doomed mountaintop community of Andartes is rife with puppy love; the island prison has a mysterious cache of ancient statues that, as if in a dream, helps liberate the boys once more. Yet Haviaras's combination runs a double risk. On the one hand, mythmaking can be carried too far, till significance overwhelms sympathy; on the other, repeated captures and escapes can become episodic, directionless.

The author solves the first problem more satisfactorily. To a certain extent his tone roughs up the Olympian impulse and keeps it in the realm of adolescent fantasy. But the greatest humanizing agent is the dialogue. The give and take of actual talk, its politics and dynamics, are never sacrificed to the on-going meditations. Even minor characters are accorded important speeches—though never in a speechifying tone. On the contrary, though from time to time the irony seems too adult, the conversation's often very funny. And what the other children have to say becomes part of the narrator's thinking; they lend an edge to his poetic languors.

The episodic quality of *The Heroic Age,* however, proves more troublesome. Haviaras does take care to repeat, to accumulate. Characters generally return from the dead, one way or another, and the closing epiphanies—on the populated island of Kalamos, near the prison—sing a strophe and antistrophe of all that's gone before. Furthermore, the author works with short chapters, many only two or three pages, thereby fitting form to episode. But there remains the occasional irksome monotony, as the latest survivors are introduced or the latest local metaphors are drawn. The worst standing around occurs, in fact, in the stonecutting chapters; the correlations made there are rather obvious (to art, as well as to history), and no substitute for dramatic momentum.

Then again, life on such a prison *is* monotonous. And the ideas raised by the stonecutting go straight to the heart of the novel's concerns. The essential meanings, after all, are adumbrated not by some flora or fauna along the way but by the main character, who from the first must suffer as one of "the unnamed." The name he was given at birth is never revealed, and he adopts, then rejects, a number of others during his years on the run. But the boy settles in the end on Panagis. The name means "all-hallowed"; it suggests that this terrible odyssey offers something greater than genocide, some purpose as transcendent and lasting as cut marble. Yet the novel's concluding scenes are ambiguous about the boy's future—they take place on an island only a stone's throw from the prison where he nearly starved to death. . . . [Not] all victims of history can so transcend their suffering. For most of this writer's generation, his novel reminds us, it's only in art that their agony will ever prove hallowed, or heroic. (p. 15)

*John Domini, "The Greek Passion," in* The Boston Phoenix, *October 3, 1984, pp. 3, 15.*

# Edwin Honig
## 1919-

**American poet, critic, translator, dramatist, and editor.**

Considered an important scholar and translator, Honig has also written numerous volumes of poetry which have received significant critical attention. Central to much of his verse is a struggle for affirmation of life and transcendence of death. This thematic concern has led some critics to compare him to the Romantics. Hayden Carruth, for example, contends that many of Honig's poems "reach back to the heart of Renaissance fear and bravery, to Ronsard and Wyatt, the cult of love and death—in short, to Romance."

Although primarily lyrical, Honig's poetry is diverse in both form and subject matter. Some of his work consists of "personal symbolic poems," as D. J. Hughes notes in his review of Honig's first major collection, *The Gazabos: 41 Poems* (1959). Other poems are long, sustained narratives with political as well as personal concerns. Laurence Goldstein described the sequence *Four Springs* (1972) as "an autobiography in the shape of seasonal meditations," later adding, "it is a historical poem—about Vietnam as much as self." Penelope Weiss notes that in much of *Survivals* (1965) "his lines are short, and the poems are spare," while L. Alan Goldstein cites in the title poem of *Spring Journal* (1968) Honig's use of "irregular meter and long lines" to create a poem "capacious enough to accommodate the flux of subjects, shifting tones and polemics that compose the journal." Some critics fault Honig's poetry for elusiveness or lack of depth; others praise the gentle rhythms and wit of his diverse poems.

Honig has also been commended for the excellence of his translations of works by Spanish and Portuguese authors. His critical contributions include literary studies of Federico García Lorca and Pedro Calderón de la Barca. *García Lorca* (1944) examines the development of Lorca's poetry and drama. *Calderón and the Seizures of Honor* (1972) explores the theme of honor in the early work of this seventeenth-century dramatist. Another of Honig's important critical works, *Dark Conceit: The Making of Allegory* (1959), is an attempt to "justify the ways of allegory to modern man," according to A. Alvarez. In this study Honig explores the presence and function of allegory throughout the ages, expanding its previously limited definition and reestablishing it as a valid and predominant literary form.

(See also *Contemporary Authors*, Vols. 5-8, rev. ed.; *Contemporary Authors New Revision Series*, Vol. 4; and *Dictionary of Literary Biography*, Vol. 5.)

## RALPH BATES

We were talking about García Lorca the other night, prompted by this excellent book ["**García Lorca**"], and we arrived at certain fairly unanimous judgments.

"Well, then. While his reputation has declined, it was formerly inflated because of political excitements. But he is, after Antonio Machado, the best of modern Spanish poets." I said this with absolute confidence in the superiority of Machado. . . .

"The 'Gypsy Song Book'?" another said, as if putting a coin on the table for inspection. . . .

"And the 'Poem of the Deep Song' and the 'Lament'. In all these feeling and imagination are one. But *not* the plays," I continued.

"Ah," said the poet, nodding agreement. Then a cunning woman, who writes mysteries and children's books, put in the difficult question: "And the 'Poet in New York'?"

"No," I answered at last. "I once thought those poems deep; nowadays I think them chiefly obscure, with more than a little banality. Their imagery is less fertile, and as verse they have less music or less beauty of language. As logic they lack the sense of necessity. They are not rigorous." The discussion that at once broke out was well served by Mr. Honig's book. I think we arrived at some sort of agreement.

I quote these judgments only because at a much larger gathering a few nights later I found that much the same views were held. Mr. Honig, who is far more familiar with the poet's work than I am, will disagree. For him, "Bodas de Sangre" ("Blood Wedding") and "Yerma" are of a stature commensurate with the best of Lorca's verse. He says, finely, "there is nothing in Lorca's poetry which does not suggest dramatic projection." It is itself a projection. Lorca's poetry is not one of immobile moods, but of a vivid procession of images that dislocate one's mental routines. But I cannot accept the author's assertion that in the plays "there is no situation or theme which does not emerge through the poetic imagination." In the first place there are at least three levels or types of poetic imagination in Lorca and the plays are not rigorous in their selection of level. In them necessities which should be grim and bare, sometimes emerge whimsy-whamsied over with refulgent and girlish moons and peasant sexual symbols tricked out with tambourine bells. (p. 570)

One is grateful to Mr. Honig for his book. It is not the last word on García Lorca, but it is a vigorous and keen-tempered approach. In it things are sometimes so well said that one puts the book down for a moment to let a remark work upon one's appreciation of the poet. In particular, the last chapter, "Image into Action," is fine and suggestive. His choice of extracts, too, is good, while the translations are luminous and secure. (p. 572)

*Ralph Bates, "The Flower in the Desert," in* The New Republic, *Vol. 110, No. 17, April 24, 1944, pp. 570, 572.*

## H. R. HAYS

[Honig's *García Lorca*] is purely a literary study. After a brief sketch of the poet's life, he covers his development chronologically in terms of style and subject matter. He stresses the dual nature of the poet's work—the blending of folk material with sophisticated modern currents and in so doing clears up a rather muddled situation in which García Lorca is alternately hailed as a surrealist and as a popular poet. (p. 225)

[Honig] points out the dramatic elements in García Lorca's early work, indicating that in all of his poetry he was groping for a more complete artistic fulfillment. It is difficult to judge the poet's dramas so long as the accepted norm in the theater remains the "well made" naturalistic play, for, while such is the case, they will never receive adequate presentation. Honig points out a certain thematic poverty in them and the tendency toward lyric rather than truly dramatic development of situation and character. Nevertheless they are certainly the most brilliant attempts at poetic theater in our time. It is also certain that it is the intrinsically dramatic quality of García Lorca's imagery which lifts even his minor poems above the work of his contemporaries.

Honig might have said much more concerning the importance of the Catholic background in Spanish poetry. Even in the case of an unorthodox thinker such as García Lorca the mystical tradition lends a special intensity to every poem. (pp. 226-27)

There are, of course, many facets to this great poet's work and much remains to be said about him. Mr. Honig has written a useful guide, particularly for those who have not read the Spanish originals. Though the book does not make any particularly profound contribution to critical thinking about García Lorca, it does touch on many provocative matters and opens up avenues to further discussion. (p. 227)

*H. R. Hays, "A Study of García Lorca," in* Poetry, *Vol. LXIV, No. IV, July, 1944, pp. 225-27.*

## ROBERT D. SPECTOR

In an age when the symbol and irony hunters have replaced the source-finders as literary critics, allegory, whose concep-

tion and methods are generally symbolic and ironic, ironically has failed to escape from the bias that has symbolized it as literature whose purpose is not primarily aesthetic. If a single book is capable of altering this critical attitude, *Dark Conceit: the Making of Allegory,* despite some serious faults, should be successful, for Edwin Honig, heavily armed with perception and knowledge, has laid waste the oversimplifications and misconceptions in the stubborn opposition.

He begins with an attack on the two central prejudices against allegory, that which arises from its use as a philosophical or rhetorical weapon (that is, its functional character) and that which comes from a traditional ignorance of its literary form. Honig at once shows its complexity and richness as a literary genre and its pervasiveness in other types. As he himself describes it, his subject may be divided into formal, generic-typical, and stylistic qualities, which open the way into an investigation of the methods and scope of allegory.

Working from an historical perspective, he traces the development and meaning of allegory from Greek mythology through Biblical, medieval, Renaissance, neo-classical, and romantic literature to contemporary writing. The way in which allegory epitomizes the values of society, measures the difference between the real and ideal, and adjusts to the demands of the age emerges from a careful study of literary and non-literary history. At times, his investigation reveals as much about literary genres, myth, and symbolism as it does about the making of allegory, but his main purpose remains clear, to demonstrate that allegory is not an imposed form, mechanically worked out, but rather "a particular kind of thinking in myth, literature, and philosophy," by which design is effectively given to fiction. As a literary type, which is "more schematic and more flexible than is usually supposed," it "engages more fully than any other [type], the symbolic uses of literature."

Then, through detailed analysis, Honig presents the varieties of allegorical fictions, showing how allegorical writers of different periods have more in common with each other than they do with their own contemporaries. (p. 108)

Had Honig done nothing more than analyze the method of allegory, *Dark Conceit* would still be an important book. But he has managed, at the same time, to give fresh readings to both standard and contemporary literature. His explication of text, particularly the first book of *The Faerie Queene,* and his understanding of the problems that create the increasing ambiguity in modern allegories are important contributions in themselves to literary criticism.

Yet Honig's book is not without its faults. Perhaps the most forgivable is the heaviness of its style, for the subject requires a use of detail that is hardly likely to be sprightly. He is burdened by the problems of literary terms that require explanation by way of illustration, and like Northrup Frye, in his *Anatomy of Criticism,* he cannot escape a pontifical tone. But there is a more serious flaw in *Dark Conceit,* one that Honig himself apparently recognizes. Early in the book he writes, "This is not to indicate that everything is allegory or to press the case for it against symbolism. . . ." Nevertheless, too often the reader feels that everything *is* allegory, and if the case is not being pressed against symbolism, that is only because allegory has consumed it. . . .

With so much to praise, however, it is surely wrong to end on a note of disagreement. Honig's book, like Harry Berger's *The Allegorical Temper,* signifies a renewed interest in allegory. More than Berger's work, which is concerned mainly with

Spenser, *Dark Conceit* opens the way not only for a careful critical revaluation of allegory but also for an encouragement of creative efforts in the form. (p. 109)

*Robert D. Spector, in a review of "Dark Conceit: The Making of Allegory," in* Western Humanities Review, *Vol. XIV, No. 1, Winter, 1960, pp. 108-09.*

## FRANK KERMODE

Mr. Honig's study of allegory [*Dark Conceit: The Making of Allegory*] is philosophic criticism in the new American manner. To write in this way it is at least necessary to read and think. The master is Northrop Frye, the method is to study the world of literature with the purpose of discovering by induction its laws. The analogy is with physics. To study allegory one observes its behaviour in as many contexts as possible; in Spenser, but also in Melville and Kafka. Mr. Honig finds that the modern disrespect for allegory in its older manifestations is founded on a misconception; for this he blames the Romantics, who destroyed the ontological basis of the old allegory and substituted for the 'divine science' of analogy 'the personal fetish of the artist.' Allegory, properly understood, is a permanent and distinctive part of the creative process, and it 'makes possible a cosmic view of the intrinsic relationships of all objects and beings.'

There are two main objections to this way of proceeding. First, it is largely concerned with the ways in which, for instance, Spenser, Melville and Kafka resemble each other, and these are on the whole unimportant compared with the ways in which they differ. Secondly it runs in places where careful walking is necessary: it is no use pretending that we are quite sure what Spenser's allegories signify, or even how they work. But this is a powerful essay, and a reminder of the seriousness with which, in America at any rate, clever men take the business of criticism.

*Frank Kermode, "Academic Discourses," in* The Spectator, *Vol. 204, No. 6870, February 26, 1960, p. 295.**

## A. ALVAREZ

Since the Romantics, allegory has been out, symbolism in. The distinction was first and most forcibly made by Coleridge. . . . Since then the whole movement in literature towards an ever increasing depth and complexity has found the simple game of allegorical correspondences at best trivial, at worst downright distasteful. . . .

Recently in America, however, the distinction between allegory and symbolism has been broken down again, and the former has prospered accordingly. A medievalist like D. W. Robertson, who is interested in Christian symbolism but not, apparently, in Christianity, a literary theorist like Northrop Frye, who writes within a powerful moral framework though he seems reluctant to say which, and a strange genius like Kenneth Burke, who uses literature as just one element among many in his *summa* on human behaviour, have all written criticism which, in its wide-ranging schematising, is like nothing so much as a highly sophisticated, intellectual and cosmopolitan cousin of the old four-fold method of allegorical interpretation. Now Edwin Honig has produced *Dark Conceit* to justify the ways of allegory to modern man by making it seem the most inclusive and subtle of all forms of writing.

Like his elder colleagues, Mr Honig does not much care for the evaluative side of criticism. Instead, he is interested in it as a comprehensive intellectual discipline which gathers under its wing anthropology, the history of ideas, politics and psychology. So, though he is at times a shrewd commentator who can demonstrate with considerable acumen how *The Scarlet Letter* or Kafka's *Metamorphosis* is organised round a single metaphor, his real interest is elsewhere.

It lies in the relationship between literature and belief. Unlike our own defenders of, say, Spenser, Mr Honig has no religious axe to grind. He is fascinated by the quality and interaction of ideas. He views allegory as a 'metaphor of purpose' which gives substance to the artist's thinking. For the artist, of course, thinking has very little to do with conceptualising. It is, instead, a matter of translating his experience of life into terms of his medium. So Mr Honig, with admirable impartiality, probes into the way in which the translations are made between experience, ethics and art, the strategies by which they are developed and maintained, the final weight of authority the work receives from them and the way in which the literary act modifies the systems from which it sprang. . . .

As a piece of literary-intellectual history, *Dark Conceit* is often peculiarly impressive. Mr Honig has a great range of reference and is a tenacious arguer. Once he gets on to an idea he will keep after it ruthlessly through the most tangled thickets of abstraction until it finally lies down and gives up. But granted his skill and persistence, it is a pity he moves so ponderously. As a quarterly reviewer, Mr Honig is a very polished performer indeed. In comparison, he seems to have written *Dark Conceit* with his boots. . . .

There is also a certain failure of judgment in the work. It is perfectly fair game for Mr Honig to extend the title of allegory to all the literature he likes. And to extend the form's realm out of the narrow boundaries of religion until it can include belief in 'art, philosophy, psychology, and science' is perhaps the only way of making allegory meaningful for us now. . . . It is one thing to justify allegory by showing that it is wider and deeper than we supposed and can tap immense subtleties of what Burke calls 'symbolic action'. It is quite another to assume that a richness of allegorical intention automatically transforms a work into major art. Mr Honig may have disposed of the old dichotomy between allegory and symbolism, but the difference in quality between *The Faerie Queene* and, say, *The Winter's Tale* remains what it was, whatever he chooses to call it.

*A. Alvarez, "Art and Allegory," in* New Statesman, *Vol. LIX, No. 1515, March 26, 1960, p. 458.*

## JACK LINDEMAN

[Edwin Honig] makes a vigorous attempt to come to grips with the poetic language of his time. He is one of the genuinely exciting young poets writing today; and though *The Gazabos: 41 Poems* is listed as his second book, it can be considered his first truly representative volume, since it includes so many poems from *The Moral Circus,* his first collection.

There are a number of detectable influences to be found in these poems—Dylan Thomas, Oscar Williams, and Lorca, for example . . . —but none of these influences ever casts a completely obscuring shadow over Mr. Honig's own impassioned voice, even in his least successful efforts. There are strong indications of an almost primitive compulsion on nearly every page, and Mr. Honig's main concern is to control and shape this seething force down inside himself, keep it from becoming a volcanic eruption, by deliberately imposing an intellectually acquired will-power upon it. Not always clear in terms of idea and circumstances out of which a particular poem was made, the language is nearly always keyed up to such a soaring tension that it alone is sufficient to keep one's mind glued to the page. *Sleepers* is such a poem. . . . This poem is full of fine imagery; and yet its subject matter is as sinister and elusive as a surrealistic detective story. (p. 112)

In the final analysis, Edwin Honig's poems contain enough rewardable density to warrant no end of return engagements. (p. 113)

> *Jack Lindeman, in a review of "The Gazabos: 41 Poems," in* Poetry *Vol. XCVII, No. 2, November, 1960, pp. 112-13.*

## D. J. HUGHES

Edwin Honig's second book [of poetry], *The Gazabos,* manifests . . . precise mastery of the medium. The hestitations and compromises of form and meaning that mark . . . [some other poets] are absent here as the struggle into clarity from "the slime, the sea, the fish, the green" emerges at last from a dark inchoateness into the accepting gesture of the title poem, the last in the book, where the poet, recalling the "gazabos" of his youth, the tough drugstore cowboys who chased him home, "a dancing, a gallumphing, a guzzling / of themselves" turns back to them, as to his necessity. . . .

["The Gazabos"] is powerful in itself and overwhelming as the outcome of the personal symbolic poems that have come before like "Sleepers," "Odyssey," "When My Sorrow Came Home," "Pray Eros," "Coralles 1948." A movement to a mastering reconciliation is certainly the major pulse of the book.

But not all the poems in *The Gazabos* lead directly here or share in this motion. As befits a marked poetic maturity, *The Gazabos* is a varied collection. Mr. Honig does not repeat himself, and the variety of forms and the exploration of many moods without ever losing that mysterious signature and blessed quiddity we call *voice* testifies to the presence of a major talent. Yet many of the poems with a strong narrative or descriptive base, "Outer Drive," "Island Storm," "Speech, Near Hope in Providence," etc., perform for the reader the same rituals of encounter and defense that the more personal poems performed for the poet. The threat that "if met / wholeheartedly would snap black lids / on everyone" is held in abeyance by a black wit and tough language. Occasionally, I think the description is too abstract or special, and the wit comes clear only after a lengthy analysis of the joke, but even the poems that do not struggle into light stir us with shadowy meanings.

Recognizing this, we can see how two more "public" poems, first-rate in their deep-breathing, "A Beauty That Rages," a character sketch of an old Italian immigrant in rock-ribbed Maine, and "Walt Whitman," the best tribute I've read to that poet, point to fresh paths. . . . These poems, together with the impressive verse drama "The Widow," that closes the volume, indicate the possibilities of new triumphs and fresh struggles. (pp. 17-18)

> *D. J. Hughes, "The Demands of Poetry," in* The Nation, *Vol. 196, No. 1, January 5, 1963, pp. 16-18.\**

## JUDSON JEROME

[American poet Bink Noll writes] about real things, things that matter, and when one untangles the sentence he finds it wraps a thought. I have not had that reassuring experience with Edwin Honig's *The Gazabos.* Lines like "A drooling silence sinks on mystery unachieved" just pass me in the night. I would not know mystery achieved if I ran across it—except in the realms of magic tricks or cosmetics. "Drooling" and "sinks" seem both vaguely contradictory and vaguely redundant. Also ugly. Perhaps mystery has been achieved. Later in the same poem, I think I understand him a little better:

> Man's wound to man is forgiven heavenward.
> Only man's wound to earth burns all creation
> And is etched forever in sullen scars,
> Compelling the trees, the fruit, the stars even,
> To retreat another fatal inch or hour
> Past imagination's swollen grasp.

It seems a strange lament. Man's inhumanity to man, whether forgiven heavenward or not, is not easily dismissed—particularly in favor of conservation. Oh, I'm not against conservation, but I'm not ready to consign ethics to heaven. Besides, nature does have a remarkable ability to cure itself. Is imagination's "swollen grasp" (whatever that is) really in danger of making the stars recede? This, I realize, is petty quarreling, but language and ideas seem wrenched with irresponsible abandon. Honig works much better in a short play, "The Widow," included in the book. The dramatic form draws him away from verbal oddity and pontification into a very human absorption in character and situation. One woman is confronting another who thinks she has lost her husband; it becomes clear that the comforter is capable of love and appreciation of this absent man, and that the widow has, in fact, killed him off in spirit long ago. It is tense, imaginative, psychologically convincing. . . . I hope that plays continue to draw him out of himself. (p. 123)

> *Judson Jerome, "A Poetry Chronicle—Part I," in* The Antioch Review, *Vol. XXIII, No. 1, Spring, 1963, pp. 109-24.\**

## WINFIELD TOWNLEY SCOTT

[Honig's *Survivals*] advances an established career. His lean, muscular style, his way of lifting a small thing into significance—these are no mean gifts. "Fall of a House" perhaps exhibits him at his haunting best. It is a theme that attracts him; he says in a later poem: "It was then / we roused to see our bodies lie down chilled together / in the last moonlight of the falling house." A poem called "The Island" ("Hurt was the first language his heart heard. / Nothing human but was alien to him.") is a remarkable instance of the way he can sustain a poem with subtle, constant music. And at the close of the book his poems of love and death are moving with an eloquence beyond rhetoric. (p. 58)

> *Winfield Townley Scott, "Music, Image, and Emotion," in* Saturday Review, *Vol. XLVIII, No. 41, October 9, 1965, pp. 57-9.\**

## PENELOPE WEISS

I have a great deal of respect for Mr. Honig as a translator, and I am sorry indeed that I don't like his poetry. His main faults seem to be an overabundance of verbs and a distinct lack of exciting turns of language or poetic ideas. Usually, his lines are short, and the poems are spare. This can be a virtue, but only, it seems to me, if there is an excitement in the conciseness. If the spareness has no depth, it cannot convey even a feeling of calmness. Mr. Honig reaches an epitome of spareness in his poem, *Absence* [from the collection *Survivals*]. . . . This poem seems to me lifeless; it says what it says and the reader is not intrigued. He senses no depth of meaning here, no excitement. Perhaps the poem succeeds by demonstrating a certain negative quality—an "absence"—but it is not pleasing.

Not all of Mr. Honig's poems are so spare. *Vehicles* moves closer to a union of verbs and nouns in the first three stanzas. . . . And in *Quarry* he begins with a short stanza that promises excitement. . . . Unfortunately, the excitement doesn't go very far, and soon Mr. Honig has lost me in his matter-of-factness. . . . (p. 63)

Again, in *Desertions*, he begins well and quickly loses the core, the interest and the quickening emotion. . . . [Its] monotonous rhythm helps destroy whatever momentum there is in the first stanza. Occasionally, there are phrases or whole passages that have merit, such as the first four lines of stanza VIII in a long poem *The Island*, but even though I've tried, I can only muster a feeble enthusiasm for the poems in this volume. (p. 64)

> *Penelope Weiss, in a review of "Survivals," in Poetry, Vol. CVIII, No. 1, April, 1966, pp. 62-4.*

## LAURENCE LIEBERMAN

[*The essay from which this excerpt is taken originally appeared in* Poetry, *April 1969 under the title "Critic of the Month, VII: A Confluence of Poets."*]

Rigorously trained in the classics, Edwin Honig's high-spirited, droll intelligence is wearing its scholarly decorations and credentials lightly in his new poems [in *Spring Journal: Poems*]. He is a formal, disciplined talent backing away from thoroughbred sophistication into an easy-going, open-ended artistry. There is enough assured firmness—an earned austerity of control—in the very accents of his cavalier, lazy-speaking lines to free him from the need for pre-given formal structures. His relaxed meters draw their surprising zest from indolence of being, a falling away into "the power of idleness." In the shorter poems, Honig is cultivating an art which is stylistically hospitable to pressing recent experience of bereavement and fatherhood—deaths and births—and he knows he can best acquire suppleness by leaning toward the raw impulse-telling of folk art. . . . Honig's new poetry is low-keyed: his lines, moving with a soft and easy quietness, catch unexpected fire from the lowbrow, unschooled rhythms of routine living. The seriousness of vision in the long title poem, **"Spring Journal,"** avoids introspective stuffiness because it is never far from spilling over into adjacent planes of easy-going, disenchantingly affable, happy being. Honig returns us from the transcendental abyss to the plain actuality that life requires us to deal with in most of our moment-to-moment frustrations. It is a poetry keeping its cool despite the worst of things, of selves, a poetry finding its nourishment and fortification in manageably confronting those worsts.

One difficulty in the long poem is that the rambling, gabby, discursive manner of the persona grows too slack, windy, in some sections of the sequence. At such times, the writing loses its texture and grows to resemble a shapeless, chopped-up prose. More usually, though, the jet stream of Honig's loqua-

ciousness is tempered by the fine cutting edge of his wit, and the interplay of these two constitutional leanings of his personality furnishes his long, spiraling verse sentences with astonishing permeability to experience. This enlivened medium is porous enough to absorb all shades of the vivid flux of lived, thought, and felt act—the ongoing and inrushing drift—of the poet's energetic daily life. (pp. 206-07)

> *Laurence Lieberman, "Edwin Honig," in his* Unassigned Frequencies: American Poetry in Review, 1964-77, *University of Illinois Press, 1977, pp. 206-07.*

## L. ALAN GOLDSTEIN

[The] typical pose of Honig's early poems [is that of] a spectator among intermittent holocausts, going about his business like Buster Keaton dodging boulders in an avalanche.

Often those early poems suggested the harrowing unhappiness that masquerades as wit, the weariness with those self-created Furies Honig called the gazabos:

> Friends, multi-
> tudes, oh lifelong shadows: are
> you my filth, my worn out longings,
> my poems that dog me
> til I die?

[In *Spring Journal*] . . . Honig turns to confront his shadows and remake his soul by casting them out. The excitement of his poem "Spring Journal" is the identification of those old demonic forces with the war-making, anxiety-making agents of history. . . . Section by section he produces snapshots . . . —McCarthyism, the Eisenhower tedium, and especially the sad exuberance of Vietnam. Gradually the stills begin to compose a workable self; the wit increases with the insistence of spring. The verse begins to reflect on itself, exalt and belittle itself as it swells and faints, "hobbles on stilts" with the pulsations of excited reverie. (pp. 640, 642)

The poem ends on a note of release, not yet discovery. According to Honig, "Spring Journal" is "the first portion of a work in progress whose final form and length are not yet determinable." Future books will have to justify the joy of . . . [the] final lines if the tone carries over, but as it stands the dance succinctly relieves a long morning of self-analysis. The irregular meter and long lines controlled by the (almost always) regular double accented short lines, make the poem capacious enough to accommodate the flux of subjects, shifting tones and polemics that compose the journal. . . .

Twenty-five short poems comprise the bulk of this collection. Remarking on Honig's early poems, the novelist John Hawkes has written: "Nearly all of these poems construct a kind of ghostly and biting double exposure, or hold in some mercurial suspension, suasion, the two deplorable and astounding processes—that of dying and that of birthing." The first part of the collection contains mostly "death poems" and the second part a number of poems about Honig's two baby sons, so Hawkes's description remains pertinent. I prefer the first section, where the intense and "ghostly" self-colloquies strain to bring the dead back to life.

Honig sometimes permits abstractions and platitudes to collapse a lyric into absolute flatness, but most often he addresses "the thinking ear" with original rhythms, and a characteristic use of metaphor that deserves an essay to itself. Individual taste will determine which poem does which. My opinion is that **"November through a Giant Copper Beech," "Her Hand," "King of Death," "Back to Tahiti," "Second Son Day,"** and **"Ah Life, this Lowgrade Infection"** have the unique life intensity of Honig's finest poems. (p. 642)

> L. Alan Goldstein, "Double Exposure," in The Nation, Vol. 208, No. 20, May 19, 1969, pp. 640, 642.

## ROBERT STILWELL

So far as I am concerned, *Spring Journal* is superior to Edwin Honig's last two books of poetry—infinitely superior to *The Gazabos* and faintly superior to *Survivals*—although I am not at all sure that such a judgment constitutes high commendation. Mr. Honig has never struck me as a poet who reaches the inmost marrows of his themes or as a poet capable of pressing his language close to its splintering limit; and I can scarcely help supposing that anyone, or at least any versifier familiar with Conrad Aiken at his watery worst, might have scribbled this typically banal passage (I excise it from Mr. Honig's title-piece, a long, loose, boringly sluggish "conversational" poem in twenty-two sections):

> The lessons of time wear out (in time all lessons
> wear out) and I
> turn back to solicit, incredulous, my own life's
> burnt-out years,
> seeing only the blinking of shutters on gutted ruins,
> the ruins all me.
> I suspect this but swear the pictures are false,
> the negatives rigged—not by me.

Mr. Honig toils at converting into verse a number of exceedingly personal, and therefore quite promising, subjects: the birth of a son, **"November Through a Giant Copper Beech,"** his meditations on the dead or on "the pale-haired fields of August," two deer glimpsed by snow-light, and so forth. His burden, however, is to persuade us to care about those subjects or, more properly, about their poetically realized analogues: and somehow I, for one, *don't* care. Despite all his admirable intentions, Mr. Honig just can't *try* exactly enough; and there's an end to't ("The lessons of time" indeed!). His poems are flaccid, decent, colorless, often derivative. The following dazzle-the-bourgeoisie reflections, which represent the whole concluding section of **"Spring Journal,"** have been uttered by other poets, with slightly different words, on at least eighty-seven thousand previous occasions:

> High noon. It's time to get up—jump into my pants
> run out and dance
> in the foggy streets of Providence, play God—
> maybe bring out the sun!

(pp. 280-81)

> Robert Stilwell, "Samples," in Michigan Quarterly Review, Vol. VIII, No. 4, Fall, 1969, pp. 278-82.*

## C. A. JONES

Used as the professional Hispanist is to explaining, if not explaining away his favourite authors to an uncomprehending world, Professor Honig provides an exhilarating shot in the arm; and not for the first time either, for his work on Lorca and as a translator of Spanish plays has established him as a forceful ally, not for any partisan reasons but because he sees

in Spanish literature an integral part of the European cultural heritage.

In face of a critical tradition which has stressed the special, esoteric qualities of Calderón, it is the universality and the modernity of the Spanish author that professor Honig underlines in [*Calderón and the Seizures of Honor*], a book which . . . is one of the most exciting and stimulating to impinge on this reviewer for some time. Honig insists, in a way which should be but is often not obvious, that Calderón was a playwright rather than a preacher (at least in his plays); interested in conflicts and the persons who become involved in them rather than in teaching moral lessons. In laying stress on the author as a practical man of the theatre Professor Honig is going somewhat against the most modern tendencies of Calderón criticism, especially in Britain; but one can accept his statement that 'because the aim of this book is to make Calderón better known to English-speaking readers of drama and not to debate with the specialists, there are no polemics in the main chapters'. (There are, it is fair to say, some traces in the introduction and conclusion.)

The studies of Calderón collected here are closely based on the plays themselves and are, as the title suggests, all related to the honour theme. . . .(p. 679)

After all the discussion on tragedy in Calderón it is refreshing to find that *comedia* is seen as the essential vehicle for the author. And moreover *comedia* means comedy: '*Comedia* as comedy is necessarily human in its resolutions, however destructive they may be'. Professor Honig would seem to question that full satisfaction can be obtained from the idea of Calderón's plays showing order upset and then finally restored, and to see instead a series of subversive attacks on honour as the prop of the establishment. (pp. 679-80)

[*Calderón and the Seizures of Honor* is] full of wise and well-expressed insights. . . . 'His plays renew for us the possibility of experiencing that glory and folly which go to make a full human being.' The best one can say of this important book is that no one better than its author has shown us how this comes about in Calderón. (pp. 680-81)

> C. A. Jones, in a review of "Calderón and the Seizures of Honor," in The Modern Language Review, Vol. 69, No. 3, July, 1974, pp. 679-81.

## LAURENCE GOLDSTEIN

A long poem. An autobiography in the shape of seasonal meditations. Readers coming to Edwin Honig's poetry for the first time may interpret *Four Springs* as a deliberate milestone, a lyric poet's philosophical summing-up. But those who have followed his verse from *The Gazabos* (1959) through *Survivals* (1964) and *Spring Journal* (1968) will see the book as a harder-fought but no more conclusive wrestling match with the exterminating angel. If anything, the Whitmanian confidence of Honig's early work has passed into its antithetical mode, in which sad memories and ghosts begin to outnumber the things of this world. In its brooding on the past, *Four Springs* really inclines toward the future—a future chronicle, a future journal which will extend, synthesize, but never completely account for the ongoing experience Honig is struggling to articulate.

In this age we are not likely to take any writer seriously who does not give a voice to his anti-self. A poet has asked, if Winter comes can Spring be far behind? A poet answers, depends what you mean by Spring. Honig turns the whole force of his imagination to the *myth* (belief and delusion) of Spring, the season of resurrection. . . . Honig has contributed something original to the elegiac use of images associated with Spring; for a condensed sample, look at the interpolated poem, **"Spring Northbound,"** which concludes the second book.

*Four Springs* incorporates many occasional poems into its ongoing reverie. Because it is a historical poem—about Vietnam as much as self—the immediate, finished responses of 1966-69 take their place as guiding flares ("thinking is a flame burning") through the latter 'Sixties. These poems in italics might almost be the obscure texts which the meditation elucidates. The effect reminds us of *Paterson*, and Honig quotes a line from W. C. Williams' epic to resonate through his own work: "A deformed verse for a deformed time." (pp. 427-28)

One shortcoming in the poem, to my taste, is that . . . [the] external pressures are described with disproportionate zeal— we hear about McCarthyism and President Johnson, but little about the less spectacular, more gruelling demons of common life. In his earlier poetry Honig has called attention to some of these; it is disappointing to find his professional work, his travels, his ambitions, his personal loves and hates so briefly alluded to in the composition of *Four Springs*. I don't mean that I miss the kind of confessional details that have made the unstable reputation of many recent poets, but that some ballast for the increasingly generalized speculations in the last section would have been welcome. The finely particularized evocation of a city fire in Book 3, which expands in metaphorical weight until it becomes the consuming, transforming fire of all life— this might have concluded the volume, sweeping more detail into its combustion.

True to his vision, however, Honig does not shower down a climactic fire; an inconclusive, bittersweet meditation on time's swiftness ends the poem. Honig's deliberate tilting of the sequence—in rhythm, myth, and dramatic action—keeps the reader off balance. (p. 429)

*shake a spear with me, john berryman* collects some new poems and a short play written since *Four Springs*. The title of one section, **"Another Orpheus"** and of the play, **"Orpheus Below"** point to Honig's continuing revisitation of the Dead World, and his location there of a beloved shade. This work is less discursive than *Four Springs,* less reflective of outward events, but it is no less philosophical. Philosophy in poetry becomes meaningful by its attachment to a dramatic myth which it informs and to which it lends fresh significance. The Orpheus myth serves Honig's elegiac needs by giving his personal distress coherence and depth. Where the poet is most objective, as in the play, he articulates in poignant speeches the yearning to recapture past happiness; where he is most subjective, as in the title section of the volume, his jagged verse lines and swallowed feelings create some confusion. (pp. 429-30)

> *Laurence Goldstein, "Honig's Elegiac Mode," in* Michigan Quarterly Review, *Vol. XIII, No. 4, Fall, 1974, pp. 427-30.*

## A. A. PARKER

In 1961 Professor Honig published translations of four plays by Calderón. . . . Nine years later he published a translation of *La vida es sueño* ("Life is a Dream"). Over this period he published in various journals separate studies of these five plays and two papers on Calderonian Honor. All this material has now been collected and adapted, with the addition of opening and concluding chapters, to form a single book on the Honor theme in Calderón's drama. (p. 173)

[Since *Calderón and the Seizures of Honor*] is confined to one theme (although one that is wide in its ramifications), and confined, moreover, to Calderón's first period, 1623-c.1640, leaving untouched the last forty years of his career, Professor Honig's book cannot claim to be comprehensive, even on the theme of honor, but it could well achieve its specific aim of making Calderón "better known to English-speaking readers of drama."

A prerequisite for this was supplied by his translations, which are here utilized for quotations from the five plays studied. How to translate Golden Age plays with their polymetrical form is a problem to which there can be no ideal solution. Professor Honig's translations read extremely well. He employs a free form of blank verse, with shorter but variable lines, having iambic tetrameter as a focal center to which the rhythm keeps returning but which it never stabilizes. This is the most successful way yet devised of rendering the various Spanish octosyllabic meters, especially the easy flow of the *romance*.

A second problem in making Calderón acceptable today is that his intellectual interests and patterns of thought and expression make him "a dramatic writer almost anathematic to Anglo-Saxon tastes." To expound his thought and to explain his art through the neo-scholastic world of baroque casuistical Catholicism is for Professor Honig to make him "parochial," with nothing to say to our age. Yet he rightly maintains that, despite all this, Calderón has an ethical vitality and a psychological penetration that can come "alive to a modern reader in fresh and basic human terms." In practice this means disregarding or minimizing nearly everything that makes Calderón a dramatist of his age, and the scholar and student of literature who wish to understand his position within the culture of his country and his contribution to the development of the European theater will not find here the guidance they are looking for.

Instead, however, of presenting this insistence on contemporary appeal as a delimitation necessitated by his special, and very proper, purpose, Professor Honig embarks in his last chapter on a theoretical exposition that would seem, in effect, to be a justification for divorcing dramatic criticism from historical scholarship, although he does not refer to the long-standing debate on this general issue. Calderón can certainly be a test case. The problem is presented in this way: "The intellectual appeal of drama on the page and its enactment on the stage are the Scylla and Charybdis confrontation no dramatic critic can escape. For the student of Calderón the job is particularly trying since the playwright's interest in ideas is indistinguishable from his interest in drama. Both seem to come together in full measure through rhetoric and imagery as well as the thematic implications of the *comedias* . . . One should not take such a metaphysician literally. He must be seen through his dramatic deeds." . . . For assessing the deeds, "craft, aesthetic theory and moral doctrine" are as secondary as the ideas. "One does not ask if a thing is Freudian or Christian or if it is well made and logically balanced, but does it work?" . . . (pp. 173-74)

One wonders whether this does not beg the question. Does a Calderonian play "work" on the stage because it succeeds in communicating the poet's dramatic vision of human life, or does it "work" because its dramatic terms can be felt to harmonize with the vision of life already formed in the reader's mind? For Professor Honig, the "dramatic deeds" through which Calderón must be seen function in this latter direction. Sometimes there is no clash, for in the case of plays like *El alcalde de Zalamea* and, perhaps to a lesser extent, *La dama duende,* the two directions coincide; but inevitably, in other cases, a distorted Calderón is seen through Professor Honig's reading of the deeds. (p. 174)

If the reader is on his guard against expecting from this book what it does not aim to offer, he will find much of interest in it. Calderón's psychological insights and his humanity will be enhanced for most readers by his "modernization," and Professor Honig has the penetration and the sensitivity needed to bring them out. He is probably right to ignore the seventeenth-century theatrical stereotyping of the code of honor and to present honor solely in modern terms as both a sense of overriding duty and the preservation of personal identity, with a potential conflict between the two; nonetheless, the exact relationship between this conception and the actions and motives of the dramatic characters is not always clear. (pp. 175-76)

> *A. A. Parker, in a review of "Calderón and the Seizures of Honor," in* Comparative Literature, *Vol. XXVII, No. 2, Spring, 1975, pp. 173-76.*

## HAYDEN CARRUTH

Edwin Honig's poems [in *Selected Poems (1955-1976)*] seem so clear and simple that no account of them is needed. There they are; go and read them. Many are beautiful. But his work is not as well known as it should be, and as for beauty—sometimes I think it must be actually despised these days, so few poets even acknowledge its possibility. I know, the times are cruel and filled with urgency, and our self-consciousness has become so frighteningly complex that we can hardly do more than pry out bits of it—which is why poets like Jean Valentine are so valuable. Yet there are other values, older but equally necessary, if life is to be worth living at all: values of song, grace, and metaphysical poignancy.

> I heard joy speak to me
> your joy and the time spent
> neither wishing nor having it
> before it came
> after it went

This is touching—I use appropriately an old-fashioned term—in its wry vision of joy as a moment in joyless time; it is fetching in its simple rhythm and spontaneous rhyme, a stanza of random harmony. But is it really random? Notice the sounds not caught in the rhyme alone: your / nor; time / came; having / after. Notice how syntax plays against the accents, no line like any other. Notice that the "neither wishing nor having" may be a kind of joy too, the before and after, since they, too, are speaking to the poet in the joy he hears. It is a Blakean innocence of perception, i.e., not innocent at all, but painful and wise. The singing is the human search for survival, whistling in the dark. I believe Honig's poems, at least many of them, reach back to the heart of Renaissance fear and bravery, to Ronsard and Wyatt, the cult of love and death—in short, to Romance. We are trying now rather desperately to free ourselves from it, and we must do so. But if in the process we jettison beauty as well, then our freedom will not be worth the having; and this, whether or not they intend it, is what poets like Honig are saying to us, their ultimate meaning. We cannot safely neglect them, nor dull our ears to their lightly antique lyric grace, for otherwise our language will be no more than

communication, somewhat refined animal barks and birdsong, and we shall have lost the component that makes words uniquely human. (p. 78)

> *Hayden Carruth, "Poets on the Fringe," in* Harper's, *Vol. 260, No.1556, January, 1980, pp. 77-81.**

## GARY ARPIN

In his poem on Walt Whitman, published in *The Gazabos* in 1959, Edwin Honig describes Whitman's task in this way: "His patent, never filed, / Was being man quixotically alive against the hoax / Of sin and dying." "'The real war,'" he quotes Whitman, "'will never get in the books,'" and Honig makes clear that "the real war" is precisely that struggle between the desire for affirmation and the "hoax / Of sin and dying." Put simply, that has been Honig's chief concern for twenty-five years as well. His poems clarify the darkness of our lives and attempt to struggle through it towards transcendence, permanence, and affirmation. The darkness—isolation, pain, sin, death—is an important part of Honig's work, most deeply felt after his first wife's death in 1963, but strongly present before that as well. Equally strong, though, is the need to oppose that darkness.

The terms of the struggle are made clear in a poem as early as **"Hamlet"** (1955). Honig's Hamlet is like Prufrock or the speaker of "Le Monocle de Mon Oncle." His problem is change, decay, mortality. . . . Honig plays on the artificiality of the play (here and elsewhere in these early pieces): in the flesh, the self is playing a role, while the true self lies elsewhere. Even at its best, life in the flesh leads only to "Ophelia's mother-masked incestuous hoax."

The alternative to the hoax lies beyond the decaying flesh, in the drive toward transcendence, toward a region "where curseless / Fathers sup from Plato's golden bowl." The language of the last stanza of **"Hamlet"** neatly reflects the movement of the poem away from the falseness of the play to the reality of the self, which speaks in spite of mortality and thus momentarily rises above it:

> O there to rise with power to divine
> The tear from torrents of delayed lament,
> And wear the motley diamond of the self
> On all one was and is, against the death
> Of speech, the shrivelling skin, and be
> Sermon on the mount of one's own
> requiem.

"Motley" changes from noun to adjective in our minds as we read the line, and in doing so changes the platitude to a truth.

The battle is clearly drawn, then—the poet fights against the death of speech and for the power to proclaim the self, to make an affirmation: "O there to rise." Honig's diction frequently rises as well during the course of a poem, moving from the colloquial or ironic to the high lyric, as it does in **"Hamlet,"** paralleling the movement from crisis to affirmation.

Most of Honig's lyrics—and the best of them—follow this Romantic paradigm, and most of the strong Romantic poets, especially Blake, Whitman, Yeats, and Stevens, stand in the background of his work. Honig returns constantly to the themes of the great Romantics, at times virtually rewriting major Romantic works. (Behind **"Island Storm,"** for example, is "Dejection: An Ode;" behind **"When My Sorrow Came Home,"** the "Ode on Melancholy;" behind **"Second Son Day,"** "Prayer for My Daughter.'') There is a strong emphasis in his work on the primacy of vision and imagination over the coldness of practicality and rationality. The poet's eye—and he puns regularly on the word—is necessarily important, and Honig's own eye is sharp. His portrayal of things as they are perceived is one of the great delights of reading Honig's work. . . .

Honig is known for his surreal touches (he has translated and written on Calderon and Lorca), but that should not obscure the fact that he is fundamentally a poet of the lyric moment. Surrealism is often used in his work to emphasize the power of that moment, as in **"Happening,"** when a house "open[s] its face, gray as a man's." He is at the same time a thoroughly conventional poet, that is, one who is at home in and can competently manipulate the language, imagery, and conventions of his time. He is not a poet who breaks through to new territory, nor does he attempt to. This is not to denigrate Honig's accomplishment, which is considerable, but it may help to explain, at least in part, why that accomplishment has been so little noticed—poets of far less ability have received far more attention. . . .

Most lyric poets have felt the constrictions of the lyric form at some time in their careers. A lyric cannot be too long, and it can include politics or history only with great difficulty. . . . Typically, what happens is that the long poem gets away from the poet, taking on a virtual life of its own, as in *The Cantos, The Dream Songs, History,* and many others. Honig's attempt, called *Four Springs,* grew beyond his control as well. Like the long poems of his contemporaries and predecessors, *Four Springs* (the echo of Eliot in the title is no doubt intentional), became a kind of prosaic matrix generating lyrics. At its best, it provided the flat plain from which a lyric moment could rise. . . .

One of Honig's great concerns is the lack of a coherent, consistent identity—a self to proclaim. He pictures himself as a person inhabited by many false selves, and "the truth is it rankles, this having / to take on somebody / else's old smell, ego-fatuous speech and smile." This concern is not simply a consequence of Honig's romanticism, but seems to be a psychological fact as well, and one of its corollaries is the great influence of strong poets on his work, at times to the point of pastiche. . . . Honig's work seems best when it resorts only occasionally to the packed alliterative language that he seems most to admire. (He uses ballad style, for example, to great effect.) The poems on his first wife's death in *Survivals* (1964) and on his remarriage and the birth of his second son in *Spring Journal* (1968) are profoundly moving, not because they are necessarily simple (they aren't), or simply because they are sincere (they are), but because there is no hint of self-indulgence in them, and his influences are kept under tight control.

The same can be said of the prose pieces which make up *The Foibles and Fables of an Abstract Man.* This volume contains meditations (some abstract and tendentious, some beautifully lyrical), descriptions, short stories, and a number of surreal, cynical, and frequently very funny fables, reminiscent, at various times, of Aesop, Ovid, and Donald Barthelme. (Or all three at once: "One day an ant, a snake, an egg, and a turd set out together on a head-hunting expedition.") The best pieces here are those that allow Honig's eye the freest rein, like **"Viewing a Leopard"** (a portrait of a young stud trying vainly to attract a married woman's attention on a Portuguese beach), or the last two sections of **"A Seed in the Sky,"** which remind one of the "Spring" chapter of *Walden.* Although the manner is slightly different here (Honig having jettisoned the restrictions of the lyric form completely), the matter is the same as

in his earlier work—the portrayal of a privileged moment. As in **"Spring Northbound"** and **"Hamlet,"** the "hoax / Of sin and dying" is once again momentarily revealed and defeated, and another temporary victory is achieved in "the real war."

> *Gary Arpin, in a review of "Collected Poems: 1955-1976" and "The Foibles and Fables of an Abstract Man," in* The American Book Review, *Vol. 3, No. 3, March-April, 1981, p. 22.*

## JASCHA KESSLER

[Suffering] preoccupies most lyric poets. . . . It occupies a good deal of their time and fills their pages: They want to tell us how it is with them, and the record of their work tells us about the stages of their attempted recovery from sad, early, and often late, damage too. . . .

Not that depression, misery, pain and catastrophe cannot evoke interesting poetry; and not that suffering doesn't often underlie even work that is relatively objective and seems to bear the burdens of its maker's life well, even jauntily, the way Kenneth Koch's does. But there are some poets who must tell us directly, always, only, obsessively as well, what they are seeing as they gaze at their past in the mirror of their art. Edwin Honig is just such a poet. For a couple of decades, I have perused his books as they came along, always finding myself curiously pondering what it was that he was grieving about so very dolorously. Clearly the music of his poetry was subtle and low, reticent and tender, sometimes seeming to withhold the full force of the pain that it was addressed to. Not that there was any mystification to his work: Honig in the 60's, as I recall him, was grieving for the wife he had married and loved and lost through her early death. There were many short poems about her, about the vacancy that death had left in his mature life. It is a curious thing, incidentally, but whereas the 19th Century was replete with poetry of such loss . . . modern medicine has removed so many of the causes of untimely death, whether it be that of children, or mature adults, through disease or infection, that the subject is not all that trite anymore, even though violent accident, warfare, massacre and genocide have killed people in our century by the tens of millions. But, precisely because the extent and magnitude of the scale of dying has been so absurdly arbitrary and enormous, the subject has also been removed from our ability to respond, and resulted in a generally-numbed silence—because the scale is not individually human. Yet Honig has persisted in the mode of grief and elegiac contemplation.

I have considered that one explanation is Honig's sensitive heart, and his deep sense of the humanness, the humaneness, so to speak, of his humanistic learning as a scholar of the Renaissance drama and as a translator from the Spanish and Portuguese poets of our time. I also knew that in middle age he had married again, at last, and become a father; and had heard that that family was dissolved by divorce. A man of sorrows and troubles, in short, plagued by the absurdity and instability of the most important of our relations. But, a new book of his poetry has just appeared, and it sheds yet another, and, for me, more penetrating light on his nature. The book is called *Interrupted Praise: New and Selected Poems,* and in it Edwin Honig has gathered poems written over a period of forty years. Instead of beginning at the beginning, however, Honig sets his newest work first, and moves backward through time, thus giving us a sense of exploring what the poetic life of a human being is like: we find the poet as he is now in his sixties, and we advance towards the past until we see his first manifestations as an utterer of woes both open and secret. What seems to have haunted him from the first was the accidental death of his younger brother when the poet was only 5—seeing and remembering the truck that crushed the child—and then a "nearly fatal bout with nephritis," when he was 9. When he was 12, his parents divorced, and he lived with his grandfather and grandmother, a woman who spoke Spanish, Arabic and Yiddish (but no English), for some years. He himself has remarked that it forced upon him the necessity to write to keep from choking, and to make sense of a world without leaving out his own fantasy. What that constellation suggests is a character that needs to reconcile the immense sense of grief, guilt and deprivation of the child, all hidden and private sufferings, with the world outside, a world that doesn't make much sense. It is from such a character that Honig has written poetry and much criticism. And neither the poetry nor the criticism pretends to objectivity. It seeks to make sense of what cannot be made sensible after all: and it all adds up to an attempt to cope with death, not at the end of life, which is the future threat conscious and self-conscious beings like ourselves try to imagine, but in Honig's case from the very beginnings of his life. . . .

Honig's lyrical study of the death-haunted depths of his emotions is seldom dreary or dull, seldom witless or self-important or burdensome. Reading his book from start to finish, that is, from the present toward the past, one comes to understand his efforts over a lifetime to say something about what is his principle subject: loss, and its accompanying grieving sadness. We come to sympathize and even suppose we can grasp what a life, an interior life, has been for this one courageous poet, for whom the only task of his creative being was from the beginning to come to terms with who he was, not what he was, for what he was is obviously a writer studying himself and the world, but always from the inside out.

*Jascha Kessler, "Edwin Honig: 'Interrupted Praise, New and Selected Poems'," in a radio broadcast on KUSC-FM—Los Angeles, CA, June 15, 1983.*

# C(yril) L(ionel) R(obert) James
## 1901-

(Has also written under pseudonym of J. R. Johnson) West Indian nonfiction writer, journalist, novelist, short story writer, dramatist, and critic.

James is a noted historian of African, Caribbean, and Soviet revolutionary movements and politics. He has recently won acclaim and recognition in North America for *Beyond a Boundary*, a classic work of sports literature. Published in England in 1963 and in the United States in 1984, *Beyond a Boundary* analyzes cricket and its popularity in England and the West Indies. James contends that the game contributed significantly to breaking down racial barriers in his native Trinidad. Critics value James's book as much for its cultural commentary and reminiscences of growing up under British colonial rule as for its graceful yet powerful presentation of the sport.

James's histories include *World Revolution 1917-1936: The Rise and Fall of the Communist International* (1937), a theoretical commentary on the upheavals within the Bolshevist movement; *The Black Jacobins: Toussaint L'Ouverture and the San Domingo Revolution* (1938), a biographical account of the leader of the Haitian slave revolt of 1791; *A History of Negro Revolt* (1938), revised as *A History of Pan-African Revolt* (1969), a survey of modern African liberation movements; and *Nkrumah and the Ghana Revolution* (1977). James has also written one novel, *Minty Alley* (1936). A recent publication, *At the Rendezvous of Victory* (1984), reprints his 1929 short story "Triumph" and several literary essays on the works of Herman Melville, Toni Morrison, and Alice Walker.

Born and educated in Trinidad, James moved to England in 1932 and worked as a journalist, particularly in the area of sports, for several years. A committed Marxist revolutionary, James came to the United States in 1938 and helped organize tenant farmers and automobile workers. He was deported in 1953 during the McCarthy era but has returned occasionally to lecture and teach.

*Val Wilmer/Format*

## G. McLURE

This most competently written book [*World Revolution 1917-1936: The Rise and Fall of the Communist International*], it may as well be said at once, presents the case of that section of the Russian Bolshevik Party which follows Trotsky, and despite its too obvious bias and its animus it deserves some serious attention from anyone who is honestly trying to understand present Russian events. For it is no mere pamphlet thrown out in the face of the Moscow trials, but a close historical study of the theoretical differences within Marxist doctrine and the bitter struggle to which they have given rise within the organization and policies of the Soviet Union. It is based too largely upon the writings of one of the chief protagonists: nevertheless it does cast some light into a dark situation....

Mr. James's thesis definitely casts Stalin for the role of villain. From his bandit origins he inherits a lust for personal power, and so uses the party machine to make himself a national dictator. The appeal to the international proletariat is dropped,

and power relations with the capitalist governments of Europe developed in its place....

Where the intelligent non-communist reader will first dissent from this argument is in its emphasis on personalities. The villain hypothesis is too simple. Surely the situation is one of tragedy rather—a genuine conflict between rights....

What is not so clear is the reason for the tactics of assassination, wreckage and treason. There a disastrous turn was taken; and Stalin has taken another with his ruthless suppression. Along that road reconciliation is impossible, and Mr. James is not enlightening about the way out.

G. McLure, "Proletariat v. the State," in The New Republic, *Vol. LXXXXII, No. 1186, August 25, 1937, p. 80.*

## CLARA GRUENING STILLMAN

The subtle interplay between the man, the circumstances and the hour forms the material of [*The Black Jacobins: Toussaint L'Ouverture and the San Domingo Revolution*], a searching historic analysis and demonstration of the revolutionary process in a specific instance. Brilliantly conceived and executed, throwing upon the historic screen a mass of dramatic figures, lurid scenes, fantastic happenings, the absorbing narrative never departs from its rigid faithfulness to method and documentation, presenting the actions of individuals and masses and clarifying social and political events in their complex interrelations with the economic forces of the age and correlating them with their counterparts of today.

Yet the purely human quality is not slighted. The amazing figure of Toussaint is always at the center, "old Toussaint," the forty-five-year-old slave when the revolution begins, steward of a plantation, knowing agriculture and men, who can read and has read to good purpose Caesar's Commentaries and the Abbé Raynal's History of the West Indies which states that liberty is the natural right of every slave. "A courageous chief only is wanted. Where is he, that great man?" Having read that passage many times and hesitated a whole month after the insurrection begins, he becomes that man. . . .

The scene shifts between the colony and France with an occasional glance at England. The trail of the abolition question through the successive French assemblies illuminates the course of the French Revolution. This question also is the touchstone for evaluating revolutionary groups and individuals.

This book is written in the light of the violent conflicts of our own age, which, says Mr. James, "enable our practiced vision to see the very bones of previous revolutions more easily than heretofore." It has therefore "something of the fever and the fret" of the present. The anatomy and the portrait of an epic struggle, it is both profound and exciting.

> *Clara Gruening Stillman, "They Struck for Freedom," in* New York Herald Tribune Books, *November 27, 1938, p. 20.*

## THE NEW YORK TIMES BOOK REVIEW

["**The Black Jacobins**"] is no mere tale of the uprising of human chattels against ill-treatment and servitude: it is a record of war and strategy, political organization and manoeuvre, which is not only studded with its own peculiar incidents, situations and personalities, but belongs with the history of the French Revolution and the rise of Napoleon. "It is impossible to understand the San Domingo revolution unless it is studied in close relationship with the revolution in France," Mr. James remarks almost casually in the course of his six-page bibliography. Yet the portrait and career of Toussaint L'Ouverture himself keep the supreme interest through this absorbing and exciting book. . . .

Mr. James is not afraid to touch his pen with the flame of ardent personal feeling—a sense of justice, love of freedom, admiration for heroism, hatred for tyranny—and his detailed, richly documented and dramatically written book holds a deep and lasting interest.

> *"The Black Jacobins of San Domingo's Revolution," in* The New York Times Book Review, *December 11, 1938, p. 7.*

## V. S. NAIPAUL

**Beyond a Boundary,** like Nirad Chaudhuri's *Autobiography of an Unknown Indian,* is part of the cultural boomeranging from the former colonies, delayed and still imperfectly understood. With one or two exceptions, a journalistic reaction to his material—cricket—has obscured the originality of Mr. James' purpose and method. (pp. 73-4)

In islands that had known only brutality and proclaimed greed, cricket and its code provided an area of rest, a release for much that was denied by the society: skill, courage, style: the graces, the very things that in a changed world are making the game archaic. And the code that came with the game, the code recognised by everyone, whatever his race or class, was the British public-school code:

> I learned and obeyed and taught a code, the English public-school code. Britain and her colonies and the colonial peoples. What do the British people know of what they have done there? Precious little. The colonial peoples, particularly West Indians, scarcely know themselves as yet. . . .

The West Indies [cricket team] captained for the first time by a black man, did great things in Australia in 1960-61. A quarter of a million people came out into the streets of Melbourne to say goodbye to the cricketers: West Indian cricket's finest moment, which Mr. James sees as something more. "Clearing their way with bat and ball, West Indians at that moment had made a public entry into the comity of nations." It is a success story, then, that Mr. James has to tell, but an odd one, since it is also the story of the triumph of the code. To Mr. James, Frank Worrell is more than the first black West Indian captain: "Thomas Arnold, Thomas Hughes and the Old Master himself would have recognised Frank Worrell as their boy."

This is the last sentence of Mr. James' book, and this is his astounding thesis. To dismiss it would be to deny the curious position of the West Indies and West Indians in the Commonwealth, to fail to see that these territories are a unique imperial creation, where people of many lands, thrown together, "came to maturity within a system that was the result of centuries of development in another land, was transplanted as a hothouse flower is transplanted and bore some strange fruit". Stollmeyer, Gomez, Pierre, Christiani, Tang Choon, Ramadhin: the names of West Indian cricketers are sufficient evidence. To be a nationalist, Mr. James says elsewhere, you must have a nation. The African in Africa had a nation; so had the Asian in Asia. The West Indian, whatever his community, had only this "system." . . . (p. 74)

It is part of the originality and rightness of Mr. James' book that he should have combined the story of his development within the system with his view of West Indian political growth, and combined that with sketches of West Indian cricketers he knew and watched develop. In the islands the cricketers were familiar to many; they were as much men as cricketers. So they emerge in Mr. James' pages, but even so they remain touched with heroic qualities, for their success, as with Constantine or Headley, was the only type of triumph the society as a whole knew. And their failure, as with Wilton St. Hill who, achieving nothing in England in 1928, remained all his life a clerk in a department store, bitter tragedy. (pp. 74-5)

**Beyond a Boundary** is one of the finest and most finished books to come out of the West Indies, important to England, important to the West Indies. It has a further value: it gives a base and solidity to West Indian literary endeavour. (p. 75)

> *V. S. Naipaul, "Sporting Life," in* Encounter, *Vol. XXI, No. 3, September, 1963, pp. 73-5.*

## ABD-AL HAKIMU IBN ALKALIMAT

[*A History of Pan-African Revolt* is] an important and challenging primer for our historical understanding of Pan-African action toward liberation. This is a valuable text for those who would move to reorganize their way of looking at the world and focus on a new Pan-African historical reality, a reality of revolt. We must come to this awareness, for then we can intelligently make historical decisions about our own action and our future direction.

This volume is a historical survey of nearly two centuries of African liberation struggle against European colonialism. It illustrates the types of revolt that African people have waged spiced with interpretive comments to probe the meaning of the revolts. James writes "The African bruises and breaks himself against his bars in the interest of freedom wider than his own."
... Brother James has focused on the Pan-African revolt to demonstrate that world revolution of tomorrow is inextricably connected with the African struggle today. He is quick with insight, as a man who works within a clearly defined ideological framework, although he chooses not to clarify the theoretical notions guiding his analysis. This work is clearly a primer for historical understanding, because James limits himself to analysis by illustration rather than comprehensive coverage of all relevant events and actions. (pp. 51-2)

[It] is clear that James is working with categories that have been generated by revolution in the West. He is concerned with how closely the African basis of social organization for struggle approximated the European proletariat, or merely the extension of a native bourgeoisie. This question is central to what constitutes the correct road to revolution, according to what James calls "fundamental laws of revolution." James appears not to be totally restricted by ideological doctrine, and suggests that so long as something is organized for the people against their oppression, to that extent it is progressive. He suggests that whatever Black organization can articulate concrete grievances of the people, demands that can be escalated to the heart of the problem ("the end to imperialist rule"), is the organization that is most progressive. This he sees as inevitably connected with the organization of the poor workers in the western metropolitan countries. However, he cites Frantz Fanon on the limitation of Black Nationalism but fails to deal with the racist colonial exploitation enjoyed by the European (white) working class. He applauds the African innovation of Julius Nyerere of Tanzania and Kenneth Kaunda of Zambia, but fits all his analysis into models of European revolution. In fact, we look at this analysis as glimpses of Black revolution as defined by James' version of Marxist-Leninism. (pp. 52, 91)

This volume calls us to develop an analysis of Pan-African action. Black people in the United States must begin to look at the world through their African eyes. . . . This is the beginning of a people conscious of their world, living in thought and emotion the everyday struggles of African people everywhere on the earth. We must be a united African people, and for that we need to have a united all-African analysis of African affairs. Brother James provides us with a provocative beginning for this new step forward. (p. 91)

*Abd-al Hakimu Ibn Alkalimat, in a review of "A History of Pan-African Revolt," in* Negro Digest, *Vol. XIX, No. 5, March, 1970, pp. 51-2, 91-2.**

### LEOTA S. LAWRENCE

This paper will attempt to characterize three West Indian heroines: one, the creation of a woman writer, the other two, of men.

The three characters, Bita in Claude McKay's *Banana Bottom* (1933), Maisie in C.L.R. James' *Minty Alley* (1936), and 'Tee in Merle Hodge's *Crick Crack Monkey* (1970), are from three different West Indian environments. Born in culturally and materially impoverished worlds, they are either given the opportunity to leave the stultifying confines of their society, or, as in Maisie's case, they actively seek a means of escape. It might be of significance to note here that most West Indian writers themselves have demonstrated that in order to be literarily creative, they had to remove themselves physically from their environment. Similarly, these three female fictional characters, in order to find themselves, so to speak, eventually leave the West Indies. (pp. 238-39)

*Minty Alley* is set in the slums of Port of Spain, Trinidad, and Maisie is a fledgling product of this real environment. (p. 242)

Maisie and the other characters live and laugh and suffer and do battle in the yard at No. 2 Minty Alley. (pp. 242-43)

Maisie, about fifteen years of age, has had the minimum of education, and is trained for nothing. Like many West Indian children, she does not live with her parents. Indeed, we learn nothing about her mother and father or her early childhood. She lives with her aunt, Mrs. Rouse, who owns the house at No. 2 Minty Alley. Maisie is the bane of Mrs. Rouse. When the young, middle-class Haynes moves into one of the rooms rented by Mrs. Rouse, he and Maisie are immediately attracted to each other. Maisie's narrow and constricting environment offers no outlet for her high spiritedness, and her frustration turns into devilment, directed for the most part against her aunt, Mrs. Rouse. . . .

Mrs. Rouse's wrath against Maisie knows no bounds when she finds out that Benoit, her common-law husband, is having an affair with the near-white Nurse Jackson, one of her tenants, under her very nose, and that Maisie is a silent conspirator. (p. 243)

Soon after . . . Haynes and Maisie become lovers. However, at no time is there any suggestion of permanence in their relationship. For Haynes is educated and middle-class, while Maisie is unlearned and lower class. Maisie is very devoted to Haynes, and whenever he is at home, she stays in his room and does not get in Mrs. Rouse's way. . . .

Maisie is uneducated and black—two very formidable impediments. Her only asset is her youth. The choices that are, therefore, open to her are rather limited. She can either become a domestic servant, and work for very low wages, or she can form a relationship with a man and hope to be supported by him. But in spite of all the odds working against her, Maisie's is an indomitable spirit. Her feelings are that securing employment will not significantly ameliorate her situation and her plans for the future do not include her present environment. Confiding to Haynes that she wants to go to America, she gives the reason that "In America you worked hard but you got good food and pay and had a fine time." . . .

But Maisie's departure does not take place until there is, in typical West Indian fashion, a resounding explosion between herself and her aunt. (p. 244)

[This] ends Maisie's sojourn at No. 2 Minty Alley, for she forthwith leaves with only the clothes on her back. Haynes meets with her the night before she leaves Port of Spain, for Maisie has indeed secured a passage to America. She explains to Haynes that she has paid twenty dollars to a stewardess who works on one of the ships which goes to New York. Acting as a procuress the stewardess will provide passage for black girls because the white officers like them. (p. 245)

Thus Maisie joins the ever increasing population of West Indian immigrants in America. The development of Maisie's character that James depicts is incisive and convincing for one can be certain that true to her word she has no intention of returning to her native Trinidad. . . . James shows Maisie's world to be bare, barren, and devoid of hope. The beauty and grandeur of the islands that the tourists rave about is lost on Maisie as it is on countless other West Indians whose main concern is where their next meal is coming from. So like many West Indian women and men in her position, Maisie chooses not to surrender to the limitations and barrenness of her environment. Her only alternative is an escape, a departure to an uncertain future, but one in which she believes that she will be materially compensated for her labors. (pp. 245-46)

For his realistic portrayal of Maisie and the other inhabitants of Minty Alley, James was soundly criticized by the "respectable" sector of Trinidad society. Unfortunately, much as one might be tempted to applaud McKay for his treatment of his heroine and to indict Hodge for hers, anyone who knows anything about West Indians would agree that McKay's Bita is a romanticized verison of West Indian womanhood, while James' Maisie and Hodge's Cynthia are realistic. In the West Indies there are many Maisies and Cynthias but very few Bitas. (p. 250)

Leota S. Lawrence, "Three West Indian Heroines: An Analysis," in CLA Journal, Vol. XXI, No. 2, December, 1977, pp. 238-50.*

## THOMAS HODGKIN

[C.L.R. James] has a special place in the history of Third World revolutionary movements. When I met him first, in late 1936-1937, he was working with the International African Service Bureau . . . and writing that wonderful book on the Haitian slave revolution, *The Black Jacobins*. To me, in my at that time somewhat sectarian state of mind, he appeared a charming and interesting, but misguided, trotskyist (he prefers the lower case), while I must have appeared to him as a no less misguided stalinist. In fact, as is clear from these writings, he combines Caribbean nationalism, Black radicalism, a once Trotskyist blend of revolutionary anti-imperialism, and the European classic tradition in an individual and potent mix.

[*Nkrumah and the Ghana Revolution*] is much the less interesting of the two, and it is not always accurate. It was mainly written, James tells us, 20 years ago, and it reads as though it was. Though a friend, comrade and profound admirer of Kwame Nkrumah, he was not closely involved in the Ghana revolution, and it would be difficult for a book written in those circumstances to throw much new light on the complex problems of that phase of history. On the absurdity and awfulness of colonial mythlogy (which continues to inform a great deal of the literature of decolonisation) James has much to say that is sensible, if also a bit repetitive. . . .

*The Future in the Present*, on the other hand, is a mine of richness and variety. James loses his tendency to pomposity and rhetoric when he is writing about themes he knows and loves—calypsos, cricket and Garfield Sobers, Picasso's *Guernica, Moby Dick*, the sharecroppers' strike in South-East Missouri in 1942. Then his language acquires a splendid simplicity. He becomes what he means to be, what he beautifully describes "the Mighty Sparrow" (Francisco Slinger, the great Grenadian

calypsonian) as being—"a man of the people, using a people's medium and cherished by the people as one of their own". I found his piece on Sparrow and the one immediately preceding it, on "The Artist in the Caribbean", dealing with the relation of the artist to his tradition, particularly moving and wise. . . .

What is excellent about James is his catholicism. He writes as perceptively about horses (which he used to ride in Trinidad and in Phoenix Park) as about the West Indian national character and its relation to West Indian class structure. It is as at his most Trotskyist, I am afraid, that I still find him least convincing. But it is not in the field of theoretical discussion that his real gifts lie; or rather, his theoretical writing is best when it is closely related to the historical realities which he understands so well—the past in the present, as well as "the present in the future." . . .

I am glad that James regards W. E. Burghardt Du Bois, whom I came to know well and respect much during his still active nineties in Ghana, as his intellectual father and "the most important name in the history of black struggles", and that he gives him an essay to himself. And I am sure his fascinating exegesis of Sparrow's "Federation" calypso is as good an introduction to the study of Caribbean politics as one could find anywhere. . . .

Thomas Hodgkin, "We Should All Be Together," in The Times Educational Supplement, No. 3267, January 20, 1978, p. 24.

## CHOICE

The first of a projected three-volume collection of C.L.R. James's voluminous published works, [*The Future in the Present*] begins very appropriately with a short story, "**Triumph**," the only piece of fiction among the 20 selections. "**Triumph**," a successful realistic story, concerns three women tenants of a "Barrack-yard" in James's native Trinidad. James is such a scholarly thinker that we need "**Triumph**" to appreciate that we are reading the work of a man who possesses the vision of an artist, one who cannot be dismissed as a doctrinaire political "out" (habitat: obscure socialist, Trotskyist-oriented publications) as some unknowing readers might otherwise suspect. It is true that the book contains excellent essays on Melville, art, the Greeks of 400 B.C., cricket; but James always gets back to socialism and sociology—and his hopes for a new world to be administered by those who produce. The essays are testimony that James's contributions of the last half-century to British, West Indian, African, and U.S. American life are of the enduring kind.

A review of "The Future in the Present: Selected Writings," in Choice, Vol. 15, No. 3, May, 1978, p. 399.

## PAUL L. BERMAN

How is it that C.L.R. James is not more celebrated in this country? There has been no better example, since the death of Trotsky, of the ideal of the Marxist intellectual: the man of action who knows no nationality or parochialism, who takes the whole of society in his scope, who writes fluently on literature, sports, international affairs, who ascends to heights of visionary speculation, yet organizes political movements that succeed in the world as it is. . . .

CONTEMPORARY LITERARY CRITICISM, Vol. 33

Nevertheless, incredibly, James has not been accorded a more general recognition here, and with the exception of his masterwork on the Haitian revolution, *Black Jacobins,* his writings have been difficult to find. Aficionados have had to keep an eye out for odd issues of the *Massachusetts Review* and other literary quarterlies, where James's work has sometimes appeared, send away for his pamphlets to mysterious little Marxist cells in Detroit, where he has always had a following, and fight one another for possession of his mimeographed book on Hegel, *Notes on the Dialectic* (James's Marxism leans heavily on Hegel).

Which makes it splendid news that [*The Future in the Present: Selected Writings* has now appeared].... Herein are tracts in favor of West Indian independence, analyses of workers' councils in Hungary, notes on the arts in the Caribbean, essays on Melville, W.E.B. DuBois, George Jackson, the slave trade, African independence, cricket, and ancient Greece. The writings are profound, sometimes; cranky, occasionally; stimulating, always. The publisher promises additional volumes shortly. Cheers to that. And long live C.L.R. James!

Paul L. Berman, "A C.L.R. James Celebration," in The Village Voice, Vol. XXVI, No. 7, February 11-17, 1981, p. 44.

## DEREK WALCOTT

George John, Arthur Jones, Josh Rudder, Piggott, Wilton St. Hill, Matthew Boardman—the roll is like a chronicle of fallen yeomen in a Shakespearean battle, but they were cricketers of African descent who brought glory to an English game in the West Indies. Their battlefields were ringed with quietly clapping spectators. Most fell victim to prejudice and neglect. They have found a grateful chronicler in C.L.R. James, whose book, **"Beyond a Boundary"** (published in England in 1963 but not here until now), should find its place on the team with Izaak Walton, Ivan Turgenev, A. J. Liebling and Ernest Hemingway, unless its author suffers the same fate as his black subjects.

**"Beyond a Boundary"** is a book about grace, about slow-bowlers with the wrists of anglers and fast-bowlers with the thunder of fighting bulls, and every one of its sentences, deftly turned, is like a lesson in that game, whose criterion is elegance.... [But] this book goes further afield than cricket. It goes behind the rusted tin forces of the barrack yards of West Indian life as far as the Periclean archipelago. And the Greek past is a lesson that Mr. James appropriates as authoritatively as blacksmiths, yardboys and groundsmen dominated the sport of their masters. He sees no difference between their achievements and those of the Athenian athletes.

Portentous as this sounds, it is what Mr. James means by civilization. It is, for him, that sweetness of disposition and that clarity of intellect that Matthew Arnold defined as culture, and Mr. James's book dramatizes its ironies as accurately as Arnold or Henry Adams did and does it not through contemplation but through action. (pp. 1, 36)

"It's just a book about cricket, for God's sake." It isn't. It is a book about cricket for the gods' sake as well. It is a book about treachery, despair and the fate of some of the best for being black, and still it is written without bitterness. Anger, yes, but no rancor. It is a noble book about poor, beautifully built but socially desperate men (one of whom begged his captain to be allowed to play the game barefoot because shoes slowed down his delivery) who made this game the next thing

to religion. Mr. James radiantly celebrates this blend of African prowess with Victorian codes. He sees how those Victorian ideals of gentlemanly conduct were ethics, even tribal ethics, regardless of race, and not a trap. (p. 36)

But Mr. James was never blinded by the plaster casts and hypocritical marble copies of the Victorian ideal. He always had a hard mind, and this book does not try to make marble from ebony. It would be laughable if it were yet another paean of gratitude, a fake pastoral with classical echoes, but it would also be incredible, since Mr. James has been a Marxist (who has broken with Russia) and, in a politically active life, has been interned on Ellis Island, out of which degradation he wrote his **"Mariners, Renegades and Castaways"**; he has also been a pamphleteer, a pioneering West Indian novelist and in **"Black Jacobins"** a historian of the Haitian Revolution. All of his life he has been known in the islands, by trade unionists as well as by writers, as a controversial humanist. But he loves cricket above everything else, not because it is a sport, but because he has found in it all the decencies required for a culture.

Then how can one be as passionate about the Russian Revolution as he is and still idealize a sport practiced by "gentlemen"? In his long life Mr. James has arrived, through this book, at a calm center. His calm is that of a meridian between two oceans, two cultures, even between radical and conservative politics, without mere neutrality. His calm is not neutrality. It has the passion of conviction, for decent conduct is the first and last thing required of men, as it is of states. He has arrived at that calm as quietly as a knight concludes a pilgrimage, and his quest has been that cup called "The Ashes," that grail of Test Cricket for which teams from South Africa, New Zealand, Australia, Pakistan, India and the West Indies have fought so that one of their captains, many of them knighted later, could hold it up to the world.

It is Mr. James's belief that there is a difference between discipline and natural grace, between relentless practice and genius. But he cherishes obedience in the Sophoclean sense, or even in the Roman way of not questioning the emperor's thumb of the umpire, if not of the empire. For him, obedience irradiates the most belligerent stroke-maker; he is appalled at the commercial anarchy of American sport. But things have changed. Cricket teams, through a certain entrepreneur, can now be bought or rented for high salaries, and black West Indian cricketers now play in South Africa. But it is the ideal that remains untarnished, not its vandals.

Mr. James's ancestors are African; why does he not find mimesis in African not Periclean sculpture when he describes the grace of his cricketers? Bodily movement is not a principle of African art, and the game is not played there on the scale of its other arenas. Proletarian in politics, patrician in taste, Mr. James should be a contradiction, but he was never a target for black radicals, rather one of its legislators, like Frantz Fanon, Léopold Sédar Senghor, Aimé Césaire and Kwame Nkrumah. His history as a polemicist, his campaigns for African and West Indian nationalism have often caused him to be blacklisted, interned and put under house arrest in his native Trinidad. And, in fact, if one thinks carefully again, **"Beyond a Boundary"** can be thought of as subversion; it undermines concepts that feel safe, it beats tradition by joining it, and its technique is not bitterness but joy.

Writers who worship a sport can sublimate their mediocrity into envy. Mr. James, who was a good bowler, has no envy. He sounds like a better bowler than Hemingway was a bullfighter or Mailer is a boxer. He had real promise and was going to make cricketing his profession. He chortles with unaffected boasting about bowling out Learie Constantine, but what remains in this book is the shadow that stained the heroes of his boyhood with colonial prejudice—the darkening future when the "gentleman's game" is over, and his blacksmiths and roundsmen split from their teammates to go their own ways.

This sense of dusk in **"Beyond a Boundary"** provides it with history, gives it a tragic enchantment, since it is both a chronicle of the sport and the decline of an empire, from colonialism to independence, from the days when black and brown cricketers had different clubs to the days of the black captaincy of Frank Worrell. It is also a book, then, about twilight, about the turning of an epoch, and yet its tone is triumphal. Most of all, for a third of its length, it is like an excellent novel. Its characters are more than biographical asides. They have their own arc, no matter how minor their roles. (pp. 36-7)

[Any] boy today as keen on cricket as Mr. James was then would be already a writer if he appreciated this passage by Mr. James himself:

"My grandfather went to church every Sunday morning at eleven o'clock wearing in the broiling sun a frock-coat, striped trousers and top-hat, with his walking stick in hand, surrounded by his family."

Fair enough, Victorian in meter, decorous in memory, then the right tingle comes: "The underwear of the women crackling with starch."

This is simply one stroke from a book whose light is as clear as a summer game's and which, as the highest tribute I can offer, every writer should read, because there, in one phrase, like the broken bottles on a moonlit wall in Chekhov, is the history of a colonial epoch: its rigors, its deprivations and its pride. (p. 37)

> Derek Walcott, "A Classic of Cricket, A Legend of Baseball," in The New York Times Book Review, March 25, 1984, pp. 1, 36-7.

## ALASTAIR NIVEN

[James] shows no diminution of his intellectual energies in [his essays in *At the Rendezvous of Victory*], which are about Solidarity in Poland and three black American women writers, Toni Morrison, Alice Walker and Ntozake Shange. It is characteristic of 'C.L.R.' to be writing on up-to-the-minute issues and people for he has done so all his life. . . . *At the Rendezvous of Victory* is the ideal introduction to James's interests for anyone who has heard of him but is not quite sure what he stands for. The only subject obviously missing is his writing on cricket. I would have liked more indication of what James was writing in the 1940s since there is only one contribution from that period, an extended preface to three essays by Marx that appeared in 1947. Throughout this book James's elegant but unmannered style, witty and relaxed when lecturing, reflective and analytical when writing for publication, always conveys a sense of his own robust, humane and giving personality. Was there ever a less polemical or more persuasive radical? . . . The collection is both vividly readable and of real archival value.

> Alastair Niven, in a review of "At the Rendezvous of Victory: Selected Writings, Vol. 3," in British Book News, May, 1984, p. 271.

## MARK NAISON

Fourteen years ago, a middle-aged community organizer from Detroit handed a dog-eared book on cricket to an S.D.S. activist from New York City who had been complaining about his comrades' lack of interest in sports and about his own inability to reconcile his love of sports with his political ideals. "Read this," the veteran told him. "It will make all the things you're feeling make sense." The S.D.S.er started reading, and images of schoolyard basketball games in Brooklyn and Harlem, of the bleachers in Ebbets Field, of heroic moments on the tennis court and of Muhammad Ali confounding the media suddenly came together. That book, at once the memoirs of a West Indian Marxist and a social history of cricket, helped the young New Yorker understand his own history and the role of sports in American popular culture better than anything he had ever read.

I was that S.D.S.er, and the book that possessed that magical quality was C.L.R. James's *Beyond a Boundary,* now reprinted for the first time for American audiences. Analyzing a sport that was, in its West Indian setting, a quintessential expression of British colonial culture, James shows how it became an instrument through which West Indians, including himself, affirmed their identity and their claims to independence. Without understanding the racial politics of international cricket, James argues, one cannot understand West Indian nationalism. And to do that, one must have respect for the power and appeal of modern sports. (p. 552)

James takes cultural critics to task for devaluing the esthetic and social meaning of sports. Cricket, he argues, can be subjected to the same standards of criticism as literature, drama or painting: its movements have comparable subtlety and complexity and require as much discipline and imagination. "The basic motions of cricket," he claims, "represent physical action which has been the basis not only of primitive, but civilized life for countless centuries. In work and in play, they were the motions by which men lived and without which they would perish."

For James, moreover, to reject the esthetic of sports has profoundly undemocratic implications. Although much of the left held that "workers were deflected from politics by sports," James rebelled against that formulation and turned his historical research to the subject. He found that the rise of spectator sports in Europe from the 1850s through the 1890s coincided with the extension of the franchise, factory legislation and the founding of socialist parties: "This same public that wanted sports and games so eagerly wanted popular democracy too." The best-known Englishman of the late nineteenth century was the great cricket player W. G. Grace, yet his name appears in few social histories of the period, even those written by socialist scholars. James sees that as the historians' failure to penetrate the lived experience of the "common people" they claim to be interested in.

*Beyond a Boundary* is a book of remarkable richness and force, which vastly expands our understanding of sports as an element of popular culture in the Western and colonial world. (pp. 552-53)

> Mark Naison, "Cricket and Colonialism," in The Nation, Vol. 238, No. 17, May 5, 1984, pp. 552-53.

## PAUL ATTANASIO

*Beyond a Boundary* is structured something like a modernist novel. It is eclectic, fragmentary—part boyhood reminiscence, part journalistic extracts, part history, part polemic. The book is best as memoir—James writes of his boyhood with an easy eloquence that recalls *Huckleberry Finn* or Willie Morris's *North Toward Home* (instead of cricket, Morris played football). . . . [James's] heroes were the DiMaggios of West Indian cricket, men like George John, Wilton St. Hill, and James's friend, Learie Constantine. When he went to the library, he was as likely to read old cricket magazines as he was to parse his Virgil.

In this way, cricket was actually a subversive influence in James's life, a way for him to rebel. And James emphasizes throughout how cricket and politics bled into each other in Trinidad. . . . Politics, in Trinidad, meant race. James tells how black cricketers were passed over for seleciton to the West Indies touring team in favor of less talented white players, how it was impossible for a black player—even Constantine—to be selected captain. James's own trial came when he had to decide which club he would play for, a difficult choice since the clubs were divided according to class, family, and skin hue. James ended up selecting the Maple Club—the team of the brown-skinned middle class—over Shannon, the club of the darker, working-class blacks.

Yet it is for Shannon, the club he passed up, that James evinces genuine enthusiasm. He writes lovingly about their intense, volatile athleticism. If *Beyond a Boundary* is structured like a modernist novel, these detailed anecdotes read like modernist prose; it is James's great triumph that, to the American reader unfamiliar with the game, such passages are both engrossing and utterly incomprehensible. . . . From recollections, James turns to a social history of cricket—how Thomas Arnold inculcated the "cricket virtues" into the scions of the ruling class at the Rugby school, and how cricketer W. G. Grace, the exemplar of those virtues and a sort of Babe Ruth of cricket, came to be, in James's mind, the most important cultural figure of Victorian England. (p. 41)

James's bias for this kind of history is based on a utilitarian notion: since more people care more deeply about sports than politics, our history books should be full of cricket, soccer, and baseball. This argument comes as a stalking horse to the main thrust of his polemic, which is that cricket is not merely socially significant popular culture, but an art form in its own right, "Not a bastard or a poor relation, but a full member of the community." In this light, going "beyond a boundary," literally a sort of cricket home run, means going beyond the artificial barriers we create between high and low culture, art and sport, social history and politics.

This echoes the now-familiar neo-Marxist critique of "liberal culture," and there's something to what James says. There's no quicker way to mummify a work of art than when it is cabined as a "masterpiece"; such low culture elements as the circus and television, for example, have brought vitality to the contemporary avant-garde theater. As Roger Angell has demonstrated, there's more of Aeschylus in a Carl Yastrzemski pop-up than there is in much of our theater, and professional wrestling, generally sneered at by intellectuals, may be the only authentic Artaudian theater of cruelty in the West.

It's hard, though, to know how far to go with this idea. All experience is not equivalent. There's a dividing line somewhere—at his most tragic, Yaz was never Lear—but it may not be worth the effort to find it. James doesn't seem to realize that all his turgid theorizing about the relation of cricket to drama and painting doesn't add one iota to his reminiscences earlier in the book which, by revealing James's depth of feeling

for the game, were themselves his best argument for considering it the equivalent of drama. By insisting that cricket be included among The Arts, he evinces that thralldom to liberal culture which he sought to criticize. "I've never understood that—about art forms," Diana Vreeland once remarked. "People say a little Schiaparelli design is an *art form*. Why can't it just be a very good dress?" (pp. 41-2)

Paul Attanasio, "Cricket and Culture," in The New Republic, *Vol. 190, No. 18, May 7, 1984, pp. 41-2.*

## WHITNEY BALLIETT

Certain autobiographical books—wayward, unclassifiable, even eccentric—seem to invent themselves. They are not so much books as indestructible occurrences. They are intensely personal, often revelatory, yet they never spill over into confession or self-aggrandizement. Their originality irradiates their form, their rhythms, their prose. Think of Sir Thomas Browne's "Religio Medici" and Thoreau's "Walden," of Gertrude Stein's "The Autobiography of Alice B. Toklas," James Baldwin's "The Fire Next Time," and J. R. Ackerley's "My Father and Myself." And now we have C.L.R. James' cool and brilliant **"Beyond a Boundary."** . . . First published in England twenty-one years ago and long considered classic, it has not appeared here before presumably because of the difficulty of its supposed subject matter—the lordly game of cricket. . . . Some knowledge of baseball—that rowdy second or third cousin to cricket—helps, and so do osmosis and James' crystal prose. By the time we are three-quarters of the way through, we know, among a good many other cricket matters, that the batter, or batsman, is allowed to hit the ball in any direction, and we hum through this passage: "The batsman can shape to hit practically round the points of the compass. He can play a dead bat, pat for a single, drive along the ground; he can skim the infielders; he can lift over their heads; he can clear the boundary. He can cut square with all the force of his wrists, arms and shoulders, or cut late with a touch as delicate as a feather." But James' book isn't just about cricket. It's partly autobiographical and partly biographical. It's full of racial, political, and social news about black Trinidad, where he was born and raised. It has slivers of literary criticism, and it tussles with Bernard Berenson. And, most important, it tells us how the black people of the British West Indies, so loose and swinging, yet so down and hopeless for so long, learned to play James' beloved cricket as well as and often better than the white man and in so doing eventually became free and equal. . . .

Activists, by and large, are not good writers, just as good writers are rarely activists. James is an exception. (p. 106)

James is not a cricket apologist—he's an ennobler. He gives us a brief history (cricket was one of the earliest organized sports, and in the eighteen-sixties became the darling first of the new middle class, then of the upper class) and brief, resonant biographies of Grace and of such black West Indian players as Wilton St. Hill, Learie Constantine, and George Headley. In due course, he tells us that cricket is an art—not only dramatic but visual. He trucks in some heavy buttressing—Berenson, Michelangelo, Aeschylus, the Greek sculptors. He compares a cricket match to a three-day performance in ancient Greece of the Oresteia. But we don't think of art when we watch a shortstop hurtle through the air after a low line drive, his body three feet up and parallel to the ground, his mitt arm a bowsprit, his other arm a wing. We don't think at all—we vibrate with admiration at such explosive physical grace and beauty. Later, we might think of strength and courage and timing, and add, as topping, the improvisatory element in all team sports, the streak of jazz. . . . Anyway, what matters in **"Beyond a Boundary"** is not James' cricket aesthetics but his description at the end of the book of his return to Trinidad in 1958. He stayed four years, and he helped the great cricketer Frank Worrell become the first black captain of an international West Indies team. The team played in Australia in 1961, and Worrell was a wonder. James writes of him, "If I say he won the prize it is because the crowd gave it to him. They laughed and cheered him continuously. He expanded my conception of West Indian personality. Nor was I alone. I caught a glimpse of what brought a quarter of a million inhabitants of Melbourne into the streets to tell the West Indian cricketers good-bye, a gesture spontaneous and in cricket without precedent, one people speaking to another. Clearing their way with bat and ball, West Indians at that moment had made a public entry into the comity of nations." . . .

We are told that James is writing his autobiography. **"Beyond a Boundary"** is a work of double reverence—for the resilient, elegant ritualism of cricket and for the black people of the world. It is also full of tantalizing autobiographical patches. To have them spread out properly in the landscape of his life is well worth waiting for. (p. 107)

*Whitney Balliett, "Mr. James and Captain Worrell," in* The New Yorker, *Vol. LX, No. 19, June 25, 1984, pp. 106-07.*

## ROBERT CHRISTGAU

In 1963, when C.L.R. James's *Beyond a Boundary* was first published, spectator sports (unlike blood sports) rarely figured in serious fiction, and they were almost never subjected to searching critical-political-historical analysis. There was good sportswriting, sure, but only within journalism's built-in limitations of space, tone, and occasion; even A. J. Liebling's *The Sweet Science*—at the time, *Beyond a Boundary*'s only full-length competition this side of Hemingway's *Death in the Afternoon*—was a collection of *New Yorker* pieces. And although there were valuable essays or chapters from the likes of Brecht, McLuhan, God help us Norman Podhoretz, and the criminally neglected Reuel Denney, not one professional thinker found the games he loved worthy of an entire book.

Of course, if you define "professional thinker" stringently, that holds true to this day; in athletics as in all other popular culture there's still a dearth of major league books. But at least this new edition, the first look U.S. fans have had at *Beyond a Boundary,* takes on all comers in a recognizable arena. And where before the book seemed a sport (a mutant, a freak, a caprice of nature: the word's etymology is far from entirely complimentary), now it has the unmistakable lineaments of a champion. With all due respect to Roger Angell and Roger Kahn and Harry Edwards, they don't belong on the same field with C.L.R. James. I'm not even sure they can share the same grounds. . . .

*Beyond a Boundary* is much more than a fond memoir. It has to be, because for James this game is much more than a locus

of personal growth—although he never quite comes out and says so, he clearly regards cricket as a human achievement on a par with dialectical materialism itself. Aesthetically, it's a "structurally perfect" enactment of a fundamental "dramatic spectacle" that in addition epitomizes the "'movement'" and "'tactile values'" singled out by Berenson as the prime constituents of significant form in the visual arts. Historically, it preserved essential agrarian values in an era of rampaging industrialization, and continues to do so, though not without the deformities struggle imposes, in the face of a "decline of the West" that James dates to 1929. Politically, it's been instrumental in bringing down racial barriers throughout what was once the British Empire. And on every level its interactions with its audience have expressed the inexorable desire of human beings for genuine democracy.

Even if you adjudge all this rather eccentric (and who wouldn't?), you have to grant it an impressive audacity. It's easy enough for centrists like Angell and Liebling to wax romantic over the symbolic competitions they treasure, because the rules of the game flatter their presumption that competitiveness is both innate and containable. James, however, almost alone among philosophers of sport, is a leftist, and not only that—he's a left historian. His all-encompassing social vision gives this book an emotional sweep and intellectual reach the centrists can't match. But unlike most left historians, who are rarely utopian-spirited enough to account gracefully for the unruly distractions of aesthetic pleasure (let alone competition or play), James enjoys that sense of connectedness to his own childhood which marks fully functional adults of whatever political persuasion. . . .

The prose of *Beyond a Boundary* combines the cultivated lyricism of someone like Hazlitt (whose boxing essays James extols) with the excitable quasi-Victorianism of the more high-tone English sportswriting, and nothing else I've seen by James equals it stylistically. But the book isn't as perfect as *The Black Jacobins,* by most accounts James's masterwork. In the usual manner of fully functional adults well connected to the lessons of their childhood, he does tend to overpraise the culture that made him what he is, and while in 1962 the description of the racial integration of West Indian cricket that occupies his last 35 pages may have seemed to work structurally, today it clearly suffers from journalism's limitation of occasion. The brief introductory "Note on Cricket" doesn't go far enough toward helping us noncolonials to understand the detailed technical analysis or (much worse) James's passionate philosophical commitment to "back play," whatever exactly that is. Since James is regarded as a prophet in some circles, it's also worth noting that, as far as I can determine, the "young Romantic" James predicted would soon "extend the boundaries of cricket technique with a classical perfection" has not yet made himself manifest. But I still don't know of a greater sports book. And more to the point, I don't know all that many works of cultural theory to match it either.

*Robert Christgau, "Dialectical Cricket," in* The Village Voice, *Vol. XXIX, No. 28, July 10, 1984, p. 39.*

# Arthur Koestler

## 1905-1983

(Also wrote under pseudonym of Dr. A. Costler) Hungarian-born English novelist, nonfiction writer, journalist, short story writer, editor, and dramatist.

Koestler is regarded as one of the leading contributors to the literature of ideas in the twentieth century. Throughout his career, he challenged and exposed the false promises of repressive political ideologies and also examined the philosophy of modern science. A prolific writer, Koestler's canon includes six novels, several autobiographies, and numerous nonfiction books and essays that depict the political, social, and technological dilemmas of modern humankind. *Darkness at Noon* (1941), Koestler's best-known work, is considered a classic political novel and has been translated from the original German into more than thirty languages.

Most of Koestler's political writings derive from his personal and professional experiences. He became interested in Zionism while studying at the University of Vienna and left school in 1926 to go to Palestine, where he worked on an Israeli kibbutz. In 1927 Koestler became a Middle East correspondent for the *Ullstein Verlag,* a distinguished chain of German newspapers. He was transferred to Berlin in 1929 and eventually became the science editor of *Vossische Zeitung.* Koestler stated that he joined the German Communist party in 1931 because "the Communist movement appeared as the logical extention of the progressive humanistic trend. It was the continuation and fulfillment of the great Judeo-Christian tradition—a new, fresh branch of the tree of Europe's progress." However, Koestler became disillusioned with Communism, particularly Joseph Stalin's leadership, which he felt distorted the party's Marxist philosophy and condemned to death many Bolshevik revolutionaries during the Moscow Purge trials of the 1930s. Koestler broke with the Communist party in 1937. While covering the Spanish civil war for a British newspaper, Koestler was arrested for espionage. He was sentenced to death by the Franco regime but was released three months later through the intervention of the British government. *Spanish Testament* (1937), and its abridged version, *Dialogue with Death* (1942), is an account of Koestler's terrifying ordeal. In 1939 he accepted an offer to work on a left-wing German newspaper in Paris and was imprisoned following the Nazi invasion of the city. Again with the aid of the British, Koestler was released and arrived in England in 1940, where he worked with the British Ministry of Information. In 1941 Koestler published *Scum of the Earth,* in which he condemned the French government for what he perceived as their failure to combat fascism. After World War II he became a British citizen and resumed his journalism career. He also worked with several organizations that aided refugees from totalitarian countries.

Koestler's early work is dominated by discussions of political issues and ethics. His first three novels, *The Gladiators* (1939), *Darkness at Noon,* and *Arrival and Departure* (1943), have been described by Koestler as his trilogy of "ends and means." *The Gladiators* is an account of Spartacus and the slave revolt in ancient Rome. In this novel Koestler contends that Spartacus was destined to fail because of his refusal to punish an outlaw general, which resulted in factional disputes that led to the

*Fay Godwin's Photo Files*

slave army's defeat. Many critics consider the novel a symbolic representation of the power struggle within the Communist party. *Darkness at Noon* is a powerful critique of Stalin and the Moscow Purges. The novel concerns Rubashov, an old Bolshevik official whose political faith is shaken after he is falsely accused of treason. Through a series of lengthy dialogues between the protagonist and his two interrogators, Koestler reveals the perverse logic behind Stalinism. Rubashov adheres to the party's rhetoric and agrees to confess publicly, rationalizing his actions as his final service to the party. Koestler described *Darkness at Noon* as a portrayal of "reason running amok in the Russian Purges, where . . . the revolution must be allowed to devour its own children if it is to triumph in the end." *Arrival and Departure* explores the psychological motives behind political action. The novel, set in the early years of World War II, portrays a party member and refugee who suffers a nervous breakdown while imprisoned by the Nazis. During psychoanalysis, he discovers that his radical beliefs derive from a childhood attempt to maim his brother; he realizes that his political activities are efforts to eradicate his guilt. In 1945, Koestler published *The Yogi and the Commissar,* a collection of essays that formally outline his condemnation of authoritarian ideologies. Koestler further examined the problems of revolutionary "ends and means" in such novels as *Thieves in the Night* (1946) and *The Age of Longing* (1951).

Koestler's rejection of Communism compelled him to abandon political issues in the mid 1950s, declaring that "I have said all I have to say on these subjects . . . the bitter passion has burnt itself out." His later works concentrate on such subjects as evolutionary theory and the behaviorial sciences. This change in subject matter prompted some critics to speculate that he was searching for the utopian state that Communism had failed to provide. Koestler insisted that such studies are crucial to an understanding of the nature of political dynamics. In such works as *The Sleepwalkers* (1959), *The Act of Creation* (1964), and *The Ghost in the Machine* (1967), he analyzes the progression of human creativity and intelligence throughout history and contemplates the dangers of developing technologies that humankind is incapable of controlling. Koestler described these books as studies of "man's glory and predicament." *The Sleepwalkers* is a historical survey of scientific thought with a strong emphasis on astronomy. The section which examines astronomer Johannes Kepler was reprinted as *The Watershed* (1960) and became a popular college textbook. *The Act of Creation* is an analytical study of human creativity which focuses on such forms of expression as philosophy and the arts. In *The Ghost in the Machine*, a study of the human mind, Koestler contends that the divided human brain is the result of an evolutionary error and is partly responsible for irrational human behavior. He suggests chemotherapy as one solution to inhibit these self-destructive tendencies. Koestler continued his study of behavior in *Janus: A Summing Up* (1978), using the two-faced Roman god Janus as a metaphor for the dualistic nature of the mind.

Koestler's literary reputation rests on his political writings. Unlike other writers of anti-Stalinist works, he carefully avoids propagandizing political issues. Koestler's direct and unequivocal expression of ideas is considered by many to be his strongest attribute. The keen analytical skills and unwavering logic of his nonfiction have been especially praised. Although some critics have accused him of generalizing and popularizing esoteric subjects, most regard his works as important commentaries on the problems of human existence. At the time of his suicide in 1983, Koestler was writing his fifth autobiographical volume, *Stranger on the Square* (1984).

(See also *CLC*, Vols. 1, 3, 6, 8, 15; *Contemporary Authors*, Vols. 1-4, rev. ed., Vol. 109 [obituary]; *Contemporary Authors New Revision Series*, Vol. 1; and *Dictionary of Literary Biography Yearbook: 1983*.)

## NAOMI MITCHISON

It is hard to write intelligently about our own times because we do not know the facts; we cannot understand how the background forces are pushing us, why we cannot behave as we intend; but the historian with a well-documented epoch can see why, can pick out significant background events and tendencies, showing, through these, what was bound to happen to the lives of individuals. This is what Koestler has done with Rome. To my mind [*The Gladiators*] is the first Marxist historical novel; there have been plenty of Left historical novels, but all have remained personal, essentially romantic. This is not personal in the old sense at all; Spartacus himself is the instrument through which the whispering of ideas is blown, to turn into action. The lawyer Fulvius who joins him is an instrument in which the whispering turns to theory. . . .

[One] reads *The Gladiators* for its political implications and questions, above all the question of doing evil that good may come. A series of dilemmas occur out of which there is no right way. In the end the Slave army, which has attempted sometimes to win and sometimes to lead the good life, is beaten; the survivors are crucified. . . . The question remains, why did Spartacus not win, when his was obviously the right side and when the Roman social system was showing every sign of developing such internal contradictions that any observer would say it was bound to crack up? The answer may be that it changed from one form of capitalism to another, organized itself as a Totalitarian Empire, and went on for several more centuries. Rome fell when it could not change from a slave economy, based on constant cheap labour, to a scientific economy, which would have replaced the human hands and enabled the whole extent of the Empire to be gathered into one bundle of power.

A book about backgrounds is bound to be rather complicated, especially when filled with people of many nationalities; sometimes too much has been squashed in, and the transitional passages among the respectable are scarcely smooth enough; here and there the general feeling is Imperial rather than Republican. But the conversations are always good; what is said is not romantic but dialectic. [*The Gladiators*] is a book which anyone who is wondering what will happen to us will do well to read.

> *Naomi Mitchison, "Marxist Rome," in* The New Statesman & Nation, *Vol. XVII, No. 421, March 18, 1939, p. 436.*

## GEORGE ORWELL

Mr. Arthur Koestler should know something about prison, for he has spent a respectable proportion of the past four years there. . . . In no case, needless to say, has he been accused of any particular crime. Nowadays, over increasing areas of the earth, one is imprisoned not for what one does but for what one is, or, more exactly, for what one is suspected of being. (pp. 15-16)

[*Darkness at Noon*] is a tale of the imprisonment, confession and death of one of the Old Bolsheviks, a composite picture having resemblances to both Bukharin and Trotsky. The events in it follow the normal course. Rubashov, one of the last survivors of the original Central Committee of the Communist Party, is arrested, is charged with incredible crimes, denies everything, is tortured by means of deprivation of sleep, etc., etc., confesses everything, and is shot in the back of the neck. The story ends with a young girl in whose house Rubashov has once lodged wondering whether to denounce her father to the Secret Police as a way of securing a flat for herself and her future husband. Almost its whole interest, however, centres about the intellectual struggle between three men, Rubashov himself and the two G.P.U. officers, Ivanov and Gletkin, who are dealing with his case. Ivanov belongs to the same generation as Rubashov himself and is suddenly purged and shot without trial in the middle of the proceedings. Gletkin, however, belongs to the new generation that has grown up since the Revolution, in complete isolation both from the outside world and from the past. . . . Ivanov does not actually believe that Rubashov has committed the preposterous deeds he is charged with. The argument he uses to induce him to confess is that it is a last service required of him by the Party. . . . Gletkin uses the same argument, but his attitude is somewhat different. It is never certain whether he believes Rubashov to be guilty or not; or, more exactly, no distinction between guilt and innocence exists in his mind. The only form of criticism that he is able to imagine is murder. As he sees it, anyone capable of thinking a disrespectful thought about Stalin would, as a matter of course, attempt to assassinate him. Therefore, though the attempt at assassination has perhaps not been made, it can be held to have been made; it exists, like the undrawn production to a line. Gletkin's strength lies in the complete severance from the past, which leaves him not only without pity but without imagination or inconvenient knowledge. On the other hand, it was the weakness of the Old Bolsheviks to have remained Europeans at heart, more akin to the society they overthrew than to the new race of monsters they created. . . .

Brilliant as [*Darkness at Noon*] is as a novel, and a piece of prison literature, it is probably most valuable as an interpretation of the Moscow "confessions" by someone with an inner knowledge of totalitarian methods. (p. 16)

> *George Orwell, in a review of "Darkness at Noon,"*
> *in* The New Statesman & Nation, *Vol. XXI, No. 515,*
> *January 4, 1941, pp. 15-16.*

**HAROLD STRAUSS**

["**Darkness at Noon**"] is the sort of novel that transcends ordinary limitations, and that may be read as a primary discourse in political philosophy. But this observation should frighten no one from the book, for it is written with such dramatic power, with such warmth of feeling, and with such persuasive simplicity that it is as absorbing as melodrama. It is a far cry from the bleak topical commentaries that sometimes pass as novels. It does not dwell on the merely circumstantial aspect of the trials, it bares no secrets, it seeks no escape in mystical generalization about oriental psychology. The trials were peculiarly Russian in their garish externals. But at their core they were a clash between programmatic absolutism and humanitarian democracy.

The accusers were men who were absolutely convinced of the rightness of their program and prepared to ride roughshod over all opposition. They sacrificed people for the sake of a job to be done, while the accused sought to limit the efficient prosecution of the program by a continuous reference to the satisfaction of the people. One comes to the book feeling that the trials were a unique and inexplicable phenomenon; one leaves it feeling that such things can recur (and have recurred) wherever men seek by force to modify the society in which they live. . . .

The men who made the revolution, having conceived its ends abstractly, had to cut themselves off entirely from the standards of traditional morality, and rely solely on faith in their own reasoning. From this arrogant faith derives that absolute dedication which makes men fanatics. They cast themselves on the lap of history and ask only for pragmatic sanctions. For such men doubt is catastrophe. . . .

Although ["**Darkness at Noon**"] is a prison novel, it does not dwell unduly on oppressive details. Rubashov was not barbarously handled. The real, the truly moving dramatic emphasis, once his guilt has been established within the Soviet frame of reference, is on the great decision whether to confess at a public trial or die in silence. The issue is in the hands of two investigating magistrates, Ivanov and Gletkin. They want Rubashov's agreement to a public confession because this is one of the great names of the Revolution, and his unexplained liquidation would have a demoralizing effect upon the people.

Ivanov himself is an Old Bolshevik who can grasp Rubashov's thought processes. He argues with Gletkin, who is young and who wants to use brutally direct methods. (p. 1)

But while outwardly Gletkin wins the duel, inwardly great changes are occurring in Rubashov. He becomes once more a human being, a man of feeling, of subjective sensibilities. While with his mind he is assenting to Gletkin, in his heart he is acknowledging that perhaps man ought not to follow the logical consequences of his thought to the end—"perhaps reason alone was a defective compass, which led one on such a winding, twisting course that the goal finally disappeared in the mist."

The magic effect of "**Darkness at Noon**" is its magnificent tragic irony. For although in a deeply moving final sequence Rubashov makes a public confession and is shot, it is he who is the real victor over his oppressors. He has learned that the word must be made flesh. (pp. 1, 18)

> *Harold Strauss, "The Riddle of Moscow's Trials,"*
> *in* The New York Times Book Review, *May 25,*
> *1941, pp. 1, 18.*

**MAX FISCHER**

I feel unable to agree with those who call ["**Darkness at Noon**"] a good novel. It lacks in epic style, in poetry, in abundance of vision. I don't even like to accept the assumption of the author that he was writing a novel. This is just a psychological study of the strange Moscow trials. Only instead of the real characters who were victims to Stalin's propaganda condemnations, Koestler for reasons of simplification presents one fictitious figure, a typical old revolutionary, persecuted by Stalin and his GPU. This study is done with a clever mind, fond of sophistry and intellectual subtlety. In this respect it is a noteworthy commentary to the politics of our times and should not be neglected by future historians. The book is written in a nihilistic, gloomy mood. A materialistic and atheistic atmosphere is the hopeless *milieu* in which the story is set; future generations, no doubt, will wonder whether its cynic wretchedness can go further or is the high point of desolation among men who have lost the knowledge of God. People of a coming religious century who read such books of our times as Valtin's "Out of the Night" and its counterpart Koestler's "**Darkness at Noon**" will certainly be convinced we lived in hell. (pp. 186-87)

> *Max Fischer, "Trials," in* Commonweal, *Vol. XXXIV,*
> *No. 8, June 13, 1941, pp. 186-87.*

**FRED T. MARSH**

["**Scum of the Earth**"] is not a literary work of that finished quality we associate with Koestler's novels. Parts of it are in the form of extracts taken from his diaries. It has been hurried through, as have most of the best books—and this is one—dealing with immediate issues and events of these terribly important times. I found it completely effective, as it is unaffected and profoundly absorbing all the way through.

In form it is simply a personal story with reflective commentary, the most moving part being the long section devoted to the months spent in the French internment Camp du Vernet d'Ariege in which Koestler describes the routine, portrays his fellow prisoners and the guards, tells a score of stories with the novelist's gift for character drawing and story-telling. But in the way of journalistic interest, it is a running critical commentary on the French governments, leaders, and attitude and thinking of the plain peoples of various interests and persuasions. The strange thing about Camp du Vernet was that most of the groups consisted of anti-Nazi and anti-Facist and anti-Bolshevik emigrés, refugees from Germany, Italy and Russia, respectively, with a sprinkling of nationals from other European countries (like the Hungarian Koestler). The camp was no Dachau . . . ; men died there, some taking their own lives, but nobody was beaten to death. But these two thousand assorted foreigners of all kind, rounded up through panic of an inept and corrupt bureaucracy or through treachery, lived under vile conditions while German prisoners of war and Nazi civilian internees were given fair treatment. . . . Goebbel's cynical humor over radio and in the press . . . , asking the refugees of the French camps what they thought of democratic liberties now, went home to some of them. One of Koestler's acquaintances succeeded in getting a transfer to a real prison camp on the grounds that he was now a Nazi.

All this is merely indicative of the many accounts and records of life in a confused, divided and unprepared France during the early months of the war, unprepared not only materially, but even more so spiritually, a condition running from top to bottom of the social scale, including political elements, right, left and center. . . . While Koestler's account is not a long and involved chronicle and moves swiftly with continuous story interest, it covers a great deal of ground both in its description and in its sharp commentary and fragments of deeply felt and mature reflections.

> Fred T. Marsh, "Personal History of an Anti-Nazi Novelist," in New York Herald Tribune Books, October 5, 1941, p. 3.

## JOHN T. WHITAKER

[The literary merit of **"Dialogue with Death"**]is unmistakable. Mr. Koestler is a writer of talent with a passion for his trade as well as for politics. Living in "the actual expectancy and fear of death," he reflected that few professional writers have an opportunity of studying these processes in the first person singular. Consequently it is the artist, not the journalist, who speaks in **"Dialogue With Death."** By declining to dramatize himself Koestler gives dramatic value to the petty, day-by-day excitements and disappointments of prison life. Thirty days and still no toothbrush. The craving for a cigarette. The mental mathematics, the imaginary conversations and other tricks to cheat time. The illusions and the hopelessness. The oppressive slowness of time in the present and the swiftness in recollection of empty hours, days and weeks once they are in the past. . . .

Koestler's brief three months' participation in the agony of the Spanish people will give Americans—still slightly in the mood of spectators—an insight into the mind of Fascism. . . . Mr. Koestler's five-year-old book is timeless, and as urgent as a dive bomber.

> John T. Whitaker, "The Agony of Spain, Prelude to World War," in New York Herald Tribune Books, July 19, 1942, p. 5.

## THE CATHOLIC WORLD

In substance [*Dialogue with Death*] is no doubt accurate, although quite obviously the author fills in details at times from his imagination rather than his memory. There can be no ques-

tion that many an injustice was committed by defenders of the Nationalist cause. But it is also true that they suffered from wanton cruelty much more than their opponents. Even assuming that Mr. Koestler's story contains no false statement . . . , it still remains a piece of propaganda.

> J. McS., in a review of "Dialogue with Death," in The Catholic World, Vol. CLVI, October, 1942, p. 120.

## CLIFTON FADIMAN

Koestler has a vision, deeper than that of any other writer I can recall, of the murky hell into which the Germans and the Germanoids, with cold enjoyment, have plunged our world. . . . But he is no inscriber of mere horrors, any more than was Dostoevsky, who is sib to him. It is the mind behind the blood-clotted club and the mass asphyxiation that interests him, as it is the mind whose body is battered and broken that arouses his most intense curiosity. I say curiosity, for he writes with deliberative detachment, as if he were not angry.

**"Arrival and Departure,"** . . . is a brief and superbly successful attempt to explain, partly—but only partly—through the insights of psychoanalysis, why a man becomes a martyr. Its hero, Peter Slavek, is a young Central European revolutionary who, despite Fascist torture, has kept the secrets of the underground and so has become a hero to his suffering countrymen. When we first meet him, he is at large in a neutral city, full of emigrés, which, though not named, is presumably Lisbon. His impulse to rejoin the movement is blocked by a number of things: a love affair, his growing doubt of the value of what he has done, the arguments Fascist sympathizers bring to bear on him, and, most important, the influence of Sonia, a woman psychoanalyst.

He falls victim to a purely functional disorder: he cannot move one leg. Sonia's attempt to cure him leads him to give a complete account of his heroic act, and this in turn leads him to a confession of certain childhood traumas which, in Sonia's opinion, adequately explain both his heroism and his neuroses.

Koestler poses the question: Is the moral validity of a great gesture annulled by one's knowledge that it is but the inevitable outcome of some childhood frustration? . . . The solution to this profound problem, central to an understanding of our time, is arrived at through the most subtle and delicate exploration of the human mind, and it is a solution which frees rather than fetters that mind. . . .

["**Arrival and Departure**"] is a book of force, which is not uncommon, but also of understanding, which is rare. It is, in addition, beautifully written, and the sinuous involvements of its plot will lead you mesmerically from the first sentence to the last. If Koestler develops, he may quite conceivably become the great writer of our generation. He has the wisdom, the passion, and the centrality, being close to the inner agony through which we are passing and still must pass. (p. 105)

> Clifton Fadiman, "Arthur Koestler," in The New Yorker, Vol. XIX, No. 40, November 20, 1943, pp. 105-06, 108.

## MALCOLM COWLEY

["**Arrival and Departure**"] is not the novel [Koestler] might have written after "**Scum of the Earth**" and "**Darkness at Noon.**" The trouble seems to be that Koestler is exclusively preoccupied with a moral problem. . . . He omits almost everything else, including the real situation in which the moral decision has to be made.

The decision is whether Peter Slavek, a revolutionist from Central Europe, is to lead his own life or to sacrifice himself for a cause about which he has many doubts. (p. 721)

What you miss in the book as a whole are the details that might explain or lend weight to Peter's decision. Everything except his inner life seems fantastically simple for a refugee. He reaches his port of refuge as a stowaway without a passport, and yet he is never once questioned by the Portuguese police. He runs out of money, and yet this problem is magically settled when [his] doctor offers him a loan. . . . An American visa was immediately forthcoming for this man with an international reputation as a Communist leader, and there was even a steam-ship ticket. . . . (pp. 721-22)

With all the real difficulties overlooked or pushed into the background, **"Arrival and Departure"** misses the color of life among the refugees. What is more important, it gives a curious picture of Peter Slavek himself. He becomes a purely passive figure, a man who is fed, clothed, lodged, healed and provided with papers while making no efforts of his own. Even his dreams are of falling, of undergoing torture, of meeting death; they are never dreams of outwitting his enemies. As a result, you simply cannot believe what Koestler says—that his name "was to become a legend for a whole generation in his country." You cannot believe that any decision taken by such a helpless and introverted character would be of importance to the world outside himself. He might become a martyr, but these are days when martyrdom is easy. There is nothing in the book to show that he could ever become a hero. (p. 722)

> *Malcolm Cowley, "Port of Refuge," in* The New Republic, *Vol. 109, No. 21, November 22, 1943, pp. 721-22.*

## PHILIP TOYNBEE

Arthur Koestler is probably the cleverest novelist writing in English to-day. In our language the word has become a slight—the quality suspect, if not odious. No honest instinct, this, but a bubble bursting on the dough of our stupidity. In itself the word has no intellectual implication, but just as there are clever salesmen and clever politicians, so there are clever intellectuals. Koestler is one of these. His attitude is profoundly and honourably intellectual in that he sees life as a series of mental and moral problems to be solved, or at least to be clearly stated. His cleverness is shown in the subtlety of his solutions and, perhaps even more strikingly, in the clarity of his expositions. His mind is dialectical in the most reputable sense of the word. Here is this attitude, here is its incompatible antithesis and here is a tentative synthesis. So it was in *Darkness at Noon* and so it is in *Arrival and Departure*. (p. 371)

Can it be said that Koestler is too cerebral? I think the answer is a qualified no, and if this review deals largely with the qualifications it assumes a high admiration shared by all who have read *Darkness at Noon* and who, it surely follows, intend to read *Arrival and Departure*. (pp. 371-72)

The book is an argument with premises and conclusion, an argument with a hundred fascinating epiphenomena on the way, rich in metaphor, simile and illustration, clear, brilliant and yet scrupulously honest. Also, and perhaps most important, it is a convincing argument. Koestler has an originality not only of thought but of vision, and the result is that one is sometimes

dazzled into acquiescence by the sheer novelty of the picture. Yet a more reflective later judgment can detect no flaw and no undignified sleight of hand. . . .

The complete novelist will one day use the great discoveries of Freud, and still more, I believe, of Jung as an integrated part of his mental equipment. This does not appear to be Koestler's aim. His interest in psycho-analysis is speculative and intellectual; instead of trying to assimilate and exploit whatever may be of value in it, he uses the theory from *the outside* as a new intellectual counter. Thus it is natural that Slavek should actually undergo an analysis and that only under these peculiar hothouse conditions is the book given new psychological depth. Briefly, Koestler's use of Freud is that of an intellectual rather than of a novelist. As an intellectual he uses him brilliantly, truthfully and imaginatively. . . .

Koestler has often expressed his horror at our insular lack of sympathetic imagination. He knows the abominations of Nazi Europe; we do not, and we make little effort to envisage them. This is certainly a horrifying quality, but I am unwilling to believe that his preoccupation with torture has a didactic motive. Yet I believe that there is little artistic justification for the sheer weight and extremity of detail which is given to these scenes. Other themes are handled as vividly but less importunately.

Finally, and in no sense a reflection on the book, I cannot avoid a certain sympathetic amusement at the persistence of Koestler's Stalinist father-imago. Here he is reduced to a mere shadow, passed from time to time in the street. All ex-members of that party, however deeply convinced of its sins and absurdities, will share the faint irrational guilt of a son towards his disreputable but legitimate parent.

I have criticised *Arrival and Departure* not as a current novel, by which criterion the faintest doubt of its supremacy would be out of place, but as the enduring work of art which I believe it may prove to be. Its qualities are not only of a high but of an extremely rare order, and its failings are the failings of an outstanding talent. (p. 372)

> *Philip Toynbee, in a review of "Arrival and Departure," in* The New Statesman & Nation, *Vol. XXVI, No. 667, December 4, 1943, pp. 371-72.*

## GRANVILLE HICKS

If we are to consider Koestler as a thinker, or at least as a man in search of a way of life, we must take into account the new collection of his essays, *The Yogi and the Commissar*. . . . [There] is certain new material, notably three closely related essays on the Soviet Union and a sequel to the essay that gives the collection its name. Mr. Koestler has at last set forth explicitly his views on Russia, and he has attempted a formal statement of his philosophy. (p. 213)

Koestler's strong language will inevitably seem dangerous not only to Communists and fellow-travelers but also to many liberals and some conservatives. We are told daily that "irresponsible" criticism of Russia is aid and comfort to the enemy, and surely, if one means by "irresponsible" what the dictionary means, this is true. On the other hand, I doubt if the interests of peace will be served by the suspension of critical judgment, which is what many political commentators seem to be calling for. After the signing of the Soviet-Nazi pact, a number of specialists on Russia came forward to tell us all the things that they had not found it expedient to tell us in earlier years, and one wonders if there will be a second outburst of true confessions on some future occasion. Actually, the suppression of honest criticism is a direct encouragement to the invention, circulation, and acceptance of rumors and lies. When there is no honest criticism, the irresponsibles have a field day.

Criticism of Soviet Russia, in other words, need face only the test that all criticism must face, and I believe that Koestler's essays can stand that test. He gives his sources, which are in most instances official Soviet documents, distinguishes clearly between fact and opinion, and sets forth the logical processes by which his conclusions are drawn from the material he cites. No one should suppose—and Koestler himself does not imply—that this is the whole truth about Russia. It is, however, an attempt to arrive at an accurate estimate of prevailing tendencies. (p. 214)

Koestler argues that Communism is a kind of substitute-religion, appealing, in his words, to the thalamus rather than the pallial cortex. It is, however, a false religion, for it rests on the inadequate view of human nature inherent in nineteenth-century materialism. So far he is in agreement with Toynbee. But where Toynbee insists that we must embrace the truth as revealed in a particular religion, Koestler believes we must look for a truth in religions—a truth that for him, but not for Toynbee, is separable from dogma. I cannot feel that Koestler has made a promising beginning in suggesting that we investigate yoga, but I think he is right in believing that the uprooted intellectuals must create their own spiritual home. (p. 219)

Koestler predicts the eventual splitting of the Left into two camps: the followers of Russia and an independent revolutionary movement. Already one sees signs of the division, and the distinguishing marks are temperamental, intellectual, and ethical as well as political. There are people who are natural Communists whether or not they ever accept the party line and the party discipline. Their strength lies in an acute awareness of evil and a determination to do something about it. The acuteness of their sensitivity, however, makes it psychologically impossible for them to be equally aware of all evils. They therefore need a myth to canalize their indignation, to keep their enthusiasm from being dissipated over a multitude of good causes. The same myth, of course, assures them that their actions are significant, and in the areas in which they operate they become hard workers.

Koestler understands the effectiveness of this type and admits his sense of inadequacy when confronted with it. . . . Nevertheless, he realizes how dangerous the type can be. He examines the dangers, however, largely in terms of the Commissar mentality—the logical extension of the type. There are also dangers on less rarefied levels. The rank-and-file Communist gets things done, but he increasingly loses his ability to evaluate what he is doing. On the one hand, he sniffs at the immediate concrete job unless he is officially told that it serves a revolutionary purpose. On the other, he forgets the ultimate goals to which he is theoretically devoted in his preoccupation with the maneuvers that are currently prescribed. At his worst he is either an unthinking tool or a make-believe Commissar, a petty manipulator. At his best he is not likely to escape from self-righteousness and Philistinism. Not only are Communist tactics incompatible with democratic humanism; the party mentality stands in the way of any thoughtful, imaginative approach to the problems of social reconstruction. (pp. 220-21)

Any talk about a new revolutionary movement, as Koestler reminds us, is purely hypothetical, and it would be fatuous to

consider programs and methods at this point. Indeed, I am not sure that we should be talking about a movement at all. One can, however, talk about an attitude. Is it not safe to say, for instance, that "realism," the sacred cow of contemporary radicalism, should be put in its place? Idealism, of course, may lead to insistence on perfection and consequent aloofness, but it need not do so if ideals grow out of a broad understanding of human experience. A revolutionary humanist, I take it, will bear in mind both the best and the worst of which mankind has shown itself capable. He will mingle with his fellows as he finds them, but with participation as his object, not manipulation. He will struggle against evils in himself as well as in the outside world. The good that he desires will seem to him the extension, rather than the negation, of existing good, and he will therefore be in some sense a conservative. But he will be revolutionary in his constant battle against apathy and self-interest and in his determination to apply to social problems the highest vision of human achievement to which he can rise.

But surely, someone will say, this mild benevolence, this gentle echo of Christian socialism, is not adequate to the situations that we see arising in the years after the war. Certainly not. I have been talking merely about an attitude, a spirit, not about the infinitely difficult ways in which it will have to manifest itself to be effective. Even as a description of an attitude what I have said is necessarily vague. Koestler has repeatedly pointed out that a new clarification must precede a new alignment on the Left. He speaks of "an irresistible global mood," "a spiritual spring-tide," "a new 'horizontal' ferment," and none of the phrases satisfies him. For myself, I am tempted to say that a new revolutionary movement must be sustained by such qualities of mind and spirit as I am conscious of when I listen to the music of Mozart and Beethoven. It must, in other words, be related to the deepest experience and the highest aspiration of which men have at any time been capable.

I express myself clumsily, and so, I feel, does Koestler, though he rises at moments to an eloquence I cannot imitate. It is hard for radicals to learn to speak a new language, but they must try if they are to give expression to a new attitude. Whether or not Koestler finds words in which to sum up the meaning of all that he has experienced in the past decade and a half, he has already succeeded in communicating something of the intensity of his hopes, disillusionments, and sufferings. Some of us, especially in America, are fortunate in not having been so drastically uprooted. We must therefore listen all the more attentively to Koestler, for his experiences are significant facts in our world. (pp. 221-22)

*Granville Hicks, "Arthur Koestler and the Future of the Left," in* The Antioch Review, *Vol. V, No. 2, Summer, 1945, pp. 212-23.*

## CLEMENT GREENBERG

Koestler's latest novel [*Thieves in the Night*] is even more negligible as art than his previous ones. But, as we know, art is not the main question with him. And yet this is not to say that the *ad hoc* novel, spot-news fiction, of which he is the most successful practitioner, has nothing whatsoever to do with art. The vulgarities and makeshifts this genre permits the novelist to get away with, even in the eyes of serious readers, contribute no little to the present decline in the general practice of the novel. (p. 580)

Koestler's is the case of a gifted reporter listening to his own remarks, which come from a man the epidermis of whose brain functions better than its core, a man highly sensitive as only the superficial can be to the changing moods of the international, up-to-date, and literate milieu in which he circulates and according to which he cuts his figure. His talent makes the best of superficiality, pretending more plausibly than those who actually do, to understand what it does not and causing his readers to feel that they understand the most precisely when they understand the least. The task of such a talent is not to illuminate our understanding and our experience but to enlighten our public emotions, to post us on the appropriate reactions of the day; it provides us with an etiquette for current events.

Koestler's way of subduing the difficult and rather impersonal material of contemporary politics is to see moral dilemmas everywhere. . . . But one of the most truly problematical aspects of modern politics is precisely that it offers so little opportunity for moral choices and independent action—in other words, so little opportunity for fiction on a high level. He who today wants to write political novels must renounce understanding and be ready to tell or condone the lies of incompleteness. Thus, in Koestler's case as much violence is done to the truth as to fiction. (pp. 580-81).

[*Thieves in the Night* begins] in 1939, the period just before and after the issuance of the British White Paper restricting Jewish immigration and land-purchases in Palestine. The hero, Joseph, is a half-Jewish, half-Anglo-Saxon pioneer on a collective farm who has identified himself with the Jews because of a painful, melodramatic, and cheaply far-fetched incident in his past. Through his and others' eyes we get quick glimpses into every corner of the Palestinian scene: the Arabs, the British, Tel Aviv, Jerusalem, an American journalist, a high-born expatriate of Mayfair, a survivor of the Socialist uprising in Vienna, a survivor of the Gestapo with a "Thing to Forget"— and so on. And it is all done with a great deal of journalistic skill, notwithstanding—or perhaps just because—almost every figure is lay and every situation stock. Since we know so little about Palestine in the flesh it is better, no doubt, to drape that flesh in all its freshness and novelty on a familiar armature taken straight from a run-down novelists' costumes and furnishings firm.

The novel comes to a climax when Joseph joins up with a Jewish terrorist organization. . . . Koestler's defense of the Jewish terrorists seems unqualified. Not only do they spirit illegal immigrants into the country, but they also keep the Arabs quiet by tossing bombs into Arab market places in retaliation for attacks on Jews. They re-assert Jewish dignity by taking fate into their own hands. The conclusive evidence as to Koestler's stand on Jewish politics is the fact that he dedicates his book to the memory of Vladimir Jabotinsky, the founder and late leader of Revisionism, a heretical Zionism that in its attitude toward socialism, the Arabs, and violence can, without distortion, be likened to fascism. Here, just where we most expect it, Koestler fails for the first time to see a moral dilemma. But just here something deeper than morality is at stake for Koestler: namely, his own Jewishness.

The chief feat of this novel and that which will some day be its only claim on our memories is that it is the first time a Jew openly confesses his own self-hatred. . . . When Jews bomb and shoot they are no longer Yids, they behave just like gentiles, they even begin to handle themselves and look like gentiles. Time and again Joseph suffers pangs of revulsion at the sight and behavior of the still unreconstructed Jews in Palestine, but when it comes to describing the junior officers of the ter-

rorist organization, Koestler likens them, in his newfound Anglophilia, to the members of an (English) officers' mess. . . . (pp. 581-82)

Koestler is entitled to his opinion of European Jews, or rather his acceptance of the majority gentile verdict on them; I myself want to take time out only to quarrel with his lack of sophistication on this score. It is possible, I want to suggest, to adopt standards of evaluation other than those of Western Europe. It is possible that by "world-historical" standards the European Jew represents a higher type of human being than any yet achieved in history. I do not say that this is so, but I say it is possible and that there is much to argue for its possibility. No one, I say further, has any right to discuss the "Jewish question" seriously unless he is willing to consider other standards than those of Western Europe. And in so far as their acceptance of the gentile verdict on the European Jew motivates so many of the Zionist leaders, I question their right to decide the Jewish question.

—Aside from all this, and beyond all this, Koestler's own egregiously false notion of what the Anglo-Saxon is (a notion that moves underneath and informs this book) disqualifies him even more profoundly. If he fails to recognize the Anglo-Saxon how can he recognize the Jew? (p. 582)

*Clement Greenberg, "Koestler's New Novel," in* Partisan Review, *Vol. XIII, No. 5, November-December, 1946, pp. 580-82.*

## PHILIP RAHV

Taken as a piece of analytical reporting on Palestine and as comment on the fate of the Jews, Koestler's [*Thieves in the Night*] is significant and wonderfully readable. Taken as a novel, however, it is not good, and that for simple and even obvious reasons.

The truth is that Koestler has very little real feeling for existence as texture and pattern or for his characters as human beings over and above their assigned roles and settings. Hence as a literary artist he is able to create an air of reality but scarcely the conviction of it. It is mostly the historic *Zeitgeist*, rather than the irreducible data of the actual behind or beyond it, that engages his imagination. As a novelist he generalizes far more aptly—and with more speed and daring—than he is able to particularize, whereas the medium of fiction demands that an author earn the right to launch generalizations precisely through his capacity to back them up by means of particulars imaginatively conceived and so presented as to brace and enhance our sense of reality.

But is it really worthwhile to go on with this criticism of Koestler in order to demonstrate that he has no great standing as a practitioner of the art of fiction? The fact is that we do not read him for the sake of the specific pleasure that a fine novel gives us; we read his fiction for the same reasons that we read his non-fiction, since in his case the two forms are virtually interchangeable. . . . Still, call it a novel or a report or a dramatized treatise, *Thieves in the Night* is, to my mind, the best book on the situation of the Jews in Palestine available in English. For Koestler has done what no other writer dealing with that situation has so far succeeded in doing: he has treated the theme of Palestine and the Jewish struggle for survival not as an isolated phenomenon, nor in a philanthropic or goody-goody way, nor from the standpoint of the sectarian Jewish tradition, but as an integral part of the modern world-theme as a whole—the theme of life in "the political ice age," *our* life with its vast, ferocious, and ambiguous social struggles, its unrestricted violence and despair, its betrayals and proscription of entire nations and societies. Thus this book engages our total attention, in the same considerable way that *Darkness at Noon* and *Arrival and Departure* did. It displays Koestler's typical virtues to good advantage: his lively temperament, his sense of irony and scepticism modulating the search for secure ideals, and above all his quality of relevance and awareness. It is for this last quality, particularly, that we like Koestler. In this period of the unmistakable loss of vitality in writing it is very rare. (p. 591)

Koestler differs from the Zionists in making it quite clear that the Arabs have a strong case in Palestine, which is not to be refuted by listing the benefits of Jewish colonization. But the Jews cannot afford the luxury of objectivity—"a race which remains objective when its life is at stake will lose it." It is the British who are mercilessly satirized in the book, for there is neither justice nor basic human need on their side.

Koestler, who is known as the spokesman of disillusioned socialists, is here for once in a position to report favorably on the results of a socialist experiment. Time and again he dwells on the contrast between the frightful results of Russian "socialism" and the achievements of the Jewish communities in Palestine.... Of course, there can be no real comparison between socialism in Russia and in Palestine, if only for the reason that in the latter country the socialists have never been exposed to the temptations bred by the possession of political power. The Jewish communes are nothing more than oases in an area dominated by imperialism. Nevertheless, one cannot but agree with Koestler that this experiment has proven that "under certain conditions a different form of human life could be attained" and that again was "as much as one could hope for."

Throughout this novel author and hero are closely identified. The fact that Joseph is half-Jewish and half-English can be taken as symbolic of Koestler's own estrangement from the Jews, his inner distance from them, and his sense of guilt and inferiority in relation to the greater Gentile world. "Since the days of the prophets," he writes, "self-hatred has been the Jewish form of patriotism." This, of course, is nothing new, though it has seldom been expressed so openly; and the melodrama of the formulation should not deter us from recognizing its basic truth. There is no need to analyze this feeling of self-hatred psychologically, for that has been done time and again and nothing has come of it. For the Jewish intellectuals in America the danger lies in their tendency to admit this feeling, not in order to enter upon a course of action that commits them more deeply to their own Jewishness, thus releasing them of its guilt and strain, but only in order to make themselves appear more interesting, that is to say, more neurotically complicated and therefore deserving of greater consideration. It is plain that this can only lead to more self-assertiveness of the wrong sort and, in the end, to more self-hatred. No, consciousness, meditation, self-analysis are not enough. The real issue is a political one, and that is the way Koestler approaches it. It is political in the sense that it compels us to ask this question: is it possible for the Jews to convert their self-hatred into a positive force for their own reconstruction? It is hatred of the sickness of his own people that turned the poet Stern into a gunman-messiah. Other Jewish poets and thinkers have followed the path of unconditional idealism and of submission to fate. Koestler is not squeamish. He admires the Jews who have tried to master

their fate much more than he can ever admire those who submit to it. That is the deeper meaning of his sympathy with the Jewish terrorists in Palestine. (p. 593)

> *Philip Rahv, "Jews of the Ice Age," in* Commentary, *Vol. 2, No. 6, December, 1946, pp. 591-93.*

## KENNETH RIVETT

*The Yogi and the Commissar* consists mainly of generalisations arising from Koestler's own thought and experience. As a contribution to political science, it suffers from the fact that he is not really typical of any group save the handful of intellectuals who, as International Brigadiers, concentration camp inmates, etc., have paid with their own bodies the price of their convictions. He seems to retain a somewhat naïve belief that there exists a freemasonry of suffering, composed in the first place of the members of this group. One of the services he has rendered is to show the enormous gulf which now separates the Continental atmosphere from that of the English-speaking world—with the result that whereas for us, Marxism symbolises the irrational forces in politics, it has, even for Koestler, the opposite significance. But his freemasonry of suffering is unreal none the less, since people differ too much to draw the same conclusions from similar experiences. His awareness of this, along with his great verbal facility, may have given some readers an impression of insincerity, but it is only the insincerity of those who are too complex to achieve honesty easily. When, indeed, he speaks of "dim realms" where "the right thing has always to be done for the wrong reasons", one does fear that he might become content with the kind of premature synthesis which he has expressly condemned. (p. 93)

> *Kenneth Rivett, "In Defence of Arthur Koestler," in* The Australian Quarterly, *Vol. XIX, No. 3, September, 1947, pp. 90-4.*

## MAX LERNER

Is terrorism ever justified? That is the root problem with which Arthur Koestler deals in his novel about Palestine, *Thieves in the Night.* (p. 51)

I agree with the reviewers who say that Koestler's Palestine story is not a particularly good novel. Joseph, the chief figure in the story, is wooden and without magic—a convenient abacus on which the author makes his moral calculations. Except in ... [*Darkness at Noon*] Koestler has generally failed in the novelist's godlike task of creating people. The fact is that he is less a novelist than a seismograph—to register the convulsive upheavals of the liberal mind and conscience. He turns ideas round and round artfully, to see how they glisten and what consequences they have for the human spirit. (p.52)

Being rooted in the liberal tradition, Koestler's terrorists are tortured at the thought of death as means. But they face the Medusa-head without turning to stone. On the road that leads to the King David Hotel there are no logical stopping-places. And in the face of Arab terrorism, British betrayal, oil power-politics, callousness about the "floating coffins" waiting outside the ports, they embrace the only language ... that is understood universally from Shanghai to Madrid, the Esperanto of the machine gun.

What is most surprising about Koestler's trend is that it seems to reverse what he has said in every book from *Darkness at Noon* through *The Yogi and the Commissar.* In those books he attacked the Communists because they acted on the principle that the ends justify any means. Yet here, as a Zionist revisionist, he is invoking sympathetic understanding for a gang which defends terrorism as a means toward the sacred end of national liberation.

There is a possible way out of Koestler's dilemma. It is to make a distinction between terror by the state against dissenting groups (as in Russia, and even more in fascist totalitarianisms), and terror by a small desperate people struggling against imperialist oppression, as formerly with the Irish, and now with the Palestinian Jews.

Another approach is to say, as Koestler does, that we live in a political ice age; and that until the ice clears away, only the glacial elements of the human spirit have any chance of surviving. . . . All war is legalized terrorism, and in an age when the preparation for war forms the logic of statesmanship and science, it is too much to expect the completed nation-states to have the monopoly of terrorism. The nation-state struggling for being is bound to be infected by it.

All this can be argued, but in the end the decision will not be made by those who stand by as observers, but by the Palestine Jews. It is they who will have to die or kill, they who will have to make the stony Palestinian earth yield enough to sustain their brothers from Europe if they can get their brothers in. (pp. 52-3)

> Max Lerner, "Koestler on Terrorism," in his Actions and Passions: Notes on the Multiple Revolution of Our Time, *Simon and Schuster, 1949, pp. 51-3.*

**PERRY MILLER**

"The Age of Longing" is a novel with a plot: an American girl in Paris, in a year that is vaguely 1955 or '56, has an affair with a Russian "cultural attaché," discovers that she hates his philosophy, tries to shoot him, and is shipped home. Meanwhile she encounters a punctiliously selected array of people, each neatly embodying a precise aspect of the present intellectual and spiritual predicament.

There is the worldly, aristocratic old cynic, the liberal intellectual disillusioned with Stalinism, the existentialist, the American colonel on a mission, the Pole tortured into madness, the Soviet poet who tries to escape and fails, the Catholic cleric, the French resistant who prepares for again resisting. And of couse there is the lover—the Neanderthal man, the man of the future, the product of the Revolution, the Russian.

Upon the heroine, at long last, nothing is lost, and on the final pages she conveniently rounds up the dramatis personae in a stream-of-consciousness inventory, ticking them off so that nothing will be lost on us. She sums them up: all are "sick with longing." . . .

The difficulty is that we have met all these characters repeatedly in recent fiction, and that here they are wooden and mechanical . . . The stage-managing is so crude that the wires creak. The American speech between the girl and her father is ludicrous. . . . Sex, the indispensable element, is judiciously ladled out. The plot develops "suspense," as would be taught in correspondence courses: the girl pulls the trigger, she has forgotten the safety-catch; then she fires, the Russian falls, and we race through the next pages until the artful author tells us that she merely wounded her target. Everyone speaks in character, and no cue is lost. . . .

What . . . nags at one's mind is how the author of **"Darkness at Noon"** can have come after eleven years to making out of the agony of our time a novel so conventional and often tedious. You are bound to perceive that he is intelligent, in fact so much so that he anticipates your mood: when the two veterans of the Resistance are about to go underground again, to hiding, hunger, and torture, one of them yawns and the other says, "The funny thing is that I too feel more bored than anything else." The liberal focuses all his wisdom into the motto that the only solution is to comprehend everything and to forgive oneself nothing. But for all Koestler's undoubted ability to comprehend the panorama of viewpoints represented by his characters, they all seem to be attitudes we find in every daily newspaper. The boredom of a man about to go into battle is not the same thing as boredom communicated to a reader. . . .

I suspect that the book will reach some such audience. . . . Still—one cannot help feeling that a writer of Koestler's stature just simply *ought* to write a better book.

> Perry Miller, "Koestler As Pedagogue," in The Nation, *Vol. 172, No. 9, March 3, 1951, p. 207.*

**R.H.S. CROSSMAN**

[*The Age of Longing*] is a conversation between Mr. Koestler and the Devil, in which Mr. Koestler gives the Devil a superb brief, but still seems surprised and resentful when the Devil proceeds to win the argument.

Diabolism of this sort—and the boastful self-pity and self-contempt which nearly always accompany it—are frequent features in first novels. The young writer "sees through Communism" and yet hankers for the Utopia he has intellectually rejected. What is unusual is that a writer of Mr. Koestler's vitality and imagination should linger in this age of longing, and present a grimace in the looking-glass as the truth about contemporary France. For the strength of France—and indeed of any democracy—resides not in abstract ideas and abstracted intellectuals, but in countless ordinary people, with the ordinary responsibilities for the ordinary decisions of everyday life. If he is to fulfil his superb talents as a novelist, Mr. Koestler should take a holiday from the politics of the intelligentsia, and learn, like Balzac, to enjoy *La Comédie Humaine.* Ex-communism is a sterile state of mind. (p. 484)

> R.H.S. Crossman, "Darkness at Night," in The New Statesman & Nation, *Vol. XLI, No. 1051, April 28, 1951, pp. 482, 484.\**

**CHARLES ROLO**

[In *Arrow in the Blue*] Koestler has analyzed more discerningly than any of the other celebrated ex-Communists the inner tensions and obsessions which, acted on by contemporary history, led him to embrace "the new faith." . . .

Koestler's primary concern is to anatomize the emotional pathology which led him and others to surrender themselves totally to the Party. His childhood, filled with "guilt, fear and loneliness," left him with a sense of isolation and the protective habit of cultivating a "false personality." . . . At fourteen, precociously well-read in science, Koestler ran up against the paradox of Infinity and it started to haunt him until it became "sheer torture." This obsession with the unsolved riddle of Infinity was the beginning of a quest which was to make him a "Casanova of Causes"; a Casanova in search of the ideal

Helena; a disciple in search of the all-knowing mentor; a pilgrim in search of Utopia—"The form of the rash changed, but the disease remained the same . . . absolutitis." Koestler defines this "disease," more specifically, as a longing for the certainty afforded by a "closed" system of belief, of which Communism is only one—a system which furnishes all-embracing answers and a logic of its own which annihilates all criticism.

Coming as it does from Koestler, this analysis has devastating implications in regard to precisely the kind of ex-Communists—the absolutists who surrendered body and soul to the Party—who have been dramatizing themselves as the oracles of our day. The symptoms change, but the disease remains the same—an all-or-nothing mentality which finds it repugnant to live in an intellectually open world. . . .

Koestler's personal history seems to me on the whole the most convincing, and certainly the most human, of his books. It has lapses into intellectual flashiness, but they are less frequent, and there is less stridency, than heretofore. V. S. Pritchett has said that Koestler gives the impression of writing with a pneumatic drill and wishing it were a machine-gun. *Arrow in the Blue* sounds as though it might have been written with a fountain pen.

*Charles Rolo, in a review of "Arrow in the Blue," in* The Atlantic Monthly, *Vol. 190, No. 4, October, 1952, p. 90.*

## EMANUEL LITVINOFF

'A typical case history of a member of the educated middle classes of Central Europe in our time' is Koestler's description of [*The Invisible Writing*]. . . . A good deal of hyperbole has been used to describe the activities of Central European intellectuals in the Thirties, but I doubt whether many were in the habit of wandering about Soviet Central Asia, of acting as full-time propaganda scribes of the Comintern, of writing encyclopaedias of sex, or of being held in solitary confinement in Spanish prison cells under sentence of death. Koestler was in all of these situations, and in others equally exceptional, and for scarcely a single moment can I be convinced that he was anything but an unusually brilliant and hypersensitive individual ranging the decline and fall of European civilisation. He was spared the total annihilation that overtook most of his generation either by a remarkable series of chances, or by a gift of personality that would enable him (almost) to keep afloat in a sea of mud. Yet if Koestler's life is not entirely a typical case history, it is one that has suffered from a universal European malady. . . .

There have been enough accounts, some genuine, some contrived, from former Communists of their adventures in chasing the devious party line, or in scurrying between the capitals of Europe on enigmatic errands for Kremlin *Apparaten* and Communist front-organisations, to leave little room for surprise. Where Koestler's book is particularly valuable is in its analysis of the mind and soul of a neurasthenic idealist during a seven years' journey through the closed system of Communist dialectics. (p. 26)

*The Invisible Writing* . . . poses an irresistible question. Are the Koestlers, the Malrauxs, the Weissbergs, and the Silones the right people to lead Western Europe to sanity? Believing in their integrity and their goodwill, I am not bold enough to offer more than a tentative answer; that perhaps these men are still convalescent after the prolonged sickness of their Communism; that until they have regained wholeness they can only express despair with conviction. As one of the most formidable ex-Communists of them all, Manes Sperber, has written: 'Mark this carefully: we stormed heaven not that we might live there, but in order to show all mankind, *ad oculis*, that heaven is empty.' (pp. 27-8)

*Emanuel Litvinoff, in a review of "The Invisible Writing," in* The Spectator, *Vol. 193, No. 6575, July 2, 1954, pp. 26-8.*

## JOSEPH G. HARRISON

As is customary with Koestler, **"The Invisible Writing"** may be said to be one-third fact, one-third psychology, and one-third speculation. Yet the result is a volume that is both interesting and instructive. Frequently complex, it is never dull. Often highly personal, it somehow manages to give a more than merely personal breadth to the author's experiences and conclusions. It has been said that there is no more interesting man writing today than Arthur Koestler. This book will not cause a revision of that view.

*Joseph G. Harrison, "A Pilgrim from Moscow," in* The Christian Science Monitor, *October 21, 1954, p. 11.*

## CHARLES FRANKEL

Novelist, essayist and political man of action, Arthur Koestler emerges in [**"The Sleepwalkers"**] as a historian of the sciences. He traces, with a comic writer's eye and a moralist's sensibility, the curious, disjointed steps by which modern astronomy forged its fundamental principles and changed man's view of his place in the universe. But if Mr. Koestler has a new subject, he continues to pursue an old theme, a theme that has been central in the moral experience of his generation and that has dominated his own many-sided career.

Mr. Koestler's **"Darkness at Noon"** was an exploration of the dilemmas, ambiguities and rationalized blindnesses that arise when men try to live by ideas they consciously adopt. His essays on politics, religion and esthetics, have had a similar concern, and have drawn their vitality from his conviction that human thinking does not change in its fundamental character, that it has the same sources and purposes, no matter in what domain it operates.

In **"The Sleepwalkers"** Mr. Koestler continues to wrestle with the old problem of his and ours. Although the book deals ostensibly with man's ideas about the heavens, its underlying theme is man's ideas about his own ideas. . . .

The "sleepwalkers" of Mr. Koestler's title are the great figures in the history of modern cosmology—Copernicus, Kepler, Galileo, Newton. They are "sleepwalkers," according to Mr. Koestler, as are, indeed, most of the creative minds in the history of science, because they never quite knew what they were doing. . . .

Mr. Koestler's favorite among the figures he discusses is the German astronomer, Johannes Kepler (1571-1630), and a remark of Kepler's catches Mr. Koestler's basic theme: "The roads by which men arrive at their insights into celestial matters seem to me almost as worthy of wonder as these matters in themselves."

This is the main burden of the story Mr. Koestler tells. It begins with an account of Greek science and philosophy, conventional in content but lively in style, in which Mr. Koestler drives home his point that there is a "common source of inspiration" behind religion and science, faith and reason. After a transitional section on the Middle Ages, in which Mr. Koestler does not hide his contempt for the fearfulness, superstition and brutality of an age which condemned the scientific impulse, there follow portraits of the personalities and intellectual achievements of the four great pioneers who cut through to the modern view of the cosmos. (p. 6)

Whatever the verdict of other historians may be on the portraits Mr. Koestler draws, Mr. Koestler's main purpose is surely achieved. He shows that there is a vast contrast between our ideals of rational thought and the actual creative processes by which the heroes of modern science came to their discoveries. It is greatly to his credit, furthermore, that he does not use this contrast to denigrate the achievements of the men whose story he tells, but uses it instead to combat the popular misconception that scientific thinking is a purely mechanical affair and has nothing imaginative about it.

Although he does not make the point nearly explicit enough, it seems plain that he accepts the indispensable distinction that must be made between the psychological processes of scientific discovery and the logical criteria by which the validity of these discoveries must be judged. Men do not come to their insights by immaculately logical processes. Their thinking moves by leaps in the dark, through fruitful errors and inchoate visions. But the truth or falsehood of the ideas to which men come by such processes can be determined only by neglecting their genesis and applying impersonal standards of logic and evidence.

Mr. Koestler, however, also argues that modern science has a "metaphysical bias" like any other view of the universe. It assigns reality only to the measurable aspects of things, and has made us take moral values less seriously. Mr. Koestler believes that the result is an "end-justifies-the-means ethics (that) may be a major factor in our undoing." Mr. Koestler is surely right to believe that there is no more reason to idolize scientists than to idolize anyone else. Nevertheless, this complaint about modern science is puzzling.

In the first place, not all of modern science is in fact mathematical. And even more to the point, the Middle Ages, whose science was neither mathematical nor materialistic, were not conspicuous, as Mr. Koestler himself makes very plain, for their moral virtue; nor were they strangers to an "end-justifies-the-means ethics." . . .

Nevertheless, Mr. Koestler has written an unusually lively and informative book. He has succeeded in bringing the astronomers down to earth. If there were more understanding of science as a human enterprise, there might be less of a tendency either to worship science as a savior or to damn it as an alien intruder on the human scene. (p. 30)

*Charles Frankel, "The Road to Great Discovery Is Itself a Thing of Wonder," in* The New York Times Book Review, *May 24, 1959, pp. 6, 30.*

## KATHLEEN NOTT

[*The Act of Creation* is about] creativity and uniqueness—the way that we are, in fact or potentially, free beings, not automata—or more justly, the way that some beings have been able to emerge, at least from time to time, from their conditioned habituality. But the book is not in itself a philosophy or counter-philosophy: it is not even exactly a psychology of aesthetics. Rather it is an attempt to discern a pattern of behavior that runs through the whole living universe and is most representatively human in art and science. So you might call it a new *myth*—in no derogatory sense, but as a premonition of what might become a science. (p. 84)

The common pattern which Mr. Koestler discerns in original scientific discovery, in painting and in music, in poetry and fiction, in both comedy and tragedy, can be seen at its most primitive in the anatomical structure of a joke. Here are the two incompatible "matrices" or contexts, in uncomplicated visibility. I quote an example, not because it is by any means the best joke . . . , but because of its compactness:

> A convict was playing cards with his jailers.
> On discovering that he cheated, they kicked
> him out of jail.

"It can be analyzed," says Mr. Koestler, "in a single sentence—two conventional rules ('offenders are punished by being locked up' and 'cheats are punished by being kicked out') each of them self-consistent, collide in a given situation." This is the bisociational pattern which Mr. Koestler . . . proceeds to track down and illustrate, not only in the mind and works of man, but throughout the living universe. . . . (pp. 84, 86)

The chief significance of [the] structural concept of matrix and code emerges when Mr. Koestler pursues his bisociational creative pattern into the non-human cosmos. Here the quality of matrix and code is developed into the concept of the hierarchical organization of all living organisms, individual and social—a concept which Mr. Koestler carries, with copious illustration, right down into the myriad varieties of motility among the minor organisms ("The lowliest creature and the highest, the moment it is hatched or born, lashes out at the environment"). The central nervous system, in other words, is not a repetitive machine—it allows local autonomy, free play on the periphery.

This holistic and purposive idea of living behavior is aimed again at the Behavioristic foe—nowhere, however, in this book, it must be emphasized, treated as an Aunt Sally, nor as an excuse for dead-horse-flogging. Mr. Koestler places himself, that is to say, on flexible terms with his opponents, in whom he is widely versed, and some of whom indeed, in the later developments of experimental psychology and learning theory, can be shown to be just about on his side. That rats running mazes can acquire a kind of "insight," a map in the head, is conceded by a number of experimentalists. (p. 86)

[Koestler] comments that 20th-century psychology of all kinds has mostly taken the "detensional" view of motivation, according to which the reduction of painful stimuli either from inside or from outside is what powers the machine. But while he himself regards this picture as "depressingly correct up to a point"—meaning, I take it, that most of us most of the time are habitual automata and copiers—he claims that here he starts from the point where the doctrine is no longer true. He is writing, in short, about geniuses, the actual examples of the original's break with habit, either his own habits of thought, or the unobserved and unreflected assumptions which he has picked up from collective existence. (pp. 86, 88)

Mr. Koestler is excellent and very illuminating on the real history of ideas, for instance on the "linear" illusion that science, at least, makes a straight progression. He has a melancholy list of mistakes, cases of "snow-blindness," when the best qualified missed the most obvious conclusions—and of the collective resistance to innovation of scientific "establishments" of all sorts. Though, unlike other "churches," the scientific establishments have not usually garbled the founding Word, they have often conveniently mislaid it—or even buried it with dark rites.

To show us the scientist as a real human being reacting to a real and very haphazard world of buzzing experiences is the main intention of the book. But although Mr. Koestler is so much better—as well as more heartening—on the subject of a pleasurable motivation than the psychological schools he attacks, his own view has limitations. He allows, and rightly, a large place for curiosity—from rats in mazes to scientists (including no doubt experimental psychologists). But the reward which is also the incentive for both scientists and artists is our old acquaintance, the Freudian "oceanic feeling" (a mystical sense of oneness with something-or-the-other). I just don't believe that this is a true description. In my view, there is a real and quite special disinterestedness in any true act of creation; it is also an act of vision which is extremely convincing and reassuring to the seer about the nature of reality, about what is *there,* and hence it is peculiarly satisfying.

While Mr. Koestler has produced an extremely vivid and comprehensive account of the *origins* of originality . . . , he seems to be somewhat weaker on its evaluation, on what validates discoveries and performances and puts them in a scale of values and gives them their rightful place in the worlds of knowledge and appreciation. [*The Act of Creation*] is too big a book in every way, however, not to have discoverable weaknesses. And we should be endlessly grateful to a writer who can manage to be stimulating on nearly every one of 700-odd pages. Mr. Koestler's "myth" is a splendid pair of spectacles for looking at a vastly enriched psychological landscape. (p. 88)

> Kathleen Nott, "The Bloom and the Buzz," in Commentary, *Vol. 38, No. 5, November, 1964, pp. 84, 86, 88.*

## LESLIE FIEDLER

[*This essay originally appeared in* The New Statesman and Nation, *October 27, 1967.*]

The title of Arthur Koestler's most recent book [*The Ghost in the Machine*] seems to me terrifyingly apt in a way he did not intend; for he himself is, and has long been, a ghost: the ghost of a man who died when his God failed. But I continue to read him—strain to hear the words he brings back from the Other Side and speaks from the shadowy periphery of the world at whose centre I am still condemned to live. . . . Koestler helped to deliver me from the platitudes of the Thirties, from those organised self-deceptions which, being my first, were especially dear and difficult to escape.

Nonetheless, I am—perhaps for that very reason—all the more dismayed to find the wisdom of [his] early works, once central to the experience of the young, re-echoed with a dying fall at a moment when it has come to seem offensively irrelevant. Bound to recapitulate the moment of terror attendant on their taking off, ghosts are inevitably bores. And such a bore Koestler proves himself, when, approaching the climax of his book, he cannot resist quoting (for publication in 1967) his own words

written in 1954 about his encounter with Stalinism in the Thirties. . . . (p. 162)

[There] is a special index to his book called "On Not Flogging Dead Horses," in which Koestler . . . argues that the horses he flogs cannot really be dead, since some men still ride them. And once more there is the compulsive allusion to Stalinism. . . . But in the land of the dead, quite obviously there are dead riders as well as dead floggers of dead beasts; and though in a pinch one would choose the floggers over the riders, best of all would be to be spared both.

To be sure, Koestler does refer occasionally to the world of the living, which is to say, the world of the young, to whom Stalin and J. B. Watson, along with Hitler and Freud, are figures quite as historically remote as Akhnaton or Napoleon; and he even cites a couple of sentences from J.B.S. Haldane in a chapter called "Evolution CTD: Undoing and Redoing" which might well have led him to the realisation that more and more the world which all of us, young or old, inhabit is precisely the world of the young. . . . But Koestler does not pause to reflect on the implication of an observation that, physiologically as well as psychologically, sociologically, mythically, youth rather than maturity is destined to become man's fate—and that this change may well represent the essential human transcendance of our animal beginnings.

The problem seems to be that Koestler is moved by a scarcely concealed hatred and resentment of the young, the envy—one is tempted to say—of the dead for the living. What else can explain the sheer nastiness, compounded by arrogant superficiality, of his offhand remark about "the hordes of screaming teenage Bacchantae mobbing Popstars, and the leering teenage Narcissi coiffured like cockroaches." Popular Culture is for Koestler as utterly contemptible as the young who produce and consume it; though in fact it can be argued that his own book represents precisely the assimilation of science to that Popular Culture. Searching for the ultimately pejorative epithet he is as likely as not to find it in the word "Pop." In one place, at any rate, he speaks of the "Pop-Nirvana" imagined by Aldous Huxley, and in another, of the "perversions of Pop-Zen" in the works of Suzuki. Huxley and Suzuki, however, are among the very few thinkers alluded to by Koestler who appeal at all to the sort of young men and women for whom the writers he admires or on whom he vents his spite scarcely exist at all. (pp. 163-64)

Koestler himself knows quite well that words, though they may kill gods, cannot annihilate devils. "Like the reader," he confesses as he prepares to conclude, "I would prefer to set my hopes on moral persuasion by word and example. But we are a mentally sick race, and as such deaf. . . ." And so he turns to pharmacology, the use of mind-altering drugs, as a last desperate hope. And here, at last, he has entered the living world, *materialised,* as the spiritualists say of their apparitions. How familiar, even fashionable, are the very terms he employs: we must turn to "the Pill" to achieve a "Final Revolution"; we must strive for the "beneficial mutation" of our species, otherwise doomed because of an imbalance between the archaic, instinctive part of the brain and the newer, more rational part. It might well be Leary himself speaking, or—to turn to the despised world of Pop-music, the Mothers of Invention, who inscribed on the jacket of their album, "Freak Out," the slogan: JOIN THE UNITED MUTATIONS.

At the very least, he seems to be seconding his own contemporary, Aldous Huxley, who, in *The Gates of Perception* and

*Heaven and Hell,* foresaw a situation, a dilemma, of whose meanings some of us even now are less aware than he was then. But Koestler hastens to assure us that he profoundly disagrees with Huxley's advocacy of "mescalin and other psychodelic drugs"—and his misspelling of the word "psychedelic," so recently invented but already so familiar, tells us even more than his statement itself about where, in the peripheral shadows, he continues to stand. Or perhaps Koestler has mis-written it deliberately as one mis-speaks the name of an antagonist one pretends to despise. But to write "psychodelic" with conscious intent as a snide reference perhaps to the mad protagonist of Alfred Hitchcock's thriller is to compound the offence. That the New Revolution, the latest Final Combat has moved from the larger world to the smaller and will be settled, with the aid of psychochemistry, inside our skulls he knows very well. But he has declared his allegiance to the Other Side from that on which such new prophets as Norman O. Brown and R. D. Laing have taken a stand—favouring not the release of the repressed archaic in us, but the restoration of a "hierarchic order," in which thought and emotion are to be united under the hegemony of thought. It is the old Freudian song set to a new tune: the hope that where *id* was *ego* will be—with the help of a Pill this time around, since the Couch has failed. But, alas, all the Pills invented or rediscovered so far are on the side of the *id;* the Freudian Pill remains still a dream. (pp. 165-66)

> Leslie Fiedler, "Toward the Freudian Pill," in Arthur Koestler: A Collection of Critical Essays, *edited by Murray A. Sperber, Prentice-Hall, Inc., 1977, pp. 162-66.*

## GRANVILLE HICKS

Koestler is one writer who has done what C. P. Snow, in *The Two Cultures,* urged all writers to do: he has familiarized himself with the methods and conclusions of modern science. He hasn't, of course, become an authority on all the sciences; Leonardo da Vinci himself couldn't do that today; my impression is that the most eminent scientist is expert in only one small part of his chosen field. But Koestler has tried to learn enough about physics, chemistry, biology, and psychology to understand what they have to say about the nature and probable future of the human race.

*The Ghost in the Machine* is a bold examination of the human predicament at the present moment. The development of science in the past three centuries, which has benefited the race in so many ways, has made possible its destruction. Koestler, indeed, is prepared to argue that extinction is certain if things go on the way they are going now. Why, he asks, are they going that way, and what can we do about it?

Koestler spends half the book in clearing the ground by attacking the Behaviorists in psychology and the neo-Darwinians in biology. . . . [He] shows how inadequate their theories are, and in doing so he offers subtler and more persuasive explanations of the development of the species and the formation of the mind. Koestler has always felt that the great discoveries of science resemble the creative acts of the great artists, and he distrusts any scientist who denies the importance of the imagination.

Having dealt with preliminaries, Koestler is ready to examine the nature of man now. According to him, the human being contains both integrative and self-assertive potentials, and, contrary to what is usually assumed, "the integrative tendencies

of the individual are incomparably more dangerous than his self-assertive tendencies." (pp. 39-40)

In order to explain how this unhappy situation has developed, Koestler begins by describing the nature of the brain. The fore part of the brain, the neocortex, has grown rapidly in recent milennia. The older part, on the other hand, has changed little since the age of the reptiles, and the great trouble is that the two parts are badly coordinated. "The Papez-MacLean theory," Koestler writes, "offers strong evidence for the dissonant functioning of the phylogenically old and new cortex, and the resulting 'schizophysiology' built into our species." Instinct and intellect have been out of step since the beginning of what we call civilization, and that is why the tremendous growth in knowledge and power threatens to destroy the race. . . . Koestler believes that, with the progress of biochemistry, a cure may be found—a drug perhaps that will bring about "a state of dynamic equilibrium in which thought and emotion are re-united, and the hierarchic order is restored."

Whatever else may be true, Koestler is a master of exposition. He uses the jargon of the specialized scientists only when it is essential to do so, and then he explains his terms. . . . As for his central argument, I am not competent to judge it, but to me, as we say when we are not too sure of ourselves, it makes sense. At any rate, Koestler recognizes a crisis when he sees one, and is conscientious enough to try to do something about it. The drug he talks about might, as he recognizes, become an instrument of tyranny, but not all scientific discoveries have been abused, and if ever desperate measures were called for, they are now. For myself, I hope that the drug is discovered in time. (pp. 40, 52)

> Granville Hicks, "A Prescription for Social Ills," in Saturday Review, *Vol. LI, No. 8, February 24, 1968, pp. 39-40, 52.*

## CHARLES I. GLICKSBERG

The emotional need that drove many intellectuals to embrace Communism was largely religious in character, though in public they explained their motives as part of a world-historical movement. Later, after casting off this pseudo-religious absolutism, the ex-Communists tried to atone for their past excesses by telling the truth about their former relation to Communism. Of the essays published in *The God That Failed,* Arthur Koestler's confession is the most poignantly revealing, the most impassioned in its repudiation of the ideology he had once sworn by, the most unsparingly documented. By the time he decided to leave the Party, he knew to what an alarming extent faith, in politics as in religion, springs from irrational sources. (pp. 277-78)

During the forties and fifties Koestler searched his conscience to discover the reasons that impelled him to join the Communist camp. His craving for the absolute of faith was so strong that he was ready for "the leap.". . . Courageously, in novels and essays, he portrayed the personality of the Communist who finally perceives that the Soviet Union is not the Earthly Paradise. Koestler turned to the depth psychology of Freud to unravel the tangled skein of unconscious motives that lead "the true believer" to choose the fate of martyrdom. In *Arrival and Departure,* he shows what happens to a revolutionary who, as the result of an inner conflict between the call of love and his desire to offer himself as a sacrifice for the Revolution, develops a "beautiful" neurosis. (p. 278)

Koestler gradually became convinced that the Revolution had been betrayed. The left-wing intellectuals were themselves responsible for this shameful betrayal. (p. 279)

Disillusioned, uprooted, bitter as he reviews the events of his past, the ex-Communist continues to feel vaguely guilty even as he goes through the elaborate ritual of atonement. He must start a new life. He has lost his former dogmatic confidence that the Revolution will automatically transform human nature. The revolutionary writer who has thrown off the ideological spell that held him so long in mental bondage must find a new, dynamic purpose in life. It is this painful experience of awakening from the messianic delusions of the past that Koestler analyzes in his anti-Communist fiction.

*The Gladiators* illustrates Koestler's obsessive theme: the ambiguous morality of politics, the pitfalls that lie in the path of those who struggle to establish perfect justice on earth. *The Gladiators* develops the paradox, which also informs Sartre's play *The Devil and the Good Lord:* that the will to do good often entails the use of evil means and hence brings about evil consequences. Spartacus sees that the revolution for which so much blood had been shed was doomed. He is trapped, forced to fight, and his slave legions are slaughtered by the Roman troops. But this disastrous defeat was foreshadowed by a series of events long before the actual massacre took place. The slaves were overcome because they had lost their revolutionary fervor. *The Gladiators* ends on a pessimistic note: freedom is not easy to achieve; men, the mediators of the revolutionary dialectic, are essentially imperfect. (pp. 279-80)

The terrible dilemma of the Communist who loses his revolutionary faith is brilliantly depicted in *Darkness at Noon*. . . . How far, Koestler asks, is the revolutionary saint perpared to go in his fanatical devotion to the utopian future? Is he willing to employ "evil" means in order to achieve desirable ends? Is he sufficiently disciplined, like the masked Comrades in Brecht's *The Measures Taken*, to end the lives of others if the millennium can thus be more quickly reached? And yet circumstances often arise when the most humane of men feel justified in killing those who are the enemies of the ideal. The utopian revolutionary is not held back by moral considerations. In *Darkness at Noon*, Ivanov the Communist is not troubled by finicky scruples about the sanctity of life. Those who oppose the Revolution are simply put out of the way. But Rubashov, who is made of different clay, wonders why hosts of innocent victims must be slain on the altars of the Revolution. Rubashov ponders this moral problem as he broods about his past: did not the needs of the collectivity justify all such actions? (p. 280)

Through [Rubashov's] eyes we behold the corruption of the regime, the spirit of ideological conformity that is made to prevail, the despotic control of the masses. Rubashov, as a revolutionary, had paid no heed to "bourgeois" distinctions between good and evil. Truth, he had argued, is identical with utility. The Party, in pursuing its ends, has had to sacrifice many men. Now it is his turn to be the scapegoat. Inwardly he is convinced that the fate of the individual is of no significance; the forward march of Communism must not be halted even if the victories it wins cost the lives of millions. . . . In the solitude of his cell it is these theories that rise up to haunt him. He sees that his past was a horrible lie. How could he have believed that the Party incarnated the will of history? He perceives that the Soviet Union no longer represents the ideals of the Revolution. It has become a dictatorship, a bureaucracy.

But if this is what Rubashov thinks, then he is indeed guilty of counterrevolutionary opposition. The Party in power affirms

its belief in truth as an expression of expediency. Whatever is conducive to "success," whatever helps to kindle the fire of faith in the masses, even though myths, painted in black and white, are specially invented for their consumption—all this is to be approved by the loyal members of the Party. Had not Rubashov acted on the assumption that the end justified the means? Rubashov, by thus probing the depths of his conscience, not only destroys his usefulness to the Party but also proves a traitor to the revolutionary cause. Ivanov argues: "The principle that the end justifies the means is and remains the only rule of political ethics . . . ." It is this Machiavellian system of ethics that Rubashov is beginning to reject. . . . If social utility is to be regarded as the sole criterion of moral value, then Rubashov realizes that he must yield to the demands of the Party, for only in that way can he be useful. Since the old revolutionaries have outlived their usefulness, they must make their exit from the stage of history. As Rubashov waits to be executed, he wonders whether it is not possible to run amok in pure reason and even to commit atrocious crimes in its name. Perhaps, he brooded, minutes before he was put to death, there lay the chief source of the evil: the elimination of the ethical standard. (pp. 283-85)

Apart from his attacks on Communism and the Soviet dictatorship, Koestler made a valuable contribution in exposing the doctrinaire fraudulence of Marxist aesthetics, which wished to exploit literature and art for the sake of hastening the proletarian revolution. In a speech delivered at the International Congress of the P.E.N. Club, Koestler described the temptations the novelist must fight against. He may decide to withdraw from the world and shut himself within his own room, where he can pursue beauty undisturbed, thus becoming a virtual Yogi of the arts. The other temptation is to open wide the window of his room and portray, if not participate in, the dynamic swirl of events going on outside. The third temptation, "the hole-in-the-curtain method," represents a compromise: the novelist leaves his window partly open and gets a limited perspective, a peephole view of the world.

According to Koestler, the perfect novel calls for a window that is open to all the winds and vistas of the world. Though the novelist should have an all-encompassing knowledge of the forces that shape his world, he must be more than a "realist." Though he must portray life against the setting constituted by the dominant tendencies of his age, these background factors—war, science, politics, labor conflicts, Communism—must be assimilated and given life in terms of the experiences the characters undergo. The novelist is not a reporter. In creative fiction, whatever is told must be imaginatively reenacted, convincingly *lived*. For that reason the writer must keep the windows of his room wide open and must take the long view.

The function of the intelligentsia is to be critical, nonconformist, a creative and therefore "revolutionary" source of protest. It is the duty of the writer to contrast the life man actually leads with the kind of life he might lead. This vision of the ideal places the artist in perpetual opposition to the society of his time, and the hostility of society deepens the process of neurotic alienation. Because of their alienation, the literati suffer from an exacerbated guilt-complex, and occupational neurosis. The case of Koestler versus the Communists is virtually closed. Though Koestler is still productive, he has stopped writing about politics. His diatribes of the forties and fifties are dated, but he was influential at the time in helping a number of writers free themselves from a closed-in system of political absolutism that repressed their creative activity. He taught them that there is more between heaven and earth and in the heart of man than is included in the philosophy of Marxism. (pp. 287-88)

*Charles I. Glicksberg, "Arthur Koestler and the Revolution Betrayed," in his* The Literature of Commitment, *Bucknell University Press, 1976, pp. 277-88.*

**MARK LEVENE**

The pre-eminent Cold War personality of the Forties, Arthur Koestler has been pronounced intellectually dead a number of times since he withdrew from political debate into what has seemed an increasingly idiosyncratic fascination with science. He was so completely identified with Europe's aborted revolutionary hopes and their bleak reflection in *Darkness at Noon* that when he began to claim prominence as a psychological and evolutionary theorist, many readers, particularly his admirers, could not make the transition with ease. In a review of *The Ghost in the Machine* (1967), Koestler's grim diagnosis of man's innate "schizophysiology," Leslie Fiedler remarks that the title is "terrifyingly apt" because Koestler, once an indispensable teacher and guide to the illusions of the Thirties, "is, and has long been, a ghost: the ghost of a man who died when his god failed" [see excerpt above]. Because he assumes that Koestler's "god" was finally buried by the German-Soviet Pact of 1939, Professor Fiedler fails to see that a distinct, if ungraceful, line extends from the early political novels to the encyclopaedic works on science. (p. 37)

Caught between his rejection of precast ideologies and the impossibility of withdrawing from the public world into the private byways of the psyche, Koestler's remarkable solution was to design his own doctrines, a compulsion that has made him perhaps the purest, certainly the most tenacious, ideologue of faith in our time.

There are both heroic and lamentable elements in his career as novelist-turned-natural philosopher. For almost half a century he has relentlessly pursued an understanding of the human condition, and we respond with startled admiration to his fierce sense of public involvement. He changed languages, forms of writing, and despite acute frustrations, he has continued to insist that his perceptions could help mankind recognize its great splendours of creativity and its more prevalent diseases. Of his contemporaries only Koestler has fought for a strategic position in the glare of the world's future redemption. Malraux withdrew into personal style and the patronage of de Gaulle; Silone returned to an unmilitant piety; and Orwell died leaving generations in fear of his vision. Our admiration for Koestler's utopian confidence is shaded with considerable regret, however. By allowing his personal messianism to develop unchecked, he relinquished the literary power intrinsic to his first novels, *The Gladiators* and *Darkness at Noon,* that rare balance of imagination and morality which marks their enduring value as political art. Spartacus and Rubashov are Koestler's objectively conceived messianic figures; through them he explores the essentially religious basis of revolutionary commitment. In the Forties, however, as the political situation in Europe accelerated through the war with Germany to the menace of Soviet expansionism, Koestler's perception of ideological faith gave way to the intense need for his own secular belief, a need that has continued to erupt not as art, but as varieties of prophecy, an almost unending series of discourses on new faiths, ethical changes, and evolutionary mutations.

But there are no suggestions of prophetic urgency in *The Gladiators* (1939). Important as the novel was for the growth of Koestler's political understanding, it has remained among the least didactic of his works. Unlike Howard Fast and J. Leslie Mitchell in their renderings of the Slave Revolt, Koestler never allows Spartacus to speak as though he were at the Finland station. Although analogies with Stalin's "revolution from above" become intrusive at points, for most of the novel Spartacus is an integral part of an authentic pre-Christian world drawn with great attention to the imaginative use of historical detail. But it is a world and a social upheaval with significant implications for an understanding of revolutionary ethics throughout history.

Although Spartacus exhibits a degree of egalitarianism in his appeals to the Italian peasantry, his first concern is the survival of his army. But when he encounters an Essene who addresses him as the "liberator of slaves, leader of the disinherited" . . . and recounts prophecies of the coming of "One like the Son of man" . . . Spartacus suddenly takes his place in the "gigantic relay race" . . . which, the novel suggests, includes Plato, Saint-Just, Lenin, and Koestler himself. Always "one man stands up and receives the Word, and rushes on his way with the great wrath in his bowels." . . . For Koestler, "the Word" is not the Logos, but a process of anointment, of conversion, by which a thoroughly secular messiah is initiated into a utopian quest. The "Word" may be the Essene's cryptic stories, the *Communist Manifesto,* or it may be Koestler's own ethical testaments as they appear in *Arrival and Departure* and *The Ghost in the Machine.* (pp. 38-9)

Koestler ascribes the entire collapse of the revolution to the refusal by Spartacus to order the massacre of a dissident tribe. In fact, the gladiator's failure was his inability to translate his own messianic feelings into a doctrine, a new religion, his followers could share. On the other hand, his clear success was in the realm of the political imagination. As the Essene prophesied, he has become a parable in the mythological structure of revolution. Nicolai Rubashov, Koestler's next moral courier, became a haunting figure within history itself.

*Darkness at Noon* (1940), Koestler's masterful novel about the consequences of revolutionary faith, prompted its readers to reaffirm or alter their own beliefs concerning the nature of politics and human behavior. . . . In the context of the power held by the postwar French Communist Party, his portrait of an Old Bolshevik's confession to fabricated charges during the Moscow Trials divided families, provoked hard-line Stalinists to malicious attacks on Koestler's personality, and compelled the non-Communist philosopher, Maurice Merleau-Ponty, to an impassioned rebuttal of the novel. Although decades later the reactions it elicits are no longer so intense, *Darkness at Noon* is still the subject of historical controversy. (pp. 39-40)

But however one regards the Trials, the novel itself apart from any external frame of reference affords an understanding of Rubashov's confession and the quality of mind he cannot repudiate. In essence, his doubts about the infallibility of a Party led by "No. 1," his fragmentary sense of conscience and selfhood, are insufficient to destroy the forty years he has devoted to the Revolution's secular messianism, too frail to erode the rationalistic habits of mind through which his faith becomes calcified. Though in speaking about the Party Rubashov alternated between mathematical terms and the language of religion, the goal he had given his identity to was not economic reorganization, but an earthly Land of Promise. Yet since man cannot lead himself or recognize the true good, he must "be driven through the desert" and prevented from "worshipping golden calves." . . . With this justification Rubashov sent dissident Party members to their death, acquiesced in the execution of one who loved him, and accepted policies which betrayed the selfless commitment of other believers.

While Rubashov's religious allusions suggest a militant, coercive faith, he is ultimately judged by a different kind of belief—a gentle morality, a compassionate grasp of human suffering represented by the *Pietà* he glimpsed on a mission in Germany, by his brief acquaintance with his silent, inner self, and primarily embodied by the old porter who served under Rubashov in the Civil War. When Vassilij hears the official account of the trial, the two objects he worships, a greasy, tattered Bible and a now forbidden portrait of Rubashov, merge in his mind: "And the soldiers led him away, into the hall called Praetorium . . . and they smote him on the head with a reed and did spit upon him; and bowing their knees worshipped him." . . . Out of compassion and love he identifies Rubashov with the suffering Christ; however, Rubashov's Christ is the heart of the Party's unyielding body: "The old man with the slanting Tartar eyes . . . was revered as God-the-Father, and No. 1 as the Son . . . From time to time No. 1 reached out for a new victim amongst them. Then they all beat their breasts and repented in chorus of their sins." . . . Symbolizing contradictory beliefs, these images of Christ mirror the static nature of Rubashov's situation. Dominated by his intellectual rigidity, he can do no more than isolate his rudimentary conscience and repent as his past and No. 1 demand. (p. 40)

One reason [Koestler] was able to approach his first novels with relative detachment was the sense of exhilaration he experienced in creating and pursuing his own mental structures after years of intellectually rigid propaganda work. Yet this imaginative freedom was itself possible because his political isolation was by no means total. Consciously or not, he transformed the religious fervour of his Communism into an emotional, diffuse belief in the development of a revitalized, independent socialist movement which in the early Forties he saw as the only force capable of reviving "the values on which Western civilisation is based." . . . [The] kind of action he envisaged was necessarily vague. . . . While his arguments clarify his distance from conservative politics in the war years, the religious note of this rhapsodic untheoretical programme originally sounded by Rubashov also marks his first movement away from historical concreteness. . . .

[Koestler] has simply never been concerned with the precise intricacies of a theoretical system. Whatever the area of debate—politics, psychology, biochemistry—and however lucid or misconceived his analyses are, Koestler ultimately measures every structure for its secular redemptive value. In his work after *Darkness at Noon* we are . . . [dealing] with incantations in the form of literature or scientific discourse. If anything, it is philosophy in a constant state of millennial anticipation. Unlike Dr. Johnson he does not kick the rock of human experience, and unlike Sisyphus he does not push it. Averting an apocalyptic shadow, Koestler jumps from stone to stone, believing all the time that each gap is a grace he is about to see. (p. 41)

The unequal battle between the prophet and the novelist begins in *Arrival and Departure* (1943). At the expense of both narrative and intellectual coherence, Koestler directs the central figure, in whom he invests considerable personal feeling, towards a new god, a new age in the life of the human race. But before Peter Slavek reaches this apotheosis, he undergoes a

process of strict Freudian therapy which reveals that his revolutionary commitment and even his heroic silence under torture were efforts to expiate the childhood guilt he incurred in trying to blind his infant brother. The novel suggests a limited endorsement of the orthodox Freudianism represented by Sonia, Peter's Junoesque analyst; Peter's unhealthy interest in boathooks clearly drives him to search for atonement through extreme political action. However, prompted no doubt by his own spiritual pursuit and urgent claims on the future, Koestler must reject not only Sonia's insistence that moral beliefs are "mere pretexts of the mind, phantoms of a more intimate reality" . . . , but also her dogmatic identification of this "reality" with neurotic motives. Just as Peter is about to leave an embattled Europe to join his lover in America, he suddenly casts the meticulous therapy aside and rushes to enlist at the British Consulate. Much to the consternation of Koestler's readers at the time, particularly Orwell, the threat Fascism poses to civilization is not the novel's overriding concern, even though Peter has actually witnessed the slaughter of aged Jews. Through Peter's intuitive compulsion Koestler affirms that transcendence and faith are inherent in man and cannot be reduced by a rationalist system of explanation.

Because both the source and goal of Peter's newly perceived realm of faith are highly ambiguous, Koestler depends upon a concentration of symbols to refute Sonia's mocking reduction of the messianic temperament. Peter is not even allowed the semblance of a rational decision. He hears the "call" . . . of a new priesthood and an enigmatic redeemer, receives his "sign," and embraces "the invisible cross" . . . which appears to him in a dream and which is no longer the emblem of the messianic revolutionary as we have known him in Koestler's earlier novels. It will become visible only with the emergence of the "global ferment" Koestler has prophesied. Just before Peter is flown behind the lines of his own country, he announces the imminent arrival of "a new god" . . . and speaking as one of Koestler's fraternity of short-term pessimists, hopes that somehow, parachuting through the night, he is assisting in its birth. What he is not permitted to realize, however, is that he is going to land in precisely the area of his country where he had watched the Jews being gassed. This striking lapse of memory eliminates an accessible morality and is the ultimate indication the novel provides of how attached Koestler has become to his recent religious intimation. (pp. 42-3)

Koestler immediately turned to challenge the "moral insanity" of postwar France and with an often terrible violence of feeling narrowed his prophetic outlook. . . . Under the pressure of what must have been intolerable frustration and disillusionment, Koestler wrote *The Age of Longing* (1951), a startling document which vilifies Europe's spiritual emptiness, its moral vulnerability, and with Rubashov only a dim memory pays a bitter tribute to Stalinist zeal.

*The Age of Longing* is less a novel than a series of uncontrolled mental projections, a prolonged rite of exorcism and compulsive revenge. Although he attempts to parody notable leftists like Merleau-Ponty, de Beauvoir, and of course Sartre pictured as the creator of "neo-nihilism," "a piquant technique of intellectual masturbation" . . . , Koestler's more effective though repellent weapon is the language of disease. He victimizes his characters with a bizarre recurrence of tics, scars, unhealthy skin, limps, heavy legs, incongruous eyes, oily mouths, and foul breath, all of which seem designed to prove a Cold War neoplatonism, that the faithless are unworthy of physical dignity. Julien is the character with the greatest assortment of afflictions and he argues, as Koestler does later in *The Ghost in the Machine*, that the nature of one's faith is the primary question, that it is preferable to have no belief than to be committed to a brutal or illusory creed.

But it is Hydie, an ex-Catholic, who voices Koestler's desperate feeling in the late Forties that any faith is stronger, hence better, than spiritual vacuity. . . . Nikitin serves the brutal Stalinist God, but since he is the only figure Koestler is prepared to recognize as capable of impersonal devotion, he escapes the metaphorical degradation inflicted on all the other characters. Neither the Son of man nor midwife for a shapeless deity, Nikitin is the embodiment of pure faith divorced from a humane messianic purpose by Koestler's own bleak longings and hatreds.

Since faith bestows on the devotee the aura of Christ and the mark of Cain, Koestler could never bring himself to give his unrepentant Parisian leftists the stature of being included among the honourable faithful. Instead, they displayed symptoms of political "masochism," "nymphomania," and sectarian "incest," aberrations that produced a dangerous "moral insanity." . . . In *The Age of Longing* Julien says almost triumphantly:

> Have you ever doubted that a hundred years hence they will discover that we have all been insane—not metaphorically, but in the literal, clinical sense? Has it never occurred to you that when poets talk about the madness of homo sapiens they are making not a poetical but a medical statement? It wouldn't be nature's first blunder either—think of the dinosaur. A neurologist told me the other day that in all probability the snag lies somewhere in the connections between the forebrain and the interbrain. To be precise, our species suffers from endemic schizophrenia . . . Our misfitted brain leads us a dance on a permanent witches' sabbath. If you are an optimist, you are free to believe that some day some biological mutation will cure the race. But it seems infinitely more probable that we shall go the way of the dinosaur. . . .

After sixteen years of attempting to reconcile his incurable optimism with the very clear shadow of the dinosaur on human history, this passage ultimately developed into *The Ghost in the Machine*. Equally important, though, is the relation of his own passions to Julien's announcement. As a man of faith, perhaps Koestler found immunity in associating madness with what he believed at the time was modern man's crippling lack of spiritual fervour. Yet it is startling that even a growing assurance of racial insanity did not give him pause to reflect upon his impulse to condemn, mutilate, and brutalize the godless. (pp. 43-5)

The concept of creative mutations not only liberated him from a strictly hierarchical perspective on social evolution, it also meant that given certain "pre-conditions," such as the "ripeness" of the times . . . , a new phase in man's development could arise spontaneously assisted by the necessary vision and visionary. Because *Darkness at Noon* became part of French political history and *Thieves in the Night* influenced members of a United Nations Commission deliberating the future of Palestine, Koestler, more than most writers, succumbed to a belief in the world's malleability. . . . If they have not yet prompted a change in social evolution, Koestler's syntheses of information from various regions of scientific theory and re-

search are expressions of a remarkable temperament and reflect his conception of the creative act itself, a drawing together of previously unrelated "ideas, facts, frames of perceptions, associative contexts." . . . (pp. 45-6)

*Mark Levene, "Arthur Koestler: On Messiahs and Mutations," in* Modernist Studies: Literature & Culture, 1920-1940, *Vol. 2, No. 2, 1977, pp. 37-48.*

**GERALD JONAS**

Of the 30 books of fiction and nonfiction that he has published in his distinguished career, Arthur Koestler is best known for his political novel, **"Darkness at Noon,"** which first appeared in English in 1941. . . . His devastating portrait of Eastern European Communism could have been written only by someone who had once been a believer; the novel drew its enormous power from a deeply felt sense of personal betrayal.

Mr. Koestler writes about science from much the same perspective. At heart he is a believer, but he cannot help finding motes in the idol's eye. . . . He appears to have been attracted to science for its promise of intellectual rigor, for its practicality and, not incidentally, because it supplied him with a body of arcane knowledge that he could reveal to awed outsiders. Yet once he decided that science, like Marxism, could not meet his demand for a coherent, emotionally satisfying picture of the universe, he set himself the task of teaching scientists how to do their own job better.

As the subtitle implies, [**"Janus: A Summing Up"**] restates themes from many of his earlier works and tries to show that they all derive from a single, unifying viewpoint—which is perhaps best described as anti-reductionism. His *bêtes noires* are scientists who insist that man is "nothing but" a killer ape, or a stimulus-response machine, or a bundle of neuroses, or the product of purely random mutations. To the contrary, Mr. Koestler argues, a human being is a "holon"—an entity that is more than the sum of its parts and, at the same time, a part of some larger whole. To symbolize man's dual nature, Mr. Koestler borrows the image of the two-faced Roman god, Janus. Each of us has strong "self-assertive" tendencies that help define us as unique individuals; we also have strong "integrative" tendencies that help tie us to one social group or another, each with its own rules and constraints. Only when these opposing tendencies are kept in equilibrium can we function successfully.

Stripped to its bare bones, the argument seems unexceptional—not unlike something that might be heard in any lively freshman philosophy seminar. But Mr. Koestler goes on to assert that man is not the only holon in the universe; in fact, everything around us (and inside us) is made up of hierarchies of holons, or "holarchies." . . .

In defending his thesis that the universe is essentially one vast chain of holarchies, Mr. Koestler writes about everything from the nature of humor to the roots of totalitarianism. Not surprisingly, he is highly selective in marshalling illustrations from the scientific literature. Less forgivable is his sometimes tendentious discussion of the facts he chooses to present. For example, he traces man's penchant for self-destruction to an evolutionary blunder: Because the new, human forebrain (where we do our reasoning) was simply stuck on top of the older "reptilian" mid-brain (which is the home of emotion), we suffer from a built-in "schizophysiological disposition." Evolution failed to integrate the new and old brains; as a result, man is often at war with himself, torn between overwhelming emotional drives and the dictates of coldly calculating reason. . . .

[Koestler suggests] that our only hope for avoiding self-destruction is to develop a pill or injection to cure our "schizophysiological disposition." Such a panacea would eliminate or circumvent the natural "obstructions and blockages" between brain structures, and "enhance the power of the neocortex—the apex of the hierarchy—over the lower, emotion-bound levels and the blind passions engendered by them." This is not only strong medicine; it is dangerously ahead of the data. The antipsychotic drugs in wide use today—which Mr. Koestler cites as precedents—were discovered by accident, and after 25 years of investigation, researchers are still trying to figure out how they work.

Passages like the above quotation leave Mr. Koestler open to the charge that he is using his knowledge of science to lend an unearned weight to his own theories about the human dilemma. Senior scientists, especially those with a keen social conscience, are often guilty of fudging the line between their professional expertise and their personal beliefs, and Mr. Koestler, who has learned much from his scientific sources, seems to have picked up this habit as well. More generally, in denigrating reductionism, Mr. Koestler fails to appreciate that the search for simple mechanisms has been, and almost surely will continue to be, an important heuristic tool for the scientist. (p. 9)

But if Mr. Koestler's antireductionist position limits his appreciation of science as a day-to-day investigative discipline, it serves him well in probing for weak points in contemporary scientific thought. For example, his summary of the current state of evolutionary theory will come as a revelation to many laymen; while the fossil record clearly shows that species evolve toward more adaptive forms (or die out), the mechanism for change proposed by orthodox neo-Darwinists is by no means universally accepted in the scientific community. (pp. 9, 16)

Perhaps Mr. Koestler's greatest service in this book is to convince the layman not to understand science too quickly. The rigidly mechanistic universe of 19th-century physics has been buried for good by the physics of relativity and quantum mechanics. We live in a universe "governed" by probabilistic laws—yet the very notion of probability, as Mr. Koestler points out, is fraught with mystery. The more deeply scientists delve into the atom and the further they let their imaginations roam in outer space, "curiouser and curiouser" grows the universe. Contemplating the unity of all being, in the mode of Henri Bergson, is not likely to provoke many useful experiments, but it may lead a future Einstein or Niels Bohr to mold experimental data from many different disciplines into an intellectually coherent, and even emotionally satisfying, world-view. (p. 16)

> Gerald Jonas, "Seeing the Universe Whole," in The New York Times Book Review, *April 2, 1978, pp. 9, 16.*

## BERNARD CRICK

[*Bricks to Babel* must be Koestler's] own view of his achievement, especially as at first glance it includes something of everything: Zionist, communist, anticommunist, philosopher, scientist, pamphleteer, deep pessimist, profound optimist, unsatisfied Yogi and frustrated commissar. Can we now judge

whether he is a bourgeois hedgehog or a natural aristocrat of foxes? Whether he should be remembered and respected more for his philosophic and scientific speculation of later years or for his earlier political writings? And did he just have two good novels in him—which came out, **Darkness at Noon** and **Arrival and Departure**—or has his abandonment of the novel as a form in favor of scientific speculations about human nature and destiny both lost him an audience and diminished his art?

In some ways, however, [**Bricks to Babel**] makes general judgments more difficult, not less. For he tries to kill two very different birds with the same stone: the omnibus is both a remarkably fair selection from his published books (including those essays republished in book form) and a substitute autobiography. It is fair because the bulk of these books fall into his postwar scientific, postpolitical period; and yet if he values them more, he still gives half of this book to the political period, in professional deference, one suspects, to the majority of his readers. It is a substitute autobiography in that the extracts, whether from novels or nonfiction, are printed in chronological order, each with an interesting headnote explaining how and why each book came to be written. But the balance of extracts is only a careful editorial compromise. It must be wrong from one or another point of view: the demands of a truthful autobiography or the demands of a good selection of what he thinks to be his own best or most important work.

So Koestler has not done the critic's work for him, or even made a clear first bid. The claim he makes on our attention is still enigmatic. . . . Indeed the alarming thought could occur, as some of Orwell's friends claimed of him, perhaps out of discomfort with the content of his writings, that it is actually the life of the man that is more memorable than the writings. To say this would obviously be to disparage Koestler's writings, but it is not a view to be dismissed out of hand. For his public life has been extraordinary. (pp. 274-75)

Why, then, has he not summed up in a full-scale autobiography, rather than this compromise volume? Or at least completed the series of the autobiographical books? . . . He anticipates this obvious question, saying that despite the pressure of friends and publishers, his life ceased after 1940 to be a "typical (sic) case history of a central European member of the educated middle class born in the first years of our century," and therefore ceased to be "of any public interest." . . . Before 1940 he was predominantly, but far from exclusively, interested in public, political affairs; and "after 1940 (although most certainly he predates the change of emphasis), predominantly interested in strange, difficult, and important borderlands of psychology, physiology, biology, and philosophy. But his shift of emphasis was far from exclusive. . . . What he really means is that his private life comes to be more valuable to him than public, political activities, and that he finds the subject matter of his new books in contemplation, rather than in action, or in reading about science, not in recounting his own experiences, as in **Spanish Testament** and **Arrow in the Blue**, or even in imaginatively reshaping them, as in **The Gladiators** and **Darkness at Noon**. And also he is probably saying, with the decent reticence of a distinguished English man of letters living in Montpelier Square, SW7, that he simply does not want to write about his private life.

In some ways one sympathizes. (pp. 277-78)

Nonetheless, it is strange that, having written so much and so interestingly in an autobiographic vein in his "red" period, he has not done so in, as it were, his "blue" period; and has, as

I've said, produced this fascinating but nonetheless compromised, commentated, chronological anthology. One sympathizes if he has a distaste for doing a Bertie Russell and writing so frankly and egocentrically about his amours, marriages, and quarrels, as well as his ideas and activities, as if the feelings of others do not matter a damn if self-revelation is complete. But if so purely intellectual, why not an intellectual autobiography? Perhaps the difficulty is not one of either writing to conceal or needing to parade a private life, but a painful uncertainty about where his real achievement lies in his public life as a writer, a contradiction between his ideal image and his actual best work. A clue may be found in his editing of the anthology: he confines himself to books or essays republished in books, so practically nothing of his vast journalistic output appears. But for most of his life Koestler has been a journalist, in Zionist, Communist, and anti-Communist phases, still an occasional reviewer, since the middle 1940s able to choose his journals and write thoughtful feature articles rather than commissioned stories, but nonetheless a journalist, reporter, professional writer, in the best senses through and through. This editing out of examples of early routine journalism may simply be because this anthology is, after all, meant to show his writing at its best. But then its chronological, quasi-auto-biographic appearance is publicly misleading, perhaps even self-deceptive. I would like to see examples of how he did write as an Ullstein journalist and then as a party hack—not to demean him, but simply because his life was so interesting. And he may underestimate the reporter's craft, as if it diminishes the thinker's status.

His prewar books told in sturdy prose fascinating stories about his own adventures. When he comes to write in English, it is a workmanlike, even at times lively, prose, occasionally even florid, but certainly with little of the vivid feeling for a new language shown by Conrad or the sharp simplicity of Orwell's use of his native tongue.... Before the war ..., he wrote well about his own experiences and matters arising from them—especially well about extreme psychological states; but he had also written, though no examples here, with some authority on scientific matters as the science correspondent of the biggest German newspaper chain in the 1920s. So when he returns to write about science, though now in books and on themes of his own choosing, he is speculative, most certainly, but not amateur or eccentric; and if he is selective in his use of evidence, he is a good reporter of what "challenging" research and theories he reads: he can both understand and popularize scientific literature. Thus, there is both more continuity in his writing than first appears to be the case or than he is prepared to acknowledge.

Add to this the fact that his novels have all dealt well with the character and ideological contradictions of a central hero or anti-hero, as well as with extreme situations, but they have shown neither psychological depth nor complexity in the interrelations of the characters. Indeed, the minor characters are all ideological or social types, neither interacting upon nor modifying each other's characters: they break or bust each other, or some escape and others remain unchanged. Reflective and revealing autobiography, then, beyond telling a good public tale of important and exciting public events, is not likely to be his strongest card as a writer. He may simply be well aware of this—no skeletons to hide, simply an old craftsman's dialectic awareness of his professional strengths and weaknesses. The one clear thread in all the variety of his themes, and linking closely his two periods, is that he has been a professional reporter of mighty themes, but always using his pen for his career, considering carefully his subject matter and his changing audiences.

This is perhaps why so many of us are still uneasy and uncertain about Koestler. His themes are great themes, but he is not a great writer, if in some sense great writing becomes, whether as political or scientific writing, an end in itself. He always demands our agreement or disagreement, not our appreciation—although we should appreciate very greatly the skill and cultural role of such writing, admitting that it is not great literature. I think of Koestler as one might think of Orwell if he had never written *Animal Farm* and *Nineteen Eighty-Four*. The claim for literary greatness could not be made, but he would still have been a figure—like Koestler—of extraordinary interest and importance.

What, however, if the content, if the message, is the thing? What emerges in his later, more difficult writings is both compelling and tantalizing. What is compelling is his humanistic tone, even at times when journalistic cadences slip in. He sees the humor as well as the seriousness of life. Life is serious, not simply in how we react to each other, a purely humanistic position, but in how we must, he still believes, search for an overall synthesis of sense of purpose in humanity. He is an individualist who has come utterly to reject hedonism or utilitarianism in favor of a long-term responsibility for improving the human species. (pp. 278-80)

So an assessment of Koestler's peculiar genius is difficult. Have any of us ever read all his books? And there is the journalism as well as the books. His own sense of achievement is shown clearly in the selection of this book. He probably disappoints his old readers or the young who read his old novels by calling fully half of *Bricks to Babel* his "Search of Synthesis," and presenting there mainly the scientific writings. But in terms of the sheer bulk of this scientific writing, the first half of the book, "In Search of Utopia," is in fact disproportionate. He would like to be remembered as a scientific thinker; but he is too good a professional writer not to realize where his greater effect and following still lie. So he presents his literary past fully and does not appear to rewrite. No Audenesque problems here.

The extracts from the novels fit in easily with the nonfictional works. The value of *Darkness at Noon* and *Arrival and Departure* is in their authenticity.... Koestler knows what he was talking about and is hard to diminish; he is easier to ignore or foolishly dismiss in New York as a nice "cold war warrior" or in London as "too clever by half." The issue in the 1940s, as the Party hacks and the fellow travelers put it, was only whether he was a liar or not. And plainly he wasn't.

This very factualness is both the clue to and the continuity in his achievement. It is not an esthetic achievement. We read his books for their matter and to learn something from them. This too links the old with the new Koestler. We should read the new scientific Koestler just as we read the earlier political novels: because he is talking about something we need to know, but all the time aware that it is a prince of journalists, a cosmic reporter, the doyen of conferenceurs, who is addressing us as an audience, mingling, like any good feature writer, personal angles with hard information. We open the quality press and we are informed, stimulated, but always on our guard. He writes columns as big and bustling as Babel, not monographs.

Whether or not Koestler himself believes that he has philosophical or scientific originality (as did Wells, alas) is irrelevant. I hope he doesn't, but it really doesn't matter. He is one of the greatest intellectual popularizers of our time, the interpreter for one set of intellectuals of the concepts of another. And his genuine cosmopolitan stance has been earned and not easily achieved. One Koestler speaks more for human unity, despite his rationalist assault on the cult of Zen and the pretensions of Gandhi, than a dozen committees of UNESCO. He deeply appreciates national cultural differences, but attaches little value to them and adopts each in turn with a kind of ironic affection. (pp. 281-83)

Ultimately, he should be pleased with himself as the super-reporter. What he has now given us is, in fact, in its temporal order and with its headnotes, a remarkably full and clear picture of the public activities of his life. The rest is silence. (pp. 281-83)

Surely it will be, rightly or wrongly, his earlier political books for which he will be best and longest remembered. He told the tale so compellingly of how a man came to look for utopias, but finally grew skeptical of political activity, except for small clear things: like abolition of capital punishment. It might fairly be objected that between utopianism and skepticism lies the whole range of practical politics, from the conservative to the democratic socialist. Orwell thought that Koestler should have explored the nature of a non-utopian political theory. But Koestler was not a political thinker. And no man, not even Koestler, can do everything. Koestler had a tendency to dramatize things to extremes, the Yogi or the commissar, and to exclude obvious mundane middles. He was a reporter of great themes, however. If there were no immediate utopias to observe in the 1950s from that Graf Zeppelin still hovering over polar extremes, he would have to report on the evolution of the species itself. I cannot evaluate his success or not in this matter, only share a common skepticism, but with a shameful sense of not being brave or rash enough to try myself. But it does not diminish or change his earlier work, and one has to hope that he himself takes this view, either at peace with himself in his old age or properly proud of all the bricks he made so skillfully and in such difficulties as a great and dedicated professional writer and superjournalist. (p. 283)

*Bernard Crick, "Koestler's Koestler,"* in Partisan Review, *Vol. XLIX, No. 2, 1982, pp. 274-83.*

# Arthur (Lee) Kopit

## 1937-

American dramatist and scriptwriter.

Kopit is an important contributor to contemporary American drama whose plays are noted for powerful social commentary and for innovations in dramatic form. Critics link Kopit's early work with the "Theater of the Absurd," a trend in modern drama characterized by experimental techniques and the philosophic view that existence is meaningless. His later plays explore such timely subjects as the media's influence on human perception and the threat of nuclear war.

In his early work, Kopit presents nonspatial, nontemporal, symbolic settings in which his characters experience the futility of attempting to make sense of the world. Kopit gained wide recognition when his play *Oh Dad, Poor Dad, Mama's Hung You in the Closet and I'm Feelin' So Sad* (1960) became popular in London and New York during the early 1960s. This play centers on a domineering woman, her overprotected son, and her dead husband, whose body repeatedly falls out of a closet during the course of the play. While Kopit satirizes American family life, he also parodies works by Tennessee Williams, Sophocles, and various Absurdist playwrights. Critics noted Kopit's extensive use of black humor, paradox, and disjointed scenes.

Kopit's next major work, *Indians* (1968), has been called one of the most important American plays of the 1960s. Kopit suggests in this play that Americans were subjected to myths created through media and literature that excused the oppression of Indians; the play intimates that myths are used similarly to condone the Vietnam War and to support white supremacy. *Indians* depicts Buffalo Bill Cody's "Wild West Show," concentrating on Cody's dilemma of feeling sympathetic towards the Indians yet contributing to their downfall in order to enhance his heroic stature.

Kopit departed from satire and absurdist techniques in his acclaimed play *Wings* (1978), which depicts the struggle of a female stroke victim to overcome aphasia. Originally conceived as a radio play, *Wings* depends on soliloquies to represent the woman's fragmented thoughts as she gradually relearns to use language. Many critics commend Kopit for his presentation of failures of communication and for his insightful portrayal of the plight of aphasia victims.

Kopit's recent work *End of the World* (1984), like *Indians,* is structured as a play-within-a-play. This drama concerns a playwright who gathers information in order to write about the prospect of nuclear holocaust. Kopit depicts the playwright as a detective investigating those responsible for nuclear proliferation. Although critics faulted the play's structure, Kopit was lauded for undertaking a drama about such a vital contemporary topic. Language as communication, a theme which informs many of Kopit's work, underlies his parody of the jargon used by military and government officials to defend nuclear arms buildup.

(See also *CLC,* Vols. 1, 18; *Contemporary Authors,* Vols. 81-84; and *Dictionary of Literary Biography,* Vol. 7.)

© Kelly Wise

## RICHARD EDER

A woman having a stroke would seem to make a difficult and resistant subject for a play. "**Wings**" mounts and soars on this resistance like the airplane that serves as its distant motif.

"**Wings**" . . . is a brilliant work; complex at first glance yet utterly lucid; written with great sensitivity and with the excitement of a voyage of discovery; and benefiting from a production whose splendor is in its imagination rather than its physical resources. . . .

It is a small play in a sense; that is it is short, it has no side plots or issues, and it is almost a dramatic monologue. But from its first moment to its last it proceeds with such intensity and with such an utter lack of padding or irrelevance that it has nothing whatever of the minor work about it. . . .

The play takes us through the stages of the stroke and the beginnings of a gradual recovery. At first [Emily Stilson] sits alone, talking brokenly of a mixture of memory of the past and bewilderment at the present. She is not sure where she is; she thinks perhaps she has been flying and has crashed in a strange country. Perhaps the doctors are Rumanians—they can't understand her when she delivers what she thinks are perfectly lucid answers to their questions; and at other times they seem to be talking gibberish.

246

Later she manages painfully to respond; the effort is huge when she indentifies a toothbrush. But we are inside her; this wry, luminous mind seems in no way deformed to us but lost, and we are lost with it. And her brief triumphs as she masters a word or a phrase are our triumphs as well.

There is a progression that gives the play dramatic as well as thematic pace. From isolation she goes to the painful beginnings of communication with the doctors, and from there to mixing with other patients and to a profound and affecting relationship with Amy, her therapist. . . .

There is a profound and profoundly beautiful scene where Emily, much recovered, walks outdoors with Amy and haltingly remembers the word for snow. Where do people get their words from, she asks, and Amy doesn't know. "How can I know, then?" she asks.

But this is much more than a play about a stroke, and the battle to recover from it. It is a play about life and death; and Emily is hauntingly suspended between the two. The great image that moves throughout the play is her memory of flying an old biplane and doing stunts on the wings.

The memories flood in on her; between her painful bouts to learn with agonizing slowness, to speak and live again, comes the sound of wind and her vision of being lost in a snowstorm. [Emily], struggling patiently and sometimes impatiently to master slow word after slow word, is like a valiant and studious immigrant.

But if she is an immigrant it is because life has become a foreign country. Death has become her home; and as the play proceeds [Emily] becomes more resonant and radiant each time she goes back into the memory of her wings.

> Richard Eder, "'Wings' Comes to Broadway: Memories of Flying," in The New York Times, *January 29, 1979, p. C13.*

**DEAN VALENTINE**

Perhaps the most important thing about *Wings* . . . is that it introduces a promising playwright. That may sound rather strange, considering that Arthur Kopit has been writing professionally for nearly 20 years and has two widely-acclaimed hits to his credit: *Oh Dad, Poor Dad, Mamma's Hung You in the Closet and I'm Feelin' So Sad* (1960) and *Indians* (1968). But the truth is that those were feeble works indeed; they testified more to a discerning eye for cultural fashion than to genuine talent.

The former, for example, was offered just when absurdism was becoming chic. The story of a piranha-like woman who keeps her husband's stuffed body in a closet and browbeats her stammering son, *Oh Dad* aped Strindberg, Dürrenmatt, Beckett, Ionesco, Giraudoux—all the right people, in short—without, however, managing to display any noticeable feeling for character. *Indians* confirmed Kopit's attachment to absurdist theater as well as his athletic prowess in jumping on bandwagons. At at time when everyone was getting down on America for exploiting and oppressing the poor, blacks and Orientals, Kopit bravely advanced the proposition that our Western myths were smokescreens concealing the rapacity of our conquest of the land and the Indians on it.

*Wings* seems to me a renunciation of the playwright's past, a renunciation that has made possible a leap forward. Where before the author was unappeasably intent on being wackily

absurd, he has now switched to a more naturalistic mode. Where before he insisted on showing us human consciousness disintegrating, he is now concerned with exploring how a woman who has suffered a stroke—and lost her capacity for language along with her sense of time, space, identity—struggles to re-establish order, to integrate. Where before Kopit kept hammering out, like a savage on a tomtom, great themes on society, he is here content merely to reproduce an individual faithfully. And where before his plays were unbearably smart-assed, full of trendy despair, *Wings* is filled with an anguished hope.

His maturity, I think, can be partially attributed to the emotional stake Kopit himself had in the play. He writes in the Preface to the text . . . : "In the spring of 1976 . . . my father suffered a major stroke which rendered him incapable of speech. . . . To what extent was he still intact? To what extent was he aware of what had befallen him? *What was it like inside?*"

To answer that question in theatrical terms is formidably difficult—it would be hard enough even if the protagonist's faculties were undamaged—yet Kopit has answered it. Moreover, for the most part, he has answered it well, by an adept use of the stage, by his meticulous research into aphasia, and by a deeply sympathetic imagination. (p. 19)

[At] the very end of the play, the memory that has been bubbling in [Mrs. Stilson's] subconscious explodes into consciousness with the force of a revelation. It is Mrs. Stilson's memory of flying in her plane and losing her way over Nebraska and Kansas. Her recitation of this trip is the most moving moment of the evening: The image of a lone woman flying about in the night symbolizes Emily's "adventure" through her aphasia; the person—the soul as it were—that remains untouched and free no matter what happens to the body or the brain; the perpetual journey of the human spirit. It is a masterful bit of writing.

All of which makes *Wings* the truest play on Broadway. Nevertheless, there are serious problems. Originally written for radio, the piece still bears too many traces of its origin. . . . [About a third of the play] would work just as well over the airwaves; there is nothing essentially theatrical to [it]. As a result, our interest is held not so much by Emily or her words as by the rather spectacular stage effects.

Another problem is perhaps inherent in the very nature of the enterprise. Kopit has gone to great lengths to make Emily believable and not a case study of aphasia. But when Emily is alone on stage a pall is cast on his efforts. Drama depends for full effectiveness on human interaction. When a solitary person is up there soliloquizing—and in a purely formal sense that's what happens in *Wings*—a certain richness is forfeited. Hence, having no one to react against, Emily often becomes merely the sum of her symptoms. Character is reduced to disease. (p. 20)

> Dean Valentine, "Kopit Earns His Wings," in The New Leader, *Vol. LXII, No. 5, February 26, 1979, pp. 19-20.* *

**JOHN SIMON**

The title *Wings* has twofold significance. It refers, first, to Emily Stilson's past, when she was a barnstorming pilot, sometimes flying her plane, sometimes performing stunts on the plane's wings. It also refers to words, which wing their way from person to person, allowing the speaker to assert his own, and experience our shared, humanity. Even as Emily was once powerful and confident with wings in her youth, now, in her old age, and after her stroke, she is first wingless, and then trying, effortfully, to recover her wings. Finally, the wings assume even a third meaning: they become tantamount to life itself, which comes to us on wings, and which we leave on the pinions of death. Emily's last words, directed presumably to the dark messenger, are: "Oh my, yes, and here it goes then out . . . there I think on . . . wings? Yes . . ." And then, after a pause, "[SOFTLY, FAINT SMILE] Thank you."

These last words are far from being coherent, but we can divine their meaning—even as Emily Stilson, after her stroke, must guess at what is going on around her in the world of people, objects, speech, all of which she perceives in a distorted fashion, just as others often cannot understand what she is inwardly formulating with perfect clarity. The perspective we get is multiple: the world as it sees Emily, and Emily as she sees herself; Emily as she sees the world, and the world as it actually is. Kopit splendidly succeeds in making these points of view coexist very nearly simultaneously, sometimes literally so. It is as if the play were a series of cinematic superimpositions and lap dissolves, the visual aspects reinforced or counterpointed by the auditory ones. (p. 78)

Kopit uses every conceivable way of splitting open or fragmenting visible and audible reality; but this is never done gratuitously. Rather, it is meant to examine what happens at the interstices of communication, visual or verbal; to explore how and why the doctors misunderstand the patient almost as much as she does them, and not through anyone's fault. A tape recorder repeats what was heard before, as Mrs. Stilson listens to a doctor's words over and over again; or Emily may be sitting downstage center in a pool of light, while upstage, doctors and nurses will be treating a prostrate figure hidden from our view by their backs—a figure that is also Mrs. Stilson, on whom they comment even while the seated woman comments on them.

Just as the play hovers between conflicting realities (partial truths all of them), the tone is tenderly balanced between sympathetic laughter and compassionate tears. In a passage where Emily's voice "is heard coming from all around; she herself does not speak," we get: "Yesterday my children came to see me. [PAUSE.] Or at least, I was told they were my children. Never saw them before in my life." . . . [When] another patient complains softly, "My foot feels sour," or when, in a group therapy session, various patients talk in language that ranges from gibberish, through quasi-Joycean distortions, to merely occasional malapropisms—how are we to react? Is our laughter an insult to these people's efforts to speak, or is it a normal though inappropriate reaction to something that—abstractly—*is* funny? And would not crying over these unusually strong intimations of mortality be, in its own way, equally inappropriate? For these awkward but noble gropings for self-expression are heroic and happy things, too: life reasserting itself. So why not laugh in an approving way? Placed as we are at the intersection of sadness and merriment, we are transported into an emotional no-man's-land that corresponds to the cognitive limbo in which the patients are struggling. The play is disorienting us into comprehension.

There are two particularly fine, unambiguously moving moments in *Wings*: one when Emily, under the kindly tutelage of Amy, discovers, in her own tears, both the word "tears" and the meaning of sadness; and the other, when Emily and Amy are gently snowed on as they sit on a wintry bench, and Amy strives to get Emily to come up with the word "snow." (pp. 79-80)

In its unobtrusive way, this scene, like the entire play, addresses itself to the questions of how, why, and when we comprehend something and can translate it into understandable utterance. The implication here seems to be that touch leads to understanding; that words, or wings, presuppose hands. Kopit wrote the play because his father had a stroke, spent time in institutions such as *Wings* evokes, had a therapist like Amy, and finally died without recovering even partially. But there were other patients for Kopit to observe, especially an old ex-aviatrix, as well as another, younger woman; and there were technical books on the subject from which to gather additional information. To ask the playwright to explain exactly what these word-wings are, and whence and how they come, would be excessive. Yet he does show the therapeutic as well as epistemological value of contact, both physical and spiritual.

If the play fails anywhere, it is in its attempt to convey the heights of language, notably in the passages in which Mrs. Stilson relives some of her flying experiences. Thus: "As I see it now, the plane was flying *backwards*! Really, wind that strong, didn't know it could be! Yet the sky was clear, not a cloud, crystal blue, gorgeous, angels could've lived in sky like that . . ." This is inadequate sub-poetical prose; but, of course, we have no right to expect Emily Stilson to be Antoine de St.-Exupéry—assuming that *he* could do justice to that ultimate experience. Still, even if the imagery is unimpressive as literature, it works dramatically: we gather that words at their most winged (Emily soaring in her airplane) occur when the person is alone—when the wings are, as it were, flying inward. (p. 80)

*John Simon, "Theater Chronicle: Kopit, Norman, and Shepard," in* The Hudson Review, *Vol. XXXII, No. 1, Spring, 1979, pp. 77-88.**

## GAUTAM DASGUPTA

When Arthur Kopit first appeared on the New York theatrical scene in 1962, he was instantly hoisted to the rank of an Edward Albee. Like his distinguished predecessor, he was proclaimed a playwright of the absurd. The critical establishment found him a true successor to the classical avant-garde and absurdist tradition of European playwriting in this century. He was more than just another off-Off-Broadway playwright; his plays resembled the works of Giraudoux, Frisch, Beckett, Ionesco, and Pirandello, all stalwarts of the modernist (and, by 1962, well-accepted) canon of playwriting. Here, in other words, was a playwright with ideas, a dramatist with a vision.

Except for minor shifts in emphasis, Kopit's fundamental dramatic premise has remained unchanged. Like the absurdists before him, he chooses to depict a horrific world where logic holds no sway. His characters are caught up in a world which is either macabre or grotesque (*Oh Dad, Poor Dad, Mamma's Hung You in the Closet and I'm Feeling So Sad*) or threatening (*The Day the Whores Came Out to Play Tennis*).

Inhabiting these worlds are a cast of characters who are equally grotesque and strange. At a loss to comprehend the world around them, they either go along with it, acquiescing to its absurd logic, or else they break out in revolt, usually with fatal consequences (*Chamber Music*). At other times, however, they fall back in quiet desperation, resigning themselves to a destiny over which they have no control (*The Questioning of Nick*).

But Kopit does not always present the world *ipso facto* as one verging on collapse. More often than not, its nightmarish dimensions are nothing more than the projections of the inner world of his characters (*Wings*). Forever in search of his identity, the quintessential Kopit character rearranges his universe in a desperate attempt to make it conform to a sense of order and to establish his own identity. But the world eludes him at every point. Continually in a state of flux, his characters find themselves stranded on an island, isolated and world-weary (*Sing to Me Through Open Windows, Indians*). No wonder, then, that the people who populate Kopit's plays talk feverishly to one another, and yet hardly ever seem to connect (except in *The Conquest of Mt. Everest* and *The Hero*).

While Kopit has rarely experimented with dramatic technique (except for *The Questioning of Nick*, his first attempt at realism, and *Indians*, an exercise in Brecht's epic style)—preferring to write in the absurdist idiom, with an occasional touch of whimsy or fairy tale-like aura—his vibrant theatrical imagination has more than made up for the deficiency. Utilizing an array of stage techniques that range from pantomime (*The Hero*) to extended monologues (*Wings*) and using to the fullest a shifting panorama of stage sets, props, lights, and sounds, Kopit creates a frightfully effective universe where both the tragic and the comic straddle each other in plays that are parodistic and serious at the same time.

*The Questioning of Nick,* Kopit's first play, was written while he was a student at Harvard. A realistic treatment of a familiar situation, it deals with the questioning of a suspect in a beating. (pp. 15-16)

Although a minor work, *The Questioning of Nick* touches upon the theme of identity which Kopit was to enlarge upon in his succeeding plays. Rather than be a nobody, Nick freely chooses to assume a false identity, thereby incriminating himself in the eyes of the law. His early defiant spirit gone, and the confrontation with his self resolved, he now finds himself unable to walk out. He becomes a victim of his own myth, a man chained down by his personal destiny. It is as if, in Kafkaesque fashion, Kopit wants us to believe that the interrogation will never be complete. The door is wide open for that inevitable stream of interrogators who will question Nick with no particular aim in mind. And he, in turn, proceeding from one myth to another, from one identity to another, will walk shakily down the path of life.

With this play, it is already evident that to Kopit the absurdity of human existence can be unveiled at the slightest provocation and in the most mundane of circumstances. But it is still a far cry from the grotesque parable of distorted identities of *Oh Dad, Poor Dad.*

In his next important play, Kopit retreats into a magical netherworld where one has few clues to the identity of the characters. *Sing to Me Through Open Windows* takes the form of a dream, with a young boy, Andrew, gradually drifting from a bare stage to an unidentifiable world inhabited by Ottoman, the magician, and his helper/friend, the Clown. Nothing is well defined in this world (even Andrew thinks he was in a classroom before he found himself in this rustic setting), and it is unclear at first whether this is the boy's dream or that of the sleeping Ottoman. Gradually, however, it is revealed that the boy visits this exotic, faraway place once a year, but the reason for his annual pilgrimage is left a mystery. And, for that matter, so is most of this play. (pp. 16-17)

Although this play rivals Pinter's works in the use of studied pauses, the sense of threat or impending disaster is entirely absent. (p. 17)

*Sing To Me Through Open Windows* is a lament on the passing of time and life. And with the motion of time, identities change. (pp. 17-18)

Although Kopit's theatrical imagination is well put to evoking a non-spatial, non-temporal landscape, the play partly suffers from being too vague. There are too many unanswered questions about who the characters are. Kopit's most metaphysical work, it suggests the impossibility of our ever knowing the universe, represented as a world of illusion and shifting planes. The staging—with objects appearing from and disappearing into shadows, and haunting sound-effects, including echoes—effectively delineates the dubious boundaries of this world.

The whimsical and strangely odd world of Kopit's earlier plays soon gives way to the harsh brutality of *Oh Dad, Poor Dad, Mamma's Hung You in the Closet and I'm Feelin' So Sad.* Subtitled "A Farce in Three Scenes," the play takes place in a hotel room somewhere in the Caribbean while sounds of outdoor festivities intrude upon the indoors. Echoing the carnival spirit outdoors, the characters of this bizarre play exist in an atmosphere of total abandon. (p. 18)

*Oh Dad, Poor Dad* belongs within the tradition of the typical American family drama now brought up to date in an absurdist setting. But unlike so much of European absurdist drama, it has a strongly psychological bias to it. The relationship between Jonathan and his mother, and Madame Rosepettle's revengeful walks along the beach shooing couples in embrace, take on Oedipal overtones. Her personal memories about Mr. Rosepettle, with Hamlet-like meditations on the nature of sex and mortality, relegate the play, at times, to a heavy-handed thesis on the psychology of the human animal.

At its best, however, the philosophizing in the play takes on an air of parody. Through a tantalizing set of sequences, each more outrageous than the one preceding, Kopit manages to theatricalize the set of futile "beliefs" about the meaning of life on which the play rests. On occasion, however, the overly intellectual preoccupation with such beliefs leads to self-indulgence and the introduction of scenes that serve little purpose. Madame Rosepettle's chance encounter with Mr. Roseabove is a setup for an exchange in French that merely points a finger at the birthplace of absurdism and corroborates the Madame's pithy statement: "Feelings are for animals, Monsieur. Words are the speciality of Man." And true to her statement, the play's premise is grounded more on what is said than on what is done. (pp. 18-19)

*Oh Dad, Poor Dad* is indeed a bizarre and monstrous indictment of the American family and its dissolution amidst the craziness of Western civilization. While the play loses in its thematics for being heavily psychological in intent and wordy in its progression, its surrealistic imagery and dramatic action gain from the realistic family situation it seeks to portray. A theatrically powerful play, it remains to this day one of the more skillful indigenous products of absurdist playwriting.

*Chamber Music,* Kopit's next play, is just as much a psychological thriller as *Oh Dad, Poor Dad* minus the overt absurdity of the latter. (p. 19)

Though the plot can hardly be termed imaginative except as a rendering of a modern day ritual, the play's structure, with its musical repetition and the intricacy that is woven around the theme of ambiguous identities, is quite compelling. But these Pirandellian devices tire after a while, particularly since the dramatic action does not get under way until halfway through the play. Kopit gets sidetracked in the beginning and the play seems more to be a study of paranoia . . . and purposeless game playing. (pp. 19-20)

In *The Conquest of Mt. Everest,* a lesser work, Kopit relinquishes his absurdist fantasies and moves toward creating a fairy tale milieu. (p. 19)

Subtitled "A Divertissement," *Everest* is a whimsical tale of romance and adventure with an undercurrent of mild satire as Kopit provokes an encounter between East and West, between a soldier and two young lovers.

*The Hero* is a play without words. Kopit has written that he was "struck dumb by the prospect of writing two plays in a single day" (the other is *The Conquest of Mt. Everest*), explaining that is why *The Hero* is without dialogue. Whether his afterthoughts are to be taken seriously or not is beside the point. It is significant, however, that both plays were written in a single outburst of dramatic energy. Their themes and situations are slightly similar. The first takes place on a snow-covered peak where characters engage in everyday chatter, the other in a sun-drenched desert where characters are reduced to silence. They both last a day, and both present a man and a woman who gradually come closer together as the dramatic action advances. (pp. 20-1)

*The Day the Whores Came Out to Play Tennis* is a reversal of the dramatic situation in *Chamber Music*. Here it is the men who are under siege by a mysterious contingent of tennis racket-wielding women in their posh Cherry Valley Country Club. The exclusive and private club is invaded by eighteen women who pull up in Rolls Royces, hastily change from lavish gowns into tennis shorts sans underpants, and proceed to play tennis on the club's courts. By the end of the play they turn the tennis balls on the club house, which soon gives way with its trapped occupants inside.

Here—even more than the clash of cultural and social values in *Oh Dad, Poor Dad* (Madame Rosepettle's snobbish air and her typical condescension toward the Caribbean natives)—Kopit brutally indicts the vacuous and helpless world of the upper classes who are reduced to total immobility within their glass house. Unable to comprehend the senseless attack on their privacy and the whimsical nature of the world around them, the men pass their time playing cards, reminiscing about their past or their families (usually with deprecating remarks about their wives), and occasionally engaging their English butler Duncan in brief altercations that point up individual limitations.

As in *Chamber Music, Whores* suffers from a belated start in terms of its dramatic development. Despite this, however, the work succeeds partly because it is less abstract than the earlier play and also because the inane conversations in which the rusty and decadent vestiges of the upper class conduct themselves develop upon the theme of the play—the collapse of a civilization barely standing on its last legs. Furthermore, the tedium that debilitates *Chamber Music* is skillfully avoided in *Whores* through a deft handling of characterization, a less self-conscious use of dialogue, and generous doses of genuine comic absurdity and humor. Permeated by a willful defiance of logic, this play uses comedy to create the overwhelming sense of chaos that threatens to engulf the characters on all sides. It is laughter in the face of defeat, a final stand before the oncoming apocalypse. (pp. 21-2)

Unlike Kopit's earlier plays, where characterization often suffered from not being adequately integrated within the plot's more generalized thematics, in *Indians* both character and plot proceed hand in hand, each setting the other in poignant relief. Buffalo Bill's inner contradictions (he feels genuinely sorry for his Indian brothers and sisters, but is caught up nonetheless in the white man's race for individual supremacy and heroism) not only shed light on the plight of the vanquished Indians but, more significantly, expose the workings of an imperialistic and hypocritical nation.

By framing the play within the structure of a theatrical show (it is a play-within-a-play), *Indians* parallels Pirandellian drama. . . . Here, true to fact, Buffalo Bill is a hero of the "Wild West Show" and—simultaneously—hero (anti-hero for the Indians) of the play and of history. His own double identity underscores with no uncertain parody the double morality of a country which, in the final analysis, is the protagonist of the play.

If Pirandellian parallels are evident in Kopit's deft handling of Buffalo Bill's character and in the continual juxtaposition of his "show" life and his life as historical fact, shades of Brecht are amply in evidence in this political drama of a nation and its peoples. Superficially, the play's Brechtian attitude derives from its refashioning of history and its devices of alienation that grow out of such techniques as narration, lack of illusionism in stage decor and plot details, and frequent recourse to song and spectacle to break up dramatic action. On a deeper level, its similarity to Brechtian dramaturgy results from an acutely developed sense of irony that continually displaces audience expectations and compounds the various threads of identity—political, social, and individual—that run through the play.

In its willingness to confront seriously the American past, and its sensitivity in handling the plight of the American Indians, Kopit's play stands out as a rare commodity for its time. And it is to the playwright's credit that this is a work of political complexity expressed succinctly in a tightly structured and theatrically endearing form.

Kopit's next major work, *Wings,* is a return to his earlier preoccupation with identity as an act of individual destiny. Reminiscent of *Chamber Music,* the play charts a voyage of self-discovery in its most basic implications for a stroke victim, Emily Stilson. Having lost her power of speech, the old woman is reduced to a state of infancy and the play depicts her uphill climb to relearn and reevaluate experiences that will confirm her sense as an autonomous human being.

Since *Wings* was originally commissioned as a radio play, the emphasis on this growth into maturity and self-autonomy rests largely on linguistic pyrotechnics. Language disorder and a breakdown of linguistic, syntactical, and semantic structures plague Emily as she tries to cope with her aphasia. Unlike the schematic plays of Peter Handke, where Wittgensteinian philosophy provokes critical discourse within their structure, *Wings* is a descriptive foray less into the *meaning* of language as it relates to human individuation than the *fact* of a language and its inseparable bond to an understanding of the world. As such, the play is quite moving in its poignant portrayal of a woman who must retrace her linguistic matrix if life is to mean anything to her at all.

*Wings* is deliberately fragmented in its structure to parallel the inner fragmentation of a woman's world. Subdivided into four sections—Prelude, Catastrophe, Awakening, and Explorations—it moves in and out of an intricate latticework of haunting images that reflect the shattered and frightful intensity of Emily Stilson's incomprehensible universe. A theatrical tour de force both in terms of setting and characterization, *Wings* shifts, mutilates, and ultimately tries to sort out the ambiguous levels of space, time, and reality.

However, *Wings* can hardly be termed a study of consciousness. Its strict adherence to clinical accuracy leads occasionally to tedium as well as a certain effectiveness. Furthermore, the deliberately descriptive nature of the protagonist's physiological crisis subtracts from the spiritual and philosophical nature of her dilemma. Kopit's concern for his victim and the issue, which is assuredly of no little magnitude, is best manifest in the poetry of the language and the overwhelmingly moving visual aura in which the play is situated. When, occasionally, the writing attempts to reach for philosophical status, it is embarrassingly poor. At best, then, *Wings* is a poetic tribute to a generalized malaise captured in the body and mind of one struggling individual who, for better or for worse, is the unarguable protagonist of this intense drama.

Though his output has been small, Kopit's dramatic oeuvre reflects a more comprehensive world view than that of many of his prolific contemporaries. In *Indians* he demonstrated that he was quite capable of acting as America's social and political conscience during the worst of times. Without being dogmatic or overly pedantic he devised provocative theatrical forms to argue his perceptive social vision. Working within the then fashionable dramatic mode of European absurdism, he had in the sixties integrated social and existential questions in a way that addressed the American way of life. In all instances, Kopit's social commentary is grounded in a cohesive dramatic and theatrical premise, a reason why his plays succeed as well as they do on stage.

Furthermore, his willingness to forego the primacy of characterization (not to mention his frequent obsession with the nature of being and role-playing) gives his work a firm sense of actuality, an attitude that rescues at times his banal plots. It is also to Kopit's credit that he has convincingly accommodated larger themes within a private mythology, imbuing his plays with a poet's imagination. Hopefully Kopit's recent success with *Wings* will prompt him to write more. (pp. 23-5)

*Gautam Dasgupta, "Arthur Kopit," in* American Playwrights: A Critical Survey, Vol. 1 *by Bonnie Marranca and Gautam Dasgupta, Drama Book Specialists (Publishers), 1981, pp. 15-25.*

## JOHN SIMON

*Nine,* the musical into which Federico Fellini's film *8 1/2* has shrunk, is a curiously titillating, enervating, engaging, and frustrating piece of work. It displays much talent, some genuine achievement, equal amounts of intelligence and foolishness, a lot of vulgarity, and more than a little grace. You want it to be much better than it is because you can sense the wherewithal for distinction; you wince at opportunities let slip and false steps taken, but you never quite give up on it. In the end, you are left in a state of mixed excitation, unfulfilled expectancy, and mild revulsion, wondering whether you are sorry you came or sad at having to go.

I was never a great admirer of *8 1/2* (as I had been of most earlier Fellini), but there is no denying that the musical's book (if that's the word for it—a few scattered and randomly reas-

sembled signatures would be nearer the mark) is an impoverishment. The movie's Guido Anselmi was a film director and lecher who also had problems with religion, mysticism, cultural politics, high finance, fathoming his childhood, and coping with his dreams; the musical's Guido Contini has real difficulties only with his women and his writer's block. Thus in Arthur Kopit's book, based on a previous version by Mario Fratti, elements that in the movie found their places among many other contrasting, reinforcing, and range-extending ones balloon into overinflated, repetitious triviality. There are also such witless lines as "A cantaloupe is a genius compared to Guido Contini." . . .

[The] exploration of the director-and-womanizer's anxieties is trifling; still more so is the dipping into his past via his mother, his wife, and his childhood self. These remain from the movie, as do the voracious mistress, Carla, and the voluminous tart, Saraghina, and a few minor Fellinian figures. . . . The stage show merely conveys the mind's elegant prison; the movie, with its frantic agitation across shifting scenery, could show us life, the world, movement itself becoming a cage. . . .

There are, moreover, two enormous lapses. [One has to do with the acting. There is also the] lack of balls as this supposedly macho, frenziedly heterosexual carnival is swathed in flagrantly homosexual sensibility. Women are dressed, made up, made to behave in ways that reduce them to subaltern or threatening grotesques or succubae; and though there was some of this in *8 1/2*, there, at least, they didn't come across as female impersonators. Consequently, we get no contest between love and lust, only shadowboxing between oversimplified stick figures and bloated travesties. Yet even in this there is enough invention and skill to alleviate some of the sham and campy crudity. (p. 88)

Kopit's dialogue does rouse itself into some tart and telling exchanges. . . . The core of *Nine* may be hollow or even rancid, but the surface is dazzlingly dressed to the nines. (p. 89)

*John Simon, "Pieces of '8 1/2'," in* New York Magazine, *Vol. 15, No. 21, May 24, 1982, pp. 88-90.\**

## BRENDAN GILL

For obscure reasons of copyright or whatever, **"Nine"** remains officially silent in regard to its relationship to the [Federico Fellini movie "8 1/2"], but the title provides a bold enough clue, and so does the name of the hero, which is Guido Contini instead of Guido Anselmi. The book is credited to Arthur Kopit (Mario Fratti having provided an "adaptation from the Italian"), but the plot, the characters, and the settings have been lifted straight from the movie; all that is missing is its spirit, which is both comic and courageous. For although Fellini's Guido is in desperate straits, his misery yields hilarious consequences; lurking back of his despair is a prospect of joy. Life, Fellini seems to be saying, is often very hard as well as absurd, but oh, how desirable it is! How eager I am to come to terms with it, and how sorry I shall be to bid it goodbye! His Guido is an artist, and out of his suffering will emerge, sooner or later, a work of art. In **"Nine,"** Guido is an overgrown baby, and out of his suffering will emerge not a work of art but a succession of melodramatic tantrums. Back and forth he rushes, between the remembered bosom of his dead mother and the extravagantly throbbing bosoms of a host of living women, and all in vain.

Tradition holds that one oughtn't to take the message of a musical too seriously, and no doubt I will be thought a humorless spoilsport for saying that I found the message of **"Nine"** a thoroughly repellent one. Bluntly put, it is that women are ornamental receptacles, capable of pleasing men by serving them but incapable of taking thought and incapable also of pleasing one another in the absence of men. They are grossly defective human beings, who, painted and perfumed, incite men to reckless bouts of lust, thereby stealing from them their most precious possession. They are, in short, *things,* seductive and dangerous in the extreme; only as mothers can they be forgiven, and then only when they are safely in their graves. (We are expected in **"Nine"** to make an exception of Guido's wife, but her supposed wifeliness is precisely the measure of her unwomanliness; she might as well be Guido's uncle.) (p. 100)

> Brendan Gill, *"Women As Things," in* The New Yorker, *Vol. LVIII, No. 14, May 24, 1982, pp. 100, 102.*

## ROBERT BRUSTEIN

The new musical *"Nine"* . . . is the work of some very talented people, organized toward a dubious goal. Nothing these days is safe from adaptation into a Broadway musical, but the notion of musicalizing Fellini's *8 1/2* seems particularly lame-brained, until the curtain parts and you realize it just might work. For the opening scenes are spectacular. (p. 25)

Arthur Kopit loses interest in his book after establishing that Guido is a creature formed by sexual needs and career pressures, and his plotting is often sacrificed to camp effects—particularly a kitsch extravaganza rendering Guido's improvised film as a screamingly Baroque seventeenth-century opera about Casanova.

The evening is not without its verbal as well as its physical pleasures, but the desultory plot is resolved in an artificially sentimental manner, with a swift, unmotivated reconciliation between Guido and his wife. There is much talent, even genius, at work in *"Nine";* I found it vastly superior to the more extravagantly praised *Dreamgirls.* But it is a celebration less of substance than of technique. I fear that Kopit unwittingly built the most accurate estimate of this musical into his own dialogue: "Visually stunning but emotionally inane—if not dishonest." (pp. 25-6)

> Robert Brustein, *"The Great Artistic Director Burnout," in* The New Republic, *Vol. 186, No. 23, June 9, 1982, pp. 24-6.*

## CLIVE BARNES

Kopit is a disquieting playwright in that he never writes the same play twice. Works like *Oh Dad, Poor Dad, Wings,* or his epic *Indians,* even his book for the musical *'Nine',* have left an uncertain impression of wayward brilliance. Now, once more [with *End of the World*], he has given us something different, in this funny, clever, thoughtful, not always completely thought-out, play.

It is a complex, vastly entertaining, half-baked play. Clearly the comic style—perversely off-the-wall—could be well compared with say, Christopher Durang.

But really for this kind of didactic dialectic, this kind of half-serious, half-humorous argument, you have to go back to Ber-

nard Shaw. There is a quizzical Shavian perversity to this play that gives it its peculiar flavor.

For the hero—part playwright, part detective—has to do his investigations among the military establishment and the power brokers, and some of these gentlemen are not so far removed from the munitions manufacturer Undershaft in Shaw's *Major Barbara.*

But of course the lingo is now different. The lingo is now the language of doomsday, and Undershaft has become something like Dr. Strangelove.

We are told such new homilies as "a bluff taken seriously is much more valuable than a threat taken as a bluff." We are informed of the benefits of "anticipating retaliation rather than preemptive strikes," the merits of "a fail-safe, built-in breakdown machine," and offered the sage military intelligence that "going first is going best—no scenario has ever shown anything else."

As our hero in search of his play wanders through his cloud-cuckoo land of death, from the subject's first commission through its mysterious and sometimes over-obvious investigation, Kopit in the last part of the play comes across his discovery.

It is the concept of man as a self-destruct mechanism—man purveying death simply because it is there as an omnipresent temptation. It is not the world "not believing what it knows"—that idea is commonplace. No, as Kopit puts it: "There is a glitter to nuclear weapons—to release the energy that fuels stars!"

The deadly glitter of destruction—this is what the play is about, and in one telling moment, with the playwright faced with his son and the very principle of the death-force, Kopit reaches his bleakly pessimistic conclusion.

The faults of the play are windiness and hysteria. The merits are logic and humor—a gaggle of events in the Russian Tea Room, a duo of crazy experts talking of destruction as if it were a cooking recipe—and his final insight of doomsday's seductive fascination. Because—merely because—its possibility is with us.

> Clive Barnes, *"Laughing All the Way to the End of the World," in* New York Post, *May 7, 1984. Reprinted in* New York Theatre Critics' Reviews, *Vol. XXXXV, No. 8, May 7-May 13, 1984, p. 277.*

## FRANK RICH

[In **"End of the World"**] Mr. Kopit alights on a red-hot subject—the specter of nuclear holocaust—and bungles it so completely that he might as well be writing about toadstools instead of mushroom clouds.

One must assume that **"End of the World"** is merely an aberration in the career of a talented writer whose distinguished credits include **"Indians"** and **"Wings."** One might also say that Mr. Kopit deserves brownie points simply for thinking about the unthinkable at a time when many playwrights look obsessively inward. (Others may feel that it's more meretricious to trivialize serious issues than to ignore them.) The author can be given additional credit for doing his homework. In the program, Mr. Kopit thanks a large, ideologically ecumencial crew of notables who have helped shape his ideas—including Herman Kahn, Richard Pipes, Freeman Dyson and Jonathan Schell. These men's views often dribble out here, at a pace as attenuated as The New Yorker's serialization of some of their famous tomes.

The play does begin intriguingly. Michael Trent, the dramatist . . . , appears in a trench coat and establishes Mr. Kopit's guiding metaphor. "A playwright is very much like a detective," the hero declares, promising to track down clues that "lead to the solution of a crime." . . . A wealthy mystery man named Philip Stone . . . turns up at Trent's office with a Faustian offer. If the playwright will create a play about "global doom," Stone will make the struggling writer as rich as the author of "Cats."

It's not long after that, however, that **"End of the World"** reaches its dead end. . . .

Mr. Kopit's craftsmanship is laissez-faire in the extreme. Little is done with the Pirandellian device of having a playwright write a play that may be the play we're watching; the notion is merely restated over and over without being woven inventively into the fabric of the work. The pulp-detective fiction affectations are also inorganic and pretentious. Mr. Kopit apparently believes that if Trent keeps babbling about puzzles and clues—and if unidentified characters wearing dark sunglasses appear periodically—then he's creating an intellectual detective story in the style of, say, Tom Stoppard's "Jumpers." But there's no suspense in the play's line of thematic investigation of coherence to its narrative; the flashing neon hotel signs, sultry saxophone riffs and hard-boiled gangsterese do little except raise false audience expectations. It's only when Mr. Kopit sends up the horrifying Newspeak of the nuclear age—in phrases such as "anticipatory retaliation"—that we feel a witty playwright is at work.

Frank Rich, "New Kopit Play: Mystery of Motive," in The New York Times, May 7, 1984, p. C15.

## EDITH OLIVER

The subject about which Mr. Kopit has had the courage to invent a comedy [**"End of the World"**] is nuclear weaponry and our continuing failure, everywhere in the world, to address the problem of its control. A hard topic to be funny about? To put it coarsely, you can say that again; and so does the author—again *and* again, and with a greater degree of success than I would have thought possible, thanks to a literary adroitness that wrings laughter from us at the very moment when, shaking our heads, we whisper darkly among ourselves that the end of the world is no laughing matter. The structure of the play takes big literary chances: the hero, Michael Trent . . . , is a playwright, making up a plot even as we sit observing it. It is a plot that requires him to assume the role of a hardboiled private eye, complete with a twittery blond secretary and a Bogart trenchcoat. Aided by a wealthy patron, he gains access to a world of highly placed political and military dunces, for whom illogic is logic; to his chagrin, he perceives that there is no need to deduce the presence of evil in a world where idiocy not only abounds but flourishes.

Yeats spoke of the savage indignation that lacerated Swift's breast; plainly, a similar indignation lacerates our playwright's breast, and he has struggled to turn this indignation into art by the means most familiar to him. A comedy that seeks to sketch within a couple of hours the folly of the entire human race is understandably difficult to give a tidy conclusion to; an enigmatic freeze-frame brings down the curtain . . . , in an im-

mobility and silence that seem to embalm the raucous hurly-burly that has preceded them. (pp. 128, 130)

Edith Oliver, "Joy and Torment," in The New Yorker, Vol. LX, No. 13, May 14, 1984, pp. 128, 130.*

## JOHN SIMON

Although bristling with imperfections, Arthur Kopit's **End of the World** is not a play to be dismissed out of the hand. It is a lean, perhaps too lean, and biting, perhaps not biting enough, second act trying to get out from under not entirely relevant and somewhat flabby first and third acts, so as to hook on to more pertinacious and pertinent material. That way lies a mordant satire on nuclear escalation and the abyss over which Moscow and Washington are dancing their soft-shoe, or soft-brain, routine. The play's dramaturgy is faulty, but there is wit, intelligence, and theatricality in it searching for a satisfying form that unfortunately eludes the author's grasp. Yet neither Kopit nor we come away wholly empty-handed.

The task was staggering. Basing his play on something that actually happened to him, Kopit tells the story of a super-rich philanthropist who comes out of the blue waving greenbacks and a four-page outline and asks the playwright hero to turn this into the anti-bomb play that might, in the nick of time, help save the world. The mysterious Maecenas, called Philip Stone, guarantees the writer, dubbed Michael Trent, a lavish, long-lasting, and remunerative production, most alluring to the younger man: "I'd been hoping to sell out for years. This could be it." Stone also informs Trent that they have met before, and eventually reveals that he chose Trent because of his knowledge of evil, all of which leaves the playwright, who remembers nothing, utterly baffled. But the real hitch is that the brief scenario is, apparently, no good, and Trent hasn't a clue about how to develop it.

The difficulty for the audience is an equation with too many unknowns: What is in that scenario? Why is it bad? Why does Trent so elaborately resist a commission he needs? (Could it be just a ploy to stretch the play into three acts?) What is this evil Trent has discovered? How does Stone know about it? We do get answers, but they are very late in coming, a bit lame, and lamentably unintegrated into the play. Integration, aside from a certain smugness, is, in fact, the chief problem here.

Kopit uses the conceit of the playwright as a mystery-story private investigator, hired in this case to investigate our government; but either the mystery format cheapens and trips up the real subject, or the author hasn't quite done his Spade work. Further, Act I is largely taken up with show-biz in-jokes, some of which are quite funny. . . . But this, too, becomes a dead end keeping the play from its goal.

In Act III, Kopit tries to link up the threat of starting Armageddon with something lurking in all of us. The story Trent tells about himself and his small, defenseless child is psychologically challenging (and was, as it happens, told me once in almost identical terms by a young mother about herself and *her* tiny son), but neither it nor Stone's self-revelation is properly wound into the main strand of the play. And perhaps it couldn't be, as long as that strand is absurdist satire, no less outrageous but more real than *Dr. Strangelove*. It is in that Strangelovian middle part that the play's best achievement and potential lie. Trent meets various atomic strategists—military and civilian, political and scientific—representing people whom Kopit actually interviewed. They talk about the need "to learn how to wage nuclear war rationally'' and about how launching it is ''a defensive act—anticipatory retaliation.'' . . . (p. 104)

But Kopit has not found the way to fuse these preposterous yet credible caricatures with his flesh-and-blood people: Stone, Trent, Trent's wife and small son. Perhaps there is no way. A takeoff on Hammett, a spoof of *All the President's Men*, a Pirandellian contrivance whereby the play to be written is the play enacted, Candide (must Trent be so naïve?) in Strangelove Country, a clinical-poetic examination of human power lust and self-destructiveness, and a lachrymose plea to save our children may be too many disparate objects for a playwright not one of the Flying Karamazov Brothers to juggle in style. (pp. 104-05)

John Simon, ''Bangs and Whimpers,'' in New York Magazine, Vol. 17, No. 21, May 21, 1984, pp. 104-06.*

## JACK KROLL

In Arthur Kopit's **"End of the World,"** thinking the unthinkable becomes dramatizing the undramatizable. And this play—impudent but honorable, frightened but courageous, playful but concerned, funny but somber—almost brings it off. Brings what off? Brings off getting you to think about the unthinkable from some kind of new angle. The unthinkable, of course, is the specter of nuclear war. Kopit was commissioned by a tycoon to write a play on this subject, and he came to realize that the only way he could write a play about the prospect of nuclear war was to write a play about a playwright trying to figure out how to write a play about the prospect of nuclear war.

Immediately, you see, Kopit is into the wonderland of inside-out logic that is the world of nuclear thinking. Step back, he's telling himself, get some distance, make it a game. Nuclear thinking, after all, is a game theory with the highest stakes imaginable. So Kopit went to a classic American genre game, the private-eye story. His mysterious tycoon . . . comes to a somewhat seedy playwright . . . just the way clients come to Raymond Chandler's Philip Marlowe. . . .

Kopit's approach may look sophomoric, but actually it's a good idea—the kind of idea that a brilliant artist-surrealist-logician like the late French writer Raymond Queneau might have made into a dazzling success. Kopit doesn't have the steel-trap control of a Queneau, but he has something almost as good—an American rock-bottom sincerity and sophisticated naiveté that make him an admirable surrogate for most of us sincere, bewildered, sophisticated, naive citizens. And he finds out a good deal, which he transmits not in thick tomes but in sharp, clever, scary scenes. Example: two young computer whiz-bangs in their kitchen cook up a gourmet meal while gleefully regaling Shea with a mind-boggling fusillade of scenarios about first strikes, anticipatory retaliation and all the deadly serious jabberwocky of nuclear strategy.

There are similar scenes with a Pentagon general and with a Russian who's an expert on Soviet jabberwocky. There's a crazy fascination to much of this—Kopit is trying to get us to listen to the ideas that are part of a whole new system of thought that's come in with the nuclear age. Although he's clearly appalled by this synthesis of Einstein and Abbott and Costello, he plays fair—this play is the most accessible synthesis we've had of Nuke-speak. And Kopit at the end has the courage (or recklessness) to express his own view of the evil that may break through the circles of logic to unleash a nuclear apocalypse. Unwieldy, uneven, garrulous, grotesque, **"End of the World"** nonetheless has guts and feeling and a fine American impertinence.

Jack Kroll, ''Nuclear Jabberwocky,'' in Newsweek, Vol. CIII, No. 22, May 28, 1984, p. 87.

# Philip (Arthur) Larkin

## 1922-

English poet, novelist, and critic.

Larkin is among England's foremost living poets. During John Betjeman's tenure as Poet Laureate, Larkin was often referred to as "Britain's *other* Poet Laureate," both because of his stature and because he is seen as a spokesman for the average person living in post-World War II England. Larkin's best-known poem is "Church Going," in which an agnostic speaker puzzles over the attraction churches hold for him. In the speaker's search for an empirical basis for his religious feelings critics have seen a metaphor for the modern sensibility. Larkin's poetry comments on contemporary life through a speaker who is self-deprecating, yet witty; cynical, yet concerned with such themes as love, loneliness, and the passage of time. Despite his specifically English point of view, Larkin's sensitive treatment of these themes has made his work universally appreciated.

Larkin's first three publications followed soon after his graduation from Oxford University in 1943. These include a poetry collection, *The North Ship* (1945), and Larkin's only novels, *Jill* (1946) and *A Girl in Winter* (1947). Although the novels are generally well regarded by critics, Larkin has said that he considers all three books to be juvenilia. *The North Ship* received little notice, and Larkin's next book, the privately published *XX Poems* (1951), was virtually ignored by critics. Larkin's reputation rests largely on his three later poetry collections: *The Less Deceived* (1955), which includes thirteen of the *XX Poems* and others, *The Whitsun Weddings* (1964), and *High Windows* (1974). Larkin said in a 1982 interview, "It is unlikely I shall write any more poems." However, he has recently published a collection of critical writings and essays, *Required Writing: Miscellaneous Pieces 1955-1982* (1983).

Larkin is linked by some critics with "The Movement" writers of the 1950s, whose work was anthologized in Robert Conquest's *New Lines* (1956). Among the authors included in this collection are Larkin, Kingsley Amis, Thom Gunn, D. J. Enright, and John Wain. These writers favored clear, rational writing in traditional forms over the highly symbolic works of W. B. Yeats, the experimental prose of James Joyce, and the obscure writing of such modernists as Ezra Pound and T. S. Eliot. Larkin himself has led a crusade against modernism, most notably in his introduction to *All What Jazz* (1970), a collection of his jazz record reviews. In this essay, he faults modernists—exemplified by Pound, jazz musician Charlie Parker, and painter Pablo Picasso—for creating works that are deliberately obscure, intrinsically unpleasant to the senses, and pretentious.

Larkin's poetic style has not always been staunchly anti-modernist. Many of the poems in *The North Ship* were modelled after the work of Yeats. Larkin subsequently rejected Yeats's influence and turned for inspiration to the poetry of Thomas Hardy, whom he still regards as his model. The poems in *The Less Deceived* and *The Whitsun Weddings* display Hardy's influence. They are rational, empirical, and rely primarily on metaphor rather than symbol. From Hardy, Larkin learned to write poetry which evokes his own experiences and their

Photograph by Mark Gerson

attendant emotions by tying them to a concrete time and place. Thus, his poetry often revolves around commonplace occurrences and settings. Although Larkin has never disavowed his opinions on modernism, many critics see a return to Yeatsian symbolism in "Solar" and several of the other nature poems in *High Windows*.

Many of Larkin's poems have been linked to a single narrative voice. Larkin's speaker is a hard-working, shy loner who leads an unremarkable life and often feels melancholy. He is a self-doubter, acutely aware of his capacity for self-delusion; thus, the conclusions he draws about the rightness of the choices he makes are tentative. For example, the narrator in "Self's the Man" contrasts his life with that of a family man and concludes, "I'm a better hand at knowing what I can stand. . . . Or I suppose I can." Some critics have noted that self-delusion is a dominant theme in both of Larkin's novels as well as in his poetry. The protagonist in *Jill*, a first-year student at Oxford, must confront the fact that reality will not measure up to his fantasy of himself and an imaginary girlfriend. In "Deceptions," a poem which appears in *The Less Deceived*, Larkin addresses a rape victim, telling her that while she suffers pain and humiliation, she is less deceived than her attacker, who anticipates fulfillment, yet will find it a "desolate attic." Many other Larkin poems also challenge "illusions" by which modern man lives: that love and society can combat loneliness, that one can make free and intelligent choices, that the passage of time is not relentless.

Larkin once said that his poetry is "too simple to profit from criticism." While his poems are structurally traditional and have clear diction, critical analysis has yielded layers of meaning in much of his work. Larkin's few detractors accuse him of insularity, narrowness, and lack of emotion in his poetry. Some grow impatient with what they perceive as his gloomy tone. However, many find hope and comfort in Larkin's writings. Stephen Hilliard wrote: "For me, his ability to face and live in a world of limited and uncertain meaning is provocative. . . . I was attracted to Larkin by the wit and beauty of his verse, but I have come to value more its clear-voiced honesty at a time when many of us conceal ourselves in rhetoric or retreat into silence."

(See also *CLC*, Vols. 3, 5, 8, 9, 13, 18; *Contemporary Authors*, Vols. 5-8, rev. ed.; and *Dictionary of Literary Biography*, Vol. 27.)


## P. R. KING

[From *The Less Deceived, The Whitsun Weddings*, and *High Windows*] there has emerged a consistency of poetic identity. It is the identity of a detached yet careful observer of the behaviour of himself and others. In many poems [Larkin] seems to turn away from the society of others and to take up a solitary stance implying a purer vantage point from which to survey life in his 'humorous, self-deprecatory and observant' way. The adoption of this role and a frequently ironic tone should not mislead the reader into assuming he is unmoved by his feelings and response to what he observes. The detachedness appears to be the necessary concomitant of his view of the artist's role. He observes and remains apart as a result of his commitment to an art which is to record and preserve life rather than to enact or transcend life. He sees this commitment as demanding above all an honesty about his own nature and, if this requires him to be on the outside looking in, it must be accepted. This is made plain in 'Reasons for Attendance', where art is seen as his way of remaining true both to himself and to what he observes. The person in the poem is looking through a lighted window to watch people dancing inside. He realizes he prefers to remain outside and he asks himself why this should be so. . . .

> What calls me is that lifted, rough-tongued bell
> (Art, if you like) whose individual sound
> Insists I too am individual. . . .
>      Therefore I stay outside,
> Believing this; and they maul to and fro,
> Believing that; and both are satisfied,
> If no one has misjudged himself. Or lied.

Although the dedication to his art is insisted upon, the final two words make it clear there is no room for self-congratulation. Larkin is aware that even this commitment of his may finally be as much an illusion and self-deception as those he exposes elsewhere in so many of his poems. Larkin seems anxious not to be taken in even by his own commitments.

The voice of this poetic identity has many tones and a variety of diction and idiom. It can be sharp and satirical ('**Vers de Société**'), quiet and almost plaintive ('**Broadcast**'), conversational and meditative ('**Church Going**'), even lyrical and mysterious ('**Coming**'), and occasionally resentful and bitter ('**Send No Money**'). In all these tones and moods the same tension is

at work: the conflict between our dreams, hopes and expectations, and the various ways in which reality serves to make them collapse. Larkin records the various ways in which man pulls the wool over his own eyes in being tempted to believe that he can achieve a paradise of money, or fame, or sex, or close relationships with others. He explores the way we 'pick up bad habits of expectancy' which is only to be destroyed eventually by that 'solving oblivion' which runs just under everything we do. He is concerned to expose our illusions and evasions so that we may stand naked but honest, 'less deceived' by ourselves before the reality of life and death.

It is this underlying concern which provides the constancy of the relatively small number of themes in Larkin's poetry: the passage of time, memory and the past, the illusory visions of man (especially the failure of the promise of love) and old age and death. But this continuity of theme should not blind the reader to the variety of tone, form and intention in the poems. The central poetic identity remains constant but does not become dull. Larkin's poetry may not develop in the sense of going through any sudden alterations of theme or style, but it rather has continued to deepen and refine his chosen concerns. He has said, 'I don't think I want to change; just to become better at what I am.' This has led some critics to be suspicious of his achievement, as if development in its meaning of change was the *sine qua non* of greatness in poetry. Since he found his mature style in *The Less Deceived* Larkin has not sought this kind of development. . . . (pp. 4-6)

At the heart of Larkin's poetry lies a constant awareness of the passing of time and a belief that man is always in thrall to time. Time strips us of illusions and is the bearer of realities which we would prefer to avoid. . . . Time is a chain that binds us to our earlier hopes and dreams which, as we grow older, we realize will never become reality. This sense of loss, of hopes blasted and ideals destroyed, pervades the poetry. In many of the poems Larkin looks over his shoulder at his own past, or indirectly considers that past by observing the youth around him, and rubs his nose in the fact that memory is cruel enough to remind us that the adult life we now experience as mundane and drab is that very same life that in our childhood and youth we invested with all possible excitement and meaning. There is a double cruelty in time: it both reminds us of what we *might* have had, and turns what we *do* have into a sense of disappointment. (pp. 6-7)

Although others might claim man can assert his will to prevent such diminishing of his hopes, the *persona* in many of these poems rules that out. He adopts a deterministic view of life whereby 'something hidden from us' destroys all attempts we make consciously to control our lives and seize our happiness. This attitude may be seen at work in '**Triple Time**', '**Next, Please**', '**I Remember, I Remember**', '**Dockery and Son**' and '**Arrivals, Departures**'. (p. 7)

Two of the best poems concerning the relationship between the past, memory and the possibilities of hope are '**I Remember, I Remember**' and '**Dockery and Son**'. Each is concerned with the memories of the poet's own past and they succeed in convincing the reader of his honesty to his feelings.

In '**I Remember, I Remember**' the poet is travelling by train with a companion when they pass through the city in which the poet was born. . . . His travelling companion asks him if the town they are passing through, his home town, is where he has his roots. . . . [The poet replies], 'No, only where my childhood was unspent'. That 'unspent' carries a world of disillusion. His honest recognition of the ordinariness of his child-hood is a deliberate defiance of all the romantic self-aggrandizing gestures of the artist and his fawning public. . . . The appeal of the poem lies in the poet's self-exposure, his own refusal to compensate for his own sense of ordinariness by sentimentalizing his past. But the reader carries away from the poem an after-feeling that someone who can so confidently assert the omnipresence of 'nothing' is unlikely to be the one to escape a sense of the dullness and futility of life.

The price that the individual may have to pay for his refusal to be under any illusions about life is the theme of **'Dockery and Son'**. It is a poem that is central to any understanding of Larkin's mixture of honesty and self-doubt which is so much a part of his best poems. Like many of these poems, the total effect of **'Dockery and Son'** is only to be understood by an appreciation of the careful manipulation of tone. It begins in a calm, unruffled manner which is soon broken by a realization of the passage of time and opportunities, and it culminates in an acceptance that our lives are ultimately controlled by powers beyond those we may influence.

These thoughts are prompted by a visit that the poet pays to his former college where the Dean tells him that the son of Dockery, one of the poet's college contemporaries, is studying there. This announcement is what leads the poet on to consider the very different ways in which individuals carve out their lives. (pp. 10-12)

Dockery, the poet assumes, must have been a man who knew early what he wanted from life. The poet finds it difficult to understand Dockery's desire for paternity. . . . This leads him to speculate on the source of our assumptions about the way our lives should be lived and his answer to this question suggests a determinism about life. It is not our ideals nor our selfishness that control our life ('Those warp tight-shut, like doors') but rather that our habits, never consciously chosen, harden with the passage of time into the only life we have. Thus Dockery's paternity and the poet's bachelorhood are equal destinies: they are both results of neither choice nor desire but simply the fact of life happening, as it were, behind their backs before they had time to realize the situation they were in. It appears that choice is one of life's major illusions. Larkin has revealed elsewhere that it is a deception that man regularly plays on himself to believe that, had we acted differently at some crucial point in our past, our present would have been changed. There is here a strong suggestion that our lives are beyond our control and that we are being continually displaced from our own possibilities by a force stronger than ourselves. . . . (pp. 12-13)

The success of the poem lies in its precise rendering of the changing tones of voice and the tension between the idea of divergent paths in people's lives and the poet's personal conviction that our lives are determined by powers outside our control. The poem betrays a strong feeling that it is time which decides all in a man's life and that the best a man can do is not to delude himself into thinking it can be otherwise. . . . Finally the poem is valuable rather for its creation of a distinct and powerful sense of a personality brooding over the facts of his experience, than for its sweeping generalization.

A desire not to be fooled by time leads to a concern to maintain vigilance against a whole range of possible evasions of reality. It is partly this which makes Larkin's typical stance one of being to one side of life, watching himself and others with a detached eye. The privilege of such an outsider's role is that

it allows him to expose the illusions of those who remain too close to their experience ever to stand back and take an objective view of themselves. In many poems the *persona* expresses an acute awareness both of his own limitations and of the illusions of those he sees around him. These poems record his refusal to be deceived into evading reality. We have already seen this in relation to time and love, but there are a variety of other evasions and deceptions and Larkin's exposure of them can often be humorous and witty.

One of the realities of life, for most people, is the need to work. In **'Toads'** Larkin displays a lively fun as well as self-awareness in his picture of the ever-present demands of the routine of work. He sees work as a huge and dirty toad squatting on our lives. . . . The poem is lightly handled, the lines alternate in a tripping rhythm of trimeters and dimeters; the rhymes are slant ('wits/louts') with a wit of their own; the language is idiomatic and lively; the toad image is amusing, and all these characteristics add up to a humorous light verse with a serious underlying self-awareness.

**'Toads Revisited'**, published in a later volume, expands the same subject. But this poem has a darker mood. It describes the poet enjoying a day off from work. He walks in the park and observes all the others there who have managed to free themselves from the toad of work. But, in contrast to the previous poem in which people used their wits to free themselves from work, the people he sees in this poem are old, ill or outcast—they are the witless. . . . This expresses the other side of the idea of work. The in-tray, the secretary, the busy routines of work are seen here as a necessary barrier to keep out loneliness, boredom and meaninglessness. Ultimately, however, even work cannot put off the inevitable, and in the poem's final couplet (which has the only full rhyme in the poem and therefore pulls the reader up with a jolt) work is seen as a mask worn to hide ourselves from death. But the poet knows no such hiding is possible:

> Give me your arm, old toad:
> Help me down Cemetery Road.

**'Poetry of Departures'** is heavily ironical. It considers this possibility of freeing ourselves from the enervating routines of a dull life. It examines the response of admiration, even approval, that we often have when we hear of someone who has really made the break and got away from it all. . . . But the poet points out that for most of us this is an easy, unthinking reaction that is part of a purely fantasy revolt against our situation.

A double use of irony is at work in this poem. The first target for it is the unthinking, escapist romanticism in our response. . . . The second target of the irony is the poet's own 'ordered life' from which he has launched his first attack on the dishonest romanticizing of those who evade their responsibilities by just clearing off. Admitting to a feeling that he detests his room at times . . . , the poet turns on himself and in the last stanza attacks his overdeveloped notion of an orderly and conventional life—'Books; china; a life / Reprehensibly perfect'.

The title **'Poetry of Departures'** is intended to suggest the fond illusion that some kind of liberation is to be discovered in throwing up the life we know for some vaguely imagined alternative. But to the poet this is an evasion. Yet the double irony works to suggest that his own refusal to be taken in by the romantic cliché may itself be another evasion. The well-ordered life might be a cowardice in the face of different ways of living. It is a cliché of another kind. The irony is a weapon against the artificial perfections of both responses to life, and it creates a self-knowledge and honesty characteristic of Larkin as a poet. (pp. 14-17)

[In some poems] Larkin employs satire and a heavy irony to expose some of the fatuities and pretensions of various attitudes.

A favourite target for satire is the cynically ambitious literary academic. In **'Naturally the Foundation Will Bear Your Expenses'** it is the jet-setting, name-dropping, trendy literary academic who is satirized for his reduction of the pursuit of truth and knowledge to no more than a hunt for the quickest means to advance his career. (p. 19)

Another strongly satirical poem is the recent **'Vers de Société'**. This attacks the conventional notion that being sociable is one of the highest virtues, and it explores the tension between solitariness and sociability, truth and hypocrisy. The poet receives an invitation to cocktails whose hypocrisy is expressed in his scornful interpretation of its real meaning. . . . Yet, even after seeing the truth of it, the poet finally accepts. This gulf between the manifest relations of the poet and the sender of the invitation and their true, hidden relationship leads the poet to speculate about the general connection of sincerity and social relations. The poet admits that he finds it difficult to be alone and seeks companionship even when he knows it to be a charade. He would prefer the courage to remain solitary but knows he lacks it. This self-awareness gives him an insight into society's attitude towards solitariness. Society hides its fear of loneliness under the guise of a false morality when it utters the clichés 'All solitude is selfish' or 'Virtue is social'. This stems from a self-centredness the very opposite of the one acknowledged: 'the big wish / Is to have people nice to you, which means / Doing it back somehow'. Being sociable is so often just playing at being interested in others. Nevertheless, having admitted all this, the poet suggests that perhaps after all the charade may in fact hint at what *should* be the reality. But, for the middle-aged poet, the truth is that it is neither loneliness nor some altruistic desire to be interested in others that provides the motive for his final acceptance of the invitation. It is his admission of a wholly human weakness:

> Only the young can be alone freely.
> The time is shorter now for company,
> And sitting by a lamp more often brings
> Not peace, but other things.
> Beyond the lights stand failure and remorse
> Whispering *Dear Warlock-Williams: Why,*
>     *of course—*

This is a poem which begins in a satirical spirit but which, through the exercise of a subtle change of tone reflecting the inquiringly self-critical mind of the poet, finally becomes a penetrating analysis of a common human situation.

In Larkin's poetry [love] is one of the supreme illusions of man. When love is present in his poems it is something either hopelessly longed for (as in **'Faith Healing'**) or cynically dismissed as just another evasion of reality (as in **'Love Songs in Age'**). **'An Arundel Tomb'** and **'Faith Healing'** make it clear that, although man clutches at his instinctive belief that only love will comfort, console and sustain him, such a hope is doomed to be denied. A lover's promise is an empty promise and the power to cure suffering through love is a tragic illusion. . . . (pp. 21-2)

**'Self's the Man'** is about marriage and contrasts that state—through the family life of one Arnold—with the bachelorhood of the poet. Arnold, the poet allows, 'is less selfish than I' because he got married and is providing for a family. But we are soon left with little doubt as to the price poor Arnold pays. . . . Any apparent sympathy for Arnold is soon lost by the insistence on the fact that 'He married a woman to stop her getting away' and that he is not really any less selfish than the bachelor because 'He still did it for his own sake / Playing his own game'. The one important difference seems to be that the poet considers himself to be better at knowing what will keep him sane. . . . It is a comic yet cruel portrait of marriage. Even [the] last line, implying that in the end the poet is not completely confident that his is the best deal after all, does not wholly overcome a rather sneering quality in the poem. It leaves a suspicion that self-justification may be stronger than any self-doubt.

**'Self's the Man'** and **'If, My Darling'** can begin to look like rationalizations of an inability to sustain a genuinely close relationship. **'Wild Oats'** gives support to this judgement to some extent. It records how the poet met two girls, one beautiful and one plain, and how he courted the plain girl, became engaged to her and then broke it off, while all the time it was really to the other girl that he had lost his heart. Finally he gains neither. He puts the loss down to his shyness and inability to declare his true love, but the real reason for his disappointment goes deeper than that: it is a result of his dishonesty to his true feelings.

**'No Road'** and **'Talking in Bed'** appear to claim that love, in any case, has little room for honesty and genuine closeness. They express an inability to draw near to someone else. (pp. 23-4)

In these poems Larkin's lover is an individual who is either afraid of love or has been made powerless to love by his corrosive honesty and self-awareness. He believes that 'that much-mentioned brilliance, love' which is 'still promising to solve, satisfy, / And set unchangeably in order' (**'Love Songs in Age'**) is totally false in the hopes it raises. Love is one of man's self-deceptions: it cannot bear all the weight of the dreams we place upon it.

Larkin's most moving expression of the relationship between love, time and truth is **'An Arundel Tomb'**. The immediate subject of this is a monument of a medieval knight and his lady recumbent upon their grave in Chichester Cathedral. The description of the monument focuses on the fact that the stone-mason has carved the couple as if holding hands. The remainder of the poem argues that what was carved as no more than a simple reminder of their marital status has been taken by our generation as a powerful symbol of undying love. It seems that because the stone has endured so long the onlooker is inclined to attribute similar endurance to the husband's and wife's love, an attribution that the poet sees as a misrepresentation of reality brought about by our too eager willingness to use the mere passage of time to uphold our sentimental hopes. . . . [The penultimate phrase] 'almost-instinct almost true' suggests both the desire to believe in love and the poet's refusal (as he sees it) to be taken in by sentimentality. Nevertheless the phrase implies that the joined hands may almost be a true statement because the mason's instinct for what would best represent his subject merges with the modern observer's example of a perennial human need to believe in love—a need the poet here acknowledges even while refusing to give his assent to it. (pp. 25-6)

The two themes this poem links are quintessential Larkin: that the passage of time may be used by man to destroy or deny the truth as he struggles to redefine his past; and that love, as one of man's supreme attempts to live an ideal, cannot support the expectations we have of it.

There are two groups of poems among Larkin's published work which strike a more positive note than many of the poems so far discussed. In the first there is a small number of poems that express a sense of fulfilment unusual to Larkin; and in the second group, a group that contains his most ambitious and successful poems, there are several which tentatively explore the possibility of positive meaning in life.

The short lyrical poems of the first group make frequent use of images drawn from nature to celebrate a sense of power and purpose, as in **'Wedding Wind', 'Coming', 'For Sidney Bechet', 'Water'** and **Solar'**. (p. 27)

[Perhaps] it is the brief and beautiful lyricism of **'Coming'** that is the most delicate expression of Larkin's rare 'epiphanies' (as John Bayley—employing a term used by James Joyce—has called those poems which celebrate the poet's infrequent moments of delight). . . . It is a perfect evocation of a mood in which every aspect of the poem contributes to its articulation. The momentary gasp of delight at the reaffirmation of spring, of the possibility of new growth—the short intermission of positive meaning—is like a sudden visitation of grace to the poet to allow him to enjoy the scene and season without his fully understanding the reasons for such an unexpected accession of delight. (pp. 28-9)

Listening to the jazz player in **'For Sidney Bechet',** the speaker of the poem experiences another moment of affirmation and happiness in which the music is 'greeted as the natural noise of good / Scattering long-haired grief and scored pity'. But the choice of 'scattering' and 'scored' creates a submerged ambiguity in its suggestion that, although the music has the power to overcome grief and express pity, it nevertheless also expresses the suffering which is the source of blues music and is therefore *scattered* in the notes that are *scored* for the player (and the experience which is their source is also *scored* in the player's personality). It is as if the affirmative mood must not be allowed to escape the realities of life.

Only in **'Solar'** does Larkin appear to express an unequivocally positive note. This poem is a brief hymn to the sun that is a 'suspended lion face / Spilling at the centre / Of an unfurnished sky'. This exuberant image with its almost physical force (a reading aloud draws attention to the alliterated sibilants which give a sense of the overflowing flood of energy and light) is typical of the complete poem. In its final part the lion-faced sun (an image born of the sun's appearance but also suggesting its fierce heat and its ruling over the whole of life) becomes a source of both delight and awe, two responses almost unique in Larkin's poetry.

The second group of poems, which could be said to represent a search for a more positive view of life, is composed of poems less wholeheartedly affirmative than these. The two most successful of this and any other group of Larkin's poems, **'Church Going'** and **'The Whitsun Weddings',** are rather tentative examinations of meaning and hope. Together with later poems like **'To The Sea', 'Show Saturday'** and **'Livings'** they represent Larkin's most balanced response to life. (p. 30)

[**'Church Going'**] is not a religious poem unless the word 'religion' is interpreted very broadly. It is a recognition that in the past the church has ministered to a perennial human need which cannot be brushed aside in a secular society. The narrator's role is to exemplify this in his own need and discovery of that 'hunger in himself to be more serious'. He is modern man who truly does not know the worth of this 'accoutred frowsty barn' but who is pulled towards it almost despite himself. The value of this poem is that it does two things at once, both of which summarize the basic dilemma of an age without faith: it reveals that age's desire to dismiss what it considers to be the spurious crutches of superstition and religion; and it reveals our continuing need to recognize and symbolize our deepest nature. It does not resolve the tensions between this scepticism and this desire to believe. The difference between them is caught in the contrasting language of the opening and closing stanzas, although the subtly achieved movements from the language of the one to that of the other through the voice of the same narrator might point to the possibility of some form of resolution.

**'The Whitsun Weddings'** may also be seen as a comment on this 'hunger to be serious' and is a poem that similarly moves from personal experience and observation, eventually to speak with the voice of a whole society. The subject of the poem is the narrator's observations of the several wedding parties that he sees boarding his train at the different stations on the way down to London one Whitsun Saturday. This situation is archetypal Larkin—several of his poems take place on journeys—because the passenger role allows the narrator to remain detached, uninvolved in the action, and yet to enter into the lines of those he carefully observes and to embrace them in a universalized meditation. His detachment does not mean he is unmoved; rather, it gives him the opportunity to 'see things as they are'. (pp. 33-4)

In the final lines [Larkin's] personal interpretation of events becomes dominant. As the various newly married couples are blended into a shared harmony in their brief journey, their common hopes of fulfilment are blessed by the narrator's affirmation. His early tone of detached amusement modulates into an earnest yet unsolemn prayer for their future. (p. 35)

This poem may be read as dealing with English society as a whole through its panorama of scenes and the couples who suggest the recurring life of a whole community, together with the traditional journey image as a symbol for life itself. In this way it becomes almost a muted prayer for the continuously revitalizing power of change in society—a forward impetus and hope of fulfilment, even if such fulfilment still remains 'out of sight'. It is perhaps as positive a view as is possible for a poet who finds such difficulty in believing in the fruition of dreams and ideals.

**'Church Going'** refers to the need for some symbolic focus for life's most serious moments, and one of these moments with its attendant rituals is the subject of **'The Whitsun Weddings'.** In some ways, it seems that Larkin can see all sorts of social rituals as bearers of a traditional sense of community and harmony. In *High Windows* several poems, like **'To the Sea'** and **'Show Saturday',** describe with loving care the communal rituals of such occasions as the annual seaside holiday and a rural agricultural show. They describe, in the same honest and unsentimental language of the description of the wedding parties in **'The Whitsun Weddings',** the 'annual pleasure, half a rite' of family holidays and communal shows. The poet knows that such occasions cannot entirely overcome time's insidious attack upon individuals and societies but nevertheless they are to be welcomed and celebrated. . . . (pp. 36-7)

In the end everyone must face the fate of time's embrace, the inevitable fact of old age and death. Throughout this poetry we have been made aware of that 'solving emptiness / That lies just under all we do' ('**Ambulances**'). It is a solving in two senses: it is death as the only certain solution to the riddle of the goal of life; and it is the awareness of the coming of death and man's 'costly aversion of the eyes from death' which *dissolves* any possibility of our dreams becoming the reality. Two poems from *High Windows* particularly express a middle-aged man's awareness of this inexorable decline towards oblivion. (p. 37)

'**The Old Fools**' is a devastating expression of the poet's feelings about the approach of age and death, its awfulness and strange otherness which will yet inevitably become the experience of us all. It enacts the middle-aged man's growing sense of time running out and his angry and bitter recognition that life can end in such a cruel and undignified way. The poet's proud determination not to be deceived here ends in a final awareness for which ignorance, in fact, could be the only palliative.

'**The Building**' reveals a more stoical acceptance of death. This poem sees the whole of life and death in terms of a busy hospital. All experiences flow together eventually in this place of life's beginning and end. The very form of the poem knits up all experience into a single strand by the way in which the carefully balanced seven-line stanzas rhyme across themselves (*abcbdcad*), overriding the stanzas' subjects, in eight-line verse paragraphs. (p. 39)

'**The Building**' and '**The Old Fools**' are chilly but honest poems which reflect the same strengths as most of Larkin's mature poems. They reveal a close observation of everyday life, they express a carefully controlled development of feeling and tone, they bear a clarity of language and immediacy of image, and, above all, they display the poet's determination not to flinch before the facts of man's frailty, failure and mortality.

Larkin's best poems are rooted in actual experiences and convey a sense of place and situation, people and events, which gives an authenticity to the thoughts that are then usually raised by the poet's observation of the scene. They frequently begin from situations we all may experience: travelling by train, watching crowds at the seaside or local show, observing mothers in a park or young people at a party, casually looking round an empty church, noticing the graffiti on a poster, speculating about the previous inhabitant of a rented room—all these give a solidity to the experiences of the poet and help the reader share in them because the mind of the poet is seen as rooted in an easily recognizable reality. The descriptions of people and events in, for example, '**Here**', '**Show Saturday**' and '**The Whitsun Weddings**' capture a whole style of life in mid-twentieth-century British society.

Joined with this strength of careful social observation is a control over tone changes and the expression of developing feelings even within a single poem (for example, '**Church Going**' or '**The Old Fools**') which is a product of great craftsmanship. To these virtues must be added the fact that in all the poems there is a lucidity of language which invites understanding even when the ideas expressed are paradoxical or complex. Larkin commands a considerable breadth of idiom, a breadth that can span from the slangy to the stately within the space of a single poem. Similarly, the diction can partake of the crudely vernacular, the simple, plain speech of conver-

sation, or the formally heightened vocabulary redolent of a more dignified age (as in the final lines of '**Church Going**').

Despite the relative narrowness of his themes, Larkin writes with a wide range of tone and feeling. It is sometimes overlooked that the poet of '**Coming**' or '**Solar**' is also the poet of '**The Old Fools**'. Although one's final impression of the poetry is certainly that the chief emphasis is placed on a life 'unspent' in the shadow of 'untruth', moments of beauty and affirmation are not entirely denied. It is the difficulty of experiencing such moments after one has become so aware of the numerous self-deceptions that man practices on himself to avoid the uncomfortable reality which lies at the heart of Larkin's poetic identity.

It is this consistent identity, recurring throughout the poems, that seems to divide critics in their final estimation of the poetry. All critics must acknowledge the subtle craftsmanship of the poetry, but those who consider Larkin's identity to be too negative come eventually to regard the poetry as suffering from limitations. They regard the identity as being too narrowly conceived and not capable of bearing the weight of universality which Larkin wishes to place upon it. There are other critics, however, who regard this identity as expressing the true spirit of mid-twentieth-century Britain.

This identity is most typically expressed as a middle-aged bachelor figure who believes we have little control over our fate and who sees us as duped by all manner of self-deceptions and wishful thinking. He seems to believe that the only honest response to life is to deny ourselves any dreams of fulfilment, and his resistance to being 'conned' by life leads him particularly to deny any possibility of lasting love. To him the role of a detached, if lonely, outsider is preferable to a false commitment in love or marriage. Honesty and awareness are his cardinal virtues. But he is no rebel: part of his recognition of man's illusions is that he sees acts of rebellion as empty romantic gestures, preferring to accept what he regards as the reality of everyday life. It is thus the identity of a disappointed man aware of life's defeats rather than the tragic identity of a man whose ideals have driven him to attempt to scale the peaks. This has divided readers and critics in their reactions to the poetry. To some such an identity speaks with the voice of experience and honesty, a voice to be valued above any frail dreams of possible fulfilment. But to others such honesty is a limited virtue which dulls the appetite for life and experience and which reneges on man's capacity to dream of ideals, to aspire to a life of larger ambitions. (pp. 40-2)

The assumption of Larkin's poetry is that anyone who does not see reality under this light must be deluding himself. There are some critics (for example, Calvin Bedient) who see Larkin's poetic identity as the spirit of our age, a spirit of scepticism and disillusionment combined with the belief that the only ideal is to have no ideals to lose. But this is to make assumptions about our own age that may, in time, prove to have overlooked something. Larkin's poetry is a poetry of disappointment, of the destruction of romantic illusions, of man's defeat by time and his own inadequacies. It could be seen as the poetry of the impotent self, unable or unwilling to risk being wrong. Yet it is a consummately crafted verse and to be valued for its skill in creating a sense of our world that we all may recognize and for its honest adherence to one man's testing of experience. The reader may be grateful for this attempt to record things as they seem to the poet, and he may acknowledge that this is the way many of us at some time view our lives. But he might yet insist that this picture of a shrunken reality—what Bedient calls 'the withering of the ideal, of romance, of possibility'—is not the total experience either of his own life or the life of our age. The great popularity of Larkin's poetry no doubt signals a delight in his craftsmanship, but it may also say as much about our age as about the poet's achievement.

We can agree with [David] Timms that part of Larkin's achievement is his refusal to compromise either the reality he personally perceives or the audience with whom he so earnestly desires to communicate. Yet it is open to the reader to feel that even such a considerable achievement as this unique body of verse none the less exemplifies the self-imprisoned limitations of an age that finds it impossible both to face reality and to retain its dreams. (pp. 42-3)

> *P. R. King, "Without Illusion: The Poetry of Philip Larkin," in his* Nine Contemporary Poets: A Critical Introduction, *Methuen, 1979, pp. 1-43.*

## GREVEL LINDOP

[The] 1970s for Larkin have been a decade of consolidation. Previous achievement has been crowned. Alone of his four small books of verse *High Windows* had from the start a large, expectant public. . . . There are good reasons for a certain mellowing in the tone of Larkin's work. Not surprisingly, *High Windows* contains fewer of the depressive or suspicious poems, of experience examined and found wanting, that characterized *The Less Deceived* and *The Whitsun Weddings*. More unexpected is the fact that it shows the re-emergence of tendencies kept carefully out of sight since Larkin's first collection, *The North Ship* (1945); and most startling of all, that poem after poem takes us towards a symbolist vision of the kind which the earlier poems were determined to exclude. (p. 47)

The Larkin of the 1970s is the Larkin of *High Windows*, and one of the most striking features of that book is its preoccupation with the past. There is much nostalgia, and seen in context **'Going, Going'** appears as one of a group of poems about the English past whose loss Larkin fears. This anxiety is justified, although certain reviewers were right to point out how little in the way of a living England is implied by the catalogue of loss in **'Going, Going'**:

> The shadows, the meadows, the lanes,
> The guildhalls, the carved choirs,

are lines that would do as caption for an English Tourist Board poster. The selection of snapshot detail is too perfectly decorative. (p.48)

[Poems which concern the past] contribute a very strong ingredient to the overall flavour of *High Windows*. In no previous collection has a concern with the social and historical past played so large a part, though Larkin has of course written numerous important poems which make full use of history: **'MCMXIV'**, for example, **'Deceptions'**, and **'An Arundel Tomb'**, to name those that come instantly to mind.

Of the other poems in *High Windows* three are satirical squibs. **'Posterity'** and **'Homage to a Government'** are forceful in a rather limited way, and **'This Be The Verse'** is a splendid exposure of facile pessimism. . . . The remaining poems are of the kind most often associated with Larkin: wry, self-critical, not hopeful but conscious of the lure of hope and of the other fine prospects which to varying degrees cheat us in life.

Yet important and surprising developments are seen at once when these poems are compared to the earlier work. The title poem, **'High Windows'**, takes on a characteristic Larkin subject—the ageing observer regarding the sexual behaviour of the young first with a touch of prurience ('I see a couple of kids / And guess he's fucking her'), next with envy ('this is Paradise / Everyone old has dreamed of all their lives') and then, seeing a parallel between their apparent sexual freedom and the religious freedom he perhaps appeared to have when he was young, getting the whole business of the human expectation of happiness into perspective. But the final resolution, if such it can be called, is not directly stated and the poem explicitly emphasizes the fact:

> Rather than words comes the thought of high windows. . . .
>
>                                                           (pp. 49-50)

[The] striking development is the turn to symbolism rather than discursive statement. The earlier poems tend to offer stated judgements: 'how we live measures our own nature'; 'Never such innocence again'; 'Life is first boredom, then fear'. But poem after poem in *High Windows* refuses to give us anything so consolingly tangible. . . . Always Larkin seems to be aiming for the symbol which will resonate in the mind, calling forth harmonies that have nothing to do with the carefully limited, scrupulously precise resolutions of most of the earlier poems. The most notable instance is probably **'The Card-Players'**, which ends with a line of exclamation—

> Rain, wind and fire! The secret, bestial peace!

as if the poet is suddenly awed to silence by his own subject.

**'The Card-Players'** is a fascinating poem in several ways. There is something factitious about it; yet it remains interesting after many readings. It suffers from a problem which besets most poems which describe pictures, in that the imagined picture communicates a static quality which is out of place in a poem. Enumerating details which we know would fit together in a pictorial composition does not produce a satisfying poetic structure. Larkin conscientiously makes his figures move and perform actions, but there remains something arbitrary about the scene. Nothing really happens, nor do the figures relate to one another in any way. There are details which seem to imply some special meaning but yield nothing. (pp. 50-1)

At the same time the poem seems to embody symbolic patterns of a kind untypical of Larkin's mature work. Great play is made throughout with the four elements, but the final line mentions only three. 'Rain, wind and fire!'—there are water, air and fire but where is earth? The answer, clearly, is that earth is represented by the men themselves. . . . Once alert to such patterns in *High Windows* one notices a surprising number. Is it without significance, for example, that **'Sad Steps'** and **'Solar'**—a moon poem and a sun poem—are on facing pages? That **'Livings'** III ends with a reference to astrology, or that the speaker of **'Livings'** II sets out 'divining-cards' after dinner, for all the world as if he expected a visit from Mrs Equitone or Madame Sosostris? Can one conceive of the Larkin of *The Less Deceived* so much as mentioning astrology or the Tarot without obvious irony?

Larkin has said on radio (in 1972) that he would like to write '*different* kinds of poems, that might be by different people. Someone once said that the great thing is not to be different from other people, but to be different from yourself' . . . , and this is what he has done. But these aspects of *High Windows* should lead us to think again about his relationship with Yeats, under whose influence his early poems were so obviously written. Yeats can be a powerful and dangerous influence—'pervasive as garlic', in Larkin's words—but in *The North Ship* Larkin's submission to his style was quite exceptionally thorough. Most commentators have been surprisingly eager to accept Larkin's apparently ingenuous account of his early poetic development, in which chance plays so large a part and choice such a small one. In the Introduction to *The North Ship* Larkin beguilingly portrays himself first as 'isolated in Shropshire with a complete Yeats stolen from the local girls' school', then as landing in 'digs' where the early sunlight in his east-facing bedroom compelled him to read something in the mornings, which something happened to be the poems of Hardy whose impact provoked an 'undramatic, complete and permanent' reaction against Yeats. Was ever a professional librarian and dedicated poet so mercilessly pushed about by a couple of stray books? Really, the story won't stand a great deal of scrutiny. After *High Windows* it begins to look, rather, as if the poetry of Larkin's 'middle period' had been a conscious, disciplined attempt to throw off the Yeatsian stranglehold: a criticism of all Yeats's attitudes and techniques as the price of poetic independence. Now, at last, something of the earlier style has been allowed to return to the surface, revealing that Larkin was never really either the narrow-minded, self-pitying moaner of his hostile critics or the hard-headed 'poet for the common man' of his admirers. The mask was meticulously constructed, but a mask it was.

Larkin's finest achievement of the 1970s, however, has been a group of poems which eschew both symbolist experiment and the limitations of satire and social criticism. A small number of poems, in particular **'The Building', 'The Old Fools',** and the uncollected **'Aubade',** have confronted the things we can hardly bear to face—sickness, old age and death—with a degree of nervous honesty rare even in poetry and virtually unknown in common life. (pp. 51-2)

Poems like these, finding their terrible subjects at the heart of mundane daily experience and presenting them with an authority almost bardic and yet quite free from romantic trappings, form a substantial achivement, and one earned by the discipline of working, during previous decades, within the limited poetic of *The Less Deceived* and *The Whitsun Weddings.* (pp. 53-4)

> Grevel Lindop, "Being Different from Yourself: Philip Larkin in the 1970s," in British Poetry Since 1970: A Critical Survey, edited by Peter Jones and Michael Schmidt, Carcanet Press, 1980, pp. 46-54.

## CLIVE JAMES

There is no phrase in Philip Larkin's poetry which has not been turned, but then any poet tries to avoid flat writing, even at the cost of producing overwrought banality. Larkin's dedication to compressed resonance is best studied, in the first instance, through his prose. The prefaces to the re-issues of *Jill* and *The North Ship* are full of sentences that make you smile at their neat richness even when they are not meant to be jokes, and that when they are meant to be jokes—as in the evocation of the young Kingsley Amis at Oxford in the preface to *Jill*—make you wish that the article went on as long as the book. But there is a whole book which does just that: *All What Jazz,* the collection of Larkin's *Daily Telegraph* jazz record review columns which was published in 1970. . . . I thought at the time that *All What Jazz* was the best available expression by the author himself of what he believed art to be. Nowadays I

still think so, and would contend in addition that no wittier book of criticism has ever been written.

To be witty does not necessarily mean to crack wise. In fact it usually means the opposite: wits rarely tell jokes. Larkin's prose flatters the reader by giving him as much as he can take in at one time. The delight caused has to do with collusion. Writer and reader are in cahoots. Larkin has the knack of donning cap and bells while still keeping his dignity. For years he feigned desperation before the task of conveying the real desperation induced in him by the saxophone playing of John Coltrane. The metaphors can be pursued through the book— they constitute by themselves a kind of extended solo. . . . (pp. 98-9)

The whole of *All What Jazz* is a losing battle. Larkin was arguing in support of entertainment at a time when entertainment was steadily yielding ground to portentous significance. His raillery against the saxophonist was merely the most strident expression of a general argument which he went on elaborating as its truth became more clear to himself. (p. 101)

The emphasis, in Larkin's admiration for [such jazz artists as Sidney Bechet, Bix Beiderbecke, and Pee Wee Russell], is on the simplicity at the heart of their creative endeavour. What they do would not have its infinite implications if it did not spring from elementary emotion. It can be argued that Larkin is needlessly dismissive of Duke Ellington and Charlie Parker. There is plenty of evidence to warrant including him in the school of thought known among modern jazz buffs as 'mouldy fig'. But there is nothing retrograde about the aesthetic underlying his irascibility.

The same aesthetic underlies his literary criticism and everything else he writes. Especially it underlies his poetry. Indeed it is not even an aesthetic: it is a world view, of the kind which invariably forms the basis of any great artistic personality. Modernism, according to Larkin, 'helps us neither to enjoy nor endure'. He defines modernism as intellectualized art. Against intellectualism he proposes not anti-intellectualism—which would be just another coldly willed programme—but trust in the validity of emotion. What the true artist says from instinct, the true critic will hear by the same instinct. There may be more than instinct involved, but nothing real will be involved without it. . . . (p. 103)

His own criticism appeals so directly to the ear that he puts himself in danger of being thought trivial, especially by the mock-academic. Like Amis's, Larkin's readability seems so effortless that it tends to be thought of as something separate from his intelligence. But readability *is* intelligence. The vividness of Larkin's critical style is not just a token of his seriousness but the embodiment of it. His wit is there not only in the cutting jokes but in the steady work of registering his interest. It is easy to see that he is being witty when he says that Miles Davis and Ornette Coleman stand in evolutionary relationship to each other 'like green apples and stomach-ache'. But he is being equally witty when he mentions Ruby Braff's 'peach-fed' cornet. A critic's language is not incidental to him: its intensity is a sure measure of his engagement and a persuasive hint at the importance of what he is engaged with. (pp. 103-04)

In Britain the simultaneous pursuit of poetry and regular critical journalism is regarded as versatility at best. The essential unity of Larkin's various activities is not much remarked.

But if we do not remark it, we miss half of his secret. While maintaining an exalted idea of the art he practises, Larkin never thinks of it as an activity inherently separate from the affairs of everyday. He has no special poetic voice. What he brings out is the poetry that is already in the world. He has cherished the purity of his own first responses. Like all great artists he has never lost touch with the child in his own nature. The language of even the most intricately wrought Larkin poem is already present in recognizable embryo when he describes the first jazz musicians ever to capture his devotion:

> It was the drummer I concentrated on, sitting as he did on a raised platform behind a battery of cowbells, temple blocks, cymbals, tomtoms and (usually) a Chinese gong, his drums picked out in flashing crimson or ultramarine brilliants.

There are good grounds for calling Larkin a pessimist, but it should never be forgotten that the most depressing details in the poetry are seen with the same eye that loved those drums. The proof is in the unstinting vitality of the language.

As in the criticism, so in the poetry wit can be divided usefully into two kinds, humorous and plain. There is not much need to rehearse the first kind. Most of us have scores of Larkin's lines, hemistiches and phrases in our heads, to make us smile whenever we think of them, which is as often as the day changes. I can remember the day in 1962 when I first opened *The Less Deceived* and was snared by a line in the first poem, **'Lines on a Young Lady's Photograph Album'**: 'Not quite your class, I'd say, dear, on the whole.' What a perfectly timed pentameter! How subtly and yet how unmistakeably it defined the jealousy of the speaker! Who on earth was Philip Larkin? Dozens of subsequent lines in the same volume made it clearer: he was a supreme master of language levels, snapping into and out of a tone of voice as fast as it could be done without losing the reader. Bringing the reader in on it—the deep secret of popular seriousness. Larkin brought the reader in on it even at the level of prosodic technique. . . . (pp. 104-06)

He got you smiling at a rhyme. **'Church Going'** had the 'ruin-bibber, randy for antique.' **'Toads'** had the pun on Shakespeare, *Stuff your pension!* being the stuff dreams are made of. You couldn't get half way through the book without questioning, and in many cases revising, your long-nursed notions about poetic language. Here was a disciplined yet unlimited variety of tone, a scrupulosity that could contain anything, an all-inclusive decorum. (p. 106)

In Larkin's three major volumes of poetry the jokes on their own would be enough to tell you that wit is alive and working.

But it is working far more pervasively than that. Larkin's poetry is *all* witty—which is to say that there is none of his language which does not confidently rely on the intelligent reader's capacity to apprehend its play of tone. On top of the scores of fragments that make us laugh, there are the hundreds which we constantly recall with a welcome sense of communion, as if our own best thoughts had been given their most concise possible expression. If Auden was right about the test of successful writing being how often the reader thinks of it, Larkin passed long ago. To quote even the best examples would be to fill half this book, but perhaps it will bear saying again, this time in the context of his poetry, that between Larkin's humorous wit and his plain wit there is no discontinuity. Only the man who invented the golden tits could evoke the black-sailed unfamiliar. To be able to make fun of the randy ruin-

bibber is the necessary qualification for writing the magnificent last stanza of **'Church Going'**. You need to have been playfully alliterative with the trite untransferable truss-advertisement before you can be lyrically alliterative with the supine stationary voyage of the dead lovers in **'An Arundel Tomb'**. There is a level of seriousness which only those capable of humour can reach.

Similarly there is a level of maturity which only those capable of childishness can reach. The lucent comb of **'The Building'** can be seen by us only because it has been so intensely seen by Larkin, and it has been so intensely seen by him only because his eyes, behind those thick glasses, retain the naïve curiosity which alone makes the adult gaze truly penetrating. Larkin's poetry draws a bitterly sad picture of modern life but it is full of saving graces, and they are invariably as disarmingly recorded as in a child's diary. The paddling at the seaside, the steamer stuck in the afternoon, the ponies at **'Show Saturday'**— they are all done with crayons and coloured pencils. He did not put away childish things and it made him more of a man. (pp. 106-07)

In Philip Larkin's non-poetic language, the language of extremely well-written prose, despair is expressed through beauty and becomes beautiful too. His argument is with himself and he is bound to lose. He can call up death more powerfully than almost any other poet ever has, but he does so in the commanding voice of life. His linguistic exuberance is the heart of him. Joseph Brodsky, writing about Mandelstam, called lyricism the ethics of language. Larkin's wit is the ethics of his poetry. It brings his distress under our control. It makes his personal unhappiness our universal exultation. Armed with his wit, he faces the worst on our behalf, and brings it to order. A romantic sensibility classically disciplined, he is, in the only sense of the word likely to last, modern after all. By rebuilding the ruined bridge between poetry and the general reading public he has given his art a future, and you can't get more modern than that. (p. 108)

> *Clive James, "On His Wit," in* Larkin at Sixty, *edited by Anthony Thwaite, Faber and Faber, 1982, pp. 98-108.*

### ANDREW MOTION

*Jill* and *A Girl in Winter* have received much less attention than Larkin's poetry and, for the last twenty-five years at least, have been placed in its shadow. But they are both novels that discuss Larkin's lasting preoccupations profoundly and at length, and they provide a graphic illustration of attitudes that determined his mature poetic language. (p.39)

Larkin left Oxford in the summer of 1943, and when he began *Jill* shortly afterwards he immediately returned there in imagination. But, while the novel relies heavily on his memories of the university, it is careful to distinguish between its unillusioned author and its ignorant maladroit hero, John Kemp. . . . He is first introduced in a train travelling from Huddlesford to Oxford in the middle of the Second World War, about to begin his first term as an undergraduate reading English. He promptly reveals himself as painfully shy. Not daring to eat his sandwiches in front of strangers, he takes them to the lavatory. When someone tries the door, he crams them out through the window and returns to his seat—only to be embarrassed by offers of food from his fellow travellers. It is a set-piece of considerable importance, partly for the symbolic value discussed below . . . and partly because it identifies insecurities that are to determine the course of Kemp's term at Oxford. It reveals him as frightened, inexperienced and—by reason of his coming from a northern industrial town—exiled from his environment, kind and class.

This isolation is intensified as soon as Kemp enters his college room, which he has been given to share with another undergraduate, Christopher Warner. Warner's minor-public-school swagger and social confidence first horrify Kemp and then impress him. They provide protection and, by appealing to a latent snobbishness, encourage him to assert himself. Another northern scholar, Whitbread, is the main cause of these brittle feelings of superiority, but by scorning him Kemp only deepens his own loneliness. He cannot belong to Warner's world—no matter how much he might want to—and deliberately cuts himself off from Whitbread's dour reminder of the past. (pp. 40-1)

In the absence of a real society, Kemp is driven to fabricate one. He invents an imaginary girl, Jill, referring to her first as a sister and then as a friend. . . . Kemp falls in love with her—not that he admits it until later. He sends her letters, keeps what he pretends is her diary, and writes a short story in her name. But, for all its ingenuity, Jill's life is a vulnerable construction. Its most serious weakness is Kemp's wish to translate his illusions into actual conditions, and when he encounters a girl [named Gillian] in a bookshop who seems to 'be' Jill he precipitates a disaster. (p. 41)

Having admitted the possibility that Jill could be found in life, Kemp is immediately obsessed by Gillian. Once he has crossed the boundary between a self-contained fantasy and the autonomous external world, he becomes the servant of an ideal he originally controlled. And, while the love he felt for Jill could afford to be as innocent as herself, his love for Gillian cannot help but be strongly sexual and deeply disturbing. Elizabeth, however, who is acting as Gillian's chaperon, is determined to protect her charge, and when Kemp invites Gillian to tea he is firmly disappointed. . . .

Kemp is prevented from brooding for too long on the implications of this rebuff by another and more literally destructive intervention. . . . Huddlesford has been bombed, and Kemp hurries home to enquire after his parents' safety. They and their house have survived intact, but it is a dismal homecoming nevertheless. Huddlesford provokes a feeling of isolation which exactly and painfully parallels his situation at Oxford. . . . His home town now looks 'like the ruins of an age over and done with' . . . , and in it, as at university, Kemp is marooned between two worlds, two classes, and two kinds of attitude to experience; but before leaving for Oxford again he at least allows himself the luxury of contemplating a fresh start. . . . (p. 42)

When Kemp reaches Oxford, he is spurred to resolve his relationship with Gillian by this new sense of freedom. . . . Kemp has nowhere left to turn for comfort except the future, but lacks the self-knowledge to govern it wisely. His dilemma is worsened by the fact that most of his hopes are invested in Gillian, who provokes him to extreme bouts of ignorant impetuosity. It is the final and most severe of these fits that ends the novel. . . . In his feverish dreams a series of incidents from his life with Jill and Gillian return and torment him—some accurate, some distorted. But in spite of their variety they all teach the same things: that, no matter how vigorously he might exercise his power to choose, he would be wrong to expect 'control over

the maddened surface of things' . . . ; and that 'love died, whether fulfilled or unfulfilled'. . . . (p. 43)

Even a rapid summary of *Jill*'s plot is enough to show that the novel explores an issue that dominates Larkin's three mature collections: the need to be less deceived. But, having established this, his commentators invariably pass on. . . . But this theme depends for much of its force on two other aspects of the book, which complement it but which have gone unregarded. The first is that *Jill* is, in a sense, a kind of cryptic literary manifesto. It is a novel about writing, about discovering a literary personality, and about the sorts of consolation that art can provide. These things are interwoven in the creation of the heroine: as Kemp brings her to life in a short story, diary and letters, he adopts various literary personalities and tests the various kinds of protection they offer from the social world. Among others, he tries the aesthetic-dandyish, the touristic-appreciative and the boorish good-living. . . . Kemp's styles are ways of disguising his failures and compensating for his disappointments. Without writing, he would be nothing—a terrified prey to Warner's whims, and overlooked by all his contemporaries. The point is made throughout the novel, implicitly by Kemp's energy as a fantasizer, and explicitly by his vacuity in the social world. When he first reaches Oxford he has virtually no character at all, and is able to make his presence felt only by imitating other people. (pp. 43-4)

While Kemp's writings are shown both to reflect and to compensate for his juvenile lack of character, they also allow him to nurture a dangerous idealism. And when he meets Gillian his attempts to transfer an imaginary 'hallucination of innocence' . . . into a specific context are violently disruptive. But what crushes the hero is a liberation for his creator: by collapsing Kemp's illusory world, Larkin completes his own fictional one, and contradicts Kemp's view of the ways in which art consoles. Although Kemp is a kind of budding novelist within the novel—a creator of characters and narratives—his procedures are the opposite of the novel's itself. Where Kemp's prose projects illusions to compensate for uncertainties, Larkin's strips them away. Writing, the novel argues, is not a refuge but an action—an attempt to understand and control. To clinch its point, it keeps its own style scrupulously plain, observant and realistic.

*Jill*'s self-consciousness is restrained: its language, structure and time-scheme are strictly traditional. For all its reserve, however, the book's preoccupation with deception produces at least one ambitious pattern of images and symbols. These are all, in one way or another, to do with food, and begin to assert themselves as soon as the novel begins. Kemp's reluctance to eat in front of his fellow travellers, and his embarrassment at being offered food when he has thrown his own sandwiches away, initiates a series of scenes in which food plays an important part, and which leave him—at least to start with—'utterly humiliated'. . . . (pp. 45-6)

The references to food amount to an exposition of awkward shyness about more than simply eating. They reveal uncertainty and ignorance about his character in general and its bodily functions in particular: they are, in other words, a means of expressing what is predominantly a sexual anxiety. Kemp spends a great deal of his time acting and reflecting on sexual motives but seldom identifies them as such. . . .

Once Kemp has encountered Gillian, he is forced to clarify the nature of his wants, and the novel's images of food change radically. They show him becoming either forceful and peremptory, or sensuously lavish. (p. 46)

There are two main causes for Kemp's sexual reticence—or, to put it another way, two reasons why the novel transforms sexual preoccupations into images of food, rather than discussing them openly. For one thing, Kemp is determined that Warner and his associates must know nothing about his fantasy life. If they discover it, it will immediately be destroyed by their mockery. For another, Kemp is tormented by the 'enormous disparity . . . between his imagination and what actually happened' in sexual relations. . . . When he has only the imaginary Jill to admire, he can persuade himself that it is innocence he cherishes; but when Gillian appears he is plunged into the world of actual desire. Whether he sleeps with her or not, she is still tyrannized by his attentions, and this makes Kemp realize that his emotions are, in essence, the same as those he finds confusing and often repugnant in other people. (pp. 47-8)

The novel's complex use of food imagery demonstrates that 'erotic fancyings' are precisely what spur a good deal of Kemp's behaviour. In his fantasy life with Jill he is too quickly embarrassed and inexperienced to admit more than a longing for innocent company, but after Gillian's appearance his feelings are easily identified. Once this has occurred, it is only a matter of time before he precipitates the novel's physical crisis: kissing Gillian. In itself this is a relatively slight sin against modesty, but its significance for Kemp is immense. (p. 48)

This is the novel's ironic climax—ironic because it is simply another kind of illusion, a nightmare, replacing Kemp's original fantasies. Its conclusions, however, are tried and proven, and part of their power derives from their connection with the book's earlier symbolic patterning. *Jill*'s preoccupation with food is here changed into a different kind of obsession, but one that is nevertheless also oral. It is an important point because it highlights and concludes Kemp's development throughout the novel from shy 'unfocused' feelings to explicit self-awareness. Although he is still in a dream, he has clarified the nature of his impulses, wishes and desires. He has acquired self-knowledge, and thereby achieved the condition to which all Larkin's speakers aspire. This represents a kind of consolation, but it does not release him from his predicament: while he has escaped the frustrations of fantasy, he has also confronted the certainty of exclusion, disappointment and loss. (p. 49)

Larkin's second novel, *A Girl in Winter* (1947), reaches precisely the same conclusion. After a long and painful process of self-discovery, the distresses of self-deception give way to unavoidable disillusionment. There are striking similarities, too, between the social isolation of its heroine, Katherine Lind, and Kemp's. But, where Kemp is shy and peripheral at Oxford, Katherine is lonely and isolated in England generally. The Second World War is, again, partly to blame: in *Jill* the bombing dramatized Kemp's separation from his past; in *A Girl in Winter* the war has forced Katherine—before the novel opens—to leave her unspecified European country of origin and seek safety in England. . . . It is, in fact, her second visit to England; as a schoolgirl she spent a summer vacation with the family of her penfriend Robin Fennel. Now, after a long interval, they are in her mind again. She has happened to notice that a child of the daughter Jane has died, and she has written a letter of sympathy. When the narrative's first section begins, she is awaiting a reply.

At this early stage, information about Katherine's past is fragmentary, partly because most of her attention is commanded by the present. . . . [A letter from Robin] reveals that he is about to arrive. . . . (pp. 49-50)

[In the second section of the narrative], attention is concentrated exclusively on the young Katherine during her first visit to England. (The novel's elliptical title suppresses the fact that it refers to a woman in winter remembering being a girl in summer.) Time, which in the first and last sections is always hurrying events out of the characters' control, now passes languorously. . . . England, and what happens to her there, is a dream—palpable and new, but always impregnated with a sense of unreality. And because it seems illusory it encourages her to develop illusions of her own. Robin is their obvious focus. . . . The more rigorously Robin maintains his reserve, the more she wants to break it down—and when he takes her out punting, and saves her from lurching into the water, she realizes that she is in love with him:

> Katherine sank down on the cushions, trembling from rage, fright, and embarrassment. The bright, almost metallic contact when he had gripped her sharply wiped away all traces of self-deception. She knew she wanted to lie with her head in his lap, to have him comfort her: she knew equally that this was not going to happen partly because he had no interest in her, and partly because Jane was specifically there to prevent it. She sat blushing.
>
> (pp. 50-1)

This unfulfilled awkwardness . . . forces Katherine into self-awareness. Jane has already bluntly told her that Robin is 'ordinary, down to the last button' . . . , but she has always resisted this possibility. Even when she cannot help noticing his dullness, she enshrines it as a 'barren perfection'. . . . In the punt, however, at the very moment that her feelings for him are most conscious and definite, Robin is unmistakably disappointing. She cannot overlook the gulf between her ideal vision of him and his indifference to her. Shortly afterwards, when Katherine discovers that it was in fact Jane and not Robin who suggested that she should stay with the family, her self-deception is destroyed altogether. . . . [Shortly before Katherine is to leave his family, Robin] takes the opportunity to give her the first sign of his affection. But, rather than confirming Katherine's original wish, his performance is ridiculous, inept and humiliating.· . . . Robin's kiss confirms the disparity between romantic aspirations and actual circumstances. It represents exactly the same lesson that Kemp learns after kissing Gillian—and, like that encounter, it is mercilessly corroborated by subsequent events. (pp. 51-3)

The bleak conclusion implied by this second section is confirmed by the third. . . . In a long, speculative passage about the value and purpose of human relationships, Katherine resolves to live without them, since they bring only pain and disappointment. . . . (p. 53)

To deny love means opting for dissatisfaction and obscurity. But, while this involves a cruel suppression of hope, it also offers (admittedly reductive) opportunities for self-preservation. In the third section of *A Girl in Winter* this ambivalence is carefully explored. By the time Robin appears, Katherine . . . has been further convinced of the value of keeping herself to herself. . . . [Robin] has slipped away from training camp with the intention of sleeping with Katherine, and his tipsy, badgering kisses threaten to damage the memory of her childhood stay with the Fennels. . . . The more he pesters her, the more completely he destroys her version of the past, and the less chance of happiness he allows.

Her final indifference is simply a hopeless kind of charity, and she can afford to give it only because she knows her isolation is complete: 'He could not touch her. It would be no more than doing him an unimportant kindness, that would be overtaken by oblivion in a few days'. . . . This is exactly the same conclusion that *Jill* describes in Kemp's realization that 'love died, whether fulfilled or unfulfilled', and, like the earlier novel, it insists that the benefits of unillusioned independence are limited. To be less deceived often has to be its own reward; self-knowledge allows fulfilment of a kind, but it is invariably accompanied by a bitter memory of pleasures and opportunities that have been irretrievably and unforgettably lost.

Although *A Girl in Winter* and *Jill* have almost identical themes, they arrive at their conclusions by radically different means. Where *Jill* is precise in its placing of characters and background, *A Girl in Winter* is deliberately vague; where *Jill* is unwaveringly—sometimes excessively—naturalistic and realistic, *A Girl in Winter* is 'a Virginia Woolf-Henry Green kind of novel'; and, where *Jill* incorporates its symbolical structures into an empirical framework, *A Girl in Winter* matches its actual observations with well-advertised symbolic intentions. It is these qualities that John Bayley summarized when he called *A Girl in Winter* 'one of the finest and most sustained prose poems in the language', and they are immediately apparent in the opening pages. The first section, like the second and third, is prefaced by a brooding meditation on the weather which is to dominate it. Life and scenery are cast into distinct but nevertheless archetypal symbolic forms. (pp. 53-5)

This emphasis on the general rather than the particular is also evident in the novel's treatment of character. Although Larkin carefully and clearly differentiates people and temperaments, he is also at pains to suggest that they are representative. This applies to a number of minor characters, as well as to Robin and Katherine themselves. (pp. 56-7)

*A Girl in Winter* is, as [one] passage says, 'an odyssey', a quest, beset by various kinds of deception. As in *Jill*, the only reliable truths are certainties of disappointment, and the only way of coming to terms with them is not to expect anything else. Living, the novels suggest, necessarily involves cultivating a self-protective pessimism. *A Girl in Winter* approaches this conclusion much more knowingly than *Jill* and—via its symbolic enlargements—with much greater determination to demonstrate it as a universal rather than a merely personal truth. But it is this which makes the novel, for all its immaculate care of writing, less compelling and forceful than *Jill*. *Jill* has all the faults of overwriting likely to exist in a novel written by a 21-year-old, but it is less self-conscious in its symbolic strategies, and more easily capable of being surprised by the world. Its language is less scrupulous but more energetic, and its theme less fully developed but more shockingly discovered. *A Girl in Winter* is a beautifully constructed, funny and profoundly sad book, but its development of 'Virginia Woolf-Henry Green' strategies has an unignorably reductive effect. Although it juxtaposes passages of rarefied writing with close attention to the familiar, the two styles convey a uniformly bleak attitude to experience. In his three mature collections the realism exemplified by *Jill* and the symbolism that dominates *A Girl in Winter* are brought into a more intimate and fruitful connection. They create a dialectic between Larkin's recurrently pessimistic impulse and his irrepressible longing for fulfilment. (pp. 57-8)

*Andrew Motion, in his* Philip Larkin, *Methuen, 1982, 92 p.*

## CLIVE JAMES

Every reviewer will say that **'Required Writing'** is required reading. To save the statement from blinding obviousness, it might be pointed out that whereas 'required writing' is a bit of a pun—Larkin pretends that he wouldn't have written a word of critical prose if he hadn't been asked—there is nothing ambiguous about 'required reading.' No outside agency requires you to read this book. The book requires that all by itself. It's just too good to miss.

**'Required Writing'** tacitly makes the claim that it collects all of Larkin's fugitive prose, right down to the speeches he has delivered while wearing his Library Association tie. There is none of this that an admirer of his poems and novels would want to be without, and indeed at least one admirer could have stood a bit more of it. . . .

If Larkin meant to avoid repetitiveness, he was being too modest: incapable of a stock response, he never quite repeats himself no matter how often he makes the same point. . . .

Jazz is Larkin's first love and literature is his first duty. But even at the full stretch of his dignity he is still more likely to talk shop than to talk down, and anyway his conception of duty includes affection while going beyond it, so as well as an ample demonstration of his capacity to speak generally about writing, we are given, on every page of this collection, constant and heartening reminders that for this writer his fellow writers, alive or dead, are human beings, not abstractions. . . .

The first principle of his critical attitude, which he applies to his own poetry even more rigorously than to anyone else's, is to trust nothing which does not spring from feeling. Auden, according to Larkin, killed his own poetry by going to America, where, having sacrificed the capacity to make art out of life, he tried to make art out of art instead.

It might be argued that if the Americanised Auden had written nothing else except 'The Fall of Rome' then it would be enough to make this contention sound a trifle sweeping. It is still, however, an interesting contention, and all of a piece with Larkin's general beliefs about sticking close to home. . . .

Lurking in double focus behind those thick specs is a star student who could have been scholarly over any range he chose. But what he chose was to narrow the field of vision: narrow it to deepen it. He isn't exactly telling us to Buy British, but there can be no doubt that he attaches little meaning to the idea of internationalism in the arts. All too vague, too unpindownable, too disrupting of the connections between literature and the life of the nation. . . .

In **'Required Writing'** the Impulse to Preserve is mentioned often. Larkin the critic, like Larkin the librarian, is a keeper of English literature. Perhaps the librarian is obliged to accession more than a few modern books which the critic would be inclined to turf out, but here again duty has triumphed. As for loss, Larkin the loser is here too ('deprivation is for me what daffodils were for Wordsworth') but it becomes clearer all the time that he had the whole event won from the start.

Whether he spotted the daffodil-like properties of deprivation, and so arranged matters that he got more of it, is a complicated question, of the kind which his critical prose, however often it parades a strict simplicity, is equipped to tackle. Subtle, supple, craftily at ease, it is on a par with his poetry—which is just about as high as praise can go. **'Required Writing'** would be a treasure-house even if every second page were printed upside down.

*Clive James, "Daffodils of Deprivation," in* The Observer, *November 20, 1983, p. 30.*

### JOHN BAYLEY

Philip Larkin is not in the contemporary sense a writer and poet, the sense in which to be those things now is to be part of the cultural entertainment industry, but a librarian who sometimes writes poetry, sometimes writes a novel or two, sometimes writes essays and reviews, all, in their different ways, of an equal excellence. . . .

The best art often does not strike us as art at all, not as 'poetry' or as 'writing', but hits us without any intermediary expectation. It conceals its art so successfully that it has many readers who don't care what art is about. It is so good that one doesn't have to think how good it is, and this is quite different from the mere efficiency of mass culture or the image of 'pop art', usually both slovenly and self-conscious. . . .

Everything Larkin writes is concise, elegant and wholly original, and this is as true of his essays and reviews [collected in **Required Writing**] as it is of his poetry. In two short essays, 'The Pleasure Principle' and 'Writing Poems,' he gives us his pungent views on the question of what poetry is for. It is for pleasure, and the poet's aim must be to please his reader. 'We seem to be producing a new kind of bad poetry, not the old kind that tries to move the reader and fails, but one that does not even try'. . . .

This is not because poets have lost their audience, but because they have gained a new one: the subsidised student of poetry. . . . The poet no longer has to be in touch with a student audience, because it is the task of that audience to put themselves in touch with him. Reading a poem is hard work, otherwise there would be no justification in being a student of it. . . .

[Larkin describes the writing of poetry as having three stages.] At first 'a man' (not 'the poet') 'becomes obsessed with an emotional concept to such a degree that he is compelled to do something about it'. In the second stage he tries to construct a verbal device that will reproduce this emotional concept in any who cares to read it, 'anywhere, any time'. Thirdly comes the recurrent situation of persons at different places and times 'setting off the device and re-creating in themselves what the poet felt when he wrote it'. (p. 36)

[The] most significant stage is the third. No true poem is born to blush unseen or 'fit audience find, though few'. . . . The poem exists if everyone who finds it finds themselves in it and becomes absorbed in it. This is to set itself the highest possible standard, which Larkin has always done, and success has justified him. So it has, in quite a different way, for John Betjeman, whom Larkin much admires, and about whose poetry he gives us here a typically incisive and perspicuous essay, 'It Could Only Happen in England'. . . .

As one would expect, some of the best of these essays are on other poets, not necessarily the sort that one might expect Larkin to like. For the impetuous Sylvia Plath, a suicide at 30, he shows the compassionate appreciation of a fellow-master, pointing out to what extent she wrote and died not out of

madness but out of a destructively compulsive ambition, the kind that kills tycoons of 40 with ulcers and coronaries. . . . But 'how valuable her poems are depends on how highly we rank the expression of experience with which we can in no sense identify, and from which we can only turn with shock and sorrow.' The Larkin criterion is absolute. The reader must identify with what he is offered if the poem is to succeed, and its purpose must be the Johnsonian one of helping us either enjoy life or endure it. . . .

Directness and swiftness give Larkin's comments on other poets their value, for example his sense that the postwar Auden, beautifully humane, superbly accomplished, none the less 'no longer touches our imaginations'. He connects Sylvia Plath and Emily Dickinson by their way of coming into the room like a scary child and putting something softly into our hand. . . . His essay on [Barbara Pym] shows how close she comes, as a novelist, to those three stages realised by a successful poet.

The key to Larkin's outlook is humour: not black humour, or wild humour, or the committed stuff used by would-be satirists, but humour which has no function beyond a sudden small redemptive glory. Pym is full of this, as are Larkin's own poems. For him it is a way of being off the edge or out of the swim. Humour is never a public possession which can result from a 'Policy for the Arts', and in that connection Larkin remarks that he 'finds the idea of other people reading my favourite books rather annoying'. (p. 37)

*John Bayley, "How Larkin Writes," in* The Listener, *Vol. 110, No. 2838, December 22, 1983, pp. 36-7.*

### BLAKE MORRISON

[We] come to Larkin for knowledge, as we don't to his contemporaries, because the tentative truths he has to offer seem hard-won and the voice that offers them a trustworthy one. What most poets know isn't worth knowing; what he doesn't, is.

Another way of putting this would be to say that Larkin is a modest poet, and not just in output. It is not that he thinks his poetry a modest achievement—the interviews in **Required Writing** suggest that he is quietly confident of its power—but that he has constructed a voice which comes clean about its failings and limitations. (p. 43)

Does reading Larkin as critic help us to read Larkin as poet? On the face of it, no, for Larkin is at pains to emphasise that poet and critic are quite different creatures: this is "required writing" (criticism and reminiscence), forced on him by the demands of editors. . . . Larkin finds it "an unexpected consequence of becoming known as a writer that you are assumed to be competent to assess other writers"; his only reason for reprinting these miscellaneous pieces is that they have "begun to be quoted out of context"—their exhumation "would otherwise hardly be justified."

Yet even as Larkin thus prefaces his criticism, we notice characteristic strategies coming into play: he runs himself down in order to build up our confidence in him. The same tone of surprise that anyone should be remotely interested in anything he might have to say also pervades two reprinted addresses here. . . . There may be an after-dinner tact and good manners about such remarks, but with Larkin they also go deeper: as in his poetry, telling us he doesn't know is the necessary prelude to showing us that he does.

What kind of critic is he? First and foremost he is a promoter: just as his poetry of the 1950s derived much of its strength from a conviction that certain tones of voice in English poetry were being neglected, so his criticism fights against the current to draw attention to overlooked or underrated figures: Hardy, Betjeman, Stevie Smith, Barbara Pym, Ian Fleming, Gladys Mitchell, a small cluster of writers who share a strong feeling for England and the English. (pp. 43-4)

He is no theorist: though at least three of his critical pronouncements are famous enough to merit a place in any future edition of *The Oxford Dictionary of Quotations* . . . , they aren't statements intended to lay down rules or alter the canon. We will find nothing in Larkin about breaking the pentameter or dissociated sensibility.

Nor is there much evidence of cosmopolitanism: it isn't just that English literature dominates to the exclusion of other literatures, but that literature dominates to the exclusion of other arts. . . . There are poets whose criticism we read for its own sake, as aesthetics, and others we read only for what their criticism tells us about themselves. Eliot and Pound are of the first category, Larkin is of the second. . . .

If Larkin strives to be a practical rather than a theoretical critic, this is in part because he associates theory with the advocacy of Modernism, and with those critics who have "bullied" the reader into "giving up the consumer's power to say 'I don't like this, bring me something different.'" His dislike of the "mystification and outrage" of the Modernist artist is famously attested to in the introduction to *All What Jazz*. . . . Affection for Larkin's criticism generally shouldn't lead one to go soft on him at points like this. It isn't just that the claims are absurd (did Picasso paint as he did because "piqued at being neglected"?) and that there's a depressing inability to discriminate between good Modernist art and bad . . . , but that Larkin is contradicting his own "pleasure principle." For what he has been unable to see is that millions of people do actually *enjoy* modern painting, modern literature, and modern jazz: they haven't been *conned* or *cajoled;* they haven't even had to *work hard at appreciation*. There are, quite simply, large areas of Modernism in which anyone can take an unaffected pleasure.

It is tempting to say that Larkin's criticism has suffered from a failure to recognise this; but that wouldn't quite be true. For one thing, he is certainly not as unlike the Modernists as he would want to think. He agrees with Pound, for example, on the desirability of "making it new", though he means something slightly different by it—not "innovation" (departure from existing practice) but "novelty" (utter originality) and even "novel-ty" (the poem having the virtues of novelistic prose). If there is one idea that *Required Writing* advances more fervently than even that of pleasure, it is that "every poem must be its own sole freshly created universe." (p. 44)

There is a further distinction here, between what both he and we secretly recognise about him, and what he hasn't recognised but we think we have. His misanthropy and child-hating come in the first category. . . . (p. 45)

Into the second, more sensitive category comes a matter such as work. Larkin is adamant about the desirability of a steady full-time job, not least for writers. But it's hard to miss the half-envy with which he writes of those who have pursued a Bohemian or hand-to-mouth existence—Edward Thomas, Francis Thompson, W. H. Davies, the Beats. To explore this contradiction candidly is difficult for Larkin: it might mean admitting, for example, that the choice he has made in life—to pursue a professional career and write in his spare time—has deprived him of the chance to produce, if not better poems, then at least more of them. . . .

This might seem to be making heavy weather of a theme which Larkin himself, in poems like **"Toads", "Toads Revisited"** and **"Poetry of Departures"**, is able to make light of. But a light treatment does not, for him, denote frivolity. In pieces here on Betjeman, Stevie Smith, and Ogden Nash, he is at pains to point to the serious elements in their work. . . .

Sadness is the great touchstone for Larkin. . . . Like Owen, who wrote (Larkin says) not about the "particular suffering" of war but "all suffering", he believes that the poetry is in the pity. Sadness has all the best cadences; Yeats's conviction that passive suffering is not a theme for poetry is called "fatuous." The burden of such passages, of course, is to suggest that sadness and passive suffering are Larkin's themes too, and to remind us that his light verse—**"Self's the Man", "Vers de Société", "This be the Verse"**—is not as light as all that. (p. 46)

***Required Writing*** is not a declamatory or confessional book, but in its own way it reveals a great deal. (p. 47)

Blake Morrison, "On Philip Larkin's Prose," in Encounter, *Vol. LXII, No. 2, February, 1984, pp. 43-7.*

## ROBERT PINSKY

As a critic, Mr. Larkin is nearly always lively and often insightful. At his best, he writes an uncluttered, funny and sensitive prose that merits comparison with work by the great common-sense poet-critics of our language, from Samuel Johnson through Yvor Winters and Randall Jarrell. At his worst, he strikes silly or repellent attitudes, suggesting a shallow attempt indeed to be himself. . . .

[The] prose in **"Required Writing"** has many of the strengths of the poems—clarity, a sense of rhythm and asymmetry, the ability to time elements like "iron lung" or "sad" and a deflating, all but despairing defiance of cant. In Mr. Larkin's verse, this tone of nearly-giving-up is sometimes reflected formally by characteristic slant rhymes, loosened iambics, broken or brilliantly fudged rhyme schemes and patterns.

Such elements in Mr. Larkin's writing seem deeply connected to two qualities of English life that often strike visitors—vulgarity and coziness. In English speech, these qualities are reflected in the savage understatement and defensive gloom Mr. Larkin has elevated to the lyric.

In his writing, the vulgar and the cozy often lead to a sense of life that is fresh, blunt and sad, with an emotional penetration almost as great as his master Hardy's. At other times, what emerges is a mean provinciality. Occasionally, Mr. Larkin affects the voice of a bluff, genially philistine reactionary who dislikes "portraits with both eyes on the same side of the nose" and resents the destruction of "happy" jazz by "Negroes" who have gone to Juilliard. . . .

This stylized, funny-paper version of himself seems to amuse Mr. Larkin, and through an odd turn of fashion, it seems to amuse others too. Perhaps it would be harmless if it didn't make a superb poet sound like a bar bore or an academic dinosaur clumsily baiting junior faculty. . . .

This leering little act parodies the view of poetry Mr. Larkin puts forward, a view that is simple, bluntly powerful and recklessly circumscribed. Poems, he thinks, should give pleasure, preferably immediate pleasure, to the "cash customers" he prefers over "the humbler squad whose aim is not pleasure but self-improvement." . . .

The modern, as embodied by Beckett, Pound and at least some of Joyce, yields only "mystification and outrage."

This view has its limits. . . . But within these limits, Mr. Larkin writes movingly and illuminatingly about such topics as his work as a librarian. He also writes wonderfully about Thomas Hardy, Wilfred Owen, Stevie Smith, Ogden Nash, Barbara Pym, Anthony Powell. Mr. Larkin casts a clear, cool eye on the post-1940 Auden, and his very brief remarks on A. E. Housman and Edward Thomas are tantalizingly rich and suggestive. (p. 9)

Toughness and insularity have led Mr. Larkin to his best works and to his worst. At this point, one could draw the conclusion that in poetry he puts to the service of vision the very qualities that sometimes cloud his judgment in prose, and so forth. But it is not that simple. . . .

Incredibly, in **"High Windows,"** on the same pages as the unforgettable title poem and **"Going, Going"** and **"The Old Fools,"** in one of only 24 poems, Mr. Larkin pauses to make [an] . . . ignorant, rather stupid joke about Jews. It is spectacularly unworthy.

My point is not that poets must be sanitary liberals or excellent people in all ways but that Mr. Larkin's judgment is terrifically deficient in vital areas. And to separate judgment about life from literary judgment, either explicitly or by finding the meaner side of the Larkin persona merely amusing, something to overlook with a grin, would be to trivialize poetry. . . .

Mr. Larkin's attitudes toward such matters as Jews, the poetry of John Betjeman, jazz, American blacks and Modernism are important only because they are his, because they help us to see the shape of what he has done. If Mr. Larkin, a superlative artist, prefers the third-rate verses of Betjeman to the writing of Beckett or if his love of Armstrong's music is knotted up by a fear of the energy in that music, that is his business. Ours, as his readers, is to understand both his best and his worst impersonations of himself. (p. 10)

*Robert Pinsky, "The Opinionated Poet," in* The New York Times Book Review, *August 12, 1984, pp. 9-10.*

# Philip Levine

## 1928-

American poet, critic, and editor.

Levine was born and raised in Detroit; his experiences growing up in the city and working in factories and other menial jobs have greatly influenced his work and resulted in a poetry grounded in the harsh reality of contemporary life. Deeply committed to the plight of the lower-class, blue-collar worker, Levine describes his poetry as an attempt to create "a voice for the voiceless." He often writes about the individual pitted against industrialism, and his narrative style typically is terse and unadorned. His tone ranges from despairing to life-affirming; although his poems often focus on personal pain, such as the childhood loss of a father, and are generally set in the grit and desolation of city slums, he also celebrates the resiliency and determination of the human spirit. As Bonnie Costello notes in her review of *One for the Rose* (1981), "the poet's soul seems to leave the body, cresting in high lyricism, but returns to a street-life hardness, often wounded in the fall, but never broken."

Since Levine's first collection, *On the Edge* (1961), later revised as *On the Edge and Over* (1976), his poetry has changed little. Although his lines have evolved from traditional meters to freer, more open cadences and his poems have become increasingly lyrical and less narrative, his concerns have largely remained the same. Some critics claim that Levine's poetry is monotonous and repetitive, but his reputation has increased steadily and many consider him among the most prominent contemporary poets. His acclaimed early volumes include *Not This Pig* (1968) and *They Feed They Lion* (1972). Levine received the American Book Award for *Ashes* (1979) and the National Book Critics Circle Award for *Ashes* and *7 Years from Somewhere* (1979). In *One for the Rose* and *Selected Poems* (1984), Levine continues to blend the personal and the political, the spiritual and the concrete, creating poetry, as Costello observes, "in which the everyday turns suddenly toward the otherworldly, dreams are mixed with the grit of Detroit, and an earthy, narrative range is cut in short, lyrical lines to let the mica shine."

(See also *CLC*, Vols. 2, 4, 5, 9, 14; *Contemporary Authors*, Vols. 9-12, rev. ed.; *Contemporary Authors New Revision Series*, Vol. 9; and *Dictionary of Literary Biography*, Vol. 5.)

© *Kelly Wise*

## DAVE SMITH

Who does not know the poems of Philip Levine? Can there be any point to reviewing his two new collections, *Ashes* and *7 Years From Somewhere,* if there is no radical, visible change? Maybe one simply likes what one likes, for my opinion is that I would as soon stop reading as give up Mr. Levine's poems. Still, what accounts for such delight? Especially when I have not altogether dismissed objections. Some have said he has written the same poem for years, that he lacks variety and vision. True, many of his poems possess one doleful cadence. True, his vision is such a relentless denunciation of injustice that he has occasionally engaged in reductive oversimplifications. For example, the political underbelly of *The Names of*

*the Lost* comes uncomfortably close to cadres of the good, the bad, and the ugly. His prose piece, **"To My Brother on the Death of A Young Poet,"** . . . seems irresponsibly blindered thinking and is, I think, reprehensible. Mr. Levine has a polemic streak which makes some of his work strident, manipulative, and at least ungenerous. And, some note, there is a level of violence in his poems few poets equal, whether it be objectionable or reflective. In spite of these objections and others, I cannot help believing his poetry is nearly a national treasure and many of the new poems are as good if not better than anything he has written.

*Ashes* contains 13 poems from the long out of print **Red Dust** . . . and 19 new poems. The former have been characterized as surreal by way of the Spanish, an influence Mr. Levine admits. The analysis is based on images and phrasings, rather than entire poems, which are more dream-like and associative than rational and linear. For example, "Blood runs to the heart and finds it locked;" or "rifles are brooding / in the closet;" or "the grave blooms upward / in sunlight and walks the roads." I suspect there is less surrealism here than a vitally alive and active landscape whose every particle possesses the ability and need to express itself and a nearly symbiotic integrity. Another way of saying this is that Mr. Levine seems to have an extraordinary capacity to sense and give witness to a man's relationship with all that exists. He is no painter of mindscapes nor a primitivist nor a canting ecologist, though dream life, fundamental states of being, and an impure world matter greatly to him. He is distinctly American, a consumer and a mensch. When he writes, ''The clouds go on eating oil,'' he indicts industrial greed as well as projects an emotional abuse beyond individual proportions. But it is the activity of his metaphor, its visual accumulation and poisoned ingestion, which causes a visceral rather than a mental response. He does not, even in *Red Dust,* rely very much on flashed and extra-worldly conjunctions but on the charged interaction of all things which he so acutely feels.

Importantly, Mr. Levine's poems always begin and remain grounded in a single, highly receptive consciousness which is a man's alone. The language, the figures of speech, the narrative progressions of this consciousness are never so private, so obscure, so truncated as to forbid less sophisticated readers. Though he takes on the largest subjects of death, love, courage, manhood, loyalty, etc., he brings the mysteries of existence down into the ordinarily inarticulate events and objects of daily life. His speaker and subject is the abused and disabused spirit of the common yet singular self. He risks the maudlin, the sentimental, the banal, and worse because he cannot live in the world fully enough; because the world is so much with us all we must sing or die of its inexpressible presence.

For me, Mr. Levine has been writing this way throughout his nine books, granted the shift from regular verse after *Not This Pig* and some slight re-orientation after *Red Dust.* With *They Feed They Lion, 1933, The Names of the Lost* and now *Ashes* and *7 Years From Somewhere,* he has shown increased technical control, a growing mastery of image and phrase, a deepened power to dramatize the suffering and potential of each moment. But there is no radical change in ''A man alone, ignorant / strong, holding the buring moments / for all they're worth.'' The style of a man's poem need not change in pace with Detroit's assembly lines. It might be said that Mr. Levine has a formula and I would answer that we should all be so fortunate, for what he has is a style patiently developed to fit his need to speak the hurt and the joy that in all of us remains unshaped and embryonic. (pp. 36-7)

> Dave Smith, in a review of ''Ashes'' and ''7 Years from Somewhere,'' in The American Poetry Review, Vol. 8, No. 6, November-December, 1979, pp. 36-7.

## PETER STITT

In terms of content, Philip Levine has always written a poetry that is generally both personal and sincere, a poetry based on the facts, feelings, and experiences of his own life. On one day last year, Levine published two books which, between them, illustrate both directions that this kind of verse can take. The poems in *Ashes* . . . show everywhere signs of the transforming power of the artistic imagination; the raw materials of experience and emotion have been converted, through metaphor, through music, into poetry. In *7 Years from Somewhere,* on the other hand, the writing is generally flat, the poems literal. At his best, Levine has always been a rhetorician, ever willing to set the devices of poetry working for him; it is a disappointment to find these elements so lacking in his most recent poems. One's sense of disappointment is all the more acute given Levine's obviously strong sense of commitment to his material. The poems are all, in one way or another, elegies—some lament the passage of time, the coming of age; some lament the deaths of friends, heroes; some lament the

progressive passing of the poet himself, the loss of his childhood and youth. These are affective subjects, possessed of considerable power in and of themselves. It is understandable that Levine often relies on this inherent strength to carry his poems, but the results here are not compelling. **"Words,"** for example, tells how time takes its toll on a family; the speaker seems to be trying, but failing, to extricate himself from a sense of depression. The poem ends: ''My wife will say nothing / of the helplessness / she feels seeing her / men rocking on / their separate seas. / We are three people / bowing our heads to / all she has given us, / to bread and wine and meat. / The windows have gone / dark, but the room is / quiet in yellow light. / Nothing needs to be said.'' The form of this poem is, in a curious way, appropriate to the subject; both reveal an endemic emptiness.

Elsewhere there is an altogether direct and artless expression of excess emotion, artistically unjustified, as in these lines: ''I did cry. I put my hands between / my legs, alone, in the room I came / to love because it was all the room / I had, and pitched forward and cried / without hope or relief, for myself. . . .'' The poems in this book are generally narrative in form and often epiphanic in structure; in poem after poem, the speaker tells of incidents in his life which led to one revelation or another. Many are good poems too—like **"Peace," "Let Me Begin Again," "You Can Have It,"** and the title poem **"7 Years from Somewhere"**—but none is as good as even the average poem in *Ashes.* There is a progression evident in Levine's work from the lush rhetorical intensity of his earlier poems to the relatively plain style of these later volumes. But Levine's natural voice is not well suited to the plain style, and that is why there is so much flatness in *7 Years from Somewhere.*

*Ashes* embodies a stylistic compromise. The pounding rhythms and insistent repetitions of the early work are largely absent here, with the formal emphasis being placed upon Levine's figurative imagination. The ability to double, to see one thing within another, to spot the latent form lurking in the block of stone—always notable in his work—is the chief feature of *Ashes.* As many critics have demonstrated, metaphor is a complicated and elusive literary device, virtually impossible to pin down and describe in all its many forms; but it is the essence of poetry, an essence of life. One kind of metaphor, sometimes called surrealism, involves ascribing to an object characteristics which in nature that object could not possess. Metaphorically, we might call this a kind of synesthesia, which itself allows a stimulation to be registered by the wrong sense, as hearing the scent of a rose or tasting the color blue. Levine's poem **"Noon"** is built of such metaphors. . . . This sort of thing can easily become too clever, but [in **"Noon"**] the purpose is admirably served.

Elsewhere Levine's images can be close to the purely descriptive, the literal, but still work brilliantly because of their profusion. . . . In his best poems, Levine reinforces his images with, and places them within, an insistent rhetorical flow. **"How Much Earth"** attempts to show man's inherent mortality through a metaphorical description of the progress of his life; it is an example of Levine at his recent best. . . . The texture of Levine's poetry has ever been emotional, revealing a strong commitment both to his subjects and his art. The feeling in this poem verges continually on the edge of an extreme, as is shown in certain crucial words (''torn,'' ''shredded,'' ''thrilled,'' ''stilled,'' ''rush,'' ''fists,'' ''startle'') and in many phrases. This kind of verbal, imagistic intensity is central to Levine's art, and the retreat from it (and from metaphor) in *7 Years from*

*Somewhere* is unfortunate. Happily, *Ashes* shows him easily in command of his full powers; it is a stunning book from one of our most powerful and masterful poets. (pp. 203-04)

Peter Stitt, "The Sincere, the Mythic, the Playful: Forms of Voice in Current Poetry," in The Georgia Review, *Vol. XXXIV, No. 1, Spring, 1980, pp. 202-12.**

## HELEN VENDLER

[Philip Levine distrusts] fantasy and invention, or perhaps I should say the look of fantasy and invention. (. . . [The] point is that everything, even if invented, has, [he feels], . . . to be made to look "real".) Lyric of course must start as the self's concentration of itself into words; but (as Keats said about Shakespeare's sonnets) a poem can be full of fine things said unintentionally in the intensity of working out conceits. What Keats meant is that the process of composition, by its own interest, intensity, and demand, often draws the poet away from the original autobiographical or narcissistic impulse, even away from the original matter that concerned the poet. The most famous modern comment on this process was made by Yeats: he wanted, in 1917, to write a poem on the Russian revolution, and took as his symbol the birth of a new era from the conjunction of Zeus and Leda. But as he wrote, "bird and lady" took over the poem, and the Russian revolution faded from his mind.

Nothing so wayward seems to happen to [Levine in *One for the Rose*]. . . . (p. 32)

[Levine believes] that realism is the only credible base for verse (even his allegories are painstakingly tailored to a realist origin, a realist frame, and a realist linear progression). Often Levine seems to me simply a memoir-writer in prose who chops up his reminiscent paragraphs into short lines. Here he is on the subject of his first suit, a brown double-breasted pin-stripe with wide lapels:

> Three times I wore it formally: first with red suspenders to a high school dance where no one danced except the chaperones, in a style that minimized the fear of gonorrhea. . . . Then to a party to which almost no one came and those who did counted the minutes until the birthday cake with its armored frosting was cut and we could flee. And finally to the draft board where I stuffed it in a basket with my shoes, shirt, socks, and underclothes and was herded naked with the others past doctors half asleep and determined to find nothing.

An American Fifties' autobiography—is there any compelling reason why it should be called poetry? Certainly it is not notably improved by being cut into the short lines in which it appears in this volume of poetry:

> And finally to the draft board
>     where
> I stuffed it in a basket with my
>     shoes,
> shirt, socks, and underclothes and
>     was
> herded naked, etc,

Levine's line breaks (unlike Williams's or Ammons's) are not particularly witty or arresting. Levine's notion of a poem is an anecdote with a flush of reflexive emotion gushing up at the end, like "that flush / of warmth that came with knowing / no one could be more ridiculous than I," with which Levine ends the tale of the brown suit. Levine does attempt poems of mythical or symbolic status, but he is not happy without his clenched toe-holds of circumstantial evidence. He is entirely aware of the division in himself between "items" on the one hand, and yearnings on the other; and he mocks his own notion (a still ineradicable one in him) that "poems"—*real* "poems"—are about love or the rose or the dew, and are sonnets "in fourteen rhyming lines."

He writes a somewhat petulant account of this affliction in a poem of thirteen adamantly unrhyming lines called **"Genius."** In it, he first enumerates a characteristic list of his sordidly and surrealistically realistic "items" ("An unpaid water bill, the rear license / of a dog that messed on your lawn," etc.) and then says that with these images "a bright beginner could make a poem / in fourteen rhyming lines about the purity / of first love or the rose's many thorns." This opposition of the squalid and the rhapsodic seems to me, even in jest, a deficient aesthetic. It owes something to Stevens's notion of making poems while sitting on a dump, using language to deny the refuse that you see; but Stevens did not linger long in that crude view.

When Levine shades off into the various forms of his sentimental endings (togetherness, doom, death, the sad brown backs of peonies, what have you) it is easy to lose faith in his good sense. The writer who thinks up these disastrous endings has never, it seems, met the writer who writes the beginnings—or indeed who writes whole poems. (p. 35)

I am not convinced that Levine's observations and reminiscences belong in lyric poems, since he seems so inept in what he thinks of as the obligatory hearts-and-flowers endings of "poems." Perhaps if he didn't think he was writing "poems" he could leave off his romantic organ tones and be truer to his stubborn earthiness. (p. 36)

Helen Vendler, "All Too Real," in The New York Review of Books, *Vol. XXVIII, No. 20, December 17, 1981, pp. 32-6.**

## DAVID ST. JOHN

By now the virtues of Philip Levine's poetry are well known: his poems are deeply humane; they are eloquently persuasive in their convictions, both personal and political; and they are fiercely concerned with their accessibility to unacademic readers. Although Levine, in his early work, exercised a variety of voices in his poems in his attempt to give voice to a whole realm of everyday working experience for which there was no voice, it has been his most recent books, *The Names of the Lost, Ashes,* and *7 Years From Somewhere,* that have fixed him in the minds of most readers. For that reason, when most readers think of one of Levine's poems, they think of a very personal first-person poem, generally serious and impassioned, sometimes gently lyrical, sometimes politically charged and rhetorically urgent.

In Philip Levine's most recent book, *One For The Rose* . . . , those recognizably *Levine* poems are present. Yet, for me, some of the most exciting poems of the book belong to those that issue out of an exuberant sideshow of voices; they are full of such sassiness and wit, such buoyancy and good humor. . . . These are wonderful, rich, and funny poems. In fact, *One For*

*The Rose* is filled with Levine's marvelous humor, at times burlesquing his subjects or speakers and at times creating a remarkable poignancy.

Yet I don't mean to slight the work in a vein more expected of Levine. Two of the poems in *One For The Rose*, **"Having Been Asked 'What Is A Man' I Answer,"** and **"To Cipriano, In The Wind,"** stand among the best poems—the most beautiful and powerful poems—Levine has ever written. And there is of course no need to feel one must choose between the poems of the personas here and the poems of the more recognizable serious-minded poet. All of these voices speak *for* the same man, just as he is speaking *in* them all. I've come to feel that *One For The Rose* is one of Philip Levine's finest, richest books. (pp. 232-33)

> *David St. John, "Raised Voices in the Choir: A Review of 1981 Poetry Selections," in* The Antioch Review, *Vol. XL, No. 2, Spring, 1982, pp. 225-34.*\*

## MARJORIE PERLOFF

In a 1978 interview reprinted in *Don't Ask,* Philip Levine remarks:

> I think Robert Bly is a poet who has become incredibly boring. I don't think he was very talented to begin with, but he was able to describe snow covered with bird shit very well. But then he became a seer, as did Gary Snyder. They became very wise men, and they got up there and they told everybody in the world how they ought to live, and they still do, and like all wise men they are extraordinarily boring.

Life, friends, is boring, as Henry Pussy-Cat knew and Levine's new book *One for the Rose* . . . testifies at almost every turn. Not that Levine was untalented to begin with. In such justly admired books as *Not This Pig* (1968) and *They Feed They Lion* (1972), he performed an impressive balancing act: the sufferings of poor people, black or white, of freaks encountered in bars, of a war victim or a **"Child Trapped in a Barber Shop,"** were recounted by a voice that responded to the destructive violence of poverty with a hard-nosed and preposterous humor. . . . [The tone was] one of grim celebration, a refusal to mourn for the "buried aunties" and "Mothers hardening like pounded stumps" and a concomitant refusal to mourn for oneself. But then Levine became a seer and a "wise man". . . .

A poem in *One for the Rose* called **"Having been asked 'What is a Man?' I Answer (after Keats)"** places the poet in the Intensive Care Unit, wired up after what was presumably a heart attack; his son "brings giant / peonies and the nurse puts them / on the windowsill where they / seem afraid to gaze out at the city / smoking beneath." The sagging here is not just that of the peonies: Levine tritely identifies with the dying flowers and then just as tritely recalls Keats's vale of soul-making and concludes with this chin-up moral:

> I will read Keats again, I will rise
> and go into the world, unwired and free,
> because I am no longer a movie,
> I have no beginning, no middle, no end,
> no film score underscoring each act,
> no costume department, no expert on color.

> I am merely a man dressing in the dark
> because that is what a man is—
> so many mouthfuls of laughter
> and so many more, all there can be
> behind the sad brown backs of peonies.

In the comparison of cardiac monitor to movie screen, there is a momentary flicker (no pun intended) of Levine's celebrated black humor, the defiant energy that made such early poems as **"Animals are Passing from our Lives"** and **"Baby Villon"** memorable. But the metaphor goes limp almost immediately in its unrelieved cuteness: heart tracings, as recorded on the monitor, have no beginning, middle, or end, nothing comparable to a musical score or costumes or color. Indeed, the tracing is everything a movie is not. In this context, the solemn assertion, "I am merely a man dressing in the dark" strikes a hollow note, and by the time we come to the line "because that is what a man is," we know Levine has joined the ranks of the Wise Men. (pp. 210-11)

[The] interviews collected in *Don't Ask* . . . are revealing. . . . Life is a holy thing, the possibilities of the human are boundless, there are a lot of terrific young people out there, teaching is fun—how do we relate these true-blue sentiments [expressed in the interviews] to Levine's political stance, which has been, from the start, Leftist (but strongly anti-Communist), Anarchist—primarily *against* everything government ("theirs" or "ours") stands for. (pp. 213-14)

Perhaps because I happened, by simple coincidence, to read [Levine's definition of a political poet] and related passages in *Don't Ask* side by side with Barthes' *Mythologies* and Guy Davenport's *The Geography of the Imagination*, my immediate reaction to Levine's "political" commentary was one of simple disbelief, almost of embarrassment that a poet as respected and honored as is Philip Levine could reduce the political complexities of our time to such banal chitchat. One reason, surely, that Romanticism in its late phase seems so desiccated, so irrelevant to the real concerns of our world, is that it often goes hand in hand with an almost willed ignorance, as if to say God forbid that a poet should have *ideas* about things, that a poet should *know* something—say, about the circumstances under which our Constitution was drafted, not to mention what that Constitution has meant to millions of refugees from countries where no such "lousy document" exists.

But, quite aside from its intellectual flabbiness, Levine's tough-guy stance is also curiously inconsistent. If our government is really nothing but a "lie," if "they" are "taking away" our water and our mountains and our air, if it's all just a rip-off anyway and the past, as we were taught about it in school, "was utter horseshit," how is it possible for the poet to be so pleasantly satisfied with his life, so happy and enthusiastic about all those "terrific" and "marvelous" people he meets on the poetry circuits? Does the holiness of the heart's affections really have so little to do with the social and cultural community in which it dwells?

At this point someone will object that it is unfair to judge a poet by what he or she happens to say in an interview, that what *counts*, after all, is the poetry itself, not the prose or publicity that surrounds it. This too, I would argue, is a Romantic position. The fact is that Levine edited these interviews himself for book publication in the *Poets on Poetry* series, and there is no reason to assume that an edited interview has a different ontological status from, say, a letter Keats wrote to his brother George in the wilderness of Kentucky. The consciousness of the poet, surely, is reflected in all he or she has written, which is not to say that all of it will be equally valuable.

A reading of Levine's political poetry will, in any case, bear out my argument. Reviewing *The Names of the Lost* (1976) . . . , Stephen Yenser called Levine "our notable heir to the radicalism of the 1930s, a descendant of Henry Roth who has read Neruda and Vallejo closely" [see *CLC*, Vol. 14]. A very apt comparison . . . but one could take it further and wonder whether the deep Latin American waters of passion can truly mix with the Detroit motor oil in Philip Levine's veins. Take an elegy like **"Francisco, I'll Bring You Red Carnations"** (*Seven Years from Somewhere*—1979), one of Levine's several poems about heroes of the Left in the Spanish Civil War years— in this case, Francisco Ascaso, who, with Buenaventura Durruti, memorialized in *The Names of the Lost,* died in the defense of Madrid in 1936.

It is a noble subject for elegy—think what Yeats might have done with it, or Lorca or Brecht—but Levine gives us no real view of the subject. (pp. 215-16)

*One for the Rose,* Levine's new book, turns from political to more personal themes, and, at least in a handful of poems, the jaunty hangdog voice of Levine's early poetry reappears: Levine as Woody Allen is always appealing. Thus, in **"The Poem of Flight,"** Levine projects himself into the role of the very first pilot (Orville Wright) flying the very first plane and crashing on the lawn of a sweet North Carolina lady who bandages his bloody hand and takes care of him. . . . This is Levine at his self-deprecating, witty best; a similar passage occurs in **"The Myth,"** in which the poet, rejected by his classically uncomprehending bourgeois family, sulks in the comfort that at least his wife has loved him. . . . Here the energy of the fable recalls *Not this Pig!,* the poet refusing to play the game according to the rules. It doesn't matter, for instance, that "everyone" tells him he was born in "a flat on Pingree in Detroit," because [in **"I Was Born in Lucerne"**] he has invented his own origins:

> in a small Italian hotel overlooking
> the lake. No doctor, no nurse. Just
> a beautiful single woman who preferred
> to remain that way and raise me to
> the proper height, weight, and level of audacity.
>
> (pp. 217-18)

These are engaging, if not arresting poems. But most of *One for the Rose* is given over to a nostalgic poetry of experience that presents Levine's now-familiar Detroit tenement world in all too pallid outline: the formula, again and again, is "This happened to me, and then that, and what I learned from it all is this, so let me tell you about it." Thus **"Roofs"** presents the child climbing the roof overlooking his own back yard, and yearning to fly down to earth, an urge that leads to a broken hand but also to the realization that he can climb up again and this time get down safely. . . . (p. 218)

Again, in **"I Wanted You to Know,"** the poet recalls how, as a young boy, he bought his mother a tiny rosebush wrapped in burlap for her birthday, only to discover, when the roses bloomed a full year later, that they were yellow, not the desired red, and that, in any case, they quickly "became four tight little blooms, eyes closed, / just touched with rain." But in his new knowledge of death, the boy has made the flowers his very own: "They were mine, / and the whole world was never the same." The truth pronounced in these final lines seems to be grafted on a pretty frail branch. (pp. 218-19)

*One for the Rose* is finally a boring book—boring in its insistent demand that we take stock response and bathos for insight. Poem after poem tells us that "This is an ordinary gray Friday after work" or "an ordinary Wednesday in winter" (**"To a New Mother"**). The reader is not likely to disagree. (p. 221)

*Marjorie Perloff, "Soft Touch," in* Parnassus: Poetry in Review, *Vol. 10, No. 1, Spring-Summer, 1982, pp. 209-30.**

### PETER STITT

The objection I had to Philip Levine's last two books [see excerpt above] . . . was that the poems were sentimental, too tied to the literal truth of the writer's life, and thus weakly written, almost garrulous. These reservations apply only in isolated cases in Levine's new book, *One for the Rose,* which seems to me a triumphant return to the high quality of his earlier work. The poems in this volume are tied together by a subtle underlying conception that determines both their form and their content. Levine surprises us in one poem, **"Roofs,"** by delivering a truth which he applies seriously to both poetry and life. After trying to fly like Superman by jumping from the roof of a garage, the speaker says: "From this I learned / nothing so profound as Newton / might, but something about / how little truth there was / in fantasy." What is remarkable about this passage is that so many of these poems are fantasies—they place the speaker in a triumphant situation which he never could occupy in life. And that of course is the point: in actual life one must never be deluded by fantasy, but in poetry the imagination may be allowed to carry us away. Thus the poem ends on a vision from another kind of roof; back on top of the garage, the speaker notices "nothing in sight but blue sky / a little closer and more familiar, / always calling me back as though / I'd found by accident or as in / a dream my only proper element."

And it is this imaginative vision of something greater, more heroic, than ordinary life that makes Levine realize all the more strongly the very nature of human life. [**"Having Been Asked 'What Is a Man?' I Answer"** is a] profound and beautiful poem. . . . (p. 683)

[Such poems as **"Into My Own"** show] Levine's powerful imagination and his considerable lyrical gifts in full flower. *One for the Rose* is an unusually strong book; its open forms are as free as the imagination can make them, but . . . we know the author is always in full control of his materials, never relinquishing his reins to them. (p. 685)

*Peter Stitt, "Poems in Open Forms," in* The Georgia Review, *Vol. XXXVI, No. 3, Fall, 1982, pp. 675-85.**

### LOUIS L. MARTZ

There is only one poem [in *One for the Rose*], **"Never Before,"** in which Levine gives way to a sense of utter hopelessness. The other poems . . . imply an amelioration through creating a deep sympathy for the human condition; thus in **"Salt"** he enters deeply into the plight of the sobbing woman left alone at night in the airport; or he remembers with affection (in **"You Can Cry"**) Old Cherry Dorn, "his black head running with gray." Levine frequently attempts to compensate for pain by an upsurge of sentiment, sometimes too baldly: "Cherry, you can cry forever and no one will know." . . . Sop it up, Levine, sop it up. But then sometimes the open burst of sentiment works. . . .

One problem with Levine's poetry may derive from the fact that he is trying to open his sensibility to all experience, like Whitman, but he is doing so in short lines that, as they lie on the page, suggest the example of William Carlos Williams, father of the modern cityscape. But the endings and beginnings of Levine's lines do not often have the firm significance and definition that one finds in Williams (and Ammons). I have the feeling that a William Everson might easily rearrange many of these short-lined poems into longer cadences, with good results. However the poems are printed, their strength does not lie in technical brilliance, but rather in Levine's acute ear for people's speech and in the range and depth of his sympathies. (pp. 69-70)

Louis L. Martz, "Ammons, Warren, and the Tribe of Walt," in The Yale Review, Vol. 72, No. 1, Autumn, 1982, pp. 63-84.*

## BONNIE COSTELLO

[In *One for the Rose* Levine] offers the pictures of a man's life, and his album . . . reveals certain mythic continuities (here registered in images of flight, rain, rose, etc.). But he is no prophet; his stories map a life, not a cosmos. His audience coincides with, but does not predicate, his verse.

The self, its identity, origins, destiny, is Levine's subject, but one he never takes for granted, scrutinizing even his name. Estranged from all such certainties, he asks, repeatedly: How did I get here? Where am I going? Where have I been in my sleep? The local resurfaces in thought, but transport or visitation renew it, sometimes as burden, sometimes as relief. In **"The Window," "Each Dawn," "Depot Bay,"** and others, the poet's soul seems to leave the body, cresting in high lyricism, but returns to a street-life hardness, often wounded in the fall, but never broken. Levine will not palely loiter in the actual, like Keats's knight; such journeys galvanize the soul against despair. Similarly, **"I Was Born in Lucerne,"** and others challenge the givens of identity, discerning a mystical center uncharted by any personal data sheet. Parable strains this concept of the inner sublime in poems like **"The Doctor of Starlight."** It is best shown as the thematic counterpart of Levine's more characteristic style, in which the everyday turns suddenly toward the otherworldly, dreams are mixed with the grit of Detroit, and an earthy, narrative range is cut in short, lyrical lines to let the mica shine.

An overdependence on rhetorical devices, in place of organic logic, weakens some of these poems. Too often Levine sets up systems of repetition that find no interior shape, so that the endings of poems tend to collapse under the relentless pattern. **"My Name"** has little but arbitrary characters to guide its dissection of identity. Similarly, **"Keep Talking"** becomes irritating with its repeated "If it ain't this, what is it," the way a child's persistent "why" can drive its parents to distraction. **"The Fox"** succeeds because Levine bases its structure in analogy: the self, like the fox, is an outcast, graceful against odds. **"Never Before"** modulates its repetitions but still wears them thin, damaging the major effect of surprise on which the poem depends. The rhetorical shape of **"Ascension"** reinforces an inner logic, moving from present, to memory, to forgetfulness, to expectation. But the language of expectation pales against the brighter language of memory, so that no true ascension takes place. The best of Levine turns around memories of new

thresholds and possibilities, looking backwards fondly at a self looking forwards. Here the launchings from local to imagined worlds, the uncertainties of place and identity, connect to a portrait of youth. **"The Radio,"** one of the least showy but most successful poems in the volume, tells very simply of fantasies a lonely youth had listening to dance music. The poem moves out from these particulars to mildly ironic, mildly nostalgic meditation on destiny. . . . Levine's fondness for this young man and for those who influenced him ("come back, Cipriano Mera, step / out of the wind and dressed in the robe / of your pain tell me again that this / world will be ours") tends to overshadow any present optimism. His will to upbeat endings leaves few poems counting their losses, but there remains a strange uneasiness about the optimism recollected, a suggestion that life has sullied the "sequined door" which "would open on something new." (pp. 108-10)

Bonnie Costello, "Orders of Magnitude," in Poetry, Vol. CXLII, No. 2, May, 1983, pp. 106-13.*

## JOEL CONARROE

[Philip Levine has] been publishing poetry of high quality for more than two decades and . . . has not yet become a household word—not that many poets have. The Pulitzer Prize, for example, has eluded him, the American Academy of Arts and Letters has not elected him, and his work is not widely anthologized. He has, however, been twice honored by the National Book Critics Circle, and he won the American Book Award in 1980. He is, if not a major figure (*are* there any major living poets?), clearly an artist worth attending to.

*Selected Poems* contains representative work from 10 collections, beginning with *On the Edge* in 1963 and ending with *One for the Rose* in 1981. Reading through the book consecutively is like stumbling through a forbidding woods finally to emerge in a sun-dappled field. Levine seems to have gone through the reverse of a mid-life crisis; I would describe it as a renaissance except I'm not sure about the "re." Call it a mid-life emergence.

His early books are grim, documenting a sensibility accustomed to failure, loss, bigotry, and violence. (p. 3)

In suggesting that the work of Levine's middle age (he is now 56) presents a more hopeful view of things, I do not want to imply that he suddenly turned into Pollyanna. Far from it. The imagery is still dark, the world still full of pitfalls. He does, though, seem to have laid to rest some of the events that haunted him for years, including his father's death when he was five. . . .

The closing lines from ["The Voice"] . . . help define his new sense of things, and of himself, revealing a singer who has found his proper pitch . . . :

> I embrace whatever pleases me,
> and the earth is my one home,
> as it always was, the earth
> and perhaps some day the sky too
> and all the climbing things between.
>
> (p. 11)

Joel Conarroe, "Poets of Innocence and Experience," in Book World—The Washington Post, August 5, 1984, pp. 3, 11.*

# Jayanta Mahapatra

## 1928-

Indian poet, translator, and editor.

Mahapatra writes in English, yet his poetry is distinctively Indian. Many of his poems feature his home, Orissa, a rural region of India. His themes are the traditional, apparently timeless concerns of his country—spirituality, hunger, death, and rebirth. Mahapatra's questioning, somber poetry evokes the Indian belief in cultural stasis and inevitability. He explains that he was raised to believe that "things happen as they do because . . . of things that have happened before, and that nothing can change the sequence of things." Thus, Mahapatra writes of immediately perceived physical and social realities without probing their causes.

A further reason for the dominance of the Indian sensibility in Mahapatra's poetry may lie in his lack of acquaintance with a world poetic tradition. Mahapatra is a physics professor who admits, "I haven't read much poetry in my life," and he did not start writing until he was almost forty years old. He produced his first volumes of poetry, *Close the Sky, Ten by Ten* (1971) and *Svayamvara and Other Poems* (1971), after briefly experimenting with writing short fiction and participating in writers' workshops. *A Rain of Rites* (1976), his first volume published in the United States, was highly acclaimed and resulted in his attendance at the University of Iowa's International Writing Program. His later verse, which includes *A Father's Hours* (1976), *Waiting* (1979), *The False Start* (1980), *Relationship* (1980), and *Life Signs* (1984), has heightened his reputation as an accomplished and prolific poet. As Madhusudan Prasad commented, "Both in quantity and quality, [Mahapatra's] poetry is amazingly impressive, almost startling."

(See also *Contemporary Authors*, Vols. 73-76 and *Contemporary Authors New Revision Series*, Vol. 15.)

## VERNON YOUNG

I doubt that the character of Jayanta Mahapatra's sad and serpentine poetry [in *A Rain of Rites*] can be adequately accounted for by the double circumstance that their creator is twentieth-century and *writes in English*. (He has never been out of India!) The manner of apprehension in his wonderful, sensate poems inevitably brings to the tongue the word, "sophistication." . . . Evident in every cadence is the long over-ripening of a sardonic wisdom, the tired consciousness of too many beginnings. . . . [In **"Now When We Think of Compromise"**] Mahapatra consistently reveals a grinding ambivalence towards the burdens of custom and revolving time with which his fellowmen are laden, sanctified, impeded, while indelibly evoking an India I recall from a glimpse in my youth: to me, then, only an exotic chaos, of ". . . bicycles, buses, idling bulls; / a whole religion framed by the land . . . Every man, every beast, trapped, dead in his own sleep . . . ruined leprous shells, leaning against one

another . . . The gods casually breezing through the air, among bones."

> A man does not mean anything.
> But the place.
> Sitting on the riverbank throwing pebbles
> into the muddy current,
> a man becomes the place.
> Even that simple enough thing. . . .
>
>                               **("Somewhere, My Man")**

Such fragments are but hints of the style that conveys the poet's melancholy overview; they tell you nothing of his command of integrated form. . . . With what art the transitive or parenthetical image corroborates the sexual thrust which is the sombre subject [of **"Hunger"**]: "I saw his white bone thrash his eyes"— "sprawling sands"—"my mind thumping"—"his body clawed / at the froth"—"opened like a wound"—"an oil lamp splayed the hours." Imposing out of all proportion to their relatively scant number and to the cultural remoteness of their author, these poems should inveigle anyone who professes a passion for the music of English. Few contemporary poems in *our* world impress me more than these. (pp. 616-18)

*Vernon Young, in a review of "A Rain of Rites," in* The Hudson Review, *Vol. XXIX, No. 4, Winter, 1976-77, pp. 616-18.*

## CHOICE

Writing in multifoliate free verse [in *A Rain of Rites*], Maha-patra evokes India in modalities ranging from stark but intense description to dreamlike webs of association—an India whose image mirrors a poetic sensibility at once alienated from and inextricably rooted in her. The poems often seem to be ad-dressed to Western audiences (sometimes with explanatory footnotes), but are far from being merely literary anthropology.

> *A review of "A Rain of Rites," in* Choice, *Vol. 14, No. 4, June, 1977, p. 543.*

## DICK ALLEN

Mahapatra, in contrast to most American poets, is most at home with poems which touch the beyond. The poetry of *A Rain of Rites* is that of a man taking up a stance against or within mysteries, sensitive to the moods of days and years. In the book's opening poem, *Dawn* is "Like a hard crossword puzzle / it sets riddles crowding against one another".... The imagery throughout the poetry is sometimes surrealistic, often ques-tioning. "With what brief magic can a little life waken?" he asks in *Ceremony*.... The questioning is important, as it com-municates the openness of this poet, the sheer quiet listening quality of his gentle lines. We are often in a dream country, a country of poetry perhaps like his *India*.... My favorite poem of this book is *The Landscape of Return,* with its lovely last stanza; and I also like *Old Palaces, A Rain,* and *Ceremony.* The book is mainly one to be absorbed as a whole, read quietly. Nothing in *A Rain of Rites* actually startles; the tone is even throughout, one of wonder sustained.

*A Father's Hours* is a short collection, containing one small poem, *Levels;* a two-page poem, *Assassins;* a seven-section poem, *Performance;* and the twenty individually-paged stanzas of *The Twentyfifth Anniversary of a Republic: 1975.* Like *A Rain of Rites,* it has poetry of question, search, wonder; the poet is tricked, puzzled, mystified, has a "bandaged mind", senses "the flowers dangling over the silence." ... In *Assas-sins* he writes, "I would loathe the goose-stepping discipline of a mind / that simply wishes to conduct one safely into the future." The assassins are here; the "coiled snakes" are "draped about our errors". The twenty-stanza poem shows his musings off to best advantage. They are serious, with imagery often consciously detaching itself from "reality" while not ignoring it. ... In both books the poetry often floats away, past its own long lines.... [Mahapatra's poetry] is bound to sky. Is it too American a response to quibble with . . . invocations that so relentlessly bring back from the beyond only the ultimate mys-terious distance? To long for more hard edges in this continual blurring? (pp. 350-51)

> *Dick Allen, "To the Wall," in* Poetry, *Vol. CXXX, No. 6, September, 1977, pp. 342-52.*\*

## CHARLES R. LARSON

It is almost impossible to describe the images that explode from Jayanta Mahapatra's *A Rain of Rites* . . . , which might otherwise be called a thunderstorm of poetic surprises.... [Mahapatra] writes with such ease and clarity of vision that many of his poems give the impression of having been animated by some private muse which exists solely to inspire him. (p. 563)

Though there are subjects here that defy classification ("**The Bare Arms in Packing Cases**"), many of the poems are rooted in pastoral themes—particularly the seasons and the land.... *A Rain of Rites* introduces a major Indian lyrical voice to Amer-ican readers. (p.564)

> *Charles R. Larson, "Anglophone Writing from Af-rica and Asia," in* World Literature Today, *Vol. 51, No. 4, Autumn, 1977, pp. 563-65.*\*

## DILIP CHITRE

Indian poets writing in English have had the singular misfortune of being the victims of rather prejudiced ridicule. Much pomp-ous ignorance goes into the derisive comments and vastly gen-eralized prohibition voiced at Indians venturing to write poetry in their former rulers' language, still enjoying the status of India's associate national language.... When the average In-dian begins to learn English, he is already besieged by and saturated in at least one Indian language. The so-called English-medium schools in India give him an obsolete model of English as a base. The slang he may speak among his peers is also based on colloquial but obsolete English and it is a strangely bastardized slang because it blends outmoded British and American vocabulary spiced with strange Indianisms.... He is hardly equipped to make love in English, get hopping mad in English or, for that matter, use English spontaneously in any situation....

A majority of Indians writing in English, as a result, become commentators on life in India rather than active participants. Many of them do not even try to face the patent paranoia of their own situation. None of them is equipped to create a living English literary tradition native to India. But such a tradition appears to be emerging now. A small number of competent, skilled and even gifted and talented Indian poets have produced significant poetry in English. They are remarkably contem-porary and unmistakably Indian. (p. 77)

Jayanta Mahapatra has a [quiet] tone, a pictorial bent of mind and, despite the sort of irony so natural to the English language giving it an unusual slant, he has a very Hindu vision of life.... [Mahapatra] is traditional in his poetic bias despite the con-temporariness of his articulation. His verse is free and moves slowly though smoothly. It is almost languid in its metaphysical poise until, suddenly, he transforms elemental visual images of Indian nature and traditional rural life into memorable met-aphors. Mahapatra is what the Indian poet writing in English is generally expected to be: an interpreter of a unique, complex and exotic culture through its landscape and people. This is the kind of role that Satyajit Ray's films have played inter-nationally.

Mahapatra's technical competence is hardly in doubt. But his vision of India could be a matter of sharp controversy among his peers and his critics in India. In this respect, he is closer to poets like [R.] Parthasarathy than to poets like [Adil] Jus-sawala whose poetry is more deeply personal but who, when it comes to the bare bones, prefer to face the ugly political implications of what they see rather than suggestively deal with its cultural complexity.... Mahapatra is at his best only when he avoids to reveal his own viewpoint or even conceals it effectively. Or perhaps it is a part of his worldview that life in India is an eternally ambiguous phenomenon and therefore reproducing each layer of it verbally is just as legitimate as peeling all those layers one after another. (pp. 78-9)

[*Indian Summer Poem,* which appears in the collection *A Rain of Rites*], illustrates the strengths and weaknesses of Mahapatra's technique and gives us a glimpse of his vision, despite his ambivalence. The choice of 'soughing' in the first line is both surprising and apt, though the adjective 'sombre' appears nearly unnecessary to me. The auditory image in the first line has another auditory image superimposed upon it in the second, plus a visual element evoked by priests. Then comes the sudden surprise:

'the mouth of India opens.'

Now the image ceases to be a mere montage of sound images with a visual element. It suddenly turns into monumental metaphysical metaphor. Meanwhile, the vowel sounds, with the deep and rounded 'o' dominating, have already produced a dark resonance, evoking the sanctum of a Hindu temple and equating it with 'the mouth of India', weaving in images of voice and devouring, and also alluding to the mouth Krishna opened to reveal the ultimate reality to Arjuna. The non-Indian reader will probably miss the last suggestion altogether, though to Hindu Indian reader, or anyone familiar with the Mahabharata and the *Bhagadvadgita,* it is a powerful recognition.

Similarly, 'the deep roar of funeral pyres' by which 'the good wife' is 'unexhausted' as she lies dreaming, is rich with suggestions of death, the chanting of the mantras of the last rites, and a true medieval *pativrata* offering to sacrifice herself on her husband's funeral pyre as a *sati.* The poem is simple and clear in its elements but has a deeper structure that is highly complex and abstract. Every image is concrete, whether auditory or visual, yet the total effect is as abstract as it is evocative, and extremely complex. All the tensions the poem produces are through an underlying metaphor. The equation of the erotic image of the wife in bed with the funeral pyre is central to the poem. Thus, while using contemporary English without a flaw, Mahapatra moves in traditional Hindu dimensions and successfully superimposes the distinct ethos of his own tradition upon the language he uses. My very Indian ear detects the incantatory rhythm of Sanskrit chants and devotional songs in modern Indian languages in his freely structured prosody. Indeed, the advantages of a double cultural heritage are efficiently realized by Mahapatra in his more successful poems, and this points to one of the main possibilities of Indian poetry in English.

Despite his strongly traditional leanings, perhaps the very choice of English as his language of self-expression gives Mahapatra a critical distance from his themes, a detachment which helps him to regard all existence as ambiguous but full of concrete detail. At times, his poems have a subtly ironical echo because of this distance. For as a writer, he belongs as much to the phlegmatic, self-doubting, emotionally inward English tradition and its more opened out, experimental and exuberant American variant as to the spiritually narcissistic and semantically elusive attitude of the elite Hindu mind. The English language and its literary culture, with all their resources and possibilities, are employed by him to describe a part of his own world and sensibility which are essentially foreign to it. There is something in this process that has close affinities with translation at its most creative and with anthropological perception. Being myself an Indian, it is difficult for me to read Mahapatra's work the same way as non-Indian, native users of the English might. Perhaps like him and like other Indian users of English I naturally compensate for the culture gap inherent in such a situation.

The poem *Myth,* which I like very much, gives us a measure of Mahapatra's awareness of this difficult distance. (pp. 80-1)

[In the last ten lines of *Myth*] we have the classic confrontation between archaic and mysterious rituals, the structure of a whole tradition, and a modern sensibility. The poet stands apart, at a distance from the myth, like a person whose caste and religion itself are doubted by the suspicious custodians of the secret. He dare not go into the dark sanctum 'where the myth shifts swiftly from hand to hand, eye to eye'. The ancient mystery of the dark sanctum has survived. It has even gained in power. 'Are you a Hindoo?' is a question full of irony, but perhaps it has more echoes than one. A slight change of pitch and intonation can alter the meaning of the question. And the poem ends with its loaded ambiguity, an unresolved tension. Is Mahapatra a religious revivalist? Is he a modern Hindu whose modernity is itself as ambiguous as his tradition? I cannot answer this question. Nor, for that matter, does the poem. I wonder how the poem would sound if it were translated into Mahapatra's native Oriya. But I suspect that the critical holding back of emotion, the ending upon an unresolved tension, and the inherent irony so central to the poem would be lost in translation into most Indian languages unless very different rhetorical devices were employed, and unless the poem were made more blatant and less contemplative. (p. 81)

*Dilip Chitre, "Poetry in the Enemy's Tongue: On Two Indian Poets Writing in English," in* New Quest, *No. 14, March-April, 1979, pp. 77-82.\**

## BRUCE KING

Many of the poems in [*A Rain of Rites* and *Waiting*] could easily find a place in an anthology of contemporary Commonwealth verse; they are carefully crafted, free-verse lyrics, making excellent use of interior assonance, alliteration and sometimes subtle end-line rhymes, in the contemporary mode in which self-awareness is achieved through sensitive brooding upon a scene, event, desire or passing experience. But perhaps this is the reason Mahapatra is not better known; each poem, though complete in itself, is a fragment of a vision which is still edging towards a more precise articulation. There are poems of uncertainty, puzzlement, humane concern, and moments of self-analysis, which need a large myth, embodiment of crisis, some position or grand architectural form to make them more than notes towards the definition of a self. Mahapatra seems aware of this problem; each of these books has a unity of tone, something like a coherence of themes, and a distinct style. But without a stronger unifying voice or structure, the unity is nominal, and the best individual poems stand out from their surroundings.

*A Rain of Rites* begins with **"Dawn,"** a poem which exhibits Mahapatra's ability to strike deeply in phrases which communicate wonder. . . . It also includes those dead, ready-made phrases that mar even his best poems: ''a distant temple bell,'' ''things suddenly found.'' Each of the poems is about some aspect of Indian life, ritual, nature, or the moods that go into poetry. Although India is very much in the poems the themes are really more the poet's relationship to the past, a tradition no longer vital to himself, to others who still lead older lives, and to the natural world as a mystery and an aspect of eternity. The poems of peasants and rituals tend to be rather simplistic exercises in sensitivity toward others; because the concern is easy and feels external, the effect is thin.

The best poems concern the self in relation to India, history, eternity. The first stanza of **"Old Palaces"** is illustrative. The opening two lines are a pleasure to read; imagination has stretched feelings into concepts and found appropriate images and sounds. . . . Unfortunately the final line of the last stanza consists of twenty-two syllables of prose which cannot be read comfortably: "Not the thought that succeeds in pushing the darkness, evil and ugliness out of my life." These are really two lines run together. (pp. 97-8)

[In *A Rain of Rites* the] sounds are patterned within stanzas, the rhymes deftly picked up throughout a poem, and the variety of techniques Mahapatra has learned to use are all impressive. Although small, meditative lyrics typical of the time, the poems exhibit an unusual range of skills, especially in line endings and internal harmonies, of the kind which distinguish the work of a poet from an amateur. Many of the poems have recognizable shapes made popular through Robert Bly and James Wright—the striking, almost surreal opening followed by an accumulation of vague, soft modifying words as the mind tries to explore a mood; the lazy, stretching gesture in surroundings which are soon observed to be filled with challenging activity or events and which concludes with the poet's withdrawing upon himself in puzzlement; and striking, if rather easily assumed, self-questioning. There are also too many tricks of diction and phrase from T. S. Eliot. But even with such reservations, *A Rain of Rites* is an interesting book with some very fine poems.

Mahapatra's *Waiting* is also focussed on images and rituals of India, the road as a symbol of life, and, more particularly, on the traditional priest, as in the last two stanzas of "Waiting," the title poem. . . . Although many of these poems exhibit characteristics similar to pieces in the earlier volume, they are less textured, less softly appealing, and, although there is the same mastery of rhymes, more bare. I have the impression that Mahapatra is trying to find his own voice by resorting less to the presently fashionable manners of Anglo-Saxon poetry; or perhaps the fashion itself has changed towards openness and a more direct speech. The poems are crafted, have form, but lines are more shaped by natural breath patterns and small syntactical groups of phrases. Many of the same gestures are there, sometimes in the same striving images and language, as in "The Earth of July." . . . But in general the poems feel more stripped down than previously. If there are fewer brilliances, the total effect is more solid. Finding one's own voice is an important step towards going beyond the lyric-of-our-time; if Mahapatra is not yet ready for grander gestures and larger forms, he is an interesting poet, well worth attention. (pp. 99-100)

> *Bruce King, in a review of "A Rain of Rites" and "Waiting," in* World Literature Written in English, *Vol. 19, No. 1, Spring, 1980, pp. 97-100.*

## FRANK ALLEN

Jayanta Mahapatra is a perfect focal point for illuminating the dilemma of the two-languaged poet. Mahapatra is from Cuttack (Orissa), a moderate size town even by Indian standards. Orissa is his intense and major subject. Rural and ancient, it is far outside the intellectual circles of Delhi, Bombay, or Calcutta. . . . Parallels to this avoidance of nervous urban distress in America would be Philip Levine, Gary Snyder, David Wagoner, William Stafford or Robert Bly, or English poets who shun the fervent self-awareness of London. Their choice of a place to write shouldn't be interpreted negatively; it's not what they want to flee, rather what they want to deepen and cultivate. The evocation and attachment to place liberates one's psyche

from the curse of masochistic Flying Dutchman wandering. This commitment to locale can be seen in Whitman's nineteenth-century New York and Camden, Hardy's Wessex (Dorset), Frost's New England, Thomas' Swansea, Williams' Paterson, Yeats's Sligo, Frank O'Hara and Hart Crane's twentieth-century New York, etc., etc.

So it would stand to reason that Mahapatra would write in Oriya, his native dialect. Except he doesn't. He explains:

> . . . I am in love with English. And then, my schooling was in English—and I learnt my language from British schoolmasters. . . .
>
> (p. 333)

Using English, Mahapatra tries to come to terms with Hindu mythology and its celebration of the belief that "the universe is boundlessly various, that everything occurs simultaneously, that all possibilities may exist without excluding each other." Hindu ritual is at once embroidery and internal symbol, surfeit and transformation, acceptance and rebellion, former existence and a timeless present. The Hindu poet is inside, trying to escape the labyrinth, like Theseus, and trying to assault the innermost godhead of the sun, like Icarus. Religious ceremony to the contemporary West, largely synonymous with dubiety and self-denial, evokes a peace that passeth understanding. To use it, the poet must struggle to free this symbolism from cultural prejudice and fantasy. Not so for India. The Hindu ethos has given all diverse human impulses, no matter how anarchic, undignified, or bizarre, a valid and accessible place in its beliefs. With disastrous consequences, the West turns them into taboos to be exorcised or sublimated.

Looking both ways for balance, like Janus, *A Rain of Rites* strives to stay free amid contradictory impulses. . . . [In "Ikons"] I see the man's pain not as frustrated energy, as though he were a Tennessee Williams unfrocked cleric, but colliding impulses allowed a maximum assertion. He must communicate with a remorseless blind phallic earth while "a museum of symbols" silences the land. An unself-conscious recognition of the rhythms of the *lingam* and the *yoni* (symbols of male and female genitals) animate and free the best of these poems, like "The Whorehouse in a Calcutta Street" and "Hunger," from stridency. If their imaginative exploration of the sexual dimension of the psyche remains perturbed and opaque, they do not at least cry out ingenuously for false heavens and false hells. The god of the lingam from antiquity has been Siva, the destroyer, simultaneously "auspicious," god of ascetics, because sexual energy, to the Hindu, is ultimately radiant spiritual energy. It is not at all that an ascetic, say like Gandhi, is squeamish about sex, but that he so comprehends his generative powers that they rise to a transcendent equilibrium.

Mahapatra bravely tries to resolve a sexual, emotional, and deeply moral crisis of belief: oversimplifying, his poems pose the question, to which alternate values can a man most meaningfully accommodate himself? (pp. 334-36)

[In "Appearances" the] old banyan is the tutelary god of India: what is more natural than to worship trees? I do it myself in spring, but these are knotted, brown, and ghostly, not lithe and virginal like Thoreau's etherealized Massachusetts trees. These gods don't have to prove anything; they've been around 2500 years. They can wait. Under them comes a student, desiring self-knowledge, from the city—from modernity, among the inscrutable elders, emblems of the trees they sit under. Possibly this refers to the four stages of life: chaste student, householder, forest-dweller, and ascetic. "Cringes of habit"—

a dynamic, assertive cringing at and in the face of earth goddesses, Indus, and Ganges.

In this land of lepers and ten-armed, six-headed deities, what is a million years since all that gives meaning appears impervious to change? Appearances: "It is difficult to distinguish one from the other." Sunrise, sunset? Out of this haze of illusion "a dead leaf stares stiffly as a scholar." Trees as gods, their leaves avatars, full of divine plentitude, blank as coins with the inscription rubbed away, stare at the scholar. Inert and mirrory, they reflect his own stiff image, so little accommodating themselves to the individual in his niche of identity.

Separate yet totally assimilated by the power of the banyan votaries, the poet sees himself passing by, student and scholar. To one defined by inputs and outputs, unified field theory and psychobabble, the gods drone like "a stupid fairy tale, where once / some holy curse changed a woman to stone." Fairy tales of the Puranas are stupid and childish yet they endure like icons. A fairy tale that demands the mature, rational person to disbelieve in it because, out of immemorial destiny, it moves down the centuries like an inherited heirloom that would take possession of one. Nor is he spared the holy curse, changing flesh to stone, condemning the people to custom. How oppressive ritual can become is illustrated in the *Kamasutra*.

Finally,

> a dream of smiling children licking
> the aging faces around; the birth for which I search
> is the death that scatters my family among the boughs.

Mahapatra has the tendency to try to fight off myth by returning to childhood innocence. This often results in a half-foggy, half-surreal blur that founders on the implicit fear of and inability to deny the turning wheel of *samsara*. (*Samsara* literally means "wandering" and represents the transmigration of the human soul through endless reincarnations in human or animal form as a result of good or bad karma [conduct].) One's self and family, wife, children, and parents, are the scattered boughs of banyan gods.

Unfortunately, this fusion of Hindu mythology with personal rage against it does not carry over in Mahapatra's recent volume, **Waiting**. Brilliant, isolated images, engulfed by abstractions, fail to coalesce into the sudden epiphany, the revelation of the sacred in the diurnal. Not that he is any less serious or disciplined in his search through the land for moral emblems.... Fertility can barely rouse the dead [in **"At the Burning Ground"**]: "the river / curls sluggishly in thick smoke...." The gods' avatars now find prophecy a mournful burden: "two grey wood pigeons as though half-awake / grope around...." The inescapable "silence" of the dead glints over the water mocking the poet's "gesture of defiance."

At least the first stanza has a certain gloomy specificity from which one garners the unappealing and hard-earned view that the dead, in cremation, reach some kind of happy oblivion. I find the language of the second stanza flat and confusingly personal. It could have been deleted. Throughout the volume there is a disappointing tone of deflation and retreat.

No, I find myself happier returning to *A Rain of Rites* where, with wondrous solidity and confidence of craft, Mahapatra gives us the sense of an entire community permeated with painfully real human and divine impulses. Awkwardness and a fumbling for symbols becomes—to take one of my favorites—in **"Sunburst"** brilliantly lucid.... (pp. 336-38)

What lovely blending of vowels and consonants [in **"Sunburst"**], especially the third stanza where the l's and o's evoke heat and a numinous atmosphere. The ostensible surface motif is the contrast between the respectable world of the schoolgirls in "white frocks and red waistbands," and the coarse rural world of the cow's owner. But then "Lost in respectability's ruse, / they stare at the road, learning to close their eyes, / to hold their keen pride." It's not until afterward that we realize how subtly Mahapatra has dramatized the paradox of the two Indias, both implacable, both determined to dominate: the post-independence modern world of survival and success, and the blank, shameless agrarian world with its polytheistic fatalism. The crowd is "friendly" but "speechless." The schoolgirls, caught between two worlds like Mahapatra himself, "learning to close their eyes" and to turn their heads away, yet "stare at the road ...," indeed, "lost in respectability's ruse...." Looking both ways like Janus.

Beneath these levels of decorum, "as the foot of propriety slips again," there is a fundamental contrast between asceticism and sensuality, control and release, human and mythical ways of looking at reality. "Two gods copulating on the warm tar ...." Western poetry, I'm afraid, is too often incapable of such infusion of pathos in the ordinary. But perhaps not. As both goddess and woman, the cow's impregnation is seen as a mysterious public icon, but at the same time a manifestation to the schoolgirls and the reader of a troubling yet inescapable identity. We experience a "sunburst" (epiphany) illuminating Hindu erotic energy, of growing up into sex, of experiencing sexual relationships in an overwhelming, undiluted dimension, which is both physical and a paradigm of the supernal. Voluptuous stone Apsarases on temple friezes gaze across the distance between the West and India with an enigmatic smile.

His poetry is somewhat circumscribed by the rhythms and themes of meditative Georgian poetry but it is unmistakably the voice of modern man estranged. The quasi-religious cast to his diction has a slightly forced quality—in an interview Mahapatra refers to the "opaque [English] language" available to Indian poets outside Bombay and Delhi—and I think at times he betrays an unfortunate distance from centers where contemporary usage vitalizes poetry. However, the valuable quality of maverick poets like Mahapatra and, say, the "Caribbean" poet Derek Walcott, is that they do not peddle the latest outrageous or trendy poetry workshop-seminar formulae in which all too often a poem is merely an excuse for a psychiatric case study.... While Mahapatra escapes Western preoccupation with urban intensity, he is too alert and accomplished to let divided loyalties become disruptive.... I see no need to "apologize" for his use of English. It is by an uncompromising dedication to his own independence, to the past and present visionary Indian landscape, to the need to sustain a direct touch with sensuous experience, that he keeps his melodic and generous poetry fresh. (pp. 339-41)

*Frank Allen, "Crisis of Belief," in* Parnassus: Poetry in Review, *Vol. 9, No. 1, Spring-Summer, 1981, pp. 332-41.*

**JAMES FINN COTTER**

Between waking and sleep, sunlight and rain, love and loss, Jayanta Mahapatra probes his own dark heart for the happiness he fails to find anywhere else. In his reflective, melancholy sixth book of poems [*The False Start*] he gropes for direction, listening and watching, but he finds few signs to enlighten his way. In several key passages, fog and storm await him, and when the sky clears only the enigmatic moon appears; more likely than not, all he finds in his heart is ignominy and ignorance. . . . These poems about false starts, failed relationships, unexplained events, and life's oppositions baffle and fascinate; they blend into one another so that the reader, mesmerized, seems to be reading the same poem over and over. Mahapatra works with archetypes rather than with specific persons, places, things. Except for an occasional temple, we could be anywhere; in **"The Moon Moments"** he asks, "Why does one room invariably lead into other rooms?" Precisely the question the reader asks. The poet has no answer other than our common fate: "We, opening in time our vague doors, / convinced that our minds lead to something never allowed before, / sit down hurt under the trees," only because we happen to arrive there in the first place. The poem ends with a cry of protest:

How can I stop the life I lead within myself—
The startled, pleading question in my hands lying in my
  lap
while the gods go by, triumphant, in the sacked city at
  midnight?

Mahapatra reaches for the heights at such moments, and at times he falls short, straining for effects, as if the polished phrase or extravagant image might be enough of a response. He loses the reader, or his metaphors grow banal with "the mist of time" and "the tree of hope." But these mysterious, unsettling lines more often draw the reader onward and inward to probe his own dark heart, to listen to the rain seep into the soil for the "art, ceremony or voice that lies / under my aimless hearing of the rain" (**"A Day of Rain"**). Even the most explicitly personal poems, **"Tonight I Hear the Water Flowing"** and **"Measuring Death,"** which meditate on the deaths of a father and a son, shun any simple solution: the poet is not fulfilled by suffering or made wiser by grief. Most mysterious of all, the last poem, **"A Certain Refrain,"** addresses the "you" that opposes all the poet says and does by pitting silence against sound, descent against ascent, darkness against light; he demands: "How far can your hand reach out, / trying to hold me back?" Finally, "something greater than darkness / passes between us," and the poet contemplates the naked seas "exhausted of all the light / which made them full of power and longing, / full of the breath that moved the world." We are back in Genesis, in the beginning, within the inner world, before history. (pp. 476-78)

> *James Finn Cotter, "Poetry of Opposites," in* The Hudson Review, *Vol. XXXV, No. 3, Autumn, 1982, pp. 471-82.*

## MADHUSUDAN PRASAD

Both in quantity and quality, [Jayanta Mahapatra's] poetry is amazingly impressive, almost startling.

Mahapatra's poetry is steeped in an authentic individuality of perception, expression and tone. His is a distinctively unsentimental voice, now conversational, now dramatic, now lyrical, now prosaic, now questioning, now searching, but always strikingly unpretentious and powerful. Earnestly committed to poetry, Mahapatra pursues his craft with an unusual care, sincerity and dexterity. He indubitably demonstrates a deep esthetic concern for both structure as well as linguistic versatility, revealing maturity and originality of a remarkably high order. In his poetry there is no symbiosis between perception and expression, between ideation and dictional ordonnance, between sensibility and imagery; instead, there is a happy fusion of all these. His symbols, rich in reverberations, and images, charged with deep emotionality, work wonders in his poetry. A skilful practitioner of the montage technique, he paints images, highly evocative and haunting, through the ingenious collocations of familiar words, which help him to achieve a remarkable effectiveness not possible otherwise. But then he capsules images with utmost care and caution; for there is no overcrowding or jumbling of chaotic images baffling the reader as is apparent in the poetry of A. K. Mehrotra. His poetic phraseology, carefully cultivated, absolutely becomes his experiential veracity and visual perceptions. His poetic rhythm, wedded to verbal frugality or extravagance, reveals an intimate tone that irresistibly charms the reader. Like Gieve Patel, he sometimes uses neutral rhythms, lacking in clear beat, verging on the prosaic. Despite the density of thought matter, he is never a difficult poet. Obviously, his poetry is never bedevilled by obscurity, stemming from academic taxidermy, that has infected the poetry of some of the contemporary poets. In him there is a surface serenity; but below the surface there is unfathomable profundity and dazzling density of material. The total effect of his careful craftsmanship and the interplay of the symbolic, the sensory, the visual, the metaphysical and the meditative in his verse is overwhelming and easily memorable.

Mahapatra's themes are varied, ranging from sex to nature, from the religious to the superstitious, from the metaphysical to the mythical, from the personal to the impersonal. But whatever his theme, there is a profound brooding, meditative quality, like that of the saint, that holds the reader hypnotized. Above all, his sensibility, absolutely uncontaminated, always remains authentically Indian, thanks to his umbilical cord *always* remaining unsevered from his motherland. Consequently, his poetry is rooted deeply in Indian socio-cultural heritage. In fact, he enjoys the distinction of being the only poet (as Raja Rao is the only novelist) who proudly interprets the glorious past of India and sincerely voices our uniquely rich and complex cultural heritage. But throughout his poetic career, Mahapatra's vision is somber, verging on the tragic. (pp. 181-82)

*Close the Sky, Ten by Ten,* which contains forty-nine poems of uneven length and varying tone and subject matter, registers Mahapatra's initial immaturity; but then immaturity is common to almost all beginners. Therefore, what matters most is the poet's progression from immaturity to maturity. In this regard Mahapatra's each succeeding volume records a remarkably fast progression towards maturity—a fact that startles the reader. Although most of the pieces in this first volume strike us as rather immature, making us feel that Mahapatra is "a poem maker," all the poems in this volume certainly reveal his early commendable capacity to mold the language like clay. It is this capacity of Mahapatra (certainly one of the basics of the poet) which has rendered these pieces poetic, although they lack a vividness of perception, a maturity of thought process and an elegance in patterning images and symbols. However, there is a poem titled **"Gandhi"** that reveals Mahapatra's early political awareness. . . . In his later poems, Mahapatra has extended his interest to contemporary life with its political connotations. In his fourth volume, *A Father's Hours,* there is a long poem titled **"The Twentyfifth Anniversary of a Republic: 1975,"** which has obvious political undertones.

There are some poems in the first volume which present striking images, well-pared. For instance, in **"Snakes"** the poet writes in an unfeigned poetic manner: "At a distance you notice they are / things like rivers, floating as / on a map, black in summertime.'' (pp. 182-83)

Mahapatra's second volume, *Svayamvara and Other Poems,* having thirty-three poems, is, like the preceding one, only experimental. It, like the earlier volume, also shows his shaky attempts at shaping words and phrases to ''make'' (rather than ''create'') poems. Most of the poems in this volume are misty, incoherent and inconclusive, and lack in the concretization of perception. Nevertheless, one comes across two good poems that reveal the promise Mahapatra fulfills in his later volumes. **''Blind Singer in a Train''** is a fine piece in which he demonstrates his capacity for evocativeness, coherence, conclusiveness and perspicuity of perception. . . .

Of all the poems in this second volume, **''Faith,''** a short poem of ten lines, is admirably poetic. One is struck immediately by its poetic qualities. The poem is singularized by the poet's concern for perspectivism, structuralism and, above all, by his emphasis on perspicuity of perception. Words, cautiously culled, conduce to the rigorous rhythm of the poem; and the images, neatly tucked in, are logically relevant. . . . (p. 183)

With *A Rain of Rites,* Mahapatra has, no doubt, taken a startling leap forward. It is certainly a mature volume of a high order and embodies some of his finest and most memorable poems, displaying the mellowing of Mahapatra's talents and the sharpening of his sensibility. Consisting of forty-nine poems, it has received lavish praises from critics abroad and has established Mahapatra as one of the major Indian-English poets writing today. (p. 184)

*A Rain of Rites* (as also his *Waiting*) reveals Mahapatra's remarkable restraint in the use of words; whereas in his other volumes he gets lost more often than not in the welter of verbiage—a malady he has not been able to get rid of till his seventh volume. Unlike all other volumes of Mahapatra, these two volumes are singularized by verbal economy required of true poetry. The poems in *A Rain of Rites* deal with rains and rivers, rites and rituals, customs and traditions charged with a profound sacred content, bringing into focus the impact of time against the timeless, of the sharply located present against the past, of waking against dream.

In most of Mahapatra's poems silence is a dominant quality and is very frequently more effectively eloquent than even some of his well-pared phrases. In his poems he perpetually tries to exploit fully the unique communicative value of silence. In a way, silence—*admittedly* symbolic of the elusive—is a recurring theme in most of his poems. . . . The word ''silence'' recurs in his poems on countless occasions—but never for nothing.

There is obviously a group of themes treated in *A Rain of Rites,* many of which are partially present in **''Ceremony''** and the concluding poem, **''Now When We Think of Compromise.''** This volume opens with the poem, **''Dawn,''** which exhibits Mahapatra's striking ability to communicate the sense of ''wonder sustained'' and the real value of silence. . . . Barring a few tame phrases, the collocations of words are in perfect harmony with the poet's ideas and the structure of the poem. The surrealistic images, carefully capsuled, do not grapple with the structure; instead, they create a strong unifying force. (pp. 184-85)

**''A Missing Person''** is indeed a fine poem. The taut, closed structure, textural richness and dictional ordonnance all do make the whole piece memorable. . . . In the poem the portrait of a village woman is painted with remarkable precision and compassion. A sharp sense of solitude and the haunting feeling of loss within the self bring a quick, sympathetic response from the reader. The fine, chiselled images extend their nuances beyond mere verbal description. The precise image created by ''drunken yellow flames'' is uniquely effective and exceptionally eloquent. (p. 186)

**''Myth''** is a fine piece illustrating Mahapatra's consciousness of double cultural heritage, which provides him with an advantageous critical distance required to assess the theme dealt with. Apart from the ample localized details, this poem presents an encounter between ancient religious rituals and modern sensibility. . . . The chanting, the incense, the crumpled leaf, the ''filthy scarlet flower,'' the stairs, the bells, the prayer and the peaks are quite significant in the poem; but the most significant thing is the question put by the brahmin at end. The poet stands at a distance from the myth not venturing to ''go / into the dark, dank sanctum / where the myth shifts / swiftly from hand to hand, eye to eye.'' The whole poem is charged with a deep irony. The poet's own suspicious attitude seems to have prompted the ''bearded, saffron-robed / man'' to put this question to him. Mahapatra has also invoked religious rituals in many poems such as **''A Ritual,'' ''A Rain of Rites,'' ''Ceremony,'' ''Now When We Come to Think of Compromise,'' ''Sanskrit,'' ''At a Ritual Worship on a Saturday Afternoon,''** etc.

Mahapatra is intensely aware of his environment and exploits the minutiae of Oriya life throbbing with religious fervor. Sometimes he endeavors to restore order to the chaos prevailing around him. In **''Dawn at Puri,''** Mahapatra depicts with a subtle touch of irony as well as pathos the incongruities he observes in the Indian landscape. . . . (pp. 187-88)

**''Indian Summer Poem''** is another example which demonstrates that there is no hiatus between the sharp sensibility of the poet and the subject matter treated. Structurally skeletal, the poem is exceptionally eloquent. . . . Undoubtedly, this poem illustrates Mahapatra's authentic Indian sensibility in a remarkable manner, although some other poems in this volume, as well as in succeeding volumes, illustrate it remarkably well also. The merger of his undiluted Indian sensibility with the mastery of his montage technique demonstrates Mahapatra's admirable poetic capability. Apart from the skeletal structure and appropriate words, the auditory and visual images employed in the poem are effectively eloquent. The auditory and visual images get transformed into a metaphor. In the very first stanza, such words as ''soughing,'' ''sombre,'' ''priests,'' ''chant,'' ''mouth,'' and ''opens'' deserve close attention. The last stanza juxtaposes the erotic image of ''The good wife'' in bed with the image of the *sati* prevalent in medieval India, when the loyal wife used to sacrifice herself on the funeral pyre of her husband. These twin images, well juxtaposed, are basic to the thematic centrality of the poem and focus on the traditional dimension of medieval Indian society. But the third line of the first stanza—''the mouth of India opens''—provokes K. Ayyappa Paniker into attacking ''the poet's over-eagerness to assert his . . . Indianness.'' He ''detects a false tone'' in the poem and remarks in a rather chiding tone, ''since Mahapatra is not interested in selling India abroad, he need not have overemphasized the Indianness in this poem. 'The mouth of India' is too vague and sweeping, even if a touch of irony is intended.'' But contrary to this comment of Paniker, this third line of the first stanza is certainly very lucid and relevant. One has got to agree with Dilip Chitre [see excerpt above] who remarks that this line alludes ''to the mouth Krishna opened to reveal the ultimate reality to Arjuna. . . .'' (pp. 188-89)

While treating sex and love, Mahapatra . . . never tickles our baser instinct, nor does he indulge in sentimental whispering, raving or blathering. His treatment of sex is indisputably delicate, unsentimental, restrained and, above all, realistic. Poems such as "**The Whorehouse in a Calcutta Street**" and "**Hunger**" merit deep consideration, as these have gained almost a unique distinction in Indian-English poetry. "**The Whorehouse in a Calcutta Street**" is precise, realistic and highly communicative, although the middle part of the poem suffers from looseness and logorrhoea with which many of Mahapatra's poems are infected. . . . The uniqueness of the poem consists not as much in the artistic components inherent in it as in the fact that the protagonist "trying to learn something more about women" gets deprived of his normal sexual response, perhaps owing to the brazenness of the whore. His body refuses to respond at all. He becomes "a disobeying toy." This realistic aspect of male sensuality has *never* been focused on by Das, Kumar, Nandy or Ezekiel, or for that matter by any other Indian-English poet so far.

"**Hunger**," the four-stanza poem, is relatively shorter than "**The Whorehouse in a Calcutta Street**." It also echoes the contour of male sensuality in realistic terms. . . . This poem, in a way, is a deeply-moving, mordant satire on India's hopeless economy. The penury of the fisherman-father compels him to let his fifteen-year-old daughter resort to prostitution for earnings. This apart, the entire poem is a masterly piece happily fusing the literal and the metaphysical. Every word, highly telling, is studded properly, contributing remarkably to esthetic effects and emphasizing the voice of silence. The very opening line, "It was hard to believe the flesh was heavy on my back," is strikingly poetic, pointing to the experiential veracity of the poet. Part of the last line, "the fish slithering, turning inside," is highly communicative symbolically. The brazen passionless attitude of the whores in both the poems has been faithfully depicted in uncompromising, realistic terms—and this aspect of sex has *never* been dealt with by any other Indian-English poet.

"**Sunburst**" is another realistic poem which depicts "A common happening" on "an ordinary day" in terms of "A black humped bull" riding "the cow" in the street while a "friendly crowd" watch the scene. Apart from the poet's mythicizing propensity, which becomes quite prominent in many of his poems, his mischievousness is worth noticing in the poem, as he makes two twelve-year-old school girls "glance surreptitiously" at the scene. (pp. 190-91)

In his slim volume, *A Father's Hours,* containing only four poems—"**Performance**," "**Levels**," "**The Twentyfifth Anniversary of a Republic: 1975**" and "**Assassin**"—Mahapatra's sensibility towards contemporary reality gets sharpened. In the twenty-section poem, "**The Twentyfifth Anniversary of a Republic: 1975**," Mahapatra makes an ambitious attempt to present the contemporary sociopolitical reality; but then the requisite intrepidity in interpreting it plainly is sadly lacking. He is aware of this lack of requisite boldness as he himself admits it in a rather apologetic tone, "In *A Father's Hours* there is a rather long poem which has political undertones, but here too I think I have not been wholly successful because of my tentative approach to things. You know, even in the freedom of my saying what we think, we are not able to say those things—and I too have been a coward that way." (p. 192)

"**Performance**," the seven-section poem, once again paints the somber vision of Mahapatra. In it his metaphysical and religious queries surface; these land the reader on the edge of

a steep precipice, compelling him to cast about for answers that are nowhere in sight. It also lays bare the agonized soul of the poet. Besides, the political undertones are once again apparent in the piece.

*Waiting,* consisting of forty-six poems, exhibits the same characterisics of Mahapatra which are seen in his third volume, *A Rain of Rites*. The pieces in this volume, like some in his other volumes, are set in Orissa and portray with sharp sensitivity and striking detail the commonplaces of the public and the private, denoting the ubiquitous reality in India. The earth, the stone, the river, the forest, the temple, the priest, the leper, the whore, the sweeper, the shopkeeper, the animal, light, blood, pain, desire and death constitute a composite world, revealing Mahapatra's intimate knowledge about the religious rituals, myths, metaphysics, superstitions and beliefs operative in the local life of Orissa. The recurring images and symbols resorted to in the poems invoke the authentic spirit of Orissa. In fact, Mahapatra's sensibility almost always converges on the Oriya, and consequently Orissa becomes a true living character in his poems. But above all, it is his brooding quality, flowing effortlessly like the river, that captures our heart. Indeed, the poems are well crafted, and the lines, having skilful verbal strategies and admirable concatenations of phrases, seem to have been shaped by natural breath patterns. (p. 194)

The terrible echoing silence in "**Nightfall**" and the improvised exorcism in "**A Country Festival**" are delicately couched in terms of remarkable vividness.

"**Taste for Tomorrow**" is undoubtedly one of the few famous poems of Mahapatra. Its taut logical structure, linguistic ordonnance, verbal laconicity and eloquent images speak volumes for the various poetic skills of Mahapatra. . . . "The one wide street / lolls out like a giant tongue" is a truly striking image that not only pictorially depicts a "giant" deserted street of Puri, but also suggests the sultry weather of Orissa. In the short structure of the poem, the poet has successfully transformed the hard reality into striking metaphors. The word "crows" used in the first line has a symbolic significance. In fact, crows, having symbolic connotations of sin, evil and destruction, figure repeatedly in some of Mahapatra's poems such as "**Crows**," "**Dawn at Puri**," "**Orissa**," "**A Summer Night**," etc., reminding us of the famous crow poems of Ted Hughes.

"**Song of the Past**" is an important poem in this volume, as it reveals Mahapatra's personal world of anxiety and apprehension, helplessness and defeat. . . . [A] brooding quality is . . . dominant throughout this poem.

"**The Faith**" is a noteworthy poem in which Mahapatra demonstrates some of his remarkable poetic qualities. Bitter irony, sharp emotions and concrete images characterize the piece. . . . The opening clinical image eloquently conveys our sick civilization and at once recalls to our minds the opening lines of T. S. Eliot's well-known poem, "The Love Song of J. Alfred Prufrock." Structurally taut, the poem is neatly divided into three stanzas and has three dramatis personae: the cripple, the priest and the speaker. The cripple dominates the first stanza, the priest the second, and the speaker the third. Words, having deep connotations, are carefully selected, and the personifying epithets (so characteristic of Mahapatra), such as "light crouched in his palms," "the furious wrinkled walls," "indulgent sunshine" and "the melting festivals," are really remarkably vocal.

**"Thought of the Future"** and **"Konarka"** are narrative poems. The former deals with a visit that the poet and his father pay to a pundit, "Fair, thick-lipped Jagannath Misra," looking "like a monsoon-month toad," to know about the future of the poet. **"Konarka"** relates a legend relating to the Sun Temple of Konarka. The legend goes that the crowning slab of this thirteenth-century temple could be fitted properly into the place by a twelve-year-old boy, the son of the chief architect, subsequent to the futile attempts made by 1200 artisans. Soon after, the boy jumped to death from the finished temple to save the honor of his father. (pp. l95-96)

**"Bazaar, 5 P.M."** is one of the best poems of Mahapatra, exhibiting his undiluted Oriya sensibility at its best. . . . Tightly structured, the poem establishes a rational nexus between the opening image, "The sunlight hurls spears," and the closing one, "the bazaar an orange ruin of limp echoes." (pp. 197-98)

The most notable quality of Mahapatra's handling of language in this volume is his transposing of metaphors representing the conceptual and the concrete, the abstract and the sensuous. For instance in **"Waiting"**: "The smell of age sticks to you innocently. / You shift years noiselessly in your eyes." Or in **"A Summer Night"**: "and my own hands tied to my need, / secretly bleating." Or in **"Shrines"**: "the heated wind / whining along the inside / of your spine, / is the mind sleeping: . . ."

*The False Start,* the sixth volume of Mahapatra, consists of forty-three poems; but its title, quite misleading, belies the power of the poet that has shaped it. This volume is related to the poet's life both in India and abroad, to his friends and people, to his land and beyond. Once again unfolding the poet's inverted sensibility and his characteristic hermit-like meditativeness, this volume, in a way, continues an exploration of the recurrent motifs, images and metaphors that have appeared in his earlier volumes. Nevertheless, it denotes a marked progression as well as mellowing of his poetic abilities.

Although the poems like **"A Day of Rain,"** **"The Rain Falling"** and **"After the Rain"** indicate Mahapatra's tendency to thematic repetitiveness, they configurate his alternating moods. For instance, *rain* in these poems acquires a metaphorical dimension that leads the poet into his own self and triggers off a chain of thoughts. These poems form the peculiar frames out of which the poet peeps at nature. (p. 199)

Mahapatra, as is noticeable in his earlier volumes, is obsessed by silence as an idea. The metaphor of silence as a living entity among the plethora of words recurs in quite a few poems in this volume such as **"Suppose,"** **"Today,"** **"Poem for Angela Elston,"** **"Women in Love,"** **"A Sailboat of Occasions,"** **"The Secret"** and **"A Certain Refrain."** The palpable power of silence in these poems holds the reader hypnotized. Silence also evokes a secret disturbance in the poet's consciousness, as is obvious in the concluding stanza of **"A Certain Refrain."** . . . (p. 200)

There are some touching poems in which Mahapatra's questioning consciousness surfaces again and again. Poems such as **"Pain,"** **"The Accusation,"** **"The Moon Moments,"** **"A Kind of Happiness"** and **"The Day After My Friends Became Godly and Great"** swarm with numerous puzzlers, denoting the disturbing inadequacy of life.

**"The Abandoned British Cemetery at Balasore, India"** is a somber piece that encapsulates the tragic vision of the poet. In it he, while questioning the meaning of history, sadly broods over the tragedy of "the dying young." . . . (pp. 200-01)

*Relationship* . . . is a clear landmark, indicating that [Mahapatra] has come a long way since his *Close the Sky, Ten by Ten.* It is a work which explores with remarkable symphonic effects his unbreakable "relationship" with rich religion, culture, rituals, traditions and myths of Orissa and, above all, with the primordial shaping influences that Konarka has exercised on him, unfolding the various stages of his own individuality. Resolved into twelve sections, this long poem is a significant corollary of his critical piety and his commendable capacity to confront and interrogate the challenges and the deficiencies of all the traditions, rituals and myths that have shaped his psyche, engendering in him a terrible sense of deprivation and defencelessness in the face of the overwhelming presence of the past. It is indisputably his profoundly serious attempt at experiential meditation on his origins and his sacred ties with Orissa.

The poet creates through numerous striking symbols and metaphors a rich "latticework" of historical truths, religious myths and legends intermingled with the present—all sharpening his questioning consciousness. (p. 202)

[In *Relationship,* the] "year's first rain" reminds the poet of the "gashed voices" of the past. Tormented by his acute awareness of the historical truth, he tries again to recreate the unforgettable painful phase of Indian history relating to 261 B.C. when Emperor Ashoka invaded Kalinga and massacred thousands of Oriyas at Dhauli, near the River Daya. He was crestfallen when he saw the river turned red with the blood of the vanquished and underwent a mighty change and had his famous "peaceful edicts" carved on the rockface for posterity. . . . (pp. 202-03)

The "burnt granite of the fallen Konarka" and the natural phenomena in general spontaneously release the poet's lyrical intensity, combined with a profound emotional warmth and a helpless surrender. The inherent elegiac symphony oozing out of the "stones of Konarka" impel the poet to a spontaneous, powerful poetic effusion. . . . (p. 203)

The questioning gesture of the poet is quite purposive. Through his questioning, he explores the purpose of the present sorry state of our existence deprived of past glories. . . . The poet in fact tries to search for some meaning, but his search only sharpens the sense of loss—and it is his awareness of the loss of past glories that introduces a touch of the elegiac in the poem. He thinks that the past glories cannot be retrieved and our existence made meaningful "until the world is made all over again." . . . (p. 205)

In order to add a justifiable significance to his poetic act, the poet considers it essential to comprehend the myth of Konarka in which is captured the unceasing rhythm of life, although he helplessly asks more than once, "But what was this myth?" Even in a mood of interrogation he thinks it proper to yield to the myth, for not to surrender to the myth is to deny one's origins. After having realized that "those who survive the myth / have slipped past their lives and cannot define their reason," he infers that survival without the myth is a sort of relegation to the futile complacence of unliving. The poet attempts to comprehend the myth apparently "in the hope of soothing myself and those others, / rummaging through the secret blood / of the wind in the pines / and awaiting the deepening nature of all things." But his attempt to comprehend the myth leads him to deliverance. . . . This deliverance is the deliverance from the sterile present which connects nothing with nothing. The poet's necessity to respond to the myth offers him a vital realization that, devoid of myth, we may have almost nothing to respond to. . . . (p. 206)

On the whole, this long poem is inconclusive, like a dream, as it offers neither any consolation nor any way out of our present impasse and fails to resolve the antinomies of life. Besides, the entire poem is loosely structured, revealing Mahapatra's poor sense of ideational ordonnance. The same ideas and images could certainly have been patterned in a better manner, demonstrating a genuine sense of structuralism, if he had been a little more cautious. This poem is disfigured at several places by excessive verbiage. No doubt, Mahapatra could have achieved a greater degree of effectiveness had he *not* been lured by the language.

Mahapatra enjoys the advantage of double cultural heritage, which offers him a critical distance required to evaluate the potentialities of his various themes. He mainly interprets in a remarkable manner the uniquely rich and complex culture of India, besides the private and the public, the national and the universal, the religious and the metaphysical, superimposed by his hermit-like meditation that holds the reader hypnotized. His poetry is singularized by a happy relationship between ideation and dictional ordonnance, between perception and articulation, and above all by his unself-conscious craft. He carefully employs images and symbols, assuming metaphorical dimensions, which never bewilder the reader. His poems are delicately constructed in tune with the nature of situations and the demands of language. His resilience, creative vitality and crafts-manship are commensurate with his vision, which is somber throughout.

Mahapatra, like Pritish Nandy, is a very prolific poet. . . . [In] a decade he has produced seven volumes, besides a number of poems (included in anthologies and periodicals) still uncollected. . . . This hasty prolificacy of Mahapatra has led him to an almost boring repetitiveness. Frequently, we run into poems treating of a similar theme. Besides, he more often than not lapses into unpleasant wordiness, which hinders him from achieving desirable poetic effects. Keki N. Daruwalla's remark that "He does not indulge in verbal excesses" [see excerpt above] is not only misleading but also indicative of his inability to see his works in totality. Also, he often jumbles up numerous ideas in a poem whose structure fails to bear them, and consequently, this leads to inelegant patterning of ideas and images. Lastly, he frequently gets lured by the language, and this results in his failure to create the proper tension in the mind of the reader—the tension which the language of successful poetry always creates. In his fifties, Mahapatra should now be fully aware of his lapses. At the height of his achievement, all he needs is to have a breather, to restrain himself, to exercise his critical capacity for control and selection, and above all, to assess critically his own merits and demerits, before he writes another poem. Writing much at a fast pace is certainly proving pernicious to him now. (pp. 206-07)

*Madhusudan Prasad, "'Caught in the Currents of Time': A Study of the Poetry of Jayanta Mahapatra," in* Journal of South Asian Literature, *Vol. XIX, No. 2, Summer-Fall, 1984, pp. 181-207.*

# Joyce Carol Oates

## 1938-

American novelist, short story writer, poet, dramatist, essayist, and critic.

A prolific and versatile writer, Oates often dwells on the violent and the macabre in her work. Her plots abound with incidents of rape, incest, and suicide, and her characters suffer as a result of their emotional weaknesses and social milieu. Although Oates is accomplished in various literary genres, including poetry and drama, critics generally agree that she demonstrates the truest mastery of her themes in her short stories. Oates has won numerous awards for her fiction, including the O. Henry Award and the National Book Award. She is also a respected critic; her essays have been collected in such volumes as *Contraries* (1981) and *The Profane Art* (1983).

Oates was born and raised in rural New York State. Her home, Erie County, is the basis for the Eden County of her first novel, *With Shuddering Fall* (1964). Eden County resurfaces regularly in her novels and short stories, serving as a microcosm for contemporary American society. Oates's second novel, *A Garden of Earthly Delights* (1967), is the first in an informal, thematic trilogy that explores the socioeconomic conditions which affect her characters. The second work in the trilogy, *Expensive People* (1968), sharply contrasts the rural environment of the first by describing the exclusive suburbs of upper middle-class America. The final volume, *them* (1969), which won the National Book Award, delves into the harsh realities of an urban slum.

Critics attribute the ambience and realistic detail of Oates's early work to the influence of such twentieth-century authors as William Faulkner and Theodore Dreiser. Oates also acknowledges the importance of Franz Kafka and Herman Melville to her literary development. Several of her recent works reflect her absorption with the lengthy novels of the late nineteenth century. *Bellefleur* (1980), her first such novel, follows the prescribed formula for a Gothic family saga. It traces six generations of a family that exploits the land amid supernatural occurrences. *A Bloodsmoor Romance* (1983) displays many of the elements of Gothic romance, including mysterious kidnappings and psychic phenomena. In *Mysteries of Winterthurn* (1984) Oates borrows heavily from Edgar Allan Poe as she explores the conventions of the nineteenth-century mystery novel. *Solstice* (1984) combines elements of the Gothic novel with a contemporary psychological mystery. The vast scope and the overriding sense of doom in Gothic literature provide Oates with an appropriate medium through which to dramatize her fascination with evil.

Oates's dense, elliptical prose style has been the source of much critical analysis. Critics debate whether Oates is deliberately vague in order to create stories of depth and complexity. The graphic violence of her works has also led to much serious commentary. In *them*, a sixteen-year-old girl awakens to the sound of her brother shooting her sleeping lover. She seeks help from a police officer, who proceeds to rape her on the kitchen table. In *Bellefleur*, a man crashes his plane into the Bellefleur mansion, killing himself and his family. Similarly

© Jerry Bauer

violent scenes are repeated throughout the majority of Oates's books. While such episodes are sometimes labeled sensationalistic, most critics perceive Oates's use of violence as attempts to graphically depict the force of evil in the world. In an essay entitled "Why Is Your Writing So Violent?" Oates explained, "serious writers . . . take for their subjects the complexity of the world, its evils, as well as its goods."

(See also *CLC*, Vols. 1, 2, 3, 6, 9, 11, 15, 19; *Contemporary Authors*, Vols. 5-8, rev. ed.; *Dictionary of Literary Biography*, Vols. 2, 5; and *Dictionary of Literary Biography Yearbook: 1981*.)

## LAURA Z. HOBSON

"It is on a windy morning in early March, a day of high scudding dizzy clouds, some nine months after their father's ignoble death, that his only children, Owen and Kirsten, make a pact to revenge that death."

These are the opening lines of *Angel of Light*, Joyce Carol Oates's 13th novel and 37th published work. *Ignoble death, revenge, make a pact*, even the *high scudding dizzy clouds*—these words and phrases somehow evoke in me an image of a vast, drear landscape pierced by an unswerving highway, and of a green-and-white roadside marker: You are entering Joyce Carol Oates country.

From her earlier novels, I know there will be violence in this dark terrain—and lightning-flash brilliance. *Angel of Light* proves me correct. In some respects, it is flawed, but its driving narrative makes it a stunner. (p. 44)

It is swift; it rings true. There [are] many . . . masterly little scenes. . . . Deft and adroit though many of them are, their frequency and timing often struck me as arbitrary and manipulative.

They awakened an uneasy sense that *Angel of Light* is flawed. Incessant repetitive sections, dialogue iterated and reiterated, and interminable rivers, torrents, spates, and avalanches of language fed that sense throughout the novel. I found also a once-over-lightly flimsiness in the author's treatment of big business, international politics, even terrorism. Thus, though the principal setting of the book is Washington at its most glittering, I found myself thinking too often: Portrait of the nation's capitol by one who has never lived there.

But for all its flaws, *Angel of Light* held me gripped. Just for the hell of it, I dug out a dozen or so reviews of her other novels: They were filled with adjectives like *weird, strange, implausible, inexplicable, nonrational, lurid, sado-masochistic, gory, obsessed, opaque, depraved.* And, of course, *violent.*

Would there be such a hullabaloo about the violence in her books if they had been written by a man? Isn't sexism crawling into many of these reviews? From her earliest books onward—when she was still in her twenties, or barely out of them—the reviewers too often struck an insulting tone of surprise: *What's a nice girl like you doing in a place like this?* Even as admirable—and admiring—a critic as Alfred Kazin permitted himself the little phrases *a woman writer* or *women writers* no less than seven times in a piece he wrote about her some years ago.

Recently Oates herself wrote that everywhere she goes she is asked, "Why are your books so violent?" She replies that in these violent times only tales of violence have reality. Well, maybe. But the critics' preoccupation with a single facet of her work ignores everything else: Her inventiveness, her insider's knowledge of college life, her evocations of nature. Above all, it ignores her ability to tell a story—to write a spellbinder like *Angel of Light.*

To me, all the harping on violence should now be declared off limits. In 13 novels, Joyce Carol Oates has staked out her own territory, and who's to question her claim to it? Or ask why she stays with it? Did critics ever ask Agatha Christie why she always wrote mysteries? (p. 45)

Laura Z. Hobson, "Oates Country," in Saturday Review, Vol. 8, No. 8, August, 1981, pp. 44-5.

**SUSAN WOOD**

Perhaps because [Joyce Carol Oates] is so prolific in so many genres—and perhaps because much of her work is so violent and obsessive—readers and critics have tended to dismiss her as a phenomenon, a freak, not to take her quite seriously, as though one who writes so much and so passionately could not possibly write well. Her new novel, *Angel of Light,* set in Washington, while as compelling and suspenseful as a thriller, demonstrates that Oates must be taken seriously indeed, for she attempts more than most of our writers dare—in this case, to explore the profound issues of evil and innocence, betrayal and revenge and atonement, as they are manifest in contemporary American experience—and to a remarkable extent she succeeds.

But *Angel of Light* demonstrates, perhaps better than any other Oates novel, what I think is the *real* reason for the critical unease surrounding her work: that she goes against the prevailing impulse in contemporary fiction toward the private and personal, a small-scale vision illustrated in the work of such a much-admired writer as Ann Beattie. As *Contraries,* Oates' thoughtful and illuminating collection of essays, makes clear, Oates' models are the 19th-century masters like Dostoevski and Conrad; like them, she is what I would call a "social" novelist, interested in creating microcosms of the world that reflect the moral and philosophical questions encountered by man as he is in conflict with society, nature, God, history. What she admires in those novelists is passion, energy, the courage to take artistic and emotional risks. . . .

[*Angel of Light*] is a complex, dense, multi-layered work that unfolds with all the profound implications of Greek tragedy—in fact, the story is a modern version of the fall of the House of Atreus. Yet Oates seems at last to have in control two of the weaknesses that have sometimes been the result of her considerable ambition and energy—a feverish, overwritten prose style and a heavy-handed use of symbolism.

The novel is the story of the Halleck family of Washington, D.C., from 1947 to 1980, and the setting of Washington not only provides the perfect backdrop for the family's tragedy but also is part of the subject itself: the betrayals of the individual characters are also the betrayals of history. (p. 5)

Oates links violent present to violent past to grapple with the novel's central question, one that was asked by Maurie Halleck when he was a boy: "To have the power to do good, how can you *be* good?" That is indeed a central question of history. . . . [The] Halleck children seek to become God's earthly agents, dispensers of justice. Putting themselves above man, they . . . come to care for no one, not even, eventually, for their father.

The plot of *Angel of Light* hinges on the unfolding of the Halleck children's pact to revenge their father's death, and it is with a horrified sense of impending doom—one of the things Oates does best is to create and sustain that feeling—that the reader is propelled forward, compelled to see it through from the very first page where Kirsten and Owen meet on "a morning of falling tumbling shadows, high above the river" surrounded by "the raucous and distracting noise of birds . . . in the leafless trees." That, it seems to me, is the first test of a novel: Does it hold our attention? And, to take it further, do we feel we *have* to read it? The answer is a decided yes. . . .

Oates has been criticized for being too bleak, too pessimistic, but that is not an accurate observation. She has always been, fundamentally, a religious novelist, like Dostoevski a mystic, and nowhere is her belief that suffering is necessary to redemption more clear than in *Angel of Light.* (p. 10)

Part of the pleasure of this novel comes from seeing the way Oates reinforces meaning. It is difficult in a review of this length to explain how the novel's structure—in sections that alternate past and present—serves this function. Like a fugue, everything doubles back. Maurie, for instance, has his doppelganger in the boarding school teacher Schweppenheiser, a flamboyant, eccentric little man who teaches the boys that "there was nothing divine about history, and particularly not American political history," who is also betrayed, who may or may not have committed suicide, who may or may not have been a spy. But in a curious way Schweppenheiser is also Nick Martens' doppelganger, for Maurie and Nick—who once saved Maurie's life and, one way or another, brought about its end— are two halves of one whole. So the theme of betrayal is echoed over and over—the betrayal of Maurie Halleck and the betrayal of American ideals by those who were supposed to uphold them. The private ceremonial apocalypse in the novel is provoked by the larger disintegration of society.

And Oates has captured that society as it disintegrates. For one who has not lived in Washington for any length of time, she seems to know it well: its casual betrayals, the chatter of its cocktail parties, the women who live in the shadows of powerful men. Even the familiar types become individualized. (pp. 10, 12)

[So] much in *Angel of Light* has the power to shock us into an awareness of our own mortality. Whatever one says about the intellectual content of the novel—and it is there in plenty— reading it is a deeply emotional experience. It is a measure of its author's passion that we are so completely enveloped that its world becomes our own. As Oates writes of Dostoevski in *Contraries,* "One has a vivid sense of [him] as a *participant* in his own tragic fiction," and it is that sense of Oates, so difficult to articulate, that makes us participate in *Angel of Light.* It is an experience far too rare in fiction; like life, it is full of pain and suffering and a kind of tragic joy that comes of knowledge, but one wouldn't want to miss it. (p. 12)

> Susan Wood, *"Vengeance in Washington,"* in Book World—The Washington Post, *August 16, 1981, pp. 5, 10, 12.*

### THOMAS R. EDWARDS

[If] **"Angel of Light"** is a philosophical novel about the impossibility of justice in a fallen, irredeemably compromised human community, the book (in a good 19th-century way) accommodates other kinds of interest too—it is at once a kind of thriller, a romance of desire and betrayal in high society, a psychological examination of alienated youth, a study of marital failure in a declining aristocracy, an uncovering of the personal roots of public violence. (pp. 1, 18)

I'm not sure that Miss Oates adds a great deal to what writers like Louis Auchincloss, Frederick Buechner, John Cheever and John Knowles have told us about the moral life in our old ruling class. Even at their most vivid moments—as when the aggressive Nick confesses a secret yearning to be not himself but just "a person," without family, history, or intentions— Miss Oates's adults may owe as much to other fiction as to fresh observation or imagining. But the story centers on Owen and Kirsten, and their search through violence for an exactitude of justice that, as Mandeville suggested, no human society could survive. In her portrayal of the Halleck children, Miss Oates achieves a fresh and frightening picture of a desire that exceeds any available attainment. Owen and Kirsten, whom Miss Oates makes descendants of John Brown of Osawatomie, strive to reconstruct reality in the image of their dream of justice, as their ancestor had once also tried to do, with equally shattering effect.

Thoreau provided the title for this novel when he called John Brown "an Angel of Light," and we may safely presume that, like Joyce Carol Oates, Thoreau was cognizant of who the first angel of light was and what befell him. One of that Lucifer's stoutest champions, William Blake, in fact presides over Owen

and Kirsten's great enterprise; they debate, with touching uncertainty, the meaning of various of Blake's "Proverbs of Hell" before finding one whose significance unarguably suits their purpose: "What is now proved was once only imagined." For them this suggests that destructive action can confirm and justify their conviction that their father was framed and killed by a wife and friend who served not only their own paltry desires but also served (somehow) a conspiracy of the power structure, whose identification of realpolitik with reality was threatened by Maurice Halleck's almost saintly probity.

We are for a while free to regard the children's imaginings as being just what they sound like, a fantasy born of grief and precarious stability. . . . If what begins to be proved is not exactly what once was only imagined by Owen and Kirsten, in a social world regulated by Evil, some uncomfortable possibilities do suggest themselves. In such a world exact proof is hard to come by—one seemingly knowledgeable source says that Nick was a C.I.A. agent, while another claims that he was an undercover Communist, and he may have been neither, or both—but such indeterminacy itself hints at moral horror. On the other hand, those who would dissolve ambiguity into single vision by an act of moral will point toward an alternative and commensurate horror—here exemplified by the American Silver Doves Revolutionary Army, a group of underemployed ex-graduate students turned Maoist terrorists who convert Owen's personal quest for justice into service in their own violent cause. . . .

**"Angel of Light"** may be another chapter in Joyce Carol Oates's ongoing exercise of the imagination, but it is also a strong and fascinating novel on its own terms. . . . **"Angel of Light"** gravitates back toward the terra firma of a novel like Miss Oates's **"them,"** where social circumstance and personal fate are closely and realistically linked. But enough mystery persists in **"Angel of Light"** to suggest that this prolific and various novelist is staking out new fictional ground. (p. 18)

> Thomas R. Edwards, *"The House of Atreus Now,"* in The New York Times Book Review, *August 16, 1981, pp. 1, 18.*

### ROBERT PHILLIPS

[Joyce Carol Oates] has published two previous collections of critical essays. *Contraries*—her third—is her most illuminating in terms of her own fictional concerns. These seven essays were prompted by personal and emotional responses and are enlivened by her own experiences as a writer. Together they give an intriguing overview of Ms. Oates's extraordinary mind.

In a Preface, she states, "We are stimulated to emotional response not by works that confirm our sense of the world, but by works that challenge it." Among the challenges Ms. Oates accepts is that of practicing a relatively new critical technique— fantasizing structures for works of literature other than those given by their authors.

The books which have moved her to literary criticism . . . are Wilde's *The Picture of Dorian Gray,* Dostoyevsky's *The Possessed, King Lear,* Conrad's *Nostromo,* Lawrence's *Women in Love,* Joyce's *Ulysses,* and the English and Scottish traditional ballads. It is tempting to remark those properties, of the authors she has taken time to study, which might have helped shape her own vision.

For instance, could the supernatural dimension and central Gothic image of the allegorical *Dorian Gray* have "influenced" her own Gothic extravaganza, *Bellefleur*, an allegorical book which (in an Author's Note), she herself describes as "a region, a state of the soul"? Is ritual violence, which she reads as so necessary to Dostoyevsky, as necessary to the integrity of an Oates novel such as *Them*? or perhaps even more so to her plays? Is her reading of Conrad, with action serving as the "barbed hook" that leads inevitably to man's destruction, a gloss on her recent novel, *Cybele*? Certainly Edwin Locke of that work follows Stein's famous imperative, "in the destructive element immerse," as does Andrew Petrie, of her *The Assassins*. Can one read her dissection of *King Lear* without reflecting upon her fascination with "the mimesis of an action 'tragic' in its intensity, involving defeat and triumph, often in inexpressible terms" (to quote from the Preface to her *Three Plays*?)

Oates's discussion of Lawrence's novella, *The Escaped Cock*, is instructive in light of her evangelical novel, *Son of the Morning*. Both share a protagonist whose love of mankind is no more than a form of egotism, perhaps even madness, which will touch and devour multitudes. And James Joyce's multivoiced compositions and wordplay surely were precursors of Joyce Oates's own *Childwold*. Her concern for Lawrence's attempts to integrate the male and female principles is reflected, perhaps, in her **"Queen of the Night,"** the first story in her latest collection, *A Sentimental Education*. (pp. 475-76)

To call a fiction *A Sentimental Education* may seem an act of folly or of hubris, recalling what for many is the favorite among Flaubert's novels. Yet the allusion is justified. Like Flaubert's chronicle of interwoven lives under Louis Philippe, Oates's title novella also depicts calf love, disillusion, futility, the passage from youth to maturity, but depicts it without Flaubert's fascination for the counterrevolutionary currents in this country's politics.

And yet Oates does depict the breakdown of a society. As Oates observes in her essays on *The Possessed*, "As society approaches crisis and breakdown, preparatory to reaffirmation of its identity, it provokes private disintegration, private ceremonial exorcism." This is the spectacle we witness as, over the course of one summer on the island, nineteen-year-old Duncan experiences erotic love for his younger cousin. Brilliant, unbalanced, and given to wild reaches of imagination, Duncan first seduces the girl and then, unable to silence her, proceeds to kill her. The act is performed at the edge of the ocean, in a secret, slimy place smelling of fish. Psychologically and symbolically Oates has rarely been more powerful. . . .

Oates's story collections are never randomly put together. The six pieces in this volume all concern individuals whose passions blind them to reality. It is their "driveness" which drives the book and makes it cohere. . . .

Each of these stories is highly dramatic, focusing upon one vital occasion in the life of a protagonist from which he or she will never adequately recover. It should not surprise, then, that Ms. Oates has been drawn to write for the stage. The *Three Plays* are **"Ontological Proof of My Experience," "Miracle Play,"** and **"The Triumph of the Spider Monkey."** . . . All three concern ceremony, ritual, and what Oates calls "the inexpressible coherence of 'fate': the disharmonious music that is torn from us at certain moments in our lives and in history." Which is merely to say that these dramas are dramatic.

Like Greek tragedies, they are also violent—among the most violent works in the Oates canon, in fact, portraying (on-stage or off) beatings, rape, machete murders, immolation, and facial disfiguration by boiling sugar water. Such violence at times supplants a surface realism and segues into surrealism. On either plane, Oates bears witness to the evils and complexities of the world in a manner usually attributed, by some critics, only to male writers. (p. 476)

> Robert Phillips, "Overview of an Extraordinary Mind," in Commonweal, Vol. CVIII, No. 15, August 28, 1981, pp. 475-76.

## DORIS SMITH EARNSHAW

*Contraries* gathers in one volume seven previously published articles reflecting the thought of the brilliant and popular novelist and short-story writer Joyce Carol Oates. . . . Her subjects include English and Scottish ballads, *King Lear* and five novels: *The Picture of Dorian Gray, The Possessed, Nostromo, Women in Love* and *Ulysses*. She exposes dramatic tensions in each work and relates the paradox or "contrary" to the author's vision of life and to the wider human predicament. (p. 342)

A fatal imbalance of elements in a character or a society is the hubris that invites the nemesis of death and destruction. In the essay on *King Lear*, a superb contemporary reading, she sees the tragedy as a confusion of masculine roles of king and father. In attempting to rule without a queen, Lear acts out a masculine predicament. Oates discusses an early essay of Freud on Lear that sees Cordelia as the masculine unconscious, the Magna Mater, the Terrible Mother and a symbol of death. She herself sees Cordelia rather as the anima, the sister, who functions as an embodiment of grace, an unwilled and unearned redemption. . . . (pp. 342-43)

In Oscar Wilde's allegory of the Fall, *The Picture of Dorian Gray*, the fatal imbalance is the delusion that art insulates the artist from other concerns. . . . Domination of the world through art or through political power, she suggests, is a doomed idea, at once Faustian and infantile. Birkin, in *Women in Love*, attempting absolute domination of the emotions, rejects his homoerotic impulses and continues his "deathly relationship" with Hermione and the "slightly bestial" prostitutes. In traditional ballads we find perishable human experience balanced by the voice of the narrator speaking for the transcendence of history, the eternally contemporary.

A hermeneutics that draws on history, psychology and literary technique requires enormous power to support its convictions. The reader who is a literary critic will find distracting flaws such as the equation of "the abstract" and "the symbolic" or the omission of Mikhail Bakhtin's work on Dostoevsky, which supports Oates's thesis remarkably well. The reader who is a social critic would like amplification of the theories of balance and social order. This said, the insights of a great storyteller on the work of her peers is full of interest and value. (p. 343)

> Doris Smith Earnshaw, in a review of "Contraries: Essays," in World Literature Today, Vol. 56, No. 2, Spring, 1982, pp. 342-43.

## GEORGE WOODCOCK

In *Contraries* Oates has gathered together a group of seven long, searching, and sometimes surprising essays written over twenty years and originally published in magazines as varied as *Southern Review* and *Critical Inquiry*. Their subjects also range over a wide field. . . . What I think united them more than anything else is that they are the work of an accomplished, thoughtful, and somewhat obsessive novelist who is looking at works of fiction (among which we must include the ballads) with a professional eye both to the unobtrusive elements of construction and to the esoteric intents that—consciously or unconsciously—may have been concealed beneath the obvious surface. As the title of her book declares, Joyce Carol Oates admits to seeing "a spirit of contrariety that lies at the heart of all passionate commitment." And it is the detection of the workings of this "spirit of contrariety" that largely but not entirely motivates her essays.

Perhaps this is why she has given pride of place in her book to what many readers will regard as a jaded and obvious book on which the last words have long been written—*The Picture of Dorian Gray.* Of course, if *Dorian Gray* had in fact been merely the facile and mechanically constructed book that is all its hastier readers discover, it would long have receded into the deserved oblivion that has overtaken the "rather silly novel" (as Oates called Huysmans's *A rebours*) that Wilde took as his partial model. But the fact is that *Dorian Gray* has provoked the curiosity and stirred the often grudging admiration of a succession of writers over the generations who have been highly concerned with the standards of their craft. More than forty years ago George Orwell wrote to me: "I particularly like *Dorian Gray,* absurd as it is in a way"; and now we have Oates—a very different writer from Orwell—taking the book with great seriousness and seeking out the "contrary" element that is responsible for its strange and lasting appeal. (pp. 467-68)

In this essay Oates is not merely uncovering the questions that Wilde raises—out of life as it were—against his own overtly defended doctrine of art for art's sake: she is stating her own rejection of "the airless and claustrophobic world of self-referential art" and also of the critical attitudes—including those of the North American academic cliques—that have sought to justify such aesthetics.

In the later essays Oates examines the other works she has chosen, to find the alternative reading, the contrary within the novel or the narrative folk poem that may reveal its deeper and fuller meaning. For example she defends the essential probability, the faith to Russian history, of Dostoevsky's *The Possessed,* and in the process, without diminishing the importance of the "possessed" characters and especially of the diabolical Peter Verkhovensky, she—rightly I believe—establishes the central figures of the novel as none of these historically plausible grotesques, but the much more passionately conceived and deeply revealed characters, Stavrogin and Stefan Verkhovensky. . . .

Both the essays I have discussed tend to increase our esteem of the writers involved—of Wilde because he could conceal under an apparent defense of aestheticism the counterarguments that life presents, and of Dostoevsky because he could see beyond the "possessions" that have so long afflicted his beloved country and could give the narration of his novel to "the unimaginative but presumably reliable Goverov, an anonymous Everyman, a survivor, a Russian whom the demons were not able to possess. *He,* and not these brilliant others, is Dostoevsky's future." (p. 469)

*George Woodcock, "Various Occasions," in* The Sewanee Review, *Vol. XC, No. 3, Summer, 1982, pp. 466-74.**

### DIANE JOHNSON

When we learn on the first page of **"A Bloodsmoor Romance"** that one of the five heroines has just been abducted "in an outlaw balloon of sinister black silken hue," we know that Joyce Carol Oates—as well as the heroine Deirdre—has embarked on a perilous course. "Well may you blink and draw back in alarm at that crude word *abducted:* and yet, I fear," remarks the narrator, a maiden lady of a certain age, "there is no other, to be employed with any honesty." And some there may be who will blink and draw back from the whole enterprise: the long, fanciful adventures of the five Zinn sisters of Bloodsmoor, Pa., circa 1870. But the reader who has no aversion to abductions and balloons and the rest will be conveyed in a manner both pleasurable and instructive (the aim, some have said, of art) through more than 600 pages of an antiromance that provides the satisfactions of a romance too. (p. 1)

This is Joyce Carol Oates's 14th novel. . . . Now, the serious modern novel as practiced by her, among others, had its origins in romances: long tales of love and picturesque adventure sometimes including knights or supernatural happenings. Since the beginning, like an ungrateful child, the serious novel has set about denying its origins, and losing in the process its birthrights of interest, wonder and surprise, surrendering these narrative gifts to the stepchildren, the genre novels about spies or detectives or spaceships. These genre stepchildren in their turn aspire to realism so that we will take them seriously and call them literature, as we call the fiction of Jack London or Dashiell Hammett or Raymond Chandler literature.

In American fiction, realism, or what passes for it, tends to violence and grim endings. Happy endings and consolatory attitudes belong to "escape" fiction; indeed the whole notion of escaping embodies the modern attitude toward the unpleasant real world. Sometimes books pretend to be serious by striking realistic poses but providing escapist endings. . . . **"A Bloodsmoor Romance"** comes out the way we want it to, but Joyce Carol Oates has found a way to assuage our Puritanical guilt about escape by writing romance that is satirical, and thus about something, but which is still successful as romance. The satirical qualities do not falsify but illumine the genre. . . .

[The subject of **"A Bloodsmoor Romance"**] is the lot of women, especially the customs and attitudes that confined and oppressed them in the 19th century, but also the present-day remnants of those conditions. Thus the book is a feminist romance with a lot of axes to grind, and it grinds them wittily till their edges are polished to a fine sharpness. Both the action of the novel and the comments of the narrator bear upon this purpose: Women are locked up, tortured by their husbands, exploited, ignored, abused and misunderstood. Their sexuality is denied them, their freedom is hard won, their brains are embarrassing to all.

The narrator often condemns the behavior of these lively young ladies. She professes to hold the most rigorous and conformist views of female conduct, and she expresses those views so pointedly that we cannot miss the novelist's intention, which is to emphasize their ridiculousness. . . . (p. 15)

This narrator is not, of course, to be confused with the author; yet so successful is the characterization, it is tempting to believe that, Victorian postures and archaic diction apart, the voice is really the voice of Joyce Carol Oates—female, clever, facetious and mischievous. One has not often heard her. In the service of the many and various literary tasks she sets herself, she is apt sternly to suppress her own voice, and that suppression has been, perhaps, the sole defect of her writing. Though one would recognize a book by John Updike from its style or one by Philip

Roth from its subject, the protean Oates is able to assume any stylistic guise and to write about anything. One seldom feels that from book to book one comes to know her better.

In this novel the author herself seems accessible, and in it she shows a relaxed and accepting attitude toward plot. As readers we tend to like plots and to admire them the way we admire the clockwork cleverness of a mechanical bank; it is intricacy, art and imitation we admire. But in the spirit of realism modern novelists have tended to conceal contrivance and to strive for the form of formless life. Joyce Carol Oates has expressed her discomfort with and attraction to plot in the past by taking plots that already exist . . . as if these plots, because they exist, are aspects of reality, uncontrived. Her interest has seemed to be in elaborating and adapting them. Satire is always implicit in the reworking of an old story or a moribund genre. But in ''A Bloodsmoor Romance'' it is explicit: The un-self-consciously plotted events are presented in a tone newly animated by the philosophical and political point of view. And the whole work is enlivened by a great deal of lore about life in the 19th century. . . . Even those who find balloon abductions thin should be satisfied by this richness of detail. (p. 16)

> Diane Johnson, ''Balloons and Abductions,'' *in* The New York Times Book Review, *September 5, 1982, pp. 1, 15-16.*

## ALICE ADAMS

[''A Bloodsmoor Romance''] is the finest novel yet by Joyce Carol Oates, the richest, the most admirably complex, and the most enjoyable; and I speak as one who has vastly admired her work, since first reading ''A Garden of Earthly Delights,'' her second book. At that time, along with my pleasure at coming upon such a remarkable talent, I also wondered how a relatively young woman could write with such absolute conviction (and convincingness) as to details, as to *feeling*, of a time that occurred before her birth. . . .

I still wonder at her talent, and ''genius'' may be the more appropriate word. I do not believe that Oates is generally envied, even, by other writers; she is out of the question, out of range, as is the beauty of Greta Garbo, say, even for the most beautiful people.

The first fact that automatically, and perhaps unfairly (it can be misleading) comes to mind about Oates is her incredibly prolific output. . . . We should not be spoiled by such a plethora of excellence. Were this new book, by some improbable stroke of literary lightning, a first novel, everyone from Madison Avenue to South Succotash would be shouting its praises.

True, Trollope wrote 47 books but much as one may love them, all sound somewhat alike. Whereas Joyce Carol Oates sounds like no one else who has ever written, nor does she sound, from book to book, much like herself—whoever that self may be.

In many of Oates' early short stories, and some of the novels, there was a young woman who is possessed of the sort of absolute passivity that pulls action, violence toward it, as a vacuum is said to do. . . . Oates receives messages, she picks up on human drama, she seems to know and to feel everything, as mysteriously as radar. (p. 1)

In addition to being a family history, [''A Bloodsmoor Romance''] is also a marvelous history of the final years of the 19th Century: Transcendentalism, Abolitionism, Theosophy.

Mme. Blavatsky, Emerson, Edison; inventions, railroad—there is even a reference to a girl named Annie Miller, known as Daisy, who is rumored to have come to a bad end, in Rome. (pp. 1, 4)

Each detail of this fabric seems absolutely authentic, all the names, the houses, the meals, the costumes, as well as the narrative tone. (Further proof that Oates possesses a sort of retrospective radar; when on earth would she have time to do research?)

Like many first-rate novels, this one gathers urgency and momentum as it goes, the first couple of hundred pages (out of more than 600) being the slowest. Toward the end of reading I began to think, Oh dear, only 100 pages more. (p. 4)

> Alice Adams, in a review of ''A Bloodsmoor Romance,'' in Los Angeles Times Book Review, *September 19, 1982, pp. 1, 4.*

## DENIS DONOGHUE

Interviewers like to ask Joyce Carol Oates, presumably in the accent of awe, how she finds time to write all those books. . . . The question isn't as innocent as it sounds. With a slight change of tone, it could come out differently, as if it asked: ''Don't you think your reputation would be even higher than it is if you took more time, let the typescripts stay on your desk for a year or two before sending them to the publisher? Think of E. M. Forster, a classic novelist on the strength of one book, eked out by a few short volumes and many years of silence.'' Oates has answered the question, in its implied second form, by saying: ''I write with the enormous hope of altering the world.'' You might as well take as many shots at that target as you think you need, especially if proof that you've altered the world doesn't come merely because you send for it. Oates might also deal with Forster by saying: think of Balzac, think of James.

The question, in any form, is a little vulgar, but it could be redeemed. There is a genuine question to be asked about a novelist who is, as Oates is, serious, prolific, and popular. Is her seriousness limited, carefully restrained to make it compatible with the demands of popularity? Is she popular because she is prolific, a success because she is already a success, the habit well formed? Or because it is attractive to see a writer as productive in her craft as, say, a successful businessman is in his? Oates has made much of a line in *King Lear* where the King says, ''They told me I was everything. 'Tis a lie,'' and she has converted it into the motto that ''the artist must act upon the frail conviction that he is everything, else he will prove nothing.'' Believing that nothing will come of nothing, she speaks again and again.

Oates's fiction is hard to describe, mainly because it is equivocal in its relation to the genres it ostensibly fulfills. *Bellefleur* (1980) comes as close as any other book to representing the quality of her work. It is a big book, a saga about an American family, already cursed and living out its doom. The generations are elaborately described, the narrative style is even more full-blooded than the blood it spills. The several stories are grandly sustained. But they are all told as if they had already been narrated elsewhere and have only to be alluded to. The strength of the novel arises from the impression, carefully maintained, that the events are now being recalled rather than imagined. In fact, we rarely feel, reading *Bellefleur*, that Oates's imagination is creatively alive; it never seems spontaneous. Even when we believe that something *Bellefleur* tells us is indeed true, we are never seized by its truth or by a conviction of its reality.

The chief quality of Oates's imagination is obedience, and what it obeys is not nature or circumstance but other fiction, especially other romances or tragedies. In *Bellefleur* the hero Gideon is not himself but any and every leonine hero from romantic fiction....

[Oates's] characters are never allowed to understand themselves or to guess that the origins of their feelings are in literature rather than in life. They think they are spontaneous, but their lives are only imitations of other fictive lives. (p. 12)

Oates knows, while preventing her characters from divining, that their lives are unconscious mimicries. Indeed, her books might have been written to justify the argument ... that spontaneous desire is a fallacy; it is a delusion if held as a sentiment, and a lie when social institutions offer it as a natural possession.... [The] characters in *Bellefleur* are allowed to think their feelings are their own; but they are kept as ignorant of the origin of those feelings as they are distraught with fears for their continuity. But I have to suggest how it comes about that the scene of Oates's imagination is the space between one tapestry and another.

To begin with, she is not a realist, except in the deep-down sense in which all writers think themselves realists. She has written serviceable pages in which she places a character in his setting and glances at a few of the circumstances of his life, but her imagination does not seem really seized by the question of self and society, by the relation between a character's indignant perception ... and the objective sources of his indignation. Oates's imagination is not circumstantial. Her subjects—politics, car racing, high life in Washington, college teaching, or whatever—are well-enough sketched, if only sketches were needed, but they are always there to be got through or got over; they are there for the sake of something else, for inner lives that are frantic precisely because they have no real connection with the objective life that surrounds them.

Raymond Williams has a telling passage in an essay on realism where he says that the typical experience, according to nineteenth-century realism, was that of "finding a place and making a settlement." In that sense, too, Oates is not a realist: her characters are never content to make settlements or to settle for the diverse experience of trying to make them. It is closer to the mark to say that she is a Gothic romancer, but that, too, is a side issue. The Gothic element in her work is her substitute for tragedy, as black farce is her substitute for comedy. But it is enough, for the moment, if we say that Oates is a psychological novelist rather than a social novelist or a realist. She assumes that one's feeling is one's truth: value consists in the intensity of one's feeling.

But I have to make a further distinction. I want to describe Oates as an essentialist. If essentialism is the doctrine that essence is prior to existence, an essentialist believes that the essence of one's life is separate from one's existence. Or even, to go back a little, that the essence of a particular life is the rift between the self and the circumstances, merely given and arbitrary, in which it appears. Essence is felt to be discontinuous with the existence assigned to it. Oates's characters are given this discontinuity as their fate: if they are conscious, they try to take the harm out of it by stirring in themselves local intensities of feeling.

Oates has referred to the rift between essence and existence, but not, so far as I know, in these terms. She has spoken rather of invisiblity and visibility, particularly in relation to the experience of being a woman.... Oates writes of invisibility as the major preoccupation of her poetry, but it applies also to her fiction. She is an essentialist, accepting a disjunction between surface and depth, the overt and the secret.... I don't doubt her enormous hope of altering the world, but I trust the tales rather than the teller, and what they say is that life is so appalling, it exhilarates. Her characters don't try to change their lives ... because they are not even aware of them as discontinuous. Intensity is the only value they recognize. So they keep themselves going in the void by exacerbating whatever incitements they are given.

The rift between essence and existence takes various forms in Oates's fiction. At its simplest, it is the rift between making a life and making a living. *Unholy Loves* is supposedly about college teachers, but the one thing they are not shown doing is teaching. *Bellefleur* is a family saga, but the one thing you don't learn from it is what the members of the family do, day by day.... (pp. 12, 14)

Another form of the disjunction is the rift between feelings, deemed to be by definition secret and complex, and any manifestation available to them.... The hectic quality of her common style is explained by the fact that her characters, knowing nothing but their feelings, and always ignorant of their provenance, have to know them desperately: their knowledge can never have the urbanity of knowing that it is typical, either in its origins or its aspiration. They know themselves only as unique: it is desolation when they suspect they aren't.

I think this accounts for the panic in Oates's heroes and, more often, heroines.... The intensity of their feelings is to themselves the only evidence that they exist. Hence the frantic sense, which occurs almost as a nervous tic in these characters, that they can't feel, or can't feel enough, so they are dead. The life of her characters depends upon the desperately asserted superiority of feeling to the world, since their sole relation is to themselves. At this point the distinction between Oates and her characters is hard to maintain. She can't trust feeling enough to let it be, or to think of it as being sheltered and protected by the words for it, or by the extension of the words into the world at large, where feeling might be transformed. So she forces words into the pretense of being feelings, and asserts as their truth the extreme reach of her rhetoric. A risky procedure; it makes much of her writing, as in the chapters in *Bellefleur* on Veronica Bellefleur's love for Ragnar Norst, sound like a parody of Daphne du Maurier.... Deprived of other sources of life, Oates's characters must be given, by way of exorbitance and self-exacerbation, whatever they need to assure them that they are alive. Having given them the empty privilege of self-identity, Oates has to pretend that their emptiness is fullness of a secret kind. (p. 14)

Oates has another way of considering this matter, apart from the question of invisibility. She often makes it a question of voice, of finding one's own or separating oneself from a defunct voice.... [Oates] asks herself: what is the voice that attends me? Excluding from *Invisible Woman* many early poems and her entire first book, she explains that "it isn't so much that I have rejected them as poems, as that I fail to recognize my own voice in them: I feel no kinship, no sense of continuity. That aspect of the past is finally *past*—and cannot be retrieved." But the explanation seems disingenuous. It is not that one aspect of the past is past, but that the voice she hears now is one she doesn't want to hear.

It is not clear from Oates's account of it what she means by voice. It could mean a writer's achieved style, something that comes at last, presumably, with luck, practice, and discipline. Does she mean voice as the only appearance, the only form of existence, in which she is willing to have her essence manifested, as if in that one instance she were willing to posit a relation between essence and existence, not as a permanent attribute but good for the time being? Her secret self, audible while the going is good? (pp. 14, 16)

It is only by thinking along these lines that I can make anything of *A Bloodsmoor Romance.* If I had never read a line of Joyce Carol Oates and merely happened to come upon this new book, I would find it almost unreadable. (p. 16)

The only way I can account for the book is by a supposition. Suppose Joyce Carol Oates, worn out with extending everybody's perimeters, were to long for a rest; to get away from the questioning of voice, her own voice, other voices, and the diverse importunities of her characters, their selves and feelings, their repetitive solitudes. Wouldn't she find it a relief to be writing a book that required nothing but the rough-and-ready allusion to other books, books that have as their chief attribute the fact, thanks be to God, that nobody is required to care about them? She could deal with the demands of her current voice by silencing them; as if to say: "I will get back to you, or to whatever lavish form your successor will take, in my next." Wouldn't it be a particular pleasure for her to produce characters who have no responsibility for the objective world, having no relation to it; and to let them rush about in the paperchase where she found them, that of Victorian popular romance?

Or so *A Bloodsmoor Romance* seems to me. To [Diane Johnson], apparently, it seems otherwise, its real subject "the lot of women, especially the customs and attitudes that confined and oppressed them in the nineteenth century, but also the present-day remnants of those conditions" [see excerpt above]. If *A Bloodsmoor Romance* were offered as a serious account of the lot of women, then or now, it would be ludicrously inadequate to its theme. I think it wholly removed from such a concern. I see no merit in forcing upon the book the social density and public ramification which Joyce Carol Oates has taken care to exclude from it. (pp. 16-17)

> *Denis Donoghue, "Wonder Woman," in The New York Review of Books, Vol. XXIX, No. 16, October 21, 1982, pp. 12, 14, 16-17.*

## RONALD CURRAN

[*A Bloodsmoor Romance*] represents Oates's incorporation of the gothic romance into her own vision of America, a kind of feminist variant attuned to the myths of social organization that informed the eighteenth- and nineteenth-century romance on both sides of the Atlantic. Women more fearsome than fearing dominate and challenge once-commanding gothic heroes. *Bloodsmoor* is both a deconstruction and a reconstruction, a creative retelling which turns the form inside out, voicing truths the gothic romance seemed always on the verge of admitting. Oates unties the narrative tongue. Her novel is the natural next step in the evolution of the form after the ambiguities of Melville's Pierre, Poe's demonic women and Hawthorne's blondes. Or we can chart the tradition even further back, across the

ocean, in the work of Walpole. . . . The violence of her phenomenological world in earlier fictions (*Them* or *With Shuddering Fall,* for instance) finds in the gothic romance a rootedness in history as well as in the interlocking social mythologies which in part define society and appropriate behavior. *Bloodsmoor* is bound to these and to their origins in medieval notions of aristocracy and male superiority, to the human struggle for power and control centered in the ego since the Renaissance and to the American forms of these same conflicts in the conservatism of the early federalists and established anti-Jacksonian families like the Kiddemasters. Oates's romances tell the same old tale with reverse English, a kind which changes both focus and direction. . . .

In *Bloodsmoor* Oates wears the form of the gothic romance as if it were a whalebone corset; she is hilarious, pious and prim, as befits the tensions inherent in so restrictive a garment. . . . The humor grows naturally from the restrictions of the literary form and the values it embodies. The tradition of the gothic romance provides a coherent social history in the light of which the phenomenology of violence, sexuality and isolation makes good sense.

It is in all an entertaining performance, dense with historical detail and mastery of literary convention, but the reader unfamiliar with the gothic tradition may see the initial third or so of the novel as an excessively tedious narrative extension of a romantic fiction that is moralistic, plot-bloated and verbose. Oates, however, is only assembling the form she plans to deconstruct. The novel is an ingenious spoof and much more. Its style recognizes the gothic's possibilities for the coherent expression of contemporary discontinuities of the kind in which notions of family, class, gender role and human values generally take on a historical coloration that makes them part of a sociocultural as well as emotional evolution. The work locates in women a more liberating and positive kind of will to power which ends toward growth rather than toward stasis, egomaniacal accomplishment or self-destruction. Unfortunately, the book's length, idiom and important relation to a specific literary tradition and to the past will restrict its appeal and obscure its intentions in misperceptions of the meaning of its obsessional nature.

> *Ronald Curran, in a review of "A Bloodsmoor Romance," in World Literature Today, Vol. 57, No. 2, Spring, 1983, p. 290.*

## ROBERT DAWIDOFF

The critical posture in these various pieces [collected in **"The Profane Art"**] depends on Oates' own sensibility and on her understanding of writing as, herself, a noted contemporary writer. Her convincing notions of what writers and writing are like authenticate many of her critical judgments. There is also a simple process of affinity that gives her writing about "Wuthering Heights," for example, a vivid, fervent quality making one imemdiately want to reread that old book and find the new and surprising novel Oates says it is. (p. 2)

At her best, Oates by the example of her own extensive reading and by her intense, almost proselytizing view of how a critic should review, makes the reader want to read what she recommends. She is evangelical rather than scholarly and a lucid advocate of making people want to read good books; her enthusiasms suit the length and purposes of a book review.

She is also antinomian. Her essays betray how completely she depends on her own views and readings and how little she respects the form and substance of the essay. Her essays are ungainly and willful. Their arguments plunge and race rather than proceed and convince. They skim and disappoint even when the ideas are good. Her enthusiasms expand and proliferate, but her arguments do not develop. Shapeless and careless, her essays serve her own views ill. Her juxtaposition of a lengthy discussion of Saul Bellow, a peculiar one of Dreiser and a rather sudden one of Anzia Yezierska under the rubric of "Imaginary Cities: America" is too typically ramshackle. Similarly her perceptive noting of an interesting intersection of popular stereotypes of women and images of women in modern novels is haphazardly demonstrated.

The conversation Oates envisions successfully about books is among friends, with whom the formalities of argument are not so important. A friend will understand and provide the context for one's enthusiasms and be guided by them. Joyce Carol Oates has earned those friends with her writing and they will understand and enjoy these essays. Those for whom her sensibility is not its own argument will find this volume nevertheless interesting, containing several excellent reviews of writers worth reading, told from the valuable and perceptive point of view of a writer who reads. (pp. 2, 5)

> *Robert Dawidoff, "Criticism: Human Conversation between Equals," in* Los Angeles Times Book Review, *May 29, 1983, pp. 2, 5.*

## DAISY ALDAN

"Invisibility" is the theme which "haunts" Joyce Carol Oates, as the word *sterility* haunted Stéphane Mallarmé. Conscious of her "invisible" role as a woman, the invisible "deepest self" which is "inward and secret," hoping that her "spiritual essence is a great deal more complex than the casual eye of the observer will allow," she sets out to reveal it and largely succeeds in convincing us that she is indeed a woman of intelligence, sensibility and vision. (p. 638)

*Invisible Woman* includes poems from previous collections as well as new works pertinent to the theme, poems she recognizes as her "own voice." In spite of the fact that part I, "Sun-Truths," with many "confessional" poems, is not entirely satisfying, each section crescendoes so that the final one, "Selected Poems 1970-1978," contains enough poems of excellence to leave one breathless. There is no doubt that Oates is at her best when contemplative, and by that I mean not only when she is questioning, as in **"Query, Not to Be Answered"** . . . , but even in the intense works which arise from personal anguish yet rise toward universality, as in **"The Present Tense."** . . .

Oates also can be lyrical, as in **"Snowfall,"** where a line like "last Sunday the snowfall of next January crystalling / in massive cloud canyons" startles one with its originality of expression and insight, or as in **"How Gentle"** . . . , where the poet is revealed in a rare mood of gentle tenderness. There are others which one would love to quote: **"Skyscape,"** with its panorama of cloud beings; **"A Report to an Academy,"** which in a few words depicts the agony of internal imprisonment; and finally, two beautiful poems side by side, **"After Terror"** and **"Fertilizing the Continent,"** the latter an apotheosis which leads us to anticipate further poems of true intuition and reverence for the Word, which so many in our generation would

debase. Oates is proving herself to be that poet "who ponders" of whom she speaks in **"The Poet."** (p. 639)

> *Daisy Aldan, in a review of "Invisible Woman," in* World Literature Today, *Vol. 57, No. 4, Autumn, 1983, pp. 638-39.*

## MICHIKO KAKUTANI

[In **"Mysteries of Winterthurn"**] Miss Oates has . . . taken on the old-fashioned detective story—a form that would seem the perfect vehicle for displaying her idiosyncratic gifts and preoccupations.

By definition, after all, the murder mystery concerns the intrusion of terrible events into ordinary life—a recurrent theme in Miss Oates's own commodious oeuvre. And the genre also gives her a chance to indulge her penchant for scenes of extraordinary violence and gore, and to re-explore a variety of social issues. . . .

Related in heavy, archaic prose that drips with symbolism and melodramatic curlicues, **"Mysteries of Winterthurn"** focuses on three cases in the career of Xavier Kilgarvan, a brilliant young detective who fancies himself an American Sherlock Holmes. The first case, "The Virgin in the Rose-Bower," concerns four murders and a suicide at Glen Mawr Manor, the family homestead of Xavier's eccentric cousins; the second, "devil's Half-Acre," the murder of five local factory girls, and the third, "The Bloodstained Bridal Gown," the ax murder of a Winterthurn minister and his adulterous lover. . . .

Obsessed with penetrating to the heart of Mystery and with his love for his beauteous cousin, Xavier is a familiar Oatesian hero—a monomaniac, whose desperate attempts to make the world conform to his internal vision lead to isolation and despair. . . .

Of course, by making Xavier a detective, who believes that "crime, if not the criminal heart itself, might someday be eradicated by the *intelligent, pragmatic and systematic unification of the numerous forces for Good,"* Miss Oates is also commenting on the old-fashioned, moralistic conventions of the mystery genre—whose tidy plots imply that order can be restored to society by the simple act of identifying and capturing a criminal—and the limitations of its philosophical outlook.

In fact, Xavier, "a child of his time," becomes a kind of symbol, for Miss Oates, of certain 19th-century ideals of enlightenment and progress. His initial belief that "what lay in the beclouded realm of the mysterious could be transposed, by the rigorous logic of detection, into the comprehensible" reflects his century's faith in reason and its view of the world as an essentially orderly place, watched over by a reasonable God. And his subsequent disillusion with these ideals—which happens to occur just before the outbreak of World War I—echoes the disillusion experienced by America during those same years.

Clearly Miss Oates has worked hard to delineate this postmodernist subtext in **"Mysteries of Winterthurn,"** but too often the effort shows. Ponderous symbols proliferate like weeds—characters have names or nicknames like Perdita and Iphigenia—and didactic passages, frequently italicized, constantly flag readers and tell them exactly what to think. For instance, of Xavier's growing skepticism about human nature, Miss Oates writes, "the assertion had begun to haunt him, he knew not from what source, that there is, after all, no innocence in Mankind; *but only degrees and refinements of guilt.*''

Given the achievement of "**Bellefleur**" and "**A Bloodsmoor Romance**,' one assumes that Miss Oates set out, with "**Mysteries**" to write a book that at once satirizes a popular genre and fulfills its own storytelling requirements. If she is heavy-handed in achieving her first objective, however, she is even clumsier with the second.

Though Xavier's failures as a detective are meant to underscore the limits of "ratiocination," the reader frequently remains as confused as the fictional sleuth—and hence derives little satisfaction from watching his thwarted efforts. Many of the strange events in "The Virgin in the Rose-Bower," for instance, simply go unexplained, for Xavier falls ill and is later unable to recall all the facts, "save in broken, jumbled and hallucinatory guise.''

As for Xavier's other two cases, we know from early on who the real murderer is—thus, even that element of suspense is missing—and we are encouraged to shrug off too many of the bizarre events as possible hallucinations. In the end, they seem like excuses, on the part of the author, simply to create atmosphere and a collection of Gothic set pieces.

*Michiko Kakutani, in a review of "Mysteries of Winterthurn," in* The New York Times, *February 10, 1984, p. C25.*

## PATRICIA CRAIG

What is Joyce Carol Oates up to? Chapter Two of "**Mysteries of Winterthurn**" . . . is entitled "Trompe L'Oeil," and it may be we're meant to infer something about the novelist's intention. What from one angle of vision looks like a plain pastiche of the 19th-century thriller, complete with hellish spectacles, romantic hero and all the rest, soon begins to show a very different design. Overlaying the pastiche is a philosophical investigation into the nature of "Mystery"—"the *mystery of personality,* and of *religious experience.*" The "detective's search for truth," you might say, is of less consequence here than the author's relish for life's incalculable mysteries. . . .

The novel has borrowed its elaborate orotundity from some wordy era of the past; however, it is pretty eclectic in style, and a good many literary modes get a showing—Gothic, Baroque, Romantic and so on. Miss Oates even creates a poetess . . . and barefacedly appropriates for her the literary manner of Emily Dickinson, as well as lumbering her with a family background as queer as Catherine Earnshaw's in "Wuthering Heights.''

Various plights peculiar to women engage the author's interest, and she makes a case for feminism by parading some ludicrously antifeminist attitudes, referring, for example, at one point, to "a particularly noisome gaggle of 'Suffragettes,' led by Miss Elizabeth Cady Stanton." These women have taken up the cause of a 17-year-old housemaid on trial for infanticide, in one of the side issues of this discursive novel that turn out not to be as inconsequential as they seem. Every instance of malign import has a part to play in establishing Winterthurn as a deadly locality; moreover, the sly insertion of one local family name or another, along with every pernicious episode, leaves hardly a family in the district untainted. "'*Here,* after all, is Hell,' the detective idly mused." . . .

As in a number of spoofs of detective fiction, we find, toward the end of "**Mysteries of Winterthurn**," an attempt to conflate the figures of detective and maniac. In this case, however, it's done to underline the impossibility of differentiating between guilt and innocence—a purpose that takes us out of the sensation mode and into metaphysics, where the novel has been tending all along.

Miss Oates endows her hero with a capacity for diguise as formidable as Sherlock Holmes's and puts him in a reddish wig at the very moment when a police search is in progress for a sandy-haired assassin. Looked at in one way, this furnishes a comment on the "Mysteries" of identity and motivation; from another viewpoint, however, Xavier's red hair is merely a red herring. True, it is difficult to discern a larky intention under all the fussiness and fervor, but one is signaled plainly enough, at intervals—in the naming of the town's outstanding doctor after a celebrated English lunatic asylum (Colney Hatch), for example, and in the striking variety of near-fatal encounters devised for Xavier and listed in a footnote. With a head as impervious to knocks as Nancy Drew's, Xavier has also warded off attacks from a man-eating sow and a giant African parrot. These straightforward comic touches, however, don't amount to a great deal. The novel, all exemplary boldness and ebullient erudition, is really too fullblooded to accommodate such playfulness with ease.

Miss Oates makes no bones about confounding the reader's expectations in the effort to reinstate "Mystery" as a kind of philosophical category. She offers no mundane solutions to her crimes, conjuring will-o'-the-wisps and cherishing ambiguity. (This is a novel with many secrets, and it keeps a number of them to itself.) It is easy enough to identify the typical lurid three-decker novel of the last century as Miss Oates's starting-point. After all, she's done this sort of thing in "**Bellefleur**" and "**A Bloodsmoor Romance.**" But at times it's unclear to the reader whether she's reproducing a 19th-century detective novel, overturning it, expanding it or sending it up.

*Patricia Craig, "Philosophical Tale of Gore," in* The New York Times Book Review, *February 12, 1984, p. 7.*

## ANNE COLLINS

In Joyce Carol Oates's previous efforts at mimicking 19th-century fictional forms, the question the reader had to ask was whether Oates had truly taken possession of the genre or has been possessed by it. *Bellefleur* (1980) and *A Bloodsmoor Romance* (1982) sprawled in looped and twisted excesses of language and plot, as if the virus of Gothic romance had infected an already fevered imagination. That her third such attempt, *Mysteries of Winterthurn,* should be greeted with trepidation is not surprising, crammed as it is with demons, star-struck lovers, macabre landscapes and heinous crimes. But in the detective story Oates has at last found a 19th-century form in which she can thoroughly entertain her reader. The pose of objectivity she must adopt to properly portray her hero, Xavier Kilgarvan, is an effective leash on florid narrative. Her mock objectivity is also a never-ending font of pleasing irony, because the true mysteries of Winterthurn are the kind that can never be solved by rational thought. . . .

Oates serves warning about the kind of quest she has set for Kilgarvan in the first "editor's note." She writes: "Our ancestors, though oft appearing less informed than ourselves, were perhaps far more sensitive—nay, altogether more astute, in comprehending Evil.'' Kilgarvan sees evil clearly but for a long time he mistakes its source, placing it solely into the hands of the powerful men and the static social order of Winterthurn. He thinks that evil is only injustice, which can be pragmatically redressed—until his last case.

In it, as in the others, he tracks the obvious villain, the one with the motive and the power to evade punishment. But Perdita has the real clue, which she told him long ago: "Angels *may* turn demon, with the passage of time—if starved of the love that is their sustenance. . . ." Kilgarvan finds evil at the very heart of his love, a deprivation that turns into a destructive power. But the word "evil" is out of use, old-fashioned, a Ronald Reaganism: people nowadays are not considered "evil" but victims of circumstance. Joyce Carol Oates resurrects an old form so that she can unabashedly resurrect the word and apply it to the destructive mysteries of the human psyche.

> *Anne Collins, "The Grotesque Face of Evil," in* Maclean's Magazine, *Vol. 97, No. 8, February 20, 1984, p. 60.*

### PUBLISHERS WEEKLY

In the title story of this new collection . . . [*Last Days*] by the fastest pen in the West, a demented Jewish graduate student afflicted by messianic delusions and paranoiac obsessions murders a rabbi and then kills himself. Why? The author's burden is to make plausible the unaccountable; and Oates unleashes upon it her identifying manner—hectic, seething, frantic, a breathlessness that omits nothing, as if a compulsive talker in a state of frenzy were pouring out an inner life and driving passion; and thereby conveys some sense of a state of mind capable of atrocious action. But not quite: finally, the story is too willed, too literary, too contrived. . . . [The stories in this collection are] excessive, overdone and overwrought, detailed beyond their natural capacity to absorb the detail they are laden with. At the same time, however, they are often compelling in a way that sets the author distinctively apart. (pp. 55-6)

> *A review of "Last Days," in* Publishers Weekly, *Vol. 225, No. 23, June 8, 1984, pp. 55-6.*

### BRANDON RUSSELL

When should a writer stop writing? When output exceeds production, or when he (or she) deliberately sets out to destroy a book's credibility. Being driven by a demon should not necessarily mean working like one, especially when one's private obsessions are no longer camouflaged by the authorial voice. What is left of Joyce Carol Oates' voice is saying 'Excuse me while I slip into something more suicidal', and it is not a pleasant sound. . . .

Like *Bellefleur* and *A Bloodsmoor Romance* which preceded it, *Mysteries of Winterthurn* is written in the style of a 19th-century romance. This last book takes for its form the detective novel and owes more than a little to Edgar Allan Poe.

But whereas Poe's stories are satisfactorily resolved, the three collected here by the book's unidentified 'Editor' are blatantly unresolved. The celebration of Mystery, in fact, is little more than an excuse to mystify the reader.

Quoting De Quincey, the Editor asks: 'Is not Murder an art-form? And does any art-form require justification?' By which means Miss Oates presumably absolves herself from future culpability and cries of 'Foul'. By the second page, it is ap-

parent that we cannot hope to take *Mysteries* at face value. . . . (p. 29)

As anyone familiar with Oates knows, she is particularly adept at creating sanguinary effects, leaving the reader and several characters feeling eviscerated, or in [the first mystery], *eaten*. No distinction is made between, on the one hand, the realities of betrayal, justice (as embodied by the law) and family ties (or otherwise), and on the other hand, paranormal voices, bodies and *trompe l'oeil* figures which are inclined to cry tears of blood at the slightest provocation.

There is a sequence of unexplained events, liberally strewn with clues, but, as in the other two tales of mystery and ratiocination, one can only finally be satisfied that Miss Oates is exercising her vivid imagination and perhaps doesn't know the answers either. . . .

Joyce Carol Oates' fascination with the depths to which humans—all humans—will sink, if the evil which resides in every brain is given free rein, leaves little hope for a positive view of the human condition. Her wilful dislocation of reader and story, coupled with her inability to separate fantasy and reality—or even to care overmuch whether such a division takes place—makes her creation itself something of a monster. (p. 30)

> *Brandon Russell, "Monster," in* The Spectator, *Vol. 253, No. 8140, July 14, 1984, pp. 29-30.*

### JAY PARINI

*Last Days* is the 12th full-length collection of stories that Oates has published—a feat in itself; it is also one of her strongest, containing two stories—**"The Witness"** and **"My Warszawa: 1980"**—that are equal to her best previous work.

**"The Witness"** is in Oates' characteristic style: swift, imagistic, breathlessly evocative. The narrator is a teenage girl on the edge of breakdown, and the hallucinatory quality found in much of Oates' writing (sometimes to the detriment of the work) is crucial to this narrative of panic and flight. The girl is poor, and her father is dying. . . . Her running away from home is used to bring the whole of her tawdry world into relief; her mind, which the narrative embodies in a seamless fashion, whirls, and the detritus of her life is caught and funneled, pulled toward the story's spinning vortex. One puts down this story exhausted, informed, and powerfully moved.

Oates achieves something of the same effect in other stories, such as **"Last Days,"** which concerns Saul Morgenstern, a young intellectual on the brink of either revelation or disaster. But there is a genuine variety here, too; **"Funland,"** for instance, is a vividly etched portrait of a father/daughter relationship that ends in a symbolic amusement park with the girl, Wendy, like a "little princess thundering along on her palomino pony" while her father rides a donkey, nailed to the floor: "He will never overtake her."

The real breakthrough story in this collection, for Oates, is **"My Warszawa: 1980,"** which won an O. Henry Award in 1983. In it, Oates sketches a haunting portrait of an American woman called Judith Horne, a prototype of the avant-garde intellectual abroad. The story, with its atmosphere of intense personal ambition and political tensions, is the centerpiece of a sequence of stories located in Soviet bloc countries that forms the second half of this excellent collection.

*Jay Parini, "Witnesses and Storytellers," in* Book World—The Washington Post, *September 30, 1984, p. 6.**

## JONATHAN YARDLEY

Of all the idiocies on the contemporary American literary scene, surely none is more idiotic than the persistent rumor that the next American to receive the Nobel Prize for Literature will be Joyce Carol Oates. . . .

To be sure, were writers to be recognized solely for their productivity, then certainly Oates would get all the prizes; they'd have to invent new ones just for her. Every other week, it seems, the door to her aerie opens and a new book gusts forth. Writers, reviewers and readers gaze at her in awe; she is, in the words they occasionally apply reverently to her, a "writing machine." It seems not to have occurred to anyone that writing is like anything else: if it is done too hastily and too profusely, it almost inevitably is done badly.

In the pungent words of the late Truman Capote, this isn't writing, it's typing. There could not be a more paradigmatic example of Oates' craft than *Solstice,* a hysterical little novel— at least, by comparison with most of her recent effusions, it has the virtue of relative brevity—that reveals itself, beneath all the noise it makes, to have nothing at all to say. It wails, it weeps, it groans, it gasps. . . .

The typewriter is on automatic pilot, spinning giddily out of control: "She was shamefaced, crying, laughing in surprised hiccuping gulps, she hadn't known until this moment, Sheila staring at her, Sheila leaning forward staring at her, what a liar she was . . . She wept, hugging herself. Her breasts were aching. Her belly, her loins." And so it goes: nearly 250 pages of overwrought, undisciplined prose more suited to the breathy encounters of a Harlequin romance than to the work of an author of high literary reputation. In the background you can hear the typewriter clacking away, like a wire-service ticker in an old-fashioned newsroom, spewing forth more words than it, or the reader, can digest.

All of this hyperactivity has to do with a youngish woman, . . . Monica, who comes to teach at a boy's preparatory school in rural Pennsylvania following the unsuccessful conclusion of her marriage. There she meets and becomes fast friends with the aforementioned Sheila, an older woman, the widow of a well-known artist and herself a painter of considerable talent. We are to believe that they are pearls cast among swine; all about them are the randy gentleman farmers of Bucks County, the self-satisfied panjandrums of the Glenkill Academy for Boys and the bubble-headed wives of both. But if these be pearls, I cast my lot with the swine.

Though Oates obviously means us to see them otherwise, neither party to this odd couple ever emerges beyond her faintest outline. Monica, who is clearly intended to be sympathetic, is merely whiny and self-pitying; Sheila, who is granted the vast license of artistic temperament, is merely abrupt and self-absorbed. There's no real characterization here because Oates is in too much of a hurry and too much involved, perhaps, in the sheer emotion of a situation that, no matter how deeply she may feel it herself, she utterly fails to convey to the reader. If we don't care about the characters because there's nothing there to care about, how on earth can we be expected to care about what happens to them?

What happens, furthermore, is not much. There's a lot of dithering, as in the passage quoted above, about Monica's abortion and her failed marriage; there's an extended episode of slumming in which the two women disguise themselves as divorcees named Sherrill Ann and Mary Beth and ply the local roadhouses in search of male company; there's a bit of suspense, if you're easy to please, involving a mysterious man who has been "making inquiries" about Monica; and there's plenty of fussing about whether Sheila will actually pull together the show she's been working on forever and then show up for its opening at a gallery in New York. There's all this *business* going on, but there's no sense or purpose to it, no evidence that it is anything more than mere stuffing for another turkey.

Judging from some rather heavyhanded hints that are laid in the reader's path, *Solstice* is meant to be a novel about the difficulties and rewards of friendship, the illusion we create for ourselves that we are in control of our lives, and the moments in life—solstices, if you will—when we pass through crisis. Those are the novel's themes; they stick out like sore thumbs, begging for our attention, but they are only casually connected with Oates' characters and themes.

Nothing in *Solstice* meshes or even connects; it's characteristic of the book's disorganization and carelessness that it is littered with parenthetical asides, some of them running to a paragraph or more, that seem to have been injected as hasty afterthoughts by a writer too hurried to pause and weave things together. *Solstice* has nothing to recommend it except thin characters, transparent themes and hyperventilated prose; surely readers, not to mention prize-givers, want more from fiction than that.

*Jonathan Yardley, "Joyce Carol Oates on Automatic Pilot," in* Book World—The Washington Post, *January 6, 1985, p. 3.*

## MICHAEL F. HARPER

Joyce Carol Oates' story of the obsessive friendship between two contemporary women ["**Solstice**"] is a Gothic novel in which the traditional Gothic machinery is suppressed, reduced to metaphor—apparently for the sake of realism. . . .

[What] is left of the Gothic is an emotional intensity, a claustrophobic sense of being trapped in a space traversed by madness, terror and desire. In "**Solstice**," this space is the mind of Monica Jensen, a pleasantly ordinary young woman who comes to Glenkill Academy for Boys in Bucks County, Pa., hoping to wash away painful memories by immersing herself in her work as an English teacher. What eventually threatens to submerge her, however, is a burgeoning friendship with the enigmatic, mercurial Sheila Trask, an artist who contemptuously holds herself aloof from most of her wealthy philistine neighbors. . . .

The story is told from Monica's viewpoint as a series of vignettes that become briefer and more troubled as the narrative hastens toward its climax. Sheila gradually comes to dominate Monica's consciousness, and as she does so, the other characters in the novel—the hearty, good-natured chaplain and his well-meaning busybody of a wife, the malicious English department chairman, the tactful and courtly lawyer whom Monica occasionally dates—all recede into the ghostly half-life of caricatures and nonentities, despite hints that they have their own depths and complexities.

Reality, Oates seems to be saying, is essentially inner and psychological, making her a strange kind of realist, making her reader wonder why she took the trouble to naturalize all that Gothic machinery. As Monica's interest in the lawyer wanes in comparison to her involvement with Sheila, he becomes ''a subject in two dimensions, a matter of affable surfaces.'' Sheila herself makes all this explicit in her painting: ''She had lost the desire, and most likely the ability, to paint subjects head on. She hadn't the faith, probably, that the subject existed; that her perception of it existed in any absolute way; that its inner being (spiritual, structural) corresponded at all to its surface.''. . .

To read **"Solstice"** is to have the illusion of being trapped in someone else's mind, and Oates has made it a powerful and vertiginous experience. The novel explores the dynamics of a friendship that becomes an obsession, of a love for another that ultimately becomes a struggle for the survival of the self. Is ''love'' to the point of madness Ariadne's thread, the only sure guide in the deep recesses of the labyrinth? Or does salvation lie in the artist's ''work and . . . her monomaniacal faith in her work?'' Perhaps they are two versions of the same thing. Anything else, Oates seems to be suggesting, is not enough: ''You took hold of it, you trusted to it, and then it snapped in your fingers.'' A somewhat discouraging conclusion for the rest of us.

> *Michael F. Harper, in a review of "Solstice," in* Los Angleles Times Book Review, *January 6, 1985, p. 3.*

# Amos Oz

## 1939-

(Born Amos Klausner) Israeli novelist, short story writer, and nonfiction writer.

Oz is acclaimed for his stories of Israeli life, particularly those set in the kibbutz, which he writes with critical affection, having been a kibbutznik himself for many years. His novel *Makom acher* (1966; *Elsewhere, Perhaps*) is a look at the singular problems and relationships experienced in such a community. It was followed by *Michael sheli* (1968; *My Michael*), a fictional psychological profile of the fantasy life of an Israeli housewife which introduces Oz's controversial contention that Jews and Arabs have ambivalent, rather than purely hostile, feelings for each other.

Oz's themes include the destructiveness of anti-Semitism upon both the hater and the hated, the interrelationship of all human experience, tensions between community and individuality, and the shifting border between the real and the surreal. In *Lagaat bamayim, lagaat baruach* (1973; *Touch the Water, Touch the Wind*), the characters are always in search of the elusive ideal, something to be found only in "another place," never here and now.

Oz creates his fiction from the political and historical heritage of Israel and its relationships with surrounding lands. A repeated motif in his novels is that of the borders which keep people together and which also separate them. Oz longs for the union of disparate peoples, though he understands the improbability of his wish. In a book of short stories, *Artsot hatan* (1965; *Where the Jackals Howl*), he uses his recurring symbol of the jackal to represent the ever-present threat to Israel from beyond its borders.

Published prior to the outbreak of Israel's war with Lebanon, the novel *True Repose* (1983) alludes to Oz's dissatisfaction with Israel's sometimes violent responses to differences with its neighbors. The constrictions of that society's expectations cause the protagonist to leave all that he loves and seek a suicidal escape in the Jordanian desert. Oz's next work, *In the Land of Israel* (1983), is a collection of interviews he conducted in 1982 with Jewish and Arab Israelis from diverse social and political backgrounds. The book concentrates on what these people think their country is and what they think it should be.

Oz is recognized as a writer of international stature, not only for his revealing portrayals of Israel, but also for the outstanding artistry of his fiction.

(See also *CLC*, Vols. 5, 8, 11, 27 and *Contemporary Authors*, Vols. 53-56.)

## ROBERT ALTER

[Israel's] two leading novelists, Amos Oz and A. B. Yehoshua, both came out with new novels just before the start of the war [in Lebanon]. Typically, Israeli intellectuals will tell you either that they couldn't finish the Oz or they couldn't finish the Yehoshua, or that both writers have ridiculously inflated reputations. Yet Mr. Oz's **"True Repose"** and Mr. Yehoshua's

© Jerry Bauer

"Late Divorce" are strong books which do certain impressive things neither of these writers has done before.

The two novels are very different in setting and style, but there is one significant link between them: Both deal with attempted flights from the constricting pressures of life in Israel. The young protagonist of **"True Repose"** abandons wife and kibbutz to head out, suicidally, for the Jordanian desert. The aging paterfamilias of "Late Divorce" returns from the American Middle West to Israel in order to sever last Israeli ties so that he can establish a new family in the United States, but his effort to escape proves to be darkened, in an oblique way, by suicidal impulses.

Mr. Oz imagines in the end a reconciliation between individual and society; Mr. Yehoshua, more concerned with rendering a portrait of familial psychopathologies, concludes on a bleaker note. I don't think either book should be read as a political statement . . . ; but both are symptomatic of the troubled connection Israeli writers increasingly feel with the realities of the Jewish state. (p. 11)

[There] is still a great deal of zest in the literary activity of this country, which produces, for better or for worse, more volumes per capita of new poetry and fiction than any other country in the world. Many writers are energetically engaged in trying to affect the future course of Israeli society through both writing and political activism.

The most remarkable document in this regard and the most widely discussed publication by a Hebrew writer in recent months has been "Here and There in the Land of Israel, Autumn 1982," a series of articles by Amos Oz that ran in the weekly magazine of the socialist newspaper Davar during December and January.... In contrast to the inclination some writers may feel to withdraw into the fastnesses of language, the Oz articles reflect a strenuous effort to go out into Israeli society and sound its depths.

The articles are a series of interviews with a variety of figures introduced by brief, effective pieces of novelistic scene-setting: two encounters with groups of West Bank settlers . . . ; a discussion with a cafe-full of Sephardic supporters of Mr. Begin in the immigrant town of Beit-Shemesh; a conversation at the home of a prosperous farmer who conceded that he would not reject the label "Judeo-Nazi" for his utterly ruthless views of current political realities; and two meetings with Arabs, one in the West Bank town of Ramallah, the other in the offices of the East Jerusalem Palestinian nationalist newspaper, The Dawn. In each instance, Mr. Oz, the ideological tourist, allows his sometimes outrageous subjects to speak memorably for themselves.

Among Hebrew readers, by and large a skeptical lot, there has been some speculation as to how much of this is transcription, how much invention. Mr. Oz indicates that he did not use a tape recorder but merely jotted down rapid notes during the conversations. Knowing assessments, however, tend to confirm the basic veracity of the articles, and if, for example, the bloody-minded gentleman farmer sounds suspiciously like one of the engaging ideological madmen of Mr. Oz's fiction, that is not in itself evidence of fabrication, only one of those startling double loops we often encounter from reality to fictional representation and back to reality again.

Though "Here and There in the Land of Israel, Autumn 1982" is conscientious reportage on the most urgent issues, the essential fact about it is that only a novelist with Mr. Oz's abilities could have pulled it off. His great success is in finding the perfect voice for each of the subjects he interviews. I say "finding" rather than capturing or reproducing to stress the advantage of the writer's selective ear over the electromagnetic tape. The little tricks of speech, the distinguishing nuances of colloquial usages are persuasively present for each speaker. But they contribute to the subtle heightening of dialogue one finds in a good realistic novel that, without diminishing verisimilitude, exposes an underlying dynamic of thought and feeling, social and political attitudes, psychology.

It should be noted that Mr. Oz does not cover the whole spectrum of Israeli reality but rather concentrates as a writer of the left on an exploration of the political Other—the Israeli right from its popular base to its extremist peripheries, as well as the Arabs. I don't mean to suggest that these pieces contain unexpected revelations, but they do manage quite impressively to put one in touch with some of the human realities that make up the explosive situation in which the Israelis are living. This is a country in which it is very hard for a writer, whatever the temptations of withdrawal, to turn his back on the political arena, and Mr. Oz's interviews strike me as an exemplary instance of a writer using his craft to come to grips with what is happening politically and to illuminate certain aspects of

Israeli society that have generally been concealed by polemical formulas. (p. 34)

    *Robert Alter, "The Writers and the War," in* The New York Times Book Review, *March 27, 1983, pp. 11, 34-5.\**

**ROGER ROSENBLATT**

In [Amos Oz's] latest work, **"In the Land of Israel,"** it seems that everyone has intentionally uncombed his hair in the author's presence, either tearing at it in some public display of anger or temper, or fluffing it out crazily as a scare tactic. On the surface, then, this is an untidy book, just as Israel is an untidy country, heaving with arguments, curses and cajolings, a country where everyone is pleading at once with hands upturned to heaven.

In fact, **"In the Land of Israel"** is brilliantly controlled, a careful if galloping report by an artist wearing a journalist's mask, who portrays his country through conversations. Last autumn Mr. Oz traveled throughout Israel interviewing and listening to people.... The voices are not types. They rise from the crowd and, having had their say, blend back in, like flights in a blues number—all except two of the voices, which do not blend in, and which may be said to represent the two souls of the book in combat.

The first belongs to a man Mr. Oz calls Z, who is not further identified. A man in his 50's, heavy-set, tan, lounging shirtless in gym shorts, Z is Israel the warrior. He derides Mr. Oz as a *Zhid*, an Uncle Tom hypocrite appeaser.... Mr. Oz says nothing in reply. The chapter is entirely Z's.

Mr. Oz does have his say—not immediately after Z, but later when he responds to Z and all his other antagonists. The author's voice is important to the book. It is necessary, to establish that he is no ordinary self-effacing reporter on a quest, but a public figure who for years has participated in major national controversies and who regularly gives his views of things to the international press, "ratting" on his homeland. It would be unnatural if he did not have a voice in this work, but his speech . . . is only tangentially political. Mainly it is a brief for humanism. That is the real battle of Israel, as Mr. Oz sees it (as Z sees it as well, from the opposite perspective)—one between humanists and nationalists. He comes out strongly for "spiritual pluralism," for a world made up not of nations but of "dozens of civilizations, each developing in accordance with its own internal rhythms, all cross-pollinating." (p. 1)

Other Israelis—mostly Jews but some Arabs—offer their opinions on the state of the nation. Mr. Oz was clever enough not to tape-record his conversations, thus freeing himself to substitute verisimilitude for replication. Whenever possible, he faithfully transcribes what people said to him, but certain choices of language and rhythm are clearly his, and Maurie Goldberg-Bartura's translation carries all the curves and edges of the original language. An urgency or despair is added to these conversations by the fact that Mr. Oz conducted them shortly after the Phalangist massacres of Palestinians in the camps of Lebanon that were under Israeli military jurisdiction. What Mr. Oz wants to know is what the world also wants to know: Who *are* these Israelis? Or, as a woman named Sarah asks near the end of the book, "What will become of us?"

In the Guela quarter of Jerusalem, where Mr. Oz began his reporting odyssey, the Orthodox Jews have no doubt about the answer as they rail against the vanity and luxury of secular

Israel. . . . They await the Messiah who alone can reveal the Promised Land. Mr. Oz notes that the only power equal to the Messiah's in this quarter is the memory of Hitler, which the Orthodox preserve to advance their case. Mr. Oz explains the polar forces: "Because of Hitler you have no right to quarrel with this sort of [Orthodox] Judaism. Because of the awaited Messiah this Jewry enchain you and threaten to reconquer what you have wrested from their hands."

The "you" is Mr. Oz, the new-race sabra, the flower of Zionism whose mere existence is a stench to the Orthodox, as is Israel itself. (p. 46)

I think Mr. Oz deliberately chooses to start his journey where, he says, Hitler and the Messiah "dominate" the wall graffiti and the souls of people "like twin pillars of fire," because he feels that Israel lies between those pillars. And Mr. Oz, like Samson, is ready to push both pillars aside, the murderous past and the crippling future, in the name of a hopeful present. Still, he implicitly acknowledges that he may have undertaken his journey because of desires he cannot fathom. He has no fellow feeling with the Orthodox railers, but he takes them seriously. The first stop on his journey thus announces that all Israel's voices will be taken seriously and honored and in the ensuing chapters, hate and love, politics and superstition, even Jew and Arab will bear the same weight.

The book then moves from voice to voice; each offers something different from the one before it, but, with the exceptions of Z's voice and Mr. Oz's own, they are not starkly different from one another. Each builds on an earlier one rather than drowning it out. After the religious zealots come the nationalist zealots in the village of Bet Shemesh, Moroccan Jews on whose political support the former Prime Minister Menachem Begin relied for much of his power. (pp. 46-7)

They are followed by Israeli settlers on the West Bank who threaten to do some "spring cleaning" if the authorities do not control the rebellious Arabs. The Arabs themselves talk of conciliation and coexistence with bitterness and confusion. Abu Haled, a writer and educator, asks, "Do you know what the hardest thing was for me to swallow? That we are two similar peoples." . . .

**"In the Land of Israel"** comes to no real end. Mr. Oz even undercuts his speech on humanism by following it with the observations of a "wise man" who tells the author that even his liberal, freewheeling (meaning heretical) views are part of God's plan for the Chosen People that Mr. Oz has ridiculed. But the sage's words only remind us that these arguments are unending. The concluding section of the book makes the same point; Mr. Oz, back home at his kibbutz, is upbraided by neighbors who read his manuscript. "Why did you suddenly decide to present our case with the rumblings of some fanatic here or some psychopath there? Aren't there any normal people left in this country?" They constitute another reminder of fluidity and continuity, which is Mr. Oz's theme. If Mr. Oz has enemies in his land, they are not just the Z's, but all the forces of adamancy and finality. In a sense, Mr. Oz refuses to end his own work, his final chapter being a list of reactions and rebuttals to the book itself, ending on the ambiguous, "So be it."

The problem all along, for Mr. Oz and those he has interviewed, is what sort of place Israel should be. For Jews the question may seem antilogical. Is there really a place, one place, for those who have been forced to wander so long that their identities have been bound to a condition of wandering,

and who now find their Diaspora confined to a single location? Is this a cause of their agitation, the turbulence in the bottle? The meaning of Mr. Oz's early novel, **"Elsewhere Perhaps"** (1966), is that only in places other than Israel do the normal laws of conduct obtain and the true Israel may always lie somewhere else. The people whose conversations are recounted in this book are also looking elsewhere, yet there is nowhere else to go. Americans will recognize the problem.

Perhaps for this reason the power of the voices in the book lies as much in things unspecified as in their rantings—in the tears, the street prophecies, the gnomic phrases, the figure of God whose name is invoked continually. Everyone agrees that "the land is God's," although there are differences of opinion on who are the preferred tenants. Still, since divinity hovers over them, these voices do not express only views, but prayers and imprecations. It is curious to find so much mystery tied to practical matters, but something spiritual and fundamental underlies this search for place, something Mr. Oz hears and wishes to express.

This is not a "fair" book, in the sense that it calls up equal numbers of bright and foolish peace-seekers and warmongers. It is not a debate, but a work in progress, and that is what Mr. Oz would have Israel be. His fellow kibbutzniks may complain that he exhibits only the freaks of the nation, the extremes, but the extremes are his main concern. . . . His final plea in this book is for patience, because in spite of everything, including their words which fly up against his, Mr. Oz believes in people. How else could he have written so stunning a book? (p. 47)

*Roger Rosenblatt, "From the Battlefield of Beliefs,"* in The New York Times Book Review, *November 6, 1983, pp. 1, 46-7.*

### GRACE SCHULMAN

When a writer's sensibility to political disorder becomes so intense as to threaten his esthetic concerns, he has several options: he may fall silent, or he may try to incorporate present human suffering into his fiction. Or, he may use a medium that calls for direct, urgent expression. Amos Oz, the Israeli novelist who creates, in heightened prose, superb fictional portraits and scenes, has turned to nonfiction to write a journalist's account of his troubled country, *In the Land of Israel.* [The book is a] report of the writer's journey through Israel in the fall of 1982, during the Israel-Lebanese War. . . .

His journey is dark, and he spares us nothing. Oz writes of widespread despair, presenting it against a background of two contrasting ideals. One is the Biblical ideal of purity and goodness; people frequently juxtapose lines from the Bible, often misinterpreted, with outbursts of contemporary opinion. The second ideal is that upon which the country was founded. Israel was established some 35 years ago not merely as a refuge for persecuted Jews, but as a nation that would set a world example for peace, for education, for the rights of minorities. Its founders, many of them intellectuals, were heroes. . . .

Amos Oz writes of a country in turmoil. He records flaming debates concerning figures such as Menachem Begin, then prime minister, and Shimon Peres, who heads the Labor Alignment, an alliance of the Israel Labor Party and the left-wing socialist Mapam, which was defeated in the 1977 election. In the Northwestern Jewish quarter of Jerusalem, Oz sees signs that read "Power to Begin, the gallows for Peres," "Death to Zionist Hitlerites,'' ''Chief Constable Komfort is a Nazi.'' In that place, Zionism—the original hope of Israel—has been rejected; instead, the people are dominated by fears of Hitler and hopes of the Messiah, both of which have produced a fierce, turbulent Judaism, dedicated to opposing Christianity and Islam. (p. 4)

Like a journey through the circles of Dante's Inferno, Oz's travels take him from despair to agony. In Tekoa, a community south of Bethlehem, he meets a diamond-processor named Menachem, who explains that his own attitude toward Arabs is not quite as extreme as that of his wife, who feels that Israel's enemies are eternal, and must be destroyed. Dr. Amiel Unger, a lecturer in political science, diminishes peace as being an American left-wing fancy. . . . (pp. 4, 14)

Probably the most devastating encounter is with a monstrous, self-styled ''Judeo-Nazi,'' who has given up any notion of morality and believes that Israel's salvation is to destroy, to be deadly and dangerous, to run wild. Hearing the man's vitriolic outburst, Oz wonders: ''Is it possible that Hitler not only killed the Jews but infected them with his poison?'' . . .

What is most compelling about this book is, I feel, less discursive and more in keeping with Oz's rare gifts as a storyteller. He writes with acuity of an Arab boy sweeping streets in Northwestern Jerusalem, of ''pious Jews in black garb, bearded, bespectacled, chattering in Yiddish, tumultuous, in a hurry, scented with the heavy aroma of Eastern European Ashkenazi cooking.'' He tells of an aging civil guardsman in sloppy uniform glaring at Arab workers repairing a school roof, suspecting them of carrying explosives. He writes of Danny, apprentice to Menachem, the diamond-processor, who has a passion for wheels that grind hard metals. Danny, a silent, intense young man who finds that hiking brings him closer to Israel, looks at the sunset, considers the empty landscape and remarks, in the context of Israel-Arab coexistence, ''There's plenty of room here.''

This book is not about Danny, though. Reading it, I have asked myself repeatedly why a writer who can create beauty of such magnitude chooses instead to write factually of a sordid, ugly reality. Oz answers this himself:

''For us, history is interwoven with biography. And not just from this morning. One can almost say that history *is* biography. Private life is virtually not private here. A woman might say, for example, 'Our oldest son was born while Joel was in the bunkers, during the War of Attrition.' Or, 'We moved into this apartment exactly one week before the Six-Day War.' Or, 'He came back from the States during Sadat's visit' . . . The genuine question is, What is the meaning of distancing oneself? Is it possible? And if it is possible—is it right?''

Unable to distance himself, Amos Oz confronts political realities and studies his land and his troubled people, hoping to find a new perspective. Despite his bleak findings, I sense that he still believes in the ideals of Israel and seeks redeeming voices of those who affirm the country's early goals. His aim is to arouse the populace to restore Israel's hopes for equality and peace.

Beyond that, his journey may be the way to an esthetic stance in which he can reconcile the conflicting demands of artistic concern and political turbulence. In one sense, the journey of Amos Oz has resulted in no new answers. In another sense, the journey itself is the answer. (p. 14)

*Grace Schulman, ''Israeli Visions of Israel,'' in* Book World—The Washington Post, *November 13, 1983, pp. 4, 14.*

## STEVEN G. KELLMAN

In his portraits of contemporary Israel, novelist Amos Oz makes no pretense of being systematic, representative, or objective. *In the Land of Israel* is a series of nine articles that originally appeared in *Davar,* an influential Labor Party newspaper. In each, Oz conveys the clamorous voices of his compatriots as they ponder Zionist dreams and realities. Oz's title refers not to the state but to the land of Israel, a biblical notion that is a focus for much of the discord he encounters. Should there be an independent Jewish state? If so, should it be held to a higher moral standard, or can it pursue its own ruthless interests like any other worldly power? In fictions like *My Michael* and *The Hill of Evil Counsel,* Oz has explored the crevices between public and private, fact and desire, and his journey through contemporary Israel dramatizes incompatible views of what it is and what it should be.

He begins in the Ge'ullah Quarter of Jerusalem, where he was born in 1939. Instead of the rich diversity he remembers from childhood, Oz now finds the neighborhood monopolized by ultra-Orthodox Jews for whom Hitler and the secular Zionist state are comparable demons. In Ofra, a settlement in the West Bank area that its Gush Emunim occupants call Samaria, Oz discovers similar zealotry, on behalf of Jewish expansionism into formerly Arab territories. In Bet Shemesh, a dispiriting new town, he listens to a crowd of resentful young Sephardim as they vent their bitterness toward a pre-Begin ''white'' establishment they contend exploited them. Near Zichron Ya'akov, 78-year-old Zvi Bachur laments the loss of pioneer idealism in a permissive, materialistic world. In Jerusalem, Arab Palestinian journalists and a Catholic priest explain their troubled senses of Israeli identity. In Ramallah, an Arab tells Oz that the situation for Arabs and Jews is ''like two people standing on a roof stuck tight together: if they don't want to fall off the roof together, they have to be careful.'' The image is as applicable to all the fractious voices—whatever the religion, ethnic origin, or political persuasion—that Oz assembles.

The most vivid chapter is the extended, strident monologue Oz attributes to a 50-year-old farmer he calls ''Z.'' Z bluntly hopes ''we've finished once and for all with that crap about the Jewish monopoly on morality.'' He is utterly scornful of the fastidiousness of assimilated Western Jews and declares his eagerness to perform whatever brutality is necessary to insure a powerful, distinctively Jewish state. Z's rhetorical performance recalls the brilliant yet deranged narrators in Dostoevsky or Camus. This section also typifies Oz's willingness to allow his forceful characters to speak for themselves, even when their ideas are antithetical to his most cherished beliefs. . . . *In the Land of Israel* is weakest when Oz . . . [follows] the frenzied tirade of an ideologue with an awkward, superfluous commentary of his own. (pp. 56-7)

Repelled by the jingoism and moral autism that have been poisoning Israeli life since the Six-Day War, he explicitly calls for toleration, patience, and respect for ''the absolute sanctity of the life and liberty of the individual.'' But Oz's vision of a pluralistic, creatively contentious society is most eloquently embodied in the very form of this book. (p. 57)

Steven G. Kellman, in a review of "In the Land of Israel," in The Village Voice, Vol. XXIX, No. 7, February 14, 1984, pp. 56-7.

## RUTH R. WISSE

The history of the state of Israel is (unfortunately) so dramatic that the great issues always threaten to obscure the subtleties of daily and individual life. Contemporary Israeli writers tend to resent this encroachment of the collective drama on private experience, and, in what may be deliberate defiance of their national fate, to concentrate on the ordinariness of ordinary men and women, on the personal scene.

This is particularly true of Amos Oz, one of Israel's finest writers of fiction and consistent demythologizers. In book after book, Oz has taken the great myths with which modern Israel is associated—the noble experiment of the kibbutz, the reclamation of the soil, the wars against the British and the Arabs, the phoenix-like rise of the Jewish spirit out of the ashes of the Holocaust—and shown us their underside: bruised, dazed, and straying characters who move in an atmosphere of almost unalleviated depression. Himself a member of a kibbutz and a soldier in Israel's citizen army, Oz in his fiction specializes in exposing the darker motives and disturbed dreams of those who must sustain these structures on which the country stands.

Now, in a sharp change of form, the latest book of Amos Oz to appear in English has entered vigorously into the public fray. (p. 68)

[In *In the Land of Israel,* some] of the voices are philosophical and calm; most, however, are pitched high with excitement, bitterness, anger. Though Oz faithfully presents the moods of the persons with whom he contends, he also remains firmly in control of the ideological terrain, guiding the reader's response to all that is placed before him.

Oz's mixture of travelogue and tract results in a book of odd contradiction. Artistically, he gives very fine expression to the views of those he meets, his antagonists in particular. . . . [The] differing points of view represented in *In the Land of Israel* demand from Oz, and by and large receive, that semblance of tolerance which, according to his own stated belief, is the wholly desirable condition of Israel's spiritual pluralism.

Yet Oz's purpose is anything but a celebration of spiritual pluralism, for he fears what is happening in his country, and has written this book to undercut the "opposition." In his running commentary he tells us how we should be reacting to all that we read; whenever his own views are threatened, he warns us against the very people he is interviewing, attempting to turn the testimony of his witnesses against them. The literary result is that when the artist triumphs, and the situations or characters are allowed to speak for themselves, Oz produces some of his most robust prose to date; whenever the ideologue intrudes, in the name of the "pluralistic" spirit, Oz reveals more than he intends about his own role in fomenting the current tensions in the land of Israel.

The central controversy, as Oz defines it, is over the nature of Zionism and the meaning of Jewish destiny. . . . Gush Emunim, the religious-nationalist "bloc of the faithful," is to him an especially dangerous element within Israel, since it purports to translate God's will into the political program of settling the territories that Israel occupied, or regained, in the war of 1967. Oz's sensitivity alerts him to the true appeal of Gush Emunim, with its genial and confident spokesmen who appear to have taken over from the early socialist pioneers their idealistic will to sacrifice, giving them the high ground in the moral debate. The danger, according to Oz, lies not so much in the group's political platform as in its spiritual strength, the very faith in the future that he and others like him often lack.

To counter the spokesmen of Gush Emunim, Oz enters "the argument on life and death" in his own person. In a multi-faceted speech that he gave at the settlement of Ofra and which is reproduced as a chapter in this book, he pleads, hectors, explains himself, but above all apocalyptically warns his auditors that by insisting on a Greater Israel, they are dragging him and his children into endless war. Oz, however, does not speak as a practical man; he never bothers to wonder how it is that the perpetual wars began long before Gush Emunim came into being, or to show how he proposes to stop them, given that the opposition to Israel's existence is not Jewish but Arab.

The problem grows thornier when Oz moves from Ofra to the offices of the daily paper, the *Arab Dawn,* in East Jerusalem. Here too Oz asks probing questions, but instead of warning his hosts about the consequences of their antagonism, as he did with the Jewish settlers of Ofra, he tips the rhetorical balance in their favor. He . . . works hard to establish a homey parallel between the Palestinian Arabs and the Jews, "two opposing peoples . . . as similar as brothers." Operating from this premise of Arab brotherliness—itself a premise of his own "humanist" outlook—Oz recites a litany to himself throughout the interview. . . . "Is it right to compare? Is it possible not to?" It is almost as if, by the force of his plaintive desire, he could will an Arab-Jewish symmetry into being.

Unfortunately, Oz's Arab interlocutors turn out to be as uncooperative in this literary attempt to maneuver them into a reciprocal framework as the Arabs in general have so far proved in politics. In the text of the interview the editors of the *Arab Dawn* are recorded as uttering relatively "moderate" sentiments, but a note at the end of the book informs us that the staff later denied many of the views the author attributes to them and accused him, "an Israeli writer who stands to the Right of Center"(!), of having set them up in a clever trap. Oz attacks the religious nationalists of Gush Emunim for presuming to interpret God's will; but if his own faith depends on thus systematically misinterpreting the Arabs' will, it can hardly be said to offer a better alternative. (pp. 68, 70)

In this book Oz reveals remarkable skills as a portraitist. When the furies are unleashed, and the author frees his subjects from the constraint of his own disapproval, the cloud of sadness that burdens much of Oz's fiction finally lifts, and the prose turns electric. Paradoxically, this study of a bitterly divided nation is the most vivid and in some ways the brightest of all his books.

Yet Oz's artistry seems to work at odds with his convictions. He cannot muster the same verve to describe what he finds admirable in Israel as he does when it comes to naming all that he dislikes and fears. He draws closest to satisfaction in writing about Ashdod, the Mediterranean port which, "not pretending to be Paris or Zurich, or aspiring to be Jerusalem," embodies the author's social ideal. (p. 70)

The prominence of negatives in [the description] is not merely a grammatical feature, it is a key to what attracts Oz to Ashdod: the absence of compelling history and ideological overlay, the very things that Israel has to the bursting point. One can sympathize with this ideal of plainness, with the secularist's need to find his own version of the Sabbath spirit in the weekday, but these pleasant generalities do not succeed in capturing our imagination as readers, as evidently they fail to capture the writer's. If we look for the center of energy and conviction in Oz's book, we simply do not find it where he would like it to be. (p. 71)

*Ruth R. Wisse, "Matters of Life & Death," in Commentary, Vol. 77, No. 4, April, 1984, pp. 68, 70-1.*

## KATHLEEN CHRISTISON

[*In the Land of Israel*] takes the reader on a non-fiction tour of Jerusalem's Orthodox quarters, Sephardic development towns, and the ultra-nationalist Jewish settlements on the West Bank. It is a sobering experience.

We do not find here the kinds of tales that Leon Uris's *Exodus*, for example, accustomed us to, of heroic young sabras, pioneering kibbutzniks, Holocaust survivors reborn in the struggle for Jewish independence, a people for whom morality and humanitarianism are instinctive. Perhaps—at least we may hope—these images are still the norm in Israel. But they are not the images Oz has projected.

Instead, we walk with him through the ultra-Orthodox neighborhoods of Jerusalem, where the pious await the Messiah and scrawl slogans against their "Hitlerite" mayor, Teddy Kollek, and where "ancient hatreds simmer and bubble." . . . We listen with Oz as North African Jews in a poor Judaean development town spew forth their bitterness against the Ashkenazim of establishment Israel; as militant West Bank settlers talk of the need to teach the Arabs who's boss on the West Bank. . . .

Oz's interlocutors are not all angry radicals. There is the shy young settler who does not have any facile answers but who knows what not to do with the Arabs: "not to kill them, not to throw them out, not to oppress them." And there is the kibbutznik who chides Oz for failing to interview "normal" Israelis who don't want to exterminate Arabs or "drag the Messiah in by his beard." There is also, throughout the book, that peculiar brand of Jewish warmth and friendliness. . . .

One suspects from time to time, notwithstanding the friendliness and the occasional moderate response, that Oz has stacked the deck a bit in his selection of interviewees. His Arabs breathe no fire and would live in peace with Israel. His Israelis are the uncompromising firebrands. But Oz does not pretend that the people he introduces us to are a representative sampling of Israelis. And he does not pretend to objectivity; he is openly pressing a point of view. . . .

Oz seldom intrudes upon the stories he presents; for the most part, they speak clearly enough for themselves. He does, however, in response to prodding from a group of West Bank settlers, devote one lengthy section to rebutting their views, and the theme of the book, if it was possible to miss it before, becomes unmistakable here. In a lucid, occasionally impassioned declamation, Oz states his deep concern that Israelis, even among themselves, can no longer differentiate between controversy and hatred, between argument and abusiveness: In their attitude toward the outside world, they have developed a hostile defensiveness that, like a self-fulfilling prophecy, will eventually assure Israel's isolation. (p. 52)

*Kathleen Christison, "A Question of Tolerance," in National Review, Vol. XXXVI, No. 7, April 20, 1984, pp. 52-3.*

# Jayne Anne Phillips
## 1952-

**American short story writer and novelist.**

**Phillips received nearly unanimous critical acclaim for her first major publication, a book of short fiction entitled *Black Tickets* (1979). Two earlier collections had been published by small presses in limited editions: *Sweethearts* (1976) and *Counting* (1978). Critics especially appreciated the longer stories in *Black Tickets*, many of which concern family relationships. In a laudatory essay, novelist John Irving commented that Phillips "seems at her deepest and broadest when she sustains a narrative, manipulates a plot, develops characters through more than one phase of their life or their behavior." However, more than half of the pieces in *Black Tickets* are, like prose poetry, very short and dense with imagery. Peopled with drug addicts, whores, madmen, and murderers, these short pieces often are excursions into the sordid side of life. Critics compared them to exercises one might do for a creative writing class and felt that they weakened *Black Tickets*. Even so, critical consensus was that *Black Tickets* marked the debut of an exceptionally talented writer.**

**In her first novel, *Machine Dreams* (1984), Phillips develops the strengths which critics discovered in *Black Tickets*. Anne Tyler noted that in contrast to *Black Tickets*, where shocks derive from either the element of horror or Phillips's brilliant prose style, in *Machine Dreams* the "shocks arise from small, ordinary moments, patiently developed, that suddenly burst out with far more meaning than we had expected." *Machine Dreams* is a family saga that spans the period from World War II through the Vietnam War. Thematic concerns of the novel include the changes wrought on a family by time and by the events of those years. *Machine Dreams* is set in small-town West Virginia, where Phillips grew up and where many of the stories in *Black Tickets* also take place. Phillips has acknowledged the influence of such Southern writers as Flannery O'Connor, Eudora Welty, and Katherine Anne Porter, among others.**

**(See also *CLC*, Vol. 15; *Contemporary Authors*, Vol. 101; and *Dictionary of Literary Biography Yearbook: 1980*.)**

© Jerry Bauer

### JUDITH GIES

Any writer whose first book can wring hosannas from both Nadine Gordimer and John Irving [see *CLC*, Vol. 15] is remarkably brave to produce a second. She is especially courageous to abandon the form of the short story over which she has demonstrated near-perfect mastery to tackle a new one: the unruly sprawl of the family saga. The father, from **"1934"** [one of the stories in *Black Tickets*], now gone broke and mad, reappears in the novel, *Machine Dreams*. It begins with the mother Jean remembering her own childhood and the early years of her marriage, and ends with the daughter Danner, 22 years old toward the end of the Vietnam war, reflecting on the erosions of time on her family and on her own psyche. . . .

At its best, the episodes add up to a thoughtful, rather sorrowful exploration of family ties and suggest the sense of bereavement that is often the price of independence. But too often, the

writing promises to lift off—we catch our breaths and wait for the rush of astonishment—only to flatten out at the last minute. Part of the problem may be what appears to be an odd kind of courtesy. There is a feeling that the tenderness toward people she knows outweighs objectivity, and as a result, the novel lacks the true, frightening clarity of the stories. . . . It's too bad. *Machine Dreams* is disappointing largely because we know what the author is capable of. (p. 34)

*Judith Gies, in a review of "Machine Dreams," in Ms., Vol. XII, No. 12, June, 1984, pp. 33-4.*

### MICHIKO KAKUTANI

[In **"Black Tickets"**] Jayne Anne Phillips stepped out of the ranks of her generation as one of its most gifted writers. Her quick, piercing tales of love and loss demonstrated a keen love of language, and a rare talent for illuminating the secret core of ordinary lives with clearsighted unsentimentality. Her first novel, **"Machine Dreams,"** not only ratifies that earlier accomplishment, but also establishes Miss Phillips as a novelist of the first order. The book will doubtless come to be seen as both a remarkable novelistic debut and an enduring literary achievement.

Though sections of "**Machine Dreams**" easily lift out and function as short stories, they have been stitched together seamlessly into a beautifully patterned novel that possesses the density of a highly ambitious work of art—a novel that succeeds in examining the intersection of public and private experience in America during the last four decades, without ever becoming didactic.

Unlike many first novels, "**Machine Dreams**" is not simply a semi-autobiographical account of coming of age, or a conventional study of character. Rather, its subject is history and the passage of time—as mirrored in the fortunes of the Hampson family, whose own dissolution reflects the dislocations suffered by this country in the wake of the 1960's and Vietnam.

Everywhere in this book there are signs that the old certainties, which Miss Phillips's characters long for, have vanished or drifted out of reach. Looking for love they end up in dissonant marriages and improvised relationships; wanting safety, they settle for the consolation of familiar habits. They look out at the landscape of West Virginia, where they grew up, and see strip mines and developments where once there were farms and trees; and the words "new" and "then" haunt their nightmares and their dreams. They even discover that family—the mystical blood bond shared by mothers and daughters, fathers and sons, brothers and sisters—is not for keeps, that it, too, is susceptible to time and death. Like the machines that Mitch Hampson once worked on, . . . their lives slowly evolve "further and further into jumbled mismatched puzzles."

Told from the point-of-view of various characters, the story of the Hampsons begins during the Depression, with the intertwining lives of Jean and Mitch; and already the sense of loss that will echo through this book is very much in evidence. Having lost her father to madness and her mother to cancer, Jean is scared of being alone, and she marries Mitch following a hasty three-week courtship. . . .

Two children, Danner and Billy, are soon born to the Hampsons, but by then their marriage has already become a sort of nonaggression treaty. . . .

The childhood of Danner and her brother Billy is drawn by Miss Phillips with the sort of precision that conjures instantly, for readers, private memories of their own youth. . . . [These] scenes of ordinary life possess the sweet-bitter nostalgia of "American Graffiti" translated to paper, and their afterimage glows indelibly in the reader's mind.

It is a world and a time—and an innocence—that will be irrevocably destroyed. . . .

Though Miss Phillips's rendition of Billy's experience in Vietnam captures perfectly the sound and feeling of that most anomalous of wars, it is her portrayal of the intimate consequences of that conflict on the Hampsons—and the collision with history that this country would suffer during those disordered years—which in the end, distinguishes this astonishing novel.

*Michiko Kakutani, in a review of "Machine Dreams,"*
*in* The New York Times, *June 12, 1984, p. C17.*

## JONATHAN YARDLEY

*Machine Dreams* is a first novel, but it scarcely seems one; in 1979 Jayne Anne Phillips accumulated so substantial a reputation and following with her collection of short stories, *Black Tickets,* that this novel seems less an arrival than the logical next step in a career already well under way. Phillips . . . has

achieved a certain early distinction because she is a literary writer who does not write about literary people or settings. In this novel as in many of the short stories, her subjects are ordinary West Virginia people who are attempting, and for the most part failing, to deal with forces and events that are beyond their control. It is an elegaic, wistful, rueful book under which runs a vein of political commentary; if these first qualities are its great strengths, this last is its most considerable weakness. . . .

Evidently the coming apart of the Hampsons is meant to be a metaphor for the coming apart of America. The parents' loving recollections of their own youthful years contrast starkly with the troubled times through which their children pass. . . .

The time when Jean and Mitch were young is portrayed as hard, to be sure, but also as characterized by community, stability and even optimism. You could tell the good guys from the bad ones in the war Mitch fought, and when you came home at the end it was to a nation in which the glittering new postwar automobiles symbolized the nation's high hopes; the machines of destruction that the men operated in the war were replaced by the machines of prosperity and "expectation," and anything seemed possible.

Possible, but not probable. *Machine Dreams* is a story of possibility gradually turning into disappointment and disillusionment. . . .

*Machine Dreams* is a heavily programmatic novel in which the various characters and their histories are meant to personify distinct aspects of 20th-century American experience. As is so often the case with programmatic fiction, ultimately the program overwhelms the people. Phillips has her ducks so neatly in a row that it is clear almost from the outset what is going to happen to whom, and when, and where, with the consequence that the novel loses much of the mystery with which Phillips means to imbue it. Further, too much of what Phillips says has acquired by now the properties of cliché: the longing for a simpler and more rooted past, the splintering of America, the traumatic effects of Vietnam—the extreme familiarity of these themes makes them seem trivial even though they are not, and the anger with which Phillips writes about Vietnam in the book's concluding pages merely shrinks those pages from fiction into political commentary.

But Phillips also has strengths as a writer, and they are abundantly evident in *Machine Dreams.* Though her prose has a tendency to become overly stylized and self-conscious, at its best it displays a fine sense of nuance; Phillips is especially skillful at giving each of the four principal characters a distinct and believable voice. With the exception of Danner, who somehow never quite comes to life, these characters are as distinct as their voices, in particular several of the women of various ages who observe and in some cases influence the fate of the Hampsons. Above all, Phillips manages to convey her love for these people and to persuade the reader to share it. Ordinary people can be extraordinary, she is saying, and what happens to them is terribly important. She is right, and the best parts of *Machine Dreams* do honor to them.

*Jonathan Yardley, "Jayne Anne Phillips: West Virginia Breakdown," in* Book World—The Washington Post, *June 24, 1984, p. 3.*

## ANNE TYLER

"Black Tickets" posed a dilemma: Was it so striking because it was so horrifying, or because it was so brilliantly written?

With "**Machine Dreams,**" we don't have to ask. Its shocks arise from small, ordinary moments, patiently developed, that suddenly burst out with far more meaning than we had expected. And each of these moments owes its impact to an assured and gifted writer. . . .

The novel takes shape as a series of voices, each family member speaking in turn. In the first chapter, Jean, the mother, talks directly to her daughter, Danner, who is probably the most important person remaining in her life. . . . Her tone is dreamy, intimate—the tone a real-life mother adopts when offering up her past to her children. . . .

The voice in the second chapter belongs to her husband. . . . Here the tone changes; it's convincingly gruff and summary, concerned with the technicalities of things—the way his people made their livings, the specifications of farms and buildings. . . .

Mitch was away at war between 1942 and 1945—long before his marriage. His letters home, which are collected in the third chapter, mark the book's turning point. "We do a lot of work here but some play," he writes his cousin Katie, but to a male friend he sends a grim account of burying Japanese corpses. . . .

It's not just war that is the great divider here, but knowledge of war as well. The men live with an awareness that the women never guess at. Mitch comes home troubled by "machine dreams," nightmares about bulldozing those decaying corpses, but he doesn't mention them to the women in his life. . . .

Danner finds a boyfriend, goes to college. Billy—a little more difficult—takes up with a "fast" local girl and begins a less successful college career of his own. And Jean and Mitch divorce, having been at odds for years. But everything that happens continues to be colored by the constant, unspoken possibility of war. We know that because of Mitch's nightmares and Billy's daydreams. . . . There's no surprise when Billy begins his inevitable drift toward Vietnam—first dropping out of college, then philosophically accepting the results of the draft lottery.

So Billy has his own chapter of letters home. "Arrived in good shape," he writes his mother. "Don't worry, I will stay light on my feet." But to Danner he describes what it's like to be fired upon by an invisible enemy. "Listen," he tells her, "I write Dad part of this and I don't write it to Mom at all." And, "I only tell you this because I know you will keep it to yourself." It's an interesting shift. At long last, women are let in on the secret. The final machine dream is Danner's own. In a book where the sexes are so deeply and painfully separated, that seems significant.

Two years after Billy is reported missing, Danner recalls their shared past in a quiet, reflective voice. She describes the emptiness in her family now that he's gone and her sense of helplessness and then—not so quietly, and perhaps less effectively—her spell of drinking too much and sleeping with too many veterans and her anger at the Government's apparent lack of interest in finding out what really became of Billy.

The story slows at a few points; at times the detailed, meticulous writing fails to achieve any sort of lift-off. But in the end, it amounts to a patchwork quilt of American voices. "A little girl with a crooked part looks like no one loves her," a mother tells her daughter, and "Better to winterize your car before snow, here is a check," a father writes his son—the unexceptional, soothing noises of everyday life.

Anne Tyler, "The Wounds of War," *in* The New York Times Book Review, *July 1, 1984, p. 3.*

**MICHAEL GORRA**

The danger with Jayne Anne Phillips's [*Machine Dreams*] is that in reading it one might mistake the will for the deed. Her intentions are both admirable and ambitious: to portray the collective life of the American mid-century through the private history of one representative middle-class family from West Virginia. . . .

Yet if Phillips's intentions are admirable, her attempt to realize them seems to me fundamentally misconceived. Most of the stories in her impressive collection *Black Tickets* (1979) were dramatic monologues, ventriloquist acts in which plot was far less important than a character's voice. In *Machine Dreams,* she gives Mitch, Jean, and Danner similar opportunities to perform themselves, and includes sections of both Mitch's and Billy's letters home during their army service as well; she interweaves this first-person material with a straightforward, third-person family chronicle. The main purpose of such split narratives is usually to create irony: one character's knowledge begins where another's ends, and by juxtaposing their perceptions a writer gives us more information about the characters than any one of them can ever know. In this novel, however, Phillips shies away from both the ironic implications of her chosen form, and what in *Black Tickets* was her own best gift, the ability to create quirkily individual voices for her characters. Jean's voice, for example, isn't interesting but bland. . . .

Laundry lists make dull reading, however "true" to life they may be. Jean's second chapter of "Reminiscences to a Daughter," . . . describes the beginning of the end of her marriage, yet provides no special knowledge that Phillips could only convey through Jean's voice, and is in no way complicated by either another character's or the author's own voice. Nothing in that chapter, that is, demands that it be told in the first person. It serves no dramatic purpose within the novel, and I can't help but suspect that Phillips has employed it only to provide an example of what an American mother of Jean's generation sounds like.

I suspect that Phillips's interest in ventriloquism got the better of her: that in the attempt to create typical figures she tried to give each character's voice the autonomy it would have had as a short story in its own right, and so denied herself the omniscience and the irony that her form requires. The consequence of that autonomy is, paradoxically, to rob her characters of the individuality that could make one care about them. Yet quirky voices inevitably conflict with and undermine each other. Her characters are emblematic of their period, but only emblematic, symbols without substance; hollow gourds from which the sustaining meat of characterization has dried and rotted away, leaving the seeds behind to rattle around inside. By "seeds" I mean the incidents and objects Phillips uses in her attempt to persuade one that her characters' lives are representative ones: sparklers on the Fourth of July, Pontiacs, breakfast foods, the parade for the town Strawberry Festival, Saturday matinees. . . . These, of course, are some of the conventional fixtures of the American novel, so much so that at times *Machine Dreams* becomes the novel as kitchen sink, in which what appears to count are the sheer number of dirty dishes Phillips can cram into it. . . .

Phillips doesn't go beyond the emblematic aspect of her characters' experiences. Her conventions and stock situations become merely clichés. It is impossible, then, to worry and wonder about what happens to Billy; impossible as well for Phillips to provide the rich imaginative synthesis of her period to which this novel aspires.

*Michael Gorra, in a review of "Machine Dreams," in* Boston Review, *Vol. IX, No. 4, August, 1984, p. 27.*

## ROBERT PHILLIPS

*Machine Dreams* is whole-cloth—an accomplished novel which is ambitious and original.

The "machine dreams" of the title ostensibly are nightmares which Mitch Hampson has after serving in the second world war. He dreams of bulldozing decaying corpses of the enemy, which he in fact had to do. But machines play important roles throughout the novel. . . . Even the Mobil flying red horse is a symbol of power, escape—as much a part of the American dream as the belief that everyone should own a home and car. The novel is "about" the American dream and how two wars destroyed it.

The first is World War II. Mitch returns from it a changed man. . . .

[The letters Mitch and his son Billy write from their wars] are some of the novel's best writing. Ms. Phillips describes basic training and combat as if she'd been there. The novel's other sections shift points of view between family members. . . . From Faulkner's *As I Lay Dying* to Shirley Ann Grau's *The Condor Passes,* it is a time-honored format for the family chronicle. With a few exceptions, Ms. Phillips handles her material skillfully. (pp. 567-68)

While one has difficulty caring much about Mitch and Jean, there is no questioning the power of the second half. The special bond of affection between Billy and Danner is the novel's most convincing and touching theme. When Billy is lost in action, the impact upon Danner is predictable but moving. She begins to think of the past only in terms of what Billy saw and knew. She begins to have dreams of Billy as he was as a young kid, before he got caught up in the machinations of men and war.

Not a perfect novel, then, but an affecting one, *Machine Dreams* is written in poetic, lyrical language—full of pastoral and precise images. One reads it knowing it is a work carefully built, sentence for sentence, page for page. With her second book Jayne Anne Phillips has earned the acclaim critics were so eager to give her the first time around. (p. 568)

*Robert Phillips, "Recurring Battle Scars," in* Commonweal, *Vol. CXI, No. 18, October 19, 1984, pp. 567-68.*

## HERMIONE LEE

Jayne Anne Phillips's stunning first novel, *Machine Dreams,* starts in the 1940s and ends in the 1970s. Before that, like something distantly imagined, there was a boy growing up on a beautiful Virginian farm. But only a few pages into the novel, the farm has been obliterated by the mines, the boy has got through the Depression and gone to fight in the American wars,

and when as a grown man he revisits the lost home, he feels as if 'I'd been asleep a long time and had wakened up in the wrong place, a hundred miles from where I lay down.'

Her reference to that veteran American myth of disorientation and dispossession, Rip Van Winkle, sets up her themes: the habitual made alien, mundane domestic histories mythologised through loss and memory, ordinary people estranged from their own country. The family story is painful, but deliberately not outlandish. . . . The story sounds predictable, but that's necessary, if we're to feel the strangeness of ordinary America.

The usual weakness of such political epics (small individuals crushed by world forces—see Dos Passos or Upton Sinclair) is that one family has to stand for too much. But Ms. Phillips avoids a crushing 'epic' feel by the delicacy and opulence of her writing, and the subtlety of her structure—a construct of self-contained narratives, linked yet separate. . . . A mesh is made between private complexities and huge, arbitrary world events, so that the angry daughter's final dilemma ('If I hated my government, shouldn't I go and live in some other country? . . . But my parents are my country.') rests firmly on the novel's weight and depth.

*Hermione Lee, "Long Lost America," in* The Observer, *October 28, 1984, p. 25.**

## GILLIAN GREENWOOD

In 1979, Jayne Anne Phillips . . . produced a collection of short stories, *Black Tickets*. The stories were highly praised for their simplicity, range and extreme sensual power. They well deserved the acclaim they received, but after reading Miss Phillips's first novel, *Machine Dreams,* some of those stories look like sketches for the substantial, eloquent work which has followed.

*Machine Dreams* is a very sad book. . . . It evokes, from different perspectives, a picture of a dissolving community, and is shot through with a kind of silent resentment at unfulfilled expectations. Such expectations were not high to begin with, or at least not in terms of materialism or political idealism. Perhaps, Jayne Anne Phillips seems to be saying, it is too much to expect to hold on to those you love. And you can rail against the State for sending your son or brother to Vietnam, and say it's their fault, but your teenage sweetheart can drop dead of a heart attack on the bathroom floor or your mother die of cancer. . . .

There is a strong sense of foreboding throughout the book. Fears, sometimes expressed in dreams, seem to come to nothing for the most part. Life's tragedies are accepted when they happen, until the final blow. This isn't an American idyll shattered, nor is there any melodrama to speak of. But it isn't quiet realism either. It is an extraordinary piece of writing which examines a recent history, recording its myths and falsehoods. . . .

The machines are only one of many themes running through the novel. No image is wasted but returns to haunt or be fulfilled. Small, unlaboured incidents occur naturally in the narrative which only later take on a greater significance. The family dog goes missing and is never found. Years later Billy finds a dog's skeleton in a ditch. He cannot be sure it is his dog, but he tells no one. It is not until we know his fate that this image comes into full play, part of a massive reverberation which is set up.

The final section of the book is concerned with Danner and her brother Billy. As the children of sad divorced parents, their bond is unusually strong. . . . Danner sees herself as her brother's protector, though he emerges as a stronger, or at any rate more accepting personality than his sister. When, at the end, she is finally left alone, she dreams of him:

> But in the dreams, Billy isn't desperate. He's just himself. I'm the one who is afraid, who knows something terrible might happen, has happened, will happen. I'm the one who can't stop it happening.

Her impotence is a cry which runs through the novel. Whatever constructions we build to conceal our isolation, nothing and no-one can stop 'it' happening.

*Gillian Greenwood, "How It Happens," in* The Spectator, *Vol. 253, No. 8156, November 3, 1984, p. 28.*

# Stanley (Ross) Plumly
## 1939-

American poet, critic, and editor.

Plumly is respected for finely crafted narrative poems in which he examines the effects of people and events on his personal life. Plumly's poems capture the sensations he felt at the moment of experience. His parents, particularly his father, are shown to be pervasive influences in his life. Although his poetry is personal and subjective, Plumly avoids self-pity and sentimentalism. Critics find much to praise in his sensitive yet disciplined verse.

In his first volume, *In the Outer Dark* (1970), Plumly uses darkness as a metaphor for the subconscious and the external world. Both worlds are presented as essentially unfathomable, but by recreating his experiences, particularly those centering on his father, who suffered from alcoholism, Plumly finds brief moments of illumination and insight. Plumly's second volume, *Giraffe* (1973), is divided into three sections represented by a giraffe, a heron, and a horse. Plumly focuses on the imagination and the poetic process in the first part, the external world and personal relationships in the middle portion, and his father's life and death in the concluding section.

With *Out-of-the-Body Travel* (1977) some critics recognized Plumly as an accomplished poet. In this volume he uses memory and dreams to explore the subconscious. His father once again appears as a dominant force. *Summer Celestial* (1983) brought Plumly acclaim as a poet of sustained artistic achievement. While he continues to emphasize memory and personal history in this volume, he is also commended for the pastoral quality of his lyrics. Several critics noted the prominence of Plumly's mother in this book, suggesting that her quiet dignity inspired spiritual reunification between the poet and his past.

(See also *Contemporary Authors*, Vols. 108, 110 and *Dictionary of Literary Biography*, Vol. 5.)

© *Thomas Victor 1984*

## S. G. RADHUBER

[*In the Outer Dark* is] a successful and promising first book of poems. . . . Mr. Plumly takes . . . chances with the language and usually can create . . . suddenly exciting lines and images. (p. 86)

One of the most exciting qualities of the book is that the poems attempt to capture sensation, not to capture it, but perhaps to re-create it, in, say, the way e.e. cummings meant his poems to "explode." . . . (p. 87)

It is not surprising that Mr. Plumly has written a poem about Seurat and his pointillist technique. . . , since Seurat's technique at its best also recreates a scene so that the viewer is swept in to it in a dazzling way.

To go further with this, the sense which operates most richly in the book is the sense of touch, and the importance of this sense is stated explicitly in a poem called **"Now the Sidewise Easing into Night,"** which however much it owes to Roethke is a good poem uniquely Mr. Plumly's. In the poem, the poet gropes his way hands out before him through the dark, and "Touch by touch I measure where I am." (pp. 87-8)

Knowing by feel is a particularly American way of knowing, and Mr. Plumly's book, in that sense, reminds me of Hart Crane, Hemingway, and Wallace Stevens.

In one or two poems the attempt to recreate experience refines itself beyond any real experience and the poems fail, for me anyway. One such poem is **"Voices."** . . . The last poem in the book, **"Killing the Whale,"** unfortunately brings to mind Galway Kinnell's fantastic poem "The Bear," against which **"Killing the Whale"** falls short some distance. But disappointments are few in this most engaging book. (p. 88)

S. G. Radhuber, "Four First Books of Poetry," in Northwest Review, *Vol. 11, No. 2, Spring, 1971, pp. 84-91.*

## ANTHONY PICCIONE

[*In the Outer Dark*] is a process of creative loneliness, as unrelenting as, if not more so than, the art of those it celebrates and advances from: Rimbaud, Rilke, Stevens, Robert Bly and William Stafford. There is no lonely dejection here; there are fifty-three pages of an often exceptional poetry leading to the awareness that, ultimately, we are each alone "in the outer darkness" of our separate existences.

Mr. Plumly's perception, and now the receptive reader's, is a blade of near-light knifing from birth to death through the darkness of the physical world which exists unexperienced and dark up until the split instant of experience, at which time that particular part of "reality" is consummated and returned to darkness (inner transformation via stored perception not being focused upon). The universe—objective external and subjective internal—is thus infinitely a darkness. There is one light, then, 1/100 of a second thick on the pinpoint of the immediate fore-front of perception doomed to exist in the past tense forever: a solitary deep-sea creature's light moving through an ocean of black.

It is within this framework—this way of vision—that the poem becomes an arrival at deep perception, and we must assume once and for all that the surface particulars (snowstorms in Ohio, dust in grass, silences in snowy fields, Mid-Western space, earth, rain, sun, et al.) are vehicles of departure for perceptual and conceptual experience recreated through the printed page. The title poem is a rather strong blend of state-ment and image embodying the poet's vision.... In a series of rapid transformations, the poem ... reaches beyond the French Symbolist *voyage* to a point where "the body of the boat in the cold blood/of time [is] moving toward one center," to the feeling of progressive absence.... It is in this last notion that creative isolation occurs in a strange sense of potential; the perception is engaged in the process of constant arrival at the center of self and experience which culminates and fades before the next new consciousness. (p. 406)

"**Study in Kore**" is a poem which embodies Plumly's external/internal notion of experience, expressed through a type of "there, not-there" image. From the moment of precise perception, the attempt to conceptualize the experience causes its destruction, leaving the poet between knowing and not knowing.... (p. 407)

In "**The Feel of a Face**" (and elsewhere), Mr. Plumly estab-lishes that eyes are the medium separating the external world from the inner consciousnesses. We are especially isolated by coded language, the rational reluctance of man to give of his inner self to another.... In this new perception of a universal situation, "the flesh" of the face will "dough up with lies." The poem succeeds in transforming reality layer by layer, end-ing in a slowly diminishing image....

"**Inside the Drop of Rain**" is a process poem composed of transformational images, each perception giving way to, being transformed anew by, the next image. The entire poem is the process and logic of perception. (p. 408)

Plumly is at his best in the image poem. His is a precise blend of ordinary language and bright new image perceptions, couched in a low-keyed voice that speaks to us all. (p. 409)

Often, the very particular voice and image create a familiar but strangely new perception.... Commonplace language also offers Mr. Plumly an entry into the near-grotesque. In "**From Athens County, Ohio**," we learn that

> Three counties over
> Great-aunt Ora
> is being eaten inside
> out by cancer.

The poet's vision of the Quaker "inner-light" burning "within a ribcage, / behind a breastbone" creates an acutely negative sense of distortion, where religous abstraction and anatomical particular meet in a kind of whimsical horror. It is from this point that the poem's intensity grows:

> Ora is transient Quaker.
> She breathes intentionally.
> And her breath reeks of shadows wound
> and winding within her body's baggage.

As in other poetries of this genre, the low-key voice delivered in a conversational language risks much. Plumly occasionally misses.... In all, though, [those] lines are overshadowed by a fresh strong vision, a poetry well and carefully aware of traditional form and its potential within the organic nature of poetry. We should be moved to watch for more of Stanley Plumly. (pp. 409-10)

> *Anthony Piccione, in a review of "In the Outer Dark,"
> in* The Southern Humanities Review, *Vol. VI, No.
> 4, Fall, 1972, pp. 406-10.*

## JOHN T. IRWIN

I saw many of the poems in Stanley Plumly's first volume *In the Outer Dark* when they originally appeared in magazines, and their minimal style did not impress me. Yet I find the volume, in which that syle is thematic, very impressive indeed. Plumly concentrates on the fundamentals of perception—the way light makes and darkness unmakes the world, the way man's round eye imposes order by the framing circle, and the way this structure is embodied in the circular still movement of the work of art. Circularity is perhaps the most important motif in the book. (p. 724)

The long-standing connection between circularity and *ek-phrasis* explains a series of poems that treats the ordering vision of painters. An example is "**For Seurat, 1859-1891.**" ... In a sense, Seurat's pointillism is painting about painting; it is an art which takes perceptual structure as its subject and as such it is an analogue of the kind of poetry that Plumly writes. Indeed, the structure of the whole volume is a series of linked analogies.... The order we find in the world is the order we put there in a circular, knowing process—one half projection, the other half introjection. Thus Plumly, in a poem like "**Ar-riving at the Point of Departure**," can suggest that the reader's movement through the volume is a circular journey toward self-consciousness of perceptual structure (introjection), and at the same time he can make that journey an analogue both of the circular still movement of the poem (the projection of that structure) and of the dramatic speaker's cyclic history, his progressive identification through the course of the volume with his dead father, an identification which ends with the speaker's return to the circle of the womb in death. This is, of course, a secular initiation rite—at once illusory death and the death of illusion. (pp. 725-26)

> *John T. Irwin, "A Nest of Tuneful Persons," in* The
> Southern Review, *n.s. Vol. IX, No. 3, July, 1973,
> pp. 720-35.**

## JAMES MARTIN

With [Plumly's] second book, *Giraffe,* we are offered a thinner, more esoteric collection [than *In the Outer Dark*]. The poems are divided into three sections entitled, "Giraffe", "Heron", and "Horse". The relationship of the bird and the animals to one another and to the poems in each section remains to be seen. While several of the poems stand well on their own, they seem to struggle against this division and placement within the organization of the book. Some of the pieces do stand on their own, and offer a more natural subtlety of statement than was presented *In the Outer Dark.* A poem like *Karate* appears all of a piece, well-conceived, contrasting raw energy with the powers of control which only experience and self-discipline can teach. . . . (p. 103)

The poems which deal with more common interactions of people and events: sleep and dreams, marriage, love-making, are those which falter. Mr. Plumly seems narrowly to avoid meeting these events head-on, and one is left with a fragment of experience. In . . . sections [of] the poems *Under Cows* and *Counting Coup,* he seems to mistrust his own voice; and we are never sure of what is happening. . . . (p. 104)

Some of the events in these poems contain true mystery—the love and wonderment of dreaming of his father on a remembered fishing trip; waking before one's lover and watching her in sleep—but in other poems the mystery seems constructed, the emotion inserted. It is a subtle mechanism; by bringing too much to a poem its true content and variety are often obscured. In the "making" of a work there is the danger of its extinction. Though some of these poems, in parts and places, lose themselves in artfulness, the best pieces do survive the book's organization and fragmentation, as they would have no matter what the arrangement. The poem *Drunk* presents a fine evocation of love for a father and has a clear, graceful closing. . . . One hopes for more of this control and this feeling in Mr. Plumly's future work. (p. 105)

James Martin, "Questions of Style," in Poetry, Vol. CXXVI, No. 2, May, 1975, pp. 103-15.*

## CLARA CLAIBORNE PARK

[In *Out-of-the-Body Travel* Plumly] plays no games, and he's anything but flashy. . . . [He] writes of the dead and the dreams which bring them back. . . . These are experiences which grope deep; they are widely sharable, and we cannot doubt Plumly's will to share them in these serious, touching poems, their subjects as immediate, as directly apprehensible as Hardy's—people working too hard, dying too soon, pain and ill luck that can be honored but not made up for. . . . How can we not respond to such genuine concerns?

Yet the poems stop short of making their personal urgencies our own. They are not, I think, well served by the obligatory indirection of their presentation; they would have benefited by the hard disciplines of simplicity. Though they are not long, they sprawl. Loosely organized, they reach in uncertain directions; rarely do they achieve that sure cadence which lets us know that only this was to be said, and only in this way. Form might increase a sense of closure, and Plumly likes to assemble lines not too dissimilar in length into groups of fourteen, though he doesn't rhyme, of course, or trouble himself with measure. The poems look like sonnets on the page, though, and one of them is even so labeled. But they merely allude cloudily to a tradition; they do not respond to the exigencies of sound and pulse which might crystallize their effects. (p. 183)

[But] Plumly doesn't deserve to be made a scapegoat. He's just a working poet, using the idiom as he finds it. It was an idiom, sixty years back, that promised a great deal—renewal of language grown inauthentic, immediacy, a new kind of participation. Above all it promised—as we still promise the

freshmen—that the effort it demanded would yield commensurate rewards. And so it did. But promises wear out, and new idioms become as habitual as those they replace. (p. 185)

Clara Claiborne Park, "Poetry, Penetrable and Impenetrable," in The Nation, Vol. 225, No. 6, September 3, 1977, pp. 182-86.*

## PETER STITT

In *Giraffe,* his second book, Stanley Plumly seems to face the problem of the confessional poets directly. This is a book with a sense of direction—and an interesting sense of direction it is, since the poems move directly away from Berryman and his brother in suicide, Randall Jarrell. As if to indicate the negative pole in this movement, Plumly has put elegies to both these earlier poets in the first section of his book. As works of art, these are not good poems, but what they promise is of great interest. The one on Jarrell makes it most clear:

> I was twenty-five and had the gun
> cocked dry in my dry mouth.
> My head was full of traffic and Chekhov.
>
> The dream said *this is too serious,* . . .

The dreaming self is correct; and not only is the suicidal pose of the young poet too serious, it is absurd and self-indulgent as well. John Berryman, perhaps the finest poet of despair in the language, led us to a dead end. Poets must absolutely reject his message if they are to go on with the business of life and of writing poems. Half of Stanley Plumly's achievement comes in this rejection; the other half comes in the positive solution which he finds for himself.

The direction in which Plumly is going to go is clearly indicated in this first section also, especially in **"Walking Out."** . . . The movement in Jarrell and Berryman is inward, into a preoccupation with the self and the problems of the self. Plumly would prefer to go outside, to become a natural creature, like the **"Giraffe"** which he describes so well. The poem is easily the best I've encountered on the subject of this animal. . . . The poem presents an appealing image of the poet as a natural creature—somewhat awkward, an observer and absorber of nature's rhythms, nature's truth. . . . (pp. 766-67)

There *is* loss, vulnerability, and pain in this volume, but, significantly, these are located not in the poet himself but in the woman he loves, his **"Heron."** She is described in the poem of that title. . . . The lines are not revolutionary, perhaps, in their rejection of self-concern in favor of concern for another, but they are refreshing. Again in **"Pull of the Earth"** it is the woman who suffers, especially at night, and the poet who comforts her. . . . (p. 767)

Plumly finds his answer to the emptiness of life in that tradition which turns to nature and to the primitive for sustenance. Natural objects, especially animals, come to serve almost a religious function, as Plumly invests them with magical overtones. The key to the magic in [the section entitled **"Horse"**] . . . is the Indian, whose very life depended upon the mystical qualities of nature. The woman of these poems is also spoken of as a horse. . . . The image of the horse is generalized later, becomes more than just the woman. In **"How the Plains Indians Got Horses,"** in fact, the horse becomes a divine creature. . . . This train of imagery has its conclusion in the postlude of the book, a passage from Kafka in which he explains his **"Wish to Be a Red Indian."** (pp. 767-68)

The value of this material to Plumly as a poet is most obvious in the penultimate poem in the book, **"The End of the Indian Poems."** Here the self is consciously left behind in favor of the nature-mysticism. . . . Plumly relies on what James Wright has called "the pure, clear word." His poems are direct and have the power of simplicity. *Giraffe* is a beautiful book. (p. 768)

> *Peter Stitt, in a review of "Giraffe," in* The Georgia Review, *Vol. XXXI, No. 3, Fall, 1977, pp. 766-68.*

## HENRY CARLILE

With the publication of Stanley Plumly's *In the Outer Dark,* in 1970, it became clear we had encountered a new poet of some importance. *Out-of-the-Body Travel,* his third book, supports that impression. Plumly has developed steadily, shaking off early influences and developing a strong, original voice. One presence, his father's, has dominated throughout. Plumly's obsession with his father, with his father's cruelty, kindness, and death, has culminated in this latest book in some of the finest father poems I have read anywhere. Though *Out-of-the-Body Travel* is really a book about family, friends, and lovers, it is the father's presence which orders and shapes this collection—in **"The Iron Lung,"** the title poem, **"Such Counsels," "The Horse in the Cage," "Two Poems," "Now That My Father Lies Down Beside Me,"** and **"After Grief."**

If Freudian psychoanalysis is something more than what Nabokov called "voodooism," this protracted scuffle with the father assumes a greater importance. The loss of one's father at an early impressionable age, or later, in the wars of adolescence, may have lasting serious consequences in the processes of individuation and the struggle for one's own identity. Plath's "Daddy" has already instructed us in the psychological costs. But Plumly is somewhat less hyperbolic, more self-possessed, if still father-haunted. **"The Iron Lung"** renders the hallucinatory confusion of father-son identities with terrifying psychological exactness. (p. 100)

The father is a drunk, a brute who "hit a horse in the face once," a sensitive man who plays the violin "so carefully as to make the music / almost visible on the air." . . . The destructiveness of a classmate's father is depicted also in **"Anothering,"** a poem about father-daughter incest and suicide. . . .

The women in *Out-of-the-Body Travel* are more benign, if less compelling. One of my favorites is **"Ruth."** . . .

Occasionally, rarely, Plumly's incantatory rhetoric plays ineffectively against an image or statement so as to render it suspect. . . . But this is one of the risks of song. In most of his poems the risk pays off. At its best, Plumly's is as fine a lyric voice as any I have heard recently. Beneath the clear, musical surfaces of these poems is an undercurrent that plays opposites brilliantly into an uneasy truce with the dominant grief of this book: the father's overwhelming presence in the psyche of the off-spring, a dangerous presence, malign and benevolent. I know of no recent book of poetry that has explored this subject more thoroughly or convincingly. (p. 101)

> *Henry Carlile, "Astral Predilections," in* The Ohio Review, *Vol. XX, No. 2, Spring-Summer, 1979, pp. 100-03.**

## PETER COOLEY

Plumly shares Lowell's obsession with a dead parent, but he never fleshes out a whole society proportionate to Lowell's New England. Nor does he join the Sexton-Plath cult of suffering-for-itself. Plumly's topography is rural Ohio in the 1930's seen through the radical simplification of a mind bringing to life not just facts of a past recaptured—his grandmother, the planting of marigolds, her death, the loss of childhood—but a struggle he plays before our eyes to apprehend and mythologize the past in its scattered pieces.

He has problems with this approach. Because of his refusal to extend the persona from personal to social interaction, Plumly builds a more limited echo chamber for the self than Lowell. He struggles, too, in accommodating the language of poems to standard forms he has chosen for their readily accessible religious and ritualistic connotations.

Most often, his poems are waking dreams reconstructed, the dreamer aware he is dreaming and reconstructing. But poems can never be dreams, only verbal representations of them, and this stance creates additional problems in form and diction. (p. 298)

In poem after poem Plumly grapples with diction problems . . . , his voices stumbling as they recreate, acutely conscious they are stumbling. What recommends *Out-of-the-Body Travel* however, and keeps us reading is this: the voices, flawed though they are, attempt to make the past new. Most of the poems successfully persuade us, at least in part, that a person, not a shadow, suffers them and wishes to share and purge that suffering. The book reads as a ceremony of expiation for a speaker who seeks to recall that stranger-who-was-his-father in all his limitations.

In prose the world of *Out-of-the-Body Travel* would be unredeemed: a farm in Ohio during the Depression, poverty, back-breaking physical work, days with little light and color—a world of abject solitude. But Plumly's recall is a telephoto lens rendering moments so intensely that little is mundane. Experience is recreated in sharp, stark contrasts of light and dark, the poems a series of family photographs shown you by someone as an intimate gesture of friendship. Though you may criticize his technique, you recognize that events leap out of the shadows, cherished by the artist's ability to bring them back "As just a moment ago." (pp. 299-300)

Though there is undoubtedly too much "I" bouncing about in it, [**"Cows"**] is successful. Its music is a harmony of past and present, the figurative language simpler than that in [**"Ruth"** and **"Rainbow"**], the structure of contrasts in time working smoothly with the sonnet form. **"Cows'"** lack of interest in fascinating metaphor is more than made up for by a language which engages us by interlaying memory and present consciousness.

To resurrect the past, Plumly often needs more radical rites than sonneteering. He finds them in those truncated litanies performed by many of the poems. Such an extraordinary work as **"The Iron Lung"** begins by talking to itself, the incantations clearing the air for a speaker who can then remember and dream. . . . Here, as in many other poems in *Out-of-the-Body Travel,* the structure, reflecting a struggle between the liturgical and the existential, is nervous, even discursive, although strapped down by syntactic parallelism. By comparison, the poems in Plumly's earlier books, *In the Outer Dark* and *Giraffe,* appear buffed up and finished off from stanza to stanza, products of a mind making poems before imagining. (pp. 300-01)

[One] of Plumly's central obsessions is a desire to incorporate his father in language so that the spirit of the past may be born again. The imaginative wish to die through his father represents his hunger to know not only Death but a foretaste of his own end. But . . . this is no simple retreat to the past. The way back is far more fractured, each poem assuming only a limited burden in the agonizing journey which shuttles between epiphany and epitaph. (p. 301)

*Out-of-the-Body Travel* moves by a structure that lunges and pulls back, side-steps and shadow-boxes. Part One sets in motion the quest inward and backward for the father, leading with key moments of the past. Part Two is more consistently successful, concerned particularly with women and sexual love, jumping from the illegitimate child of Alma Schultz to the speaker's mother and sister and finally to three love poems. That lying down with his father in death, which consumes the speaker in Part One, is transmogrified into [a] radical extension of self through sexuality. . . . (p. 302)

[In "Sonnet"] Plumly has loosened the structure and the texture, each line disjunctive yet impressing itself with the force of a refrain. Rich with spliced-in phrases, the poem's consistency derives from a recurrent aphoristic humor and violent juxtapositions in parallel phrases. Who made the original statement on which the poem is based we never find out. Nor would we expect such exasperated dismissal to be a root for the poem-to-come. And the third line is a surprising cliché, amusing considering the radical body-soul and life-death couplings and uncouplings to follow. For if, as the poem insists, the soul is present in us as an open grave, we scarcely own our soul at all. (pp. 302-03)

That Plumly should include the simple "I love you" just one side of the poem's center and reintroduce the girl, a jarring detail, are further unexpected touches. . . . A kissing cousin to those love poems building in sonnets little rooms, this Plumly poem reflects in its final line that obsession to cross over into another life which the speaker registers elsewhere. Plumly continues to play with the narcissism of "Sonnet" throughout the remainder of Part Two.

Part Three is directly obsessed with Father. If earlier he was seen in all his weaknesses, he now assumes mythic and totemic proportions. He is a kind of Hercules, a good angel and eternal comforter in this arrested moment that is childhood as a man experiences it. . . . Father is larger than nature now, and, as if anticipating us, Plumly himself evokes Whitman when the father's situation as worker and man is mythically extended to a nation of men at work in "Two Poems." Even dying, the father is maker and doer; the speaker voices a nightmare, a myth.

By comparison with *Out-of-the-Body Travel,* Plumly's early books, though concerned with fatherhood and death, are pale fire with but occasional forays into the crags and bogs of the psychic landscape excavated here. His voice is not yet accustomed to the dark, and the words he throws out to it often echo against each other, his volume too high for the melodies, the pitch not quite right for the subject he has taken up. One can only hope, however, that Plumly continues to write out of that dark cave of the mind into which this book has thrust its torch. With such books as *Out-of-the-Body Travel* Plumly may well be at the real beginning of a long voyage backward into darkness and light. The entrance is auspicious, even if his foothold is sometimes shaky. (pp. 303-04)

Peter Cooley, "I Can Hear You Now," in Parnassus: Poetry in Review, *Vol. 8, No. 1, Fall-Winter, 1979, pp. 297-311.**

## PETER STITT

Prepublication blurbs, a charming way writers have of paying off debts to one another, are, at best, generally misleading to the prospective reader. But Robert Penn Warren is in a different, higher, category from most writers, and the comment which he has offered on Stanley Plumly's [*Out-of-the-Body Travel*] is in this transcendent realm also: "Plumly has established," he says, "a new sort of ratio between the poet and his subject—or even his poem. It's a new turn of mind, behind the turn of language, in haunting, visionary pieces." This seems to me very wise. Plumly's subject matter is not new—the death of the father has, indeed, become something of a cliche. The way he handles this preoccupation, however, is striking; like the good poet in any age, Plumly has succeeded in "making it new." Our immediate poetic heritage comes from that maudlin, self-indulgent group called the Confessional Poets—John Berryman, who surely set a new standard of excess in writing of *his* dead father in *The Dream Songs,* Robert Lowell, Sylvia Plath, Anne Sexton. Something was in the air that made certain poets write of themselves and their sorrows in a way that left them trapped in the fatal web of solipsism.

But while the matter of Stanley Plumly's poems is similar to that of these earlier poets, his handling of it is remarkably different; we find "a new sort of ratio between the poet and his subject." Gone is the pathos of self-pity; what replaces it is a sense of spirituality which allows the father to remain with the son, an abiding, enduring, spiritual essence. . . .

One could argue, of course, that Plumly's sense of spiritual optimism is not new on the face of the earth; but it is relatively new in American poetry of the twentieth century. Similarly, the lyricism of these poems is also far from revolutionary, though it is certainly startling, and refreshing, in these days so heavily dominated by the plain style. . . .

I am tempted to say that many of the poems in this book are inspired—they are that good, in rhythm, in language, in imagery, in structure. Plumly is one of those unusual cases—a poet whose progress, whose movement from one level of achievement to another, is obvious and demonstrable. His earlier poems are good, as most reviewers have readily recognized. But rereading them after the new ones, I cannot help but find them pale and flat. Perhaps it is the spiritual dimension of the new poems that makes them seem inspired; more likely it is the new level of excellence that Plumly has achieved in his artistry. . . .

This high level of artistry helps to separate Plumly from the crowd. Although his subject matter is subjective and personal, he has not allowed it to seduce him into careless writing, as is too often the case in Confessional and post-Confessional Poetry. Because of the way Plumly has universalized his personal vision, he has been able to stand above it, creating, modulating, manipulating his words and themes into crafted objects. And he manages to avoid the other extreme as well—where the poem is all clever craft and devoid of felt meaning. The poems stand up well to repeated exposure; with most good volumes there comes a time during the second or third reading when you begin to yawn and think about another cup of coffee or a game of tennis. But this book continues to draw my attention—and I have read it six or eight times now. (p. 16)

It certainly does seem to me, as Warren says, that there is a "new turn of mind" present in Plumly's "visionary pieces." I don't know whether to call Plumly a mystic or just a transcendentalist. But whatever term we choose, the effect is the same—his sense of an abiding and mysterious spiritual essence lends a depth to his work that is rarely found anywhere. And this vision is itself reflected within the very texture of the poetry—in image, in language, in rhythm, Plumly manages to communicate the same surprising and magical quality. His objective and universalizing stance allows him to control the ultimate subjectivism of his theme; emotion in its turn is held in check by a classical use of craft. The book is all of a piece, a giant step forward for Plumly and an enduring source of delight for his readers. (p. 17)

> Peter Stitt, "On Stanley Plumly: That Enduring Essence," in The American Poetry Review, Vol. 9, No. 2, March-April, 1980, pp. 16-17.

## DAVID BROMWICH

In the heyday of the Georgian movement in England (1910-1920), the cant of criticism was to describe any poem one liked as "beautiful." The word implied "vivid," "in earnest," "purged of all disagreeable elements" (and of much else besides). Most of Stanley Plumly's poems are beautiful in just that sense. . . .

"Summer Celestial" is Mr. Plumly's fourth book of poems, but his procedure and characteristic emotions are still those of a youthful poet; indeed, his work appeals most through its evident ambition to be greater and larger than it is as yet. With the sort of language a reader may love (and find that he has memorized half-unwillingly) Mr. Plumly's shares one important feature: a groundnote of seriousness. His syntax and his use of line breaks are consciously various. But his ideal is an incantatory eloquence too decorous to reveal its motive; he has none of the turns or sudden emphases that can surprise a poet who is possessed by his subject.

The best things in this book are landscape pieces. The worst are the frankly literary poems: one about Keats's last days and a more ambitious one about Whistler's portrait of Carlyle. "Carlyle," says Mr. Plumly, "is tired, beyond anger, and beautiful." Beautiful, however, Carlyle never was, and beyond anger not even Whistler has imagined him. It is a pleasant-sounding line without a particle of truth.

In a poem like **"Chinese Tallow,"** his style embalms every grace within the reach of craft. (p. 12)

["Chinese Tallow" illustrates] both the enchantment of Mr. Plumly's writing and its imprecision. The cadence is sure and has a life of its own. "Bright with small dark leaves" seems to be a paradox for which the poet does not hold himself answerable. And things do not necessarily shine "in first light," if by first light is meant simply dawn; whereas if something else is meant, the poem fails to suggest what that could be. (p. 13)

> David Bromwich, "Remembered Gestures," in The New York Times Book Review, October 9, 1983, pp. 12-13, 18.*

## DAVID ST. JOHN

[In *Summer Celestial*] the grace of the natural world seems to balance every line. There is a calm, insistent integrity in Plumly's poems which echoes their composure and maturity. As in his previous book, *Out-of-the-Body Travel*, Plumly uses the landscapes of his childhood, the Ohio and Virginia countryside, as the backdrops to his poems of the family. In *Out-of-the-Body Travel* the dominant presence was that of the poet's father, a rough and sometimes drunken man, whose dark, troubling form shadowed many of that book's poems. In *Summer Celestial* the presiding spirit is that of the poet's mother, who is both soothing and calming. . . . Plumly's concerns are often those of generation and regeneration, in both the family and the natural world. . . .

Plumly loves to regard that natural world, its wildflowers and open fields, its rampant foliage and ground birds. . . . The wild beauty of the world is sketched with such precise delicacy, it seems to acquire, in Plumly's poems, its own personality and cunning. . . . Plumly sees in the orders and cycles of nature a healing, regenerative power. He sees something basic and spiritual (that is, *of* the spirit) in the landscapes which surround him. The conflict, of course, is that the world, in its natural (which is to say *unnamed* and *unnameable*) state, necessarily resists the activity of the poet.

There is a deceptive simplicity to the poems of *Summer Celestial,* yet their grace and resonance show that Stanley Plumly's descriptive forces have never been more powerful. His meditative poems unravel slowly, allowing the reader to discover their quiet, spiritual undercurrents, and his poems of maternal legacy convey a rare familial tenderness.

> David St. John, in a review of "Summer Celestial," in Book World—The Washington Post, December 25, 1983, p. 8.

## ROBERT McDOWELL

*Summer Celestial* records the continuation of Stanley Plumly's attempt to get back to the terms of an old agreement. There is much sadness here . . . , but it is not wholly the sadness of defeat. Rather, it is the sadness inherent in one who knows that revelation will not return lost innocence. Suffering exacts its price. The anchors of childhood (grandmother, father, summer resorts, our mother's feet) vanish, and we can never get them back. In poems, we return to them by honoring them, by creating other things. We become aware of death working, and we confront that moment of awareness again and again. That is the beauty of memory. That is its curse, too, and Plumly knows it well.

He knows it so well that in some of his previous volumes he has constructed a number of accomplished poems in service to this essentially romantic impulse. In this book, too, we find the quantitative pentameter and internal rhyme, the echoes of Roethke upon the terraces of childhood. In addition (and especially in the poems of the latter section), *Summer Celestial* unveils a widening set of concerns. The historical impulse is awakened, and joining hands with the romantic and mimetic, develops the most ambitious poems Plumly has written. **"Blossom"** exemplifies this breakthrough. Beginning with the description of a disturbed war veteran whose "head was a rose," the poem evolves into a comment on blacks in Winchester, Virginia in 1945. . . . Then memory calls forth the vision of the National Guard marching eleven German prisoners of war through the town. Blacks and whites line up to watch. The moment when autobiography, biography, history, and romance recombine is at hand. . . . (pp. 123-24)

This is the breadth of vision that commands attention. (p. 124)

Robert McDowell, "Recombinative Poetry," in The Hudson Review, *Vol XXXVII, No. 1, Spring, 1984, pp. 115-31*.*

### DAVID WOJAHN

The strengths of Stanley Plumly's recent work result not only from his finely tuned lyric voice, but also from his ability to construct *books,* not mere miscellanies. *Out-of-the-Body Travel* . . . was a powerful sequence of poems charting the poet's relationship with his contentious and alcoholic father. While perhaps only a third of the poems specifically dealt with the character of the father, his presence was felt everywhere. In its shadowy enactment of the Oedipal struggle, the book's tone repeatedly shifted from the reportorial to the mythic, from painstakingly recreated vignettes of a Forties childhood in Ohio to a kind of sweeping, mock-Biblical incantation. Remarkably, these dictional shifts were always superbly modulated. . . . A major factor in the book's success was its disciplined technique and structure. Plumly worked mainly in variants of iambic pentameter, juxtaposing his longer, more narratively based poems with more purely lyrical, sonnet-like efforts. Both the arrangement and formal rigor of the book enhanced its elegiac concerns.

But *Out-of-the-Body Travel* is elegiac not merely because it mourns the poet's father. Like Wordsworth, Plumly views the experience of recollection itself as a form of loss. Furthermore, he understands that apparently insignificant events from the past are often the most resonant ones, that memory rarely establishes a logical protocol. Thus, most of the scenes recalled in the book are quotidian—the drunken father singing to his cows, the mother at her doorway calling her children—made significant because they carry an inexplicable importance for the writer; they become what Proust calls "involuntary memories." . . . [The] purpose of the book is cathartic. The events recalled are not meant to be understood, only to be exposed in the hope that the poet will then be able to free himself of their obsessive hold.

What distinguishes *Summer Celestial* from its predecessor is the new book's desire to come to a more lasting understanding of involuntary memory, and to grasp how the present is imbued with memory itself. This collection seems meant to be read as a companion piece to *Out-of-the-Body Travel,* exploring the earlier collection's concerns more thoughtfully and acceptingly. While it lacks the passion and fortuitous revelation of the earlier volume, it is finally a more controlled and affecting effort. Just as the figure of the father dominated the poems of *Out-of-the-Body Travel,* the figure of the mother looms everywhere in *Summer Celestial.* . . . By changing the emphasis of the collection to the mother, Plumly has also changed his concept of the past and of ancestry. While the father of the earlier collection symbolized a past that must be struggled with and overcome, the past of *Summer Celestial,* usually represented by the presence of the mother, is a source of nurturing and

continuity. This is not to say that the book is conventionally nostalgic; instead, Plumly has abandoned his *quarrel* with memory in favor of a *dialogue* with it. He has not denied the past's hold on him, but neither has he resigned himself to it.

This new attitude permits a wider range of subject matter and emotion than Plumly has been capable of before, and the poems establish the connection between past and present in some surprising ways. "**After Whistler**" begins with a description of Whistler's portrait of the aged Thomas Carlyle. Suddenly the emphasis shifts to a carefully wrought reminiscence of the poet's relationship to his grandmother. . . . In the collection's title poem, Plumly even more ambitiously weaves seemingly disparate concerns, achieving a sestina-like repetition of his favored leitmotifs—thumbnail portraits of his parents, fragmentary childhood memories, and at last a scene of transcendent reverie. . . . While portraits of parents and family form the core of the collection, the pastoral lyrics that are interspersed with them also play a significant role. There were similar poems in *Out-of-the-Body Travel,* and some, like "**Peppergrass**," are among Plumly's best. But these short lyrics seemed at odds with the book's principal concerns. It is otherwise, however, in *Summer Celestial,* not only because the lyrics are longer and more ambitious, but also because they are meant to complement the primary emphasis on memory and family history. . . . The conclusion of "**Tree Ferns**," the lyric that opens the collection, aptly introduces us to Plumly's themes. . . . Plumly's technical prowess here, as in the book's other poems, is impressive. Even more so than *Out-of-the-Body Travel,* this volume repeatedly makes use of a rather fluid blank verse line. While Plumly is not rigid in his adoption of iambics, the formality of the poems is befitting of their themes. . . . Ever the Wordsworthian, he seems genuinely to believe that poetry is "emotion recollected in tranquility."

Perhaps the only real shortcoming of *Summer Celestial* has to do with such polish and tranquility. Although it is a wiser and more accomplished book than *Out-of-the-Body Travel,* many readers will miss the earnestness and fervor of the earlier book. Plumly sometimes seems older and more avuncular than he should be—and more presentable. A friend of mine recently told me that the book's only failing was that "there's not a hair out of place in it," and there's some accuracy in this statement. But the exhaustiveness with which *Summer Celestial* approaches its subjects also indicates, I think, that Plumly's cycle of poems on family and childhood is now complete. He seems to have thoroughly explored the realm of his memory, and I would imagine that Plumly's future work will be highly different from anything of his that has come before. Plumly is one of our most skillful and convincingly visionary writers; his achievement is already impressive, and will surely continue to be so. (pp. 492-96)

*David Wojahn, in a review of "Summer Celestial," in* New England Review and Bread Loaf Quarterly, *Vol. VI, No. 3, Spring, 1984, pp. 492-96.*

# Peter (Neville Frederick) Porter

## 1929-

Australian-born English poet and scriptwriter.

Porter is considered one of the most significant poets to have emerged in England during the 1960s. He has experimented with various verse forms and has focused on such diverse topics as personal experience, mythology, history, and contemporary society. Porter's work has been included in several important anthologies, and the publication of his *Collected Poems* (1983) has prompted reassessment of his entire literary output.

With his first two volumes of poetry, *Once Bitten, Twice Bitten* (1961) and *Poems, Ancient and Modern* (1964), Porter established a reputation as a satirist both of modern commercialized culture and the hedonistic subculture of "swinging London" in the 1960s. Although Blake Morrison claimed in a 1983 retrospective that Porter lacked the ruthlessness necessary for effective satire, many critics praised Porter for accurately mirroring the often petty and materialistic outlook of urban culture in that era. Critics compared Porter with W. H. Auden for his detached and ironically humorous criticism of the pressures of modern culture. With *A Porter Folio* (1969) and *The Last of England* (1970) Porter began to comment more objectively on modern society through allusions to the cultural heritage of Europe. His extensive knowledge of art, music, literature, and history added depth and complexity to the poems in these volumes.

*Living in a Calm Country* (1975) helped solidify growing critical recognition of Porter as a serious and resourceful poet. With this volume he began to develop a more personal expression, in contrast to the detached, satiric tone of much of his earlier work. In *The Cost of Seriousness* (1978) and *English Subtitles* (1981) he refined this new style while continuing to blend social commentary with allusions to European cultural heritage. Critics have observed that this technique frees Porter to voice personal concerns without resorting to the confessional mode of poetry, contributing a dimension of social significance to his work. In many of the poems in these two volumes Porter attempts to come to terms with his memories of his wife, who died in 1974. The elegiac tone of such poems, which many critics found affecting, reflects Porter's willingness to experiment with all types of verse. Critics were especially impressed with those poems in which Porter ruminates on the role of art in dealing with serious personal themes and the ability of language to express deep emotions without trivializing them. "An Exequy," in which he develops these ideas, is considered by some critics to be Porter's finest poem. Despite the generally pensive tone of Porter's later pieces, many contain the witty turns of phrase and wry social criticism that characterize his early work.

Many critics have stated that Porter's *Collected Poems* reveal him to be a poet of continued development and sustained achievement. Several accord Porter the status of a major contemporary poet on the basis of this volume.

(See also *CLC*, Vols. 5, 13 and *Contemporary Authors*, Vols. 85-88.)

*Photograph by Mark Gerson*

## DONALD DAVIE

[Peter Porter is Australian. But in *Once Bitten, Twice Bitten*] this is a matter only of subject-matter, almost of local colour—and only in certain poems. In style, attitude and tone he is undistinguishable from much of the better British verse of the Fifties. One thinks of the first collection of Thom Gunn—but Porter is much shaggier, a much rougher workman than Gunn. His clumsy metres and approximate rhymes give an impression of violence and power, but the violence is only implied, . . . so that before long we stop believing in Porter's violence as anything more than querulous rancour. All the same, he's a promising poet, especially when he names things, such as himself 'Eight years old drinking Schweppes in bed.' That comes from a poem called '**A Christmas Recalled**,' which is spoiled by its pointlessness in gesturing towards a metrical and rhyming regularity which it can only approximate. Why bother? This sort of very interesting material would surely go much better into naked and jagged unmetred verse like Robert Lowell's in 'Life Studies.' (p. 417)

*Donald Davie, "Australians and Others," in* The Spectator, *Vol. 206, No. 6926, March 24, 1961, pp. 416-17.**

## EUGENE IONESCO

[Porter belongs to a] group of poets who meet every Friday in a Chelsea drawing room, and this has matured and extended a powerful natural talent. He now steps forward at the age of thirty-two with an excellent first book [*Once Bitten, Twice Bitten*], though of significantly uneven merit. In the earlier poems he's capable of a murky tortuousness. . . . In Porter's later work this relentless obscurity has gone. And there are more and more poems bitten out with a vitriolic clarity. . . . There's a distillation of a highly subtle and original social conscience in this kind of writing. And in poems like '**John Marston Advises Anger**', '**Lament for a Proprietor**' and '**Phar Lap in the Melbourne Museum**' the wit, the envy and the wry pity fuse into a sustained personal style. There are about fourteen too many poems in this book; but there are about sixteen which hit the jackpot and these establish Porter as perhaps the only poet under thirty-five who has seriously grappled with the same issues as John Osborne, Arnold Wesker and Alan Sillitoe. (pp. 81-2)

Eugene Ionesco, "*Some Recollections of Brancusi*," translated by John Russell, in London Magazine, *Vol. 1, No. 1, April, 1961, pp. 80-2.**

## MARTIN DODSWORTH

Peter Porter's verse [in *Poems Ancient and Modern*] establishes a norm of abnormality in rhythm as in everything else. These brilliant poems are puzzling in so far as the things they catalogue . . . seem to elbow the particular manner of expression out of the way. One wants to call the poems baroque, because such details crowd the structure on which they stand out of sight. It is easy to feel that you are faced by a heap of unorganised particulars, but this is quite a wrong feeling. Mr. Porter's subject is civilisation in decline, and he evidently relishes the implicit parallel of his "ancient" poems between the corrupt civilisation of the Roman Empire and our own. He is attracted by the equivocal in human behaviour, or, rather, it is the favourite object of his loathing. . . . These *Poems Ancient and Modern* are permeated with the sense that life is being lived for us. They are packed with the description of objects because objects are pushing men out of their own world. "Spending money is the kindest orgasm," and possession is "**Nine Points of the Law**," the title of the best sequence in the book. There are four beautiful poems "**Changed from Martial's Epigrams**"; Mr. Porter's likeness to Martial lies not only in the scene he describes, but also in his unwilling involvement in it. "**The Sins of the Fathers**" begins by contemplating cruelty to animals, turns to reflect that

> somewhere every second occurs
> Some unswervable agony,

and ends by picturing the relation of child to parent as that of the trap to the tortured beast. In the middle of this disturbing poem, which reduces love to the guilty admission of sins, the poet says of himself that he "welcomes" guilt. It is just this fact, that guilt is welcomed along with so much else that one would have thought unequivocally bad, that gives the poems their deepest force. . . . This comic, pathetic, horrific obstinacy amazes yet appals. And it is there, perhaps, rather than in Mr. Porter's dazzlingly inventive and repulsive catalogues, that the puzzle lies. (pp. 85-6)

Martin Dodsworth, "*Puzzlers*," in Encounter, *Vol. XXIV, No. 3, March, 1965, pp. 83-6.**

## ANTHONY THWAITE

Porter is an extremely learned poet, without benefit of supervision at Hull, Oxford, Liverpool, or indeed any university. Italian opera, the more modern goings-on at Darmstadt and Donaueschingen, the life and work of Rilke, Carthaginian history, Jacobean drama, Martial's verse—Porter moves through these seemingly disparate worlds with the same ease that he uses to negotiate the more facile terrain of Twiggy, Sotheby's, Heal's, Simon Raven, PROs and advertising campaigns, the *Daily Express* and the Festival Hall bar; and he makes all of them engage and mesh. There is an unbroken line of development from *Once Bitten Twice Bitten* (1961), through the new work in the Penguin Modern Poets selection (1962) and *Poems Ancient and Modern* (1964), to *A Porter Folio,* which shows him gradually extending and perfecting his *personae;* he has never been one for the beseeching ego-based lyric or the winsome true confession. It is a body of work that is highly personalised without being personal, from the early '**Reflections on my own Name**' to '**Porter's Metamorphoses**', '**The Porter Song Book**', and the very title of this new volume [*A Porter Folio*]; and when—rarely, as in '**Five Generations**'—he makes a less oblique move, his characteristic sardonic voice seems muffled.

There is a deliberate irony, of course, in all this self-reference, since what it adds up to is evasion and sleight of hand, the ingenious chameleon taking his colour from his context. Porter is a set-faced illusionist, creating scenes, monologues, charades, all of them dense with proper names of people, places, titles, identifiable things; and yet the creator, like Joyce's artist, is withdrawn. . . . For those who have stopped reading new poetry because it seems to lack the inventiveness, the human *stuff* that is fiction's province, Porter's poems should persuade otherwise. Auden has it, and Auden has obviously meant a lot to Porter, sometimes to the extent of sounding like ventriloquising (e.g., the third of the '**Three Poems for Music**'). But it is an influence that on the whole has suggested possibilities rather than dictating pastiche. (p. 53)

Anthony Thwaite, "*Ingenious Chameleon*," in New Statesman, *Vol. 78, No. 2000, July 11, 1969, pp. 53-4.*

## BRIAN JONES

*A Porter Folio* is an intriguing book. It shows Peter Porter to be concerned with what every good professional at times is concerned with—the mastery of new skills, so that when the time comes for the next real challenge to the capabilities, he will be ready for it. There are a number of fine poems here, mainly, like the one in memory of W. F. Bach, in one of the styles he has been evolving over recent years, a style close to that of Auden in his later work—talking and relaxed and tightening into the aphoristic statement. . . .

[Porter's] sharp satiric tongue is also in evidence, but the poems in this vein lack the shocked initiate's vituperation to be found in his earlier work. Here, the edge seems turned a little by too close and long familiarity with what he is attacking. There are also, here, some successful uncomfortable-reminiscent poems, in a style we remember from *Once Bitten Twice Bitten*, but mainly, as I said, this seems an interim book, full of promise for the next period. He is mastering and perfecting some interesting techniques—the technique, for example, of eclectic wandering among European culture, a technique which he uses, not to suggest, like Eliot, estrangement, but to hint at confederation and the extension into the present of the wisdom and follies of the past. Porter also, in shorter poems, shows himself to be working at a tighter, more elliptical utterance. A volume, then, in which achievement and experiment make interesting bedfellows. . . . (p. 97)

*Brian Jones, "Black Feathers," in* London Magazine, *Vol. 9, No. 7, October, 1969, pp. 95-9.\**

### NEIL RENNIE

In the way that the copy of some advertisements is becoming more 'poetic', some poetry begins to read like an advertisement. Porter's poetry is part of the overwhelming homogeneity of a society where everything insidiously becomes like every other thing. Perhaps this explains why it is so frequently unevocative. Nothing need be suggested because it is all included. The poetic function of indicating relationships between objects/ideas has been superseded by an attempt to produce an exhaustive catalogue. . . .

Like a good piece of advertising copy of the 'soft sell' variety, Porter's quality derives from such devices as schoolboy juxtapositions ('. . . the Grail filled with orange cup'), and above all from his own amusement; his synthetic laughter at the synthetic society of which he is a practising member and a very typical part. His amusement (which comes with the poetry like the instructions on a thoughtfully packaged product) he shares generously with the reader who is, by proxy, amused, and pleased to feel secure in his awareness of the plasticity of life. . . .

Porter enjoys detecting clichés (thus enjoying them) and, like a person who has found something pleasantly disgusting, he cannot resist displaying them in his poetry—where they consequently abound. (p. 93)

As Porter lists clichés, he celebrates them, forming part of the machine (of which I have myself, just become another part) that makes clichés forgetting that detecting clichés is the obsession of a neophiliac, forgetting that detecting clichés is a cliché.

The poetry is built around trendiness. . . .

Where it is satirical, and not simply comic, Porter's writing is often guilty of a variation of the paradox which ensnared Wittgenstein and his ladder. It is the object of its own satire. . . .

In a couple of poems [in *The Last of England*] Porter manages to escape his twentieth-century obsessions by burrowing into history. (p. 94)

Some of the other poems in the collection are a list of jokes which lean too heavily on a single theme. Part 2 of **'Job's Discount'** is a series of descriptions of God based on the premise that anything funny you say is funnier if you say it about God. . . . **'A Consumer's Report'** also suffers from this rather tiresome elaboration of one idea (in itself rather amusing): that life is a consumer product. The amusement wears thin, however, and by the time the poet has bounced 48 lines off the conceit, it has somewhat lost its initial resilience. . . .

The saddest thing about the 'bad' poetry in this book is that Porter can, and does, write 'good' poetry. . . . [In **'Diana and Actaeon'** there are] original and striking images, perfectly cadenced and infinitely evocative, where thought is allowed to flow unimpeded by logjams of reference, or by over-writing.

Also there are signs that Porter is not going to be left at the wayside by recent neosurrealist, quasi-impressionistic developments in poetry and this collection contains some fine throwaway lines. . . . There is plenty of variety in these poems (although the number 57 comes to mind) for they are the work of an experienced and versatile poet. They are as clever, as quick, and sometimes as ephemeral as the society they reflect. . . . Witty, amusing, amused, erudite but not intellectual. Almost completely vacuous. A best buy. (p. 95)

*Neil Rennie, "A Best Buy," in* London Magazine, *Vol. 10, No. 12, March, 1971, pp. 92-5.*

### MICHAEL SCHMIDT

Of the London poets least heard of in the United States, for my money the most impressive is Peter Porter. His recent book, *The Last of England,* establishes him as far more than the "social poet" he is usually labeled. . . . His world includes allusion to present urban realities, the polluted pastoral, to music in all its styles, to literatures from many languages and ages, to various religions and to many histories, myths, and legends: a formidable store of information deployed with an almost unerring intelligence. The speed and suppleness, and yet the complexity of allusion, and the consistent structure of implication as it were external to or unstated in the poems, the truth to voice as well as truth to form, make this poetry not far short of major. As satire, it plays through time as well as space, implicating history as the conditioning agent and the future as conditioned, or at best predictable. As in Randall Jarrell's poems, the varied general inheritance of past histories works through the individual, but the final destination is the particular—death—no matter how he works to hide or evade it. Porter's poems are prophetic in a concrete way; his "I", even in the *Sanitized Sonnets* which are ostensibly about the poet himself, is evanescent. He is a situation, not a poet at confession. If his soul is withered, it is not his soul but the withering situation that needs looking to. This selflessness is his most valuable asset. It consists of an ability to generalize the particular fate, as Auden could in his heyday. Porter is perhaps more local than Auden, less confident, more tentative. But he has a power to coordinate allusion. One does not sense in the middle of his poems, as one does in Auden's, the gap between the detail and the generality, the sense that the images, the units, don't support the moral or intellectual weight placed on them. (pp. 177-78)

*Michael Schmidt, "A Defence," in* Poetry, *Vol. CXX, No. 3, June, 1972, pp. 170-81.\**

### COLIN FALCK

Porter can beguile our emotions with a doom-laden cultural allusiveness which one would have to beat one's way reductively and analytically back through if one wanted to make personal contact with the poet at the centre of it all. Porter established himself in the *ur*-years of Swinging London with some Swiftianly terse or MacNeiceishly resigned annotations of the carnal and spiritual vanities of that scene, as well as with some fiftiesish deprecations of his own carnal and spiritual inability to be part of it. Putting both sides together one could sense a dimension to his poetry which wasn't always obvious in the neatly satirical tags ('Love goes as the MG goes'; 'The name of the product I tested is *Life*') or neatly satirical whole poems (his nuclear alert piece **'Your Attention Please',** say) which it looked as though he was going to be remembered by in the anthologies. With so much quotability behind him it must have been difficult for Porter to abandon his hard-nosed role as the thinking man's pop poet and to try—as he soon did—to come to terms with himself as some kind of exemplary cultural victim or sufferer. But if leaving his early stylishness behind made him seem a raggeder and more wasteful poet, it also brought him nearer to his peculiar strengths.

What really comes over in Porter's verse, for all its glisteringly or blisteringly contemporary surfaces, is an inability to assimilate the modern world at all. Unwilling to permit that world anywhere very near his pulses, let alone to prove itself on them, the poet allows his deeper feelings to leak through on to the page only indirectly, almost symptomatically—just as he writes about his own past only when it seems far enough away to be somebody else's. The effect this adds up to is of someone in a state of never-quite-recovered-from cultural shock; and though poetically one would trade in a good many pages of Porter's edgy erudition for a single clean image or heartfelt rhythm, this general smokescreen effect of flustered ebullience is the real basis of his genuineness. Behind his frenziedly cultural gesturing one senses classical, urbane, ironic (but also humane and sensual) affinities in a state of rout; or—from another angle—the responses of an Australian poet to a world seemingly post-Edenic to the point of irrecoverability. What holds Porter to life, meanwhile, is a lingering, disinherited humanism, a wishing-it-could-be-true loyalty to our (and his) ordinary dreams and longings: it was this incompletely disillusioned side of his nature which made his early satires such ambivalent love-hate rhapsodies and some of his fantasy-pieces—particularly the erotic ones—so enticingly readable.

Porter's new book *Living in a Calm Country* has touches of his old crispness and it also has at least one poem (**'An Australian Garden'**) where the tone goes so far in the opposite direction as to be almost elegiac. But stateliness isn't Porter's *forte*, and his best moments here are where his European *Angst* is granted its usual place at the centre of things but—instead of being merely indulged satirically or just wryly put up with—finds itself being tellingly played off against some of the mutely reproachful composures of nature or art. . . . Porter's calm—as and when he achieves it—is more likely to be an inward composure than any kind of outward approximation of his verse to more ceremonious models. It may leave him as egocentric a poet as he always has been—but simply a more trustingly imaginative one. Some of the more self-revealingly autobiographical flashes in these recent poems suggest that he may be winning through to it at last.

> Colin Falck, in a review of "Living in a Calm Country," in The New Review, Vol. III, No. 26, May, 1976, p. 58.

## JAMES LASDUN

Stylish nay-saying, a delighted disgust with all the nastier details of contemporary life, and a public voice learned partly from Auden and partly from classical satirists, were the hallmarks of Peter Porter's earlier volumes. With the personal tragedy [his wife's death] that lay behind the poems in [*The Cost of Seriousness*], Porter's gaze began to turn inwards, and in his new collection *English Subtitles* he seems to have arrived at something of an impasse, wherein private melancholy frequently finds itself at odds with a style that was developed for public vituperation.

The wealth of vividly imagined particulars that gave weight to the rancour of those earlier poems . . . is sadly lacking in these more solipsistic pieces [in *English Subtitles*]. Without it, Porter's characteristic gloomy catchphrases . . . seem merely attempts to endow a personal unhappiness with a larger significance than it possesses.

A corollary of the poet's introversion is a certain self-obsession about the poems themselves. Porter repeatedly interrupts himself in this volume with remarks—usually defensive—about the poem he is writing:

> What we need are stories. Regard this
> Poem up to now as preparation. . . .
>
> (p. 21)

This kind of self-reference is a sure sign that all is not well with the poet, and indeed, the impression that much of this volume gives is of a writer going through a crisis of confidence. It is only towards the end of the book that this impression is fully relieved. The last three poems not only show a return to the pithy, outward-looking intelligence of the early work, but also, in their complex treatment of history, myth and place, reflect a complexity in the world which was not often admitted in that early work. **'Landscape with Orpheus'**, in particular, where Porter's own bereavement is sublimated in myth, contains those qualities of poised discursiveness and elegiac pace one associates with a fine poet in his maturity. (pp. 21-2)

> James Lasdun, in a review of "English Subtitles," in The Spectator, Vol. 246, No. 7971, April 18, 1981, pp. 21-2.

## DAVID WILLIAMS

For many readers of contemporary poetry the name Peter Porter tends still to produce the automatic reaction 'satirist'. Certainly his satires are effective, particularly those on trendiness in contemporary culture, but concentration on Porter the satirist has tended to filter attention away from areas where much of his best poetry is to be found. His poetry, as the recent *Collected Poems* makes clear, has always been preoccupied by pain as experienced in the individual life and in history. In his most recent books, particularly since the death of his wife in 1974, loss and bereavement have become more and more central to his work, finding their deepest expression in *The Cost of Seriousness* (1978) and *English Subtitles* (1981).

In these books the earlier, more grotesque, treatment of death has been replaced by an elegiac and meditative vein which can encompass the direct transcription of grief or the more reflective appraisal of the relationship between art and death. In some of the most affecting poems in *The Cost of Seriousness* Porter tries to come to terms with his wife's death, remembering their life together or lamenting her loss. . . . But, alongside these poems, and sometimes within the same poem, Porter is able to move from the details of suffering to meditations on broader aesthetic questions such as the competing claims of art and life, the adequacy of art in the face of death and the ability of language to describe extreme feelings. It is typical of Porter that, in the midst of grief, he should use his intellect to explore problems like this, trying to resolve these questions within the confines of the poem. In poems like **'The lying art'**, **'The cost of seriousness'** and **'A lecture by my books'** he raises the whole question of the adequacy of poetry and we follow the twists and turns of his argument as he is forced to reevaluate the importance of art. . . . On the other hand, Porter's arguments sometimes lead him to an eventual acceptance of the necessarily feigning nature of art, especially when art is compared with the blankness of death. . . . One of the most characteristic features of Porter's work is this split-level perspective on experience, by which he can portray feelings of loss and unhappiness whilst at the same time exploring the intellectual implications of those feelings.

In some of the poems in *The Cost of Seriousness* there is a momentary loss of confidence in the adequacy of art when confronted with grief. But more typical of Porter's work as a whole are the poems which show his immense indebtedness to specific works of art, and to European civilisation as a whole. When Porter writes about his favourite artists or works of art it's as if he's talking to them and we're overhearing him expressing his gratitude. . . . Throughout the *Collected Poems* the reader is struck by the sincerity with which Porter describes the delight and consolation which he experiences before certain works of art; they do not exist as touchstones against which to set contemporary works for satiric comparison, but rather as objects which have been absorbed into his emotional and intellectual life.

In his latest book *English Subtitles* some of the best poems portray a different aspect of loss: the psychology of bereavement, and, in particular, the dangers and temptations in bereavement. These poems often involve a dialogue in which Porter's natural feelings of guilt, self-pity or resentment are answered by a corrective viewpoint which enables him to bear loss better. In 'The Werther level', for example, this corrective advice is put into the mouth of Goethe's Werther, who speaks authoritatively on the dangers of self-pity. . . . In other poems the example of his wife, and all she stood for, serves to chasten any tendency to linger in the more insidious emotions of bereavement. In **'Talking to you afterwards'**, for instance, Porter imagines a conversation between his wife and himself in which the sanity of her attitudes stands as a reproach to any maudlin self-abasement. . . . Also in **'Alcestis and the poet'**, a poem which uses the mythological figure of Alcestis to represent the voice of a dead wife, Alcestis tries to reconcile the poet to the inevitability of death and dispel his feelings of persecution but, this time, despite her reassurances, the poet remains unconsoled, and the poem ends with Alcestis regretfully 'looking back' at him. . . . With these poems Porter was able to stand back from his own emotions and analyse some of the dangerous falsifications implicit in his reactions to bereavement. But these falsifications are not teased out in an arid or mechanical way but, instead, are 'placed' for him by a wiser view of life and death which is often represented, most movingly, by the figure of his dead wife.

Another feature of *English Subtitles* is the way in which a more general sense of unhappiness is realised through the indirection of landscape. Like Auden, Porter has always been fascinated by *paysages moralisés*, where landscape is used to comment on aspects of human life. He has often used the metaphor of landscapes or 'countries' to represent the varying states of the self. . . . In 'The garden of earthly delights' we are presented with a landscape of self-deception; the people of the town are given over to a naive hedonism which seeks to hide from the reality of pain and death, but those realities continually intrude despite the attractions of the town. . . . Several of the best poems in *English Subtitles* have [a] surreal, dream-like quality as landscapes are suffused with feelings of inadequacy. Through these allegorised maps Porter was able to represent that diffused and unfocused sense of unhappiness which lies behind *English Subtitles*.

Some of the poems do, however, justify a major criticism of his work: the allegation that he is sometimes perversely obscure. Part of the problem stems from Porter's delight in ideas, and by 'ideas' I mean not only theories or arguments, but also insights, perceptions and intuitions. His poems often enact a mental process in which he examines the ambiguities of his attitudes or follows the implications of a train of thought. Sometimes, however, Porter is unable, or perhaps unwilling, to define the nature of the initial scene, object or feeling which sets the succession of ideas into motion, and it is often extraordinarily difficult to follow the sequence of thought. . . . (pp. 55-60)

Porter's allusiveness also lies behind some of the criticisms that can legitimately be made of his work. His allusions are sometimes unhelpful and obscure, gesturing towards a meaning which he has felt, but been unable to convey. This tendency to produce allusions which are unassimilated into the overall meaning of the poem, when combined with a certain arbitrariness of phrasing and a habit of making sudden transitions of thought which do not seem to have an underlying intellectual or emotional connection, can produce impenetrably difficult poetry. . . . (p. 60)

At his best, however, Porter is able to use fragments from literature and music in a readily comprehensible way which is woven closely into the meaning of the poem, putting into condensed form the import of the preceding lines and bringing relevant experience from art to bear on the dilemmas of life. Often his allusions perform a talismanic function, recalling lines of music or poetry which have had a consoling effect in the past and which enable him to face the difficulties of his life now. At the end of 'An exequy', for example, the final line of the poem, 'Fürchte dich nicht, ich bin bei dir' (the title of a Bach motet) is beautifully integrated into the mood of the preceding lines, giving a feeling of calm reassurance in answer to Porter's uncertainties: . . .

> Then take my hand and lead me out,
> The sky is overcast by doubt,
> The time has come, I listen for
> Your words of comfort at the door,
> O guide me through the shoals of fear
> 'Fürchte dich nicht, ich bin bei dir.'

The sensitivity with which that final line is inserted shows how Porter can use the allusion to create particularly poignant effects in which it seems to comment directly on the events of a life. The sureness with which Porter handles the allusion in that poem is another example of that union of artistic control and intensely realised grief which is so typical of his confrontation with loss in his recent poetry, and which makes [*The Cost of Seriousness* and *English Subtitles*] so continuously moving and stimulating. (p. 61)

*David Williams, "'A Map of Loss': The Recent Poetry of Peter Porter," in* Critical Quarterly, *Vol. 25, No. 4, Winter, 1983, pp. 55-62.*

**TIM DOOLEY**

Peter Porter, like his contemporaries Thom Gunn and Ted Hughes, finds himself in the rather ambivalent position of being most known for poems which reached a wider audience than might have been expected, either before or since, as an accidental result of the economic and educational climate of the middle to late nineteen sixties. To an occasional reader of contemporary poetry, Porter has remained the poet of **'Your Attention Please'** or **'Annotations of Auschwitz'**—as Hughes has been the poet of 'Hawk Roosting', or Gunn of 'On the Move'. A result of this has been to inhibit awareness of the affective concerns of his work: it still makes sense to read Gunn as an ethical poet with an exact eye for the implications of social trends; to see Hughes as a poet whose insights into animal behaviour have strong implications for the way we live our lives is perhaps to do him too great a favour; to see Porter as a social poet—a man with a talent for summarising great issues in an acceptable, marketable way—is to maintain a limited view of his talent in particular, and of the proper usefulness of poetry as an art in general.

On one level, Porter's work of the 'sixties presents a figure typical of that period: an autodidact and outsider with no easy respect for established authority—one of the self-confident 'new men' determined to take advantage of the openings offered by a false boom. . . . One does not have to look far, however, to find Porter questioning fashionable assumptions as readily as established conventions. 'I am only the image I can force upon the town', says the figure in the Daks suit in **'Metamorphosis'**, but by the end of the poem he admits to being 'horrible, far / below the collar'. **'John Marston Advises Anger'** looks at the mores of a new 'Elizabethan Chelsea set' and finds social attitudes on the King's Road less radical than they first appear. . . .

A tone that was to become characteristic of Porter's poetry also appeared in early poems: a sense of waking nightmare, and an acute susceptibility to images of suffering—so that he could, for instance, be reminded of the victims of Auschwitz by the closing of doors on an underground train or the rotation of a chicken on a spit. (p. 27)

It is Porter's humanist responsibility—his sense of the seriousness of [the] struggle between life and death—that fuels the anger of his satirical writing. His highest contempt is saved for those willing to settle for an easy response to serious questions, who are too egotistical to question their own motives or who comply with a society that trivialises life by reducing everything to the level of a commodity. . . . [In] the volumes which have appeared since *The Last of England,* the threats to security come from much nearer home than before. . . . (p. 28)

His poems of the 'seventies not only show the skull beneath the skin; they move deeply inside the mind, exploring parts of the personality that the will might wish to deny. A changed attitude to language accompanies the more reflexive focus of Porter's work. As his metrical control has tightened, so he had deliberately loosened the grip of syntax and logic, surprising the reader with 'words that fall down if they're leaned on' (**'The Giving Vein'**).

A side-effect of this process may be occasional obscurity, but Porter has gained, as Ashbery has, by allowing some of the confusion of contemporary reality into the closed world of the poem.

Other shifts that have taken place in Porter's work during the 'seventies have been more contingent: the unavoidable results of growing older and of knowing personal loss. . . . The death of Porter's wife in 1974 was followed by writing of extraordinary clarity and control. Formal, literary poems like **'An Exequy'**, or **'The Delegate'** (with its echoes of Hardy), are balanced by poignantly plain recollections of shared experience such as **'Roman Incident'**. It is to be hoped that the publication of his *Collected Poems* will draw wider attention to the considerable achievement these poems represent. (p. 29)

> *Tim Dooley, "Acting Against Oblivion," in* Poetry Review, *Vol. 73, No. 1, March, 1983, pp. 27-9.*

## GEORGE SZIRTES

Lord Byron once described himself as 'Methodist, Calvinist, Augustinian'. In other words he knew the devil and gave him his due, or as Peter Porter might have said, whatever his other organs were doing he kept his nose to the moral north. Porter's own verse might be described in the same terms. Both poets left their native country in their twenties and took up residence elsewhere. Both were travellers. Both tried to resolve the tension between their romantic and classical instincts through humorous and conversational verse. Both are known for their loquacity and both have left behind sharp sketches of their milieux: one can talk about the world of Porter much as one talks about the world of Byron. Porter's world is a racy but guilt-ridden complex and his new *Collected Poems* lays every part of it before us. There are no carefully guided tours or recommended beauty spots—the book includes everything in the previous collections in plain chronological order (apart from the version of Martial at the back) and leaves out only limited edition ventures like **'The Lady and The Unicorn'**. The reader must follow his own nose and that would be well advised to keep to the above mentioned moral north, for even the decision to include everything was taken by the poet on moral grounds as he makes clear in his short preface: 'Reading through the many pages of this book I have often been visited by feelings of disapproval of my gauche or cocky past self, but I do not want to act the prig to the man who wrote these poems.' Almost incidentally he is staking an important claim to be more than the sum of his best poems.

The comparisons with Byron are premature: Byron's airy manner is not quite in Porter's line, and despite the latter's often expressed admiration for 'Don Juan' many other influences have shaped his career. . . . [His] first book, *Once Bitten, Twice Bitten* was published in 1961. At thirty-three Porter was a slightly late starter but he immediately established, if not exactly a tone of voice, then a recognisable complex mode. The book begins with a group of poems about his childhood in Australia. (p. 34)

There are hints in the Australian poems . . . of an early loss of security but these remain no more than hints. Soon a new, re-made Porter takes over, one equipped to deal with the new world on its own terms. His experience as a copywriter enables him to become what he later calls 'a philosopher of captions', that is to say, someone who makes phrases. The title of an early poem, **'Syrup of Figs Will Cast our Fear'** is an example of this, and from **'Metamorphosis'** onward such captions begin to populate the poems. . . . The book then takes us on a tour of the consumerised sixties menaced by cancer, coronary and Bomb. Porter shows a sharp, novelist's eye for detail but the fictions he creates here—and fiction is probably the Porter style *par excellence*—give glimpses between the captions of an almost morbid delicacy at work. There is a microscopic view of the disagreeable in body and spirit, a disgust like Rimbaud's with the natural functions. Indeed it is a desire to shock that prevents Porter's ruthless ironies from ever sliding into gentility. These poems are neither gentle nor genteel: they tend if anything towards high-camp.

But it is worth returning to the subject of captions for much of his immediate authority derives from them. Sometimes these are aphoristic in character, other times they take the form of a claim, or a directive or they simply deal out information. In mode of address they are between the oracular and the demotic and they are usually memorable. There are probably more quotable lines in Porter than in any other contemporary poet: 'Of all God's miracles, death is the greatest', 'There should have been fictions to be real in', 'Now go quickly to your shelters': the stock is endless. . . . At their best such devices open out quite majestically to a world of general ideas where miracle, art and history are constantly available to comment on each other. But the ground beneath us is always shifting and occasionally we are left awkwardly in mid-air.

Part of this sense of unsteadiness is due to the strong element of burlesque in Porter's captions. The captions themselves are usually located within stretches of deceptively prosaic writing. 'God will be verbose', says Porter in the title poem of *Preaching to the Converted,* and he goes on to create God in his own image. God is not only a compulsive talker but also an excellent mimic. He is also a crucified God who is for ever questioning the reality of His own pain and His own voice. Porter's fictions are related by miscellaneous voices. Browning may well be the inspirer of the dramatic monologue but the burlesque is Porter's own. (pp. 34-5)

Porter's conversations with God are never abstract. General ideas are always met with specific instances drawn from as wide a field of experience as possible. But the most trodden field is that of the fine arts. Porter's habit of wearing his erudition on his sleeve is more than simply showing-off or deflecting criticism, it is an aspect of his drive towards particularity for one thing and a way of tackling God on his own ground. It can be irritating of course: at worst it becomes a ridiculous mélange of name-dropping, self-consciousness and sloppy metrics, but that is a price we have to pay for the frequent times that Porter breathes new life into old longings and aspirations, or at least puts them through their paces.

If he is hard on God, he is also hard on himself. We do not tend to look for simple lyricism in Porter, and it is true that there are few purely lyrical poems in the *oeuvre,* yet there is room for delicacy. Although parts of *A Porter Folio,* the 1969 volume, seem rather declamatory in their surrealism, there are also tender, almost crystalline examples of observation on a small scale in poems like **'Seahorses'** and **'St Cecilia's Day'**. It is perhaps his most dazzling collection and contains one of his finest sequences, 'The Porter Song Book', which represents to me all that is most attractive in a typical Porter poem. Here, as elsewhere he uses the first person singular as interlocutor but his voices are most subtly blended.

'The Porter Song Book' describes the relationship between a man and a woman. *The Cost of Seriousness* of 1978 contains and is animated by a number of meditations on the premature death of his wife, Jannice, in 1974. Despair finds its focus here and this results in the straightest and most moving verses in the *Collected Poems*. Perhaps they are not the most representative in technique but poems like **'An Exequy'** and **'The Delegate'** sound a new *de profundis* which Porter in another mood might have distrusted. But there is no false note. Nor false colours: even his comedies, **'Three Transportations'** and **'Talking Shop Tanka'** are bathed in the same cool sad light. 'Trying to be classical', he says in the title poem, 'can break your heart'. But here is a succession of poems that achieves the dignity of classicism in sorrow. (pp. 35-6)

[Porter] is a very difficult poet to classify because only one pigeon-hole fits him and that is the one he himself has made. It is almost easier to define his work in negatives. He is to start with not a properly Anglicised writer, his loyalty is more to Europe and the Classical-Romantic tensions in its artistic heritage. There is therefore nothing parochial in his writing, no traditional English sense of place. There is no gentility, nor Oxford smartness or insularity, he is in fact almost classless. On the other hand he is the most self-conscious and introspective of our major poets and the most sensitive to what Aldous Huxley once called 'the inner weather'. There is something reckless in the way he attacks a subject, something reckless too in his decision to reproduce all his published work. He has quite willingly given many hostages to fortune. Those people who are maddened by his mannerisms will find plenty to annoy them here. But they will be surprised just how many first-rate poems he has written and how many individual lines will remain with them after a particular poem is forgotten. Yet however we may admire the Horatian beauties of his verse, the overall effect is astringent. And the astringent works because the application is humane. His true landscape is the human body taking risks on behalf of the human soul. Like Pope, 'His rows / of blooms had their grotesques but they / took the place of music.' (p. 36)

George Szirtes, "Humane Astringencies," in Poetry Review, *Vol. 73, No. 1, March, 1983, pp. 34-6.*

### STEPHEN SPENDER

There is, I think, a distinction between poets who start off their poems through an intoxication with words and those who do so through an intoxication with ideas which they can express only in poetry.

Peter Porter, an Australian who for the past 30 years has lived in London, at first sight strikes me as belonging to the latter category. His **'Collected Poems'** produce, above all, the impression of an immensely fertile, lively, informed, honest and penetrating mind, pouring out ideas about people and things observed, social manners, books and their authors, history, travel and music. Music, especially, he is both intelligent and passionate about. And there are many poems here that are observant, informative, critical or satiric.

At a second glance, though, I find Porter the former kind of poet—so gifted in language and rich in vocabulary that his words have an intoxicating effect on the reader. At times he is like someone who seems to be drinking glasses of the purest, most transparent water, but who as he goes on drinking and conversing makes one think that the water has turned into vodka—purest alcohol. How can language be so clear and yet so baffling, one finds oneself asking. . . .

The most personal thing in these mostly impersonal poems is the sense of loss in his relations with others. Memories of loneliness in childhood are described in many of the early poems—catalogued, even, in **'The View from Misfortune's Back'**—though when Porter seems nearest to writing confessional poetry (which I am sure he despises) it would be wrong to assume that he is writing about himself and not inventing fictions to fit himself into. In a few poems he is marvellously successful in objectifying the pain that hurts the poet into poetry, most notably in **'An Anthropologist's Confession.'**

There are influences of other poets, those he admires: Eliot, in the early poetry (particularly 'Gerontion'), Stevens, . . .

Auden *passim*, a bit of Graves, a pinch of Ewart. Influences of painting and music also get into this very civilised poetry. They do not weigh heavily however.

The feeling of strangeness underlying these poems is difficult to analyse. Perhaps it is Australian. I think of those Australian painters from Nolan on, lonely figures, painting landscapes in which wooden shacks float on light reflected from the desert as though they were standing on stilts. Perhaps it is the Australian light which keeps this lively, witty, allusive, sometimes mysterious poetry a few feet above the ground.

> Stephen Spender, "*Wakeful Dreaming,*" *in* The Observer, *March 27, 1983, p. 33.*

## JOHN LUCAS

I opened Peter Porter's *Collected Poems* with a feeling of some uneasiness. Years ago I lost my copy of his first volume, *Once Bitten Twice Bitten,* and I was nervous in case some of the poems which I could now only hazily recall turned out to be less good than they had seemed in 1961. I needn't have worried. The best of them come up fresh as paint, witty, uncharitably acute. If you want to know what much English life felt like a quarter-of-a-century ago Porter's early poems will tell you. They will also tell you how people talked, what they ate, drank, how they dressed. . . . It was a world of espresso bars . . . , in which there was a newly fashionable concern with discussing cancer and the bomb. And Porter set it all down. . . .

But for the most part Porter is our best satirist of *moeurs contemporaines*. He has a kind of disenchanted, tough relish for the world he observes, and it is easy to understand why he so admires Rochester. As with Rochester, a dark seam of cheerlessness is always threatening to break through the surface wit of his poems. 'Unhappiness is real as turning round', he says in **'Between Two Texts'**, but on the other hand he knows that 'real pain is never art' (**'Ode to Afternoon'**), and at his best he is therefore a very inventive poet. The famous modesty which he wears like a mask and which has too often been taken at face value should not lead anyone to assume that he is careless about his craft. He may not be formally very adventurous—though the **'Sanitised Sonnets'** sequence is managed with a proper *insouciance*—but his way with language is masterly. Anyone who can accommodate 'claggy' and 'matutinal' within the one poem (**'Down Cemetery Road'**) gets my vote. In fact, the worst thing about that poem is its title, and this is odd because Porter is usually so good in this respect that you feel required to read one of the poems simply to see whether it can measure up to its start. (The answer is mostly yes.) It is true that he can occasionally produce a groan-making title such as **'Diana and Actaeon'** with the result that you find yourself murmuring ungratefully, 'but *anyone* can write that sort of a poem'; but then when you read Porter's you realise that the solemnity is merely a way of having you on. *His* **'Diana and Actaeon'** is a teasing, characteristically wry and original inspection of the conscience. . . .

Porter has more exuberant imagination than he's sometimes given credit for. He is also more wide-ranging. In fact, I can't think of any other contemporary poet who is so consistently entertaining over such a variety of material. (p. 21)

> John Lucas, "*A New Daks Suit,*" *in* New Statesman, *Vol. 105, No. 2715, April 1, 1983, pp. 21-2.*\*

## PETER LEVI

If you take poetry now as a serious entertainment, which satisfies curiosity and bemuses you with newness much as modern music does, then you must admire Peter Porter. Other poets have admired him greatly since 1961. There is no comfort and little instruction to be had from him. His strength is technical. He is the furthest point of distance from Tennyson or from Milton that English poetry has ever reached. He is sharp, sarcastic, and egg-bound with culture. . . . His style often resembles late Roman satire, full of grit and gravel and sudden baroque soarings, and bespattered with vinegar. His translations of Martial, usefully reprinted [in *Collected Poems*], have the right morbid brilliance.

It is said that Matthew Arnold in his generation introduced poetry as a substitute for religion; by comparison, Peter Porter's poetry is a believing man's substitute for atheism; there is something bright and Sixtyish inside much of his work, though he is too deep a poet to be dogmatic about a modern view of life. His mind is disappointed, angry and alive, 'to all it suffered once a weeping witness'. He is almost never boring, very seldom impertinently obscene. He can hardly have lost a reader in his career. And yet something must be wrong, because in 22 years I have never learnt a poem by him by heart, and after constant re-readings over that period I find few familiar phrases except for titles. Maybe he is simply too demanding for the way we use books, as modern music is for the way we use the wireless. These collected poems offer a new kind of opportunity; they stand well together and reveal a continuous human strength.

What lasts in literature as in alcohol, as some ancient critic remarked, is a dryish taste verging on the formidable. That would include Peter Porter, though personally I prefer Herrick or Cotton for everyday use. But Porter's foundations are sound; he has been able to express more about the world than most writers since 1961. It may be that his career has been one long experimentation: to incorporate Auden's cleverness and aridity, Larkin's sourness, the concentration of Wallace Stevens, the fire of John Marston who advises anger, the surrealism of Christopher Smart, the simple and truthful baroque of Henry King. Peter Porter's most convinced fans find in the poems of grief for his dead wife . . . , particularly in *An Exequy,* based on Henry King's, a leap forward of his style, an admirable breakthrough of straightforwardness and grief. Certainly these poems are moving, but they could not possibly have been written without a long and varied series of experiments. They are just one mood, one model, among many, and Peter Porter's most recent poems have departed in other directions. . . .

But some of his informal and syllabic rhythms lose in the memory more than they gain in the attention. Too much cleverness undoes him, and his recent admiration for John Ashbery adds a further depressing element. There has been a certain obstinate dullness at the bottom of the souls of many greater writers in this century, more so in England than America no doubt, and more so in Dorset and Hull than in London to be sure. And yet what a relief towards the end of such a century to read completely intelligent, absolutely modern poems. . . . At the least, Peter Porter is an antidote and a reviver.

The label of satiric verse applies mostly to his early manner, which reaches a climax in a series of sarcastic sonnets exploding like barrels of smooth gunpowder, his *Sanitized Sonnets* published in 1970. Since that time his experiments have involved a broadening of range and a trial of confident tones. Some of the poems are occasional and deflating, but some attempt a new range and are more direct. They do seem, by hindsight, to lead towards *An Exequy* four years before that event. Even if we disallow simple grief and prefer complexity, two benefits tilt Peter Porter's account heavily into credit. He is a true poet's poet; to other poets his experiments always look worthwhile. And he is often extremely funny. . . .

Greatness is surely a kind of dishonesty, unless one is born Shakespeare, and Peter Porter seems to refuse it. What he attains is depth, the best that art can do. He does so by bravura with his technical means, by irony and contrast of many kinds.

> *Peter Levi, "Funny Poet," in* The Spectator, *Vol. 250, No. 8076, April 23, 1983, p. 24.*

## DOUGLAS DUNN

Porter's vision (in his own words it could be called a 'consumer's report' on life/God) is demandingly bleak. It is rhetorically engraved, frequently diverting, often funny in spite of its insistent seriousness. To spend a few days with his *Collected Poems* is to begin to see Porter as a large-minded classical fantasist, or fantasy classicist, whose imagination has the superiority to be both realistically moral and consistently original.

As a result many readers are happier than they should be with the comfortable notion that Porter is a 'social poet'. It is understandable, even if it simplifies the complexities of Porter's writing. Earlier poems such as **'John Marston Advises Anger'**, **'The World of Simon Raven'** and many others sketch an amusingly disdainful picture of foolish odds and ends of the contemporary scene. Satirical particularity runs through his work. By his three most recent collections [*Living in a Calm Country, The Cost of Seriousness,* and *English Subtitles*], however, his satirical impulses are put away, remaining, perhaps, as a general tough-mindedness. (pp. 74-5)

To call Porter a social poet avoids attending to the meaning of his poetry. His commitments are cultural and human; he is social only in the sense that an author to whom urbanity is an ideal inevitably finds the human condition(s), past and present, of greater immediate fascination than spiritual guesswork, botanical and zoological analogues or a tidily aesthetic purism. It would be wrong, though, to suppose that Porter's poetry neglects the mystery of being. What has always been impressive in his work is an irritated gnawing at how that mystery is fudged, and misrepresented by those who, claiming it is everything, pass over the book of reality as well as ignore the humility through which the unknown and unknowable are to be acknowledged. There is a near-religious feeling in Porter's seriousness which, if vexed and doubtful, is present for all that. Besides that respect (it may follow naturally from a respect for the rituals of art) to write with apparent conviction that 'only imagination is yourself' (**'Hints from Ariosto'**) puts a wide distance between Porter and those whose definitions of reality are materialist and allegedly rational.

Even so, the real world is abundantly present in his verse, in, for example, its diction as well as its occasions. More than any poet now writing (more so than Larkin, if only because there is much more of Porter) Porter allows his poems to appropriate words and images which more fastidious poets would shun. In Porter's poetry you will find Harrods and Heals, Matt Munro, Pat Boone, the Dunciad on Ice, spin-driers, cat-food, paddipads and plexiglass, 'the Fit City warm with mini-praise', Hi-Fi, tights, brand names, the world over which trundles an American machine 'with Hot Gothic printed on its brow'. A

line like 'A firework of freeloaders day-tripping by the burgher's sea' is characteristic of how what amounts to a mixture of high and low styles can work. There are many poets in whose poems I cannot imagine the word 'freeloaders' appearing other than as an embarrassment. . . . That Porter can get away with journalistic diction, without any loss of authenticity, is, I feel, an indication of at least one of his particular and important literary virtues. He has not accepted poetry as an ideal language in the sense that in obedience to the bias of poetic tradition it must recoil from the usages of mass society—a society which Porter's culture defies, but not his humanity, which is omniverous if also, of course, ironic. Temperamentally, he is too unrespectable for a satire of prissy distaste, one of unwholesome superiority. For all the witty erudition and witty historical anecdotage of his verse, he is brave, too, in his colloquial candours, lively, and unlikely to be lined up with those whom he calls 'Laureates of Low Spirits'. (pp. 75-6)

Curiously, Porter's mastery of rhyme and metre became assured after about three or four books. At one time, if I remember correctly, he admitted in print that he felt himself weak in the rhythmical side of poetry. While that characteristically candid admission ought to be disputed, it is true that there are instances of clumsiness in his earlier work. But a productive poet can survive a few blemishes here and there. . . .

Porter's wife died lamentably young. . . . A poet has little choice but to write about what happens; there are events in life which make the gift of poetry seem like a curse instead of a delight, although in these times it is seldom a happy art for its practitioners unless for those blinkered or complacent enough to see universal misfortune in a mood of remote dismay. It is bad to live through anguish; it is worse, much worse, to have to write about it.

So gifted a balance of realism and fantasy, knowledge and feeling, reasonableness and an informed admission of the irrational, lend Porter's elegies a movingly unsentimental scope. **'Old Fashioned Wedding'**, for instance, has something of the touch of a poet writing from the pain of his own grief.

In its grievous, rhymed iambic tetrameter couplets, **'An Exequy'** dispenses with erudite referencing. Taking its place is a simple strength of mind. The poem's solemnity, its dignity, is braced by it. **'An Exequy'** strikes me as an authentic funeral monument, a poem as likely to last as long as the elegy by Bishop King whose form it imitates. (p. 77)

[If] his work is seldom mellow and reassuring, it is certain at least in its own undoubted veracities, defiant in its faith in literature and its love of painting and music.

> I haven't enjoyed life. I don't want to die.

That line of antithetical remorse and fear amounts to more than a mordant joke. It is a token epitomizing the wit and realism that many readers will associate with sanity and talent. (pp. 77-8)

> *Douglas Dunn, "A Piece of Real," in* London Magazine, *n.s. Vol. 23, No. 3, June, 1983, pp. 74-8.*

## DICK DAVIS

There used to be an anthology of modern verse for schoolchildren that contained the sentence (more or less, I quote from memory): 'Peter Porter's subject is the decadence of Western capitalist society; he works in an advertising agency.' I don't know whether this juxtaposition was deliberate or not, but it does indicate the source of that slight unease which reading [*Collected Poems*] can give—the sense that you are watching a man profoundly given to having his cake and eating it too. The feeling is reinforced by the juxtapositions in the poems themselves, 'Green stamps for the furnishings of Heaven', 'Consider the lilies and the talcum of the field', 'talks on God are issued as supplements', 'God in aspic', 'the Grail filled with orange cup', 'Owing so much to God and the National Trust' and so on. Where does the poet stand? The question seems irrelevant, but if some kind of moral alternative is not being presented in these phrases, what *is* being presented? Again, I think we sense disgust in such formulae, but if the disgust is directed against the paraphernalia of a superficial consumer society—as it seems to be—what are the verities against which this superficiality is weighed by the poet and found wanting?

Well, the word 'God' appears fairly frequently, as can be seen from my quotations (though Porter at one point describes himself as an atheist), as does, though rather less often, 'Heaven'. Both are left unexplained, and largely unexplored, as are the two other words he uses most frequently when he appears to be about to own up to an emotion unqualified by irony—'hell' (a word he is very fond of, and one of the few nouns he is not driven to quirkily qualify every time it appears) and 'death'. Of the four, death is the word which he comes closest to discussing, and it indicates a subject he returns to obsessively; death is the fact which he approaches with most persuasion and authority. Reviewers have praised his recent poems on the death of his wife but the sense of death which, it seems to me, he more successfully conveys is a metaphorical one connected with the whole culture in which he feels implicated, and by extension with the mind that by observating and recording that culture absorbs its values. . . .

Porter's mentor has clearly been Auden. I mentioned above his apparent need to define his nouns with self-consciously unexpected—often abstract—epithets . . . ; and this is a device Auden made his own, using it to create a very idiosyncratic sense of dislocation between the perceiving mind and the perceived world. Auden also liked to sum up a culture or time or scene by slightly bizarre and seemingly random vignettes presented in quick succession and Porter obviously finds it quite difficult to get through many poems without resorting to the same device.

In Auden's poems we feel that this examining and crowding of particulars refer back to a pressure and magnanimity of mind, a sense of quest and desire for meaning, an inability to rest in the given; but in Porter's poems the vision, or even the need

for vision, which the reader feels would justify this whimsical itemising and poring over quotidian reality, seems to be simply absent—or at best indicated by the laconic buzz-words God, Heaven, hell, death.

Without such a defining perspective, or some intimation of what it might be, the cultural references and kaleidoscopic little scenes from contemporary life can drift dangerously close to being not much more than the higher chat. At times you feel that Porter is manifesting those very mores the poems appear to have set out to condemn. . . . It is very well done, and many of the jokes have worn well, but the reader has an almost continuous feeling that the poet's considerable energies and talents have been committed to evasion and distraction, and it is difficult to believe that lastingly satisfying poetry can be written out of so earnest a wish not to look beneath the surface of things, beguilingly horrid though that surface may be.

*Dick Davis, "An Absent Vision," in* The Listener, *Vol. 110, No. 2822, August 18, 1983, pp. 20-1.*

## ALAN BROWNJOHN

[Porter's *Collected Poems*] is currently the best volume of its kind, the most substantial and impressive one, since those of Auden, MacNeice and Roy Fuller.

It is a less approachable *opus* than theirs. Porter stands to Auden rather as Michael Tippett stands to Benjamin Britten: lacking the sheer range, technical adroitness and felicity of his inventions, yet possessing an emotional and intellectual force which takes hold on the imagination more gradually, and finally seems compelling and memorable. Fashion has treated Porter variably; but then the metropolitan literary universe to which some would consign him is really an unfortunate isle itself, surrounded by oceans infested with syllabuses and grudging prejudices. Although one famous poem, **"Your Attention Please"**, has been taken up by a rock group, he is not very widely studied and quoted; a steady groundswell of interest among readers here and abroad may alter that.

His poetry is a poetry of harsh intelligence, and unswerving responsibility to the standards of the art. The 300 pages of the *Collected* offer something for which we should be grateful: writing which is honestly and searchingly addressed to the major concerns of art and civilisation in our time. It is a book for anyone who cares for, and about, English poetry in the post-War years. (p. 84)

*Alan Brownjohn, "From the Eighth Floor of the Tower: The Collected Peter Porter," in* Encounter, *Vol. LXI, No. 2, September-October, 1983, pp. 80-4.*

# Thomas (Ruggles) Pynchon (Jr.)

## 1937-

American novelist, short story writer, and nonfiction writer.

Pynchon's novels are often described as encyclopedic and labyrinthine. He develops an aura of great mystery and incorporates ideas from an array of disciplines in both the natural and social sciences in order to explore values of contemporary Western society. Pynchon's use of sophisticated ideas is balanced by his verbal playfulness; black humor, puns, slapstick, running gags, parody, and songs are among the elements included in his fiction. Through this blend of serious themes and comedic inventiveness and the combination of documented fact and fabulous creations, Pynchon simultaneously suggests and denies that hidden meaning lurks beyond mundane reality. Pynchon's protagonists typically undertake vague yet elaborate quests to discover their identity and to find meaning and order within the chaos of modern life; this chaos is mirrored in the fragmented structure of Pynchon's novels. While Pynchon's works have met with mixed critical reviews, they have been the subject of many scholarly exegeses and have proven to be especially popular among young people.

Pynchon's literary career began with the publication of several of his short stories in various periodicals. Five of these early works are collected in *Slow Learner* (1984), a volume that is uncharacteristically introduced by Pynchon, who strictly maintains his anonymity and rarely makes public statements outside of his fiction. Although Pynchon's short stories have been negatively received, they offer useful insight into his thematic and stylistic development. Pynchon's initial novel, *V.* (1963), was praised as an exemplary work of black humor. Like works by such authors as Joseph Heller, William Burroughs, Kurt Vonnegut, and John Barth, *V.* is characterized by experimental form and absurd humor. *V.* relates the obsessive search by Herbert Stencil to discover the identity of a person or thing referred to as "V." in his father's diary. Stencil's quest is complicated by a superabundance of clues which he feels compelled to follow. During his travels, Stencil comes in contact with a group of people known as "the Whole Sick Crew" whose decadence and aimlessness are considered representative of the moral, social, and cultural decline of the West. Pynchon contrasts the energetic Stencil with the moribund state of the Whole Sick Crew as part of an extensive investigation into the nature of the animate and inanimate. Some critics consider this novel to be an overelaboration of simple themes. However, others were impressed by the vast historical scale of *V.*, particularly its multi-perspective view of twentieth-century events and the intricate network of referents that continually expand the implications of Stencil's quest.

Pynchon's second novel, *The Crying of Lot 49* (1966), is regarded as his most accessible work due to its concise development. In this novel Pynchon uses the Second Law of Thermodynamics, a law of physics that describes entropy, or energy loss, as a metaphor for the forces that contribute to social decline. *The Crying of Lot 49* centers on Oedipa Maas, who is named executrix of the will of Pierce Inverarity, a California real-estate mogul who had been her lover. In executing Inverarity's will,

Oedipa comes upon a number of clues that suggest the existence of a centuries-old communications system secretly operating as a rival to the present-day United States Postal Service. However, like many of Pynchon's characters, Oedipa is unsure whether her perception is valid or a result of either her own paranoia or the manipulation of her thoughts by others. In his fiction, Pynchon repeatedly alludes to paranoia, through which many of his characters attempt to assign an organizing principle to what they consider a random, meaningless world. Like all of Pynchon's works, *The Crying of Lot 49* ends before the protagonist's quest is resolved. Critics have offered many interpretations of this novel but generally agree that Pynchon's use of entropy as a metaphor for the decline of civilization is effective and that the mystery is well developed. Several critics have suggested that Oedipa is a surrogate for the reader.

Pynchon's third novel, *Gravity's Rainbow* (1973), which received the National Book Award, is an immensely complicated work that provoked controversy among critics. Pynchon's detractors attack this novel as obscene, nihilistic, and incomprehensible. On the other hand, many critics consider *Gravity's Rainbow* a masterpiece, contending that Pynchon achieves a work of dazzling artistry and profound implications by exploring a wide variety of human activities and ideas and connecting them with the mass destruction of World War II. This novel, which has been described as an extended meditation on death, offers several perspectives of historical events. Pynchon suggests that Western society actively promotes a culture of death by perfecting such weapons as the German V-2 rocket, and he links advances in science and technology, historical patterns, political, economic, and social values, and international cartels in their contribution to the war effort. *Gravity's Rainbow* is considered Pynchon's finest literary achievement and is regarded by his supporters as among the most important novels in American literature.

(See also *CLC*, Vols. 2, 3, 6, 9, 11, 18; *Contemporary Authors*, Vols. 17-20, rev. ed.; and *Dictionary of Literary Biography*, Vol. 2.)

## ROBERT SKLAR

If fiction has not completely lost its relevance as an art form to creative young people, then it languishes in a period of biding time; since fiction is tied more closely to events and ideas than other arts, perhaps it stands in a fallow period, assimilating new configurations, as happened in the mid-19th century after Darwin and the early 20th after Freud. In this perspective, Thomas Pynchon is far more than, dutifully recognized, the only known and therefore leading writer of the under-30s; for more than any other contemporary American novelist he has succeeded, in two interesting, intelligent and serious novels, in absorbing and transforming new scientific and philosophical perspectives within his art. (p. 277)

The critical point in Pynchon's career so far lies in the radical shift in literary focus he undertook to make from *V.* to *The*

*Crying of Lot 49*. To say that the second novel is a better and more important novel than the first is not simply a way of scoring an easy victory over dull reviewers or doggedly insisting on a principle of growth. To grasp the nature of Pynchon's shift, for its artistic and intellectual value, and as a liberating gesture in its own right, is to take the measure of his wider significance for contemporary American fiction.

As a liberating gesture, Pynchon's shift from *V.* to *The Crying of Lot 49* broke him free from the constricting limitations of belonging to a "school" and writing in a genre. One reason the second novel proved disappointing to some admirers of the first, in fact, was its failure to fulfill the stereotyped expectations they had held for him. Yet even if *V.* wears a "black-humor" label, and stands as one of the most intricate and elaborate novels in that genre, it accomplishes a good deal more than that. One who rereads *V.* in the light of *The Crying of Lot 49* may come to feel that *V.* is itself a liberating gesture, a gesture of liberation from nearly all the styles and forms of fiction that have preceded it.

As *Catch-22* may be the first American novel truly to have attained a Cubist form in its treatment of space and time, so *V.* may be the first American novel of collage, an abstract composition put together with parodies of spy novels, political novels, adventure novels, decadent novels, romances, utopias and whatever other category the ingenious mind can find. . . . [The] attentive explicator will find that one of the principal subjects of parody in *V.* is the "black-humor" style itself.

Read in the light of *The Crying of Lot 49*, then, *V.* does not appear as a launching platform for a style or a subject but rather as an isolated object or as an ending. That novel published in 1963 seems in 1967 not so much a contemporary work as a historical work, a novel that reflects the moods of the late fifties in America and the style of the early sixties. Part of this feeling, if it is an accurate one, may be attributed to a stylistic trait of the novel common to many works in the "black-humor" genre, a style deliberately constructed to put a distance between the reader and the work, as if the novel were a game drawing on the reader's mental faculties but deliberately excluding his emotions. (pp. 277-78)

*V.* is like a riddle that once correctly answered never taxes the mind again; *The Crying of Lot 49* is founded in an emotion of mystery, an emotion which remains, inviolate and mysterious, even when the outward mystery is solved. *V.* is a complex novel that gets simpler with each rereading, *The Crying of Lot 49* a simple novel that reread grows more complex.

*V.* is chiefly memorable for what its earlier admirers called its vast warehouses of information, its immense knowledgeability, its prodigies of research. If one function of the novel, as Mary McCarthy once suggested, has been to provide facts, to let the reader know how to catch a whale or cut a field of hay, Pynchon's *V.* may rank as one of the most encyclopedic founts of facts in the history of the novel. In *V.* the reader may find out how to perform a nose operation; how the Germans wiped out the native population of South West Africa before the First World War; how British espionage agents operated in the Middle East since the time of Kitchener; a good part of the history of Malta in this century, and much more. How much one may care to rely on Pynchon's facts is another matter. . . . [Given] Pynchon's propensity to parody the fictional styles which have conveyed this sort of subject in the past, it might be wise not to make any bets on the basis of what one reads in *V.* In any case the truth of Pynchon's details, or even their significance, is not a matter that deeply engages the reader's concern.

Form and style in *The Crying of Lot 49* combine to give a far greater resonance to facts. . . .

Nevertheless, Pynchon has created in *V.* an aura of formidable intellectual competence, and nowhere more significantly than in his mastery of scientific and technical subjects, particularly physics and electronic technology. It may be that no American novelist before Pynchon—science-fiction writers not excepted—has brought so thorough and so prepared a scientific intelligence to bear on modern life, and this capacity to include in the novel the pervasive scientific and technological aspects of our day-to-day lives rather than to neglect them through ignorance, may make *V.* a landmark of the novel in yet another sense.

It is true, though, that Pynchon dissipates this competence by expending it on a theme beloved of science-fiction writers and their cousins among black humorists, the battle between men and machines, between the power of animation and the power of the inanimate. . . . At the heart of Pynchon's imagination lies not science and technology, nor the parody and wild humor which are so much a part of his style but a sense of mystery, a vision of fantasy, that expresses itself in dualisms, in images of surface and depth, of mirrors, of secret societies and hidden worlds.

The prime mystery of *V.*, of course, is the mystery of V. herself, as a woman in many guises—Victoria Wren, Hedwig Vogelsang, Veronica Manganese, a mysterious woman in Paris, the Bad Priest killed in Malta—as a bald cipher that is charged with greater resonance with every repetition, until the eye responds to every captial letter V as if it were inked in red. . . . Who is V.? The British espionage agent, Sidney Stencil, one of her lovers, in 1899 had written in his journal: "There is more behind and inside V. than any of us had suspected. Not who, but what: what is she? God grant that I may never be called upon to write the answer, either here or in any official report."

Pynchon, however, does feel called upon to write the answer, and he raises few mysteries in *V.* for which he does not quite openly and obviously provide the solution. But to answer who she is in her many masks is not to answer Sidney Stencil's question, what she is, and that question Pynchon leaves to his exegetes. (p. 278)

Pynchon's radical shift in literary focus from *V.* to *The Crying of Lot 49* took the shape not of new themes and images but rather changes in form and tone that significantly altered the value of old themes and images. His verbal playfulness, puns and jokes are reduced in quantity rather than intensity, and are made to serve the movement of the novel. Factual materials remain as important to the second novel as to the first, but where in *V.* the facts seemed to have been real but not necessarily true, Pynchon quite obviously invented the "historical facts" in *The Crying of Lot 49* for the purpose of the novel and thereby made them more plausible, artistically more true. The form of *V.*, moreover, exaggerated the sense of mystery and the aura of an exotic unknown, though Pynchon too often broke in and disengaged the mystery by providing explanations. In *The Crying of Lot 49*, the form of the novel centers on the normal and the everyday: strange events are explained earnestly and straightforwardly, yet the aura of mystery obstinately grows. And finally, whatever sense of mystery remained in *V.* was focused and contained by the past, where in *The Crying of Lot*

*49* the feeling of mystery that will not down comes inexorably to rest in the present and the future.

*The Crying of Lot 49* is the story of how Mrs. Oedipa Maas discovers a world within her world, an anti-world, an adversary world—or invents one in her imagination. (pp. 278-79)

Oedipa comes upon her new magic—to adopt language which Pynchon's reference to religion validates—in an immanent world which gradually becomes more and more imminent.

The adversary world reveals itself to Oedipa through the symbol of a muted post horn and also by signs bearing the initials WASTE or w.a.s.t.e. These signs and symbols represent an underground postal system which operates parallel to or in direct subversion (through forged stamps and cancellations) of the U.S. Post Office. Oedipa pursues the long history of this secret system through investigations into the arcane byways of bibliography—a good part of the novel centers on the performance of a mock Jacobean revenge play, *The Courier's Tragedy,* and the tracing of its various texts and editions—and philately, giving Pynchon an opportunity to display his intellectual ingenuity in two fields he neglected to cover in *V.*

But the backbone of Pynchon's intellectual structure in *The Crying of Lot 49* as in *V.* is science, and in the second novel he develops a scientific metaphor far more rich and more original than the animate-inanimate dichotomy he borrowed or parodied in *V.* . . . Pynchon set down the new theme even more precisely in a preliminary short story, **"Entropy,"** of which however, only the theme carried over to the novel. In physics the term entropy applies to the second law of thermodynamics. It describes loss of energy, or the amount of energy unavailable for use in a thermodynamic system. Henry Adams borrowed this idea for his essay, "The Rule of Phase Applied to History," in which he calculated the running down of intellectual energy on earth—Thought would reach the limits of its possibilities, he postulated, in the year 1921.

Henry Adams' concept of entropy lies at the core of Pynchon's story of that title, but the concept of entropy most important for *The Crying of Lot 49* derives from communications and information theory, particularly as that term was discussed by the mathematician Norbert Wiener. In *The Human Use of Human Beings* and in *Cybernetics,* Wiener argued against the pessimism which the second law of thermodynamics had engendered in Henry Adams and others. He agreed that the universe's energy would surely run down some day, but at a given moment in a given part of the system there were forces powerful enough to decrease entropy, to increase the amount of available energy in that part. "We may well regard living organisms," Wiener wrote, "such as Man himself, in this light." In *The Crying of Lot 49* Pynchon takes up not only the scientific significance of Wiener's viewpoint but its obvious social and political significance as well. The w.a.s.t.e. system puts to use moral and human energies that the surface system—the United States Government and the dominant American mode of life, as Pynchon makes explicit—lets go to waste.

*The Crying of Lot 49* is a radical political novel. Where in *V.* . . . Pynchon tossed out an idea of political apocalypse with bravado and as if to scare the liberals, in *The Crying of Lot 49* he never uses the word "apocalypse" but rather builds a concept and a structure of revolution right into the form of the novel. Unexpectedly Oedipa runs across a Mexican anarchist she and Pierce had once argued with in Mexico. The anarchist says to her:

You know what a miracle is. Not what Bakunin said. But another world's intrusion into this one. . . . Like the church we hate, anarchists also believe in another world. Where revolutions break out spontaneous and leaderless, and the soul's talent for consensus allows the masses to work together without effort, automatic as the body itself. And yet, señá, if any of it should ever really happen that perfectly, I would also have to cry miracle. An anarchist miracle.

*The Crying of Lot 49,* too, in this sense, is an anarchist miracle, a novel which not only postulates another world but creates with the truth of art another world's intrusion into this one.

It is perhaps idle to talk of American tradition in the novel, but one of the unmistakable virtues of *The Crying of Lot 49* is its success in making new and contemporary a traditional concern of the great American novelists—the creation, through the style and form of their fiction, of a social system more true to their national ideals than the existing political and social system. *The Crying of Lot 49* ends with Oedipa Maas awaiting the auctioning of the lot of postage stamps which will prove whether the muted post horn symbol and the w.a.s.t.e. signs form only a web to snare her paranoia or, in truth, the communication network of another world.

For all his philosophical and scientific competence, for all his revolutionary political inclinations, Pynchon is above all an artist; and the ending of *The Crying of Lot 49* makes clear what the Argentine Jorge Luis Borges meant when he wrote in an essay, "that imminence of a revelation that is not yet produced is, perhaps, the aesthetic reality." One would like to say of *The Crying of Lot 49* what T. S. Eliot said of *The Great Gatsby,* that it represents the first step forward for American fiction in some time; for if the road ahead for fiction lies in the direction Borges in his stories has pointed, toward greater philosophical and metaphysical sophistication, Pynchon surely ranks as the most intelligent, most audacious and most accomplished American novelist writing today. (pp. 279-80)

> Robert Sklar, "The New Novel, USA: Thomas Pynchon," in The Nation, Vol. 205, No. 9, September 25, 1967, pp. 277-80.

## EDWARD MENDELSON

Pynchon's anonymity—like his books—calls into question the familiar modes of modern writing and the styles of modern authorship. Just as his books take little interest in the interior psychological labyrinths and the narrow domestic landscapes which are the fields of this century's fiction, so his minimal personal presence in the literary world, the vacancy he offers to the eye of the camera and the interviewer, deliberately rejects all the varieties of artistic heroism which the romantic and modernist traditions have created. Pynchon's books try to be seriously *there*; while he himself is somewhere else entirely.

The aggrandizement of the self-conscious artist, the conflation (as in Joyce) of his person into his work—or, conversely, the cultivation (as in Beckett) of a detachment so complete and serene that it lifts the artist entirely away from the world of his subjects—are both consequences of the change in sensibility which marked the end of the eighteenth century, whose effects are still with us. That change established self-consciousness (or its corollary, the self's consciousness of a world important only to the extent that it is perceived) as the central fact of human existence and as the central subject of art. It transferred the significant aspects of history from the stable generalities of the human race to the dynamic particularity of individual nations and individual minds. The romantic era hardly invented self-consciousness, but until then it had been a *problem* only for the exceptional—only for the rare Oedipus or Hamlet whose self-conscious isolation could be watched with pity and fear by audiences who were secure in the knowledge that they would never share it. (pp. 1-2)

Pynchon is one of a few, as yet a very few, major writers for whom self-consciousness is a central problem only in their early work, a problem they eventually manage to put aside. In these writers' maturity, self-consciousness becomes only one of many possible channels of perception, and not the most important one. (Brecht is another such writer; Auden is a third.) To the methods of reading and criticism which the past two centuries have developed in order to domesticate romantic and modernist literature, the work of these writers is almost opaque and impermeable. But those methods of reading have reached the point of diminishing returns. Pynchon suggests this in *Gravity's Rainbow*. The one character whom the book presents through the techniques of self-conscious modernism ends in disintegration and dissolution. He literally falls apart, diffuses. This character is Tyrone Slothrop, the reflexive, isolated, mysteriously inspired charismatic who attempts a quest for an understanding of his own uniqueness. His literary modes of being, the means through which he exists on the printed page, are private perspective and interior monologue—the central literary modes of the great Moderns. Slothrop's failure and disappearance dramatize Pynchon's conviction that these modes are no longer sufficient to the tasks of literature. The work of self-discovery which they were designed to perform has now been done. For Pynchon there are other tasks, and other methods. . . . (pp. 2-3)

In its attention to the interior landscape, recent fiction has forgotten the density of the exterior one. Modernism prefers to speak of the world of politics and ethics in personal and aesthetic terms. Pynchon does the opposite. In his books, character is less important than the network of relations existing either between characters, or between characters and social and historical patterns of meaning. Pynchon also tries to attend to the force with which history, politics, economics, and the necessities of science and language shape personal choices and are in turn shaped by those choices. To see in this a deliberate turning away from novelistic realism, as some readers have done, is to confuse certain mediating literary conventions with unmediated reality. For most of this century, fiction has located the origins of human action in the depths of personal psychology. Pynchon comes up for air and looks elsewhere. What he finds seems cold and abstract only to the extent that it remains unfamiliar in literature and art (if nowhere else).

Pynchon's realism, in short, is built on an attention to realities ignored by the fiction that we have come to accept as "realistic." That is, Pynchon has begun to develop or revive a repertory of conventions that can render aspects of non-literary experience that Modernist conventions are unable to comprehend. To choose a small but significant example: the characters in *Gravity's Rainbow* are among the very few fictional characters whose thoughts and actions are affected by the work they do. In the world outside fiction, anyone can recognize that there is a connection between one's work and one's idea of the world, but Modernism never found—and necessarily could never have found—a way of making use of this recog-

nition. In part, this is because Modernism itself had no work to do, no *use* or *occasion* that demanded its existence, no function in the world beyond its self-declared claims to significance.

In *Gravity's Rainbow* Pynchon begins to find work for his fiction. He tries to respond to an occasion created for his book by the conditions of recent history; that is, he recognizes the changes in modern culture that have created, as other changes have done in the past, a felt need for an encyclopedic fictional survey of the new conditions. Pynchon's book tries to fulfill a public function. From the perspective of *Gravity's Rainbow*, his earlier books, *V.* and *The Crying of Lot 49,* have the appearance of preparatory exercises for this public work; but they have their own importance as well. *V.* served in part as a preliminary essay in organizing vast quantities of data into a coherent literary form. As a piece of apprentice-work it is already mature in technique, but it also has clear signs of the later depths and range. *The Crying of Lot 49,* Pynchon's most attractive and accessible book, was his first effort, in a narrow field, at detailing the kinds of relationships and responsibilities he would explore massively in his third book. (pp. 4-6)

The problem of responsibility, which arises mostly by indirection in *V.*, makes a direct appearance in *The Crying of Lot 49.* This may be why the second book, although much shorter than the first, is far more substantial. . . . There is generally no doubt, in the world of *V.*, that a process of decline is universal, but it is the reader—and not any of the characters—who is in the privileged position of having no doubt about the matter. In *The Crying of Lot 49,* the status of reader and character is altered. Again there is a universal historical process, but now the reader and the book's central character, Oedipa Maas, have equal knowledge of it—and not only equal knowledge, but equal doubt, and comparable responsibility for its existence or non-existence. There is no certainty in *Lot 49* (as there is in *V.*) that the book's historical process is "really" (by which, in speaking of fiction, I mean "virtually") there: the book ends with both the reader and Oedipa in doubt. The reader is left not with a puzzle to be solved, as in *V.* or *Ulysses,* but with a radical and insoluble problem of interpretation. *V.* leaves its reader secure in his superiority, once he has found the key to all its mysteries of detail. *Lot 49* leaves its reader caught in an irreconcilable ambiguity, one which takes on a disturbing moral weight. The book ends with Oedipa left alone to decide whether the events she has witnessed do in fact cluster together to point to a "reason that mattered to the world" or whether they simply amount to a chaos which her own paranoia has set into a spurious, projected order. The book offers an analogue of this choice to its reader as well: Is the book in part an ethically disturbing parable of the choices he must make in interpreting the world, or is it merely an aesthetic structure? The book challenges its readers to choose their relation to experience. Either, like the romantics and Modernists, they will project their private aesthetic order onto what they perceive as the malleable or ultimately inaccessible objects of the world, or else they will accept responsibility for and to the order which exists already in the world of which they are an active part. This choice is one that everyone confronts at every moment; but great works of art, those works which both rebuke and console, can make the issues vivid and memorable.

By the time Pynchon wrote *Gravity's Rainbow,* there was no longer any doubt about the difficulty of this choice. Responsibility was now real. Everyone in the book is inextricably implicated in complex patterns of meaning, in large historical processes which at once limit freedom and are themselves established by individual acquiescence and choice. In direct addresses to his readers, Pynchon tries to implicate them also in the choices the book itself includes—either passive acceptance and impersonal detachment, or ethical resistance and personal love. *Gravity's Rainbow* is in part a second-person novel which periodically addresses "you." When a question of interpretation—and its ethical consequences—arises, like the question Oedipa must face at the end of *Lot 49,* Pynchon poses the alternative responses and asks, "Which do you want it to be?"

This is more than a rhetorical stance, more than an artist's self-important pose. Pynchon's questions and challenges to his readers have force—in part because in *Gravity's Rainbow* he himself has changed his literary status from *author* to *institution*. Few authors ever undergo this transition; only one or two who achieve it have ever desired it; and some have endured it who wished it had never happened. But when an author becomes a monument in his own lifetime, the history of his work becomes entangled with the history of his readers and his culture. (pp. 7-9)

Critical industries tend to organize themselves around a special variety of book (or author) which is encountered only rarely in literary history. A useful term for such a book is *encyclopedic narrative;* and one can speak also of an *encyclopedic author.* Not all books that establish industries are authentic narratives of this kind . . . , but all encyclopedic narratives are eventually recognized not only as books which have industries attached to them, but also as *national* books that stand as written signs of the culture of which they are a part. The industries devoted to Dante, Shakespeare, Cervantes, and Goethe are not restricted to the academy; they are national industries as well.

All encyclopedic narratives . . . are metonymic compendia of the *data,* both scientific and aesthetic, valued by their culture. They attempt to incorporate representative elements of all the varieties of knowledge their societies put to use. . . . All encyclopedic narratives contain, *inter alia,* theoretical accounts of statecraft, histories of language, and images of their own enormous scale in the form of giants or gigantism. They are generally set a decade or two before publication, so that they can include prophecies of events that actually occurred in history. All are polyglot books, and all are so determined to achieve encyclopedic range that they exclude from their plots the single centripetal focus that develops when a narrative records a completed relation of sexual love. These books usually appear at the moment when a national culture begins to recognize its uniqueness—at that cusp (to use a word from Pynchon) dividing the pre-history of a national culture from its history, its potential from its actual achievements and failures. At least six such books are familiar to literary history: Dante's *Commedia,* Rabelais' five books of Gargantua and Pantagruel, Cervantes' *Don Quixote,* Goethe's *Faust,* Melville's *Moby-Dick,* and (a special case) Joyce's *Ulysses.* Shakespeare's plays . . . hold a comparable place in English culture, as do Pushkin's works in Russia. (pp. 9-10)

The genre of national encyclopedic narrative is severely exclusive in its numbers but massively inclusive in the contents of its individual members. *Gravity's Rainbow* offers itself as the latest member of the genre. The book proposes itself as the encyclopedia of a new international culture of electronic communication and multi-national cartels. Whether or not Pynchon's historical conceptions will eventually correspond to our culture's perception of itself, at least those conceptions have an urgent plausibility. *Gravity's Rainbow* is a book which hopes

to be active in the world, not a detached observer of it. It warns and exhorts in matters ranging from the ways in which the book itself will be read, to the way in which its whole surrounding culture operates.

With some exceptions, critics seem uncomfortable with *Gravity's Rainbow*'s efforts at *agency.* Like generals who are ready to fight the last war but not the next one, critics who dislike *Gravity's Rainbow* try to read it as if it were another *Ulysses.* But to read it this way is to mistake its purpose and its role. (pp. 10-11)

[Joyce] acknowledged that his book focuses on its own structure, and that an understanding of the world outside *Ulysses* is of little use in understanding the world within it. No other major work of art is at the same time so extreme in its factuality and yet so tenuous in its relation to its historical setting.

The inward turn of *Ulysses,* the circularity of its narrative, is among the late consequences of the romantic and modernist sensibility whose triumphant achievement is a literature which exists finally only for itself. Such literature may claim a public function or an unacknowledged legislative role, but these are claims best honored when left untested. (p. 11)

In short, the romantic quest is the image of romantic literature's own condition: purposeless, aspiring to a goal it can never achieve or define. And in *Ulysses,* the circular journey of Bloom, turning in an endless and purposeless repetition, is the culminating disillusioned image of that same condition.

It is different in Pynchon. There is a quest-without-object in *Gravity's Rainbow*—the journey of Tyrone Slothrop—but Pynchon knows that it must lead only to disintegration and dissociation. Pynchon faces, possibly for the first time, the consequences of the romantic quest. Outside the disintegrating Slothrop, the book insists on calling attention to real tasks and purposive choices that cannot be evaded. In *Ulysses,* all ends in resigned forgiveness; from its vast final perspectives, no single event in human history matters very much. But as *Gravity's Rainbow* nears its end, Roger Mexico finds himself approaching a dilemma which he must somehow resolve, a decision from which he cannot turn aside, one which will have irreversible consequences. "It is not a question he has ever imagined himself asking seriously," Pynchon writes. "It has come by surprise, but there's no sending it away now, he really does have to decide, and soon enough. . . . He has to choose between his life and his death. Letting it sit for a while is no compromise." And in raising problems like this one, Pynchon never suggests any comforting possibility that the solutions can be simple or painless.

The ethical problems in *Gravity's Rainbow* have analogues in the linguistic and interpretive problems it raises as well. Language for Pynchon is not a system complete in itself but an ethically and socially performative (his word is "operative") system, one which can be altered by deliberate acts. The model of language in *Ulysses,* on the other hand, is characteristically self-enclosed. For Joyce, the history of language is, in effect, an embryological history (in the chapter known as "Oxen of the Sun"), a version of an unconscious cycle unaffected by personal or social choice. *Gravity's Rainbow*'s history of language (in the episode set in the Kirghiz) is instead political, "less unaware of itself," determined by conscious decisions. Consistently, *Gravity's Rainbow* refers outside itself to the cluster of problems raised by political and ethical conditions, and insists that "letting it sit for a while is no compromise."

In Pynchon, unlike Joyce, the surface details are often incredible and baroque, while the underlying organization is all too plausible and disquieting. Beneath the fantasies and the paranoia, Pynchon organizes his book according to historical and scientific theory—according, that is, to an order independent of *literary* imagination, an order derived more from the realms of politics and physics than from the self-conscious Modernist reflexivities of language and literature. *Gravity's Rainbow*'s large vision of political connectedness has domestic analogues in its vision of sexuality perverted by local varieties of compulsion and control. And, similarly, the book's vision of Slothrop's personal *dis*connectedness (what the book calls "antiparanoia") has its correspondences in the political chaos of the post-war German Zone—a chaos that is about to be ordered once again into bureaucracies, just as the vacancy left by Slothrop's disintegration will be filled with comforting explanations and organized memorialists.

Serene in its vision of unalterable cycles, *Ulysses* ends just before its beginnings, and closes with its tail in its mouth. *Gravity's Rainbow* devotes its final hundred pages not to a return on itself, but to an effort at finding ultimate beginnings and endings. *Ulysses* ends in an eternal return, *Gravity's Rainbow* in the dangerous facts of a moment of crisis—which is, always, our present moment. (pp. 13-14)

[The] special challenge that Pynchon offers to critics and readers is the challenge to become aware—and publicly aware—of their motives and, in the political sense, of their *interests*. This challenge is never made by modernist literature, which, like romanticism, imagines that it establishes its own value, and uses only its own terms to question itself.... *Gravity's Rainbow*, when intelligently read, gives little comfort to the interpretive legions who would rationalize and restrain. And the book has no tolerance for their unacknowledged social motives. (pp. 14-15)

It would be satisfying if one could report that Pynchon's challenge has been met by his critics, but for the most part this has not been the case. There is, of course, nothing that requires a critic to think as his author does—literary history would be in chaos if there were—but when an author questions the basis of a critic's enterprise, then that critic ought at least to acknowledge that the question has been raised. Pynchon's challenge to confront the motives of criticism, his insistence that readers consider the *effects* of interpretation in the world of ethics, is precisely the challenge that criticism must face if it is to escape at last from the centripetal, reflexive momentum of romantic and Modernist writing and of the literary theory that such writing has engendered. Recent critical theory, especially in its philosophical branches, merely extends the hermetic self-referentiality that his already brought literary Modernism to its unmourned dead end.

Pynchon's challenge to literary studies offers one means of turning away from this dead end—there are other means available as well, of course—and to turn instead to methods of reading that have (as Oedipa Maas imagines in a similar context) "a reason that mattered to the world." As with criticism, so with the act of reading itself: Pynchon challenges his readers to participate, not merely in the linguistic and philosophical puzzles of his books' interpretation, but in the choices that those books make plain. It is a challenge with special urgency, for it is offered by a writer who—in the judgement of this reader, and of many others—is the greatest living writer in the English-speaking world. (p. 15)

*Edward Mendelson, in an introduction to* Pynchon: A Collection of Critical Essays, *edited by Edward Mendelson, Prentice-Hall, Inc., 1978, pp. 1-15.*

## JOSEPH W. SLADE

[*The essay from which this excerpt is taken originally appeared in a different form in* Thomas Pynchon *by Joseph W. Slade, Warner Paperback Library, 1974.*]

"**The Small Rain,**" Pynchon's first story, is his most conventional, the product of an undergraduate perhaps drawing on his military experience. Yet it introduces a character type and a theme that will become constants in Pynchon's fiction: a potential "redeemer" who fails to rejuvenate a waste land because, like the paranoids of *Gravity's Rainbow,* he wants "to perfect methods of immobility." Immobility in Pynchon's world is the schlemiel's defense against entropy, the paranoid's means of coping with randomness, the decadent's denial of motion; it is, finally, the romantic's false notion of transcendence, the stillness at the apogee of a rocket's parabola. The comic, passive figure in "**The Small Rain**" is Nathan "Lardass" Levine, a pudgy graduate of CCNY gone deliberately to seed as an army recruit at Ft. Roach, Louisiana, partly as a protest against the phoniness of intellectuality. In contrast to most of his buddies, Levine enjoys the torpid mindlessness of army routine, which relieves him of responsibility.... Levine is temporarily jostled from inertia by a hurricane that has devastated the bayou country of southern Louisiana. His communications unit is ordered into rescue operations with the National Guard.

From the college campus where the army sets up headquarters, Levine surveys a literal waste land whose metaphoric value is underscored by Pynchon's references to T. S. Eliot. Levine is the symbolic redeemer come to the swamps that now contain sterility and death. Whenever he appears someone exclaims "Jesus Christ!" A communications expert, Levine dreams of all humanity on "a closed circuit." ... "Everybody on the same frequency. And after a while you forget about the rest of the spectrum and start believing that this is the only frequency that counts or is real." His is a longing for human community without the diversity that would make the community human, and it attests to his incompetence as a healer. The July sun beats down on the swamp, but Levine is a "seed that casts himself on stony places, with no deepness of earth." He helps pick up corpses, tries to succor, and thinks of lifegiving rain, but lacks fertility himself: he is a "Wandering Jew" without "identity" or potency. Even in what should be an oasis in this figurative desert, the college campus, there is no potential for salvation, only the trivial intellectuality Levine despises. Here Levine meets and sleeps with a coed who calls herself Little Buttercup and who has no "capacity to give." Having been conditioned by pornographic novels to regard women as objects, Levine can offer this "swamp wench" neither fertility, love, nor involvement; their union ends in stasis. In what is his first statement about modern society's sexual love of death, Pynchon has Levine remark after intercourse, "In the midst of great death ... the little death." (pp. 69-70)

Although "**The Small Rain**" does not explore, as Pynchon will explore later, the cultural forces that oppress the modern world, its theme is clear: man has lost the capacity to revivify his landscape. Given the limitations of Pynchon's early methods, chiefly the near-audible clicks of motifs falling neatly into place, the story is fine and workmanlike. If it is a trifle superficial and a bit too sluggishly paced, Pynchon will learn, in his later fiction, to add historical dimension and to animate his plots with the excitement of lunatic quests.

In **"Mortality and Mercy in Vienna,"** Pynchon alludes again to Eliot—and to Shakespeare and Conrad as well—so that while the setting, Washington, D.C., becomes a figurative waste land, it can also be thought of as the lawless Vienna of *Measure for Measure* or as the chaotic jungle of "Heart of Darkness." To a party in Washington comes another redeemer, Cleanth Siegel, a young diplomat recently returned from Europe. Part Catholic, part Jewish (an amalgam that will recur in Benny Profane of *V.*), Siegel's divided nature has apparently unbalanced him and caused him to equate healing with destruction. The party-giver, a strange Rumanian named Lupescu, startled by his *Doppelgänger*-resemblance to Siegel, deputizes the latter as his host and abandons the party to him with these instructions: "As host you are a trinity: (a) receiver of guests '—ticking them off on his fingers—'(b) an enemy and (c) an outward manifestation, for *them,* of the divine body and blood." (p. 71)

Siegel is not surprised when one by one the party guests tell him of his similarity to Lupescu and corner him in the Rumanian's "confessional," a bedroom decorated with crossed Browning Automatic Rifles on the wall. This mock priest hears confessions of decadent love affairs and emotional entanglements that increase his hysteria and convince him that the waste land is blighted indeed.

The instrument of healing turns out to be Irving Loon, an Ojibwa Indian himself on the verge of hysteria. When Siegel sees the Indian standing in the apartment like a "memento mori," he recalls from his computer-like memory banks a Harvard anthropology professor for whom "all cultures were equally mad." According to the professor, the Ojibwa live so perpetually on the brink of starvation that the Indian brave succumbs to paranoia, convinced that the forces of nature are arrayed against him. The paranoia culminates in a peculiar psychosis, a personal identification with the "Windigo," a destructive, cannibalistic spirit. (pp. 71-2)

By whispering "Windigo" in Irving Loon's ear, Siegel triggers an irreversible chain of events which will lead to "a very tangible salvation" for the party guests. . . . At this point the allusions to Eliot and Conrad begin to swell. Eliot's waste land requires the imposition of a new mythology, a new religion, before it can be cleansed and healed of its sterility. Ironically, the machine-like Siegel perceives in Irving Loon's primitive paranoia just the kind of healing the waste land needs. It will be a religion of retribution, of apocalypse—a destruction after the manner of Conrad's Kurtz, who wants to exterminate all the brutes. (p. 72)

Pynchon possesses the enviable ability to blend fact and fantasy in such a way that the facts seem less credible than the fantasies. The Windigo psychosis is well documented by anthropologists but appears more preposterous than Lupescu's leaving his party to a stranger or hanging BAR's on his walls. As Pynchon becomes more adept at incorporating his wide knowledge into his stories, the line separating the real and the ridiculous will grow thinner. . . . While Irving Loon is probably the most extreme, other paranoids in Pynchon's fiction seem almost reasonable. In an insane world, call it waste land or whatever, paranoia represents an attempt to establish sanity, to create order out of chaos. To believe, however wrongly, that the world is hostile is to acquire a basis for action. A second motif is an

assumed moral superiority of "primitive" cultures over the decadent, "civilized" type. Superseding the Ojibwas in later stories will be Maltese and Africans, from cultures which have been abused by colonialism but which still retain vitality. A third motif is a human penchant for annihilation as an alternative to a blighted world. Like Conrad's Kurtz, Cleanth Siegel suffers from a void within, made unbearable by the perception of a void without; Siegel and his successors in Pynchon's work cannot tolerate such a vacuum.

Still another redeemer appears in Pynchon's third story, **"Low-lands,"** an explicit parody of *The Waste Land*. Dennis Flange, the protagonist, resembles both Lardass Levine of **"The Small Rain"** and Benny Profane of *V.;* More accurately, he is the prototype for Roony Winsome and Mucho Maas, the disaffected husbands of *V.* and *The Crying of Lot 49*. Another figure, Geronimo Diaz, a mad psychiatrist, prefigures the zany shrinks of the novels. **"Low-lands"** also marks the debut of Pig Bodine, the ubiquitous all-round pervert and good-natured if slightly sinister slob that his name suggests. And for the first time Pynchon makes use of what will become virtually a trademark: underground passages. Throughout his work tunnels serve as psychological and metaphysical arcs, as negative parabolas that will have positive counterparts in the flights of the V-2 in *Gravity's Rainbow*.

In **"Low-lands,"** Dennis Flange's marriage is going sour. Behind the failure is his passivity. Since his days in the Navy he has retreated almost to a fetal state in his womb-like house on Long Island, in order to avoid responsibilities he vaguely associates with the sea. So strong is Flange's affinity with the sea that he cannot even talk about it. . . . (pp. 72-3)

Flange has come to think of his life as a flat surface, with "an assurance of perfect, passionless uniformity"; what he fears most is a convexity, a bulging of the planet's curvature that would leave him exposed. This vision of a flat surface, of course, is of a sea without water—in short, Eliot's waste land, arid and sterile. . . .

When Flange's wife throws him out and tells him not to come back, he and Bodine fetch up at the city dump, a waste land ruled over, in lieu of Eliot's Fisher King, by a Negro named Bolingbroke (Shakespeare's Henry IV). Flange immediately perceives a predictable correspondence: the dump is a "lowlands," a flat surface slowly rising into convexity as garbage fills it. By the time Pynchon writes *Gravity's Rainbow,* the accretion of debris or detritus will serve as his principal metaphor for the history of civilization. It is a frightening image: the waste land, in this case a literal one, sifting deeper and deeper in accumulated sterility. (p. 74)

Eliot's waste land suffers from failures of communication and love. Similar failures afflict Flange, and the dump, Pynchon's waste land, symbolizes his life. The dump is not, however, a particularly good paradigm for Flange's condition, if only because we know too little about him; but it does represent an amusing and imaginative attempt to unite the motifs of water and waste made so vivid by Eliot's poem. (p. 75)

If the story is pleasantly nutty, and considerably richer in its imagery than **"The Small Rain,"** **"Low-lands"** is much less accomplished than **"Mortality and Mercy in Vienna."** In the latter, Pynchon's literary allusions bear the weight of his ambiguity without effort. In **"Low-lands,"** because he too closely adapts Eliot's motifs, themselves highly complex and ambiguous, the result is fuzziness. Moreover, the story is essentially static; at the end Flange returns full circle to a fetal state, so that the plot does not advance, although it can be argued that from it Pynchon learns to use multiple plots to carry his themes. In any case, elements of **"Low-lands"** presage motifs and incidents in Pynchon's later works: failures of communication, underground networks, oddballs who enjoy Vivaldi, loving females, images of history, midgets. Considered together, the first three stories exemplify the extremes of response to the waste land of modern civilization: a desire for annihilation, for one's self or for others; and a desire for withdrawal, in order to protect one's self against the waste land's encroachment. (p. 76)

Compromise is the theme of **"Entropy,"** Pynchon's fourth and most mature short story. With **"Entropy,"** Henry Adams displaces T. S. Eliot as Pynchon's principal literary creditor, although references to de Sade, Faulkner, and Djuna Barnes crop up as well. If **"Low-lands"** demonstrates that the saturation of one's work with allusions is tricky business, **"Entropy"** reestablishes the method as a valid artistic approach. Here Willard Gibbs and Ludwig Boltzman are juxtaposed brilliantly with Henry Adams and Henry Miller. From Miller Pynchon takes a metaphor; **"Entropy"** begins with an epigraph from *Tropic of Cancer* in which Miller speaks of our age's depressing cultural and metaphysical climate as inclement weather. With this metaphor Pynchon associates a second, from *The Education of Henry Adams:* the concept of entropy as historical process. (pp. 76-7)

Complicating Pynchon's story is his introduction of communication theory. Within a communication system, many things can cause information to deteriorate; the effect of distortion and noise, as when two people are speaking on a telephone, can act like friction or conduction of energy within a thermodynamic system. In communication theory, then, entropy can represent loss and decay. It can also be a measure of information, and here the ramifications of the term grow complex. Later, in *The Crying of Lot 49,* Pynchon will explore the abstruse relationship between communication theory and thermodynamics; in **"Entropy,"** the term entropy in communications serves merely as counterpoint to the term as applied to the running down of the universe and society.

**"Entropy"** is skillfully constructed around the interlocking metaphors of weather and entropy in its double sense. Its structure can be visualized as parallel vectors pointing in opposite directions—tracks that provide compression and tension for the narrative. On one floor of a Washington, D.C., apartment house, Meatball Mulligan's lease-breaking party, now in its second day has been disintegrating into a chaos steadily augmented by arriving guests.... By contrast, on the floor above a man named Callisto has perfected an ordered existence in a hermetically-sealed, ecologically stable flat at the cost of isolation from the world. In fact, Callisto's apartment is a small-scale jungle, a "hothouse" in which he lives with a girl named Aubade, of French and Annamese ancestry—by which Pynchon may be hinting at exploitation by a technological colonialism. They do not go out, since Callisto fears the outside. He worries about the "heat-death" of the universe, a fixation abetted at the time of the story by the weather. For three days it has been 37 degrees outside; the weather will not change. Paranoiacally, Callisto seizes on the phenomenon as an omen of the end.

The significance of the story's title is amplified in Callisto's ruminations, which Pynchon intersperses with the events of the party below. Outside his room, Callisto believes, a decadent society has reduced people and things from healthy "differ-

entiation to sameness, from ordered individuality to a kind of chaos." ... Callisto tries to resist entropy with love, manifested in his affection for a sick bird and for Aubade. It is the first such linkage of love and power in Pynchon's fiction; but, unlike his creator, Callisto does not realize how feeble a power love is, especially when it is coupled with stasis.

While Callisto treads his mental paces, below stairs Meatball Mulligan's party rollicks on. Meatball's guests range from the weird to the aimless, most of them pseudo-intellectuals, most of them employed by the government in some form of communications. Dominating the rest are the Duke di Angelis quartet, a spaced-out group of musicians sporting sunglasses and smoking marijuana—thoroughly decadent. (pp. 77-9)

As the "system" of his party continues to decay, Mulligan does what he can to keep things functioning—not at top efficiency, but through compromise. Saul is dropping waterbags out the window, a girl is drowning in the bathtub, drunks are fighting, and horny sailors are gate-crashing in the belief that they have found a whorehouse. Unlike Cleanth Siegel at a similar chaotic party, Meatball responds humanely. He has two choices: he can crawl in a closet and wait till everybody leaves, or he can "try to calm everybody down, one by one." The former option is tempting, since the latter involves hard work, but Pynchon is suggesting that hard work is the only legitimate means to combat entropy in social systems. Hard as the job is, Meatball does restore order to his apartment. (pp. 79-80)

**"The Secret Integration,"** the first of Pynchon's stories to appear in a large-circulation magazine, is perhaps his least successful. Published after *V.*, it suffers from the very qualities that make the novel so engaging. *V.* is discursive and loose, but its diffusion is appropriate to its global setting. Equally loose, **"The Secret Integration"** is set in Mingeborough, Massachusetts, the Berkshire Mountain hometown of Tyrone Slothrop, protagonist of *Gravity's Rainbow*; and the small community cannot contain the multiple motifs of the plot. Nevertheless, **"The Secret Integration"** has its moments, and, more important, has elements of considerable relevance to Pynchon's other work. As one might expect, paranoia, technical terminology, and communication and its failures are prominent issues here. (p. 81)

Pynchon's fascination with junkheaps furnishes a focus for **"A Journey into the Mind of Watts,"** his 1966 study of the slums of Los Angeles. The essay is a skillful piece of journalism in which Pynchon traces the ironies and absurdities of black life in a prosperous white city. It is an excellent tonic for the reader daunted by the difficulty of Pynchon's fiction. Although as journalism it is unremarkable, from the standpoint of continuity within Pynchon's work it is important, for it offers a sober and concise view of the Los Angeles he treats comically in *The Crying of Lot 49.* Pynchon constructs his essay around a real junkheap, a landmark in Watts erected by an Italian immigrant named Simon Rodia, who for thirty years gathered scrap and waste into "his own dream of how things should have been: a fantasy of fountains, boats, tall openwork spires, encrusted with a dazzling mosaic of Watts debris." Rodia's heap becomes a metaphor for the wasted lives in the waste land of the black ghetto. (p. 83)

Several aspects of the article are germane to Pynchon's novels, not least of which is his grasp of authentic human suffering. For all his humor, Pynchon exhibits in his fiction, as he does here, an astute and sympathetic understanding of social and political realities that anchors his imagination and turns it toward the complex and very tangible dilemmas of this century. Systems—social, political, religious, economic—become his major concern, as do the paradoxes those systems generate. How is it possible, he will ask, for isolation and inhumanity to persist in the midst of the greatest potential for human community in history? The "media" in **"A Journey into the Mind of Watts"** hint at the approach he takes in his novels. In a sense, Pynchon is the world's first genuine technological novelist: he has evidently read, assimilated, and synthesized Lewis Mumford, Marshall McLuhan, and other theorists of the Second Industrial Revolution. In company with McLuhan in particular, he is preoccupied with all forms of communication, from language and mathematics to television, computers, films, and transportation, and with energy *as* communication, the definitive characteristic of the technological era. Pynchon knows that this energy is different from the energies of earlier eras, that it has disrupted our culture, but he knows also that historical momentum is powerful. While technological communication has the capacity not only to integrate Los Angeles but also to convert the entire planet into McLuhan's "global village," the historical forces of a linear, entropic, western culture fragment, divide, and disinherit. Rather than rejuvenating moribund systems, technology has been perverted to foster fantasies, "mindless pleasures." Technology, be it an alternative system of communication in *The Crying of Lot 49* or the flight of a rocket in *Gravity's Rainbow,* is Pynchon's ultimate "redeemer" for the waste land. So far, like all his other redeemers, it has failed; but the potential is still there. (pp. 85-6)

> Joseph W. Slade, "'Entropy' and Other Calamities," in Pynchon: A Collection of Critical Essays, edited by Edward Mendelson, Prentice-Hall, Inc., 1978, pp. 69-86.

## TONY TANNER

To argue on behalf of Pynchon's importance as a writer would be supererogatory. Placing him in a larger context is more difficult. More difficult, because he seems aware of all the literature that preceded him as well as the writing that surrounds him. From one point of view, he emerges from that extraordinary proliferation of experimentation in the novel which so deeply shaped the direction of American fiction during the 1960s and 1970s. Thus he takes his place in a period of American writing that includes such authors as William Burroughs, Joseph Heller, John Hawkes, John Barth, Robert Coover, Rudolph Wurlitzer, Ishmael Reed, Norman Mailer, Saul Bellow, and many others. The aesthetic funds alive at this time were various, but in particular I believe he was affected by the work of William Gaddis, whose novel *The Recognitions* (1955) exerted a general influence that has yet to be fully traced. This generation of American writers was in turn influenced by many European and South-American writers—in particular, Jorge Luis Borges and Vladimir Nabokov, but also Samuel Beckett, Italo Calvino, Gabriel García Márquez, Alain Robbe-Grillet and Günter Grass. That list could be extended; but suffice it to say that Pynchon was writing his novels during an extraordinarily rich time of ferment and innovation in the contemporary novel, and quickly became one of its essential voices.

However, looked at from another angle, Pynchon's work takes its place in that line of dazzlingly daring, even idiosyncratic American writing which leads back through writers like Faulkner to Mark Twain and Hawthorne, and above all to Melville and *Moby-Dick*. And, taking yet another view, we might want to cite *Tristram Shandy* as an earlier experimental novel that

lies behind him; but then Sterne points us in turn back to Rabelais, and both bear the mark of *Don Quixote* (as does Pynchon)—which is, in a manner of speaking, where the novel as we know it in the West began. Few major modern writers have not in some fashion returned to these origins, and thus we can see Pynchon continuing that series of radical shifts and innovations in fictional technique which was started by Conrad and James, and continued by Joyce—all of whom are more or less audible in his work. Which is all to say that he is both creatively eclectic and unmistakably original. From one point of view, the novel from its inception has always been a mixed genre with no certain limits or prescribed formal constraints; Pynchon, then, is in no way an 'eccentric' novelist, for the novel has no determined centre. Rather he is a key contemporary figure in the great tradition of those who extend the possibilities of fiction-making in arresting and enriching ways—not in this or that 'Great Tradition', but in the great tradition of the novel itself. (pp. 90-1)

> Tony Tanner, in his Thomas Pynchon, Methuen, 1982, 95 p.

## CHARLES CLERC

The word *classic* is bandied so freely these days that it has become virtually meaningless. It is a favorite in the bloated repertoire of hype, and hype, as we all know of contemporary culture, almost never delivers the goods promised. Nevertheless, the word still must be taken seriously when the genuine article comes along. The important criterion for a novel, beyond its own aesthetic accomplishments, is that it will have enduring significance and worth, a work of art to be read and discussed and analyzed with ever renewing enjoyment, understanding, and enrichment by generations of readers.

In these respects, Thomas Pynchon's *Gravity's Rainbow* is destined to become a classic of literature. (p. 3)

It would be unreasonable to expect that any single novel could provide sufficient materials for a liberal education, but certainly *Gravity's Rainbow* comes closer to that goal than any other work of fiction produced in America. It is a dazzling pioneer work in its utilization of manifold subject matter: history, war, mythology, literature, film, culture (whether canonical or pop), religion, philosophy, the military-industrial complex (whether in peace or war), psychology, politics, geography, cybernetics, sex, death, comedy, scatology, music, international cartels, engineering, ballistics, mysticism, plastics, and many more. Further, some of these areas have their own subdivisions; for instance, science, which includes specific uses of chemistry, mathematics, biology, physics, and cosmology. As a multi-topic novel, it thus makes many demands of its readership. . . .

*Gravity's Rainbow* should be experienced, in the best sense of the word. It is a novel to be enjoyed and endured, fought with and agonized over in the zone of intimacy between reader and page. (p. 9)

Whatever interpretations are brought to bear, there is no mistaking the historical foundations upon which the novel is built. Although wonderfully inventive and imaginative, it pays scrupulous attention to verifiable factual details. As historical fiction, one of its chief intentions is to reflect inheritance of the past in the present. The major historical symbol that unifies the four parts of the novel and many of its seventy-three unnumbered chapters and that also resonates into multiple meanings for our own time is the German A-4 rocket, known more commonly as the V-2. The terrible reign of these flying bombs shattered Britain during the latter stage of the war. The Rocket is a symbol that betokens modern civilization's obsession with technology, whether devising, building, or launching the weapon, or pursuing the secrets of its mysterious potency. As a gigantic destructive phallus, it couples sex and death and links to other related obsessions. (p. 11)

*Gravity's Rainbow* is the kind of artistic work that needs to be read slowly, thoughtfully, and persistently in small chunks, without distraction, and then read again and again. Many of its passages are so extraordinary that they ought to be read aloud. Such suggestions may seem unwarranted, perhaps pointless, because the same can be said of any challenging literature. But in this case the advice is emphatically necessary because the reader must surmount obstacles that grow fiercer along the way. To complicate matters, the author puts on an intellectual light show of such erudition that its beams bedazzle rather than clarify. Thus the reader may often be prevented from knowing where he or she is going. . . .

First, the novel's enormous cast is difficult to keep track of, especially in the moiling rush of their entries and exits. Some of the principal characters do not appear until the middle third of the novel. The unsuspecting reader may be thrown off by the initial twenty pages devoted to minor characters. Some incidental characters occupy long later passages; others will merely trip in and out of a paragraph or even a sentence. Furthermore, an important character may be dropped, not to reappear for hundreds of pages, or simply dissolve. (p. 12)

Besides the difficulty of keeping all the characters straight, the reader encounters difficulty following the lines of action. Just as Pynchon abandoned some traditional notions of characterization, he also dispenses with some of the standard and familiar guidelines for constructing plots. In a novel filled with schemes, conspiracies, spying, networks, conglomerates, the plotting cannot be disentangled with any ease, nor should it be. The same holds true for the intricate path-crossings of individuals, all in search of something or other: a rocket, relatives, lovers, power, secrets, drugs, kicks, or their own identity. (p. 15)

Although treatment of characters and plot may seem initially overwhelming, like a parody of an internationalized soap opera . . . , the two problems can be surmounted. Many novels of the past—typical social novels or family sagas from Russia, Britain, Scandinavia—have had huge casts and multiple story lines. But Pynchon's ways of telling his story require some readjustment by even the most practiced readers. His narrative methodology confirms that the timeworn critical tactic of affixing convenient plot, characterization, motives, and so on may be in large measure an inappropriate enterprise. The episodic, discontinuous structure manages to work effectively for conveying varied modes of experience, and, in turn, for reflecting the chaos of fragmenting cultures. The swift movie-cutting, the mixture of styles, the picaresque movement, the sporadic pacing, the emphasis on poetic evocation, the crazy quilt of subject matter, historicity, and the outright subversion of that same historicity by comedy and surrealism, amply reveal that the reader who is used to the staples of consistency, causality, credibility, and unity of effect is in for many surprises.

One of them is digressiveness, which allows Pynchon to pursue any tangent, whether a scientific discourse or the history of generations behind a character. . . . Unquestionably, some of the detours are long and self-indulgent. Creative genius may

on occasion give way to excess, particularly when the artist is a put-inner, like Pynchon, rather than a take-outer. Once begun, the putting-in process becomes difficult to stop, a problem clearly evident in, say, Joyce's later fiction, in Jean-Luc Godard films, in the music of Stravinsky. Although this novel might have profited from greater selectivity in places, the detours eventually come to be regarded as within the itinerary. In fact, upon reflection most are found to be integral, and a few are positively brilliant. . . . Overall, the digressions contribute rather than detract, so that in the end—to use Pynchon's words from another context—"It was worth the trip, just to see this shining. . . ."

The narrative voice is extremely flexible. Of indeterminate gender, it often stays detached to maintain an objective third-person point of view, but it also rises in protean ways to become involved, intimate, even paranoid. It speaks pointedly to the reader ("You will want cause and effect. All right."), makes frequent other uses of second person ("You have to be on your toes for this: you trade four-line stanzas. . . ."), and on rare occasions gives parenthetic advice, like its recommendation that the reader check out Ishmael Reed. . . . Whenever objectivity is set aside, the flexibility of the voice makes possible various uses. Among examples, it can be didactic to settle a score (although Pynchon almost never delivers overt messages); it can be lyrical to convey emotions; it can be deeply concerned, in which case Pynchon may skirt character to address the reader directly, sometimes seeming to embrace humanity as he does so; it can be ambiguous, provoking diverse streams of thought in the reader. In these shifts the voice may give the impression of being many and haphazard, but it is singular and quite in control. Even punctuation becomes a manipulative instrument. Ellipses are liberally used to suspend action, to pause, to suggest prolonged continuance or repetition, to trail off, to interpolate, and conversely to join, ideas. And undercutting is achieved by glibly nimble phonetic shortenings, such as *sez* for *says*.

Like the mercurial voice, the tone also refuses categorization. It can be tender and compassionate, hard and ruthless, witty, sensitive, jolly, obscene. It can dynamically shift from straightforward scholarly data to jaunty hyperbolic cartooning, from graphic realism to sophomoric tomfoolery to elegiac beauty. (pp. 16-18)

Additional proof that Pynchon loves to play with mood, as he loves to play with language and ideas, may be seen in his use of interruptive-supportive songs and poems, which number close to a hundred and range in length from a couplet to some fifty lines. They cover a wide diversity of types: from macaronic to limerick to haiku, from cadenza to Broadway show tune; they come in varied languages, mostly English, but also German, Latin, Middle Dutch, Spanish, Japanese; their rhythms change from beguine to fox-trot to sea chanty, from rumba to jazz to Hawaiian beat. One beguine, "Pavlovia," is sung by laboratory rats and mice doing a Busby Berkeley dance routine. A few more are equally as silly. . . . They work in a manner equivalent to songs in musical comedy, except that often their presence is oxymoronic. They are used to change mood and focus, to spoof, to extrapolate, to underscore action while at the same time achieving distance from it, to show a lighter underside to horror or ugliness or futility, to hint at the illusion behind the reality or vice versa. Notably, the songs, as if in spite of themselves, also lend support to an ironic affirmation. (p. 18)

This juxtaposition of the apocalyptic and the comic is a sure sign of Pynchon's ambivalence. For all the novel's forbidding concerns with waste, fragmentation, destructiveness, victimization, and death, life is sustained. Much of that very sustenance derives from humor, the unquenchable human capacity to laugh at ourselves. *Gravity's Rainbow* is a very funny book, laden with sight gags, practical jokes, zany chases, and pratfalls. Its puns are deliberately egregious: "I Ching feet," "Unto thee I pledge my trough," "For DeMille, young fur-henchmen can't be rowing." (p. 19)

Although one of the most serious novels ever written persistently attempts not to take itself too seriously, its seriousness is magnified—for the same reason that an image of giving the finger can be inverted and overblown to become an atomic bomb blast. So we are never able only to laugh, not with a book as concomitantly visceral and discomforting as this one. There is no way to avoid being moved by the homages to nature, by sadness for the passed-over Preterite, by pain of loss, especially of the young like Ilse or Bianca, because the author's sympathy for children comes through so genuinely. Nor is there any escape from the squirm of shock brought on by vivid details of sadomasochism and coprophilia. On the comic side of the spectrum, Slothrop falls naked through a tree using a purple bedsheet as a parachute; on the tragic side, Blicero sends Gottfried hurtling off to a fiery ritual suicide in the Rocket. It is not always easy to reconcile these disparities of low comedy and high tragedy. By the same token, Pynchon's narrative methodology is often so indirect and tortuous that the reader may be uncertain of what is going on. (pp. 19-20)

Beams flashing the brightest in *Gravity's Rainbow* generate from Pynchon's own erudition. They cause us to blink and squint and grope because he knows so many subjects we may know little about: quantum mechanics, the Beveridge Proposal, the five positions on the launching switch of an A-4 rocket. His reconditeness encompasses tarot cards, the Cabala, mandala, Qlippoth, the Wheel of Fortune, delta-t, double integral, yin-yang, a mathematical equation for motion under yaw control. He dips into Orphic, Norse, and Teutonic myths, and divines with ease necessary detritus of pop culture: Wonderwoman, German movies, zoot suits, Plasticman, King Kong, the Wizard of Oz, Carmen Miranda's hats.

By authentic quotations and paraphrasing, Pynchon makes serious use of mathematicians, scientists, philosophers, sociopolitical thinkers like Leibniz, Kekulé and Heisenberg, Max Weber, Wernher von Braun, and Teilhard de Chardin. He dredges up Patrick Maynard Stuart Blackett's buried remark that "the scientist can encourage numerical thinking on operational matters, and so can help to avoid running the war on gusts of emotion," which appeared in the obscure *Scientists at the Operational Level,* published in 1941.... As is Pynchon's customary playfulness, these authoritative citations are counterbalanced by imaginative flights: his Proverbs for Paranoids, his excerpt from *Neil Nosepicker's Book of 50,000 Insults,* his fragment from the Gospel of Thomas: "Dear Mom, I put a couple of people in Hell today." A plethora of allusions from literature, art, opera, film, science, music, and scripture beckon the cataloger to Gilbert and Sullivan, Käthe Kollwitz, Conrad, *Moby Dick,* Tannhäuser, Prometheus, *The Waste Land,* Hänsel and Gretel and the Witch, Fritz Lang, the Bible, Elena Petrovna Blavatsky, the Niebelungen Saga, Jakob Ackeret. He authentically quotes Emily Dickinson on decay and death and parodically injects a monosyllabic "What?" from Richard Nixon. A mournful dirge is played by Rainer Maria Rilke's *Duino Elegies,* which recurs again and again.

The allusions have a way of reinforcing their new context and enlarging the situation. Moreover, they can be symbolic or analytical, and, most importantly, they can contribute by enriching thematic meaning. (pp. 20-1)

The keenest probe among the beams of erudition is historical: it emanates from Pynchon's sound knowledge of the organization of international cartels, life in London during the Blitz, inner workings of Peenemünde and Nordhausen, intricacies of the German black market. Down to the trivia of prison camp jargon, an American B movie, comic book action, radio shows, including who played what on the organ for BBC, it is a brilliantly researched novel (overlooking a few minor errors), all the more remarkable because, as a child during World War II, Pynchon could bring no firsthand knowledge of the period to his book.

These ramifications of esoterica and research suggest that the reader be sufficiently literary and intellectual to want to pursue the references, the puzzles, the allusions, the concatenations. However, the appeal is not meant to be strictly elitist. A sensuous, unschooled vulnerability may be just as important as trained critical faculties. Put another way, the reader ought to be quite nonliterary too—open, responsive, amenable to radical form and diverse content. In either case, some powers of discernment are needed because Pynchon has a way of writing history as if it didn't happen, when it did—or vice versa. The reader is probably better off for knowing the difference.... Pynchon makes no concession to an audience to whom a more readable, clear-cut novel might otherwise appeal. Here, then, is a writer determined to go his own way, to present the universe as he sees it.

What is the nature of his vision in *Gravity's Rainbow*? The reader is forewarned on the very first page of "a progressive *knotting into*—." That entanglement becomes a cultural and historical emblem of Western traditions. The culmination of "knotting into" is the massive gargoyle of modern society malformed by war and political-industrial-technological chicaneries, all extensions of past malaise. Although authorial reach is necessarily vast, it is also selective in its fixations upon origins, values, hierarchies, upon superficialities, fantasies, and endings. Furthermore, the novel is tenaciously concerned with a mysterious supernatural world beyond the empirical ordinary one we know. (pp. 21-2)

The complexity of Pynchon's vision is spun out by webs of motifs, images, and symbols each identifying with some theme or fragment of theme. (p. 22)

These and other thematic subjects emerge out of the brilliant conceptual stroke of creating a war novel that is less about war than it is about how a world was and is wrought. It fixes upon a moment in history when the world was poised at apparent teeter-totter balance—the past on one side, the future, including of course our own time, on the other. At a barely distinguishable fulcrum, a chaotic war ends, a chaotic peace begins, Europe is divided up, new allegiances are formed, and the dark, age-old magnetism points the weapons across the deadly playground all over again. Their firing must perforce follow the rainbow of gravity—if they fire. That basic tension is subjected to a series of interrelated dialectical tensions.... Some are dramatic contrasts that do not necessarily provoke any authorial judgement: like German-American (or Russian-American, etc.), mind-body, cause-effect, war-peace.

The last duality reminds us again of the consistent unusualness of Pynchon's vision. In his view, there is virtually no difference in conditions of our existence in either peace or war. The teeter-totter hardly moved; nothing much happened at the fulcrum. Put another way, the same forces remain at work upon humanity when a war is over. This is one reason why almost no significance is attached in the novel to the ending of World War II.

Other tensions represent decidedly negative and positive poles: control-freedom, rationality-fantasy, determinism-randomness, mundaneness-magic, supernature-nature, stasis-flux, repression-uninhibitedness, "modern analysis-savage innocences," frigid north-tropical climes, fragmentation-connectedness, white-black, Elect-Preterite, They-We. Pynchon's attraction to the positive poles in all these instances is clearly discernible. His sympathies go out to little people, clowns, rebels, children, endangered species (man or animals), victims, rapscallions who are endearing because they either resist the System or disdain it by their carefree attitudes. (pp. 23-4)

The resolution of one dispute will probably continue to remain tantalizing: ascertaining whether Pynchon is ultimately a diabolic prophet of doom or a humanistic visionary. At first, critical response to the novel seemed to favor the former, but in recent years the pendulum has swung toward more humanistic readings. Which is probably as it should be, since even in an apparent dead heat optimism will win out over pessimism. The writer, after all, is on hand to give alarm signals, not death knells. Otherwise, if the decline of civilization were irreversible, one must wonder the point of even writing about it. The issue merits continued debate. Meanwhile, artistry always matters more than polemics anyway, and we can be indebted to Pynchon for the richness of his created worlds and, we must hope, others to come. (p. 24)

Charles Clerc, in an introduction to Approaches to "Gravity's Rainbow", edited by Charles Clerc, Ohio State University Press, 1983, pp. 3-30.

## CHRISTOPHER LEHMANN-HAUPT

In an introduction to [the five stories collected in **"Slow Learner"**] that is funny and wise enough to charm the gravity from a rainbow, Thomas Pynchon indicts his early writings for sins both juvenile and delinquent. They are guilty, he contends, of racism, sexism, proto-fascism and even an occasional plagiarism. They lack an ear and they try to be overliterary.

Worst of all, he insists, they are ignorant. . . .

What is it like to read the stories after this bombardment? Well, forewarned is disarmed, predictably enough, and what we notice most are their virtues, not their shortcomings. All five of the pieces, which appeared originally in various magazines, have unusual narrative vigor and inventiveness. Each establishes its own special mood—whether it is the sultry tension of the hurricane in **"The Small Rain,"** the junkyard chaos of **"Low-lands,"** or the slightly paranoid fantasy world of the children in **"The Secret Integration"**—and each contains its moments of Pynchonesque comedy—the miming musicians in **"Entropy"** or Porpentine's tumble down the stairs in **"Under the Rose."**

Pynchon's ear may be off in recording the accents of Tidewater Virginia in **"The Small Rain,"** but it is marvelously on in the ramblings of an alcoholic black musician in **"The Secret Integration."** And if there is something a little cute about making his A. A. partner a 9-year-old reformed beer drinker, or about inserting into the story characters with names such as Etienne

Cherdlu and Hogan Slothrop, the good-naturedness of the story far exceeds its tendency to show off.

**"Slow Learner,"** then, as well as being "illustrative of typical problems in entry-level fiction, and cautionary about some practices that younger writers might prefer to avoid," has certain virtues to celebrate. In fact, if it is as much of a failure as Mr. Pynchon insists, then it makes failure as a writer positively inviting.

All the same, it is a slightly risky game that Mr. Pynchon is playing here. For one thing, there's an element of egotism in coming down upon oneself so hard, a sense of undue self-importance already apparent in the author's passion for anonymity. More significantly, Mr. Pynchon's self-needling distracts us from a deeper problem in his early writing. This is a contempt for the world created by grown ups—a contempt that is charming in **"The Secret Integration,"** which after all is overtly about children, but is slightly insidious in **"Under the Rose,"** which treats the background of World War I in the tone of comic opera.

One finds oneself wondering if something about the insouciant, loose-jointed style of Mr. Pynchon's later novels doesn't reflect an unwillingness on his part to take the past seriously. In the light of the stories in **"Slow Learner,"** each of which condemns in some way the world handed down to its protagonists, one has to wonder if underneath it all the author's attitude toward European history in **"V."** and **"Gravity's Rainbow"** isn't just plain snotty.

Actually, I plan to stand by my admiring judgment of these later novels, and of his novella **"The Crying of Lot 49."** I'm assuming that their author had grown by the time he wrote them. But considering how in his introduction he turns his back on his earliest stories—how he even disparages **"The Crying of Lot 49,"** "which," he writes, "was marketed as a 'novel,' and in which I seem to have forgotten most of what I thought I'd learned up till then"—I have to wonder if he isn't eventually going to leave me out on a limb with my admiration.

Christopher Lehmann-Haupt, in a review of "Slow Learner: Early Stories," in The New York Times, March 29, 1984, p. C24.

## PETER S. PRESCOTT

If [**"Slow Learner"**] were Thomas Pynchon's new book, we'd have to reckon it a major disaster, the kind of book that sends critics reeling back to their warrens to reassess its author's earlier work. Fortunately, it's not new—so call it a minor disaster. . . .

Each [story] fails in its own way, but over all an arty aura looms. Either Pynchon is, as he admits, forcing his characters and events to conform to "a theme, symbol or other abstract unifying agent," or he's whipping his prose into a viscous pudding. Sometimes he does both at once. The story **"Low-lands,"** for instance, is a good example of the forcing process. . . . Now anyone who went to college in the '50s, as Pynchon did, knows exactly what he's reading: he's reading a prose variation of "The Waste Land." Eliot's imagery, somewhat translated, mounts as . . . well, as rubbish does in a dump; it finally smothers the story.

Of the earliest story in this lot [**"The Small Rain"**], the less said the better. It's about disaster, death, sex and the military—just the kind of thing you expect to find in a college magazine.

Lest any reader be so dull as to miss its labored point, Pynchon spells it out clearly at the end. The latest story ["**The Secret Integration**"], written after "**V.**" appeared, shows Pynchon jettisoning what he had learned about writing fiction to produce a plastic artifact for The Saturday Evening Post. The plot involves some prankish schoolboys who treat a "colored" boy just as if he were one of them—which their parents won't do. A coy performance, it's sentimental, much too long and has a trick ending reminiscent of Ray Bradbury on one of his windy days. (p. 100)

It's no sin for a writer to begin with stories like these. But why, after his novels have made him justly admired, would he want to resurrect them? Pynchon's groupies, and the graduate students who even now are hacking out dissertations on Pynchon's use of 19th-century physics, will doubtless want to paw over each of the master's shards, looking for signs of better things to come. The story called "**Entropy**" will give them what they want: two models of the world grinding to a halt, one cerebral, the other instinctual; allusions to Henry Adams; some college humor; some chatter about communication theory . . . and entropy. . . . Pynchon is right on target when he writes of the "bleakness of heart" he experiences when he rereads "**Entropy**"—it's as crisp and tasty as a salad left overnight in the refrigerator.

This collection omits a story called "**Mortality and Mercy in Vienna**" that critics have sometimes discussed. Nor does Pynchon mention it in his introduction; it's as if it never existed. Curious, but then this entire enterprise is curious. (pp. 100-01)

> *Peter S. Prescott, "The Collegiate Pynchon," in* Newsweek, *Vol. CIII, No. 15, April 9, 1984, pp. 100-01.*

## MICHAEL WOOD

It's always an occasion when the invisible man comes to dinner. Thomas Pynchon, like J. D. Salinger, is a writer who has been hiding away for years, and in "**Slow Learner**" he cautiously paints himself back into the public view. Indeed, he makes more of an appearance than he has ever done, since the volume not only collects five early works but offers an easygoing, seemingly vulnerable 20-page introduction by the vanishing author himself. . . .

This introduction had me worried for a while. Was this man of such patient discretion about to crumble and cry, to spill his soul on the confessional page? It would be like the Scarlet Pimpernel having a breakdown. Why was Mr. Pynchon presenting these pieces if he didn't like them? But my worry soon subsided. There is no confession, only the reflections of a writer looking back over ground traveled, and a very engaging, informal history of an odd American time, the tag end of the 50's, too late for bop and beat, too early for the hippies. (p. 1)

In his introduction to "**Slow Learner**" Mr. Pynchon . . . says of his generation: "There were no more primary choices for us to make. We were onlookers: the parade had gone by and we were already getting everything secondhand, consumers of what the media of the time were supplying us." It was the generation of students Lionel Trilling became very worried about; they were receiving Kafka's despair and Conrad's anguish as commodities, dished out in literature courses among other requirements.

What is admirable about Mr. Pynchon is that, knowing this, he doesn't give up or set out to become a lumberjack, searching

for fabulous, untainted writerly experience. He writes with the resources that writers always have, but will not always use: memory, imagination, curiosity, access to accumulated funds of knowledge. This approach paid off particularly in "**Gravity's Rainbow**" (1973), where Mr. Pynchon impeccably describes details of life in wartime England—and speculates, amid a densely imagined postwar Europe, not on the personal quests and panics of his earlier novels, but on the possible master connections of modern history: the links between rocketry and Puritanism, for instance, or between language and death; between race and sex, and sex and class; between the anonymous cruelties of economics and the things we are now (but were not always) prepared to do to each other. . . . We may quarrel with or fail to comprehend whole chunks of this difficult book but there can be no doubt that it is here to stay, a major work whose local liveliness is such that its parts make us want to bet on the whole.

The faults of his early stories are just what Mr. Pynchon says they are—"bad habits, dumb theories," purple prose and a portentousness that crops up in all his writing. What he doesn't talk about, although it is a perfect answer to our question about why he is publishing this book, is how extremely good the stories are for all their faults, how quickly they carry us into their scruffy, variegated, wonderfully imagined worlds. . . .

"**The Small Rain**" centers on one Nathan "Lardass" Levine, a sort of ancestor of Benny Profane in "**V.**", and an enlisted man who is sleeping his days away at Fort Roach, La. He is a college grad who takes the army as a refuge from feeling and thought, from what a character in "**V.**" calls "the acquired sense of animateness." He is sent out on a detail helping to clear up after a hurricane, and one day, without being ordered to and without knowing why, he joins a group collecting corpses from the flood. . . .

Does Levine find his way back to life because of this encounter with death? Perhaps. At the end of the story he is asleep again. The hovering presence of T. S. Eliot's "The Waste Land" in this text is a little tiresome, to use Mr. Pynchon's word. All these characters are waiting for rain, see, rootless soldiers in a dry and then soaked land. (p. 28)

The landscape of "**Low-lands**" moves steadily toward fantasy. The scene changes from a Long Island house full of sewers and cellars and "innumerable tunnels, which writhed away radically like the tentacles of a spastic octopus" to a nearby dump . . .; beneath its blasted surface the dump is honeycombed with tunnels and secret rooms, the work of a 30's terrorist group. Dennis Flange, a well-off ex-navy man, is thrown out of his home by his wife and finds in the dump a romantic, diminutive rescuer in the shape of a lovely girl called Nerissa, only three and a half feet tall. . . .

Flange, like Levine, is hiding in various ways from life's entanglements, and perhaps little Nerissa, as Mr. Pynchon suggests in his introduction, is a picture of what Flange thinks he can manage. . . . What Flange fears is "eventual convexity," the rising wave, the dump filled in so that the plain becomes a hill, "so that he would be left sticking out like a projected radius, unsheltered and reeling." These moral landscapes are metaphors for his need, and the impossibility of his position is part of Mr. Pynchon's implied argument.

Flange meets Nerissa at "a desolate hour somehow not intended for human perception," and this, in many ways, is Mr. Pynchon's hour. Amid a shuffling, funny, amiable life, the 50's behaving as if they would last forever, someone sees what he was not supposed to see, as if the heart of darkness were to open up in Nassau County. The story brings us very close to **"V."**, which has the same mixture of austere thought and broad but enjoyable bad jokes. By the time of **"Gravity's Rainbow,"** of course, the ordinary world is not so amiable or funny to start with; it has fallen into war and its aftermath, and is mined with conspiracies, like the dump in **"Low-lands."**

**"Entropy"** is the best known of Mr. Pynchon's stories, much anthologized and commented on. It gains from being placed in the company of the other early pieces, because its characters, like those in the other stories, can be seen searching for images, means of arranging their lives in their minds. Thus Callisto in **"Entropy"** seals himself in his room, "a tiny enclave of regularity in the city's chaos," thinks about entropy and awaits the end of the world, the moment when all temperatures, inside and out and everywhere, will be the same, and so no heat of any kind will be transferred. (pp. 28-9)

Critics are fond of this story, with its neat antitheses—the death wish in one place, the disorder of life in another. . . . But I find that **"Entropy"**'s abstraction makes it rather pale in comparison with the other pieces in **"Slow Learner."** Still, I treasure the crazy communion of those silent musicians. What difference does it make, if there is nothing to hear, whether one of them is playing the wrong tune, or no tune? How could they even know? It makes all the difference, I would say, and that is how we know a lot of what we know—like whether we are loved, and when people are lying to us. It's all a matter of "inference," of "imaginative anxiety," as Mr. Pynchon says in **"V."** We can get all sorts of things right by those means. Wrong too, of course, but nobody's perfect. . . .

Thomas Pynchon was a cult figure in the mid-60's. Copies of **"V."** were passed around and annotated amid the Dylan records and the beginning of the end of the Beatles. He was then taken up in a big way by the academy and must be now among the most written about of contemporary authors. I have the highest opinion of Mr. Pynchon's work myself, but what I miss in the figure he has become for scholarly critics, in the difficult, meditative writer who is thought to put all merely lucid or entertaining practitioners to shame, is the sense of a man in a particular time and place, and of a living author whose faults as a writer are not to be extricated from his great virtues. This is just what **"Slow Learner"** helps to restore. (p. 29)

*Michael Wood, "The Apprenticeship of Thomas Pynchon," in* The New York Times Book Review, *April 15, 1984, pp. 1, 28-9.*

## J. O. TATE

No longer will these stories [collected in *Slow Learner*] (except for one of them) be merely the dusty objects of the sublimated lusts of malnourished graduate students and tendentious professors, photocopied obscurities to be pondered by cultists; nor are they either the piracies and rip-offs that (having occurred in England, the grapevine asserts) provoked the publication of this book. The question is, was this pre-emptive strike necessary?

The answer is somewhat mixed. On the one hand, there's as much here to bore or annoy the common reader as there is to mystify, to tease, to entertain, or to enthrall. On the other

hand, Pynchonites will be far from the only ones who will be fascinated by these works in themselves, such as they are. The alert reader who is accustomed to studying technique, to pondering the effects of tone, and to meditating on the cultural imperatives of post-modern literature will have plenty to work with. Remarking that Pynchon seems to hold his worst story, **"The Secret Integration,"** in the highest esteem, the reader would then have also to remark its original publication in *The Saturday Evening Post* (December 1964). The juxtaposition of the bizarre and chilling demands of Pynchonismus cheek by cheek with the coziness of Norman Rockwell is an association that may liberate, for some, an insight into Pynchon's social agenda, which, in this story, collapses from the surreal to the sentimental and, finally, to the cutesie-poo. It is curiously refreshing to watch the Big Boy fall flat on his face.

**"Under the Rose"** is better apprehended in context as the transmogrified chapter three of Pynchon's first novel, *V.* (1963). **"Low-lands"** is a take-off on *The Waste Land;* **"Entropy"** alludes to Henry Adams explicitly; **"The Small Rain"** echoes Hemingway. These stories have already been discussed in essays, monographs, and books, for Pynchon's pack-rat propensities, his skill at insinuation, and his disarming manner are backed up by a seriousness and an erudition worthy of comparison with the Joyce who declared he would "keep the professors busy for centuries." But what also will inevitably be remarked is the "personal appearance" of Pynchon, who, in his Introduction to most of his own apprentice fiction, casually "drops in" or "by" with all the frigid spontaneity of a jaded night-club singer who just happens—his schedule and reservations booked months in advance—to turn up in front of those television cameras dominated by Johnny Carson.

This appearance would not be nearly so remarkable coming from anyone else, for Pynchon's notorious or celebrated self-effacement has begged comparison with the reclusiveness of B. Traven and J. D. Salinger. Yet the hermit yearns, finally, to reveal himself, and in doing so he puts at least one reader in mind of the aging ecdysiast who was greeted with the cry, "Put it back on!" (p. 54)

This is not the first time in the history of American letters that playing the game of Meet the Author has led to embarrassment—no doubt mutual. And that's the reason why many have respected Thomas Pynchon for staying in the closet. . . . *Gravity's Rainbow,* now—undoubtedly Pynchon's greatest work—is a dazzling and profound "encyclopedic narrative" that, more than any other recent fictional achievement, effectively represents the horror and the absurdity of the conditions of contemporary existence—a work that is, for its complexity, eccentric wit, and magical realism, worthy of being mentioned in the same breath with *Moby Dick,* "Heart of Darkness," and *Absalom, Absalom!* . . . [Pynchon should perhaps] have refused the opportunity to introduce his early-stories-but-one, and let them simply speak for themselves. Instead, straining to recapture his adolescence while approaching fifty, Pynchon forces the question of whether, having doffed one mask, he has only revealed another; and the question of why the man whom Professor Edward Mendelson of Yale has called "the greatest living writer in the English-speaking world" feels such a need to be considered a jerk. (pp. 54-5)

*J. O. Tate, "Slow Burner," in* National Review, *Vol. XXXVI, No. 22, November 16, 1984, pp. 53-5.*

# David (William) Rabe

## 1940-

American dramatist and scriptwriter.

Rabe is best known for his award-winning trilogy of Vietnam plays: *The Basic Training of Pavlo Hummel* (1971), *Sticks and Bones* (1969), and *Streamers* (1976). In these plays, stark images, strange, lyrical language, black humor, and symbolic devices provide the context for alienated characters who often express themselves through rage. Several of Rabe's plays culminate in sensationally violent incidents. In addition to his exploration of the effects of the Vietnam War on young soldiers, Rabe has examined such topical issues as exploitation of women and the deleterious effects of drug use.

After serving in Vietnam, Rabe made an impressive theatrical debut in 1971 when his first two plays were produced on Broadway and prompted enthusiastic, if mixed, critical response. *The Basic Training of Pavlo Hummel,* which won an Obie Award, centers on the title character, a teenager estranged from his family who seeks companionship and meaning in his life by becoming a good soldier. In Vietnam he observes a lack of respect for humanity, participates in violence, and dies a senseless death. Rabe uses several expressionistic devices, including a character who voices Pavlo's inner thoughts, to create a surreal atmosphere. *Sticks and Bones,* written in 1969 but produced on Broadway after *The Basic Training of Pavlo Hummel,* is a symbolic presentation of society's refusal to acknowledge the horrors of the Vietnam War. The play concerns David, a blinded, embittered Vietnam veteran who returns home to his prototypical "all-American" family. His parents, Ozzie and Harriet, and brother, Ricky, are deliberate caricatures of the family depicted in "The Adventures of Ozzie and Harriet," a popular television series of the 1950s and 1960s. The family appears unable to sympathize with David, who is haunted by his war experiences and by memories of the Vietnamese prostitute with whom he fell in love. *Sticks and Bones* was awarded the Antoinette Perry "Tony" Award for best play.

*Streamers* won the New York Drama Critics' Circle Award for best play and is considered by some critics to be Rabe's most accomplished work. This play focuses on three soldiers, two white and one black, who live together in barracks while awaiting transport to Vietnam. The uneasy camaraderie of the threesome is disrupted by the intrusion of a bitter black soldier. The play erupts in violence as the men react to their fear of death, to racial tension, and to the repressed homosexuality of one of the characters.

In his other plays, Rabe dramatizes the deterioration of moral standards in contemporary American society. *Boom Boom Room* (1973) and its revised version, *In the Boom Boom Room* (1974), center on a female go-go dancer who is repeatedly humiliated and exploited by men. *Hurlyburly* (1984) is set in a Hollywood home where four men associated with the entertainment industry pass time by taking drugs and having sex with women whom they do not respect. The characters spend much of their time in drug-induced stupors, speaking in clichés and employing popular psychology in their banal philosophizing about life. Rabe dramatizes how drugs, liquor, loveless sex, and

Copyright 1985 Thomas Victor

cultural kitsch have infected and undermined individual intelligence and morality in the Southern California lifestyle and, by extension, in American society.

(See also *CLC,* Vols. 4, 8; *Contemporary Authors,* Vols. 85-88; and *Dictionary of Literary Biography,* Vol. 7.)

## RICHARD L. HOMAN

*The Basic Training of Pavlo Hummel, Sticks and Bones* and *Streamers,* often referred to as Rabe's 'trilogy' though they were not conceived as such, exhibit not only [a] progression from an experimental style to realism, but also Rabe's extraordinary use of language. (pp. 74-5)

The progression of Rabe's style in this trilogy ultimately allows him to treat with clarity his chosen theme: our struggle to comprehend violence and death. Throughout these plays, Rabe shows this as a personal struggle, involving the value of sexuality and life, while, at the same time, suggesting through his military settings the national struggle to comprehend the horror of U.S. involvement in Vietnam. For each play Rabe chooses a situation in which the horror of violence can be juxtaposed with the assumptions of everyday life. In the first two plays he tends to personify normal life in his civilian characters and the horror in his military characters with a resulting sense of ridicule toward both. In *Streamers,* Rabe makes no such distinction: all are military, and all maintain their civilian identities and values. Thus, all participate internally as well as externally in the struggle to reconcile their contradictory impulses toward sexuality and life on the one hand and violence and death on the other.

In the first play of the trilogy, Rabe shows us, as the title states, *The Basic Training of Pavlo Hummel.* In the transformation of a young man into a soldier, we see a fellow with problems of a civilian sort—the need to impress an older brother, the need of a father figure with whom to identify, the need of a reputation for acts of daring as well as sexual acts—seeking and accepting solutions of a military sort. Rabe successfully uses language and situations verbatim from his military experience to sketch the personal struggle of his hero. He suggests the incompatibility of Pavlo's military way of life with his civilian life through the juxtaposition of scenes and speeches from both lives in simultaneous settings. However, though this collage technique is effective, it allows only for personifications; character development and sustained dramatic conflict are impossible. Therefore, although Rabe achieves a vivid statement of his theme, it remains crude: as if 'the military' really were an impersonal force for which no one is responsible.

In *Sticks and Bones,* Rabe dramatises the intrusion of the horror into ordinary life through the situation of a blinded soldier, David, returning to his parents' home. His unceremonious arrival in dark glasses, carrying a long white cane shocks his parents. David's disturbance of their happy, normal life proceeds with each revelation of what he did and what was done to him in Vietnam, and climaxes with his showing of some movie film he shot while over there. His family protests that it is blurred, showing nothing, while David insists it shows the torture and murder of a Vietnamese man and woman. Throughout the second act, the family grows more frantic in their efforts to understand their eldest son, until, on the initiative of the younger son, they lead David through a ritual suicide.

Rabe sets this play in a realistic interior, but his treatment of the theme remains nearly as crude as in *Pavlo Hummel,* because the characters remain, to a large extent, personifications. The names of the parents, Ozzie and Harriet, and the sons, David and Ricky, are identical with the names of the perfect, average American family, The Nelsons, from the television series of the 1950s, and Rabe's characters act accordingly. Furthermore, Rabe introduces another personification which creates a stylistic anomaly. The young Asian woman, who enters the house unannounced, never speaks and we are left to guess whether Ozzie, Harriet and Ricky really cannot see her or choose to ignore her. Rabe must rely on this sort of expressionistic device because he still, on the whole, dramatises the problem as one of opposing forces. Only in the characters of Ozzie and Harriet does Rabe begin to realise the struggle of individuals to comprehend the contradictions within them. Though their names make them figures of ridicule, they do not simply personify the mindless civilian, wilfully ignorant of the horror of war, because they do not ignore David. Rather, they actively question him and his truth throughout the play, even if, after discovering that truth, they trivialise it through the language they use.

In *Streamers,* Rabe gives us a cast of characters who simultaneously feel themselves to be citizens and soldiers, and who struggle to comprehend the contradiction within themselves. Consequently, the play proceeds simply through the interaction of the characters, without need of unrealistic conventions. Rabe chooses a situation perfectly suited for exploration of the contradictory sides of his characters. The three who share a cadre room at an army base in the U.S. have finished their training and are waiting to be assigned. On the one hand, the war exists only as an awful rumor: in the first act, they out-do one another telling stories of what they have heard about jungle warfare. On the other hand, civilian life exists for them only as a fading memory: each treasures the 'civies', the civilian clothes kept neatly in the locker, donned with pride for the night on the town.

Each struggles desperately to retain his former identity, and to justify it to the soldier he himself has become, as well as to his fellow soldiers. This brings them into conflict. Billy, a college boy from Wisconsin, flaunts his masculinity in a manner which suggests some unresolved urges within him. Ritchie, who has admitted his own homosexuality, responds to Billy's displays and occasional threats with kindness, sarcasm and an open resolve not to deny what he is. Roger maintains a tenuous peace by providing them various means of ignoring the difference between them. He readily supplies the clownish hyperbole, or the hasty, military jargon. (pp. 75-7)

Two intrusions turn this uneasy household into a battleground. Cokes and Rooney, career military men of the World War II generation, initiate the rookies into the rites of the 101st Airborne Division, the 'Screaming Eagles'. Their elaborate pantomime demonstrates the swashbuckling adventure of a parachute jump but concludes with a solemn singing of 'Beautiful streamer', a hymn to the man whose parachute failed to open. Also, Carlyle, a transient soldier, comes looking for the companionship of a black brother, and finds it, in different forms, with all three. Returning from a night of drinking and whoring with Billy and Roger, Carlyle makes homosexual advances toward Ritchie. When Billy refuses to allow them to proceed and refuses to turn his back as Roger advises, the confrontation is at hand. Billy pauses and declares, '. . . . I'm thinkin' about comin' up behind one black human being and I'm thinkin'. . . . I wanna cut his throat. THAT IS RIDICULOUS.' . . . In this moment of discovery, Rabe achieves a synthesis of what in the previous plays were opposing, impersonal forces. Yet, despite Billy's discovery, the play climaxes with a good deal of violence. (pp. 77-8)

With the unified characters of *Streamers,* Rabe creates an understanding of the use of violence and death to ignore the irreconcilable differences between us. He illustrates that violence on a personal scale, or on a national scale through military involvement, is a way of evading what troubles us most, and therefore is an extension of our little evasions through language. (p. 78)

*Richard L. Homan, "American Playwrights in the 1970s: Rabe and Shepard," in* Critical Quarterly, *Vol. 24, No. 1, Spring, 1982, pp. 73-82.**

## MEL GUSSOW

[*On May 8, 1982, in* The New York Times, *Rabe disavowed the production of* "Goose and Tomtom" *reviewed in this excerpt. He claimed that he had attempted to have the play closed before its premiere.*]

David Rabe has disavowed the production of his play, **"Goose and Tomtom."** . . . Perhaps it would have been more judicious of him to disclaim the play. It is difficult to believe that the author of the searing **"Basic Training of Pavlo Hummel"** and

"Streamers" could have created such an impecunious caper comedy.

While one has to honor the attempt of a talented artist to break out of his mode—in this case to do a kind of vaudeville turn—it is necessary to acknowledge the fact that **"Goose and Tomtom"** lacks a light touch. The author has achieved his reputation as a dramatist with a strong sense of morality, but even his most serious efforts have had their comic interludes, for example, the barracks-room ribaldry of **"Streamers."**

Goose and Tomtom (no explanation for their names) are a pair of jewel thieves, a couple of wrong guys, who in collaboration with a lady named Lorraine have amassed a swag of gems, only to have the booty ripped off by a rival gang. The play is a whodunit that leaves the theatergoer thinking, who cares? . . .

The language is unlike Rabe without being Runyonesque, and relies far too much on repetition, as in the line "Are you saying you don't know what you're saying?" Breaking rules of burlesque, neither Goose nor Tomtom is a straight man. They are Hardy and Hardy, two portly, pistol-packing buffoons. In short, there is no give and take. The two are mirror images of each other, with only a slight difference in characterization, and that contrast is more of dress than of conduct. . . .

With the arrival of Bingo, the evening almost awakens. He has been pictured as the meanest gun in the East, but when he arrives . . . he is meek and soft-spoken. Bingo rambles on—and soon becomes boring—about his life in crime, issuing comments on the "concrete" guys and the "iron" facts that he knows. Those two adjectives polarize one's feelings about the play. The evening, fragmented by abstraction, would benefit from an addition of "iron"—and of irony. The play is so formless that it could float right off the stage, and that is approximately what happens.

**"Goose and Tomtom"** could be considered a long-delayed exploding cigar, a slow burn followed by a single anticlimactic pop.

*Mel Gussow, "'Goose and Tomtom' Opens," in* The New York Times, *May 8, 1982, p. 17.*

### PHILIP D. BEIDLER

In the most important contributions to the dramatic literature of Vietnam during the period 1970-75—David Rabe's *The Basic Training of Pavlo Hummel* and *Sticks and Bones,* the first two plays in what, with the addition of *Streamers* in 1977, would become a major trilogy—the principle of bringing the war home evolved into a central thematic issue. Similarly . . . , the attempt to explore the effects of Vietnam on actual American life would also come to suggest the degree to which the war's horror had been implicit in the American character from the outset, a collective tragedy waiting to happen, a prophetic curse hiding at the heart of a whole mythology of culture.

The range and ambition of Rabe's endeavors are suggested in the two plays by the large formal challenges he poses for himself. In both *The Basic Training of Pavlo Hummel* and *Sticks and Bones,* he deals in visions of pure hackneyed Americana, opts for the mode of the almost oppressively quotidian and familiar. In the first, he works (as he will again in *Streamers*) the old American ground of boot camp and barracks, the world of *See Here, Private Hargrove* and *Sands of Iwo Jima* and *No Time for Sergeants,* and later on of Ernie Bilko and even Beetle Bailey. In the second, his broad-ranging debts to domestic and

popular lore are equally evident. The blinded veteran, David, returns to his family, including Ozzie the father, Harriet the mother, and Rick the younger brother, who hops about with a snapshot camera and asks plenty of vaguely cute, witless questions. At issue in these plays, then, is not only the experience of Vietnam but also the nature of what passes for reality in America, and how the war is precisely the function of a culture holding fast, against a whole accumulation of geopolitical evidence to the contrary, to a sentimental, even banal complacency in some idiot sense of its own goodness and right.

The size of the risk is repaid again and again by the enduring quality of the accomplishment. *Pavlo Hummel* and *Sticks and Bones* bring the war home in all the immediacy of spectacle and even affront that modern drama in its greatest strength can produce. In these plays, like a sore or a boil or an encysted anger that can no longer be kept in, Vietnam spills its hot burden across the whole reach of our collective existence as a people.

*Pavlo Hummel* is a mad, inexhaustible pastiche of the American experience of Vietnam in the fullness of its commingled banality and terrifying waste. It is a collection of master images. The play opens with Pavlo in a Saigon bar, stinking, foul-mouthed, high-school drunk. . . . Then, like all drunks feeling sorry for themselves in a strange place, he begins to tell the usual sad story, sloppy, stumbling persiflage about lost love and other confidings. . . . Appropriately, just as he has begun to spill his guts in a figurative sense, a grenade is thrown into the bar. Pavlo gets his real chance. In an enactment of the worst fear of every GI in the war, he wakes up dead. . . . (pp. 112-14)

Afoot on the landscape of death, and accompanied by Ardell, the black comrade who serves as his slangy, irreverent GI Virgil, he now voyages in retrospect through the last stage of the American life that has eventually brought him to his moment of second-rate apotheosis. With him, we get to see the basic training as the *basic* training of Pavlo Hummel, the means whereby he learns, as the author notes, "only that he is lost, not how, why, or even where." If he has time to work up a talent, it is only the one he already has "for leaping into the fire." . . . (p. 114)

Pavlo does not survive. David, in *Sticks and Bones,* has managed it, barely. One wonders what he has achieved in the bargain. He is blind, self-pitying, bitter, guilt-ridden. Yet that, as they would have told him in the army, is a personal problem. As a casualty, we learn quickly, he is but one of many. (p. 115)

David's problem, moreover, albeit the stuff of collective national tragedy, remains largely personal even when he is brought back to "the family home." It is not easy for "the perfectly happy family" in America, the playwright tells us, when a son comes home from Vietnam "no longer lovable." . . .

The household of *Sticks and Bones* is the "image" . . . of that family, so much the image that it is nearly a caricature of itself. Hence the condition of ugly, unreal tension that creates itself when the peevish, maimed, strange-acting David returns from Vietnam, with his talk of Zung, his yellow whore, and of the squalor and suffering he has seen, and forces the people who used to call him son and brother, Ozzie and Harriet and Ricky, to confront the whole American mythology of a happy life on which they depend for their very existence.

The story of the play is the family's attempt to remain ignorant of that challenge. Rabe has said that this work was meant to be a combination of "farce, horror movie, TV situation comedy." . . . Effectively, he runs out the combination in reverse order. The sitcom is the image of happiness that is its own parody; the horror movie is the reality of a war coming home; the farce is the attempt to dodge that reality.

The farce is Ozzie's constant recourse to a wondrous store of platitudes he has always used to clear away the jitters. (p. 116)

The farce is family snacks, family movies, family horseplay, and family priest, a whole set of clichés marshaled against realities that will not go away: a blind, unlovable lump up in his bedroom; the spectre of his yellow whore just outside the living room archway. When the clichés fail, there are also more desperate measures. (p. 117)

Only one problem remains: what to do with David.

Suddenly, the answer is there like some sweet, inescapable revelation. David will quietly commit suicide. . . .

It is as if nothing has ever happened at all. A living American dream, the "image of how the perfectly happy family should appear" settles back again into the everyday business of being perfectly happy. (p. 118)

In *The Basic Training of Pavlo Hummel* and *Sticks and Bones,* the domain of the creative artifact has served as an autonomous, "open" precinct of vision where it has been possible at once both to suggest a sense of the awesome, harrowing reality of Vietnam as experience and also to address that reality in terms of something like collective mythic consciousness as well. So with *Streamers,* a play effectively completing a trilogy. Precisely to the degree, in fact, that it enacts the visionary design of *Going after Cacciato* essentially in mirror image—the country that is the war extended backward, so to speak, to incorporate the stateside barracks room, a vision of what may happen becoming in effect the determinant of much that actually does happen—it reveals the unique serviceability of that design as a centralizing mode of literary response. To put this in more familiar terms, just as the self-consciously literary and even "mythic" quality of *Streamers* seems predicated on some strange interplay between memory and imagination in an essentially aesthetic sense, so it is precisely by being about that interplay that the drama also achieves its intense air of human actuality.

Indeed, if *Streamers* is "about" anything, it is about the effects of a "memory" of something called Vietnam upon a group of soldiers mainly who have never been there, who have to conceive of its threat as almost pure imaginative projection, and who in turn allow imaginative projection to turn itself most deadly real in bitter experiential fact. Conversely, the bearer of this "memory," the one character in the play who has already been out there, is an aging, boozy, career NCO, lost almost completely in his own world of make-believe, of dreams of better wars, of the camaraderie of the airborne, of heroism in Korea, of anything but what his most recent war just was.

The war is there, then, in *Streamers,* as some weird amalgam of memory and imagining, at once a curse and a terrible prophecy. The Army that died a good deal of the time in Vietnam of its own self-torturing misery, its enlistment in the service of random, multiform violence to no discernible end, finds itself imaged in microcosm and contained in a single squad bay about to explode of its own awful inside tension. Macho posturing jangles with homoerotic threat and insinuation. Lifer and draftee, officer and enlisted man, black and white, hold together in a tense, fragile symbiosis only a soul's breath away from horror.

The horror comes in the person of Carlyle, a hard, sullen, violent black draftee. Strutting his mean, ugly anger, he brings out the dark latencies that in each of the play's other characters have for the moment been lying barely submerged. He confronts Roger, another black, whose closest friend has been a white soldier named Billy, with the easy fiction of his hunger for white acceptance, and taunts him with the prospect of his fate as a black man in a white man's army. With an overt homosexual come-on, he exploits the fears and miseries of the edgy, epicene Richie, who has previously divided most of his time between emotional backbiting and worrying about being "queer." This grotesque, almost demonic preying of Carlyle's on Richie in turn draws out the violence hiding in Billy, an average, decent, even thoughtful boy. (pp. 179-81)

The melting-pot, macho army, the repository of old marching songs, of patriotic slogans, of a whole accumulated legacy of warrior myth, hemorrhages to death in a frenzy of internal convulsion. What is left at the end of *Streamers*—after the MPs have come and gone with their predictably officious lieutenant—is a tired old drunken NCO ("they" say he has leukemia, but he thinks he keeps falling down just because he drinks so much) home from a war he cannot even understand enough to talk about, and a couple of scared privates, one black, of dubious racial identity, and the other white, of equally dubious sexuality. They are the remaining specimens of American manhood. (pp. 181-82)

*Philip D. Beidler, "In the Middle Range, 1970-1975" and "The New Literature of Vietnam, 1975 to the Present," in his* American Literature and the Experience of Vietnam, *The University of Georgia Press, 1982, pp. 85-136, 137-92.\**

**DOUGLAS WATT**

They snort coke, pop 'ludes, swill vodka, smoke pot, and have sex (though one wonders how or why) in David Rabe's new play, **"Hurlyburly."** . . . Dwellers on another planet called the Hollywood Hills, they are, as their most concerned and articulate member puts it, "spin-offs from prime time . . . just backgrounds for each other." The play, consisting in large part of elliptical dialogue spinning at a great rate, is a downer.

It all takes place in the house shared by two casting directors, Eddie . . . and Mickey . . . , the one severely troubled by the world around him as described by the daily news events, and the other as flip and laid-back as a movie producer after two big scores.

Almost buried in all the glib talk, full of buzz words and the sort of stoned philosophizing endemic among college seniors after cramming 24 hours straight for finals, is the thread of a plot involving Eddie and Phil . . . , an ex-con with delusions of talent and the hope of landing a part in a TV series. It isn't entirely clear why Eddie cares so much about Phil, who is dangerous, and even articulate in that reasonable manner his kind adopts between flareups. But Phil is a useful character through which Rabe can vent his horror and anger at an entertainment industry that makes use of such authentic hard types as Phil to lend background credence to pure bull. In the second of the three acts, a tragedy occurs that is at least an excuse to keep Rabe's verbal momentum at a steady pace.

The three men—add to them . . . Artie, a scriptwriter who is older and, if anything, even more depraved than his companions—are all fathers who have long since left wife and kids and who treat their parade of girlfriends like tramps; the women, in turn, behaving as such. . . .

Rabe's game is social comment, a lashing out at the mores of the entertainment colony. A scriptwriter himself for a few years, he obviously detests everything about the place except the money.

While Rabe's talk can be dazzling (though self-satisfiedly so) when it isn't running about in circles, he has failed to relate this weird crowd to others. . . .

**"Hurlyburly"** is a play that seems about to lift us with every line, but lets us down instead—all sound and fury and, yes, signifying nothing but the author's hurt.

> Douglas Watt, "'Hurlyburly': A Vicious View of Hollywood," in Daily News, New York, June 22, 1984. Reprinted in New York Theatre Critics' Reviews, Vol. XLV, No. 10, June 25-July 1, 1984, p. 235.

## CLIVE BARNES

[*Hurlyburly*] is probably the first play to make a dictionary its hero. It is all, as Hamlet said, words, words, words. The play itself bears as much resemblance to a well-made play as an unmade bed does to a museum four-poster. It is a Hollywood landscape, full of mist and words, a wasteland of lost meanings and psychological probings for "stuff under stuff."

The characters in these episodes from a Hollywood life are ripped to their rib-cages with dope, coke, and booze. . . .

Words, words, words—or as Rabe and Eddie would put it: "Blah, blah, blah!" The play is a celebration of the articulate inarticulate. Jargon—much of it psychologically inclined—and a cool, laid-back, bent-over gobbledegook, introspective and obscurantist, amusingly dominate the work.

The picture of Hollywood is bleak. Remember the last Hollywood expose play, Clifford Odets's *The Big Knife*, just 35 years ago. That was pure innocence compared with this jungle whose zombie denizens seem preoccupied, in Mickey's words, "with pharmaceutical experiments testing the parameters of the American dream."

It is a world of narcotic anesthesia, treadmillingly recreational sex, and, Eddie puts it best, "semantic insanity." Introspection and dope as a way of life.

Rabe has written a strange, bitterly funny, self-indulgent, important play. . . .

The dialogue crackles in a strange Californian way—the way a prune might crackle. I do not believe that anyone ever says things like "gloom and doom have come to sit in my household like some kind of domestic appliance," but I appreciated Rabe's artistic deception that they might. . . .

Rabe has here written what is, I think, his first linear play. There are no overtly symbolic overtones or undertones, but Rabe's concept of linear is not necessarily a straight line, and the play with all its tortuous locutions is more of a picture than a story. . . .

"I know what I am saying, but I don't know what I mean." Another quotation from this bleakly amusing play: "It's great when people know what people are talking about."

This is Western society's 20th-Century dilemma, and Rabe is pinpointing it, although at times it is like sticking the tail on a donkey.

I was entertained, horrified, intrigued, and disturbed by *Hurlyburly*.

> Clive Barnes, "Rabe's 'Hurlyburly' Pins Hollywood to the Wall," in New York Post, June 22, 1984. Reprinted in New York Theatre Critics' Reviews, Vol. XLV, No. 10, June 25-July 1, 1984, p. 236.

## FRANK RICH

Until it crash lands at midpoint—halfway through the second of three acts—**"Hurlyburly"** offers some of Mr. Rabe's most inventive and disturbing writing. . . .

**"Hurlyburly"** is set in the Hollywood Hills—seemingly a world apart from the Vietnam-era Army base of . . . **"Streamers."** But the tropical villa . . . might as well be a barracks, and the battles haven't entirely changed. Mr. Rabe remains a dynamic chronicler of the brutal games that eternally adolescent American men can play. When his buddies aren't assaulting one another, they're on search-and-destroy missions against the No. 1 enemy—the women they invariably refer to as "broads," "ghouls," "bitches" or worse. . . .

At his impressive best, Mr. Rabe makes grim, ribald and surprisingly compassionate comedy out of the lies and rationalizations that allow his alienated men to keep functioning (if not feeling) in the fogs of locustland. According to one character, television "cuts the truth out of stories and leaves only the surface." Mr. Rabe's people live in a similar manner, with dense, contorted language to match. They dismiss depravities as "whims," try to "maintain a viable relationship with reality" and hope to sell their "marketable human qualities." They work in an industry so corrupt that its only honest executives are those who openly admit that they lie.

Amid the ebb and flow of the drug-sotted bull sessions and requisite Hollywood gags are some inspired set pieces. . . .

Mr. Rabe's pièce de résistance is his first act curtain scene—in which [Eddie and Darlene] decide to have sex only moments after their "relationship" had seemed permanently kaput. . . . The couple's ever-phonier declarations of sentiment are belied by ever lewder acts of disrobing.

The evening's collapse begins not long thereafter, once Mr. Rabe has finished diagnosing the anesthetized, unhinged and unfocused lives in view. As in **"Streamers,"** one man is a psychotic waiting to detonate. When the explosion comes—in successive acts of automotive violence—**"Hurlyburly"** sputters out irrevocably. Suddenly, those characters in any remote touch with their anguish start to emote about "desperation"— and, as they do, the speeches buckle and the tears flow. . . .

The ensuing revelations aren't terribly revealing—"I don't feel loved," cries [Eddie]—and the tributes to the tough guys' previously hidden vulnerability are banal. At the end of both Acts II and III, it's sentimentally demonstrated that the men are at least capable of offering paternal, if not romantic, affection to the opposite sex.

This is a paltry, amorphous payoff to the strong buildup, and it's unaccountably larded with intimations of nuclear apocalypse. . . . Perhaps a latent concern for the world's fate will at last allow [Eddie] to connect to other people—and to stop bouncing around the "vague hurlyburly" of his anomic existence. But we feel instead that the playwright is floundering and fudging. By imposing grand, crowd-pleasing significance on his characters, Mr. Rabe avoids the painful task of facing his own conclusions about them.

*Frank Rich, in a review of "Hurlyburly," in The New York Times, June 22, 1984, p. C3.*

### JACK KROLL

David Rabe's new play, **"Hurlyburly,"** is a powerful permanent contribution to American drama. . . .

There's no doubt that **"Hurlyburly"** is a challenging work. Starting out as a tough, funny play about some Hollywood wise guys, it swerves, darts and drives deep into a darkness shot through with the emergency lights of anxiety and despair. . . . Can these people be important?

They are—they're representative Americans of this moment, a moment compounded of cultural kitsch and forebodings of apocalypse. The messy living room is strewn with copies of Psychology Today and The Hollywood Reporter; the English muffins are stale but the Bolivian coke is fresh. And what seems like heartlessness is a stylized desperation. Eddie, Phil and Mickey have broken marriages; they are casual failures as husbands and fathers. Artie, hanging on to his Hollywood youth through these younger studs, brings them a "care package," the teen-age Donna, whom he's found living in an elevator— "just to stay in practice in case you run into a real woman," he tells his buddies. Eddie thinks he's found a real woman in the gorgeous Darlene, but Mickey outmaneuvers him to take possession of her, then returns her in a scathingly funny scene of movieland casuistry. Phil is a sensitive Neanderthal, a brooding self-doubter who beats up strangers and his wife but harbors grandiose ideas that range from beating the casinos in Las Vegas to solving the international situation.

What may seem like random elements of human chaos are really sharply observed details that Rabe shapes into a microcosm of spiritual dislocation. These perpetual adolescents who look at women and see only bimbos, these delectable women who make a virtue out of their susceptibility to male meanness, are drawn with a merciless compassion. We are seeing the breakdown of values through Hollywood jive; the brutal funniness of this play draws blood. Working on their scripts, their shows, these guys are professional junk artists and they know it (with different degrees of rationalization). Junk looms over this play like a Moloch of the technopop age; Rabe sees the human spirit itself in danger of turning into spiritual junk. (pp. 65, 67)

One of the strongest things in the play is Rabe's vision of wasted intelligence. Eddie and Mickey are smart guys, but their intelligence floats uselessly in a moral void. Rabe has a marvelous ear for their speech; masters of b.s., they take pride in snakelike sentences that are arabesques of evasiveness, showbiz sophistry turned into a dialectic of nihilism. The women, too, are affected by this hollowness: Darlene says, "Everything is always distracting me from everything else." Intentionally or not, this is an echo of T. S. Eliot's "Four Quartets": "Distracted from distraction by distraction." Rabe shares Eliot's vision of a world of intelligent nervous wrecks who've lost their moral center and, not knowing where to turn, turn everywhere. The climax, with its casual, nutty, almost comedic violence, has a frightening inevitability.

Rabe's vision of the wasteland may not be impeccably structured, but it has a savage sincerity and a crackling theatrical vitality. . . .

This deeply felt play deserves as wide an audience as possible. . . . **"Hurlyburly"** is going to be seen all over America for a long time. (p. 67)

*Jack Kroll, "Hollywood Wasteland," in Newsweek, Vol. CIV, No. 1, July 2, 1984, pp. 65, 67. Reprinted in New York Theatre Critics' Reviews, Vol. XLV, No. 10, June 25-July 1, 1984, p. 238.*

### JOHN SIMON

After *Goose and Tomtom,* I feared not just for David Rabe's talent, but even for his sanity. With the current *Hurlyburly,* however, the author of the deservedly acclaimed Vietnam trilogy reclaims, and even adds to, his reputation. The increments are chiefly in the area of humor; though Rabe has been funny before, I doubt if his previous work possessed such passages of sustained comedy, verbal and visual gags topping one another in a riotous *gradus ad Parnassum.* True, there are fairly painful longueurs in the more than three hours of this dark comedy, yet there is also some sort of payoff even in the overlong, arid stretches. And although *Hurlyburly* emerges (unintentionally) as a play more or less about nothing, that nothing ascends, in its better moments, to a philosophical nothingness, which has a sorry dignity of its own. Unfortunately, the play also tries, or seems to try, to become seriously concerned—it is extremely hard to distinguish between irony and naïveté in some of its passages—and this does not work at all. (p. 42)

[The] play's first half is better, mainly because it does not drag in quasi-serious philosophizing. Still, it is not as if all *Hurly* were good and all *burly* bad. Snappy bits keep surfacing throughout, and the ending is even moving in its emotionally twisted, strangulated way. In fact, only one long scene involving anagrams tries one's patience beyond endurance. There are, however, problems with language as well—several characters, but especially Eddie, speak in too long sentences with overassertive paragraph structure. But the chief difficulty is Eddie himself: Rabe seems to be divided, indeed riven, about him. To the extent that he is part of the ghastly Hollywood scene, Eddie is guilty; but to the extent that he is Rabe's alter ego, he is meant to be deeper, more sinned against, more likable. The split is beyond mending, and with Eddie in patches, the play, too, falls apart. In the end, we can tell no more than Rabe can whether we are beholding shallowness posturing as existential trauma or stature eroded by parental, societal, political iniquities. (pp. 42-3)

Rabe has been accused of misogyny in this play, and his men are indeed beastly to and about women. Yet if *Hurlyburly* has any Pyrrhic winners in it, it is the women who, as mothers and daughters, wrest a tiny victory from their defeat as lovers and wives. (pp. 43-4)

*John Simon, "War Games," in New York Magazine, Vol. 17, No. 28, July 16, 1984, pp. 42-5.**

### ROBERT BRUSTEIN

I had the unusual opportunity to read David Rabe's new play, *Hurly Burly,* in typescript before I saw the production. It was then called *Spinoff* and so powerfully written that I sent a letter to the playwright, whom I had never met, congratulating him on his achievement. I had not been kind toward some of Mr. Rabe's previous work, characterizing it as formally linear, thematically manipulative, morally self-righteous—smug mechanisms for producing guilt. This new play was either a major departure for Rabe or I had been wrong in my previous assessment. Either way, I felt obliged to write an apology, hoping thereby to encourage the playwright in what was bound to be a difficult progress toward the stage. (p. 27)

The text of **Hurly Burly** is 152 typewritten pages, which makes it as long as a late play by O'Neill, and equally repetitive. Like O'Neill's, however, Rabe's repetitions have a purpose, if only to expose the audience to the same ordeal as the characters. Structurally, they form a centripetal pattern, bringing us closer and closer in diminishing circles to an explosion at the center. In cutting this lengthy four-hour work to manageable length, [director Mike Nichols] has spared the audience's buns but left us wondering just what in hell the evening is all about.

What the play is about, I believe, is how the disintegration of American values has created a sense of anomie and a pronounced loss of purpose. Rabe's metaphor for this is cocaine. . . . Like O'Neill, who achieved greatness only when he adopted an unadorned Ibsenian realism, Rabe's style is now informed by the implicit *verismo* of David Mamet rather than the tendentious exhortations of Arthur Miller.

**Hurly Burly** takes place in the Hollywood Hills home of two casting agents, Eddie . . . and Mickey. . . . Both are divorced, and their house is a center of casual sexual encounters and male friendships. . . . [These] are not males with a capacity for abiding relationships; their strongest connections are with other men.

Or, more accurately, with drugs. From the very first moment of the play, which starts in early morning, everybody is "getting ripped" through a wide variety of orifices on a wide variety of narcotics, among them cocaine, marijuana, mushrooms, and Quaaludes. . . . People converse, but in a stream of meaningless talk, a species of underwater conversation, about broken marriages, sexual betrayals, blighted careers. . . . The language of the play grows ritualistic—repetitions of "blah-blah-blah" and "rapateeta" become a form of incantation.

The only plot concerns Phil, whose behavior grows increasingly erratic as the drug fog closes in ("Phil has got violent karma," says Eddie, "that's all, it's in the cards"). He has beaten up his estranged wife; he has mauled a stranger just for looking at him; teaching Donna to play football (a scene cut from the production), he butts her in the head. When he takes the balloon dancer out for a quickie, he throws her out of her own car. Eddie's affection for Phil is inexplicable; perhaps, as Artie says, it is because Phil is "safe"—"no matter how far you manage to fall, Phil will be lower." Whatever the case, Eddie excuses every instance of his friend's inexcusable behavior until, in the second act climax, he turns on him, brutally

destroying Phil's already shaky belief in his acting "potential" ("They just use you to make the bullshit look legitimate").

Eddie quickly reconciles himself with Phil, but in the final act his doomed friend fulfills his inevitable destiny by killing himself in a car crash. Eddie, wiped out by guilt and drugs, feeling somehow responsible, begins analyzing Phil's suicide note for anagrammatic messages. He is trying to establish coherent causal connections between his own state of mind and the state of the world, but whenever he comes up with reasons, Mickey ridicules him. . . . Still, Eddie's bitter reflections on television brainwashing, the neutron bomb, and the Nestlé formula milk invasion of Africa are apparently intended as serious social indictments (they are the only remaining traces of Rabe's former accusatory style and uncharacteristically explicit). At the end, Eddie is blowing coke in front of his television set, talking back to Johnny Carson, and blearily confessing himself to the bubble-headed Donna.

Mike Nichols has excavated all the humor available in the text, and added a considerable degree of satire, but in providing so much laughing gas, he has anaesthetized the toothache. Under his direction, the all-star cast sniffs out the jokes like truffles, but I don't think Rabe conceived **Hurly Burly** as such a madcap romp, nor were the three women originally intended to be such Nichols and May caricatures. . . . [One] ends up feeling it is the playwright, rather than his male figures, who has no understanding of women. (pp. 27-8)

Rabe has conceived Eddie as fully in his bitter elegiac desperation as any character since O'Neill's James Tyrone Jr. in *A Long Day's Journey Into Night*. (p. 28)

I think Rabe intended something a great deal deeper than [this production exhibits]. Besides displaying a dazzling new technique—not just a flawless command of dialogue, but an improved understanding of the nuances of human conflict—he has documented a chronicle of post-Vietnam War American life as pieced together from the shards of our shattered beliefs. Probing the social-metaphysical secrets revealed to only the most visionary playwrights, he has correctly seen that the plague of cocaine, which has infected virtually the entire entertainment industry, is less a disease than a symptom of a much larger malaise that is infecting virtually the entire country, thus giving us insights into our fall from grace, if not into our capacity for redemption. Not much of this is now evident on the stage . . . , where **Hurly Burly** remains a dramatic masterpiece in search of a faithful uncut production and an audience less eager to gape at Hollywood stars. But just to see it produced in the same year that featured *Glengarry Glen Ross* suggests that 1984 may very well go down in theater history as a watershed of American playwriting. (pp. 28-9)

*Robert Brustein, "Painless Dentistry," in* The New Republic, *Vol. 191, No. 6, August 6, 1984, pp. 27-9.*

# Christopher Reid

## 1949-

**English poet.**

**Reid belongs to a generation of British poets who emerged in the late 1970s and whose poetry exhibits a keen sense of imagination. Reid combines strange metaphors and archaic nouns to produce entertaining poems. One of the effects achieved through the comparison of disparate objects is the transformation of the ordinary into the exotic. These poems contain riddles that, when solved, offer fresh impressions of the familiar world. Such impressions have led critics to place Reid in what has been termed the "Martian School" of poetry. The phrase was inspired by poet Craig Raine's collection *A Martian Sends a Postcard Home*, in which Raine describes commonplace things as if he were seeing them for the first time.**

**Reid's two volumes of poetry, *Arcadia* (1979) and *Pea Soup* (1982), received mixed critical response. Critics generally praised his clever and inventive style; however, some found his poems lacking in depth and in concern for human conflicts. Yet Reid's intention does not appear to be to explore moral or social dilemmas. According to critic John Bayley, "Reid's chief excellence, which makes him one of the best poets of our times for some things, is for making a basic simplicity of theme work itself out through a highly visual and tactile pattern."**

Courtesy of Oxford University Press, Oxford

### BLAKE MORRISON

Fear of the imagination may not be something we'd normally expect of poets, but it would be hard to deny that in British poetry since 1945 that fear has been prevalent. Imagination has come to be associated with the unleashing of dark forces, and those forces, in turn, with the traumas of 20th-century history—fascism, the concentration camps, Hiroshima. It is hard to trace the origins of this idea. . . . But the assumption has grown that imagination is in some way dangerous, undemocratic, and that a level or moderate tone in poetry is more 'responsible'. Few poets feel happy with their low-keys and half-lights, but until now there has seemed little possibility of a way out.

It is too early to say yet whether the poetry of Craig Raine and Christopher Reid is the breakthrough we've been waiting for: so far there are only two first collections, Raine's *The Onion, Memory* and now Reid's much slimmer *Arcadia,* on which to form an impression. But already there can be no doubt of their literary-historical significance: Raine and Reid are the first mainstream British poets since 1945 to embark on a programme which makes imagination its priority, but which does so without lapsing into the shamanism and bardolatry commonly assumed to go along with it. For them imagination is *play*—the mind enjoying itself on life's surfaces rather than burrowing beneath. And though the world of appearances that they unfold is not without its darker elements, it's usually well protected from anything that—as Reid's **'A Whole School of Bourgeois Primitives'** has it—'might prove dangerous'. . . .

It is at times a rather too twee and comfortable world, but then comfiness is part of Reid's manner: the various leisurely poses in which we find him in *Arcadia*—on holiday, at dinner, in the park, visiting the zoo—imply that there's a time for poets

to have done with dramatic intensities, and to relax and have fun instead. The Reid persona gets an unashamed pleasure out of life . . . , and many of his poems are constructed as riddles which it is pleasurable to solve. These hedonistic structures are certain to irritate anyone looking for moral or political engagement. But they are not quite the poems of a dandy or aesthete: after reading *Arcadia* you feel that the world is a stranger, richer, more various place than you'd supposed, a feeling which it takes commitment of a kind to produce.

Play not only figures largely in the tone of *Arcadia* and in its subjects (a weightlifter, horse-jumping, rugby), it is also Reid's dominant metaphor. Like the mirror in his poem **'Patience'**, which 'says *Snap!* / to the wallpaper opposite', Reid turns up parallels and correspondences where they're least expected. A can-opener becomes 'a twirly dragonfly', . . . a whippet 'a framework for another dog'. Religious metaphors also figure largely, both for ironic contrast (these earthly flanks of pork, 'strung with ribs', as against angelic harps), and to locate sacred moments within the everyday. The other key metaphor is language itself, with Reid, 'a bookworm in the kitchen', discovering 'improbable fictions' wherever he looks. . . . The analogies come thick and fast, inviting the objection that this is obsessiveness, metaphor as illness. But now that structuralism has forced attention on to signs and decoding, Reid's basic method of misreading—getting things wrong in order to get them right, using a mock-innocent eye to make us see life afresh—seems a timely one. Comparisons with Craig Raine are inevitable. Both poets share the belief that a poetry which begins at home can nevertheless be exotic. But Reid's treatment of people is cooler, even crueller, than Raine's.

Blake Morrison, "A Bookworm in the Kitchen," in *New Statesman, Vol. 98, No. 2521, July 13, 1979, p. 64.**

## ANNE STEVENSON

[Artificiality] abounds in Christopher Reid's first collection, somewhat inappropriately called *Arcadia.* For . . . Mr Reid is thoroughly down-to-earth and up-to-date. . . . Christopher Reid has set up shop in Craig Raine's metaphorical amusement arcade. The object of this poetry is to entertain us, test our knowledge of classically derived vocabulary, and generally persuade us to mock the exalted.

Reid's poems seem harmless enough, and they abound in clever images. . . . But they are not quite funny. They are, in fact, oddly uncomfortable. Why? Maybe because, instead of laughing with his readers, Reid seems to laugh, if not at them, over their heads. A more likely explanation is that, taken as a whole, the poems in *Arcadia* leave an impression not unlike that created by a group of clever, smug public-school boys. You are only a fool, they seem to say, if you take anything seriously. Sadly for Mr Reid, any such trivialising of the sacred backfires. The gods will not be mocked. In the end, most of these poems are simply silly. (p. 220)

Anne Stevenson, "Poems, Dressed and Undressed," in The Listener, Vol. 102, No. 2624, August 16, 1979, pp. 220-21.**

## ALAN BROWNJOHN

Christopher Reid has been linked with Craig Raine (whose own first volume, *The Onion, Memory,* was published last year) in a two-man school of the New Fantasticals. His own debut, with *Arcadia,* shows him bent on the same sort of enterprise with metaphors—neatly capping the ordinary with extraordinary resemblances . . .—but he wonders about it more; enough to acknowledge that he is playing somewhat frighteningly at alternatives to reality, that successful play can be paradise but if it is too successful (too complete?) it can verge on nightmare. The child in the delicately and accurately fashioned title-poem about a child's drawing . . . may also be the child who often imagines, or dreams of, "an Edwardian bicyclist, / a roly-poly man with a walrus moustache", who *must* remain balanced on his machine. This particular obsession suggests a quiet but real horror lurking behind the toy world, and this is something different from Raine's . . . manner of squaring up to things.

Reid looks at first sight a more casual and relaxed dabbler with objects than Raine; but he could turn out (he already has a little more formal variety and dexterity on this showing) the more sensitive and accomplished poet of the two. He is not always so mathematically exact in his comparisons as Raine . . . yet his intertwining of fun and disquiet can sometimes be more haunting. Diners may sit down to a eucharistic joint of meat, their table "graced by a single chorister—salt in a fluted sur-

plice''; but the butcher's shop is a disagreeable "heaven" where pigs' heads

> relax on parsley and smirk about
> their newly-disembodied state.

But what about the idea that this kind of writing represents a new release of the imagination in English poetry? There's certainly a novelty in the thoroughness with which the technique is used, even if far-fetched comparisons of this sort have been the stock-in-trade of a MacNeice . . . , or (in America) a Richard Wilbur and an X. J. Kennedy. . . . Yet one can't help feeling that it could be a retreat into a defensive irony masquerading as a fertile, exuberant aestheticism. If the Movement verse of the '50s looked at the menace of the post-Hiroshima world with tight lips and tight verse forms, how else to exorcise the bourgeois families, homes and gardens of Mrs Thatcher's England other than with ironical fancies . . . ? I suspect that this ironical stance can't be kept up indefinitely, that reality kept at bay with "intoxicating discoveries" will keep coming back, and that Raine and Reid will need to move on from these very entertaining and promising beginnings. (pp. 72-4)

Alan Brownjohn, "Cosmic, Comic, Casual, Careful," in Encounter, Vol. LIII, No. 5, November, 1979, pp. 70-7.**

## JOHN BAYLEY

Decoration in poetry traditionally has a purpose: to embellish the story of the Faerie Queene or of Venus and Adonis, to ornament with appropriate curlicues the exposition of order and harmony in a poem like Sir John Davies's *Orchestra.* In what might be called the new decorated style, or modern Elizabethan, the decoration has become an end in itself, serving only to embellish the sense of time passing, water dripping, bells ringing, clothes flying on the line. . . .

[New Decorated contains] a language code in which art can try to reveal nothing but itself, its own message as a great deal of medium.

In the hands of brilliant performers such as Christopher Reid, John Fuller or Craig Raine, the results can be extremely variegated and highly satisfying. . . . The art is to surprise by a Zen-like defamiliarisation, the upshot of which, however, is not so much to startle us into seeing something simple afresh as to add a solid little cube of satisfaction to the Rubik language. Christopher Reid has a poem [in *Pea Soup*] in which a

> lordly fellow
> who cuts and stripes
> the Council's grass
>
> surveys a terrain
> of meticulous damage.

His 'haruspication of pods' in the title poem **'Pea Soup'** are green victims who cascade their entrails to a jab of the thumb 'like so many plump suspension-dots'. The pretty epanorthosis of 'meticulous damage' would have been appreciated by readers of *The Shepheard's Calender,* connoisseurs of tropes such as Sidney's 'sweet enemy': but in traditional Elizabethan such a rhetorical flourish was fitting itself to a larger design. Reid's pea-pods and Council grass are for themselves only.

Given the nature of poetry, given the tendency of the words in it to lead on to other unspoken words and stories and perspectives, that is quite an achievement, even if a negative one.

This is where Decorated styles begin to diverge. For all their charm, Reid's poems are singularly lacking in implication, of the kind cumulatively possessed, for instance, by the stanzas of Craig Raine's poem 'Flying to Belfast 1977'. . . . [However], it could well be argued that a great part of the success of Reid's poetry comes precisely from the skill with which he has blocked off implication and afterthought. . . .

Again and again [with Reid], poetry and meaning meet the moments of our present time head-on, and the resultant collision is intensely exhilarating for the spectator. A marvellous example is **'Dark Ages'**, which celebrates quasi-affluent urban squalor—'our heraldry of dirt'—in the terms and images appropriate to allegorical design, and to the ages of faith or enacted stability which talked and pictured in its terms. . . . The extensions of the conceit are worked out [in the poem] as thoroughly as in any of the old Elizabethans, and in a fashion that would have delighted them. A policeman with his neat little RT 'obeys the rasp of airborne voices' like Joan of Arc. . . . Newspapers enfold the knees like supplicators; the hippy is a holy man staring at panties and tights doing a dance round the maypole of a clothes-line. And here these worked-out conceits are implications too: of a particular kind and quality exclusive to Reid's verse. By the sharpness with which they are themselves, they suggest something of the slackness, the indifference and pathos of their subjects, the lack of sense and form in urban manners.

Something similar happens in **'Magnum Opus'**, a poem of splendid virtuosity about the cornucopia of absurdities, both tangible and liturgical, that constitutes today the huge heap of a cathedral. Again Reid makes his own kind of poetic order out of something that to the ordinary eye has ceased utterly to make sense. . . .

Reid's chief excellence, which makes him one of the best poets of our time for some things, is for making a basic simplicity of theme work itself out through a highly visual and tactile pattern. Like Craig Raine, he has the gift of defamiliarisation which demands the familiar knowledge of the reader's eyes. Raine has a delightful image of the urinals in the Gents calmly sucking their peppermints, a glimpse instantly at home, even if only with half the poetry-reading public. In practice, this technique is probably as old as poetry, consisting as it does, not of an idea and object abstractly yoked for exemplary purposes, as in the Metaphysical conceit, but of two objects magicked into a coincidence that produces not visual fantasy but homely truth. . . .

Reid's simpleness starts with his acceptance of total contingency, abruptly made the trademark of emphasis. Our empty eye has had to register that 'supermarket-till cartouche looping inanely' before we can recognise it in its new livery, just as we have had to register the antiseptic cubes in the glugging urinals. This is a poetry of peculiar topos, which as handled by Reid has an unexpectedly wide variety of uses, though seldom or never that of directly moving us. And yet it does so in its own way, as in **'Bravura Passage'**, a poem Hardy would have liked, which assembles the contingent aspects of a dingy day by the London Thames, and then spots a motor-launch, 'abounding in chutzpah', which symbolises

> your adventurous beauty
> in the midst of things.

The technique is modishly intellectual in **'The Exotic Nouns'** and in **'The Naive Reader'**, which threads in brilliantly Audenian metre the cliché-paths of popular fiction. It is amusing when it titups round the clichés of anthropomorphism in the aquarium, where the turtle, the old buffoon of the zoo, is your departed uncle trying to 'come through' from another world, 'and not drowning but waving . . .' But the best use is perhaps for the portraits, 'after Turgenev', which spring all too credibly into life. Here is the beggar, once a soldier,

> who, in a seaport
> near the Equator,
> possessed a young girl
> as glossy as an aubergine,
> with a curious perfume
> both fecal and sweet.
> A cap like a puddle
> now lies at his feet,
> to receive the odd penny.
> He wheedles his harmonica—
> a horrible sound.

Among the delicate verbal springes and mines of this verse that plain dead end in the last line does touch the heart: for, in contrast to the curious perfume, the horrible sound expresses a life outside the usual coding of the poetry.

*John Bayley, "Decorations and Contingencies," in* London Review of Books, *September 16 to October 6, 1982, p. 14.*

### PETER PORTER

Christopher Reid's achievement in **'Pea Soup'** is to be attractively stylish while staying human and approachable. The skill and dazzlement of the 'New Nasties,' the Martians, and the Metaphorists are made to serve the cause of refreshment and humanity. Reid is not really a virtuoso. In this, he differs from the captain of his black band, Craig Raine, who has a Lisztian fondness for fireworks.

Both Raine and Reid have done poetry a service by trying to make it as interesting as prose. They are out to entertain, to regain poetry's lost readership. They imply that verse can compete with space-invaders, documentaries on the box, gossip from starland, that it need not be a vision of the seasons, a confession wrapped in foreboding, or a résumé of myth. In their hands, it startles by comparisons, adopts wilful metaphors and is unapologetic about being clever. But it is also set in the real world, and, as likely as not, in domestic and everyday scenes. If the worst 'Martian' poem is little more than a scenic wisecrack, the best carries the liberal injunction of 'only connect' into regions of mystery and marvel.

One of the simpler poems in **'Pea Soup'** shows Reid's method at its most characteristic—**'Dark Ages.'** The mess and menace of our decaying cities is invoked by the opening—'This is our heraldry of dirt.' Thereafter three stanzas of likenesses develop a recognisable picture of urban life. . . .

**'Pea Soup'** is more accomplished and entertaining than Reid's first book, **'Arcadia,'** and that was a prize-winning volume. He has added strange stories to his life studies and pictures: **'The Traveller,' 'The Inspector'** and **'The Ambassador'** are all variants of science fiction daydreams. A trip to Japan shows him, as you would expect, an alert observer, but also a neat de-mystifier of Zen. Looking at the minuscule marine life of a Japanese island-shrine, he offers a feeling prayer: 'You Nothings, bless / me in my next-to-nothingness.'

The wit in these poems does not defuse the emotion—instead it expands that over-pious motto 'No ideas but in things.' In Reid's work, things and ideas have a brotherly love for each other. Sometimes the metaphors don't earn their keep. In **'Business as Usual,'** the poem never really recovers from its dud start—

> Flashing their lamps by daylight,
> the police are like Diogenes
> in full cry after an honest man

—though there are good things thereafter. **'Pea Soup'** shows that Reid has plenty of ambition for his poetry, beyond accuracy and skill.

> *Peter Porter, "The Human Face of Mars," in* The Observer, *October 3, 1982, p. 32.\**

## JOHN MOLE

The kind of poetry Christopher Reid writes offers dozens of neat little hostages to those who don't warm to his particular brand of snappy wit. It is easy to take phrases from [*Pea Soup*], as "in the playground of impromptu metaphors" or "the tiny boudoir-church / that is my favourite", and stick them as labels on his poetic baggage. Nor is it hard to single out his "grave rumpuses, flytings / of fanfare and frugal whoopee" and see him as a dinky Wallace Stevens. This would be to do him some injustice, though. His poems are pleasantly inventive, beatitudinous charms, or they are mischievously disconcerting like verbal/visual equivalents of Satie or Milhaud—"a saxophone / oozing into / efflorescence." What I find disappointing about them is—again to take one of his perfectly wrought phrases, of which there are perhaps just too *many*—that they don't amount to more than "tokens of possible eloquence." I've read somewhere that Reid is an admirer of the potter Lucie Rie, so he'll remember a comment she made about the moment when she opens her kiln being "not a revelation—a surprise." Reid's work is full of surprises—his pots are splendidly turned and immaculately glazed—but it never moves me to more than a feeling of wistful tenderness or a recognition that the world, viewed from a certain angle, does after a fashion look like that. The church painting where "heaven itself / is graced by an off-centre patch of damp" is typical of the Reid frisson—that *graced* preparing for a delicious coup of witty bathos. Robert Frost observed that a good poem begins in delight and ends in wisdom. Reid's poetry, however serious its implications, begins and ends in delight. (p. 64)

> *John Mole, in a review of "Pea Soup," in* Encounter, *Vol. LX, No. 1, January, 1983, p. 64.*

## MARTIN BOOTH

Christopher Reid's second book of verse [*Pea Soup*] furthers his emerging reputation as darling of the new poetocracy, the movement that seems to draw its inspiration from the technique of metaphor, even at the expense of emotion, that core of verse-making, and which is rapidly succeeding in its takeover bid for contemporary British poetry. His work is characteristically shallow in its observation and depends much upon a witty modernity for its impact, seeking to study as it does the world of today. . . .

Much of the poetry in the book is somewhat posturing, indicating a lingering on in the poet's mind of the dictates of his academic background which militate against his abilities to explain feelings in poetic terms; even his love poems are singularly distant and coldly analytical in an oblique fashion. In some respects, Reid's poetry is akin to the early work of Auden, more a stretching of limbs within the confines of words than a release of ideas through the excitement of language. The work is abundantly clever but distinctly artless. Yet it is typical of what is flowing from the new generation of British poets and they are certainly a reflection of the current trend against beauty and towards the uglier aspects of human activity.

> *Martin Booth, in a review of "Pea Soup," in* British Book News, *February, 1983, p. 117.*

## MICHAEL HULSE

Christopher Reid is often mentioned together with Craig Raine, and the two men have a lot in common, sharing the Oxford background, a publisher, and (twice) the *New Statesman* Prudence Farmer Award. "His strength is the innocent trustfulness of his eye," Peter Conrad wrote of Reid, adjudicating the 1980 Prudence Farmer Award, and certainly it is true to say that Reid's poetry is more often ingenuous and uncynical than Raine's. This said, we find that the actual mechanics of image making in the two poets are very often strikingly similar. The main structural principle of Raine's work is the simile, and the same is true of Reid's poetry, where "like" and "as if" also abound. . . . Most of Reid's images, like Raine's, are visual, finding equivalents for one shape or movement in another, as if the whole world were being seen through new eyes. This means that literally anything can serve as the subject of a poem, and in the same way ironies and almost metaphysical meanings can be hung on the peg of almost any insight. So in one way the poetry is simple and transparent, but at the same time it is dense and fully-textured.

Reid's [first] volume . . . is significantly titled **Arcadia,** and the label is rich in the ironies so dear to the poet. Clearly it is the vehicle of excuse for the other-world removed from everyday reality (one poem in the book is in fact called **"A Holiday from Strict Reality"**) which characterizes the perspectives of Reid's would-be unknowing image-making. . . . In addition, it invites us to consider the poems in the book as idylls; but, though the sheer pleasure of celebration of the things of this world is rich in the collection, there is also many a hint that the "peaceable kingdom" is no more than a figment of the language, that the idylls we posit as ideals sooner or later prove to have only the remotest connection with "strict reality." So in fact Reid's poetry often has a profound underlying pathos, for all its wit. (pp. 23-4)

> *Michael Hulse, "The Dialectic of the Image," in* The Malahat Review, *No. 64, February, 1983, pp. 20-7.\**

# Danny Santiago

## 1911-

(Pseudonym of Daniel James) American novelist, dramatist, and scriptwriter.

*Famous All Over Town* (1983) is the first novel by Danny Santiago, who as Daniel James coauthored several Broadway plays during the 1930s and 1940s and worked on the script of Charlie Chaplin's film *The Great Dictator*. James was blacklisted in 1951 after being implicated as a Communist by the House Committee on Un-American Activities. The authenticity of *Famous All Over Town* derives from James's experiences as a volunteer social worker in the Mexican-American district of Los Angeles during the 1950s and early 1960s. Described by John Gregory Dunne as "a lunatic success, a Chicano *Bildungsroman*," the novel elicited critical interest as a lively, poignant account of growing up in an impoverished barrio. Through flashbacks, the narrator remembers himself at age fourteen, when death, sexual awareness, and urban renewal changed his life and the lives of his family and friends. Critics especially praised Santiago for his adept use of Chicano street slang.

### KIRKUS REVIEWS

[Danny Santiago's *Famous All Over Town* contains episodic] memories of growing up Mexican-American in the Los Angeles barrio: a talented debut by a writer whose distinctive delivery—brash but wistful, streetwise but genial, selectively broken-Englished—usually works better in the comic moments than in the more serious ones. Rodolfo M. Medina, Jr., a.k.a. "Chato," recalls himself some years back at age 14—when everything pretty much went wrong for him. Ordered to kill his first chicken by his noisy father (a coming-of-age privilege), Rudy can't quite manage the knife—and shoots the chicken in the throat with a .45 instead. . . . Bright but distinctly underachieving at school, Rudy gets genuine encouragement from a Jewish counselor—but his one classroom display of smarts just gets him in trouble. His sexual yearnings for neighborhood women are rudely deflected. His attempt to defend his older sister's honor (against the attentions of a wetback suitor) turns out to be highly unnecessary. And Rudy winds up spending most of his time with his two-bit gang—until a night of joyriding ends with a buddy being shot dead by an over-eager cop. . . . [The] book ends with the parents split, the old neighborhood about to be razed . . . and Rudy starting his writing career in "Juvy," after being arrested for covering the Bank of America with graffiti. More a series of vignettes than a sustained coming-of-age novel—but bright, sassy recollections overall, full of unprettied-up local color (a brawling wedding reception, a grimly riotous funeral), ironic social observations (the strivings toward middle-class-dom), and substantial flashes of comic inspiration.

A review of "Famous All Over Town," in Kirkus Reviews, *Vol. LI, No. 3, February 1, 1983, pp. 126-27.*

Photograph by Abe Aronow. Courtesy of Danny Santiago

### SALLY ESTES

[*Famous All Over Town* is a] compelling coming-of-age novel set in a Los Angeles barrio where the Mexican American residents are drawn together by their shared values and traditions. At a crossroads in his life, Rodolfo ("Chato") Medina recalls the year he was 14, a time of turmoil and change for him, his family, and friends. . . . The author fleshes out his characters with verve and wit, and while a sense of the absurd pervades, the narrative's underlying tone is one of poignancy and sadness, revealing sympathy for people caught between two cultures and welcomed in neither.

Sally Estes, in a review of "Famous All Over Town," in Booklist, *Vol. 79, No. 15, April 1, 1983, p. 1016.*

### DAVID QUAMMEN

[It] is cheering to be able to report that Danny Santiago is a natural. . . .

"Famous All Over Town" is full of poverty, violence, emotional injury and other forms of major disaster, all vividly and realistically portrayed, yet, like a spring feast-day in a barrio, it is nevertheless relentlessly joyous. Best of all is its language; narrated by Chato, the novel employs a rich street Chicano

English that pleases the ear like sly and cheerful Mejicana music.

"**Famous All Over Town**" is an honest, steady novel that presents some hard cultural realities while not for a paragraph failing to entertain. I am totally ignorant of the Chicano urban experience but I have to believe this book is, on that subject, a minor classic. And Danny Santiago is good news.

> *David Quammen, in a review of "Famous All Over Town," in* The New York Times Book Review, *April 24, 1983, p. 12.*

### THE NEW YORKER

The language [in "**Famous All Over Town**"] is an expressive mixture of Mexican Spanish and American English, the events—frictions at home, macho strivings, unrequited sexual pangs, trouble (by way of a friend in a stolen car) with the police—are strongly imagined and told with vivacity, and although there are many moments of real poignancy, there is also much real humor here, and even joy. The ending is not really satisfactory—abrupt, inconclusive, and dangling—but Mr. Santiago (or, rather, Chato) seems to promise a sequel. (p. 129)

> *A review of "Famous All Over Town," in* The New Yorker, *Vol. LIX, No. 11, May 2, 1983, pp. 126, 129.*

### MARGARET WIMSATT

The country is full of problem kids, and ghettos and barrios produce many of them, as do Indian reservations. New York City might claim title as the most productive, but Los Angeles is certainly in the running. It is the setting for [*Famous All Over Town*]. Seldom has the topic of juvenile delinquency been approached with such loving and knowledgeable irony.

Problem kids, as we all know, come from problem families and backgrounds, and Rudy M. Medina, Jr., (Chato) tells the story of his. Aged twenty-eight, he looks back on the summer of his fourteenth birthday. (p. 309)

That was an exciting summer on Shamrock Street, though maybe not anything out of the ordinary.

Language is the eye of thought, and to be bilingual doubles the vision. But to be, as it has been described, illiterate in two languages, creates the problems Santiago's characters face. Ignorance of, and disdain for, Norte-Americano ways got Chato and his friends into scrapes with The Law. It lost for the Shamrock Street residents their homes and their satisfactory way of life. Of course it also gave them a sense of community which while it lasted was feudal and chivalric—and funny, to the outsider, as Don Quixote's world has always been to its readers. This sense of the tragi-comic gives the novel its power. . . . All this is told in a complex language brew: murdered Spanish, murdered English, combine on the page to be intelligible, even eloquent. "My fingers slided back and forth." "It costed me nothing." "He never once discriminated me." "Seldom if never." "No quieras un free shoeshine." Language as tool, as means to an end. (pp. 310-12)

The author's eyes and voice provide an insight into the sad funniness of life. Danny Santiago has written a love letter; in Chicano. With music, it would make a fine scenario. (p. 312)

> *Margaret Wimsatt, "Wild Ride, Wild Language," in* Commonweal, *Vol. CX, No. 10, May 20, 1983, pp. 309-12.*

### GEORGE KEARNS

[Danny Santiago] will be read more for his subject, life among Mexican-Americans, than for his art, although he's an artist with a very sure touch. You'd have to be a dedicated highbrow (in the sense of "dedicated wordprocessor," it can't do anything else) not to catch the pleasure Santiago takes in his writing and the energy he brings to every page of his first novel, *Famous All Over Town*. Fiction could not be less pretentious, nor more confident in its mimetic power: there's an amazing world out there, and words can do a lot to capture it. The center of Santiago's world is . . . a Mexican neighborhood in Los Angeles about twenty years ago. . . . [Chato, his narrator] has returned, "slow, law-abiding and drunk," to the place where his "skinny little house" used to stand, with a "famous '55 low-mileage Buick" in front of it. He then turns the narration over to himself at the age of fourteen, and Danny Santiago's triumph is in the language he finds for the teenage Chato. The language carries the book, for I suppose that without it all that would be left would be sociology. There's a good deal of sociological observation, of course, but the verve of Chato's language leaves the Social Sciences far behind. It's a language that moves rapidly from one emotion to another, as Santiago renders it without much dialect, just light, expressive indications of the kind of syntax and Spanglish that are used in Chato's world. . . . A lot happened in Chato's fourteenth year, including the way he made himself famous all over town, by writing [his name in graffiti style, "a 4-color job with letters 2 feet high outlined in gold"]. . . . *Famous All Over Town* is structured as a series of short, rich, adroitly-shaped sketches. Danny Santiago's warmth and affection for a resilient, deracinated people he knows very well makes this, for all the trouble it records, a very sweet book. (pp. 559-60)

> *George Kearns, "World Well Lost," in* The Hudson Review, *Vol. XXXVI, No. 3, Autumn, 1983, pp. 549-62.\**

### JOHN GREGORY DUNNE

[*Famous All Over Town* is about] a fourteen-year-old street-smart kid with an IQ of 135, resisting assimilation by a voracious Anglo culture he sees as dominated by the Southern Pacific Railroad, which wants to buy up and pave over his block in the interest of better freight management. He is equally divorced from the rural Mexico of his grandparents, a Valhalla he deprecates as a place where "they milk each other's goats."

Chato lives by his considerable wits on that brink where the comic adventure can easily flip into casual violence. With quick tongue and sharp eye, he is ever the observer of his family—his spirited sister Lena (christened Tranquilina, but never tranquil), his placid, preoccupied baby-machine mother, and especially his blustery, ham-handed father: "My father is very loud in stores speaking Spanish, but in English you can barely hear him."

The Medinas exist in a secondhand way: "Day-olds from the bakery, dented tomato cans, sunburned shirts from store windows, never two chairs alike and lucky if one shoe matched the other." They buy their clothes from the "As-Is" bin at the Goodwill, "fishing through boxes raw off the trucks before anything was washed or fumigated.'' But Chato is never a victim of his circumstances. He is a victor, a vivid historian of his own life: ''There's my cousin Cuca and my cousin Kika and Lalo and Lola and Rosario the boy and Rosario the girl and my Uncle Benedicto that the priest put a curse on him for what he done in the bell tower.''

Given my rooting interest, I found *Famous All Over Town* a lunatic success, a Chicano *Bildungsroman* by a septuagenarian ex-Stalinist aristocrat from Kansas City. There is no trace of the didacticism of **Winter Soldiers** [a play written by Santiago under his real name, Daniel James, during World War II], no hint of the author's history, either of his communism or his apostasy. This is not social realism, not a proletarian novel; James's Southern Pacific is not Frank Norris's octopus. *Famous All Over Town* takes the form of a classic novel of initiation, and Chato Medina could be read as a Hispanic Holden Caulfield. His weapons against the world are brains and humor, his language an eloquent and scrambled mixture of Spanish and English. (p. 26)

*John Gregory Dunne, "The Secret of Danny Santiago," in* The New York Review of Books, *Vol. XXXI, No. 13, August 16, 1984, pp. 17-18, 20, 22, 24-7.*

# Helen Hooven Santmyer
## 1895-

American novelist, essayist, short story writer, and poet.

Santmyer gained attention in literary circles for her chronicle of small-town life, "*. . . And Ladies of the Club*" (1982). Originally published by Ohio State University Press, the novel was largely ignored until it became a Book-of-the-Month Club selection a year later. The book was conceived as a defense of the type of people satirized by Sinclair Lewis in his 1920 novel *Main Street*. Critical reaction to "*. . . And Ladies of the Club*" was divided: some critics argued that the novel was being praised only because of Santmyer's advanced age, while others contended that this fictional account of the town of Waynesboro, Ohio, from 1868 through 1932 is rich in domestic detail and includes fully developed characters. Another charge against Santmyer was that she depicted her Jewish and black characters in a racist manner. However, several critics defended her by pointing out that the viewpoints of her protagonists toward these characters realistically reflects an attitude of that era.

Santmyer had published three books prior to "*. . . And Ladies of the Club.*" Her first two novels, *Herbs and Apples* (1925) and *The Fierce Dispute* (1929), display several elements found in her later novel: attention to detail, a straightforward narrative style, and insight into the lives and ambitions of her female characters. *Ohio Town* (1963) is a memoir of Santmyer's hometown of Xenia, Ohio. In this work Santmyer contrasts the town's past with its present and focuses on the importance to the townspeople of such buildings as the church, the courthouse, and the library. *Ohio Town* has recently been republished. Santmyer has also contributed essays, poetry, and short stories to several publications, including *Atlantic, Scribner's,* and *The Antioch Review.*

(See also *Contemporary Authors,* Vols. 1-4, rev. ed. and *Contemporary Authors New Revision Series,* Vol. 15.)

Charles Steinbrunner/Dayton Newspapers, Inc.

## THE NEW YORK TIMES BOOK REVIEW

["**Herbs and Apples**"], Helen Hooven Santmyer's first novel, is a dignified piece of writing, whose seriousness of purpose bears a promise for the future. But, like most first novels, it is overcrowded with minutiae. Written in biographical form, it deals with the life of Derrick Thornton, a Middle-Western girl brought up in a small farming community in Ohio. More than half the thick volume is devoted to detailed description of incidents in her childhood, adolescence and college life.

The impression received is that Miss Santmyer has delved into her own personal reminiscences. She seems to have been afraid of omitting something that, to her, seemed vital to the psychological development of her heroine. . . .

The tale would have gained in power and emphasis had the author deleted at least one-third of the events described. For there is sufficient material in the first 200 pages to furnish substance for another book. Later, the story broadens and becomes more tense and gripping. There is no imbroglio until the third section. It is merely a recital of passing days and

years. Then comes the war to furnish motive for the heart complication. But Derrick's fiancé, Jack Devlin, is only a shadowy figure and, after his departure for France and the trenches, disappears from the pages. (p. 17)

[At] the age of 10 Derrick has already planned her life. Her ambition is to write books, to be famous, "as great as Louisa May Alcott," and to have the world admire and wonder at her genius. However, the novel proves that ambition can be destructive to one's own happiness and to the happiness of those one loves. And in the end the girl gathers up her few herbs and apples and, in renouncing, learns that duty accomplished is the only thing that brings real peace.

"Pleached Gardens," the second section, is devoted to Derrick's college years. Here she and five other girls form a close corporation in friendship, spending their leisure hours dissecting their emotions. Problems that have baffled the greatest brains have no terrors for this wise sextet. They are what youth has been since the world began: to itself omniscient in all that relates to life and its meaning. And so they utter their opinions with a finality that precludes discussion. . . .

In "The Sky That Holds Them All," by far the most interesting part of the book, the college chums come to New York to make a career for themselves. Alice, Frances and Derrick share a flat on a cross-street off Third Avenue. The converted brownstone mansion, with its cheap window boxes, its narrow, bare, uncarpeted hall redolent with the odor of stale boiled cabbage, the high-ceiled rooms, the long windows, the housekeeping inconveniences—all these are real. . . .

Derrick finds a position as private secretary to the book review editor of a big New York daily. After a year she is promoted to writing reviews, to refusing manuscripts, to accepting poetry. But a writer's life holds no more charm for her. . . .

All through the volume are scattered samples of Derrick's poems. She frankly says that editors have refused them because they are poor. She is right. Perhaps this is one reason why she clutched at herbs and apples instead of straining after the elusive laurel wreath of the successful writer. (p. 19)

> *"Ambition Compromises," in* The New York Times Book Review, *September 13, 1925, pp. 17, 19.*

## THE SATURDAY REVIEW OF LITERATURE

The pathos of a weak talent succumbing to the inertia of native circumstance after a few of its green fruits had been gathered is the theme of ["**Herbs and Apples**"]. The heroine, Derrick Thornton, a prodigy of a small Ohio town, is exhibited in the short course that her gifts enable her to run from an eccentric girlhood at home, through the fame of the undergraduate literary "genius" in an eastern college and the favorable notice of the frequent contributor to magazines and reviews in New York City, back again to the Ohio household and a dutiful womanhood. Neither the duty nor the talent are exigent enough to make pathos moderately deep, and the theme is smothered in a welter of irrelevancies. These, to be sure, are the most interesting part of the book, showing as they do, consciously and unintentionally, how a certain type of young woman—the recent graduate of a woman's college who comes to New York with an eager literary ambition or simply a desire to win and keep independence—feels and thinks and lives. It would appear that she remains at the surface, spreads herself rather thinly, as the author of this book herself has done in her presentation of the type. Under the facetious dialogues, the patter about books and ideas and the career, one can detect the wistfulness and sentimentality of an ungrown emotional life necessarily unfruitful in art. There is something in the air of these associations of Derrick Thornton's that keeps her at the level of wistfulness—a wistfulness concealed beneath a bright film of jocosity and cynicism *a la môde*. Derrick begins and ends her "career" in this undeveloped state of the emotions, and for this reason it is hard to sympathize with her defeat, her need to hurry her talent. She has not tried hard to make a place in actuality for her dreams.

> *A review of "Herbs and Apples," in* The Saturday Review of Literature, *Vol. II, No. 16, November 14, 1925, p. 301.*

## THE NEW REPUBLIC

The pattern of a woman's life has ever been a lure to the pen of the novelist. Miss Santmyer believes in the dignity of unsuccess met firmly. A not unworthy motive—but [in *Herbs and Apples*] Miss Santmyer is lacking in the ability to sift her material so as to make it sustain her theme, and the narrative drags accordingly. Her backgrounds also are uneven. Her Tecumseh, in its haze of golden dust, its fields and hillsides, is wholly vivid and beautiful. Her New York is drab and flat. And be it said in mournful candor, her college atmosphere is

juvenile and dreary. Yet scattered through this oddly compounded book are passages of a breath-taking delicacy and poignancy, of insight and power beyond cavil.

> *E.B.H., in a review of "Herbs and Apples," in* The New Republic, *Vol. XLV, No. 579, January 6, 1926, p. 198.*

## NEW YORK HERALD TRIBUNE BOOKS

[In "**The Fierce Dispute**"] Miss Santmyer tells the story of the struggle, obstinate rather than fierce, between widowed and well-to-do Margaret Baird and her daughter Hilary over the training of the latter's child, Lucy Anne. Hilary's marriage with an Italian musician had been unfortunate because of his polygamous habits, and she had returned to her mother. Mrs. Baird, strongly disapproving of all Bohemian tendencies, had received her on condition that Lucy Anne be kept in ignorance both of her father and of music in all its forms.

The narrative unrolls mainly from the child's point of view. Lonely, deprived of companions of her age, she peoples the old house with imaginary playmates. The musical instinct awakes in her despite all precautions. . . . In the end, Hilary triumphs through causes, natural and supernatural, which the reader may be left to discover.

With an unobtrusive artistry, Miss Santmyer envelopes the situation in an atmosphere akin to a musical mood of which the charm is emotionally definite and intellectually elusive. It is in terms of tones and timbres that one recalls her work rather than in pictorial images. Her style is unadorned, and at times almost naive in its simplicity. She writes on a quiet plane, and her few departures into dramatic angularity are less effective than her habitual serenity.

> *"Hilary Triumphs," in* New York Herald Tribune Books, *April 28, 1929, p. 25.*

## THE NEW YORK TIMES BOOK REVIEW

The warfare of two women over the possible future of the child who is the daughter of one and granddaughter of the other is "**The Fierce Dispute**" of Helen Hooven Santmeyer's title. It is a dispute which, though it contains moments of effectiveness and even of beauty, seems neither reasonable nor probable. For it all hinges on the fact that Hilary Baird, some years before the novel opens, had married a musician, an Italian named Paolo, whom she left because he was unfaithful to her. Hilary returned to her mother, bringing her little girl, Lucy Anne, with her, but though pride had induced her to leave her husband she still loved him so much that she was not able even to think of her little daughter. . . . Because of Paolo, Mrs. Baird, Lucy Anne's grandmother, hated music and musicians, though why she, a practical sort of woman, not especially imaginative, should have felt so intense a detestation it is difficult to understand, since she does not seem ever to have cared two straws for Hilary. Had she been an adoring mother, heartbroken over the spoiling of her daughter's life, her resentment, though still rather far-fetched, would at least be intelligible; but all her love is given to Lucy Anne. Hilary, for her part, shows no touch of either past or present affection for her mother. Mrs. Baird was determined, at all and any costs, to prevent Lucy Anne from becoming a musician; Hilary was no less determined that a musician the child should be. . . .

Lucy Anne herself is sympathetically and charmingly drawn. Her loneliness, her fanciful re-creation of the children who had been her grandmother's playmates, her feeling for the old house and its haunting memories, are all portrayed with insight and even beauty. She is the book's outstanding character.

> *"Women at War,"* in The New York Times Book Review, *May 5, 1929, p. 7.*

### THE SATURDAY REVIEW OF LITERATURE

["The Fierce Dispute"], belying its title, is a quiet, dignified novel. It tells the story of only three people—two women and a child—unfolded against a single background. It is a struggle of years carried on under one roof and seldom expressed. The two women, a mother and daughter, completely isolated from the world, fight for the happiness, as each sees it, of one little girl. It is an excellent situation with untold possibilities. But it fails here because it is not made to seem sufficiently inevitable. . . .

Moreover the story is badly manipulated. Death and disease have to be called in to end a struggle which should have had a psychological solution. Spiritually the two women end where they started. True, there is a last hurried attempt to satisfy the reader. But it seems to come like an after-thought—an attempt to tie together the loose strings. Life is not like that. Nor, if you see the pulling of the strings, is art like that.

Yet there is a good deal to be said for **"The Fierce Dispute."** There is great charm in the measured dignity of its writing and the quiet of its scene. The whole picture seems to come out of the past, it has none of the earmarks of a "costume" novel. Its faults, on the whole would seem to be faults of inexperience. The understanding and sincerity in the character-study of the child alone, save the story. And the simple, straightforward manner in which the whole morbid tale is told, raises it to the ranks of the significant. It comes as a pleasant antidote to most of the more ostentatious present-day American novels.

> *A review of "The Fierce Dispute,"* in The Saturday Review of Literature, *Vol. VI, No. 3, August 10, 1929, p. 41.*

### ELDON C. HILL

[*Ohio Town*] mingles undocumented history and personal memories in a nostalgic effort to evoke the past of Xenia, Ohio, and contrast it with the town at present. The result is a lively account that entices the reader's attention from the first page to the last.

As Miss Santmyer says in her "Acknowledgments": "The following sketches are drawn mostly from memory, mine or my elders'; the passage of time may have colored some events to the detriment of accuracy." Perhaps this is so. Yet one feels that, though she may be unwittingly at times a bit unfaithful to the facts, the broad truth of the narrative remains. . . .

In all, Miss Santmyer presents thirteen of these sketches, centering on the chief landmarks of Xenia. . . . She writes with understanding and affection of the unusually large Negro population concentrated in the East End. Indeed, the author's deepest interest throughout the book is in the people, from the "leading citizens" and the millionaires, who were not quite sure how they were expected to behave, to the lowliest servants, who seemed to feel no stigma in performing the most menial tasks. (p. 294)

She sees all the persons and places in her book with the double vision of a small girl experiencing and a grown woman remembering and revisiting. Often she writes with poignant regret of the changes industrialization has wrought in the little city whose freedom she enjoyed in childhood and adolescence. Of her characterizations I liked especially those of Miss McElwain, the old-time librarian who ruled with strictness her little kingdom, and of Dr. Will, the general practitioner who always took time to visit in a leisurely manner with his patients. Interesting likewise is her mention of the interurban lines, now entirely faded from the scene, and of the shrill whistle of the steam locomotive which interrupted the famous Joe Jefferson and lesser players in performances at the Opera House before giving way to the low moan of the Diesel.

Miss Santmyer has not only a retentive memory and a quick eye for the interesting anecdote; she has also an admirable literary style, a fact not particularly strange since she has published two novels. She expresses herself with particularity and vividness. (pp. 294-95)

Somewhat carried away with her subject, the author asserts, "The town is Winesburg and Spoon River, it is Highbury and Cranford, it is even Illyria and Elsinore." . . . Miss Santmyer's Xenia, however, bears little resemblance to any of these fictional places, each of them unique. Her book, rather, recalls the work of another novelist who once lived near Xenia. I refer, of course, to Wılliam Dean Howells and his *A Boy's Town*, which also happens to chronicle the life of another southwestern Ohio town, Hamilton. To say that it deserves a place on the same shelf with Howells' interesting book is to indicate the chief merit of *Ohio Town*. (p. 295)

> *Eldon C. Hill, in a review of "Ohio Town,"* in Indiana Magazine of History, *Vol. LIX, No. 1, March, 1963, pp. 294-95.*

### JAMES IVERNE DOWIE

*Ohio Town* is not a formal history in terms of fact and statistic carefully documented, but it is a lively history pulsating with memories, local lore, and landmarks "as familiar as bread and butter." Here is the nostalgic account of Xenia, Ohio. Helen Hooven Santmyer has written the story of any Ohio town or, more exactly, of any town in mid-America. *Ohio Town* is another Grover's Corners. Within the familiar and at times hackneyed environs of the little town there exists the universal.

Unlike Thornton Wilder, who left the stage largely empty of properties, Santmyer has concentrated upon the stage settings. The table of contents sounds formidable with chapter titles such as "The Courthouse," "The Church," "Streets and Houses," "The Library," and "The Opera Hosue." But these pages contain more than an inventory of town real estate. The author has a veritable genius for developing historical narrative through sensitive descriptions of familiar landmarks. (p. 217)

In the hands of a less able writer the materials which make up the core of *Ohio Town* could well sink into the commonplace and dingy trivia. But here the prose is handled with charm and perception. There is no tawdry self pity or apology for a life spent within the confines of a little town. Though Helen Hooven Santmyer has the requisite skill to write history, her primary concern is to tell a story: ". . . how many of the old houses stand today, to remind us of another time, no one can ever write a book based on the lives spent under their roofs. To know about those lives you must be child, grandchild, great-grandchild of the town. . . .'' Despite her diffidence, Helen Hooven Santmyer has written a book which is not only concerned with architecture and places but with the lives of the folks who live and have lived in *Ohio Town.* (p. 218)

> *James Iverne Dowie, in a review of ''Ohio Town,''
> in* History News, *Vol. XIX, No. 13, November, 1964,
> pp. 217-18.*

## GENE LYONS

[There] are literary events and there are publishing events, and it is a critic's not always pleasant duty to make the distinction. In just about every way one can imagine, **''. . . And Ladies of the Club''** fits into the latter category. Less a novel than a chronicle devoted to ancestor worship, the book treats in sometimes fascinating but more often enervating detail 64 years in the lives of the very proper members of the Waynesboro (Ohio) Woman's Club, from its founding in 1868 until the awful day the lights went out in 1932 with the election of Franklin Delano Roosevelt. . . .

While Sinclair Lewis's small-minded villains were mostly boosters on the make, Santmyer's heroes and heroines are local nobility—judges, physicians, Presbyterian ministers, captains of industry and their wives. And though a handful of scenes—mainly those describing the deaths of important characters—have undeniable power, few readers will get that far. Santmyer's style, while competent, is undistinguished by either gravity or wit; her third-person omniscient narration too often leaves the reader hanging in mid-air. . . .

Santmyer's larger theme is ''the relentlessness of time,'' but she also devotes an amazing amount of space to what can only be described as Republican apologetics: our author seeks to give the presidency of Ulysses S. Grant the restored eminence some wish for Richard Nixon. There are detailed, one-sided harangues (nobody who'd disagree has the pedigree requisite for club membership) on the gold standard, the iniquity of labor unions and the undesirability of Eastern European immigrants.

By the standards of their class and time, Santmyer's characters are idealists, not only decent by their own lights but obsessed with ''decency'' to the exclusion of almost every other moral value. It's not shocking that they are snobs and bigots; what's remarkable is that their creator displays not a particle of irony about it. A parade passes: ''gaping Negroes grinned and shouted.'' Every one of the several black characters is shiftless, credulous as a child and talks ''unintelligible'' darky gibberish. . . . Despite the ladies' temperance crusade, ''the Irish, unable to find work to do, or perhaps not trying very hard,'' stick to their ''grogshops.'' **''. . . And Ladies of the Club''** is suffused with this stuff from beginning to end. It's not at all pretty.

> *Gene Lyons, ''Sunny Side of the Street,'' in* News-
> week, *Vol. CIII, No. 25, June 18, 1984, p. 93.*

## VANCE BOURJAILY

In the spring of 1868, Abraham Lincoln was three years dead and not much talked about. The young men, home from the battlefields, hospitals and prisons of the Civil War, were getting started in life. The young women were waiting for them.

**''. . . And Ladies of the Club''** begins with the graduation of two such young women from the Waynesboro Female College in the small city in Ohio in which almost all of the events of this long novel take place. The two are Anne Alexander, the doctor's daughter, and Sally Cochran, the banker's. Each has her young man pretty well picked out. Anne's is to be John Gordon—a moody young doctor now fallen away from medicine because of the wartime horrors—when John decides to return to his profession. Sally has her eye on Ludwig Rausch, a rising entrepreneur, energetic, good-hearted and shrewd. Both marriages will take place; the brides will be lifelong friends.

They will also be lifelong members of the Waynesboro Woman's Club, founded to keep some of the town's educated women intellectually alive. . . .

The novel re-creates an American period—the post-Civil War era in the North—I, for one, yearned to know more about. This is done with a combination of delicacy and candor as far as the intimate psychological and sexual relationships are concerned, though it deals much more often with routine matters. It is written in workmanlike prose, sometimes—perhaps by design—a little stilted, but by no means primitive.

Each chapter chronicles one or more years in the lives of certain Waynesboro families. Each chapter is preceded by a list of current members of the Woman's Club, which changes gradually as new members are added, their names changing too, sometimes, as they marry. Those whom they replace are listed ''In Memoriam.'' The lists are more than a unifying device. They are a running summary of the book, and readers impatient with a narrative pace as slow as day-to-day life itself may find themselves looking ahead to learn from the membership list what is going to happen.

For many readers the appeal of **''. . . And Ladies of the Club''** will be quite personal. For those whose antecedents were, wholly or in part, middle-American, genteel, white, Protestant—and Yankee in their Civil War connection, hence Republican—it will be like reading family history. Though the specimen families dealt with most consistently are Anne's and Sally's—the Gordons and the Rausches—there is a universalizing factor. The book is more often ethnographic than novelistic; it is, in large part, an affectionate catalogue of the homes and happenings, ways and means, of that social segment named above—middle-American, genteel—during the 19th century.

Even the storytelling is generally ethnographic rather than plotted. A problem comes up. Counsel is taken. A remedy suggested by custom and common sense is agreed to. The problem's outcome is predicted. Things work out that way.

It is details that give the book charm. . . .

[The women] paid regular, formal calls on one another, leaving cards when the person called upon wasn't at home. For dessert they served floating island. For their children's parties they had taffy pulls. The Fourth of July was as grand a holiday as Christmas. Their doors were answered by devoted black maids. They rode in horsedrawn carriages, which were got ready and often driven by black coachmen. Post-bellum life in the victorious North seems to have looted some of the graces of the defeated South, but it was not mindless. The ladies might gossip and make matches, but they campaigned effectively, some for women's rights, some against the abuse of alcohol, some to establish free libraries. They were genuinely educated, and the club presented an intellectual challenge every fortnight. . . .

Although the book is primarily about women, adequate attention is given to the concerns of their sons and husbands, which are chiefly business, the economy, politics and technological and scientific advances to be put to use. . . .

Helen Hooven Santmyer is not an inexperienced writer, and if her book is sometimes told artlessly, this is as often offset by a repeated mild irony—the observation that, to her people, the important matters are marriage, birth, illness and death, that the affairs of the Captains and the Kings are quite secondary.

There are some affecting stories within her story, along with some pat and sentimental ones. The most haunting is that of the lonely death of an old schoolmistress, a club member from whose little day school the children have had to be withdrawn. Trying to fight off the pains of aging, she has become addicted to laudanum, then a legal opiate. It causes her to dream away the class periods, while the children sneak off. She is given pension enough for food and fuel but—whether by calculation is ambiguous—not enough to pay for her drug. She cannot survive the forced withdrawal, which seems to her an incomprehensible cruelty. In the most sentimental story, a child who has just learned to be happy dies of polio. It seems relevant to point out that the first of these stories takes place during the first two-thirds of the book—the 19th-century part. In the 20th-century part, the span of years is the same, 32, but the condensation is greater, and the author, recognizing perhaps a decline in the freshness of the material, tries harder for plot and complication.

In her concluding pages, she introduces a character whom we read as herself as a young woman writer. She has published a couple of novels, set in Waynesboro. Now she means to write "a long one, covering several generations of life . . . an answer to Sinclair Lewis, whose 'Main Street' had made her so angry."

A book like "*. . . And Ladies of the Club*," with its sincerity and exhaustiveness, may be a fit rebuke to a satirist, but it is not a complete account of a town's life. There are darker things, more absurd things, a greater incidence of tragedy and violence in any period if the more sophisticated, the deprived, the failures, the strange ones and the restless are included along with the upper normal. It's to be supposed that Miss Santmyer is too wise not to know this and that she has been willing to sacrifice the goal of completeness for something that means more to her—that is, to defend the women themselves whom Lewis attacked. This she does. Anne and Sally and the others are not fools. They are not pretentious. They are not shallow. They are convincingly drawn as decent, caring people, with rigorous ethical senses, the best of them with enough compassion to balance it. And they are endowed, particularly in the character of Anne, with natures sufficiently strong and philosophical to endure real sadness and loss. "To live happily is an inward power of the soul," Anne quotes from Marcus Aurelius. As things will go, we shall not, it's implied, see her like again.

> Vance Bourjaily, "*The Other Side of 'Main Street'*," *in* The New York Times Book Review, *June 24, 1984, p. 7.*

## MICHAEL MALONE

["*. . . And Ladies of the Club*"], in industry lingo, has legs.

It has legs without the sex or shootouts or glitz that usually accompany such limbs. It has legs without the grace of style or joy of creativity that occasionally accompany such limbs. Its legs have nothing to do with its enormous body (it's longer

than *War and Peace*), nor its circumscribed soul. *Ladies* is an earnest, intelligent, stolidly written, leaden-crafted, Sears, Roebuck catalogue of the lives of a great many earnest, stolid, well-off, white Protestant Republican citizens who reside in a small southwestern Ohio town and think its values the center and circumference of the moral universe. The book is village Victorian; the legs are modern Manhattan. Having legs means a novel will walk briskly off the shelf to the cash register, like any other successfully promoted product. Just as literature need not be bad (or good) to fail—Thackeray's *Vanity Fair* was rejected eighteen times—so it need not be bad (or good) to succeed with a helping leg up. (p. 52)

["*. . . And Ladies of the Club*" is a] discursive, repetitious and often exhaustingly dull four and a half pounds of paper. . . . I am not a particularly slow reader, and it took me months to trudge my way dutifully through its wrist-wrenching bulk. Moreover, I love long novels with lots of characters, like *War and Peace*, I love Victorian town novels, like *Middlemarch*, I love Great Middle American Novels, like *My Antonia*, I love fat pedestrian family sagas, like *The Forsyte Saga*. I love *Gone With the Wind*. Had *Ladies* been anywhere near as good as the least of these, I would have loved it. But it wasn't and I didn't. (pp. 52-3)

Santmyer is a defender, like the President, of "Old America"—that mythical Eden where happy, decent, solvent, paternalistic, family-faithful, Good Christian People of the Middle Class live protected by white picket fences from the soot of the fallen world. "Such is our comfortable tradition and sure faith," as Lewis says in the preface to *Main Street*. It is interesting to see journalists contrasting Santmyer's Waynesboro with Lewis's "embittered" Gopher Prairie, Anderson's "twisted" Winesburg and Masters's "morbid" Spoon River—as if we'd slid back a half century and "revolt from the village" literature was freshly shocking. Of course, we *have* slid back, and the conservative character of Santmyer's book is a key to its success. Raised a Calvinist Republican, the author gives every indication of sharing the political views of her protagonists. . . . Her heroine, Ann (symbol of devoted loving-kindness), regrets dying and leaving the country in the hands of "that bland patronizing demagogue," F.D.R. "Where did all those votes come from? Poor white trash must have crawled out like worms from under stones."

The novel is loosely centered around sweet brunet Ann and saucy blond Sally, and their Civil War veteran husbands, John (a good but gloomy doctor) and Ludwig (a benevolent industrialist). The politics of all four, from age 17 to 70, are as right as Reagan. John: "I didn't fight to set the nigger free." Ludwig: "Our labor force probably doesn't know the meaning of the word [union], and we could replace them easily enough anyway." Sally (after her son gets "an Irish washerwoman's child" pregnant): "What is the use of money if we can't use it to get out of mistakes like this?" Woodrow Wilson is a "pusillanimous pedagogue"; Eugene Debs, a "jailbird"; Populism, "incredible folly"; and, according to these victors of the Civil War, "Negroes would rather fish than work anyday."

The women pass their days paying calls, retiring to have babies, planning theatrical Christmas parties and subscription libraries, writing literary papers for their Women's Club and talking politics, on which subject they are quite *au courant*. . . . In comparison, Carol Kennicott, with her yearning for romance and her interior-decorating notions of revolution against Main Street, seems astonishingly innocent. An inordinate amount of *Ladies* is given over to secondhand nitty-gritty convention politicking, for Ludwig, Mark Hanna's pal, is a bigwig among delegates. We need to remember that, during the postwar years, various gangs of Ohio Republicans were running the country. . . . That the Ohioans (from the Whiskey Ring to the Teapot Dome) were as inept and/or corrupt a bunch of mediocrities as ever sat in the Oval Office now occupied by Harding's true heir is a view vigorously pooh-poohed by Santmyer's Waynesboroeans. What's good for the G.O.P. is "for the good of the country." Bad times (the Panic of 1873, the Depression) are ultimately troublesome only because they temporarily threaten Ludwig's cordage factory. Of Ohioan Coxey's March to Washington with thousands of unemployed, we hear nothing. Presumably, those sorts would rather fish than work. For the rest, prosperity always triumphs in the end.

But it is as a writer and not as an apologist for reactionary nostalgia that Santmyer must be judged. Indeed, she has wisely judged herself in the person of a novel-writing young woman who appears toward the book's end, her heart set "on being famous," ready to "do a long book about the 60s, 70s, and 80s, covering several generations of life in a small midwestern town." "She laughed at herself ruefully. She was no Galsworthy, much less . . . a Proust."

Exactly so. And while this novel is a prodigious feat of endurance and, in a way, an act of bravery, the result is work and not art. Much has been made of its "thick-textured tapestry of life," but I found the attention to setting curiously sporadic and diffuse—like blurred and spotted rotogravures. Naturally in so long and minutely paced a domestic saga, historical particulars do add up. Slowly, sewing machines, public schools and horseless carriages appear. If not an artist's selective eye for the revelatory detail, Santmyer has a research librarian's eye for the accurate detail, the "iron-gray faille, whose skirt had a deep box-plaited flounce, an overskirt of lilacs foulard." This parenthetical facsimile of life (how a class of people dressed, wed, celebrated, died, worshipped) has in itself the interest (if not the liveliness) of the Lisle Letters or Mary Chestnut's diary. But as Santmyer devotes far more descriptive space to Ludwig's rope factory (her father ran one) than to anything else, we learn rather more about hemp delivery and cable-lay than most readers will find riveting.

More troublesome, she lacks a writer's ear and consequently, her characters lack voices. The middle class speak the writerly prose of the narrator, rather formal even among intimates. . . . The faithful blacks speak Uncle Remus: "Res' yo'se'f on yonde' chair." Conversations are repeated again and again as if the author as well as the characters had forgotten they'd already said all this. Talk swings from the mundane . . . to the philosophical . . . to the sociological. . . . Dialogue is used in awkward ways to refresh the reader's memory. Why should Sally need to tell Ann, whom she has seen almost daily for fifty years, that her son "seems to be doing very well as a customer's man in the brokerage firm where his father-in-law's a partner"?

Santmyer has listed among her own favorite writers Dickens, Twain, Balzac and "the Russians." Those are good choices. I wish she could have learned from them extravagance and passion and proportion. In her *Comédie Humaine,* life is kept in ledgers, summer to fall, winter to spring, year by changeless year. It's not that nothing happens; there are immense events—fires, floods, polio epidemics—and domestic calamities—infidelity, divorce, drug addiction, runaways, a probable lesbian's suicide—social scandals and endless deaths, both sudden and lingering. But there are so many of them and most are so patly foreshadowed and so matter-of-factly fulfilled that our

response is blunted. Santmyer's detached, summarizing approach works most effectively, and movingly, on her portraits of the cramped, dwindled valiant lives and solitary deaths of three spinsters. There are secondary characters (an elderly suffragette and temperance activist, a bright socialist lawyer, a wry newspaper owner) who struck me as far more interesting than the central figures but who get short shrift. Santmyer also has a talent for the caustic riposte which I wish she had allowed herself to indulge, especially as so much of the book is gossip of a not especially good-hearted kind, among folk with the "universal desire to be the first with the news, particularly bad news."

Fellow members of the real Xenia Women's Club have described Helen Hooven Santmyer as "reticent and austere." Something of that quality stiffens her pen in "... And Ladies of the Club." She said she worried people wouldn't think the book dramatic because there wasn't enough violence in it, "nothing hysterical." In fact, it isn't dramatic because there isn't enough drama in it; the author seems to shy away from scenes, not squeamish about their subject matter so much as their fictive nature, as if fiction-making itself were a bit silly. "These things don't happen except in cliché-filled banal novels." "A novelist couldn't have worked things out better," is the embarrassed response to a coincidence. But the great novelists were no more afraid of life's continual clichés and coincidences than they were tempted to use fact to justify fiction. (pp. 53-4)

Michael Malone, "... And Ladies of the G.O.P." in The Nation, Vol. 239, No. 2, July 21-28, 1984, pp. 52-4.

**JOHN BASKIN**

Miss Santmyer, fresh at 89 from her best seller, . . . *And Ladies of the Club,* has just reissued *Ohio Town,* which was written 22 years ago, and while she is more memoirist than historian, I think of her in the company of those good folk . . . who struggled with their time and geography without much hope of reward or readership. . . .

*Ohio Town* is a more successful book than *Ladies.* A nonfiction account of a small Ohio town in the early part of the century, it is told from the viewpoint of a child and through the references of a woman who chose to remain there. The town is, of course, Miss Santmyer's home, Xenia. . . .

She writes about the town institutions—church, library, opera house, school—and her language is decorous, measured, and somewhat distant. It is as though one institution were writing about another, which is understandable for she, herself, has *become* one of the town institutions.

While her book requires patience, Santmyer is a better journalist than novelist, and there are good, clear scenes that bring the fallow stretches to life. There is a chapter on the railroad, which ran down Xenia's principal street only feet from the opera house, where the locals fit the train's passing into the onstage drama, and through the detail in Miss Santmyer's observation and emotion, it becomes a good essay about the power of the train on the imagination.

Her chapter on the East End, the black side of town, is an odd mixture of good scenes and people—some of the best people in the book—and a hint of some of the smoky, hidden life there, but also a naiveté that will likely have her pronounced racist. In observing her East End, Miss Santmyer is always affectionate, yet the reader is constantly aware of her position of privilege.

It is this quality of a rather innocent woman-child watching that informs Miss Santmyer's memoir. Her good scenes are visible through a certain calm air, over distance, the way hot weather produces mirages down country roads. . . .

In between the good scenes are sections that list and catalogue, testament to Miss Santmyer's years as librarian, and there the reader's tendency is to drive faster, looking for the mirages. Lulled by this innocent, kindly, tedious world, Xenia appears as the gift of taxidermy, Winesburg-as-travelogue. And yet she sums up her place well: "The town has had no high moment of beauty and perfection to lay an obligation on us to preserve it as a museum. It encourages no glamorous illusion that life once was wholly fair; it is a background that makes no demands on its children; it does not sustain in them any extravagant hope. In these streets, under these roofs, they are free to dream their dreams in peace; they are also free to forget them when they must, without bitterness, and to accept instead the humdrum daily life of the generations of mankind. . . ."

> John Baskin, "The Sunny Side of the Street," in Book World—The Washington Post, September 2, 1984, p. 10.

### FRANCIS X. MARNELL

One of the characters in ". . . *And Ladies of the Club*" contemplates writing a long book describing small-town Midwestern life, by way of a riposte to Sinclair Lewis's *Main Street*. Evidently such a bout of contemplation produced *Ladies*. At any rate, *Ladies* reverses many of *Main Street*'s perspectives on their common subject. A great part of Lewis's fun in *Main Street* consists of contrasting the ignorant self-satisfaction of the citizens of Gopher Prairie, Minnesota, with the superior savoir-faire of the inhabitants of Paris, Chicago, and Minneapolis. Miss Santmyer, in *Ladies*, does not let her attention or that of her characters stray to faraway cities; she keeps it firmly fixed on Waynesboro, Ohio, from 1868 to 1932. Lewis's concern is Gopher Prairie's unwitting provinciality. Provinciality is not at issue in *Ladies;* one of the givens of the novel is Waynesboro's centrality. Miss Santmyer's acceptance, sometimes resigned and sometimes celebratory, of small-town life is not an answer to Lewis's undermining satiric contrasts; it is a different way of looking at things. The question in judging it is whether its way of looking enlightens.

The early reviews mostly declared that it does not; that *Ladies* is too long, too little dramatic, and bigoted as well. These criticisms are partly accurate, but on the whole so unjust that one is tempted to argue too much on Miss Santmyer's behalf. Several things, however, do need saying.

In the first place, the perception of bigotry in the novel is due to two confusions: a confusion of narratorial with authorial voice, and a confusion of sociological observation with moral judgment. Many of the characters assume that the Irish are naturally inferior, and the blacks more so; Miss Santmyer records these assumptions. Insofar as Miss Santmyer finds it necessary to judge racism, she opposes it. But racism is not her subject; her most conspicuous position on the topic of bigotry is that the Reformed Presbyterians are too rigid. To write about something other than racism does not constitute racism.

*Ladies* is more difficult to defend from the charge of excessive length. Miss Santmyer sometimes forgets she is writing a novel.

Charm but also tedium resides in, for instance, noting the successive impractical fashions of hoop skirts, bustles, and leg-of-mutton sleeves. A more serious indulgence of the reportorial impulse, as opposed to the narrative or the dramatic, occurs in roughly the second half of *Ladies,* when the current of the novel, having run strongly in stories of its most central characters, Sally Rausch and Anne Gordon, is weakened by being divided up among numerous relatives and connections over too many years.

Capaciousness, however, has its compensations. *Ladies* gives us good accounts of the development of the Rausch and Gordon families over three generations; this would have been difficult to do in a small space. (p. 54)

Although the Rausch and Gordon families are treated most fully in *Ladies,* others are described with sufficient attention to take on individual life. Miss Santmyer's abilities in domestic history are considerable. Bringing to life so many distinct private arrangements is no small task in itself. In addition, Miss Santmyer succeeds in giving us a good idea of what domestic life must have been during the period her novel covers. This is not always a drily historical or nostalgically heart-warming accomplishment. Few death scenes since the Victorian era are so good (which means so heart-wrenching) as several in *Ladies*. The effects of aging on the old and on the young around them, and the consequences, physical and social, of bearing children in the nineteenth century, are described with hard-headed intelligence and understanding.

Despite, then, unfortunate stretches lacking realized dramatic purpose, *Ladies* sensibly and calmly describes the world of a small American town several generations ago, and serves, if not as an answer, at least as a counterpart to *Main Street*'s sometimes petulant ridicule. (p. 55)

> Francis X. Marnell, "Main Street Revisited," in National Review, Vol. XXXVI, No. 19, October 5, 1984, pp. 54-5.

### CYNTHIA GRENIER

The summer of 1984 was certainly the appropriate time to publish ". . . *And Ladies of the Club*," celebrating as it does several generations worth of "rock-ribbed Republicans" in Ohio, the state which has given this nation seven distinguished Republican Presidents.

It is thus not by chance that this book has been the object of reviews in the liberal press ranging from the mildly disparaging to the downright hostile. The 88-year-old author Helen Hooven Santmyer has been accused of being "insensitive," racist, and anti-Semitic. Nasty charges designed to put off as many readers as possible—charges, interestingly enough, that are without foundation. . . .

The omniscient voice of the author rarely intrudes upon the narrative of this book. Primarily Miss Santmyer is concerned with reflecting as faithfully as possible the sensibilities and *mores* of another age. It would be artistically misplaced to insert godlike pronouncements of a Yuppy sensibility into the narrative, lamenting, say, the plight of blacks (termed Negroes throughout in keeping with period usage) or yearning for affirmative action and quotas.

As for the charge of anti-Semitism it comes down, we find, to the one-time use of the term "huckster" on page 93 to describe the profession of a minor, sympathetic Jewish character. The word is being used in the longtime meaning of peddler, itinerant salesman. It is perfectly clear from the context that no defamatory intent is meant, which makes criticism of the author on this point not merely excessive but in downright bad faith.

As for the novel itself, Proust it indeed is not, as its author is aware, but perhaps a comparison with Galsworthy is not far off the mark. . . . [The author] is concerned more with "the relentlessness of time" than with producing a conventionally plotted novel designed to keep the reader turning pages ever faster. There is no golden glow of a more innocent past, nor is there any vision of a perfect utopia coming one day on earth. "To live happily is an inward power of the soul," one of the quotations from Marcus Aurelius used by Miss Santmyer, might well be the message of the book. People draw on their own moral strength or on religion to see themselves through difficult and trying times. If there can be no easy solutions, the characters know how to bear their troubles with courage and dignity.

Reading *Ladies* is rather like being transported by a time machine to witness the daily life, small dramas, and occasional tragedies of another age. . . .

What makes Miss Santmyer's novel unusual . . . is not really what happens to her protagonists, but rather the way she presents so much of the lives of her secondary, often minor characters. Almost without exception they are women—women who sometimes die young or live out very long lonely lives. They come alive on the page with an extraordinary vividness. Most are poor, struggling to maintain themselves in a society in which they are largely marginal. Just as the changing fash-

ions in dress and decor are meticulously recorded for the Gordon and Rausch homes, so are the sagging stockings, bustle-less gowns, and drab quarters described for society's orphans. Victims or rebels they are to a woman unself-pitying, and if not always strong are most assuredly stoic in their attitude to life. . . .

The author seems to understand these women intimately, viewing them with a compassion that never once falls into sentimentality. Indeed, her writing in these passages becomes remarkably energized. Her critics, secure in their unassailable sense of virtue, manage to ignore these admirable portraits of the injured, lonely, and damned.

No less distasteful to these critics doubtless is the strong sense of patriotism underlying the book. The memory of the Civil War hovers over the whole story. The men who experienced it forever feel its traces, remembering it not as a time of glory but as a time of testing of their souls. There is a sense that war is a terrible thing, but that sometimes it is necessary to risk dying for your country. (p. 46)

One can only wish Miss Santmyer many years to enjoy this late-coming fame and good fortune. One thing seems sure: She at least will not have to despair like her 82-year-old heroine faced with the election of FDR, "I don't want to die and leave the country in the hands of the Democrats!" That, Miss Santmyer, I think you need not worry about. (p. 47)

*Cynthia Grenier, in a review of "'. . . And Ladies of the Club',"* in The American Spectator, *Vol. 17, No. 11, November, 1984, pp. 46-7.*

# Shiga Naoya

## 1883-1971

Japanese short story writer, novelist, and essayist.

Shiga is considered an important contributor to the evolution of modern Japanese fiction. His only long novel, *An'ya Kōro* (1937; *A Dark Night's Passing*), is regarded by many Japanese scholars as the masterpiece of the Taishō period, and some of his short stories are models of the genre. Shiga's association with the *Shirakaba* (White Birch) literary group, whose name derives from the arts journal that they published, was important to his development as a writer. The young, well-to-do authors who made up the group opposed the pessimistic naturalism prevalent in Japanese literature during the early twentieth century. Instead of the social and economic determinism implicit in naturalism, the *Shirakaba* group espoused an idealistic humanism, an almost romantic belief in individual effort. Although differing in this important respect from other writers of the period, the *Shirakaba* group, and particularly Shiga, shared with them the tendency to base fiction on autobiographical material. These authors, known as the I-novelists, became the narrator-protagonists of novels which focused on themselves and their emotional development. *A Dark Night's Passing* is praised as a major I-novel.

Nearly all of Shiga's work is autobiographical. Central to much of it is the long period of antipathy between Shiga and his father first described in the novelette "Wakai" (1917) and developed in greater detail in *A Dark Night's Passing*. The latter, written over a twenty-five-year period, chronicles the hero Kensaku's life—his upbringing by indulgent grandparents; his mother's death; and the conflict with his father, who disapproves of Kensaku's renunciation of many Japanese traditions and is especially opposed to his son's determination to be a writer. The novel also covers the eventual reconciliation of father and son, Kensaku's marriage, and several personal crises. The ambiguous ending portrays a Kensaku who finally seems able to accept himself and his life.

Although there are some variances between his life and his fiction, Shiga explained, "Kensaku the hero is by and large myself. I would say his actions approximate the things I would do, or would wish to do, or actually did, under the given circumstances." This comment also illustrates the introspective, psychologically probing quality of Shiga's writing, for the author is constantly exploring his own feelings. Events are episodic and secondary and other characters are viewed from the perspective of the author-narrator.

Along with his novel, Shiga's short stories are considered a vital part of his work. Many of the stories deal with the same episodes covered in his novel. Several seem wholly fictional, although they continue to examine the psychological complexities of the main character. For instance, "Han's Crime" intricately probes the motives of a man who, after years of conflict with his wife, kills her during their knife-throwing act. Another sketch, "The Old Man," written while Shiga was young, is an acclaimed portrayal of a man who comes to terms with old age and death. "Sibei's Gourds," "The Good-Natured Couple," and "The Apprentice's God" are notable for their careful structure, precise detail, and evocative, poetic

Photograph by Setsuzo Katayama. Courtesy of Iwanami Shoten, Publishers

language. As Phyllis Birnbaum commented, Shiga's prose conveys the "quiet nuances of feeling long cherished in Japan."

(See also *Contemporary Authors*, Vol. 101, Vols. 33-36, rev. ed. [obituary].)

## FRANCIS MATHY

Shiga Naoya's most ambitious autobiographical work and his only long novel is *Journey Through Dark Night*. Though it lacks the perfection of his best short stories, it is generally considered to be his finest and most representative work. (p. 83)

In a postscript written for the first publication of the novel as a whole, Shiga gives considerable information concerning the circumstances of its composition and his aim in writing. The first part, he writes, caused him the greatest difficulty. He began it in 1912 at the age of thirty when he was living in Onomichi, and he took as his subject matter the long-continuing conflict with his father. The difficulty in writing arose in great part from his desire to transcend personal emotion and to write something that would not embarrass his father. After their reconciliation in 1917, his interest in the novel, especially in the theme he had chosen, diminished, all the more since he had already written an objective account of the affair in "**A Certain Man and the Death of His Sister.**"

Then he recalled that one night at the height of the conflict with his father when he had not been able to get to sleep, many thoughts had rushed into his mind, among them the fantasy that he was not his father's son but his grandfather's. He had dismissed the notion for the fantasy that it was, but later when he saw his novel disintegrate for lack of material, he suddenly saw the possibility of restructuring it about this fiction. He would write about the vicissitudes of fortune that might attend a hero born under such infelicitous circumstances, circumstances known to everyone but himself. It was at this point that the novel *Tokito Kensaku* became *Journey Through Dark Night*. (p. 91)

From beginning to end *Journey Through Dark Night* presents the various stages of feeling experienced by the hero in his long struggle to the light. The two seductions, whose effects the author purports to explore, form the central axis of the plot and serve to give a semblance of structure to this long, highly subjective novel, but they are never really of central concern. The focus all the way through is upon the spirit of the hero as he reacts to external events. Moreover, it is not even true to say that the novel depicts the "movement" of the hero's spirit. There is little or no movement depicted; the novel is extremely static. Rather it is the successive stages that are depicted, without showing them as developing from one stage to the next.

In general, four distinct stages of Kensaku's changing consciousness are presented in the course of the novel. The first two, which appear in Parts I and II, alternate rather than succeed each other. They are the stage of confidence in self, in his work, and in the ability of man to prevail over his dark fate; and the stage of depression, of complete spiritual impoverishment, and of deep pessimism concerning his own future and the future of man. In Part III he has found a peace that is only partially disturbed by the death of his infant daughter. In Part IV he is plunged once again into the lower depths because of what happens to his wife, Naoko, but in the end he achieves enlightenment and comes to enjoy a still deeper peace than before. (pp. 92-3)

Kensaku takes an attitude of confrontation toward everything— other people, nature, fate, man's history—and he is filled with a mighty ambition. As an artist, he is determined to accomplish an immortal work, "a work that will contribute to the happiness of the entire human race, a work that will advance mankind along the direction which it must take." . . .

This is the attitude of Shiga himself at the high tide of his conflict with his father. . . .

The attitude of confrontation was extremely superficial and was never really able to sink deep roots into Kensaku (Shiga). It was little more than the product of the excited irritation caused by external conflict. It was an attitude easy enough to confide to a journal, but one difficult to realize in daily life. (p. 94)

Unlike the attitude of confrontation, [the] poverty of spirit manifests itself everywhere in Kensaku's actions. He progressively degenerates until he is completely enslaved to his carnal instincts. This process is vividly described in some of the finest passages to come from Shiga's pen. Nakamura Mitsuo points out that never before in Japanese literature—despite the vast amount of writing that is centered on the pleasure quarter— had man's sexual instincts been presented so baldly as a perfectly natural phenomenon not in need of apology. He goes on to state that this is the best book to put into the hands of a young girl preparing for marriage to show her what it is to be a man. At the same time, he adds, no Japanese novel has ever made a more forceful presentation of the dark melancholy that accompanies the kind of profligacy that has as its only object the satisfaction of lust.

The events in Shiga's life that lie behind these passages are his own struggle until marriage with the despotic demands of the flesh and the series of misfortunes that befell him between the years 1912 and 1917, the year of his reconciliation with his father: the continuing discord with his father, further aggravated by his marriage; the grave injury sustained in the streetcar accident; his wife's nervous condition; his continued inability to write; and the death of his first child.

Despite the darkness of Kensaku's experiences of this time, there are already glimmers of the light that harmony with nature will eventually bring. (p. 95)

Even in his dark excursions to Yoshiwara there is the suggestion that in yielding himself to his sexual instincts, he is in fact yielding himself to nature, trusting that nature in her good time will release him from his bondage. (p. 96)

There is only a short time lapse between the end of Part II and the beginning of Part III, but the reader is ushered into an altogether changed world. Kensaku has been in Kyoto for a month and is convalescing from his spiritual illness.

"For the first time he had somewhat the feeling of being saved." The influences of ancient landmarks, ancient temples, and ancient art have a therapeutic effect on him, and he goes "from temple to temple, enjoying the flush of well-being of a convalescent and a feeling of calmness and humility." . . . The account of his meeting and marriage with Naoko is presented as a kind of romantic idyl. Their life together is extremely peaceful and pleasant. But even so, Kensaku experiences a strange melancholy and is still unable to write. Soon they are looking forward with joy to the arrival of their first child. The child is safely delivered but dies shortly after birth. (pp. 96-7)

In writing this section Shiga was recalling the events and feelings of his early married life, especially of the years 1915 and 1916. Shiga had found peace of a sort, but a peace lined with a deep melancholy. It was the period shortly before his reconciliation with his father, when he had lost the will to assert himself strongly, but had not yet reached a full harmony with nature. The death of his daughter plunged him once again into darkness, but not so deep a darkness as before. . . .

Kensaku finally concludes his long journey through dark night in the final section of the novel. But before that he is forced, as a result of his wife's misfortune, to experience the darkest trial of all. The first step toward the enlightenment on Mt. Daisen is the realization of his own shortcomings. (p. 97)

On Mt. Daisen he first loses his apprehension about the fate of man and his earth and learns to contemplate with equanimity and resignation the destined extinction of both. (p. 98)

Finally he achieves the crowning enlightenment on the top of the mountain. (p. 99)

If *Journey Through Dark Night* is judged according to the critical standards ordinarily applied to Western novels, its defects are all too obvious. In the first place, it has—as even its greatest admirers readily admit—but one character, Kensaku. All the other characters are sketched in so lightly that they seem little more than the stage setting for the dramatization of the hero's internal struggle. This is true even of Naoko, who is, in the words of Hasegawa Izumi, "like a doll tossed about on the waves of Kensaku's feelings."

Moreover, apart from the hero's immediate circle of relatives and friends, no external world is allowed to intrude upon his solitude. The time of the action of the novel is that of the First World War, of the rice riots, of the growing disenchantment with capitalism and the rise of proletarian thought, of great social unrest occasioned by wide unemployment, of new currents of writing in reaction to the above. But no hint of any of this finds its way into the novel. The outside world is ignored completely.

A more serious defect is that the hero himself remains largely abstract due to the fact that the reader learns much about his feelings but little about his concrete circumstances, and almost never sees him in action. Contributing to this impression of abstractness is the fact, already mentioned, that the transitional stages between the hero's states of feeling are not well depicted. (p. 100)

The drama of Kensaku's journey through dark night, then, is an internal one. Real interaction with other people is lacking throughout the novel. Some critics, however, make much of the fact that at the end, finally, for one brief moment, Naoko comes alive and Kensaku looks upon her with new eyes. Edwin McClellan thinks that here for the first time Kensaku comes to have understanding and respect for another and thus is finally able to enter into his true self. In McClellan's interpretation, Shiga is making "the simple yet profound statement. . . . that it is through discovering objective reality outside of oneself and coming to terms with it that one can come to terms with oneself." When Kensaku eats spoiled fish and becomes ill, it is not only the poison in his stomach that he rejects, but also the poison in his soul. His illness is a complete catharsis. At the end he receives his wife with love, and in a silence like death there is the powerful affirmation of human dignity. "And death, even if it should come to Kensaku, seems not to matter in the face of this affirmation." This, McClellan asserts, gives the novel a moral context and the power to move us.

A Western reader is very much tempted to read this final scene in this way, especially since it is an axiom of modern psychology that self-definition cannot take place in isolation from others. But this is not, we think, the correct reading. The novel has an Eastern conclusion, not a Western. It is in the depths of his own psyche that Kensaku reaches the resolution to his problems. He goes to Mt. Daisen to get over the repulsion he feel towards his wife because of what has happened to her. He does indeed get over it, but not in such a way that he can go down from the mountain and take up his daily life with her again. What he discovers on Mt. Daisen is that nothing in the world of men really matters. All men, he himself included, are part of nature; the boundaries that have served to distinguish self from other, whether human or nonhuman, have melted away, and he has the strong feeling of having been purified in body and spirit. Let death come, he is ready for it. He has transcended the distinction between life and death. By the same token he has transcended the boundaries of human relationships. There may be love in his eyes as he looks upon Naoko, but it is the look that he bestows now upon all of nature, a look that can no longer distinguish between human and nonhuman. Shiga leaves his hero poised between life and death, not caring which it will be; and he assimilates Naoko to Kensaku's state of feeling. She understands that he may not recover. "Strangely enough, though, this thought did not really make her sad." The reader may well ask: "Why shouldn't this

thought make her sad?" The answer is obvious. It is not Naoko's consciousness that we are being shown here, but Kensaku's still. He may wear the mask of Naoko but there is no mistaking his identity.

Kamei Katsuichiro also points out that in this last scene there is no question of any kind of conversion on the part of Kensaku. There is only the action of nature upon him. He covers over his wife's "fault" with the heart of nature, and the condition that made this possible was the very real possibility of death. "It is not a question of the happiness of family. There is merely a light which nature suddenly bestows upon him—a light which he had not expected and which indeed came to him only with the approach of death." (pp. 101-03)

In real life the Daisen experience had been for him only a point of enlightenment, not a solution or a conclusion. It was the world of one person, not the realization of reconciliation. Therefore it could not very well effect a reconciliation between Kensaku and Naoko. The reader is moved by the scene, but it is neither a conclusion nor a resolution.

*Journey Through Dark Night* can best be read as a lyrical novel. Tanikawa Tetsuzo, one of Shiga's greatest admirers, admits that from the point of view of the Western novel, this work cannot be thought of as a novel. It is more like a picture scroll (*e-maki*) that unfoldes one frame at a time. Edward Seidensticker suggests that it be read as a kind of *uta-monogatari*, such as *The Tales of Ise*, a sequence of poetic flights held together by the cement of prose.

Certainly it helps to think of the novel in this way. There is much to please us in individual parts, and in lyrical writing we do not expect to find much development, interaction, and cause and effect. Many of the parts of *Journey Through Dark Night* are excellent when taken as lyrical statement. No writer is more skillful than Shiga in interweaving nature with the moods of the hero. Moreover nature is always something concrete, the nature of a particular place at a particular season of the year. His nature is so localized that Japanese readers claim to be able to recognize the scene at once. In this novel we also find the same spare style we find in his best short stories. In a few words he is able to evoke a mood or describe a place or situation.

But the fact remains that in *Journey Through Dark Night* Shiga was making use of material that required dramatic development as well as lyrical, and this was not given it. Shiga, after all, does pose basic problems of human relationships—especially that between man and wife, of the meaning of life and death, of the effects of sin and human error. After having been presented with such weighty problems, how can the reader be content with Shiga's final answer: "Forget about these problems, live sincerely, be faithful to self, entrust yourself to nature and live with her in full harmony"? (pp. 103-04)

> *Francis Mathy, in his* Shiga Naoya, *Twayne Publishers, Inc., 1974, 187 p.*

## PHYLLIS BIRNBAUM

Western readers of Oriental literature will shudder to discover that the Japanese regard [*A Dark Night's Passing*] . . . as a modern classic and its author as "the god of the novel." The thin plot—a rare fictional touch and clearly a burden—turns on the protagonist's discovery that he is the offspring of an illicit alliance between his mother and her father-in-law. Kensaku's attempt to comprehend the meaning of his birth might have made a revealing, if melodramatic, search for self-discovery. But Kensaku is loath to reveal anything more psychologically precise about himself than that he feels "an emptiness inside him." Instead, the author uses the novel to record without comment the minute physical details of his own life. So we are only told that Kensaku travels, meets his friends, and drinks with geisha. Theme and character quickly disappear in this abundance of diary notation.

Discursiveness, limp characterization, and a monotonous focus on the hero would seem flaws enough to disqualify this novel from serious consideration. Yet its success assured the domination of the autobiographical novel in Japan. Fiction was scorned, and the "I-novelists" strained to equal Shiga's "sincerity" by writing objective accounts of their personal experiences. . . .

Shiga's undeniable achievement is a plain but subtly resonating prose style. Descriptive passages delicately mix natural images with empty, unspoken spaces. The poetic evocations of smoke atop valleys, moss-scented air, light in the forest, and herons' cries convey quiet nuances of feeling long cherished in Japan.

> *Phyllis Birnbaum, in a review of "A Dark Night's Passing," in* Saturday Review, *Vol. 4, No. 6, December 11, 1976, p. 70.*

## MAKOTO UEDA

In writing about his own works, Shiga was preoccupied above all with the question of their factuality. In almost every instance, he wanted to tell his readers to what extent the work was fictional. As it turned out, a large number of his stories were based on his own experience; many of them, indeed, purported to be faithful records of actual events. . . . When a certain critic made some derogatory remarks about his novelette *Reconciliation,* Shiga defended himself by saying that it was true to fact. He had written it, he said, not to present a moral thesis but to vent a "more immediate sentiment" of his—namely, "the joy of having arrived at a reconciliation [with my father] after a long period of estrangement." He concluded: "I simply kept on writing down the facts as they were, without any artifice, and I ended up producing a work of art. That is the strength of this work." Underlying all these comments is Shiga's idea that literature is in the last analysis a record of events that actually took place in the author's life. A literary work, he thought, should be autobiographical in the strict sense of the word; that is, it should be a conscious effort at self-revelation. (pp. 85-6)

The fact remains, however, that Shiga was primarily a novelist, not an essayist or a diarist. His main creative energy went into writing works of fiction—a novel, three novelettes, and a sizable number of short stories, which include such obviously imaginative tales as **"Han's Crime," "Claudius' Diary,"** and **"Akanishi Kakita."** Why did he think fiction was the best mode in which to record the facts of his own daily existence? His answer can be found in his notes on *Voyage Through the Dark Night.* "Kensaku, the hero, is by and large myself," he wrote. "I would say his actions approximate the things I would do, or would wish to do, or actually did, under the given circumstances." The prime function of a diary, like most other genres of personal nonfiction, was to record only what one actually did. A work of fiction, on the other hand, could present what one "would do, or would wish to do" in various imaginary situations. It described man not only as he had been or was, but as he might be or might want himself to be.

Likewise, in Shiga's view, a novel presents facts not only as they are but also as the novelist imagines they are or as he would wish them to be. He might, indeed, write down things contrary to actual fact, if they seemed imaginatively more convincing to him. Once, on devising a scene for a short story, Shiga placed the moon in a geographically impossible position, but knowingly let the description stand because that was the way he had long visualized the scene in his mind. . . . Shiga also tells of instances in which his imagination seemed to sense an event before it actually happened, despite the fact that he had no foreknowledge of the circumstances. On one occasion, he was writing a short story and was trying to visualize a scene in which a barber kills his customer with a razor. By coincidence, one of his next-door neighbors committed suicide with a razor just about the same time. . . . [This instance] seemed to him to substantiate his idea that some imaginary facts are just as valuable as, or even more valuable than, actual facts.

What kinds of facts, whether actual or imaginary, are most suitable for a work of fiction? Ordinary facts would not do; they would merely provide material for a chat, or for a popular novel at best. . . . Fiction above the popular level was different: it presented an event in the way the author thought most "natural." A serious writer of fiction presented men and women who behaved themselves more "naturally" than the average person. . . . (pp. 87-8)

Exactly what did Shiga mean by the word "natural"? The obvious answer, as we have seen, was that he used it to mean the opposite of "commonsense" or "conventionally accepted." . . . At a deeper level, however, the term assumed a more positive value for him. To be "natural" meant to be true to nature. A person who behaved "naturally" was not a mere eccentric who pays little attention to conventional norms; he was a person who, having awakened to his innermost nature, was trying to return to it. When Shiga said a work of fiction presented things that he would do or would wish to do, he meant the things that were most natural to him in this sense. With such a creed, a writer of fiction becomes a seeker after his own and others' true nature. (p. 89)

As against some of his literary colleagues, who tended to see human nature as founded on sexual drives, [Shiga] believed that man possessed a kind of instinctive wisdom so deep-seated that it sometimes overrode even his sexual impulses. It was almost an animal instinct, an instinct that maintained man's physical and mental health. In **"Film Preview in the Morning,"** another of his autobiographical pieces, Shiga called it "the law of nature." The narrator of the story, obviously Shiga himself, is walking along the street with a male dog of his called Yone, when a neighborhood dog, a female, happens to come by. Yone becomes excited and goes up to her, but calmly leaves on discovering that her mating season has passed. The narrator is impressed to see that dogs act according to "the law of nature." He recalls a film, *The Charterhouse of Parma,* that he saw a week ago. The film's characters had become embroiled in a tragic crime of passion. "In the world of dogs a male would never kill a female for love, no matter how much they were at odds," Shiga wrote. "But in the human world, men have been known to kill women for precisely this. Man, by his wisdom, should be able to avoid such senseless tragedies." Man has impulses; Shiga would not deny that. Yet man has wisdom also, instinctive wisdom given him by nature for his own health and survival. Shiga advised that every man be attentive to it, understand it, and follow it; this was the way to return to nature. A work of art should present a man doing just that, under the specific circumstances in which he happened to have been placed. In short, a novel should describe a "wise" man....

Many of Shiga's ... stories depict such people. Explaining the theme of his lone full-length novel, he said: "Everybody, wise or foolish, has misfortunes that are due to fate; it is impossible to avoid them. Yet one should wish to tide oneself over them as wisely as possible. That is the theme of *Voyage Through the Dark Night*." The novel's hero, Kensaku, suffers two misfortunes that he was powerless to prevent: his incestuous birth and his wife's rape (though Shiga preferred to call the latter incident adultery). Shiga's three novelettes, which he once compared to three branches of a tree, combine to tell the story of how a man, in trying to be faithful to his inner feelings, arrives at a tragic clash with his father because of their basic difference in personality, and how he eventually reaches a reconciliation with the latter in a way acceptable to them both. The same type of hero appears in many of Shiga's short stories; his progress is always from disaster to recovery.... In some stories, like "The Razor," "Claudius' Diary," and "Kuniko," the disaster part is heavily emphasized. In others, like "A Snowy Day," "The Fires," and "Yajima Ryūdō," a more peaceful mood prevails, since the protagonist has completely recovered from a disaster as the story begins. Also falling into the last category are many short prose pieces that deal with animals, birds, and insects.... It is hardly surprising that Shiga, who recognized true wisdom in dogs, was so much at ease with so many other members of the animal kingdom.

Shiga's adverse criticism of certain literary works can also be explained in terms of this highly individual view of human nature. He did not like *Othello, Hamlet,* or *Romeo and Juliet* because they were, in his opinion, tragedies caused by human folly. He felt that, in each case, the tragedy could have been averted if the protagonists had been "wiser" in the sense already discussed. He also disliked naturalist writers, because the characters they described had nothing beautiful about them. (pp. 91-2)

Shiga's idea of artistic imitation thus assumes a didactic character. Literature should be factual, he believed, but that did not mean a writer should present all facts indiscriminately. Some facts were more "factual," more "natural,"and therefore more convincing than others. Autobiographical facts were an important source of material for fiction, but only insofar as they resulted from the natural, instinctive behavior of the person in question.... Fundamentally, man was a wise being. It followed that a novel, if it was to be as factual as possible, should prove him to be so. In this way, the reader would be awakened to the fundamental wisdom lying dormant within himself.

Ultimately, Shiga's theory of literature is limited in the same way as his view of human nature. Even if it be granted that man has some basic animal wisdom such as Shiga recognized, it may be argued that he was being too optimistic.... He never seems to have visualized himself in an extreme situation; certainly, few of his heroes have been in them. To be born of an incestuous mother, to have one's wife raped, to live with a stubborn, domineering father—these are lesser disasters than, say, to be born crippled, to be born of an insane mother, or to have one's marriage forcibly broken up. Shiga's characters are never faced with such agonizing choices as either eating human flesh or starving to death. His theory seems reasonable enough as long as it maintains that literature must be true to

fundamental human nature. But to make wisdom, or anything resembling it, the very essence of human nature seems a little far-fetched. Inevitably, much of his fiction seems far-fetched as well, as far as its philosophical implications are concerned.

If a novel's primary purpose is to depict the life of a man who, having met with a catastrophic misfortune, recovers from it by his innate "wisdom,"it seems that the novelist would do well to become such a man himself.... It follows that there are two prerequisites for being a novelist: first, one must be somewhat disaster-prone, whether by circumstances or by character; second, one must have the physical and mental vigor to rebound from a disaster. There is sufficient evidence to show that Shiga thought this was so.

Shiga's concept of the artist as a disaster-prone person is best expressed in his short story "Kuniko." The heroine, named Kuniko, is married to a playwright who is suffering from writer's block because his family life is too peaceful. She of course likes things to be that way; she cannot understand how he could sit at his desk and work if his home were not peaceful. Her husband, however, thinks of himself as having been rotting "like a peach" during those peaceful years. Finally he starts having an affair with a flighty young actress. When the affair is picked up by the newspapers as a juicy piece of scandal, news of it reaches his wife. The happy atmosphere of the household is completely shattered. At the same time, however, the playwright regains interest in his craft and begins work on a large-scale play. Kuniko, on the other hand, is utterly crushed by this turn of events. Having lost all hope of saving her marriage, she commits suicide.

While it would be rash to identify Kuniko's husband completely with Shiga, there is no doubt that Shiga was similarly exercised by the basic predicament of the artist's personal life. (pp. 92-5)

Why does an unhappy personal life stimulate the writer to write, while a happy life does not? Shiga's answer, as might be expected, is that an unhappy man has a stronger motive for expressing himself, suffering as he does from frustrations that he cannot contain. A person may be unhappy because he believes he is right but few people sympathize with him; he therefore appeals to their sympathy in words. (p. 95)

Characteristically, however, Shiga thought of creative writing as something that, while it might help to relieve tension, did not necessarily restore mental equilibrium. Venting one's frustrations in the form of a novel did not remove the cause of the frustrations. Literature was, after all, an inferior substitute for life, not life itself. The cause of one's unhappiness has to be dealt with and overcome in the sphere of one's actual life; this was as true of novelists as of ordinary people.... A novelist, he thought, should have enough vitality to rebound from any misfortune he might have to face. Most of the artist-heroes in Shiga's stories have such vitality and do rebound from their misfortunes. The most striking example is the young novelist-hero of *Reconciliation*, who has a violent clash with his father and is disinherited as a result. The novelist, however, does not yield to defeatism; he is determined to fight on, and even imagines a scene in which he engages in a mortal duel with his father.... For Shiga, the ultimate goal in life was to become a man of moral strength. This was a logical conclusion for a writer who considered literature as at best an inferior substitute for life. Problems in life had to be solved in the realm of life; the solutions offered by art were, in the final analysis, no more than substitutes for real solutions, dreams that might or might not be fulfilled. The artist, Shiga thought, should not be a mere dreamer; he had to have vigor and strength to make his dreams come true in real life. He had to lead a "vigorous life" in a "positive frame of mind."

Shiga actually seems to have attained the goal he set for himself. The protagonists of his later works (say, after 1928), easily identifiable as Shiga, are by and large "free, natural, honest, vigorous, and carefree" persons. In fact, they are so vigorous and carefree that they hardly ever allow anything untoward to happen. When it does, it rarely amounts to more than a ripple on calm waters. In **"Kuma,"** for example, the "disaster" that befalls the hero is that his family dog goes astray for a few days.... It seems that, as time progressed, Shiga succeeded in establishing his own and his family's well-being on such a firm basis that no serious misfortune could ever befall them again. Inevitably, given his view of literature, he lost the urge to write; he had no frustrations to vent, no disasters to rebound from. He wrote less and less frequently, his yearly production dwindling to fewer than five short prose pieces—normally two, one, or none—after 1928. Very likely he could not have cared less. (pp. 96-8)

In Shiga's view, then, the ideal novelist is an inactive novelist, a writer who feels no urge to write. For if he remains active, he is forced to lead an ambivalent existence, keeping a delicate balance between his disaster-prone character and his strength to recover from disasters. If he is too disaster-prone, he will make a good poet (like Verlaine) but a bad novelist (like Dazai). If his character is too wholesome, he will hardly meet with any real misfortunes, and will therefore have little motive for writing a novel. In his younger days Shiga managed to keep this balance, and produced some fine pieces of literature as a result. But as he got older he lost it, and remained largely inactive as a writer. For most other writers this development would have constituted a painful setback. For Shiga, it was progress.

Ideally, what kind of impression should a novel give its readers? ... Although it would be impossible to list all the qualities that go into such an impression, at least three can be singled out as important—natural beauty, vigor, and spiritual elation.

An impression of natural beauty comes from observing a man who conducts himself honestly, in accordance with his inmost feelings.... A man fighting for his survival was beautiful, beause he was, if nothing else, pure in his motives. A fight for material gain or for lust was ugly, but a fight for bare existence, physical or mental, had its own dignity.

It goes without saying that natural beauty is also to be found in the behavior of an animal, bird, or insect following its instinct for survival. Shiga's short prose pieces on such little creatures—and there are a great many of them—all speak of this.... Shiga's sketches of children have the same quality; a characteristic example is **"My Youngest Child,"** which describes his little daughter's carefree behavior.

Shiga may have had a special feeling for natural beauty, but nature in the conventional sense—flowers, trees, mountains, rivers, etc.—seems to have meant little to him.... Shiga was not impressed by the beauty of mountains and rivers because they had no life and did not struggle for survival. Similarly, he was not much attracted by Japanese flowers because they seemed too passive in asserting their right to live. Shiga's works of fiction are generally lacking in descriptions of beautiful natural scenes.

The only notable exception is the most celebrated scene in the entire Shiga canon, the climactic episode of *Voyage Through the Dark Night* in which the hero spends a night on Mount Daisen. At dawn, he looks down on the world below. The beauty and tranquillity of the scene enable him to overcome his fear of death; finally, as he becomes absorbed by it, he feels ready to die at any time. This is a rare moment in Shiga's works, which seldom show man's vitality overwhelmed by the forces of nature. Here, inanimate nature is almost personified; in fact, Mount Daisen is a holy mountain in both Buddhism and Shintoism. This, of course, makes it more suitable as an opponent. To Shiga's hero, inanimate nature is beautiful in this instance precisely because it is not passive; instead, it works on him and transforms him, so that he becomes the passive one. This explains what many critics regard as the novel's most serious flaw: the abrupt change of viewpoint in the last few pages. Hitherto, nearly everything has centered on Kensaku. But now, without warning or explanation, his wife takes over. Shiga later explained that he had done this deliberately, and claimed that the average reader would hardly be bothered by it. A more convincing explanation is that since Kensaku has now become ill, and so lost much of his vitality, he is disqualified, in Shiga's eyes, as the novel's narrator-hero. The person who takes his place has to be his wife, who is beginning to recover from her misfortune. Thematically, however, the novel ends at the point where Kensaku regains his mental equilibrium and feels readiness for death. Shiga chose to write further, and had therefore to find a new protagonist.

Natural beauty—the beauty of powerful creatures living violent lives—gives an impression of vigor and strength. Things that are strong are beautiful, and when they become protagonists the stories create a powerfully beautiful impact. Shiga, in sharp contrast to Tanizaki and Kafū, made nearly all his protagonists men. They are all healthy, with firm confidence in their body and its functions. (pp. 98-101)

Shiga said little about plot. This is understandable, in view of his emphasis on spontaneity in creative writing. Constructing a plot is basically an intellectual undertaking, far removed from the sphere of impulse. It is also an area in which the novelist's desire to accommodate his readers is often only too obvious. An intriguing plot, Shiga thought, might be necessary for a popular novel, but it did nothing but harm to a genuine work of literature, whose prime purpose was to convey the author's vigorous rhythm of life. A fascinating plot made the reader read the novel for the plot alone, neglecting its thematic content.

Shiga especially disliked a story that built up suspense by hiding facts from the reader....

Another reason, Shiga thought, why a story that depends too much on plot is second-rate is that no one would want to read it again after finding out how it ends. (p. 104)

Shiga's devaluation of plot in storytelling makes sense ..., but as a yardstick it has to be applied with caution. Of course, a story that has nothing to offer except an entertaining plot is an inferior work of literature by any yardstick. Yet plot can be used to enforce theme; indeed, it would seem incumbent on every good novelist to do just that....

However, Shiga's remarks on plot would seem to be well taken as long as he is talking about the *ich-Roman*, or "I-novel." In this type of novel, the hero obviously has to evoke as much sympathy as possible. If the author holds back too many facts, readers will find it hard to identify with him. He is better off taking the first opportunity to tell them all the essential facts about himself. (p. 105)

Shiga's view, then, was that a novelist did not have to pay much attention to plot, since if he had a vigorous rhythm of life the story would develop one of itself. Plot, in other words, marched to the rhythm of the author's own life. If that rhythm of life was weak, the plot would refuse to develop; the author, then, would have to make up the story by using his brains. The story should spontaneously "flow" out of the author; it should not be imposed on the material. In short, it had to be natural, as the author's life had to be natural. (pp. 105-06)

It is easy enough to imagine Shiga's ideal novelist and his style. The style would be, above all, powerful, reflecting the vigorous rhythm of his life. The sentences would be powerfully short and concise. There would be few conjunctions, so that the sentences would look even shorter than they actually are. The words and phrases would be sonorous in sound and clear in meaning; vagueness would be avoided at all costs. Visual images would predominate over auditory ones. Chinese characters would be used plentifully, because they create a more powerful, masculine impression than Japanese letters. In brief, Shiga's idea of a "natural" style has all the attributes of Tanizaki's "laconic style." And this was Shiga's own style, too, as Tanizaki rightly pointed out. (p. 107)

Shiga's style has been widely admired as the best in modern Japanese prose. Whereas Tanizaki's style is inimitable, samples of Shiga's prose appear in every school textbook. A number of professional writers have succeeded in writing very much like him. In fact, it has been pointed out that all top students in Japanese composition classes write like Shiga. This fact probably has little to do with the intrinsic value of Shiga's style. But at least it is ample proof that his style is a "natural" one, since it lies within a range attainable by a great many Japanese, including students in elementary school. (p. 108)

*Makoto Ueda, "Shiga Naoya," in his* Modern Japanese Writers and the Nature of Literature, *Stanford University Press, 1976 pp. 85-110.*

**KENNETH STRONG**

A long, intensely 'private' story of the search for inner stability by a young man who, he admits, has 'always allowed his emotions to tyrannize over him', [*A Dark Night's Passing*] offers little in the way of 'action', or of genuine, two-way human relationships, and the protagonist's own development, such as it is, proceeds quietly through numerous small incidents only loosely strung together. Shiga's total identification with his hero precludes irony or the complexity that a more detached point of view would permit. Even the immediate cause of Tokitō Kensaku's instability—the shock of the discovery that he is the child of his mother, who died when he was six, and of the grandfather whom he despises—while certainly dramatic in its impact, is too bizarre a circumstance to enable the reader to enter very readily into Kensaku's state of mind. The novel's great reputation in Japan depends to a considerable extent on its style, characterised by Professor McClellan in his Introduction as 'the language of the traditional Japanese poet translated into modern prose . . . not a language that is precise in any intellectual, analytical sense': a style that in the subtlety of its nuances of feeling and atmosphere inevitably defies translation even into a language as rich as English, and even at the hands of so experienced and sympathetic a scholar as Professor McClellan. Style apart, there are leading critics in Japan, even,

who vigorously decry Shiga's 'self-centredness', the narrowness of his range. (p. 88)

When we realise that Shiga had the greatest difficulty in finishing *A Dark Night's Passing* at all—the final chapters having been written nearly seventeen years after the first—and that this was the only full-length novel he ever managed to write, we might be forgiven for wondering what all the fuss is about.

Yet there is much to be said to commend the novel to the English-speaking reader—more, indeed, than Professor McClellan is willing to claim in his brief and too-modest Introduction. To start from the drier, more purely academic end of the book's spectrum, *A Dark Night's Passing* reflects accurately important aspects of the intellectual history of Taishō and early Shōwa: the new determination to live independently of the constraints imposed by family and convention, the alternating moods of optimism and insecurity that had succceeded the more disciplined, unquestioning drives of Meiji. *A Dark Night's Passing* is as firmly rooted within its time as the novels of Sōseki; and as with them, this is paradoxically one reason for its permanence. It presents too, in the descriptions of Kensaku's dealings with his family and friends, and towards the end with his wife . . . , a picture of the ordinary intercourse of Japanese people with each other which those who live in Japan will recognise as in the highest degree authentic: the sensitive, brooding characters spar with each other, never giving much away and always taking refuge in silence when the danger of exposure, for either party, is too great. Whether this tentativeness in dealing with one's fellow human beings, this unwillingness to commit oneself too readily, makes in the long run for unsatisfactory relationships (fictional or in real life), or for a greater sensitivity, may be arguable; but Shiga conveys the atmosphere of such exchanges to perfection.

More importantly, if *A Dark Night's Passing* is in a sense certainly 'self-centred', Shiga's treatment of Kensaku is remarkable in that it manages to combine unfailing sympathy for his hero with a total honesty, almost Sophoclean in its clarity, in regard to his failings. Gradually, as one reads through the long placid narrative, one responds to Shiga's 'sincerity', his consistent determination to give a truthful account of his hero's feelings, which in so many respects are also his own. It is this quality, one imagines, which most of all endears Shiga to his Japanese readers. But beyond this peculiarly Japanese virtue of sincerity, there is a universality—and again it makes itself felt only slowly, with a cumulative effect—in this quiet portrayal of the self-centredness of the maturing process human beings have to go through. This, surely, is how most of us *do* feel most of the time at that stage in our lives, if we are courageous enough to admit it. Only the fact that our own fiction has not chosen to explore this area very thoroughly makes it seem strange at first.

But Kensaku is not merely a seeker after inner stability: he is a finder too. The famous concluding section of the book, where Kensaku leaves his young wife and their baby to go and spend some weeks in a mountain temple, is exceptionally interesting. The climax, Kensaku's mystical experience of 'merging' with nature, is handled with a beautiful restraint. . . . (pp. 88-9)

[The mountain episode underlines] the whole theme of the novel. We all start with the self, and if we can't cope with that—to adapt a more earthy saying of Dr Johnson's—we are not likely to be able to cope with anything satisfactorily, let alone relationships with other selves. . . . The book has the limitations of its time. Shiga could probably not have conceived the possibility of the *wife* acting in the way that Kensaku acts. But that apart, *A Dark Night's Passing* presents, in the last analysis, the traditional Oriental emphasis on the prime importance for growth of facing the self—which is not necessarily the same thing as self-centredness. Seen in this light, it may have a special appeal to contemporary Western readers, as in Europe and America increasing numbers turn to look more closely inward. (p. 90)

Kenneth Strong, "Salvation through Selfishness," in Monumenta Nipponica, Vol. XXXII, No. 1, Spring, 1977, pp. 87-91.

## EMIKO SAKURAI

The first half of the four-part novel [*A Dark Night's Passing*] was reworked from a composition started in 1912. The last half was begun in 1921, and the concluding chapters were completed in 1937, when Shiga was fifty-four. It was inevitable that there was unevenness in the work. The first half is particularly cluttered with insignificant and often tedious details, such as vapid conversations and games with geishas. The last part moves more rapidly, but in general Shiga's desire to show Kensaku's reactions to people and incidents and to record his psychological development—which was his main concern in the novel—resulted in the inclusion of a number of irrelevant incidents and characters.

The story zigzags from one episode to another without an apparent overall design and without passion, suspense or drama. Some of the chapters or clusters of chapters, published as separate installments in a magazine before the book's completion, show more symmetry and cohesion than does the novel as a whole. The prefatory chapter is undoubtedly one of the best short stories ever written in this genre. The characters come alive in a few pages of reminiscence, and the tension between father and son is compellingly evoked in a childhood memory.

In his ability to re-create sensuous impressions and convey nuances of the human condition in a few imagistic lines, Shiga is still unexcelled. As a prose master also, he has had few peers. . . .

Besides the excellence of style, *Anya Kōro* has been admired for the creation of its hero. Kensaku, however, is no King Oedipus but "a sort of average student," as his housekeeper views him. When Kensaku is near death, his wife is not particularly chagrined. And neither is the reader. Clearly Naoya Shiga was not God of the novel, only a favorite of the muses.

Emiko Sakurai, in a review of "A Dark Night's Passing," in World Literature Today, Vol. 52, No. 1, Winter, 1978, p. 181.

## HISAAKI YAMANOUCHI

Japanese literature during the period immediately after the death of Sōseki may be represented by Shiga Naoya and Akutagawa Ryūnosuke, two writers who can be profitably compared in many respects. Shiga Naoya (1883-1971) was a member of a congenial group of writers called Shirakaba-ha (White Birch School), named after the magazine they published. . . . [One] feature of this group of writers was that through the writings of Tolstoy they became champions of idealistic humanitarianism. (p. 82)

The initial objective of the Shirakaba-ha group may be summed up as a conscious reaction against the Japanese naturalists who had become a major force in the preceding period. The Japanese naturalists had formed an exclusive clique called *bundan* (literary circle). These writers had to belong to this narrow circle, partly because the act of writing was necessary for their livelihood. The subjects of their writings were limited to the narrow sphere of their own lives, which were in most cases poor and miserable. Very often they dramatised their misery and poverty with more than a little masochism, and some even deliberately led a life of misery so that they could render it in their work. From this derived . . . the peculiarly Japanese literary institution of the I-novel, or *watakushi-shōsetsu*.

The Shirakaba-ha group shared this reliance on the personal life for writing fiction, as the autobiographical works of Mushanokōji and Shiga show. However, there were far more differences than similarities between these two literary factions and their contrasting life styles. First, the writers of the Shirakaba-ha group could remain detached from the *bundan*. Secondly, they had no need to write for money. Thirdly, due to their bourgeois and even aristocratic backgrounds, the writers of the Shirakaba-ha group cultivated a wider scope of aesthetic sensibility than that of the poverty-stricken naturalists. Fourthly, unlike the frustrated naturalists, they espoused a positive, optimistic attitude to life or at least retained some resilience with which to surmount their predicament.

Shiga Naoya is often regarded as a virtuoso of the short story form, since throughout his career he produced innumerable masterpieces in this genre. His short stories are either fictional tales or brief accounts of episodes taken from his own life, written with a compact organisation, delicate sensibility and lucid prose style. For instance, **'At Kinosaki',** which is one of the most popular anthology pieces for Japanese school texts, depicts the psychological process by which the author, while convalescing from an accident that could have cost him his life, awakens to the mysteries of life and death. The fact that in twenty-five years he produced only one lengthy novel, *A Dark Night's Passing* (*Anya Kōro*, 1921-37), suggests various possibilities: that he had a certain preoccupation which he needed to express in his work; that the subject was extremely difficult to handle; and that he persistently kept on tackling it despite difficulties. What then was Shiga Naoya's preoccupation with which he dealt in *A Dark Night's Passing* as well as in his shorter works? In brief it was the conflict with his father and his need to be reconciled. (pp. 83-4)

**'Ōtsu Junkichi'** (1912) [also] reflects to a great extent . . . aspects of Shiga Naoya's own life, in the way the protagonist's forbidden love for one of the maid servants leads him into conflict with his father and causes his estrangement from the family. This subject matter is coupled with another of Shiga's major concerns. Although he was never baptised into Christianity, in 1900, at the age of eighteen, he became and remained until 1907 a follower of Uchimura Kanzō's reformist Christian sect, the *mukyōkai-ha* or 'non-church' movement against the established church. Under Uchimura's influence the protagonist of the story (like Shiga Naoya himself) is obsessed with the fear of committing adultery. So far he has suffered from the split between his spiritual faith and his frustrated physical desires. Now, unless he consummates his love in the form of marriage, his relationship with his maid servant is strained by the stigma of adultery. There is, then, the urgent need for him to marry her, an act which is inevitably bound to bring about a clash with his father.

While 'Ōtsu Junkichi' is thoroughly autobiographical, 'The Diary of Claudius' ('**Kurōdiasu no Nikki**', 1912), written about the same time, has a fictional structure. As the title suggests, it deals with the relationship between Hamlet and Claudius, looked at not from the prince's but from his uncle's point of view. While drawing on the framework of the well-known play, the author deliberately distorts Shakespeare's text. First, Claudius pleads not guilty to the alleged crime of fratricide. Secondly, he shows utmost sympathy with Hamlet's self-imposed sufferings. Thirdly, however, in Claudius' view Hamlet's suspicion of him is nothing but a morbid phantasy. And, finally, despite Claudius' solicitude for his nephew, Hamlet turns out to be intrinsically self-centred and not sympathetic at all. What could these features of the story imply? First, by siding with Claudius and belittling Hamlet, the author seems implicitly to give warning of the danger of Hamlet's Oedipus complex, and his hatred of Claudius as a usurper of his mother. Furthermore one may hazard a guess that the author is critically judging his own hatred towards his father. Secondly, Claudius' solicitude for Hamlet may be interpreted as the author's hopeful desire for his father to soften his attitude. These implications suggest that the author was searching for a reconciliation.

In the same year that he wrote '**Ōtsu Junkichi**' and '**The Diary of Claudius**' Shiga Naoya launched another autobiographical project, *Tokitō Kensaku*, which was later to become *A Dark Night's Passing*. It was an attempt to elaborate in extended form his personal conflicts. (pp. 84-5)

*A Dark Night's Passing* distinguishes itself from such works as '**Ōtsu Junkichi**' and '**Reconciliation**' in the degree to which the author transforms the facts of his own life. The prologue, Kensaku's recollection of his childhood, presents the key factors of the whole novel. First, Kensaku's estrangement from his father is suggested by the *sumō* wrestling episode. The father throws his unyielding child again and again until he ties up the child with his belt. The child eventually bursts into tears. Secondly, his close links with his grandfather is shown: he is brought up in his grandparents' household and remains there, looked after by the grandfather's widowed mistress. Here, however, one notices a modification from the author's own life. While his own grandfather was a man of integrity and intelligence, who had a profound influence on him, Kensaku's grandfather is portrayed as somewhat repellent. Each of the four organically constructed chapters of *A Dark Night's Passing* represents a different phase of Kensaku's life, in which he suffers a different kind of ordeal and attains maturity by surmounting it. (p. 86)

At the end of the novel he has fallen ill and is suffering from fever and exhaustion, thus leaving the reader uncertain whether he will survive or not.

Despite this ambivalent ending, there emerges from *A Dark Night's Passing* a sense of catharsis, reminiscent of the Shirakaba-ha's forward-looking attitude. The works of the naturalistic I-novelists were often replicas of the petty reality in which they dragged out their lives. There was scarcely any way out of this morass for either the created characters or the author himself. The protagonist of *A Dark Night's Passing*, based on the author's own self and yet adequately equipped with the autonomy of a fictional character, is sufficient evidence that the author has survived his own predicament. (p. 87)

*Hisaaki Yamanouchi, "The Rivals: Shiga Naoya and Akutagawa Ryūnosuke," in his* The Search for Authenticity in Modern Japanese Literature, *Cambridge University Press, 1978, pp. 82-7.**

## WILLIAM F. SIBLEY

[In] his own country Shiga has at various times over the past sixty years been exalted as a master craftsman of the modern literature and a special spokesman for the genius of the nation (*bungaku no kamisama*, "the lord of literature," is the journalistic tag he was given late in his career), and has alternately been excoriated, particularly in the years after the Second World War, as one of those most responsible for the stunting of modern Japanese fiction.

In an often cited sweeping comment on much of modern Japanese fiction, Kobayashi Hideo stated, "Since Tayama Katai learned from Maupassant the literary value of daily life itself, no writer has succeeded as well as Shiga has in boldly, even violently, wresting from his own life a work of art; no one has adhered so scrupulously as he has to the approach of the personal novel (*shishōsetsu*), in which the logic of everyday life becomes the logic of literary creation."

Less grandiosely, Akutagawa Ryūnosuke, a contemporary, greatly admired Shiga for his ability to write what Akutagawa called "stories without stories" (*hanashi no nai hanshi*). But he too takes on an almost reverential tone when he further observes, "Shiga Naoya is the purest writer among us. His works are first and foremost those of a man who lives a fine life . . . by which I mean a morally spotless life."

As if in reply to Akutagawa's homage, Dazai Osamu wrote of Shiga some twenty-five years later, "What everyone says is so 'fine' in his works amounts to nothing more than the man's conceit, the courage of a bully. . . . If he writes that he has farted it will be published in large print, and we are supposed to read this with the utmost solemnity. What nonsense!"

Looking at Shiga's works themselves, one finds the most prominent, recurring themes to be obsessive memories of childhood; fantasies of murder and parricide, sometimes acted out on the stage of the narrative, elsewhere imagined by the narrator or the central character through evident substitutions; a deeply ambivalent attraction to alternately protective and destructive older women; and ultimately, the incest wish and the death wish, which appear in various partially displaced or sublimated forms. The evidence of his relatively slender oeuvre, the only evidence of interest, leads one to the conclusion that, whatever Shiga was as a man, as a writer he has been neither so banal and literal-minded as Kobayashi's remarks (contrary to his intention) would suggest, nor so "pure" as Akutagawa would have us believe, nor finally so consumed with self-importance, relentlessly self-involved though his writing surely is, as Dazai's diatribe makes him out to be.

Shiga is an author who (to paraphrase William Gass on D. H. Lawrence) wrote of nothing, in story, tract or letter, ever, but himself. "Anything can be made into fiction," Shiga himself once commented. "Whether a particular subject turns into a story or novel, an essay, biography, or diary depends entirely on the author's attitude as he writes rather than on the material itself." . . . The interchangeability of such different genres in Shiga's mind, not excluding even biography, is a clear expression of the subjectivism bordering on solipsism that characterizes all of his writing. He has indeed been both canonized and castigated as the most successful (in Kobayashi's view) and most intransigent (in the eyes of his detractors) practitioner of those curious subgenres that so dominate Japanese literary-historical treatments of the first half of the twentieth century: the *shishōsetsu* ("I novel" or, better, in Henri Peyre's more broadly based terminology, "personal fiction") and the *shinkyō shōsetsu* ("the novel of mental states"). (pp. 1-3)

If Shiga did indeed start from the doubtful premise that, in Kobayashi's words, the "logic of everyday life" may serve as "the logic of literary creation," he has carried this formula to its often illogical conclusion. It hardly requires a trained psychologist to recognize that on a deeper level of reality our days are filled at least as much with irrational impulses and inchoate emotions as with orderly social intercourse and articulate thoughts. It is this sort of reality, bound up with and triggered by the external trivia of "everyday life" but having a separate life of its own, that Shiga has taken as his prime subject. Like various other writers both in Japan and the West, he has arrived independently at a wholly intuitive kind of psychoanalytical consciousness. . . .

Whatever the subject, when his "attitude" has determined that his work is to be fiction (that is, a *shōsetsu*), the focus is most often inward and backward, introspective and retrospective. As is the case with all deeply subjective fiction, much of Shiga's raw material is unmistakably rooted in his own inner experience, we may conclude; for he could scarcely know another's mind so thoroughly. But one may not find very interesting or particularly germane the dubious game of correlating closely the outward events of his life with the representation of psychological effects supposedly produced by them, the game so vigorously played by the biographical critics. . . .

Dreams and elusive "psychological states"—moods, feelings, impulses, are finally what is most real in Shiga's fiction, together with concrete impressions, the sights and sounds that are fused with these things. Attempts to tie this intangible stuff directly to what we "know" about his life and times are not entirely convincing. (p. 4)

Shiga does of course eventually succeed in giving some outward form to his inner experience. He does this through vivid concrete images . . . , detailed descriptions of dreams (nature's contribution to the process of visual objectification), and in general through the elaboration of a restricted symbolic vocabulary that includes elements borrowed from various established lexicons, fixed idioms that are frequently invoked in a sense peculiar to Shiga, even occasional neologisms.

That Shiga was in a general way a writer of personal fiction is borne out by a common-sense reading of the works and need not be confirmed by protracted exercises in biographical criticism of the most literal-minded kind. . . . [The] recurring events that form the narrative kernel of most of his major works are in any case most often non-events, rooted in "chimerical thoughts" whose actual occurrence in Shiga's mind are unknowable. . . . What distinguishes Shiga from several other Japanese writers who, in the first decades of the century, set about writing various kinds of both personal and psychological fiction is his motive for undertaking the project in the first place, and the transparency with which, both in the works and outside, the motive is revealed. In a story entitled *Wakai* (Reconciliation, 1917), Shiga's hero, who is himself a writer, describes a kind of autotherapy which he has practiced in his works behind a thin veil of fiction: "I would write about [my own problems] from the point of view of the impersonal author. . . . Through putting down on paper various unpleasant events which might well occur in my own life . . . I hoped to prevent them from actually happening to me. As I set down each episode I would imagine that I had escaped acting out an identical situation myself." . . . And after he had completed a

large portion of his major works, Shiga reminisced: "It strikes me that in those years there was something pathological in me [as well as in my writing]. Lately, my interest in sick states has diminished. But I still cannot deny that one derives a certain élan from such sickness—an excitement which permits one to experience and to express things not accessible under normal conditions of sanity." . . . These words cast considerable light both on Shiga's idiosyncratic practice of the craft of fiction and on what might be called his ulterior motives for writing in the first place. (pp. 5-6)

It is above all, and in some cases nothing but, style which, as "incitement pleasure," draws the reader into Shiga's works. Shiga's indifference to the larger formal features of narrative craft is often striking. Apart from the special vocabulary and the terse, rhythmical style which he has painstakingly created, there are few formally satisfying elements in his works, a minimum of well-constructed plot, dramatic incident, "big scenes," and sustained dialogue. If one's perspective stresses such larger formal attributes of the genre, as does that of Edward Seidensticker in his discussion of Shiga, one would no doubt agree with him that Shiga's only successful works have been a handful of short stories. But, as Seidensticker himself has pointed out, the modern Japanese temperament has not yielded many sturdily built novels laid out on a grand scale in the classic nineteenth century European manner. (p. 7)

In addition to being personal, subjective, and often intuitively psychoanalytical (with an eye to autotherapy), Shiga's approach to fiction is . . . also highly fragmentary. In an effort to grasp some of the "whole" which eluded Shiga, or which . . . he deliberately eschewed, one would want to emphasize those elements in his individual works that contribute to some unity linking all of them. Chief among these, beyond the consistent surface of his well-honed style, is surely the single central character who, in one guise or another, appears in nearly all of Shiga's stories and novels, and whose viewpoint, with occasional interventions by the omniscient author, predominates in the great majority of his narratives.

This character is given a number of different names in the various works where he appears, and often speaks to us directly in the first person. We encounter him at several different stages in his life and in a variety of social roles. But in his inner life he is recognizably the same figure throughout Shiga's works. Although one need not be concerned with exact correlations and literal identifications, this created character and the microcosm he inhabits can no doubt be closely associated with the creating author and his world. . . . And so it will be useful to refer to Shiga's recurring protagonist in all cases (except for two early, openly confessional stories) as the Shiga hero, to distinguish this persona, alter ego, surrogate, etc., from Shiga's "real self," who is unknowable.

We recognize the Shiga hero precisely because his inner identity is always shifting. He is most often portrayed in the act of transforming his view of himself, of others close to him and of his immediate surroundings, social and natural. But the reader comes to discern certain patterns in these subjective transformations and, in large outline, a kind of cycle that recurs with inexorable regularity.

There are of course numerous subordinate characters, who are revealed to us from the hero's point of view and who take on a provisional reality through him. Also vivid images and wonderfully spare settings, often drawn from the realms of dreams and nature, which sometimes fulfill roles as important as the characters'. But it is first and foremost the single figure of the Shiga hero, both constant and protean, that gives some unity to the individual works and the entire oeuvre. We come to depend on him for our bearings in the often amorphous world of Shiga's fiction. (pp. 7-8)

*William F. Sibley, in his* The Shiga Hero, *The University of Chicago Press, 1979, 221 p.*

## LOUIS ALLEN

[In *A Dark Night's Passing* the range of Shiga Naoya's] observation is not wide, but the style is evocative and full of nuance, and it is style which counts—not idea or plot, with neither of which is Shiga much concerned. He said himself he cared less what his characters *did* than for what they felt when they did it. So there is no question of the build-up and resolution of a conflict, which the horrendous nature of Kensaku's birth might lead you to expect, but rather the possibility of sharing an experience, an autobiographical one if autobiography is taken to include fears and fancies as well as lived fact. *A Dark Night's Passing* has been called the supreme example in modern Japanese literature of the *watkushi shōsetsu*, or 'I Novel'. In a fairly tight society, Shiga succeeded, through self-exploration, in writing quite openly about sexuality, not only his private dreams but the sexuality of others. But the revelation is an interior one. Where many modern Japanese novels give us a good grasp of Japanese society, this one explores the inwardness of an individual Japanese soul. (p. 88)

*Louis Allen, ''The Geishas and the Jellyfish,'' in* The Listener, *Vol. 105, No. 2695, January 15, 1981, pp. 87-8.**

# Wilbur (Addison) Smith

## 1933-

**South African novelist.**

Smith writes novels of adventure, romance, and intrigue that are usually set against the landscape and history of Africa. His plots revolve around such exploits as daring rescues, blood rivalries, sinister schemes, and tragic misunderstandings. Smith liberally supplies other elements as well. In *The Sunbird* (1972), for example, he blends politics, archaeology, and ancient magic into a tale which becomes part scientific present and part mythical past. Although Smith has been faulted for relying on stock characters and other clichés, critics generally consider his work entertaining in the best pulp and potboiler tradition.

Among the exotic quests undertaken in Smith's novels are the search for gold in *Gold Mine* (1970), undersea treasure in *The Eye of the Tiger* (1974), and oil in *Hungry As the Sea* (1977). *Cry Wolf* (1975) is set in Ethiopia during Mussolini's invasion in 1935. Smith has also written two trilogies. The novels of the first, *When the Lion Feeds* (1964), *The Sound of Thunder* (1966), and *A Sparrow Falls* (1976), take place between the 1860s and the 1930s and include some of the historic and political events of that period in South African history. The second trilogy, consisting of *A Falcon Flies* (1979), *Men of Men* (1980), and *The Angels Weep* (1982), involves the Ballantyne family, a prominent clan which challenges the power and ambition of Cecil Rhodes during the establishment of Rhodesia. Like Smith's earlier trilogy, these works include much realistic detail, including descriptions of slave trade and conflicts within various factions of Rhodesia during this era.

(See also *Contemporary Authors*, Vols. 13-16, rev. ed. and *Contemporary Authors New Revision Series*, Vol. 7.)

© *Jerry Bauer*

## MARTIN LEVIN

Gold and corn are the by-products of ["**Gold Mine**," a] novel about South African mining operations. When two-fisted, hairy-chested Rod Ironsides becomes the youngest general manager of the Sonder Ditch mine, little does he know that he will be drawn into two underground complications. One concerns industrial sabotage. The other involves a mine director's wife. . . . Mr. Smith, an adventure writer disdainful of subtleties, blasts his way to a finale strewn with broken bodies and orange blossoms.

> Martin Levin, in a review of "Gold Mine," in The New York Times Book Review, October 25, 1970, p. 58.

## MARTIN LEVIN

I had thought that such 120-proof moonshine as ["**The Diamond Hunters**"] had gone the way of Black Mask magazine and the wonderful world of Street & Smith. But, lo, here . . . is a writer who can crank out a line like "Benedict had placed himself beyond the laws of man." And mean it!

The potpourri Wilbur Smith has assembled is rife with lifelong misunderstandings, undying hates, unbelievably nefarious

schemes and nick-of-time rescues—delivered with the deadpan sincerity of the pulp greats. It all begins, as they used to say, when young Johnny Lance fails to earn the love of his stepfather, a South African diamond magnate, but gains his stepsister's instead. Rugby star, top scholar, crack geologist—Lance finds nothing that will win the Old Man's heart. His only legacy is the financial straits of the family diamond-mining operation and the hatred of Benedict, his tricky stepbrother.

Will his mountain of debits destroy Lance, as the Old Man planned? Or will Lance retrieve his fortunes with Kingfisher, his fantastic new diamond-dredging vessel? Read on, adventure fans.

> Martin Levin, in a review of "The Diamond Hunters," in The New York Times Book Review, April 23, 1972, p. 41.

## MILES DONALD

[*The Sunbird*] is a simple tale of superhuman folk. The hero, a hunchback South African Jew called Ben, speaks 15 languages, is the world's most enterprising archaeologist and has very strong arms. He is the occasional lover of his glamorous assistant Sally who also carries on a clandestine affaire with Louren Sturvesant, huge, blond, preternaturally strong, one of the world's 20 richest men . . . , and a virility symbol in much the same measure as Everest is a tall mountain.

Under Louren's patronage, and with the help of some agreeable bushmen, Ben and Sally uncover and excavate the ancient Carthaginian city of Opet—discovering in the process an entire history of the people and place by the Opet poet Huy. Dotted throughout the various events there are some heavy hints that the characters Have Been Here Before, and while I gritted my teeth against Mr Smith's tying a knot in this loose thread I certainly wasn't prepared for his weaving it into an abridged version of the Bayeux tapestry. For he actually sets the entire second half of his novel in bygone Opet, and gives the characters—hunchback, millionaire, beautiful assistant and all—equivalent former selves. Only instead of dealing merely with the world's most brilliant archaeologist and the world's biggest virility symbol, they are now High Priest and King as well.

Still if you are going to have wish-fulfilment you might as well have it big, and there is no doubt that Mr Smith can buckle and swash with the best of them. He . . . is out to tell a story and that story gets well and truly told. There is a consistently fine use of detail so that each event—an archaeological dig, a battle, an attack by wild animals—is, quite simply, interesting in itself. It is principally for this reason that Mr Smith's narrative is maintained against all the odds. Although I didn't believe a word of it I wanted to know what happened next. In fact I wanted to know what happened next even when I didn't *care*.

It is for this reason—[he tells] stories—that people will actually buy [his] works. . . . [This novel is] full of baloney, but [it has] spirit.

> Miles Donald, "Spirited Baloney," in New Statesman, *Vol. 84, No. 2170, October 20, 1972, p. 568.*

## MARTIN LEVIN

The lost Phoenician city of Ophir—if I remember my research correctly . . .—was discovered by Tarzan. [In **"The Sunbird"**] Wilbur Smith . . . has now dispatched his own expedition to the area headed by a South African archeologist, Dr. Benjamin Kazin. Maybe it's just as well, because Dr. Ben hits paydirt and a bonanza of excitement.

Some of this is archeological, some political and some romantic. . . . Just when the action levels off, and Kazin is able to confound the doubting Thomas of the Royal Geographic Society, he falls victim to an ancient hex. . . . And we are off into a book-length sequel: a hallucinatory, mirror-image trip to the dying city of Opet, with a cast of thousands. You can't say Mr. Smith's twofer doesn't give the reader his money's worth.

> Martin Levin, in a review of "The Sunbird," in The New York Times Book Review, *July 29, 1973, p. 13.*

## RONALD BLYTHE

It is all go in *Eagle in the Sky,* as one might expect. Images, incidents and action establish themselves, brightly and briefly like the expert suggestions in polished advertising. Speed, sun, sex, freedom, joy, plus all the toys and pleasures of the electronic age, flash past entertainingly until, with a gruesome interruption by the old moral-purpose warning system, we are forced to contemplate a death's head. It is poor David Morgan's head, once amazingly beautiful, now something to flinch from,

due to a flying accident. Debra, the girl he met during the Israeli war, alone stares straight back at the dreadful sight and continues to love him. And if this isn't enough, he has to be present when she undergoes brain surgery. Wilbur Smith can certainly hurry the adventures along, but his eroticism is agonising.

> Ronald Blythe, "Proconsuls and Postmen," in The Listener, *Vol. 91, No. 2349, April 4, 1974, p. 444.*

## NEWGATE CALLENDAR

["**The Eye of the Tiger**" is] a good adventure story, even if much of it is written as though by formula. It has every tested tried-and-true device. Here is a book about treasure under the sea that has a brave adventurer . . . , miscellaneous bloodthirsty villains, scuba diving, coral poisoning, fights with sharks, hand-to-hand encounters with human monsters. Smith has not missed a trick.

But he has put everything together in the most skillful manner. Smith is a good writer who has the knack of making his bigger-than-life situations believable. So his hero is a kind of superman. Yet we can identify with him, he is the kind of he-man we all want to be. At the end of the book, Smith presents the reader with a bit of suspense, something like an unresolved dominant at the end of a classic symphony. But just as the ear readily supplies a missing tonic chord, so the emotions tell us exactly how Smith's admittedly artificial situation is going to be resolved. Most of **"The Eye of the Tiger"** is fairy-tale stuff. But it's almost impossible to resist.

> Newgate Callendar, in a review of "The Eye of the Tiger," in The New York Times Book Review, *May 30, 1976, p. 13.*

## RICHARD FREEDMAN

While it may lack High Seriousness, **"Cry Wolf"** is so well-researched and filled with desperate action that one [can imagine] John Wayne and David Niven [as] the two heroes: an American engineer and an English soldier of fortune who ferry four battered armored cars to the besieged Ethiopians out of purely commercial considerations. Accompanied by a ravishing American newspaperwoman who spends her time between dispatches bathing languorously in jungle streams and being attacked by lions and lusty tribesmen, the two heroes end up committed to fighting for her favors and against the Fascist invaders.

Among the invaders, actual historical figures like the Italian General Badoglio put in an appearance. The author even quotes the notorious description by Mussolini's son Vittorio of the sensuous pleasure he felt dropping a bomb in the midst of a defenseless Ethiopian crowd. . . . Another Italian, Count Aldo Belli, cuts a fine comic figure in his combined bluster and cowardice.

In fact, only the major characters tend to be constructed out of movie clichés of the 30's, but with someone like John Huston directing, the inevitable film of **"Cry Wolf"** could well be another "African Queen."

> Richard Freedman, "Pirates, Soldiers of Fortune and Spies," in The New York Times Book Review, *September 4, 1977, p. 10.*

## PEGGY CRANE

Wilbur Smith novels are almost impossible to find on library shelves—and there is always a long waiting list for his latest book. It is hardly surprising, for his novels are almost as compulsive reading as Ian Fleming's tales of James Bond were a decade or so ago. Indeed, some of his heroes could well be styled the Bond of the Bush. The difference is that Bond plays out his adventures against a backdrop of espionage; Smith heroes play out theirs in the glow of southern Africa's magnificent landscapes.

Sean Courtney, the old hero in Wilbur Smith's latest book, *A Sparrow Falls,* is an almost perfect example of the genre. This is the last in a trilogy that spans Courtney's life in South Africa from the 1860's to about 1930. As with Fleming, the writer's expertise—whether it be about hunting, gold mining or death by rabies—brings a sense of reality to extravagant feats of derring-do particularly when, as here, the story touches the fringes of history; Isandhlwana, Rorkes Drift and the first gold rush on the Witswatersrand in the first of the trilogy, *When the Lion Feeds;* the Anglo-Boer War with the siege of Ladysmith and Spion Kop in *The Sound of Thunder* [published in the United States as *The Roar of Thunder*]; and the white miners' strike on the Rand in 1922 in *A Sparrow Falls.*

The heroes are usually of British stock; the Afrikaners, when they appear, are big, sturdy men, tough but kindly, if sometimes misguided. And the African—or Bantu as Mr Smith still prefers to call him? He is always—at least in the books I have read—depicted as a most noble savage. There is Mbejane, descendant of the famous Zulu King, Tshaka, who hitches up with Courtney at Isandhlwana, saves his life and never leaves him until death. The equal in the bush, he is the servant in the town; he prefers his loin cloth and his spears; sings digging in the gold fields, leaves his wives and children to follow his master to war; is always wise, is always on hand when he is needed. Pungushe, in *A Sparrow Falls,* is also of royal Zulu blood. His life entangles with Mark Anders, a young man in whom Sean sees the sons he has lost, and the black man/white man relationship, though somewhat updated, is essentially the same. In *Gold,* King Nkulu is the great Shangaan who, in his free time, likes to prance in his feathers and leopard skins, but who heroically dies saving his employer's flooded mine. All splendid people whose image would be tarnished if they resented the white men taking their land or their cattle or, because of pride, refused to accept him as the natural leader.

As with Bond, the backgrounds differ, but the core of the stories remain the same. The heroes are splendid men, tall, of magnificent physique, brave, quick-tempered and highly sexed. The women are supremely beautiful, fiery, intelligent and femininely challenging. Their passions getting the better of them, the hero, surprisingly often (and unlike Bond), manages to implant a baby in these paragons of women before fate removes such dreary obstacles as husbands or other hindrances from the scene. Storm is conceived in a storm—hence her name—on a mountainside in a night of passion between Sean Courtney and Ruth; later Ruth's husband is conveniently killed off in the Boer War. Storm, in her turn, has a passionate affair with Mark Anders, conceives his child but, to hide it from him, marries someone else, finally divorcing him. Thus, through death or divorce, the lovers meet again and live in marital bliss with their offsprings forever after. Life may deal them hard blows, but the bond remains fast. Set against the splendid landscape of an earlier South Africa, it is the perfect fairy tale. No wonder Wilbur Smith has such an avid readership. (pp. 42-3)

Peggy Crane, "The James Bond of the Bush," in Books and Bookmen, *Vol. 23, No. 3267, December, 1977, pp. 42-3.*

## THE VIRGINIA QUARTERLY REVIEW

A generation ago Evelyn Waugh wrote the definitive satire . . . on the Italian invasion of Ethiopia in his biting and hilarious novel *Scoop.* He must now yield to Wilbur Smith, whose treatment of the same theme [in *Cry Wolf*] is as good as his, if not better. It took courage, if not gall, for the author to challenge Waugh on the same turf, but he has pulled it off successfully.

A review of "Cry Wolf," in The Virginia Quarterly Review, *Vol. 54, No. 1 (Winter, 1978), p. 24.*

## PIERS BRENDON

[*Wild Justice*] deals with terrorism and the efforts of an international organisation, named Atlas, to combat it. Smith's book has more pace and fewer pretensions than [Morris West's novel *Proteus*]. It contains a number of exciting set-pieces; the storming of a hi-jacked aircraft and the attack on the hero's Maserati, for example, have an authentic Dornford Yates quality. But there is much involved and unlikely cloak-and-dagger skulduggery. There is an Ian Flemingish concern with the appurtenances of high living—Gucci shoes, etc. And the characters, Saint-Laurent dummies to a man, converse in the compulsory risk business idiom: 'I have put Mercury on condition Alpha'; 'Somebody has blown Atlas; this is going to be a living and breathing bastard'. (p. 54)

Piers Brendon, "Blockbusters," in Books and Bookmen, *Vol. 24, No. 7283, April, 1979, pp. 53-4.\**

## NEWGATE CALLENDAR

["**Hungry As the Sea**"] is a big book about a lot of big subjects: the sea, oil tankers, salvage tugs, heroic seamen, ecology, financial manipulation, greed, romance. It tries for an epic sweep, and there are indeed some exciting things in it. When Mr. Smith sticks to the sea, he does just fine, even with his one-dimensional characters, even with the clumsy construction of the book. It is really two books in one, the first being a long account of a salvage operation in Antarctica.

But as a writer, Mr. Smith can be very tacky. At moments of emotional stress, his characters fall back on the worst soap-opera conventions.

Newgate Callendar, in a review of "Hungry As the Sea," in The New York Times Book Review, *February 24, 1980, p. 30.*

## ROGER MANVELL

Set in Africa and around its coasts in 1860, this admirable and extremely detailed novel [*A Falcon Flies;* published in the United States as *Flight of the Falcon*] concerns the adventures of a British naval captain and his sister and their virtually single-handed campaign against the still prevalent slave trade. The author, who seems to possess an unrivalled knowledge of his subject, writes with an impressive authenticity, as if he had himself taken part in these varied actions a century and more ago. The central character, Robyn Ballantyne, is a pioneer woman doctor, daughter of a celebrated explorer-missionary of mythic reputation who has disappeared into the African hinterland; her brother, the captain, is disapproved of by his superiors because of his high-handed action at sea against the slavers. . . . The action involves a whole series of set pieces—such as the raiding of a slave-ship and the release of its human cargo amid scenes of incredible suffering, or the hunting of wild game, in particular elephants, every minute detail of which is recorded. While Robyn is equally dedicated to the welfare of the hideously exploited natives and to the discovery of her long-lost father, Zouga, her brother, is more concerned with the opening-up of the rich hinterlands of Africa, of which his father has left tantalizing and mysterious accounts. As a result, brother and sister undertake with incredible fortitude an extraordinary expedition into unknown territory, the outcome of which is totally astonishing. Wilbur Smith must surely be considered an author in the grand tradition of the picaresque novel of travel and adventure to which he brings a modern quality of research.

> *Roger Manvell, in a review of "A Falcon Flies," in* British Book News, *August, 1980, p. 504.*

## NEWGATE CALLENDAR

**"The Delta Decision"** deals with international terrorism and the secret head of it all, a mysterious force known as Caliph. It is a dreadful book. . . . It starts with a cliché on page one: "She moved with the undulating grace of one of the big predatory cats . . ." It ends with another on page 393: "Even through the weakness of his abused body, Peter could feel a deep well of strength and determination within himself . . ." Characters mouth things like "You bloody monster." The plot goes from contrivance to mere silliness, and at the end Caliph is revealed as the person any elementary-school reader would have guessed him to be.

> *Newgate Callendar, in a review of "The Delta Decision," in* The New York Times Book Review, *April 26, 1981, p. 38.*

## HENRY STANHOPE

[*Men of Men* is an] adventure yarn "of spellbinding action and romance" in nineteenth century Southern Africa where men are men . . . and women have "limbs as long and supple as a heron's neck". Even the rain manages to fall as a "slanting curtain of silver arrow shafts". Thus the red-blooded prose flows through Matabeleland engulfing witchcraft, suicide, rape and almost every other kind of violent animal behaviour beneath the shade of the mopani trees. . . . By and large it confirms Wilbur Smith's reputation as a professional wordsmith of the airport bookstall school. I see from the blurb that he has previously been described as lying somewhere between Alistair Maclean and Nicholas Montserrat. I would not dissent from that view.

> *Henry Stanhope, in a review of "Men of Men," in* The Times, *London, April 30, 1981, p. 19.*

## JOHN BROSNAHAN

Smith's cross-generic hybrid [*Flight of the Falcon*] —a tempestuous historical romance set in the mid-nineteenth century—finds Robyn Ballantyne, a young female medical missionary, on an arduous trek across Africa with her brother in search of their missing father. On her sea voyage from England Robyn

has met a handsome slave trader whose moral character she has judged as spiritually repulsive but who has stirred her on a purely physical level in a strange yet fascinating manner. Meanwhile, Robyn's brother loses sight of his original altruistic quest and instead becomes entranced by the possibility of the great riches lying hidden in the middle of the continent. Smith lets out all the stops in this florid-hued, broadly painted pot-boiler of considerable appeal as Robyn chooses between respect and passion, between charity and greed. All the risky entanglements, treacherous enemies, exotic locales, impetuous desires, and high-spirited action make for a fine stew of adventure and lust.

> *John Brosnahan, in a review of "Flight of the Falcon," in* Booklist, *Vol. 78, No. 8, December 15, 1981, p. 522.*

## DAVID COREY

Sentimentalists and students of gerontology will be happy to know that Wilbur Smith continues to provide work for the particularly long-in-the-tooth band who populate the jungle-outpost adventure novel. *Shout at the Devil*, however, may lead some humane readers to lobby vigorously for a mandatory retirement age. One certainly experiences an empathetic weariness as these tired veterans of yesteryear's pulp fiction go through their all too familiar paces. There are, for example, Flynn Patrick O'Flynn, the gin-drenched, swaggering soldier of fortune; Sebastian Oldsmith, a dim-witted, innocent of good family who is drawn into a ring of ivory poachers; and Rosa, the love interest and victim of this genre's barely sublimated sado-masochistic convention of placing a helpless female among some variety of moral savage—in this case, the German colonials, criminal expatriots and natives of Zanzibar in 1912.

Although one hopes that long service in the genre will have provided these characters with a somewhat philosophical view of their situations and surroundings, on the contrary, each new dilemma allows Mr. Smith to orchestrate an emotional storm for them. At no point are they granted a flash of comforting insight or intelligence; only the reader knows that there can be no real danger in the comedic realm of self-parody.

Ivory poaching is clearly serious business for a hero who, when not gulping gin, is known to "gulp with excitement," "tremble," or be "breathless with wonder." And poor Rosa, after making her difficult way up through history from the romances of the Middle Ages, and coming out of retirement for a second career in the Gothic novel, she parades once again in the old uniform: her "long night-dress," made to feel the "rough stone and thorn beneath her bare feet," forced to grapple with "senses over-wrought by her terror." Rosa's senses, however, are by no means the most overwrought element in this novel. . . .

*Shout at the Devil* is what might have been produced if Joseph Conrad had spent his nights at sea reading *Real Man's Adventures* instead of Shakespeare and *The Bible*.

> *David Corey, in a review of "Shout at the Devil," in* The Reprint Bulletin Book Reviews, *Vol. XXVII, No. 1, 1982, p. 20.*

## KIRKUS REVIEWS

[*Men of Men* is a] sprawling, exotic sequel to *Flight of the Falcon* (1981)—with the far-flung Ballantyne family heavily involved in the South Africa of the 1880s: diamonds, colonialism, missionary work, tribal warfare, and treasure-lust. The opening 200 pages or so are best, with the focus firmly on elephant-hunter Zouga, now a widower with two young sons, still dreaming of native loot up north, but working a sorry diamond-mine claim to get money for a new trek to Zambezia. Son Ralph pitches in earthily . . . ; he'll eventually take off on his own trade/treasure expedition, reaching the court of Matabele king Lobengula—where his missionary-medic Aunt Robyn, with husband and daughters, is a court adviser. Meanwhile, Zouga's other son Jordie, a castration-inclined homosexual, becomes "secretary" to Cecil Rhodes, who's voraciously extending his land/mineral empire. And as the novel swarms its way up to and past 1890, the focus slips around from subplot to subplot. Robyn's devilish old flame Mungo St. John reappears, with tough mistress Louise . . . ; Ralph woos one cousin but weds another . . . ; Zouga goes to work for Rhodes and finds Louise near death in the wild; Ralph defies ancient curses to seize tribal treasures. And, in the final 100+ pages, despite peacemaking efforts by Robyn and . . . Zouga, there's war between Rhodes' colonials and the Matabele—with Zouga battling . . . , Robyn's husband a massacre casualty, the Robyn/Mungo lust re-flowering, and Bazo swearing tribal revenge. Veteran Smith makes no attempt to shape these promising materials . . . ; none of the major characters is developed or sympathetic enough to provide a center. But—with diamond-mine details, ritual glitter and gore, and plenty of outdoors action—this is sporadically engrossing as adventure, if not as family saga; and it's certainly an improvement over the lurid excess of *Flight of the Falcon.* (pp. 1311-12)

*A review of "Men of Men," in* Kirkus Reviews, *Vol. L, No. 23, December 1, 1982, pp. 1311-12.*

**WILLIAM BRADLEY HOOPER**

Smith can certainly keep a pot boiling. This third installment of the Ballantyne family saga [*The Angels Weep*] follows *Men of Men* . . . and is every bit as action-packed as its predecessors. Greed is the theme that has linked the individual novels of the trilogy, specifically the greed for African gems and minerals that reduced so many British imperialists to moral midgets, indifferent to the destruction of land and people that their pursuit of riches unfailingly entailed. *The Angels Weep* counterpoints the exploits of the family in 1895, when gold in Rhodesia was uppermost on their minds, with their business as it stood in 1977, when a further generation of Ballantynes are fighting ruthlessly to maintain white supremacy in the face of black nationalism. All three of Smith's Ballantyne books combine adventure and melodrama with sex and violence on a grand scale—a time-honored formula for bestsellerdom.

*William Bradley Hooper, in a review of "The Angels Weep," in* Booklist, *Vol. 79, No. 22, August, 1983, p. 1422.*

**MICHAEL HEALY**

In two of his previous novels, *Flight of the Falcon* and *Men of Men,* Smith fashioned his fiction around the development of Cecil Rhodes's empire and the destiny of Rhodesia. [*The Angels Weep*] continues the story, focusing on the Ballantyne family, whose daring and ambition rival Rhodes's. The conflict between these characters combines with the uprising of the Matabele natives to subvert their destinies, as well as their nation's.

The novel's two sections explore the Ballantyne family's conflicts in 1895 and in 1977—the beginning and the end of Rhodesia. This structure shows all too clearly that the more things change, the more they remain the same. The colonialists compete with each other for wealth and power while the natives fight a guerrilla war to gain independence. No matter what the era, the whites are gorgeous, wealthy, healthy, and sexy to just this side of gross mythologizing. . . . The natives are fierce, proud, noble, yet still savage. . . . In fact, the suggestions of the Old West's adventure, violence, and opportunism may crowd out the fact that the setting is Rhodesia.

Smith should not have to slant his story. Born in Zambia, he has always lived in Africa. But because his characters are types, he has only the historical allusions to place his story. The effort is weak, despite clear writing and lucid storytelling.

Still, this is that old story of conflicting ambitions destroying all, including the prizes. Friends become enemies; their violent means so overwhelm their lives that their ends are always lost. Yet the toll on those who suffered under the imperialists and their legacy in Zimbabwe makes this a story that deserves more than trivializing and stereotyping.

*Michael Healy, in a review of "The Angels Weep," in* Best Sellers, *Vol. 43, No. 9, December, 1983, p. 322.*

**PUBLISHERS WEEKLY**

In this long, action-propelled novel [*The Leopard Hunts in Darkness*], the author . . . pits a tough, best-selling English novelist and a beautiful American photographer against an African official greedy for power and produces a richly textured adventure story that will leave readers limp but satisfied. When writer Craig Mellow, covertly employed by the World Bank to determine the political intentions of the government of Zambezi, returns to that troubled land to rebuild his grandfather's ranch, he becomes embroiled in the war between the government and scatterings of guerrillas. Peter Fungabera, Minister of Internal Security, is at first friendly, but then betrays Mellow, accusing him of being in the employ of the CIA and, with the support of a Russian operative, sets out to destroy him. . . . Readers may be disquieted by the utilitarian killings of innocents, and especially by the scenes of torture, but those who persevere will be treated to a thriller of high-speed excitement.

*A review of "The Leopard Hunts in Darkness," in* Publishers Weekly, *Vol. 225, No. 19, May 11, 1984, p. 261.*

# Anne (Katharine) Stevenson

## 1933-

**English-born poet, critic, and dramatist.**

Stevenson's poetry is noted for its attention to rhythm, its strong sense of place and detail, and its themes of love, loss, and solitude. Although she usually explores commonplace settings or circumstances, she often develops a sense of ambiguity in her work by investigating the subject in a new or inventive way. As Harry Marten has remarked, "[Stevenson] renders the familiar suddenly unfamiliar—sometimes frighteningly alien, sometimes funny or inviting, almost always surprising." The sense of transience that pervades Stevenson's poetry can be traced to her background. An American citizen, Stevenson was born in Cambridge, England, was educated in the United States, and since 1962 has lived mostly in Great Britain.

Stevenson's first volume, *Living in America* (1965), was praised for its sensitive treatment of such themes as love and death and for the way in which her poems vary in structure yet develop a cohesive world view. *Reversals* (1969) extends the themes of *Living in America* and displays an acute sense of place in many of the poems. This becomes increasingly important in Stevenson's later volumes. *Correspondences: A Family History in Letters* (1974) is a poetic examination of a New England family from its European roots to the present and contrasts the lifestyles of both the countries and the generations. In *Enough of Green* (1977) Stevenson's poems evoke physical isolation yet glory in the wonders and the beauty of imagination. Many of these poems were written while Stevenson lived on the Tay estuary in Scotland; the influence of the bitter and desolate coastline is clearly evident.

With *Minute By Glass Minute* (1982) Stevenson leaves the coastal isolation of Scotland for the plush landscape of South Wales. It echoes *Enough of Green* in its concentration on nature and description. *Minute By Glass Minute* also recalls an earlier collection of selected poems, *Travelling Behind Glass* (1974), in its use of glass as a metaphor for the objects and thoughts that distance and distort reality.

(See also *CLC*, Vol. 7; *Contemporary Authors*, Vols. 17-20, rev. ed.; and *Contemporary Authors New Revision Series*, Vol. 9.)

## DOROTHY DONNELLY

That the author of *Living in America* speaks with her own voice is apparent from the first poem, "Love." Love, she says, "is to its season as a Ferris wheel / to its fair," and she unfolds her theme through the extended image of the intoxicatingly revolving wheel. It is clear at once not only that she has things to say about life in the world, but that her eye is on the poem rather than on some extraneous external such as what-is-everybody-else-doing.

Less immediately noticeable is her concern for form; her thoughts for the most part seem to flow naturally through the lines and to have no need of strict metrics or the more elaborate schema. Form is there just the same, but more often understated than emphasized. Actually, almost half the poems are rhymed, but

except when clearly regular as in poems like "**In Winter,**" or "**The Traveller,**" with its "skin" and "in," or "rose," "froze," and "rows," the rhymes tend to be muted. "**Dreaming of Immortality in a Thatched Hut,**" for example, which at first reading gives the impression of being rhymeless, uses end rhyme throughout, perfect in "nightfall" and "all," imperfect in "sleeves" and "knees," almost imperceptible in "hut" and "regret," and the especially pleasing final "pine" and "rain."

The image, in a sense the touchstone of the poet's imagination, can in itself bestow form of a kind as well as distinction on a poem. The form of the poem "**After a Death**" derives in part from its underlying image which might be described as the sleep of things, or the familiar entranced, the "book," for example, "oblivious to the deepening snow, / absorbed in its one story." The image casts light on the impermanence of the personal "subject" and the permanently impersonal "object," on their inescapable separateness. It reveals the pathos of the human being in relation to time and the world of things, recognizing the distance between them. The sharp, pictorial image presented in the first lines of "**In Memoriam Miss B.**"

> Strained through the four
> Royal petals of the clematis, sunlight
> Transfigures the flowers; they become four
> Bladed propellers made of stained glass

advances the poem by the transformation indicated in the last clause. The final lines of the same poem not only surprise and please with the comparison of the plane's wake of light and the sun's, and with the beautiful image of the sun "trailing an exhaust like roses," but they suggest again the mysterious separateness of the person and the things with which he has to do. The pilot is "Left out of the light he causes"—an illuminating observation.

What flowers are to a bouquet, what paint is to the picture, words are to the poem. How, once the right word is found, it is manipulated in conjunction with the other right words to construct a personal and poetic yet natural and not poeticized speech, determines the distinction and individuation, the textural effect, the brightness, and much of the pleasure of the poem. Anne Stevenson's poems manifest considerable perception in the choice and handling of words and in well-put, well-placed phrases. (p. 298)

Green is a magic word and always has been, from Shakespeare's "Sing all a green willow," and "summer's green all girded up in sheaves," to Marvell's "green thought in a green shade," and Wallace Stevens's "Her green mind made the world around her green." It is a word of endless evocations. In these pages there are "green peacocks," and love's "green delirious way," but the word is used with finest effect in the poem, **"This City!"** which takes issue with the notion

> that love love love
> is the only green in the jungle.

She says a great deal, and says it strikingly, in a few words.

What one sees, or thinks one sees, forming these poems is the firm intention not to stop at the surfaces of things but to penetrate to their interior meaning, and along with this the avoiding of stereotypes and clichés of "grown-up" life. . . .

The tone conferred by her particular vision might, I think, be designated as an affectionate sadness, not the dour sadness of pessimism, but regret at the transience of things and people and the discrepancies between expectations and actualities. The sadness is not negative, not a denial, but a form of affirmation of the good. . . .

We can only be grateful to the author for all the bad things she does not do. She does not show off nor try to gain attention by shock tactics; she does not invite us to share a private "nausea" at the world, nor does she bare the intimate details of her personal life, nor take the stance of the professional liberal, beating the propaganda drum and pointing out how rightly he is on the right side. She writes with candor out of her own experience, and her attitudes, integral to her poems, emerge quite clearly.

**"Love"** and **"The Grey Land,"** the first and the last poems in the book, illuminate each by their crosslight. The first poem celebrates the "happening," the now, the breathtaking surprises of being in love, though with the reminder in the last line, that "tomorrow the fair will be gone." **"The Grey Land"** is the tomorrow of that now. It is a sober and memorable poem. . . .

[Poems], to be good, need not always be deep or serious, and there is one here that makes me smile with pleasure each time I come on it. Its form fits it like a skin, and sheer vividness, élan, surprise, and a sense of action about to break loose make it stand out. It is called **"In March."** . . .

The author has what Henry James calls "sensibility to the scenery of life," and her poems have added considerably to the scenery of our own landscapes. (p. 299)

*Dorothy Donnelly, in a review of "Living in America," in* Michigan Quarterly Review, *Vol. V, No. 4, October, 1966, pp. 298-99.*

### DANIEL HOFFMAN

Introducing Anne Stevenson's [*Living in America*], X. J. Kennedy writes, "if a man or woman is a poet whatever he writes will reflect a poet's way of looking at the world, whether it be scannable in trochees or whether it obey rules evident only to itself." . . . [Miss Stevenson] writes in both regular meters and in lines whose shape is the natural expression of their own meaning. . . . [Her] regular meters do not seem a superseded phase, an apprenticeship successfully transcended, but are rather a set of strategies on which she is able to draw when the needs of a particular poem demand them. She need not depend upon traditional structures, however, for on other occasions she can discover the inherent rhythms and design in the experience her poem creates. . . . Best of all perhaps is [**"Love"**], in which the simile with which it begins is kept in dizzying motion, the meter swooping and falling, the jerky, swaying motion of the lines beautifully evoking both the literal and the figurative movement, the motion and the emotion fused together. . . . To make such disparate experiences not only coincide but enlarge our understanding of each other is the work of an accomplished poet, the earned reward of her expertise. Miss Stevenson's work encloses a welcome range of reality. She can communicate fantasy and nightmare in a diction and a rhythm identifiably her own. Her personal poems are honest and convincing, with a probity that precludes the pinchbeck exhibitionism of some recent verse by others in this confessional vein. In her apparently easy commerce with both formality and freedom, Anne Stevenson seems to have solved, for her own work, the identity problem that has wrenched the careers of many contemporaries. If she has made painful repudiations of her earlier selves, these are not visible here; instead she has evidently absorbed her apprenticeship and built upon it. *Living in America* is a slender book of only thirty-two poems, but these are enough to announce the arrival of a new poet for whom fine things should be possible. (pp. 233-35)

*Daniel Hoffman, "Meter-Making Arguments," in* The Southern Review, *n.s. Vol. IV, No. 1, Winter, 1968, pp. 220-35.**

### CRAIG RAINE

Anne Stevenson's [*Enough of Green*] is full of pleasing things . . . , yet in certain poems influential voices drown out her own, making it seem frail and a little uncertain. To be really good, you have to make yourself heard in the Hallelujah chorus. Her **'North Sea off Carnoustie'** is a powerful expression of something dangerous and barely comprehensible, just beyond us on the frontiers of consciousness: 'The sea is as near as we come to another world.' It has a strong appeal, a kind of inchoate grandeur that makes our mundane certainties seem trivial. Finally, though, the oyster-catchers, 'doubtful of habitation', weeping, are replaced by a blackbird asserting individuality: '"You, you," he murmurs, dark purple in his voice.' The familiar earth is chosen, dissolution rejected, and the poem closes beautifully with the image of lighthouses as 'candles in the windows of a safe earth'.

As a poem it is accomplished and yet that 'dark purple in his voice' is *echt* Wallace Stevenson and the second stanza is too reminiscent in its line breaks of Lowell's imitation of Montale's 'Dora Markus'. **'A Summer Place'** shows, in the same way, how powerful a voice Robert Frost has in comparison with that of Miss Stevenson. All the same, *Enough of Green* succeeds in that most difficult area, the love poem. (p. 192)

*Craig Raine, "With Many Voices," in* New Statesman, *Vol. 95, No. 2447, February 10, 1978, pp. 192-93.\**

## JAY PARINI

Stevenson's new book is *Enough of Green,* a collection of tense, ironic lyrics of surpassing skill. In a prefatory poem, **"To Be a Poet,"** she says: "You must always be alone. / But don't beg a soupscrap of charity / or birdcrumb of tolerance. / Shift for yourself." It is this rare weather of aloneness which hangs over these poems, many of which conjure the landscape and climate of eastern Scotland with its chilly coast and chastened atmosphere.... Stevenson's strategy in [**"Fire and the Tide"**] is consistent with the others in *Enough of Green;* she establishes a landscape, bitter, usually autumnal, and this setting rapidly becomes metaphorical, a *paysage moralise,* a mental terrain wherein various possibilities for existence can be discerned. The fire in **"Fire and the Tide"** represents all these energies within us beyond rational control; the tides, likewise, can hardly be controlled. The imagination is like both natural forces, scarring the predictable mudscapes of our lives. It is a sign of great skill that the poet never gives in to the abstractions upon which the poem depends; she keeps shifting, movingly, between tenor and vehicle, as in the last two lines, the image of the birds "pulled raggedly over November" and the emotional tug-of-war between "now and the way you will not escape." This clarity, this attention to concrete detail and awareness of the metaphoric potential of everything in the natural world is characteristic of her work.

The Scottish poems interest me most, ones like **"North Sea off Carnoustie," "The Mudtower,"** and **"With my Sons at Boarhills."** The landscape here is hard-bitten, clenched.... The poet, repeatedly, confronts the "serious ocean" of reality, tries to withdraw or escape, but returns from "the planet ocean" with perspective; the lighthouses become "candles in the windows of a safe earth." One thing this poet always skirts is despair; she is willing to live with a world of imperfection, confident of the final triumph of imaginative order over chaos. Even the mudtower, in contrast with the lighthouses, has its meaning: "Its lovethrust is up from the mud it seems to be made of."

The poems which make up the rest of this book are set, occasionally, in Oxford, where the poet now lives. Many of them are satirical, sometimes whimsical. All of them display a rare lyrical bent, a fundamentally skeptical yet generous nature, an impulse toward clarity and compression. Most of the poems are short and epigrammatic.... There is everywhere in **"Cain"** the aura of verbal chastity, of fierce intellectual precision, of self-restraint. These virtues have always been rare in poets, today perhaps even more so. The only poet writing in the U.S. who equals Anne Stevenson in these respects is Elizabeth Bishop. ... *Enough of Green* is a welcome extension of a continually fascinating corpus of work. (pp. 209-11)

*Jay Parini, "On Anne Stevenson," in* Ploughshares, *Vol. 4, No. 3, 1978, pp. 209-11.*

## HARRY MARTEN

[*Enough of Green*] is anything but typical in its handling of domestic territory or personal voice. While the poems are generally first person observations, Miss Stevenson does not dissolve the world of things into impressions of the inner eye. She refuses equally to allow the sense of self to vanish into objects observed. Offering neither clicks of a camera, nor moments of self-consuming private awareness, her acts of attention to thoughts and things make clear the ways in which individuals make, and are made by, the worlds they inhabit. She reads for us the signatures written in domestic relations and she makes us acknowledge the borders that contain our day to day activities; yet even as she does so she shows us, often with distressing suddenness, the impossibility of defining perceptual systems that work or physical edges that bind.

From early lines in the first poem which announce that "Bare boughs in their cunning / twist this way and that way / trying to persuade by crooked reasoning" ... she renders the familiar suddenly unfamiliar—sometimes frighteningly alien, sometimes funny or inviting, almost always surprising. As in the novels of Dickens, inanimate objects spring to life and animate beings are abruptly deanimated. In **"The Exhibition"** perceptions of human models and created artifacts are rendered so as to confuse and bemuse us.... (pp. 147-48)

Many of the poems were written while Miss Stevenson was living in a cottage on the Tay estuary, and present a record of daily observations of life lived in that "outer" area where man's domestic patterns, while strongly felt, have not completely dispelled the influence of a still uncontrolled natural environment. In fact, we are made to realize that domestic circumstances are not readily separable from those energies which define the expanses of nature that household walls are intended to shut out. Even tight little islands of limited space can constitute vast territories in the recesses of the inhabitant's mind.... Images persist of lives that never were lived, but which nonetheless stubbornly stay with one always. And the domestic scenes are ghosted by memories which collapse bounded spaces.... (pp. 148-49)

Miss Stevenson's remarkable ability to combine the outsider's voice (the detached observer) with the insider's (caught in the experience of the moment) and the mediator's (aware of both watcher and thing watched as part of a continuum) guarantees the success of this representation of complicated interior and exterior spaces. Because our guide through *Enough of Green* enables us to share her tri-focal perspectives, we are assured of seeing broadly and feeling with narrow intensity, all the while being made to realize that, paradoxically, in these powerfully wrought Scottish and English landscapes and interiors, subjects and objects entwine. These clean and clever poems, finally, are not as much about individuals or places as about continuities, about the forces which move around and through us all.... (pp. 149-50)

*Harry Marten, "Finkel, Stallworthy, and Stevenson," in* Contemporary Literature, *Vol. 21, No. 1, Winter, 1980, pp. 146-58.\**

## DICK DAVIS

[The] poignancy that suffuses Anne Stevenson's poetry arises from a sense of the constantly dissolving, ungraspable transience of experience.... [*Minute by Glass Minute*] introduces a new tone into her work, an almost mystical sense of particulars transfigured by imagination and love—but there is still, as there always has been in her poems, a stubborn respect for the particulars as things in themselves. This tension is the hallmark of the book's most interesting poems (largely concerned with family relationships, a subject peculiarly susceptible to treatment in these terms), notably **'The Mother', 'Poem to my Daughter'** and the marvellous concluding **'Transparencies'**, which is one of the finest poems she has published. (p. 23)

Dick Davis, "Private Poems," in The Listener, *Vol. 108, No. 2791, December 16, 1982, pp. 23-4.**

## JOHN LUCAS

The temptation with Anne Stevenson's new volume is to do nothing but quote. *Minute by Glass Minute* contains a number of poems which are so good, so flawlessly pure, that beside them most other contemporary poetry looks patched, clumsy or scuffed. Although she can work to a small scale, the imagination and art that go into her work are very considerable. She can transform the world through an ecstatic, visionary quality. . . . Wallace Stevens is behind Anne Stevenson's recognition of the need to see the world with an ignorant eye. Thus there are poems of serious wit, like **'He and It'**, about the aggressive desire of a certain kind of imagination to humanise the world, which means in effect losing it: 'How comfortably it fits the creator / is what he describes'. **'Small Philosophical Poem'** and **'The Figure in the Carpet'** argue and tease out themes of art and reality with a panache that Stevens would have admired.

At the centre of the volume is a long poem, **'Green Mountain, Black Mountain'**, which I am unable to like. It feels to have been so heavily worked over as to have become petrified; yet she has perfect poetic pitch, an unfakeable sense of how a poem *sounds,* and how rhythm depends on sound.

John Lucas, "Ignorant Eyes," in New Statesman, *Vol. 104, No. 2700, December 17, 1982, p. 45.**

## JOHN MOLE

Anne Stevenson's recent poems are at the same time anxious and generous, brittle yet open to a wide range of experience which sometimes overwhelms them. *Minute by Glass Minute* is puritan and celebrant, and the glass that Anne Stevenson keeps looking through (the title of this new book is reminiscent of the earlier *Travelling Behind Glass*) both separates her from the world and irradiates it. "When we belong to the world/we become what we are", she asserts at the end of **"Poem to my Daughter"**, but she knows that consciousness, the self-awareness of her art, is a holding back. . . . She keeps hearing what her mind says, and she answers back with litanies of the actual. Several poems in the book weave their way philosophically in and out of exact, sensuous transcriptions . . . but there is a strenuous, mannered air about the way Anne Stevenson registers her doubts and tentative certainties. **"Burnished"** is an interesting poem in this respect. It begins:

> Walking out of Hay in the rain, imagining Blake
> imagining the real world into existence,
> I suddenly turned on him and said with energy—
> How dare you inflict imagination on us!
> What halo does the world deserve? And he—
> Let worlds die burnished, as along this bank.

"What halo does the world deserve?" The question is rhetorical and has a double edge; it is recriminating and, at the same time, hesitantly affirmative. At its centre is the quarrel out of which Anne Stevenson makes an authentic, if somewhat befuddled poetry. The tug between what, in the long poem **"Green Mountain, Black Mountain"**, she defines as "ghost-pull" and "animal pull" leaves rather too much unresolved although it's fascinating as oblique autobiography and as an exploration of the contrasts between her New England upbringing and her more recent experience.

An incidental strength in Anne Stevenson's work is her acute feeling for moments of pain in human relationships—there's a world of horror and compassion in the portrait of her dying mother ("she was dying at us")—but in the same poem she can be modishly whimsical in her excessive use of simile. Stanzas 11-13 of section five of **"Green Mountain, Black Mountain"** announce the Martian invasion of Vermont. (p. 72)

John Mole, "Respectable Formalities," in Encounter, *Vol. LX, No. 4, April, 1983, pp. 69-75.**

## SARAH WHITE

Stevenson's exercise of word craft has been devoted and sustained. Her four previous volumes reveal scarcely an untuned or an unintelligent line, though [*Minute by Glass Minute*] surpasses the others in strength and spareness. She has sure but varied, always appropriate, rhythms. . . . She has an instinct for the click of words against each other, rhyme that isn't rhyme. . . . Because she understands the resonance of her metaphors, the collection, not always visionary, sometimes wry and familiar, develops and coheres. Glass, especially, characterizes her unifying air. It gives her work transparency and an uncanny feeling of pre-Socratic time, as her birds fly through air "breaking through it minute by glass minute." Glass also helps convey a chastening sense of nature's nonsympathy and nonmalice; dissolution is never far off: "Alder, silently glazing us, the dead."

In 1966, Stevenson published a strong study of Elizabeth Bishop. In her essay on Bishop's nature description, we can discern Stevenson herself deciding what to do about the pathetic fallacy, lyric poetry's claim that landscape may be described as possessing human temperament or wishes. We know it's an insult to plants and animals to depict them in these terms. Yet to sing and to paint, we almost have to; and, finally, what other terms are there? Some of Stevenson's solutions to this problem (which becomes a nonproblem in a powerful elegy like **"The Man in the Wind"**) may be found in **"Swifts."** For one thing, she sings in truthful ways of how spring-starved humans feel about swifts by directly quoting a spring-starved human: "Face to the sun like a child / you shout 'The swifts are back!'" For another, she acknowledges the swifts' indifference to her joy in a passage which restricts itself to sound, motion, and form: "Swreeeee. Swreeeee. Another. And another. / It's the cut air falling in shrieks on our chimneys and roofs." She takes advantage of the fact that the swifts are observed in Britain by a poet permeated with British thought, history, legend: "These are the air pilgrims, pilots of air rivers." This, in turn, gives rise to a lovely myth which relates the swifts' peculiar motion to their imaginary personal foibles. Then she leaves the fable aside and moves to a contemporary assessment—"We have swifts, though in reality not parables"—without losing the breath of her enthusiasm. Though creatures live in a separate part of the universe, they remind us of things experienced through our own needs, rhythms, language: "A way to say the miracle will not occur. / And watch the miracle."

Numerous lyrics like this one draw the reader, line by idiosyncratic line, into a generous, educated, feelingful world of life in surrounding air. There is an interpenetration of self, time, and things: "When we belong to the world," she says in a poem about bearing a daughter, "we become what we are." Stevenson's personal geography gives her roots in both America and Britain. Many of her poems have been concerned with alternating between countries, and with how New England, say, and South Wales are alike and how different (as in **"Green Mountain, Black Mountain"**). Still, readers with different geographies will resonate to her regional descriptions, never over-enchanted, and to the tension and originality of her diction. It isn't original out of self-conscious formal experimentation; that would seem intrusive and irrelevant. Authenticity has come from digging deep into her own way of seeing, her aloneness.

Not only has she thought about whether we can plausibly take comfort in nature (the query is explicit and witty in **"He and It"**), she has posed the same question, and it really *is* the same question, about language. A number of comical, though not brittle, poems show that she knows academics and intellectuals, is up on their topics, and maintains a dialogue, open or internal, with a seductive and, to her, somewhat silly World of the Intellect. She comments on people, including herself, who, so

to speak, make a living in language: "How lucky we are / to have a room in language. We / who are known take pride in our hotel." But even these little epigrams usually return to life's true misery and how we fend it off, lamely or ingeniously as the case may be. Even the drolleries address a real problem: that of nature and history, which, though real, can only be framed in a glass of language, befogged by our living, our weeping, our rages, "the steamed, squeezed / eye of her kitchen window" (**"The Garden"**).

Some of the poems are like short stories; they describe people who can't see through the window at all but know only their own texts. Yet the most effective of the poems located in people's minds depict a mind much like Stevenson's, one that breathes, reads, and dreams plants (**"The Holly and the Ivy"**), animals (**"Whose Goat?"** a jewel), and months (the prodigious **"Sonnets for Five Seasons"**). These are her mind's and body's home, her witnesses to what preceded and what follows. Strong commitment to what follows emerges in **"The Fish Are All Sick"** and in poems where a woman poet says good-bye to her grown children. In the last piece, glass returns as the **"Transparencies"** of the poem title, then as the windows of a bus, as a film, as ice on a river, and as a lens which the poet struggles to focus on inexorable contradictions: the growing distances between kin and the wish for continued nearness.

*Sarah White, "Anne Stevenson's Weather Reports,"*
*in* The Village Voice, *Vol. XXVIII, No. 47, Novem-*
*ber 22, 1983, p. 48.*

# Carl Van Vechten

## 1880-1964

American novelist, critic, essayist, journalist, editor, and photographer.

Van Vechten was an important literary figure during the early decades of the twentieth century. He was an advocate of avant-garde literature and music and a supporter of ethnic art; these interests inform his fiction and his later work as a photographer. Van Vechten is best known as a patron of the Harlem Renaissance, an era of unprecedented excellence in black American art and literature during the 1920s and 1930s. However, his influence with the artists and writers of the Harlem Renaissance was seriously marred by controversy following the publication of *Nigger Heaven* (1926), a novel of life in Harlem that continues to elicit interest among contemporary critics.

Van Vechten was born into an affluent family in Cedar Rapids, Iowa. He attended the University of Chicago and graduated in 1903. Remaining in Chicago for the next three years, he was a reporter for *The Chicago American* before moving to New York City to become assistant music critic for *The New York Times*. Van Vechten also spent two years in Paris working for that newspaper as a cultural correspondent. Upon his return to America, he briefly served as a drama critic for *The New York Press*. The publication of his first book, *Music After the Great War* (1915), ensured his influence on American culture. He was one of the first American critics to praise such dancers as Isadora Duncan and Anna Pavlova and was credited with accelerating the popularity of modern dance in America. His series of articles on jazz, Negro spirituals, and blues, published in *Vanity Fair,* helped to establish their importance as legitimate musical forms. In addition, Van Vechten introduced to American readers the early works of Gertrude Stein.

Van Vechten's interest in black American culture began while he was a student in Chicago. He first became acquainted with the New York black intellectual set through Walter White, a respected essayist and a high-ranking official in the National Association for the Advancement of Colored People, and the poet James Weldon Johnson. Through his literary contacts Van Vechten aided many promising black writers, including Langston Hughes, whose first book of poetry was published by Van Vechten's own publisher, Alfred A. Knopf. Van Vechten reviewed many works written by blacks and wrote several articles featuring black entertainers. In addition, he served as a judge for several literary competitions sponsored by the NAACP and The Urban League. The parties given at his home became focal points of the Harlem Renaissance, and several professional relationships were initiated between black writers and influential editors and publishers at these events. Van Vechten was also popular among the nonliterary blacks in Harlem. He was a frequent patron of many businesses and speakeasies and was often asked to escort white celebrities and foreign dignitaries to Harlem's famous nightclubs. Despite his efforts to encourage black culture, many people questioned his sincerity, and some charged that Van Vechten was a dilettante.

Van Vechten's fiction is heavily influenced by the works of Ronald Firbank and Oscar Wilde. His novels, described by Joseph Warren Beach as "veritable guide books to Paris and New York," are satires of the leisure class. Van Vechten's fiction features lavish settings, frivolous characters in search of escape from the constraints of traditional society, and, in the words of Beach, "a mania for verbal virtuosity." Van Vechten's first novel, *Peter Whiffle: His Life and Works* (1922), is based on his travels to Paris and satirizes young American expatriates living in Europe. *The Blind Bow-Boy* (1923) dramatizes the reckless behavior of young, wealthy New Yorkers through the experiences of a spoiled and pampered young man. Iowa is the location of Van Vechten's third novel, *The Tattooed Countess* (1924). Set in a small town similar to that in which Van Vechten was raised, the novel concerns a well-to-do woman who returns to her hometown after years of living in Europe. In *Firecrackers* (1925) and *Nigger Heaven* Van Vechten returns to the fast-paced world of Manhattan. His last novel, *Parties* (1930), evokes a different mood from that of his earlier work. The novel depicts the despair of a couple who turn to alcohol as a shelter from reality.

*Nigger Heaven* launched a series of highly publicized debates within the Harlem community and the literary establishment. One of the major objections to the novel was its title, which some black critics defined as a "copyrighted racial slur." Van

Vechten insisted that "nigger heaven" was an ironic label used by Harlem blacks to describe the district; it also refers to the practice of admitting black patrons only to the upper balconies in theaters. Van Vechten defended *Nigger Heaven* as the story of a "boy from a small town . . . unable to meet the demands made on his character by life in a big city." He said it "gave readers a microcosm of American Negro life" and maintained that it was written as if "the characters had been white." Van Vechten strongly believed that *Nigger Heaven* would help generate better race relations by his portrayal of blacks as ordinary people. Although most white critics praised the book, D. H. Lawrence concluded that Van Vechten wrote it for shock value. Black critical opinion was sharply divided. James Weldon Johnson hailed Van Vechten as "the only white novelist . . . who has not viewed the Negro as a type." The distinguished activist and founder of the NAACP, W.E.B. DuBois, led the opposition to the book, describing its plot as perverse. Others charged that the book reinforced racial stereotypes and that Van Vechten exploited his relationships with blacks in order to capitalize on the conception of Harlem as decadent. Nevertheless, *Nigger Heaven* attained popular success and was translated into several languages.

After 1930, Van Vechten devoted his energies to philanthropic concerns and photography. Despite the furor over *Nigger Heaven,* the majority of his photographs were of black celebrities and others who made significant contributions to the arts. Van Vechten stopped writing altogether except for occasional introductions to books; he also served as Gertrude Stein's literary executor. Although his own fiction was written during the jazz age, Van Vechten never received the serious critical attention given to such contemporaries as F. Scott Fitzgerald and Ernest Hemingway. However, Van Vechten's novels enjoyed a loyal audience, and many now credit him with capturing the sophistication and rebelliousness of his generation.

(See also *Contemporary Authors,* Vols. 89-92 [obituary] and *Dictionary of Literary Biography,* Vols. 4, 9.)

## RANDOLPH BOURNE

Mr. Carl Van Vechten is [one of those writers who believe that to do a light essay all one needs is a light subject]. So in *The Merry-Go-Round* . . . he writes on Music and Cooking, De Senectute Cantorum, and then stuffs his pages with the most deplorably indigestible facts and anecdotes imaginable. For he is of that school of which James Huneker is the grandfather and H. L. Mencken the honored immediate sire. They are a curious crowd. They combine the utmost ferocity of conviction against the academic and the puritanical with a pedantic fondness for the ragbag of facts. They are, or have been, most of them, musical and theatrical critics or inveterate reviewers. And it is, of course, good for critics to be erudite. As reviewers their minds require and receive continual fertilization of after-the-play suppers and convivial glasses. . . . So into their writing, little by little, the facts do creep, the mere historical rubbish of the profession, and you get light essays like those of Mr. Van Vechten, delineating every instance where musicians and food have come into contact or reciting lists of the musical comedies he saw in his younger days. . . .

[To] read their work is as uncomfortable as taking out the stuffing of a sofa-pillow to rest your head against. And yet Mr. Van Vechten's intentions are evidently all for the light essay—for the bright unconventional sauntering about the mu-

sical, dramatic, and literary fair. But like the others of his school, his gustatory capacities are too enormous. He can swallow any amount of bad plays, and any number of pseudo-decadents like Edgar Saltus and Erik Satie. When he chooses out Feydeau and Mirbeau and Avery Hopwood and Philip Moeller to praise in the theater, you feel that hatred of puritanism has thrown his taste, as it has that of Mencken's, askew. His essay In Defense of Bad Taste argues in favor of sincerity, and that is good. But the trouble with his school, with the Menckens and the Nathans, is not that their taste is bad but that it is all disintegrated. They mire themselves in facts because their learning is not assimilated to their tastes. Neither are their tastes harmonious with each other. These critics appreciate the second-rate, not because they do not know any better, but because the whole slant of their judgment has tended to take up the defense of whatever the puritan mind most violently objects to. They have, one feels, let their taste be determined rather by negativing the puritan than by positively asserting a strong modern harmony of appreciation.

Mr. Van Vechten however deserves some mitigation of these strictures. He is always as sprightly as his intellectual dough will allow him to be. Where he can resist the clutch of facts, as in the little piece called Au Bal Musette, he is graphic and amusing. Here he has the light essay trembling on the very verge of the short story, and you find him writing with a power that you wish he would oftener avail himself of. He leaves the impression elsewhere of a talent that has been somewhat coarsened either by too much use or by a following of minor prophets. What saves him in the end is the freshness and warmth of his appreciations. The Impressions of the Theater, the notes on Mimi Aguglia, Isadora Duncan, and the Spanish dancers of The Land of Joy are fine pieces of discerning admiration. In a merry-go-round of criticism it is, after all, this fine cordiality of liking that the reader himself warms to. (p. 420)

*Randolph Bourne, "The Light Essay," in* The Dial, *Vol. LXV, No. 777, November 16, 1918, pp. 419-20.**

## MARY TERRILL

"In the Garret", by Carl Van Vechten, is the essay set to the music of dish-rattling in a table d'hôte restaurant. Mr. Van Vechten, one of the most readable and breeziest essayists of the day, refuses to sit in any chair. When he writes he runs. If he does sit for a moment, it is on the bar in some old tavern or on top of a trolleycar at Forty-seventh and Broadway. Therefore he writes. He eats and gallivants; therefore he lives.

He is a connoisseur of the vivid and the odd, of the flashing and the grotesque. His essays are the Midnight Frolics of a joyous, pagan soul. He is what Bohemia ought to be—Burgundy, charlotte russe and cymbalum. He has a magnificent way of being unimportant. His touch is light and artistic. His culture is Hunekeresque. His scholarship is musicianly, sometimes jazzy. **"In the Garret"** is a full meal—from soup to "nuts". (p. 193)

*Mary Terrill, "About Essays, and Three," in* The Bookman, *New York, Vol. LI, No. 2, April, 1920, pp. 192-95.**

## CARL VAN DOREN

There may be a line which separates fiction from biography, but it is a metaphysical affair about which no one need worry much. . . . [In **"Peter Whiffle"**] Carl Van Vechten has crossed the two literary forms fascinatingly. His hero has a *fin de siècle* look about him, as if he were, perhaps, a version of Stephen Crane or of one of his contemporaries. When Peter first dawns upon his biographer he has in mind to beat such decorative geniuses as Edgar Saltus at the art of producing fine effects by the sheer enumeration of lovely or definite things: he will make his masterpiece the catalogue of catalogues. Later, he has shifted to the mode of Theodore Dreiser, having been converted by "Sister Carrie," and is a revolutionist wedded to the slums. Eventually he turns to the occult and the diabolical and ends in about that spiritual longitude and latitude. Does Peter suggest some of Max Beerbohm's men too much? The question will be asked. At least it is certain that he is piquant, arresting, brightly mad. Whether in Paris or in New York he glitters in his setting. And that setting is even more of a triumph than the character of Peter. Mr. Van Vechten, however he made up his protagonist, has taken his setting from life: actual persons appear in it, actual places. He deals with it now racily, now poetically. He is full of allusions, of pungencies, of learning in his times. He knows how to laugh, he scorns solemnity, he has filled his book with wit and erudition. He is a civilized writer.

> Carl Van Doren, "The Roving Critic," in The Nation, Vol. CXIV, No. 2966, May 10, 1922, p. 569.*

## EDMUND WILSON

[*The essay from which this excerpt is taken was originally published in* The Dial, *October 1923.*]

Mr. Carl Van Vechten, in *The Blind Bow-Boy,* has tried his hand at a kind of burlesque fiction of which we have had all too little in America: the satiric iridescent novel of the type of *Zuleika Dobson* and *La Révolte des Anges;* and, though at times a little less fantastic, a little less surprising than one could wish, he gets away with it, on the whole, very well. You must remember that he has had the hardihood to go to New York for his rococo *Satyricon;* and you may imagine whether New York is recalcitrant. The result, in spite of all the green orchids and the rose-jade cysts for cosmetics that the author finds in East Nineteenth Street, may come closer to the prosaic reality— or conventional reality of fiction—than Mr. Van Vechten perhaps intended. The marriage of the hero, Harold, with the rich, boring, well-bred Alice Blake might almost have taken place in the New York of Edith Wharton. It is rather the figure of Campaspe Lorillard who exists on a high comic plane, and I am inclined to believe that the book should have centered about her rather than Harold. Campaspe craves no other activity than the luxurious enjoyment of her mind, thoughts and sensations, the play of an exquisite taste and the exercise of a ruthless intelligence; she snubs her husband with a regal kindness, yet declines any other attachment, and sees as little of her children as possible, thereby trebling their interest in her. The only member of her family who interests *her* is her mother, whom she calls by her first name. She is Mr. Van Vechten's most successful achievement. (pp. 68-9)

> Edmund Wilson, "Late Violets from the Nineties," in his The Shores of Light: A Literary Chronicle of the Twenties and Thirties, Farrar, Straus and Giroux, 1952, pp. 68-72.*

## JANET FLANNER

[The jacket on] *The Blind Bow-Boy* warns the reader that the contents are neither romantic, realistic, life, art, fantasy nor satire. . . . Conscious of the necessity for caution, the reader starts the first chapter like a child to whom the ice cream and cake at a party cannot be expected completely to make up for the strain of required good conduct.

Once in company with those of *The Blind Bow-Boy,* however, the reader's misapprehension ends. It is a lively crew. There is a tremendous rattle of rare china going on in the book, noisy before a vast parade of lovely continental loot on which the reader's queer hosts and hostesses make foreground and talk nights through. . . . It is a cartoon of the 1920's: locale, New York. And in America, as unique as a painted Trojan horse.

Its sad and conquering central figure is Harold Prewett, who comes of age, as the legend opens, in a Shavian situation. He meets for the first time his father, rich, eccentric, a victim of the cloak and suit trade. By him Harold is handed over to be tutored by a man who has answered the paternal advertisement demanding a person without morals. (pp. 259-60)

It seems to be a cartoon of orientation. And the consistent and sad development of Harold holds it in such good shape that the whole seems a sketch for a more than fair drawing, for the moment underestimated. Mr. Van Vechten has a talent, granting an erotic circumstance to each character, to hold the character to its own premise, thus letting each one, as Jurgen said, "deal fairly" by itself. Not one novelist in forty has such a talent. And if the characters, so far as wit goes and talking all the time, have better success in their house decorations, theirs is indeed a very human frailty. And even pretty houses are rare.

Such a type of book, gladly started by the author here in America, demands perfect writing as a perquisite. . . . It demands good writing as a city woman reasonably demands clean gloves. Ronald Firbank, whose corpulent Varmouth duchesses were presented here, direct from London, by Mr. Van Vechten, shows an interesting indifference to haste, or opinion, and has suavity in his result. America's precious writers, beginning with Huneker, are a little behind the British, what with the delay our culture suffered here, fighting Indians, British, and later, railroads.

If one may be allowed the flight of fancy—and only by taking it can one appreciate the historical picture Mr. Van Vechten has outlined and its peculiar veracity—there is, let us say, not far from the healthy skyscrapers of Manhattan, a floating island, visible particularly at night, from which glamorous lights, more glamorous new music and new speech signal back to the mainland. On this island dwells a group which once liked to épater la bourgeoisie but is now, in its higher sophistication, indifferent even while it shocks the intelligentsia. It is an island of habitual novelty, nerve ends and sensory obligations. On it, inventiveness produces no new machines for the home, pleasure no permanent privilege. There "male and female flutes," syncopation of the senses, love for beauty, and delight are normal. Pleasure is something to be thought out in advance, like a speech for a banquet. It is what is left of London's 1890's. It is our 1920's. Both are still periods of brilliance and decay. This island produces a shrill minute sound of civilization whose report, at a distance, is like hearsay of an overtone. Its disappearance will be as exciting a topic to a few of the succeeding generations as the problem of the lost Atlantis. (p. 260)

> Janet Flanner, in a review of "The Blind Bow-Boy," in The New Republic, Vol. XXXVI, No. 465, October 31, 1923, pp. 259-60.

## J. W. KRUTCH

There is a kind of romance, midway between sentiment and cynicism, which no American has ever yet written well. In stories of true love we have long been at home, and lately we have come to treat the drama of illegitimate passion without the more obvious sort of moralizing. But the latter is still, with us, a matter too serious for sentiment, and we are still too little familiar with it as an accepted social institution to take it lightly. . . . Passing as we just have from the age of innocence into the first excitement of disillusion we still look for great passions, legitimate or illegitimate, and we have come not yet to the point where, like some of the older, wearier peoples, we can accept sex and gallantry which are veiled only by exquisite manners as the most that man can well expect and as having in their own consciousness of their incompleteness a wistful charm.

It is this fact, perhaps, which explains the comparative failure of "**The Tattooed Countess.**" Mr. Van Vechten has wished, I think, to write a completely sophisticated novel, and he has certainly chosen a completely sophisticated plot, telling of an American countess who leaves Paris in middle age and returns to her native village in Iowa in the hope of forgetting there a love affair with a provincial opera singer. When she, snatching at love once more as her youth ends, becomes passionately enamored of a village boy, and when he, not because he fails to realize the temporary nature of his love but because he sees in her an escape, runs away with her to Paris, Mr. Van Vechten means that we shall see these actions not as mean but as wise. . . . In spite of all his grace of style and his wit the book is hardly more than a very clever stunt, an effort to capture a spirit which the author admires, but which he has learned instead of finding bred in his bones.

Various defects might be pointed out. It might be remarked, for example, that the author's knowledge of the world is too obviously paraded, that many tricks of style, including the use of strange words like "sciapodous" and "egrimoncy," give sometimes the impression of intolerable preciosity, and that the solemn references to fashionable places and things amount sometimes to snobbery. But most serious of all, perhaps, is the fact that, like nearly all Americans who are "advanced" in their literary ideas, Mr. Van Vechten suffers from the Main Street complex. Having brought the countess and the boy together he cannot resist the impulse to do a thing absolutely fatal to the non-moral romance, namely, to attempt to justify them. He must prove, what no thorough sophisticate would dream of thinking worth his while, that the life of the village is narrow, bigoted, and morally worse than the great world, and as a result we are treated to one more description of the sewing circle and the gossip party, the speech of the booster and the pronunciamentos of the villagers on the subject of art. The result is a mixture of styles which not even Mr. Van Vechten's skill can hold together. Indeed it is not difficult to detect three manners and to suspect that the mood of the book changed as the author wrote it. The fantastic title seems to belong to the opening portion, which is written in the style of rather extravagant satire; next comes the homely realism of the Gopher Prairie school of fiction, and finally the drama of disillusioned passion.

In spite of the fact that there are not infrequent passages of wit and that, as a whole, the book is amusing reading, it remains one which obviously did not grow but was made, and its artificial character is revealed by many things, including, for example, the rather clumsy documentation which leads the author to mention, one would guess, at least two hundred names of books, authors, pictures, etc., and to rely to a preposterous extent upon the opinions of his persons upon works of art to illustrate their characters. He has proposed to himself the writing of a certain kind of novel, highly sophisticated and stylistically elaborate, but the essentially literary character of his inspiration is evident in almost every line, and he has produced a book which seems constantly more in contact with other books than with life.

> *J. W. Krutch, "Artifice," in* The Nation, *Vol. CXIX, No. 3087, September 3, 1924, p. 241.*

## R. M. LOVETT

There is nothing tattooed about Mr. Van Vechten [in **The Tattooed Countess**]. He changes his spots as he might change his spats. After the whimsical extravagance of *Peter Whiffle* and the urbane persiflage of **The Blind Bow Boy,** with almost preternatural gravity he addresses himself to the well known problem of the return of the native. It is the cosmopolitan Countess Nattatorrini who returns to the provinces of her youth in Maple Valley, Iowa. There are the usual aspects of the situation, the homely reality of the midwestern American scene, the comedy of incomprehensible interests and incommensurable standards, the pathos of home ties broken by foreign intrigue, but Mr. Van Vechten does not seem greatly excited by them. . . . Mr. Van Vechten is a virtuoso who improvises variations upon well known themes with a technique which, in the total absence of feeling, is itself finely contemptuous. Yet there is an air of good faith about the performance which is disarming. Doubtless when Mr. Van Vechten is gathered to the snows of yesteryear some critic will discover that this is his first novel, and bears his haughty challenge: My foot is on my native heath, and my name is Van Vechten.

> *R. M. Lovett, in a review of "The Tattooed Countess," in* The New Republic, *Vol. XL, No. 510, September 10, 1924, p. 53.*

## THE SATURDAY REVIEW OF LITERATURE

"**Red**" is a collection of twelve papers of very uneven interest. Music critics, stodgy music of stodgy American composers, Stravinsky, orchestral programs, and chamber music are some of the subjects of [Van Vechten's] praises and discontents. There are engaging moments of spirited attack on established things. Mr. Van Vechten, like many concert goers, rebels against the ceaseless repetition of music that has long since said its last word. But he feels too wonderfully advanced because seven years ago he wanted to hear Stravinsky. Many, many others were of the same mind even longer ago than seven years. Does the author imagine that Stravinsky came to his regular place because of this seven-year-old clamor?

The book is entertaining, witty, clever, and quite unimportant. The style is diluted Huneker with a dash of Mencken. "Cordite for Concerts," the concluding essay, is wholly enjoyable. With a deft touch Van Vechten reviews much of the music we hear too often in concert, and arranges the composers in amusing categories.

The most amusing thing about "**Red**" is that it isn't red. It is a pleasant and inoffensive pink that will not enrage anyone.

A review of "Red: Papers on Musical Subjects," in The Saturday Review of Literature, Vol. I, No. 39, April 25, 1925, p. 711.

## DONALD DOUGLAS

Whenever Carl Van Vechten brings out a new novel I read "Alice in Wonderland." Mr. Van Vechten called "**The Tattooed Countess**" a romantic novel and now he calls "**Firecrackers**" a realistic novel, and by those legends he sends me to "Alice in Wonderland." It isn't at all that his definitions are lacking in absolute truth. It is only that "**The Tattooed Countess**" is less romantic than "Alice in Wonderland" and "**Firecrackers**" is less realistic than "Through the Looking Glass." Of course if you look carefully you will find something of George Moore and something of Oscar Wilde in the works of Carl Van Vechten, but most of all you will find the deliberate method and procedure of "Alice." What else can you say when you find Mr. Van Vechten collecting fantastics and bringing them together for the purpose of wit and verbal escapades? They have nothing in common with one another except that they live in the same book. They do not develop the plot by the slow groundswell of a complicated harmony. They meet in scenes and lives disjoined and they perform an antic of words and a fantasy of lives. If only Mr. Van Vechten were as inspired in his creative capacity as he is correct in his method of "realism" he might some day invent a character as witty as the Mad Hatter or as charming as Alice or as implacable as the Red Queen. He never quite gets there. His firecrackers sizzle and flare but they do not burst into red and blue and green, and as often as not something seems to have poured cold water upon their fuses. "**Firecrackers**" is one of those obscure performances which leave the beholder puzzled to explain exactly the presence of so many damp squibs. (p. 492)

It may be that the characters in Mr. Van Vechten's books spring too rapidly full-blown from the head of their creator. None of them except Campaspe seem to have had time for birth and growing pains and substance and nourishment from the blood of their own life. Even as fantastics they lack the completion of such individual portraits as the Red Queen, the White Knight, and the Duchess. They do not so much explode like firecrackers as shine like pale, pleasant ghosts in fashionable drawing-rooms of the intellectually unemployed. (p. 491)

Donald Douglas, "Damp Powder," in The Nation, Vol. CXXI, No. 3147, October 28, 1925, pp. 491-92.

## JOSEPH WARREN BEACH

Mr. Van Vechten is the Baedeker of the intelligentsia. His novels are veritable guide books to Paris and New York, with the stars on everything that Baedeker leaves undistinquished and E. V. Lucas ignores. In "**Peter Whiffle**" he devotes many solid pages to a list of the things he did in Paris during his visit there in his twenties. He concludes with the modest declaration: "In short, you will observe that I did everything that young Americans do when they go to Paris." It is a very modest declaration. What he means is that he did very much more than other young Americans do, having inside information, and that other young Americans will do well to profit by his suggestions. . . . They can follow Mr. Van Vechten to lunch at the Deux Magots in the company of unidentified artists presided over by the two bland grotesques. They can learn from him where to get their perfumery and dresses, if they are women, what bars and music-halls to frequent, if they are men, where,

in either case, to find Brittany china-ware and impressionist paintings. They can learn to speak easily of Dranem and Max Dearly, André Gide and Jeanne Bloch.

In the later chapters of "**Peter Whiffle**," Mr. Van Vechten does much the same things for New York, and in "**The Blind Bow-Boy**" again, the scene is New York. . . . The cultural specialty of the book is perhaps the many detailed descriptions of interiors anything but banal in decoration; the reader has but to turn the leaves to learn what pictures and bibelots are the last word for the salon of a lady, the bedroom of a duke, or the boudoir of a kept (a very well-kept!) woman. (p. 66)

The reader who likes to be "in the know"—and who of us is exempt from this pardonable, nay, this intellectual aspiration?—must perforce be grateful to Mr. Van Vechten for his useful hints. It may seem ungracious to suggest that the thing is overdone. But indeed it does smack a bit of ostentation. Our author seems in such a hurry to pluck his flowers, to bring in his armful of novelties, as if he feared that some one might get ahead of him. He is so much concerned to avoid the commonplace, to deal solely in the caviare. He loses no opportunity to present a list of things,—of pictures, music, books. He catalogues the libraries of his friends. He reminds us of the hostess who gives to the newspapers a complete list of her guests.

There is a passion for things of the mind, and there is another passion for being in the know. Most widespread of all ambitions of young men is the ambition to order the right drinks. (p. 67)

In literary theory and in his own practice Mr. Van Vechten displays the same passion for the last word of modernity. The word which he finds is the word sophistication and the evidence of sophistication is, in his view, a light ironic manner. In "**The Blind Bow-Boy**" the mouthpiece of his ideals is a New York society woman who for all feeling and for all sentiment seems to have substituted a lively set of opinions on esthetics. She has, for one thing, no patience with the heavy manner of Waldo Frank and Theodore Dreiser. . . .

> The tragedies of life, she reflected, were either ridiculous or sordid. The only way to get the sense of this absurd, contradictory, and perverse existence into a book was to withdraw entirely from the reality. The artist who feels most poignantly the bitterness of life wears a persistent and sardonic smile. . . .

What indeed could be more up-to-the-minute than such sophistication, such disillusion, such a sense of the tragic futility of life? It is particularly prevailing, particularly natural, in war-disordered Europe. One cannot read such books as "La Négresse du Sacré-Coeur" or Paul Morand's "Fermé la Nuit" without receiving a dismal impression of a world bewildered, in which not merely destiny but even man is without aim, without hope, without values. One receives the same impression from a show of paintings in which the artists have deliberately renounced all charm of line, all splendor of color and light, from a concert of music made up of nervous jerks and snarls and ending forever off key in a whimpering question. There is a certain character to much of this work, a deal of ingenuity and erudition, and it seems indeed the sincere expression of a characteristic view of life. It is the art of our time in Europe, and as such must be respected. (pp. 67-8)

In Mr. Van Vechten's books the serious things are certainly well hidden. An amusing creation is Peter Whiffle, this runaway from Toledo, who has exhausted all the force of his will in escaping from the mediocrity of his father's bank and espousing vaguely the life of art, this irresolute artist who can never make up his mind on any question, and who drifts from one absurd theory of writing to another without ever putting any into practice. But he does not seem to stand for anything more significant than futility in the abstract. It might be supposed at times that it is all intended for a satire on the type of writing represented by Mr. Van Vechten, only it is too evident that his creator shares with him his enthusiasm for literary ideals out of the common road, no matter what, so long as they are surprising and *not* shared by the vulgar.

"**The Blind Bow-Boy**" appears to be intended for a study in disillusion. But disillusion implies the loss of ideals, and Harold Prewett is not known to have had any ideals to lose. The story serves actually as an occasion for the author to parade such figures as Campaspe and the Duke of Middlebottom,— people whose aim in life is to seek out new gratifications for their esthetic vanity. One remembers the words of Flaubert: "I seek new perfumes, larger flowers, pleasures untried." But there is none of the holy passion of Flaubert in these lives, there is little but the complacency of Flaubert's contemporaries whose aim in life was to shock their neighbors, *épater les bourgeois*. And they and their discovery, the child of nature, Zimbule O'Grady, give the author his opportunity to shock the bourgeois a little on his own account,—an exercise which, for the rest, has now at last its market value in America.

It is clear from many indications that the great models of Mr. Van Vechten are George Moore ( of the "Confessions of a Young Man") and Huysmans (of "À Rebours"),—men who so loved to swim against the current of their time. It is a bit ironic indeed to consider that, of this author so proud of bringing us ever the last word in the arts, they should say now on the rue de l'Odéon that, compared with Waldo Frank, he is old-style, still walking in the track of "À Rebours." "À Rebours" is verily the bible of those who follow the cult of the rare, of the *au delà de l'art*. But we find in Van Vechten none of the heat and depth of feeling of the hero Des Esseintes, who, when he had to return to vulgar Paris from his aristocratic seclusion, addressed his fervent prayer to a god in whom he did not believe. . . . We know that, beneath the crust of vanity, of snobbishness, there was in Huysmans the profound love of a cultivated man for whatever is rare, the patience and tenacity of a scholar, and the desperation of a man bent on saving his soul, who in the end did save it in the one way he could conceive.

In his American disciple we tap the crust of vanity in anxious and uncertain hopes of finding something solid underneath.

As for the disciple of George Moore, we should acclaim him with enthusiasm if he gave promise of some day presenting us with an "Esther Waters" or an "Evelyn Innes." . . . Already in those early days Mr. Moore had achieved a style strong, supple, and above all simple. He was already an English purist of the school of Oscar Wilde,—another of Mr. Van Vechten's admirations. It was from the best French models that these men learned to write such impeccable English, in a classic manner worthy of Congreve and Addison. Very different is the ideal of Mr. Van Vechten as set forth in the preface to "**Peter Whiffle**." In his testamentary letter to his friend Van Vechten, Peter Whiffle explained how difficult it was to recover the lucid moments of vision when he was potentially an author. . . . It is perhaps a pardonable vanity on the part of the author to claim for himself a success which has been so gen-

erally accorded him by the critics. London and New York unite to grant him, as his dominant quality, glitter, and New York has added the revealing judgment that "he has some very happy hits in verbal virtuosity."

The phrase is most appropriate, reproducing so well in its alliterative and slightly facetious turn some of the means by which Mr. Van Vechten produces his effect of glitter. He is for one thing, a diligent collector of rare words from the most out-of-the-way places, and his pages sparkle with outlandish terms as the diadem of an actress sparkles with apocryphal gems: koprologniac tastes, adscititious qualities, fragrant acervation, dehiscent jaw, pimpant and steatopygous figures, pinguid and amblyoptic gentlemen. There is to be sure nothing new in this. It has long been a recognized device of humorous writing in English—not the humor of Swift or of Max Beerbohm—to provoke the reader's smile by saying simple things in elephantine periphrasis. And Mr. Van Vechten is fond of the sort of wit which consists in saying "paronomasia" where he means a play on words, "vocatively adjured" where he means severely prohibited, "impinging on her consciousness" where he means coming into her mind, and "a feline death scene" where he means the death of a cat.

But such individual flowers of rhetoric give but an inadequate idea of the quality of his style when he is most conscious of the call for verbal virtuosity. (pp. 68-70)

A captious reader might complain of such an intemperate use of alliteration as passing the bounds of discreet humor and verging on the burlesque. He will open the book at random and come upon phrases like this, "moodily occupied with such morbid meditations," and sentences like this: "These wasters, apparently, incessantly staggered about seeking sensation." And a reader versed in the virtuosity of Meredith or Lamb is inclined to wonder whether he should not attribute to the awkwardness rather than the cleverness of the author these jaw-breaking series of adverbs, "apparently incessantly staggered," "a particularly ornately constructed sofa;" these staggering series of infinitive phrases, "to look back at this figure who seemed to be pretending to be unaware," "to get on sufficiently well to enable him to support his wife."

A writer less enamoured of the capricious style would have asked himself whether there was no way to avoid these awkward combinations. And he would have seen at once that, in avoiding the awkwardness he might at the same time contribute to the lucidity and forcefulness of his writing. George Moore would never have said, "to get on sufficiently well to enable him to support his wife." He would have said simply, "to get on sufficiently well to support his wife." Oscar Wilde would never have said, "completely confident that his father was certainly more terrified," but simply "confident that his father was more terrified." It would be to say everything that Mr. Van Vechten says and to spare us both of the offending adverbs.

It is not fashionable in our day, and it may be thought pedantic, to point out the habitual misuse of English in popular writers. But when it is a question of an author who has a reputation for style, it might be a consideration of real value in determining whether his reputation is deserved. The unit of musical excellence is the musical phrase. The unit of excellence in English style is the English word. (pp. 70-1)

And so when I find myself inclined to question the formula of Mr. Van Vechten, when I am in doubt how much to allow for certain amusing inventions in an author who strikes me as rather flashy, I say it may be helpful to take into consideration the elementary features of style. And it seems to me not without significance that he is constantly misusing English words: that he uses betray when he means discover ("Only once did Harold betray what he thought was a trace of affectation in the Duke"), that he uses withal when he means although ("withal this taste was somewhat bizarre"), communication where he means communion ("he held daily communication with himself"), aggrandize where he means increase ("a suspicion which seemed to aggrandize with every new opportunity"), and scantily where he means hardly or slightly (a man "scantily past thirty," i.e. insufficiently past thirty—when was ever man insufficiently past thirty?); and that all this he does in one of the latest of his ten published volumes, and one that represents presumably the maturity of his style. And it seems not without significance, too, that these slips are generally made in the use of words a bit archaic, or rare, or otherwise showy, as where, again, he says of the Duke that he "seemed free from a mania for exhibitionism." He means simply exhibitionism, or a mania for making a show of himself. But exhibitionism is a somewhat technical word, and the author betrays himself a little in his mania for verbal virtuosity.

But there is always, one says, the glitter. And one thinks of Meredith, one thinks of Anatole France. One is prepared for the pointed phrase, the flashing figure of speech, sharp as a sword, the amusing paradox, the intellectual illumination. Here at least, one says, there will be no truce with cliché, no compromise with the banal, no drab and messy figures, no flavor of the bromide. And one opens the book on such gems as these: "Friendship, indeed, is as perilous a relationship as marriage; it, too, entails responsibility, that great god whose existence burdens our lives;" where the precious stone of thought is so innocent of the cutter's tool, so little disengaged from its native ore. Or such an epigram as this: "I think it is Oscar Wilde who has written, only mediocre minds are consistent. There is something very profound in this aphorism." I find it hard to believe that Oscar Wilde should ever have let go so flat and unfashioned a saying. Perhaps Mr. Van Vechten is thinking of Emerson's more pointed version: "With consistency great souls have nothing to do." (pp. 71-2)

And one wonders whether, if this be not actually the last word of modern style, it may not be perhaps the "limit" of the banal. (p. 72)

*Joseph Warren Beach, "The Peacock's Tail," in* American Speech, *Vol. I, No. 2, November, 1925, pp. 65-73.*

## EDWARD DAVIDSON

Mr. Van Vechten has chosen to excavate in some very sandy soil. Most of his pits are shallow and the winds of a season will easily level out the earth he has disturbed. His avowed purpose—[in **"Excavations"**]—to provoke the reader of his essays to share his enthusiasm for certain obscure figures in the worlds of literature and music—would be excellent but for the fact that so many of his enthusiasms are not worth communicating. His literary judgment, in general, is ill-considered and immature. His manner is at once knowing and mellow but it cannot disguise the superficiality of his literary tastes nor their exceptionally restricted character. He has no real sense of literary values and almost less of what may be called "life-values." . . .

Mr. Van Vechten's enthusiasms are not those of a critic and man of letters at ease among his books so much as they are

the enthusiasms of a rather neurotic mind searching for the exotic and the bizarre. The paper on Edgar Saltus, for instance, might well have laid more stress on that author's wit and skill and less on his abnormal and pornographic leanings. Mr. Van Vechten, here and elsewhere, pauses a little too often to lick his lips over such amiable themes as cicisbeism and incest. The spectacle is more dull than disgusting. And nothing is proved in Ronald Firbank's cause by his admirer's cheap sneer—"These novels are not suitable for public libraries and Brander Matthews and William Lyon Phelps will never review them." Mr. Van Vechten has yet to learn how to be effectively supercilious. When he can do the thing as well as it has been done by some of his literary heroes, Oscar Wilde, Ronald Firbank, *et al.*, literature will know how to welcome him. At present his pretentiousness is altogether out of proportion to his achievements as a man of letters. In the meantime, praise is due for the essays on Dedications, and an ingenious discussion of the later works of Herman Melville. He cannot patronize Ouida in any way that carries conviction to the reader. Mr. Van Vechten's ingenuity is rather destroyed by his lack of ideas. There is too much allusion and too little real thought in his book. Under the mask of the essayist-critic (for we are not to be fobbed off by his statement that these are not essays in criticism) appears the mere dilettante. The crying need in modern America is for a reasoned and sober, if not authoritative criticism of the arts, particularly of literature. Mr. Van Vechten has his opportunity, but there is little in [**"Excavations"**] to suggest that he will profit by it.

*Edward Davidson, "Peter Whiffle Incognito," in* The Saturday Review of Literature, *Vol. II, No. 26, January 23, 1926, p. 507.*

## EDWIN CLARK

It must be confessed that Mr. Van Vechten has never apparently had the modern serious attitude for literature, though he is much occupied with nuance, charm, and humors. So naturally enough, in this light, his new novel, **"Nigger Heaven,"** while a pioneering effort in its study of the negroes in their Harlem district, is hardly a startling variation.

To the old theatrical term for the top gallery he has brought a new significance, for his title, **"Nigger Heaven,"** stands for the haven that the Harlem district has provided for the new negro. Here, within the City of New York, the negro has a miniature city of his own-making—"a City of Refuge." Here there is a society of various strata that is variegated, racy, stolid and very much like the composition of other social orders elsewhere. In the course of his novel, Van Vechten runs the gamut from low life to high life. Here the questions, the social problems of race and color, are living incidents, subjected to the quirks of humanity rather than logic. . . .

[The hero of **"Nigger Heaven,"** Byron Kasson,] wanted to be a writer; yet he found he had little to say. He was under the delusion that he had been educated at college and was now ready to conquer. He hadn't any money except what his father gave him. He was extremely sensitive—his shyness was such that he lost poise in society—and his touchiness brought down upon his head many imaginary slights that hurt him. At heart he was a snob and felt superior. Still, he was race-conscious and proud; his racial pride, however, was so lacking in humility that he found it difficult to see his brother in the more primitive negro. Between his imaginary obstacles and the actual, life was difficult. His pride was such that it kept him from going to those older who would have directed him. His color made it difficult for him, on his own, to find any employment but manual labor. Brooding over his troubles pulled his nerves taut and made him more susceptible to weaknesses and impulsiveness. The inferiority complex had a perfect feeding ground in Byron. On top of that he fell in love.

Mary Love was the daughter of a middle class, educated negro. She was a librarian. She perceived the life about her through her intellect rather than her emotions. . . . Her life of books, concerts, theatre-going, friendly acquaintances with the new writers, was in it itself sufficient. She was a retiring, soft spoken, golden brown girl, into whose life Byron brought change.

As is usual in a Van Vechten novel, there is a divided interest. In his prologue he introduces his background and a few characters that are woven in and out of the subsequent narrative. He also introduces Mary and Byron to each other at a weekend house party of the smart set on Long Island. Book I gives the emphasis of the story to Mary. Book II is Byron's story. This technique is a variant of the old wheel method. Mr. Van Vechten continues to put his foot through all the rules of narrative, and by his sheer skill in handling situations and style of writing, carries off his effects with entertaining and satisfactory results. He has also effected through the medium of interpolated verses and songs an element of refrain that serves in the manner of a Greek chorus. . . .

The story of Byron is that of disintegrating character. He loses his own self-respect. He is inarticulate. He demands too much of himself. He is so sensitive and proud that his ambition muddles his groping thought and makes him too suspicious. Absurdly and humanly he wants to begin at the top, instead of working up from the bottom. . . .

Turning to the night life of the Harlem cabarets for escape, Byron becomes the prey of a rich, predatory widow. The fascinating Lasca Sartoris, ingratiating and corrupt to the limits of civilized decadence, takes Byron for her momentary plaything. Taking him away from Mary gratifies her sense of power and her purpose in life of getting everything she desires. In the gaudy background which she offers, Byron is but a child trusting in the kindness, the reliance of a beautiful, diabolical Cytherea. In the inevitable crescendo of disillusion, bitterness, psychologic and melodramatic travail, the story comes to a vivid and dramatic close under gaudy and jazz circumstances.

Striking characterizations deftly drawn abound in this novel. The Scarlet Creeper, Anatole Longfellow, the bullying and picturesque procurer, is a lively character who is indirectly entangled with the fate of Byron. There is the worldly ex-diva of the music halls, sympathetic and kindly to Mary, who tries to marry her off to the self-made, crude, good hearted Mr. Pettijohn, the Bolito King. Then there are the Sumners, wealthy and respectable, who entertain Gareth Johns, the novelist, also Campaspe Lorillard and Edith Dale from earlier Van Vechten novels. For contrast we have Hester Albright, middle-aged spinster, and her mother, who find the society of Harlem much inferior to that of Washington. They do not approve of the new negro and the literature of the new negro. They feel that the primitive art of the African is best forgot. A smug, conservative respectability is their ideal. Life in Harlem, strangely enough, is revealed in universal terms, with its younger generation and the frills thrown in.

Mr. Van Vechten has written a novel of absorbing interest. Its psychology is quite remote from the obvious, its candor is searching. He has observed the scene in the whole and shrewdly set down with more than good reporting what he has seen. And the novel has other interest than the stimulant of a new subject. Doubtless flaws may be found in his conception, but in the main his contentions are basically sound. It is in understanding and insight into varied personalities that he has performed with such capital skill. The effect of class psychology, the color taboo and its reaction are all adroitly placed and considered in his human motivation. His style in general is simpler, limpid and light; its attractive capacity for the picturesque and exotic is given play, but limited to the occasional need.

> *Edwin Clark, "Carl Van Vechten's Novel of Harlem Negro Life," in* The New York Times Book Review, *August 22, 1926, p. 2.*

## JAMES WELDON JOHNSON

Whether you like it or dislike it you will read [*Nigger Heaven*] through, every chapter, every page. Mr. Van Vechten is the first white novelist of note to undertake a portrayal of modern American Negro life under metropolitan conditions. Mr. Van Vechten is also the only white novelist I can now think of who has not viewed the Negro as a type, who has not treated the race as a unit, either good or bad. . . .

It was inevitable that the colorful life of Harlem would sooner or later claim the pen of Carl Van Vechten. He has taken the material it offered him and achieved the most revealing, significant and powerful novel based exclusively on Negro life yet written. A Negro reviewer might pardonably express the wish that a colored novelist had been the first to take this material and write a book of equal significance and power. Mr. Van Vechten is a modernist. In literature he is the child of his age. In *Nigger Heaven* he has written a modern novel in every sense. He has written about the most modern aspects of Negro life, and he has done it in the most modern manner; for he has completely discarded and scrapped the old formula and machinery for a Negro novel. He has no need of a *deus ex machina* from the white world either to involve or evolve the plot. There is, of course, the pressure of the white world, but it is external. The white characters are less than incidental. The story works itself out through the clashes and reactions of Negro character upon Negro character. Its factors are the loves, the hates, the envies, the ambitions, the pride, the shamelessness, the intelligence, the ignorance, the goodness, the wickedness of Negro characters. In this the author pays colored people the rare tribute of writing about them as people rather than as puppets. This representation of Negro characters in a novel as happy or unhappy, successful or unsuccessful, great or mean, not because of the fortuitous attitudes of white characters in the book but because of the way in which they themselves meet and master their environment—a task imposed upon every group—is new, and in close accord with the present psychology of the intelligent element of the race. The only other full length novel following this scheme that I can recall at this moment is Jessie Fauset's *There Is Confusion*. It is a scheme for the interpretation of Negro life in America that opens up a new world for colored writers.

There are those who will prejudge the book unfavorably on account of the title. . . . Indeed, one gauge of the Negro's rise and development may be found in the degrees in which a race epithet loses its power to sting and hurt him. . . . [The] title of *Nigger Heaven* is taken from the ironic use of the phrase made by the characters in the book. But whatever may be the attitudes and opinions on this point, the book and not the title is the thing. In the book Mr. Van Vechten does not stoop to burlesque or caricature. There are characters and incidents in the book that many will regard as worse than unpleasant, but always the author handles them with sincerity and fidelity. Anatoles and Rubys and Lascas and number kings and cabarets and an underworld there are as well as there are Mary Loves and Byron Kassons and Olive Hamiltons and Howard Allisons and Dr. Lancasters and Underwoods and Sumners and young intellectuals. There are, too, Dick Sills and Buda Greens, living on both sides of the line, and then passing over. It is all life. It is all reality. And Mr. Van Vechten has taken these various manifestations of life and, as a true artist, depicted them as he sees them rather than as he might wish them to be. But the author, again as a true artist, deftly maintains the symmetry and proportions of his work. The scenes of gay life, of night life, the glimpses of the underworld, with all their tinsel, their licentiousness, their depravity serve actually to set off in sharper relief the decent, cultured, intellectual life of Negro Harlem. (p. 316)

The book is written with Mr. Van Vechten's innate light touch and brilliancy, but there is a difference: Van Vechten, the satirist, becomes in *Nigger Heaven* Van Vechten, the realist. In every line of the book he shows that he is serious. But however serious Van Vechten may be, he cannot be heavy. He does not moralize, he does not over-emphasize, there are no mock heroics, there are no martyrdoms. And, yet—Mr. Van Vechten would doubtless count this a defect—the book is packed full of propaganda. Every phase of the race question, from Jim Crow discriminations to miscegenation, is frankly discussed. Here the author's inside knowledge and insight are at times astonishing. But it is not the author speaking, he makes his characters do the talking, and makes each one talk in keeping with his character. If the book has a thesis it is: Negroes are people; they have the same emotions, the same passions, the same shortcomings, the same aspirations, the same graduations of social strata as other people. It will be a revelation, perhaps, a shock to those familiar only with the Negro characters of Thomas Nelson Page, Thomas Dixon and Octavius Cohen. It is the best book Mr. Van Vechten has done, and that is saying a good deal when we remember *Peter Whiffle*.

*Nigger Heaven* is a book which is bound to be widely read and one which is bound to arouse much diverse discussion. This reviewer would suggest reading the book before discussing it. (p. 330)

> James Weldon Johnson, "Romance and Tragedy in Harlem—A Review," in Opportunity, Vol. 4, No. 46, October, 1926, pp. 316-17, 330.

## ERIC WALROND

"Nigger Heaven" is the epic of a mood. At the outset there is much in it to excite and erupt, be one black or white, for it abounds in objectivity and truth. A deeply subjective study, from an exotic Nordic viewpoint, of an ebony Paris, it yet has its moments of racial fidelity and abiding reality. Here, despite a deceptive prologue, is no low-lifed darkey cabaret tale; no plaintive Negro tragedy of flight into virgin Northern wastes. Here is no jazz pæan to the musty rodents of an Upper Fifth Avenue basement. Mr. Van Vechten's concern is of a soberer kind. With the mantle of a showman and the sagacity of a journalist he has anticipated the mob and enthusiastically explored the glimmering summits of High Harlem. There he found, shrouded and gay, a Negro dream-world enchanting in

its bewilderments. Its complex vastness, its eternal varieties left him excited and chaotic. His sympathies, however, following a tradition begun in "The Blind Bow-Boy" and "The Tattooed Countess," took him above the "lower Negro depths" to an austere colored upper crust.

Going above One Hundred and Twenty-fifth Street, Mr. Van Vechten was careful to be armed. His coat was of sparkling mail; his passions studied, distilled. But Striver's Row is the one flexible spot in the engaging chrysalis that is Harlem and yielded much in excess of Mr. Van Vechten's wildest dreams. Among its dark-skinned aristocracy he expected to find, presumably, evidences of "culture," the source of jazz, swaggering opulence, "instinctive" gayety; but hardly, I gather, heirlooms of a pale, dim ancestral past, mulatto aversion to black, a dominant tribal spirit, snobbishness, delightful crudity, neuroses, intellectuality. For all these Mr. Van Vechten found, and more. . . .

The reaction to "Nigger Heaven" will be varied and tremendous. Colored people, who for the most part object to its title, will outlaw the lush lingo and the decadent cabaret passages on the ground that a white man wrote them and that "they do not show the race at its best." On the other hand, the majority of white people will prefer the Creeper's slinking cruises on the Avenue to the glowing glimpses of splendor among the dusky Harlem smart set.

In the last analysis, however, "Nigger Heaven" will be pointed to as a frontier work of an enduring order. As literature with a strong social bias it prepares the way for examination of the fruits of a cultural flowering among the Negroes which is now about to emerge.

And no colored man, adept as he might be at self-observation and non-identification, could have written it.

> Eric Walrond, "The Epic of a Mood," in The Saturday Review of Literature, Vol. III, No. 10, October 2, 1926, p. 153.

## W.E.D.B. [W.E.B. DU BOIS]

Carl Van Vechten's "Nigger Heaven" is a blow in the face. It is an affront to the hospitality of black folk and to the intelligence of white. First, as to its title: my objection is based on no provincial dislike of the nickname. "Nigger" is an English word of wide use and definite connotation. As employed by Conrad, Sheldon, Allen and even Firbank, its use was justifiable. But the phrase, "Nigger Heaven," as applied to Harlem is a misnomer. "Nigger Heaven" does not mean, as Van Vechten once or twice intimates, . . . a haven for Negroes—a city of refuge for dark and tired souls; it means in common parlance, a nasty, sordid corner into which black folk are herded, and yet a place which they in crass ignorance are fools enough to enjoy. Harlem is no such place as that, and no one knows this better than Carl Van Vechten. . . .

I find this novel neither truthful nor artistic. It is not a true picture of Harlem life, even allowing for some justifiable impressionistic exaggeration. It is a caricature. It is worse than untruth because it is a mass of half-truths. (p. 81)

The author counts among his friends numbers of Negroes of all classes. He is an authority on dives and cabarets. But he masses this knowledge without rule or reason and seeks to express all of Harlem life in its cabarets. To him the black cabaret is Harlem; around it all his characters gravitate. Here is their stage of action. Such a theory of Harlem is nonsense. The overwhelming majority of black folk there never go to cabarets. The average colored man in Harlem is an everyday laborer, attending church, lodge and movie and as conservative and as conventional as ordinary working folk everywhere.

Something they have which is racial, something distinctively Negroid can be found; but it is expressed by subtle, almost delicate nuance, and not by the wildly, barbaric drunken orgy in whose details Van Vechten revels. There is laughter, color and spontaneity at Harlem's core, but in the current cabaret, financed and supported largely by white New York, this core is so overlaid and enwrapped with cheaper stuff that no one but a fool could mistake it for the genuine exhibition of the spirit of the people.

To all this the author has a right to reply that even if the title is an unhappy catch-phrase for penny purposes and his picture of truth untruthful, that his book has a right to be judged primarily as a work of art. Does it please? Does it entertain? Is it a good and human story? In my opinion it is not. . . . "Nigger Heaven" is to me an astonishing and wearisome hodgepodge of laboriously stated facts, quotations and expressions, illuminated here and there with something that comes near to being nothing but cheap melodrama. Real human feelings are laughed at. Love is degraded. The love of Byron and Mary is stark cruelty and that of Lasca and Byron is simply nasty. Compare this slum picture with Porgy. In his degradation, Porgy is human and interesting. But in "Nigger Heaven" there is not a single loveable character. There is scarcely a generous impulse or a beautiful ideal. The characters are singularly wooden and inhuman. . . . [Van Vechten's] women's bodies have no souls; no children palpitate upon his hands; he has never looked upon his dead with bitter tears. Life to him is just one damned orgy after another, with hate, hurt, gin and sadism. (pp. 81-2)

All he hears is noise and brawling. Again and again with singular lack of invention he reverts to the same climax of two creatures tearing and scratching over "mah man"; lost souls who once had women's bodies; and to Van Vechten this spells comedy, not tragedy. . . .

I cannot for the life of me see in this work either sincerity or art, deep thought, or truthful industry. It seems to me that Mr. Van Vechten tried to do something bizarre and he certainly succeeded. I read "Nigger Heaven" and read it through because I had to. But I advise others who are impelled by a sense of duty or curiosity to drop the book gently in the grate and to try the *Police Gazette*. (p. 82)

> *W.E.D.B. [W.E.B. Du Bois], in a review of "Nigger Heaven," in* The Crisis, *Vol. 33, No. 2, December, 1926, pp. 81-2.*

## D. H. LAWRENCE

*[The essay from which this excerpt is taken was originally written in 1926.]*

[*Nigger Heaven*] is a nigger book, and not much of a one. It opens and closes with nigger cabaret scenes in feeble imitation of Cocteau or Morand, second-hand attempts to be wildly lurid, with background effects of black and vermilion velvet. The middle is a lot of stuffing about high-brow niggers, the heroine being one of the old-fashioned school-teacherish sort, this time an assistant in a public library; and she has only one picture in her room, a reproduction of the Mona Lisa, and on her

shelves only books by James Branch Cabell, Anatole France, Jean Cocteau, etc.; in short, the literature of disillusion. This is to show how refined she is. She is just as refined as any other "idealistic" young heroine who earns her living, and we have to be reminded continually that she is golden-brown.

Round this heroine goes on a fair amount of "race" talk, nigger self-consciousness which, if it didn't happen to mention it was black, would be taken for merely another sort of self-conscious grouch. There is a love-affair—a rather palish-brown—which might go into any feeble American novel whatsoever. And the whole coloured thing is peculiarly colourless, a second-hand dish barely warmed up.

The author seems to feel this, so he throws in a highly-spiced nigger in a tartan suit, who lives off women—rather in the distance—and two perfect red-peppers of nigger millionairesses who swim in seas of champagne and have lovers and fling them away and sniff drugs; in short, altogether the usual old bones of hot stuff, warmed up with all the fervour the author can command—which isn't much.

[*Nigger Heaven*] is a false book by an author who lingers in nigger cabarets hoping to heaven to pick up something to write about and make a sensation—and, of course, money.

> *D. H. Lawrence, "Literature and Art: 'Nigger Heaven'," in his* Phoenix: The Posthumous Papers of D. H. Lawrence, *edited by Edward D. McDonald, 1936. Reprint by William Heinemann Ltd., 1961, p. 361.*

## EDWIN CLARK

At the moment we have enjoyed a goodly number of smart, sophisticated novels. Mr. Van Vechten has written blithely and wittily. But in Hollywood he has found a background for one of his original character creations that brings spontaneous merriment and a rare gayety all too uncommon in light fiction. "Spider Boy," with its satirical basis founded on the antics of the cabots, is always good-natured. His panorama of Hollywood at work and play is a Neroesque circus—where nobody dreams, but bunk comes true, and sin is exciting and at the same time pure. Here satire is only burlesque and there is nothing to do except laugh.

The spider boy of the title is a dramatist who at the beginning of the novel had written the best play current on Broadway. That he should be in Hollywood is odd; still, writers have been known to adventure. This, however, is another story. (p. 5)

Mr. Van Vechten, since "Peter Whiffle," has been a virtuoso of novel technique. He always had his discursive interludes of comic idiosyncrasies. Never before have they dovetailed in such a perfected pattern as is displayed in this roistering farce of a mummer's wonderland. The studded style is restrained to apt usage, and the crackle of his simplified prose gives an ingratiating movement that sends the story spinning on from laugh to laugh. It is the grandest joke that has come to a people who pride themselves on knowing what is funny. Not the least of its many gay merits, its comic temperaments, is the sheer good nature which never permits a smirk and carries off a madcap extravaganza to a wedding that is beyond belief and an opening night that is a nightmare. (p. 12)

> *Edwin Clark, "Mr. Van Vechten Presents a Hollywood Farce," in* The New York Times Book Review, *August 19, 1928, pp. 5, 12.*

## CLIFTON P. FADIMAN

Mr. Van Vechten would be very happy if he had attained his object [in *Spider Boy*], which was to concoct a witty and fantastic satiric extravaganza out of the absurdities of Hollywood. He has not attained it. He has not even manufactured a passably farcical situation. His satire is without sparkle or good nature and is so obvious that the attentive reader (who will be a rare phenomenon) scents it twenty pages ahead. On the whole, Mr. Van Vechten is a mediocre reporter of the smart cracks of five years ago and a fairly good purveyor to the appetites of upper-class fourteen-year-olds. His prose, which had a whipped cream and champagne quality in *Peter Whiffle*, has in *Spider Boy* gone flat and stale. Whoever wishes to attain an English style, coarse but not familiar, and smart but not sophisticated, must give his days and nights to the volumes of Van Vechten.

> *Clifton P. Fadiman, in a review of "Spider Boy," in* The Bookman, *New York, Vol. LXVIII, No. 2, October, 1928, p. 223.*

## FLORENCE HAXTON BRITTEN

Undoubtedly Mr. Van Vechten writes for Posterity—for Posterity and the Old Lady from Dubuque. For **"Parties"** is so meticulous a report of the New York speakeasy, 1929-30, that the wistful old lady from the West may save her railroad fare; and the social research worker of the 1980's need but turn to this one novel to find massed for his use all he needs to know of the functioning of contemporary Manhattan bars, both public and private—or, better, paying and non-paying—under prohibition. Of course, **"Parties"** neglects the economic background and wastes no time in low dives that sell poison for a quarter. But Mr. Van Vechten's observations throw a brilliant floodlight on the class of speakeasies and luxurious apartment house bars frequented by that tentatively despairing group who were once our wild younger generation—and who now, grown older, titillate and assuage their thirst for life with (according to Mr. Van Vechten) copious tumblersfull of gin, rye, brandy, vermouth and absinthe, mixed. . . .

Nobody can deny that Carl Van Vechten has a talent for observing and setting down surfaces, at the same time, alas, robbing them of their significance. Of the brief, pungent characterization that reads like a bit of brilliant vivisection and reveals almost nothing, he is master. And of the striking *non sequitur*. Certainly this world of ours is full of unrelated accident—and of coincidence, if you are willing, as Mr. Van Vechten is, to make the most superficial of connections establish the relationship. But his faculty for discovering slight resemblances is so intense as to make him generally irresponsible concerning anything beyond the scintillant surfaces, and to relieve him at all times of probing for sources and meanings. He comments on contemporary life in **"Parties"** rather as a man going through a gallery of Rembrandts might remark that "Old Lady Paring Her Nails" resembled "Diana the Huntress," who used to adorn the top of the old Madison Square Garden, and the "Portrait of the Artist by Himself" looked precisely like a tramp he once observed staring up at the goddess.

It is not that the subject matter Mr. Van Vechten presents in **"Parties"** is essentially trivial: Dorothy Parker, Ernest Hemingway and Aldous Huxley have done memorable jobs with similar materials. It is merely that Mr. Van Vechten is an incurable smart Aleck who would rather be witty than wise,

sophisticated than genuine, facile than fine. And he gets his wish. . . .

Mr. Van Vechten is still a phrase maker of no mean talent, with an exultant pleasure in subtle—and not so subtle—vulgarities. But the tricks that he used in his earlier books do not here produce the same results. They are almost as good—but they have become routinized, and the ringmaster who cracks his whip over them seems a bit weary. The gay mischievousness of **"The Blind Bow Boy"** and the hot color of **"Nigger Heaven"** are wanting. I would hazard a guess that Mr. Van Vechten is pretty tired of the sort of party his particular literary gifts provide him, but that—like the persons in his novel—having no better place to go, he orders another round.

> *Florence Haxton Britten, "Those Tired Sophisticates," in* New York Herald Tribune Books, *August 17, 1930, p. 3.*

## GEORGE DANGERFIELD

*Parties* promises entertainment, but offers something quite different and far more important. It should confound a certain dilettantist criticism which maintains that Van Vechten is an American love-child compounded between Firbank and Huysmans, with certain engaging qualities, but no originality. And it should establish what one believes to be the truth—namely that the body of Van Vechten's work, whether good, bad or indifferent, represents in its own way a modern comedy of manners; and that the same fate has befallen it which overtook an earlier comedy of manners; that it has been forced from the unmoral to the moral, not by outside influence . . . but by inner compulsion.

The surface of this story is not unlike that of his other novels. Many of the characters are easily recognizable, their entrances brilliantly managed, their background cleverly constructed. The manner again is extravagant, and exaggerated, and witty, and somewhat satirical. But if the manner which presents the story is familiar, the emotion which informs it is unfamiliar; it is painful and violent and essentially moral; and because of it Van Vechten is more definitely creative than before, and the reading of his *Parties* an experience, not an entertainment.

The core of this story lies in the relationship between David and Rilda Westlake, always drunk, hardly seeing each other except at parties, but cursed, whatever they do and however they do it, with a "damnable fidelity"; and in this tortured relationship all the other characters are more or less involved. While the circumstances that surround it are fluid enough, the pattern that these characters form among themselves is like that of a *caelum stellatum*—a fixed motion. It is a matter of disgust and escape from disgust and disgust with the form of escape—on and on; in this path the more important characters are forced to go, and the others to follow, either because they wish to keep up with them, or because having drifted in they find it easier to stay where they are. The atmosphere—which is simply the difference between certain people who are confined to the same limited space—is almost to the end tense and powerful and rather disgusting. (pp. 71-2)

*Parties* is a failure because it is incomplete; but a failure significant enough to place Van Vechten once and for all among the more important of contemporary novelists; and significant enough for us to speculate about his future, when we had come to expect nothing more from him than a repetition of his past. (p. 72)

*George Dangerfield, in a review of "Parties," in* The Bookman, *New York, Vol. LXXII, No. 1, September, 1930, pp. 71-2.*

## JOHN CHAMBERLAIN

We think of Carl Van Vechten as a novelist of the '20s who swam with the surface currents of the years that were only yesterday, and whose descent over Niagara as an artist coincided rather patly with the descent of the stocks of the Electric Bond and Share Company and Radio common. His **"Peter Whiffle,"** published in 1922, was a work of naïve charm, playfully naughty in spots, but still wearing an innocent expression. But as the cry went up for madder music and for stronger wine Mr. Van Vechten was faithful to his public; the rogueish mode was transmuted into the febrile; and from the sophistication of the Paris of George Moore to the simulated primitiveness of **"Nigger Heaven"** Mr. Van Vechten made his inevitable pilgrimage. He had promised us his autobiography for 1932, but evidently he has thought better of it; at any rate, he has been satisfied to jot down a few notes for an autobiography on Page 225 and thereafter in **"Sacred and Profane Memories."** One would not be surprised to discover Mr. Van Vechten taking a totally new tack in the future—in which case, of course, his autobiography, when it is finally written, will be very different from the one he would have written in 1932.

And why, pray, one can imagine the reader asking, may one expect a new tack? Because, as this collection of sacred and profane memories proves, Mr. Van Vechten is no better—and no worse—than his times; a new social atmosphere stirs in him new tastes, new manners. A majority of the papers that compose this book were written before 1920—and the tone is that of—James Huneker's "Steeplejack." Every one who has read it will remember the innocent gusto of "Steeplejack," with its delight in all fresh things, its sounding talk of Nietzche, of George Moore, of great names in a time when all the names were new. There is the same innocent gusto in **"Sacred and Profane Memories."** . . .

So completely are these papers of the "Steeplejack" era, and so completely were Mr. Van Vechten's novels of the jazz age, that one looks up from the last page of this book with entire confidence that, whatever the style or mood of the future, one will find Mr. Van Vechten riding the crest of the newest fashion. Hasn't Mr. Van Vechten himself said that it is useless to go against the currents of one's time?

*John Chamberlain, "Van Vechten's Memories," in* The New York Times Book Review, *May 1, 1932, p. 12.*

## ALFRED KAZIN

Carl Van Vechten was granted a less distinguished but more functional role in what threatened, as the twenties ran out, to become a movement. For beginning as its playboy, Van Vechten ended as its historian. He had been a music critic and he had a flamboyant knowledge of the world. It was he who brought the Charleston to literature, took the esthetes on slumming parties through Harlem, retailed the gossip, memorialized the fads, and—a sardonic Punch to the last—brought one dream of the twenties to a close by writing its obituary in *Parties* before he gave up writing for photography. As a stylist he proved so dextrous that he came uncomfortably close to ridiculing himself. . . . What saved him and gave him his signal

importance at the moment, however, was the range of his facile cynicism. As the novelist of the speakeasy intelligentsia, he carried sophistication to its last possible extremity by refusing steadfastly to admit the significance of anything west of Manhattan Island. He represented the Jimmy Walker era in literature as Mr. Walker represented its politics, Texas Guinan its pleasures, and George Gershwin its music. In a series of novels that proceeded with becoming regularity from *Peter Whiffle* (1922) to *Parties* (1930) he meticulously detailed the perversions, the domestic eccentricities, the alcoholism, the esthetic dicta, and the social manners of ladies and gentlemen who did nothing, nothing at all. The world he so amiably described was careless, violently erotic, and cheerfully insane. Written up in Van Vechten's snakelike prose, it boasted an extraordinary appetite for evil; if there was no evil his characters played at being evil. (pp. 244-45)

Like most of the Exquisites, Van Vechten thrived on his own affectations. He began and ended his career as a novelist on a good, heartily satiric note, but there were times—notably in *The Blind Bow-Boy*—when he took such pleasure in his freaks that they seemed to climb all over him. A nudging good sense, of course, never deserted him; he giggled steadily at his own pretensions for eight years. But at last the eroticism became more perverse, the alcoholism more opulent, the lechery for nonsense uncontrolled. It was but a step from the buffoonery of *Peter Whiffle,* in which Van Vechten demolished a whole school of poseurs, to the carnival of idiocy represented in *The Blind Bow-Boy.* There, superintended by the gorgeous Campaspe . . . Van Vechten's aristocratic perverts and idlers enjoyed their last triumph. . . . Ineffably bored with their own pursuits, his characters then turned to Harlem, which, as Van Vechten described it in the torrid pages of *Nigger Heaven,* was a place where colored folk slashed each other merrily and had fun.

The final word came in *Parties.* . . . Unhappily, it was amidst the detonations of a falling stock market and an expiring culture that Van Vechten had gathered his creatures for the last party and the last exquisite sensation of extravagance and futility.

"It's just like the opening chorus of an opera-bouffe," one character laughs. "Somehow it's more like the closing chorus," replies another. "I think we're all a little tired." *Da capo.* (pp. 245-46)

*Alfred Kazin, "The Exquisites," in his* On Native Grounds: An Interpretation of Modern American Prose Literature, *1942. Reprint by Harcourt Brace Jovanovich, Inc., 1963, pp. 227-46.\**

## HUGH M. GLOSTER

Perhaps the most popular novel of Negro life during the 1920's was Carl Van Vechten's *Nigger Heaven* (1926), a work which not only dramatized the alleged animalism and exoticism of Harlem folk but also influenced the writings of Negro Renascence authors. Appearing at the proper time, when the Negro was making considerable headway as a stellar performer in the entertainment world as well as when white Americans were inordinately curious about so-called picturesque and primitive facets of Harlem society, *Nigger Heaven* enjoyed widespread popularity and became a sort of guidebook for visitors who flocked uptown seeking a re-creation of the African jungle in the heart of New York City. The songs and blues selections by Langston Hughes which Van Vechten incorporated in the novel not only augmented the appeal of the book but also drew general attention to the rising young *literati* of Manhattan's black ghetto. (p. 310)

On the crowded canvas of *Nigger Heaven* Van Vechten presents many colorful aspects of Harlem life. He gives an account of a lavish week-end party at the Long Island estate of Adora Boniface, an ex-music hall diva who also maintains a luxurious residence on Striver's Row on West 139th Street. He essays to present *bourgeois* respectability in the life of Mary Love, who associates with young writers and other professional men, frequents dinner and bridge parties, attends plays and musical entertainments, reads the best books (including Gertrude Stein's *Three Lives,* which made a deeper impression than any of the others), and appreciates African sculpture. He describes the Charity Ball, a mammoth paid dance sponsored annually by a group of socially prominent colored women, and gives the opinions of Negroes concerning Harlem sightseers, passing, miscegenation, inter- and intra-racial color prejudice, and many other subjects.

But, with more gusto than he does anything else, Van Vechten paints Harlem cabaret life. He is particularly fascinated by the barbaric rhythms of Negro jazz, the tom-tom beat of the drum in the band, and the melting bodies of intoxicated dancers swaying to sensuous music. Contemplating the cabaret, Van Vechten surmises that Negroes are essentially primitive and atavistic. In the singing of spirituals and jazz, black folk are described as "recognizing, no doubt, in some dim, biological way, the beat of African rhythm." (pp. 310-11)

Ever the painter of the exotic and fantastic, Van Vechten took particular delight in emphasizing—even in exaggerating and distorting—the primitive aspects of his *milieu.* To him the Harlem cabaret was a transplanted jungle, and Negroes were creatures of impulse and emotion, atavistically yearning for the animalistic exhibitions of Africa. This stress upon the Negro as a child of nature did at least three things: first, it increased the influx of white visitors to upper Manhattan; second, it created a furious controversy among Negro intellectuals; and, third, it made American publishers and readers eager for more works with a similar emphasis. (pp. 311-12)

While *Nigger Heaven* was generally received with favor by white critics and readers, it aroused a storm of controversy among Negro intellectuals. . . . Voicing nearly all of the dissenting reactions to the novel, DuBois argued that *Nigger Heaven* is "a blow in the face," "an affront to the hospitality of black folk and to the intelligence of white" [see excerpt above]. . . . Reflecting the sentiments of Negroes who liked the novel, James Weldon Johnson insisted in his review . . . that *Nigger Heaven* is "an absorbing story," "comprehends nearly every phase of life from dregs to the froth," and ranks as "the most revealing, significant and powerful novel based exclusively on Negro life yet written" [see excerpt above]. (p. 312)

The modern critic, viewing *Nigger Heaven* nineteen years after it was published, submits that the novel's proper evaluation is at a point somewhere between the appraisal of DuBois and that of Johnson. In stylizing the primitivism of the Negro and the jungle atmosphere of the Harlem cabaret, Van Vechten was doing no more than Langston Hughes had done a year earlier in *The Weary Blues* (1925). . . .

Van Vechten, who knows or should know that the Negro is no more primitive and atavistic than any other racial group in America, was merely a literary faddist capitalizing upon a current vogue and a popular demand. . . . He probably did not deserve the vitriolic criticism of DuBois, for he frankly set out to exploit what he considered to be the exotic and animalistic elements in Harlem life. At the same time, however, he did not merit the high praise of Johnson, who called *Nigger Heaven* a mosaic of Harlem and the first work by a white novelist in which the Negro is considered as an individual rather than as a type. There were many significant phases of Harlem life which Van Vechten did not apparently know and therefore could not describe; and surely Gertrude Stein, T. S. Stribling, Waldo Frank, DuBose Heyward, and several other white predecessors of Van Vechten in the use of Negro subject-matter made departures from the stereotyped presentation of colored characters. (p. 313)

Being primarily a fad, the Van Vechten Vogue was doomed to fall before the first violent shock or the next new rage. The inevitable reaction came in the form of the Wall Street *debacle* of 1929 which, as Langston Hughes wittily remarks, "sent Negroes, white folks and all rolling down the hill toward the Works Progress Administration."

The fatal mistake of the Van Vechten school was to make a fetish of sex and the cabaret rather than to give a faithful, realistic presentation and interpretation of Harlem life. In spite of this error, however, the Van Vechtenites helped to break away from the taboos and stereotypes of earlier years, to make self-revelation and self-criticism more important considerations in fiction by Negroes, and to demonstrate to publishers and readers that Negro authors have an important contribution to make to the nation's cultural life. (p. 314)

> Hugh M. Gloster, "The Van Vechten Vogue," in PHYLON: The Atlanta University Review of Race and Culture, *Vol. VI, No. 4, 4th Quarter, 1945, pp. 310-14.*

## CARL VAN VECHTEN

[*The essay from which this excerpt is taken was originally published as an afterword entitled "A Note by the Author" in the 1950 paperback edition of* Nigger Heaven.]

[The] plot of *Nigger Heaven* is one of the oldest stories in the world, the story of the Prodigal Son, without the happy ending of that biblical history. In my book a boy from a small town is bewitched, bothered, and bewildered by a big-time Lady of Pleasure and is unable to meet the demands made on his character by life in a big city. Paul Laurence Dunbar had previously employed this plot in a very bad novel called *The Sport of the Gods,* a title which fits *Nigger Heaven* like a glove. . . .

There have been those who have objected to the title. These objections have usually come from people who have not read the novel. The title is symbolic and ironic, even tragic. Before the book was published I had submitted the manuscript to two prominent Negro literary men, James Weldon Johnson and Rudolph Fisher, for their approval or disapproval and also to check up on errors. After it had passed this test successfully, it was submitted to the world. . . .

[What made the book important] was the fact that it gave readers a microcosm of American Negro life and habits from the rich and intelligent figures at the top, to the exotic misfits at the lowest round of the ladder. And, as one reviewer sapiently pointed out, it is written . . . [without] condescension. The story is related exactly as I would have written it if the characters had been white. (p. 80)

[So] far as psychology and behavior are considered in the book, Negroes are treated by me exactly as if I were depicting white characters, for the very excellent reason that I do not believe there is much psychological difference between the races. The local color was the local color to be found in Harlem in 1925. Dunbar's world of 1900 was obsolete. Even the scenes in my novel are laid in a different quarter of New York, an essential change due to the fact that Negroes had moved in the interim from one part of the city to another. Just as now in 1951, much that I discussed or pictured has also happily become obsolete.

One of the games frequently played by the public after the publication of a novel is the guessing game of the identity of the characters. In 1926, this was played with *Nigger Heaven* up to the hilt. All the characters of a novel naturally are imagined from the novelist's experience, but it should be stated sternly that any resemblance or fancied resemblance to living persons by the characters in *Nigger Heaven* is purely coincidental. A few of the characters may have possessed some of the superficial traits of persons then living, but unless an author takes his characters from books this would be true of any novel. I must repeat, however, that any fancied resemblances to be found in *Nigger Heaven* are purely accidental and coincidental. In the round the characters are imagined, and only exist in real life in certain aspects or attitudes. What is more important is that the book itself is true, at least *was* true, to actual existence in Harlem. (pp. 80-1)

> Carl Van Vechten, "'Nigger Heaven': A Belated Introduction," in his "Keep A-Inchin' Along": Selected Writings about Black Art and Letters, edited by Bruce Kellner, Greenwood Press, 1979, pp. 78-80.

## EDWARD LUEDERS

Van Vechten's most valuable asset as a commentator on his scene was his ability to identify himself with the society in which he moved, while at the same time remaining an interested, detached observer of its performances. He was a singular example of the one-man show; besides being one of the actors on stage, he was also occasionally its director, and at all times its audience. His motive, consistent with the mood of the time, was an escape from boredom in the pursuit of novelty and amusement. Unlike so many restless souls in the Twenties, he found it and captured it in the very comedy of the chase.

The critical unrest and intellectual wanderlust that served as a prelude to the Twenties is present in Van Vechten's early work. His critical essays on music and the arts establish his place in the revolt of the young intellectuals. In anticipation of Mencken and his henchmen, he could declare, "The ironclad dreadnoughts of the academic world, the reactionary artists, the dry-as-dust lecturers are constantly ignoring the most vital, the most real, the most important artists while they sing polyphonic, antiphonal, palestrinian motets in praise of men who have learned to imitate comfortably and efficiently the work of their predecessors." Peter Whiffle echoed the sense of intellectual isolation that made the sensitive individual an uneasy, inarticulate prophet in the Waste Land. Like T. S. Eliot's frustrated Prufrock, Peter shook his head vainly at conventional answers to his questions: "I thought you would say that but that's not what I meant, that's not at all what I meant." (pp. 103-04)

The twenties in the United States produced an adolescent, imitation *decadence* that is peculiar in a historical sense. The word sits uneasily on the era, but it is nonetheless applicable to many aspects of its society. It featured contempt for the standards, morals, traditional restrictions on thought and conduct, and the sense of wholeness inherited from the past. It bred national neurosis and a dedication to the pleasures of the moment. It asserted individual freedom from cultural and moral taboos, and it fostered in art an inversion of the aesthetic which had previously demanded classic decorum, simplicity, order, and unity. It sought in art and life the ideal symbolized by Dionysus, an ideal related to both love and intoxication, either of which promises momentary ecstasy as its ultimate reward.

That it was not real decadence, that it was the product of impetuosity and revolt rather than of age and maturity, that its presence in the nation-at-large was never secure, all these observations are true, but they are also misleading. The generation that reflected postwar bohemia in its fads and philosophy was seldom aware that this was only a reflection. In the excesses of the Twenties, in the veneer of release and the inability to dispense with the conscience even while ignoring it, the era practiced willful self-deception. But in their more subtle modulations these same elements in our society led the nation to a new maturity and self-realization that would not have developed without the impetus of revolt and experiment. On the surface, the movement was one of running away, but within the headlong race was the motion of running toward. (p. 108)

Van Vechten maintained a precarious balance. Bohemian himself by inclination and association, he wrote of people devoted to the uninhibited moment, but his affection for them did not prevent his exposure of their follies. Instead he made the amusing exposition of those follies the basis of his books. Peter Whiffle exhausted the possibilities of aesthetic realization and found himself, instead. The sophisticated characters of *The Blind Bow-Boy* and *Firecrackers* outdid each other in their attempts to banish boredom through perverse and novel pleasures, but over them reigned the detached super-sophisticate, Campaspe, whose more stable pleasure came not from her own participation, but from the detached observation of the others. . . .

Except for *Parties,* and, to a lesser extent the preceding novels, *Nigger Heaven* and *Spider Boy,* the line separating Van Vechten from the milieu of his characters is a tenuous one. Campaspe displays an awareness above that of her companions, but she is disturbingly unaffected and supreme in her lack of conscience. Her ego is admissable, but it is undisciplined by any super-ego. At best, it observes with aloofness what it chooses to call "comportment" rather than evoke the morality of the term "deportment." The reader is shocked not so much by the characters' immorality as he is by the author's unmorality. . . . With the last three novels, however, the balance was reaffirmed. Still picturing the excesses of bohemianism, *Nigger Heaven* made them the tools of a tragedy. *Spider Boy* applied its own antic disposition to the outlandish West Coast imitation of the real thing. *Parties,* at the end of the era, described the clientele of the Wishbone, the speakeasy in which harried, abandoned sophisticates clustered almost in mutual protection from reality, as cosmopolitan. (p. 109)

Evidence of the popular move toward sophistication, toward "class," is found in both the cultural and the commercial life of the Twenties. At some levels, the war on pretentiousness and frippery was being successfully waged. American taste improved steadily in the pictorial arts during the Twenties. Simplicity and functionalism made rapid headway in the fields of architecture and design. Taste in the fine arts, the "lively" arts, and the domestic arts became more thoughtful, more sophisticated, and more cosmopolitan. But in almost all respects, American taste was guilty of overindulgence. . . . (p. 110)

In such a society, sophistication is easily lost in its own popular counterfeit, but it is no less desirable for that. The art of living comfortably and contentedly in the midst of one's accessories is sought by the many, but known only to the few. A regard and affection for these accessories reflecting pleasure *in the things themselves,* rather than reflecting extraneous motives for their possession, is even more rare.

To as fine a degree as anyone writing in America during the era, Joseph Hergesheimer and Carl Van Vechten utilized this epicurean art of taste and of charming living. (p. 111)

The décor in Van Vechten's books was more lively, more variable, more personal, and more vulnerable to imitation than Hergesheimer's, but the personal sense of atmosphere was just as evident. Individuality was the keynote, and the reflection of its owner's personality was the creed. . . . In his novels, Van Vechten revealed characters through the self-expression (or the lack of it) to be found in their surroundings, in the furnishings they had chosen to live with. Peter Whiffle, of course, is the outstanding example; each new dedication to a way of life and a means to art in Peter's restless career is signalled by a new abode and a new set of personal appurtenances. Only cats, Van Vechten's symbol of the philosophy which Peter gradually discovers as the goal of his quest, accompany Peter through all his settings. Gareth Johns and Lennie Colman in *The Tattooed Countess,* Mary Love in *Nigger Heaven,* and others are revealed, in a similar fashion, through the choice of their surroundings. Even Mrs. Alonzo W. Syreno, the unimaginative pretender among the weary sophisticates of *Parties,* employs an English decorator who gives her home the stamp of "a permanently uninhabited English house," and betrays her lack of both taste and imagination in its alien character. (pp. 111-12)

Any author who indulged his whims and thrived on novelty was in tune with the Twenties. A society which immediately caught up anything novel, strange, or modern, and just as quickly dropped it for the next item in the series, could accept as its own the writer who was likely to discover some new field or exciting interest with each new book. In an age of fads, Van Vechten was one of the leading faddists. He introduced new composers, the emotions of the blues, Gertrude Stein, the Harlem vogue, strange and exotic figures in literature, and the lively performers of stage entertainments. To him the unusual experience was the most satisfying, although not necessarily the most lasting. (p. 113)

In joining the national passion for novelties and fads, however, his disregard for confining consistency once again enabled him to participate in the amusements at the same time as he pointed out their ridiculous features. His novels consistently satirized the aberrations and characteristics of the same public that received them so enthusiastically. The antics that endeared American society to Van Vechten, and provided subjects for his novels, were shown to their perpetrators in the light of their pretentious foolishness, but were accepted more often than not as amusing caricatures of others. To Van Vechten this must have been the most grotesque, and therefore the most entertaining, twist of all. Much the same thing happened with Sinclair Lewis's satires of middle-class America, but there was tragedy in the readers' reluctance to identify the characters with themselves. For the satires of Carl Van Vechten, the situation served only to heighten the comedy. (pp. 113-14)

Van Vechten's fiction reflects [the problems associated with the new moral "freedom" of the jazz age] with his customary give-and-take ambivalence. He reserved comment on Prohibition, virtually ignoring both its motives and its manifestations, as, indeed, most of America had, until *Parties.* There it was offered as an integral part of the tragedy of the whole decade. . . . For the characters who haunted American speakeasies, crowded in upon themselves in their attempt to escape, liquor was their only means. (p. 120)

In matters of sex, Van Vechten's novels were notoriously emancipated. *Peter Whiffle* was uninhibited, but maintained a decorous charm in what the readers of 1922 called its indiscretions. *The Blind Bow-Boy,* however, treated even the perversions of sex with a flippant intimacy that was shocking in 1923 and still seems the least palatable of his erotic trivia. The reputation of *The Tattooed Countess* has been celebrated by Sinclair Lewis's *Gideon Planish* in a fictitious episode that turns on the contemporary reception of its "improprieties." *Firecrackers* employs the peccadillos of the *Bow-Boy* to more serious purposes. *Nigger Heaven* and *Spider Boy* continue this trend, the first exploiting the author's most erotic sequences for both artistic and moral ends, and the second passing over them so lightly that entertaining innuendo carries the weight of the author's purpose. *Parties,* once again, is the most searching treatment of a social ill. Sex is rampant and free in this final book, but its consequences for the characters and for the reader are deeply disturbing. The frustrated lives caught in the conventions which grew out of a revolt against earlier conventions are tragically lost in a new transition. (pp. 120-21)

Van Vechten's novels are peculiarly childless. Only two children are given speaking roles in the seven books, and each of them is unique. Consuelo Everest of *Firecrackers* is so modern and sophisticated that her mother (whom she addresses "Maman") despairs of catching up with her; in these respects, the child surpasses everyone else on the scene but Campaspe Lorillard. Regent Westlake, the other, enters the final chapter of *Parties* with no previous hint of his existence, to ask in eight-year-old confusion that Hamish Wilding try to keep his mother and father from drinking so much. (p. 121)

Aside from these two, children are either non-existent or off-stage. Campaspe and Cupid Lorillard have two boys, but they are kept at the comfortable distance of a boarding school so that their mother can escape the responsibilities and bother of having them under foot. Her marriage, appropriately, has been maintained since their birth solely as a convenience and a means of financing her extravagant whims. She has declared herself free of all encumbering affection and responsibility, and insists that her husband leave her alone. What he does, in turn, is no concern of hers. . . . (pp. 121-22)

This wish to lead a weightless existence free from distracting alliances is almost thematic in Van Vechten's tales. It appeared first in *Peter Whiffle,* where it is even applied to friendship, which unfortunately entails "responsibility, that great god whose existence burdens our lives." Only the more realistic scenes of *The Tattooed Countess* and *Nigger Heaven* present marriage and the home as anything more than a means of placing amusing or contrasting personalities in juxtaposition, and even these books, along with the perpetual crisis of the Westlakes' marriage in *Parties,* describe tragic misunderstanding within the constraint of the family unit. (p. 122)

The one-word title of Van Vechten's last novel symbolized perhaps the most typical manifestation of the Twenties' demand for diversion. Parties gave society personal and vital occasions for escape, occasions through which the moment could be filled with the amusement, the excitement, the tension and the challenge of personalities at close quarters. Time and life were measured in terms of these spirited entertainments; time spent not at a party was time spent in impatient anticipation of one. What *Parties* recorded in 1930 was the violent anachronism of this habitual escape at a time when escape was no longer possible. The bewilderment and disenchantment of the party-goers at the end of the decade is the undertone of tragedy that is heard like an insistent pedal point beneath the capricious scherzo of their parties. It is very much the same stark disappointment and shock that meet a person who has escaped in the artificial darkness of a matinee to the high life of the stage or screen, when he steps out of the theater into the glaring reality of daylight and the ant-like scramble of the city street. But while the performance went on inside, it was quite a show. (pp. 128-29)

The vitality and the capacity for pleasure which marked the Twenties are still a part of Van Vechten, but the irresponsibilities of that era are behind him. When he emerged from the darkened theater and the ten-year matinee of amusement and escape, he realized he had seen a last performance. But he brought along with him into the sober daylight of succeeding years some of its most serviceable and memorable scenes.

Later decades may well censure the wayward emphasis of an era that set out, as every era does in its own way, to conquer boredom through some appealing pattern of life. But there is a certain element of inevitability that conditions the choice. If they had been choosing in 1920, or 1925, or even 1928, the chances are they would have chosen the same riotous pattern. They may not, however, have had the impudent honesty or the careless foresight to echo Peter Whiffle's impertinent defense of his folly, "It was all gay, irresponsible and meaningless, perhaps, but *gay.*" (pp. 131-32)

> Edward Lueders, *in his* Carl Van Vechten and the Twenties, *University of New Mexico Press, 1955, 150 p.*

## NATHAN IRVIN HUGGINS

Of all the whites to become associated with black Harlem in the 1920s, Carl Van Vechten was the undisputed prince. He had the reputation of knowing Harlem intimately, not only the places of entertainment but also the important people. He not only enjoyed Harlem, but he also catered to Harlemites by maintaining a kind of downtown salon to which Negroes were welcome as important guests. Indeed, he almost made a career of promoting, socially and professionally, Negro artists and performers. He counted James Weldon Johnson as one of his closest friends; Countee Cullen, Langston Hughes, Richmond Barthé, the sculptor, Ethel Waters and Paul Robeson were befriended by him. He listened, without weariness or apparent condescension, to Negro writers and artists. He read and viewed their work, urged their interests before publishers and producers, made the important introductions, and, in that way, acted as a kind of midwife to the Harlem Renaissance. Even Langston Hughes, who had slight patience with patrons, welcomed Van Vechten's friendship and supported and defended him against his Negro critics. Beyond this, Van Vechten was responsible for the gathering of Negro manuscript materials at Yale University, encouraging James Weldon Johnson to contribute the nucleus of the collection. Still, it is open to question how well, or in what way, Van Vechten served Harlem and the Negro.

It is at least as important, however, to ask how Harlem and the Negro served him. (p. 93)

[Van Vechten] had a career that was not only long but varied. While his interests were always cultural, he exploited them in many different ways. Critic of music, art, drama, and literature, journalist, novelist, and photographer, he followed his mind and talent through successive changes of interest and fascination. And while at each point he demonstrated exquisite taste and potential, he never found anything wholly absorbing. Van Vechten was a dilettante in the best sense of the term, excelling where he had the talent, and pulling it off where he did not. Through all of the change, however, there was consistency. He was a collector of rare *objets d'art* and of rare people; rare, in both instances, because no one had stopped to see or think about them properly until Van Vechten showed them how. He enjoyed the discovery, and he enjoyed the display, as any collector would. He thrived in that thin, dangerous, and exhilarating atmosphere where one makes *approving* critical judgments about the very new and the very off-beat. (pp. 93-4)

Of course, Van Vechten did support and promote writers who would not be recognized today, novels that enjoy the same oblivion as his own. It was more than a simple matter of literary judgment that caused his appreciation of writers like Edgar Saltus and Ronald Firbank, the British author; Firbank, at least, was a writer of consummate imagination and skill. Rather, here was further evidence of Van Vechten's penchant for collecting the exotic and his fascination with decadence. For both Firbank's and Saltus' novels were fantasy creations. Firbank's artificial worlds, which could seem more real than reality, contained the strong flavor of evil and decay that had thrilled the late Victorian readers. It is not surprising that, when Van Vechten concocted his own novels, they too would have the heavy odor of *fin de siècle* decadence. (p. 95)

Van Vechten's most controversial novel, *Nigger Heaven* (1926), exemplified this inversion of values and fascination with the exotic. That work was a high point in Van Vechten's long interest in Negroes. (p. 98)

It was in 1922, after the publication of *Peter Whiffle,* that Van Vechten, to use his words, became "violently interested in Negroes." "I would say violently," he emphasized, "because it was almost an addiction." Walter White had just published *Fire in the Flint,* and Van Vechten got to know him through Alfred Knopf. Walter White took him everywhere—parties, lunches, dinners—introducing him to everyone who mattered in Harlem. (p. 99)

He had almost been brought into a new life by the Negro and Harlem. He was thrilled by it all and devoted much of his energy to being a midwife, a patron, an interpreter of Negro culture. It "soon became obvious to me that I would write about these people, because my feelings about them were very strong." The novel he wrote about them was *Nigger Heaven.* Most of the Negro commentary on that novel must have made them appear very insensitive, very ungrateful, to Van Vechten.

*Nigger Heaven* tried to make two points. In the first place, it wanted the reader to know Harlem as a social microcosm of New York City. The reader had to reject definitions of the Negro as a type. There was a wide variety of characters, tastes, and values. You could witness as many kinds of social experiences—parties, intellectual salons, elegant dinners, brawls, and bashes—in Harlem as you could in the rest of New York. Harlem was no monolith, and the Negro fit no stereotype. Yet, at the same time, the reader was expected to accept the Negro as a natural primitive. Where he was true to himself, he was saved from civilized artificiality, and had preserved his mental health. Indeed, the novel seems to argue that the Negro "civilizes" himself at great cost. These rather contradictory assumptions are never reconciled. Present-day readers, however, should not underestimate the daring of the first point. Until the publication of *Nigger Heaven*, no generally read novel had chosen the Negro as its subject and abandoned the stereotype. It was not for many years after 1926 that the other popular medium, the movies, could dare to do the same. Whatever the novel's faults then, it was a historic event. (pp. 102-03)

Those reviewers who liked the book, and there were many, insisted that one of the novel's strengths was its restraint from propaganda, from making sociological points. Edward Lueders, Van Vechten's literary biographer, concurs in that judgment [see excerpt above]. In the sense that the novel does not probe very deeply into race relations (or racism) or engage the reader in any fundamental moral problem, this assessment is correct. But propaganda and sociological points the book makes. . . . Carl Van Vechten goes to great lengths to show that besides the Scarlet Creepers and the Randolph Pettijohns, Harlem has some very cultured and intelligent people. Mary Love reads everything that is up-to-date and illuminates her bedroom with a single, framed reproduction of the "Mona Lisa." Stravinsky is a part of her life, as well as the blues and spirituals—it is all culture. Mary quotes, from memory, poems by Wallace Stevens and, if that were not enough, about a page of "Melanctha" from Gertrude Stein's *Three Lives*. A dinner at the wealthy Aaron Sumners' allows Van Vechten to employ his talent for description of rich furnishings and appointments. It also permits the famous author, Gareth Johns, to be openly astonished by the refinement of Negroes. They have read his books. They know Paris. One of the guests, Leon Cazique of the Haitian consulate, allows the conversation to drift into French, in which language Mary talks about an authentic African sculpture exhibit that she has arranged and, at another point in the novel, discusses Cocteau, Morand, and Proust with M. Cazique, who turns out to be something of an expert on modern French literature. In short, culture abounds. On reading *Nigger Heaven*, it is impossible to escape the feeling of being forcibly drawn to acknowledge these facts of Negro life, which have little, if anything, to do with the story. They are *obiter dicta* and no less propaganda because they condescend to the reader.

The reader is also instructed about the "Blue Vein Set" and "passing." The problem of Negroes' being served in downtown restaurants or seated in the theaters is explained, as well as the advantages of light-skinned over dark-skinned Negroes in almost every walk of life, and other social differences among Negroes. Often, characters' conversations are mere lengthy disquisitions on these subjects. The points of view are authentic enough, but they are designed to instruct the reader more than to develop the novel. Lest the reader draw racist generalizations from Byron Kasson's failure, Van Vechten is careful to contrast it with the success, after long struggle with frustration, of Howard Allison, the fiancé of Mary's apartment mate. The presentation of statistics on the number of Negroes who pass every year is gratuitous. Often, speeches are no more than whimsical fantasies about how the "problem" will disappear, for instance through interbreeding. Van Vechten, throughout the novel, amuses himself by commenting upon the joke on the white world that "passing" is. All of this is propagandistic and sociological in petty ways. What is missing in the novel

is a clear moral or intellectual perspective that might engage the reader in the dramatic issues of Negro life.

The essential limitations that frustrate Mary and Byron are personal rather than societal. Racial problems form a backdrop for, indeed, inform everything they think or do, but it is character that makes them fail to be their best selves. They suffer, in fact, two varieties of the same malady. They are alienated from their ethno-spiritual roots but are unable to be anything else. Mary is plagued with her inability to be passionate, essential, primitive. Although spirituals or Clara Smith's singing the blues can bring her to tears, she cannot abandon herself to men or to the Charleston until she meets Byron. She is said to be cold, and she has doubts about her priggishness and her persistent propriety. Her inhibitions keep her from what she really wants. When Lasca Sartoris charms Byron at a dance, Mary's inner rage and jealousy make her want to kill Lasca. But she is reduced to priggish impotence by Lasca's deft, feline verbal slashes. Mary is proper and polite; she has just witnessed two women fighting and screaming over a man and was revolted by the scene. Her impulse to act is throttled by her civility. Her inability to act on her feelings defeats her.

Byron, on the other hand, is a very spoiled young man who has no nerve for the struggle forced on Harlem Negroes. He was educated in a white college, and he has lost all contact and sensitivity with Negro people. He despises the rich Negroes because he thinks them snobs. He resents the young, successful professionals and writers because they make his failure evident. He abhors the poor blacks because they shame him. Except for small checks from his father, he refuses help from anyone, turning down a good job when he learns that Mary had arranged it. His writing will be worth something, he is told by a magazine editor—a thinly disguised H. L. Mencken—if he observes what is around him, if he looks at Harlem life close up, and writes about it. Of course, Byron could not bear to look at Negroes, and he could not really see anything else. Rejected and defeated at every turn, he leaps into the arms of Lasca Sartoris. She uses him and rejects him after unmanning him.

Present-day readers would be likely to interpret Mary's and Byron's problem as race-hate and self-hate. Neither of them can accommodate to the blackness they see around them and the suggestion of the blackness within them. Rejecting the Negro that they see, they must also deny themselves, which makes them less than whole. But Carl Van Vechten, true to his nineteenth-century influences, treats the matter differently. Both Mary and Byron, in characteristic ways, drift away from the primitive, natural, and intuitive springs of the race. Mary can only be abandoned in her dance as a result of her rage over Byron's obvious receptivity to Lasca's charms. Byron's sexual passion turns to mere lust. And he lacks—as is made clear in a letter of advice from his father—that intuitive sense that has allowed the Negro to survive: the acceptance of the humble portion for the moment, the expectation of being helped and patronized, and the desire to be useful. In the end, neither Mary nor Byron can find the words, because of pride, to say what can reconcile them and avert tragedy. Pride is their fault. To Carl Van Vechten, their tragedy is that they have become civilized. (pp. 105-08)

The sad thing about *Nigger Heaven* is that Mary and Byron, although the core of the novel, are not the most interesting characters. Mary is a sad little thing; one might feel sorry for her ineptitude; her problem is not fully enough understood to feel more than that. As librarian, Mary's difficulties could as well be an occupational stereotype as anything, and Carl Van

Vechten does not develop them enough for the reader to know. Byron, on the other hand, is too miserably weak; the reader is moved to disdain too quickly for any sense of tragedy to develop. Perhaps excepting Peter Whiffle, all of Van Vechten's strong characters have been women, and emasculating women at that. Here, again, in this novel, the truly strong character is Lasca Sartoris. (pp. 108-09)

Lasca Sartoris is a true Van Vechten female character. Like Campaspe Lorillard, she has all the right ingredients: self-centeredness, self-indulgence, moral inversion, indifference, and abhorrence of boredom. "She has found what she had wanted by wanting what she could get, and then always demanding more, more, until now the world poured its gifts into her bewitching lap." That is Byron's assessment. Her apartment, like herself, is richly and sumptuously decadent. Those chapters she shares with Byron are the most lively in the book. (p. 109)

[Although perverted, the Scarlet Creeper, a pimp introduced at the beginning of the novel,] and Lasca are permanent, endurable, and perversely heroic because they have accepted without qualification their primitive and predatory natures—civilization, respectability, propriety, manners, and decorum are for others, for "niggers." Try as he might to illustrate that Negroes were much like other people, Van Vechten's belief in their essential primitivism makes him prove something else. It stands to reason, after all. Had he thought Negroes were like white people, he would not have adopted Harlem the way he did. His compulsion to be fair to the race while he exploited the exotic and decadent aspects of Harlem caused the novel to founder. (pp. 111-12)

Criticism of the book by blacks apparently stung Van Vechten, because much of his interview for the *Columbia Oral History* was taken up with a discussion of the novel; and most of that with the title. He meant the title ironically, he reiterated, and only "emancipated people" like George Schuyler, James Weldon Johnson, Mrs. Alice Dunbar, and Langston Hughes understood that. Other Negro journalists complained about the title and charged that the author had exploited his friends in Harlem to get material for this highly commercial and sensational book. The problem was irony, "and irony," he at last told his interviewer, "is not anything that most Negroes understand, especially the ones who write for the papers." And Langston Hughes joined him in that judgment. Unfortunately, most of those who accepted Van Vechten's view were too close to him to make free judgments. Van Vechten had both Hughes and Johnson read the manuscript for authenticity, and he discussed with these men his intentions. The same, too, can be said for Edward Lueders, who had the privilege of interviews with the author as well as correspondence. Surely, Van Vechten could be convincing about his intentions. The problem is, however, that they are not clear in the novel, where it counts. It is not irony that the reader, then or now, comes away with. Sensation is a better word. (p. 113)

*Nathan Irvin Huggins, "Heart of Darkness," in his* Harlem Renaissance, *1971. Reprint by Oxford University Press, 1977, pp. 84-136.**

# Gore Vidal

## 1925-

(Born Eugene Luther Vidal, Jr. Has also written under pseud-onym of Edgar Box) American novelist, essayist, screenwriter, dramatist, short story writer, and critic.

The body of work Vidal has produced in a career that spans almost forty years is remarkable for its volume, its range of genre and subject matter, and the critical debate it has often sparked. Controversy has focused on the artistic merits of Vidal's work, on his frankness in discussing such topics as homosexuality, and on his outspokenness in satirizing social mores and institutions. Vidal is considered a stunning stylist; Peter Ackroyd called him "[a] person whose words turn each page into a tray of jewelry." His gift for language enables him to be incisive in his satire and to be entertaining even in those novels faulted for being either insubstantial or polemical. He has been praised for his accomplished use of classical plot structure, his adept social criticism, and, above all, his wit. While critical reception of Vidal's novels has varied, his essays on politics and his literary criticism have been widely admired, and many critics contend that he is a better essayist than novelist.

Although his first novel, *Williwaw* (1946), was acclaimed by critics, Vidal was not able to maintain his positive reputation during what he has termed his "apprenticeship." During this period, which ended with *A Judgment of Paris* (1952), he pub-lished a novel nearly every year. Vidal has disowned three of his apprenticeship novels because he had not yet found his "own true voice and pitch," but these likely did less to damage his reputation than did publication of *The City and the Pillar* (1948). One of the first novels written about homosexuality, *The City and the Pillar* was considered by some critics to be sensationalistic and pornographic. Vidal contends that critics and advertisers, reacting to *The City and the Pillar,* deliberately ignored his next few novels. Consequently, Vidal turned to writing plays for television, many of which, particularly *Visit to a Small Planet* (1957), were quite successful. Vidal also wrote several plays for the Broadway stage, and he penned three detective novels under the pseudonym of Edgar Box. He re-turned to writing novels under his own name with *Julian* (1964). *Julian* is a work of historical fiction, a genre in which Vidal has had many critical and popular successes. Vidal's first col-lection of essays, *Rocking the Boat* (1962), was followed by several other volumes culled from articles he had written for a wide variety of periodicals. Vidal has also aired his political and social ideas on many television talk shows and has twice run for Congress.

Vidal once referred to himself as being "thematically monot-onous" and went on to say, "It's all part of a search for the Self, and it took . . . six novels—before I found my Self." His early works center on young protagonists, often travelers, struggling with questions of freedom and identity and often involved in romantic relationships and rivalries. Vidal wrote *Williwaw* while he was in the army, confined for a long period to a transport ship in the Aleutian Islands. The novel is set in a similar situation, and the conflicts result from the boredom of confinement, a severe storm, and a sexual rivalry between two of the characters. Critics compared Vidal's writing in

*Williwaw* to Hemingway's spare style. Some maintained that Vidal demonstrated a degree of control unusual in a first nov-elist, evoking character and setting without flooding the reader with an abundance of emotion, philosophy, or convolution of plot. Vidal's next novel, *In a Yellow Wood* (1947), concerns a veteran of World War II who chooses the security of a good job over an exciting love affair. This is one of the novels that Vidal disowned, along with the autobiographical *A Season of Comfort* (1949) and his first work of historical fiction, *A Search for the King* (1950).

Vidal's third novel, *The City and the Pillar,* brought him the first widespread notice of his career and the most outraged response. The novel tells the story of a young man's awakening to his homosexuality and examines the homosexual lifestyle. The novel became a best-seller, but some critics considered it too sexually explicit and didactic and its ending melodramatic. Vidal may have agreed with some of these assessments, for when he published *The City and the Pillar Revised* (1965), it was less philosophical and included a different ending. By today's standards the sexual element in *The City and the Pillar* is relatively modest, and the book is now recognized as a se-rious attempt to treat homosexuality as a natural and attractive choice.

Vidal has examined themes of politics and power in many works of historical fiction. He is a tireless researcher and anchors his novels in the reality of the times depicted. *Julian* is the story of Julian the Apostate, the fourth-century Roman emperor who tried to stop the spread of Christianity. Some critics contend that *Julian* is the novel in which Vidal finds his literary voice as a dispassionate commentator on the follies of humankind. *Messiah* (1954), *A Search for the King*, and *Creation* (1980) are also set in the ancient past, but Vidal's strongest historical interest has been in American political history. His American history tetralogy comprises *Washington D.C.* (1967), a portrayal of the Washington milieu from 1937 through 1952; *Burr* (1973) and *1876* (1976), both narrated by the fictional historian Charles Schuyler; and *Lincoln: A Novel* (1984), in which Vidal reconstructs Abraham Lincoln's character through the comments of his political associates.

Vidal has also written several humorous novels satirizing contemporary society, including the well-known "Breckinridge" novels. In *Myra Breckinridge* (1968) the protagonist undergoes a sex-change operation. The kinky sexual episodes which ensue were abhorred by some reviewers; others, however, read the book as a campy satire on sex, politics, and Hollywood values and applauded Vidal's wit and inventiveness. Although *Myra Breckinridge* is a comic novel, it reinforces a belief that Vidal has voiced in some of his other novels and essays: that all people are inherently bisexual and androgynous. A sequel, *Myron* (1974), although not as successful as the earlier book, is notable for its fantastic shifts of time and place. *Kalki* (1978) and *Duluth* (1983) also are satiric novels in which fantasy plays an important role.

Written in the satirical tone he favors in his novels, Vidal's essays also reflect many of his fictional concerns. His observations on history, sexual mores, and literature are wittily recorded, but he saves his most devastating remarks for the American political machine. Vidal's collections of essays include *Rocking the Boat, Reflections Upon a Sinking Ship* (1969), *Homage to Daniel Shays: Collected Essays 1952-1972* (1972), *Matters of Fact and Fiction: Essays 1973-1976* (1977), and *The Second American Revolution* (1982).

(See also *CLC*, Vols. 2, 4, 6, 8, 10, 22; *Contemporary Authors*, Vols. 5-8, rev. ed.; *Contemporary Authors New Revision Series*, Vol. 13; and *Dictionary of Literary Biography*, Vol. 6.)

## CHRISTOPHER LEHMANN-HAUPT

To judge from this latest nonfiction collection, **"The Second American Revolution"** [published in Britain as **"Pink Triangle and Yellow Star"**], Mr. Vidal . . . is some sort of genius at making connections. How else is it possible for him to air once again all his now-familiar obsessions and at the same time cover such an entertaining variety of subjects as the screenwriting of "Ben Hur," the satirical novels of Thomas Love Peacock, the sensibilities of LaBelle Lance and the gossip surrounding Alice Roosevelt Longworth's affair with Senator William Borah. . . .

How else could **"The Second American Revolution"** wax by turns outrageous, witty, nasty, amusing, poisonous, shrewd and silly, yet still leave one feeling that it was written by a man of taste and seriousness?

Part of what is stimulating about these essays is the way they challenge the reader to make his own connections. For example, how is one to reconcile Mr. Vidal's tireless defense of homosexuality with the anti-estheticism he betrays in his sneering denigration of the "serious-novel" that is "a word-struc-

ture that deals only with itself" (as opposed to the novel that "deals with the human condition"), or the contempt he expresses for the auteur theory of cinematic creation. . . .

[One] would have thought of a man whose fundamental outlook appears to be based on his self-identification as an outcast, that he would have been inclined to embrace the vanguard of experimental art and to hold with the view of the artist as rebel and outsider. Yet he has always sneered at high-falutin' theories of esthetics and inclined toward the traditional mainstream. . . .

Is his esthetic traditionalism perhaps connected with his radical, anti-elitist politics? Or is it simply the result of his experience both as a working Hollywood screenwriter and as a novelist who has never been taken very seriously by the academic critics . . .? The answer, I suppose, depends on how seriously one is willing to take Mr. Vidal.

This too is not always easy to decide. Can he mean it when he declares that "very little of what" F. Scott "Fitzgerald wrote has any great value as literature" and that "Fitzgerald was barely literate"? Is he serious when he calls Thornton Wilder "one of the few first-rate writers the United States has produced" and Christopher Isherwood "the best prose writer in English"? Is this intentional hyperbole? Or has Mr. Vidal lost his sense of responsibility?

Just when you think he has he is likely to pull the rug out from under. The fourth essay from the end, "The State of the Union Revisited (1980)," is a tired rehash of standard leftist-conspiracy theory, blaming the Chase Manhattan Bank for everything that is wrong in the contemporary world. This is Mr. Vidal lazily going through the motions, and it tempts one not to bother to read any further. But he follows this piece with the title essay, a probing, knowledgable analysis of what may well have gone wrong in the unfolding of American constitutional history and what might be done to ameliorate certain current problems.

Finally, in "A Note on Abraham Lincoln," he offers us a sensitive appreciation of the 16th President. While it makes too much of an insubstantial rumor that Lincoln may have had syphilis, it goes far to dispel the Disneyland image that we have grown accustomed to. Thus one closes **"The Second American Revolution"** feeling simultaneously annoyed and stimulated by this brilliant gadfly of a writer and social critic.

> *Christopher Lehmann-Haupt, in a review of "The Second American Revolution and Other Essays," in* The New York Times, *April 27, 1982, p. C11.*

## DENIS DONOGHUE

[In the title essay of **"The Second American Revolution,"** Gore Vidal proposes] that the U.S.A. should adopt the British system of government. . . .

On the margin of his main theme, Vidal has many things to say, and to repeat, about drink, Hollywood, religion ("particularly the Judaeo-Christian variety"), the C.I.A., and how rough life is for homosexuals, whom he sometimes prefers to call homosexualists. . . .

Vidal is a famous novelist and, for readers who care, an equally famous stylist. In his book reviews he writes a more glittering prose than anyone else who goes in for the Revlon Look. (p. 7)

Vidal can be very funny, even when he tries. He is quite funny when he goes after Midge Decter, sexually harassing her along the Fire Island Pines. But he can also avoid being funny. In his review of Doris Lessing's "Shikasta" he says that "at best, Lessing's prose is solid and slow and a bit flat-footed." Envying her these merits, Vidal tries to achieve them for himself, and now and then succeeds. . . .

When Vidal wants to be lively, he goes in for hyperbole and the pointless comparison. . . .

But when he wants to be boring, he resorts to a few standard themes: the absurdity of literary scholarship, the evils of the Chase Manhattan Bank, the similar evils of Christianity. When he wants to say nothing, he says it about Mary McCarthy. When he wants to praise Christopher Isherwood, he calls him "the best prose writer in England," without examining a line of his prose.

Still, Vidal is a witty man, at his best a fine novelist and, even on an off-day, a lively person. **"The Second American Revolution"** is not one of his choice works. . . . It is best read as a function of Vidal's personality, taking the reviews and essays as particles of that substance. If you already like the substance, you'll like the current particles. If not, not. (p. 35)

*Denis Donoghue, "Odds and Ends by Gore Vidal," in* The New York Times Book Review, *May 2, 1982, pp. 7, 35.*

**THOMAS MALLON**

[In *The Second American Revolution and Other Essays (1976-1982)*] the reader will find enough of Gore Vidal's familiar peeves and idiolect to make him feel thoroughly at home. All the bees are still hiving under that brilliant bonnet, swat as their keeper will at them. The "hacks of Academe," "Christers," writers of mere description, Truman Capote, those "hustler-plagiarist" directors acclaimed as *auteurs,* "book-chat"—even the use of "shrill" as a verb: they're all back for another beating.

The really new bee is Vidal's preoccupation in a number of these pieces with the need for a second constitutional convention, at which he would no doubt play George Mason, the political figure (with the possible exception of Nero) to whom he must feel closest. So eager is he to see the birth of a "Fourth [American] Republic" (never mind about the second and third) that he is willing to throw in his lot with the National Taxpayers Union and extreme Right-to-Lifers if that will mean the convention gets called. . . .

The spectacle of Gore Vidal government-building with the Reverend Jerry Falwell could have its pleasures, but I would not wish to witness it other than from a safe distance in the afterlife. If Vidal would rather write constitutions than novels at this point, I don't think he should be encouraged. Let not even his admirers be bulled by Gore on this one.

And an admirer I certainly am. No one else in what he calls "the land of the tin ear" can combine better sentences into more elegantly sustained demolition derbies than Vidal does in some of his best essays. . . . Sometimes the witty line gets smeared into a cheap graffito ("a Catskill hotel called the Hilton Kramer"), but the real *élan* Vidal—the wicked conspiracy of syntax and diction—is more often in evidence. (p. 1035)

[Most] of the literary (as opposed to "political") essays in this volume are celebrations. Christopher Isherwood, L. Frank Baum (the author of the Oz books, "a truly subversive writer"),

Thomas Love Peacock, Leonardo Sciascia, and V. S. Pritchett are, along with [Edmund] Wilson, praised, not nuked. Vidal's specific judgments proceed from his long holy war against the sterilities of academic criticism and "word-structure" novels that are written to be taught instead of read. These are very big bees, and for years of flailing against them Vidal deserves—however little he would like it—to be blessed. He has gone after literary insects not for the mere joy of the killing, but because he is trying to clear the air around the books he loves. The long piece on Baum shows him willing to be tender. . . . Indeed, in a number of the essays on writing in this volume the famously mean lizard of page and tube comes very close to being positively sweet.

Vidal is by now getting a little sentimental about his own cynicism. He says he believes that "there is no more certain way of achieving perfect unpopularity in any society than to speak against the reigning pieties and agreed-upon mendacities." This is of course not so. After decades of listening to him direly proclaim "these last days of empire" just "as things begin to fall apart," one feels a sort of familiar affection for him. The *enfant* isn't quite so *terrible* any more; the spleen seems a little avuncular. I strongly suspect the apocalypse is much farther away than he thinks; the flames are, after all, not currently much higher than they were when, all those decades ago, his fiddle started to fan them. But—and here "but" is everything—the strings remain wonderfully in tune. (pp. 1035-36)

*Thomas Mallon, "Catching a Buzz," in* National Review, *Vol. XXXIV, No. 16, August 20, 1982, pp. 1035-36.*

**DAVID MONTROSE**

Gore Vidal, essayist, began as a novel-reviewer who sometimes wrote about politics. Over the years, and the collections, the second string expanded until, in *Matters of Fact and of Fiction* (1976), fact (usually American politics) outweighed fiction (writers and critics). In *Pink Triangle and Yellow Star,* the ratio of politics to literature is lower. Nevertheless, matters of fact set the tone more strongly than ever.

Above all, Vidal is a polemicist, ever-prepared to ride his hobby-horses one more time. His essays are purposeful arrangements of major and minor preoccupations: an aside in one, or more, becomes the crux of another. . . . This arrangement is particularly evident in the political essays, which tend to be digressive and compendious, reading like permutations on a single campaign speech. In a way, they are: everything converges in 'The State of the Union Revisited (1980)', a useful anthology of Vidal's political thought and the foundation of his lecture-circuit pitch. Repetition is a necessary ingredient of polemic; as literature, though, Vidal's programme is now somewhat familiar, like his advocacy of bisexual promiscuity as psychological cure-all.

Repetition should be more avoidable in literary territory, where Vidal has only one real crisis: that the Hacks of Academe operate critical procedures—geared solely to career advancement—which are killing literature. Even so, this lone preoccupation bobs up throughout the matters of fiction. . . .

Although Vidal's political and literary crises are entirely distinct, they share a grounding in conspiracy theory. The Hacks are all in it together; American society is run for the benefit of The Bank. Now Vidal's conspiracies certainly have some existence outside his imagination, especially when he detects an orchestrated manipulation, by the New Right, of sexual issues to replace the Red Menace, whose potency has waned, as electorate-frightener and vote-catcher. Increasingly, though, he explains all injustice in such terms. . . .

[Everything] boils down to one neat equation that's so much more attractive than the dull 'There are no easy answers'. Conspiracy theory imposes pattern, providing reasons for the state of things and, however vaguely, someone to blame. The problem is: there usually are no easy answers. . . .

Inevitably, readers will come to this volume principally for Vidal's prose; his subjects are a lesser attraction. This happens with all major essayists. Vidal, however, consciously puts the cart before the horse: one's awareness is primarily of reading Vidal, only secondarily of reading about Christopher Isherwood's autobiographies or Cecil Beaton's diaries. Chesterton wrote that 'a good novel tells us the truth about its hero; but a bad novel tells us the truth about its author'. If a similar rule applies to essays, those in *Pink Triangle* ought to be very bad indeed; but Vidal invariably carries off his high profile. Most of the pieces included here are review-based. In this collection Vidal sticks closer than usual to the books: to excellent effect in his consideration of Doris Lessing's *Shikasta*, much less so when *The Thirties*, a selection from Edmund Wilson's journals for the period, and Pritchett's *The Myth Makers* come up for scrutiny. Mind you, the essays proper are, 'The Oz Books' excepted, a little disappointing. . . .

On the other hand, Vidal's talents as a populariser of American history remain undiminished. His method is to re-present in synopsis (with Vidalian commentary) a work of academic muckraking that might otherwise be little noticed, finishing off with his personal conclusions. Biographies of Lincoln and Theodore Roosevelt are so treated; but the outstanding performance disseminates Ferdinand Lundberg's *Cracks in the Constitution*, which diminishes the revered makers of that document and traces the dubious histories of the Supreme Court's power to review legislation and of Presidential executive orders.

*Pink Triangle* is a less satisfying collection than *Matters of Fact and Fiction*. The pieces are generally shorter and the factual matters especially have a flavour of second pressings. There are even some infelicities of style! But the vineyard is still *grand cru classe*. Vidal is an astute literary critic—as his firm placing of Fitzgerald demonstrates—and a stimulating, if not entirely reliable, political pundit. He is formidably well-read and invariably entertaining, even if he does, these days, limit himself to one-liners, eschewing hilarious routines like the preamble to his exposition on Walter Annenberg (*Collected Essays*). If only he would put his hobby-horses out to grass for a while or at least refrain from rounding them up inside hard covers.

> David Montrose, "Riding His Hobby-Horses," in New Statesman, *Vol. 104, No. 2683, August 20, 1982, p. 18.*

## ROBERT F. KIERNAN

Vidal is a difficult writer to categorize because he is a man of several voices. He has brooded over ancient empires in several novels, as though he were possessed by the spirit of Gibbon, yet he has also written about the American *crise de virilité* and managed to sound a good deal like Hemingway. He has sent young Americans in search of Old Europe, as a dutiful son of Henry James, but he has also written novels about the American political system and acknowledged a debt to Henry Adams. In his essays he often seems like Lord Macaulay, magisterial and urbane, while in the Breckinridge novels he evokes Ronald Firbank, irrepressible and playful.

Nevertheless, there are aspects of Vidal's writing that are constant. Syntactically elegant sentences are a trademark, certainly, and understated structures and a coolness of tone are too. More than anything else, however, we have learned to expect amplitude from Vidal. We have learned to expect that his narratives will be enriched with gossip, incidental satire, self-mockery, and philosophical and historical asides, very much in the eighteenth-century mode of Laurence Sterne and other giants of the early English novel. Concomitantly, we have learned to expect antique literary forms from Vidal, as if they were necessary to accommodate this old-world amplitude. Thus, his writings include historical fiction, moral essays, nonsense tales, mythography, and apocalyptic parables.

But Vidal is as much prankster as pundit, and his elegance, coolness, and learning derive a special piquancy from a wit always at the ready. "I am at heart a propagandist," he has written of himself, "a tremendous hater, a tiresome nag, compacently positive that there is no human problem which could not be solved if people would simply do as I advise." There, in a sentence, is the Vidalian manner: the arrogance of the pundit solemnly and unabashedly put forth but undercut and put in amenable focus by the prankster's wit. (pp. 10-11)

Although Vidal had several early successes, he was almost two decades into his career before he discovered his most successful voices and the literary forms that would best accommodate them. The novels . . . and short stories that he produced en route to those discoveries bear the scars of experimentation, but they merit brief attention inasmuch as they are the workshop in which the Vidalian manner was forged. (p. 118)

*The Season of Comfort* [1949] is interesting for its stylistics. Even though they are generally unsuccessful, they show Vidal breaking away from the hard-boiled manner of his early Hemingway style, in search of a more experimental style. The early chapters, for instance, attempt a stream-of-consciousness effect, with elaborately triggered flashbacks and long passages of third-person narration which might as readily be in the first person, so closely do they follow the mental processes of individual characters. The penultimate chapter even attempts to represent simultaneous monologues on facing pages, with the verso pages belonging to Bill, the recto pages to Charlotte. The gimmick is appropriate to the alienation between Bill and his mother at that point in the story, but it is too clumsy a device to be accounted successful.

The most damaging of Vidal's stylistic experiments in *The Season of Comfort* are his experiments in tone. He strives for an arch tone early in the novel by employing a great many clichés in the stream-of-consciousness passages, thus making the point that his characters think in clichés, but belaboring the point. In his use of transitional and linking devices Vidal tries too hard to be clever. . . . Yet archness of tone and elegant transitional devices are hallmarks of the mature Vidal style. *The Season of Comfort* should therefore be understood as a transitional novel, marking the end of Vidal's use of the Hemingway style and marking a serious attempt to devise a voice of his own.

*A Search for the King* (1950) is a very different sort of book, set in the twelfth century and recounting the tale of Blondel de Néel, a French troubadour alleged to have been a friend of Richard Coeur de Lion. (pp. 123-24)

Because *A Search for the King* is Vidal's first novel in a historical mode, it must be seen as another experimental work, a giant step away from the Hemingway manner. But there is much about the novel that suggests a mature achievement. Its prose style is assured, its narrative pace is brisk, and its characterizations are lucid. Vidal displays no taste for the trumpery ornament or the quaintly period language that vitiates so much historical fiction, and he does not even poke fun at the medieval world in the way we might expect. The werewolves, vampires, and giants in the novel are taken seriously, although their treatment has just the right latitude to accommodate a modern understanding of how such folk beliefs developed. Vidal's werewolves are essentially highwaymen dressed in wolfskins who merely call themselves werewolves, exploiting the popular belief in such creatures. Similarly, Vidal's characters are credited with an entirely realistic sense of their world. (p. 125)

If the historicity of *A Search for the King* points toward the great historical novels of Vidal's maturity, this straightforwardness in the novel seems to point backward to the unadorned realism of *The City and the Pillar* [1948]. As a result, the novel seems to many to be inexplicably positioned in the *oeuvre*, more contrary to the general lines of Vidal's development than otherwise. I prefer to emphasize the relevance that *A Search for the King* has to the *oeuvre*. Specifically, the motif of the two males, one of whom grounds his existence in the other, is as fundamental to this novel as it is to such novels as *The City and the Pillar, Washington, D.C.* [1967], and *Burr* [1973]. In fact, Vidal never renders the motif more affectingly. When Blondel finds himself without a center and the world itself without a center point after Richard's capture, his disorientation echoes our romantic impression that the medieval world enjoyed a centricity that we have lost. We share profoundly in Blondel's heartache, as a result, and it is tempting to use our understanding of the two male figures in this novel to gloss all such pairs in Vidal's fiction, although Vidal never again depicts the relationship between two men in quite so charming (and asexual) a manner.

*Dark Green, Bright Red* (1950, revised 1968) emerged out of Vidal's experience of living in Guatemala in the late 1940s. Set in an unnamed Central American country, it is the story of an abortive revolution waged by General Jorge Alvarez Asturias. . . . (pp. 125-26)

Like *A Search for the King, Dark Green, Bright Red* is an experimental work in which Vidal tests the ability of a minor genre to accommodate his interests and voice. Specifically, he experiments with the novel of tropical intrigue, as developed by Joseph Conrad and Graham Greene. Like those earlier novelists, Vidal dilutes the elements of adventure in his narrative with monologic passages that are weary in tone, and those passages turn what might have been a simple tale of adventure into a study in *Weltschmerz*. The novel fails to engage the reader in its weary mood, however. Peter Nelson, whose eyes control what we see in the novel, has the curious ability to turn dark green and bright red into monotonal drab, and Nelson is himself utterly without color. We never know why he was court-martialed by the United States Army, for instance, and we never glimpse any feeling in him for Elena or for his friend José. His *Weltschmerz*, therefore, seems simple dullness, a world-weariness born not of jadedness but of disengagement.

Many of Vidal's novels show a marked inability to create rounded characters, but this inability is never more damaging than it is in *Dark Green, Bright Red*, for the novel has no psychological interest whatsoever. (pp. 127-28)

*Messiah* (1954, revised 1965) is the first of Vidal's novels to affect the guise of a written testament. (p. 129)

In many ways, *Messiah* marks Vidal's coming into his own as a writer, for it seems to be the novel in which he developed the formula of his most successful fiction. Specifically, it was in *Messiah* that Vidal explored the possibilities of the fictive memoir and discovered that it is a genre which perfectly accommodates his sudden flashes of wit, his interest in revisionist ideas, and his occasional taste for a recherché syntax. At the same time, he no doubt discovered that the fictive memoir requires little in terms of character and plot development, those typical failings of his art. . . . Vidal's gift has always been for the quick effect rather than for sustained development, and because the form of the memoir is so amenable to discontinuous effects, Vidal's voice seems more assured and more wholly his own in *Messiah* than ever before. It is as if the tendency to a grandiose rhetoric that Vidal has said he fears in himself were kept at bay by the intimacy of the memoir form, as it was earlier by the Hemingway manner. It is as if Vidal were able to expose himself full voice only under the pretense that he speaks sotto voce.

Vidal's minor works include seven short stories. Six of them were written in the late 1940s and early 1950s, published variously, and collected under the title *A Thirsty Evil* (1956). "Pages from an Abandoned Journal" was written somewhat later, expressly for the publication of *A Thirsty Evil*. "The audience for the short story so shrank in my lifetime," Vidal has said, "that it would have taken a dedication of the sort I lacked to keep on." The short stories were seminal in Vidal's development as a writer, however, because they developed his feel for first-person narration, and Vidal's best work is all in the first-person mode.

"Three Stratagems," in fact, employs *two* narrators. The first part of the story is narrated by a young prostitude named Michael, and the second and third parts by an aging widower named George Royal, who picks up Michael one day on the beach at Key West. . . . "Three Stratagems" is a wonderfully neat and efficient story, sharp and effective in its plotting and understated in its theme. The device of the double narrator is the obvious key to its success.

"The Robin" is a slighter tale and not nearly so successful in its mode of narration. It begins promisingly with a sardonic narrator who describes how he and his friend Oliver took pleasure in all sorts of unpleasantness when they were nine years old. . . . But when the boys discover an injured robin one day, they fail to measure up as sadists, for they burst into tears after clumsily dispatching the bird. The narrator's tone unfortunately shifts as abruptly as the boys' psychology, and the shift to a sentimental point of view undercuts a number of passages in which childhood is seen with a nicely disillusioned eye. The story seems trivial and emotionally false as a consequence, as inept a tale as Vidal has ever told.

Like "The Robin," "A Moment of Green Laurel" is a first-person story which looks back on childhood, but it succeeds where the earlier story fails. The narrator is a young man who has returned to Washington after World War II. He walks out to his childhood home in Rock Creek Park, and there he meets a twelve-year-old boy who is gathering laurel to weave into

Roman wreaths, just as the narrator had done a dozen years before. . . . The man has stumbled upon the ghost of his own childhood, we understand, and there are many suggestions that the man and his youthful *Doppelgänger* are Vidal himself. The story is as nostalgically sentimental as "The Robin," but its sentiment rings truer because the tone of the narration is consistently dreamlike and remote and because the narrator's responses are artfully blunted, as if wrapped in the cotton wool of sleep.

"The Zenner Trophy" is another story about homosexuality, narrated from the point of view of Mr. Beckman, a teacher in a New England preparatory school. Beckman is given the uncongenial task of expelling the school's top athlete because he was caught *in flagrante delicto* with another boy. . . . To Beckman's surprise, the boy is not in the least ashamed of his homosexual activity, only annoyed that the school has chosen to worry his parents with it. The boy's ability to take the reins of his life in hand wins the teacher's respect, for Beckman is not even able to take in hand the reins of their conversation. The story is interesting enough so far as it goes, but the boy's quiet confidence and the teacher's diffidence are simplistic, and the shock value they had in 1950 is no longer able to compensate for the lack of psychological depth in the story.

The narrator of "Erlinda and Mr. Coffin" is an impoverished Southern gentlewoman who rents one of the rooms in her Key West home to the title characters. . . . The tale is rather giddily contrived, and it can hardly be taken seriously as a work of art, but its histrionics are fun, and the voice of the gentlewoman is carried off with panache.

"Pages from an Abandoned Journal" is a more serious story. Its narrator is a failed Ph.D. candidate who attends a party on the rue du Bac in Paris and finds himself introduced to a world of homosexuality and drugs presided over by one Elliott Magren. . . . The world of Elliott Magren . . . is replete with prostitution, opium addiction, and the *gendarmerie,* and because Magren's world contrasts so invidiously with the narrator's, the latter earns no points for merely discovering himself to be homosexual. It is a curious story, filled with contempt for the effeminate sort of homosexual and best understood, perhaps, as Vidal's antidote to the pieties of "The Zenner Trophy."

"The Ladies in the Library" is the last story in *A Thirsty Evil*—appropriately, a death story. Walter Bragnet, a middle-aged writer, and his cousin Sybil are the last remaining members of the Bragnet family, and they spend a sentimental weekend at the old family home in Virginia, the house now owned by a Miss Mortimer. Three childhood friends, the Parker sisters, are invited to lunch, and Walter overhears them argue about his death as they work at their knitting in the library. As soon as they agree that he is to die from a heart attack, one sister cuts the knot in her yarn, and Walter is suddenly conscious of a massive constriction in his chest. He sees Miss Mortimer smiling at him, "a familiar darkness in her lovely eyes." Death itself inhabits the house of Bragnet, in other words, while the Three Fates conspire in the library. The story works surprisingly well, given the difficulty of domesticating allegorical figures. The third-person viewpoint ·of the story allows us just the right degree of access into Walter's mind to pull off the allegorical stunt, and the tone of the story is pitched exactly right, neither offensively cute nor darkly mysterious. Vidal is obviously very skilled at this sort of fantasy, as "A Moment of Green Laurel" and *A Search for the King* bear out. One regrets that he has not written more stories in the mode. (pp. 131-36)

Because Vidal is a writer with many voices, his career seems a history of elaborate feints and passes. His first novel, *Williwaw,* was hard-hitting in the best Hemingway tradition, but *The City and the Pillar* applied the Hemingway manner to a homosexual theme and delivered a limp-wristed uppercut to our expectations. A series of undistinguished novels in the 1950s convinced us that Vidal was one of those writers whose careers peak early, but 1964 served up *Julian,* an intimidating novel in terms of both scholarship and aesthetics. The trilogy *Washington, D.C., Burr,* and *1876* followed shortly in tandem with the Breckinridge confections, and once again Vidal proved difficult to categorize, for the trilogy is a formidable overview of American history, while the Breckinridge novels are the purest camp. *Kalki* disinterred the apocalyptic theme we had thought abandoned with *Messiah, Creation* disinterred *Julian*'s interest in ancient history, and *Two Sisters* came out of nowhere, its autobiographical dazzle wholly unexpected. Vidal's performance is nothing less than ventriloquistic.

Yet there are performances of which Vidal seems incapable. The formal discipline of modernism seems beyond him, for instance. Faithful instead to an eighteenth-century aesthetic of the novel, Vidal crams gossip, journalism, sociology, philosophy, history, and literary parody into a narrative hopper and christens the mix a novel in the name of the god Vitality. Also beyond him is the high-romantic pretense that interpersonal love is the ultimate adventure. A more traditional respect for self-love claims his allegiance, and all his major characters are estimable narcissists. Is Vidal a reactionary? Is he a classicist in his tastes and values, stepping back over the nineteenth century as over something unpleasant on the footpath? Is he a Petronius, as he has several times been labeled, casting a dispirited eye over the last days of the American empire? Is his vaunted radicalism a radical traditionalism? Yes. And he plays that role, like his others, with panache.

Vidal is also a *farceur,* of course, and insouciance and insolence regularly join forces in his rhetoric. The seriousness of his reactionary stance is therefore open to question. It is entirely possible that his celebrated distaste for modernism and his fulminations against romantic love are simply apologias for the glaring incapacities of his fiction, a policy of attack or be attacked, as it were. But apologias aside, the weakness of Vidal's larger structures and his general inability to make his characters come alive are *defining* incapacities of his fiction—importantly so, because they define him as an artist of the middle rank. . . . Vidal is an artist of the middle rank primarily because his talent is for the small scale: for the anecdote, for the scene, ineluctably for the sentence.

Pointing out this limitation in Vidal's art does not constitute an attack. Vidal's anecdotes and scenes are not so much line drawings as richly conceived impasto, clotted with intelligence, layered with wit, and worked to the substantiality of bas-relief. And Vidal's prose . . . is very fine. His deft touch with syntax, his marvelous ear for cadence, and his adroit sense of tone are entirely masterful. If even his best characters are not quite flesh and blood, they are, like Cleopatra, fire and air. (pp. 142-44)

The great charm of Vidal's writing is its auctorial audacity. The risqué, the demotic, and the left wing always threaten to bring down his elegant prose and mannered sophistication, and a devilish wit always counterpoints his angelically lucid style. It is a bravura performance withal, and in a sense Vidal is less a storyteller than a performer. His fictions do not tend to establish self-contained worlds independent of his mediation; rather, they constitute a juggler's feats, with Vidal compounding the most extraordinary materials not for the art of jugglery alone but for the opportunity to wear an audacious face. We are always aware of that face in Vidal's mature fictions. A quip, an outrageously sentimental *glissade,* an autobiographical indiscretion—all turn his jugglery into a performance, a *celebration* of auctorial selfhood. (p. 144)

Robert F. Kiernan, in his Gore Vidal, *Frederick Ungar Publishing Co., 1982, 165 p.*

## ANGELA McROBBIE

Just imagine what Derrida might do with *Dallas.* Consider for a moment what might be Gore Vidal's relationship to each of these, dare I say it, signifiers. *Duluth* ('Love It Or Loathe It, You Can Never Leave It Or Lose It') could well be seen as an answer. Both Vidal and Barthes before him have commented on the practice of summarising a text as a kind of re-writing: not a claim most critics in their modesty would make. In any case, *Duluth* almost denies the possibility of its own summary.... I find this book one of the most brilliant, most radical and most subversive pieces of writing to emerge from America in recent years.

Its view of America focuses on the private obsessions and fantasies which, in Vidal's view, have come to motor the whole political machinery. Duluth is a fine example. It has of course no real or authentic existence but is precisely the sum of, in this case, the fictions Vidal weaves around it. There is *Duluth* the new television series, there is that *Duluth* described by pulp novelist Rosemary Klein Kantor, who ... depends on a word processor for her scripts, and finally there is the meta-version provided by the author himself. *Duluth*'s characters are suspended somewhere between the necessity for each of these narratives to move, and their own personal, media-inspired fantasies....

Vidal has always engaged with the excesses of mass culture, with soft porn, soap opera, sex 'n' violence, and rough humour. It might even be said that his status as a serious writer has suffered from this very American addiction. (Everyone in Duluth is addicted to something.) He is also a vengeful writer, one who has closely observed the marginalisation of the radical critic in his own country by the New Right, and is compelled to hit back. Denounced by the pro-family lobby, the anti-ERA campaigners and the 'fag-haters', and bereft of the support of a Left culture (he once claimed there was no Left in America), Vidal's is a lonely voice. No wonder he responds so ambiguously to the 'death of the author' structuralists, who would also write him out of the picture. *Duluth,* the novel, is a nasty, demented reply to both. It's a ruthless account of a population stupefied by its own projected and desired self-image—a self-image drawn from those sub-literary genres which grace our screens. It's a fearful account because it shows how this white, middle-class section of the community and those non-stop visuals together can invade and win over the hearts and minds of those groups and classes who might just otherwise have represented an alternative.

And to those who tell him that all words and all language are prescribed and that you don't write it, it writes you, then, goddamm-it, Vidal will lay down his pen or at least he will pass over his word-processor to somebody else—allowing her, notionally, the last word. It's up to bug-woman Tricia vengefully to consign Duluth to the past tense. So be it, except that, though Vidal may cynically and wittily preside over this social removal, he won't willingly write himself out of history or culture

altogether. He is not a man prone to sentiment, but I do think he feels and he certainly continues to signify.

*Angela McRobbie, "Sign Language," in* New Statesman, *Vol. 105, No. 2720, May 6, 1983, p. 24.*

## JONATHAN YARDLEY

Gore Vidal means to amuse in *Duluth,* a flamboyant satire in the manner of *Myra Breckinridge,* and from time to time he does. At its most penetrating, Vidal's wit is agreeably malicious; he has selected here a long list of targets that ache for demolition—among them avant-garde fiction and its academic critics, the oratorical style of Ronald Reagan, the vocabulary of psychobabble, and the hegemony of television—and he leaves many of them in pieces on the floor. There can be no question that Vidal had a grand time writing *Duluth,* and some of that pleasure is passed along to the reader.

But there's a funny, or not-so-funny, thing about Vidal. He is arguably the most accomplished and authoritative essayist in the United States; he is a person of indisputable sophistication and *savoir vivre;* he is equally at home in a literary salon or a public-policy debate; he is all of these things, yet he is capable of—no, he relishes—retailing a brand of witless, slapstick humor that would cause a sophomore to blush. There is much at which to laugh in *Duluth* but there is even more, alas, at which to wince. His crudity can be astonishing....

[Certain passages are funny] in the way that the graffiti on a men's room wall or the maunderings of a living-room comic are funny; we laugh not because any genuine wit is present but because we have encountered the *appearance* of humor, even if in its rudest form. Over and again, Vidal indulges himself in wordplay of the most strained, yet obvious, variety: formulaic romantic novels are set in "Regency Hyatt England," public television is the "Petroleum Broadcasting System." Surely Vidal can do better than this.

As, of course, he can. When a writer of Vidal's gifts fires off as many rounds as he does in *Duluth,* a few at least are bound to find their targets....

[*Duluth* is] not so much a novel as a long succession of gags, asides and invectives. Duluth, the Minnesota city of the title, is indeed in Minnesota, but it borders Lake Erie on one side and Mexico on the other.... This city called Duluth is, in other words, an American Everycity as imagined by Vidal, to whom "there is no lie so great that it will not be taken at face value in Duluth."

This is Vidal's politics; he offers an ample serving of it in *Duluth,* just as he did in *Myra Breckinridge.* He also offers some amusing divagations on the subject of illusion and reality as experienced in the age of television, and he conjures up several characters who, though fashioned entirely from cardboard, are nonetheless entertaining; a good word certainly must be said for Darlene Eck, the libidinous cop, and Rosemary Klein Kantor, who is not merely "queen of romance, Harlequin-style," but also "the acknowledged heiress—as well as plagiarist—of the late Georgette Heyer."

*Duluth* is Vidal's 20th novel; like most of its predecessors, it demonstrates nothing so much as that Vidal is an essayist, not a novelist. His grasp of fictive structure is insecure, his gift for characterization is exceedingly small, his tendency is to wander off on tangents. Yet he has a large and presumably appreciative audience for his fiction, and no doubt that audience will lap *Duluth* right up. This is, on the whole, a mystery.

> Jonathan Yardley, "Throwing Firecrackers Down Main Street," in Book World—The Washington Post, *May 15, 1983, p. 3.*

### CHRISTOPHER LEHMANN-HAUPT

[In **"Duluth"** Gore Vidal has created] a Duluth that is the whole of America collapsed into its essential nonsense like a constellation of humanity into a crippled white dwarf. . . .

I hesitate to burden you in this brief space with all . . . that is going on in Mr. Vidal's novel. It isn't even his Duluth; it belongs to Rosemary Klein Kantor, the Wurlitzer-Prize winner (sounds like "Pulitzer Prize" if slurred) who, according to the law of fictive relativity and its corollary, the simultaneity effect, is able to create at the same time the novel "Duluth," a TV serial "Duluth" and romances set in the Regency-Hyatt era of the Napoleonic wars, all because she hunts and pecks on a word-processor containing the plots of 10,000 previously published novels.

Is this getting confusing? Not in the hands of Gore Vidal it isn't—who, in the madcap mood that produced **"Myra Breck-inridge"** and **"Myron,"** is kidding everything from heterosexuality to J. Edgar Hoover, but most particularly "those abstract verbal constructions so admired by the French and boola-boola Yale!" In Mr. Vidal's hands it's all very clear, and it zips along so smoothly that inertia, if nothing else, carries us through to the end.

It's also rather funny for a while, with its outrageous wordplay—"mucho macho," the comparison of petite flaring nostrils to "a *pomme souffle* getting its second wind," or an announcement by Calderon, a Mexican terrorist, that, "In the absence of an agreed-upon moral consensus, the categoric imperative is self-interest." . . .

By and by, the bright brittleness of **"Duluth"** begins to pall a little. But by then, Mr. Vidal has something other than amusing us in mind. He's warming up for his usual apocalyptic indictment of the human race. I won't give the ending away. But think of Mr. Vidal's familiar peeves and crotchets. Think of his curiously contradictory dislike of experimental art and traditional morals. Think of his disgust with nuclear families and his horror of overpopulation. Think of a world overrun with mindlessly procreating beings. Then you'll have an inkling of how this savagely inhuman comedy winds up.

> Christopher Lehmann-Haupt, in a review of "Duluth," in The New York Times, *May 20, 1983, p. C32.*

### GEORGE STADE

[The] middle American way of life is the subject of **"Duluth,"** a novel set in a city you will not find on any map. . . .

Politically speaking, Mr. Vidal's Duluth occupies all of Middle America: "Every society gets the Duluth it deserves." Morally speaking, its locale is "the wide empty spaces of the human heart." . . .

The main targets of Mr. Vidal's derision this time out . . . are Middle America's political and sexual practices, its cultural pretensions and its literary preferences, which do not seem to include novels by Mr. Vidal. In that respect, at least, **"Duluth"** is not true to life. . . .

The various Duluths in "Duluth" intersect at all angles, so that a character in one may discover that he is also a character in another. Edna Herridge, for example, dies early in the novel "Duluth," but lives on as the actress Joanna Witt, who plays Hilda Ransome in the television serial "Duluth," out of which she speaks directly to her brother Mayor, who is lounging in his living room in the city of Duluth. There is a lot of this sort of thing, which gives Edna, and not only Edna, a migraine.

The moral of these shufflings of characters and fictions, I suppose, is not only that writers repeat themselves and each other, but also that readers imitate characters as they daydream themselves in and out of fictions, there being nothing else. All the world's a plagiarist. One of the Duluths in **"Duluth"** is the novel "Duluth," for this is one of those fictions that refers to itself—often, but not with derision. It is the kind of fiction lately called "a self-consuming artifact," in that it takes itself in as it cancels itself out. It ends with an apocalypse of sorts, not with a bang, but an eraser. (p. 3)

[Mr. Vidal] is not at his best here, mandibles clacking with venom and glee. There is an uncharacteristic lack of zest to his malice, elsewhere so edifying. Bergson remarked that comedy depends on an anesthesia of emotions, and in that respect **"Duluth"** qualifies, but for the most part it is more footloose than funny. Maybe Mr. Vidal noticed along the way that his targets were easy, that they were already in tatters and scarcely worthy of his aim, which is by no means unerring. (p. 37)

> George Stade, "The Duluth We Deserve?" in The New York Times Book Review, *June 5, 1983, pp. 3, 37.*

### CHRISTOPHER LEHMANN-HAUPT

Anyone with a benign outlook on the course of American history would seem to have reason to be nervous about the publication of Gore Vidal's new novel, **"Lincoln,"** the fourth and latest book in his fictional tetralogy, of which **"Burr," "1876"** and **"Washington, D.C."** were the previous three entries.

After all, Mr. Vidal, our most accomplished and commanding historical novelist, has not been especially kind to American history in general or to such icons as Thomas Jefferson, John Marshall, or Ulysses S. Grant in particular. Moreover, in an essay on Lincoln that he included in his most recent collection of nonfiction writing, **"The Second American Revolution,"** Mr. Vidal managed to work in everything unsavory that is known about the Great Emancipator. . . .

But behold, it is a well-founded, complex, very nearly heroic portrait of Lincoln that Mr. Vidal presents in his lengthy chronicle, which confines itself to the years of Lincoln's Presidency. To be sure, there are the blemishes present. The log cabin, rail-splitting legend is debunked. Billy Herndon shows up, gets drunk and talks about Lincoln's whoring adventures as well as the likelihood of his having picked up an infection somewhere along the way. And considerable attention is focused on Mary Todd Lincoln's emotional and financial difficulties, if those can in any way be counted among Lincoln's shortcomings.

But far overshadowing his faults are Lincoln's dignity, his self-deprecatory wit, his endless patience and restraint and his inexhaustible supply of folksy, slightly long-winded stories. The major personal drama of "**Lincoln**"—as opposed to the historical one—is the gradual revelation of Lincoln's deep vision and iron determination, as seen from the point of view of men who judge him at first to be weak and manipulable. . . .

Unfortunately, it is almost as if Mr. Vidal had been stunned into narrative paralysis by the figure of Lincoln. For where the earlier books in the tetralogy, particularly "**Burr**" and "**1876,**" were narrated with high style and a swagger, "**Lincoln**" is sodden in its lack of pace or focus. The viewpoint switches arbitrarily and unpredictably among a half-dozen characters. . . . The details pile up so haphazardly and hectically that it's often difficult to keep one's mind on the story.

What can Mr. Vidal possibly be up to in "**Lincoln**"? Did he set out to write an antihistory of Lincoln and then change his mind in midstream? . . . Or is Mr. Vidal striving for the ultimate in historical authenticity now that he has proved in his earlier novels that he can write historical caricature? . . .

Whatever Mr. Vidal is up to, something is lacking in the effort. The Civil War and the Lincoln years were a turning point in American history, one that consolidated the industrial future of the country and set it on a course that Mr. Vidal himself has been complaining about for years. Yet the narrative sorely misses a mouthpiece to articulate that point of view. The bile seems to be gone from Mr. Vidal's writing. . . .

Perhaps Mr. Vidal only wishes to edify in "**Lincoln.**" Certainly he has deromanticized the era. There are no illusions of a war fought to free the slaves, or of Lincoln's faith in a viable future for the Negro in American society, or of an end to political backstabbing, or to corruption and financial chicanery. But compared to the author's usual fare, it is all so mellow and responsible and, I am afraid, finally dull. One misses the hiss of acid.

> *Christopher Lehmann-Haupt, in a review of "Lincoln," in* The New York Times, *Section III, May 30, 1984, p. C20.*

### JOYCE CAROL OATES

Mr. Vidal's "**Lincoln**" with its necessary but somewhat misleading subtitle, "A Novel," [is] certain to be a controversial work among literary critics, if not among historians (surely the history cannot be faulted, as it comes with the imprimatur of one of our most eminent Lincoln scholars, David Herbert Donald of Harvard), or among readers with a temperamental distrust of fiction's usual strategies (they will love "**Lincoln**"). (p. 1)

[Mr. Vidal's portrait of Lincoln] is reasoned, judicious, straightforward and utterly convincing, less dramatic, perhaps, than the inspired portrait of Aaron Burr in Mr. Vidal's "**Burr**," but even more compelling. In his ongoing chronicle of American history . . . , Mr. Vidal is concerned with dissecting, obsessively and often brilliantly, the roots of personal ambition as they give rise to history itself. If there are very few idealists in Mr. Vidal's fiction, it should be remembered that there are very few idealists in history. . . .

So mythologized has Lincoln become over the decades, it is startling to learn that, at the time of his inauguration, his fellow politicians considered him too uninformed, inept and naïve to handle his office. Running the country would be the responsibility of Secretary of State William Henry Seward, the party's national leader and its most famous man—the wily Seward to

be "premier to Lincoln's powerless monarch." Eventually, of course, Seward has his moment of shuddering epiphany: . . .

"[Lincoln] had been able to make himself absolute dictator without ever letting anyone suspect that he was anything more than a joking, timid backwoods lawyer, given to fits of humility in the presence of all the strutting military and political peacocks that flocked about him."

Lincoln's dictatorship is gradual, and always justified in terms of "inherent powers." One by one, traditional liberties are abandoned in the exigencies of war. . . . Yet Lincoln's power is such that he is to be easily confused, up to the fall of Atlanta and the turning point of the war, with one or another mediocre President, like James Buchanan and Franklin Pierce, who preceded him.

These are dramatic ironies, which Mr. Vidal handles with exquisite tact and skill. His Lincoln is not a debunked portrait by any means–no hint is given here of the man's penchant for telling obscene stories, or Negro dialect jokes—and, as the novel runs its course, he emerges as a truly outstanding man. At the novel's heart, however, is the shrewd judgment made of Lincoln by his defeated rival, Stephen Douglas, that, at the young age of 28, Lincoln had already fantasized dictatorial powers. . . . Lincoln's ambition, Douglas charges, is for greatness—whether at the expense of "emancipating slaves, or enslaving free men." And this would appear to be Mr. Vidal's judgment as well.

Though "**Lincoln: A Novel**" is an obsessively political work, covering in exhaustive detail the bumpy course of the Civil War as viewed from the White House, its narrative pace is slow and leisurely; multitiered rather than sweeping, it accommodates a variety of characters in orbit about the President, or, like young David Herold (a potential co-conspirator of John Wilkes Booth), stationed across the street from him, in a pharmacy. Since it is the author's strategy to keep Lincoln mysterious and secretive, we are never privy to his thoughts, as we were to Aaron Burr's; but, by degrees, we come to know him well through the eyes of his witnesses. (p. 36)

One of the most satisfying aspects of "**Lincoln: A Novel**" is Mr. Vidal's presentation of the incalculable complexity of his subject—the evolution of Lincoln's attitudes toward slaves, slavery, Negroes, compensation for slaveholders, colonization of Negroes abroad, for instance; the development of Lincoln as a wartime President, head of what has become, as if overnight, "the largest military power on earth"; the ceaseless strain and conflict of politics. Alexis de Tocqueville remarked that the passions of democratic men either end in the love of riches or proceed from it, which "gives to all their passions a sort of family likeness, and soon renders the survey of them exceedingly wearisome." In Mr. Vidal's imagination, however, fueled as it is by men's quest for power throughout history, political triumph, and not mere money, is the goal. But this too can become wearisome.

The novel breaks off with disconcerting abruptness after Lincoln's assassination, with only a final chapter in which, rather chattily, [John] Hay sums matters up for the advantage of two fictitious (that is, author-invented) characters. With Lincoln's death this particular tale must end. The novel is likely to be . . . controversial, since it so closely follows historical studies . . . and imposes no unusual novelistic structure or language on its material. . . .

"Lincoln: A Novel" is not so much an imaginative reconstruction of an era as an intelligent, lucid and highly informative transcript of it, never less than workmanlike in its blocking out of scenes and often extremely compelling. No verbal pyrotechnics here, nothing to challenge a conservative esthetics biased against the house of fiction itself. By subordinating the usual role of the novelist to the role of historian-biographer, Mr. Vidal acknowledges his faith in the high worth of his material, and in this, he is surely right. John Hay's succinct judgment of Lincoln will speak for our own: "Mr. Lincoln astonished us all." (p. 37)

*Joyce Carol Oates, "The Union Justified the Means,"
in* The New York Times Book Review, *June 3, 1984,
pp. 1, 36-7.*

## WALTER CLEMONS

[In "Lincoln,"] Vidal has accomplished something no other popular novelist has even attempted in dealing with the Civil War. Gone are the swirling hoop skirts and full-scale battle scenes. Instead, the focus is squarely on the political issues of the conflict. Most of the key scenes take place at the cabinet table in the Executive Mansion.... The book's cumulative power resides in its revelation of Lincoln as a man possessed by an idea no one around him shares—the indissolubility of the Union.

Instead of the sentimental icon of Carl Sandburg's homespun biography, Vidal's Lincoln is a canny politician whose opponents underestimate him at their peril.... [While researching this book, Vidal wrote], "The official Lincoln is warm, gentle, shy, modest ... everything a great man is supposed to be in Sandburg-land but never is.... The actual Lincoln was cold and deliberate, reflective and brilliant."

In demonstrating the brilliance of a reserved and secretive man, Vidal makes a shrewd novelistic decision: never presuming to plumb Lincoln's inmost thoughts, he enters his head only once, near the end, when the president dreams of going downstairs in his nightshirt to find mourners filing past his body in the East Room—a dream Lincoln did in fact describe to close associates shortly before his assassination. Everywhere else in the book he is seen by witnesses with their own biases.... (pp. 74-5)

Vidal has undertaken a more difficult task here than in "Burr" or "1876." Aaron Burr and Samuel Tilden were sideline figures; speaking in the vivacious fictional voice of Charlie Schuyler, Vidal was able to light American history from familiar angles. In "Lincoln," facing the central mythic figure in our history, Vidal surrenders his gift for impersonation. His inventiveness is limited to creating a fictional life for young David Herold, a member of the Booth conspiracy. The plain chronicler's prose of "Lincoln" sometimes descends to commonplaces Vidal would never commit when speaking in his own voice.

But this is his most moving book. He sympathetically reimagines Mary Lincoln as an intelligent woman going mad before our eyes. Her charm is palpable; she can never again figure in the reader's imagination as a shrew.... Lincoln himself enlarges Vidal's imagination. The novel becomes a meditation on power, which Lincoln exercised to a degree that makes Hay's final comparison of him with Bismarck plausible. We think how lucky we were that Lincoln happened to be a good man. (p. 78)

*Walter Clemons, "Gore Vidal's Chronicles of America," in* Newsweek, *Vol. CIII, No. 24, June 11, 1984, pp. 74-5, 78-9.*

## RHODA KOENIG

Vidal the novelist has written the sort of book that Vidal the critic would pulverize with a well-pitched wisecrack. *Lincoln* has a cast of hundreds, but they are all marionettes whose strings Vidal tweaks with a jaded air.... Vidal has not exerted himself in matters of character and plot ... and in the matter of dialogue this is also a novel of record, with stick figures striking poses to analyze political tactics and military campaigns. About the only suspense in *Lincoln* is in wondering whether any of the puppets will listen too closely to the others and drop dead of boredom....

*Lincoln* is a very lazily written book, in its sleazy tropes (guests at a buffet are compared to locusts, applicants for office to pigs at a garbage heap) and its overall design. Characters drop into whorehouses, have a little sex between paragraphs, and leave without advancing the plot. A supremely dull drugstore clerk mooches through 500 pages of the novel, sighing about how he wants to do something exciting, until (surprise!) he joins the conspiracy led by John Wilkes Booth.

At the cold heart of *Lincoln* is a void, that left by the absence of its tragic and tormented hero. Vidal has assembled a great deal of material about Lincoln's actions and beliefs during the course of the Civil War, but there is no animating spirit to make him more than a talking head. Every so often he disarranges his hair or makes a homely remark ... ; then it's back to the history lesson about the *Trent* affair and the Treasury notes. Throughout, we are in the position of the secretary who "wondered what the President was thinking; as usual, he did not have the slightest clue."

Vidal once wrote that "American men do not read novels because they feel guilty when they read books which do not have facts in them," and he sympathized with them to a degree, saying that "facts, both literal and symbolic, are the stuff of art as well as of life." But the facts in *Lincoln* remain only stuff—yard goods, raw material that has not been molded and transformed into a life of its own. The only interesting question about *Lincoln* is, Whom has it been written for? American men—and women—who like facts will be better off with a straight history that spares them all the forelock tugging and teacup tinkling. American ladies will prefer novels that spend less time on foreign policy and more in the whorehouses. I'm afraid the sad and cynical answer is that *Lincoln* is for those who want to impress their guests or themselves with a large, thick book with two big names on the cover. As Abraham Lincoln himself said, in his excursion into literary criticism, "People who like this sort of thing will find this the sort of thing they like."

*Rhoda Koenig, "Meissen Men," in* New York *Magazine, Vol. 17, No. 25, June 18, 1984, p. 74.*

## MALCOLM BRADBURY

At 657 pages, ['Lincoln'] is ... a hyper-novel, in the sense that a large supermarket is a hyper-market. But its formal characteristics are those which readers of the previous novels in Vidal's Washington sequence ... will readily recognise. This is fictionalised American national history told from the standpoint of the State Rooms and the drawing-rooms, and seen through the eyes of 'characters' who are personages from the history books. . . .

The fact is that Vidal has already shown himself a very strong if conventional fictional historian of the oligarchies and the opportunisms of American political life. And the story of Lincoln, the 'Original Ape,' and his Administration over the crucial years of the Civil War is a natural subject for him. Vidal has a taste for some of the genre's heavier machinery, and his characters are less bearers of consciousness than politicking sources of utterance, with a way of regularly inspecting one another's haircuts and dress for the historical benefit of the reader.

The machinery makes his narrative methods slow, and his subtleties lie elsewhere. It is the telling portrait of Lincoln, the often naïve but politically cunning father-figure steering his course among Abolitionists, Secessionists, the reefs of politicking around him and the crises in his own family, in order to preserve the Union of the Disunited States of America, that makes the new book another cornerstone in an already powerful sequence. . . .

Lincoln's rivals for office—Vidal is always good on rivals— are many. His generals side with them and hide from him the conduct of the War, much of it close enough to Washington to enter immediately into the action. By slow social interweaving Vidal gradually brings all this to dramatic form—a drama angular to the great national drama we already know.

Vidal's Washington is a world where history takes a devious course through the deviousness of men. What should happen is not what does. . . . The human being is an unremitting, self-seeking political animal.

Perhaps it is so. As a novelist, Vidal has a flamboyant and experimental reputation. But it is the novelist as painstaking, socially knowing workman, tackling the largest themes from well-accumulated evidence, that creates this book, with its radiating dead Lincoln, the great victim and the Bismarck of his country.

> Malcolm Bradbury, *"In the Hot Seat," in* The Observer, *September 23, 1984, p. 22.*

# Eudora (Alice) Welty

## 1909-

American short story writer, novelist, essayist, and memoirist.

Welty is often designated as one of the most notable Southern regionalists, along with such writers as William Faulkner, Katherine Anne Porter, and Flannery O'Connor. However, critics stress that if there is such a thing as a "Southern School" of writing, Welty has remained independent of it. She has lived all of her life in Jackson, Mississippi, and nearly all of her fiction is set in the American South. In an essay entitled "Place in Fiction" (1954), Welty contends that grounding works of fiction firmly in a particular location aids the achievement of universality; she claims that "*feelings* are bound up in place." Critics agree that her restriction of setting has aided Welty in writing fiction that is universal in its relevance and appeal. They point out that the universality of Welty's fiction is due in part to her ability to look beneath the surfaces of even her most comical characters and honestly present their emotions. Welty's fiction is further broadened by her versatility: she writes of the historical South as well as the contemporary, of the Southern aristocracy and the common people, in comic as well as serious tones. Her style at times is very straightforward, at other times so lyrical that it is almost impressionistic.

Welty has distinguished between two styles in her writing, which she labels "inside stories" and "outside stories." The inside stories are introspective, and the thoughts and emotions of her characters are clearly delineated. Modeled after the writings of Anton Chekhov, Virginia Woolf, and Elizabeth Bowen, Welty's inside stories include the novels *Delta Wedding* (1946) and *Optimist's Daughter* (1972) and many of the stories included in *The Wide Net* (1943) and *The Bride of Innisfallen* (1955). A sense of mystery pervades many of her inside stories, and their tone is quiet and reflective. Outside stories are those in which the reader has no access to the characters' thoughts. Characterization is achieved through dialogue, storytelling, and action. Like the work of Mark Twain and Ring Lardner, Welty's outside stories, including *A Robber Bridegroom* (1942), *Ponder Heart* (1954), *Losing Battles* (1970), and most of *A Curtain of Green and Other Stories* (1941), are often humorous and light, although not without messages. While these categories are not exclusive, they do reflect Welty's deliberate exploration of different narrative techniques.

Critics often note Welty's capacity to delight the reader through her ability to capture the colorful patterns of Southern speech and through her imaginative evocations of Southern life. According to a set of lectures on how she "became a writer," published as *One Writer's Beginnings* (1984), Welty has been a voracious reader and an avid listener since early childhood. Her ear for dialect and her sense of the ridiculous have enabled her to create such memorable characters as Edna Earle Ponder, the garrulous hotel manager who narrates *Ponder Heart*, and Sister, the young woman whose family does not understand her in the story "Why I Live at the P.O." (1941). The fruits of Welty's wide reading appear in much of her work, most notably the novella *The Robber Bridegroom*, which incorporates elements from fairy tales, folklore, classical myth, and legends of the Mississippi River and the Natchez Trace during pioneer days.

The South works well as a location for Welty's stories and novels for several reasons. Southern speech is a rich resource for a writer as attuned to colloquialism, dialect, and local color as Welty. Further, the South has a tradition of oral history and folklore; Welty has described these attributes of her home as "a treasure I helped myself to." One of Welty's favorite subjects is family life, the continuity of which is particularly strong in the South. Several of her novels focus on family and community ceremonies and rituals, such as weddings, reunions, and funerals. Welty's longest novel, *Losing Battles*, takes place at a family reunion, where the family history is retold. Set in a backwoods area, the novel is based in part on stories Welty heard about her mother's childhood in rural West Virginia. Welty said, "I needed that region, that kind of country family, because I wanted that chorus of voices, everybody talking and carrying on at once. . . . Those people are natural talkers and storytellers, in a remote place where there was time for that." While Welty's novels celebrate many aspects of family life, they also examine the foibles to which families, especially large clans, are prone. She has written of the tendency of the family to squelch individuality, to ostracize outsiders, and to resist improvement. This is often dramatized in Welty's novels by a marriage between a member of a clannish family and an outsider, a situation that figures prominently in *Delta Wedding* and also occurs in *Losing Battles* and *Optimist's Daughter*.

Welty's willingness to look at the destructive aspects of family love is one example of her fascination with multiplicity. As Clement Musgrove of *A Robber Bridegroom* tells his daughter, Rosamund, "All things are double, and this should keep us from taking liberties with the outside world. . . ." *A Robber Bridegroom* is a fanciful exploration of the concept of doubleness. The hero has a dual identity: by day he is the gentleman, Jamie Lockhart; by night he is Rosamund's lover, "the bandit of the woods." The novel is also a study in the contrasts inherent in the transition from the rough-and-tumble Old Southwest to the more refined New South. The tolerance and affection with which Welty treats even her least appealing characters is due to her ability to see elements of love in hate, hope in despair, and good in evil. The concept that nothing is exactly what it seems, that life is essentially mysterious, is one which Welty's writing celebrates.

Welty has been warmly accepted by critics from the time of her discovery and promotion in the late 1930s by magazine editors John Rood of *Manuscript* and Cleanth Brooks and Robert Penn Warren of *The Southern Review*. Her first collection of stories, *A Curtain of Green*, was graced with an introduction by Katherine Anne Porter, who praised Welty's "extraordinary range of mood, pace, tone, and variety of material." Forty years later, this same quality was applauded by Maureen Howard, who wrote in a review of *The Collected Stories of Eudora Welty* (1980), "Her range is remarkable—her way of telling us that stories are as different as human faces, that beyond the common features of plot and narrative, there are discoveries to be made each time. . . ." Welty's many literary achievements have been acknowledged by a Pulitzer Prize, a Gold Medal from the National Institute of Arts and Letters, and numerous O. Henry Awards for her short stories.

(See also *CLC*, Vols. 1, 2, 5, 14, 22; *Contemporary Authors*, Vols. 9-12, rev. ed.; and *Dictionary of Literary Biography*, Vol. 2.)

## KATHERINE ANNE PORTER

Being the child of her place and time, profiting perhaps without being aware of it by the cluttered experiences, foreign travels, and disorders of the generation immediately preceding her, [Eudora Welty] will never have to go away and live among the Eskimos, or Mexican Indians; she need not follow a war and smell death to feel herself alive: she knows about death already. She shall not need even to live in New York in order to feel that she is having the kind of experience, the sense of "life" proper to a serious author. She gets her right nourishment from the source natural to her—her experience so far has been quite enough for her and of precisely the right kind. (p. xiii)

[There] is a trap lying just ahead, and all short-story writers know what it is—The Novel. That novel which every publisher hopes to obtain from every short-story writer of any gifts at all, and who finally does obtain it, nine times out of ten. . . . Miss Welty has tried her hand at novels, laboriously, dutifully, youthfully thinking herself perhaps in the wrong to refuse, since so many authoritarians have told her that was the next step. It is by no means the next step. She can very well become a master of the short story, there are almost perfect stories in [*A Curtain of Green and Other Stories*]. It is quite possible she can never write a novel, and there is no reason why she should. . . . There is nothing to hinder her from writing novels if she wishes or believes she can. I only say that her good gift,

just as it is now, alive and flourishing, should not be retarded by a perfectly artificial demand upon her to do the conventional thing. (pp. xviii-xix)

These stories offer an extraordinary range of mood, pace, tone, and variety of material. The scene is limited to a town the author knows well; the farthest reaches of that scene never go beyond the boundaries of her own state, and many of the characters are of the sort that caused a Bostonian to remark that he would not care to meet them socially. Lily Daw is a half-witted girl in the grip of social forces represented by a group of earnest ladies bent on doing the best thing for her, no matter what the consequences. Keela, the Outcast Indian Maid, is a crippled little Negro who represents a type of man considered most unfortunate by W. B. Yeats: one whose experience was more important than he, and completely beyond his powers of absorption. But the really unfortunate man in ["Keela, the Outcast Indian Maiden"] is the ignorant young white boy, who had innocently assisted at a wrong done the little Negro, and for a most complex reason, finds that no reparation is possible, or even desirable to the victim. . . . The heroine of "Why I Live at the P.O." is a terrifying case of dementia praecox. In this first group—for the stories may be loosely classified on three separate levels—the spirit is satire and the key grim comedy. Of these, "The Petrified Man" offers a fine clinical study of vulgarity—vulgarity absolute, chemically pure, exposed mercilessly to its final subhuman depths. Dullness, bitterness, rancor, self-pity, baseness of all kinds, can be most interesting material for a story provided these are not also the main elements in the mind of the author. There is nothing in the least vulgar or frustrated in Miss Welty's mind. She has simply an eye and an ear sharp, shrewd, and true as a tuning fork. She has given to this little story all her wit and observation, her blistering humor and her just cruelty; for she has none of that slack tolerance or sentimental tenderness toward symptomatic evils that amounts to criminal collusion between author and character. Her use of this material raises the quite awfully sordid little tale to a level above its natural habitat, and its realism seems almost to have the quality of caricature, as complete realism so often does. Yet, as painters of the grotesque make only detailed reports of actual living types observed more keenly than the average eye is capable of observing, so Miss Welty's little human monsters are not really caricatures at all, but individuals exactly and clearly presented: which is perhaps a case against realism, if we cared to go into it. She does better on another level—for the important reason that the themes are richer—in such beautiful stories as "**Death of a Traveling Salesman**," "**A Memory**," "**A Worn Path**." Let me admit a deeply personal preference for this particular kind of story, where external act and the internal voiceless life of the human imagination almost meet and mingle on the mysterious threshold between dream and waking, one reality refusing to admit or confirm the existence of the other, yet both conspiring toward the same end. This is not easy to accomplish, but it is always worth trying, and Miss Welty is so successful at it, it would seem her most familiar territory. There is no blurring at the edges, but evidences of an active and disciplined imagination working firmly in a strong line of continuity, the waking faculty of daylight reason recollecting and recording the crazy logic of the dream. There is in none of these stories any trace of autobiography in the prime sense, except as the author is omnipresent, and knows each character she writes about as only the artist knows the thing he has made, by first experiencing it in imagination. But perhaps in "**A Memory**," one of the best stories, there might be something of early personal history in the story of the child on the beach, alienated from the world of adult knowledge by her state of childhood, who hoped to learn the secrets of life by looking at everything, squaring her hands before her eyes to bring the observed thing into a frame—the gesture of one born to select, to arrange, to bring apparently disparate elements into harmony within deliberately fixed boundaries. But the author is freed already in her youth from self-love, self-pity, self-preoccupation, that triple damnation of too many of the young and gifted, and has reached an admirable objectivity. In such stories as **"Old Mr. Marblehall," "Powerhouse," "The Hitch-Hikers,"** she combines an objective reporting with great perception of mental or emotional states, and in **"Clytie"** the very shape of madness takes place before your eyes in a straight account of actions and speech, the personal appearance and habits of dress of the main character and her family.

In all of these stories, varying as they do in excellence, I find nothing false or labored, no diffusion of interest, no wavering of mood—the approach is direct and simple in method, though the themes and moods are anything but simple, and there is even in the smallest story a sense of power in reserve which makes me believe firmly that, splendid beginning that this is, it is only the beginning. (pp. xix-xxiii)

> *Katherine Anne Porter, in an introduction to* A Curtain of Green and Other Stories *by Eudora Welty, Harcourt, Brace and Company, 1941, pp. xi-xxiii.*

### CLEANTH BROOKS

*[The essay from which this excerpt is taken was originally delivered as a lecture at a symposium honoring Eudora Welty at the University of Mississippi in 1977.]*

[Eudora Welty] is the author of works that make use of the resources of our language at its highest level. The interior life, the world of fantasy and imagination, is the subject matter of much of her fiction. . . . But what I want to stress . . . is Miss Welty's treatment of the folk culture of the South. She evidently knows that culture intimately, and her stories make it plain that she is fascinated by it. Nevertheless, she views it with an artist's proper detachment. Like the good artist that she is, she never condescends to the folk culture or treats it with anything less than full artistic seriousness. (p. 3)

[The] acuteness of Miss Welty's ear for dialect is astonishing. For example, I had for years thought that I was alone in having noticed that many Southerners pronounce *isn't* as *idn't* and *wasn't* as *wadn't,* turning the standard *z* sound into a *d.* . . . Imagine my surprise, therefore, to discover in reading **"The Petrified Man"** that Miss Welty had unerringly picked it up and recorded it, and for good measure had elsewhere recorded another curious *z* to *d* shift, one that I had failed to notice—*business* pronounced *bidness.*

Now, I'm not trying to turn Miss Welty into a dialect specialist, much less a scientific phonetician. She has had far more important business in hand than that. But her grasp of the Southern dialect does have its importance for her literary artistry, and that is one point I have wanted to establish. (p. 7)

I should point out that pronunciation is the least part of Miss Welty's interest and concern. She is far more interested in matters of vocabulary and of metaphor and idiom. She means to bring Southern folk speech alive on the page in all of its color, vigor, and raciness.

The finest instances of her handling of the speech of the Southern folk are to be found in *The Ponder Heart, Losing Battles,* and *The Optimist's Daughter.* They constitute at least the great sustained examples of her rendition of that speech. But I'm not forgetting some of her short stories—for example, **"Why I Live at the P.O."** or that wonderful story, **"The Petrified Man."**

The action of this last-named story is set in a small town. The speech that we hear there is raffish and vulgar in a pseudo-citified way. It is the chitchat of a rather cheap beauty parlor. The language in *Losing Battles,* on the other hand, is not at all vulgar or cheap. The characters in *Losing Battles* are rustic and unlettered, but each of them is as genuine as a handmade hickory kitchen chair, not in the least common or trashy.

On the other hand, the beautician named Leota who dominates **"The Petrified Man"** is wonderfully vulgar, but she is also wonderful to listen to in the same way as are some of the shabbier characters in Chaucer's *Canterbury Tales.* If the beauty parlor as the town headquarters for female gossip has cheapened and coarsened Leota's mind and spirit, her moving into town has not yet quite sapped the vitality of her country-bred language. It surges on triumphantly, and Eudora Welty has reproduced Leota's manner to a nicety. (pp. 8-9)

Eudora Welty's delicate but powerful grasp of the speech of the country people of the South reminds me of what William Butler Yeats, the great Irish poet, remarked in an essay entitled "What Is 'Popular Poetry'?" Yeats carefully distinguished between popular poetry and the true poetry of the folk. Popular poetry, he argued, did not, in spite of all its pretenses, issue from the folk at all. . . . The audience to which this popular poetry appealed was composed of "people who have unlearned the unwritten tradition which binds (together) the unlettered . . . (but) who have not learned the written tradition which has been established on the unwritten." It's a very acute discrimination. Popular poetry in this bad sense appeals to people who have discarded the age-old oral tradition of the folk ballad and the folk tale. But in repudiating the heritage of the unlettered, they have not taken the trouble to master the written tradition of the truly literate reader. Yeats believed that both the oral and the written tradition could be expected to yield literature. What he denied was that true literature ever could issue from that group which was neither one nor the other. . . .

Yeats here is not condescending to the literature of the folk. "There is only one kind of good poetry," he insists, and poetry both of the oral *and* the written tradition belong to it, for both are "strange and obscure, and unreal to all who have not understanding." (p. 10)

I believe that Yeats has a genuine point here, and one that applies to the folk literature of the South. The Southern folk culture is still vibrant and alive, and affords rich material for the gifted professional writer who respects it and knows how to make use of it. The dangers are two: first, that the writer will exploit folk material for cheap laughs and so produce merely a succession of Little Abners and Daisy Mays, caricatures that are appropriate to an Al Capp comic strip but have no place in genuine literature. The other danger is that the folk speaker in actual life, the country-bred man or woman who is steeped in the oral tradition, will become merely half-educated and lose the values that he now possesses without acquiring the virtues of true literacy. (p. 11)

Leota, I would judge, has already picked up some of the triviality and cheapness of her rather scruffy beauty parlor life.

But she still keeps her hold on a live and vigorous tradition of expressive English. If it is not quite what Spenser called "a well of English undefiled," neither is it yet a mere mud puddle.

Wanda Fay, in *The Optimist's Daughter,* by contrast, has been severely damaged. But perhaps she was flawed from the first. To have come out of a folk culture is no guarantee of virtue. Indeed, one of the fundamental religious tenets of the Southern folk culture is the doctrine of Original Sin: nobody is saved naturally; we have all fallen and come short. At all events, Wanda Fay is clearly a shallow little vulgarian. (pp. 11-12)

We shall miss the point, however, if we conclude that Miss Welty means to disparage the yeoman whites as a class or even the lowly poor white. Wanda Fay is really awful: "common poor white trash" would scarcely seem too harsh a term to apply to her, and Wanda Fay's sister and mother are of the same stripe. But Miss Welty does not allow that even this family is wholly corrupted. Wanda Fay's grandfather, old Mr. Chisom, seems genuine enough, a decent old man. . . . (p. 13)

The best testimony, however, to Miss Welty's respect for and even a certain affection for the genuine folk culture is to be found in *The Ponder Heart* and especially in *Losing Battles.* *The Ponder Heart* is comic, even merrily absurd; *Losing Battles,* though it has its own comedy too, and closes with a qualified happy ending, is more deeply grounded on the inexorable facts of life.

*The Ponder Heart* is in its presentation one long unbroken monologue issuing from the lips of Edna Earle Ponder, the proprietress of the Beulah Hotel, the main hostelry of Clay, Mississippi. . . .

Edna Earle is uncommonly good company. In her exuberance and in her earthy complacency, she reminds me of Chaucer's Wife of Bath. Like the Wife, Edna Earle is perceptive, on occasion even witty, and always the complete mistress of her own little domain. And like the Wife of Bath, how Edna Earle can talk! (p. 14)

Edna Earle compels a hearing even as Coleridge's Ancient Mariner did, and like the Ancient Mariner she evidently does all the talking. Whether her victim eventually leaves her as a wiser and a sadder man, we do not learn. But one fact becomes plain: Edna Earle is clearly not a devotee of Yeats's written tradition. Reading just puts your eyes out. She is a high priestess of the oral tradition. (p. 15)

Eudora Welty is an artist, and she has permitted Edna Earle to be a kind of artist too. (p. 16)

*Losing Battles* is Miss Welty's most profound and most powerfully moving account of the folk society. In it we listen to a whole clan gathered for the birthday of its matriarch, great-grandmother Vaughan, and we hear them talk from the dawn of one day to near midnight and later on into the afternoon of the following day. It is wonderfully rich and exuberant talk and there are a variety of voices: male and female, gentle and quiet or aggressive and domineering, querulous and argumentative or ironic and conciliatory; but they are all voices of the folk and speak the characteristic folly or wisdom, joy or melancholy, of such a community.

In emphasizing the wonderful talk to be found in this novel—its quality and its quantity—I may have given the impression that nothing happens—that the novel is all just talk. Nothing could be further from the truth. All kinds of things happen. (p. 17)

The truth of the matter is that *Losing Battles* is in spirit a kind of Tall Tale of the Old Southwest. Indeed, the action is so violent and some of the coincidences so improbable that it needs its folk language and sayings and ways for the actions depicted to pass muster as credible. Pass muster they do, for by virtue of its folk characters and the language they speak, the novel strikes the reader as being itself a kind of folk tale—bardic, outrageously strange, almost epic in its happenings.

A second qualification that I want to make is this: in spite of the seriousness with which Eudora Welty takes this folk culture, she does not sentimentalize it. She does not make it too good to be true. If the clan loyalties of the Beechams and the Renfros are admirable and excite the envy of us modern readers who tend to be alienated, lacking in family ties, and lonely in our unhappy self-sufficiency, Miss Welty makes it plain that the pressure of this great extended Renfro family can be suffocating. (pp. 19-20)

This counter note, this glimpse at the other side of the matter, is the necessary pinch of salt. The strength of family ties is touching, and the loyalties of the clan may well rouse in the modern a certain homesickness for a world that many of us have lost. But Miss Welty is not writing a tract in defense of the extended family. Rather, she is dramatizing such a family, and in doing so she is telling the truth about it. The virtues are there, but the Renfros have the defects of their virtues.

One of their defects is a kind of naiveté. Jack is good-hearted, impulsive, loyal, essentially kindly, though very jealous of what he regards as his masculine honor. It is his naiveté which first gets him into trouble, and in the course of the day and a half that we watch Jack's actions we see that his guileless simplicity continues to get him into trouble. (pp. 20-21)

Some of Jack's aunts and uncles and cousins are more worldly-wise than he. Yet in a sense Jack Renfro's special vulnerability does hint at the vulnerability of the folk society itself. It is genuine, sincere, strong in integrity, resolute, and capable of suffering without whining. But its chief virtues are those that can be handed down in a simple and basically unlettered society. Book learning, after all, does provide virtues too—very important ones—and these the Renfros tend to lack.

The folk society is a bit skittish about book learning. It is natural that it should eye with a certain suspicion the world of books and the rhetoric of false grandiloquence that goes with it. A little learning is indeed a dangerous thing, and on this point the suspicion manifested by the folk makes a certain sense. But the folk are even more afraid of profound learning—for this smacks of a strange and unfamiliar world filled with abstractions.

Miss Welty has made this point subtly but very forcibly in *Losing Battles.* Though we never see Miss Julia Mortimer, the school teacher who has made her impact on so many lives in Banner, the bailiwick of the Renfros, her name comes up again and again throughout the novel. (p. 21)

Miss Julia had been a great teacher and a formidable power in the community. . . . Yet in the talk that we hear from the Renfro clan, we note a certain uneasiness and suspicion. They respect Miss Julia and even take some pride in having weathered their experiences in her schoolroom. But they think of schooling as a necessary evil, and their awe of Miss Julia is mingled with a certain fear. She was the dedicated priestess of what was for them an arcane mystery. They were never really comfortable with her.

A folk community is usually uneasy in the presence of those who exalt the written word, and in this regard Miss Welty's Banner community is not special. Other Southern writers have made the same point.

Such is the uneasy truce that is struck between the representatives of the oral and the written traditions. And I can be sympathetic with the fears that plague the child of the oral tradition. He has good reason to guard his innocence. Thus the Renfros, who instinctively flinch from the sophistications of the great world outside, see the school teacher as the prime agent of that studiedly artificial world. As we have earlier remarked, Yeats believed that members of the unwritten oral tradition had cause to be wary in the presence of the evangelists of the printed word. But Yeats knew also that the genuine artist does not threaten the oral tradition of the folk.

The genuine artist, though aware of the limitations of the unwritten tradition, respects it. He appreciates its honesty and its other basic virtues. He knows that these virtues are not really antagonistic to the virtues of the great written tradition. He remembers that Homer, the father of the poetry of Western civilization, was himself a poet of the oral tradition, even though he was to become the very cornerstone of the written tradition.

The genuine artist not only respects and admires the oral tradition; he knows how to use it, how to incorporate it into the written, and thus how to give it an enduring life.

Eudora Welty is just such an artist, for in her work one finds a true wedding of the two diverse but not hostile traditions. (pp. 23-4)

> Cleanth Brooks, "Eudora Welty and the Southern Idiom," in Eudora Welty: A Form of Thanks, edited by Louis Dollarhide and Ann J. Abadie, University Press of Mississippi, 1979, pp. 3-24.

## CHARLES E. DAVIS

Eudora Welty's first novel, *The Robber Bridegroom,* is one of her richest and most complex in terms of the variety of themes it explores—the general history of a region, the effects of the steady passage of time, the question of personal identity, the inability to distinguish between reality and fantasy, and the dual nature of both man and the world he confronts. This complexity has been generally overlooked, perhaps primarily because of the disarming and deceptively simple method of Miss Welty's presentation. The style is elemental, almost child-like, as she combines a number of fairy tales from the Grimm brothers with Southern folk humor and legend. More important to the development of the multiple themes, however, is the author's use of the tradition of the Old Southwest humorists.

While one of the purposes of these humorists was quite simply to provide comic entertainment for themselves and for their audience, they were also attempting to capture a short-lived period in the history of the southern United States and its people—a period whose time and character were rapidly passing out of existence. On the surface the scenes and the individuals in their sketches are comic, often hilarious; but while the reader laughs, he also feels the tremendous gap between his own time and that of an innocent, fabulous world that, if indeed it ever existed, is forever lost to him. It is this aspect of Southwest humor, this tension between the comic and the serious, that Miss Welty so effectively utilizes in *The Robber*

*Bridegroom* to develop her concept of the duality of all things— man, the wilderness, time, history, and reality. (p. 71)

That Miss Welty is extremely conscious in this novel of the Southwest humor tradition, there can be little doubt. . . . Certainly the strong local color element in the tradition is captured in Miss Welty's description of the Old Natchez Trace, the wilderness, and the outlaws and adventurers who inhabited that world. The comic exaggerations and comic comparisons associated with the Southwest humorists also find their way into the novel with amazing regularity. For example, we are told that the simple-minded boy Goat is so named "because he could butt his way out the door when his mother left him locked in, and equally, because he could butt his way in when she left him locked out." . . . (pp. 72-3)

The significance of [the Southwest humor tradition] for the reader of *The Robber Bridegroom* lies in the humorist's essentially dual vision of the frontier world, his blending of the humorous and the serious, his comic treatment of a now-vanished era. The "lost fabulous innocence" that [Alfred] Kazin had spoken of in 1942 finds its chief exemplar in the person of the frontiersman-planter Clement Musgrove, "an innocent of the wilderness" . . . who "had trusted the evil world." . . . That he realizes the time of innocence has passed is cleary evident in his musing that "the time of cunning is of a world I will have no part in." . . . Even the delightful tall tales of Clement's daughter Rosamond and of the riverboatman Mike Fink reinforce the reader's sense of separation from this fabulous world. (p. 73)

The dual nature of the Southwest humorist's attitude toward his material is heightened by a deliberately established distance between himself and the world he is depicting. . . . Looking at the sketches from the standpoint of a reader, Pascal Covici states that the total effect "is to insulate him [the reader] from any emotional involvement or identification with events, characters, or region." Miss Welty, like the Southwest humorists, establishes a distance between herself and her story. Alun R. Jones describes her attitude toward her material as "detached, even ironic. . . ." Such an attitude allows Miss Welty to treat the horrors of murder, decapitation, torture, and rape—at least on the surface—as comic. The humorous depiction of death and decay and of cruelty and sadism, that is so much a part of the tradition of Southwest humor, is amply evident in *The Robber Bridegroom.* But despite the lighthearted treatment, death, after all, remains death; cruelty remains cruelty. The matter-of-fact recounting of Jamie Lockhart's rape of Rosamond Musgrove must not blind us to the fact that it is still a rape. (pp. 73-4)

With both the relationship between the Southwest humor sketches and *The Robber Bridegroom* and the primary significance of that relationship established, the complexity of Miss Welty's vision of the frontier in this novel becomes more apparent. The doubleness of all things, the inextricable commingling of the pathos and the absurdity of life, allows man to see and comprehend very little either of himself or of the world. Neither Jamie Lockhart nor Mike Fink can effectively establish and maintain a single identity; Clement Musgrove is confounded by events that occur, apparently without his volition, in his own life; Rosamond Musgrove is forced to fantasize because the reality of her existence with her stepmother is intolerable; all the characters are helpless before the forces of time and change. As the detached narrator of these events, Miss Welty suggests through the entanglements of the personal lives of her characters the monumental task that confronts the twentieth-century mind that attempts to piece together and interpret the general history of a region.

The essential doubleness of all things most certainly includes man himself. Every man has, on the one hand, a private self—what Miss Welty calls a "who I am"—that he presents to the world. Only when he is in his proper time can he effectively unite these two selves. Mike Fink, for example, thinks of himself as a heroic part of the frontier, and as long as that frontier remains a reality, he insists upon his complete identity—insists, that is, upon both who and what he is. . . . Like Mike, the notorious outlaws, the Harp brothers, identify completely with the wilderness, and they insist at the end of every robbery upon calling out as they ride away, "We are the Harps!" . . . As long as the frontier remains wild and free, people like Mike Fink and the Harps can follow their natural inclinations, but when the frontier begins to disappear, to become civilized, they are lost. The Harps, of course, die, their deaths corresponding to the closing of the frontier. But Mike lives, and unable to assimilate himself into the changing world, he becomes a man out of his time. When we last see him, he is, of all things, a mail rider, a position which places him as a link between person and person, between town and town, as a representative of civilization and communication. Unwilling to accept this new position forced upon him, he insists upon being "an anonymous mail rider." . . . In good comic fashion Miss Welty assures us that Mike's "name was restored to its original glory," . . . but the implication is, I think, that only in legend can he again be who and what he once was.

While Mike and the Harps immerse themselves totally in the life of the frontier, the bandit Jamie Lockhart feels a distance between himself and the wilderness. That is, his identity as a man must remain separate from his identity as a bandit. Early in the novel Jamie says to Clement, "Say *who* I am forever, but dare to say *what* I am, and that will be the last breath of any man." . . . With this kind of rift between his public and private selves, Jamie does indeed lead a double life in the woods with his bride, Rosamond. . . . (pp. 74-5)

Just as the men of the wilderness have this dual nature, so also does the wilderness itself, at one moment being peaceful and gentle and at the next, savage and foreboding. . . . Is the wilderness a garden generously providing man his basic needs, or is it a dark and evil place where the unwary will be swallowed up? This is the question that plagues Clement as he muses over the nature of man and the world. . . . (p. 76)

Clement's reflection about time and place sounds what is perhaps the most persistent theme in the book—the relationship between the past, the present, and the future. Man's identity is tied inextricably to his attitudes both toward the past and toward the future. For Clement his old life before the death of his first wife, Amalie, at the hands of the Indians is infinitely more desirable than his present life with his second wife, Salome. But the past is forever closed to him except in his dreams. . . . For an individual like Clement, then, the distinction between reality and fantasy is difficult, even undesirable, to ascertain. As for Mike Fink, the riverboatman turned mail rider, he yearns for the world of "the old days" when he was a "big figure in the world." . . . When Rosamond, who is much more concerned with the future than the past, tells him she has a message for Jamie "from another world"—that of the future—Mike immediately assumes it to be "a message from out of the past. . . ." . . . Both Rosamond's use of the phrase "from another world" and Mike's erroneous assumption point out poignantly the enormity of the gap between the

way of life associated with the past and that offered by the future. Before his change from bandit to merchant Jamie thinks he has "it all divisioned off into time and place, and that many things were for later and for further away. . . ." . . . But in the world of *The Robber Bridegroom* life is not so neat and man does not so easily control his own destiny. Only after his acceptance of the future offered by Rosamond, only after his acceptance of the new world and his place in it can Jamie have "the power to look both ways and to see a thing from all sides." . . . For some, then, the passage of time brings a new and better world. For others the future brings only a world into which they cannot assimilate themselves. (p. 77)

As has already been stated, the old Southwest humorists had been concerned with chronicling the life of a frontier period that even in its heyday was in a state of rapid transition. Maintaining a detached attitude, they could present this world, despite the flux that characterized it, essentially as a comic one. Adopting the same disinterested stance, Miss Welty, too, depicts the history of a frontier continually undergoing change. . . . The history of the white man's intrusion into this world is traced by Clement as he recounts to Jamie the details of his own personal history. . . . His transition from pioneer to planter, his change from wanderer and explorer to owner and tiller of the land, is . . . puzzling to him. The cost of his move from Virginia has been great: the loss of his first wife, his son, his friends, and his happiness. The shrewish Salome insists that he own more and more land, clear more and more of the forest, and build bigger and better houses. Her attitude toward the land obviously parallels that of the rapacious plantation owners who came to ravage the wilderness. . . . Clement believes, however, that man's attempt to carve from the wilderness such large monuments to himself are futile, that permanence is merely illusory. . . . Jamie also acknowledges the transition, for he knows that "the bandit's life is done with. . . ." . . . His metamorphosis from outlaw to respectable merchant is perhaps most clearly exemplified by the religious ceremony complete with priest when he marries Rosamond, presumably for a second time. Fulfilling Clement's prophecy that the merchant will come after the planter, Jamie settles with Rosamond into a routine and reputable life in New Orleans.

Because of the fairy-tale atmosphere maintained by Miss Welty throughout this book, one might be tempted to assume that the young couple will live happily ever after. But the general tenor of the novel will not allow such an interpretation without considerable qualification. The suggestion of doubleness, the blending of the comic and the serious which is prevalent in so many of the Southwest humorists' sketches in general and in *The Robber Bridegroom* in particular, depends in part upon the reader's realization that the characters and deeds depicted are so short-lived, so subject to the passage of time. If the times of the hunter and planter pass rapidly, there is little reason to believe that the time of the merchant will be substantially different. (pp. 78-9)

Careful examination of the novel and the major tradition which lies behind it makes it difficult to understand those who see in it mainly an exuberation of Miss Welty's spirits and a fairy-tale celebration of the history of her region. These elements are certainly there. But humor, as we all know, is a vehicle through which the pathos, even the tragedy of human experience can be revealed. The humorists of the old Southwest, writing primarily between 1835 and 1860, captured both the comedy and the pathos of an era that, even as they observed it, was quickly passing away. Miss Welty, approximately a century further removed from that era, has, like those humorists before her, traced with both a loving and an ironic hand the essential doubleness of the life and times of her subjects, has depicted that blend of the comic and the serious that is human existence. The result, I think, is one of her most rewarding and significant works. (p. 80)

Charles E. Davis, "Eudora Welty's 'The Robber Bridegroom and Old Southwest Humor: A Doubleness of Vision,'" in A Still Moment: Essays on the Art of Eudora Welty, edited by John F. Desmond, The Scarecrow Press, Inc., 1978, pp. 71-81.

## ROBERT L. PHILLIPS, JR.

[Eudora Welty] did not begin with myth and fantasy and make them native to Mississippi; rather, she found that fantasy and myth are expressions of things she found "around (her) in life."

Welty has experimented with different ways to present the mythic dimension which she finds in the rich texture of human experience.... That myth and fantasy are not used in the same way or for the same purposes in each story or novel becomes apparent when one examines Welty's fiction from a structural perspective. Allowing for the facts that there are always exceptions to rules and categories, that confining Welty's fiction to a formula is the last thing she and her stories will permit, and that one story or novel may fit more than one category, allowing for all that, it is helpful to the understanding of Welty's accomplishment to observe three categories of myth and fantasy in her fiction. The three categories we may define in terms of character and narrative point-of-view. In the first, the narrator uses allusions to traditional myth and fantasy to enhance realistic characters and settings; thus the reader's task is to interpret the third-person narrator's insight or, with some first-person narrators, to interpret passing allusions that the speaker does not seem to notice. In the second category, the narrator defines character and setting almost entirely in terms of myth and fantasy so that the reader's understanding develops from the narrator's arrangement of allegory and symbol. In the third category, however, some characters consciously experience the rich, imaginative dimension of myth and fantasy; therefore, the reader must deal with the character's as well as the narrator's insight.

Welty's narrators often use myth and fantasy to present characters to their audience, sometimes without seeming to be aware that they are doing so. Welty is a master of narrative technique; her first-person narrators—Edna Earle of *The Ponder Heart*, the postmistress of the China Grove P.O., Mrs. Rainey of **"Shower of Gold"**—are oral story tellers of the first order. But for most first-person narrators the mythic dimension is as unconscious as it is with most characters. Allusions to the mythical past are for the readers to notice. Mrs. Rainey in **"Shower of Gold,"** the first story in *The Golden Apples*, is a good example.... The references in [the story Mrs. Rainey tells] are to the classical stories of Danae and Leda, but she does not know that.... [The allusions] make the reader's experience richer, for the reader can sense that [the couple in Mrs. Rainey's story] have transcended the limitations of everyday, ritual-bound, gossip-ridden Morgana to experience freely the primal joys of a fertile marriage.

Old Phoenix in **"The Worn Path,"** one of Welty's most famous characters, has a mythic dimension. The story's rich allusions give archetypal depth to the old black woman's annual journey to Natchez to obtain medicine for her grandson. The genesis of the story was not the phoenix story, which certainly contributes to its significance, but rather, as Welty explains in "Is Phoenix Jackson's Grandson Really Dead?" it was one day seeing "a solitary old woman like Phoenix" walking "in a winter country landscape."... From that grew the story of Phoenix's journey through the winter landscape.... Phoenix's act of love and compassion is primary to the story: the "deep-grained habit of love," says Welty is what gives the story its "emotional value."... Allusions to myth and fantasy amplify the events for the reader so that Phoenix is, first of all, the bird of the legend who rises from her own ashes.... The story is rich in [other] allusions, but old Phoenix is not aware that she is acting out patterns as ancient as the imagination itself. She knows only what she sees and feels to be important. The frozen earth, the hunter, the scarecrow, the dogs and birds she encounters are to Phoenix parts of the world, not symbols of the ancient past. In **"The Worn Path"** the rich texture of allusion and symbol is there for the reader and the critic to enjoy.

The technique which was important in **"A Worn Path"** and **"Shower of Gold"** is also found in a later novel, *Losing Battles*. Myth is fundamental to the novel; yet just as in **"A Worn Path"** its significance is found in the relationship between narrator and reader rather than between character and character or a character and himself.... Jack Renfro's mythic consciousness is simply not intellectual; it is not something that Jack himself explains to us. Rather, it is something the narrator of [*Losing Battles*] explains, using all the tools of metaphor and symbolism at her command. The complexity in the novel is not created by the characters' verbalized and intellectualized understanding of the myth and fantasy that define their conditions. That is the narrator's understanding.

*The Robber Bridegroom* and **"The Wide Net"** are examples of the second way in which Welty uses myth and fantasy, which differs from the first category in that we more clearly and distinctly leave the world of concrete reality and encounter instead the world of romance.... In the second group of stories we enter the world of fantasy itself; the landscape is likely to be inhabited with strange creatures—goblins, devils, elves—and to display strange phenomena—burning trees, strange lights or winds. (pp. 58-61)

William Wallace Jamieson, the central figure in **"The Wide Net,"** has an experience that strongly resembles that of [Hawthorne's] Goodman Brown. The time is October, and William Wallace's wife Hazel is three months pregnant. At the outset, he has stayed out all night drinking ... and comes home to find a letter from Hazel in which she says she has jumped into the Pearl River. Dragging the Pearl for Hazel's body is no ordinary affair; the setting is that of romance; the landscape is mythical. The wide net used to drag the river resembles the nets of silver and gold that Wynken, Blynken and Nod used to fish in their "river of crystal light" in Eugene Field's nursery rhyme.... The "King of the Snakes" swam past while the searchers were eating a lunch of fish on the banks and then a thunderstorm came. Lightning struck a tree which "seemed to turn into fire before their eyes"; another tree "split wide open and fell in two parts." William Wallace dove into the very deepest part of the Pearl River "where it was so still that nothing stirred, not even a fish, and so dark that it was no longer the muddy world of the upper river but the dark clear world of deepness."... William Wallace believed that if Hazel were not in this deepness "she would not be anywhere."

After the storm the searchers do not find Hazel but they go into the village of Dover anyway, where, carrying their strings of fish, they bring new life to the dead town. . . . Eventually William Wallace returns home, where he finds Hazel waiting for him; she has been hiding there all the time. **"The Wide Net"** celebrates fertility; the landscape is not that of Phoenix Jackson's wasteland, but it is not a realistic landscape either. It is a landscape in which characters encounter unusual events and creatures.

Welty has identified some of the elements of myth and fantasy that figure in *The Robber Bridegroom*—Grimm's *Fairy Tales*, the legend of Cupid and Psyche, Claiborne's history of Mississippi, and the frontier tales of Mike Fink and the thieves along the Natchez Trace. In *The Robber Bridegroom* are characters whose roles are taken from legend and who are more appropriate to romance than to realistic fiction. Rosamond is the beautiful daughter, Clement Musgrove is the innocent, kind father, Salome is the wicked stepmother, and Jamie Lockhart, the robber bridegroom, is the prince charming. (pp. 61-2)

The landscape and characters in *The Robber Bridegroom* are the ingredients of fantasy and romance, but there is also allegory. Clement learns that there is a fundamental "duality" in nature, that if he kills the famous robber Jamie Lockhart he also kills his daughter's bridegroom. The country around the Natchez Trace is symbolic and in it are characters and details that represent aspects of the psyche. The narrator is in a position to define meaning for us, but we have left the world of material reality for an inner, symbolic world where characters do things we dream of doing. Respectability and the claims of the community have no hold. Rosamond runs away to Jamie Lockhart's cabin and enjoys the freedom of unrestrained passion. Evil is also here in the persons of Goat, Big Harp and Salome. These are the spirits of the earth who must be overcome. Unlike Hawthorne's Young Goodman Brown, whose "dying hour was gloom," Rosamond's journey is successful. She finds fulfillment in passion she can experience and accept as the natural expression of her psyche.

The structure of the more allegorical group of tales does not differ in kind from the group of more realistic tales, but rather in degree. Drawing absolute distinctions between the two is perhaps impossible. The narrators in the second group of tales are in positions to define meaning for us, but we have left a world of real landscapes for a symbolic, even allegorical, landscape full of mythical men and strange beasts. The framework built of myth and fantasy is far more visible. Characters can reach new levels of understanding—William Wallace understands the quality of love; Clement Musgrove learns that life has greater complexity than he imagined. But while the reader is able to define the heightened level of awareness in terms of myth and fantasy, the character himself is not. With these stories, too, it is not so apparent that the genesis of the story is Mississippi life; yet *The Robber Bridegroom* is firmly based in Mississippi history, as Welty has pointed out, and the mythical Pearl is the name Mississippians gave one of their rivers.

The third type differs from the first two in that some characters develop an awareness of a dimension of myth and fantasy. The more successful or admirable characters come to understand themselves as parts of a long tradition that reaches back to the origins of the psyche. One can come to understand oneself in these terms. Two stories in *The Golden Apples* are appropriate for comment here.

The stories ["**June Recital**" and "**The Wanderers**"] take place in Morgana, or have to do with people from this small Mis-

sissippi town. Here two contrasting levels of experience can be identified: the manners, gossip, folkways, and respectable behavior of the citizens of Morgana define one level; the dimension of myth that transcends experience available through the five senses defines the second. (These two might better be called "gradations," but for the purposes of discussion the term "levels" is more serviceable). There are in Morgana those characters who never deal with anything beyond the level of immediate perception and understanding; one or two delve into the depths; and some fall into various grades in between. For Virgie Rainey knowledge of the deeper dimension may come in an experience which has elements of the mystical. Music and sex are also portals through which one may see or enter this dimension of other time.

The significance of the dimension of myth and fantasy can be seen in the roles assigned to Cassie Morrison and Virgie Rainey. The names themselves are emblematic of a distinction between a character who is afraid and rejects the understanding and freedom of life in its deeper dimension and one who accepts it. Cassie as Cassandra can cry out the woes of the land, but she is only a Morrison. Virgie, however, is a Rainey and certainly by the second story in the series not a virgin. (pp. 63-4)

Virgie differs from Cassie in that she accepts . . . freedom. In . . . "**The Wanderers**," we sense that Virgie consciously defines and understands herself in terms of the permanence of myth and fantasy. Morgana, ever oppressive with its schedules and formulas, embodies a limiting understanding from which Virgie escapes or which she transcends. (p. 66)

[On her way out of town after her mother's death, Virgie recalls a picture that] "showed Perseus with the head of Medusa." As she considers the picture she comes to understand her own experience in terms of the myth. Virgie identified with Perseus in that she too faced the terrible risk of becoming as lifeless and stone-like as the statue of the angel Cassie had bought to mark Mrs. Morrison's grave. One glimpse of the head of the Medusa would turn the unfortunate beholder to stone. Virgie saves herself from that fate; she escapes to life in another dimension. (p. 66)

Virgie's is a heroic imagination we can admire. Her world is very much a real world. . . . Morgana could be a small Mississippi town of the mid-1920s; the Big Black River which flows near Morgana is a river in Mississippi famous for its catfish. The artist, Welty, can see the richness of life in Mississippi small towns and describe that richness in terms of myth and fantasy; the artist can also see the shallowness and vacuity of small town existence. Virgie, like her creator, is an artist.

*The Golden Apples* can be seen perhaps as a merger of Welty's realistic method with the allegorical, but the notion hardly seems to do justice to so fine a book. It is more helpful to think of Welty's use of myth and fantasy in terms of three methods defined from a structural perspective. The demands she makes on her readers' imaginations are great no matter which sort of structure may be found. Her narrators may use myth and fantasy to define character; or with fantasy she may imaginatively create the interior of a mind or an allegorical landscape to investigate "the truth of the human heart"; or, finally, she may create characters who, like Virgie, are as aware of the dimension of myth and fantasy as the reader is asked to be. (p. 67)

Robert L. Phillips, Jr., "*A Structural Approach to Myth in the Fiction of Eudora Welty*," in Eudora Welty:

Critical Essays, *edited by Peggy Whitman Prenshaw,*
*University Press of Mississippi, 1979, pp. 56-67.*

## SARA McALPIN, B.V.M.

[An] emphasis on family, as one of several essential defining
features among southerners, is consistently evident in the literature produced by authors whose origins lie in the American
South; significant among these writers in the twentieth century
is Eudora Welty of Mississippi. Like her southern colleagues,
Welty repeatedly explores in her writing the nature of the family: its origins, structures, growth, influence, enmities, affections, and complexities.

Unlike certain of her contemporaries, however, Welty rarely
engages in extensive, meditative searchings into the long, entangled past of family in order to discover forgotten secrets,
to reveal unexpected and violent realities, or to interpret obscure facts about personal identity and familial relationships;
nor is she primarily concerned with the burdens which family
in the present must bear as the result of actions of family in
the past. Although she is consistently *aware* of family development for several generations, she most often concentrates
on family in the present involving, directly and typically, two
generations and their immediate past. While interesting additional comparisons and contrasts can certainly be made between
Welty's imaginative presentation of family and that of other
southern writers, my concern here is simply to suggest the
existence of such distinctions, before concentrating more fully
and specifically on Welty's unique use of family in her fiction.

Although she focuses on family throughout her work and deals
with it in a variety of ways, Welty's concentration on family
is most explicit in two novels separated by a quarter of a century
in her extensive, distinguished writing career: her first full-
scale novel, *Delta Wedding,* published initially in the *Atlantic
Monthly* in 1945 and her longest novel, *Losing Battles,* published in 1970.

Each of these novels concentrates not only on a single, extended
family, but also on a traditional family occasion. *Delta Wedding*
concerns the relatively commonplace but frenzied activities of
the comfortable Fairchild family of Shellmound Plantation,
located in the Delta community of Fairchilds, Mississippi; the
action occurs in 1923 during the week leading up to the wedding
of Dabney Fairchild, second oldest daughter in the family, to
the plantation overseer, Troy Flavin, considered by several of
the Fairchilds to be an unknown intruder and distinctly unworthy of such intimate admission into the family. *Losing
Battles* concerns the incessant activity and talk of the large,
impoverished Vaughn-Beecham-Renfro family, whose members live on or near a depleted farm just outside the northeastern
hill community of Banner, Mississippi; they are gathered on
an August Sunday in the 1930s for an annual reunion to celebrate the ninetieth birthday of the family matriarch, Elvira
Jordan Vaughn, "the last Vaughn in the world." (pp. 480-81)

I am . . . concerned with an exploration of precisely how Welty
presents family, how family functions in her fiction, particularly in *Delta Wedding* and *Losing Battles*. Since family is
obviously an influential force in her creation of fictional worlds,
a limited investigation of its presentation and function in these
novels should offer certain insights into Welty's more encom-
passing vision of reality.

One's initial response after reading *Delta Wedding* and *Losing
Battles* is to conclude that family in Welty's fiction is basically

a nurturing and supportive force for the group itself and for its
individual members. Indeed, this impression is bolstered by
countless features in both narratives, significant among them
Welty's vivid demonstration that she shared with Jane Austen
the gift which Welty described in her admiring essay on the
earlier author's work as an awareness "that the interesting
situations of life can take place, and notably do, at home."

With obvious relish, Welty brings to life the relatively commonplace activities of two unsensational families and celebrates their existence by emphasizing a variety of pleasing
familial characteristics: enthusiasm and vigor with which families gather to celebrate; generous and thoughtful gift giving;
lavish contributions of advice, assistance, and food to the success of family enterprises; expressions of genuine empathy of
various family members for others in both joy and sorrow;
stout defense for the actions of individual family members;
constant communal awareness and sharing through direct conversations and subtle gestures. All of these dimensions of family existence, as well as others which might be noted, underscore Welty's presentation of the family as a truly caring,
indeed loving, group and as a source of sustenance and affirmation. (pp. 483-84)

While not denying any of the warm, positive, celebratory aspects of family as presented by Welty, one is at the same time
reminded, when reading these two novels, of Clement Musgrove's comment in *The Robber Bridegroom* that "all things
are double," as well as of Welty's repeated emphasis both in
her fictional and nonfictional works on the "mystery" of human existence. While on the one hand, that is, recognizing the
abundant warmth of family in both novels, on the other hand,
one recalls also, when reflecting on these narratives, Dabney
Fairchild's judgment that "people are mostly layers of violence
and tenderness—wrapped like bulbs." When exploring carefully Welty's portrayal of family in these works—unwrapping
various layers—one becomes increasingly aware that the family
is not *only* a nurturing and supportive force; just beneath the
glowing, even mellow, surface of *Delta Wedding* and the exuberant, sometimes courageous, surface of *Losing Battles,* the
family functions also as a decidedly restrictive and diminishing
force.

One of the most obvious ways in which the family wields
restrictive power is in its merciless categorizing of people, both
implicitly and explicitly. As noted by several recent critics,
especially Lucinda MacKethan and Carol Moore, both families
tend to define certain people as insiders and others as outsiders.
To the Vaughn-Beecham-Renfro clan, anybody not bearing one
of those names is automatically a suspect stranger; such a
character, like the valiant schoolteacher Julia Mortimer, is frequently reduced from a person to a mere label or to a communally created caricature, when seen from the self-protective
viewpoint of the family. (p. 484)

[Legitimate] members of the family also often endure the condition of not "belonging." Like Robbie Reid Fairchild and
Gloria Renfro, Troy Flavin will join the family through marriage but will never be totally accepted into it. One can be
fairly certain in this judgment because even Ellen Fairchild,
though she has been an extraordinarily devoted and loyal wife
to Battle and borne him eight children with a ninth expected
soon, remains to the end an outsider. . . . (p. 485)

The tendency of the Fairchilds and Beechams to categorize
people narrowly and absolutely is further stressed by their com-
placently limited conviction that the entire world is satisfac-

torily encompassed within their own geographical locations. Although Vaughn Renfro boasts of knowing the distance to Parchman and other remote places because, as he says, "I've been to school! I seen a map of the whole world!" the fact remains that he has "never been out of Banner!" When Judge Moody suggests that Jack and Gloria might move to Alabama, Jack replies incredulously: "Cross the state line! . . . You want me and Gloria and Lady May to leave all we hold dear and that holds us dear? Leave Granny and everybody else that's not getting any younger? . . . Why, it would put an end to the reunion."

Similarly, in *Delta Wedding* there is the conviction that "everything came to Shellmound. . . . When people were at Shellmound it was as if they had never been anywhere else." When Laura indicates to her cousins an awareness of a world outside the plantation, she receives a typical reaction: "In the great confines of Shellmound, no one listened." Obviously, knowledge of the world outside their residence is rare for these people, and when such knowledge is claimed it is often ignored or discredited by the family rather than encouraged and admired.

It is, in fact, Welty's emphasis on the tendencies of both families to limit, categorize, distort, even deny, certain realities, which causes a reader to reconsider the somewhat deceptive surface of the novels and to see family functioning in more negative ways than are perhaps at first perceived. Isolated and enclosed within itself, each family tends to view reality as it chooses; that is, the family as a unit demonstrates the collective power to ignore, alter, avoid, contradict, or accept reality according to its own view. In thus ordering reality, the family often functions as a restrictive and diminishing force for individual members of the group.

In *Losing Battles,* for instance, the family agreement that "now that Jack has come home to stay, everything's going to look up" and when he "jumps out in those fields tomorrow, he'll resurrect something out of nothing," simply denies the reality that the farm is dying and that no human effort can bring it to fruitful productivity. Familial expectations here decidedly do not acknowledge individual capacities. (pp. 485-86)

The harshest attempt of family members to alter reality according to their desire occurs when they explore communally the parentage of Gloria, who defines herself as an orphan. In an effort to give her blood connection with the family, several of its members agree, on the basis of extremely questionable evidence, that Gloria is actually the child of Rachel Sojourner and the dead Sam Dale Beecham. Not wanting to be smothered in the family by accepting an identity fabricated by it, Gloria strongly resists this flimsy link: "I don't want to be a Beecham! . . . I won't be a Beecham." . . . Gradually, "all the aunts and some of the girl cousins" crowd in on Gloria, force her to the ground and, pushing a freshly opened watermelon into her face, engage in a primitively violent initiation ceremony. . . . (p. 487)

Although this is a rather extreme example of the family compulsion to force reality into its desired mold, the Vaughn-Beecham-Renfro clan has several other means of bending truth to its liking, one of the most obvious and defensive of which is the long ritualistic recounting of family history, which is the core event of each annual reunion. . . . Throughout the elaborate telling of the history, various members of the family feel free to correct, challenge, expand, or minimize any details which fail to please them. The result is a carefully revised and edited version of history which, as critic Bessie Chronaki notes, members of the family have "colored to give a desired impression of themselves." (pp. 487-88)

In *Losing Battles* talking, like remembering, also appears as a basic and vital aspect of staying alive. In this novel, even more than in *Delta Wedding,* talk is incessant. Consistent with her expressed desire "to *show* everything and not as an author enter the character's mind and say 'He was thinking so-and-so'," Welty presents the entire novel from outside her characters, allowing them to reveal everything we learn about them only through their conversation and action. Talking, however, like remembering, serves the family as a device for hiding or ignoring certain aspects of reality, and often reinforces the impression that family exerts a restrictive and negative influence. For all their talk and ostensible sharing with each other, for example, there is very little sense in the novel that individuals succeed in genuinely communicating with each other. (p. 488)

[The] characteristic result of the cascade of talk throughout *Losing Battles* is to mold reality according to the speakers' desires. As Louis Rubin has commented, the people in this novel "do not talk *to,* they talk *at.* Part of the reason that they talk is to communicate, but part of the reason is to dissemble, to mask, to hide. They converse obliquely, chattering away all the time but never entirely revealing themselves or saying what they think; and the barrier, the mystery that results, lies at the center of the high art of Eudora Welty."

The same kind of oblique, masking talk pervades *Delta Wedding.* Like the Vaughn-Beecham-Renfro family, the Fairchild family has its own devices for ordering reality as it chooses, occasionally contributing to negative consequences for individual members. In *Delta Wedding,* however, primarily because the narrator has access to several minds and is not limited to dramatic presentation as in *Losing Battles,* the distortions of reality occasionally appear somewhat more subtle. Typically, though not exclusively, in *Delta Wedding* it is through the private reflections of a single character, rather than in overt conversations or actions, that we learn how the family functions to limit or alter reality.

In a minor but telling instance, for example, Ellen Fairchild reflects on Battle's "determined breaking of her children's left-handedness," a specific suppressing of an individual characteristic under familial demand. A more general tendency of the family to fashion reality according to its wishes is underscored at the wedding dance toward the end of the novel, when Ellen considers her husband's insistent questioning of their daughter: "'Are you happy, Dabney?' Battle had kept asking her over and over. How strange! Passionate, sensitive, to the point of strain and secrecy, their legend was *happiness.* 'The Fairchilds are the happiest people!' They themselves repeated it to each other. She could hear the words best in Primrose's gentle, persuading voice, talking to Battle or George or one of her little boys."

Just as the Fairchilds convince themselves of their general familial happiness, they also cast individuals into roles which are assuring to them. The most salient recipient of their efforts to mold is George Fairchild. Although the reader never enters his mind, every significant character in the novel reflects upon George at one time or another, normally to glorify him, to emphasize his many virtues. The result is that the individuality of George is somewhat buried in familial expectations imposed upon him. (pp. 489-90)

Although overt challenges to the family's ordering of reality are relatively rare in *Delta Wedding* and are largely unheeded, there are numerous suggestions that the family's eagerness to maintain its communal view of reality has restrictive, diminishing consequences for certain members of the family, forcing them to mask or deny their individual differences. Laura McRaven, for example, frequently reflects upon the pain and unhappiness caused by her isolation and the failure of the family to accept her fully; yet, when she is at last warmly invited to stay and live at Shellmound, she experiences ambivalent responses, feeling that "in the end she would go—go from all this, go back to her father. She would hold that secret, and kiss Uncle Battle now."

Shelley Fairchild similarly protects her own secrets; rather than reveal some of her most private and intimate reflections to others, she hides them for herself in her diary. . . .

Sharing some of Shelley's ambivalence, Dabney also reflects privately that she and others are seldom dealt with individually by members of the family, who tend, rather, to maintain an embracing, unruffled view of reality. As her wedding approaches, Dabney takes a fresh look at the family around her: ". . . [They] simply never looked deeper than the flat surface of any tremendous thing, that was all there was to it. They didn't try to understand *her* at all." (p. 491)

So long as the family as a whole insists upon seeing exclusively the outside and fashioning reality according to corporate desires as is the case in both *Delta Wedding* and *Losing Battles,* little of the inner life of individuals is allowed to develop, emerge and reveal itself. In the tendency to avoid and adjust reality as it chooses, the family prevents its members from coming to the kind of realization gradually gained by Ellen Fairchild: "Not her young life . . . but her middle life . . . had shown her how deep were the complexities of the everyday, of the family, what caves were in the mountains, what blocked chambers, and crystal rivers that had not yet seen light." Insofar as the family stifles such realization, it may indeed function as a safe refuge and supportive force for its members, but it operates at the same time to restrict and to smother them. While the family may often be a restorative and nurturing force in Welty's world, then, she clearly demonstrates that it is also at times narrow, insensitive, selfish and limiting, even harsh, repressive, and cruel.

I have emphasized the latter function of family not in an effort to disprove the obvious fact that Welty celebrates the sustaining value of family, nor to undermine the validity of that presentation; rather, I have been concerned with demonstrating in this exploration that Welty's portrayal of family is much more ambivalent than is usually noted by readers. In *Delta Wedding* and *Losing Battles,* the family is both nurturing and stifling, affirming and negating, supportive and destructive.

Such ambivalence, however, enriches rather than diminishes Welty's final presentation of family, and emphasizes the fundamental conviction which she has consistently reiterated: "The sense of mystery in life we do well to be aware of." The fact that mystery in human existence, individual and familial, cannot be reduced to an easily explicable pattern, is persuasively reinforced in Welty's imaginative creation of family in these two novels.

Moreover, the vivid demonstration of overt and subtle ambivalence in her portrayal of family also underscores Welty's extraordinary sensitivity to the complexities of ordinary human beings, as well as her profound respect for the value of each individual person. Indeed, she thus illustrates in her own fiction a fact which she notes in *The Eye of the Story* about the work of both Cather and Chekhov: "In the whole population of Chekhov's characters," she writes, "every single one, the least, the smallest, the youngest, the most obscure, has its clear identity. No life is too brief or too inconsequential for him to be inattentive to its own reality."

While it is clear in her rich creation of characters in both *Delta Wedding* and *Losing Battles* that no single life is unworthy of Welty's careful attention, however, in these two novels her primary focus remains on individuals within a group: her focus is on the family. "At all times," she says, "I'm interested in individuals . . . and in personal relationships, which to me are the things that matter; personal relationships matter more than any kind of generalizations about the world at large." Even more specifically, she declares, "Family relationships are the basis for all other relationships."

In her concentration on family relationships in *Delta Wedding* and *Losing Battles,* Welty implicitly juxtaposes herself to Willa Cather who, writes Welty admiringly, "*contended* for the life of the individual . . . This contending was the essence of her stories." In her own two novels, I think, Welty *contends* for the family. For her, as for numerous other southern authors, the family, linked by inseverable bonds, is the arbiter of behavior and action. Under the family the individual is to a large extent subsumed; what any individual ultimately does is chiefly determined by the collective authority of family.

Ambivalently wrapped like a bulb in "layers of violence and tenderness," then, the family functions in *Delta Wedding* and *Losing Battles* both to nurture and to suppress its individual members. As a force within each novel the family provides the source not just for viewing and ordering reality, but finally, for *shaping* reality. Functioning with considerable ambivalence, which underscores the mystery of both the individuals within the family and the group itself, the family in each novel twists, trims, and expands reality sufficiently to understand it, cope with it, live with it, survive it. (pp. 492-93)

*Sara McAlpin, B.V.M., "Family in Eudora Welty's Fiction," in* The Southern Review, *Vol. 18, No. 3, July, 1982, pp. 480-94.*

## ANATOLE BROYARD

In "One Writer's Beginnings," Miss Welty presents her life as if it were one of her stories, so that the book is something more than a brief autobiography. It's a lesson, by one of our best writers, in how to look at a life, how to see it as an art form, not a chronicle, but a drama. She shows us how close we all are to literature, if we only knew it. After reading her book, we might go back and re-examine our lives and feel better about them. Even if they were miseries, they were inevitably filled with metaphors, scenes and moments of transcendent appeal. . . .

When Miss Welty began to read, she was disappointed to discover that books were written by people, that they were not natural wonders. Later in life, she did her best to make her own books natural wonders, as if they were written by a time and a place and a whole race of people. She tells us that, from the beginning, she always *heard* the stories she read. In her own writing, she says, "The sound of what falls on the page begins the process of testing it for truth." . . .

When she got new shoes, Miss Welty remembers, her father would score the soles with his knife so that she wouldn't slip. His strategem seems to have worked: There isn't a single slip or false note in **"One Writer's Beginnings."**

Anatole Broyard, *"Life As a Drama," in* The New York Times, *February 18, 1984, p. 15.*

## C. VANN WOODWARD

**"One Writer's Beginnings"** is not a misleading title. It takes two-thirds of the book to bring the author down to age 10, and yet this and the remaining part are all addressed to the origins of a writer and her art. [Miss Welty] manages, in her informal and self-deprecatory way, to be quite informative about her real subject. "Children, like animals, use all their senses to discover the world," she writes. "Then artists come along and discover it the same way, all over again." An early interest in painting and in photography, a passion for words and for reading and a precocious gift and eagerness for listening are all relevant here. . . .

Since Mississippi, the poorest state, with the poorest schools, has produced a remarkable number of first-rate writers, some of whom have also clung to their native soil, Miss Welty regularly gets lumped with them as a member of the Mississippi School or the Southern School. Actually, there are no such schools, and if there were, Eudora Welty would have doubtful claim to membership, given the attributes usually put forth to define or characterize them.

One of the attributes most persuasively advanced is what Allen Tate called "the peculiarly historical consciousness of the Southern writers," which produced "a literature conscious of the past in the present." Tate had in mind a variety of things and examples too numerous to elaborate on here, but the past he meant was essentially a Southern past, and the writers' link with it was hereditary. And it was not just any part of the past but particularly the South of slavery, secession, Civil War, defeat, reconstruction, decline, Yankeefication and all that. . . .

Those burdens are not to be found in the fiction of Miss Welty. Her first section, "Beginnings," provides some understanding of their absence. The hereditary link is missing. Her parents moved to Mississippi from "outside"—her father from rural Ohio and her mother from West Virginia—a few years before her birth in 1909. As a child, she got to know her Northern kin very well. . . . Traces of those Yankee and border-state relatives can be found in her fiction.

But Welty stories are almost entirely filled with Southerners, Mississippi Southerners, as authentically Southern as they come in their idiom, their gestures, their moods, their madnesses, everything to the finest detail. Black and white both, though mostly white. There are no Compsons or Sartorises, no hero with a tragic flaw, no doomed families with ancestral ghosts. With few exceptions—one thinks of **"The Optimist's Daughter"**—they are unsophisticated and very plain people. Some are as objectionable as the Snopeses, but they are never types, only individuals. They never speak for the author, only for themselves or the community. Miss Welty writes with detachment and sympathy but without identification. She has no fictional spokesman. "I don't write out of anger," she says, for "simply as a fiction writer, I am minus an adversary." It could be said that she is apolitical, nonideological, perhaps even ahistorical.

It is not that she is indifferent to history. The Natchez Trace runs right through her world. She even introduces historical figures—an imaginary encounter of Audubon, Lorenzo Dow, the evangelist, and John Murrell, the outlaw, in **"A Still Moment,"** for example. Aaron Burr turns up in Natchez. But they appear from a legendary past, not as regional symbols or as "the past in the present." She passes over the Civil War with only one short story, and that as seen through the eyes of a totally uncomprehending slave girl. If the distinguishing "historical consciousness" were going to appear, it would be in **"Delta Wedding,"** but it doesn't. Whole families pass in review, several generations of them, trailing no clouds of destiny, no hereditary curse, no brooding guilt or racial complications or torments of pride and honor. They are located in time and place but are never seen as the pawns of historical or social forces. That is not the Welty way. As much as she may admire that way in works of her contemporaries, she has left it to them.

She has her own way, and it would be a mistake to push her into any traditional category. Her fiction is often enigmatic, elusive, elliptical, difficult. Much is said between the lines or in the *way* it is said. Distinctions between love and hate, joy and sorrow, innocence and guilt, success and failure, victory and defeat are often left vague. So are the lines between dream and reality, fantasy and fact. One critic was brought up sharp by the suspicion that the whole story in **"The Death of a Traveling Salesman"** was hallucination on the part of the main character. The same sort of suspicion arises in that gem of a story **"A Worn Path"** or in **"Powerhouse"** or in **"The Purple Hat."** The author keeps her counsel. She records but never judges and often leaves enigmas enigmatic and mysteries mysterious. . . .

Miss Welty seems at her best with sprawling families assembled for rituals, ceremonies or reunions. For example, the riotous romp and clatter of the Renfros and Beechams and the Banner community through **"Losing Battles"** or the familial convulsions and hilarities of **"The Ponder Heart"** and **"Delta Wedding."** In these novels, comedy, satire, tragedy, pathos, irony and farce are blended, often indistinguishably, by the disciplined spontaneity and exuberance of an artist who tells us, believably, that "the act of writing in itself brings me happiness."

In **"One Writer's Beginnings,"** we find that in a turbulent period when authors commonly wrote in anger, protest and political involvement and many of them had reason to do so, one of them led a sheltered, relatively uneventful life, never married and always made her home in a provincial community. The same could have been said of Jane Austen.

*C. Vann Woodward, "Southerner with Her Own Accent," in* The New York Times Book Review, *February 19, 1984, p. 7.*

## WILLIAM MAXWELL

Dream, illusion, hallucination, obsession, Eudora Welty says [in **"One Writer's Beginnings"**] "and that most wonderful interior vision which is memory have all gone to make up my stories, to form and to project them, to impel them." It is because of this, and not because she was born in Mississippi, that she is as quintessentially Southern a writer as William Faulkner or Flannery O'Connor or Walker Percy. . . .

From the age of two she was read to by her mother. . . . Many children have loved to be read to who didn't become writers. There has to be something else, a kind of fermentation. "In my sensory education," Miss Welty says, "I include my physical awareness of the *word*. Of a certain word, that is; the connection it has with what it stands for. . . ." (p. 133)

[In "One Writer's Beginnings"] thoughtful attention is given to a great many experiences of one kind or another: ideas and attitudes she was exposed to as a child, visits to Ohio and West Virginia, family stories, old letters, train rides—whatever opened her ears and eyes and mind to the life around her and revealed to her the nature and material of what was to become her fiction. It is all wonderful. . . . And she does it from a carefully calculated distance, as if she were taking pictures with a camera. But one has finally the feeling that the crucial thing was her own sensibility, which she was, of course, born with. . . . Surely nothing on God's green earth could have prevented [her] . . . from devoting her life to a study of the connections of all sorts of relationships and kinds that lie in wait of discovery.

The parts of the book that are about her family, her immediate family and going back for two or three generations, are by turns hilarious and affecting. They are a kind of present . . . from Miss Welty to her audience. (pp. 134-35)

> *William Maxwell, "The Charged Imagination," in The New Yorker, Vol. LX, No. 1, February 20, 1984, pp. 133-35.*

## SHIRLEY ABBOTT

The lectures [which comprise *One Writer's Beginnings*] are autobiographical but do not quite make an autobiography. In "Listening," "Learning to See," and "Finding a Voice," as the pieces are called, Welty specifically defines how her early childhood formed her sensibility as a writer and shaped her habits of perceiving the world. She is not, needless to say, indulging in self-advertising or tortured confessions. Each lecture has the structure, the economy, and the concreteness of a good short story—and the same flashes of illumination. Such qualities should suffice for any book, but this one transcends its modest purposes and by some miracle becomes a volume of many uses, many mysteries, and universal appeal. . . .

Because Eudora Welty has drawn us a map (a partial map) to the sources of her creativity—which lie in and around Jackson, Mississippi, and in her childhood there—a reader not yet acquainted with her work could use these essays as the perfect introduction to the stories and novels. A teacher of English could use them as a literary handbook. Yet they also go beyond the literary, portraying in delectable detail a kind of American culture of the 1920s: the comfortable, decent, rooted existence of the middle-class white South. . . .

Anyone who remembers this world, or who cares about the textures of the American past, will savor this aspect of the book. There are, in addition, unforgettable passages about train and automobile trips young Eudora took with her family in the days when voyagers crossed rivers by ferry. She recounts these trips not primarily as reminiscences but because they became a lifelong sourcebook for her fiction. "The trips were whole unto themselves. They were stories." Thus, when she began to write, "the short story was a shape that had already formed itself and stood waiting in the back of my mind." This is an aesthetic revelation and along with it, free of charge, comes

the sound of the train and the sensations of going to sleep in a Pullman berth. . . .

In its 104 pages, Welty's book leads to reflection on a dozen other subjects as well: the assets and drawbacks of a sheltered childhood, the importance of sexuality (a subject barely alluded to but somehow present by its absence), the role that grade school teachers play in American intellectual life. . . .

For better or worse, [Welty] has always been a favorite among writing teachers, and my writing teacher at the Texas female college I attended made me read some Welty every week. I say "for worse" because Welty's elaborately crocheted syntax, her reaching for images, is a dangerous model for a beginner. Moreover, I read her grudgingly. In perpetual emotional turmoil as I then was, I thought good writing ought to be about suffering. What else was worth writing about? Luckily I lived to grow up, and came to understand that Jane Austen, as well as Charlotte Bronte, has something to offer the world.

Yet I still think an iota of justice is on my side. "Of all my strong emotions," Eudora Welty says in her first lecture, "anger is the one least responsible for any of my work. I don't write out of anger. For one thing, simply as a fiction writer, I am minus an adversary—except that of time—and for another thing, the act of writing brings me happiness." What are we to think of such an attitude? Is it saintly or merely timid? The only story, she says, that she did write in anger was **"Where Is the Voice Coming From?"**—a monologue, in the killer's voice, about the murder of Medgar Evers in Jackson in 1963. The story may be singular, but it brings a needed urgency and passion into Welty's work. If I had to pick one story as her masterpiece, this would be it. . . .

The ultimate pleasure of these lectures is that they give all writers great and small the chance to meet this extraordinary woman of letters. No writer, of however meager accomplishment, can encounter her without making a few personal comparisons. Eudora Welty felt her calling early, strongly. She had loving, intelligent parents who encouraged her in her vocation, who cherished her in every aspect. . . .

Miss Welty chose a path most writers are not at liberty to take—actively avoid, in fact. Is she better off for never having had to scrape up rent money or change diapers or contend with a spouse or scheme a course through the thickets of insolvency? More to the point, what if she had cultivated her anger, turned her talents to tragic themes? Is the sheltered life still possible these days? Is suffering, as I once imagined, the only fit subject for a great writer? There are no answers to these questions, or at any rate, Eudora Welty's stories and novels are the only answers we have.

This book is an essential work, provoking thought and recollection. It nourishes and comforts. If there is any literary prize Eudora Welty has not won, I hope this will bring it home. As I write, the book has hit the best-seller list—a fact to make all civilized persons in the nation rejoice.

> *Shirley Abbott, "Eudora Welty's Southern Comforts," in Boston Review, Vol. IX, No. 3, June, 1984, p. 25.*

## MARGARET WIMSATT

[Eudora Welty] is one of a renowned crop of Southern writers: William Faulkner, Walker Percy, Katherine Anne Porter, Elizabeth Spencer, and Flannery O'Connor among them. A

"Southern School" they of course do not form, unless from their work one wishes to conclude that Southern writers are idiosyncratic. Her fiction is most often set in the South, in Mississippi scenes she knows, and their tone is personal—often first person.

A reader of her short stories and novels . . . might piece together some of the material in [*One Writer's Beginnings*]. She draws, as a writer must, on her own experience, but not directly, as she explains. Here she is speaking autobiographically (one hopes no official biography will be attempted) and from the heart. It must have been painful as well as pleasant to record for the public so many details of daily living, so many private facts, about herself and her forebears. Of course this does not mean that she is rattling skeletons better left in peace. She comes from a family exemplary in outward matters and warmly united at home. (p. 342)

The whole book is engaging. It is the record of a person, a family, a town, and an era. . . . It is, of course, an artful book—written with love and craft, and with one art, the fiction writer's, at its heart. Eudora Welty was educated before "writing" became a college subject. She learned from listening, to that inner voice, and to the storytellers around her. She learned, she says, from her own mistakes. She does not theorize—as in her stories, she presents. She gives us the materials to decide for ourselves why, from the many cared-for children of her time, her milieu, only one of them grew up to be Eudora Welty. (p. 343)

*Margaret Wimsatt, "Listening, Seeing, Finding a Voice," in* Commonweal, *Vol. CXI, No. 11, June 1, 1984, pp. 342-43.*

# Morris L(anglo) West

## 1916-

(Has also written under pseudonyms of Julian Morris and Michael East) Australian novelist, dramatist, essayist, and journalist.

West is an author of popular novels whose characters struggle to find a moral guide in a complex and troubled world. West studied in a seminary and often writes from a Christian perspective; several of his novels examine the operations and bureaucracy of the Catholic Church. In addition to dealing with religious concerns, West explores such political and ethical dilemmas as war and starvation. He sometimes places his characters in circumstances where they must confront a moral problem. For example, in *The Big Story* (1957; published in the United States as *The Crooked Road*), a journalist anxious to expose a corrupt public official must reconsider when he discovers that his story will harm many others, including himself. West has also written several suspense novels, and he employs the techniques of intrigue writing in all his fiction.

West first gained critical attention for *Children of the Sun* (1957; published in the United States as *Children of the Shadows*), a nonfictional examination of the slums of Naples. His first major success as a novelist, *The Devil's Advocate* (1959), relates the story of a dying priest sent to investigate the life of a proposed saint. In examining the case the Monsignor meets various unfortunate people and develops true compassion for them, thereby renewing his ebbing faith in humanity and the Church. One of West's best-known books, *The Shoes of the Fisherman* (1963), tells of the struggle of a Ukranian pope to mediate political disputes between Russia and the United States in order to prevent the outbreak of World War III. *The Tower of Babel* (1968) is a spy story set against the growing tensions preceding the Six Day War in the Middle East. *Harlequin* (1974), a crime thriller, is another of West's popular mixtures of entertaining narrative and Christian moralizing.

West's later novels maintain this characteristic combination. *Proteus* (1979), a thriller involving a network that attempts to free political prisoners around the world, also examines oppression and terrorism. *The Clowns of God* (1981) concerns a pope who is forced to abdicate because he plans to announce his vision of the imminent end of the world. *The World Is Made of Glass* (1983) departs somewhat from West's earlier work in its concentration on human sexuality. The novel develops an actual case history described by the famed psychoanalyst Carl Jung. The narrative alternates between Jung and his patient, allowing West to explore the psychological conflicts within both characters.

(See also *CLC*, Vol. 6 and *Contemporary Authors*, Vols. 5-8, rev. ed.)

## FREDERIC MORTON

Morris L. West shares with Graham Greene a preoccupation with mystery in its religious as well as its whodunit sense. He, too, probes the riddle of faith with an austerely disciplined literary craft; he, too, stands on the Catholic premise even while viewing the world with almost Puritan acerbity. And he,

© Jerry Bauer

too, wants to discern in the carnal chaos of emotions a higher order.

All this Mr. West did with vivid success in **"The Devil's Advocate."** . . . Now in **"Daughter of Silence"** he returns to similar themes, using a similar point of departure. Again a strange occurrence in a small Italian village triggers the story. Again some men of acute sensibility arrive to investigate this strangeness, to articulate it in terms of good and evil—and again they discover that in trying the matter at hand they put themselves on trial. . . .

It's a meticulously adjusted clockwork of a plot. Mr. West oversees its forward motion with a shrewd sense of pace. The opening is a troubled pastoral, featuring noon bells and sundrowsed vineyards—and abrupt bloodshed. Then the high-colored landscape calms and recomposes itself under Mr. West's astringent Anglo-Saxon cadences. The middle piece, dealing with trial preparations, sees a series of confrontations and transmutations. . . .

The courtroom drama does very well for a climax. In uncovering the dark antecedents of the murder, Carlo eventually unmasks the roots of his own weakness. And the verdict quarried from the evidence not only judges Anna, but, in diverse ways, affects nearly every other figure in the book.

Mr. West skillfully renders the inquisitorial pomp of Italian trial procedure. In a way the book is an illustration of a telling insight: justice must be a pageant, not just a principle, if it is to minister to popular understanding. "Every court," says Mr. West, "has something of the aspect of a theatre. . . . The principals are in costume. The movement is stylized. The dialogue is formal and traditional so that, as in all theatre, reality is revealed through unreality and truth, by a mummer's fiction."

This describes more than the dramaturgy of the law. It is, above all, a good definition of Mr. West's novel. And there's the rub. The courtroom manner imprisons the whole story. Its people may argue on a villa terrace, chat in an outdoor cafe, make love among cypresses and nightingales. No matter where, they address each other in succinct summations, in clever arrangements of statement and retort. **"The Devil's Advocate"** at its best used the genuine echoes of a folk tale. **"Daughter of Silence,"** though similar in structure and intention, is largely the exercise of an urbane, accomplished rhetorician.

Some of the things Mr. West says are subtle and intriguing; many are brilliant. Yet it is much too patently *he* who says them, his characters being an elegant waxwork obstruction between him and the reader. He has dosed the story cannily with suspense. He has made it sonorous with aphorisms and ideas clanging in well-rehearsed tournament. But it misses all the ambivalences and half-tones, the dumb irregular eloquence of life.

        *Frederic Morton, "Everyman Is on Trial," in* The New York Times Book Review, *November 26, 1961, p. 5.*

### NEWSWEEK

Novelist Morris L. West stood on the sidelines last season while Dore Schary dramatized his **"The Devil's Advocate"** for a moderately successful run. The stage version of **"Daughter of Silence,"** which came to Broadway last week only a week before the novel's publication, is the work of novelist West himself, and it demonstrates that, though he is still a novice in the theater, he is learning the tricks of the trade.

Once again the writer sets the scene in his beloved Italy; this time the quiet of a little Tuscany town is suddenly shattered as a beautiful, wide-eyed young girl . . . crosses the village square and calmly, almost methodically, pumps three bullets into the local politico who was responsible for her mother's death in the Partisan underground of World War II. The institution of vendetta is both understood and feared by the villagers, and the fact that this girl, who waited almost a dozen years to avenge her mother, must be a little deranged seems obvious to everyone, including the insecure young attorney . . . who undertakes her defense. . . .

At its best moments . . . **"Daughter of Silence"** is an effective courtroom spectacle, and it has its calculated surprises.

        *"Frayed Nerves," in* Newsweek, *Vol. LVIII, No. 24, December 11, 1961, p. 65.*

### HAROLD CLURMAN

Not having read Morris L. West's novel *Daughter of Silence,* I cannot say what "point" it makes. I am in no happier state about the play he has adapted from his novel. . . . It is certainly an earnest effort, and its material promises complex as well as colorful drama. Yet the play created no positive impression on me.

The plot deals with the assassination of Rosati, the mayor of a small Italian town, by a girl of eighteen, Anna Albertini. . . .

I was not sure of the playwright's purpose. It may be that he wishes to demonstrate the awful consequences of silence and inaction in regard to wickedness—since Anna's crime might have been avoided if those who knew its cause at the outset had had the courage to denounce Rosati. It is much more likely that the play purports to show the mysterious ways in which God moves. . . .

The fact that the play's point seems unclear need not in itself be regarded as a major fault. Many masterpieces have no *exact* meaning. The play fails to convince because its wholly literate writing is unfelt, bloodless. The characters speak as if someone were explaining them, not as if they were animated by their own impulses. This is deadly in a realistic play; in a "stylized" (a poetic) play the writer's fire kindles life in the characters, so that even when they speak with their creator's voice they take on the passion he has lent them—and we are moved. This does not happen in *Daughter of Silence.*

        *Harold Clurman, in a review of "Daughter of Silence," in* The Nation, *Vol. 193, No. 21, December 16, 1961, p. 500.*

### JOHN SIMON

Since there could be such a thing as a *Son of Lassie,* it is perhaps not altogether surprising that a *Daughter of Silence* should have come along. Let me see if I can figure out exactly how this out-of-wedlock accident occurred. At one point in the play, an Italian lawyer who from an impecunious peasant rose to a prince of jurisprudence, and who is given quite unaccountably, to quoting Palgrave's *Golden Treasury,* utters the line "Thou still, unravished bride of quietness." I can assume only that Morris L. West, the Australian playwright, misread this beloved verse as "Thou *still* unravished bride of quietness," and hastened to make amends for this neglect by raping hell out of the unfortunate lady. So much for the genealogy of *Daughter of Silence.* . . .

In the course of the play, our hero brilliantly uncovers the truth, moves the judges, and wins the girl's near-acquittal. He also wins his young client's love, but must give it up because she proves as demented as a Donizetti heroine and because we have a Catholic playwright. But starting with the case (I refer to the trial, not to the hapless girl), he goes right on winning: his wife's ardor, his father-in-law's admiration, his own self-respect. Under the circumstances, it would be asking too much to expect him to win over the critics and audiences as well. To convey the nature of the writing, I give you three prototypical specimens: "Well, I know too there are women who need to rob their lover of his manhood!" "Well, then you must know what a rough one he can be!" which probably sounds better in the original Australian. Lastly, "I'm going to follow you into whatever twilight country you're living in now and I'll drag you back with me." . . .

[*Daughter of Silence* is] the most boring and pretentious play of the season so far. . . . (p. 15)

        *John Simon, in a review of "Daughter of Silence," in* Theatre Arts, *Vol. XLVI, No. 2, February, 1962, pp. 14-15, 74.*

ARNOLD L. GOLDSMITH

Coming at the very end of the decade, Morris L. West's prize-winning novel, *The Devil's Advocate,* may prove to be one of the best novels published in the last ten years. It is a richly textured, finely constructed story with all of the ingredients of a literary classic. Unlike those contemporary novelists who apparently feel that they must assert their individuality and challenge the reader with startling idiosyncracies of style, Morris West tells a complicated story in simple language. To a strong plot situation, he adds sharp social criticism, credible and deep characterization, effective suspense, and layers of symbolic suggestiveness. Like Nathaniel Hawthorne in his famous novel of psychological analysis of Puritan character, West is able to blend the personal with the local and the universal, giving us not only the memorable portrait of a deeply disturbed theologian, but also a wider view of the troubled soul of a church, a country, and the world.

*The Devil's Advocate* is the story of Monsignor Blaise Meredith, sent by the Vatican after World War II to the twin cities of Gemello Minore and Gemello Maggiore in southern Italy to investigate the proposed canonization of a new saint. As the devil's advocate, Monsignor Meredith must interrogate witnesses, take testimony, and investigate the events indicating sanctity before writing his report and recommendations to the Church. Above all, the devil's advocate must look for "the element of conflict. It was an axiom in the Church that one of the first marks of sanctity was the opposition it raised, even among good people. Christ himself had been the sign of contradiction. His promise was not peace, but the sword. No saint in the Calendar had ever done good unopposed." An equally important quest of the devil's advocate is for "the tangible good or evil that sprang from the life, works and wonders of a candidate for saintly honors. There was an axiom here too: the Biblical axiom that a tree is known by its fruits. Sanctity in one man leaves its imprint like a seal on the hearts of others. A good work reproduces itself as the seed of one fruit grows into another. A miracle that produces no good in a human heart is a pointless conjuring trick unworthy of omnipotence."

These two passage are among the most important in the novel, not only because they help explain the objectives of the protagonist and arouse the reader's curiosity, but also because they reinforce the novel's central theme ("contradiction") and foreshadow the spiritual rebirth of the central figure. The tree of Giacomo Nerone, the candidate for sainthood, can be known by the fruit of Blaise Meredith's regeneration.

West does a brilliant job of weaving together the antithetical strands of the theme of contradiction. Blending thesis with antithesis, he comes up with a synthesis that finds eternal meaning and hope in the midst of a world of confusion, perversion, and tragedy. This subtle blending of opposites results in a tapestry which records the spiritual pilgrimage of a dying man who is trying to rediscover his faith. (pp. 199-200)

Blaise Meredith has suddenly realized that he is a hollow man. He, who has faithfully followed all of the rules, is now for the first time aware of the shallowness of his faith. "He had kept the rules all his life: all the rules—except one; that sooner or later he must step beyond the forms and conventions and enter into a direct, personal relationship with his fellows and with his God." (p. 200)

Meredith's problem is intensified by his ill health, and here are two more contradictions. While the cancerous growth is destroying his body, spring has come to Italy. "In the midst of all this life—the thrusting grass, the trees bursting with new sap, the nodding of crocus and daffodil, the languid love-play of youth, the vigor of the early strollers—he alone, it seemed, had been marked to die." This contrast is more than a rejection of the pathetic fallacy, of course; it is a symbolic foreshadowing of the protagonist's rebirth.

The use of seasonal symbolism is a commonplace in literature, but West goes beyond the obvious and adds another contradiction, this time on the national level. This was an Italian spring. New grass is sprouting where before there was erosion, rain has washed clean the stucco housefronts, new moss covers ancient ruins of Roman aqueducts. . . .

There is even another contradiction here—that the Vatican should select for the arduous task of devil's advocate in the mountains of Calabria a monsignor whose body is weak and racked with pain. But Blaise Meredith's immediate supervisors are aware of the man's spiritual unrest and hope that in discovering the truth about Giacomo Nerone, he will rekindle the embers of his faith.

Here again Morris West goes from the personal to the national, from the specific to the general. The Church at Rome is faced with a dilemma, a contradiction that threatens its unity. There are bishops like Aurelio of Valenta, who thinks that the Church's mission in the twentieth century should be social, that Italy needs fewer saints and more social workers. The opposite view is represented by the methodical Eugenio Cardinal Marotta, who, at the novel's end, having finished the report of the Bishop of Valenta, leaves for the Prefect of the Sacred Congregation of Rites to discuss with "His Holiness the Pope . . . among other things, the beatification and canonization of servants of God." (p. 201)

In Gemello Minore Blaise Meredith finds the opposition he is looking for. As he investigates the life of Giacomo Nerone, he discovers that the people of this village betrayed and murdered the man, whose body was secretly buried near the twin city, Gemello Maggiore. Since the betrayal, Gemello Minore, the Italian home of Nerone while he lived, has sunk into ruin and poverty, while Gemello Maggiore, his resting place, has prospered. There are those who think Nerone a saint, and those who consider him a devil. All the more confusing and contradictory is the information that Nerone was an army deserter, lived with the village whore, and deserted her when she was pregnant with his child.

From this apparent confusion, from these conflicting views, gradually appears the truth which gives Morris West's novel its unity, intensity, and force. As Meredith uncovers the true nature of Giacomo Nerone, he rediscovers his own faith, enhanced now by a sincere love for his fellow men. His reformation proceeds through each stage of the investigation. (p. 202)

Meredith uses the little time left him to complete his investigation. Gradually, he learns all he has to know about Giacomo Nerone from the three villagers who played the most important part in his life and death: the Countess Anne Louise de Sanctis, whose love he scorned; Dr. Aldo Meyer, his good friend who signed his execution papers; and Nina Sanduzzi, the village whore who became his love and gave birth to his son, Paolo. But the character who offers Blaise Meredith the greatest challenge and temporary setback in his search for his faith is Nicholas Black, the homosexual painter living with the Contessa.

Village gossip has it that Nicholas Black is seducing Paolo Sanduzzi, who is modeling for him a picture of Christ crucified on an olive tree. Blaise Meredith takes it upon himself to save Paolo from the evil of Black, but the young painter correctly accuses Meredith of condemning him without knowing the facts, without having any compassion or understanding. . . .

Blaise Meredith makes one more attempt to help Nicholas Black. He foils Black's plan to take Paolo to Rome where the artist claims that he wants to educate the boy and prepare him for a brighter future than he would ever know among the superstitious and ignorant peasants of Calabria. Meredith, of course, and all the others, are convinced that his intentions are immoral. But Nicholas Black corrects this misconception, this contradiction, when he explains the irony to Meredith. Sincerely denying his sexual interest in the boy, he explains, "I've seen in him everything that's been lacking in my own nature. I wanted to take him and educate him and make him what I could never be—a full man, in body, intellect and spirit. If it meant denying every impulse to passion and every need I have for love and affection, I was prepared to do it. But you'd never believe that, would you?"

Here is a crucial test of the sincerity and strength of Blaise Meredith's regeneration at this point, and he fails. Forgetting Bishop Aurelio's sage advice to work with his heart and not his head, he makes "the most brutal remark of his life. . . . 'I might believe you, Mr. Black, but you could never do it—not without a singular grace from God. And how would you ask it, not believing?'"

This cold logic in place of the warm sympathy he craves drives Nicholas Black to suicide. Before he hangs himself from the same olive tree on which Giacomo Nerone was executed, he slashes to bits his painting of the Crucifixion. The title of this important picture is the theme of Morris West's book: "The Sign of Contradiction." To Meredith it was blasphemy for a homosexual painter to use as a model for Christ a young boy who is accused of being a willing object of the *femmenella's* love-making. To Nicholas Black it is ironic that the one time in his life he has tried to do a decent thing, involving a suffering and asceticism to him as excruciating as Christ's, he is denied the opportunity by a Church that preaches forgiveness and love. This peculiar blending of the sensual and the ascetic is, as West points out, a contradiction inherent in the two greatest symbols of Catholicism: the Madonna suckling her child and Christ on the cross. From the contradictory appeal of these two symbols comes one of the world's great religions; from Morris West's use of the theme of contradiction comes one of the last decade's most memorable books.

With the suicide of Nicholas Black, Blaise Meredith considers himself a failure. He thinks of himself as "what he had been at the beginning; an empty man, devoid of humanity and godliness." But this, too, is a contradiction. The truth of the matter is that Monsignor Blaise Meredith has done a great deal of good. He has removed Paolo from danger, made Father Anselmo repent, and talked the nymphomaniac Contessa into seeking medical and psychiatric help in London. For himself, he has discovered the truth of Giacomo Nerone's philosophy that "one should educate the heart first and the head later." True, in his relations with Nicholas Black he momentarily slipped and let the head rule the heart, but he has learned an invaluable lesson which still comes in time to redeem him. From the papers of Giacomo Nerone, who forgave his enemies and friends for their part in his execution, Blaise Meredith feels a new peace and tranquility. Giacomo Nerone has taught him that "The only thing that dignified man and held him back from self-destruction, was his sonship with God and his broth-

erhood in the human family." As he dies, Blaise Meredith asks to be buried in Gemello Minore because "here, for the first time, I have found myself as a man and a priest."

A final contradiction is the one with which the novel ends. Blaise Meredith, in his death, has personally reconciled the conflicting interests within the Church. While advocating the canonization of Giacomo Nerone, Meredith himself has discovered the importance of brotherhood and the need for the Church's social conscience. In the Christian symbol of the fish and the loaves of bread, on an amethyst stone given Meredith by Bishop Aurelio, there is seen Christ, the fisher of men's souls and the need of bread to nourish the bodies of these men. The two opposite extremes of the Church are here united in the successful completion of Blaise Meredith's mission as the devil's advocate. (pp. 203-05)

*Arnold L. Goldsmith, "The Value of Contradiction in 'The Devil's Advocate'," in* Renascence, *Vol. XIV, No. 4, Summer, 1962, pp. 199-205.*

## MARTIN LEVIN

Somewhere south of Papeete, in a phosphorescent sea under a perpetual cloud, there is an uncharted island where the great Polynesian chiefs and navigators paddle out to die. So goes the legend of an ancient cult, and so goes the career of anthropologist Gunnar Thorkild, who subscribes to it. His colleagues at the University of Hawaii won't offer tenure and an endowed chair to a nut who believes in navigation by second sight.

Thorkild's predicament [in *The Navigator*] is the springboard for two of Morris West's specialties: a sense of adventure and an aversion to materialism. One is served when Thorkild launches a marine expedition to find the island; the other develops when their ship arrives and is wrecked upon it. The shipwreck of a Noah's Ark full of survivors gives Mr. West a fine opportunity to manipulate social and spiritual values. The castaways become a kind of instant tribe, dominated by the religious significance of the island as a place for dying. West shows them coping with the unknowable and with one another, with the largesse of nature and with its dangers.

*Martin Levin, in a review of "The Navigator," in* The New York Times Book Review, *August 29, 1976, p. 20.*

## HUGO WILLIAMS

*The Navigator* might have been a jolly South Sea yarn until killjoy West introduced his mystical theme to the adventurers, a bizarre cocktail of Pacific voodoo and Jesuit mumbo-jumbo, enough to becalm a ski-boat. Those under the influence set off on a voyage to find some legendary island. The trip is disguised as anthropology, but really it's about what they call 'finding out who you are'. Barely have we embarked for this enchanted paradise (Sex? Shame!) than Writer West pops in to explain the book is really nothing to do with undiscovered isles: it's about his hulking hero Gunnar Thorkild's choice of soul-mate. The poor thing can't choose between Martha the mad artist, Sally the doctor, Ellen Ching the dyke or Jenny the pregnant 17-year-old, and one has to sympathise with him. The book stops suddenly, as if West realised too late that he'd said too much, and the surprise ending comes as too much of a surprise to salvage such a wreck of improbable unreadability. Who *buys* these people?

Hugo Williams, "Home Front," in New Statesman, Vol. 92, No. 2376, October 1, 1976, p. 456.*

## TIME

Many people dream of escaping the world and fleeing to some unspoiled tropical isle. Most of them settle for a couple of weeks in the Hamptons or a package tour to Puerto Rico. Not Gunnar Thorkild, the half-Polynesian, half European hero of Morris West's latest novel [*The Navigator*]. The grandson of a great Polynesian navigator as well as an instructor at the University of Hawaii, Thorkild publishes a paper claiming that even in this day of earth satellites and up-to-date hydrographic charts, there exists in the vastness of the Pacific an island known only to Polynesia's traditional navigators. He is promptly denied tenure for this temerity.

Thereupon, with a pickup crew that somewhat resembles a World War II movie platoon . . . the professor sails west searching for the mysterious island that will convince his colleagues that he actually deserves full professorship.

Thorkild instead wrecks his boat and maroons himself and his crew, setting up the same situation that William Golding once exploited so skillfully. Indeed, *The Navigator* might more accurately be called *The Lord of the Fleas*. The castaways elect Thorkild chief and play at being survivors, pairing off in various combinations and permutations, cultivating taro and learning how to make stone axes.

How people endure *in extremis,* whether on Andean mountaintops or in concentration camps, is a popular theme in an overpopulated age preoccupied with lifeboat survival theory. But West's characters clump about mouthing lines like, "We have all stepped back in time," or pondering jejune perceptions. Sample: "Relative values change." The book itself seems to be a compendium of South Sea clichés containing, in addition to the mandatory paean to the Polynesian way of life, a tidal wave, a tropical storm and a run-in with a poisonous stonefish—a great relief to readers who had been expecting a shark. One thing Thorkild proves, though: there is no tenure in paradise.

A review of "The Navigator," in Time, Vol. 108, No. 14, October 4, 1976, p. 96.

## PAUL GRAY

In the tiny group of consistently best-selling novelists, Morris West qualifies as the brains of the organization. That will give you, as Groucho Marx used to say, some idea of the organization. Still, West's popular fictions, like *The Devil's Advocate,* have regularly favored byplay over foreplay, concepts over jet-set conceits. Rather than reading the public mind, West has specialized in suggesting what it ought to be thinking.

[In *Proteus*] his premise is grim and all too true. Innocent people are being kidnaped or blown up by terrorists, tortured and murdered by repressive regimes of all political stripes. West's question may be old, but it is nonetheless urgent: Is it possible to combat violence without becoming violent?

No, at least not in the pasteboard parable that West contrives. John Spada, an Italian American, runs his multinational conglomerate in the style of a medieval prince, but he is also, in the best potboiler parlance, "a man living a double life." When not wheeling and dealing, he heads Proteus, an apparently vast and clandestine club that liberates political prisoners. Proteus prefers handing out carrots to achieve its ends, but will use the stick when other means fail. Spada's crusade becomes a vendetta when his daughter and her Argentine husband are arrested in Buenos Aires and brutalized by security police. He manages to rescue them both, and then, for reasons not entirely clear, is put on the hit list of any number of nasty organizations. In retaliation, Spada secures a toxic substance sufficient to hold the entire world for ransom. In short, he becomes the most terrible terrorist of them all.

If it is possible to ignore the moral issues that West himself raises and then drops, *Proteus* can be clear sailing. Connoisseurs of page-turners will feel right at home in a world where a woman can still be described as a "leggy redhead," where grins are "crooked," where a Jewish character says "oy vay" and a Scotsman says "aye."

Escapists will revel in the hero, whose power and wealth lead to freedom that is the stuff of fantasy, and fantasy-fiction. . . . West's people may converse in bromides ("Let me put it this way," one observes. "It's lonely at the top"), but they get them wrong often enough to sustain suspense: "Men get drunk in high places. Sometimes they get illusions of grandeur."

West's neatest trick, though, is reserved for the end. One of the things that Spada demands, as the price for not poisoning mankind, is permission to address the General Assembly of the United Nations. In real life, of course, he could do so and no one would notice, but West ignores this for the sake of his artifice. The resulting episode is thus one of the neatest bits of whimsical invention since A. A. Milne created the heffalump.

Paul Gray, "Pasteboard Parable," in Time, Vol. 113, No. 4, January 22, 1979, p. K6.

## PETER HEINEGG

Morris West's latest novel [*Proteus*] looks at first like just another modish thriller (terrorism, torture, foreign intrigue), but it's straining to be something else: an angry moral fiction denouncing the inhumanity of world politics. Camus might have brought off this mix of entertainment and philosophical vision, but West cannot. His story strains credulity at every step while it fudges on real political issues. He aims at tragedy and ends up in a made-for-television melodrama. (p. 140)

[West's] wisdom on the political problems of our time seems to be exhausted by his simplistic Manichaeanism: good guys fighting bad guys for control of the planet. All parties lie, especially Fascists and Communists, and they all employ ruthless hit-men. It comes as no surprise that someone like Mike Santos, who preaches ecology, pacifism and sharing the wealth (not your typical corporate hack), proves to be a monster. It's the old story: You can't trust anybody outside the inner circle of relatives and confidants. That may be good enough for the Mafia (or cinematic versions thereof), but not for grown-up readers. (p. 141)

Peter Heinegg, in a review of "Proteus," in America, Vol. 140, No. 7, February 24, 1979, pp. 140-41.

## MARTIN LEVIN

Morris West fans know what to expect, and [in *Proteus*] they will get it. Namely, a hero who is a surrogate for the author's own ideology and a story designed to punch home the author's moral values. This one is inclined to lumber along a bit heavily for my taste; the reader is expected to have the same faith in Spada that he has in Clark Kent. Despite the plot complications, the action is painted in primary colors. But Morris West is a disarming storyteller whose narrative skill helps to gloss over a few of the rough spots.

> *Martin Levin, in a review of "Proteus," in* The New York Times Book Review, *March 4, 1979, p. 13.*

## PIERS BRENDON

Before [Morris West] became what the blurb of *Proteus* calls 'one of the most successful' authors in the world, he wrote rather well. True he had a somewhat unfortunate penchant for the purple patch; I seem to remember, in *The Devil's Advocate*, Tuscan 'cypresses growing out of the mouths of dead princes'. Otherwise the book was admirable. Now Mr West, evidently feeling that he must appeal to buyers both here and in America, writes in a pompous, vapid Midatlanticspeak. It owes something to big business (terms like 'adversary situation') and something to television (clichés like 'No way!' and, used in response to an insult, 'I love you too'). People do mouth remarks like that, of course. Indeed, as Mr Auberon Waugh has shrewdly pointed out, the glottal-stop-swallowing presenters of Blue Peter do nothing else. But a novelist ought to mould his own prose rather than retail the pre-fabricated, mass-produced verbiage of illiterate media-persons, *Proteus* reads like the script of 'Wonder Woman'.

And it has similar cosmic preoccupations. For, with audience ratings at stake, neither the television series nor the aspiring best-seller can waste time on peripheral issues. There is no percentage in nuances. So Mr West conjures up a monstrous 'multi-national corporation' which acts as the front for a secret society called Proteus, dedicated to freeing political prisoners all over the globe. Of course, world-wide companies which trade with dictators do not run clandestine amnesty operations on the side, but the gross implausibility of his plot does not seem to strike Mr West. And the intellectual power which went into the making of his novel may be measured further by its sententious dedication: 'For The Prisoners of Conscience of whom to our shame there are far too many'. (How many would be an acceptable figure?) Similarly discussions on the morality of violence and the final solution adopted by the head of Proteus, to fight state terrorism with his own brand of terrorism, germ warfare, are saloon-bar stuff. For that reason, no doubt, *Proteus* will sell well in the suburbs. (p. 53)

> *Piers Brendon, "Blockbusters," in* Books and Bookmen, *Vol. 24, No. 7283, April, 1979, pp. 53-4.\**

## ROBERT KAFTAN

Early in his career, Morris West wrote two novels on religious themes, *The Devil's Advocate* and *The Shoes of the Fisherman*, both popular successes. His new novel may be added to the list.

*The Clowns of God* has a fascinating premise: the pope is forced to abdicate to prevent him from disclosing an apocalyptic vision of the end of the world. The pronouncement would be too dangerous. The world, already in turmoil, would be further, perhaps hopelessly, divided. And, more to the point, Gregory XVII's vision may not be real. It may simply be the hallucination of an exhausted, ailing pontiff. (p. 594)

[West's] portrait of the world at the edge is chilling and disquieting, and it is by far the strongest part of the novel. West manages to convey the paranoia of the great and the fears of the common folk, all trapped by forces clearly out of control. . . .

The novel finally becomes a cross between an adventure story and a utopian fantasy with the appearance of a character who may be far more than he seems to Father Barette [the former pope], who knows him first as a physical therapist.

It would be a pleasure to recommend this novel wholeheartedly, because it takes up so many serious issues and because its message is so timely and necessary for human survival. But the adventure elements and West's insistence on a complicated, ever-active plot result in splitting *The Clowns of God* in two. There is so much going on in every direction that the characters become so many pieces to be manipulated to propel the story forward.

One would like to know the pope and his friend Carl Mendelius better, but they are pawns of the action, as are all the other— too many other—characters who rush through the novel.

The atmosphere of disaster in *The Clowns of God* is superb, the adventure familiar, the fantasy consoling; beneath it all there are some serious issues—religious, social and political— that get lost. (p. 595)

> *Robert Kaftan, "Apocalyptic Vision," in* The Christian Century, *Vol. XCVIII, No. 18, May 20, 1981, pp. 594-95.*

## DIANE CASSELBERRY MANUEL

Hollywood loved Morris West's best-selling novel **"The Shoes of the Fisherman."** As a 50-year-old veteran of Soviet labor camps, Anthony Quinn was a marvelously gutsy Ukrainian Pope. . . .

One wonders what Hollywood would do with West's latest novel of papal intrigue, **"The Clowns of God."** This time his pope is a 65-year-old Frenchman who's also facing the prospect of a nuclear holocaust. . . .

Jean Marie Barette, lately Pope, has been forced into abdication because the cardinals don't know how else to cope with his apocalyptic vision of the approaching end of the world and the second coming of Jesus Christ. What follows, as he sets off on a lonely pilgrimage to find a way to proclaim his vision without sending his cherished world into a tailspin of chaos and hysteria, makes for a novel that is a journey in its own right: There are dramatic peaks, subtle valleys, and a few pretentious cliffs.

At his best, author West is a skillful storyteller who knows how to build suspense into every twist of the plot. Will Jean Marie's closest friend, former Jesuit scholar Carl Mendelius, believe him? And what role will the CIA's nasty agent-in-place play?

The most perplexing question may well be how anyone who knows Jean Marie could mistrust him or wish him evil. West's novel is remarkable among much of today's fiction for its decent, well-meaning characters, and the relationships he builds among them are at the heart of this work. . . .

In intimate, realistic conversations . . . , West can talk of love and faith and hope without sounding mawkish. But when his characters launch into soulful interior dialogues with themselves—or with the world—one has the uncomfortable feeling that he's reaching too far and is about to lose his grip on believability.

West has great faith in the power of faith, but little tolerance for the bureaucratic wranglings that often seem to accompany organized religion. In a day when the traditional churches are losing clergy and congregations while the cults continue to flourish, his moral examinations of church hierarchy strike a timely note.

Readers may not agree with West on many of the theological points he puts forth, especially his resolution of a coming final judgment. But at a time when millenarianism appears to be making a comeback . . . , West is at least raising thought-provoking issues.

> Diane Casselberry Manuel, "Fine Blend: Suspense, Decency," in The Christian Science Monitor, August 10, 1981, p. B3.

## EDMUND FULLER

Popes, prelates and princes of the church always have been fascinating subjects for fiction and drama, even to the unbelieving—sometimes especially to them. Many bestsellers, occasionally oddly prescient, have been built around such figures. In 1963 Morris West gave us "The Shoes of the Fisherman," about a first Slavic Pope from the Communist world. . . . Now Morris West returns to the See of Peter with the boldest papal novel of them all, "The Clowns of God" . . . , the extent of his daring to be seen only by those who read it to its tense conclusion. Will it prove prescient or not? . . .

Many current books show the fast growth of a "pop" doom mystique focused on the approaching turn of the century. In harmony with that, Mr. West predicates worldwide despair at a threatening onrush of global nuclear war which all political and diplomatic resources seem impotent to avert. This brings a political dimension to the former Pope's vision. Powerful international forces, ranging from governments to terrorist groups, seek to suppress the matter. The lives of both Mendelius and the former Pope are imperiled and blood flows. As melodrama it is tautly absorbing in its doom-threat genre.

Yet the book far transcends that aspect, for Mr. West is an intelligent, thoughtful writer with knowledge of the ecclesiastical and theological issues that are the essence of his tale. The reader wonders—it is a secondary kind of suspense in itself—what possible way Mr. West can find out of the problems of this story. Often he seems to have painted himself into a corner but always extricates himself with reasonable plot credibility.

It irritates me that the worst villain is a CIA agent, for this has become an anti-American and anti-agency cliche—one that I can forgive more easily in the Australia-born, Europe-dwelling Mr. West than in many American writers. He is also too cute in the "Johnny-the-Clown" persona assumed by Jean Marie for a series of epistles to the world. Such flaws are small, measured by the book's merits both as melodrama and as reflections on power and faith.

> Edmund Fuller, "The Coming of the Millennium or Madness?" in The Wall Street Journal, August 24, 1981, p. 12.

## RICHARD A. BLAKE

[Morris West] has chosen to peg his church-fiction to characters and situations in novels like *The Devil's Advocate* and *The Shoes of the Fisherman,* while leaving the pea-soup explosions of exorcism, sadomasochism in the convent and episcopal skul-duggeries to dimmer bulbs on the literary rialto.

*The Clowns of God* promises to be a superb novel before it collapses under its own contrivance. After the actor-pope nearly wrecked the church by trying to centralize too much authority in his own person, the cardinals elected a French mystic, Jean-Marie Barette. This gentle man was supposed to provide a respite, but instead he has the poor taste to have a vision of the end time as he is making his annual retreat at Monte Cassino. . . . Too much! The cardinals declare him insane and elect a nice, safe bureaucratic Italian to restore normalcy. But the prophet must proclaim his message. . . .

Events of the times add credibility to the revelation: Terrorists rule the streets, Russian armies are poised for the attack to obtain grain and oil, national leaders speak coldly about culling the population. When such events are read against the background of Scripture, the nuclear holocaust can be nothing other than the end time, the Second Coming of the Messiah.

This haunting and provocative parable sadly falls apart in Book II, when Mendelius disappears from the narrative and the ex-pope falls into the grasp of a well-meaning team of publicists, who will use the modern means of communication to proclaim his message. The concept of an electronic Jeremiah, complete with cassettes, film strips and syndicated column, trivializes the theme. In a terrible miscalculation, West has chosen to reproduce some of the columns Jean-Marie writes as a warning of the end of the world. At best, these are Saint-Exupery; at worst, Jean-Marie Livingston Seagull.

Still, when all the clutter is swept away, West has succeeded in creating a fascinating and believable character in Mendelius and in raising the most significant questions of human survival in a very human and religious context. West is a prolific writer; there is always hope that the next novel will build on the strengths of *Clowns of God* and evade the pitfalls of its slick, pop-religion solutions.

> Richard A. Blake, in a review of "The Clowns of God," in America, Vol. 145, No. 5, August 29-September 5, 1981, p. 100.

## PHILIPPE VAN RJNDT

Morris West's latest novel, **"The World Is Made of Glass,"** may well be the standard against which all his previous works will be judged. What makes his achievement all the more impressive is the success with which he combines the historical novel and the psychoanalytic character study.

The setting is Europe in the days before World War I. The central male character is the eminent psychoanalyst, Carl Gustav Jung, a man who has arrived at a crossroads in both his personal and professional lives. He has become estranged from his wife and taken a former pupil, Antonia Wolff, as his lover. Professionally, Jung recognizes that the philosophic differences between himself and Freud have become intractable. He has no choice but to make his stand clear before the fledgling psychoanalytic profession. This situation precipitates a breakdown that will last four years.

Mr. West's female protagonist, herself a physician, is the passionate, demonic Magda von Gamsfeld. When her partner in sado-masochistic coupling succumbs to a heart attack in Berlin, Magda flees to Paris and is referred to Carl Jung as the one man in Europe who might be able to help her. In the course of her analysis she unveils various stages of her life, each more furious and tempestuous than its predecessor, and we learn that Magda's sexual appetite is such that only savagery will arouse her. . . .

Magda von Gamsfeld is Mr. West's most impressive creation. And as she mingles with fictional and historical characters, we sense through her portents of the coming war. Yet, for all the cruelty Magda inflicts and receives, her struggle towards redemption demands our respect and compels our fascination.

> Philippe Van Rjndt, in a review of "The World Is Made of Glass," in The New York Times Book Review, *July 3, 1983, p. 9.*

## NICHOLAS SHAKESPEARE

I once crossed the Atlantic on a ship where one could drink as much red wine at dinner as one wished. This I did. It was only after a week I realised that successive carafes, although pleasant in their way, were having very little effect. In fullness of bladder rather than of mind, I traced the wine to its source and discovered the reason. It was powdered. Morris West's novel [*The World is Made of Glass*] is of a similar vintage. What seems plausible at the time of reading is retrospectively ridiculous. What appears to be the intoxicating encounter between a man and a woman who explore "the nature of evil" and "the complicated logic of guilt" turns out to be a boggy twilight where Dennis Wheatley gropes for D. M. Thomas. . . .

*The World is Made of Glass* is solidly researched and professionally written, but it does not go to the head. I have a suspicion it is not aimed there, and that Morris West is tackling universal themes with Universal Pictures in mind. . . .

> Nicholas Shakespeare, "Hallo Jung Lovers," in The Times, *London, July 14, 1983, p. 11.**

## FRANCIS KING

The best way to describe [*The World Is Made of Glass*] in a sentence is to say that it stands in the same relationship to D. M. Thomas's *The White Hotel* as *The Mikado* to a Noh play. There is no doubt as to which work projects the higher artistic pretensions or imposes the more insistent demands; and, equally, there is no doubt as to which work is the more fun.

Thomas's novel describes how a deeply disturbed woman consults Freud; West's, how a woman even more deeply disturbed consults Jung. . . .

It is odd that a book that concentrates almost exclusively on what is darkest in human nature should at its conclusion leave so bracing an impression. The reason is that, though Morris West is a brilliant story-teller and an erudite man, he never convinces one that he is any more capable of making the imaginative leap into the tormented spirits of a woman capable of incest, sadism and murder and of a man of genius at the frayed end of his mental tether, than Agatha Christie into those of her culprits.

As his heroine is painted by Klimt, falls in with Schnitzler, Oscar Wilde and Richard Burton, and finally, as *directrice* of

a refuge for fallen women in Paris, meets her gruesome death by cheese needle at the hand of a Corsican assassin hired by Zaharoff, the book increasingly distances itself from life as even criminal psychologists know it. But for relaxed reading on the lawn or the beach in a heatwave, it can be strongly recommended. 'It starts with incest and builds up to murder . . . Hand me your copy of *Psychopathia Sexualis* and I'll mark the relevant passages.' Magda's own words sum it up. What more can one ask?

> Francis King, "Jung As You Feel," in The Spectator, *Vol. 251, No. 8088, July 23, 1983, p. 20.*

## REGINALD HILL

[*The World Is Made of Glass*] is the story of a gifted woman's psychological disturbance and sexual obsession seen partly through the eyes of one of the earliest great practitioners of psychiatry and set against a background of Europe tottering on the brink of a cataclysmic world war. It is not, however, *The White Hotel*. The woman is a Hungarian countess, the psychiatrist is Jung, and the world war is the First. Nor does the lack of resemblance end there, for by the end of the book I found I cared very little about Magda or indeed any of the characters and the nearest I came to a cathartic experience was a shudder of horror at the prospect of being unwell and falling into the hands of someone like Jung.

But perhaps the comparison is odious and certainly Mr West is far too experienced at the writing game not to offer pleasures and profits of his own. . . .

The novel is told in the alternating first person narratives of the countess and the analyst. The sudden switch of viewpoint is sometimes effective, especially during the analysis sessions, though perhaps less than it might have been because it is a switch from one area of disturbance to another rather than from a storm to a calm. On the whole, however, the twin narratives produce a split which weakens the whole structure of the novel. Psychoanalysis, the exploration of the subconscious, the interpretation of dreams, are fascinating, particularly, let it be admitted, when they relate to sexual behaviour. Equally fascinating is the private life of the famous, particularly when it is in some way at odds with the public persona. Best sellers are made of bent bishops! But the combination of the two here, of the disturbed woman and the mad analyst, of the fascinating fiction of Magda's life and the fascinating fact of Jung's, produces rather too rich a mixture. Morris West rarely does what he sets out to do less than well. The problem here is that his purpose is less than clear. And the result is a book which is less than satisfying, though no doubt its subject matter and Mr West's deserved reputation will combine to make it a popular success.

> Reginald Hill, in a review of "The World Is Made of Glass," in Books and Bookmen, *No. 335, August, 1983, p. 30.*

## PATRICIA OLSON

Readers familiar with the works of Morris West may be jolted with surprise by the violent sexuality at the center of his latest novel, *The World Is Made of Glass*. Known for his realistic narration, his sensitive character portrayal and his concern for modern religion, West has never before presented such melodrama, such passionate characters, or such a critique of conventional Christianity as he does here, in a novel about Carl

Gustav Jung and his patient of one visit, Magda Liliane Kardoss von Gamsfeld. . . .

In his "Author's Note," West explains that his novel grew out of a case history that Jung briefly sketched in *Memories, Dreams, Reflections*. Jung wrote that a woman came to him anonymously for one visit to confess her crimes, that he never heard from her again, and that, if her story were true, she could have been driven ultimately to suicide. West's intent is to tell that story, to pour forth the confession in the context of Jungian analysis—stressing the complexity of human experience for both Magda and Jung—and to point toward the possibility of a profoundly personal "new birth" issuing from the analysis.

West succeeds remarkably in bringing to light elements of the "collective unconscious" in Magda's story. Jung's own favorite animus / anima pair, folktale figures, water and animal symbols, as well as the dominating womb-and-tomb / life-and-death images help unify this double-visioned story and give it its absorbing power. Equally absorbing is the encounter that sustains its telling, the effective "transference" which arouses and enrages the patient and analyst equally.

West concludes his novel with four pages of "Fragments in Epilogue," properly ending his imagined story of Magda, and properly leaving to history the end of Jung's. The real impact of this neatly structured novel is in its demonstration of the important Jungian insight that religion, sex and suffering make up the most constant trinity of human experiences. (p. 914)

*Patricia Olson, in a review of "The World Is Made of Glass," in* The Christian Century, *Vol. 100, No. 29, October 12, 1983, pp. 912, 914.*

# Donald E(dwin) Westlake

## 1933-

(Also writes under pseudonyms of Richard Stark, Tucker Coe, Curt Clark, and Timothy J. Culver) American novelist and short story writer.

Westlake is best known for his popular crime novels, which range from simple farce to harsh drama. He usually focuses on criminals and their escapades rather than detectives or policemen. Under his own name Westlake has written several comic novels, including *The Hot Rock* (1970) and *Why Me* (1983), which follow the bungling criminal John A. Dortmunder. For Dortmunder and his gang the caper always goes awry. In contrast, the novels written under the pseudonym of Richard Stark feature Parker, an unsentimental, cold-blooded professional thief. Works such as *Slayground* (1971) and *Butcher's Moon* (1974) are spare and often violent tales of vengeance and high-stakes criminal action.

*Dancing Aztecs* (1976) and *Castle in the Air* (1980) typify another Westlake genre, which Jerome Charyn labels "the screwball thriller." These novels feature complicated yet farcical crime plots. Westlake has written fiction that does not focus on crime, most notably *Up Your Banners* (1969). This novel centers on a love affair between a white male teacher and a black female colleague and is set against a background of racial tension at a high school in a Brooklyn slum. He has also written science fiction, sometimes using the pseudonyms Richard Stark and Curt Clark. Westlake received an Edgar Allan Poe Award for *God Save the Mark* (1968), and several of his books have been adapted for film.

(See also *CLC*, Vol. 7 and *Contemporary Authors*, Vols. 17-20, rev. ed.)

© Joyce Ravid

## ALLEN J. HUBIN

The most recent of Donald E. Westlake's comedies of crime is **"Somebody Owes Me Money."** . . . Westlake's strategy here is simple: take an innocent citizen—like cab driver Chester Conway—naive, spasmodically intelligent, continuously cowardly, and stubborn about his rights. Toss him a girl, a winning bet on a horse, and a very murdered bookie (before Chester can collect his money). Add two gangs of Runyonesque New York hoods, engaged in a territorial dispute. Put Chester right in the middle, and you've got the makings of a fine romp—and, I suspect, a fine movie.

Allen J. Hubin, in a review of *"Somebody Owes Me Money,"* in The New York Times Book Review, *December 28, 1969, p. 17.*

## ALLEN J. HUBIN

["**The Hot Rock**"] comes awesomely close to the ultimate in comic, big-caper novels; it's so filled with mocking style and action and imagination that if it isn't filmed within 18 months at the outside my respect for Hollywood's judgment will undergo a further precipitous decline. There's this emerald, you see, worth half a million, on exhibit in New York. It belongs to one-half of a recently subdivided African nation. The other

half wants it, and hires Dortmunder and colleagues to procure it. These sturdy felons, nutty and brilliant and all (it would seem), born under the wrong batch of stars, carry off an inspired scheme, which proves, unexpectedly, to be just the prelude. (pp. 32-3)

Allen J. Hubin, in a review of *"The Hot Rock,"* in The New York Times Book Review, *July 19, 1970, pp. 32-3.*

## NEWGATE CALLENDAR

Even if, as it turns out, it has nothing much to do with the book, Donald E. Westlake's **"I Gave at the Office"** . . . is a very funny title, just as the contents provide a very funny book. It is narrated by a real schnook, a loser type. Guys drink his liquor, but he never gets the girls, he falls overboard, and nobody misses him; things go wrong, and he is the patsy. Yet there is something endearing about him, for he is essentially pure.

He gets mixed up in a gun-running caper to a Caribbean island presided over by a Papa Doc kind of dictator. Up to then, the most dangerous thing he has ever done in his life is interview celebrities on a TV quiz show. . . . Basically, **"I Gave at the Office"** is a farce, but a farce with bite in it, like a chihuahua with the teeth of a tiger. . . . Nothing is sacred in Westlake's world. And he writes like a dream—naturally, wryly, amusingly. You can't do much better than this.

> Newgate Callendar, in a review of "I Gave at the Office," in The New York Times Book Review, May 16, 1971, p. 40.

## HASKEL FRANKEL

Mr. Stark's bad-guy hero, Parker, is back again [in **Slayground**], the only one of his gang to escape a car crash after a successful armored auto heist. He finds himself trapped on Fun Island, an amusement park closed for the winter, by a small army of crooks and crooked cops who are out to kill him and take his satchel of loot. . . . Although Richard Stark is working here within the confines—one problem, one setting—more suited to the short story than the novel, he has injected plenty of action into his one mouse-many cats setup. (pp. 38, 40)

> Haskel Frankel, in a review of "Slayground," in Saturday Review, Vol. LIV, No. 39, September 25, 1971, pp. 38, 40.

## NEWGATE CALLENDAR

[Richard Stark's **"Plunder Squad"**] attempts an external kind of verismo. Parker, the "hero" of so many previous Stark books, is back. Parker, you will remember, is the tough, dangerous professional thief who murders when necessary and who lives completely in the underworld.

**"Plunder Squad"** is really two books. The first half is a manhunt story; the rest is the description of an art caper. All this is told in Stark's seemingly objective style. Seemingly, for these books are highly manipulative, and they all have a tendency to read the same way. Stark wants to demonstrate that a top professional criminal works as hard as anybody else, has certain extra built-in hazards and has to tread warily in his jungle. And after all the planning, work and daring, things as often as not go wrong. With Parker, however, things always seem to be going wrong, through no fault of his own. Stark has this formula down pat, and he does write very well. But it still remains a formula.

> Newgate Callendar, in a review of "Plunder Squad," in The New York Times Book Review, January 7, 1973, p. 35.

## NEWGATE CALLENDAR

Richard Stark has created a large reputation (including screen credits) with his novels about Parker, the professional thief and killer-if-necessary. And he does these books very well, even if a few in the series strain credulity. One such was **"Slayground"** (1971), in which Parker takes on a whole police force in an amusement park shootout and makes his getaway.

But things improve in the latest Parker, **"Butcher's Moon."** . . . It has a tie-in with **"Slayground"**: in the earlier book, Parker had left some money hidden in the amusement park. In **"Butcher's Moon"** he goes back to retrieve it after a job has gone sour. . . .

Parker the super-tough, Parker the super-suspicious, Parker the super-lethal, Parker the super-ingenious. . . . [It's] all nonsense. But what is not nonsense is Stark's admirably controlled writing—as tough and spare as Parker himself is. Stark deals only with the criminal subculture. His is an unsentimental world and a fatalistic one. Life means absolutely nothing. Men are governed only by greed, power or lust. There is no such thing as honesty, and everybody, everything is to be distrusted. Parker himself is a curiously vague figure. Stark is not much on characterization. But the world in which Parker prowls is made very real thanks to Stark's considerable gifts as a writer and storyteller.

Curiously, Parker is not an anti-hero. He is bigger than life; and nobody was ever like him or ever will be.

> Newgate Callendar, in a review of "Butcher's Moon," in The New York Times Book Review, September 15, 1974, p. 44.

## MARTIN LEVIN

If criminals were anything like the happy hooligans invoked by Donald Westlake, we'd all be safe in our beds. . . . [**"Jimmy the Kid"**] is the third caper of the Dortmunder gang, and it is every bit as much a comic fiasco as the others.

**"Jimmy the Kid"** is an inventive switch on "The Ransom of Red Chief." In this updated version, a 12-year-old in the genius class is kidnapped and held for ransom in an abandoned farmhouse. . . . Jimmy is not a rotten kid like O. Henry's hero; he is just fearfully clever, a few jumps ahead of both his captors and his rescuers. He is also nice. Everybody is nice. This archaic deportment enhances the charm and in no way encumbers the action. (pp. 52-3)

> Martin Levin, in a review of "Jimmy the Kid," in The New York Times Book Review, November 17, 1974, pp. 52-3.

## JOHN CROSBY

**"Dancing Aztecs"** is very humorous indeed in a 1940's "See Here, Private Hargrove" sort of way. It's all innocence and mirth and nobody gets damaged beyond a black eye. The Dancing Aztec of the title is a solid gold figure with emerald eyes worth a million dollars, and about two score scallywags . . . are trying to lay their hands on it—which leads to wild bedroom farce, Mack Sennett chases and good old-fashioned vaudeville blackouts. A lot of this made me laugh out loud, which few books do anymore.

I'm a bit shamefaced about laughing at this old-fashioned hilarity but, there it is, it's funny. Donald Westlake writes about women, blacks and homosexuals as if Women's Lib, Gay Lib and Black Power had never been invented or, at least, he had never heard of them. Some of the black blackouts are pure Uncle Tom, and I'm sure Mr. Westlake will get a few letters telling him so.

But, as one character says, "Enough was enough," and 374 pages of this is just about 150 too many.

> John Crosby, in a review of "Dancing Aztecs," in The New York Times Book Review, October 31, 1976, p. 34.

## ROBIN WINKS

Donald Westlake knows how to write. . . . The trouble is, he has long since abandoned his early style (except in a near parody form as Richard Stark) which by now might well have supplanted Chandler for many, and he has made the "madcap caper" virtually his own. To read him is to feel one is back at Mohonk Mountain House with all those people who have gathered together at Murder Ink's invitation; too funny by half. Perhaps Westlake has told too many of his stories to Hollywood by now, and if the success of *Bank Shot* and *The Hot Rock* didn't spoil Rock Hunter they have at least spoiled Carey Thorpe. [In *Enough!*] Thorpe is a movie critic who weaves in references to every obvious movie in the Steinbrunner-Penzler encyclopedia. He is a murderer who finds himself playing the roles associated with detective fiction, from Least Obvious Suspect to Amateur Detective to the Innocent Accused. Everything is spelled out in capitals, like here, in *Enough!* It certainly is.

> *Robin Winks, in a review of "Enough!" in* The New Republic, *Vol. 176, No. 12, March 19, 1977, p. 37.*

### NEWGATE CALLENDAR

"Enough!" by Donald Westlake . . . contains two entries. One, "A Travesty," is a short novel; the other, "Ordo," is a long short story. "A Travesty" is a crime novelette in Westlake's typically frenetic vein. But "Ordo" is a strange companion piece. There is no real mystery involved, no crime. Rather, it is a story of a sailor who goes to Los Angeles to see the girl he married during the war. She is now a movie star and a sex goddess. "Ordo" is written skillfully enough, but what it is doing in this book is anybody's guess.

As for "A Travesty," it is in constant motion. Westlake is very good at this kind of thing. It is the story of a man who kills his girlfriend during an argument. He covers up everything nicely, or thinks he has, but discovers that he has to keep on killing. In the meantime, he finds himself working with the cops to solve the original murder and a few others that have nothing to do with his case. He proves to be a detective with a Holmesian aptitude for solving murders. There is a twist at the end, as there so often is in Westlake's novels. "A Travesty" is good, though not top-notch Westlake. Too bad the companion story in this book did not have more relevance.

> *Newgate Callendar, in a review of "Enough!" in* The New York Times Book Review, *April 17, 1977, p. 58.*

### KIRKUS REVIEWS

[*Castle in the Air* is another] fairly funny, very busy Westlake caper—and, as usual of late, the telling is really more cinematic (quick-cutting scenes) than novelistic. This time an international brigade of thieves—organized by master criminal Eustace Dench—sets out to heist every piece of a stone castle. . . . Too many lead characters for a little novel (at least a dozen heisters) and too much purely physical action—but the comic dialogue is cannily timed . . . and fans of caper-action at its cartooniest will find veteran Westlake in rousing good humor, if not exactly top form.

> *A review of "Castle in the Air," in* Kirkus Reviews, *Vol. XLVIII, No. 3, February 1, 1980, p. 163.*

### JEROME CHARYN

Donald E. Westlake, author of "**The Hot Rock**," "**Bank Shot**" and "**Dancing Aztecs**," seems to have established a new genre for himself: the screwball thriller. Mr. Westlake's books are quite different from the classical mystery and espionage novels of Graham Greene and John le Carré: There's none of the terror or the brutal psychic landscape of "Brighton Rock" or "The Spy Who Came in From the Cold." Mr. Westlake shoves cartoons at us, instead of characters we might love, fear or despise. There are no murderous boy gangsters like "Pinky" Brown, or pathetic drunken spies to remind us of Alec Leamas. But we do have energized masks that babble at us in all sorts of crazy tongues, come alive for a minute, and then return to their normal frozen position. This allows Mr. Westlake to push his narrative along at a tremendous pace, and supply his masks with the marvelous illogic of a cartoon world.

"**Castle in the Air**" has all the shifting scenery and bumpy play of Krazy Kat and the Katzenjammer Kids. It's naughty, lunatic fun, childish and perverse. (p. 9)

Mr. Westlake gives us a thieves' tour of Paris, with hidden barge canals, abandoned metro stations, tunnels and spooky parks. At times, however, his language lapses into a kind of hyperbole that threatens to destroy the rhythm of the book: "The rain poured down, it lashed, it drenched, it fell in sheets and buckets and cascades, it plunged down from the sky as though God, having just finished His bath, had pulled the plug on the celestial tub." And when Mr. Westlake writes about the French con man, Jean LeFraque, his cartoon style slips into pure mannerism: "Storm clouds were crossing Jean's face now, and his moustache was at half mast."

It's this exaggeration that often dissipates the book's energy. The pacing is lost, and Mr. Westlake's cartoons begin to trip over themselves. Nonetheless, he is a master of madcap larceny: Vito Palone, a retired criminal, laments throughout the novel that Eustace's "Italian Connection" had him kidnapped from his jail cell to join the party of thieves. "I was in retirement," Vito insists. "I had my flowers. I was writing my memoirs."

These words of sanity provide a perfect counterpoint to the whole screwy disorder of the novel, the slapstick and the crumbling landscapes. Despite its cheerfully mindless ways, "**Castle in the Air**" is a very funny book. (pp. 9, 27)

> *Jerome Charyn, in a review of "Castle in the Air," in* The New York Times Book Review, *April 13, 1980, pp. 9, 27.*

### EDWARD BARTLEY

Reading a book like [*Castle in the Air*] is like eating peanuts or potato chips. Once you start, no matter how badly you want to, you can't quit until "fini."

*Castle in the Air* is not badly written nor is it offensive. Westlake has a way of hinting at naughtiness without a detailed account of the proceedings. He also has a whimsical humor that is good, but rather old hat. On the whole then, the book is better than average, but the time spent reading it could be put to better use. . . .

The final go-around would be beautiful on a two hour television show as a summer replacement for "BJ and the Bear" or anything of that ilk. Old timers would call the ending a Mack Sennett comedy finish.

My valedictory is, "ventured, nothing gained."

> *Edward Bartley, in a review of "Castle in the Air," in* Best Sellers, *Vol. 40, No. 4, July, 1980, p. 131.*

## NICHOLAS SHRIMPTON

*Castle In The Air* is not a book which permits itself even the briefest excursion into philosophical argument. It offers, none the less, a new and valuable insight into the laws of chance. If a hundred monkeys with typewriters were to strike the keys at random for a thousand years they would produce a novel as good as this roughly once every 25 minutes. A leaden caper story full of stereotyped comedy criminals, it commits the unforgiveable sin of losing faith in its own central conception.... Much is made of the linguistic difficulties of the criminals, who have the misfortune to be five different varieties of monoglot. One word in one language sums up the book in which they appear: rubbish.

*Nicholas Shrimpton, "Situation Ethics," in New Statesman, Vol. 101, No. 2599, January 9, 1981, p. 21.\**

## JOHN LEONARD

The only thing wrong with Donald E. Westlake's ambitious new thriller ["**Kahawa**"] is that Mr. Westlake twice uses the word "disinterested" as though it means "indifferent." It means, instead, "unbiased." Such a minor transgression against the English language would be forgivable, by everybody except John Simon, were it not for the fact that Mr. Westlake at one point employs "uninterested" and does so correctly. Therefore, he knows better and should be ashamed of himself.

Otherwise, "**Kahawa**" is such splendid huggermugger that if you don't like it, there's something wrong with you. Mr. Westlake has specialized in the crime caper, a cocktail with a sardonic twist. In "**Kahawa**," he goes big time—what could be bigger than Africa?—and while he retains his sense of humor, his catty wit, he is angry. Idi Amin, after all, was not a buffoon. Idi Amin was a buffoon who drank blood.

Kahawa means coffee. Mr. Westlake asks us to imagine a coffee-bean crisis in Brazil in 1977, a consortium of "venture capitalists" who would abolish that crisis by an airlift from Uganda, a $6 million heist by an unlikely gang of expatriated Asians and American mercenaries, and enough betrayals to confuse a corkscrew.

The gang intends to steal a train—not to rob it, but to steal it, and then after emptying each car of its coffee bags, to drop pieces of that train, as if they were pebbles, down a gorge and into Lake Victoria, plop. Before this gang succeeds, in the usual pyrrhic fashion, members of it, black, white and caramel, will be threatened with scissors, hit with tire irons, shot at by gunboats, stabbed and seduced....

Amin, thuggish and cunning, dominates. Mr. Westlake hates him and yet is charmed, as if by a clever obscenity, a kind of pornographic waltz step. Small of foot, big of gut, long on grudge, Amin steals the novel. "His mind was like an anthill, the busy self-involved thoughts scurrying along narrow channels." And yet his suspicions are rewarded, and Mr. Westlake makes us understand that there is a portion of Idi Amin in every power-grub, a cleverness entirely strange to scruple. He is, according to this persuasive version of him, Stalin with bells....

Mr. Westlake has many things to say while he jerks our strings. He will deliver such history as we deserve on kalah, a pebble game that resembles the Japanese game of go; Port Victoria "like a failed person," Africa divided up as though the colonizers drew boundaries in order to insure smuggling, the source

of the Nile. He will entertain: we learn the Swahili word for "foot" and the Kikuyu word for "venereal disease" and watch an Amin "as though Henry Kissinger at his most ponderous had been crossed with Muhammad Ali at his most butterfly-and-bee." He will frighten, as if like Frank in "his Kabuki demon costume," he intends to be "the very ideogram of rage."

But Mr. Westlake also has bigger beans to grind. He wants us to think about language as magic, black and white. He wants us to understand that Swahili, an "African Yiddish," has something to say about the Asians Amin booted out of Uganda, those "African Jews." He is trying to connect Hitler and Stalin and Amin in a book that is amazingly persuasive as it enters so many different minds inside so many different pigments of skin.

And he is writing an essay on heroism. Everybody in "**Kahawa**" keeps talking about heroes, even though everybody is in the unheroic business of stealing coffee. Mr. Westlake refers, with wonderful irony, to "Treasure Island" and Tom Swift. Nevertheless, as though his publisher had told him at the last moment to shape up and fly right, he ordains a superperson. At least, she is female. He couldn't help himself, I suppose. In a thriller, good guys prevail, even if they must be girls. No reader that I will ever want to meet should dare complain. Nifty is the word I'm looking for to describe this book.

*John Leonard, in a review of "Kahawa," in The New York Times, March 5, 1982, p. C25.*

## RANDY HOGAN

Donald Westlake's thick adventure novel ["**Kahawa**"] is a bit of a surprise from the author of such slight, amusing caper novels as "**The Hot Rock,**" "**The Spy in the Ointment**" and "**Bank Shot.**" It is a full-dress international intriguer with all the usual trimmings....

Westlake is an old hand at huggermugger, and for the most part he manages to transcend the limitations of pulp fiction by his skillful use of atmospheric detail. Occasionally, however, the intrusion of Westlake's little index-card lessons in African history are annoying....

Practically every character in the book is awarded a turn at being omniscient narrator, which is amusing rather than annoying, but Westlake severely tries the reader's patience with long stretches of dialogue rendered in dialect....

Donald Westlake's peculiar brand of anthropomorphism is also bothersome: "The locomotive dropped, on the right side, about an inch, lurching as though it had been shot. Lew lost control of the throttle, and when he grabbed to regain it he pressed down too hard. The wheels spun with that grating, roaring sound, but then the right side lurched up again and the locomotive lunged forward onto the old spur track like a bear hurling itself away from thin ice."

Still, despite this sort of thing, "**Kahawa**" is entertaining in its adult comic-book way.

*Randy Hogan, "African Intrigue," in The New York Times, Section VII, May 16, 1932, p. 19.*

## HERBERT GOLD

*Eeeepp, snnnarrrkkk, plok-chunk, chook-whirrrr, chick-chick, hum-pah, guk-ick, plink, thup thup* and *ptak* are some of the onomatopoeic inventions that Donald E. Westlake sprinkles through **"Why Me"** to express various disturbances in telephones and telephone devices, doors and vaults, teeth, F.B.I. men and other adverse conditions in and about the life of the bumbling burglar John A. Dortmunder. While they don't always have the perfect rightness of Vladimir Nabokov's description of the sound made by a pencil sharpening—*Ticonderoga, Ticonderoga*—they are usually appropriate and stimulate a smirk of recognition. In general, accurate naming is a steady Westlake virtue; for example, the "unreeling" silence of an answer tape, the "furry" silence of a disconnection.

**"Why Me"** is a Dortmunder book, further adventures of the lost soul who also appears in **"The Hot Rock,"** **"Bank Shot"** and **"Jimmy the Kid."** While the plight of this small-time heist and malaprop artist who finds difficulties in getting a pizza delivered to a street corner in New York is not so deep as the troubles in some of Mr. Westlake's other novels, the concept achieves a nagging sense of kinship for this reader. Dortmunder accidentally burgles a ruby that the police, the F.B.I., the Turkish ambassador, many other governments and national liberation movements and religious fanatics and finally even the amalgamated crooks of New York desperately require to be returned to some more rightful owner. The action is securely zany, but its unraveling is filled with sly and satisfying observation, fast, efficient and convincing, and I found myself racing along with pleasure and gratitude.

Those rare, special, by-yourself laughs are not all. Mr. Westlake is playing with metafiction, or surfiction, or parody of the genre, which becomes clear in his dealing with the up-tight, low-IQ F.B.I. man Malcolm Zachary, who utters: "A third potentialism would be a transactage by a dissident factor within the Turkish populace." Agent Zachary also commands: "Just speak it out in clear and simple terminology. We have infiltratory specialists, men carefully trained to blend into any environmentalism."

**"Why Me"** is such innocent, intelligent fun that I even forgave the chain-smoking of Dortmunder's moll, the ash-dropping May. (pp. 13, 31)

Herbert Gold, "Cops and Robbers," in The New York Times Book Review, *January 9, 1983, pp. 13, 31-2.\**

## JEAN M. WHITE

*Why Me?* is another hilarious Westlakean romp from the opening pages when Dortmunder tangles with a telephone-answering machine. Ma Bell should be grateful for its court-ordered divestiture of local telephone service after Kelp, one of Dortmunder's sidekicks, demonstrates the wonderful possibilities of modern gadgetry in foiling police traces on calls. A squad of cops, disguised as winos, garbagemen, and chess players,

stake out an empty phone booth, in one of Westlake's funnier scenes. . . .

The charm of Dortmunder and his merry gang is that they are not silly bumblers of the Maxwell Smart set. It's bad luck, rather than incompetence, that gets them in a pickle. They may be losers but they are shrewd enough to be survivors. And they have panache and style even when the fates conspire against them. Dortmunder, picked up in the police roundup, can't get the ruby off his finger as he is carted off to the police station. So he twists the stone to his palm and banters with the police about his wedding band.

Westlake is *the* comic novelist of American crime fiction. The genuine comic crime story is a rare delight (we can dismiss parodies and buffoon detectives). What Westlake does is take a well-planned crime and turn it into a boisterous comic caper. He proceeds on the premise that things can go wrong for scamps and scalawags as well as for other people as they go about their business.

So it does for the Dortmunder gang. In *The Hot Rock,* our luckless thieves break *into* a jail, a prison, and an insane asylum in an attempt to retrieve a stolen emerald swallowed by a colleague as he is arrested. In *Bank Shot* . . . , the gang plans an ingenious theft of a bank itself (housed in temporary quarters in a mobile trailer at a shopping mall).

*Why Me?* is another high-spirited outing for Dortmunder. It may not be his "greatest triumph" but it is very funny indeed.

Jean M. White, in a review of "Why Me?" in Book World—The Washington Post, *January 16, 1983, p. 10.*

## KIRKUS REVIEWS

Between 1959 and 1964, before he discovered a remarkable talent for suspense-comedy, Westlake wrote five very un-comic magazine stories about Detective Abraham Levine of Brooklyn's Forty-Third Precinct—some of them under the influence, he readily acknowledges, of Evan Hunter/Ed McBain. Levine, middle-aged and stocky, has a heart condition, is preoccupied with death—and has a heavy idealistic streak. In two of the stories [in *Levine*] . . . , Levine rages against suicide—and uses his rage to save a would-be ledge leaper. There's a creepy, if implausible, *Bad Seed* variation (with still more suicide) and, best of all, **"The Feel of the Trigger"**—which puts the ailing Levine into an emotional duel with a teenage killer. . . . And the final two episodes, one written especially for this collection, offer Levine in decline and quasi-martyrdom—with sentimentality rising, a little uncomfortably, to the fore. Still, even without laughs, Westlake is a crisp, tangy, no-fat storyteller—and fans of old-fashioned police drama (psychological, social, with echoes of earnest 1950s teleplays) will find this a welcome resurrection.

A review of "Levine," in Kirkus Reviews, *Vol. LII, No. 7, April 1, 1984, p. 329.*

# C(harles) K(enneth) Williams

## 1936-

**American poet.**

Williams is considered an original stylist whose poetry is characterized by bleak descriptions of people and situations in American life. His poems project a hostile universe and are often filled with anguish, helplessness, and despair. Williams's disparate images often appear to be chosen for their shock value rather than their literary content. As a result, some critics find his spare poetic vision less powerful than he intends. Others, however, insist that Williams's wrathful observations, together with his unstructured verse, create a sense of urgency.

In his first collection, *Lies* (1969), Williams lashes out at the alienation and deception that he sees as central to contemporary life. These poems are written in short, elliptical lines that jump from image to image. The concluding poem, "A Day for Anne Frank," with its epigram, "God Hates You!," sums up Williams's despairing vision. *I Am the Bitter Name* (1972) covers many of the same topics as *Lies*. Many critics conclude that this volume is a period piece, for its anger is expressed in a series of protest poems focusing on the political and social turmoil of the late 1960s. "A Poem for Governments" rages against involvement in the Vietnam war, and "In the Heart of the Beast" has as its epigram "May 1970: Cambodia, Kent State, Jackson State."

*With Ignorance* (1977) marks an important change of direction in Williams's work. Instead of using the short lines of his earlier volumes, here Williams begins to write long, prose-like lines and to emphasize character and dramatic development. Critics note that these poems about the vagaries of human behavior have more universal appeal than his earlier work as a result of their sympathetic portraits of believable characters. In *Tar* (1983) Williams continues to use long lines in his creation of scenes from urban life. Williams also returns to topical issues; for example, the title poem concerns the threat of nuclear warfare. Although several critics found disappointing the long concluding poem, "One of the Muses," which is more abstract and allegorical than his other recent work, *Tar* is generally considered Williams's most accomplished volume.

(See also *Contemporary Authors*, Vols. 37-40, rev. ed. and *Dictionary of Literary Biography*, Vol. 5.)

## RICHARD HOWARD

Venturesome, C. K. Williams' publisher has asked Anne Sexton . . . for an advance comment on his first book [*Lies*], and she has provided just the right one; she has said, "C. K. Williams is a demon." And his poetry . . . *is* truly demonic, is dead set *against itself,* reminding us that hell cannot win its war with heaven because, as Claudel greatly said, *"le mal ne compose pas."* Infernal poetry—committed to the energies of decreasing, decreating, doing in—appears a contradiction in terms, for does not poetry, the word itself, mean composing, a matter of making and shaping? Yet it would be a sentimentality to think so without the diastole, the converse, the opposition, to fail to see the necessary energies of the negative as wielded by Mr. Williams; and though he himself is often

sentimental when he condescends to the dreadfulness of it all, he can make us rejoice and celebrate with him, make us see the good of gainsaying. . . . (p. 134)

Everything comes of nothing, as Shakespeare knew . . . , and Mr. Williams knows it too. The very titles of his litanies of unbeing—"Loss," "What Is and Is Not," "Trash," "Giving it up," "Don't," "Downward"—and his formal procedures which jettison rhythmical constants, repetitions, rhymes, capital letters, all semblances of propriety—his refusals of procedures, in fact—are concerted to achieve, by the ultimate holocaust of denial, the ultimate assertion. . . . The garbage and pain of the world, the disasters of our history and the holding-actions of our crude hope: that is the landscape and weather of these poems, seemingly endless and certainly craving an end. Williams' necessary versification being a nullifying one, allowing for lots of blanks, silences, cancellations: it is only fair, as well as foul, that the poem which does end this astonishing book, **"A Day for Anne Frank,"** with its awful motto from St. John Chrysostom, "God hates you!" should itself come to an end with the *physis* of unmaking. . . . Has it not always been said, among us, that the Devil is the father of *Lies*? (pp. 135-36)

*Richard Howard, "Some First Volumes," in* The Kenyon Review, *Vol. XXXII, No. 1, 1970, pp. 130-37.**

## FRED MORAMARCO

[*Lies*] by C. K. Williams is a mature and exciting first volume of poetry. For some, those two adjectives ("mature" and "exciting") may seem antithetical, but it is precisely in the tension between these two qualities that Williams' poetry operates. The maturity involves the experiential dimension of his work—the depth of a vision which sees life as **"The Long Naked Walk of the Dead,"** to cite one of his titles. These poems sound the grim notes of the *Songs of Experience,* but at the same time there is a vitality, an ingenuousness here that constantly surprises and clashes with the somber and sobering vision of the whole. The first of these surprises occurs in the title itself, which is commonplace enough, but causes us to think again when we associate it with a collection of poetry. If "beauty is truth," then what indeed are we to make of *Lies*? A paradox, to be sure, and paradox is a quality central to almost each poem in the volume. The term which comes most easily to mind in connection with Williams' poetry is "metaphysical." The abrupt openings, the ingenious metaphors, the deceptive colloquial ease of the diction—all techniques we associate with Donne, Herbert, et al., are abundantly present in *Lies.* This is of course simply to say that he is very much a *modern* poet, with an alert awareness of the major directions of contemporary poetry. (p. 203)

> Fred Moramarco, "A Gathering of Poets," in Western Humanities Review, *Vol. XXIV, No. 2, Spring, 1970, pp. 201-07.\**

## ALAN WILLIAMSON

[In *Lies*] C. K. Williams is as hard-boiled as Louise Gluck, but less intimate, and derives from the confessional group mainly in his need to imagine the unimaginable horrors of modern war, his feeling that they are relevant to his most private moods and fancies. He often risks becoming homiletic and grandiose on these subjects; the poor-man's existential note appears at its worst in a poem comparing God to a farmer who "can't leave and goes sullen and lean / among the rusting yard junk." Elsewhere, Williams seems to listen more closely to his own real feelings, and to come up with a tone, compounded of paranoiac bluster and wounded tenderness, in which he can be passionate without being embarrassed by his rhetoric. It is a tone in which one can state, with irrefutable authority, such metaphysical truths as

> It's horrible, being run over by a bus
> when all you are is a little box turtle.

The same tone, combined with a complete refusal, except in one section, to approach the impossible subject directly, makes **"A Day for Anne Frank"** a surprisingly moving poem, one of the best in the book.

Williams is not an exceptionally evocative poet, visually or aurally, and he frequently depends for his total effect on the cleverness of his extended metaphors. The wildness of these metaphors reminds one somewhat of a fellow apocalyptic poet, W. S. Merwin; yet Williams' method is the opposite of Merwin's, an almost Metaphysical precision in elaboration, rather than ellipsis and mystery.

This anomaly sometimes creates problems: when, in **"It Is This Way With Men,"** the correspondences are switched around twice, and each time spelled out equally thoroughly, the illogic of the shifts bothers me, because no general atmosphere of strangeness excuses (or uses) it. The metaphors are often the most powerful and poetic element in Williams' work; but he has not found a way of presenting them that is at once weird and logical enough for the needs of his temperament. (pp. 92-3)

> Alan Williamson, "The Future of Confession," in Shenandoah, *Vol. XXI, No. 4, Summer, 1970, pp. 89-93.\**

## M. L. ROSENTHAL

The most interesting poems in . . . *Lies* consist of elusive, even vanishing, notations of delicate terror or pity. A poem like **Even If I Could** or **Trappers** is like Dylan Thomas in intaglio, restrained and inward despite a proliferative overlay of images. They have none of Thomas's assertiveness; it is as though [Williams] had revised *And Death Shall Have No Dominion* to read, in title and refrain, *In Death's Subtle Dominion.* The images of **Even If I Could** are certainly energetic: "you're always oozing around the edges", "the fire-cloud", "rage howls in your arms / like a baby", "shadows / merging like oil", "the angels ride / in their soft saddles". But the idiom of the whole poem is of surrender to the hopelessness of trying to come through. **Trappers** is another poem of psychic paralysis despite the need to make contact whether with someone loved or with reality or God or oneself. Its music is gentler and more exquisite than that anywhere else in the book. . . . (pp. 101-02)

[The] beginning, with its romantic, distantly erotic, sentimental promise, is quickly followed by more violent effects. The second stanza evokes mountaineers trapped and stifled by snow in the Rockies. The final stanza presents a nightmare shift from the "old song" of the beginning to "an awful drone, / a scab" of sound and total loss of touch with the initial romantic image. **Trappers** crystallizes a whole history of collapsing cultural morale, but its center of focus is the speaker's inner yearning for an unattainable relatedness. When, in other poems like *It Is This Way with Men,* Williams puts his thought more baldly, a certain poverty of conception is revealed. One then notices, too, that certain rhythmic characteristics—the short lines, the sparse distribution of caesuras, for instance—are not altogether functional. A depressively exacerbated state is what we are keyed in to at Williams's best; when he does not explain himself, we are free to read certain further implications. These are symptoms, not discoveries. (p. 102)

> M. L. Rosenthal, "Plastic Possibilities," in Poetry, *Vol. CXIX, No. 2, November, 1971, pp. 99-104.\**

## MORRIS DICKSTEIN

C. K. Williams is a newcomer to the strain of surreal bitter humor and indignation that characterized the best protest poems of the sixties. In his very impressive first book, *Lies,* published in 1969, this was scarcely one mood among many: despite its title the book was personal, relaxed, spacious and various in tone, full of boyish starts of affection and empathy. Its view of pain had more of wonder and discovery than pure horror. . . . Every poem is a piece of growing up. Every crushing blow, every pain, indeed every experience, is an opening toward life, an accretion of fresh feeling. In **"Faint Praise,"** a poignant poem on a dead friend, he tries at first to imagine the horror, the physical decomposition of death, but soon turns to describe the wonder of his own survival. . . . (pp. 125-26)

Sex provides the model for this sort of opening up, this flowing outward toward an unknown, and the poet gets almost a sexual pleasure out of existence itself, for all its dark uncertainties.

But towards the end of the book another note begins to intercede, a deeper grief, a guilt, as in the poem **"Penance."** . . . The poet continues this litany of regret until it reaches out to include every redemptive possibility—every joy, ecstacy, or tranquility—that lies behind the bitter world of appearance. The book stoops at last to justify its title and denounces all consolation as sham. . . . (p. 126)

This note of despair and demystification, of guilt at one's own sensory and imaginative longings, is also present in the last and longest poem of the book, **"A Day for Anne Frank,"** where Williams tries to embrace and console the child-victim who obsesses him, but also tells her the world is empty and senseless, "God hates you!," "there is nothing." The movement of the poem's ending imitates the halting disjunctiveness of its vision. . . . (p. 127)

[This] unfortunately imposes a breakdown of poetic language, a renunciation especially of the natural and dramatic richness that makes most of the poems in the book so full and human. In the new book, *I Am the Bitter Name,* this distrust of poetry and language is more marked. Williams eliminates punctuation of any sort: capital letters, commas, periods, all but an occasional question-mark or exclamation point. He breaks lines at points that conflict with the sense and runs them on when the meaning dictates a halt, as if only the inflections of the voice could salvage the sense without betraying it into mechanical periodicity or eloquence. Not surprisingly, many of the poems sound better from the poet himself . . . than they read on the page. This isn't simply because his cadenced, heightened monotone serves the poems so well, but because he has lost faith in any meaningful, objective syntax of poetry and experience, unless (as with Anne Frank) he can intervene with his personal gift of comfort, forgiveness, and love.

In most of the poems of the new book this just cannot be done. The poet has been bitten by the bug of the age, which for ten years has envenomed us all with public disasters—assassinations, civil wars, genocide, subhuman terrorism, anti-personnel savagery—that are as real and inescapable as our own private tragedies. Yet how helpless we all are, how little we can do except shout, as the poet repeatedly does, "stay where you are! . . . don't die on me!"

Like all good protest poets, of which there are so few, Williams succeeds in conveying the personal meaning of the public fact. In the best poems of *I Am the Bitter Name* he seems to tap unspoken sources of private unhappiness that feed and vivify his response to the larger horrors of the time. This convergence of feeling, at once illicit and utterly authentic, enables him to write three or four of the best antiwar poems—and they are real poems!—since Bly's *The Light Around the Body* (1967). But the book as a whole falls far short of *Lies.* The tonal range and emotional nuance of the earlier book get narrowed into bitterness and anger. Though only a handful of the poems allude directly to politics the whole book is pervaded by a spirit of protest and self-immolation.

What saves the better poems is a rueful irony, a childlike sense of the marvelous that refuses to be stamped out by history, that continues to move the poet beyond hatred to wonder. Read **"The Beginning of April,"** or the two best poems, **"The Rabbit Fights for his Life the Leopard Eats Lunch"** and **"The Spirit the Triumph,"** the latter of which speculates in Hamlet's wistful, incredulous vein on what a piece of work man is. It begins with the homely magic of learning to tie your shoes or ride a horse, or of "getting your hand under a girl's sweater." With

gasps of astonishment that "we are the crown of all that exists" it moves dialectically into a maimed world of mechanical limbs and physical horror, with no break in the wide-eyed, gee whiz tone. Finally,

> we men! aren't we something? I mean
> we are worth thinking about aren't we?
> we are the end we are the living end

What keeps this from being a piece of spiritual Grand Guignol is that Williams really means it: the title is less than half ironic. In the end the poems are all offerings of love, renunciations of the scorn that dehumanizes all it touches. Thus the long concluding poem on the Kent State massacre, **"In the Heart of the Beast,"** begins harshly with a refusal to forgive or understand, but the poem is soon waylaid by unexpected complications of feeling. . . . He discovers that he doesn't want to call anyone "pig," that he feels a human kinship with cops and hard-hats and haters, that he yearns to take them in his arms and wrestle them into awareness and love, quite as he had wished to comfort the others, the victims, Anne Frank, or the bloated, starving children of Biafra, or the Kent State girl who is screaming on the front page of the *Times*.

But he knows that the girl in the paper "will be screaming forever / and her friend will lie there forever." The fragile, wasted bodies of the Biafran children are almost palpable to him but they explode under his touch, they elude him. Finally they are only television images, newspaper images, explosions in some corner of his mind. The public fact in itself is finally distant and untouchable, immune to the interventions of love.

As poet he is alone and makes nothing happen—his final refuge is outside politics entirely, in his nostalgia for the energy and innocence of growing up, for the unspoiled pleasure of awakened love and true knowledge. Though bombarded by history the poet of *Lies* survives in his successor's insistence on honest emotion, however idiosyncratic or uncomfortable, and in his disconcerting empathy for the Enemy. . . . In the end his politics is a revulsion from *mere* politics, an application of the human standard, a reassertion of the human presence. Amid fantasies of the Revolution he continues to yearn for the blessings of the quotidian—"to know there is something marvelous / and not pay attention," to gulp a draught of the dailiness of life. (pp. 127-29)

*Morris Dickstein, "Politics and the Human Standard," in* Parnassus: Poetry in Review, *Vol. 1, No. 1, Fall-Winter, 1972, pp. 125-29.*

## JOHN VERNON

C. K. Williams certainly doesn't shun the bad taste of things. If concrete poetry doesn't take enough risks, he takes, if anything, too many. But this is infinitely preferable. In his second book, *I Am the Bitter Name* . . . , as in his first, language rides on a crest of energy, and is shaped by that crest, rather than by concepts of visual design, as in concrete poetry. If concrete poetry is small and well confined, Williams' poems are expansive, urgent, and breathless. . . . At first I thought that many of these poems could be edited or pruned, but now I realize that's an inappropriate response. If the poems succeed it is because of the quickness of their gestures, a quickness that embodies hesitations, false starts, and a frantic sort of casting around. They can no more be "improved" than Rodin's quick studies in clay, because, like those studies, their form expresses the act of composition. This refusal to plan and deliberate, to choose or reject words carefully (again, the opposite of concrete poetry) is strengthened by the moral urgency of the poems. Williams' attitude seems to be that in the face of public events as tragic and frightening as Kent State, the process of selecting and censoring bits of language is hypocritical, and defers the moral rage that the poem should be expressing. This is the problem that all political or "committed" poetry faces. At his best, Williams is enough of a poet so that his rage seems naturally to hit upon most of the right words as it flails around. At his worst, as in the long final poem, **"In the Heart of the Beast,"** the poetry has become too naked a gesture and the emotion too undigested, so that the language is like a whip that lashes out but takes hold of nothing. . . . Williams is better in shorter poems, perhaps because the apocalyptic sense in the book requires short, quick bursts. When the feeling is that time is closing its door in your face, the most natural response is to squeeze everything into the little space that's left. . . . The breathless energy of thought in these poems is also the energy of a scream, one that tries to sustain its maximum volume as long as it possibly can, in order at least to insult the silence that it can't fill. The trouble is, the more Williams writes, the less time there is to write in; the more he screams, the weaker his voice is bound to get. Even if you can't accept the feeling of apocalypse floating around these days, you know in reading these poems that for Williams at least the apocalypse *is* coming. How long can someone continue to squeeze poems into a rapidly diminishing space and time? The gesture of squeezing itself makes space and time all the smaller. Williams is going to have to be quiet, and that will be his apocalypse. And then he'll have to begin again, post-apocalypse, if the world lets him. (pp. 103-05)

John Vernon, "A Gathering of Poets," in Western Humanities Review, Vol. XXVII, No. 1, Winter, 1973, pp. 101-10.*

## JASCHA KESSLER

*I Am The Bitter Name* is meant by C. K. Williams to stand for Death; perhaps the poet wants us to know that he is its Prophet. A very tall order indeed, but at least it focuses his energies on defining his own voice, which he uses consistently throughout, and which is easily identifiable by his manner of speaking, which is simply a breathless or pauseless run-on continuum— as though monotone is the medium or ground against which the individual poems have occurred, possibly by deft excisions or by having been scooped out, the writer merely fishing with a net in the stream of his own violently-flowing self and thus not altogether responsible for what he flings over his shoulder at us. I think Williams is willing to take the responsibility, however, for what he doesn't throw back. . . .

Williams is really quite varied in the shapes of his poems, given his method, but I am not sure this isn't more than an arbitrary visual manipulation of his findings, or accidents, I mean *merely* arbitrary. For, taken as a whole the book blurs, and one is aware constantly of suffering a vertigo while reading it: is it possible that the world is *that* indiscriminate a collection of phenomena, or phenomena in the forms of feelings and opinions about things? Williams is very feeling, very angry, and utterly frank in declaring himself and the world he seems to see us all in, which is a revolting world, to say the least. But—it hasn't occurred to this poet that the world, seen any way you will, is both far more terrible than he can manage to describe for us, for real horrors beggar any description which is direct expression of them, and far more complex and beau-

tiful than his breathless run-on syntax poems are able to suggest. The hell he speaks of, like all hells, is that of his own vision, which is, I think, the case for each of us. What I would hope, that being so, is that Williams will grow more skilful at *thinking* about his poems, without losing the energy he needs to write them out. One never knows, except in his most editorial poems, where Williams is going from moment to moment, or how to relate his beginnings with his endings, or the passage in-between, for that matter. Or else, I find it too difficult really to bother. I hope that this book is a phase. . . . (p. 300)

[*Crawl*] shows Williams' defects and strengths as they are: the simplicity, clarity of diction, haste and jumbling of his thought by the unremitting stroboscopic, kaleidoscopic pulsing of a voice from thought to speech to image to unvoiced thought. I may have my values upside-down, or inside-out, and the reader may think just the opposite about Williams' work; but I am going on my gut response, which tells me that I am both impressed by what is a collection of real poems and disoriented by the work, and yet know they come from a source that is not vacuous or false. Maybe the voice Williams is using here is his best attempt to cope with an overwhelming flux of insupportable experience, and thus renders the subworld of the demonic in the only way he can acknowledge and so contain, if not master it. (p. 301)

Jascha Kessler, "Trial and Error," in Poetry, Vol. CXXI, No. 5, February, 1973, pp. 292-303.*

## JAMES ATLAS

[C. K. Williams's] first two books, *Lies* and *I Am the Bitter Name,* were vitiated by a shrill vehemence and sentimentality. The absence of capitals or punctuation made the poems blur and sprawl. Their dominant note was of agony; there were welts of inchoate feeling. His new book, **With Ignorance,** is likewise flawed, but his poetry has come to possess an eerie incantatory power that salvages it from confession. . . . Williams is writing parables, plain tales about men and women in extreme situations: a laborer at home with his family, and the inarticulate tensions that tear him apart; a friend who went mad; a Vietnam veteran in a bar, tormented by the murders he committed, both in the war and as a small-time mobster later on; and in other poems, "my wife, my child . . . my home, my work, my sorrow." . . . [He] borrows the cadences of ordinary speech, vigorous and utterly without refinement, depending on a litany of charged rhetoric to transform prose into poetry.

Some of his poems *are* prose. . . . The lines are so long that the book had to be published in a wide-page format, like an art catalogue. The limitations of such a style are self-evident; Williams is writing in haphazard strokes, and with such apparent haste—or perhaps deliberate casualness—that he even disposes of grammar on occasion. . . . Eager to blurt out his feelings, he rushes from one sad incident to another, pouring forth woe in a hectic, rude, indignant voice; what comes to mind is the Italian gesture of slapping one's forehead with an open palm.

Still, in other poems his lines are Biblical in their sonority, and resonate with a dire prophecy reminiscent of "Howl." . . . Williams achieves a memorable intensity in the title poem, where the longing to survive, to transcend the dross of experience and to discover its essence culminates in a stunning evocation of "history, power, grief and remorse"—sensations that converge on the speaker and threaten to annihilate his imaginative life, the only life that promises to survive. (p. 765)

*James Atlas, "The Poetry of Mere Prose," in* The Nation, *Vol. 224, No. 24, June 18, 1977, pp. 763-66.\**

## MORRIS DICKSTEIN

With his penchant for tucking a credo into a wisecrack, Ezra Pound once insisted that poetry should be at least as well written as prose. Throughout the history of English poetry, revolutions have been made by poets who envied the suppleness, fluency and vigor of good prose. Chaucer, Dryden, Wordsworth, Eliot and Pound were all reacting in one way or another to the florid, gorgeous poeticism of a previous generation. . . .

Even a cursory glance at C. K. Williams's third book of poems, **"With Ignorance,"** shows us how firmly it belongs to this anti-poetic tradition of poetry. The first thing that's distinctive about the book is its physical shape, tall and wide, very wide, almost square. This is surely meant to accommodate a long and lanky verse line, the longest I've seen in recent poetry, yet the lines repeatedly elude the design and run on, run over. The poems themselves are equally outsized, stretching from two to seven pages. In his first two books, **"Lies"** (1969) and **"I Am the Bitter Name"** (1972), Williams was a poet of trim anecdotes, fragmentary phrases and brutal metaphors; here he's traded in a staccato lyrical rhythm for the cadences of a storyteller. The excitement is tremendous, as it always is when we see a pungent talent emerging to find its own form and voice.

In its way Williams's last book, **"I Am the Bitter Name,"** was a characteristic document of the early Nixon years. Its largely unpunctuated language was violent, fragmentary, forced by rude enjambment, torn by rage and frustration. The Vietnam war was very much on Williams's mind then, and it released shadowy springs of private desperation to create a surge of anger and horror. The wistfulness, nostalgia and boyish passion of **"Lies"** had narrowed to a savage irony; a deeply playful poet had turned bitter and sardonic. . . .

The new voice we hear in **"With Ignorance"** strikes us not for this sort of raw sarcasm, this stupefied amazement at human foibles, but for its colloquial intimacy. (p. 14)

[Williams] is like a more self-conscious but still affable barroom companion, always about to sail off into another monologue, another tiff with the everyday world. Yet the stories usually go off the rails—suddenly he's gazing inward; they lose their anecdotal shape and turn ruminative, self-lacerating, revelatory. The poet becomes a drinker of ecstacies, and he hunts for secrets that promise him salvation.

Like A. R. Ammons, Williams is intrigued by the ordinary world but always in quest of a "radiance" that will transfigure it, an intuition that might irradiate his life. In one poem, **"The Cave,"** he remembers his belief that the mad had access to such secrets. He recalls his fantasies about a man and woman he had visited in a madhouse. . . . (pp. 14, 30)

With its dovetailing of Plato's cave, that great metaphor for the elusiveness of knowledge, and the tortured life in the mental hospital, shot through with illusions of vision and wisdom,

**"The Cave"** is a masterful poem, leavened by the comedy of the poet's eager, acquisitive innocence. Williams finally lets go of his romantic image of madness; he discovers that the secret, the mystery, "isn't lost in the frenzy of one soul or another, but next to us, in the touch, between," in the intimate and trivial encounters of daily life.

As testimony to this recognition the book contains something rare in contemporary poetry, a bustling number of other people: a blue-collar worker and his family, the author's children, a lonely old grocer, wives, lovers, the friend who goes mad, the famous writer drinking himself to death, and so on. Williams approaches these people with a mixture of tenderness and curiosity that usually outflanks his powerful reserves of desperation. Only in the long unsatisfying title poem, **"With Ignorance,"** is he overcome by a vague ruminative bleakness, a feverish disgust, which looks morosely inward and puts the actualities of life in limbo.

Elsewhere, the solid realism, the clash of contending feelings and human interchange, give the book its most signal quality, its emotional range and intensity. . . . (pp. 30-1)

By bringing poetry closer to prose Williams has also brought it closer to the dramatic complexity and personal directness of fiction—the book has its crackerbarrel side. His main aim is not storytelling, but stories happen along the way, and his sinuous lines have the breathless rush, the rapid shifts of nuance and inflection, that characterize good talk. Williams's poems sacrifice eloquence for energy, epigram for affect, song for speech. I find them deeply inspiriting. (p. 31)

*Morris Dickstein, "Sacrificing Song for Speech," in* The New York Times Book Review, *July 10, 1977, pp. 14, 30-1.*

## STANLEY PLUMLY

The named obsession is one thing, the unnameable another. The fourteen poems of C. K. Williams' *With Ignorance,* alternating between a sort of street talk storytelling and incandescent lyricism, seem to end where they begin, at the peripheries of speech and naming, with ignorance. The difference, of course, is that his book moves from a negative to a positive pole, from "a mouth full of nails" to "a silence rising through light." It is inevitable that a poet preoccupied with the inarticulate and inarticulated should fill the page with lines as long as prose, in pursuit of a right hand margin. . . . Williams' lines eventually enjamb or turn back to recover breath, good sense, or hope. And yet they read as if determined to turn into silence, or light. The poems themselves in this third volume, posing story against song against story in a cause-and-effect pattern, accumulate much as the individual lines do, *toward* something more than *to* something. Rhythmically, it is a book about momentum as much as meaning. Even so Williams is fond of interrupting himself with gestures like "This is going to get a little nutty now" or "There's another legend" or "I was dreaming about the universe." Occasionally he interrupts himself at the start of the poem—"This is a story." Still, the rhythm of the book as a whole is no horizon line. The moments of the emphatic lyric, such as **"Spit"** or **"The Race of the Flood"** or **"Near the Haunted Castle,"** offer the stories a place to get to and leave, as if the emotional life being freighted in the narrative moments had too much left over and some accounting had to be made.

"The first language was loss, the second sorrow," Williams says on his last page. Almost every line, every image up to and including that page rehearses that knowledge, a knowledge exercised again and again against ignorance. But ignorance here suggests something deeper than unknowing; it speaks from a position of primacy, from "the gut cave, the speech cave," from "the hide, the caul, the first mind." That is why the voice throughout the book is so consistent, so complete. It comes from an absolute source, an emotion so exposed as to call into question the very idea of artifice. No wonder, then, the technique of Williams' total fiction is to hesitate or spill over, interrupt or repeat, pledge doubt or reassurance. *With Ignorance* is predicated on one of the most dangerous cliches in literature, that to recreate the condition one must imitate its origin. The artist, not the man, rescues that cliche. The artist in Williams recreates the *condition of ignorance,* "not to know how silently we knell in the mouth of death," in its full voice, the voice of letting go, letting out, letting alone, the pure voice of the prose lyricist.... Here is a poetry that proves that meter and metaphor are not necessarily symbiotic, that the music must be in the source before it can be in the sound of the line. The feeling of and a feeling for things, the empathy is in the very length of the line, the inevitability of the line, beyond the ability of the music—"then the gates of the local bar unlaced and whoever was left drifted in out of the wall of heat"—and beyond, almost, the endurance of the page. It is not simply that Williams' lines are long, but that they contain so much, carry so much, say and say.

*With Ignorance* is about a man in trouble, but thank God it is real trouble.... Williams is not returning to anything. Ever the urban dweller, his poems normally begin at street level and end up on the side of the mountain. Ever the actualist, he picks up the detritus lying in front of him, peopling it with friends, locals, his wife, his son and daughter, the drunk on his front-step, and then he takes all this literal data and places it in a configuration, in a series of configurations, in a sequence of near-allegories in which everything is at stake and everything can be lost. What is remarkable about Williams' tone of voice, the commitment of his line, the relentlessness of his music is the extreme to which it all takes us without leaving us there. One comes away from his text feeling filled up, tested, yet emptied too.... The arc of the emotion is nearly the same from poem to poem not simply because of the obsessive nature of the search, but because of the singular and continuing appeal to archetypes—and one purpose of the length of the line and poem is to insure that transformation from street level is made. The force field of Williams' page is tremendous because the rhythms and images are so inexorably located in the first mind of their maker and are articulated from that first voice he calls silence. His poems are dreamspeech, he their dreamspeaker. (pp. 31-2)

*Stanley Plumly, "Chapter and Verse," in* The American Poetry Review, *Vol. 7, No. 1, January-February, 1978, pp. 21-32.\**

### ROBERT COLES

These new, chosen poems of C. K. Williams [included in *With Ignorance*] beg for a wider audience than they are likely to get. In substance they reach out to the ordinary hum-drum world, and doing so, remind the reader how self-centered writers (and reviewers) can be, and how provincial some of us are who have staked out certain academic territory, and every day bare our teeth, past which go the hisses and growls: the cranky, condescending, self-serving and always self-displaying words that make up *hauteur*. Maybe, one day, those of us who love poems such as Mr. Williams has wrought and offered us, will pay the poems a different kind of tribute than the critic's; will, instead, take the poems down the street, read them to people like the ones who appear, speak, grumble, curse, whisper, smile, embrace, question in *With Ignorance*....

[One] speculates that he is deadly serious when he draws upon Soren Kierkegaard for the title of the book, and its longest poem: "With ignorance begins a knowledge the first characteristic of which is ignorance." The sad, sharp-tongued Danish theologian had no use for intellectual pomposity and arrogance.... He turned on his own brilliance with a skeptical humility that was, clearly, hard won. Ignorance for him was the result of a sacrifice of sorts—maybe the psychological equivalent of the biblical sacrifice Abraham was willing to offer. (p. 12)

C. K. Williams has, for his own reasons, made a similar gesture of self-restraint, self-criticism. He does not come to us with answers, programs, weighty and all too knowing pronouncements. (He does not, alternatively, make of himself, his thoughts and ideas, a precious, demanding, slyly exhorting but thoroughly aloof if not untouchable literary presence.) Like Kierkegaard, he stays in the world, watches, hears, keeps trying to straddle the boundary of affection and disapproval, compassion and scorn. Like Kierkegaard, he also moves inward, groping for truths that may be lying around in his head—truths, however, that have to do with experience, and that have a certain moral worth, rather than abstractions, generalizations meant to conquer the world. There is no "pure" emotion, he knows, as did his 19th century spiritual friend. They both demonstrate an Augustinian capacity for self-scrutiny, and at times, consequently, have to acknowledge despair—as in the ending of **"Near the Haunted Castle,"** with the line "In the beginning was love, right? No, in the beginning . . . the bullet . . ."; or, as in the ending of **"Hog Heaven,"** with the words "it stinks and it stinks and it stinks and it stinks."

But there are other moments, too: the poet daring to narrate; daring to speak loud and clear about the things of this world; and daring to affirm the various kinds of love he feels—without, however, making too much of them, of himself.... But because we know what goes on below the mind's surface does not mean we need deny ourselves a look at what actually is— what has been won, however precariously. C. K. Williams has achieved in these poems a humble intelligence, able and willing to acknowledge its severe limits ("ignorance"). It is a risky path he has chosen—not only for the interior (psychological, moral, spiritual) difficulties, but for what may be waiting on the outside along the way: some scold, brandishing a ruler, waving a list of essentials, demanding compliance—or else. (pp. 12-13)

*Robert Coles, in a review of "With Ignorance," in* The American Poetry Review, *Vol. 8, No. 4, July-August, 1979, pp. 12-13.*

### LOUIS SIMPSON

For a generation, American poetry has been stuck in the first person like a truck spinning its wheels. A few poets, however, have gone beyond the confessional and, in writing about themselves, have made up stories. The "I" in the poem is treated as a character, and life is given a more dramatic, satisfying shape. That is the way Robert Lowell wrote "Life Studies," and in **"Tar,"** C. K. Williams appears to be transforming the worlds of adolescence and early manhood in the same fashion.

He uses a long line with eight stresses—at least by my count—that carries the action steadily forward, allows for the inclusion of details and creates a music apart from what the writing is about. You are conscious of the pace and sound of verse, though the material is the kind you expect to find in a novel. . . .

Mr. Williams is a realist. Reading **"Combat,"** which describes the narrator's frustrating and unforgettable affair with a young woman who is a German refugee—an affair encouraged by her mother—we feel this is how it must have been because it is grotesque. The grotesque is the sign of truth in our time.

His realism spares us nothing. If you want to know what a cripple looks like with his pants down, Mr. Williams will tell you. But if you want the breath of spring on parted lips, you're out of luck. The muse of poetry Whitman saw arriving in the United States has been with us for some time, as Whitman said, "install'd amid the kitchenware," but I am inclined to think the Graces haven't arrived and, given our Puritan hatred of beauty, never may.

Several of Mr. Williams's poems make a point about suffering and doubt and the moments of expanded consciousness that suffering and doubt occasionally produce. One of his memorable successes is the title poem, **"Tar"**—perhaps because the material is so resistant to poetry and yet he manages to make poetry out of it. . . . How can removing an old roof and the near catastrophe of Three Mile Island be connected? The poem manages to connect them. . . . (p. 13)

["Tar"] is Mr. Williams's fable for the nuclear age, his statement of faith in perdurable, blundering humanity. It is also a statement of faith in the art he practices—poetry "scribbled with obscenities and hearts" and as hard as lumps of tar. A number of poets are putting characters and incidents in their poems and reclaiming territory that had been abandoned to the novel. C. K. Williams is in the front rank of the movement. (pp. 13, 32)

*Louis Simpson, "Dramas and Confessions," in* The New York Times Book Review, *November 27, 1983, pp. 13, 32.**

### CLAYTON ESHLEMAN

C. K. Williams' poems [in **"Tar"**] don't look like much on the page. All have extremely long 20- to 25-syllable lines which must be indented as runovers. Page after page, the identical type-grid evokes the monotonous sameness of urban tenement districts, which are the settings in which many of the poems occur. Curiously, the negative impression that the pages initially convey becomes, as one reads along, psychologically relevant to the neighborhoods and events that Williams is scrutinizing. With the scrupulous attention to detail of fine metal engraving, Williams is writing some of the truest—and most stinging—poems that I know about becoming a man in America.

More than half of these 17 poems have a particular strategy of construction that reminds me of Kafka's story, "The Country Doctor"; labyrinthine twists of events climax, about two-thirds of the way through, with the sudden revelation of a gaping,

wormy wound in the patient's side that had been camouflaged by the earlier demands on the doctor's attention. Once this monstrosity has been fixed as the "center" of the labyrinth, Kafka's task is to get the doctor out.

In a similar fashion, Williams' gentle and generous curiosity peers around the contours of his many human figures and with an inevitable, awful accuracy discovers the central suck in the sluggish whirlpool of their lives. He then withdraws, often in an almost aimless drift of associated memories; and without any dramatic "conclusion," the poem is over. . . .

[Most] of the poems . . . strike me as being fully realized if we accept them on the poetic terms that Williams proposes. I think we should do this, but I also think we should be willing to read a poet as good as Williams against what we imagine his poetry of the future could become. Some readers will feel that the writing in **"Tar"** is too descriptive, and that the poems sometimes become too storylike and predictable. Williams himself seems to have an eye on his own development: The final poem is an attempt to do something more cerebral and mythically ambitious. In **"One of the Muses,"** all the perceptive exterior description is emptied out, and without it, Williams' language becomes laborious and opaquely abstract. It becomes a poem about a vision that has no vision in it—but I am not put off by its failure; Williams, who has already carved out a territory and mastered it, is willing to risk failure in order to take on new, more widely challenging materials.

*Clayton Eshleman, "The Poetry of Central Wounds, Gaping," in* Los Angeles Times Book Review, *January 22, 1984, p. 3.*

### DAVID WOJAHN

Although the manners of C. K. Williams and Stanley Plumly are highly different, the poets emphatically share a desire to capture the visionary within the everyday, perhaps more so than any other two figures of their generation. . . . Both poets have spent a long while preparing their new books [*Tar* and *Summer Celestial*], but neither writer has used his new collection for a significant departure of style or concern. Instead, they have refined their approaches and deepened their authority.

The most obvious change that C. K. Williams's work has undergone over the years is a formal one. The terse, shortlined, vernacular lyrics of his first book, *Lies,* reminiscent of Alan Dugan and David Ignatow, have gradually been replaced by increasingly longer poems and a much longer and more wideranging line. But in lengthening his line, Williams has become, almost paradoxically, a more careful prosodist; he is surely in no way a writer of "prose poems." Since *With Ignorance,* his lines have often contained twenty or more syllables, but have avoided the laxness of prose through a preponderance of stressed syllables, numerous caesuras, and a Whitmanesque endstopping. Rather than lulling, the effect of these techniques is staccato and percussive, a music so discordant that the reader's attention rarely lags. Like a good jazz musician, Williams knows that virtuoso technique is not always elegant. . . . Williams never varies this technique, and yet it remains successful throughout the book. Despite the brutality of Williams's sonics, the effect grows almost incantatory, the most apt vehicle to illustrate his concerns. Pavese—another virtuoso of longlined verse—referred to his poetic method as "restless meditation," and the same phrase might be applied to the poems of *Tar.*

Continually bewildered, continually in doubt of his ability to rid himself of his obsessions, Williams's speaker approaches despair in each of his poems, not because the world he dwells in overwhelms him, but because he feels overwhelmed by the need to articulate his experience. But in his effort to give our essential inarticulation a voice, Williams must discard any rhetoric he regards as false or artificially soothing. Clarity of vision and expression becomes a goal of nearly mystical proportions, and his pursuit of such clarity almost always incorporates a narrative investigation of specific memories, and a faltering, stream-of-consciousness method of disclosure. Given this program, it's no wonder that Williams seeks to recapture events from his past that bring him unease and regret.... The situations he recalls are likely to be grotesque ones—a crippled Vietnam vet's wheelchair overturning, an adolescent visit to a Times Square prostitute, repeated encounters with a woman as she curbs her howling, cancerous dog. His recollections of youth and adolescence permit a sort of self-conscious ignorance, but nothing akin to innocence.... Despite epigraphs from Heine, Wittgenstein and Plato, these poems are determinedly anti-literary, for Williams wishes to deny that art has any real power to give us solace. Epiphanies come not through knowledge, but through reduction and renunciation. Again and again, the poems seek to recall their characters to a kind of preliterate state of vulnerability and inarticulation. But by diminishing us to our most basic needs, Williams also establishes our commonality.... Lurid scenes of urban life ... are something we're familiar with in the work of many of Williams's contemporaries—Levine and Ignatow immediately come to mind. But in Williams we see none of the posturing that sometimes mars their work. The speaker of the poems refuses to glamorize the events he witnesses and remembers, and similarly refuses to glamorize his personal disclosures. There's little of the nervous sensationalism of confessional poetry here. Williams admits his failings in a manner that's embarrassed, even awkward, and perhaps this is why personal history is never misused in the book. Despite the unflinching honesty of Williams's approach, his continual self-questioning works to give his poems the effect of *discretion* rather than effusiveness.

I'm always a bit perturbed when readers of Williams accuse him of simply writing undigested prose. He has picked a style so difficult to excel in, one that so closely aligns itself to his sensibility, that the frequency of his success is remarkable. Although the poems of *Tar* are all too long for useful quotation or explication here, the volume contains a number of very notable efforts—**"From My Window,"** **"My Mother's Lips,"** **"The Dog," "Floor,"** as well as **"Gas Station"** and the title poem. The book's only real failure is, unfortunately, its longest and most ambitious poem, **"One of the Muses,"** a fifteen-page opus that appears deliberately to eschew everything that Williams is best at. Abandoning narrative and realistic biography for a highly allegorical piece of obsessive abstraction, it's the only instance in the book where Williams's self-questioning gives way to self-indulgence. Longer efforts such as this have tempted Williams before, but **"One of the Muses"** is far less successful than the long title poem of *With Ignorance*. Still, *Tar* is Williams's finest book to date—he's become one of the best, and certainly one of the most iconoclastic, figures of his generation. (pp. 489-92)

*David Wojahn, in a review of "Tar," in* New England Review and Bread Loaf Quarterly, *Vol. VI, No. 3, Spring, 1984, pp. 489-92.*

## DAVID ST. JOHN

In *Tar* ..., C. K. Williams's fourth book of poems, there is a muscular, prosaic density that invites us to see his poems as small novellas, or perhaps as parts of the greater novel that is the body of his poetry. Like his fine (and mysteriously undervalued) third book, *With Ignorance, Tar* presents us with poems whose nominal subjects include varying extremities of experience—extremities of sexual hunger and disease, of dissipation and neglect—that could easily approach melodrama. Yet it is the victory of these poems that the serious witnessing that becomes each poem's meditative action never spares the witness—the speaker, the poet—in its own self-examination. These poems are both testimony and testament. The nominal subjects of these poems might seem unpleasant and even grotesque, but it is the resilience of the human spirit that is the true subject of these poems. It is the activity of memory (of memory's reclamation and revivification of the past) that provides the speaker's faith—its depth and resonance—and that allows his spirit to *understand* and then to go on. It is the prosaic quality of the poems in *Tar* that makes possible their comprehensive descriptiveness. They offer their "realism" and ask to be seen as the poetry of nonfiction. But, in fact, at their cores these poems reflect again and again upon the nature of consciousness, the nature of sensibility and its transformations throughout a lifetime, especially a creative lifetime. The poems all hold to the locus of the self. The poet (his sensibility) is the lens that mediates the "reality" culled in *Tar,* and it is by its clarifying focus that the inner and outer darknesses of the poet emerge. (pp. 372-73)

*David St. John, "Raised Voices in the Choir: A Review of 1983 Poetry Selections," in* The Antioch Review, *Vol. XLII, No. 3, Summer, 1984, pp. 363-74.\**

## BRUCE BAWER

C. K. Williams is, among other things, a storyteller. Each of the seventeen long and lovely and lush poems in *Tar* presents a personal anecdote, a "small history" drawn from the poet's life. These poems (which are as reminiscent of the stories of, say, Flannery O'Connor or Peter Taylor as they are of the work of any contemporary poet) recall Pound's dictum that poetry must be as well written as prose: their language is rich and resonant, their sentences beautifully composed. Their lines may be long—between fifteen and twenty or so words apiece—but they are far from Whitmanesque; Williams's lines are quieter than Whitman's, radiating not energy so much as warmth and intensity of feeling, and reflecting not egotism but an exquisite sensibility which is as sensitive to the distresses of others as to its own.

For Williams is not only a storyteller but a portraitist. His poetry is engagingly, magnificently human, and one has the feeling, unusual when reading today's poets, that he is truly interested in the lives around him. He has known alienation and misery—but he also knows that other people have known them at least as intimately as he.... [It is with] pathetic, near-grotesque victims of war and poverty, time and nature, that Williams's poems are concerned. Some of these poems communicate, and quite effectively too, his dismay over the Vietnam War and nuclear power and the decay of American cities; but the strength of these poems lies in Williams's resistance of the temptation to write shrill, preachy protest verse or to escape into the mountains to commune with (and list) every flower, bird, and tree in sight. People—not issues, ideas, or inert images—are at the center of his poetry.

Among the best poems in *Tar* are **"Waking Jed,"** a vivid, three-page description of the poet's son (one assumes) coming to consciousness in the morning, and **"The Color of Time,"** which seems to derive from the poet's childhood. The latter poem (which is told entirely in the third person, but which one cannot help reading as a memory poem) illustrates Williams's rare gift for unostentatiously bringing out every bit of beauty and meaning in a simple, seemingly unremarkable episode. . . . With every line, *Tar* reminds us not only what poetry is all about, but what life is all about. It is a beautiful book. (pp. 353-55)

*Bruce Bawer, in a review of "Tar," in* Poetry, *Vol. CXLIV, No. 6, September, 1984, pp. 353-55.*

# A(ndrew) N(orman) Wilson

## 1950-

English novelist, biographer, critic, and editor.

Wilson writes farcical novels in which politics, religion, sex, and middle-class mores serve as targets of satire. In spite of their humor, many of his works present a bleak vision of contemporary British society. Wilson's fiction has been commended for its verbal wit, powerful irony, and sharp observation of human character—features characteristic of the early fiction of Evelyn Waugh, who is often cited as a literary influence.

Wilson's first novel, *The Sweets of Pimlico* (1977), sets the pattern for his early works. In these novels, which revolve around complicated plots and absurd situations, Wilson comments on social institutions and examines how people react to them. An underlying motif reflects Wilson's interest in sexual behavior. In his fourth novel, *The Healing Art* (1980), Wilson shifts from traditional farce to a poignant study of how two women react to terminal illness. *Wise Virgin* (1982), Wilson's first novel to be published in the United States, explores a blind scholar's growing acceptance of the things he cannot change.

Wilson is also recognized as a talented literary biographer whose creative approach in analyzing the lives and works of Hilaire Belloc, John Milton, and Sir Walter Scott is highly praised. His meticulous scholarship and his interpretive skills are regarded as instructive as well as entertaining. Wilson is currently the literary editor of *The Spectator*.

(See also *Contemporary Authors*, Vol. 112 and *Dictionary of Literary Biography*, Vol. 14.)

© *Jerry Bauer*

## SUSANNAH CLAPP

*The Sweets of Pimlico* supplies a . . . quizzical account of manipulations and affections . . . , but does so with little thumping home of points and no sense of a quest being undertaken.

Evelyn Tradescant likes reading Darwin, has little time for aesthetics and, confronted with the 'soupy' looks of those around her, considers with some interest the possibility that '"falling in love" was not part of her repertoire'. At the beginning of the novel, Evelyn is chiefly interested in beetles . . . ; by the end, she has committed incest, been present at the bombing of the National Gallery, gained money and a fiancé, and even acquired a bemused concern for other people. The novel's more dramatic events confirm rather than precipitate its real concerns, which are sensible and sensibly handled—to do with the disconnectedness of people's lives and the heady attractions provided by enormous wealth and purposeful mysteriousness. The last are ushered in by Theo Gormann, an exuberantly enigmatic OAP who picks Evelyn up in Kensington Gardens. By displaying intense inquisitiveness about her (rather colourless) life while elaborately shielding his own . . . , he manages to take Evelyn over. One of the acutenesses of this alert novel is to show that 'taking over' involves not only the pinioning of a person's time and preoccupations . . . , but also, and more trappingly, imitation: as Evelyn becomes more tantalised by

Mr Gormann's manoeuvres with his friends and money, she becomes more manipulative; obsession with her friend's secretiveness breeds her own brand of concealments.

Susannah Clapp, "Whirligig," in New Statesman, Vol. 93, No. 2410, May 27, 1977, p. 719.*

## JEREMY TREGLOWN

[Both of A. N. Wilson's novels] have a simple but impelling narrative movement which in *Unguarded Hours* is supported by a comic touch whose sureness confirms the predictions critics made, I thought over-confidently, on the evidence of *The Sweets of Pimlico*. The new novel is about an at first ineffectual and inexperienced hero, Norman Shotover, betrayed in his first love and sacked from his first job, who drifts into a kind of *Carry On Curates* theological college. It's a very skilled conflation of Chaucer's *Troilus and Criseyde* and Evelyn Waugh's *Decline and Fall* (Auberon Waugh is detectable, too, behind many of the clerical bits). But it manages to be more than the sum of its parts, the story's optimism and domestic geniality off-setting the queasier comic episodes; and a delightful comic creation is present in Norman's friend Mungo, the Dundee of Caik, with his impulsive aristocratic certainties. 'I don't hold with the Lake District,' he says of Norman's father's painting *Near Ullswater*. 'Why not?' Norman asks. 'It just makes me angry.'

Jeremy Treglown, "All Clear?" in New Statesman, Vol. 95, No. 2458, April 28, 1978, p. 566.*

## JOHN MELLORS

A. N. Wilson writes about 'ritual observances' that make people 'behave with the most abandoned irresponsibility'. The narrator in **Unguarded Hours** is a drifter who decides to become a C of E clergyman because he cannot think of any other career at which he would be more successful. Also, he happens to have been ordained deacon, priest and archimandrite, all in one evening, by an alcoholic Wandering Bishop. The latter is one of Wilson's funnier eccentrics, a retired electrician addicted to gin and *Magic Roundabout;* he elopes with an epicene youth from Silchester Theological College, a Dotheboys Hall in more senses than one. Unfortunately, too many of Wilson's selected targets are only sitting-ducks. It is easy enough to make fun of a radical dean who writes books called *Chuck It, God* and *I Can't Get No Satisfaction*. Effeminate male homosexuals, and girls who run health food shops but deep down inside want to be chained to the kitchen sink, are equally easily mocked. (p. 619)

John Mellors, "Buried Treasure," in The Listener, Vol. 99, No. 2559, May 11, 1978, pp. 618-19.*

## PATRICIA CRAIG

A. N. Wilson's central character [in **Kindly Light**—a] young man uncertain about his future—is prone to startling changes of direction, a fact which is reflected in the somewhat chaotic structure of the novel. To begin with it seems as if the author's primary target is the Catholic church and its ridiculous attempts to turn itself into a modern institution, but this promising theme is promptly swamped by a number of others—international intrigue, the behaviour of watch committees, common-room rivalries, kidnapping, misunderstandings of various sorts. Even the hero fails to provide a fixed central point, since he's characterised by little more than his successive occupations: priest, schoolmaster, grapefruit picker, film extra, research assistant to a mystic. Though much of the scenario is very funny, the book appears seriously strained by its excess of material.

Patricia Craig, "Gory," in New Statesman, Vol. 97, No. 2514, May 25, 1979, p. 762.*

## PAUL ABLEMAN

I enthused mightily about A. N. Wilson's first novel **The Sweets of Pimlico**, missed the second and now, confronted with his third, feel let down. It's not so much that [**Kindly Light**] doesn't work—although it doesn't—as that the way in which it nearly works is an unaspiring one. Was it Lord Hailsham who remarked just before the recent election that David Steel had progressed from white hope to elder statesman with no intervening phase? Something similar, in the sphere of letters, seems to be happening to young A. N. Wilson. He is writing not exactly as if he had abruptly evolved into old A. N. Wilson but like a fully established novelist in secure possession of a mature style. The trouble is it's not really his style at all. It's partly P. G. Wodehouse's and partly early Aldous Huxley's and preeminently Evelyn Waugh's. And yet **Kindly Light** is not, in the crudely pejorative sense, derivative. Mr Wilson has

fully assimilated his sources but has he really earned the right to exploit them? It must always seem suspect, as it is inevitably dispiriting, when a young man endowed with as much creative vitality as Mr Wilson elects to base his view of the world upon a tradition of literature rather than upon his own observation. If observation had been informing his pen, Mr Wilson could not have failed to perceive that not only is the world now drastically different from the one that Huxley and Waugh romped through in that prelapsarian age before man tasted the atom but also, and as a direct consequence, it can no longer be satirized in such simplistic terms with much hope of success.

**Kindly Light** is a satire directed largely at the Roman Catholic Church, a target not exactly unfamiliar with onslaughts of this kind, and in particular at that branch of it, the Society of Jesuits, here masquerading as the Catholic Institute of Alfonso, which bristles so densely with satirical shafts as to be almost invisible beneath them.

The opening is brilliantly funny and might easily have come from a previously-unpublished early novel by Waugh. Norman Shotover, the hero, is a reluctant priest whose call was rather thrust upon him when 'having been illegally ordained by a wandering bishop of the Eastern church', and having joined the Church of England, he 'got himself tangled up with a lot of girls and finally jumped off the tower of a cathedral with a hang glider' only to land in the 'garden of the Institute's retreat house in Sussex'. . . .

[Three years later, he] has lost his faith and wants to leave the church but can't quite bring himself to declare his intended apostasy to Father Cassidy, the formidable Provincial. What Norman does not know is that Cassidy, most scheming of fictional Jesuits, has long ago decided that Norman is some kind of spy and traitor. . . . In the approved tradition of farce, every move Norman makes is interpreted by his superior as further proof of immeasurable cunning while in reality our hapless hero is scarcely motivated at all. Such little will as he retains—and it is often forgotten that the anti-hero was really a Twenties rather than a Fifties invention—is devoted to abortive attempts to get himself sacked from the church. But his would-be outrageous conduct backfires and he finds himself a celebrity, temporarily reconciled to the cassock because of the social and ego perks that go with his new role of media publicist.

Norman's inveterate innocence, however, soon procures his renewed downfall and Cassidy tries to pack him off to South America with his alcoholic chum, Lubbock. However, both priests abscond at the air terminal. Their paths separate and they only meet again years later as teachers at the same private school. . . .

[By] now the book is coming apart at the seams. Too many characters, too tenuously connected, jostle in its confines and their activities are forced out of the civilized pavilion of satire into the scrubland of desperate contrivance. The pages creak with the dismal sound of the author churning out strawless bricks. Finally, Wilson, quite arbitrarily, bundles everyone off to Israel for a would-be grand finale. But by this time the game is lost. . . .

For all its sophistication and urbanity what this work chiefly exhales is an air of literary exhaustion. And yet A. N. Wilson undoubtedly has a huge talent. It would be splendid if he could now demonstrate that it extends beyond mastering the craft and technique and—most depressingly—outlook of an obsolete mode of fiction.

*Paul Ableman, "Outmoded," in* The Spectator, *Vol. 242, No. 7873, June 2, 1979, p. 26.*

## FRANCIS KING

If I had not been obliged to review it, [*The Healing Art*] is not a novel that I should have read to the end. In writing this, I am condemning, not A. N. Wilson—whom I regard as one of the most promising of our younger novelists—but my own squeamishness. People often say, 'I am not in the least bit afraid of death but I dread the whole process of dying.' I have the same feelings about death and the whole process of dying in fiction. I can happily weep buckets at the passing of some such character as Steerforth; but I am glad that Victorian writers, usually so specific, spare us all the vomit, excrement and blood of the average death-bed in the modern novel.

*The Healing Art* is brutal in its specifics from its very beginning—when, on page one, two women wait together to learn the results of their mastectomies. Pamela is a fortyish, beautiful, upper-middle-class Oxford lecturer; Dorothy (Dolly) is a fiftyish, plain, lower-middle-class housewife. Pamela is told that her prognosis is bad; Dolly that she has nothing to worry about.... Pamela is persuaded by her Anglican priest to go with him on a pilgrimage to Our Lady of Walsingham, in the hope of a miracle cure. She then takes off for the States, on a farewell visit to John, her closest male friend; and she there learns, to her amazement, that she is totally free of cancer....

Meanwhile, back in England, Dorothy has mysteriously begun to break her bones, despite her clean bill of health. Mr Wilson spares the reader no detail of her frightening deterioration; and it was here that I found that I had to force myself to read on.... (p. 20)

When Pamela returns to Oxford, she meets up with Dorothy; and she at once realises, such is the other woman's state of emaciation, that what took place was not the miracle that she had supposed but merely an error. The surgeon must have muddled up their cases.

This theme of the apparently doomed man or woman reprieved through some miracle drug or operation or, as here, through the discovery of a wrong diagnosis, has, of course, been common enough in both the novel and the film for a long time. But Mr Wilson has cleverly sophisticated it, firstly with the possibility that the miracle may have been divine, and secondly with the fact that, so far from reacting to the news of her imminent death with terror or rage, Pamela has calmly welcomed it.

This author has a penchant for characters whose sexuality is either muted to the point of extinction or else precariously ambivalent. Pamela has never slept with John, though they have holidayed together; during his visit to the States, John sleeps with an androgynous girl, Billy; Pamela falls in love with Billy, in the euphoria of learning that she is not to die, and has an affair with her. Dorothy is half in love, though she does not realise it, with Pamela; and though Dorothy's adored son has a girl-friend, he is really homosexual....

What I shall chiefly remember from this novel is not (I hope) its plot, much of which I should prefer to forget as soon as I possibly can, but its wit, its intelligence and the delight of such scenes as dinner at the High Table of an Oxford College, a visit to Blenheim, and Billy's American academic describing the latest of his elephantine Victorian biographies....

Though his range is far wider, Mr Wilson might best be described as a male Barbara Pym. There is the same spiky churchiness; the same adroit use of literary allusions; and, under all the fun, the same melancholy of people constantly at emotional cross-purposes with each other. (p. 21)

*Francis King, "Reprieves," in* The Spectator, *Vol. 244, No. 7924, May 24, 1980, pp. 20-1.*

## SIMON BLOW

The setting for A. N. Wilson's new novel [*The Healing Art*] is a spired and quadrangled university town like, we assume, Oxford. A town mellow with architecture, learning and tradition; but Wilson's subject matter is less pleasant. Pamela Cowper, an attractive, unmarried lecturer of 39 is told she has advanced cancer. Frankly, only a few months remain. However, if she accepts the doctor's recommendation to take a course of the euphemistically termed 'cocktail drug' she may have her life prolonged by several years.... Pamela declines the treatment and does not die. On the other hand, her wardmate, Dorothy, who was pronounced clear when she was declared moribund, weakens daily. Is it possible then that the testy Doctor Tulloch, his mind distracted by thoughts of a salmon-fishing holiday, has muddled the X-ray plates?

The suspicion that Doctor Tulloch is guilty of carelessness provides A. N. Wilson with his spring-board for a menacing intake of error. As the novel unfolds, the ratio of human carelessness broadens and multiplies far beyond the consulting room. There is Pamela's academic chum, John Brocklehurst, living with the vision of a defunct marriage that has staled him of loving. Sex Brocklehurst continues to need, but emotion no. Purely for sex he has used Billy, a sugary and androgynous American girl who would have preferred love. But Billy in her turn is to use Pamela, who is to be as deceived by Billy, as Billy was by John. (p. 854)

Doctors may well be offenders in the healing art but so, all too frequently, are we. Whether the fault lie with the ego or elsewhere, invariably we fail the goals of love and caring that we so pride ourselves to reach. Why did the moment have to slip forever between John and Pamela? and what more terrible reminder to care than Dorothy's servile bequest to Pamela of the fairground piece: a china lady in a crinoline? And yet, deeply tragic as the implications of this novel are, A. N. Wilson is a master at playing black comedy that can make us laugh just when we should cry. Thus, as Brocklehurst thoughtlessly sets alight his college, reducing to ashes two dear friends, Wilson transmutes his dreadful honesty to a comic nightmare. Employing farce and shock tactics Wilson has created a holocaust of avoidable errors where few remain standing, and those who do must settle for compromise, which is, perhaps, the final lesson reserved for the diminished ego. A. N. Wilson's triumph is to make his devastating and truthful material so instantly acceptable. (p. 856)

*Simon Blow, "Cocktail Drugs," in* New Statesman, *Vol. 99, No. 2568, June 6, 1980, pp. 854, 856.**

## HILARY CORKE

Michael Holroyd, in his *Augustus John*, suggests: that 'many of the greatest artists ... appear miraculously to translate all their energy into work, leaving little for the biographer to use.' But Scott, as Mr Wilson points out [in *The Laird of Abbotsford: A View of Sir Walter Scott*], for all his incredible output, devoted the major parts neither of his life nor of his energy to literature. He began to write verse at 31, fiction at 43. In the three last years of his forties he certainly produced seven huge novels and furlongs of essays and reviews; but he was simultaneously pursuing a full professional life as Clerk to the Edinburgh Court of Sessions and Sheriff of Selkirk. . . .

Still less do we lack 'the facts'—one need look no further than Lockhart's *Life*, so useful for piling up and standing on when reaching to the top shelf for other books. We have the facts; and they don't help. Almost certainly nothing would help. 'Wonderful man!' wrote Byron, 'I long to get drunk with him.' Precisely. And next morning one would have no more notion than the night before of what Mr Wilson calls 'Scott's private self—the solitude which he enjoyed when he took a bannock and a piece of cheese to the wood'.

This defensive silence, broken only by the odd remarkable intimate flash in the *Journal* . . . , tantalises us the more in that the works themselves are also difficult of access for us today. 'Written at the gallop, they are intended to be read at the gallop,' says Mr Wilson: and that is not our way. Scott himself advocated 'the laudable habit of skipping'. His attitude to his writings was in fact cheerfully cynical—indeed, reviewing the anonymous 'Author of Waverley', he singles out for peculiar disapprobation the spinelessness of his own heroes. By all the rules these potboilers, scribbled slapdash for cash, should be worthless. Since they so obviously are not, one asks, in a somewhat appalled fashion, whatever kind of person it can have been who could casually throw off *Old Mortality* or *The Heart of Midlothian* while busily really thinking of something else? But the question is merely met by a consideration of Scott's personality, not answered; for he wished to be seen to extend exactly the same detached wry amusement to himself. . . . (p. 120)

Mr Wilson addresses himself to all these questions, and many more, in this spare monograph. He has the fragrance of the Senior Common Room about him, but there are worse smells than that. He has not only the seriousness but also the skittishness of the Good Don. He doesn't hesitate to swing a few highly unfashionable haymakers. I feel he could hardly have got it more wrong when he stigmatises Forster as 'rather unintelligent', Waugh as 'embarrassingly sugary', and Austen as having 'much more in common with the vulgar, silly and selfish people in her books than she did with the moral heroes and heroines'; but it's amusing to see such things trenchantly said. And I enjoy his comment on Ballantyne's initial reaction to *Waverley*:

> With typical publisher's percipience, he saw that there was no future in such a book.
>
> (pp. 120-21)

*Hilary Corke, "Muzzled Passions," in* The Listener, *Vol. 104, No. 2671, July 24, 1980, pp. 120-21.*

### DONALD SULTANA

[*The Laird of Abbotsford: A View of Sir Walter Scott* by A. N. Wilson] is an illuminating survey of Scott's life and works, designed to make the many facets of his genius better understood by present-day readers and to revive interest in the Waverley Novels. Although not a long book . . . , it ranges widely over different aspects of Scott's personality and environment, relating them to his poetry, novels and celebrated journal. Moreover, it reinterprets them in the light of present-day at-

titudes in a lucid and engaging style that only occasionally strays from accurate scholarship or indulges in sweeping, if not contentious, generalizations. . . .

[Wilson] achieves the distinction of sustaining an original and perceptive commentary on the more technical features of Scott's art, including his development from poet to novelist, his various working formulae for his heroes and heroines, and his blend of a historical sense with realistic dialogue in a Shakespearean gallery of characters. The author also relates Scott to his age, touches on Scott's extraordinary impact on European culture (particularly in opera and the Gothic Revival) and discusses some of the pronouncements on Scott by influential critics. . . .

Although the book tends to gloss over some of Scott's literary weaknesses, it is pervaded by a highly intelligent mind combined with a cultured and humane outlook that seems to have found in Scott a congenial, perhaps even something of a kindred, spirit. As a biographical and critical introduction to Scott, including a reappraisal of a large selection of his novels and poems, *The Laird of Abbotsford* performs an excellent service. . . .

*Donald Sultana, in a review of "The Laird of Abbotsford: A View of Sir Walter Scott," in* British Book News, *September, 1980, p. 567.*

### NICHOLAS SHRIMPTON

Eye of Twiggy, toe of Conran, wool of Hulanicki and tongue of Sandie Shaw. Put that little lot together in the cauldron, along with reputation of Marianne Faithfull, and you've got a heroine of our time. A. N. Wilson does just that in [*Who Was Oswald Fish?*], a book which finds him working with characteristic self-assurance in the Tom Sharpe territory of topical and Rabelaisian farce. Against a backdrop of Mrs Thatcher's 1979 election campaign he sets the conspicuously untidy life of one Fanny Williams, a model turned pop-star turned fashionable chainstore proprietor, who is suddenly bitten by a craze for architectural conservation. . . .

So, when her new Birmingham warehouse turns out to be a crumbling brick church, and its creator an enthusiastic Goth of the early 1890s, it is not altogether surprising that she should wish to embark on wholesale restoration. What is surprising is the chaos which this innocuous decision unleashes. Mild municipal lawyers, meek art historians and even gay, black, Old Etonian barristers are drawn into an egoistical labyrinth. A positive Fonthill of hopes and desires is erected with crazy speed. And at the end of the book, in the best slapstick manner, the literal and metaphorical walls come duly crashing in.

Farceurs, like cabinet-makers, are judged by the neatness of their joints. Mr Wilson makes very nice joints indeed and puts a high polish on his veneers while he's about it. His portrait of life in contemporary Chelsea is wickedly apt and he handles his large cast of characters with marvellous dexterity. But this glittering sense of the present is only the surface of *Who Was Oswald Fish?* Fish was in fact the Victorian architect who designed St Aidan's, Purgstall Heath, and his uninhibitedly priapic diaries are accidentally discovered by Fanny's grandmother just as Fanny herself acquires his neglected masterpiece. The quotations from his journals form a stylistic counterpoint to the brittle picture of how we live now. And the complicated couplings which he describes with such relish turn out to involve the 20th-century characters in a strangling web of intimate blood relationships.

This is the sort of book in which the heroine is discovered to be a close relative not only of the Birmingham council official whose job it is to foil her plans with a compulsory purchase order, but even of the char who cleans the corridor outside his office. As a joke about coincidence in fiction it functions very well. What is less clear is whether or not it is meant to have any thematic significance. Mr Wilson's epigraph is 'the whirlygig of time' bringing in his revenges, from *Twelfth Night,* and the revenges in question seem mostly to involve the sins of the fathers being visited upon the children. But the extent of those sins, and the principles for which they stand, remain obscure. At one moment St Aidan's and its surrounding terraces appear as a model of social coherence, altogether preferable to the concrete filing-cabinets and sterile Community Centre with which they are to be replaced. At the next they are merely the tip of an iceberg of capitalist exploitation. Is the current state of British urban society, in other words, the inevitable consequence of Victorian social and economic assumptions or the result of a divergence from them?

A. N. Wilson's uncertainty about this historical question blunts the point of his simultaneous juxtaposition of farcical fiction with contemporary reality. When the book ends with Mrs T's famous St Francis of Assisi quotation on the steps of Number 10 it is genuinely hard to know how little or how much we are meant to make of it. Such fastidious reservations, however, should deter nobody from reading *Who Was Oswald Fish?* As a farce it remains as deft, delightful and disturbing a book as anyone has published this year.

Nicholas Shrimpton, "Well Jointed & Highly Polished," in New Statesman, Vol. 102, No. 2640, October 23, 1981, p. 22.*

## ANGELA HUTH

*Who was Oswald Fish?* is a veritable spaghetti of plots, spiced liberally with extraordinary coincidence. These coincidences are so numerous that one might be forgiven for sneering a bit, or complaining it is just not like that in real life. But then Mr Wilson makes no pretence of either creating real life, or reporting without exaggeration. His novelist's licence a-dancing in his hands, he has written a very high-class strip cartoon which induces sudden laughter and painful sympathy. His prose is swift, understated, clear: his humour oblique and quite original. . . .

The hero, the mysterious Oswald Fish, is a long-deceased randy Victorian architect to whom, by devious means, other disparate characters are linked. They are, indeed, a rum group, sparkling in their peculiarities and dreadful clothes. (A. N. Wilson is the only male novelist I can think of who is good on clothes and their importance.) Fanny Williams, to whom most of life is 'flipping', is an affectionate portrait of a middle-aged muddle-headed sexy lady, a well-known pop singer in the Sixties, whose deepest feelings now are for her obnoxious corgis. She has a part time lover-lodger, Charles Bullowewo, a black Old Etonian, who picks up an Old Wykehamist in a public lavatory the night before the book begins and makes him one of the merry band—which includes two of the nastiest children in fiction, about whom even the author is half-hearted. They all live in London. Meanwhile, in Birmingham, Fred Jobling and his lustreless wife suffer their grating lives while waiting for the long arm of coincidence to bring Fred and Fanny together.

*Their* desire, uncontainable, takes them to Kensal Green cemetery early one morning. Fanny's breast 'heaved with excitement'. . . . And their coupling is hilarious.

A. N. Wilson is too wise to indulge in such enjoyment all the time, and lest we might take him for a constant joker he allows us some pauses for breath and serious thought. This he does by means of extracts from Oswald Fish's diaries; sad journals, most elegantly written. They made me yearn a little for a whole book in their vein. But that is not a complaint: I marvel, rather, at Mr Wilson's adeptness in both styles, and it is nice to think that when the laughing has to stop he can switch confidently to an even more satisfying, deeper prose.

Angela Huth, "Good Gusto," in The Listener, Vol. 106, No. 2735, November 12, 1981, p. 584.*

## STANLEY REYNOLDS

Wilson's *Wise Virgin* is a splendid novel. This is the intellectuals' comic novel about a blind scholar who has devoted all his life to one slim medieval treatise, an early thirteenth-century book of advice to virgins.

One is disinclined to say much about the plot. Not in case one might give the game away but because it is all rather esoteric and, indeed, might seem rather dull. Nothing could be further from the truth. . . . [Mr Wilson] has a cruel and very cutting, donnish sort of humour and a complete grasp of English, able to make all sorts of jokes, bookish ones full of literary allusions or more simple, common one-liners.

He also knows about people. With one or two exceptions—and these are only very minor characters—none of his characters is wooden or stereotyped. His portrait of the blind scholar's teenage daughter is an exceptional piece of writing.

In a time when feminist writers produce grotesque stereotyped male characters and when male novelists create wooden ladies, it is amazing to read a young English novelist who has the old-fashioned ability to breathe life into all his characters. (p. 602)

Stanley Reynolds, "Passing Theroux," in Punch, Vol. 283, No. 7404, October 13, 1982, pp. 601-02.*

## JOHN SUTHERLAND

With *Wise Virgin,* A. N. Wilson continues his bleak investigation of trauma. . . . *Wise Virgin* takes the life term and solitary confinement of bereaved blindness. It's played out with Wilson's customary geometric neatness of design. Giles Fox, as the novel's retrospect finds him, was once a fulfilled man—someone who could have represented the happy ending of some other story. He is a librarian and a scholar (his 'period' is 'somewhere between 1213 and 1215'), and the best efforts of his intellectual maturity have been happily applied to editing a Medieval text, the 'Tretis of Love Hevenliche', a work eventually destined for the dusty glory of Early English Texts Society publication. . . . The treatise celebrates the anchoretic life: or the wisdom of virginity as the path to true marriage with Christ. For all his obsessed attention to his text, Fox had lived the life of its antitype. He was worldly, carnal and atheistic. . . . Then, in the way of Wilson's world, there fell on him a rain of shattering blows. His wife died in childbirth with her baby. He went blind. His second wife, a Moorfields nurse, was run down and killed by a hit-and-run driver (the miseries in Wilson's narratives are invariably the acts of a God who may perhaps just be an insurance company fiction). Giles remained, a sightless scholar blundering uselessly in his library. As we encounter him, he is attended by two virgins: his luscious teenage daughter Tibba and his dowdy amanuensis. Miss Agar (PhD, failed). With all this wretchedness stacked behind it, the novel opens: '''Marry me,'' said Louise Agar.' Will he?

The monstrously tragic prelude (given in terse and intermittent flashback) permeates **Wise Virgin** with a kind of post-operative exhaustion. It is as if the writer had aimed at a juicy plot, missed and hit the epilogue instead. But, of course, depression is the level Wilson has chosen for his novel: its mood swings in the narrow range between glum stoicism and the suicidal. The action, slight by comparison with Fox's earlier trials, re-volves around Agar's proposal. Should he try again for fleshly gratification, or should he retreat into his dark, ascetic cell, tended only by Tibba? . . .

As used to be said of Thomas Hardy, Wilson turns his screw of misery once too often. The end of the novel has Giles alone: a Milton, Oedipus or Lear without even a daughter by his side (and Tibba's devirgination is anyway imminent). Miss Agar has been turned away. The great edition of the little book has finally been dispatched to Oxford. But after years of heroic effort, the general editor of the EETS finds it philologically wrong, critically out of touch and inaccurately transcribed. It will not be published. The last scene moves us to the solitary Christmas celebrations of Captain de Courcy, the mysteriously romantic object of Tibba's virginal passion. He is discovered to be a bewigged, homosexual con-man. It would be unbearable if Wilson's narrative were to let us feel. But response is an-aesthetically frozen by the Arctic objectivity of it all.

> John Sutherland, ''Dark Places,'' in London Review of Books, *November 18 to December 1, 1982, p. 19.*

**ALAN WATKINS**

By modern standards, Mr Wilson is better equipped than most to write about Milton. He loves English; knows Latin; is a professing Anglican; possesses strong—perhaps over-confi-dent—views on theology; and writes always clearly and often wittily. He is less sure-footed on 17th-century political history; but one cannot have everything. In his interesting biography [**The Life of John Milton**], he hints several times that Milton is something of a lost cause. He implies that this is a conse-quence of the decline in educational standards of the past de-cades. Mr Wilson, though he has many admirable qualities, is a bit of a professional young fogey.

He may be right about the decline in standards. But I doubt whether Milton has been fully comprehensible throughout this century and for most of the preceding one. Both the class, and the overlapping religious distinctions in society have made him hard to grasp. . . . This centuries-long decline in knowledge of a certain kind has been accompanied by a correlative ascent in knowledge, to which Mr Wilson gives insufficient credit.

Like most good books, Mr Wilson's has a point of view. This is that Milton was always a C of E man, with most of the virtues which this category implies. He was reasonable, and liked the good things of life in moderation. . . . Above all he was a Renaissance Man. He was studious but not gloomy, prudent but not mean, a social climber but not a truckler to authority. He wanted to enjoy life; would have enjoyed it but for the terrible misfortunes—unsatisfactory wives, a dotty child,

dead children, blindness—which befell him and which he bore with admirable stoicism.

It is an attractive picture, a partially convincing one. It is certainly more convincing than the former Master of Balliol's portrait of Radical Jack Milton, roaming the ale-houses of London, carousing with his revolutionary comrades. Mr Wil-son deals scornfully with this vision, as Lord Dacre dealt with it, even more scornfully, in a review at the time. But Milton as an apostle of reason, freedom and toleration—it will not really wash.

Mr Wilson has no difficulty in showing that the pamphlet on divorce was not brought about by prolonged marital unhap-piness. . . . He has more difficulty in squaring the virulence, the nastiness of tone, of the pamphlets generally with his picture of a learned, tolerant poet. His way of resolving the difficulty is to depict Milton as having a bit of fun, indulging in jolly japes, rather as if he were some 17th-century precursor of Mr Auberon Waugh. The better answer is that Milton wrote in this way because this was the way controversy was conducted. It relied on largely bogus appeals to scriptural or other authority and on personal abuse. The notions of evidence, of reasoned argument, came much later. What we have lost in graphic immediacy we have gained in truth. This is what I meant earlier when I wrote about the ascent in knowledge to which Mr Wilson gave insufficient credit.

Mr Wilson is a religious man, but he is not—cannot be—religious in the same sense as a man of the early 17th century. There is something else. Our two greatest essays on Milton are by Johnson and Macaulay. Mr Wilson often mentions each, depreciating Johnson to the advantage of Macaulay. Yet from internal evidence, and not only internal evidence, I believe that Mr Wilson's general views are closer to Johnson's melancholic Anglican Toryism than they are to Macaulay's optimistic Evan-gelical Liberalism. This dissonance does not detract from the great merits of the book. It is always instructive, and sometimes entertaining, to look at someone making out a case. Ten or so years ago a reviewer, the late A. P. Ryan, writing about the most recent biography of C. J. Fox, said that it was the life of a rake by a prig. Mr Wilson's is the life of a Roundhead by a Cavalier. It is nevertheless well worth reading. (pp. 21-2)

> Alan Watkins, ''Cavalier View,'' in The Listener, *Vol. 109, No. 2796, January 27, 1983, pp. 21-2.*

**LAURENCE LERNER**

No one wants a new biography of Milton that simply tells us where he was in each year, or what he published when, but once one begins to interpret his marriage, his career, and his political views [as does A. N. Wilson in **The Life of John Milton**], the subject becomes as elusive as a Shakespeare son-net.

Not that this need lead to scepticism or hesitation. A. N. Wilson is a boldly opinionated biographer, but his very boldness, like that of the interpreter of poems, is a kind of admission that others may see—and have seen—the same things differently. He uses the biographer's conditional from time to time: e.g., of Milton's time at Cambridge, ''how dull it must have been to have to listen to some not very intelligent don, droning on about the rules of medieval disputation.'' Lest that seem all too reminiscent of the vapidity of so much biography, I will add that Wilson then goes on to suggest that translating Plato into Latin must have been one of the more attractive tasks for an undergraduate, and this leads him to suggest that if Milton had stayed on and become a don, he would have been one of the Cambridge Platonists. There's a good deal of neo-Platonism in Milton's early poetry, and I share Wilson's high estimate of its imaginative power in Renaissance art and poetry, so it seems churlish to remark that there's no real evidence for this speculation. (pp. 87-8)

Mr Wilson is scrupulous about showing when he knows and when he's guessing, and what he has written can be described as a scholarly biography with speculation added. And perhaps that is what we want. The effect of merely scholarly biographies is to make one feel one would rather just have read the documents oneself.

How does a biography of a poet differ from a biography of anyone else? Clearly, it must talk about poems; but if the sections on the life simply alternate with self-contained sections on the work, then we have not got a literary biography, but a critical book and a life bound up in the same covers. On the other hand, if the poems are used as material for the life . . . then we may watch sadly as they are dismantled into not very reliable evidence, instead of being treated as poems.

Mr Wilson cannot escape from this dilemma any more than anyone else, but I found him never less than entertaining about the poems, and he seldom says what you would expect. It is refreshing to read a discussion of *Paradise Lost* that stresses its joyfulness, and on *Paradise Regained* his interpretation is very similar to that of Professor Lord ("Folklore and Myth in *Paradise Regained*") in the Martz *Festschrift*. Both of them point out that Satan presents the richness of a cultural tradition which had been Milton's own, and which the Son austerely rejects; though whereas Lord the scholar presents this, rather speculatively, as a rejection of myth and epic in favour of the simple hero of folk-lore, Wilson the novelist sees it in more orthodox terms as the rejection of Greek in favour of Hebrew culture, and reminds us (a happy use of biographical material) that Milton read the Hebrew Bible every day. (p. 88)

When one of our wittiest younger novelists writes a biography, you would expect him to be a bit tendentious. It wouldn't be much fun if he wasn't. Mr Wilson is not sparing of controversial asides—from which I learn that he dislikes revolutions, progressive education and (so it seems) both modern Christian apologists and agnostics. . . . He also dislikes Cromwell intensely, and one element in Milton he cannot stomach is his apocalyptic enthusiasm for the Puritan cause.

On this he is less scrupulous than usual. He quotes the famous sentence "Methinks I see in my mind a noble and puissant nation rousing herself like a strong man after sleep, and shaking her invincible locks''; and follows it with an atrocity story of how Cromwell burst in on a very old clergyman called Wilson (an ancestor, perhaps?), abused him, and tortured his son. Now I share Mr Wilson's dislike of revolutionary bullying, but there is no reason to connect this story in any way with Milton; and no justification whatever for saying twenty pages later that "Cromwell's torturing of aged clergymen seemed to Milton a certain sign that God was revealing himself." At this point I wish Mr Wilson did regard 17th-century politics as more of a shard or a blurred hieroglyph. (p. 89)

Laurence Lerner, "Shards and Blurred Hieroglyphs: Seventeenth-Century Studies," in Encounter, Vol. LXI, No. 1, July-August, 1983, p. 83-9.*

## FRANCIS KING

It is on the sad detritus of past political scandals that this highly entertaining novel [*Scandal*] has been constructed. The central character, Derek Blore, is a vulgarly pushy politician who, in a bad year, might conceivably become the leader of his party. Married to a woman socially and morally his superior, he is in the habit of taking himself off to a flat in darkest Hackney where, disguised as a schoolboy, he submits to pleasurable chastisement at the hands of an embarrassed, dim-witted tart with the unsuitable name of Bernardette. . . .

All at once, Blore finds events closing in on him from all sides, as in one of those horror-stories in which walls, floor and ceiling all simultaneously begin to approach nearer and nearer. There are tapes of his indiscretion; worse, there are photographs. . . .

Mr Wilson is a wonderfully funny writer in his wry, downbeat way. The final scene is a good example. Blore, determined to brazen out the scandal with vigorous denials, takes part, disguised as a Viking, in the Patronal festival of his local parish church, of which he is churchwarden. At the buffet which follows evensong, he is foolish enough to embark on a speech, in which he appears totally to have forgotten that he has been exposed as a lecher, liar, traitor and accessory to a murder. Mr Wilson has already described the absurdity of his fancy-dress: 'He clanked noisily in his boots and breast-plate. His grave bespectacled face was framed by a bronze helmet from which horns jutted out dramatically above his ears.' It is in this preposterous get-up that, deprived of any dignity, he is charged and arrested in the presence of his family, friends, fellow churchgoers and a mob of pressmen.

But though so many of its scenes are farcical, the book as a whole is intensely serious. Almost all its characters are guilty of betrayal. . . . Clearly Mr Wilson, in common with most people in this country, has a low opinion of politicians and an even lower one of the press.

The one unsatisfactory aspect of the novel is its jocular treatment of the underworld of prostitution into which Bernardette is sucked. Mr Wilson, one guesses, is here venturing into territory familiar to him only from newspapers and other novels. . . . There is no reason why a writer should not encompass imaginatively things of which first-hand knowledge has been denied to him; but in this case the Bernardette passages have all too patently been concocted in a looser, more off-hand manner than anything else in the book. (p. 25)

It is in describing the consequences of Blore's folly and ambition that Mr Wilson is at his formidable best. At school, Blore's son is tormented openly by his fellows and subtly by the staff. The Prime Minister grimly faces the prospect of one of his senior Cabinet colleagues being put on trial for conspiracy to murder. Blore's wife prepares herself to embrace the vocation of the courageous little woman who sticks by her husband in his hour of shame. Friends are variously embarrassed, supportive or alienated. Those who can make money by selling their stories to the press, do so.

The surface of the narration is so sparkling that, at first, one is hardly aware of the dark, choppy currents of misanthropy beneath. Morally, Mr Wilson makes clear, at least half-a-dozen of the characters ought to be in the dock along with wretched Blore. (pp. 25-6)

Francis King, "A Wonderfully Funny Novel," in The Spectator, Vol. 251, No. 8096, September 10, 1983, pp. 25-6.

## PAT ROGERS

A. N. Wilson had raised the issue of political scandal in an earlier book, *Who was Oswald Fish?* (1977). But he got out of the situation by ensuring that his Honourable Member was too dim to be dishonourable, so that the heroine Fanny junked him by the end of Chapter One. This time [in *Scandal*] Wilson addresses the matter head-on—that is to say, full-frontally. At the centre of the story stands Derek Blore, 'next Prime Minister but three', an unimaginative careerist who happens to have a sexual kink and an understanding wife. . . .

There is the usual excellent feeling for place: Wilson, who can make artistic sense out of Birmingham, gets the unreal atmosphere of Westminster here. . . . But there isn't so much comedy as in earlier books, and the novel lacks the underlying metaphor (the profession of healing, Victorian architecture, Medieval legend) which has sustained its three predecessors. Again, though the author shows his habitual skill in the union of knowing social observation and hidden spiritual exploration, there is a little too much of his weaker side—for example, patronage of those who like Somerset Maugham. . . . It is not hard to see what people dislike in Wilson: his basilisk eye on human weakness, his super-efficient plotting, his grim affection for the melodramatic. Yet he is surely the most talented novelist of his generation in this country, and his J. T. Edson scale of productivity confirms rather than negates his ability. (p. 19)

> *Pat Rogers, "Tristram Rushdie," in* London Review of Books, *September 15 to October 5, 1983, pp. 19-20.\**

## BRUCE ALLEN

[By the time the plot of **"Wise Virgin"**] has run its course, Wilson's characters—and his readers—have received a comic and serious "instruction" on how to live in the world and how to make the best of one's imperfect nature. It is thus a comedy about the most serious matters imaginable, and a nimble entertainment that keeps on resonating in your head long after you've finished reading it. (p. 33)

We know from the beginning—the long opening chapter which details the background of Giles's and Tibba's life—that we're in the hands of a novelist who knows his business. And, besides continuing evidence of Wilson's verbal and satirical skills, we're treated to such elegant pleasures as his droll capsule history of the survival down through the centuries of that medieval manuscript and his virtuosic use of parallelism—counterpointing Giles's amatory confusions against stern excerpted injunctions from the "Tretis," and also balancing Giles's slow emergence from his shell of self-regard with Tibba's gradually more willing exchange of innocence for experience. These delicious conflicts climax with a Christmas Day visit that's a complete surprise and offers a totally believable and satisfying happy ending.

Yet, admirable as it is, the plot is not *the* thing in this formidably skillful book. What keeps us engrossed is the depth and range of its characterizations. We see each of the important characters in terms of his and her feelings about all of the others, and the way these feelings keep changing is charted for us in revealing and moving detail. . . . The charming Tibba proceeds quite credibly from docile repression through a tentative discovery of the world outside her father's living room

to a rapturous comprehension that love is "more beautiful than anything in books could have prepared one for."

Giles himself is a marvel of genuine mental complexity. Both his unpleasant egoism and his touching physical awkwardness are vividly described, as are the changes that slowly, surely, come over him. . . . Giles changes before our eyes into a more thoughtful and compassionate man than we would have believed him capable of becoming. That is almost as much of an achievement in a novel as it is in life.

A. N. Wilson has been compared to Evelyn Waugh, Angus Wilson, and other masters of serious farce. Such comparisons certainly hold, but I'd say that his emphasis on his characters' psychological and moral growth also links him closely with such analytical comic writers as Iris Murdoch and Joyce Cary. What's beyond argument is that he is one of the best English novelists at work today. (pp. 33-4)

> *Bruce Allen, "A Trim Tale of Blossoming Out of Cloistered Academic Life," in* The Christian Science Monitor, *November 29, 1983, pp. 33-4.*

## JOHN GROSS

Hilaire Belloc was an unpleasant man and at first sight A. N. Wilson might seem well suited to be his biographer. Nor is such an expectation altogether misplaced. Mr Wilson, as readers of his novels will know, is something of a specialist when it comes to writing about squalid behaviour, and he is too enterprising a storyteller to let slip the rich opportunities in this line that Belloc presents him with. . . .

[In **'Hilaire Belloc,'** Mr Wilson] makes no attempt to disguise how unscrupulous Belloc could be in controversy; he faithfully records—perhaps too faithfully—his more offensive personal habits; he can be unsparing in his account of episodes which even the most uncritical admirer of Belloc would probably prefer to forget. . . .

At the same time Mr Wilson wants us to take Belloc very seriously indeed. He insists that he was a genius. . . . And here he is less persuasive. There is a gap between the claims that are made and the evidence that is put forward; the details are vivid, but they do not add up to a coherent picture—not, at least, on the terms that Mr Wilson proposes.

To the world at large Belloc's most memorable achievement is his light verse, and from what I know of his other writings the world at large is right. . . . [It] is very much overdoing things to assert, as Mr Wilson does, that the best of his serious verse puts him 'in the A. E. Housman league,' and absurd to speak of him in the same breath as Dr Johnson, as Mr Wilson does more than once.

Mr Wilson has surprisingly little to offer by way of critical illumination even about those works of Belloc he most admires, such as 'The Four Men.' . . .

There are aspects of Belloc's religious life which almost any outsider is likely to find baffling. Mr Wilson provides a clear and helpful exposition of his beliefs. He shows how indebted he was to Cardinal Manning, particularly for his social ideals, and how irrevocably he was a child of the First Vatican Council, with its 'triumphalist' Catholicism—'baroque, certain, glorious and hard.' But while true believers are allowed their jocosities, it is difficult to reconcile this adamantine faith with the reason Belloc gave for his reluctance to accept a Papal knighthood—he wondered why anyone should want to be honoured by 'some greasy monsignore'—or his cart-before-the-horse avowal that he only revered Christ because the Church told him to. . . .

It is no secret that Belloc was rabidly anti-semitic. Even so, readers of this biography may well be surprised to learn how obsessive his prejudice was, as liable to show itself in spluttering about alleged Jewish calumnies of Marie-Antoinette as in rejoicing that Moscow (when he visited it for six hours in 1912) seemed to be *Judenrein*. . . .

While Mr Wilson dissociates himself from this side of Belloc, he sometimes seems out of his historical depth when discussing it. And while in all likelihood he is right in putting down Belloc's hatred of 'financiers' to his disappointment when he was 17 at discovering that he was not, as he had thought, going to inherit a fortune, it can hardly be the whole story. If one is looking for a psychological explanation there are, for one thing, his other hatreds to be considered—his revulsion from 'the stench of Protestantism,' for example.

> *John Gross, "Roman Spleen," in* The Observer, *April 22, 1984, p. 22.*

### RONALD BLYTHE

Some men take to loud-mouthing to hide their complex souls, and in Belloc's case nobody has ever doubted that behind his lifelong hunger for a row and his robust polemics, some of them so grisly that it would be charitable to call them mad, there existed a more important and more intriguing figure than the author of *The Bad Child's Book of Beasts*. Here he stands, incomparably more interesting in himself than any reference to him in a history of 20th-century English literature would allow, and casting a deal of light on it into the bargain. Treading not so much delicately as knowingly into the always ramshackle, often deplorable but also frequently brilliant Bellocian edifice, Mr Wilson has been able [in *Hilaire Belloc*] to reveal

how both its virtues and its cracks have to be understood if we are to understand many of the more subtle elements in British society. He seeks neither to reinstate Belloc nor to dissect him, but to show him. It is not a pretty sight, but always a fascinating one—the quarter-French Sussex countryman for whom dogma was holy writ and who yet remained a wild one. (p. 22)

Early in his biography Wilson has to decide what to do about Belloc and 'the Jew question', which confronts him with what he calls a serious technical difficulty. Yet he must chronicle it. He surmises that Belloc's frightful, obsessional interest in Jews began when he was doing his French military service and was confirmed by the Dreyfus case. However it began, it seems to have lasted him for life. In 1922 he published *The Jews*, 'my admirable Yid book', a work which Wilson found too upsetting to be read today, but which is also prophetic about Israel. Even allowing for the pre-Holocaust permissive anti-Jew language of his youth, Belloc goes far beyond such commonly held opinions and into his own squalid fantasies. Wilson is too good and true a writer to let this side of Belloc off as 'aberration' and uses it to throw a beam of murky light on Britain's attitude towards its Jews this century. . . .

This remarkable portrait concludes with Belloc's ponderous, slow-motion demise. Senility is a fragment of life and when a man like Belloc has a decade of it, it has to be taken into account. Wilson uses it as Belloc used the death-bed scenes he was so impressive at rendering, as a grand passing of a subject from his attentions and of a spirit from the earth. There he goes, Manning's disciple, whose religion was 'triumphalist, baroque, certain, glorious and hard', and who was 'a pioneer in exposing the fundamental absurdity of the Whig view of history'. (p. 23)

> *Ronald Blythe, in a review of "Hilaire Belloc," in* The Listener, *Vol. 111, No. 2855, April 26, 1984, pp. 22-3.*

# Snoo Wilson

## 1948-

(Born Andrew Wilson) English dramatist, screenwriter, novelist, and nonfiction writer.

In his plays Wilson explores extremes of human behavior and the social contexts that contribute to deviancy. He employs surreal images, nonlinear progression, and black humor to investigate individual psychology and to comment on social, moral, and political influences that repress individuals. He deemphasizes plot and often presents varying temporal and spatial perspectives to blur the distinction between the interior world of the mind and external reality.

Wilson is one of several respected British playwrights who emerged from the "Portable Theater" of the early 1970s. The Portable Theater was part of the "Fringe Theater" movement in the London area and provided an alternative, noncommercial forum for experimental plays which often expressed radical political and social views. David Hare and Howard Brenton are two other playwrights who developed their individual styles in the Portable Theater.

In his early plays Wilson cast violent, dreamlike, and animalistic images in the midst of naturalistic scenes to ironically underscore his themes. In *The Pleasure Principle* (1973) two characters search for pleasure, each according to separate ideals. Within this framework, sudden strange events, including the appearance of two dancing gorillas, help counter the obsessive rationalism of the protagonists.

Following *The Pleasure Principle* Wilson's plays began to center on the pseudosciences and the occult, focusing on the charismatic personalities of several cult leaders. In *The Beast* (1974) and its revised version *The Number of the Beast* (1982), Wilson examines Aleister Crowley, a proponent of black magic. *The Soul of the White Ant* (1975) takes its title from a book by the Afrikaans writer Eugène Marais, a visionary morphine addict. In this play Marais appears in a South African bar, where he and other characters represent various attitudes toward apartheid. Critics were impressed with Wilson's criticism of apartheid, particularly his use of a queenless termite colony as a metaphor for South Africa. In *The Glad Hand* (1978), a fictional South African fascist recruits a strange mix of people to sail with him to the Bermuda Triangle, where he hopes to pass through a time warp and do battle with the Antichrist.

In *Spaceache,* a play (1981) and novel (1984), Wilson satirizes various social practices and scientific concepts by projecting them into a future totalitarian state. Critical reaction to this work is typical of the general response to Wilson's writings. While the structure of *Spaceache* was faulted by some for being disjointed and ineffective, others applauded Wilson's original treatment of controversial topics.

(See also *Contemporary Authors*, Vols. 69-72.)

## MICHAEL BILLINGTON

This bilious little play [*Pignight*] by Snoo Wilson provides the most savage and disenchanted portrait of rural life we have

seen since *Afore Night Come*. It is nowhere near as good as Rudkin's black and terrifying work; but it shows a comparable Genetesque influence and makes one similarly glad to be living in the relative comfort and security of a crowded metropolis.

Set in a large Lincolnshire pig farm, it contrasts the hygienic boredom of assembly line farming with the personal viciousness and cruelty that country life allegedly fosters. On the one hand, this is a world of vacuum-sealed ham and freeze-dried giblets awaiting delivery to the supermarket; on the other hand, it is a place where dogs get wantonly speared with hayforks, bestiality and sado-masochism diurnally flourish and the values of the piggery are finally triumphant. If I reveal that, as the audience leaves the theatre, human flesh is supposedly frying in a pan onstage you will gather that Mr. Wilson's view of rural life is not exactly Wordsworthian.

The trouble is his central argument is illogical; for if the countryside is suffering from the spread of urban values and factory methods, then surely the specifically rural vices that thrive on a sense of social isolation must be on the decline. Also his obvious distrust of sequential plot development leads him to shuffle characters and scenes with a frequency which leaves one bewildered rather than mentally liberated. But if the piece is deficient in argument and technique it does at least project a very strong personal nightmarish vision of the countryside and is directed by the author himself with a nice feeling for poisoned atmosphere.

Michael Billington, in a review of "Pignight," in The Times, *London, March 5, 1971, p. 9.*

## IRVING WARDLE

[Wilson] is a hard, impersonal writer, with a strong practical sense for what can be achieved with the minimum theatrical resources. . . .

He writes like an outsider who has surfaced in Britain and started compiling reports on our inhuman tribal habits; picking some custom, like intensive meat production, and documenting it from numerous angles. The result is intentionally dislocated. Society is at once inter-related and dispersed; and better an honest incoherence with every detail cutting like flint, than phoney logic with everything tied up into neat linear sequence.

*Blow-Job* opens with an extremely funny scene in a northern working men's club where a couple of London skinheads, up in the area to crack a safe, are sharing a crate of beer with a lady-like Scottish security man who mistakes their criminal disguise for a drag act. This scene alone, with its rapid shifts between vulnerability and menace shows Wilson to be a performer with steel in his fingers. The action then moves on to a factory yard where the security man is plaintively trying to get a girl trespasser down off the wall.

As the piece develops, a certain brutal pattern takes shape. At one end of the scale are the two boys, both products of self-perpetuating criminal backgrounds. At the other is the girl, with her head stuffed with social statistics and pronouncements from R. D. Laing.

My faith in this play would be greater if it did not contain certain passages—as where the girl admires the flies feasting on a corpse's eyelids—that betray a taste for the coarsely sensational; and if the criminal and drop-out figures had not been forcibly brought together for implausible confrontation. None of which diminishes the play's authentic sense of horror; nor its intermingling of physical outrage and savage farce.

Irving Wardle, in a review of "Blow-Job," in The Times, *London, November 11, 1971, p. 12.*

## PETER ANSORGE

[*The Pleasure Principle*] employs a three-act structure which contains three contrasting settings and variations on a theme. The play focuses upon the unspoken relationship between Robert and Gale whose opposing ideas of pleasure prevent them from actually sleeping together until the final act. . . . Each of the acts reflects the characters' search for particular kinds of pleasure. Act one is an account of a holiday undertaken in Ireland which ends in Robert's breakdown; the second act is set in Gale's flat where she finds her future husband despite the interferences of . . . burglars; while act three takes place in the circus where Robert retreats from the rat race to embrace poverty and 'the pleasure principle.'

As in Wilson's previous works as much confusion as clarity tends to emerge through the course of the evening. We first see Gale and Marien (Robert's wife) on holiday together in Ireland picking up a menu in a Wimpy Bar and finding that it contains a bomb warning. Robert then joins the women for a picnic (he enters waltzing with his chauffeur to the tune of *Je*

*ne Regrette rien*). This is followed by a brilliant scene in which the characters' views of pleasure (they are on *holiday*), rest subtly under the control of Robert's aggressive defence of capitalism. Robert (who describes himself as 'a big tiger with a mouth full of credit cards') is in fact going mad—hopelessly entertaining an ideal that the whole world will soon be like 'California' instead of the oil-starved desert which is currently being threatened. Gale in the meantime remains in her dream-world bound to an erotic vision of Robert seducing her in a swan (which is duly wheeled on stage). In this scene Wilson manages to weave themes from contemporary politics and psychology in an imaginative account of human breakdown and isolation. He then reveals Robert and Gale to be swopping priorities in life. While Robert enters an asylum, gives away his money and retreats to his life in a circus tent—Gale accumulates a husband, abandons writing her novel and chooses a life of indifferent affluence. But in the final scene Robert seduces Gale in her swan—though even this act turns into an anti-climax for at least one of the partners. The play ends with the entrance of a Grand Magic-Circus style of French group cheerfully claiming Robert as one of their own.

None of the writing quite fulfils the promise of the first act but [it] . . . is a finely-judged evocation of the search for the pleasure principle. The theatre is decorated with sadly-decked images of carnival, during the interval . . . gorillas inform us that we shouldn't expect too much from life, and there are scattered references (always ironic) to the sexual theories of Wilhelm Reich. It would seem that Wilson is on the side of Freud rather than WR in his view of sexual freedom; civilisation must always experience its discontents and the reality principle triumph over the pleasure seekers. It's certainly this underlying strain of melancholy . . . that marks off *The Pleasure Principle* from many fringe [theater] celebrations of an orgiastic life-force.

Peter Ansorge, in a review of "The Pleasure Principle," in Plays and Players, *Vol. 21, No. 4, January, 1974, p. 55.*

## JOHN FORD

No doubt about it, Snoo Wilson's *The Beast* is a good play. . . . Wilson's enjoyment of the ludicrous and dangerous extremities of human behaviour had already been shown by his previous plays, especially *Pignight, Blowjob* and *Vampire*. . . .

The angular, butted construction of [*The Beast*] surprises and jolts; but ultimately it works in keeping a sufficient distance from Aleister Crowley to develop a critique of both him and the values of the society he rejected. Wilson starts from the primary notion of Crowley's credo—'Do what thou wilt under the law; love is the law, love under the will.' Then he places the man in a series of situations and endows him with a raging rhetoric and self-deflating wit which reveal the contradictions of The Beast. Here is a charlatan who is on to something; a Cambridge man and a gentleman who chooses to live by 'the left-hand way', smothered in skunk oil; an urbane lunatic whose 'sex magic' can wreck an hotel but fails to prevent the death of his daughter. Crowley's new religion can obfuscate with the apocalyptic force of the Book of Revelations, or it can be urged with a limpid colloquialism. . . .

The play steers clear of a linear narrative, and the portrait of Crowley is built up like a jig-saw. The device is simple: past scenes are the subject of conjurations for the benefit of a Belgian hotelier, a retired magician, who wants to learn about sex magic. Full portraits of others in Crowley's life are realised with an incisive wit and economy. Most of the others are there largely to provide a frame for the various excesses of Crowley's inspired madness. Only Laria, The Beast's Scarlet Woman, is given equal attention, and she emerges with a pathetic clarity.

It is when the play is considered as something more than a biographical fantasy—or an explanation—that it falls short. Crowley does not achieve the universality of a Faustus or a Prospero, nor would the author wish him to do so. But beneath the razzmatazz Wilson does seem to sound a bass line concerning the nature of history in the 20th century—perhaps about the legacy of Victorian puritanism, or the need for a romantic imagination in an increasingly explicable universe. The clues are there throughout the text, but somehow they fail to connect. That is why **The Beast** is a good play, but not a great play.

> John Ford, in a review of "The Beast," in Plays and
> Players, Vol. 22, No. 4, January, 1975, p. 33.

### JONATHAN HAMMOND

Snoo Wilson is one of the most talented playwrights in Britain today; a view amply justified when one considers the surrealistic imagination wedded to audacious theatrical techniques at work in **Vampire, The Pleasure Principle** and **The Beast**.

Compared to these three, **The Everest Hotel** is a *divertissement*, but one that contains the same flow of weird images, cultural cross-references and striking juxtapositions arising out of a multi-layered central situation. Three girls, Deidre, Tracy and Sandra, seem to be situated at the top of Mount Everest and seem to be nuns out to break Communist domination and inspire a religious revival in countries like Russia and China. I say 'seem' because it is not clear whether they are what they say they are, or whether in fact they are schoolgirl delinquents indulging in a prolonged fantasy. They divert into several side fantasies—like enrolling to be a CIA agent, registering for the dole, one of the girls pretending to be a guerrilla and so on. Of the cultural influences in the play, Uri Geller and The Who jostle with Freud's concept of the superego, Tom Jones and Acker Bilk. Images and situations flow into and out of each other with rapidity and ease.

In essence, the play is an exercise in ironic contrast between the hard, objective social realities we inhabit and the kind of lunatic thoughts and aspirations inspired in us by old habits of religious belief and other residual cultural leftovers; and the frequently absurd ways in which these two kinds of reality interact, causing damage and havoc to the psychologies of the people involved. The idea of trying to turn Russia and China on to religion (à la Solzhenitsyn) is at once absurd, funny and touching; and so is Wilson's play.

I have said the play is a *divertissement* and indeed in many ways it is only an entertaining sketch for a more extended work. But I have rarely seen an hour so chock-full of ideas, conceits and images. Wilson's own production, interspersed with musical interludes, moves at a sparkling pace and deliberately plays up the ambiguities of both character and situation. . . . (pp. 34-5)

> Jonathan Hammond, in a review of "The Everest
> Hotel," in Plays and Players, Vol. 23, No. 6, March,
> 1976, pp. 34-5.

### STEVE GRANT

It is sometimes said of Snoo Wilson by his detractors that beneath an admittedly brilliant surface lies a barren subsoil, composed of form without content, argument without matter, and, to put not too fine a point on it, that Wilson's imagination is a riderless horse, that the intellect is divorced from emotional involvement; that the playwright is a brain on a stick.

Such detractors (and they exist) would do well to . . . [see **Soul of the White Ant**]. Its hallmark *is* intelligence, and though Wilson has never visited the country in which it is set, South Africa, it is this intelligence combined with a good deal of funny, moving and powerful substance which accounts for the play's inexorable achievement. It is a measured, penetrating but, above all, a completely original look at white-ruled South Africa, not through the eyes and mouths of its more obvious victims, but through the deadening lifestyles of its unenviable red-neck Van der Meuwes and their mates. It is Athol Fugard seen from the other end of the telescope, but despite that, its intentions and effects are very much the same, be the audience 'closet' black, Ku Klux white, or plain floating voters.

Its title derives from one of several books purportedly written by Eugène Marais, an Afrikaans poet, self-styled anthropologist and pseudo-scientist, who died by his own hand in 1936 after years of morphine addiction, mental illness and professional controversy. Revered in his own country, and exposed throughout the world, Marais is a compelling metaphor for the conflicting attitudes and emotions which constitute Apartheid South Africa. . . .

The ambiguity [of the play] lies in choice: the choice that Wilson's characters are faced with; to comply to a male chauvinist or female-subjugated lifestyle based on brutality or apathy, or to go slowly but inevitably insane with horror at the limited and cruel society around them. Mabel, a raunchy bar-owner opts for drink, murder, and eventual lunacy; Edith and June, a pair of hopeless office-party dowdies, opt out of choosing; Pieter de Groot, a pig-headed, arrogant journalist, opts for phrenology and dreams of film production and world rugby domination, and Julius for being a white man's cop in a white man's small town.

Into their world, first as an earth-covered Gothic corpse and, finally, as a dazzling commercial traveller-cum-miracle-man-cum-abortionist, steps the figure of the resurrected Marais, obsessed with his ant-heap that is racist society's corporate soul, and with the personal frustrations and addiction by which the mind-termites which bring about that society's decay are engendered. Playing opposite Marais is the inverted Ant Mother figure of Mabel, who murders her houseboy in her men-only bar because his carefully-collected sperm is filling up her deep-freezer. . . . It is Wilson's ability to leap from moments of ladies-lav naturalism and exposition to flights of supreme Surrealistic terror which enable the final punches to be delivered with such easy menace. . . . (p. 36)

> Steve Grant, in a review of "Soul of the White Ant,"
> in Plays and Players, Vol. 23, No. 7, April, 1976,
> pp. 36-7.

### RANDALL CRAIG

Except for the title and for the fact that one of the characters was called Marais, there was nothing to indicate how much Snoo Wilson's play **The Soul of the White Ant** owed to The

*Soul of the White Ant* by Eugene Marais, the South African journalist, lawyer and entomologist, who killed himself in 1936.

Some of Marais's ideas are put into the mouth of the character Marais but, more important, the conception of the play depends on them. The rottenness of South African society is effectively presented through the image of a queenless termite colony. The earth on the floor of the stage helps to physicalise the analogy, while the insanities and inanities of the characters—hard-boiled and soft-boiled looking alike inside a fragile shell—add up to convey an impression of general frustration, directionlessness and sterility. A bizarre focus is thrown on it by Mabel's habit of keeping her black houseboy's sperm in a deep-freeze, so that it can be sent to the wife, who is not allowed to join him. When Mabel kills him, the white policeman is casually willing to connive at the murder but disgusted at the presence of the sperm, which is promptly thrown into the river. In a characteristic sequence of Snoo Wilson comedy, two white women who have bathed in it are late with their periods.

This is probably Snoo Wilson's best play to date. His knowledge of South African society is laconically but deftly projected into a relaxed sequence of assorted episodes which combine sympathy with stringent irony. Tinged with alcohol and desperation, the conversations all have a tone of authenticity—not least when the three women are alone together. . . .

[There is, however, a] major structural weakness. There is too little to connect Marais's first appearance with his second, or to make the disconnection into an advantage. It would be unfair to say that all Snoo Wilson's energy has gone into local comic effects, because the disparate episodes do, for the most part, work well together, but his failure with Marais is part of his failure with [Marais's book]. He should have made either more use of it or less.

*Randall Craig, in a review of "The Soul of the White Ant," in* Drama, *No. 121, Summer, 1976, p. 79.*

## MICHAEL COVENEY

[Time] has not diminished [the] power and originality [of *Vampire*]. Mr Wilson may well argue that we are all, after a fashion, 'vampirised' by social conditioning and the cruel march of history. The play itself operates on that assumption and weaves a spell-binding magic throughout its three acts: the first set in the rural Wales of the mid-19th century, the second in the Home Counties at the outbreak of the First World War, while the third is suspended somewhere between a droning cargo plane over the Atlantic and the pagoda in Kew Gardens, 1977. . . .

Structurally, the play is all middle, each moment playing a strong and independent part in a superbly achieved mosaic of sex, fantasy, violence, repression, melodrama, leather, cricket and bestiality. No other play in London has, it could be said, so much to offer.

How does it all work? Wilson's insistence that theatre need not be confined by a plot, a moral purpose or even a logical narrative progression is, in itself, an outrageous proposition that would be doomed to total failure were he anything less than sincere. And the sincerity can be gauged by the successful maintenance of an over-riding tone. . . . [The] superb, imaginative production supports this tone, so the company switch effortlessly from the Welsh parsonage to a phoney clairvoyant's parlour to an Edwardian cricket pavilion and still work towards the same sort of ironical points and jokes. In every locale we see characters strait-jacketed by their environment bursting forth, reflecting in anger and unleashing dark forces. . . .

The production is little short of mesmeric. . . .

*Michael Coveney, in a review of "Vampire," in* Plays and Players, *Vol. 24, No. 8, May, 1977, p. 29.*

## JEREMY TREGLOWN

*The Glad Hand* is so unpredictable, so hilariously and richly fantastic, that any description is bound to distort it in some way, either exaggerating these qualities or over-emphasising the underlying coherence and simplicity of what Snoo Wilson actually has to say. It's . . . an absurdist drama which cares about the world we live in, a surreal work of social realism. . . .

A South African dabbler in the occult called Ritsaat has got together a varied group of people on a ship bound for the Bermuda Triangle. The group is particularly varied because Ritsaat's advertisement mentioned Cowboy Fun—a blunder by this hopelessly obsessive anti-deviant, who meant it literally. Convinced that the Anti-Christ is coming in the form of world Communism, and equally convinced that it will be invincible, Ritsaat means to confront it in an earlier manifestation, the 19th century labour movement as represented by an archetypally oppressed group that went on strike in the very heartland of capitalism: the American cowboys who took action in the 1880s. The proposed confrontation will happen, he believes, by means of a time-warp, the Bermuda Triangle operating with various other mystical triangles and pyramids and with the help of an (in fact fraudulent) occult scientist he has hired. Ritsaat's team prepare themselves for it by rehearsing a play enacting the cowboys' strike, being written by an (in fact unproductive) author he has engaged.

The interpretation of fictional and symbolic levels in all this is very funny and intriguing—for all the obvious theatrical debts, it belongs more to the world of Vonnegut's and Brautigan's novels—and *The Glad Hand* is further complicated by the copious off-stage lives Wilson gives his characters, and the coincidental connections these lives often turn out to have with one another. The play is full of lines that briefly open up whole new unwritten comedies. . . . And within this wonderfully proliferating, anarchic, allegorical world of the ship and its ill-treated inhabitants . . . another, similarly lawless drama, in many ways resembling the 'outer' play, gradually takes shape.

It begins almost randomly with a number of moments building up an atmosphere of casual ruthlessness. (p. 18)

[Apparently] unrelated details help set the mood for the strike itself, in which the cowboys' leader . . . is deserted by one after another of his supporters as the employers' bribes take hold, and is left to lie down alone in front of a train, as an act of protest. His legs are cut off, and the scene, like those which follow it, is done with a recklessly indifferent kind of humour that forces out any possible sentimentality. But the capitalist victory it rawly depicts represents only one of the possible outcomes, of course, and in the other action alternative forces are at work—forces moving towards the kind of solution which, according to the play's view of history, has to be found if the sacrifices of the past are to be made worthwhile. . . .

The meaning is simple enough, then, for the most part; perhaps too simple, if the play itself were not so independently, organically and completely alive. (p. 19)

*Jeremy Treglown, in a review of "The Glad Hand," in* Plays and Players, *Vol. 25, No. 10, July, 1978, pp. 18-19.*

## BENEDICT NIGHTINGALE

*Flaming Bodies* has its farcical moments . . . , many of them couched in the gaudy-gothic style which has made Snoo Wilson something of a cult; but it also has . . . bite. A podgy Lesbian . . . haunts the office of the movie entrepreneur who has, she claims, stolen from her a scenario about a female Christ. So far, so clear; but before long a secretary has disappeared over the balcony in a puff of smoke, a stuntman has driven his garish auto through the window, a fridge has been transmuted into a space rocket, the ghost of [the lesbian's] father has materialised, the ashes of her mother have been stickily devoured, and all is hectic imagery and lurid hubbub.

What we're visiting, it seems, is the free-associating brainbox of a paranoid schizophrenic, itself an amalgam of amusement arcade, chamber of horrors and junkyard, an internal jungle parallel to and no doubt created by the civilised jungle beyond.

It's a trip which mercifully few of us have made in reality, and hence rather hard to judge by orthodox criteria. On the one hand, the invention seems a bit arbitrary at times, some of the effects self-conscious, the tone a trifle facetious; on the other, Wilson's derring-do imagination visibly carried the audience with it, teasing, disorienting, amusing, and finally sobering.

*Benedict Nightingale, "Lurid Hubbub," in* New Statesman, *Vol. 98, No. 2543, December 14, 1979, p. 952.\**

## JOHN RUSSELL TAYLOR

[*Flaming Bodies*] concerns this overweight lesbian screenwriter who has had the brainwave of making a film about Christ based on the hypothesis that He was a woman. Or at least had a sex-change somewhere along the way. We are to presume that this notion is so dazzlingly original, and commercially viable, that her uppity gay English boss at once fires her to steal it for his own. . . .

From there Snoo Wilson's script takes off into a series of freewheeling fantasies, mostly undergone by the heroine, Mercedes Mordecai, while suffering the pangs of hunger as she haunts her old office, hiding in the broom-closet and only daring to come out after dark to plot her revenge. Since the first, symbolic move of her ex-employer is to wheel away her giant refrigerator, she has to make do with the odd slice of apple she finds lying on the floor and a bite or two of the oversized hard-boiled egg and salami with which the mad scientist means to fuel the rocket ship that is going to counter the comet signalling Christ's birth.

How did he get in there? I thought you would never ask. Well, you see, after Mercedes had had this unsatisfactory talk with her telephone psychiatrist in New York, tried a couple of times, unsuccessfully, to tell her mother she is a lesbian, and coped as best she may with the car which crashes through the window of her thirtieth-floor office bearing a dying driver and a green-haired, black-leather-clad girl who announces, improbably, that she is just a stand-in stunt-girl and makes a heavy play for Mercedes, it seems only natural that her ideas for revamping the New Testament should begin to take on bodily form.

They include, as well as the aforementioned mad scientist, a Herod played exactly like a bearded Mae West and a pregnant Joseph as well as a pregnant Mary desperately trying to push the ass in the direction of Bethlehem. . . . The American term for Wilson's imagination would be sophomoric, which is probably flattering it by a few years. If the play were really sharp and sophisticated (and about half the length) it might come off as deliciously campy. But as it is, it seems mostly childish, saying ya-boo to a collection of social and religious bogey-men who have long since vanished from the scene.

*John Russell Taylor, in a review of "Flaming Bodies," in* Plays and Players, *Vol. 27, No. 4, January, 1980, p. 24.*

## BENEDICT NIGHTINGALE

*Space Ache* is a bit of a shambles, . . . but never meant to be plausible, involving (as it does) a trip through the solar system aboard a freighter seemingly concocted from old car seats and kitchen foil. Personally, I prefer my sci-fi satirical; and Snoo Wilson obliges, first with an Earth that concentrates the unemployed and other no-hopers into Campbell soup cans and leaves them to hover deep-frozen in space until a better time, second with a Neptune upon which the rich and fashionable treat themselves to gratuitous spare-part surgery and the sensation-seeking get their orgasms from obliging fruit-machines. It could all be much tougher, more concentrated and pointed: which is, I suppose, only to say that it has more in common with *The Hitchhiker's Guide to the Galaxy* than with *Gulliver's Voyage to Laputa*. (p. 33)

*Benedict Nightingale, "Green Tongues," in* New Statesman, *Vol. 100, No. 2593, November 28, 1980, pp. 32-3.\**

## JAMES BIERMAN

Snoo tends to write about subjects which cannot be "known" in any definitive manner, but rather must be explored in such a way that their mystery is penetrated rather than explained. The subject matter of such plays as *The Beast, Vampire, The Glad Hand, Flaming Bodies* leans toward the occult, the mysterious and the unknown. Dreams, psychic healings, astral union, astrological events, sex magic, the Bermuda Triangle, vampirism and black magic, play roles in his plays, drawing attention to the mysterious workings of the human psyche and their projection outward on the universe of the plays or vice versa. Snoo finds such subjects particularly appropriate to the theatre because it is a domain of illusion. (pp. 425-26)

In keeping with this activity at the edges of the unknown, the central characters of a Wilson play are likely to be madmen or madwomen, visionaries, morphine addicts, or tormented and possessed individuals. This is particularly true of the plays which have strong central characters, such as *The Beast* and *Flaming Bodies*. While the subjects of these plays may be said to be representative of Snoo's plays, the structure is not. Prior to *The Beast* . . . , none of Snoo's "mature" plays were structured around a single character. . . . More commonly, Snoo's characters are involved in a complex and often outrageous chain of events of their own making, but not their conscious intention. *Blowjob* . . . offers an excellent example of such a work. In it, two skinheads (one in drag) attempt to rob a man they are holding captive in a bathtub. Their attempts to blow open the man's safe are foiled by the appearance of a night guard and an attack dog who get blown up along with the safe when the dog picks up the explosive in his mouth and takes it to his master. These events are mysteriously catalyzed by a young woman whose name is ironically the one the Greeks gave to fate—*Moira*. Here, Wilson's characters are appealing bunglers. When the explosives go off, as they do also in the first act of *The Pleasure Principle* and at the end of *A Greenish Man*, they go off under unsuspecting victims of an intrigue far too arbitrary or far too sophisticated for them. Characters like McVittie in *Blowjob*, Troy Philips in *A Greenish Man* and Easey in *Space Ache* are overwhelmed by the events they help to create.

Snoo Wilson's plots tend to have all the complexity and fortuitous tuning of a Feydeau farce. After *Pignight* . . . , Snoo abandoned the linear arrangement of time in his work and created a kind of refraction which allows for multiple viewing of a given event from several perspectives. (pp. 426-27)

As with time, so with space. The versatility of staging effects in Snoo's plays allows him to shift locations frequently and with ease, or permits the settings to transform themselves as part of the action. Such plays as *Blowjob, Vampire, A Greenish Man* or *The Pleasure Principle* make use of simultaneous settings, leaving two or three locations accessible to the performers at any given time. Others like *The Everest Hotel* and *Pignight* employ a mutable stage that may serve as many places at once or transform itself with ease. . . . It seems strange that critics should cite Snoo Wilson for his abandonment of the conventions of naturalistic drama, since the reaction against that idiom is almost as old as naturalism itself. Nonetheless, his work does draw that sort of reaction as a result of the boldness of its staging. (pp. 427-28)

What most polarizes the reactions to Snoo Wilson's work is the forceful and often intentionally outrageous quality of the staging. In this theatre, the author acts as a master of magic who is always ready to amaze his audience with stunning *coups de théâtre*, amazing events or theatrical sleight of hand. His stage is frequently occupied by a menagerie of real or re-created animals—gorillas, pigs, goats, swans, donkeys. Often such creatures emerge from within an otherwise traditional dramatic situation and cast it into an entirely different context. An excellent example can be seen in *The Pleasure Principle*, where two gorillas emerge out of the dream of one of the characters and then take on a regular presence on the stage. [As Wilson explains:]

> In the play, the gorillas are like factotums to push the idea that as you move through the "reality" it's being rolled up after you by rather strange stage-hands. They provide a deliberately temporary home for the action, because the people in *The Pleasure Principle* are ultra-rationalistic. They're class authoritarians. The audience has the gorillas to show a version of what goes on.

Characters are as likely to saw their way into a scene through a plaster wall (as Robert does in *The Pleasure Principle*) as to enter through a door. But such staging is never entirely for the effect alone. Often it serves as an external manifestation of internal states of mind. Dreams, nightmares, madness, trances: all find physical analogues on the stage. (p. 429)

Throughout Snoo's work there is a tension between the environment of the setting and people moving within it. This is particularly manifest in the play-within-a-play situations found in *The Glad Hand*, where a cowboy strike of 1886 in Wyoming is re-enacted inside the belly of an oil tanker, or in *Flaming Bodies*, where a mock-heroic feminist revision of the Nativity is presented within the context of a Los Angeles office building. Another fine example of the tension between the events and their setting appears in the third act of *The Pleasure Principle*. What has all the trappings of a domestic psychological drama is set in a circus storage tent. The resultant disorientation internalizes the drama, setting it for the subconscious mind. . . . (pp. 430-31)

Snoo Wilson's dramaturgy is enormously refined. His characters are at times awesomely intelligent. Others display great comic genius in their speech. What is most impressive about his writing is the organization of events so that they resolve themselves with greater and greater moment. Often incidents are organized so as to be literally explosive as they come together with incredible comic timing reminiscent of a Feydeau farce. An excellent example can be seen in Act I, Scene I of *Vampire*, where Ruth and her sister Jesse conduct a séance in one location while another sister, Joy, makes love to Ruth's fiancé, Reuben, in an upstairs room which is set in another pool of light on stage. The sounds of lovemaking build, and Jesse, concluding that they have raised a devil, runs to find their father, a Welsh parson, while Ruth succumbs to a fit of hysterics. In the second scene of that act, Joy works at Mrs. Sugg's Clairvoyant Parlour (also a brothel). She appears as a staged apparition for Mrs. Sugg in a séance for a man who turns out (unbeknown to her) to be her father. By the time the scene comes to its rapid conclusion, five bodies are piled on stage as a result of thwarted attempts at incest, sadism, trickery, and blackmail. The pandemonium comes as a result of a smooth progress of causes and effects leading to an outrageous conclusion to the act in which the prolonged deaths of three of the characters serve as a pathetic backdrop for a recognition scene for the battered remnants of the central family. (pp. 431-32)

As might be expected, Snoo Wilson's plays frequently end with explosive *coups de théâtre*—an explosion literally concluding *A Greenish Man*. Other plays (e.g., *The Glad Hand* and *Salvation Now*) end with the deaths of visionary characters central to them, but these endings have an *ex machina* quality which some people find unsatisfying. The most satisfying endings are unexpected and bring about an ironic reversal to the action. . . . (p. 432)

Throughout his writing, Snoo Wilson eschews any didactic postures. He does not attempt to demonstrate a strong position on social and political issues in his work, and avoids any role as an "expert" or "authority." . . . As a result of his disinterest in instruction, Snoo Wilson's plays tend to reflect a process of exploration. They re-create odd moments in history and places their author has never visited. While *The Soul of the White Ant* or *A Greenish Man* are set in the arena of political issues, they do not address those issues directly, but rather explore the cultural and social contexts in which they exist. Snoo is constantly aware of the matrices within which ethical decisions are made and chooses to deal with them. . . .

The exploration of the ethical context for action is as alive in seemingly nonpolitical plays as it is in the ones set in South Africa or Northern Ireland. In this regard, both *Flaming Bodies* (set in contemporary Los Angeles) and *Space Ache* (centering around a space voyage to Neptune) are akin. In both, central characters voluntarily face necessity and choose to go on living with optimism after surviving a battle with despair. Although *Space Ache* is set in the future, it is, like most science fiction, written in a future-present tense. It projects present-day horrors and absurdities into the future, expanding and distorting dominant aspects of contemporary life. . . . In *The Soul of the White Ant,* a South African barkeeper, Mabel, has collected the sperm of her houseboy in her freezer. When it is discarded into a river, it impregnates two women bathing there. Similarly, in *Space Ache,* an active cryogenic program freezes people today and reduces them for storage in small canisters which are deposited in outer space for future life. These are seeds of a future life which are at present frozen—rendered lifeless through repression. Snoo Wilson's drama melts the edges of that repression. In it, dreams, sex, magic, and mystery come alive, often producing shock and surprise. It is these surprises which remind us of our own aliveness by reawakening us to it, with a resultant sense of liberation. (pp. 432-34)

> *James Bierman, "Snoo Wilson: 'Enfant Terrible' of the English Stage," in* Modern Drama, *Vol. XXIV, No. 4, December, 1981, pp. 424-35.*

## ROWENA GOLDMAN

How simple life would be if one could be frozen in the natural state and transported headlong half a million years hence, and, hopefully into a better world. This is the theme that Snoo Wilson's *Space Ache* explores. . . . But although it begins with this interesting premise the play degenerates into a flabby mixture of "Close Encounters of the Cryogenic Kind" and "Biggles Flies Undone". Why is a futuristic spaceship being manned by a crew dressed in war-time flying gear? The plot centres upon schoolgirl mother, Christine, who urgently requests the deep-freeze process so that she can awaken in a happier age when there will be no such thing as unemployment or crime. But things go wrong when she is accidentally ignited before her time, only to emerge in a reconverted state as a mermaid on board a spaceship zooming towards Neptune. In the futuristic age where Mr. Wilson places the action, sexual fulfilment is achieved via machines called 'mouthies', there are brain transplants, and aborted foetuses are sold off at a high price. Some sort of interplay is built up between the luckless heroine and the alcoholic space-captain and his crew, but the play goes nowhere fast. This is partly because Mr. Wilson's ideas are still only in the melting-pot stage where they need to congeal, and partly also because . . . stagecraft does not adequately express the range of Mr. Wilson's imagination. (p. 48)

> *Rowena Goldman, in a review of "Space Ache," in* Drama, *No. 139, 1981, p. 48.*

## MEL GUSSOW

Snoo Wilson is, along with David Hare, Howard Brenton, Howard Barker and others, one of a wave of young, politically aware English playwrights. However, in contrast to his peers, he is a Surrealist and a fantasist. His plays, such as **"The Soul of the White Ant,"** . . . are filled with turnabouts, the theatrical equivalent of reverse somersaults.

"The Soul of the White Ant" is also the title of a book by Eugene Marais, that strange South African naturalist, Afrikaans poet and drug addict. Marais's suicide in 1936 does not deter Mr. Wilson from making him a character in his contemporary play. As a cynical journalist sips a beer in a local bar in a Transvaal town, the dirt-encrusted Marais returns from his grave and strolls into the bar. The journalist convivially treats him to a couple of rounds.

Such bizarre events repeatedly occur in **"The Soul of the White Ant,"** and they are regarded as everyday occurrences. A dead body festers behind the bar, two women become pregnant after bathing in a local river—and no one takes notice. On the other hand, Mr. Wilson can make the everyday seem absurd. When the owner of the bar allows women to drink in her all-male establishment, that decision becomes a subject of heated controversy. Killing people—if they are black and of the servant class—is acceptable, but nothing should be done to upset the established social order.

The play . . . is a brief, hectic affair, the kind of grotesque comedy that might be more enjoyable in a pub or a cabaret. But there is no denying Mr. Wilson's mordant sense of humor or his resolute moral position. He has apparently never been to South Africa, a fact that does not stop him from perceiving many faces of prejudice. The termite reference is intentional. The world, as he sees it, is a festering mound crawling with deceit, and, indicates the author, unless the situation is rectified, the structure will be eroded from the inside.

The author's most compelling image is Marais cupping his hand over an imaginary ant heap, swarming with unseen creatures—a microcosm of a self-consuming society—and showing it, on the sly, to that journalist. The scene reminded me of that horrifying moment in Mark Twain's "The Mysterious Stranger" when the satanic title character molds an army of people in miniature. Marais becomes Mr. Wilson's devil ex machina. . . .

In his diabolical comedy about the evils of apartheid, Mr. Wilson operates as both ideologue and iconoclast.

> *Mel Gussow, "Surrealistic 'Soul of the White Ant'," in* The New York Times, *January 28, 1982, p. 19.*

## BENEDICT NIGHTINGALE

[*The Number of the Beast* is] predictably unpredictable. The first act offers us the Beast on his uppers, scrounging a living from the improbable acolytes who people his run-down Sicilian sin-bin, and wanly perpetrating 'sex-magic' with an American sailor in hopes of saving the wasted baby he and his Scarlet Woman have co-parented; the funny, downbeat writing . . . [helps] to create the impression of a deluded loser, half-mad victim of the bourgeois values he earnestly works to affront. But in the interval he's deported, and the second act finds him in Boulogne, making apparently authentic magic with a lady hotelier who claims to have been the Whitechapel Ripperette. How are we to see him, then—as an up-market Manson, a down-market Merlin, or what? As the incarnation of some of our repressed power-lusts? I enjoyed having my expectations subverted and my mind disoriented by Mr Wilson's curvilinear craft; but the rectilinear in me did end up ploddingly wondering, well, what was the *point* of it all.

> *Benedict Nightingale, in a review of "The Number of the Beast," in* New Statesman, *Vol. 103, No. 2657, February 19, 1982, p. 30.*

## ROWENA GOLDMAN

[Writing] and production are of an equally high standard in Snoo Wilson's *The Number of the Beast.* . . . Mr Wilson marks his return to the fringe with this new version of his play *The Beast,* which looks at a few hours in the life of the extraordinary Aleister Crowley. . . .

Crowley was known as a black magician who practised the occult and dabbled in the supernatural to find "the self". In fact, he preferred to consider himself as more of a prophet and a philosopher, who indulged in curious rituals to summon spirits and create deistic power.

Wilson concentrates on a particular period in Crowley's life when he and his disciples took over the Abbey of Thelema in Sicily before being expelled by Mussolini's government in 1923. The playwright's anarchic imagination is given plenty of scope, for Crowley was a truly remarkable character. . . . Snoo Wilson's achievement in this play . . . is that he shows us a man who was a brilliant enigma and who possessed that indefinable quality, charisma; just as he becomes fascinating and we begin to understand him a little the playwright whisks him away. The play's weakness lies in the final part where the introduction of the Boulogne hotel proprietress is no more than a contrived theatrical device to map out Crowley's ideas. Consequently the play drags towards the end, but nevertheless it is an intriguing work. . . . (p. 32)

> *Rowena Goldman, in a review of "The Number of the Beast," in* Drama, *No. 144, Summer, 1982, p. 32.*

## ANTHONY THWAITE

Contemporary science fiction often seems to teeter on the brink of self-parody. . . . Snoo Wilson's **"Spaceache"** is described as 'part spoof SF, part acid political satire.' The spoof element is, I suppose, clear enough. It's as if a bunch of punks and half-remembered characters from wartime comedies had been scabrously put into orbit by a member of what has been called the Genital Herpes school of fiction. The acid political satire, on the other hand, doesn't bite into anything deeper than villainous ermine-robed judges. We have been here before, proles and all. It's high-spirited, self-assured, but unwisely launched in the Year of Orwell.

> *Anthony Thwaite, "Dickensian Underworld," in* The Observer, *February 19, 1984, p. 25.\**

## JOHN BROWNING

The terrain [of *Spaceache*] is disarmingly familiar to urban refugees of *Clockwork Orange*—a bleak wasteland subtly yet utterly dominated by the State. Though it is a brutal age foreseen, when barbarism is refined into media events, the scenario is not without its humour.

*Spaceache* is littered with fragments of witty insight which float loosely around the central character Chrissie who, at sixteen, surrenders her future to the Cryogenic programme. . . .

Meanwhile, enemies of the State are target-launched straight to the sun, where before the televiewing millions, the victim implodes and splatters into helios. The author singles out the legal profession for particularly harsh treatment, as grossly decadent media stars like The Burning Judge televise their courtroom procedures, complete with a jury of 'impartial' computers programmed by the State. Are we so far away?

As a collection of witty vignettes with a singularly acid vision, Snoo Wilson's *Spaceache* succeeds in bemusing and disturbing its audience; a tighter control of language and characterization would certainly qualify Wilson's work for cult status. The brighter ideas of this startling book hover as in a parking orbit, waiting for developments on earth to catch up, before re-entry into the demands of high satire, chief of which might be control and technical plausibility. Nonetheless, this is a book which could only happen in 1984.

> *John Browning, in a review of "Spaceache," in* Books and Bookmen, *No. 343, April, 1984, p. 35.*

# Stephen Wright
## 1946-

**American novelist.**

**Wright's critically acclaimed first novel, *Meditations in Green* (1983), is one of the many Vietnam War novels written by veterans which have appeared in the past several years. Like James Griffin, the protagonist of the novel, Wright served in Vietnam for a year as a military intelligence officer. In *Meditations in Green* Wright interweaves a third-person account of the tedium and horror of the war with a first-person account of Griffin's traumatic readjustment to civilian life. Griffin's battle with drug addiction is a central feature of both periods. The color green symbolizes Griffin's difficulty in putting the war behind him; his memories of the greens of Army fatigues and the Vietnamese jungle compete with his efforts at peaceful meditation on the green of plants.**

### PUBLISHERS WEEKLY

[*Meditations in Green*] is not only a startlingly good first novel . . . , but possibly the best story yet to come out of the Vietnam War, the most imaginatively conceived and executed, the most painful and hard-hitting.

Spec. 4 Griffin, whose special task is to interpret aerial photos for his intelligence unit, enters the war hoping to get through it detached and unscathed. He leaves it heroin-addicted, psychologically blown apart, patiently awaiting the injury or death that will be his ticket home. Searing war scenes alternate with others depicting the postwar Griffin. . . .

It's a savagely clear-eyed study of soldiers escaping from horror into cynicism, hysteria or madness, of an army so demoralized its officers have reason to fear assassination by their own men, of a nightmare that was real. Wright is bursting with talent, and it's not possible to forget either his story or his characters.

*A review of "Meditations in Green," in* Publishers Weekly, *Vol. 224, No. 7, August 12, 1983, p. 54.*

### TOM CARHART

During the 1960s, a few tentative novels set in Vietnam appeared, but however accurate or enlightening, America just wasn't ready for them. Through the 1970s, more were published, but still we averted our national attention and seldom focused on the lessons available from that experience.

Today, Vietnam remains an undigested lump in our national belly. By this autumn, however, enough time seems to have passed for books on the subject to appear suddenly like mushrooms after a country rain.

Stephen Wright's novel, "**Meditations in Green**" . . . is one of these, and he brings the advantage of a first-hand perspective, having served in Vietnam himself. But while his personal experiences bolster much of his narration, his efforts to concoct a credible story fail miserably in the execution.

The main character is Spec. Four James Griffin, and we follow him through the war as he toils at interpreting aerial photo-

© Jerry Bauer

graphs. . . . There are also two minor themes that regularly interrupt the narration as somewhat disjointed chapters: Griffin assisting a buddy after the war in his attempts to murder a sergeant once harsh to him in Vietnam, and Griffin as either— it is unclear which—a botanist or a plant.

One expects a resolution of these unconnected story lines at the end, their final interconnection in a denouement satisfactory to the reader. Unfortunately, Mr. Wright doesn't even try this, and the ending has Griffin either—once again, it is unclear which—over the deep end on drugs or actually turning into a plant.

In all settings, Griffin and friends are constantly frying their brains, first with marijuana, then later with heroin, but this creates a painfully inaccurate picture. Sure, illicit drugs abounded in Vietnam, but their use was guarded. . . . The constant emphasis on drug use running through the book only adds an uncomfortably phony aura to the tale. . . .

Mr. Wright paints . . . tedium very well . . . and his descriptions of people, places and things sometimes take one's breath away with vivid, almost electrifying imagery. But in order to convey a convincing case of his presence in a war, he takes inappropriate literary license.

Normally, such license might be used to emphasize by exaggeration actual circumstances and compress saga reality into easily swallowed bites. Unfortunately, Mr. Wright raises stereotypes to ludicrous stature and offers them at face value as justification for the eventual communist triumph. . . . And it drags on, all the Southeast Asian war stories ever concocted showing their faces. . . .

You name it, this story flashes it, however unconvincingly. And of course at the end the war breaks into the protected rear. The compound where Griffin lives and works is overrun and all his friends are killed. But the event is without context and so without story meaning: All of a sudden, the unknown, unseen enemy arrives from "out there," kills everyone and then disappears. It's not even climactic.

Well, I guess photo interpreters were fighting the war too, and perhaps one of them can write our "Catch-22" as well as anyone else. Mr. Wright often shows a startling skill in weaving descriptive words into compelling snapshots. Unfortunately, I don't believe many readers, in 1983, will agree with what seems to be his basic philosophy in this book: Drugs solve everything. One of the last chapters ends with a sentence that perhaps best explains **Meditations in Green**: "None of this ever really happened." That says it all, better than this reviewer can.

> Tom Carhart, *"Taking Literary License with Vietnam,"* in The Wall Street Journal, *October 13, 1983, p. 26.*

## WILLIAM BOYD

In the iconology of the Vietnam war, drugs occupy as significant a role as B-52s, napalm, free fire zones, and Charlie Cong. This may be an inescapable fact but it's a grave disadvantage for novelists, especially for those with pens loaded with purple ink: drug trips, hallucinogenic dreams, zonked-out introspections take the biscuit when it comes to boring reading. . . .

[Detailed passages about drug use] pop up all through **Meditations in Green** to mar, though not critically, what is otherwise an uneven but on the whole impressive debut and addition to the canon of Vietnam war novels. . . .

[**Meditations in Green**] charts in a series of sustained flashbacks the tour of duty of one Spec. 4 Griffin. We move to and fro in time between Vietnam and Griffin's drug-hazed present. These twin chronologies are demarcated also by a change in pronoun. The Vietnam sequences are in third-person omniscient narration; the present earns the subjective viewpoint of a narrative "I." The mix is further complicated by intersections of brief meditation (hence the book's title). (p. 3)

It has to be said that although these various sections with their pronoun changes and fractured chronology make the book seem more complicated and critically *à la mode*, they actually contribute little to the novel's impact and effect. **Meditations in Green** belongs to that category of Vietnam novel that includes *If I Die in a Combat Zone* (Tim O'Brien) and *Close Quarters* (Larry Heinemann): namely the thinly fictionalized memoir. It's a tradition with a long and respectable heritage. . . . In such books one is moved and appalled by their documentary truth—and **Meditations** is no exception. Its portrayal of the U.S. military machine and mind at their most brutally callous and complacent is a terrifying indictment.

But it's when one comes to consider this type of book's status as a work of fiction—as a product of the writer's imagination—

that certain doubts are raised and certain needs unsatisfied. Documentary truth is some remove from imaginative vision, and it's in this last department that most war novels fail, and in which the whole genre of "war novel" is surprisingly deficient.

I would suggest that it was in an effort to provide this that the drugged-present sequences and the meditative interludes were supplied. One applauds the motive, but it seems to me that it is in the eyewitness testimony which Wright supplies that the novel is most admirable. It's a real bonus too that Griffin's job is ancillary to the main effort of the war. (pp. 3, 11)

All the stupidity and chaotic mess of warfare are convincingly portrayed in the unit's squalid, apathetic life. But from time to time it seems that the novelist feels that this type of meaningless quiescence is insufficient and decides to go gung-ho. Consequently we get ambushed patrols, Griffin taking over from a wounded door gunner in a helicopter, Griffin volunteering for a dangerous mission and an apocalyptic attack on the base itself.

But why should this detract from the effectiveness of the novel? The answer is that it moves it into another category—that "war is hell." Since the great poets and novelists of the First World War, action sequences in war novels have been subject to the law of diminishing returns. One can only describe blood and guts all over the place in a limited number of ways and they have to be essayed with either a very specific motive in mind or with exceptional stylistic verve to succeed.

Wright, it's true, handles his action sequences very competently, but one example will have to suffice for the sort of dilemma he finds himself in. The sequence of the ambushed patrol seems to me to be one of the best subjective viewpoints of what it must be like to be under fire that I have read. The only trouble is that the person experiencing all this is a virginal, inept rookie out on his first patrol. As the rookie—one Claypool—sets off with immense trepidation all the clichés of the war novel genre lead us to expect that he's going to run into danger. And sure enough he does. The fact that it's all brilliantly described is undermined by the extreme familiarity of the situation.

Most war novels written by ex-combatants suffer from the same weaknesses. The urge to "tell it how it was" makes the necessary art and artifice required in writing a work of fiction all too apparent, and therefore unsuccessful. It's no surprise that the two best novels about the Vietnam war, are, on the one hand, the most fanciful and absurd (*Going After Cacciato*) and, on the other, the most removed (*Dog Soldiers*). Wright's novel—flawed and impressive—makes a serious claim to join these two exemplars. But we're still waiting for the classic. (p. 11)

> William Boyd, *"The War That Won't Go Away,"* in Book World—The Washington Post, *October 30, 1983, pp. 3, 11.*

## JOHN A. GLUSMAN

"Meditations in Green" is of particular interest not because of its plot, of which there is little, but because of its form and the way it reflects the author's attitude toward the war. "This is not a settled life," the protagonist, Spec. 4 James Griffin, observes early on, and the structure of the novel tells us as much. If "The Naked and the Dead" was concerned with the upholding of discipline in the face of adversity, **"Meditations in Green"** is about the breakdown of order, the loss of control, the deterioration of character. Its multiple perspectives convey the fragmentation of experience, the shattering effects of war. Catastrophe, Wright impresses on us, lacks coherence.

It is really three stories in one. Wright precedes each chapter with a "meditation," recalling Hemingway's technique in "In Our Time." Told from the point of view of Griffin, a disabled vet strung out on dope, they are reflections on plant life—specifically the poppy—that lead into Griffin's recollections of Army life, which in turn help explain his present predicament. The horrors of war are thus seen in vivid contrast to the life cycle of a plant, which must nevertheless survive the hazards—both natural and artificial—of the environment. . . .

The meaninglessness of the United States mission, the arbitrariness of chance, provoke savage laughter among Wright's characters. . . . In a touch worthy of "Catch-22," one soldier stages his private battles for a home movie; another observes the action from a guard tower as if he were watching such a movie. But the humor conceals fear; Wright's sarcasm resounds with a seriousness of intent. . . .

Griffin escapes with only a leg injury, but the real damage is psychic. **"Meditations in Green"** is as much about the war as it is about its traumatic aftereffects. "I was a bad seed," Griffin believes. To cope with the pain, to forget the past, he turns to drugs. He learns how to meditate, and he also turns to gardening full time, cultivating life, not destroying it as he did in the war. . . .

Griffin's "Meditations in Green" lends coherence to his wartime experience, but the organic metaphor is at first misleading. Man seems to be too much an instrument of fate, a pawn at the hands of nature, as if he were neither responsible for, nor the victim of, his own actions.

But that is precisely the author's point. Wright, who served in Vietnam from December 1969 until November 1970, explains that "Most of the time, people in the novel are pretending to do something, which was the sense we had over there. We thought no matter what you did or had accomplished, what did it matter in the end?" The structure of **"Meditations in Green"** may at times be disconcerting, and Wright, like many first novelists, can be seen straining after effect. But it is this consciousness of Vietnam as an abstraction, the recognition of US policy there as stagecraft, that makes his work such an important—and disturbing—contribution to the literature of the war.

John A. Glusman, *"Bringing the Field to Us: Superb Novel about Vietnam,"* in The Christian Science Monitor, *November 4, 1983, p. B10.*

**WALTER KENDRICK**

Late in **"Meditations in Green,"** lying on his bunk blowing smoke rings, Specialist 4 James Griffin experiences transcendence. . . . He has found the one escape from pain and horror, an escape that neither logic nor religion nor even psychosis can promise, an escape waiting for him all along in the green, growing things of nature. Specialist Griffin has discovered heroin. . . .

Stephen Wright makes no attempt either to condemn or defend Griffin's heroin addiction, even when, after a painful withdrawal and 10 years off the stuff, Griffin returns to it. Throughout **"Meditations in Green,"** chapters on Griffin's Vietnam experiences alternate with accounts of his later life as a slightly disabled veteran in a large unnamed American city too hectic and violent to be any but New York. Both plots culminate in heroin. Though ignorance and panic might excuse the first addiction, the second is entered on deliberately, with full knowledge of the consequences. If judgment is to be passed on Griffin or the society that made him what he is, the reader must do it unaided by Mr. Wright, who narrates the lunacy of war and the euphoria of drugs evenhandedly.

This brilliant, scarifying first novel contains many materials familiar to readers of Vietnam fiction. Drugs are omnipresent, in every form from plants to powder. Torture, mutilation and murder are frequent, often so vividly described that the reader has trouble keeping his eyes fixed on the page. And as in most Vietnam novels, the influence of Joseph Heller's "Catch-22" is strong—perhaps because Heller's technique of multiple, intertwined subplots, each centered on a different type of war-induced insanity, is the only way that a writer can give form to a subject so abysmal and mind-numbing. (p. 7)

The absurdity of other wars has provoked humor, but Vietnam was so extreme that laughter immediately escalates into a shriek. The reality of the experience could not be faced directly; it seemed that everyone it touched, from the policy makers to the lowliest private in the field, fled into fantasy and stayed there. To narrate events coolly, with humor and detachment now, would be the wildest madness of all.

There is little humor in **"Meditations in Green,"** except for an occasional death's-head grin, and no detachment whatever. The novel is lurid, extravagant, rhapsodic and horrific by turns—sometimes all at once. Its structure is needlessly complicated, and its superheated prose often gets wearisome. Yet for all its self-conscious excesses, it has overwhelming impact—the impact of an experience so devastating that words can hardly contain it.

Some of the excess of the book can be ascribed to its being a first novel, mulled over for at least 10 years. It tries to do too much—to describe the war, its aftereffects, the psychology of drug addiction and (most murkily) the role that green plants play in all these matters. Mr. Wright strains after poetry and scatters literary echoes like shrapnel. His talent is impressive, though unruly. . . . Certainly a novel of the caliber of **"Meditations in Green"** is a promising start for a young novelist. Yet even if Griffin's postwar story were not told in the first person, the novel's brutal intensity would suggest that Mr. Wright—who, like his protagonist, was an "image interpreter" in Vietnam—is Griffin. Vietnam is the only story that Griffin has to tell; we can only hope that Mr. Wright departs from Griffin here, that this first display of Mr. Wright's extraordinary talent will not be his last. (p. 24)

Walter Kendrick, *"Drugged in Vietnam,"* in The New York Times Book Review, *November 6, 1983, pp. 7, 24.*

**TOM GRAVES**

[*Meditations in Green* wavers] between a gripping, no-nonsense, eye-level look at the war and a William Burroughs-like mush of verbiage that serves the reader little. . . .

Wright does cut through the creative writing class nonsense often enough to forcefully recall the psychological ravages Vietnam wrought on so many Americans—the debilitating stretches of boredom combined with anxiety that led to heroin addiction, for example, among other acts of self-destruction.

But he sabotages even the heart of his story with disorienting shifts in the narrative voice. . . .

[The protagonist's] wartime experiences, told in the third person, are introduced as flashbacks from a first-person account of the fractured life he lives after returning home. The transitions are numerous and abrupt, muddying the sequence of events and ultimately distancing the reader from it. . . .

As Wright's focus drifts backward, we see that Griffin, like most of our soldiers in Vietnam, began his tour of duty as a reasonably patriotic young man who believed he had been sent to this remote country to defend America and democracy. The highminded sentiments fade quickly, and he comes to be concerned with little except his supply of narcotics. (p. 14)

Probably Wright's least successful character is the CIA man, Kraft. The author seems unclear about what he wants to do with his spook. . . . [Kraft] interacts little . . . with anyone else in the novel. He simply drifts about out-of-synch. In a book with an already sprawling ensemble, one has the impression that Kraft has been jammed in because the author wants to be sure he has included all the prominent types in Vietnam. . . .

Wright integrates the growing plant motif into the war sketches with frequent ruminations on the unconquerable Vietnamese jungle—which he writes about brilliantly both on its own terms and as a symbol for the Vietnamese people, whom no amount of American military technology will ever "pacify." In that overgrown land, pitted against those implacable guerrillas, he demonstrates, our Hueys and Puff-the-Magic-Dragons were no more capable of conquest than a swarm of angry wasps.

Wright's treatment of drug abuse also deserves high commendation. The smell of the dope pipes and the late-night acid trails are reported in ferociously vivid prose that avoids stooping to sensationalism. The author makes it easy for us to understand how so many veterans came home addicts, and easy to give them our sympathy.

While the Vietnam masterwork remains to be written, one can certainly admire *Meditations in Green*. Wright, moreover, is young, and it is hard to believe he could have exhausted all his material on the war. One hopes he will cure himself of his propensity for low-grade film editors' tricks, and then have another go at it. (p. 15)

Tom Graves, "A Checkered Novel of Vietnam," in The New Leader, *Vol. LXVI, No. 22, November 28, 1983, pp. 14-15.*

# Appendix

The following is a listing of all sources used in Volume 33 of *Contemporary Literary Criticism*. Included in this list are all copyright and reprint rights and acknowledgments for those essays for which permission was obtained. Every effort has been made to trace copyright, but if omissions have been made, please let us know.

**THE EXCERPTS IN CLC, VOLUME 33, WERE REPRINTED FROM THE FOLLOWING PERIODICALS:**

*African Literature Today,* No. 11, 1980. © Heinemann Educational Books 1980. All rights reserved. Reprinted by permission.

*America,* v. 140, February 24, 1979 for a review of ''Proteus'' by Peter Heinegg; v. 145, August 29-September 5, 1981 for a review of ''The Clowns of God'' by Richard A. Blake; v. 150, May 26, 1984 for a review of ''The Autobiography of LeRoi Jones/Amiri Baraka'' by Joyce Ann Joyce. © 1979, 1981, 1984. All rights reserved. All reprinted with permission of the respective authors./ v. 126, April 22, 1972. © 1972. All rights reserved. Reprinted with permission of America Press, Inc.

*The American Book Review,* v. 3, March-April, 1981; v. 5, May-June, 1983. © 1981, 1983 by *The American Book Review.* Both reprinted by permission.

*The American Poetry Review,* v. 7, January-February, 1978 for ''Chapter and Verse'' by Stanley Plumly; v. 8, July-August, 1979 for a review of ''With Ignorance'' by Robert Coles; v. 8, November-December, 1979 for a review of ''Ashes'' and ''7 Years from Somewhere'' by Dave Smith; v. 9, March-April, 1980 for ''On Stanley Plumly: That Enduring Essence'' by Peter Stitt. Copyright © 1978, 1979, 1980 by World Poetry, Inc. All reprinted by permission of the respective authors.

*The American Spectator,* v. 17, November, 1984. Copyright © *The American Spectator* 1984. Both reprinted by permission.

*American Speech,* v. I, November, 1925.

*The Antioch Review,* v. XXIII, Spring, 1963; v. XL, Spring, 1982; v. XLII, Summer, 1984. Copyright © 1963, 1982, 1984 by the Antioch Review Inc. All reprinted by permission of the Editors./ v. V, Summer, 1945. Copyright © 1945, renewed 1972, by the Antioch Review Inc. Reprinted by permission of the Editors.

*Ariel,* v. 13, July, 1982. Copyright © 1982 The Board of Governors, The University of Calgary. Reprinted by permission.

*The Atlantic Monthly,* v. 190, October, 1952; v. 205, January, 1960; v. 211, June, 1963; v. 252, October, 1983. All reprinted by permission.

*The Australian Quarterly,* v. XIX, September, 1947.

*Best Sellers,* v. 28, November 1, 1968. Copyright 1968, by the University of Scranton. Reprinted by permission./ v. 35, November, 1975; v. 40, July, 1980; v. 42, May, 1982; v. 43, May, 1983; v. 43, December, 1983. Copyright © 1975, 1980, 1982, 1983 Helen Dwight Reid Educational Foundation. All reprinted by permission.

*Negro Digest*, v. XIX, March, 1970.

*New England Review and Bread Loaf Quarterly*, v. VI, Spring, 1984. Copyright © 1984 by Kenyon Hill Publications, Inc. Both reprinted by permission.

*The New Leader*, v. LXII, February 26, 1979; v. LXII, November 3, 1980; v. LXVI, November 28, 1983; v. LXVII, June 11, 1984; v. LXVII, June 25, 1984; v. LXVII, July 9-23, 1984. © 1979, 1980, 1983, 1984 by The American Labor Conference on International Affairs, Inc. All reprinted by permission.

*New Quest*, n. 14, March-April, 1979. © Indian Association for Cultural Freedom 1979. Reprinted by permission.

*The New Republic*, v. XXVI, October 31, 1923; v. XL, September 10, 1924; v. XLV, January 6, 1926; v. LXXXXII, August 25, 1937; v. 110, April 24, 1944; v. 127, July 7, 1952./ v. 186, June 9, 1982 for "The Great Artistic Director Burnout" by Robert Brustein; v. 191, August 6, 1984 for "Painless Dentistry" by Robert Brustein. © 1982, 1984 The New Republic, Inc. Both reprinted by permission of the author./ v. 136, April 22, 1957; v. 143, November 14, 1960; v. 152, May 8, 1965; v. 154, May 28, 1966; v. 162, January 31, 1970; v. 170, January 19, 1974; v. 175, November 20, 1976; v. 176, March 19, 1977; v. 177, November 26, 1977; v. 178, June 24, 1978; v. 179, December 9, 1978; v. 187, October 18, 1982; v. 189, October 10, 1983; v. 190, May 7, 1984; v. 190, June 11, 1984; v. 191, October 22, 1984. © 1957, 1960, 1965, 1966, 1970, 1974, 1976, 1977, 1978, 1982, 1983, 1984 The New Republic, Inc. All reprinted by permission of *The New Republic*./ v. 109, November 22, 1943 for "Port of Refuge" by Malcolm Cowley. © 1943 The New Republic, Inc. Renewed 1971 by Malcolm Cowley. Reprinted by permission of the author.

*The New Review*, v. III, May, 1976. © TNR Publications, Ltd., London. Reprinted by permission.

*New Statesman*, v. LIX, March 26, 1960; v. 78, July 11, 1969; v. 84, October 20, 1972; v. 92, October 1, 1976; v. 93, May 27, 1977; v. 95, February 10, 1978; v. 95, April 28, 1978; v. 96, December 1, 1978; v. 97, May 25, 1979; v. 98, July 13, 1979; v. 98, December 14, 1979; v. 99, March 7, 1980; v. 99, June 6, 1980; v. 100, November 28, 1980; v. 101, January 9, 1981; v. 102, October 23, 1981; v. 103, February 19, 1982; v. 104, August 20, 1982; v. 104, December 17, 1982; v. 105, March 4, 1983; v. 105, April 1, 1983; v. 105, May 6, 1983; v. 107, January 13, 1984; v. 107, April 6, 1984. © 1960, 1969, 1972, 1976, 1977, 1978, 1979, 1980, 1981, 1982, 1983, 1984 The Statesman & Nation Publishing Co. Ltd. All reprinted by permission.

*The New Statesman & Nation*, v. XVII, March 18, 1939; v. XXI, January 4, 1941; v. XXVI, December 4, 1943; v. XLI, April 28, 1951; v. LII, August 18, 1956./ v. 74, October 27, 1967. © 1967 The Statesman & Nation Publishing Co. Ltd. Reprinted by permission.

*New York* Magazine, v. 14, December 14, 1981; v. 15, May 24, 1982; v. 17, April 2, 1984; v. 17, May 21, 1984; v. 17, June 18, 1984; v. 17, July 16, 1984. Copyright © 1981, 1982, 1984 by News Group Publications, Inc. All reprinted with the permission of *New York* Magazine.

*New York Herald Tribune Book Review*, November 21, 1954; September 7, 1958; April 26, 1959; January 10, 1960; May 29, 1960. © 1954, 1958, 1959, 1960 I.H.T. Corporation. All reprinted by permission.

*New York Herald Tribune Books*, April 28, 1929; August 17, 1930; November 27, 1938; October 5, 1941; July 19, 1942. © 1929, 1930, 1938, 1941, 1942 I.H.T. Corporation. All reprinted by permission.

*New York Post*, July 15, 1982; May 7, 1984; June 22, 1984. © 1982, 1984, New York Post Corporation. All reprinted from the *New York Post* by permission.

*The New York Review of Books*, v. V, January 20, 1966; v. XXVIII, December 17, 1981; v. XXIX, October 21, 1982; v. XXXI, February 2, 1984; v. XXXI, August 16, 1984; v. XXXI, December 6, 1984. Copyright © 1966, 1981, 1982, 1984 Nyrev, Inc. All reprinted with permission from *The New York Review of Books*.

*The New York Times*, s. VII, April 19, 1959; February 2, 1972; July 17, 1978; January 29, 1979; November 1, 1981; January 28, 1982; March 5, 1982; April 27, 1982; May 8, 1982; s. VII, May 16, 1982; s. II, June 27, 1982; May 20, 1983; August 22, 1983; November 9, 1983; December 6, 1983; January 23, 1984; February 10, 1984; February 18, 1984; March 29, 1984; May 7, 1984; May 11, 1984; May 21, 1984; s. II, May 30, 1984; June 12, 1984; June 22, 1984. Copyright © 1959, 1972, 1978, 1979, 1981, 1982, 1983, 1984 by The New York Times Company. All reprinted by permission.

*The New York Times Book Review*, September 13, 1925; August 22, 1926; August 19, 1928; May 5, 1929; May 1, 1932; December 11, 1938; May 25, 1941; December 9, 1945; September 28, 1947; October 4, 1953; October 7, 1956; April 19, 1959; May 24, 1959; September 25, 1960; November 26, 1961; November 4, 1962; January 3, 1965; May 2, 1965; November 28, 1965; May 8, 1966; November 30, 1969; December 28, 1969; July 19, 1970; October 25, 1970; May 16, 1971; April 23, 1972; August 6, 1972; January 7, 1973; July 29, 1973; June 30, 1974; September 15, 1974; November 17, 1974; December 21, 1975; May 30, 1976; August 29, 1976; October 31, 1976; April 17, 1977; July 10, 1977; September 4, 1977; September 25, 1977; April 2, 1978; March 4, 1979; June 24, 1979; February 24, 1980; April 13, 1980; November 9, 1980; April 26, 1981; June 7, 1981; August 16, 1981; November 22, 1981; January 3, 1982; May 2, 1982; August 29, 1982; September 5, 1982; December 12, 1982; January 9, 1983; March 27, 1983; April 24, 1983; June 5, 1983; July 3, 1983; October 9, 1983; November 6, 1983; November 27, 1983; December 11, 1983; January 22, 1984; February 12, 1984; February 19, 1984; March 25, 1984; April 15, 1984; May 20, 1984; June 3, 1984; June 10, 1984; June 17, 1984; June 24, 1984; July 1, 1984; July 15, 1984; July 22, 1984; August 12, 1984. Copyright © 1925, 1926, 1928, 1929, 1932, 1938, 1941, 1945, 1947, 1953, 1956, 1959, 1960, 1961, 1962,

1965, 1966, 1969, 1970, 1971, 1972, 1973, 1974, 1975, 1976, 1977, 1978, 1979, 1980, 1981, 1982, 1983, 1984 by The New York Times Company. All reprinted by permission.

*The New Yorker,* v. XIX, November 20, 1943 for "Arthur Koestler" by Clifton Fadiman. © 1943, renewed 1970, by The New Yorker Magazine, Inc. Reprinted by permission of the author./ v. LVIII, May 24, 1982 for "Women As Things" by Brendan Gill; v. LX, February 20, 1984 for "The Charged Imagination" by William Maxwell; v. LX, May 14, 1984 for "Joy and Torment" by Edith Oliver; v. LX, May 14, 1984 for "Boo!" by Edith Oliver; v. LX, June 25, 1984 for "Mr. James and Captain Worrell" by Whitney Balliett. © 1982, 1984 by the respective authors. All reprinted by permission./ v. XXXV, June 6, 1959; v. LIX, May 2, 1983. © 1959, 1983 by The New Yorker Magazine, Inc. Both reprinted by permission.

*Newsweek,* v. LVIII, December 11, 1961; v. CII, August 29, 1983; v. CVI, September 17, 1984; v. CIII, January 30, 1984; v. CIII, April 9, 1984; v. CIII, May 28, 1984; v. CIII, June 11, 1984; v. CIII, June 18, 1984; v. CIII, June 25, 1984; v. CIV, July 2, 1984. Copyright 1961, 1983, 1984, by Newsweek, Inc. All rights reserved. All reprinted by permission.

*Northwest Review,* v. 11, Spring, 1971. Copyright © 1971 by *Northwest Review.* Reprinted by permission.

*The Observer,* October 3, 1982; March 27, 1983; November 20, 1983; February 19, 1984; April 22, 1984; June 24, 1984; September 23, 1984; October 28, 1984. All reprinted by permission of The Observer Limited.

*The Ohio Review,* v. XX, Spring-Summer, 1979. Copyright © 1979 by the Editors of *The Ohio Review.* Reprinted by permission.

*Opportunity,* v. 4, October, 1926.

*Parnassus: Poetry in Review,* v. 1, Fall-Winter, 1972; v. 3, Spring-Summer, 1975; v. 8, Fall-Winter, 1979; v. 9, Spring-Summer, 1981; v. 10, Spring-Summer, 1982; v. 11, Spring-Summer, 1983. Copyright © Poetry in Review Foundation. All reprinted by permission.

*Partisan Review,* v. XIII, November-December, 1946 for "Koestler's New Novel" by Clement Greenberg; v. XLVII, 1980 for a review of "Zip" by Lynn Luria-Sukenick; v. XLIX, 1982 for "Koestler's Koestler" by Bernard Crick. Copyright © 1946, 1980, 1982 by *Partisan Review.* All reprinted by permission of *Partisan Review* and the respective authors.

*People Weekly,* v. 22, July 23, 1984. © 1984, Time Inc. Reprinted by permission.

*PHYLON: The Atlanta University Review of Race and Culture,* v. VI, 4th Quarter, 1945. Copyright, 1945, renewed 1973, by Atlanta University. Reprinted by permission of *PHYLON.*

*Plays and Players,* v. 21, January, 1974 for a review of "The Pleasure Principle" by Peter Ansorge; v. 23, April, 1976 for a review of "Soul of the White Ant" by Steve Grant; v. 25, July, 1978 for a review of "The Glad Hand" by Jeremy Treglown; v. 27, January, 1980 for a review of 'Flaming Bodies" by John Russell Taylor. © copyright the respective authors 1974, 1976, 1978, 1980. All reprinted with permission of the respective authors./ v. 22, January, 1975 for a review of "The Beast" by John Ford; v. 23, March, 1976 for a review of "The Everest Hotel" by Jonathan Hammond; v. 24, May, 1977 for as review of "Vampire" by Michael Coveney. © copyright the respective authors 1975, 1976, 1977. All reprinted with permission of the publisher./ n. 352, January, 1983; n. 356, May, 1983. © copyright Brevet Publishing Ltd. 1983. Both reprinted with permission of the publisher.

*Ploughshares,* v. 4, 1978 for "On Anne Stevenson" by Jay Parini; v. 5, 1979 for a review of "When the Tree Sings" by Anne Bernays. © 1978, 1979 by Ploughshares, Inc. Both reprinted by permission of the publisher and the respective authors.

*Poetry,* v. LXIV, July, 1944 for "A Study of Garcia Lorca" by H. R. Hays. © 1944, renewed 1972, by The Modern Poetry Association. Reprinted by permission of the Editor of *Poetry* and the Literary Estate of H. R. Hays.

*Poetry,* v. XCVII, November, 1960 for a review of "The Gazabos: 41 Poems" by Jack Lindeman; v. CXVI, July, 1970 for "Transparencies" by Stephen Berg; v. CXIX, November, 1971 for "Plastic Possibilities" by M. L. Rosenthal; v. CXX, June, 1972 for "A Defence" by Michael Schmidt; v. CXXI, February, 1973 for "Trial and Error" by Jascha Kessler; v. CXXIII, November, 1973 for "Dealing with Tradition" by Jonathon Galassi; v. CXXVI, May, 1975 for "Questions of Style" by James Martin; v. CXXIX, January, 1977 for "Art or Knack?" by Richard Howard; v. CXXX, September, 1977 for "To the Wall" by Dick Allen; v. 133, November, 1978 for "'Fool', Said My Muse to Me . . . ," by Alan Williamson; v. CXLII, May, 1983 for "Orders of Magnitude" by Bonnie Costello; v. CXLIV, September, 1984 for a review of "Tar" by Bruce Bawer. © 1960, 1970, 1971, 1973, 1975, 1977, 1978, 1983, 1984 by The Modern Poetry Association. All reprinted by permission of the Editor of *Poetry* and the respective authors./ v. CVIII, April, 1966. © 1966 by The Modern Poetry Association. Reprinted by permission of the Editor of *Poetry.*

*Poetry Review,* v. 73, March, 1983 for "Acting Against Oblivion" by Tim Dooley; v. 73, March, 1983 for "Humane Astringencies" by George Szirtes. Copyright © The Poetry Society 1983. Both reprinted by permission of the respective authors.

*Publishers Weekly,* v. 221, June 25, 1982; v. 223, February 11, 1983; v. 224, August 12, 1983; v. 225, March 2, 1984; v. 225, April 27, 1984; v. 225, May 11, 1984; v. 225, June 8, 1984. Copyright © 1982, 1983, 1984 by Xerox Corporation. All reprinted from *Publishers Weekly,* published by R. R. Bowker Company, a Xerox company, by permission.

*Punch,* v. 283, October 13, 1982. © 1982 by Punch Publications Ltd. All rights reserved. May not be reprinted without permission.

**THE EXCERPTS IN CLC, VOLUME 33, WERE REPRINTED FROM THE FOLLOWING BOOKS:**

Achebe, Chinua. From *Morning Yet on Creation Day: Essays*. Anchor Press/Doubleday, 1975. Copyright © 1975 by Chinua Achebe. All rights reserved. Reprinted by permission of Doubleday & Company, Inc.

Aidoo, Christina Ama Ata. From an introduction to *The Beautyful Ones Are Not Yet Born: A Novel*. By Ayi Kwei Armah. Macmillan/Collier Books, 1969. Copyright © 1968 by Macmillan Publishing Company. All rights reserved. Reprinted with permission of Macmillan Publishing Company.

Beidler, Philip D. From *American Literature and the Experience of Vietnam*. University of Georgia Press, 1982. Copyright © 1982 by the University of Georgia Press, Athens, GA 30602. All rights reserved. Reprinted by permission of The University of Georgia Press.

Bigsby, C.W.E. From *The Second Black Renaissance: Essays in Black Literature*. Greenwood Press, 1980. Copyright © 1980 by C.W.E. Bigsby. All rights reserved. Reprinted by permission of Greenwood Press, a division of Congressional Information Service, Inc., Westport, CT.

Bradbury, Malcolm. From *Saul Bellow*. Methuen, 1982. © 1982 Malcolm Bradbury. All rights reserved. Reprinted by permission of Methuen & Co. Ltd.

Brooks, Cleanth. From "Eudora Welty and the Southern Idiom," in *Eudora Welty: A Form of Thanks*. Edited by Louis Dollarhide and Ann J. Abadie. University Press of Mississippi, 1979. Copyright © 1979 by the University Press of Mississippi. All rights reserved. Reprinted by permission.

Brown, Lloyd W. From *Amiri Baraka*. Twayne, 1980. Copyright 1980 by Twayne Publishers. All rights reserved. Reprinted with the permission of Twayne Publishers, a division of G. K. Hall & Co., Boston.

Clerc, Charles. From an introduction to *Approaches to "Gravity's Rainbow."* Edited by Charles Clerc. Ohio State University Press, 1983. Copyright © 1983 by the Ohio State University Press. All rights reserved. Reprinted by permission.

Conradi, Peter. From *John Fowles*. Methuen, 1982. © 1982 Peter Conradi. All rights reserved. Reprinted by permission of Methuen & Co. Ltd.

Cox, Martha Heasley and Wayne Chatterton. From *Nelson Algren*. Twayne, 1975. Copyright 1975 by Twayne Publishers. All rights reserved. Reprinted with the permission of Twayne Publishers, a division of G. K. Hall & Co., Boston.

Dasgupta, Gautam. From *American Playwrights: A Critical Survey, Vol. 1*. By Bonnie Marranca and Gautam Dasgupta. Drama Book Specialists (Publishers), 1981. Copyright © 1981 by Bonnie Marranca and Gautam Dasgupta. All rights reserved. Reprinted by permission.

Davis, Charles E. From "Eudora Welty's 'The Robber Bridegroom' and Old Southwest Humor: A Doubleness of Vision," in *A Still Moment: Essays on the Art of Eudora Welty*. Edited by John F. Desmond. The Scarecrow Press, Inc., 1978. Copyright © 1978 by John F. Desmond. Reprinted by permission of the author.

Fraser, George. From "The Man within the Name: William Empson As Poet, Critic, and Friend," in *William Empson: The Man and His Work*. Edited by Roma Gill. Routledge and Kegan Paul, 1974. © Routledge & Kegan Paul 1974. Reprinted by permission of Routledge & Kegan Paul PLC.

Fraser, Robert. From *The Novels of Ayi Kwei Armah: A Study in Polemical Fiction*. Heinemann, 1980. © Robert Fraser 1980. Reprinted by permission of Heinemann Educational Books Ltd.

Glicksberg, Charles I. From *The Literature of Commitment*. Bucknell University Press, 1976. © 1976 by Associated University Presses, Inc. Reprinted by permission.

Grebstein, Sheldon Norman. From "Nelson Algren and the Whole Truth," in *The Forties: Fiction, Poetry, Drama*. Edited by Warren French. Everett/Edwards, Inc., 1969. Copyright © 1969 by Warren French. All rights reserved. Reprinted by permission.

Hayman, Ronald. From *British Theatre Since 1955: A Reassessment*. Oxford University Press, Oxford, 1979. © Oxford University Press 1979. All rights reserved. Reprinted by permission of Oxford University Press.

Heywood, Christopher. From *Nadine Gordimer*. Profile Books Ltd., 1983. © Christopher Heywood 1983. Reprinted by permission.

Howard, Richard. From "A Note on Frank Bidart," in *Golden State*. By Frank Bidart. Braziller, 1973. Copyright © 1973 by Frank Bidart. All rights reserved. Reprinted by permission of George Braziller, Inc., Publishers.

Phillips, Robert L., Jr. From "A Structural Approach to Myth in the Fiction of Eudora Welty," in *Eudora Welty: Critical Essays*. Edited by Peggy Whitman Prenshaw. University Press of Mississippi, 1979. Copyright © 1979 by the University Press of Mississippi. All rights reserved. Reprinted by permission.

Pinsky, Robert. From *The Situation of Poetry: Contemporary Poetry and Its Traditions*. Princeton University Press, 1976. Copyright © 1976 by Princeton University Press. All rights reserved. Excerpts reprinted with permission of Princeton University Press.

Porter, Katherine Anne. From an introduction to *A Curtain of Green and Other Stories*. By Eudora Welty. Harcourt, Brace and Company, 1941. Copyright, 1941, renewed 1968, by Eudora Welty. All rights reserved. Reprinted by permission of William Morris Agency, Inc. on behalf of author.

Richards, I. A. From "Semantic Frontiersman," in *William Empson: The Man and His Work*. Edited by Roma Gill. Routledge & Kegan Paul, 1974. © Routledge & Kegan Paul 1974. Reprinted by permission of Routledge & Kegan Paul PLC.

Sibley, William F. From *The Shiga Hero*. University of Chicago Press, 1979. © 1979 by The University of Chicago. All rights reserved. Reprinted by permission of The University of Chicago Press.

Slade, Joseph W. From " 'Entropy' and Other Calamities," in *Pynchon: A Collection of Critical Essays*. Edited by Edward Mendelson. Prentice-Hall, Inc., 1978. Copyright 1974 by Joseph W. Slade. Reprinted by permission of Joseph W. Slade.

Taylor, John Russell. From "Art and Commerce: The New Drama in the West End Marketplace," in *Contemporary English Drama*, Stratford-Upon-Avon Studies, No. 19. Edited by C. W. E. Bigsby. Holmes & Meier, 1981. © Edward Arnold (Publishers) Ltd., 1981. All rights reserved. Reprinted by permission of Holmes & Meier Publishers, Inc., IUB Building, 30 Irving Place, New York, NY 10003.

Ueda, Makoto. From *Modern Japanese Writers and the Nature of Literature*. Stanford University Press, 1976. © 1976 by the Board of Trustees of the Leland Stanford Junior University. Excerpted with the permission of the publishers, Stanford University Press.

Van Vechten, Carl. From "A Note By the Author," in *Nigger Heaven*. Avon Books, 1950. Reprinted by permission of Avon Books, New York and Robert B. Wyatt.

Wain, John. From "Ambiguous Gifts: Notes on a Twentieth-Century Poet," in *The Penguin New Writing*. Edited by John Lehmann. Penguin Books, 1950. Reprinted by permission of Penguin Books Ltd.

Wolfe, Peter. From *John Fowles, Magus and Moralist*. Bucknell University Press, 1976. © 1976 by Associated University Presses, Inc. Reprinted by permission.

Yamanouchi, Hisaaki. From *The Search for Authenticity in Modern Japanese Literature*. Cambridge University Press, 1978. © Cambridge University Press 1978. Reprinted by permission.

# Cumulative Index to Authors

This index lists all author entries in the Gale Literary Criticism Series and includes cross-references to other Gale sources. References in the index are identified as follows:

**AITN:** *Authors in the News,* Volumes 1-2
**CAAS:** *Contemporary Authors Autobiography Series,* Volume 1-2
**CA:** *Contemporary Authors* (original series), Volumes 1-113
**CANR:** *Contemporary Authors New Revision Series,* Volumes 1-14
**CAP:** *Contemporary Authors Permanent Series,* Volumes 1-2
**CA-R:** *Contemporary Authors* (revised editions), Volumes 1-44
**CLC:** *Contemporary Literary Criticism,* Volumes 1-33
**CLR:** *Children's Literature Review,* Volumes 1-8
**DLB:** *Dictionary of Literary Biography,* Volumes 1-38
**DLB-DS:** *Dictionary of Literary Biography Documentary Series,* Volumes 1-8
**DLB-Y:** *Dictionary of Literary Biography Yearbook,* Volumes 1980-1983
**LC:** *Literature Criticism from 1400 to 1800,* Volume 1
**NCLC:** *Nineteenth-Century Literature Criticism,* Volumes 1-9
**SATA:** *Something about the Author,* Volumes 1-38
**TCLC:** *Twentieth-Century Literary Criticism,* Volumes 1-16
**YABC:** *Yesterday's Authors of Books for Children,* Volumes 1-2

Author Index

Author Index

**Author Index**

Author Index

**Mann, (Luiz) Heinrich**
1871-1950................ **TCLC 9**
See also CA 106

**Mann, Thomas**
1875-1955............. **TCLC 2, 8, 14**
See also CA 104

**Manning, Olivia** 1915-1980 ..... **CLC 5, 19**
See also CA 5-8R
See also obituary CA 101

**Mano, D. Keith** 1942-.......... **CLC 2, 10**
See also CA 25-28R
See also DLB 6

**Mansfield, Katherine**
1888-1923................ **TCLC 2, 8**
See also CA 104

**Marcel, Gabriel (Honore)**
1889-1973................... **CLC 15**
See also CA 102
See also obituary CA 45-48

**Marchbanks, Samuel** 1913-
See Davies, (William) Robertson

**Marinetti, F(ilippo) T(ommaso)**
1876-1944................ **TCLC 10**
See also CA 107

**Markandaya, Kamala (Purnalya)**
1924-........................ **CLC 8**
See also Taylor, Kamala (Purnalya)

**Markfield, Wallace (Arthur)**
1926-....................... **CLC 8**
See also CA 69-72
See also DLB 2, 28

**Markham, Robert** 1922-
See Amis, Kingsley (William)

**Marks, J.** 1942-
See Highwater, Jamake

**Marley, Bob** 1945-1981 ..........**CLC 17**
See also Marley, Robert Nesta

**Marley, Robert Nesta** 1945-1981
See Marley, Bob
See also CA 107
See also obituary CA 103

**Marquand, John P(hillips)**
1893-1960................ **CLC 2, 10**
See also CA 85-88
See also DLB 9

**Márquez, Gabriel García** 1928-
See García Márquez, Gabriel

**Marquis, Don(ald Robert Perry)**
1878-1937................. **TCLC 7**
See also CA 104
See also DLB 11, 25

**Marryat, Frederick** 1792-1848 .... **NCLC 3**
See also DLB 21

**Marsh, (Edith) Ngaio**
1899-1982.................... **CLC 7**
See also CANR 6
See also CA 9-12R

**Marshall, Garry** 1935?- ..........**CLC 17**
See also CA 111

**Marshall, Paule** 1929-............ **CLC 27**
See also CA 77-80
See also DLB 33

**Marsten, Richard** 1926-
See Hunter, Evan

**Martin, Steve** 1945?-............. **CLC 30**
See also CA 97-100

**Martínez Ruiz, José** 1874-1967
See Azorín
See also CA 93-96

**Martínez Sierra, Gregorio** 1881-1947
See Martínez Sierra, Gregorio and Martínez Sierra, María (de la O'LeJárraga)
See also CA 104

**Martínez Sierra, Gregorio** 1881-1947 and **Martínez Sierra, María (de la O'LeJárraga)** 1880?-1974 .... **TCLC 6**

**Martínez Sierra, María (de la O'LeJárraga)** 1880?-1974
See Martínez Sierra, Gregorio and Martínez Sierra, María (de la O'LeJárraga)

**Martínez Sierra, María (de la O'LeJárraga)** 1880?-1974 and **Martínez Sierra, Gregorio** 1881-1947
See Martínez Sierra, Gregorio and Martínez Sierra, María (de la O'LeJárraga)

**Martinson, Harry (Edmund)**
1904-1978................... **CLC 14**
See also CA 77-80

**Masefield, John (Edward)**
1878-1967................... **CLC 11**
See also CAP 2
See also CA 19-20
See also obituary CA 25-28R
See also SATA 19
See also DLB 10, 19

**Mason, Bobbie Ann** 1940- ........ **CLC 28**
See also CANR 11
See also CA 53-56

**Mason, Tally** 1909-1971
See Derleth, August (William)

**Masters, Edgar Lee**
1868?-1950................ **TCLC 2**
See also CA 104

**Mathews, Harry** 1930- ............**CLC 6**
See also CA 21-24R

**Matthias, John (Edward)** 1941-......**CLC 9**
See also CA 33-36R

**Matthiessen, Peter**
1927-................ **CLC 5, 7, 11, 32**
See also CA 9-12R
See also SATA 27
See also DLB 6

**Maturin, Charles Robert**
1780?-1824................... **NCLC 6**

**Matute, Ana María** 1925-..........**CLC 11**
See also CA 89-92

**Maugham, W(illiam) Somerset**
1874-1965............. **CLC 1, 11, 15**
See also CA 5-8R
See also obituary CA 25-28R
See also DLB 10, 36

**Maupassant, (Henri René Albert) Guy de**
1850-1893................... **NCLC 1**

**Mauriac, Claude** 1914-.............**CLC 9**
See also CA 89-92

**Mauriac, François (Charles)**
1885-1970................. **CLC 4, 9**
See also CAP 2
See also CA 25-28

**Mavor, Osborne Henry** 1888-1951
See also CA 104

**Maxwell, William (Keepers, Jr.)**
1908-........................**CLC 19**
See also CA 93-96
See also DLB-Y 80

**May, Elaine** 1932-................**CLC 16**

**Mayakovsky, Vladimir (Vladimirovich)**
1893-1930................. **TCLC 4**
See also CA 104

**Maynard, Joyce** 1953-.............**CLC 23**
See also CA 111

**Mayne, William (James Carter)**
1928-........................**CLC 12**
See also CA 9-12R
See also SATA 6

**Mayo, Jim** 1908?-
See L'Amour, Louis (Dearborn)

**Maysles, Albert** 1926-
See Maysles, Albert and Maysles, David
See also CA 29-32R

**Maysles, Albert** 1926- and **Maysles, David** 1932-........................**CLC 16**

**Maysles, David** 1932-
See Maysles, Albert and Maysles, David

**Mazer, Norma Fox** 1931-..........**CLC 26**
See also CANR 12
See also CA 69-72
See also SATA 24

**McBain, Ed** 1926-
See Hunter, Evan

**McCaffrey, Anne** 1926- ...........**CLC 17**
See also CA 25-28R
See also SATA 8
See also DLB 8
See also AITN 2

**McCarthy, Cormac** 1933-...........**CLC 4**
See also CANR 10
See also CA 13-16R
See also DLB 6

**McCarthy, Mary (Therese)**
1912-............. **CLC 1, 3, 5, 14, 24**
See also CA 5-8R
See also DLB 2
See also DLB-Y 81

**McCartney, Paul** 1942-
See Lennon, John (Ono) and McCartney, Paul

**McClure, Michael** 1932-........ **CLC 6, 10**
See also CA 21-24R
See also DLB 16

**McCourt, James** 1941-.............**CLC 5**
See also CA 57-60

**McCrae, John** 1872-1918........ **TCLC 12**
See also CA 109

**McCullers, (Lula) Carson**
1917-1967........... **CLC 1, 4, 10, 12**
See also CA 5-8R
See also obituary CA 25-28R
See also SATA 27
See also DLB 2, 7

**McCullough, Colleen** 1938?- .......**CLC 27**
See also CA 81-84

**McElroy, Joseph** 1930-.............**CLC 5**
See also CA 17-20R

**McEwan, Ian** 1948-................**CLC 13**
See also CA 61-64
See also DLB 14

Author Index

Author Index

Author Index

Author Index

# Cumulative Index to Critics

Critic Index

**Critic Index**

Critic Index

Critic Index

**Critic Index**

Critic Index

**Critic Index**

**Critic Index**

Critic Index

**Critic Index**

Critic Index

**Critic Index**

Critic Index

*Critic Index*

Critic Index

Critic Index

Critic Index

Critic Index

Critic Index

Critic Index

Critic Index

Critic Index

Critic Index

Critic Index

**Critic Index**

Critic Index

Critic Index

Critic Index

Critic Index

Critic Index

**Critic Index**

Critic Index

*Critic Index*

Critic Index

Critic Index

**Critic Index**

Critic Index

Critic Index

Critic Index

Critic Index

Critic Index

**Critic Index**

Critic Index

Critic Index

**Critic Index**

Critic Index

**Critic Index**